ADRIAN S

THEY MADE GREAT BRITAIN

THE MEN AND WOMEN
WHO SHAPED THE MODERN WORLD

ADELPHI

COUNTIES OR COUNTRIES OF BIRTH FOR THE FIFTY MEN AND WOMEN, BORN OR WHO CHOSE TO BECOME BRITISH, WHOSE LIVES MADE PERHAPS THE MOST DIFFERENCE TO THE MODERN WORLD

British Isles showing county boundaries in 1965

- Scotland
- England
- Wales
- Northern Ireland *(since 1922)*
- Republic of Ireland *(since 1949)*
- Isle of Man and Channel Islands

1.	Alfred the Great, King of Wessex	849–899	Berkshire
2.	Austen, Jane	1775–1817	Hampshire
3.	Brunel, Isambard Kingdom	1806–1859	Hampshire
4.	Burns, Robert	1759–1796	Ayrshire
5.	Carnegie, Andrew	1835–1919	Fife
6.	Cecil, 1st Lord Burleigh, William	1520–1598	Lincolnshire
7.	Churchill OM FRS *(1953)**, Sir Winston Spencer	1874–1965	Oxfordshire
8.	Churchill, 1st Duke of Marlborough, John	1650–1722	Devonshire
9.	Clive, 1st Baron, Robert	1725–1774	Shropshire
10.	Cochrane, 10th Earl of Dundonald, Thomas RN	1775–1860	Lanarkshire
11.	Cook, Captain James RN	1728–1779	Yorkshire
12.	Crick OM FRS *(1962)**, Francis Henry Compton	1916–2004	Northamptonshire
13.	Cromwell, Oliver	1599–1658	Huntingdonshire
14.	Darwin FRS, Charles Robert	1809–1882	Shropshire
15.	Dickens, Charles John Huffam	1812–1870	Hampshire
16.	Drake, Sir Francis	*1540*–1596	Devonshire
17.	Edward I, King of England	1239–1307	London
18.	Elgar, 1st Bt. OM, Sir Edward William	1857–1934	Worcestershire
19.	Elizabeth I, Queen of England	1533–1603	London
20.	Faraday FRS, Michael	1791–1867	London
21.	Fleming FRS *(1945)**, Sir Alexander	1881–1955	Ayrshire
22.	Händel, Georg Friedrich *(naturalised* 1723)	1685–1759	Germany (Halle)
23.	Henry II, King of England	1133–1189	France (Maine)
24.	Henry V, King of England	1387–1422	Monmouthshire
25.	Henry VII, King of England	1457–1509	Pembrokeshire
26.	Keynes of Tilton, 1st Baron, (John) Maynard	1883–1946	Cambridgeshire
27.	Kipling *(1907)**, (Joseph) Rudyard	1865–1936	India (British)
28.	Law of Lauriston, John	1671–1729	Edinburgh
29.	Lawrence ("of Arabia"), Thomas Edward (T.E.)	1888–1935	Caernarvonshire
30.	Livingstone, David	1813–1873	Lanarkshire
31.	Lloyd George of Dwyfor, 1st Earl, David	1863–1945	Lancashire
32.	Marshal, 1st Earl of Pembroke, William	1147–1219	Wiltshire
33.	Maxwell FRS, James Clerk	1831–1879	Edinburgh
34.	Nelson, 1st Viscount, Horatio RN	1758–1805	Norfolk
35.	Newton PRS, Sir Isaac	1642–1727	Lincolnshire
36.	Pitt, 1st Earl of Chatham, William	1708–1778	London
37.	Raffles, Sir (Thomas) Stamford	1781–1826	Jamaica (British)
38.	Rhodes, Cecil John	1853–1902	Hertfordshire
39.	Robert I (de Bruce), King of Scotland	1274–1329	Essex
40.	Scott, 1st Bt., Sir Walter	1771–1832	Edinburgh
41.	Shackleton, Sir Ernest Henry	1874–1922	Clare
42.	Shakespeare, William	1564–1616	Warwickshire
43.	Smith, Adam	1723–1790	Fife
44.	Smuts OM FRS, Field Marshal Jan Christiaan	1870–1950	South Africa (British)
45.	Turner RA, Joseph Mallord William	1775–1851	London
46.	Tyndale, William	*1494*–1536	Gloucestershire
47.	Walpole, 1st Earl of Orford, Robert	1676–1745	Norfolk
48.	Wellesley, 1st Duke of Wellington, Field Marshal Arthur	1769–1852	Dublin
49.	William I (the Conqueror), King of England	1027–1087	France (Normandy)
50.	Wren FRS, Sir Christopher	1632–1723	Wiltshire

OM: Order of Merit; PRS or FRS: President or Fellow of the Royal Society; RN: Royal Navy; * Nobel Laureate *(date)*

Dedication

THIS BOOK IS DEDICATED TO THE UNKNOWN WARRIOR

At the chapel in Saint Pol near Arras, on 7 November 1920, the body of "a British warrior who fell in the Great War" was chosen from four coffins draped with Union Flags, brought there from an unknown battlefield by Brigadier-General L.J. Wyatt and Lieutenant-Colonel E.A.S. Gell: to serve as a symbol for all the unknown dead "known unto God", wherever they fell. Marshal Foch saluted the coffin as it rested under a guard of French soldiers at Boulogne, whence it was taken across the Channel on HMS *Verdun*, to be received with a Field Marshal's 19–gun salute from Dover Castle.

At 8:32 p.m. on 10 November the coffin arrived at Victoria Station, where it rested overnight. On Platform 8, each year at 8:32 p.m. on 10 November, a bugler sounds *The Last Post*, followed by a two-minute silence and a reading of Laurence Binyon's words: "They shall grow not old as we that are left grow old. Age will not weary them nor the years condemn. At the going down of the sun and in the morning, we will remember them".

On Armistice Day, 11 November 1920 the coffin was drawn on a gun carriage through immense and silent crowds to Whitehall, where the Cenotaph, designed by Sir Edwin Lutyens, was unveiled by King George V.

The magnificent oak coffin, donated by the British Undertakers Association, was interred in Westminster Abbey beneath six barrels of earth from Flanders fields and a marble slab: "They buried him among the kings Because he Had done Good toward God and Toward His house". The coffin had an honour guard of 100 holders of the Victoria Cross.

On 17 October 1921 the US Medal of Honour was conferred on the Unknown Warrior by General Pershing. On 11 November 1921 the US Unknown Soldier was awarded the Victoria Cross. A total of 1,356 Victoria Crosses have been awarded for valour to known recipients, the last in October 2006. In December 2010 only six were still living (three British, one Australian and two Gurkha), together with one holder of the VC for Australia and one holder of the VC for New Zealand.

On entering the Abbey on 26 April 1923 to be married to Prince Albert, later King George VI, Lady Elizabeth Bowes-Lyon spontaneously laid her bouquet at the Tomb of the Unknown

Warrior, a gesture which every royal bride since has copied; though some have chosen to do this on the way back from the altar rather than to it.

The tombstone of the Unknown Warrior is the only one in Westminster Abbey upon which it is forbidden to walk.

"The Lord knoweth them that are His"

A RATHER DIFFERENT INTERPRETATION OF THE WORDS "THE LORD KNOWETH THEM THAT ARE HIS"

In 1209, during the 'Albigensian Crusade' against the Cathar heresy in southern France, the forces of Orthodox Catholicism besieged Béziers. Finally the walls were breached and the crusaders prepared to storm the town. Their commander, Simon de Montfort, 5th Earl of Leicester [father of the powerful 6th Earl of the same name (1208–65), who led a revolt against King Henry III and called the first elected English parliament in 1265] observed that not everyone in the city was a heretic: some of them were good Catholics – so how should the inhabitants be treated when the town was taken?

A monk who was present at the siege recorded the answer given by the Papal Legate, Arnaud-Amaury, Abbot of Citeaux to the Crusaders: *"Neca eos omnes. Deus suos agnoscet"* ("Kill them all. God will know his own").

The Crusaders took his advice and killed everyone in Béziers.

Foreword

BY PROFESSOR NORMAN STONE

My university in Turkey, like so many the world over, teaches in English. Every year I ask the students not just why this should be so, but why they wear clothes, listen to music, play a sport, and even eat fast-food, all of them Anglo-American in origin. That gets them thinking, especially when you throw a difficult one at them: why was England the first country to abolish slavery and the last to abolish serfdom (we can take 1772 and 1922 as roughly appropriate dates)? The really good ones understand that serfdom had become a formality, that it had to do with a sort of labour rent and hence property law, whereas slavery was an infringement of individual rights, and therefore fell into the 'you can't do that there here' category, to which George Orwell referred. Even in 1772, with the Mansfield judgement, slavery had been ruled out in England (I am deliberately saying 'England' because Scotland's history is significantly different).

Not so long ago, intelligent Russians and Germans, from of course quite different perspectives, wondered why their countries were not like England. 'Mounya' (later Professor Sir Michael) Postan, by origin a Russian, looked at English agriculture in some amazement: where were the peasants with the square-faced bottles? He became an expert on what he regarded as the decisive period, that of the Black Death, when English farming became different (he also wrote about the British economy in the Second World War and handled economic relations with the USSR). Germans also wondered, and asked why English institutions, though ancient, never the less provided Enlightenment without despotism. There was no political revolution in modern times; and a German historian, Otto Hintze, said that England consisted of living fossils: if you looked at the way it worked, it was a feudal system which had vanished everywhere else. The Church of England for instance, represented a sort of pre-Counter Reformation Catholicism, which did not burn people, though it might burn books. Parliament was a *parlement*, but was not the sort of protection racket that it became in eighteenth-century France. In property law there was a concept, freehold: which, though you can translate it into French (*nue propriété*) or German (*Freibrief*), no one really understands. A freeholder on the Continent (as partly in Scotland too) does not have the rights his English equivalent has, which accounts for the straightness of Napoleonic roads. Even, until not so long ago, an English freeholder could refuse any unsolicited inspection of his property-deeds in the Land Registry. Or rather, we can say here 'his or her' because another peculiarity of English history is that women were registered as property-owners even in Anglo-Saxon times. I might set for my Turks an exam question: which battle do you wish England had lost. There is a very strong case for saying 'Trafalgar', because the oddities and the inefficiencies of England can be quite maddening. But the place works; and her history is endlessly interesting.

This splendid book is a gigantic *Cabinet des Antiquités* and, if you have an interest in English history, it ought to accompany you on any journey or in any waiting room. It kept telling me things that I did not know, details that light up a large surrounding area. It is fair, and of course cannot avoid being in some degree encyclopaedic, but it is more interested in people and events than in the world of Evelyn Waugh's Hooper who 'had no illusions about the Army – or rather no special illusions from the general, enveloping fog from which he observed the universe. He had come to it reluctantly, under compulsion, after he had made every feeble effort in his power to obtain deferment. He accepted it, he said "like the measles". Hooper was no romantic. The history they taught him had few battles in it but, instead, a profusion of detail about humane legislation and recent industrial change'. Jonathan Clark's recent *A World By Itself* is a very efficient survey, with much the same periodisation as this volume, and it carried me without effort from Istanbul to Stansted and then in the bus to Oxford; and if you want an old classic, Trevelyan's *England in the Age of Queen Anne* which I have been reading in the watches of the Ankara night, is endlessly rewarding – though I fear rather smug. But this book of makers and shakers is fun; and you can dip in and out, back and forth.

The British do history very well, in some fields (e.g. the two World Wars) obviously better than others; and quite often foreigners are taken aback by this: why is history so popular at, say university level, whereas Political Science rather languishes? In many countries (Turkey not excluded) history is a subject for would-be primary-school teachers; and in Germany, around the turn of the last century, men (and some women as well, such as Hannah Arendt) deliberately substituted Political Science for a History which they thought was just degenerating into a rubble of meaningless articles and anecdotes. It had no Theory to it and stood condemned. The record of Political Science in predicting has not however, been very good. The late Philip Windsor, who taught at the LSE, had it right when he observed the fall of the Berlin Wall on that famous night and remarked that it was the end of an empire. He was asked: you mean the Soviet Union? He replied no: Political Science, which had so plainly failed to spot the most important development of the century's second half. Historians at least do not claim superior wisdom; though, at a very superficial estimate, I should have said that they were much less wrong than others. But, whatever its virtues, it is also endlessly interesting.

The immediately attractive thing about this book is simply the voracious enthusiasm with which it assembles things that you like me, probably did not know. They are there on every page. I found the early part particularly interesting, because that is the area I know least well: who were the Picts, for instance? They survive with place-names (thus, 'pit', as in Pitlochry, means 'part of'). They seem to have been Ancient Britons, displaced by speakers of a different sort of Celtic or Gaelic. It is curious that the Scots had their own Norman Conquest – names such as Fraser or Menzies or Maxwell (de Mesnières) have a French root; and Urquhart, with a modest change, could be the name of a Channel fishing village. Their ancestors must have been a sort of Norman 'B team', picking up Scottish scraps after the Mowbrays and Courtenays had taken the best bits. On this sort of subject, why is Auchinleck pronounced 'Affleck' and Strachan 'Strawn' (to the polite bewilderment of Continentals, in dealing with the outstanding historian of the First World War). Mysteries. The language is also a mystery, if you judge it from a continental perspective: a sort of cod-German, with a mad system of spelling. According to

Geoffrey Lewis, the great expert on Turkish languages, there was an effort, around the time of the Hundred Years War, to reform English and get rid of the Franco-Latin words. Some monk wrote a work, 'Remorse of Conscience' which, patriotically (and this in pre-printing days) he re-titled 'Inbyte of Inwit'. The English intelligentsia have many vices, many, but no one has ever said they lacked a sense of humour. A shout of laughter went up over London: and language-reform has never been heard of again. Very different from French or German, where the academies got to work – in the German case, imposing a rather literal-minded version of classical Greek on the written language: such that today, Germans sometimes have to read Kant in English to make sense of him. Kant, by the way, had a Scottish grandfather.

There is one expression in German which, applied to English history, makes sense: the old East German ministry of education's *fruhbürgerliche Revolution*, meaning 'early-modern bourgeois revolution'. The English were cashing cheques and enclosing peasants and beheading monarchs in the seventeenth century, where other countries started later: Henry VIII, in this view, was a sort of sawn-off Napoleon. There is something to it just the same. Things were half-modernised, a striking achievement for the era, and it was often enough an enlightenment from below: encouraged by a great aristocracy that was not rendered supine by a Versailles-style monarchy. 'Common Law' does not mean the laws of the Commons: it is a version of *jus commune*, the law common across the Roman Empire, which fell into desuetude in the barbarian invasions; but carried on in England, though roughly. It could be adapted above all to guarantee property, and so Trust Law came up, around 1600, to keep predatory hands off private property (it should really be called 'Mistrust Law', but this is not the only case of a word's meaning its opposite – as for instance, with 'public schools', originally charity schools that were hi-jacked).

Alan Macfarlane (like so many of the best commentators on England, born abroad – in his case, as with the author of this book, in India) made his reputation with a demonstration that this early-modern bourgeois revolution had happened, if at all, in Anglo-Saxon times: property was property, and even women had rights long ago. The continuity of English history is in other words the explanation for so much. Macfarlane came under heavy fire back in the days when the done thing was to say that the English Civil War was indeed a sort of early French Revolution: but nowadays we have gone back to explaining it in terms of religion, which after all is the language that the civil warriors themselves talked, and Macfarlane has established himself again. Anglo-American civilisation is indeed a world of its own; and deserves to be treated as such. Maybe its central trick is to have feudalism without peasants. It is certainly true that the records of English history have survived in extraordinary width and depth, such that there is a vast amount to keep historians busy.

Geoffrey Elton was probably right to put the Tudors at the decisive point. He grew up in Central Europe, with a (not very) Jewish background, and (like Lewis Namier) looked at England from that perspective. Why and where had Germany (and Austria even more so) gone wrong? It is intelligent to look at the Thirty Years War and before that to the Reformation; and so you come to a question, why England got Anglicanism, a sort of pre-Counter-Reformation Catholicism, which burnt books (a good idea, come to think of it) and not people. The dissolution of the monasteries, the confiscation of a third of the land, was at the centre of that change; and though the fashion is to lament what happened, it did transfer resources to productive effect. All such land, held in other countries under the well-named system of *mortmain*, which ruled out sale and therefore also credit, usually meant backward agriculture. To Tim Blanning's *Pursuit of Glory* I owe the reminder that a system in France known as *vaine pâture*, meant to let an old woman's cow graze freely, but also meant that turnips were chewed when half-grown: such that the turnip revolution never worked in France. Did turnips give England 1832 rather than 1789? Arguable.

One thing that the dissolution of the monasteries did do was to finance Trinity College, Cambridge. The famous Holbein portrait of Henry VIII is there, a picture of Asiatic cruelty (I learn from this book that he weighed 30 stone when he died), as also a batty Mary Tudor – and Trinity did well from the connection. Apparently, if it had been a country, the college would have been fifth on the Nobel Prize list; and Cambridge overall outranks France. The survival of those Colleges is characteristic of the development of England. Everywhere else they just became halls of residence, where they did not fall down. In England they survived with their own funds, as little universities, and were extremely productive in the early-modern period (this book is very good indeed on Newton, the star of Trinity), though famously less so in the eighteenth century. I wonder what their future is, just the same. Some just do not have the money; and governments will always harass them for this or that reason. The only College in Oxford that is in financial health is All Souls, which does not take undergraduates at all.

I have written 'England' throughout, missing out Scotland. It is significantly different, for a start poorer, and it had a harsher Reformation. Public authority had to do more because the private world was weaker and more backward than in England: so towns are planned and schools concentrate on essentials. No wonder that Edinburgh and Glasgow contributed more than their due share to the English story. It was not painless. The Master of Stair was responsible for a very nasty episode, the massacre of Glencoe in 1692. His father had written *The Institutions of the Laws of Scotland*, by all accounts a very spirited effort to up-date the system (getting somewhere to live in Scotland is still much less of an ordeal than it is in England). The younger Stair, ambitiously attacking England in the manner of the piranha fish that should have been in the family crest, did not want to know about backward, thieving and disloyal Macdonalds in Glencoe: and had some three dozen of them treacherously killed in the depths of winter. It counts as one of the Scottish moments of martyrdom; and this book points out, rightly, that it was done by Scots. The Stairs got their punishment, in that their daughter and sister respectively was *Lucia di Lammermoor*, of mad scene fame. And this book is good on Scott as well. It is good on a great many things.

Norman Stone
July 2011

Preface

BY THE AUTHOR

THE TELEGRAPH REPORTED THE RESULTS OF A SURVEY CONDUCTED ON 13 MAY 2009:

● British people know more about their favourite celebrities such as David and Victoria Beckham than key historical events, according to a new study ● Nine out of 10 adults knew the names of the Beckhams' first three children, Brooklyn, Romeo and Cruz, but less than half knew that John Major was Prime Minister during the First Gulf War ● A third of Britons thought the previous General Election took place in 2008 rather than 2005, but more than eight out of ten knew Chelsea and England footballer Ashley Cole's wife was X Factor judge Cheryl ● It also emerged that three quarters of the 3,000 surveyed know Kerry Katona's first husband was Bryan McFadden, but 20% don't know 29 February was a Leap Day – one in 10 thought it was either 30 or 31 February ● One in 10 thought Winston Churchill was Prime Minister during the First Gulf War, with four in 10 thinking it was Margaret Thatcher ● The quiz also showed that one in five had no idea that D-Day was in the 1940s. Five per cent of people mistakenly thought that the Pearl Harbour naval base bombed by the Japanese in 1941 is in Ireland.

SKY NEWS REPORTED THE RESULTS OF A SURVEY OF 3,000 PEOPLE ON 8 FEBRUARY 2008:

● The % of Britons who thought the following are mythical: King Richard I (47%); Winston Churchill (23%); and Florence Nightingale (23%) ● Charles Dickens, Gandhi, Cleopatra, Sir Walter Raleigh, Bernard Montgomery and Boudicca were all thought to be characters dreamed up for films and books. However 58% thought that Sherlock Holmes and 33% that Biggles were real people.

ON 24 NOVEMBER 2002 THE BBC COUNTED MORE THAN A MILLION VOTES IN A SURVEY TO NAME BRITAIN'S 100 MOST SIGNIFICANT HISTORICAL INDIVIDUALS, AFTER A TWO-HOUR DEBATE ON LIVE TELEVISION:

- The winner was Sir Winston Churchill, with 447,423 votes. He beat his nearest rival, the engineer Isambard Kingdom Brunel by more than 56,000 votes. So far, so good: but Princess Diana came third, ahead of Darwin, Shakespeare and Newton. John Lennon came seventh
- It was the depressing result of this survey that provoked me to research a list of my own. This book is the result.

The Devil's Dictionary, a satirical reference written by Ambrose Bierce (a San Francisco-based columnist) in 1911, defines "history" as: "An account mostly false, of events mostly unimportant, which are brought about by rulers mostly knaves, and soldiers mostly fools". There is not much truth in this tongue-in-cheek observation, but enough for history taught at schools to have become almost a pariah subject. Where Bierce is right, is that history is principally about people; and **They Made Great Britain** tries to tell it through short biography.

The book was originally titled **Made in Britain** because, within the author's lifetime, this statement implied quality of design and manufacture – and reliability. In 1943 the German Reichsmarschall Hermann Göring said: "In 1940 I could at least fly as far as Glasgow in most of my aircraft, but not now! It makes me furious when I see the Mosquito. I turn green and yellow with envy. The British, who can afford aluminium better than we can, knock together a beautiful wooden aircraft that every piano factory over there is building, and they give it a speed which they have now increased yet again. What do you make of that? There is nothing the British do not have. They have the geniuses and we have the nincompoops. After the war is over I'm going to buy a British radio set – then at least I'll own something that has always worked". Today, the jackboot is firmly on the other foot.

PRICE COMPARISONS OVER THE CENTURIES

Whenever a price or cost has been made mentioned in this book, a contemporary value has usually been bracketed beside it. These comparisons are necessarily approximations: there are various ways of calculating changes in value, the methodology of all of them is inexact; and the method chosen may not always be the most appropriate.

There are five principle ways of attempting to put a present day or 'relative' value on an historical amount: the retail or "consumer" price index (RPI); the gross domestic product (GDP) deflator; "average earnings"; per *capita* GDP; and GDP itself. There are problems with them all, depending on context, and none can claim to be "correct".

The RPI, often used carelessly, measures a basket of goods and services purchased by average households at the time. This is useless over long periods: bread and meat were vital in the 14th century; when insurance, mortgages and mobile telephones did not exist. The GDP deflator, a broad index of inflation, is the best measure for complex products; but it underestimates, sometimes spectacularly, modern values of almost everything else. Per capita GDP is effective in computing the relative values of income and capital; but a better measure of these is "average earnings". Even this index however, can throw up anomalies: Doctor Johnson's dictionary would have cost £6,500 using "average earnings", against the RPI's more believable £560.

GDP, the total output of goods and services in an economy in money terms, is the best measure for large scale government expenditures: such as a castle or a warship or especially, the cost of waging a war. The last full year of WWI is estimated to have cost Britain £2.5 billion in 1918 money: as a share of GDP, this would equate to £840 billion today (UK GDP in 2008 was about £1,553 billion). This gives a more telling impression of the terrible cost of the "war to end war" in specie, as well as in ruined lives, than the RPI (£104 billion) or even "average earnings" (£555 billion).

In 1875 Benjamin Disraeli borrowed £4 million from the House of Rothschild, to buy 44% of the Suez Canal from the cash-strapped Khedive of Egypt. The RPI would value this amount today at £280 million; the GDP deflator at £376 million; "average earnings" at £2.1 billion; and GDP at £4.6 billion – much the most realistic figure, assuming such a transaction could possibly occur in the modern Middle East.

> Lionel Rothschild asked Disraeli's private secretary, "What is your security?". He was told, "The British Government" – to which Rothschild replied: "You shall have it".

GDP is hopeless however, when used to work out the modern price of something too small to configure in these terms. In most cases, "average earnings" is the most accurate and consistent yardstick over the centuries, even over relatively short periods.

The *Daily Mail* cost half an old penny (1/2d) in 1896, its first year of publication: the RPI would price this today at 18 (decimal) pence; the GDP deflator, at 22p; and *per capita* GDP, at £1.24. "Average earnings" would suggest 99p (the weekday cost in 2010 was 50p, but 80p on Saturday). It is the method used throughout the book – although by far the most logical, readers should nonetheless view the results with some caution.

From this last example, it is clear that any government which links state pensions to the RPI, rather than "average earnings", is guilty of knowingly short-changing pensioners.

A RHYME TO HELP SCHOOLCHILDREN REMEMBER THE KINGS AND QUEENS OF ENGLAND

Willie, Willie, Harry, Steve,
  Harry, Dick, John, Harry Three,
Edward One, Two, Three, Dick Two,
  Henry Four, Five, Six, then who?
Edward Four, Five, Dick the Bad,
  Harrys twain and Ned, the lad.
Mary, Lizzie, James the Vain,
  Charlie, Charlie, James again.
William and Mary, Anne o'Gloria,
  Four Georges, William and Victoria.
Edward Seven, Georgie Five,
  Edward, George and Liz (alive)

Acknowledgements

The first and by far the most important person that I must thank is my friend of over
fifty years, Richard Raynsford. He has been more than a colleague in the writing of this book.
Without him, I doubt whether I would have undertaken the project at all, let alone finished it.
My gratitude knows no bounds: for his skill and hard work in the preliminary drafting of many
of the articles; and for his humour, optimism and inspiration.

I must thank too, his brilliant daughter-in-law Clemmie Raynsford for researching much
of his material.

Another old friend who gave me enormous help and motivation was Jeremy White.
Nigel Cartwright, Jon Connell and Christopher Wilkins were very kind too.

Special thanks must go to Helen Stirling, who drew all forty of the clear and beautiful
maps; to Isambard Thomas for the elegant design of the book; to Nicole Harley; and to my
publisher David Campbell. I am grateful to Henry Strutt for introducing me to the latter.

My thanks also to Rothschild Wealth Management, for the generous support and
encouragement the firm gave me.

I wish I could thank individually the many other friends who helped me, but I hope that
they will know who they are. Their advice was always valued and often followed.

Finally I must thank my family for their patience over the last five years. My son Sam spent
hours programming my computer, showing me how to use and make the most of it; and much
else besides. I cannot thank him enough.

They Made Great Britain is bound to contain errors, all of them mine. It is subjective,
sometimes extremely so, and inevitably there will be omissions: as it is not a proper history, but
a book to entertain, perhaps that will not matter.

Adrian Sykes
19 June 2011

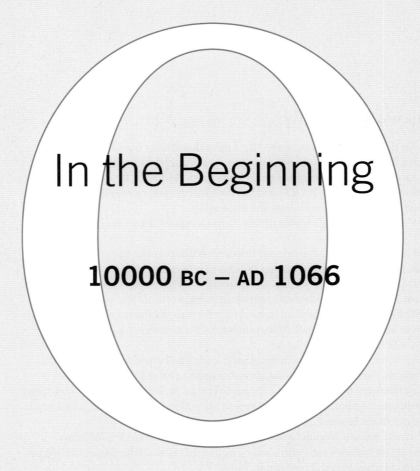

In the Beginning

10000 BC – AD 1066

Principum amicitias!

THE BRITISH ISLES IN 1965
(showing all the county boundaries before changes made in 1974)

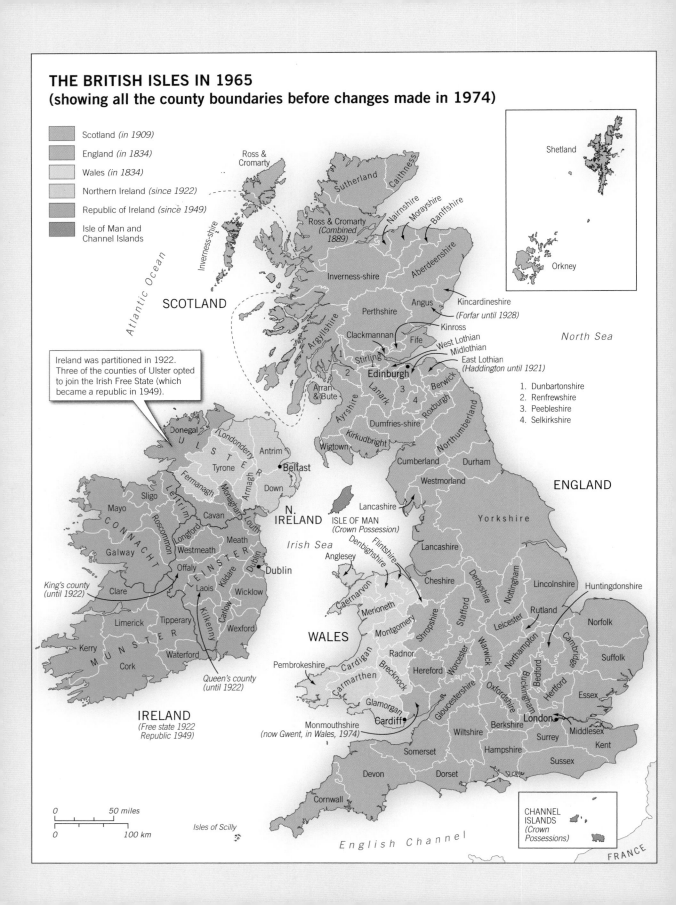

Scotland *(in 1909)*

England *(in 1834)*

Wales *(in 1834)*

Northern Ireland *(since 1922)*

Republic of Ireland *(since 1949)*

Isle of Man and Channel Islands

Shetland

Orkney

Ross & Cromarty

Inverness-shire

Atlantic Ocean

Sutherland

Caithness

Ross & Cromarty *(Combined 1889)*

Nairnshire

Morayshire

Banffshire

SCOTLAND

Inverness-shire

Aberdeenshire

Perthshire

Angus

Kincardineshire *(Forfar until 1928)*

North Sea

Clackmannan

Kinross

Fife

West Lothian

Midlothian

East Lothian *(Haddington until 1921)*

1
2

Stirling

Edinburgh

Argyllshire

Arran & Bute

Lanark

3
4

Berwick

Roxburgh

Northumberland

Ireland was partitioned in 1922. Three of the counties of Ulster opted to join the Irish Free State (which became a republic in 1949).

Ayrshire

Dumfries-shire

Kirkudbright

Wigtown

1. Dunbartonshire
2. Renfrewshire
3. Peebleshire
4. Selkirkshire

Cumberland

Durham

ENGLAND

Westmorland

Donegal

U L S T E R

Londonderry

Antrim

Tyrone

Belfast

Fermanagh

Down

Yorkshire

Sligo

Leitrim

Monaghan

Armagh

Louth

Lancashire

Mayo

Roscommon

Longford

Cavan

N. IRELAND

ISLE OF MAN *(Crown Possession)*

Lancashire

CONNACHT

Westmeath

Meath

Irish Sea

Denbighshire

Flintshire

Lincolnshire

Huntingdonshire

Galway

Offaly

Kildare

Dublin

Anglesey

Cheshire

Derbyshire

Nottingham

King's county *(until 1922)*

LEINSTER

Laois

Wicklow

Dublin

Caernarvon

Merioneth

Montgomery

Shropshire

Stafford

Warwick

Leicester

Rutland

Northampton

Norfolk

Clare

Kilkenny

Carlow

Wexford

Cambridge

Suffolk

Limerick

Tipperary

WALES

Radnor

Worcester

Hereford

Oxfordshire

Bedford

Hertford

Essex

Kerry

MUNSTER

Waterford

Queen's county *(until 1922)*

Pembrokeshire

Cardigan

Carmarthen

Brecknock

Gloucestershire

Buckingham

London

Middlesex

Cork

Glamorgan

Cardiff

Berkshire

Surrey

Kent

IRELAND *(Free state 1922 Republic 1949)*

Monmouthshire *(now Gwent, in Wales, 1974)*

Wiltshire

Hampshire

Sussex

Somerset

Devon

Dorset

CHANNEL ISLANDS *(Crown Possessions)*

0   50 miles

0   100 km

Isles of Scilly

Cornwall

English Channel

FRANCE

Dublin

Dublin

In the beginning

A BRIEF HISTORY OF THE BRITISH ISLES

The British Isles (French: *Îles Britanniques*; Irish Gaelic or Erse: *Oileáin Iarthair Eorpa;* Manx: *Ellanyn Goaldagh*; Scottish Gaelic: *Eileanan Breatannach*; Welsh: *Ynysoedd Prydain*) consist of two sovereign states: the United Kingdom of Great Britain and Northern Ireland and the Republic of Ireland. The British Isles include the crown dependencies of the Isle of Man and the Channel Islands, the latter only by tradition and association as they are not physically part of the main group of islands.

More world travellers, explorers, surveyors, voyagers and navigators have started out from the British Isles than from any other country in recorded history. In the 20th century it was established that the islands themselves had drifted across the surface of the planet over the last 3 billion years almost as much as the people who later came to inhabit them.

They have moved from well south of the equator to the far north and back again; separated; joined up; moved across the Atlantic from left to right; encompassed huge mountain ranges; been covered by equatorial forests, swamps and deserts; and been submerged beneath oceans that came and went. The geological endowment of this peregrination has given a significant advantage to the people of these islands over the last thousand years (it is said that Britain is an enormous coal field floating in a sea of oil), but all histories have to start somewhere – and ours begins around 15 million years ago, during the Miocene period (23 to 5 million years ago), when North America and Greenland separated from Eurasia, leaving the British Isles as a peninsula of Europe.

Cranium of Homo heidelbergensis

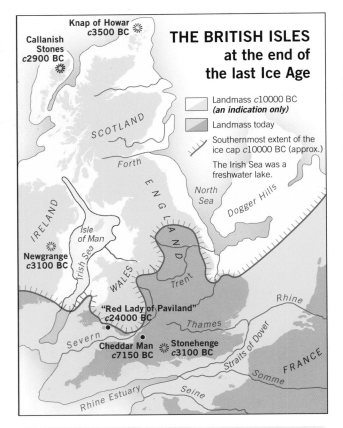

THE BRITISH ISLES at the end of the last Ice Age

Knap of Howar
c3500 BC

Callanish
Stones
c2900 BC

SCOTLAND

Forth

IRELAND

Isle
of Man

Newgrange
c3100 BC

Irish Sea

WALES

E N G L A N D

North
Sea

Dogger Hills

Trent

Rhine

Thames

"Red Lady of Paviland"
c24000 BC

Severn

Cheddar Man
c7150 BC

Stonehenge
c3100 BC

Straits of Dover

FRANCE

Somme

Rhine Estuary

Seine

Landmass *c10000 BC*
(an indication only)

Landmass today

Southernmost extent of the
ice cap *c10000 BC* (approx.)

The Irish Sea was a
freshwater lake.

Several ancient civilizations in the Middle East record a catastrophic inundation, first mentioned in the Sumerian *Epic of Gilgamesh* and later by the Babylonian priest Berossus, which is described in *The Bible (Genesis)* as the Great Flood – even the Koran refers to it, albeit two thousand years later.

The event most likely to have inspired these accounts is thought to have been the collapse of the land barrier separating the Mediterranean from the Black Sea (then a huge 4,000 feet deep freshwater lake), creating the Bosphorus. The suddenness of the breach, the surge and the volume of water (400 times that of the Niagara Falls) destroyed all the towns on the southern, now Turkish coast of the Black Sea. Traces of these Neolithic (New Stone Age) settlements have been found over 400 feet underwater, perfectly preserved. At that depth the Black Sea is almost sterile, impregnated with hydrogen sulphide – without oxygen and the bacteria that would have destroyed all remains of human life.

Mount Ararat lies less than 200 miles south-east, giving some plausibililty to the story of Noah's Ark. The timing of this disaster has been dated to around 6000 BC. It is possible that it occurred at much the same time, and for the same reason, that the English Channel was created: a 400 foot rise in global sea levels.

The next period (the Pleiocene), lasting from 5 to 1.8 million years ago, was followed by the Pleistocene which lasted from 1.8 million to 10,000 years ago – the end of the last Ice Age. The Earth has been, and still is, in an interglacial (a period of relative warmth) known as the Holocene for the last 10,000 years.

Some 750,000 years ago when the islands were still joined to continental Europe, *Homo erectus*, the first hominid to leave Africa, brought Palæolithic (Old Stone Age) tool use to the south-east of modern England. About 250,000 years later *Homo heidelbergensis,* ancestor of Neanderthal man, followed with more advanced tools, like those found at Boxgrove in West Sussex. Modern humans appeared with the Aurignacian culture about 30,000 years ago, evidenced by the "Red Lady of Paviland" (in fact a man, discovered in south-west Wales in 1823), carbon-dated to about 24000 BC.

He and his kind, nomadic hunter-gatherers, had followed the retreating ice sheets in search of mammoths, mastodons, aurochs (bison) and enormous deer during a previous interglacial, only to be driven south again when the ice returned.

The last ice age ended around 10,000 years ago. Mesolithic (Middle Stone Age) hunter-gatherers had fanned out to all parts of the islands, now warmed by the Gulf Stream, within 2,000 years when rising sea levels cut them off them from the European continent. Immigrants chiefly came from the ice age refuges in the Pyrenees and Iberian peninsula. Most ancestors of the present British Isles population arrived on this tide of immigration. As the ice cap over northern Europe finally began to melt at the end of the Pleistocene period, the Irish Sea became a lake and the Thames a tributary of the Rhine. By 6500 BC the Irish Sea had flooded, separating Ireland from Britain; and the North Sea had burst through the Straits of Dover. Britain too had become an island and the 'land bridge' from Europe had gone forever.

The earliest permanent inhabitants of the British Isles arrived shortly before the Channel was breached. Settlements and monuments, over 5,000 years old and widely separated, had in common (however bleak the environment) one important feature: a lack of trees, which would have been impossible to clear with tools made only of flint and antler. Traces of primitive agriculture have been found on bare hillsides and in

The Scots Pine was one of the few trees to survive the last Ice Age and once covered Scotland in the Caledonian Forest

breaks in the heavily forested downlands from Orkney to southern England. Recent genetic studies of Y-chromosome (male) distribution prove conclusively that the blood of these Neolithic (New Stone Age) settlers continues to course through most of the modern population of the British Isles.

Around 6,500 years ago, agriculture spread throughout the newly created British Isles with the Neolithic (New Stone Age) Revolution. The western seaways also brought megalithic (building with large stones) culture. The earliest existing stone house in northern Europe (3500 BC), is at Knap of Howar, in Orkney. Maes Howe, also in Orkney, Newgrange in Ireland and Stonehenge in southern England are similar to megalithic monuments in France and Spain – "henge" means "hanging rock" and is only applied to Neolithic stone monoliths found in Britain. Further cultural changes in the Bronze Age (2000 BC) were followed by the construction of numerous hill-forts and trading links with continental Europe during the Iron Age (700 BC until the Roman occupation)

Around 325 BC Pytheas, a Greek metal trader from Massalia (present day Marseilles), who wrote the earliest account of the British Isles, mentions a number of Celtic tribes. The names *Priteni* or *Pretani,* were used to describe the whole of the British Isles. *Hiberni* was the name given to the inhabitants of Ireland and *Albiones* to those of Britain. It is unlikely however, that these "Beaker folk" (so called from their pottery) identified themselves with any social group larger than their own tribes.

The Celts are thought to have originated as neolithic farmers in Anatolia (modern Turkey), who travelled westwards through southern Europe from about 7000 BC. Modern analysis of the male Y-chromosome indicates that the Brythonic-speaking tribes who settled in Cornwall and Wales had inhabited the Pyrenean or Basque Ice Age refuges of south-west France; whilst their Goedelic-speaking (Irish and later, Scottish) cousins came from further south, having migrated to Spain from the near east, probably Greece. Both groups would have had swarthy skins and dark curly hair.

Drifting northwards from about 3200 BC (the early Bronze Age) along the Atlantic 'façade' or west coast of France, both Celtish groupings followed the western coastlines of Britain and Ireland (the earliest copper mines in Ireland date from around 2450 BC). The Goedelic and Brythonic language subdivision is thought to have occurred between 900 and 500 BC. Genetic testing however, indicates that far from eradicating the earliest inhabitants, Celtic influence was mainly cultural and linguistic. In the Scottish Highlands, the Caledonians or *Picti* (Latin for "the painted people") spoke a language that is now extinct but presumed to have been Brythonic.

At **Knap of Howar**, on the Orkney island of Papa Westray, a Neolithic farmstead has been wonderfully well preserved. It is claimed to be the oldest stone house in northern Europe. Radiocarbon dating shows that it was occupied from 3500 BC to 3100 BC – 400 years earlier than similar houses at Skara Brae, also in Orkney. Primitive agriculture was only possible where there were no trees to fell with only stone axes.

Newgrange *(Dún Fhearghusa)* is one of the passage tombs of the *Brú na Bóinne* complex in County Meath, one of the most famous prehistoric sites in the world. Newgrange was built in such a way that at dawn on the shortest day of the year, the winter solstice, a narrow beam of sunlight for a very short time illuminates the floor of the chamber at the end of the long passageway. It was built 200 years either side of 3100 BC . It is more than 500 years older than the Great Pyramid of Giza in Egypt; and is roughly contemporary with the earliest stage of Stonehenge.

Newgrange lay hidden for over 4,000 years until in the late 17th century men looking for building stone uncovered it – and described it as a cave. Newgrange was excavated and considerably restored between 1962–75.

Silbury Hill is a 130 foot high mound in Wiltshire. It is the tallest man-made mound in Europe and one of the world's largest.

Composed principally of chalk excavated from the surrounding area, the mound covers about 5 acres. It is a display of immense technical skill and prolonged control over labour and resources. Archæologists calculate that Silbury Hill was built about 2750 BC; and that it took 18 million man-hours, or 500 men working 15 years to deposit and shape 8.75 million cubic feet of earth and fill, on top of a natural hill. The base of the hill is circular and 550 feet in diameter. No one has any idea why and by whom it was built.

Almost a century after Julius Cæsar made a reconnaissance in force (54 BC), Aulus Plautius landed at Richborough in Kent in AD 43: and proceeded to transform Celtic Britain into a province of the Roman Empire called *Britannia*. The Romans governed most of the island of Great Britain: but, despite Agricola's defeat of 30,000 Picts led by Calgacus at Mons Graupius (in Aberdeenshire) in 84, never subdued the highlands of *Caledonia* (Scotland) – probably deterred by the Scottish midge. Around 180 the Romans withdrew to Hadrian's Wall, ensuring that friendly tribes provided a buffer zone

The Uffington White Horse in Oxfordshire is a 374 feet long stylised hill figure cut into the turf, dating back some 3,000 years. It is the only chalk figure generally accepted as 'prehistoric'.

further north to the Antonine Wall, between the Firths of Clyde and Forth. Roman interaction with Ireland was limited to a minimal trade. From the 5th century, raids on Roman Britain by Germanic tribes escalated and many Britons migrated to *Armorica* (Brittany), which was already Brythonic-speaking from trade and religious links, to escape them. The Romans renamed Armorica *Brittania* (presumably to differentiate it from *Britannia*).

The abrupt departure of the Roman legions in 410 was followed by the formation of a number of Anglo-Saxon kingdoms. Vikings from Norway first raided Lindisfarne, Iona and Ireland in the 790s; with further raids settling Orkney and Shetland – followed by the Western Isles, Caithness, Sutherland (a southern land to a Scandinavian), the Isle of Man and Galloway. Danish Vikings attacked Northumbria, East Anglia and Mercia; establishing their capital at Jórvík (York). Norwegians founded the Irish cities of Limerick, Waterford, Wexford, Cork, Arklow and Dublin. The kingdom of Wessex finally blocked Danish expansion in England and united the heptarchy of seven Anglo-Saxon kingdoms into one in 937; which was subsequently ruled by both English and Danish kings until 1066.

In 889 Donald II became the first King of Alba rather than just King of the Picts. Constantine II and his successors amalgamated the kingdoms north of the English border into the Kingdom of Scotland – and fixed its southern border on the Tweed in 1018 (little different to the Anglo-Scottish border today). Following Roman abandonment of Britain, Wales was divided into a number of Brythonic kingdoms, achieving unification for only one short spell in about 942.

Ireland, having evolved into ten provincial kingdoms by the tenth century, was virtually unified by Brian Boru early in the eleventh. Norwegian Viking settlements were checked in 980 by the Battle of Tara; and, following the Battle of Clontarf in 1014, those Norsemen that remained were expelled from Ireland or entirely assimilated. Brian Boru's death in the battle caused a power vacuum and a series of bloody factional wars. The Norwegians fell back on Scotland and the Western Isles – while in 1016, the English throne was taken by the Danish King Cnut ("the Great").

Stonehenge dates from *c.*3100 BC

Callanish Standing Stones, Isle of Lewis, a cross-shaped setting of standing stones (erected *c.*2900 BC)

Celtic crosses (AD400–800) are especially identified with the Picts of Highland Scotland

Maiden Castle is the largest Iron Age hill fort in Europe, covering an area of 47 acres. 'Maiden' may derive from the Celtic *Mai Dun*, meaning "great hill". It is two miles south of Dorchester, in Dorset. After more than 2,000 years, the earthworks are still immense, some ramparts rising to a height of 20 feet. Construction of Maiden Castle probably began around 3000 BC.

In the late Stone Age or early Bronze Age a massive ditch and bank some 600 yards long were constructed. The hill fort that has survived dates from *c.*450–300 BC.

Seahenge is a Bronze Age monument discovered in 1998, just off the coast of of Norfolk at Holme-next-the-Sea.

It is possible to date the creation of Seahenge very accurately. The date of felling the oaks was in the spring or summer of 2049 BC.

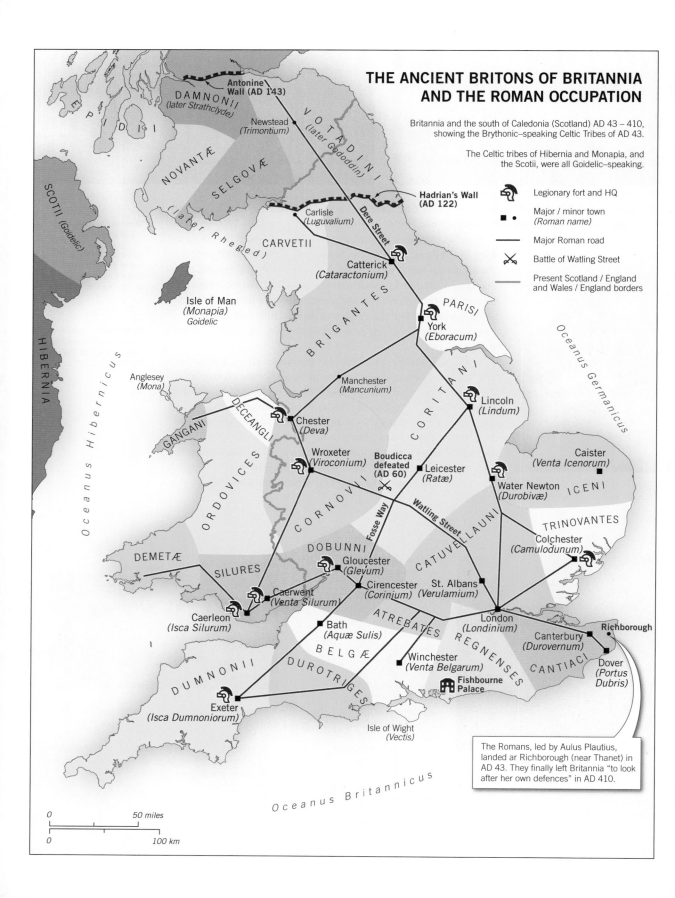

THE ANCIENT BRITONS OF BRITANNIA AND THE ROMAN OCCUPATION

Britannia and the south of Caledonia (Scotland) AD 43 – 410, showing the Brythonic–speaking Celtic Tribes of AD 43.

The Celtic tribes of Hibernia and Monapia, and the Scotii, were all Goidelic–speaking.

Legionary fort and HQ

■ • Major / minor town
(Roman name)

Major Roman road

✕ Battle of Watling Street

Present Scotland / England
and Wales / England borders

The Romans, led by Aulus Plautius, landed ar Richborough (near Thanet) in AD 43. They finally left Britannia "to look after her own defences" in AD 410.

Tribes / regions:

EPIDII

DAMNONII
(later Strathclyde)

NOVANTÆ

SELGOVÆ

VOTADINI
(later Gododdin)

Antonine Wall (AD 143)

Newstead
(Trimontium)

Hadrian's Wall
(AD 122)

Carlisle
(Luguvalium)

CARVETII

Dere Street

SCOTII
(Goidelic)

Catterick
(Cataractonium)

BRIGANTES

PARISI

York
(Eboracum)

Isle of Man
(Monapia)
Goidelic

HIBERNIA

Oceanus Hibernicus

Anglesey
(Mona)

DECEANGLI

GANGANI

Manchester
(Mancunium)

Chester
(Deva)

Wroxeter
(Viroconium)

CORITANI

Lincoln
(Lindum)

Oceanus Germanicus

Caister
(Venta Icenorum)

Boudicca
defeated
(AD 60)

Leicester
(Ratæ)

ORDOVICES

CORNOVII

Water Newton
(Durobivæ)

ICENI

Fosse Way

Watling Street

CATUVELLAUNI

TRINOVANTES

Colchester
(Camulodunum)

DEMETÆ

SILURES

DOBUNNI

Gloucester
(Glevum)

Cirencester
(Corinium)

St. Albans
(Verulamium)

London
(Londinium)

Caerwent
(Venta Silurum)

Caerleon
(Isca Silurum)

Bath
(Aquæ Sulis)

ATREBATES

BELGÆ

Winchester
(Venta Belgarum)

REGNENSES

Richborough

Canterbury
(Durovernum)

CANTIACI

Dover
(Portus Dubris)

DUMNONII

DUROTRIGES

Fishbourne
Palace

Exeter
(Isca Dumnoniorum)

Isle of Wight
(Vectis)

Oceanus Britannicus

0   50 miles

0   100 km

CARATACUS (OR CARACTACUS)

In the first century AD, Caratacus, son of the Catuvellaunian king Cunobelinus (Shakespeare's Cymbeline) encroached westwards into the territory of the Atrebates. Verica, King of the Atrebates was expelled, fled to Rome and appealed to the emperor Claudius. This appeal was used by Claudius as a pretext to launch his invasion of Britain in 43 (a *casus belli* was needed even then).

Cunobelinus had died before the invasion: leaving Caratacus and his brother Togodumnus, employing guerrilla tactics, to organise the defence of the country against Aulus Plautius's legions. They were defeated however, in two crucial battles on the rivers Medway and Thames. Togodumnus was killed and the Catuvellauni territories were overrun: but Caratacus survived and carried on a determined resistance further west.

In his *Annals*, Tacitus identified Caratacus, now as the leader of the Silures and Ordovices (in Wales), resisting Plautius's successor as governor, Publius Ostorius Scapula. In 51 Caratacus was finally defeated in a set-piece battle somewhere in Ordovician territory. He escaped capture and fled north to the lands of the Brigantes (in modern Yorkshire). The Brigantian Queen Cartimandua found it in her interest to stay loyal to Rome and handed him over in chains. Caratacus was sent to Rome, where Tacitus records his address to the senate: "If the degree of my nobility and fortune had been matched by moderation in success, I would have come to this City as a friend rather than a captive, nor would you have disdained to receive with a treaty of peace one sprung from brilliant ancestors and commanding a great many nations. But my present lot, disfiguring as it is for me, is magnificent for you. I had horses, men, arms, and wealth: what wonder if I was unwilling to lose them? If you wish to command everyone, does it really follow that everyone should accept your slavery? If I were now being handed over as one who had surrendered immediately, neither my fortune nor your glory would have achieved brilliance. It is also true that in my case any reprisal will be followed by oblivion. On the other hand, if you preserve me safe and sound, I shall be an eternal example of your clemency".

He made such an impression that he was pardoned and allowed to live peacefully in Rome. After being freed, according to Dio Cassius (a Roman historian), Caratacus himself was so struck by the city of Rome that he said: "And can you then, who have got such possessions and so many of them, covet our poor tents?".

In 1960 workmen in Sussex, installing a water main, discovered a spectacular Roman building. The size of Buckingham Palace, it had under-floor heating, a separate bathhouse and 50 rooms with mosaics. **Fishbourne Palace**, near Chichester, was one of the most luxurious buildings in the Roman Empire. It was built around AD 60 – probably for Cogidubnus (died *c*.70), king of the Regnenses, as a reward for his help during their invasion.

Hadrian's Wall

HADRIAN'S WALL

Hadrian's Wall was built between AD 122–130, as a defensive fortification to protect the northern frontier of the Roman province of Britannia against Pictish invasion. The wall stretched 73 miles from Wallsend, near Newcastle to Bowness, on the shores of the Solway Firth. The wall consisted of a ditch 10 feet deep and 20 feet wide, fortified every mile with eighty small, gated forts, manned by a dozen troops; with pairs of intermediate turrets used for observation and signalling.

A *vallum* (rampart), running behind the southern side of the wall, was used as a military road. Three Roman legions built the wall within eight years. Hadrian's Wall, garrisoned by around 10,000 auxiliary troops of the Roman army and not by the legions, remained in use until the Romans abandoned Britain in 410. The Wall was declared a World Heritage Site in 1987 (there are 28 in the United Kingdom).

ENGLISH WINE

The Romans introduced the grape vine to *Britannia* – and glass, for bottles. When Emperor Constantine made Christianity Rome's official religion in 312, wine production in England was encouraged, for use in religious ceremonies – which ceased with the departure of the Romans in 410. When St Augustine arrived in Britain in 597 however, it is likely that there was a modest revival of wine making.

But it was not until the 950s, 75 years after the Vikings were defeated by King Alfred, that vineyards flourished again, in Somerset. By the time of the Domesday book (1086) there were forty-six vineyards in southern England. In the 1200s religious orders were using wine from Kent across southern England to Herefordshire. When Henry VIII came to the throne in 1509 there were at least 130 vineyards in England and Wales – 11 of them owned by the Crown, 67 by noble families and 52 by monasteries.

A relatively warm period ended *c*.1530; and a 'little ice age' set in for 300 years – oxen were roasted on the Thames in the 1660s. Vineyards did not disappear completely, but ceased to be profitable: until 1951, when the first modern vineyard was planted at Hambledon, in Hampshire. In 2008 there were 416, mostly in the south of England.

THE HERBARIUM

Most plant species in the British Isles were wiped out in the last ice age, though many had found their way back again from Europe before the arrival of the Romans. With the devotion to good food that they bequeathed modern Italy, the Romans also brought with them to Britain: parsley, borage, chervil, coriander, dill, fennel, mint, thyme, garlic, leeks, onions, rosemary, sage, savory, sweet marjoram, radishes, turnips, carrots, cabbages and peas. They also, in addition to the grape vine, brought apples and pears – and stinging nettles, to rub their limbs with to keep warm.

THE ROMANS ENRICHED BRITAIN'S WILDLIFE TOO

Marcus Terentius Varra (116–27 BC) stated that the legions bred rabbits for the table in Spain. The oldest rabbit remains in Britain, found at Lynford in Norfolk (*c*. AD 100), are clearly

Roman. Coney, the Old English word for rabbit, which comes from the Latin *Oryctolagus cuniculus* gave its name to Coney Island in the US – and, via the Gaelic *Coineagan*, to the district of Renfrewshire and surname, Cunninghame. The Romans also introduced the common pheasant, *Phasianus colchicus*, to Britain. Until recently it was thought that the Normans introduced fallow deer *(Dama dama)* to England, but finds at Fishbourne Palace make clear that it was in fact, the Romans.

VORTIGERN

Vortigern (*Gwrtheyrn* in Welsh), was a legendary 5th century Romano-British king about whom very little is known – except that he gave away his kingdom. Vortigern is described as the *superbus tyrannus* ("proud tyrant") by the 6th century writer Gildas, who invited the Angles to settle the eastern half of England, in exchange for protection against Pictish invaders from Caledonia in the north. The Angles accepted his offer – but overwhelmed Vortigern and set up their own kingdoms.

From *c.*455, pagan kings of Kent held power over a territory roughly the same as the modern county, until King Æthelbert I (died *c.*616) was converted to Christianity by St Augustine in 597. The traditional founders of the Kentish royal house are the two Jute brothers Hengist (died *c.*488) and Horsa (killed *c.*455). Bede identified them as the leaders of the Germanic forces invited to Britain by Vortigern, as described by Gildas, and he calculated that they had arrived in 449. That such mercenary captains should turn on their erstwhile employers is highly plausible. The chronicle relates that Hengist and Horsa fought Vortigern at Ægelesthrep (Aylesford) in 455, with the result that Hengist became king. Horsa was killed in the battle – Bede reports that a monument bearing his name was erected in east Kent. In spite of such details it is probable that Hengist and Horsa were mythical figures. Their alliterative names invite comparison with other founders in Indo-European legend, such as Romulus and Remus. Their names mean "stallion" and "horse".

KING ARTHUR

It is doubtful that King Arthur (supposedly *c.*480–*c.*550) ever existed as an identifiable individual. The earliest references to "Arthur" are in a 6th century poem by Aneirin; in the *Historia Brittonum*, by the "unrestrainedly inventive" but obscure Welsh historian Nennius; and in the *Annales Cambriæ* a century later.

Nennius describes Arthur not as a king but as *dux bellorum* (war-leader) who fought twelve battles against the Anglo-Saxons, culminating in a great victory at Mons Badonicus (Mount Badon). The *Annales Cambriæ* also describe Arthur's victory at Badon, "in which Arthur carried the cross of our Lord Jesus Christ for three days and nights on his shoulders: and the British were victors"; as well as reporting another Arthurian victory at Camlann in 537, "in which Arthur and Medrawt fell". The contemporary writer Gildas, says that the date of the battle of Badon was in the same year as his birth (*c.*516). Extraordinarily, although Badon certainly took place, no one has ever been able to prove where it was.

Gildas is the first to mention Medrawt, or Mordred; but it is unclear whether Arthur and Mordred were allies or enemies, or even whom Arthur

Nennius (died 809) was a shadowy figure, possibly a student of Elfodugww, Bishop of Gwynedd, who in 768 is said to have persuaded the early Celtic church in Wales to celebrate Easter on the same date as the rest of the Church in Britain.

Annales Cambriæ (Annals of Wales) is a body of Celtic-Latin texts dating from before the 10th century. The annals are not peculiar to Wales but also describe events in Ireland, Scotland, England, Cornwall and France.

Gildas, an early Celtic saint (died 570), wrote *De Excidio et Conquestu Britanniæ* ("On the Ruin and Conquest of Britain"): in which he records the battle of Badon but makes no mention of Arthur. He states that Ambrosius Aurelianus (or *Emrys Wledig* in Welsh), said to have been a 6th century warrior, was the "battle-leader".

The Arthurian legend, which took root in the 12th and 13th centuries developed the theme of Arthur as a champion of Christianity and soon embraced his association with the Holy Grail. Camelot is the fictional castle and court associated with him. Later romances depict it as the fantastic capital of Arthur's realm, from which he fought many of the battles and pursued the quests that made up his life. Camelot as a place is associated with ideals of justice, bravery and truth, the virtues Arthur and his knights embody in the romances. It is absent from the early material; and its location, if it even existed, is unknown. Thus most modern academic scholars regard it as being entirely fictional, its vague geography being perfect for writers of romantic fiction: the Arthurian scholar Norris Lacy commented that, "Camelot, located nowhere in particular, can be anywhere".

The Winchester Round Table was first recorded in 1463. Tree-ring and radiocarbon dating methods and a study of carpentry technique indicate that the table was constructed in the 1270s, at the beginning of King Edward I's reign. The table was probably used at the many tournaments which Edward liked to hold. These were sometimes known as 'Round Tables'.

The little that is known about Malory is intriguing. He was probably born *c.*1420 (maybe as early as 1405). He died in March 1471, soon after finishing *Le Morte d'Arthur*. Malory was twice an M.P. but was also accused of a number of serious crimes during the 1450s: including burglary, rape, stealing sheep and plotting to kill the Duke of Buckingham. He escaped from gaol twice, once fighting his way out and once by swimming a moat – but he was never brought to trial or convicted. In the 1460s he was pardoned by Henry VI, though Edward IV regarded him with less favour. Malory wrote at least part of *Le Morte d'Arthur* in prison.

Dozmary Pool on Bodmin Moor in Cornwall, "deep, cold and lifeless", is supposed to be the lake into which Sir Bedivere threw Excalibur after Arthur's death. In the droughts of 1859 and 1976 the pool proved to be shallow when it dried out – with no sword, or the arm that was said to have risen from the surface to catch it.

was fighting. It is likely that both accounts derive from the same sources, since the *Historia Brittonum* also refers to Arthur carrying the "image of Holy Mary ever virgin upon his shoulders". This imagery may well hark back to the victory of the Christian Emperor Constantine in 312 at the Milvian Bridge near Rome, where he won control of the Roman Empire. Before the battle, Constantine had emblazoned the shields of his soldiers with the Cross of Christ.

These sparse references made in the *Historia Brittonum* and the *Annales Cambriæ* provide the only evidence for an historical 6th century Arthur. Both texts originated between one and two hundred years after the events they describe.

Over the next two hundred years these bare facts, particularly popular in Wales, fed legends, stories and romances – summarised as "the matter of Britain" by Geoffrey of Monmouth in 1135. Chrétien de Troyes, writing fifty years later and drawing heavily on Welsh myth, elaborated the legend of a great leader, by focusing on Arthur. He hypothesised an adulterous love affair between Lancelot and Arthur's wife Queen Guinevere, together with the concept of a search for the Holy Grail. By 1225 these embellishments had been gathered together in the Vulgate Cycle which introduced the panoply of Arthurian legend, including the fictitious Merlin and the sword Excalibur; and the pilgrimage undergone by Sir Lancelot's son, the pure knight Sir Galahad – which culminated in his vision of God.

In 1470 Sir Thomas Malory capitalised on the Continental fascination with the Arthurian legend in his chivalrous romance, *Le Morte d'Arthur* (Death of Arthur). This was the first work of prose to be written in English; and, in 1485 was one of the first to be printed by William Caxton. It became an immediate best-seller.

Malory drew heavily on French chivalrous romances for his inspiration, but *Le Morte d'Arthur* is distinguished from these sources by emphasis on the Round Table fellowship of knights and the conflict of loyalties which eventually destroyed them.

ANEIRIN

Aneirin (or Neirin) was a Brythonic poet from the late 6th century, possibly employed at the Cumbric-Brythonic kingdom of Gododdin, with its capital at Edinburgh. His most celebrated work is *Y Gododdin,* a series of elegies (laments for the dead) written in Old Welsh for the warriors of Gododdin who fell in battle against the Angles of Deira and Bernicia (the two kingdoms of Northumbria), at the Battle of Catraeth (probably Catterick in North Yorkshire) *c.*600. The first known reference to King Arthur is found in one verse: as an exemplar of honour and bravery, with whom one valiant British warrior who was killed is compared.

Dumbarton Rock

Aneirin wrote *Y Gododdin* in Dumbarton Castle, which stands on a plug of volcanic basalt that rises above the river Clyde. *Dùn Breatainn* (the Gaelic for "fortress of the Britons") has the longest recorded history of any stronghold in Great Britain. Its strategic position and virtual impregnability made it the natural capital of the (Old Welsh) Strathclyde Britons, who founded (and named) Glasgow, from the 5th century until the ninth.

There had been a settlement on the site at least since the Iron Age, whose inhabitants traded with the Romans, and possibly much earlier. The first written mention of the fort is in a letter from Saint Patrick to King Ceretic of *Alt Clut* in the late 5th century asking him to stop kidnapping Christians and selling them into slavery.

In 870 the Vikings besieged Dumbarton (as *Alt Clut* was now called) for four months, eventually taking the fortress when the well ran dry. King Olaf returned to the Viking city of Dublin in 871, with two hundred ships full of slaves and treasure. Olaf was celebrated in Icelandic Sagas as the "greatest warrior-king in the Western Sea". Dumbarton, together with the kingdom of Strathclyde, was subsumed into Constantine II's new kingdom of the Scots in 908.

In mediæval Scotland, Dumbarton was an important royal castle. It sheltered King David II (Robert the Bruce's son) after the Scots were crushed at Halidon Hill in 1333. In 1548, after the equally disastrous Battle of Pinkie, the castle protected the infant Mary, Queen of Scots for several months before her removal to safety in France.

The castle's importance declined after Oliver Cromwell's death in 1658, but new defences were constructed to meet threats posed by Jacobites and the French in the 18th century. The castle remained a military garrison until WWII.

Joseph of Arimathea
by Pietro Perugino

GLASTONBURY

The Gospels state that Joseph of Arimathea took Jesus's body after the crucifixion. Some legends insist that he was Jesus's uncle; and had visited Britain years before with Jesus, in pursuit of his interests in the tin trade. There was a strong Jewish presence in the west of England at that time; and some miners may have been Jewish settlers.

When Jesus died, Joseph thought it prudent to flee Palestine. Eventually he found his way to Britain, with a company of followers. He brought with him the Holy Grail, the cup used by Jesus at the Last Supper. Some versions of the legend have it that the Grail contained two drops of blood captured from Jesus's side when he was wounded on the Cross.

On arrival in Britain, Joseph was granted land at Glastonbury by the king of the Durotriges. Joseph stuck his thorn staff in the earth, whereupon it rooted and burst into bloom. A cutting from that first tree was planted in the grounds of the later Glastonbury Abbey, where it continued to bloom every year at Christmas time. There is still a thorn tree in the Abbey grounds, of a variety native to the Holy Land – and, unlike any other thorn bush in the country, it flowers every Christmas.

Joseph was said to have established the first church in England at Glastonbury; and archæological records show that there may well have been an extremely early Christian church there. Legend has it that Joseph buried the Holy Grail at the foot of Glastonbury Tor; whereupon a spring of blood gushed forth from the ground. There is still a well at the base of the Tor, Chalice Well: and the water that issues from it does have a reddish tinge (from the iron content of the water).

The hymn *Jerusalem*, is a short but wonderful poem by William Blake (1757–1827) from the preface to his epic *Milton* (1804). It was set to music by Sir Hubert Parry (1848–1918) in 1916; and has stirred English hearts ever since:

The Fortingall Yew, possibly
the oldest tree in Europe

And did those feet in ancient
  time walk upon England's mountains green?
And was the holy Lamb of God
  on England's pleasant pastures seen?

The text was inspired by the legend that the young Jesus had accompanied Joseph of Arimathea to Glastonbury. This is linked to the "Second Coming" in the Book of Revelations, in which Jesus establishes a new Jerusalem.

THE SCOTTISH GLASTONBURY

Very close to the exact geographical centre of Scotland, stands a remarkable yew tree, believed to be over 5,000 years old. The yew is in Fortingall (which translates from the Gaelic *Feart-nan-Gall* as the "Stronghold of the Strangers") churchyard, seven miles west of Aberfeldy in Perthshire. Thomas Pennant (1726–98), the naturalist and traveller, visited the yew tree in 1771 and recorded a girth of over 56 feet. It has long since stopped growing.

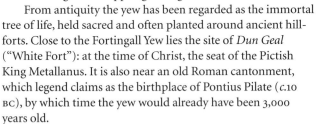

The Royal Scots was, until amalgamation into the 1st Battalion Royal Regiment of Scotland, the oldest regiment in the British Army, raised by Charles I in 1633. It was dissolved on 28 March 2006, 373 years to the day since its formation. After a 17th century boasting contest with the French Regiment of Picardy, who claimed that prior to the Resurrection it had guarded Christ's tomb, the Royal Scots was nicknamed "Pontius Pilate's bodyguard".

From antiquity the yew has been regarded as the immortal tree of life, held sacred and often planted around ancient hillforts. Close to the Fortingall Yew lies the site of *Dun Geal* ("White Fort"): at the time of Christ, the seat of the Pictish King Metallanus. It is also near an old Roman cantonment, which legend claims as the birthplace of Pontius Pilate (*c.*10 BC), by which time the yew would already have been 3,000 years old.

Pilate's father was an ambassador sent by the Roman Emperor, Cæsar Augustus to exact tribute from King Metallanus. His mother was said to have been a native Pict.

SCHIEHALLION

Schiehallion is a 3,554 foot high mountain in Perthshire. The name is derived from the Gaelic *Sidh Chailleann*, meaning "Fairy Hill of the Caledonians" or, more convincingly the "Maiden's Pap" (the two translations demonstrate the versatility of Gaelic). A 'Munro', Schiehallion is almost precisely in the centre of Scotland. Holy to the Picts, it is 5 miles north of Fortingall where three ley lines intersect: between Eilean Isa (Isle of Jesus) and Holy Island (Lindisfarne); between Tobermory ("Well of Mary") and Marywell; and between Holy Island (Iona) and Montrose ("Mount of the Rose").

A Munro is a Scottish mountain with a height over 3,000 feet. They are named after Sir Hugh Munro (1856–1919), who produced the first exhaustive list of them, known as *Munro's Tables*, in 1891. A 1997 revision identified 284 Munros and 227 further subsidiary tops. They are all in the Highlands, north of the "Boundary Fault".

'Ley lines' are hypothetical alignments of at least three places of geographical significance, such as ancient monuments and megaliths. Their existence was suggested in 1921 by the amateur archæologist Alfred Watkins (1855–1935).

FORTINGALL: SCOTLAND'S GLASTONBURY

Map of the ley lines intersecting at Schiehallion

Schiehallion's isolated position and perfect shape led Nevil Maskelyne (1732–1811), the Astronomer Royal, to use the deflection caused by the mass of the mountain to estimate the mass of the earth, in an ingenious experiment carried out in 1774. Following Maskelyne's survey, Schiehallion became the first mountain ever to be mapped using contour lines.

One of the major oil fields on the UK's continental shelf is named Schiehallion. Discovered in 1993 and operated by BP, it is 110 miles west of the Shetland Isles.

Schiehallion

PICTISH BROCHS

A Broch is a circular, dry-stone tower found only in northern Scotland, particularly in Caithness and the Northern Isles. The Hebrides and Sutherland enjoy a smaller concentration, with a scattering on the borders in Dumfries and Galloway. Carbon dating has established that most originate from the last century BC to the first century AD. There are nearly 600. Whether intended for offensive or defensive purposes, as little is known of their origin as of their Pictish builders. The Picts survived as an independent race for only another 600 years, before being entirely subsumed by the Scots.

Dun Carloway broch, Isle of Lewis

**Anglo-Saxon helmet
from Sutton Hoo**

SUTTON HOO

Sutton Hoo was discovered on the Bawdsey peninsula, near Ipswich, on the eve of WWII and was given to the nation by Mrs Edith Pretty (1883–1942). The find reminded England at least, of its early Anglo-Saxon roots and was exploited by the government to prepare the country to defend its freedom.

Sutton Hoo (*Hoo* means "spur of land" in Old English) was the undisturbed site of a ship-burial dating from *c*.624. Its significance cannot be overstated: for the light it sheds on burial ritual in the 7th century; for its size and completeness; and for the magnificence and quality of its treasure, now in the British Museum. It is a priceless narrative of early English history.

It is believed to be the grave of King Rædwald of the East Angles, who ruled *c*.599–*c*.624. He converted to Christianity: but from the nature of his burial, was clearly equivocal in his beliefs. From *c*.616 Rædwald was *Bretwalda* or overlord of all Anglo-Saxons.

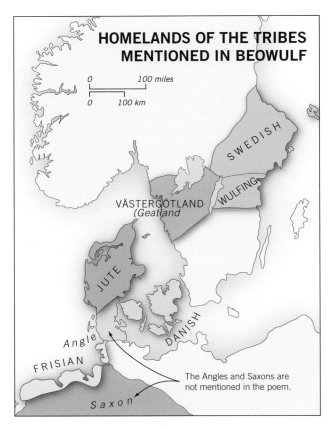

BEOWULF

Beowulf is an anonymous Anglo-Saxon heroic epic poem, composed in Old English between the 8th and 10th centuries. The only surviving manuscript, with 3,183 lines, has been dated to *c*.1010. It is a major national treasure and is in the British Library.

The events described in the poem take place in the late 5th century, after the Anglo-Saxons had begun to migrate and settle in England – but before the migrations had ended, a time when the Anglo-Saxons were either newly arrived or still in close contact with their Scandinavian and North German kinsmen. The East Anglian royal dynasty, the Wulfings, were also descendants of the Eastern Geatish Wulfings ("wolf clan") described in *Beowulf*.

In the poem Beowulf, a hero from the royal house of the Geats, battles three antagonists on behalf of the Danish king, Hrothgar: Grendel, a deformed monster, who attacks the Danish mead hall called Heorot and its inhabitants; Grendel's unnamed mother (*Grendles modor* in Old English); and, after returning to Geatland *[in red on the map]* as king of the Geats, in place of Hygelac and his son Heardred who had both died, an unnamed dragon. He was mortally wounded in the final battle and buried in a barrow (a long mound) in Geatland by his retainers.

Beowulf was released as a 'motion capture' film in 2007. It grossed over $200 million.

**The first page of the
Beowulf manuscript**

**Map showing the regions
of the tribes mentioned in
Beowulf [The Angles and
Saxons are not mentioned
in the poem]**

**HOMELANDS OF THE TRIBES
MENTIONED IN BEOWULF**

0   100 miles

0   100 km

SWEDISH

WULFING

VÄSTERGÖTLAND
(Geatland)

JUTE

DANISH

Angle

FRISIAN

Saxon

The Angles and Saxons are
not mentioned in the poem.

"FROM THE FURY OF THE NORSEMEN, GOOD LORD DELIVER US"

Between the 8th and 12th centuries, exploding out of Scandinavia as a result of population pressure, the Vikings ("one who came from the fjords", from *vik*, meaning a bay or fjord – as in Wick in Scotland and Berwick in England) literally encircled Europe.

In England the Viking Era began with a raid on Lindisfarne in 793 and ended at Stamford Bridge in 1066. By the 9th century they had settled large parts of the British Isles. By the 10th, Normandy ("land of the Northmen") had been accepted as a duchy by the King of France; Iceland and Greenland had been colonised; and the Rus or "Red-haired men" (who gave their name to Russia) had reached the Black Sea.

The Vikings were the finest shipbuilders and most daring seamen since the Phoenicians 1,500 years earlier. They were the first Europeans to discover North America – 400 years before Columbus. Naming Maine Vinland ("land of Vines") suggests that the global warming that fed the increase in Scandinavian population lasted until the 1100s.

Aside from dialect and place-names, the Vikings, especially their Norman descendants, left England two legacies of great importance (characteristics of which can still be seen in the way Nordic countries ensure social cohesion, by taxing and spending heavily): democracy and the rule of law. The world's oldest parliament (itself a Norman-French word) is the Icelandic Althing, established in 930 but suspended during periods of Danish rule. The Isle of Man's Tynwald is the oldest parliament in continuous existence: informally established before 900, formally in 979. The Normans lost some of their egalitarianism from exposure to Frankish feudalism in France, but the rudiments lived on in the *curia regis*, or King's court, which replaced the Witan in 1066.

A Viking longship

Map showing the extent of Viking raids, conquests and settlements

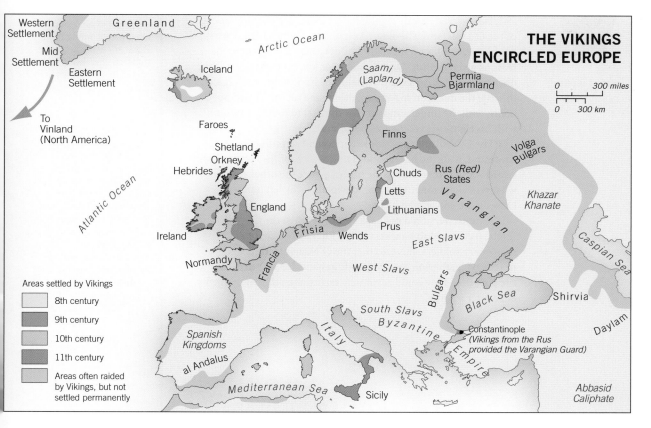

Western Settlement
Mid Settlement
Eastern Settlement
To Vinland (North America)

Greenland
Arctic Ocean
Iceland

THE VIKINGS ENCIRCLED EUROPE

0 — 300 miles
0 — 300 km

Saami (Lapland)
Permia Bjarmland
Finns
Faroes
Shetland
Orkney
Hebrides
Chuds
Rus (Red) States
Volga Bulgars
Letts
Varangian
Khazar Khanate
England
Lithuanians
Prus
Atlantic Ocean
Frisia
Wends
East Slavs
Ireland
Caspian Sea
Normandy
Francia
West Slavs
Shirvia
Bulgars
Black Sea
Daylam
Spanish Kingdoms
South Slavs
Byzantine
Constantinople (Vikings from the Rus provided the Varangian Guard)
al Andalus
Italy
Empire
Mediterranean Sea
Sicily
Abbasid Caliphate

Areas settled by Vikings
- 8th century
- 9th century
- 10th century
- 11th century
- Areas often raided by Vikings, but not settled permanently

The Lewis Chessmen

The Red Hand of Ulster

THE LEWIS CHESSMEN

Mediæval chess sets are rare and the finding of the "Lewis Chessmen" by Malcolm "Sprot" Macleod, at the head of the Bay of Uig on the west coast of Lewis, in the Outer Hebrides in 1831, was exceptional. They were probably made in Trondheim, north Norway in the 12th century.

Most of the ninety-three 1½ to 4 inch high pieces are carved from walrus ivory with a few made from whale teeth. Except for the pawns which resemble gravestones, the figures are all sculpted human figures. The knights are carved sitting on tiny horses, clutching spears and shields. The figures wear deeply gloomy expressions, apart from four warders (rooks or castles) which represent berserkers – ancient Norse warriors who fought in a frenzied state of blood-lust.

The chessmen were exhibited in 1831 at the Society of Antiquaries in Edinburgh. Eighty-two pieces were acquired by the British Museum and eleven are in the National Museum of Scotland. They are amongst the most important antiquities ever found in Scotland.

THE O'NEILL HAS THE OLDEST NON-ROYAL PEDIGREE IN EUROPE

Niall means "champion" in Irish Gaelic (Erse) and the Ó means "grandson of", so O'Niall means "Grandson of the Champion". The surname O'Neill was probably first used by Domnal O'Neill (died 980), supposedly Ireland's 158th monarch and who claimed descent from the Egyptian Pharaohs – the last O'Neill High King of Ireland.

The O'Neill can trace their family history back to AD 360, a rare feat even among the royal families of Europe. They are descended from the royal family of Tara, who were kings of Ulster and titular monarchs of all Ireland from the fifth to the eleventh centuries. The two other most important Irish families were O'Brien and O'Conor.

The severed bloody right hand of Ulster is a prominent part of the O'Neill family heritage. As with every other Irish story that has been embellished through the ages, there are a number of reasons given for this. One of the better known is that there were once two chiefs disputing ownership of some land. They agreed to settle the question in a competition: and set out in two open boats, with the understanding that the first to touch the shore with his right hand could claim the land.

The O'Neill ancestor saw his opponent stepping onto the shore and, realising he was about to lose, cut off his hand with his sword – and threw it on to the beach, before the other realised what was happening. This legend explains why left handed O'Neills are considered lucky.

Another version dates back to a time when the O'Neill forebears are said to have served the Pharaoh of Egypt as mercenary soldiers. It is said that the O'Neill introduced the practice of gathering severed hands in hand-baskets to deliver to the scribes so they could accurately record the number of enemy dead after a battle.

The "Hill of the King" (*Teamhair na Rí*) at Tara, near the River Boyne in County Meath, is the site of a number of ancient monuments dating from 2000 BC. According to tradition, Tara was the seat of *Árd Rí na hÉireann*, or the High King of Ireland.

An Irish legend explains how Lough Neagh, the largest lake in the British Isles, was formed: a mythical giant Fionn mac Cumhaill, sometimes known as Finn McCool, scooped up a lump of earth and tossed it at a Scottish rival. He missed; and the chunk of earth landed in the Irish Sea – creating the Isle of Man.

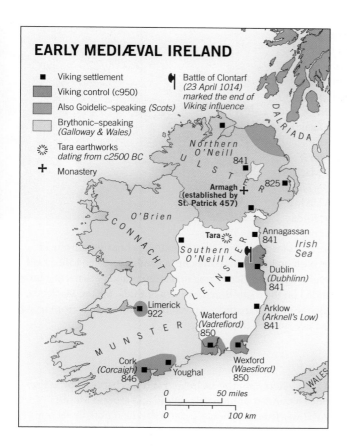

EARLY MEDIÆVAL IRELAND

- ■ Viking settlement
- Viking control (c950)
- Also Goidelic–speaking *(Scots)*
- Brythonic–speaking *(Galloway & Wales)*
- ☀ Tara earthworks dating from c2500 BC
- ✚ Monastery
- ⚔ Battle of Clontarf *(23 April 1014)* marked the end of Viking influence

DALRIADA

Northern O'Neill

U L S T E R

841

Armagh ✚ 825 ■
(established by St. Patrick 457)

O'Brien

C O N N A C H T

Tara ☀
Southern O'Neill

Annagassan 841

Irish Sea

L E I N S T E R

Dublin *(Dubhlinn)* 841

Limerick 922

Waterford *(Vadrefiord)* 850

Arklow *(Arknell's Low)* 841

M U N S T E R

Cork *(Corcaigh)* 846

Youghal

Wexford *(Waesfiord)* 850

WALES

0   50 miles

0   100 km

Map of Ireland pre-1169. with provincial divisions and Viking Settlements: Pytheas "of Massalia" referred to Ireland as Ierne, *c.*325 BC. The inhabitants of Ireland consider themselves Milesians (Mil Espáine) or Celt-Iberians and claim a mythological descent from Goidel Glas, an heroic ancestor from the Spanish peninsula who was descended from the Pharoahs. Be that as it may, whilst the Irish language (or Erse, which is Goidelic or Q-Celtic) is different from the Brythonic (P-Celtic) spoken the other side of the Irish Sea, they are closely related. The Romans never tried to invade Ireland. The native Irish were able to maintain an ancient Celtic culture and Christian society; which had little secular interaction or trade with other parts of Europe – unlike the Celtic tribes in Britain. This misty dreamland was abruptly disturbed by Viking raids from Norway, which began in AD 795. However the Vikings founded important towns, notably Dublin; and most Vikings were assimilated peacefully over the years. Those that were not, with their Ulster and Leinster O'Neill allies, were routed at the Battle of Clontarf by Brian 'Boru', King of Munster and High King of Ireland (who was killed after the battle). The leading septs of Ireland were then left alone, free to feud amongst themselves again – until one chieftain issued a fateful invitation in 1169.

THE MACLEODS WERE NOT TO BE OUTDONE BY ANYONE EITHER

Forty miles west of South Uist, in the Outer Hebrides, lies the tiny island archipelago of St. Kilda, the remains of an extinct volcano. Stormbound for eight months of the year, with no trees, no horses, cats, rabbits or even rats (though there are a species of wren and mouse) – and crucially, no harbour – a fluctuating population of up to 180 people eked out a precarious existence on Hirta (1,656 acres), the main island, for at least 2,000 years.

They lived on potatoes and sea birds, speaking only Gaelic; and for months on end there was no contact with the outside world. 'Sea Messages', in stout waterproof boxes, were thrown from the cliffs (at 1,400 feet, the highest in the United Kingdom) and carried by the prevailing winds to the Hebrides: where they might be found. One determined islander, Donald MacLeod left St. Kilda in the 18th century to join the East India Company army, retiring as a Lieutenant-Colonel.

In 1931 St. Kilda was sold by Sir Reginald MacLeod to Lord Dumfries. On 29 August lifeboats carried 36 passengers, of whom only two were men, through the surf to the sloop, HMS *Harebell*. 590 skinny highland cattle and sheep had to swim. They were to be resettled, at their own request, in Morvern on the mainland. Volunteers now work on the islands in the summer months, to restore the ruined buildings the islanders left behind. There has also been a small military base on Hirta since 1957. In 1986 the islands became the first place in Scotland to be designated a UNESCO World Heritage Site. The islands are a breeding ground for gannets, puffins and fulmars.

It is hard to imagine why anyone would wish to own St. Kilda (or *Hiort* in Gaelic), but legend has it that two clans were once prepared to go to great lengths to win it.

Macdonald of Uist challenged Macleod of Harris to a race in their respective *birlinn* (tough little boats descended from Viking longships) from the Hebrides to St. Kilda. The first to touch the shore would take possession of the islands. In a close race, Macdonald's *birlinn* was about a boat-length ahead when nearing Village Bay on Hirta. With no hope of catching up, a young crewman called Coll Macleod drew his claymore and severed his hand. Screaming in triumph (and perhaps in a little pain), he threw the hand, which landed on the rocky beach – to win St Kilda, for the Macleods. This story suffers from a possible charge of plagiarism; but, given the detail, benefits from being marginally more believable than the tale spun by the O'Neill.

The village street after restoration (2006)

The Book of Kells (Trinity College, Dublin), probably made on Iona (*c*.800), is Ireland's greatest treasure

SAINT BRENDAN

Saint Brendan was born in 484 in County Kerry, southwest Ireland and was baptised by St Erc. Between 512 and 530 Brendan founded a number of monastic cells in and around Mount Brandon and Shanakeel in Kilkenny. It was from south-east Ireland that he reputedly set out into the Atlantic, with sixty companions and three unbelievers, on his famous, seven year voyage to the "Land of Delight".

Not to be outdone, the Welsh have the legend of Prince Madoc, possibly a son of Owain Gwynedd. He is said to have sailed to Florida or Alabama in 1170 and that his companions intermarried with local Native Americans.

Brendan is best known for his legendary expedition to the "Isle of the Blessed" *(Tir nanÓg)*, described in the 9th century *Voyage of St Brendan the Navigator,* the tale of how he found North America. If true, his discovery predates Bjarni Herjolfsson and Leif Erikson's by 400 years and Columbus's voyages to the Caribbean by nearly 1,000. On this expedition Brendan is supposed to have seen a blessed island covered with vegetation, which turns out to be a giant sea monster called Jasconius or Jascon.

The Brendan legend shares much with those of Jonah and the Whale, Sinbad the Sailor and Pinocchio. St Brendan is also credited with undertaking pilgrimages to Brittany, Orkney and Shetland. He is the patron saint of sailors, travellers – and whales.

THE STONE OF SCONE

The Stone of Scone or *Liath Fàil* ("the speaking stone" in Gaelic) was used for centuries in the coronations of Scottish kings. It is a rectangular block of red sandstone, decorated with a Celtic cross, 26 inches long by 16 inches wide and 10.5 inches high, weighing 336 pounds. The top surface is scarred by chisel gouges and there is an iron ring at either end. The Stone was taken to Dalriada (Argyllshire) from Antrim in Northern Ulster by the Gaels. In *c.*500 Mortough, an O'Neill ancestor, is said to be the first Christian to have been crowned king while sitting on it. It may have been used later by St Columba as a travelling altar.

After 450 years at Dunadd, or possibly Dunstaffnage in Dalriada, Kenneth MacAlpin brought the Stone to Scone (pronounced "Scoon"), near Perth in *c.*847. King of the Picts and Scots (843–58), he was the first Scottish king to have sat on it during his coronation.

The Stone was kept at Scone Abbey until 1296, when Edward I ("Hammer of the Scots") seized it and took it to London – to symbolise his claim to be "Lord Paramount" of Scotland, with the right to approve its king. The Stone was placed under the Coronation Chair at Westminster Abbey. It was subsequently used at the coronation of every English monarch (except Queen Mary I) until 1714 when, following the Act of Union (1 May 1707), George I was crowned King of Great Britain.

On Christmas Day 1950 four students took the Stone from Westminster Abbey to return it to Scotland. In the process of removing it from the Abbey, they broke it into two pieces. It was repaired by a Glasgow stonemason and left on the altar of Arbroath Abbey on 11 April 1951. Prime Minister John Major decided to return the Stone to Scotland. On 15 November 1996 it was taken to Edinburgh Castle – with a promise that the Stone will be returned to Westminster Abbey for all future coronations.

Legend has it that Robert the Bruce gave a sliver of the Stone to Cormac McCarthy, King of Munster in gratitude for his support at the Battle of Bannockburn in 1314 – and, kept at **Blarney Castle** in County Cork, it became the Blarney Stone. Since Edward I had seized the Stone in 1296, this may safely be dismissed as 'Blarney'. The Blarney Stone, or "Stone of Eloquence" is said to bestow on anyone kissing it, the gift of silver tongued persuasion and sweet-talk.

1066 and All That (pub. 1930) referred to the stone as the Scone of Stone.

BAGPIPES

The earliest mention of the bagpipe in history is about 400 BC, when Aristophanes, the Athenian poet and dramatist, recorded that the pipers of Thebes (with whom Athens was at war) blew pipes made of dog skin, with chanters made of bone. Nearly four hundred and fifty years later, Suetonius described the Roman Emperor Nero as a player of the *tibia utricularis*. Pipes, in one form or another, were common in most mountain societies.

Before the 12th century, only a few Pictish and Irish stone carvings record the existence of bagpipes in the British Isles; but finds of statuettes of pipers in archæological digs suggest that they were introduced by the Romans.

Bagpipes have been in use since the 12th century in Scotland. Although *Hey Tutti Taiti* (the tune used by Robert Burns for *Scots Wha Hae*) is said by Sir Walter Scott to have been played as Robert the Bruce's troops marched to the Battle of Bannockburn in 1314, it was not until the late

16th century that pipers playing the Great Highland Bagpipe (*A' Phìob Mhòr* in Gaelic) started to displace harpists, who had been the chief Celtic musicians since the Roman occupation.

Highland regiments were present at many of the battles fought to expand or protect the British Empire in the 18th and 19th centuries; and are often remembered specifically for the sounds of their pipes. No other instrument, as the survivors of the siege of Lucknow (1857–58) later attested, can lift the spirits and imbue martial ardour as the bagpipe – nor equal the tearjerking melancholy induced by laments played on it.

The bravery of bagpipers is legendary: George Findlater VC of the 2nd Battalion Gordon Highlanders, from Turriff in Aberdeenshire, who continued to play *Cock o' the North,* under fire from a sitting position, despite being shot through both ankles, at Dargai in Afghanistan in 1897; and Kenneth Mackay of the 79th Cameron Highlanders, from Tongue in Sutherland, who left the protective square at Waterloo and played *Cogadh ná Sith* ("Peace or War"), are two. The slaughter of WWI is remembered for heroes like James Richardson VC of the Canadian Scottish at the Somme in 1916; Daniel Laidlaw VC of the King's Own Scottish Borderers at Loos in 1915; and especially for Robert Mackenzie VC, from the same regiment and in the same battle, who played until he died of his wounds, aged sixty.

The large numbers of pipers trained for military service in the two World Wars spread the popularity of the instrument around the Empire. All the old Dominions, the US and the Gurkhas have their own pipers; and are rightly proud of them. The bagpipe is the only musical instrument to be determined a Weapon of War in a Royal Court.

The Lindisfarne Gospels (*c.*700)
British Library

THE LINDISFARNE GOSPELS

The Lindisfarne Gospels are a huge illuminated Latin manuscript, written on sheepskin, of the four gospels. The manuscript was produced on Lindisfarne (Holy Island) in Northumbria in the late 7th or early 8th century. It is generally regarded as the finest example of the kingdom's unique style of religious art: a style that combined Anglo-Saxon and Celtic themes, now called Hiberno-Saxon, or Insular art. The manuscript is complete (but lacking its original cover), and is astonishingly well-preserved. The Gospels are richly illustrated in the Insular Style (the finest example of which is the Book of Kells), and were originally encased in an ornate leather binding, covered with jewels and metals. A new cover was made in 1852.

In the 10th century Aldred, Provost of Chester-le-Street, translated the Gospels into Old English. He inserted a word-for-word gloss between the lines of the Latin text – the first known translation into English. They were taken from Durham Cathedral during the dissolution of the monasteries; and were acquired by Sir Robert Cotton.

THE "VENERABLE" BEDE

Bede – also St Bede, the "Venerable Bede" or in Latin, *Beda* (*c*.672–25 May 735), was a Benedictine monk at St Peter in Monkwearmouth and at its companion monastery, St Paul's in Jarrow – then in the Kingdom of Northumbria, later in County Durham. His *Historia Ecclesiastica Gentis Anglorum* (The Ecclesiastical History of the English People), written in Latin, gained him the title "the father of English history". It traces the history of England from Julius Cæsar's invasion of Britain in 55 BC to AD 597, particularly recording the conversion to Christianity of Britain's Anglo-Saxon tribes. Bede invented the *Anno Domini* (AD) method of dating events from the year of Christ's birth, a system he used throughout his monumental *Historia Ecclesiastica*.

ST ALBAN

Alban is the earliest Christian in Britain who is known by name. He is also the first British martyr. A Roman soldier stationed at *Verulamium*, now St Albans, he gave shelter to a Christian priest, fleeing from persecution, who then converted him. When officers came to Alban's house, he dressed himself in the garments of the priest and gave himself up. Alban was tortured and martyred on the hilltop where the Cathedral and Abbey Church of St Alban now stands. The traditional date of his martyrdom is *c*.303, but modern research suggests that it was as early as 209.

The site of his martyrdom soon became a shrine. King Offa of Mercia established a monastery there in about 793; and in the Middle Ages St Albans ranked as the premier abbey in England. The great Norman abbey church, begun in 1077, now serves as the cathedral of the diocese of St Albans, established in 1877. It is the second longest church in England (Winchester Cathedral is the longest, by six feet); and it is built on higher ground than any other English cathedral.

The Venerable Bede described Alban's trial in his *Ecclesiastical History of the English People*. His feast day is observed on 22 June.

ST URSULA

The legend of St Ursula (a "small female bear" in Latin) is almost entirely unsupported by historical evidence. However she was accorded a feast day in the Roman Catholic calendar (21 October) and is regarded as the patron saint of students.

Ursula is said to have been a Romano-British princess, born a year or two after St Alban's death, in *c*.305. At the request of her father, King Donaut of Dumnonia (Devon and Cornwall), Ursula sailed to join her future husband, the pagan Governor Conan Meriadoc of Armorica (Brittany), along with 11,000 virginal handmaidens. A miraculous storm brought them across the Channel in a single day, to a Gaulish port, where Ursula declared that before her marriage she would undertake a pilgrimage through Europe.

She headed for Rome with her followers; and persuaded the Pope, Cyriacus (who is unknown in the pontifical records) and Sulpicius, Bishop of Ravenna, to join them. Reaching Cologne, which was being besieged by Huns, all the virgins were beheaded in a dreadful massacre. The Huns' leader is said to have shot Ursula dead with arrows himself. The legend suffers from two inconsistencies in particular, which rather spoil the story: the supposed date of her death in 383 would have made her a very old marriage prospect indeed (about seventy-eight); and rather than having 11,000 virgin companions, the Roman numerals in the

St George and the dragon by Gustave Moreau

description of the event can just as easily, and a great deal more believably, be interpreted as only eleven.

Today the story of Saint Ursula is usually regarded as fiction. Nonetheless, Christopher Columbus named the Virgin Islands after her and her unfortunate associates. After a long and dangerous voyage across the Atlantic, with no women on board, he can hardly be blamed for wishful thinking.

ST GEORGE

England is the only country in the British Isles whose patron saint was not an evangelist. St George was supposedly born around 275, the son of a Roman soldier from a Greek-speaking Christian family in Nicomedia, now the Turkish city of Izmit. His mother was from Lydda, in Palestine (now Lod, in Israel). She returned, with her young son, as a widow to her native city, where he was educated. George joined the Roman army as soon as he came of age; and proved to be a good soldier. By his late twenties he had been promoted to *tribunus* (Tribune), then *comes* (Count), and was stationed back in Nicomedia as a member of the personal guard attached to the Roman Emperor Diocletian.

In 303 Diocletian issued an edict authorising the systematic persecution of Christians across the Empire. Rather than participate, George confessed to being a Christian himself and criticised the imperial decision. An enraged Diocletian ordered his torture and execution. George was lacerated on a wheel of swords and beheaded on 23 April 303. His body was returned to Lydda for burial, where Christians soon came to honour him as a martyr. Despite a wealth of detail provided, probably invented, by hagiographers later in the 4th century, George remains a semi-mythical character.

The legend of St George and the dragon (representing evil) was brought back to England from the Holy Land by Crusaders, who wore his red cross, in the late 12th century. In the reign of King Edward III (1327–77), who founded the Order of the Garter in 1347, St George came to be recognised as the patron saint of England.

St George's Chapel at Windsor Castle is both a royal peculiar (it falls directly under the jurisdiction of the monarch) and the chapel of the Order of the Garter. It was substantially rebuilt between 1475–1528 in the Perpendicular Gothic style, as an expansion and rededication of the 13th century Chapel of St Edward the Confessor.

One of Shakespeare's most famous lines is the climax to King Henry V's address to his army before Agincourt on 25 October 1415: "Cry God for Harry, England and Saint George". Shakespeare himself was both born and died on 23 April – St George's Day.

The English and Scots are less enthusiastic about their patron saints than the Irish, who celebrate St Patrick's Day with unabashed delight; and even the Welsh show more interest in theirs. In part this is a reflection of national character, but in the case of England it might also be because George was decidedly foreign, largely imaginary and above all, not especially appropriate. Indeed, George is also the patron saint of of Aragon, Canada, Catalonia, China, Ethiopia, Georgia, Greece, Montenegro, Palestine, Portugal, Russia, and Serbia, as well as the cities of Amersfoort, Beirut, Ferrara, Freiburg, Genoa, Ljubljana, and Moscow. Doubtless he was a splendid fellow, but the East Anglian king, St Edmund the Martyr will always be more suitable as England's patron saint – as he once was. Since St Patrick was British and St Andrew was a Jew, only St David of Wales was a national of the country he represents.

ST NINIAN

The Romano-British Saint Ninian (*c*.360–*c*.432), the first Christian missionary to Scotland, is credited with converting the Picts. Although veiled in myth, it is probable that Ninian was born in Brythonic Cumbria and was the first bishop of Galloway – where he established his see at Whithorn in 397 and built a whitewashed stone church. Whithorn, derived from the Anglo-Saxon *Huitaern*, or *Candida Casa* ("white house") in Latin, became a leading monastic centre. Ninian's influence is enshrined in the many churches throughout Scotland and northern England dedicated to him. His missionary work laid the ground for St Columba in the 6th century.

ST PATRICK

Patrick, patron saint and founder of the church in Ireland, was born *c*.390, possibly in the south of Scotland. A Romano-Briton, he was kidnapped aged about sixteen, and taken to Ireland as a slave. After five years he escaped; but returned *c*.432 to convert the Irish to Christianity. He died *c*.461, having established his see at Armagh (*c*.457), monasteries, churches and schools. He was said to have rid Ireland of snakes; and used a shamrock to explain the mystery of the Trinity. There have been no snakes in Ireland since the last Ice Age (nor moles): "snake" is an allegory for "serpent", a reference to evil. Patrick's feast day is 17 March.

St Mary's Abbey, Iona

ST COLUMBA

Columba, also known by the Old Irish name of *Colmcille*, meaning "Church Dove" was born *c*.521, supposedly in Gartan, County Donegal. His paternal relations were the Uí Néill, already emerging as Ireland's dominant royal dynasty. Columba was therefore born into the highest rank of Irish nobility. He was ordained in 551.

Having founded several religious establishments in Ireland, with the help of twelve disciples, Columba built a church and monastery on the island of Iona in the Inner Hebrides, west of Mull. Iona became the springboard for the Christian conversion of Scotland; and St Mary's Abbey on the island contains the graves of many early kings of Scotland – as well as kings from Ireland, Norway and France.

St Columba, his followers and his successors did more than any contemporary to spread Christianity throughout the British Isles. He died on 9 June 597, aged seventy-six, and is buried in an unknown grave on Iona. His mother's grave, with its Byzantine cross, is still visible on one of the Gavellachs. His feast day is 9 June.

Pelagius was an English or Irish monk who rejected the orthodox Christian view that a predisposition to sin was an innate human weakness: he held that God had created man with the free-will to choose for himself between good and evil. In a modern context, this hardly seems an heretical opinion.

ST DAVID

St David's life is almost completely opaque. The Welsh scribe Rhygyfarch ap Sulien, writing an hagiography of the Welsh patron saint nearly 500 years later *c*.1070, identifies his father as the chieftain Sant who raped David's mother, St Non (supposedly a niece of King Arthur). He was born near St Bride's Bay, Pembrokeshire in *c*.520. David (or Dewi) was apparently educated at the monastery of Henfynyw in present day Cardiganshire. David was an implacable foe of Pelagianism.

David, clearly in a senior ecclesiastical capacity (probably as a bishop), moved the seat of Church governance from Caerleon to *Moni Judeorum* or Mynyw (now known as St David's or *Tyddewi*: "The House of David"). David also founded at least fifty churches throughout South Wales, all named after him.

A lifelong vegetarian, David was possibly over eighty when he died *c.*601. He was buried at St David's Cathedral (Britain's smallest), where his shrine soon became a popular place of pilgrimage. He was canonised a Saint in 1120 by Pope Callistus II and 1 March (the date of his death) was declared his feast day.

He was quickly recognised as the patron saint of Wales. Pope Callistus II decreed that two pilgrimages to St David's in Pembrokeshire would be deemed as one to Rome.

One of St David's best-known teachings was that people should "do the little things" in life *(gwnewch y pethau bychain mewn bywyd)*.

OTHER FOUNDERS OF THE CHRISTIAN CHURCH IN THE BRITISH ISLES

The next wave of Christian conversion of Britain was led from Rome, by St Augustine of Canterbury who founded the Christian Church in southern England. Of aristocratic birth and born sometime in the middle of the 6th century, Augustine was prior of the Benedictine monastery of St Andrew in Rome, when Pope (later Saint) Gregory I "the Great" (*c.*540–604) selected him to lead a mission of 40 monks to convert pagan England to Christianity.

They landed on the Isle of Thanet in the spring of 597 and were well received by King (later Saint) Æthelbert I of Kent, who accommodated them in Canterbury and allowed them to preach. Æthelbert and his wife Bertha were amongst the first to be converted, to be followed on Christmas day 597 by thousands more. Augustine was consecrated bishop of the English. In 601, he received more help from Pope Gregory in Rome: from the future saints Mellitus, Justus and Paulinus. Augustine founded Christ Church in Canterbury, establishing it as his cathedral; as well as the monastery of St Peter and St Paul nearby – which became the second most important Benedictine monastery in Europe. Canterbury, established as the prime see of England, was followed by London in 604, then by Rochester in Kent. Less successful were Augustine's efforts to unite the Celtic churches of north Wales with his new English churches. He died in Canterbury on 26 May 604 and was buried in the monastery church of St Peter and St Paul. The present Archbishop, Rowan Williams is the 104th.

There are no sources revealing the pagan religions of ancient Britain which Christianity replaced, other than Roman records of the Druids. In the centuries immediately following the Roman evacuation in 410, only a handful of missionaries met the daunting challenge of evangelising 'Dark-Age' Britain; and progress was slow. However, by the 7th century each Anglo-Saxon kingdom had one bishop – with the exception of Kent, which had two, centred on Canterbury and Rochester. All missionary work was organised by the bishop from the Episcopal see.

According to Bede, Pope Gregory said *"Non Angli, sed Angeli"* ("They are not Angles, but Angels"), when he first encountered blue-eyed, blond English boys in a slave market – which led to St Augustine's mission to convert England.

Druids were members of an educated monotheistic priesthood, who acted as teachers and judges among the ancient Celtic tribes of Britain and France. They taught young men, arranged sacrifices, sat in judgement and exacted punishment. They studied verse, natural philosophy, astronomy and religious tradition: believing in the immortality of souls and their transmigration. Druids practiced human sacrifice in extreme situations of imminent danger. In the first century AD, the Romans suppressed the Druids, who declined rapidly thereafter and became extinct with the coming of Christianity.

The Romano-British population of Britain had heard the Gospel well before AD 300; but in the 5th and 6th centuries, waves of pagan invasion from the Continent by Angles, Jutes and Saxons, forced the Celts into what is now Wales, Cumbria and south-west Scotland. Celtic missionaries launched attempts to convert the heathen newcomers to Christianity in the north and west; with the Church in Rome conducting initiatives in the south and east. Roman and Celtic (Irish) practices did not differ in doctrine, but varied greatly in detail – such as the date of Easter and the proper habit and haircut (tonsure) for a monk. It was obviously vital that Christians throughout Britain celebrated Easter, the most important feast in the Christian calendar, at the same time.

Saint Mellitus, third Archbishop of Canterbury (died c.624) was born into a Roman noble family. In 601, while Abbot of St Andrew's monastery in Rome, Pope Gregory I sent Mellitus to England as a missionary, to support Augustine. He carried instructions to destroy Anglo-Saxon idols; though not to destroy their pagan sites of worship, but to convert them into churches. He was also to preserve pagan festivals by transforming them into Christian observances – as had been done in the 4th century, when the Roman feast of *Sol Invictus* (which was on 25 December, the Winter Solstice in the Julian calendar), had been turned into Christmas – no one, then or now, has any idea of precisely when Jesus was born. This adroit, diplomatic approach did much to make Christianity more acceptable; and greatly advanced the cause of the early Christian church in England.

Saint Justus (died c.631), the fourth archbishop of Canterbury, was another of the missionaries sent by Pope Gregory to England in 601. With Mellitus, his predecessor at Canterbury, he made an abortive attempt to persuade the Celtic church to adopt the Roman method of calculating the date of Easter.

In 601, Paulinus (c.584–c.644) was a well-born monk at St Andrew's monastery in Rome when Pope Gregory I sent him to join Mellitus and Justus in a second group of missionaries to England. He remained in Canterbury until 625 when he was consecrated bishop by Justus. He then accompanied Æthelberg, the sister of King Eadbald of Kent, to Northumbria where she was to marry King Eadwine (c.586–633). Paulinus converted Eadwine and his court in 627 at York, built a church and remained in Northumbria, expanding the church, until Eadwine's death in battle in 633. Paulinus retired to Rochester where he spent the remainder of his life as bishop.

In 653 a young Northumbrian thegn of King Oswiu (Oswald's younger brother), Benedict Biscop (c.625–689), with a later bishop and saint called Wilfrid of York (634–709), went on a pilgrimage to Rome. They were the first northern clerics to establish a close relationship between the English church and the papacy. Wilfrid introduced Benedictine Rule to Northumbria.

On their return to Northumbria, Biscop and Wilfrid devoted themselves to promoting Roman Christianity. Up to this point Northumbria had followed the Irish church; but King Oswiu and his court, deeply influenced by Biscop's and Wilfrid's fervent evangelism decided, at the Synod of Whitby in 664, that Northumbria would henceforth observe Roman and not Irish religious practices.

Wilfrid was the first to propose a liturgy that included music and employed a Roman cantor to instruct his clergy in church music. He also introduced the practice of bringing back from Rome saintly body parts as holy relics.

St Benedict (480–547) founded a monastery in 524 at Monte Cassino, 80 miles south of Rome (it was destroyed by US bombers on 15 February 1944). The Benedictine Rule eventually became standard European monastic practice.

The Rule forbade personal property and established a probationary year before a novitiate took the vow of obedience and residence for life. Benedict carefully ordered each monastic day: with five hours of liturgy and prayer, five hours of manual labour and four hours for scriptural reading.

St Hilda, Abbess of Whitby (614–680), was the great-niece of King Eadwine of Northumbria. She was baptised in 627, when the royal household became Christian. In 647 Hilda became a nun and, under the direction of St Aidan and funded by Oswiu, founded several monasteries, the most important being Streaneshalch, which hosted the Synod of Whitby in 664. This monastery, unusually, housed a mixed sex community divided by a chapel: with Hilda as governor of both congregations. Hilda strongly supported the Celtic Church (possibly the reason she so disliked Wilfrid). Streaneshalch became the most famous abbey in Northumbria and was home to Cædmon, the earliest English Christian poet.

In 668 Biscop made his third journey to Rome, where pope Vitalian asked him to accompany and mentor the newly appointed Archbishop of Canterbury Theodore of Tarsus, a Greek who had never been to England.

Saint Theodore of Canterbury (602–690) became the seventh Archbishop of Canterbury in 668. Arriving in Canterbury, Theodore established a famous monastic school, before organising and centralising the early English Church. Bede wrote of his archbishopric: "Never had there been such happy times since the English first came to Britain". In 672, he convened the Church's first national synod after Whitby, at Hertford: whereby Celtic (Irish) procedure was discarded and Roman church doctrine was affirmed.

Saint Ceolfrith (c.640–717), a Northumbrian aristocrat, was Bede's mentor. He became Abbot in 686, of the twin monasteries of Wearmouth and Jarrow, after Benedict Biscop.

He amassed a library of over 300 volumes, the largest in Anglo-Saxon England; and his greatest achievement was the creation of three, single volume editions of the bible. The only surviving copy is the *Codex Amiatinus*. Ceolfrith died in France, while attempting to discharge his promise to the pope to deliver a copy to him personally. He was almost eighty.

The *Codex Amiatinus* is the earliest surviving manuscript of the complete Bible in the Latin Vulgate, or official version. It was produced at the turn of the 8th century in Northumbria and is considered to be the most accurate copy of St Jerome's text. The *Codex* is also a fine specimen of mediæval calligraphy. It is now kept at the Biblioteca Medicea Laurenziana in Florence.

Biscop returned home with John the Archcantor, the head of liturgy in Rome, to teach his monks liturgical practice. He also brought paintings of the Virgin, Apostles and famous biblical incidents, so that the illiterate could be inspired and learn from these images. He also obtained a letter of exemption from Pope Agatho, guaranteeing the independence of the monastery from external interference.

In 680 Biscop admitted Bede as a young initiate. In 681, on receiving an endowment of 40 hides from King Ecgfrith, he founded the monastery of St Paul's in Jarrow. Returning to Rome for four years in 682, Biscop arrived back in Northumbria with another rich haul of books, vestments, relics and religious art for his monasteries – and a strict list of rules regarding the election of abbots, including dire warnings against the common practice of hereditary succession. On 12 January (his feast day) 690, St Benedict Biscop died at the age of 62 at St Peter's Wearmouth, having established the Roman church in Northumbria; and having created the social and religious climate in which monks like the Venerable Bede could flourish in safety.

The Chapel of **St Peter-on-the-Wall, Bradwell-on-Sea**, Essex is the oldest Christian church in England still in regular use. It was built in AD 654 by St Cedd on the foundations of the abandoned 'Saxon Shore' fort of Othona. From the 14th century it was used as a barn and thus not vandalised or used for building materials. It was reconsecrated in 1920 as a chapel.

The eventual triumph of Roman Catholicism over western Europe was assured by Wilfrid's advocacy at the Synod of Whitby in 664; and the arrival of Theodore of Tarsus in 668. In 672 the Synod of Hertford mirrored the success of the early English church by increasing the number of new bishoprics. These first English bishops resembled secular lords with temporal responsibilities as well as spiritual ones. Anglo-Saxon society put bishops above the nobility and expected them to behave accordingly. It was perfectly accepted that the church should take a third of all booty won in war.

By the 8th century, the Christian church in Britain was an ascetic mix of dynamic teaching and monastic contemplation. Monasticism was a compound of Irish and Benedictine influences: sprouting centres of outstanding learning and substantial wealth. From rude, wooden churches to the mighty basilican cathedrals, abbeys and minsters, established in all Britain's principal towns, the early Christian church had become, after the king, the most important, influential and enduring institution in the land.

St Botolph (died c.680), a much loved abbot, patron saint of travellers and farmers, gave his name to over 70 churches – and Boston (St Botolph's-town) in Lincolnshire, after which Boston in Massachusetts was named. The Lincolnshire Boston has been declared to have the highest clinical obesity rate of any town in Britain (31%). Until recently the population kept slim, or at least fitter, by working the Lincolnshire fields where much of the country's vegetables are grown. Over the last few years however, immigrant labour has largely replaced the local workforce but the Boston high-calorie, full-fat diet has remained the same.

The synod also determined, in favour of the Roman church, that Easter (Pascha), the most important feast in the Christian liturgical year, should be celebrated on the Sunday following the first full moon on or after the spring equinox (21 March). The earliest date that Easter can occur is therefore 22 March and the latest is 25 April.

THE SYNOD OF WHITBY

The Synod of Whitby was a crucial meeting held by the Christian church of the Anglo-Saxon kingdom of Northumbria, to decide whether to follow the Celtic (Irish) or Roman religious practice. The synod was summoned in 664 to Saint Hilda's double monastery of Streaneshalch, later called Whitby Abbey.

The case for adopting the Roman way was led by St Wilfrid and Biscop. They were strongly opposed by

The ruins of Whitby Abbey

St Colmán of Lindisfarne, representing the Celtic missionaries who had largely converted Northumbria. King Oswiu however, chose in favour of Rome. Oswiu, appears to have been persuaded that the Roman church most closely followed the teaching of St Peter, "Holder of the Keys to Heaven" – and the "Rock", on which Christ had proclaimed he was to build his church.

The Synod of Whitby united the English Church, bringing it into closer communion with the rest of Europe.

Lindisfarne Castle

**Folio 27 of the
Stonyhurst Gospel**

ST CUTHBERT OF LINDISFARNE

Cuthbert was probably born in Northumbria *c.*634. He began life as a shepherd until he had a vision in 651 of St Aidan being borne aloft to heaven by bands of angels. He entered Melrose monastery but unaccountably left to spend several years as a soldier. By 661 Cuthbert was back in the monastic world acting as *præpositus hopitum* (receptionist) at the new monastery at Ripon. In 661 Melrose was struck by plague. Cuthbert and the prior were both afflicted, but Cuthbert survived to succeed him.

It was at this time that Cuthbert realised his gift of healing. He toured the countryside as far as the west coast of Scotland, miraculously restoring plague victims. His fame in the region lingers still, enshrined in the Scottish county of Kirkcudbrightshire: "the church of Cuthbert's county". Cuthbert attended the Synod of Whitby in 664.

In 676, by inclination a recluse, Cuthbert retired to the islet of Inner Farne, building himself an oratory and cell, where he devoted himself to contemplation and prayer. Cuthbert also took a great interest in an Eider duck colony and other birds which populated the Farne Islands. He instituted laws for their protection, becoming perhaps the world's first conserver of wildlife – hence the Northumbrian name "cuddy duck" (Cuthbert's duck) for the Eider duck.

In 684 King Ecgfrith of Northumbria appointed him Bishop of Hexham, a see which he exchanged the next year for Lindisfarne. In 687 Cuthbert finally returned to Inner Farne where he died. A tiny 14th century chapel marks his grave. His body was subsequently exhumed to protect it from Viking raids.

In 999, after a twelve year meander, being variously deposited at Melrose, Chester-le-Street and Ripon, Cuthbert was interred in Durham Cathedral. His tomb became a popular pilgrimage site until its destruction by Henry VIII in 1538. In 1104 Cuthbert's coffin was opened to reveal that Cuthbert had been buried in an exotic vestment made of Byzantine "Nature Goddess" silk – indicating a thriving 7th century silk trade across Europe. Cuthbert's feast day is 20 March.

The St Cuthbert Gospel of St John (formerly known as the 'Stonyhurst Gospel') is a small Anglo-Saxon pocket gospel which belonged to Saint Cuthbert of Lindisfarne. The book was discovered in 1104 when Cuthbert's tomb was opened so that his relics could be moved to a new shrine behind the altar of Durham Cathedral. It passed to collectors in the dissolution of the monasteries; eventually being given to the Jesuits by the 3rd Earl of Lichfield. At only three and a half by five inches the Stonyhurst Gospel is one of the smallest surviving Anglo-Saxon manuscripts. It was written at the monastery of Monkwearmouth during the abbacy of Ceolfrith (before 717).

The original tooled goatskin binding is the earliest surviving Western binding in Europe; and a very rare example of "Insular" leather work. It is now in the British Library.

ANGLO-SAXON AND IRISH MISSIONARIES IN EUROPE

Less than 250 years after their pagan Anglo-Saxon forebears had migrated to England, Englishmen returned to Holland and Germany as missionaries. Together with Irish members of the Celtic Church they converted north-western Europe to Christianity.

ST WILLIBRORD, THE "APOSTLE TO THE FRISIANS"

One of the earliest evangelists was Willibrord, an Anglo-Saxon bishop of Utrecht, who became patron saint of Holland. Born *c.*658, his father was a hermit, later Saint Wilgis; who sent him to

Charles Martel (688–741), is best remembered for defeating Umayyad invaders (the Moors) from Spain at the bloody but decisive Battle of Poitiers (sometimes called the Battle of Tours) on 10 October 732 – saving Christian Europe from Islam. His grandson Charlemagne (742–814), who ruled from 768, was crowned on Christmas Day 800 as the first Holy Roman Emperor.

the Benedictine monastery at Ripon under Wilfrid of York. In 690 Willibrord, after twelve years in Ireland, was sent to evangelise the Frisians. In 695 the pope re-named him Clement.

He established a monastery at Utrecht; and another at Echternach, in Luxemburg. He made vigorous attempts to convert the Danes as well as the Frisians. He also baptised Charlemagne's father; but failed to convert King Radbod of Frisia (Frisia extended along the Dutch and German coasts almost to Denmark). Radbod refused baptism at the last moment, when he was told that after conversion he would not be reunited with his friends and relations in Heaven. Radbod apparently told Willibrord that he would prefer to spend Eternity in Hell with his ancestors, rather than in Heaven amongst complete strangers. In 716 Radbod ordered the murder of missionaries and the burning of churches throughout his kingdom.

Willibrord greatly enhanced Roman influence over the Frankish Church. From 719–22, protected by Charles Martel, King of the Franks, and assisted by Wynfrith, later St Boniface, Willibrord instituted a training programme for the Frankish clergy. Rome's bond with the Frankish court lasted until Charlemagne died in 814.

Willibrord was the first to create a formal church hierarchy, appointing bishops under the authority of an archbishop. He also persuaded the Franks to adopt the Christian dating system introduced by Bede. He died in 739, was buried in his abbey of Echternach and swiftly canonised. His feast day is celebrated on the continent on 7 November; but by special dispensation from Pope Leo XIII, on 29 November in Britain.

Statue of St Willibrord at Echternach

ST BONIFACE, THE "APOSTLE OF GERMANY"

Boniface, whose original name was Wynfrith ("friend of peace"), was born to a noble Saxon father and British mother at Crediton in Devon, around 675. Having received an outstanding education at the Benedictine abbeys of Exeter and Nursling near Southampton, he became a Benedictine monk and was ordained when he was about thirty – having produced the first grammar ever published in England. Between 716 and 722 he made two attempts to convert the Frisians, but was thwarted by King Radbod.

On returning to England he discovered that Abbot Winbert had died and he had been elected his successor, a promotion he declined in order to persevere with his missionary vocation. In 718 he accompanied a group of pilgrims to Rome where he met Pope Gregory II who invited him to lead a mission to convert the pagans east of the Rhine – insisting that Boniface used the Roman rather than the Celtic (Irish) rites. Gregory also required him to change his name to Boniface ("maker of good deeds"). In 719 Radbod died and Boniface was diverted to help his fellow Anglo-Saxon, Bishop Willibrord who had evangelised much of Denmark, Heligoland and Frisia.

In 722 Boniface was recalled to Rome by Pope Gregory and given letters of introduction to Charles Martel, whose support was to play such a vital role in Boniface's future. Without Martel's crucial protection, as Boniface himself owned, he could: "neither administer

Heligoland comprises two small German islands in the North Sea. Formerly Danish (1714–1807) and British (1807–90) possessions, the islands (population 1,650) are located 44 miles from the German coast. On 18 April 1947 the Royal Navy detonated 6,800 tons of explosives, the biggest single non-nuclear detonation in history, to destroy German wartime fortifications.

his church, defend his clergy, nor prevent idolatry". The reason why Boniface found such a staunch ally amongst the Christian Frankish leaders was because their interests matched. The Franks wished to defeat their pagan, Saxon rivals and absorb their territory into their own empire: which coincided nicely with Boniface's drive to extinguish German paganism and destroy their holy places. Pope Gregory appointed him bishop of the German territories he was endeavouring to evangelise.

In 723 Boniface faced down large numbers of pagans at Geismar, in Hesse. He seized an axe and felled an oak tree dedicated to the god Thor, while challenging Thor to strike him dead. When Thor failed to respond, the Hessians converted: and the "Felling of Thor's Oak" marked the beginning of German Christianisation. In 732 Boniface travelled once again to Rome, this time to receive the *pallium* (a woollen vestment conferred by a pope on an archbishop), with jurisdiction over all Germany. So effective was Boniface's administration that in 737 he was anointed papal legate for Germany. Tradition credits Boniface with the adoption of the Christmas tree, inspired by the tiny fir tree he discovered amongst the roots of Thor's felled oak at Geismar.

St Boniface, Baptising and Martyrdom from the Sacramentary of Fulda

This image moved Boniface to offer the Germans his famous prayer: "This humble tree's wood is used to build your homes: let Christ be at the centre of your households. Its leaves remain evergreen in the darkest days: let Christ be your constant light. Its boughs reach out to embrace you and its top points to Heaven: let Christ be your Comfort and Guide". A German historian wrote of him: "Everything which has developed afterwards [in Germany] .... is established on the foundation laid by Boniface, whose tomb should be more sacred for us than the tombs of the patriarchs were for the Jews, because he is truly the spiritual father of our people. Boniface has given us, as well as our successors, more than any of our great emperors and kings has been able to contribute". He is the patron saint of Germany.

Despite his successes elsewhere in Germany, Boniface had never given up his desire to convert the Frisians, who had remained impervious to every evangelical approach. In 754, he set out for Frisia with a small band of followers. On 5 June 755, whilst baptising a large number of Frisians at Dokkum, a hostile crowd, enraged by his destruction of their shrines, hacked the old archbishop to death. His feast day is 5 June.

ST KILIAN

Kilian (Cilian) was born *c.*640 at Mullagh, County Cavan into a noble family. A precocious child with unusually studious and pious inclinations, he entered a monastery. In 685, he set out with ten companions for the Continent to convert the pagan tribes of north-east Europe. After travelling through eastern Gaul (France), they sailed up the River Rhine and its tributary the Main, arriving eventually at Würzburg in Franconia (northern Bavaria), which was ruled by the pagan Frankish Duke Gosbert. Here their nerve failed and they turned back: travelling on to Rome instead. Arriving in Rome during the autumn of 686, they received a missionary commission from Pope Conon, who stiffened their resolve to continue with their evangelical journey.

On their return to Franconia the group split: Kilian and two Irish companions, later Saint Colmán (or Kolonat) and Saint Totnan, made Würzburg their base. The other eight spread out through East Franconia and Thuringia. Kilian converted Gosbert in a large wooden tub. Unfortunately, he discovered after the Duke's conversion that he was married to his brother's widow Geilana (whom Kilian had failed to convert), an irregularity forbidden by the Christian canon. Gosbert obligingly agreed to put her aside, before departing on a military expedition.

Geilana did not take to this new arrangement. As soon as Gosbert had departed, she plotted with the castle cook to kill Kilian, Colman and Totnan. The pair apparently seized the three missionaries on the night of 8 July 689 and beheaded them, burying them within the castle precincts along with all their vestments, books and regalia. Retribution was not long in coming. On the Duke's return, Geilana denied any knowledge of the missionaries' disappearance – until the cook went mad and confessed.

In 752 Burchard, Bishop of Würzburg transferred the missionaries' bones to his cathedral where he inlaid their skulls with precious stones. Every year, on 8 July (Kilian's feast day), they are paraded through the streets of Würzburg in a glass case. A strong Kilian cult sprang up and spread as far as Vienna and Ireland, where he is revered today. *Kilianfest* is one of the best-known festivals of German-speaking peoples everywhere, including German-Americans. Kilian is the patron saint of rheumatism.

ST WALPURGA

Walpurga (or Walpurgis, Walburge, Valborg, Valpuri or Vappu) was born in Wessex in 710. Together with her brothers, the later Saints Willibald and Winibald, she became an Anglo-Saxon missionary to Franconia (present day Rhineland-Palatinate, Baden-Würtemburg, Hesse and Bavaria) to help her uncle, St Boniface. Eventually she became a nun, settling at the convent of Heidenheim near Eichstadt, which had been founded by her brother Willibald; and where she died on 25 February 779. Her claim to posterity lies in the celebration of Walpurga's Night, especially in Germany's Harz Mountains (as *Walpurgisnacht*), on 30 April – the day before her relics were re-buried.

A legend maintains that witches and other occult emanations celebrate during the dark hours before May Day: before they are banished by the dawn of Walpurga's feast-day.

> Adolf Hitler and Joseph Goebbels, with the Russians closing in on their bunker, committed suicide on *Walpurgisnacht* in 1945. It was a significant day for them to die. 30 April is the most important date in Satanism – an appropriate moment perhaps, for the powers of darkness to recover two of their own.
>
> US Special Forces killed the terrorist Osama bin Laden on 2 May 2011. It would have been more fitting if they had brought forward the operation by 48 hours.

TWO GREAT EARLY EUROPEAN SCHOLARS, ALCUIN AND ERIUGENA

No one better exemplifies the spirit of 8th century Anglo-Saxon humanism than Alcuin (*c.*732–804). Born in York and educated at the Cathedral School, he became headmaster in 778. In 781, Alcuin went to Italy and met Charlemagne who invited him to his court at Aachen, where he was assembling the leading scholars of the day, to teach at the school which he had attended. Alcuin introduced English learning systems, reorganised the curriculum and encouraged the study of the liberal arts, the better to understand doctrinal hair-splitting. In 796 Alcuin left Charlemagne's court to become abbot of St Martin at Tours; where he further refined Carolingian 'minuscule script' (the Romans wrote in capitals). Alcuin's contribution to the development of the Roman Catholic Church in Europe was profound. He revised the liturgy of the Frankish church while introducing the Northumbrian practice of singing the creed. He established a system of votive masses offered in fulfilment of a vow for each day of the week, a practice still followed today. He re-edited the Vulgate, the official biblical text of the Roman Catholic Church. His influence endured well into the Middle Ages: yet he remained only a deacon and, in spite of being known for great piety, was never included in the canon of saints. Alcuin is said to have taught Charlemagne how to hold a knife and fork.

Alcuin

John Scotus Eriugena (810–877) was an Irish theologian (*Scotus* in the Middle-Ages was the Latin term for Irish or Gaelic). He followed the humanist path blazed by Alcuin: but whereas Alcuin was essentially a schoolmaster, Eriugena was a philosopher and Greek translator – able to integrate texts of the Greek philosophers with Christian doctrine.

Eriugena had a lighter side and an earthy sense of humour. King Charles the Bald once asked him *"Quid distat inter sottum et Scottum?"* ("What separates a sot from a Scot?"). Eriugena replied, *"mensa tantum"* ("only a table").

BLOOD REALLY IS THICKER THAN WATER

Enormous progress has been made in the last twenty years in genetic profiling: and some startling facts have emerged. These comprehensively debunk ingrained opinions concerning the ethnic origins of the British and Irish populations prior to post-WWII immigration – largely into the UK from the Commonwealth and recently, the EU.

Far from the generalisation that the English are Anglo-Saxon, with a dash of Norse and Norman; and that the Irish, Scots and Welsh are almost totally Celtic, of one sort or another: it turns out that about 75% of the population of these islands born before WWII are descended from the hunter-gatherers who arrived *long before* the neolithic farmers (Celts) who migrated from the Pyrenean ice refuge after 3500 BC. It is now thought that 88% of Irish blood, 81% of Welsh, 79% of Cornish, 70% of Scots (including the islands) and even 68% of English blood derives from the nomads who followed the retreating ice sheets long before the historical period, up to 30,000 or more years ago.

The so-called invasions in the Christian era (Anglo-Saxon, Viking and Norman) were largely cultural, with little physical violence once the initial landings had been absorbed. The Irish have been least affected by non-indigenous immigration, as English and Scots 'colonists' of Ireland were themselves of similar genetic make-up. Shetland Islanders have 20% matching gene types from Norway and Orcadians have 17% but Manxmen have only 10% – and both western Islanders and Ulstermen have less than 8%.

Amazingly, it seems that only an average of 3.8% of British male gene types have matches in the Anglo-Saxon homelands of north-west Europe: this rises to 5.3% in England (up to 20% in parts of Norfolk). Overall, Anglo-Saxon gene flow was modest in terms of numbers, although

It should be important to future harmony, between so-called Celtic or Anglo-Saxon groupings in the British Isles, for historical protagonists to accept that between 70% and 90% of all genetic matches within the Isles are now known to be of a common, indigenous origin – not from northern Europe, Iberia or anywhere else.

It could be argued that Iceland should be regarded as one of the British Isles. It was first settled from Norway by Ingólfur Arnarson in 874, followed by migration from the Faroes ("sheep islands"), Shetland, Orkney and the Hebrides. The vast majority of these early colonists were males: who, if there was to be any lasting settlement, needed wives from whom to breed. The solution was to raid the British Isles for female slaves – much the same as a wife from a Viking point of view.

The resulting population mix today is that, while 75% of Icelandic males are of Norwegian origin and 25% British or Irish, only one third of the females in Iceland are of Norwegian stock and fully two-thirds are descended from willing or unwilling females seized over two hundred years from the British Isles. With nearly half of Icelandic blood being British or Irish, the relationship with the British Isles is extremely close – as is Iceland itself, less than 400 miles away.

Abergele, near Llandudno in North Wales, is an odd little pocket of DNA nonconformity. Copper was mined in the district from the early Bronze Age until the 19th century; and Roman legions from North Africa and Eastern Europe were stationed nearby from about AD 100–400. Celtic mine workers from Spain had brought their skills to the area 1,800 years earlier; and their blood would have been similar in genetic make-up to that of soldiers from the Balkans. The resulting 30–40% concentration of the Y-chromosome haplogroup E3b in Abergele compares with no more than 5–10% of this chromosome elsewhere in Wales. 29% of the present population of Abergele is fluent in Welsh: but perhaps this small town's second language should be proto-Spanish, or even Serbo-Croat.

the cultural impact was profound. Genetic markers from Norway and Denmark are much more significant. Even so, no more than 30% of gene types in England derive from modern Scandinavia, Germany or Holland. The largest north European gene concentrations are 41% around Fakenham in Norfolk (of which 19% is Danish) and York (with an even higher percentage of Danish matches) – but Castlerea in County Roscommon has only 7% and Llangefni in Wales just 4%.

The population of England at the time of the Domesday census, completed in 1086, is thought to have been a little over two million, though estimates vary considerably. This was not much more than half of the population of *Britannia* at the time of Roman withdrawal in 410, reflecting the mayhem of the 'dark ages' which followed. Total Norman immigration following the Conquest in 1066 was in the low ten thousands, perhaps one or two percent of the population – compared with five percent or so from all of northern Europe over the previous 650 years. The cultural, linguistic and economic effects of the Conquest were however, much more devastating than anything that had gone before it: estates previously owned by over 2,000 noble Anglo-Saxon families now belonged to fewer than 200 Norman barons.

THE ENGLISH LANGUAGE IS DERIVED FROM THE ETHNIC COMPOSITION OF MEDIÆVAL ENGLAND (AN EARLY 'UNITED STATES OF EUROPE')

Virtually all the words that modern English has inherited from the earliest inhabitants of these islands are themselves derived from ancient Indo-European roots. Contrast these to see how closely linked numbers and basic words are in different languages.

ENGLISH	one	two	three	four	five	mother	father
GREEK (*PHONETIC*)	*ena*	*duo*	*tria*	*tessera*	*pente*	*mitera*	*pater*
LATIN	unus	duo	tres	quattuor	quinque	mater	pater
FRENCH	un	deux	trois	quatre	cinq	mère	père
GERMAN	eins	zwei	drei	vier	funf	mutter	vater
HINDI (*PHONETIC*)	*ek*	*do*	*teen*	*char*	*paanch*	*ma*	*bap*
PASHTU (*PHONETIC*)	*yao*	*dwa*	*dre*	*salor*	*pinza*	*mor*	*plar*
RUSSIAN (*PHONETIC*)	*adeen*	*dvah*	*tree*	*chetyreh*	*pyat*	*mahma*	*pahpa*

PRE-ROMAN CELTIC	bin, cairn, combe, crag, full, loch; and place or topograhical names – Dover and Kent are both Brythonic;
ROMAN (SECULAR)	cheese, cup, kitchen, plant, street, wine; Saturday (Saturn was the Roman god of agriculture, which became Sæternesdæg in Old English);
ANGLO-FRISIAN	83% of the 1,000 **most often used** words (but only 23% of all words); Sunne (sun)-day and Mona (moon)-day; Eostre (Easter);
LATIN (RELIGIOUS)	abbot, acolyte, altar, angel, candle, lily, martyr, mass, monk;
NORSE	both, cake, call, cut, egg, fellow, flat, get, hit, husband, leg, odd, rag, scar, scorch, scrape, scrub, sister, skill, sky (most words beginning with 'sc' or 'sk'), take, their, them, they, ugly, want, and window. The Norse gods Tiu, Woden, Thor and Frigg gave their names to Tuesday, Wednesday, Thursday and Friday;
NORMAN-FRENCH	art, crime, joy, justice, law, marriage, money, ornament, parliament, pleasure, rent. From a list of the 100 most often used words in English, *number* is the first derived from French – it is 76th. Some 29% of **all** English words however, come from Norman or later French, which should help our proud neighbours come to terms with the retirement of their own language to the kitchen.

The cliché that English words for farm animals are those of the Anglo-Saxon serf in his hut (*hutta* in Old German) who nurtured them, whilst those for the meat they produced were coined by the Norman-French noble in his manor house (*manoir*) who ate them, is broadly correct. Ox, bull, cow, calf, stot and bullock become beef (*boeuf*) and veal (*veau*); swine, pig, boar, hog, sow and gilt turn into pork and bacon (*porc et bacon*); lamb, ram, tup, ewe, even goat become mutton (*mouton*); and deer becomes venison (*venaison*), a word derived from the chase. However the words were often interchangeable until the 18th century. Doctor Johnson referred to "a beef being killed for the house", as late as 1775. It was his great dictionary (1755) that gave impetus to the harmonisation of modern English spelling. The following examples give the origins of some commonly used words.

Honourable mention must also be made of Italian. Virtually all musical expressions have been purloined by English as 'loanwords': from *allegro* (brisk) to *sforzando* (emphasised). In matters culinary too, as with French, English unashamedly uses dozens of Italian words: from *al dente* (slightly undercooked) to *zucchini* ('courgette', itself yet another French word to describe an item of food). It remains a mystery that Yorkshire pudding, Irish stew and haggis have yet to be translated into Italian.

ARABIC	200,000
GERMAN	190,000
JAPANESE	116,000
FRENCH	100,000
HEBREW	100,000

The 1989 Oxford English Dictionary (20 vols.) contains 616,500 word-forms; and in June 2008 the Global Language Monitor forecast that the millionth word in English would be coined on 29 April 2009. This compares with the languages above – all now described as "dead", in that they have ceased to "grow" new words of their own.

The versatility of English is to a great extent due to there being so many alternative usages from source words in the different root languages. This can lead however, to repetition of meaning in mixed language phrases: an extreme example being Cumbria's *Torpenhow* Hill, or *Hill-hill-hill* Hill, in four languages (Cornish, Welsh, Old Norse and modern English). More often than not, English verbs are of Old German origin; while nouns are from Norman-French – combining the simplest and best of both languages.

Nor does English need stresses or accents, diacritical marks or unpronounceable combinations of consonants – no *grave* or acute accents, diareses or *umlauts, tildes,* circumflexes, rings, slashes, cryptic symbols like þ and ð and ß; or combinations of letters like GLH, LLW, TG or TX. Though words such as diphtheria, diphthong, ophthalmology and naphtha are unusual, they are taken straight from the Greek.

Peter Mark Roget FRS (1779–1869), a doctor of Swiss extraction who co-founded the Manchester School of Medicine, compiled a *Thesaurus* ("treasury") of 15,000 words in 1805 (the year of Nelson's death); and published it in 1852 (the year of Wellington's death). The entry for the word "wood" (in its collective sense) is revealing: grove, copse, shaw, thicket, trees, timberland, weald, woodland, brake, chase, clump, coppice, cover, covert, holt, jungle, stand, growth, orchard, plantation, spinney and of course, forest. Some of these are clearly more precisely defined than others: jungle, orchard and plantation are specific. In its usable, decorative or in any material sense, the list is endless: rosewood, deal, plank, spar, joist and so on (leaving aside lumber, logs and kindling, golf clubs and musical instruments).

English is practical: there is usually an exact description to be found; and often a much shorter one than in other languages – it is pleasing however, that there is no one-word definition of the German *Schadenfreude* (enjoyment taken from another's misfortune). Apart from the influence of the US in its promotion, this is the principal reason for the international adoption of English in the world of information technology, medicine and (above all, literally) air traffic control. Another useful quality is the ease with which new words can be coined: for example by returning to Greek roots for scientific terms (as in "technology") or Latin: in law, literature and plant classification. English has no pride to overcome in adopting words or phrases from other languages: unlike the French, who still insist on *chemin de fer* ("road of iron") for a simple railway, when the English know it only as a game of chance. Many 'loanwords' are from countries within the British Empire, notably India, as in: Blighty, bungalow, candy, cashmere, catamaran, cheroot, chintz, chutney, cot, dinghy, doolallie, dungarees, ginger, gymkhana, juggernaut, jungle, jute, khaki, lacquer, loot, pyjamas, shampoo, thug, tickety-boo (*tikai babu*) and verandah. Others come from one language by way of another: from Persia via Turkey came *kiosk* ("shade-maker") and *tabby* (a cat from Tabas); from Russia via France, *bistro* ("quickly"). Two celebrated misunderstandings of loanwords are: "It's like *déjà vu* all over again" ("Yogi" Berra); and "the trouble with the French is that they have no word for *entrepreneur*" (President George W. Bush).

In 1500 a working man's vocabulary amounted to some 500 words (in the 21st century it is about 2,000 – with another 1,000 to 2,000 for a university graduate). Despite this, between the years 1500–1659, some 30,000 words were added to the English language.

George Bernard Shaw once described Britain and the US as "two countries divided by a common language". It is a commonly, but wrongly held opinion that the American usages of some words are either American inventions or simply bad English: "fall" for autumn is an example of the former, "gotten" (instead of got) of the latter.

There are indeed, many American neologisms (new words), often describing animals, trees or native life that the colonists found on arrival in North America that did not exist in England: such as ground-hog, hang-bird, hickory, hominy, live-oak, locust, opossum, persimmon, pone, succotash, wampum and wigwam. There are also words or phrases that are pure American: good examples are belittle, lengthy, lightning-rod, to darken one's doors, to bark up the wrong tree, cold snap, pay dirt and small potatoes. There are also words that have taken on a new meaning in the US: such as card, clever, fork, help, jelly, penny, plunder, raise, rock, sack, smart, ticket and windfall. Finally, there are any number of nouns formed from verbs by adding the French suffix '-ment', as in franchisement, releasement and requirement.

To return to words like "fall" is to go back to 17th century English – and words which have become obsolete in Britain. Roger Ascham, Queen Elizabeth I's tutor wrote: "Spring tyme, Somer, Faule" in 1545; Walter Raleigh too, "A honey tongue, a heart of gall: is fancies Spring, but sorrows Fall". The Scottish historian, Thomas Carlyle, as late as 1851 recorded that: "His first child .... was born .... in the fall of that year".

Gotten (past participle of "get"), obligate, doghouse, rider (for "passenger"), sidewalk (for "pavement"), faucet, spigot, coverall, necktie, range (for "stove"), letter carrier, attorney (for "lawyer"), misdemeanor (in law), teller (in a bank), crib (for a child), plat, pillow (for "cushion"), pocketbook, monkey wrench, night table, station house, wastebasket, skillet, raise (a child) and diaper were all words that Shakespeare would have recognised – or recognized with a "z", a genuinely different US spelling; as is also found in words like "color", "honor" or indeed, "misdemeanor".

To be fair, whilst there is little added economy or meaning in *démarche* for "manoeuvre" (tactic), *cul-de-sac* for "dead-end", *tête-à-tête* for "head-to-head" (quiet chat) or *savoir-faire* for "savvy" (street-wise), there is no language to match French for intuitive, *soigné* ("elegant and sophisticated") description. *Lèse-majesté* (an affront or crime towards a ruler), *jolie laide* ("pretty ugly", but attractive), *sangfroid* ("cold blooded", or composure under stress), *tête à claque* ("the face you want to slap") or *cinq à sept* ("five to seven", meaning the opportunity to be used for sex on the way home from the office) are *sans pareil* ("without equal").

There are of course, plenty of modern words used in the US that are different to British English for describing the same things: cookie (biscuit), movie (film), mailman (postman), closet (wardrobe), trunk (boot), hood (bonnet), gas (petrol), elevator (lift), apartment (flat), pants (trousers), suspenders (braces), eraser (rubber), vacation (holiday), realtor (estate agent) and yard (lawn).

The origins of some well-known roads and places in London are intriguing. Pall Mall hosted games of *paille maille* (a sort of 17th century croquet); Rotten Row in Hyde Park, established by King William III, may be a corruption of *Route du Roi*; Portobello commemorates the capture of Porto Bello in Mexico from the Spanish in 1793; Piccadilly is named after "picadil", a stiff collar sold there by a tailor called Robert Baker; Soho was a grazing area and comes from the hunting call "soho!"; Faulke's Hall, later Foxhall, eventually became Vauxhall. Pimlico is more obscure: it may have received its name from Ben Pimlico, a publican famous for his nut-brown ale.

William Tyndale (*c*.1494–1536) was born in North Nibley, Gloucestershire. A scholar and early Protestant reformer, he is considered to be the "father of English prose". While a few Old and Middle English translations had been made from the 7th century onward, Tyndale's was the first in early Modern English; the first to draw directly from Hebrew and Greek texts; and the first to take advantage of print, allowing a wide distribution. In his Bible (1525) and the

There are only eight nations in the world without an official language: Britain, Pakistan, Costa Rica, Ethiopia, Somalia, Eritrea, Bosnia-Herzegovina and the US

William Tyndale

Tyndale worked on his translation in Little Sodbury in Gloucestershire: one of only 24 confirmed, but possibly up to 31, "Thankful Villages" identified by Arthur Mee in the 1930s – because all those who left to fight in WWII returned safely.

Pentateuch (1530), Tyndale added over 1,700 words to the English language on his own. The King James, or Authorised Version of the Bible (1611), the work of 54 independent scholars but to a large extent based on Tyndale's translations, contains 791,328 words – adding another 800.

He coined such words as "beautiful", "peacemaker", "long-suffering" and "scapegoat"; and phrases such as: "the apple of his eye", "the salt of the earth", "the powers that be", "east of Eden", "my brother's keeper", "lick the dust", "a law unto themselves", "filthy lucre", "how are the mighty fallen" and "fight the good fight". For his efforts to spread the word of God, Tyndale was strangled and burned at the stake in Flanders, a brutality connived at by King Henry VIII.

John Heywood (1497–1580), a contemporary of Tyndale, was a poet, playwright and epigramist from Hertfordshire. He too contributed greatly to the prodigious flowering of colloquial English in the 16th century. All of the following are found in *The Proverbs of John Heywood* (first printed in 1546), the earliest book of proverbs in English:

"When the sun shineth, make hay"
"Look ere ye leap"
"Two heads are better than one"
"Beggars should be no choosers"
"All is well that ends well"
"The fat is in the fire"
"I know on which side my bread is buttered"
"One good turn asketh another"
"A penny for your thought"
"Rome was not built in one day"
"Better late than never"
"An ill wind that bloweth no man to good"
"The more the merrier"
"You cannot see the wood for the trees"
"This hitteth the nail on the head"
"Out of sight out of minde"

Then there is the "Immortal Bard": William Shakespeare, who was born and died on 23 April, St George's day (1564–1616). Accurate details of his life are so few and the subject of so much disagreement that it is best simply to let his unique contribution to the English language speak for him.

Shakespeare used 15,000 words in his plays and another 7,000 in his poems, 22,000 in all – not bad for someone who never went to university. He invented about 1,700 commonplace words: accuse, addiction, advertising, amazement, arouse, assassination, backing, bandit, bedroom, beached, birthplace, blanket, bloodstained, barefaced, blushing, bet, bump, buzzer, cater, champion, circumstantial, cold-blooded, compromise, courtship, critic, dauntless, dawn, deafening, dwindle, epileptic, equivocal, elbow, excitement, exposure and eyeball.

After a pause for breath, to continue with: fashionable, fixture, flawed, frugal. generous, gloomy, gossip, green-eyed, gust, hint, hobnob, hurried, impartial, invulnerable, jaded, label, lacklustre, laughable, lonely, lower, luggage, lustrous, madcap, majestic, marketable, mimic, monumental, moonbeam, mountaineer, negotiate, noiseless, obscene, obsequiously, ode, olympian, outbreak, pander, pedant, premeditated, puke, radiance, rant, remorseless, savagery, scuffle, secure, skim milk, submerge, summit, swagger, torture, tranquil, undress, unreal, varied, vaulting, worthless, zany; and so on. We take many of his sayings as commonplace today – indeed, he is sometimes

The Cobbe portrait of William Shakespeare by unknown artist (*c.*1610)

derided by wiseacres for using so many clichés: "into thin air", "what the dickens (*devil*)", "fair play", "foregone conclusion", "in my mind's eye", even (anticipating Aldous Huxley's novel published in 1932) "Brave New World" – and hundreds more.

No other language has been so enriched by so many poets, dramatists and authors.

Punctuation in such a grammatically simple, versatile and exuberant language is clearly vital to meaning – especially where words are repeated. Without becoming distracted by the enormous and often comical scope for misunderstanding in the absence of any formal 'stops', there are few languages that can bemuse a reader with a splendid little sentence like this: *[The landlord of the Cock and Bull refused to pay for a new pub sign, because]* "there was too much space between Cock and and and and and Bull".

There is a world of difference between being just comprehensible (in various forms of creole or pidgin, or simply shouting at someone in Shanghai) and in flawless, idiomatic English; but the real give-away between those who grew up speaking English and those who learned it later in life, is accent.

To speak British English undetectably as a foreigner is extremely difficult. This seems odd, given that there are more regional accents within the British Isles themselves than in any other similarly sized part of the world; but then the Islanders know their neighbours, even if they cannot understand a word they say. It must be harder still for a foreigner to make sense of a broad Scouse, Geordie, Glasgow or Belfast accent – to say nothing of the many dialect words used throughout the Isles (especially in Scotland). There is an irony in the Hollywood use nowadays of actors with cut-glass English accents as seriously evil villains, when once it was a sign of innate good breeding and behaviour. The Sheriff of Nottingham has much to answer for.

The flat vowels of New England originate from East Anglia, where the first colonists came from; the longer, drawling Southern accent comes from the West of England.

Many Old English words, derived from the same Indo-European roots (often shared with Sanskrit, the classical language of Northern India), have split and developed into quite different spellings and meanings in modern English. The following is just one example of thousands that have separated, some of them mystifyingly so: the first word describes the largest indigenous wild animal in the British Isles today, the Red deer.

"Deer" is from the Old English: *déor* > Old Frisian (the language closest to English): *dier* > German: tier > Old Norse: *djur* > Icelandic: *dyr* – and so on, becomes *dær* or *der* in Middle English and was used in general for "animal" (Shakespeare speaks of "mice and rats, and such small deer" for Edgar's diet in King Lear). This might be described as the North European 'route' back to the mother tongue from which all European languages descend – except Basque, Magyar (Hungarian) and Finnish.

In southern Europe the Greek word for a wild animal is pronounced *thier* (hence "feral"), which evolved into *thieriaké*, used to describe an electuary (a medical preparation made into a paste with honey or syrup) against a venomous bite. By various journeys, via the Provençal: *tiriaca* > Old French: *triacle*, it became *triacla* in Spanish. The Spanish used *triacla* to describe the uncrystallized, sweet and sticky juice from a tall, stout grass they took to the New World

The name Pakistan was coined (in 1933) from the first letters of **P**unjab, **A**fghania, **K**ashmir, **I**ndus valley and **S**indh. Happily, *pak* also means "pure" in Persian.

originally from New Guinea. This word was adapted into the English "treacle". Thus, "deer" and "treacle" are derived from the same root. The suffix '-stan', as in Tajiki-stan, Turkmeni-stan and Waziri-stan, is formed from the old Iranian root *sta-*, meaning "to stay". In this context it describes "the place where one stays", i.e. homeland or country. Iranian is descended from the same 7,000 year-old Proto-Indo-European (known as PIE) family of languages as English.

"Stan" occurs in English in many other forms such as "stand" and "steady".

English is the first language of about 400 million people, second only to Mandarin Chinese (about twice as many), but a little more than those who speak Hindi and Urdu; a third more than Spanish; twice as many as Russian; nearly three times as many as Arabic; four times as many as German; and five times as many as French.

As the second language of perhaps another 1.1 billion however, English is understood, if not spoken fluently, by a total of some 1.5 billion people. It is therefore the official language of the United Nations, European Union and (unsurprisingly) the Commonwealth. English has indeed become the world's first *lingua franca* (in Latin, naturally).

Over a quarter of all Nobel prizes for literature have been awarded to authors who wrote in English. Eight out of the ten Eurovision song contest winners in the decade to 2007 sang in English – despite no entry from the UK itself being successful.

THE VAGARIES OF ENGLISH PRONUNCIATION

I take it you already know
  Of tough and bough and cough and dough?
Others may stumble, but not you
  On hiccough, thorough, slough and through.
Well done! And now you wish perhaps
  To learn of less familiar traps?
Beware of heard, a dreadful word
  That looks like beard and sounds like bird.
And dead: it's said like bed, not bead;
  For goodness' sake, don't call it "deed"!
Watch out for meat and great and threat
  (they rhyme with suite and straight and debt),
A moth is not a moth in mother –

  Nor both in bother, broth in brother.
And here is not a match for there,
  Nor dear and fear for bear and pear.
And then there's dose and rose and lose.
  Just look them up – and goose and choose.
And cork and work and card and ward,
  And font and front and word and sword.
And do and go, then thwart and cart –
  Come, come, I've hardly made a start.
A dreadful language? Why, man alive!
  I'd mastered it when I was five!
And yet to write it, the more I try,
  I'll not learn how 'til the day I die. (Anon.)

A THORNY PROBLEM

It may come as a disappointment, but "Ye", as in "Ye Olde Curiositie Shoppe", should be pronounced "the" – as its use in this context suggests.

The voiced dental fricative "th" sound was originally represented by a single Old English (and Icelandic) letter called "thorn" – derived from a rune, which was a symbol of an obscure and obsolete Scandinavian alphabet. It was also used in mediæval Swedish, but was later replaced with the digraph "th". Early printers' type fonts, imported from Italy or Germany, did not include the letter "thorn". Instead the letter "Y" was used, sometimes with a small "e" superscript – as in Ye.

The last vestige of thorn, in the form of a "Y", survives to this day only in the "Ye" pseudo-archaic representation of "the". In all other usages it had died out by 1700.

LALLANS

Lallans (an abbreviation of the Scots word "lawlands" meaning the lowlands of Scotland), was once used to refer to the Scots language as a whole. Recent scholarship however, suggests that it refers only to the dialects of south and central Scotland. Doric (Greek for "rustic"), a term once used to refer to Scots dialects in general, is now used only to describe those of north-east Scotland. It is also known as the "Moray Claik".

Robert Burns and Robert Louis Stevenson used Lallans as the "Scottish language":

> *They took nae pains their speech to balance,*
> > *Or rules to gie;*
> *But spak their thoughts in plain, braid lallans,*
> > *Like you or me.*

Robert Burns in *Epistle To William Simson*

> *What tongue does your auld bookie speak?*
> > *He'll spier; an' I, his mou to steik :*
> *No bein' fit to write in Greek,*
> > *I wrote in Lallan,*
> *Dear to my heart as the peat reek,*
> > *Auld as Tantallon.*

Robert Louis Stevenson in *The Maker to Posterity*.

Before the Treaty of Union in 1707, Lallans was the state language of Scotland and it was used for all government business. Even after the Union, Lallans continued in use by the Scottish courts for much of the 18th century. In Ulster, the word Ullans has been coined to refer to the revived literary output of Ulster Scots. The magazine of the Ulster-Scots Language Society is also named *Ullans*.

ENGLISH PLACE-NAMES

-ENDING(S)	EXAMPLE(S)	*MEANING*	LANGUAGE
borough, bury	Scarborough, Salisbury	*fort*	O English
bourne, burn	Eastbourne, Blackburn	*stream*	O Frisian
by	Grimsby, Derby, Whitby	*farmstead*	O Norse
caster, cester, chester	Ancaster, Leicester, Winchester	*castle*	Latin/OE
don	Hendon, Maldon, Croydon	*hill*	O English
ea, ey	Battersea, Pewsey, Anglesey	*island*	O English
ham	Chobham, Grantham, Durham	*manor, house(s)*	O English
hithe, hythe or eth	Rotherhithe, Lambeth	*landing place*	O English
holm(e)	Barholm, Axholme	*island*	O Norse
hurst	Wadhurst, Midhurst	*wooded hill*	O English
leigh, ley	Hadleigh, Henley, Wembley	*clearing, glade*	O English
minster	Westminster, Upminster	*monastery*	Latin/OE
ness	Skegness, Dungeness	*headland*	O Norse
thorp(e)	Althorp, Scunthorpe	*outlying farm*	O Danish
thwaite	Armathwaite, Bassenthwaite	*remote meadow*	O Danish
wick, wich (vicus)	Warwick, Howick, Ipswich	*house(s), farm*	OE (Latin)
worth	Tamworth, Petworth, Lulworth	*enclosure*	O English

The earliest place or topographical names that we use today were bequeathed us by the Welsh or Brythonic-speaking Celts. For all that we will ever know, they may have inherited them from even earlier inhabitants of Britain (the Celts were relatively latecomers themselves). There are a surprising amount, including most rivers: Aire, Avon, Colne, Dee, Derwent, Don, Esk and Exe (the same word), Kennet, Ouse, Severn, Stour, Tay, Tees, Test, Thames, Trent, Wey and Wye (the same word) and Yare. The Celts also named Cannock, Leeds, Malvern, Thanet and Wight (which can mean "man", so there are actually **two** "Isles of Man") – and the majority of places in Cornwall, which was not colonised by the Anglo-Saxons until 926.

Invaders and other incomers then 'scent-marked' the landscape, usually obliterating the names that had been coined by previous generations of Britons – and often showing little originality. Without dwelling on the obvious meanings of suffixes such as bridge (Cambridge), church (Hornchurch) or kirk (Oswaldkirk), field (Driffield), ford (Oxford), hill (Edgehill), mere (Ellesmere), mouth (Plymouth), port (Southport), water (Bayswater), wood (Brentwood) and so on, there are a considerable number of less straightforward place-name endings covering Britain in their thousands, especially England.

Suffixes can equally be used as prefixes (Bournemouth, Chesterfield); stand alone (Bury, Thorpe, Chester); or be used together (Burnham, Wickham, Leyburn, Thorpeness). Often both parts of the name contribute to the meaning: Chelsea (from *Chesil-ea*) means "gravel-island"; and Chiswick and Keswick, both of which mean "cheese farm".

In the centuries before telephone operators, a number of places were pronounced in ways that were difficult to reconcile with their spelling: as in "Cicister" for Cirencester, "Stukey" for Stiffkey, "Daintry" for Daventry and "Hunston" for Hunstanton. In a few cases there was an historical reason: Pontefract (in Yorkshire) used to be known as "Pomfret", because the original name was *Pont-freit* (from the Latin *Fracti-pontis*), or "broken bridge". Awkward or overly-long place-names were often shortened too: Brighton was once Brighthelmston and in Scotland Bo'ness was Borrowstounness.

Some Scottish pronunciations remain defiantly counter-intuitive: "Aflek" for Auchinleck, "Coolain" for Culzean and "Mull-guy" for Milngavie are simply unguessable.

The Romans left little mark on English place-names. Latin was the language of administration, not of daily life. However here are some splendid examples to be found:

Colchester (*Camulodunon* to the Celts, *Camulodunum* to the Romans), meaning "Castle on the river Colne", 56 miles north-east of London, is considered to be Britain's oldest town – having served as the first Roman capital of *Britannia*. The town's near two mile-long walls were built between AD 65–80, after it had been destroyed by Boudicca. Colchester Castle was the scene of Humpty-Dumpty's "great fall" in 1648.

It would be hard to guess the origin of Baldock, in Hertfordshire. *Baldac* is the Old French name for Baghdad; and it was given to the town by the Knights Templar (who held the manor in the 12th century), to commemorate the Crusades.

Eleanor crosses were 12 lavishly decorated stone monuments, three of which survive intact, in a line down the east of England. King Edward I had the crosses erected (1291–94) in memory of his wife Eleanor of Castile, marking the route of her body as it was taken from Hartby in Lincolnshire to London.

Eleanor's last resting place before burial in Westminster Abbey was Charing Cross. The word Charing is said by romantics to come from the French *chère reine* ("dear queen"). Disappointingly, it probably comes from the Anglo-Saxon word *cerring* (a "bend"), as Charing Cross stands on the outside of a 90° bend in the River Thames. The original cross stood at the top of Whitehall on the south side of Trafalgar Square – the official centre of London, when measuring distances from the city.

The Romans measured all distances in Britannia from the "London Stone". It is now set within a stone surround and iron grill on Cannon Street, in the City of London.

• **Victorian replica at Charing Cross**

Barton in Fabis, Ryme Intrinseca, Toller Porcorum are three. While village names followed by Magna and Parva (large and small) are not uncommon in the Midland counties, Lincoln (Lindum Colonia) is unusual in its wholly Latin origin.

The Normans seized and bled the countryside, but most places had been named long before. Those that are of Norman origin usually relate to ownership and often involve two words (Wootton Bassett, Mallet Montague, Cricket Malherbie); but not always (Herstmonceux). Descriptive names include: Belvoir for "beautiful view" (pronounced "Beaver"), Beauly ("beautiful place") and Devizes ("straddling a boundary"). Battle (the supposed site of the battle of Hastings) is, not unreasonably, from the French *bataille*.

Britain would not be the country it is without names of places reflecting the originality and quirkiness of its polyglot forebears.

SURNAMES

In the 12th century most people in Britain lived in small farming communities. Everyone knew their neighbours and there was little need for more than one name. Geoffrey of Monmouth (died 1155), William of Malmesbury. or Elias of Dereham (died 1245), who oversaw the building of Salisbury Cathedral, were typical of the way people once referred to each other. But as the population increased and the towns grew, it became necessary to differentiate between two people of the same first name. It took over two hundred years before everyone had a surname, because change in the countryside is embraced slowly and no laws were ever passed to speed things up.

Expectant parents will discover that every first name has a meaning: from Amanda ("she who must be loved") to Zachariah ("the Lord Remembers") – so do surnames.

There were four principal sources used to choose, or have chosen for you, a second name; none more important than another. The first was a patronymic (the father's name): Johnson, Richardson, Williamson are straightforward. Less obvious are Anderson (Andrew), Dawson (David), Harris or Harrison (Harry), Henderson (Henry), Nixon (Nicholas), Patterson (Patrick), Simpson (Simon) and Tennyson (Dennis). 'Kins', after the father's name, was a diminutive: Tomkins, Wilkins and Perkins; or 'lett' as in Bartlett (little Bartholemew) and Hewitt (little Hugh) – much the same as Hudson (Hugh's son). 'Cock' meant "young man", as in Wilcock or Wilcox.

In Scotland and Ireland, Gaelic speakers often put 'Mac' or 'Mc' (meaning "son of") in front of a father's name to obtain the same result: hence Macdonald or Macgregor. In Ireland, a variant of 'Mac' was 'Ó', meaning "grandson of", which led on to countless variations from Ó Baire (Barry means "blonde" in Irish) to Ó Tuathail (O'Toole, or Tully means "ruler"). Some Norman names in Ireland synthesised over time into more Irish sounding ones: de Burgh became Burke and de St Aubyn became Tobin. In England, as well as in Ireland, the French for son (*fils*) became 'Fitz' (as in Fitzwilliam or Fitzgerald). This prefix was often a euphemism for a royal bastard, as in Fitzroy (the family name of the Dukes of Grafton, descended from Charles II).

In Welsh, instead of 'Mac' (Q-Celtic), 'Map' (P-Celtic) means "son of", usually shortened to 'ap'. Over time 'ap' became elided into the father's name: ap Evan became Bevan, ap Rhys became Price, ap Owen became Bowen, ap Hugh became Pugh, ap Harry became Parry, ap Richard became Prichard, ap Robert became Probert and so on. The Welsh saw no reason to use surnames until two hundred years after they were adopted in England, so only a relatively small number developed. As a result, Jones ("son of John") is the second most common surname in

Britain, after Smith – followed by Williams (also of Welsh origin), Brown, Taylor and Wilson.

The second source of surnames was to describe occupation or office – an endless choice, but invariably simple to understand. Baker (or Baxter), Butler, Carpenter, Clerk, Cooper, Farmer, Faulkner (Falconer), Foster (Forester), Gardener, Miller, Shepherd, Smith, Cartwright and Wainwright (both mean the same) and Weaver are all explicit – as is Hooker, for a hook-maker (its earliest use in reference to a prostitute was in 1845).

The third source was from physical characteristics: White (Blunt came from "blond"), Black (Blake), Green, Brown, Red (Read, Reed , Reid and Russell), Long, Short, Stern, Stout (as in "brave"), Peacock (not so flattering), Palmer (as in "pilgrim", for those who went on pilgrimage always returned with a frond of palm), Little or Armstrong. Bastard means what it says too; but Hoare should not be taken as it is pronounced: spelled this way it means white or grey, as in "hoar".

Blond (or blonde) is one of the few adjectives in English differentiated by gender.

The final source was residence. It was least used to identify an actual place, for it scarcely narrowed the field if you were a Londoner: but examples can be found from Ashby, Blofield, Colchester and Darby, by way of Murray (Moray) to Winchester, York and Zealand. De'Ath, not a name to conjure with, simply means "from Ethe" in Flanders or "Eth" in northern France. Sometimes names were taken from descriptions of property: as in Barnes, Granger, Hall and House. Usually though, names were simple associations with noteworthy features or the physical characteristics of where they lived: as in Birch, Hazel or simply Tree; and Bank(s), Brook(e), Cliff(e), Dyke (or Syke), Field, Heath, Hill, Lake, Marsh, Meadow(es), Moor(e), Mountain or Wood(s).

The nobility of course, usually took their titles from places (once it especially described those they actually owned): Earl of Surrey, Marquess of Blandford, Duke of Norfolk and so on. The Normans, Huguenots and other French emigrés introduced the particles (as they are called in French) 'de', 'du' and 'de la'; and the Dutch brought the preposition (as it should be called) 'van'. Both mean "of" or "from". Some surnames have elided into one word: as in Debrett, Defoe and Dupont or Vanbrugh, Vancouver and Vansittart. Most French names however, still retain the separation – as they also do in the Anglo-Norman Channel Islands (De la Rue is a Guernsey name).

Retaining the 'particle' shows little advance from the days of Elias of Dereham. As we have seen though, French is impervious to new word formations of any kind.

The *Empire Windrush* arrived at Tilbury on 22 June 1948, carrying 492 passengers from Jamaica wishing to start a new life in the United Kingdom. The passengers were the first large group of West Indian immigrants to the United Kingdom after WWII. However, they all arrived with conventional British first names and surnames. By an unpleasant quirk of history, it was as though they had wound the clock back a few hundred years and had no need of a fresh identity in a foreign land.

The Scots were especially partial to nicknames: examples include Cameron for "crooked nose", Campbell for "crooked lip", Kennedy for "ugly head" and Cruikshank for "crooked leg".

Cornwall (Kernow) was not absorbed into Wessex until 926: and, to judge from some surnames native to the county, it remains a land of mystery and magic. Trelawney ("farm in a clearing") and Boscawen ("house of the elder tree") are well-known and recognisably Cornish names. Others are less so: Andrewartha ("upper homestead"), Baragwanath ("bread"), Cadwalader (a Welsh saint), Kitto ("Christopher's children"), Tangye ("fire dog") and Vellanoneth ("new mill").

Winston Graham's twelve books about *Ross Poldark* and his family in Cornwall (also a 1970s TV series) were exciting and popular – but the surname is not Cornish.

Passengers disembarking from Empire Windrush
Science & Society Picture Library

The vile reality behind this was of course, slavery. Although some of the new arrivals, and more who followed them from British colonial possessions in the Caribbean, were blood descendants of plantation owners or overseers, many more were not.

Their ancestors had simply been issued with new names by the slave-masters who had bought them (usually their own); and unwittingly, they bestowed on free men and women a helping hand towards an easier life in Britain two hundred years later.

Recent immigrants from the Sub-Continent brought with them surnames more akin to the clan names of the Scottish Highlands than anything else. Patel (meaning "village headman" in Sanskrit) is the twentieth most common surname in Britain today; whilst Singh ("lion" in Sanskrit) is seventy-sixth. Singh really is unusual, in that the name was conferred on all Sikhs by their tenth guru Gobind Singh in 1699, to eliminate the possibility of caste within the ranks of his *Jat* (Punjabi farmer) followers. Women are known as Kaur, meaning "princess". Singh is therefore the surname of a virtual nation.

Though Khan (meaning "prince" in Turkish and Arabic) is overwhelmingly Muslim, it also means "wise and learned man" in Persian and is occasionally used by non-Muslims. It is common throughout India, Pakistan and Bangladesh; and now in Britain too.

None of these surnames imply any blood connection; and presumably subdivision into family or more specific names will evolve at some point, possibly driven by the introduction of identity cards. Until then two or more first names, or honorifics will continue to be used to differentiate between individuals with the same 'surname'.

ANCESTRY

Most families used to be satisfied with one first or Christian name; but over time, many started to add another, or even more, to increase individuality and aid precise identification. In the US, within some families, it has become a tradition to name the son after the father, using the addition of "Junior" to differentiate between them. The Courtaulds of Halstead, in Essex have gone one further. The popular historian George Courtauld (born 1967), son of George Courtauld (born 1938), is the eighth of his line to be given the name George – and no other. It must be confusing, to say the least.

Most families concentrate on the father's line, anxious to preserve the continuity of the Y chromosome inherited only by sons, as well as the surname. A rare exception is to be found in Jewish families, which are matrilinear – a practice that arose because only the mother can ever really be sure who the father was.

Dedicated genealogists try to research all the lines in their families, male and female, as far back in time as possible: but they rapidly come across the staggering effects of simply multiplying by two with each generation. One person has two parents, four grandparents, eight great-grandparents, then 16 > 32 > 64 > 128 > 256 > 512 > 1,024 > 2,048 > 4,096 and so on. After a mere fifteen generations, a person has over sixteen thousand forebears (male and female) to identify. This is just comprehensible as an ambition, but quite impossible to achieve in practice. After twenty generations the number grows to over 500,000 – and that is still eleven generations short of 1066.

There are 30 years to a generation, so to draw a 'complete' family tree back to the Conquest (thirty-one generations), in grinding theory a person will have well over a billion ancestors. Of course, long before this ridiculous total is reached, forebears will have interbred: indeed the Quakers very often married their first cousins and, each time they did so, they halved the number of ancestors that they shared. It is only possible to guess at how many people have ever lived in the British Isles, but a number that has been suggested is perhaps 200 million (the population of England was about 1 million in AD 43, 2 million in 1066 and still only 8 million in 1800). Divide 1,000 [million] by 200 [million] and the implication is clear: everyone whose family has lived in these islands for more than, say 250 years is related to each other a minimum of five times over. Thousands of people, as it is, can quite easily trace their ancestry back to Henry III (died 1272) and beyond: indeed so could everyone else, had they the documentation to prove it – with countless lines of descent. This ought to stop snobbish affectation about pedigree (from the French *pé de grue*, or "crane's foot") in its tracks. The reason that it does not, is that it is the paperwork that counts: and not many have that much of it, given the violent upheavals over the centuries – and the illiteracy of all but the lucky few.

RED HAIR

Approximately 1.5% of the human population has red hair. It occurs more frequently (about 4% of the population) in northern and western Europeans and their descendants. It originated in Neanderthal Man, who lived in Europe for 260,000 years before being replaced by modern man, who arrived from Africa only 40,000 years ago.

Red hair appears in people with two copies of a recessive (non-dominant) gene on chromosome 16, which causes a change in the MC1R protein. It is associated with fair skin, freckles and sensitivity to ultraviolet light, as the mutated MC1R protein occurs in the skin and eyes rather than the darker melanin. It often skips generations.

Red hair is associated particularly with parts of the British Isles: matching the movement of the Celts, as they were pushed west and north by the Anglo-Saxons, as well as the pattern of Viking settlement. Vikings had significant numbers of redheads too: memorably Erik the Red (950–*c*.1003), who first settled Greenland. King William I ("the Lion") of Scotland and his son Alexander II both had red hair.

Scotland has the highest proportion of redheads in the world (13%) and as many as 40% carry the recessive red hair gene. Ireland has the second highest (10%), with an estimated total of 46% carrying the gene. Brythonic Wales and Cornwall; and Northumberland, Nottinghamshire and Yorkshire (in the Viking Danelaw) also have significant proportions of redheads. Queen Elizabeth I had red hair too.

In the United States, 2 to 6% of the population is estimated to have red hair. This would give the US the largest population of redheads in the world (6 to 18 million), with approximately 650,000 in Scotland and 420,000 in Ireland.

Redheads are supposed to be quicker tempered, more able to tolerate pain and highly sexed. Jonathan Swift satirised redheads in *A Voyage to the Country of the Houyhnhnms*: "It is observed that the red-haired of both sexes are more libidinous and mischievous than the rest, whom yet they much exceed in strength and activity".

The colour "titian" takes its name from the artist Tiziano Vecelli, known as Titian. Sandro Botticelli's celebrated painting *The Birth of Venus*, depicts her as a redhead. The Pre-Raphaelites especially favoured redheads too, as did the Italian Modigliani and the Viennese Gustav Klimt. Ellen Terry (1847–1928), the celebrated Victorian actress, had stunning red hair. According to a Clairol *Color Attitudes Survey*, redheaded women see themselves as "fearless and street-wise". However fair-skinned redheads lack the melanin needed to prevent sunburn – the reason they are found more in Northern Europe than in Africa.

Red is a respected colour of hair in Islam. The Prophet Mohammed dyed his hair red, using henna (paste from a flowering plant found in Africa, South Asia and Australia).

Boudicca, Queen of the Iceni, was described by the historian Dio Cassius as: "tall and terrifying in appearance .... a great mass of red hair .... over her shoulders". Tacitus also mentioned the "red hair and large limbs of the inhabitants of Caledonia".

THE SCOTS ARE ROMANO-BRITISH, IRISH, ANGLO-SAXON, NORSE AND ANGLO-NORMAN, BUT HAVE NOT BEEN "SCOTTISH" SINCE ABOUT AD 850

SOME SCOTS FAMILIES OF NORMAN OR NORMAN SPONSORED DESCENT

NORMAN NAME	SCOTTISH NAME	DATE
de Aigneaux	Agnew	
de Annesley (in Nottinghamshire)	Ainslie	
de Bailleul (-Neuville)	Balliol (King of Scotland)	
de Bosville	Boswell	
de Brix (or de Brus)	Bruce (King of Scotland)	1124
de Comines (nicknamed "Cummin")	Cumming (Comyn)	1144
(from Flanders)	Douglas	*temp.* David I
(from Flanders)	Fleming	
de Fresles (nicknamed "Fraises")	Fraser	1160
Gor-dun (Old English "great hill fort")	Gordon	1320
de Graegham (Old English "Gray Home")	Graham	
le Grand (the "Big One")	Grant	1264
de Hambledon (in Leicestershire)	Hamilton	1200
La Haye (Norman "stockade")	Hay	1160
(from Flanders)	Innes	
de Limesay	Lindsay	1086
de Montalet	Maitland	*temp.* William I
Marcus (then Maccus-ville)	Maxwell	
de Malleville	Melville	1155
de Mesnieres	Menzies	1249
de Montgommerei (Mons Gomeric)	Montgomerie/y	*temp.* David I
de Ramesai (in Huntingdonshire)	Ramsay	
de Rots (or Ros)	Ross (in the Lowlands)	
Saint-Clair (-sur-Elle)	Sinclair	1162
Fitz Alan ("the High Steward")	Stewart (Kings of Scotland)	1141
de Tournbeau	Turnbull	

Many Scottish clan and family names have their roots in Normandy; and many Norman knights left families of the same name in England, moving freely between the two countries – Robert "the Bruce", King of Scotland (1306–29), was also Earl of Huntingdon. King David I spent many years in England; and invited many young and ambitious knights to make their fortunes in Scotland.

Anglo-Norman and Plantagenet knights left their mark on almost every facet of Scottish life: from *Sheriffs* and *Procurator Fiscals* who administer justice, to *feu duty* paid on land. In

This map shows Alba (Scotland) and Northern England in *c.*700 with later Viking occupants (9/10th centuries). Anglo-Norman and Plantagenet incursions and settlements followed, usually by invitation, in the 11/13th centuries. By the middle of the 9th century the original inhabitants of Scotland, the Picts (Latin for "Painted People"), had ceased to exist. The muddled, exaggerated nationalism inspired by the inaccuracies and bad history of the US film Braveheart (1995) is ironic: the hero William Wallace was a man of Wales (Wealas); and all three of the main contenders for the throne (Bruce, Comyn and Balliot) were Anglo-Norman knights.

THE MAKING OF THE SCOTS

The Scots are Romano–British, Irish, Anglo–Saxon, Norse and Anglo–Norman,
but have not been Caledonian (Pict) since about AD 850.

- Occupied by Vikings from Norway (9/10th century)
- Occupied by Vikings from Denmark (9/10th century)
- Present Scotland / England border
- ● Capital
- ✝ Monastery
- Battle

SHETLAND
(Earldom of Orkney)

0   25 miles

0   50 km

ORKNEY
*(Earldom
of Orkney)*

KINGDOM OF THE ISLES

NORTHERN
PICTS

CALEDONII

The Romans, led by
Agricola crushed the Picts
led by Calgacus in AD 84.

Mons Graupius
(AD 84)

FORTRIU
Kingdom of the Southern Picts
(Brythonic–speaking Celts)

The Picts were extinguished before
AD 850, through intermarriage or
conquest, by the Scots (Irish Gaels)
from Dalriada.

Iona
St. Columba (AD 563) ✝

DALRIADA

Dunnichen
(AD 685)

Perth ●

The Picts destroyed
the Angles.

Dunadd

Dalriada
Kingdom of the Scots
(Goidelic–speaking Celts).

Dumbarton

Antonine
Wall
(AD 143–180)

Edinburgh

Din Eidyn (Brythonic) or Dun Eideann
(Gaelic), captured and renamed
Edinburgh by the Angles in AD 638.

Holy Isle
(Lindisfarne)
St. Aidan (AD 635) ✝

STRATHCLYDE
BRITONS
(Brythonic–speaking
Celts)

Bamburgh

NORTHUMBRIA
(Angles)

SCOTII
(Irish Gaels)

RHEGED BRITONS
(Brythonic–speaking Celts)

CUMBRIA

Hadrian's Wall
(AD 122)

Armagh ✝
St. Patrick (AD 457)

Whithorn ✝
St. Ninian (AD 397)

The Danelaw was
Anglo–Saxon, but
occupied by Vikings
from Denmark.

E R I N

ISLE OF
MAN

THE DANELAW

● York

short order, this small group achieved a virtual take-over of Scotland: and were rewarded with land, titles – and the throne. It was an astonishing achievement.

The remarkable Norman ability to be assimilated into the indigenous population, whilst retaining power and privilege, was very much what happened in Ireland too – but, because the king and many of his nobles had substantial possessions across the Channel to protect, it took much longer for the Normans fully to integrate in England. The de Burgh family claims descent from Clovis (*c*.466–511), the first king of the Franks, who conquered and occupied present day France. William FitzAdelm de Burgh (1157–1206) followed the invasions of Richard de Clare ("Strongbow") and King Henry II to Ireland in 1175. Henry appointed him Governor of Limerick and gifted him vast estates in Leinster, Munster, and Connaught. One of William's descendants married the heiress daughter of de Lacy, Earl of Ulster – a family that is mentioned frequently in Chapter I, playing pivotal roles in the history of mediæval England and Ireland. The surname eventually synthesised into Burke.

SCOTTISH PLACE-NAMES

PREFIX(ES)	EXAMPLE(S)	MEANING	LANGUAGE
Aber	Aberdeen, Abergavenny (Wales)	*river junction*	Brythonic
Blair (from *Blár*)	Blairgowrie, Blair Atholl	*place (battle)*	Gaelic
Cairn or Carn	Cairngorm, Carnoustie	*rocky hill*	Gaelic
Clach or Clack	Clachnacuddin, Clackmannan	*stone*	Gaelic
Drum or Dum	Drumbeg, Dumbarton, Dumfries	*ridge (fort)*	Gaelic
Dun	Dunfermline, Dundalk (Ireland)	*mound (fort)*	Gaelic
Inch (Irish: *innis*)	Inchnadamph, Innisfree (Ireland)	*island*	Gaelic
Inver (from *inbhir*)	Inverness, Invergordon, Inverurie	*creek*	Gaelic
Kil (from *caell*)	Kilmarnock, Kilcreggan	*cell (church)*	Gaelic
Kin	Kintyre, Kinloch, Kinross	*at the head of*	Gaelic
Pit	Pitlochry, Pittenweem, Pitsligo	*part, share*	Pictish
Strath	Strathblane, Strathmore	*wide valley*	Gaelic

-SUFFIX(ES)	EXAMPLE(S)	MEANING	LANGUAGE
burgh (*borough*)	Edinburgh, Jedburgh, Roxburgh	*fort*	O English
haven (from *hythe*)	Stonehaven, Newhaven	*landing stage*	O English
haugh or heugh	Phenzhopehaugh, Maxwellheugh	*water meadow*	O English
ness	Caithness, Bo'ness, Inverness	*headland*	O Norse
wald or wall	Tinwald, Dingwall, Tingwall	*parliament*	O Norse
wick (from *vik*)	Berwick, Wick, Lerwick	*bay, inlet*	O Norse

Aber is Welsh and clearly Pictish too (where rivers meet or reach the sea): as in Arbroath (*Aber-Brothaig*), Aberfeldy and Aberdeen – it is common in the old Pictish heartland of north-east Scotland. Irish (Erse) and Scottish Gaelic share many place-name origins, both being Goidelic. Prefixes are often Gaelic; name-endings, usually not.

The Celts named the A'an (Avon), Annan, Clyde, Forth, Spey (probably meaning hawthorn), Ythan (meaning gorse) and many other rivers in Scotland.

Place-names beginning with Ben (hill), Glen and Kirk (Kirkcudbright means the church of St Cuthbert, an English saint), or ending with brae (hillside) and muir (moor) need little explanation. A number of less straightforward ones do: Dumbarton is *Dùn Breatainn* in Gaelic (meaning "fort of the Brythons"); Elgin is Irish (*Elg* is Ireland in Irish Gaelic, Elgin its diminutive: little Ireland); Glasgow is Welsh (*glas cau*, or "green hollow": and Glesca, is the correct pronunciation); Lanark is Welsh too (*llanerch*: "forest glade" or "clearing"); Skye is Gaelic (*sgiath*: "wing", to reflect the winged or divided shape of the island); and Stornoway, which is from the Old Norse, *Stjornavagr* (for "steering bay"). Many place-names in the north end with beg (*beag*) and more (*mhor* or *mòr*) – simply meaning "small" or "large", as in Drumbeg and Strathmore, in Gaelic.

John o'Groats takes its name from Jan de Groot, a Dutchman who had the rights to operate a ferry to Orkney, which had been recently acquired from Norway by King James IV, in 1496. Gretna is obscure, possibly from *greten ho* ("at the great hill"). A few common, but not especially obvious in their meaning, prefixes and suffixes are set out on the previous page.

OFFA, KING OF MERCIA (REIGNED 757–96)

Offa (died 796), the most powerful king of Anglo-Saxon England of his time, became King of Mercia in 757, having seized power in a civil war. He began a ruthless campaign of conquest, subjugating and unifying most of southern England. Offa brought his new territories to the highest degree of political cohesion ever seen in Britain. He married off his daughters to the kings of Wessex and Northumbria, at the same time opening a diplomatic dialogue with the Frankish court of Charlemagne – with whom he concluded a commercial treaty in 796, the year of his death. Offa's status was established when Charlemagne addressed a letter to him as "Brother", clearly regarding him as a monarch of equal rank. Offa allowed Pope Adrian I to increase his dominion over the English church. In return, Adrian acceded to Offa's request for the creation of a new bishopric at Lichfield: freeing the Mercian church from the control of the Archbishop of Canterbury, Offa's implacable enemy. Offa's most enduring memorial was the construction of "Offa's Dyke," a massive earthwork, protecting Mercia from Welsh incursions. Offa was also the first Anglo-Saxon king to introduce headed coinage.

There was a revival of coinage, in common usage by the Roman-British, during Offa's reign, particularly in silver coins, linked to an increase in trade – leading to a demand for sea ports and more mints. Gold coinage was rare, used more for ornamental purposes or for high value luxury items, land transactions and international trade. Each coin bore an image of the King's head and the name of the moneyer who minted it, a practice that endured for several hundred years. Charlemagne was the first early mediæval king to use coins as a medium to project royal authority.

A mysterious coin was procured by the Duc de Blacas in Rome sometime before 1841; and has been in the British Museum

Offa's Dyke is the greatest single fortification known in European history, a colossal feat of organisation and engineering for an Anglo-Saxon king. The only reference to the Dyke is contained in Asser's *Life of King Alfred*, where he mentions a *vallum magnum* (great wall) from sea to sea between Britain (Wales) and Mercia. The dyke stretches some 170 miles from the Severn near Chepstow to the Dee estuary. Offa built it to fortify the boundary between Mercia and the Welsh tribal territories.

It consisted of a plain, earth-filled berm, in some places over 25 ft high; and a ditch 12 ft deep, pierced by a number of gaps and gates implying an agreed frontier. The time, labour, expense and technical knowledge required would have been on an unimaginable logistical scale. The Oxford historian of Anglo-Saxon Britain, Patrick Wormald (1947–2004) describes Offa's Dyke, as "marking not the first great public work of English government; but the last great prehistoric achievement of the inhabitants of Britain, in a tradition stretching back thousands of years".

since 1922. Struck in Kent, it was issued in perfect Arabic Kufic script bearing Koranic verses, along with the name of King Offa of Mercia. It was dated (AH) from the Islamic Hegira: 157 (AD 779).

ST EDMUND

Edmund the Martyr (841–20 November 869) was King of East Anglia, which had been independent of Mercia and the Danes for nearly fifty years. He succeeded to the throne while still a boy. The earliest and most reliable accounts state that Edmund was descended from Rædwald (who was buried at Sutton Hoo) and the Wulfing kings of East Anglia.

In 869 the Danes, who had wintered at York, marched through Mercia into East Anglia and encamped at Thetford. Edmund engaged them fiercely in battle; but the Danes under their leaders Ubba Ragnarsson and his brother, Ivar "the Boneless" (he may have had 'brittle-bone' disease) won the day and killed King Edmund.

Edmund is said to have died as a martyr, tied to a stake and killed by arrows, when he refused to renounce Christ. The story dates from soon after the event. The king's body was ultimately interred at Beadoriceworth, the modern Bury St Edmunds; where pilgrimage to his shrine was encouraged by the 12th century enlargement of the church. Edmund's popularity among the Anglo-Norman nobility helped justify claims of continuity with pre-Norman traditions – a banner of St Edmund's arms was carried at the battle of Agincourt in 1415. There are churches dedicated to his memory all over England, including Christopher Wren's St Edmund the King and Martyr in London.

There are a number of colleges named after St Edmund. He is seen as a patron saint of various kings, pandemics, torture victims and wolves – and specifically, England.

The king with his witan (c.1050)
The British Library

THE WITAN

The Witanagemot (or Witan, more properly the title of its members) was a political institution in Anglo-Saxon England, between the 7th and 11th centuries. The name derives from the Old English for "meeting of wise men" (*wita:* wise man or counsellor, nominative plural *witan*, genitive plural *witena;* and *gemot:* assembly). It was the remnant of the ancient tribal general assembly, or folkmoot, which had developed into a convocation of senior clergy, ealdormen and leading thegns, speaking to the king.

The witan had its origins in the Germanic assemblies summoned to witness royal grants of land. Before the unification of England in the 9th century, separate witanagemots were convened by the kings of Essex, Kent, Mercia, Northumbria, Sussex and Wessex. Even after Wessex became the dominant power in England, supplanting the other kingdoms, local witans continued to meet until as late as 1067.

The Witan was in some respects a predecessor to Parliament, but had substantially different powers and some major limitations: such as a lack of a fixed procedure, schedule, or meeting place. The Witan could prevent autocracy and carry on government during interregnums. But while the king must answer to Parliament, the Witan answered to the king. It only assembled when he summoned it.

The best-known sitting of the English witanagemot was on 5 January 1066, which approved the succession to the throne of Harold Godwinson, following the death of Edward the Confessor. Fifty years earlier in 1016, it had approved the splitting of the kingdom between the Saxon Edmund Ironside and the Danish Cnut.

This arrangement ended when the Normans invaded in 1066, replacing the witanagemot with the *curia regis*, or King's court.

ROLLO THE NORSEMAN BECAME ROBERT OF NORMANDY

Rollo (*c.*860–*c.*932) was the founder and first ruler of the Viking territory in what became Normandy. He is also known as Robert I of Normandy. His nickname *Ganger* ("walker") came from being too big, or heavy to ride a horse.

Rollo was a minor chieftain in the Viking fleet which sailed up the Seine in 885 under Sigfred, to besiege Paris. In 886 Sigfred retreated in return for tribute from King Charles "the Fat" of France: but Rollo stayed and was paid by Charles to harry Burgundy.

Charles's nephew, Charles "the Simple" realised that he could not buy off Rollo when he returned to raid the lower Seine; and gave Rollo the coastal lands he occupied, on condition that he defend them against other Viking raiders. In the Treaty of Saint-Clair-sur-Epte (911), Rollo pledged feudal allegiance to the king, changed his name to Robert and converted to Christianity.

Initially Rollo stayed true to his word and defended the coast of Normandy; but in time, responding to the land hunger of his followers, he allowed them settle further inland, between the Epte and Risle rivers, and made Rouen his capital.

Around 927 Rollo gifted Normandy to his son, William "Longsword" and died soon afterwards. The historian Adhemar stated that before he died, Rollo lost his reason and had a hundred Christian prisoners beheaded in honour of the gods whom he had once worshipped. He hedged his bet however, by giving a hundred pounds of gold to the Duchy's churches, in honour of the true God in whose name he had accepted baptism. Though nominally a Christian, Rollo never quite shook off his pagan roots.

Rollo was the great-great-great-grandfather of William the Conqueror.

KING CONSTANTINE II OF SCOTLAND (REIGNED 900–43)

Constantine, nicknamed *An Midhaise* ("the Middle Aged"), born *c.*874, was a contemporary of Rollo. He was a grandson of Kenneth MacAlpin (*Cináed mac Alpin*), ruler of Dalriada in western Scotland from 840; and the first Scottish King of the Picts from 843 till his death in 858. Constantine succeeded his cousin Donald II, the first *Rí Alban* or King of Alba. He laid the foundations of Scotland's political and ecclesiastical structure for the next 500 years; and established part of Scotland's modern border with England. He was the first Scottish king to pay homage to an English king – Edward "the Elder", father of Æthelstan.

The realistic King Charles "the Simple" granted Rollo a small part of his province of Neustria, to the west of Rouen, renamed it Normandy and made him its duke (a word taken from the Latin *dux*). It is said that, when required to kiss the foot of King Charles to conclude the treaty, Rollo refused: ordering one of his men to do so in his place. The warrior, standing upright, lifted Charles's foot up to his mouth so that he fell over.

- **Rollo's tomb in Rouen Cathedral**

The *Clameur de Haro* (an ancient legal injunction of restraint employed by a person who believes he is being wronged) is said to have been an appeal to Rollo. It survives in the Channel Islands as a fully enforceable law to this day. It is more likely though, that it is derived from "harrow" meaning "give chase", which was commonly used in mediæval England and France as a cry for help in arresting a criminal. It survives on the hunting field as "Halloo".

In 900 Alba constituted only the territory between the Forth in the south, the Spey in the north and the coast on the east; its western limits are still uncertain. Constantine defeated the Vikings at Strathearn in 904; and four years later he withstood further attacks led by Rognwald, the Viking King of Dublin, who laid waste to Dunblane. In 914 he fought Rognwald to a standstill on the Tyne – which discouraged any further Viking attacks on his kingdom for over half a century.

In 906 Constantine re-established the Scottish church, which had been suppressed by the Pictish kings, centred on the bishopric of St Andrews on the east coast of Fife.

In 908, on the death of Donald, King of the Britons of Strathclyde, Constantine secured the election of his own brother Donald, as King of Dumbarton. This gave him control of virtually the whole of mainland Scotland.

With the Viking King Guthfrith of Dublin and the Strathclyde Britons, Constantine invaded England in 937 – only to suffer a crushing defeat by Æthelstan, King of Wessex, at Brunanburh. In 943 he abdicated his throne in favour of his cousin Malcolm I. He died in 952 as Abbot of St Andrews – where he is buried.

In 1510 the *Aberdeen Breviary* stated that St Rule (or St Regulus), shipwrecked off Fife in the 7th century, had carried with him relics of the Apostle Andrew (the younger brother of St Peter), who had been crucified at Patras in Greece. St Andrew had begged not to be crucified on the same shape of cross as Christ.

He was duly crucified on the X-shaped cross (or saltire) which became his symbol. By AD 1000 St Andrew had become the patron saint of Scotland. The saltire is the oldest sovereign flag in the world, having been continuously in use since AD 832. St Andrew's feast day is 30 November – not a public holiday in Scotland.

HYWEL DDA, KING IN WALES

Another contemporary of Rollo and Constantine II was Hywel Dda (*c.*880–950), known in English as "Howell the Good". Already King of Deheubarth, in south-west Wales, he added Gwynedd, in the north-east, to his realm on the death of King Idwal Foel in 942.

Hywel is remembered as one of the most successful native Welsh rulers prior to the Norman Conquest – and was known as King of the Britons. His name is particularly linked with the development of the Welsh laws, known as the Laws of Hywel.

Opinions vary as to the motives for Hywel's close association with the court of Æthelstan. He may have been an anglophile and admirer of the kings of Wessex or simply a pragmatist who recognised the realities of power in mid-10th century Britain. It is notable that he gave one of his sons an Anglo-Saxon name, Edwin. His policies with regard to England were evidently not to the taste of all his subjects. A Welsh language poem entitled *Armes Prydein*, possibly written in Deheubarth during Hywel's reign, called for the Welsh to join a confederation of all the non-English peoples of Britain and Ireland to fight the Anglo-Saxons. The poem may well be linked to the alliance of Norse and Celtic kingdoms which challenged Æthelstan at the Battle of Brunanburh in 937. Hywel however, was careful to remain neutral.

In about 945 Hywel held a conference, almost a parliament, at Whitland in south-west Wales, to modernise Welsh law. The outcome, *Cyfraith Hywel* ("the laws of Hywel"), was codified and recorded in writing. Following Hywel's death in 950, his kingdom

Hywel's reign, uncharacteristically for the time, was a peaceful one, and he achieved an understanding with Æthelstan of England. Such was the friendship between the neighbouring countries that Hywel was able to mint his own coinage in the English city of Chester. He was the only Welsh ruler ever to produce coinage. His study of the English legal system and a pilgrimage to Rome in 928 encouraged him to formulate new procedures for government and the administration of justice.

was soon split into three. Gwynedd was reclaimed by the sons of Idwal Foel, while Deheubarth was divided between Hywel's sons. However, his legacy endured in the form of his effective and enlightened laws, which remained in use throughout Wales until Edward I's conquest. The remnants were finally replaced by Henry VIII, an English king of Welsh descent – but not until the 16th century.

THE ANGLO-SAXON CHRONICLE

The Anglo-Saxon Chronicle is a collection of annals in Old and later, Middle English narrating the history of the Anglo-Saxons. They were created late in the 9th century, almost certainly in Wessex, during the reign of Alfred the Great. Multiple manuscript copies were made and sent to monasteries across England – and were then independently updated.

Peterborough Chronicle
The British Library

Nine manuscripts survive in whole or in part, though none is an original version. The oldest seems to have been begun towards the end of Alfred's reign, while the most recent was written at Peterborough Abbey after a fire in 1116. Uniquely the Peterborough Chronicle was maintained until 1155 – recording events said to have taken place since 449.

Almost all of the material in the chronicle is in the form of annual digests: the earliest of all being for the year 60 BC. Regular annals follow, to the year in which the chronicle was actually written: at which point contemporary records begin. These manuscripts collectively are known as the Anglo-Saxon Chronicle.

The Chronicle is not unbiased: there are occasions when comparison with other mediæval sources makes it clear that the scribes who wrote it omitted events or told one-sided versions of stories; there are also places where the different versions contradict each other. However, taken as a whole, the Chronicle is the single most important historical source for the period between the departure of the Romans and the Norman Conquest. Much of the information given in the Chronicle is not recorded elsewhere. In addition, the manuscripts are important sources for the history of the English language; in particular, the later Peterborough text is one of the earliest examples of Middle English in existence.

Seven of the nine surviving manuscripts are owned by the British Library, all of which had been gifted to the nation by the heirs of Sir Robert Cotton.

The last two MS are kept in the Bodleian Library in Oxford and the library at Corpus Christi College, Cambridge. The latter also contains a priceless collection of over 600 mediæval texts – most were bequeathed to the College in 1574 by Matthew Parker (nicknamed "Nosy" Parker), the second Anglican Archbishop of Canterbury.

The Cotton Library was assembled by Sir Robert Bruce Cotton M.P. (1571–1631), an antiquarian and bibliophile. It is a unique collection of books, manuscripts, coins and medallions – many of which he acquired from Thomas Walker, Clerk of the Parliaments, who had recovered them during the dissolution of the monasteries. Cotton's Library is the single greatest body of literature written in Old and Middle English. Several well known works such as *Beowulf*, the poem *Pearl*, and the *Lindisfarne Gospels* only survive today because of Robert Cotton. His collection was seized and sealed after he had publicly criticised the policies of King Charles I. His family regained possession of it on Cotton's death: and in 1700 presented it to the nation. The Cotton Library is of inestimable importance and is the basis of the manuscript collection in the British Library.

KING ALFRED "THE GREAT" OF WESSEX (REIGNED 871–99)

Alfred (or Ælfred) fought three invading Danish armies to a standstill and united most of southern England under his crown. He promoted literacy and education as well as promulgating an effective body of law. His military, administrative and diplomatic achievements justifiably earned him the byname of Alfred "the Great". Alfred is the only British king to be styled "Great" (Cnut was Danish).

Anicius Manlius Boethius (*c.*480–524) was a Roman-born Christian philosopher – executed by Theodoric "the Great", a Gothic ruler of Italy. Alfred translated his *Consolation of Philosophy* from the Latin; and added a summation of his own personal beliefs. These would be remarkable in any age: in the 9th century they are without parallel.

Alfred wrote that: "Desire for and possession of earthly power never pleased me overmuch …. nevertheless I wished for tools and resources for the task …. that I should virtuously and worthily guide and direct the authority which was entrusted to me ….The king [must] have his land fully manned: he must have praying men, fighting men and working men …. He [must provide] their means of support: land to live on, gifts, weapons, food, ale, clothing, and whatever else is necessary for each of the[se] three classes of men …. because every skill and every authority is soon obsolete and passed over, if it is without wisdom …. for whatever is done unthinkingly, cannot be reckoned a skill. To speak briefly: I desired to live worthily as long as I lived, and to leave after my life, to the men who should come after me, the memory of me in good works".

Alfred was the son of King Æthelwulf of Wessex (died 858), an Anglo-Saxon kingdom in south-west England, and his queen Osburh. His grandfather Egbert (802–839) was the first of his line to become King of Wessex and *Bretwalda* (Overlord) of England. He was the youngest of at least six children and never expected to become king, preferring the life of a scholar. His three brothers Æthelbald, Æthelbert and Æthelred were all successively Kings of Wessex before him. His sister Æthelswith was married to King Burgred of Mercia, a kingdom occupying the land between the Thames and the Humber. In 868 Alfred married Ealswith (died 902), daughter of a Mercian noble.

Statue of Alfred "the Great" at Wantage

Asser (died 909) was a Welsh monk who became King Alfred's principal advisor, teacher, confidant and biographer. He was a monk at St David's Abbey in Pembrokeshire where he acquired a reputation for learning. In 886 Alfred summoned Asser to his court in Wessex, to teach him Latin. So successful was this experiment that Alfred made Asser abbot of the monasteries of Congresbury and Banwell in Somerset, before raising him to the bishoprics of Devon, Cornwall and finally Sherborne in Dorset. Asser wrote a biography of Alfred (*Vita Ælfredi regis Angul Saxonum*) in 893, drawing heavily on The Anglo-Saxon Chronicle for historical data, particularly for accounts of the Danish invasions and subsequent battles. The only copy of the MS, held in the Cotton library, was destroyed in a fire in 1731; earlier transcriptions however, enabled the work to be reconstructed.

Alfred, born in Wantage in Berkshire in 849, was brought up as a warrior – as were all nobly born young Saxons. He accompanied his brothers on two visits to Rome in 853 and 855, when he spent time at the Frankish court. He first saw military service in 868 when he joined his brother Æthelred I on campaign with their brother-in-law King Burgred to repel a Danish invasion. In 865 a powerful Danish army had landed in East Anglia and marched north to settle Northumbria. The Danes refused to fight preferring to make peace and retain the territory they had occupied.

In 860, Æthelbald died childless, to be succeeded by Æthelbert. In 865 Æthelbert died and Æthelred replaced him, producing two sons before he too died in 871. Alfred then became king, the first in 9th century northern Europe successfully to combine the life of both warrior and scholar. According to Bishop Asser who wrote a life of Alfred, his mother Osburh gave her son a book of Saxon poems, a reward for having learnt them by heart.

In the autumn of 871 the Danes invaded Wessex. Alfred fought an indecisive battle at Wilton, in present-day Hampshire before signing a truce. Alfred's resistance convinced the Danes that further aggression, in the short term at least, was not worth the trouble.

In 871, the year of Alfred's accession, the Danish army was reinforced by another led by Guthrum. In 876, launching maritime raids on Exeter and Wareham and operating from a base in Cambridge, Guthrum advanced through Wessex. He nearly captured Alfred by using his knowledge of the Christian calendar. He surprised Alfred's carousing, unprepared army near Chippenham during the Christmas festivities. In disorder, Alfred retreated to the Somerset wetlands: where he built a heavily fortified base, to conduct a guerrilla campaign against Guthrum's army of occupation.

From wherever Alfred drew his inspiration, it was effective: by May 878 he had gathered enough of an army to defeat Guthrum at Edington (or Ethandun), possibly in Wiltshire but more likely in Somerset. Guthrum surrendered: and with Alfred standing as his sponsor, was baptised a Christian with thirty of his lieutenants. The Danes then retired behind their East Anglian boundary.

Yet a third Danish army had by now landed in East Anglia. On learning from Guthrum's defeated troops of the fierce resistance likely to be encountered from Alfred's forces, these most recent invaders sailed on to France to take advantage of the disintegrating Frankish kingdom. In 892 they returned, but this time the Danes found a Wessex transformed into a series of strategic strong-points called burghs, rivers made impassable by fortified bridges, a formidable navy of large, 60-oar ships built to Alfred's own design; and a flexible, well organised peasant army: the fyrd. Nevertheless, it was not until 896 that the Danes gave up and returned to the Continent: to establish the future duchy of Normandy – the springboard for a rather more successful invasion of England in 1066.

In 885 Alfred repelled yet another Danish invasion. He reacted to the collaboration of the East Anglian Danes by taking London, a success that persuaded all Anglo-Saxons not under Danish rule to accept him as

Danish invasions were conducted at two levels: quick raids for treasure and slaves; and coordinated attacks under determined leaders aimed at conquest and settlement. The three Danish invasions in 865, 871 and 878 were of the latter, most dangerous kind. In 866, under Ivar the Boneless and his brothers Halfdan and Ubba, the Danes overran Northumbria and killed its king. East Anglia followed in 869 and Mercia was reduced to an enclave between 872–4. It was Viking policy to dominate, rather than destroy, existing political structures; to seize land on which to settle; and to extract treasure from the local population, with which to fund new colonies. If regional resistance proved too troublesome, they would move on to find a more welcoming environment. Alfred understood the Viking psyche and cunningly exploited its weaknesses.

A popular legend tells how, when he first fled to the Somerset Levels, Alfred was given shelter by a peasant woman. Unaware of his identity, she left him to watch some cakes that were cooking on the fire. Preoccupied with the problems of his kingdom, Alfred accidentally let them burn: and was taken to task by the woman when she returned. Upon realising the king's identity, the woman apologised profusely, but Alfred insisted that any apology should come from him.

A burgh was a garrisoned fort built by Alfred within 20 miles of every major Wessex town; and wherever possible, constructed on old Roman or Iron Age defensive sites. Chains of forts were erected along the Wessex coast and the main river systems. They were maintained by "Burghal Hidage" and *Trinoda Necessitas*.

Burghal Hidage was a system which determined the maximum amount of men and materials that could be supported by a unit of land. Each fort (burgh) was allotted a number of "hides", in effect the soldiers needed to man a given length of defensive wall. Some of these burghs were no more than emergency strongpoints: whereas the larger ones, like Winchester, developed into townships with churches, markets and mints. Under this sophisticated scheme, Alfred could mobilise nearly 27,000 men. *Trinoda Necessitas*, a threefold tax, was raised to meet the costs of maintaining Alfred's burghs, including road and bridge construction, and providing enough men for military operations.

The fyrd was the Saxon militia, or standing army. Divided into two, half the fyrd's strength was operational, ready for battle: while the other half attended the fields and protected their families – a very effective arrangement.

The *Anglo-Saxon Chronicle*, covering the year 896 describes the ships in Alfred's new fleet as being much larger than contemporary design, with 60 oarsmen. The *Chronicle* describes how unwieldy the new ships were, running aground during their trials, with the crews floundering in the mud. The Anglo-Saxons, once great seafarers, had to relearn their nautical skills. However they persevered; and for the following five reigns, 60-oar ships remained the model. It is fair to describe Alfred as the "father of the Royal Navy".

king. With London as a firm base, Alfred's son Edward the Elder was later able to re-conquer all the Danish territories.

Alfred is sometimes described as *Rex Anglorum*. In fact it was his grandson Æthelstan who was the first King of all England, with the exception of Cumbria.

The key to Alfred's military success lay in his establishment of a competent administration, as evinced by the highly successful burghal hidage system, reinforced by attention to lawmaking and social cohesion. Compared with the number of charters (royal decrees) of the preceding reign and his successors, Alfred issued relatively few, perhaps a testament to the beleaguered state of his kingdom for much of his reign. Those charters that he did promulgate were prepared on the premise that the English could and should be a holy people, answerable for their shortcomings to God. His laws covered divers offences: ranging from stealing from the Church, adultery, felling trees without permission, penalties for a Welshman killing an Englishman, rape of slave-women, regulations controlling dogs – and rules of behaviour to be observed during Lent.

There was a limited relationship between Alfred's defence programme and his educational reforms. Alfred, a keen disciple of Mosaic Law, shared the contemporary view that the Danish invasion was a divine infliction incurred through the ignorance, hence ungodliness, of his people. Having eventually defeated the Danes, his priority was to remedy this defect through education. He understood too, that his thegns would provide much more effective leadership if they were properly educated. Thus able to understand God's word and inspired by the Church, they might be more inclined to fight the pagan Dane.

A thegn was an Anglo-Saxon military nobleman, granted land by the king. In the social order, a thegn ranked between a freeman and an hereditary noble.

Alfred's most important innovation concerned the keeping of "oath and pledge," to be sworn by "the whole people", that obedience was due not only to the king's law but also to the law of God. This principal above all others, distinguished English Law from the many strains of Roman law applied elsewhere in northern Europe.

Alfred was strongly influenced by the Frankish approach to education. The system Alfred evolved however, was distinguished from that of Charlemagne by his insistence that schools should be open to all ranks and established at his court: rather than the Carolingian practice of founding them in churches, only for the nobility. Alfred also decreed that all lessons took place in English, rather than Latin. His purpose was: "to lay the foundations on which Latin learning could then be built in those continuing to higher rank". The result was that English became a written language – which was key to its survival during the 300 years after the Norman Conquest, when only Latin and French were spoken by the ruling classes.

Unlike Charlemagne, Alfred actually wrote down his thoughts; and, having learned Latin, from 887 translated Latin manuscripts into English. His translations, and those of the scholars he invited to his court, made available English texts of "the books most necessary for all men to know". Alfred believed that kingship mandated an obligation to seek wisdom through knowledge – and that the correct balance to a successful ruler's *hubris* was internal contemplation. He expected, perhaps naively, that this precept would also be followed by his advisors and administrators.

Alfred read all the works of Bede; and the *Seven Books of Histories Against the Pagans* by Paulus Orosius, a 5th century theologian, which attempted to identify a divine purpose in earthly events. In addition to Boethius's *Consolation of Philosophy*, Alfred translated the *Pastoral Care of St Gregory I*, which laid down rules governing priestly behaviour; the first 50 Psalms;

and the *Soliloquies* of St Augustine of Hippo (whose *Confessions* have remained in print for 1,500 years).

Alfred attempted to establish monasticism in England, founding both a monastery and a convent. His efforts were premature however – a hundred years would pass before the monastic movement spread to England from the Continent.

It is clear from Asser's *Life of Alfred* that the king suffered all his life from bouts of a painful disorder now tentatively identified as Crohn's (inflammatory bowel) disease. It is all the more remarkable that Alfred managed to achieve so much by the time of his death, aged about fifty, on 26 October 899. He was buried in Winchester Cathedral.

Alfred was succeeded by his son Edward "the Elder" – an unusual event in the 9th century. Edward re-buried his father in his own New Minster Abbey, in 901.

ÆTHELSTAN, THE FIRST KING OF THE ENGLISH (REIGNED 925–39)

Ethelstan, the first *Rex Anglorum* or King of the English, was another contemporary of Duke Rollo of Normandy, King Constantine II of Alba and Hywel Dda, King in Wales. The heirs of these four rulers were to become the architects of modern Great Britain.

Ethelstan was the first West Saxon king to exert effective control over the whole of England, except Cumbria. He was born around 895, the first child of King Edward "the Elder" (870–924) and his mistress Egwina (or Ecgwyn). Edward had inherited Wessex from his father Alfred, but had to kill a Danish client-pretender Ethelwald in 902 to secure his throne. Edward then conquered all five Danish Boroughs south of the Humber, namely Leicester, Stamford, Nottingham, Derby and Lincoln, establishing eleven new forts in the process. In 918 Edward absorbed the crown of Mercia on the death of the queen, his sister Ethelfleda, and by 920 had subdued Northumbria. When Edward died, Æthelstan was elected King of both Wessex and Mercia. He was crowned King of all England at Kingston-upon-Thames on 4 September 925.

Although Offa of Mercia had styled himself *Rex Anglorum*, and was certainly the most powerful king in England, his power was confined to the Midlands and East Anglia; and died with him. King Alfred almost earned the title; but again, his authority never reached Northumbria, to encompass the whole country. The first king to consolidate his rule from the Scottish border to the English Channel and from the Welsh Marches to the North Sea was Æthelstan, King Alfred's grandson – one of the most overlooked, but most important 10th century figures.

In 927 Æthelstan annexed the Viking kingdom of York and occupied Northumbria, becoming the first West Saxon ruler to share a border with Scotland. Ten years later, in 937 Æthelstan's suzerainity was challenged when Constantine of Scotland, King Owain of the Britons of Strathclyde and Olaf Guthfrith, the Norwegian King of Dublin (and claimant to the kingdom of York), joined forces and invaded England. Æthelstan defeated this coalition at Brunanburh (probably near Rotherham in South Yorkshire, but possibly at Bromborough on the Wirral), where five kings and seven earls died in the battle – including the son of the Scottish king, Constantine II. As a result of this resounding victory, Æthelstan became overlord of the Celtic kingdoms in Cornwall, Wales, Cumbria and Scotland.

Brunanburh *(Dún Brunde)*, was reported in the *Annals of Ulster*: "a great battle, lamentable and terrible was cruelly fought .... in which fell uncounted thousands of the Northmen .... and on the other side, a multitude of Saxons fell; but Æthelstan, the King of the Saxons, obtained a great victory".

Ethelstan was an inspired lawgiver, though only six of his law codes survive. He made the first concerted attempt in England, not only to reduce

King Æthelstan's tomb,
in Malmesbury Abbey

theft and punish corruption, but also to recognise the problem of young offenders by mitigating their punishment. He also made provision for the relief of the destitute. Æthelstan promulgated his laws effectively through a corps of skilled clerks based at Winchester Cathedral, the forerunner of a highly efficient early English mediæval civil service. He reformed the coinage by establishing regional mints. His charters and his coins all bore the proud legend *Æthelstan Rex totius Britanniæ* – "King of all Britain".

Transcending his military achievements, centralisation of the administration, firm control of the coinage and robust charter (legal) protection, Æthelstan was the first English king to pursue a recognisable foreign policy. The extent of his diplomatic reach and the energy with which he encouraged and gathered European intellects to his court was an exceptional feature of his reign. He married off three of his sisters to Frankish dukes – and one, in 930, to the Holy Roman Emperor Otto I.

William of Malmesbury recorded that "the whole of Europe sang his [Æthelstan's] praises and extolled his merits to the sky".

An intensely pious man, Æthelstan died on 27 October 939 in Gloucester. He is buried in Malmesbury Abbey in Wiltshire, which he had richly endowed. Having never married, he was succeeded by his half-brother, Edmund ("the Magnificent"): who, aged sixteen, had fought valiantly at his side at Brunanburh.

TWO GREAT MEDIÆVAL HISTORIANS

Malmesbury Abbey (1180)

Henry of Huntingdon (*c.*1088–1157) was archdeacon of Huntingdon and an historian best known for his dramatic *Historia Anglorum* (History of the English), covering the period from the Roman invasion in AD 43 to the accession of Henry II in 1154. Much of the content was pirated, forty percent or so from the Venerable Bede alone; but the years 1126–54 are undoubtedly Henry's own work, since he witnessed many of the events described, especially the anarchy of King Stephen's reign.

The *Historia Anglorum* was popular, influential and rigorous – despite its plagiarism. Henry divided his history into the five great invasions of England: by the Romans, Picts, Anglo-Saxons, Vikings and Normans. He was the first to record the celebrated story of King Cnut and the waves, which supposedly took place at Bosham in Sussex, near the Roman palace at Fishbourne.

William of Malmesbury (*c.*1090–1143) was born in Wiltshire to a Norman father and Saxon mother. He too wrote a well-received English history (in Latin), based on Bede's *Historia Ecclesiastica Gentis Anglorum*. William's best known works are *Gesta Regum Anglorum* (Deeds of the English Kings) from 449–1127, followed by *Gesta Pontificum Anglorum* (Deeds of the English Bishops) in 1125. William's *Historia Novella* (New History), recording events since 1125, breaks off abruptly at the end of 1142, presumably when he died.

William was observant, reliable and shrewd. John Milton praised him as, "by far the best of all" the 12th century chroniclers, "both for style and judgment".

Map of Anglo-Saxon Britain
with the "Heptarchy" and
"Danelaw" marked

THE MAKING OF THE ENGLISH
(the Anglo–Saxon Heptarchy)

CALEDONIA
(The Scotii had replaced
the Picts by 850)

Dunnichen (685)

Perth

The Picts
destroyed
the Angles.

DALRIADA

Largs (1263)
Ended Viking rule
in Scotland

Edinburgh
(captured by Angles
in 638)

Holy Isle (Lindisfarne)
St. Aidan (635)

Bamburgh

Bernicia

SCOTII
(Irish Gaels)

Gaels raid and
settle Dalriada
370–600.

BRITONS

NORTHUMBRIA

North Angles (subdued by Wessex 927)

Jarrow
(681)

Strathclyde and
Rheged (Cumbria)
combined in 573
but were subdued
by Wessex and
granted to Malcolm,
King of Alba
(Scotland) in 945.

ISLE OF MAN
(Gael until c800
then Norwegian
until 1266)

Deira

Whitby Abbey
(657)

York

Stamford
Bridge
(1066)

East Anglia was:
– conquered by Mercia (794)
– independent (827)
– taken by the Danes (870)
– subsumed into Wessex (920)
– Danish again (1017)
– finally part of England (1042)

Clontarf (1014)

Dublin

THE

D
A
N
E
L
A
W

Brunanburh (937)
(actual site is unknown)

Offa's Dyke
(785–96)

Tamworth

Cymry (Wealas) as Wales,
was finally subsumed into
England in the Statute of
Rhuddlan (1284).

CYMRY
or
WEALAS
(meaning
"Foreigners"
to Anglo-Saxons)

M E R C I A
(subsumed into
Wessex 918)

(886)

North–folk

EAST ANGLIA
Bury St. Edmunds

South–folk

East Saxons

ESSEX

Sutton Hoo
(c624)
Anglian
ship burial

0   25 miles
0   50 km

BRITONS

Ethandun (878)
(actual site is unknown)

Maldon
(991)

London

Ebbsfleet

KENT

Jute

Canterbury (597)

Aylesford (455)

Kernow (Cornwall) was
subdued by Æthelstan
by 926.

Glastonbury

Winchester

South Saxons
SUSSEX

Hastings (1066)

KERNOW

W E S S E X
West Saxons

Alfred "the Great" (871–99) routed the
Danes at Ethandun (they were baptised and
confined to the Danelaw). His grandson,
Æthelstan became the first "Rex Anglorum".

Kent (Jute), Sussex (South
Saxons) and Middlesex
(Middle Saxons) were
seized from Mercia and
absorbed into Wessex (825).

Britons from Cymry and Kernow
migrated to Brittany (Armorica)
between 450–600

Occupied by Vikings from
Norway (9/10th century)

Raided by Vikings from
Norway (9/10th century)

Occupied by Vikings from
Denmark (9/10th century)

Present Scotland / England
and Wales / England borders

●   Capital

✝   Monastery

⚐   Battle

ST SWITHUN

St Swithun (or Swithin) was born *c*.800, possibly in Hampshire, certainly in Wessex and died 2 July 862. He was an early English Bishop of Winchester, now best known for a popular British proverb forecasting the weather – if it rains on Saint Swithun's feast day (15 July) it will rain for 40 days and 40 nights:

St Swithun's day if thou dost rain
*   For forty days it will remain*
St Swithun's day if thou be fair
*   For forty days 'twill rain na mair*

Swithun was buried out of doors, rather than in his cathedral, apparently at his own request, so that the "sweet rain of heaven" could fall on his grave. In 971 it was decided to move his body to a new indoor shrine. It is said that the ceremony was delayed by 40 days of torrential rain, a sign of Swithun's displeasure at the move. Unsurprisingly, Swithun is regarded as one of the saints to whom one should pray in the event of drought.

THE CUTTING EDGE OF EARLY MEDIÆVAL SURGERY

There was little hope for anyone who fell ill until the 14th century: death or full recovery were the only realistic outcomes. This did not stop people attempting desperate remedies. Hugh de Orival, consecrated Bishop of London by Archbishop Lanfranc in 1075, who suffered from leprosy, resorted to the drastic "cure" of castration. He died on 12 January 1085, still a leper – but now also a eunuch.

KINGS OF ENGLAND (ALBION) TO 1327 AND SCOTLAND (ALBA) TO 1329

The Regents of the young King Edward III of England gave up any claim to the throne of Scotland at the Treaty of Northampton (3 May 1328). This effectively deferred union between the two countries for another 378 years (and 362 days). No tribal leader merits the description of king of either country before AD 802.

The Scottish *Albainn* (Alba) for "Highlands" probably derives from the same Indo-European source as the name for the Alps and Albania. Alternatively, it may derive from the Indo-European root *Albho* meaning "white", also the source of Albion, the ancient name for England. *Picti* means "the Painted people" in Latin.

BRIAN BÓRUMA (BRIAN BORU)

Brian "Boru" (*c*.941–1014), High King of Ireland, was born at Kincora near Killaloe in County Clare. He was the son of Cennétig, "royal heir to Cashel" or Munster. His mother was Bé Binn, daughter of the King of Uí Briúin (O'Brien) Seóla in Connacht. He was nicknamed *Bóruma* (anglicized as "Boru") from the Old Irish *bóruma*, meaning "of the cattle tribute", or perhaps "of Béal Bóruma", a fort north of Killaloe.

Brian was significant chiefly because he overthrew the centuries-long domination of the

The Rock of Cashel *(Carraig Phadraig)*, also known as Cashel of the Kings and St Patrick's Rock, is in County Tipperary. It was the traditional seat of the Kings of Munster for several hundred years before the Norman invasion and dates from *c*.1100. Cashel is said to be where St Patrick converted the King of Munster to Christianity in the 5th century. It is a remarkable combination of Celtic art and mediæval architecture.

HOUSE OF WESSEX (SAXON)

Egbert. *Bretwalda*	802–839
Æthelwulf (*d*.858)	839–855
Æthelbald	855–860
Æthelbert	860–865
Æthelred I	865–871
Alfred "the Great"	871–899
Edward "the Elder"	899–925

KINGS OF ENGLAND (SAXON)

Æthelstan. *Rex Anglorum*	925–939
Edmund "the Magnificent"	939–946
Edred	946–955
Edwy "the Fair"	955–959
Edgar "the Peaceful"	959–975
Edward "the Martyr"	975–978
Æthelred II "the Unready"	978–1013
	1014–1016
Edmund II "Ironside"	1016–1016

DANISH

Sweyn "Forkbeard"	1013–1014
Cnut or Canute "the Great"	1016–1035
Harold I "Harefoot"	1035–1040
Harthacnut or Hardecanute	1040–1042

ANGLO–SAXONS

Edward "the Confessor"	1042–1066
Harold II (Godwinson)	1066–1066

NORMANS

William "the Conqueror"	1066–1087
William II "Rufus"	1087–1100
Henry I "Beauclere"	1100–1135
Stephen of Blois	1135–1154

ANJOU (PLANTAGENET)

Henry II "Curtmantle"	1154–1189
Richard I "Lionheart"	1189–1199
John "Lackland"	1199–1216
Henry III	1216–1272
Edward I "Longshanks"	1272–1307
Edward II	1307–1327

Edward II lost his claim to the throne of Scotland at Bannockburn in 1314

PICTS AND SCOTS (MACALPIN)

Kenneth I, *Rex Pictorum*	843–858
Donald I	858–862
Constantine I	862–877
Aed	877–878
Giric	878–889

KINGS OF ALBA

Donald II, *Ri Alban*	889–900
Constantine II (*d*.952)	900–943
Malcolm I	943–954
Indulf "the Aggressor"	954–962
Dubh (or Duff)	962–967
Cuilén "the White"	967–971
Amlaib	973–977
Kenneth II "the Fratricide"	971–973
	977–995
Constantine III	995–997
Kenneth III "the Chief"	997–1005
Malcolm II "the Destroyer"	1005–1034
Duncan I "the Sick"	1034–1040
Macbeth	1040–1057
Lulach "the Foolish"	1057–1058
Malcolm III "Canmore"	1058–1093
Donald III "the Fair"	1093–1094

KINGS OF SCOTLAND

Duncan II, *Rex Scottorum*	1094–1094
Donald III (restored)	1094–1097
Edgar "the Valiant"	1097–1107
Alexander I "the Fierce"	1107–1124
David I "the Saint"	1124–1153
Malcolm IV "the Maiden"	1153–1165
William I "the Lion"	1165–1214
Alexander II	1214–1249
Alexander III	1249–1286

Regency for Margaret, Maid of Norway (d.1290), who was never crowned or ever set foot in Scotland

	1286–1290
Competition for the Crown	1290–1292
John de Balliol	1292–1296
Edward I of England	1296–1306
Robert I ("the Bruce")	1306–1329

kingship of Ireland by the Uí Néill. Building on the achievements of his father, Cennétig mac Lorcain and brother, Mathgamain, Brian first made himself King of Munster: then subjugated Leinster, making himself ruler of the south of Ireland.

The Uí Néill (O'Neill) King Máel Sechnaill, abandoned by his northern O'Neill kinsmen, reluctantly acknowledged Brian as High King, at Athlone in 1002. In the next decade, Brian campaigned against the northern Uí Néill, who had refused him homage; against Leinster, where resistance was endemic; and against Dublin, a Viking enclave. On Good Friday 1014 Brian confronted the armies of Leinster and Dublin at Clontarf, near Dublin. The resulting battle was bloody: with Brian, his son Murchad and Máel Mórdha, King of Leinster, among the dead. Máel Sechnaill seized the opportunity to resume his interrupted reign, as the last Uí Néill High King.

It is likely that Brian was killed by Brodir, a Viking mercenary, while praying in his tent after the battle – and was probably buried near St Patrick's Cathedral in Armagh.

CULINARIA

Anglo-Saxon vegetable plots were called "leek-gardens" and a gardener was a "leekwarder". The Old English *leak* referred to any member of the onion family, including garlic (*garleac* in Old English). Amongst others: Leighton Buzzard, Laughton and Leckhampstead are named after the leek.

The cucumber, cultivated for at least 3,000 years in Northern India, was introduced by the Romans. Called "cowcumbers" in the Middle Ages, cucumbers were treated with suspicion in England, until they had been trained to grow straight. In 1663 Samuel Pepys recorded in his diary that, "Mr Newburne is dead of eating cowcumbers".

The Jerusalem artichoke, "neither came it from Jerusalem or out of Asia but out of America", stated John Gerard (1545–1611) in his 1597 *Herball*. Its large yellow blossom is similar to the Sunflower Artichoke, *Girasole Articiocco* in Italian – and "Jerusalem" is thought to be a corruption of "girasole". Runner beans are also native to central America and were first grown in England in the 17th century.

In the Middle Ages the church imposed a large number of 'fish days', when 'flesh' (animals and birds) could not be eaten. The whole of Lent and all Fridays and Saturdays were fish days – indeed, eating fish on Fridays is a tradition still observed in many households today. For centuries 'fish' included beavers, seals and the barnacle goose.

In 1617, at Hoghton Tower in Lancashire, King James I is said to have enjoyed a cut of beef so much that he conferred a knighthood on it – known ever since as "sirloin".

"THE OLD ONES ARE THE BEST"

The *Codex Exoniensis,* a 10th century book of poetry held at Exeter Cathedral, reports that Ethelred the "Ever-Funny" (his stage name) cracked a joke at The Worksop Inn in Nottinghamshire in 959: "What hangs at a man's thigh and wants to poke the hole that it has often poked before?" The answer to this early stab at humour was, "a key".

The audience's response to such an hilarious quip is not recorded – but it is good to know that the British sense of humour has changed little in over a thousand years.

ST DUNSTAN OF CANTERBURY

Dunstan was born into an aristocratic family in Glastonbury in 924, where he was educated by the Abbey's Celtic monks. He was first employed by his uncle, Archbishop Æthelhelm of Canterbury and then at the court of King Æthelstan.

Dunstan withdrew to live as a hermit at Glastonbury, until summoned by Æthelstan's successor, King Edmund "the Magnificent" in 943, to be one of his counsellors. Appointed Abbot of Glastonbury, Dunstan developed the monastic school into a leading institution. King Edmund's successor Edred (946–55), a keen proponent of clerical reform, effectively made Dunstan his chief minister of state: with a brief to consolidate royal authority, reform the clergy and improve relations with the Danelaw.

Dunstan was dismissed by Edwy "the Fair" (955–959) and outlawed. He fled to Flanders and entered a monastery in Ghent, where he took note of Continental monastic practice. King Edgar "The Peaceful" (959–975) recalled him in 959, as Bishop of Worcester and London; and shortly afterwards, appointed him Archbishop of Canterbury. Dunstan presided over a period of intense intellectual activity, reforming several important monasteries and organising a missionary expedition to Scandinavia.

In the reign of Edgar's son, Edward "the Martyr" (975–978), the nobility resisted Dunstan's controversial monastic reforms; and, when Ælthelred "the Unready" succeeded his murdered brother, his career went into eclipse. Having served six Wessex kings faithfully, Dunstan retired to Canterbury: where he lectured at the Cathedral school for ten years, dying in 988. His feast day is 19 May.

EDWARD "THE CONFESSOR" (REIGNED 1042–66)

Edward, known to history as the "Confessor" (any saint who lived, rather than died, for Christ can be called a "Confessor"), is the only English king to have been canonised. He was the penultimate Anglo-Saxon King of England and the last of the House of Wessex. Edward's image is of a weak

King Edward "the Confessor", depicted in The Wilton Diptych
National Gallery, London

and ineffectual king, in thrall to his powerful nobles. England however, remained at peace and prospered during his 24-year reign. Through his lineage, Edward united the Saxon and Norman blood lines; and his close ties with Normandy prepared the way for the conquest of England by William, Duke of Normandy – later King William I.

Edward was born at Islip in Oxfordshire around 1002. He was the son of King Æthelred II and his second wife Emma, daughter of Duke Richard I ("the Fearless") of Normandy.

Æthelred, usually known as Ethelred "the Unready", or Æthelred Unræd (c.968–1016) had succeeded to the throne aged about ten, after his half-brother Edward's assassination – in which he was almost certainly implicated. Ethelred's nickname "the Unready" is a mistranslation. *Unraed* means "the recipient of bad advice".

England had experienced over sixty years of peace after King Alfred's son Edward "the Elder" (Ethelred's grandfather) reconquered the Danelaw in 918. However, a new wave of raids from Denmark began in 980, which culminated in the destruction of the Anglo-Saxon forces at Maldon in Essex, on 10 August 991.

An incompetent ruler and an inept military leader, Ethelred devised a tax called the Danegeld. The money raised was used to bribe the Danes to withdraw. Needless to say, each payment had to be larger than the last and served only to tempt them back again.

On 13 November 1002 Ethelred's desperate and foolish reaction was to massacre some Danish settlers, which provoked a devastating response from Danish armies led by King Sweyn I ("Forkbeard"), Olaf Tryggvason and Thorkill "the Tall", who burned Oxford in 1010. Finally, in 1013 English resistance collapsed, Sweyn conquered the country and Ethelred fled to Normandy.

Edward's formidable mother Emma (c.985–1052) took Edward to Normandy for safety. Following Sweyn's unexpected death in 1014 and Ethelred's in April 1016, civil war broke out between Ethelred's son by his first marriage, Edmund "Ironside", and Sweyn's son Cnut (Canute "the Great"). Edward fought bravely at the side of his half-brother, but Edmund died in November 1016 – allowing Cnut to seize the throne.

Though fourteen year-old Edward was obliged to return to Normandy, where he remained in exile for the next 25 years, his pushy mother Emma returned to England and married Cnut. She cared little that Cnut was thirteen years her junior and already had a "handfast" wife, Ælgifu of Northampton – who had borne him a son called Harold "Harefoot" (because of his speed) in 1015. Cnut and Emma's son, Edward's half-brother, Harthacnut was born in 1018. In November 1035 Cnut died and his Danish empire began to unravel.

Cnut left England at the shire level in the hands of three powerful earls: Leofric of Mercia, Siward of Northumbria and, the most influential, Godwin of Wessex.

Emma's favourite son Harthacnut was in Denmark fending off an invasion led by King Magnus of Norway. His absence made it difficult for Emma to sustain his claim to the English throne against the increasing popularity of her stepson Harold Harefoot. Impetuously, Emma appealed to her English sons Edward and Alfred for help. Edward crossed the channel and

Cnut (c.998–1035) brought together the English and the Danes in a golden age of cooperation. He reinstated the Laws of King Edgar to allow for the constitution of a Danelaw and the safety of Scandinavians at large. He also made existing laws fairer, notably on *Inheritance in cases of Intestacy* and on *Heriots and Reliefs* (a form of inheritance tax). He strengthened the currency, introducing a series of coins of equal weight to those used in Denmark. Markets grew and the economy of England expanded, bringing a period of peaceful prosperity. The story of how Cnut used his failure to turn back the waves to demonstrate the futility of pitting human power against the forces of nature (i.e. God), is thought to be true.

sailed up the Solent to establish a base on his mother's estates in Hampshire, but was easily driven off. His younger brother Alfred, sailing a little later, fared less well. Captured by Godwin, Earl of Wessex, he was handed over to Harold Harefoot, who had the luckless Alfred blinded. Alfred died from his ordeal and was buried as a martyr in Ely Cathedral. In 1038 Harold Harefoot banished Emma from England. She fled to Bruges, where she urged her surviving sons, Edward and Harthacnut to plan a military invasion of England, carelessly proposing that both should share the throne.

Obediently, but forgetting his mother's history of recklessness, Harthacnut arrived off Flanders with a small fleet in 1039. Fortunately, while he was gathering reinforcements, on 17 March 1040 Harold Harefoot died, enabling Emma and her favourite son to land in England unopposed.

Edward was invited to join his mother and half-brother in England in 1041. On 8 June 1042 Harthacnut, childless like his half-brother Harefoot, died suddenly of convulsions at a wedding party. The English throne was now vacant. Both Magnus, King of Norway and Harthacnut's cousin, Sweyn Estristhson of Denmark made claims: but the succession was settled when Earl Godwin of Wessex, the most powerful of the English magnates, supported Edward. On Easter day 1043 Edward was crowned King of England by the archbishops of Canterbury and York at Winchester Cathedral – where both his stepfather Cnut and his half-brother Harthacnut were buried. He was thirty-nine at the start of his reign, an age which few of his predecessors ever attained.

Edward immediately sequestered all his mother's lands. He had long borne Emma a grudge for supporting his brothers and believed that she had attempted to frustrate his succession. It quickly became apparent that Edward was able to rule only with the cooperation of Godwin, the real master of the throne. In 1045 the pragmatic Edward married Godwin's daughter Edith, but the marriage was probably not consummated.

Edith's mother, Gytha was King Cnut's sister-in-law. Edith was at least twenty years younger than Edward: "she seemed more like a daughter than a wife, not so much a spouse as a good mother".

In 1051 Edward, at loggerheads with Godwin, outlawed the Earl and his family and dismissed his queen. He then filled many of the senior government posts with Norman officials, causing great resentment. A year later Edward, under unbearable pressure from Leofric, Siward and the Witan, but with no letting of blood, restored Godwin to his estates, recalled his wife and dismissed his Norman advisors. On Godwin's death in 1053, his son Harold emerged as a highly competent soldier and virtual crown-prince.

Although Edward's reign was inherently peaceful, Wales and Scotland caused occasional concern. In 1063 Godwin's sons Harold

Lady Godiva (died 1067) was the Anglo-Saxon wife of Leofric, Earl of Mercia (died 1057), celebrated in legend for her naked ride through the streets of Coventry. Godiva, troubled by the heavy taxes burdening the people of Coventry, nagged her husband to reduce them, until the exasperated Leofric promised to do so if she rode naked through the market-place. Godiva did so, her body decently covered by her long hair. Leofric kept his word and lifted all taxes except those on horses.

One version of the legend maintains that Godiva rode through the market-place on the condition that all the people of the town remained indoors. The embellishment of "Peeping Tom", a tailor who could not resist looking out of his window (whereupon he was struck blind or dead), did not become part of the legend until the 17th century.

In 1043 Godiva and Leofric founded a Benedictine monastery at Coventry. Godiva was recorded as a pre-Conquest landowner in the Domesday Book.

• **Lady Godiva** by John Collier (c.1898)

King Edward "the Confessor" by unknown artist (18th Century)
National Portrait Gallery, London

S. EDVARDVS. Confessor.

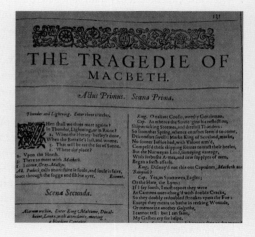

Earl Godwin, or Godwine (c.1001–53), was noble born but a self-made man. After two advantageous marriages to Danish noblewomen, the second of whom was Cnut's sister-in-law, Cnut made him Earl of Wessex in 1019. An astute politician, he cultivated Cnut's friendship so skilfully that at the time of Cnut's death he was in a position to influence the succession. Twice he failed to back Edward, having been responsible for the death of Edward's brother Alfred, but finally did so in 1042 – marrying his daughter Edith to Edward in 1045. Earl Godwin remained resolutely opposed to Edward's propensity to advance Normans to high positions; and in 1051, proved to be too powerful to defy.

Earl Godwin's second son Harold (c.1022–66) was good looking, charming, brave and ambitious. In a brilliant campaign against the Welsh in 1063, he proved himself an able soldier. He did so again in Brittany in 1064 where he was knighted by Duke William of Normandy; and again at Stamford Bridge in September 1066. His psychopathic elder brother Sweyn died in 1052, leaving Harold as the outstanding English claimant for Edward's throne.

Harold II was anointed the day after Edward's death. It is possible that he was the first English king to be crowned in Westminster Abbey, but this is uncertain. His ability and courage remain unquestioned, but in accepting the crown of England he had probably perjured himself – and he paid for it at Hastings. After the battle Harold's mistress, Edith "Swanneck", was called to identify the body (the face had been destroyed), which she did from the tattoos pricked into his chest, with the words "Edith" and "England" – he was almost certainly killed in hand-to-hand fighting at close quarters. Harold's body was buried under a pile of stones overlooking the shore. He was later interred in his church of Waltham Holy Cross in Essex, which he had refounded in 1060.

Isabella, wife of Edward II, was a direct descendant of Harold through his daughter Gytha. She reintroduced the bloodline of Harold to the Royal Line of England (and Scotland) through her son, the future Edward III, in 1312.

• **Harold's death, detail from the Bayeux Tapestry (11th Century). It is extremely unlikely that he was killed by an arrow in the eye**

Macbeth, probably a grandson of Kenneth II, was married to Kenneth III's grand-daughter Gruach. In 1031 Macbeth succeeded his father Findlaech mac Ruiaidri, as Mormaer (provincial ruler) of present day Morayshire. Macbeth usurped the throne by killing his cousin Duncan I in battle near Elgin, on 14 August 1040. Five years later, he defeated and killed Duncan's father Crinan, Abbot of Dunkeld.

In 1046 Siward, Earl of Northumbria, unsuccessfully attempted to remove Macbeth in favour of Duncan's son, Malcolm Canmore. By 1050 Macbeth had evidently secured his position to the extent that he felt confident enough to embark on a pilgrimage to Rome, the only reigning Scottish king ever to do so. In 1052 Macbeth registered another first by recruiting Norman mercenaries into his service. Two years later, pressure from Siward forced Macbeth to cede territory in southern Scotland to Malcolm Canmore: who, with English help defeated Macbeth at the bloody battle of Dunsinane Hill, near Scone. Macbeth escaped but was killed by Malcolm on 15 August 1057 at Lumphanan, near Mar in Aberdeenshire. In spite of being an usurper, Macbeth is said to be buried on the island of Iona, the traditional resting-place of Scottish kings.

Macbeth was succeeded by his stepson Lulach, who was killed in an ambush on 17 March 1058, at Essie in Aberdeenshire – leaving Malcolm the uncontested King of Scotland. His dynasty, the House of Dunkeld, ruled Scotland for the next two centuries.

Shakespeare relied upon Cheshireman Raphael Holinshed's *Chronicles of England, Scotland and Ireland* (published in 1577) for source material used in some of his historical tragedies. His low opinion of Macbeth is not justified by the facts, most of which he appears to have made up.

• **The first page of Macbeth from the First Folio (published in 1623)** and Tostig launched an overwhelming, two-pronged attack on the Welsh, resulting in the subjection of all Welsh territory and the vassalage of most of their princes. The Welsh leader, Prince Gruffydd ap Llywelyn was killed by his own men and his head was presented by Harold to Edward in person.

In 1054 Edward ordered Siward, Earl of Northumbria to remove the Scottish usurper Macbeth. On 27 July Siward and Malcolm ("Canmore") defeated Macbeth at Dunsinane, north of the river Tay in Perthshire. Malcolm was Siward's nephew and the son of King Duncan I, whom Macbeth had defeated and killed in battle.

Throughout his reign, individuals in a position to pose a threat or to embarrass Edward died at convenient moments; and this was especially true of his last thirteen years. His mother Emma died in March 1052; in September, his brother-in-law Sweyn died at Constantinople while returning from a pilgrimage to Jerusalem; and in April 1053, his father-in-law Godwin died at court. This left the four Godwinson brothers Harold, Tostig, Gyrth and Leofwine effectively running all of England save Mercia, as highly capable governors and generals – an arrangement which suited Edward very well.

Edward always kept for himself the power to make ecclesiastical appointments. With the rare exceptions of the venal Stigand and the conniving Norman, Robert Champart who fell out with Earl Godwin, as Archbishops of Canterbury (both were removed from office), Edward's choices were respectable and wise. Many of his appointments were reformers; and one, Wulfstan of Worcester was later canonised. As he grew older Edward interested himself in monastic affairs, building Westminster Abbey on a scale unprecedented in northern Europe – painstakingly recorded in the Bayeux tapestry.

Edward respected old English laws, codified by Cnut and subsequently left unchanged by William the Conqueror, enforced and added to them. From 1052–65 England, though heavily taxed, enjoyed prosperity and peace. The French-speaking Edward was on good terms with most of the precarious alliances on the Continent. His administration was competently run, underpinned by effective tax collection and an efficient mint. He deferred to the Witan and maintained its political and advisory power. There was only one cloud on the horizon, but it was an ominous one: the celibate Edward had no heir.

In 1054 Bishop Ealdred of Worcester was sent to the court of the Holy Roman Emperor Heinrich III, to find the only English ætheling (prince) who might be accepted by the Witan as Edward's heir. The son of the Confessor's half-brother Edmund Ironside, known as Edward

Edward founded his church at Westminster (with St Paul's and Canterbury Cathedrals, one of the three most important ecclesiastical buildings in England) on the site of an old Benedictine monastery. Westminster literally means the church to the west (of the City of London). Edward had originally earmarked the funds to honour a vow to make a pilgrimage to Rome, abandoned because of the security risk. Reflecting his admiration for all things Norman, the Abbey was built between 1045–50, in the Norman style; and consecrated in 1065, when Edward was dying.

In 1245 Henry III kept the nave but pulled down the rest of Edward's church and rebuilt it in its present Gothic style. A new nave was begun in 1376 but only completed in the 16th century. Henry VII built his own chapel there in 1503, remarkable for the magnificence of his renaissance tomb and the delicate fan-vaulting of the roof. Nicholas Hawksmoor (1661–1736) designed and John James (c.1673–1746) completed in 1745 the last additions, the western towers. William the Conqueror was the first king known to have been crowned at Westminster. He was followed by every English, then British monarch – except for Edward V (who was murdered in the Tower of London by his uncle Richard III) and Edward VIII, who abdicated.
• **The western towers of Westminster Abbey**

Edgar Ætheling was acclaimed King for a brief period after the battle of Hastings. He survived in a modest role in the Anglo-Norman world into the 1120s. His daughter Margaret, later St Margaret (died 1093), married King Malcolm III of Scotland.

The Bayeux Tapestry is a 1.6 by 230 foot long embroidered cloth. It depicts the events leading up to the Norman Conquest, with details of the invasion itself. Probably made in England (Anglo-Saxon needlework, or *Opus Anglicanum*, was famous across Europe) and completed *c*.1077, the tapestry is exhibited today in a special museum at Bayeux in Normandy.

Ætheling or Edward "the Exile", had married Agatha, a German-Hungarian princess, and had attained high office at the Hungarian court. Edward and Agatha had three children: Margaret, Christina and Edgar, who was only five years old. Edward the Exile was induced to come to England with his family, as the Confessor's heir – but he died on arrival.

Another initiative, unreported until after the Norman invasion, was Harold's secret mission in 1064 to the court of Duke William in Normandy, possibly to confirm a promise made by Edward in 1051 to make William his heir. On the way, Harold was captured by one of William's vassals. Released, perhaps because William had paid his ransom, Harold was invited by William to accompany him on a campaign into Brittany – where Harold was alleged to have sworn an oath, over concealed holy relics, to uphold William's claim to the English throne. Harold's violation of this oath was represented by William in 1066 as his moral justification for invading England.

In 1065 Harold and his brother Tostig quarrelled. A rebellion in Northumbria against Tostig's high-handed governance was supported by Eadwine and Morcar, Earls of Mercia and Northumbria; and covertly by Harold, who cemented the alliance by marrying their sister Ealdgyth. Edward was now confronted by a *fait accompli*. To his great distress, he found himself forced to exile a friend and ally. Tostig and his family were banished and took refuge in Flanders. Edward then suffered a series of strokes, dying on 5 January 1066 – a week after the dedication of his new church at Westminster on 28 December 1065.

Edward was buried before the high altar of Westminster Abbey on 6 January 1066: but he was not allowed to rest in peace. In 1102 Henry I, at the insistence of his wife Edith, caused her great-uncle's tomb to be opened as part of the process of canonisation. The corpse was duly reported to be uncorrupted, a sure sign of saintliness. Bishop Gundulf of Rochester, who assisted at the opening, was said to have plucked a souvenir hair from Edward's long white beard, earning himself a severe reprimand from the Abbot of Westminster. Edward's coffin was again opened by Henry II, who removed his burial robes and a pilgrim's ring. Edward was canonised in 1161.

He was disturbed again when his admirer Henry III rebuilt Westminster Abbey. On 13 October 1269 he removed Edward's body to a new shrine, which became the centre piece of the new building. Henry himself assisted in carrying the body to its new resting place, a popular pilgrimage site throughout the Middle Ages. Edward's shrine was desecrated by Henry VIII during the dissolution of the monasteries, but restored by his devout Catholic daughter Queen Mary I.

In 1685 workmen dismantling scaffolding used during the coronation of James II dropped a beam on Edward's sarcophagus, smashing the lid. A crucifix and chain were found under the corpse's right shoulder and presented to James. When he fled the country in 1688, the relics were stolen by the crew of the vessel taking him to France.

It is likely that the dying Edward bequeathed his kingdom to Harold and his queen Edith, both of whom attended his deathbed. Not even the most vocal Norman apologist ever suggested that Edward had named William as his heir.

The Anglo-Saxon Chronicle's record of Edward's life is pure hagiography. There is little doubt that elsewhere his reputation would have been better sustained had Harold not been killed at Hastings. As it was, Norman propagandists enjoyed free rein to distort the reality: projecting Edward as a political and physical weakling; and an unworldly, pious recluse. This was far from the truth: Edward was brave, resourceful and energetic. Although sometimes cruel and impetuous, he was a great survivor. Throughout the chaos and perils of 11th century European politics, Edward safeguarded his realm as an island of relative peace and prosperity, free from foreign invasion.

The cult of St Edward the Confessor started almost immediately after he was canonized in 1161. Although Edward was never venerated as a saint in England, he was admired by all mediæval kings, especially Henry III – who named his son and heir after him. Henry was the first English king to have been "touched for the King's evil", a custom harking back to a miraculous cure said to have been performed on a scrofulous (a form of tuberculosis) woman by Edward the Confessor. This practice endured for five hundred years, ending only with the accession of the Hanoverian George I in 1714.

KING HAROLD II RULED ENGLAND FOR ONLY TEN MONTHS (1066)

The Confessor's legacy was a country on the doorstep of nationhood: peaceful, rich and firmly Anglo-Saxon. The population had doubled, to about two million, between AD 43 and 1066 (though it had been some 3.5 million in 410). However England's fertile farmlands, temperate climate and settled borders fed covetous ambitions from Norsemen and Normans alike.

Harold Godwinson, self-styled King Harold II, was now unchallenged within his kingdom; and his dynasty appeared to be secure. He had six children by his mistress Edith – and twin sons by his wife Ealdgyth were born a month after his death.

Across the channel however, Duke William of Normandy was preparing the diplomatic and religious justification – and assembling an army from all over northern France, Brittany and Flanders – to win himself a kingdom.

Harold proved more than a match for the Norsemen, when he faced 7,500 led by their King Harald Hardrada ("Stern Ruler") and Harold's exiled brother Tostig. After a five-day march of 180 miles, Harold and another brother Gyrth, leading an Anglo-Saxon army of 7,000, surprised the Norsemen on Monday 25 September 1066 at Stamford Bridge, near York. Hardrada, Tostig and 7,000 Norsemen were killed, for the loss of 2,000 Anglo-Saxons. The Norsemen never returned.
- **The Battle of Stamford Bridge by Norwegian artist Peter Nicolai Arbo (1831–92)**

The Normans and the Plantagenets

1066–1485

NRICVS.   II.

William I, King of England

"THE CONQUEROR"

William, Duke of Normandy (1035–87), known as "the Bastard", and King of England (1066–87), known as "the Conqueror", left an indelible stamp on English history: as the creator of a strong and independent nation state that has endured for nearly 1,000 years.

William was born at Falaise in Normandy c.1027. He was the only son of Duke Robert II of Normandy and his mistress Herleva, the daughter of Fulbert, a tanner and undertaker. Herleva subsequently married Count Herluin de Conteville, by whom she had two sons. The eldest, Odo was appointed Bishop of Bayeux aged only sixteen.

In 1035 Duke Robert died returning from a pilgrimage to Jerusalem; and William, aged seven and despite his illegitimacy, succeeded his father as Duke of Normandy.

William's accession to the dukedom as a young bastard triggered a general collapse of authority throughout Normandy. Anarchy prevailed while warring factions of nobles competed for power. Before he reached adolescence, three of William's regents died violently and his tutor was murdered. His uncles were of little use since they too plunged into the chaos, hoping to profit by William's death. He was saved only by the cunning of his mother, who frequently hid him in peasant hovels during these dangerous years.

Knighted at fifteen by Henry I of France, William began to take an interest in his inheritance. From 1046 to 1055 William was engaged in putting down a series of baronial rebellions, mostly led by members of his family. Often in grave personal danger he had to rely on the support of Henry I, but it was during these hazardous years that William developed an unshakeable

> Odo, Bishop of Bayeux (1033–97) was William's half-brother – and an incorrigible rogue. He attended the Battle of Hastings and commissioned the Bayeux Tapestry to commemorate it. William created him Earl of Kent in 1067, making him responsible for the defence of the south-eastern approaches to his new kingdom. In 1095 Odo joined the First Crusade, dying at Palermo on his way to Jerusalem.

> The dukedom of Normandy, previously a province of France called Neustria, had been ceded in 911 to the Viking chieftain Rollo by Charles "the Simple" (meaning "straightforward"), in return for Rollo's homage and fealty. The descendants of Rollo, now known as Duke Robert I, intermarried with the area's previous inhabitants, becoming the Normans – a French-speaking mixture of Scandinavians, Hiberno-Norse, Orcadians, Anglo-Danish and indigenous Franks and Gauls.

King William I "the Conqueror" The Bayeux Tapestry

resolve to replace anarchy with firm governance. At Val-ès-Dunes near Caen in 1047 William, in alliance with Henry I, defeated an army of rebel barons – the first evidence of his instinctive military ability.

For the next five years William was occupied with assisting Henry I in a series of campaigns against Geoffrey de Martel, Count of Anjou. By 1054 the tables had been turned. William was now confronted by an alliance of Henry and Martel, as well as a dangerous rebellion which had flared on his eastern border. Had Henry, Martel and the rebels co-ordinated their attack against William, he would not have survived: but his inspired leadership, and favourable circumstances, enabled him to suppress the rebels and defeat Henry and Martel decisively at the Battle of Mortemer. By 1057 William was the undisputed ruler of Normandy, a position secured even further in 1060, when both Henry and Martel died. In 1063 William conquered the Duchy of Maine and became the dominant ruler in northern France.

In 1064 Edward the Confessor, King of England, sent his brother-in-law Harold Godwinson as an emissary to Normandy, supposedly to confirm his recognition of William as the heir to the English crown. Harold was shipwrecked on the way and imprisoned by the Count of Ponthieu. When William ransomed him, Harold confirmed Edward's resolve to make William his heir. Despite this, Harold was crowned King of England the day after the Confessor died. Norman propagandists later insisted that Harold had sworn an oath, over concealed holy relics, promising to uphold William's succession. It was Harold's perceived violation of this oath that provided William with the pretext for invading England.

Having gone to considerable lengths to establish the legality of his claim to the throne, William drew up plans to invade England. He moved rapidly to secure his own kingdom of Normandy and to win the international support he believed critical for the venture. He made his wife Matilda and son Robert regents and placed his most loyal supporters in key positions. He petitioned Pope Alexander II and received both his support and that of Archdeacon Hildebrand, the future Pope Gregory VII. At the same time William raised an international army composed of Norman, Breton, German, Frisian, Flemish and French knights. He also had to assemble a fleet and coordinate the supplies required to launch an amphibious operation across the notoriously unpredictable English Channel, dangerously late in the year. Astonishing by any standards, especially those of the 11th century, in a few short months William accomplished a most remarkable military, logistic and diplomatic success – unmatched for 900 years, until the invasion of Normandy by the Allies in 1944, sailing in the opposite direction.

While William was preparing to invade England, King Harald Hardrada of Norway, who also opposed Harold's claim to the English throne, together with Harold's exiled brother Tostig, landed on the coast of Northumberland. Harold marched north to meet the invader. On 25 September 1066, in a bloody encounter at Stamford Bridge near York, he defeated and killed both Tostig and Hardrada, who was killed by an arrow through the neck. Harold promptly plunged south to meet the threat from William, who had landed near Hastings on 28 September. Despite strong advice to rest his exhausted army in London, Harold set out for the Sussex coast on 12 October. The most crucial battle in English history was at hand – and Harold was in no fit state to fight it.

William's interest in England derived from an alliance made in 1002: when King Ethelred II of England married Emma, sister to William's grandfather, Duke Richard II of Normandy. Emma's eldest son, Edward ("the Confessor") was William's first cousin once removed. During his exile in Normandy Edward would have met the young William, who supported him after his accession in 1042. Edward's marriage was barren, encouraging William to aspire to become Edward's heir and King of England.

By mid-August William had assembled a large fleet at the mouth of the river Dives. Embarking in mid-September, William's fleet was driven by a gale up the Channel and he was forced to re-assemble his ships at Saint-Valéry on the Somme.

Unknown to William, the militia army left behind by Harold to defend his south coast had dispersed in order to bring in the harvest, which had left Kent and Sussex unprotected. On 27

THE NORMAN CONQUEST (September to October 1066)

Map of the Norman
Conquest: September
to October 1066

September, after several days of wind and rain, William's fleet set sail and landed in Pevensey
Bay the following day. His force of nearly 7,000 cavalry and infantry secured a beachhead and
moved swiftly to occupy the towns of Pevensey and Hastings. William's army was still
positioned between the sea and the densely wooded Weald when, just before dusk on 13
October, Harold emerged from the forest to defend Senlac Hill, a ridge six miles north-west of
Hastings. At dawn the next day William attacked, before Harold had been able fully to deploy
his weary troops.

The Battle of Hastings took place on the 14 October 1066. It lasted all day, an unusually
long time for a battle in the early Middle Ages – and an indication that the sides were evenly
matched. The battlefield presented difficulties for both: while the English had the high ground,
requiring William's troops to advance up a steep slope, Harold's ability to manoeuvre was
constricted by the surrounding forest. The battle was fought between armies quite different in
composition, training and tactics. Harold's relied principally on the Saxon *fyrd*, a military levy
deriving from the Norse practice of raising militias from free farmers (*leidangr*) and developed
in England by Alfred the Great. By 1066 the *fyrd* was raised from all able-bodied men in districts
threatened with attack. Service lasted as long as the threat existed and each man provided his
own arms and provisions.

The shock troops of Harold's army were provided by the housecarls, household troops who
formed a standing army of professional soldiers, whose primary duty was to act as bodyguard

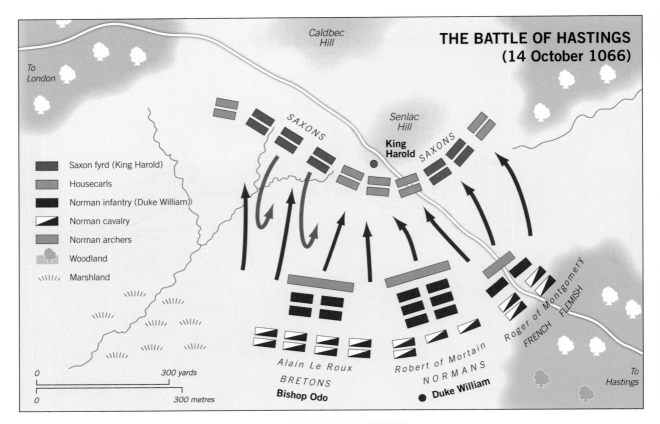

THE BATTLE OF HASTINGS
(14 October 1066)

Caldbec
Hill

To
London

SAXONS

Senlac
Hill

**King
Harold**

SAXONS

Roger of Montgomery

FRENCH

FLEMISH

To
Hastings

Alain Le Roux

BRETONS

Bishop Odo

Robert of Mortain

NORMANS

● **Duke William**

■	Saxon fyrd (King Harold)
■	Housecarls
■	Norman infantry (Duke William)
◩	Norman cavalry
■	Norman archers
■	Woodland
\\\\\\	Marshland

0   300 yards

0   300 metres

The Battle of Hastings and the ensuing Norman conquest were illustrated in an embroidered tapestry. It was almost certainly commissioned by Odo, Bishop of Bayeux, and woven in the 1070s: for it was discovered in Bayeux Cathedral, founded and built by Odo between 1070–76. It is embroidered in eight different colours of woollen thread on coarse-woven linen cloth, using two methods of stitching: outline or 'stem stitch', for lettering and figure silhouettes, and couching or 'laid-work' for the detailed infill. The tapestry is 231 feet long and 20 inches wide.

The Bayeux "tapestry" is not, in the strict sense a tapestry at all. It is made up of 79 panels, scored in Latin, with ornately decorated borders, in the manner of illuminated English manuscripts. There are good grounds for assuming that it was woven in England, specifically in Kent – where Odo had his power base. The text contains hints of Old English; and both the embroidery style and vegetable dyes are similar to those used in Anglo-Saxon needlework, or *Opus Anglicanum*, renowned throughout Europe at that time.

The tapestry was hung in Bayeux Cathedral until Napoleon removed it to Paris in 1803: to promote his own, ultimately aborted invasion plans. During WWII it was hidden from the Nazis in the basement of the Louvre. It was returned to Bayeux after the war; and is today displayed in a museum attached to the Cathedral.

• **Detail of the Bayeux Tapestry showing outlines in stem or outline stitch and fillings in laid work**

to the king. Housecarls were proficient in a wide range of weapons including the one-handed sword, the throwing-axe and the 'long-bearded axe' (*Skeggox*). Although practised in the defensive tactic of the shield-wall, a phalanx of interlocking shields against arrow volleys and attacking cavalry, the housecarl was trained principally to use his great axe to cleave the forelegs of an attacking war-horse. While William's cavalry led their horses into line to keep them fresh, the housecarls did the opposite: by riding to battle, dismounting and fighting on foot.

Throughout the day William's large contingent of archers fired volley after volley into the Anglo-Saxon lines, obliging the housecarls to adopt their traditional shield-wall defence: which made it impossible for them to attack. So intense was the rain of arrows that William's army nearly ran out of ammunition. Each volley was followed up by a charge from William's knights. Without any archers of their own, the Anglo-Saxon lines recoiled but held firm against these repeated charges: until William ordered his knights to feign retreat. This tactic encouraged the headstrong Anglo-Saxons to break ranks in pursuit. William's knights swiftly turned about and attacked the unprotected foot soldiers chasing them. Early in the battle Harold's brothers were killed. As night fell Harold himself, surrounded by his housecarls in a classic Anglo-Saxon fight to the death, was cut down – having been wounded by an arrow but probably not in the eye. Harold's army disintegrated and gave up the fight. The events leading up to William's invasion of England and its aftermath were recorded in the Bayeux Tapestry.

William, fearing that the English might rally and isolate his army in hostile country, moved rapidly to protect his rear, by securing the towns of Dover, Canterbury and Winchester. On Christmas Day 1066 William was crowned in Westminster Abbey.

William had arrived in England well versed in the art of creating order out of chaos. In Normandy, over the previous twenty years, he had crushed rebellion, recovered territories, stamped out private feuding and laid down precise terms of the service he expected from his vassals. By placing only those of unquestioned loyalty in key positions, peace and stability were established and the Norman Church flourished. In England he replaced all the Anglo-Saxon bishops with Norman clerics and replaced the corrupt Archbishop of Canterbury, Stigand with his trusted advisor Lanfranc. English monastic life was transformed by an influx of Norman monks and abbots.

William was in Normandy throughout 1067, when he had to return to England to face a serious rebellion in the north of the country. The rebels were assisted by a large Danish army under King Sweyn Estrithson, which had razed York. By 1071 he had suppressed the insurrection, making the northern counties temporarily uninhabitable by burning homesteads and devastating the land, in a terrible campaign which became known as the "Harrying of the North". William descended to a level of savagery, remarkable even by the cruel standards of the day. In the immediate aftermath, William introduced the Norman practice of castle construction, beginning with Chepstow in 1067, Warwick in 1068 and Richmond in 1071 – the Tower of London dates from 1078.

In 1072 William invaded Scotland; and then Wales in 1081, building a ring of protective castles in the "Marcher" counties to secure England's frontiers.

After 1075 William spent most of his time in Normandy, leaving the governance of England to Archbishop Lanfranc. Earlier that year William had to confront a rebellion (the "Revolt of the three Earls") raised by Ralph, Earl of Norfolk, Roger, Earl of Hereford and the last surviving

Lanfranc (1010–89), Archbishop of Canterbury (1070), was born in Pavia in Italy. A scholar, he settled in Normandy and entered the Benedictine Monastery of Bec, later becoming Prior. William made Lanfranc his personal advisor, appointing him to be the first Abbot of St Stephen's at Caen. As Archbishop, Lanfranc completely reformed and reorganised the English Church on Gregorian principles. In 1075 Lanfranc uncovered a conspiracy against William led by his eldest son Robert – which secured the throne of England for his second son William Rufus.

Richmond Castle in North Yorkshire, stands on a breathtaking position above the River Swale. It was constructed in 1071, as a direct result of the slaughter of the Norman garrison at York in 1069, by one of William's most loyal followers: Alain Le Roux ("the Red") de Ponthievre of Brittany. Alain (c.1040–93) is probably the richest man who has ever lived in the British Isles. He left £11,000 at his death (over 7% of GDP), some £81 billion today.

Having given its name to Richmond-upon-Thames, Richmond ("strong hill" in French) has become the most mimicked overseas settlement of any British town. There are at least 56 Richmonds worldwide: 31 in the US, 5 each in South Africa and Australia, 4 in Jamaica, 2 each in Canada and Grenada, and one apiece in the Bahamas, New Zealand, Trinidad, St Vincent and the Grenadines.

In 1083 William's beloved wife Matilda died. This was a great loss to him personally and to his kingdom. She had performed admirably the role of a traditional mediæval queen: representing William during his many absences, arranging his households, distributing alms and keeping his extended family together. They had married c.1050 and had four sons and five daughters.

English earl, Waltheof of Northumbria – who had enlisted the support of the Danes. The Danish fleet never appeared and the rebel forces, prevented by William's deputies from uniting, were defeated. An appalling retribution was exacted by William. Earl Roger lost his hands and was imprisoned, his followers horribly mutilated and exiled. Earl Waltheof was beheaded. At Salisbury in August 1082, William took oaths of allegiance from the England's leading landowners – and knighted his youngest son Henry.

William's last years were spent in conducting a series of complex political and military manoeuvres, all directed towards securing the borders of his duchy.

William's movements during 1083–85 are unclear. He was certainly in England during 1084: when a tax of six shillings was levied on every hide of land to fund the cost of meeting an impending Danish and Flemish invasion, led by King Cnut IV of Denmark.

William returned yet again in 1085 to arrest his half brother Odo, who was raising an army without permission, in preparation for a march on Italy to place himself on the papal throne. In 1086 William commissioned an economic survey of all English land tenures – which became known as the Domesday Book.

In 1087 William attempted to seize back the towns of Mantes, Chaumont and Pontoise– all of which had been occupied by Philip I of France since 1077. In July, in a surprise attack on Mantes in the Île-de-France, William's horse stumbled and fell while crossing a ditch. The armoured pommel of William's saddle crushed his abdomen. He was taken to Rouen where he lay lucid, but dying in great pain, for five weeks: contemplating his possible choice of heirs. Eventually William decided to give England to the most loyal of his sons, Rufus; and Normandy to the eldest, Robert Curthose. Henry, the youngest was given substantial funds and a huge grant of land. At dawn on the 9 September 1087, William died from a massive internal haemorrhage. He was sixty years old.

In 1961 a thigh-bone disinterred from his tomb in St Etienne Abbey, which he himself had founded, indicated that he was a tall man for his day, at five foot nine

Published in 1086, **The Domesday Book**, the Book of Winchester or more accurately, "The Description of England" is an original record and summary of William I's survey of England. It was planned in considerable detail and executed with remarkable speed, making it the most extraordinary administrative achievement of the Middle Ages. Deeply unpopular and resented at the time, the survey was carried out by eight panels of commissioners, each panel devoted to a separate group of counties. The aim was to compile a detailed account of the King's estates and those of his tenants-in-chief, who held their lands in exchange for their loyalty to the crown. From these accounts a summary was assembled which, by the mid-12th century, had become known as the Domesday Book.

Dom is an Anglo-Saxon word meaning "reckoning". One of the main purposes of the Domesday Book was to raise taxes. There was no appeal on assessments by the commissioners, which became law. It was written in Latin, was highly abbreviated and included Anglo-Saxon words where necessary. It was published in two volumes.

Little Domesday, actually the larger, includes Norfolk, Suffolk and Essex. Great Domesday covers the rest of England – except for four northern counties still under Scottish control. London and Winchester were also omitted, probably because of their size and complexity.

Each English county was visited by several Royal commissioners called *legati*. The proceedings were attended by barons and representatives from the local towns.

The focus of his investigation was the Hundred, an administrative subdivision of the county. The return made from each Hundred was affirmed by a jury composed of six Englishmen and six Normans.

The Domesday Book was concerned with the valuation of rural estates – the sole source of national wealth at the time. Each manor was assessed on its area of arable land and plough-teams of eight oxen needed to work it: then river meadows, woodlands, pasture, fisheries, water mills and salt pans – concluding with the numbers of peasants it supported. This not only enabled the King to keep track of his barons' possessions but importantly, the identity of any under-tenants he had engaged. William intended that these under-tenants should be available to serve as soldiers when required and should, through their Lord, swear direct fealty to the crown. The enquiry also concentrated on sources of revenue, so that the King could readily tax them when he needed to raise money.

inches. He was immensely strong, able while galloping a horse to draw a bow that most men on foot could not even bend. In his last years however, he became extremely fat: to the point where his body had to be broken in order to fit it into his stone sarcophagus.

William's passion for hunting, extremely effective in maintaining peak fitness for war in the 11th century, resulted in the creation of the New Forest as a royal hunting preserve in *c*.1079. It was designated a National Park in 2005.

William is among the most significant figures of mediæval English history. From precarious beginnings, through unflagging determination, an iron will and outstanding courage he transformed his duchy from an anarchic *mêlée* into the most powerful state in northern France.

The White Tower is the central tower of the Tower of London. The great keep was started in 1078 by William the Conqueror. He ordered it to be built inside the south-east angle of the City walls, adjacent to the Thames – as much to protect the Normans from the people of London as to protect London from outside invaders. The Tower was built of Caen stone, imported from Normandy: and Gundulf, Bishop of Rochester was appointed as architect. The tower was finished around 1087 by his sons, Kings William "Rufus" and Henry I.

His strong support for the Church as a pillar of authority, expressed by his reform of monasteries and bishoprics, won him the unswerving loyalty of the Church fathers. After the invasion, his uncompromising 'Normanisation' of the English Church both reinvigorated it and enabled it to benefit from the monastic and religious developments that were burgeoning on the Continent. He also imposed a new culture and a French-speaking order of aristocracy on the old Anglo-Saxon hierarchy: transforming the English language and England's literature, art and architecture for ever.

William remained deeply involved in the politics of Europe which brought an inward-looking England more into the mainstream of international affairs. He replaced the English hierarchy of land ownership and recorded the changes in his great land survey. This in turn, created a strong feudal structure of nobles and tenants whose loyalty was assured – because all of them ultimately derived their power from the king by holding his land in "fee simple". Massive castle keeps now studded the landscape, ensuring that no Englishman would forget that the Normans were there to stay.

HEREWARD "THE WAKE"

Hereward the Wake was known in his lifetime only as "the Outlaw" or "Exile". In Old English, 'Hereward' means "guardian of the army". The name may have been ascribed to him by the Wake family, Normans who claimed Hereward's estates after his death, to imply kinship and to legitimise their claim to his lands. An Anglo-Saxon, Hereward is thought to have been born *c*.1035, in or near Bourne in Lincolnshire.

Hereward is said to have rebelled first against Edward the Confessor, whom he saw as aligning England with the Normans. Having been outlawed, he became a mercenary in Flanders, before returning to England after the Conquest. In 1069 the Danish King Sweyn Estrithson sent a small army to establish a camp on the Isle of Ely. He was joined by many

Some remarkable men have come from the small town of Bourne, which has a population of less than 12,000. Robert Manning (*c*.1298–*c*.1338), who translated *The Handling of Synne* from the French in *c*.1330 was one. He was the first poet known to have written in English – his preface states: "For men unlearned I undertook, in English speech to write this book". William Cecil, 1st Lord Burghley was another; as was Charles Worth (1825–95), who went to Paris in 1846 and founded French *haute couture* (the House of Worth).

Raymond Mays (1899–1980), also born at Bourne, founded British Racing Motors (BRM) in 1949 and made racing cars there in the 1950s and 1960s – Graham Hill (1929–75) drove a BRM in 1962, the first all-British car to win a world championship.

Ely was once an island, rising 70 feet above the fens: named for the eels that were once abundant in the surrounding waters. In 673 Æthelthryth (or Etheldreda), daughter of the King of East Anglia and wife of Ecgfrith, a Prince of Northumbria, founded a monastery on the Isle of Ely. Canonised as St Audrey, she gave her name to a fair held at Ely each year in her honour. The cheap trinkets sold there were described as "tawdry". The monastery was sacked by the Danes in 870.

Construction of the present Cathedral was started by Abbot Simeon in 1083. The central octagonal tower was built after his original crossing-tower collapsed in 1322. It rises 142 feet to a wooden "lantern", the only Gothic dome in the world.

• **The Octagon "Lantern"**

Westminster Hall, the oldest surviving part of the Palace of Westminster and one of the oldest halls in Europe, was built by Rufus in 1097. King Richard II modernised the structure in 1395, with the finest hammer beam roof in the world. Designed by the royal master mason Henry Yevele (died 1400) and made by the master carpenter, Hugh Herland (died 1406), it is the largest unsupported mediæval roof in England: measuring 68 by 240 feet. The chestnut timber-work was framed at Farnham in Surrey.

Englishmen, including Hereward. In 1070 they sacked Peterborough Abbey, supposedly to save the abbey's treasures from the Normans.

In 1071 he made a final stand on the Isle of Ely. More factual than legend is the story that the Normans built a mile-long timber causeway, but it sank under the weight of armour and horses. They bribed the monks of the island, to reveal a safe route across the marshes instead, and captured Ely. Hereward escaped into the inaccessible fenland.

The 15th century *Gesta Herewardi* states that Hereward was pardoned by King William.

KING WILLIAM II ("RUFUS") OF ENGLAND (REIGNED 1087–1100)

William "Rufus" was born *c.*1056 in Normandy. He became King of England in 1087. He was a brutal and tyrannical ruler, called Rufus for his puce complexion. He was probably homosexual, possibly bisexual. William II's reign is remembered only for a series of military successes against England's neighbours, short-lived in their importance though they proved to be, and his barons – whom he usually treated with contempt.

Within a year of acceding to the throne he had to put down a rebellion by barons loyal to his elder brother Robert "Curthose" (short stockings), who had inherited the duchy of Normandy. William took control of Normandy when Robert mortgaged his duchy to join the First Crusade (1095–99).

In 1095 he crushed another rebellion led by Robert de Mowbray, Earl of Northumberland, with great cruelty; and exiled the saintly Anselm, Archbishop of Canterbury. In 1093, having defeated and killed Malcolm III of Scotland at the Battle of Alnwick in Northumberland, he reduced the Scottish kings to vassalage. Five years later he subdued Wales. On 2 August 1100 William was killed when hunting in the New Forest – said to have been shot with an arrow in the back by Walter Tirel, Lord of Poix, in an accident that was quite possibly arranged by his brother Henry.

DURHAM CATHEDRAL

The Cathedral Church of Christ, Blessed Mary the Virgin and St Cuthbert of Durham, usually referred to simply as Durham Cathedral, is over 900 years old but still used for daily worship. It is one of the finest examples of Norman architecture anywhere in Europe. It is also a UNESCO World Heritage Site – along with Durham Castle which it faces across Palace Green, towering above the River Wear.

Durham Cathedral from across the River Wear

The Cathedral houses the shrine and relics of Cuthbert of Lindisfarne, the head of St Oswald of Northumbria and the remains of the Venerable Bede. There are 325 steps to the top of the 217 foot-tall tower. Durham is an early example of the Gothic architecture of cathedrals built in Northern France by the same Norman stonemasons a decade or two later, although the style of architecture is more accurately described as Romanesque.

The Cathedral was designed and built by the first Prince-Bishop, William of St Carilef. Construction began in 1093. William died in 1096, before its completion in 1135.

Durham is the fourth in importance of the "five great sees" in the Church of England hierarchy, ahead of Winchester but after Canterbury, York and London.

KING HENRY I OF ENGLAND (REIGNED 1100–35)

Henry, known as "Beauclerc" (good scholar) or "Lion of Justice", for the attention he brought to the administrative and legislative machinery of England, was born in 1069, probably at Selby in Yorkshire. He was the youngest son of William I. He seized the throne on the death of his elder brother William "Rufus". His eldest brother, Robert "Curthose" returned from the First Crusade in 1101, but Henry bought him off by returning Normandy to him. Five years later however, Henry took Normandy back, because of Robert's misrule, and imprisoned him. There was nothing cuddly about Henry: in 1124 he had 94 mint workers castrated for producing substandard coins.

On 11 November 1100, an easy date to remember, Henry married Edith, daughter of King Malcolm III ("Canmore") of Scotland and Margaret, great-niece of Edward the Confessor. She changed her Anglo-Saxon name to Matilda on becoming queen – which united the Norman and Anglo-Saxon lines of kings. Matilda died in 1118. Desperate for an heir, Henry married a second time in 1121 but the marriage was childless. It is ironic that Henry left only one legitimate child, as he holds the English royal record for fathering the largest number of acknowledged illegitimate children: between twenty and twenty-five. He had many mistresses and identifying which mistress was the mother of which child has proved impossible.

Henry was tough, wily and pragmatic. He is chiefly remembered for effective government, judicial and financial reform and for reconciling Anglo-Saxons to Norman rule. He died on 1 December 1135 of food poisoning from eating "a surfeit of

The Romanesque St Magnus Cathedral, at Kirkwall in Orkney (begun in 1137) is another fine example of Norman architecture. It was built by masons from Durham Cathedral. The diocese was originally under the authority of the Archbishop of Nidaros in Norway – Orkney was Norwegian until being annexed by King James III of Scotland in 1468. Earl Magnus of Orkney, a pious and gentle man, was murdered by his cousin Håkon's cook, Lifolf on 16 April 1116.

Henry's only legitimate son, the seventeen year-old William Adelin (or the Ætheling) drowned on the *White Ship*, which sank off Barfleur on 25 November 1120. "No ship ever brought so much misery to England", wrote William of Malmesbury. When the ship set off in the dark, it struck a rock (which can still be seen from the cliffs of Barfleur) and quickly capsized. The passengers and crew had been carousing all evening and the helmsman was drunk.

The oldest Livery Company in England, the Weavers was established in c.1130; and the second oldest, the Bakers in c.1155 – both over 850 years ago. None were formed between 1709–1926. Post-1926 companies are called "Modern". The 108th was the Security Professionals, who were granted Livery in 2008.

In 1515 the precedence of the 48 Livery Companies then in existence was settled. Of the "Great Twelve", the Mercers is first: followed by the Grocers, Drapers, Fishmongers and Goldsmiths. Every Easter the Merchant Taylors and the Skinners exchange sixth and seventh place – the origin of the phrase "at sixes and sevens".

lampreys", in Normandy – having made his barons swear to accept his only surviving child, the Empress Matilda, as his heir. His remains were sewn into a leather shroud, to preserve them, and interred at Reading Abbey – which he had founded in 1121.

THE "ANARCHY", WAR BETWEEN MATILDA AND STEPHEN (1135–54)

Matilda, or Maud, was born in London in 1102. In 1114 she married the Holy Roman Emperor Henry V. He died in 1125 and Matilda married Geoffrey of Anjou – which found little favour with Norman barons who regarded Anjou as their enemy. On King Henry I's death, Matilda's first cousin Stephen of Blois (1097–1154), whose mother Adela was William the Conqueror's youngest daughter, seized the English throne and crowned himself on 26 December 1135. Anarchy prevailed, despite Stephen's defeat of Matilda in 1141. Good-natured and well-meaning, he found maintaining order impossible while his imperious cousin was left in possession of most of western England. Matilda finally retreated to Normandy in 1148, having never been crowned.

Matilda's son Henry of Anjou however, invaded England in 1153: and by treaty with Stephen, became king after Stephen's death in 1154. Matilda remained a close advisor to her son, now King Henry II, until her death in Rouen on 10 September 1167.

KING HENRY II OF ENGLAND (REIGNED 1154–89)

Henry was born at Le Mans in Maine on 5 March 1133 and was educated by the greatest Norman philosopher of the day, William de Conches. He was known variously as Henry Plantagenet, Henry "Curtmantle" (short robe), Duke of Normandy (1150), Count of Anjou (1151) and from 1154, King of England. He was the son of Geoffrey Plantagenet, 5th Count of Anjou and the Empress Matilda, daughter and heir of Henry I.

Henry's mother Matilda, who had lost her claim to the English throne to her cousin Stephen, was the first powerful woman in Henry's life. In 1152 Henry married Eleanor of Aquitaine, the divorced wife of the French King Louis VII: she was the second.

Alienor (anglicised into Eleanor) of Aquitaine was born in 1122 in Guyenne in southwest France. In 1137, aged fifteen and having inherited the duchy of Aquitaine from her father, she married the dreary French Dauphin Louis – heir to the French throne, but heir to little more of modern France than Eleanor herself. She was the richest woman in western Europe – also a beauty, strong-willed, highly-sexed and capricious.

As Duchess of Aquitaine, Eleanor insisted on accompanying Louis to the Holy Land on the Second Crusade (1147–49). Her scandalous behaviour, which probably included an affair with her uncle Raymond of Antioch, drove Louis to annul the marriage (on grounds of consanguinity) in 1152. Her two daughters were, however, declared legitimate.

Despite being eleven years his senior and more closely related to him than she was to Louis, Eleanor immediately proposed to Henry Plantagenet, soon to become King Henry II of England. One of Eleanor's rumoured lovers had been Henry's own father, Geoffrey of Anjou, who strongly advised his son not to marry her.

When joined with Henry's inheritance of England and Normandy, Eleanor's dowry united the whole of western France under the English crown. She bore Henry five sons including Richard "the Lionheart" and, when she was forty-four, John "Lackland" – both later kings of England. She also produced three daughters, all of whom Henry married strategically into leading European royal families. Eleanor maintained a magnificent court at Poitiers which was celebrated for its troubadours.

Late in Henry's reign Eleanor encouraged her sons to rebel against their father. When these rebellions failed Henry imprisoned her. Released on his death in 1189, Eleanor acted as regent for Richard I during his absence on the Third Crusade. After Richard's death, whenever his brother John was in England, she defended Anjou and Aquitaine competently against French incursions. This formidable woman retired to the monastery at Fontevrault, where she died on 1 April 1204 – and where she is buried. Having had ten children, her age of eighty-two was remarkable in the 12th century.

Throughout his reign Henry was preoccupied with the defence of his vast Angevin empire. The term "Angevin" (of Anjou) refers only to Henry II and his sons Richard I and John. Thereafter, until Richard III was killed in 1485, the dynasty is described as Plantagenet.

Henry's possessions derived unity only from his overall sovereignty, consolidated through a subtle combination of conquest, diplomacy and the marriages of his children – which extended his influence to Germany, Spain and Sicily. He was on familiar terms with the principal Continental monarchs, Frederick Barbarossa of Germany and Louis VII of France, as well as Pope Alexander III. As a result, he was able to add the long-disputed Vexin in southern Normandy to his territories when his eldest surviving son, also Henry married Marguerite, Louis VII's daughter by his second wife Constance of Castile. Henry could have ridden over 900 miles from the Scottish border to the Pyrenees without leaving his estates – other than when crossing the English Channel, the strip of water which would ultimately divide them from each other for ever.

Early in his reign, Henry compelled King Malcolm IV of Scotland to pay homage to him and to return the lost counties of Westmorland, Northumberland and Cumberland. This commitment was continued by Malcolm's brother and heir William "the Lion". In Wales, Henry was also able to exact homage without conquest. Finally, in 1155 Pope Adrian IV announced that he had granted Ireland to the English crown, a dubious award that Henry was surprisingly slow to act upon. When he did so, he despatched an expedition led by Richard de Clare, Earl of Pembroke ("Strongbow") from the south of Wales. It landed at Wexford on 1 May 1169 and rapidly established an Anglo-Angevin enclave in Leinster.

In 1162 however, Henry's impressive military, territorial and diplomatic achievements were marred by a fierce dispute with his Archbishop of Canterbury, Thomas Becket.

Thomas Becket was born in 1118 on Cheapside in London. Both his parents were Norman, his father a textile merchant. Commonly known as à Becket, although the prefix is nonsense, he was an outstanding administrator and diplomat. A trusted king's counsellor, promoted by

Troubadours were a class of well-born lyric poets and musicians. They charmed and amused the ladies of all the principal courts in southern France, northern Italy and Spain for two hundred years from the 11th century. They used the dialect of south-western France, the *langue d'oc* (soft speech), in a style of expressive poetry of complex rhyme and metre, extolling the virtues of courtly love.

Henry even sent his eldest son Henry to live with Becket (the custom then was for well-born children to be fostered out to other noble houses). The younger Henry is supposed to have said that Becket showed him more fatherly love in a day than his father ever had in his entire life.

WALES

ENGLAND

London

Thames

English Channel

FLANDERS

Calais
⚔ Bouvines (1214)
Cambrai

ARTOIS
• Amiens

Château Galliard 🏰
Rouen
Seine
Gisors 🏰

Reims ✝

CHAMPAGNE

Paris
ÎLE-DE-FRANCE
Marne
Troyes •
Seine

NORMANDY

BRITTANY

Rennes •

MAINE
• Le Mans

Nantes •
Angers •
ANJOU
Loire
Tours •
TOURAINE

✝ Fontevrault Abbey

BLOIS

NEVERS

BURGUNDY
Dijon •

Orléans •

Bourges •

Saône

POITOU
• Poitiers

BERRY

MÂCON

LA MARCHE
Loire
Lyons •

Châlus-Chabrol 🏰
• Limoges

LIMOUSIN
Clermont •

AUVERGNE

Rhône

PERIGORD

A Q U I T A I N E

Bordeaux •
Garonne

GASCONY

Albi •
TOULOUSE
Toulouse •

Nimes •

Marseilles •

Rhône

H O L Y   R O M A N   E M P I R E

CASTILE

NAVARRE
Ebro

ARAGON

BARCELONA

FRANCE 1166

Territories possessed by
King Henry II of England (1133–89)

	911	Viking Settlement
	1151	Angevin (Anjou) legacy
	1152	Aquitaine (by marriage)
	1154	England (from 1066)
	1166	Brittany (by conquest)
		Vassal

Retained by England until 1453. All but Bordeaux and part of Gascony were lost by King John after Bouvines in 1214

Royal Domain of France

	987	Possessed by Hugh Capet
		Possessions or vassals of King Louis VII (1120–80)

🏰 Castle
⚔ Battlefield
✝ Abbey / Cathedral

0   100 miles
0   100 km

After his marriage to Eleanor, Duchess of Aquitaine at Poitiers in 1152, King Henry II of England controlled more of France than the French King, Louis VII.

Henry in 1155 to be his Lord Chancellor, Becket served his king with zeal and efficiency. He became a courtier of style and cheerful worldliness.

In 1162 King Henry appointed Becket Archbishop of Canterbury, in which office he expected Becket to do his bidding. Far from remaining Henry's obedient placeman however, Becket embraced his ecclesiastical duties seriously and devoutly. In 1164 Henry proclaimed the Constitutions of Clarendon, unequivocally laying down royal prerogatives over the Church. When Becket refused to comply, Henry attempted to arraign him – who fled to France. In 1170 however, he returned to Canterbury; where he was murdered in his cathedral by four misguided knights seeking royal favour. They are said to have responded to Henry's furious, and almost certainly apocryphal, question: "Who will rid me of this turbulent priest?". Becket was buried in Canterbury Cathedral, where his tomb became a focus of devotion to pilgrims: the most important of whom was Henry – who had himself flogged on 12 July 1174, as part of his penance. Canonised in 1173, Saint Thomas Becket's feast day is 29 December. All four of Becket's murderers were dead within four years.

The damage done to Henry's reputation by Becket's murder paled into insignificance when compared to his feuding with his family. Henry's complete refusal to compromise frustrated his designs, endangered his life and finally destroyed him. Though he fathered at least four bastards with four mistresses, Henry enjoyed sufficiently good relations with his wife Eleanor for her to bear him eight children.

Henry's sons, Henry, Geoffrey, Richard and John, became deeply embittered as a result of their father's refusal to entrust them with any real authority. Eleanor shared their frustrations and encouraged her sons to conspire against their father. In 1173 Henry angrily placed Eleanor in custody, where she remained until his death in 1189.

By the early 1170s Henry's fortunes were at a nadir. He was faced with rebellions both in England and Normandy, insurrections that were respectively supported by William "the Lion" in Scotland and inevitably, Louis VII of France. Henry reacted with great vigour: and by 1174 had managed to restore stability to his sprawling kingdom. The Scots had been defeated at Alnwick and he had put down the rebellion in Normandy.

The next crisis erupted in 1181 when his sons, Henry (known as the "Young King", following his coronation in his father's lifetime) and Richard, fell out over the ownership of Aquitaine. This resolved itself in 1183, when the Young King died; but Richard then turned on John who had been authorised by his father to take over the province from Richard. The threads of Henry's life began to unravel. He found himself opposed by a coalition between Richard and the shrewd, capable young Philip II Augustus of France, who had succeeded his father Louis VII. Henry was at last overwhelmed and obliged to surrender when he heard the news that John too, had joined his enemies. Henry died of a fever, a broken man, at Chinon Castle near Tours on 6 July 1189.

One of the knights, Richard Brito (or Le Breton) is said to have had a personal reason for murdering the Archbishop, crying out as he struck Becket down: "Take that, for the love of my lord William, the King's brother!" and broke his sword when he delivered the fatal blow. He had been in the employ of William FitzEmpress, Count of Poitou, Henry II's brother: and it was believed by William's friends that the Count died of a broken heart after Thomas Becket refused to allow his marriage. Brito retired to the island of Jersey. Seven hundred years later Lillie Langtry, the "Jersey Lily" and mistress of Edward VII, claimed him as an ancestor.

Eleanor's complete opposite and said to be the love of Henry's life was Jane Clifford, known as "the Fair Rosamund". Daughter of a Marcher baron, Henry met her whilst campaigning in Wales in 1166, when she was twenty-six: and so flaunted her that, after her death in 1176, it was rumoured that Eleanor had poisoned her.

Site of Martyrdom of
St Thomas Becket in 1170,
Canterbury Catherdral

King Henry II by unknown artist (c.1620)
National Portrait Gallery, London

Able, energetic, intelligent, ruthless but possessed of a near manic temper, Henry effectively restrained the powers of his nobles by confiscating their lands and destroying nearly a hundred of their castles. His feud with Thomas Becket however, blocked any progress in Church administration for many years.

His reform of Anglo-Saxon and feudal law created a professional class of lawyers, tax-collectors and civil-servants which rapidly evolved to serve a dynamic royal bureaucracy. Through his skill in waging war, diplomacy and in arranging dynastic marriages, Henry acquired more European territory than any other English king – but he spent barely fourteen years in England during a 35-year reign. Henry's claim to greatness though, was seriously undermined by his tragic relationships with his wife and sons, whose antagonism finally destroyed him.

HENRY II'S GREATEST LEGACY TO ENGLAND

Henry established Anglo-Saxon common law as the law of England. He also introduced circuit courts and trial by jury, to replace the primitive ordeal of trial by combat.

Early in his reign, Henry adapted existing institutions to cope with the aftermath of the war of succession fought between his mother and King Stephen. Most important was the King's Council of Barons, which had replaced the Anglo-Saxon Witan – and especially an inner circle of ministers, who acted as both judges and tax collectors. They sat at the Exchequer and were charged with accounting for revenues raised and paid in by the King's local representative, the 'sheriff' (from shire and *reeve*, a magistrate).

In 1166 Henry laid down the principles and practice of criminal justice in the Assize of Clarendon, which followed the method of enquiry used to compile the Domesday Book. In each shire leading citizens were sworn (*jure*) to report to the sheriff all crimes committed since the last visit of the King's justices, on "eyre" or circuit. A *grand* jury decided if the evidence warranted an indictment; and a *petit* jury of twelve men sat in judgement during a trial. In 1215 the grand jury was recognised by King John in *Magna Carta*. England abandoned grand juries in 1933 but they are still used in the US.

Henry provided the stability that made possible the establishment of secure property rights – which still pertain 850 years later and allow capitalism to thrive. Henry achieved this by establishing writs that could be presented to a Possessory Assize court.

The Possessory writ was an order from the Exchequer directing a sheriff to convene a sworn local jury at the petty assize court, in order to establish the fact of an unlawful dispossession. If confirmed, the sheriff would reinstate the defendant until his case could be heard at the grand assize. These writs gave an immediate remedy, although they were subject to appeal. The fees generated by them produced a rich stream of income for the Exchequer – and extended the King's authority into every corner of the land.

The "Exchequer" itself was a 10 feet by 5 feet cloth laid over a large table, with a lip on the edge of 4 'fingers', on which counters were placed representing various values. The name referred to the resemblance of the cloth to a chess board.

Chess, invented in the Punjab in the 6th century, reached England early in the 11th. Black was considered the lucky colour, so white was allowed the first move. Howard Staunton (1810–74) remains Britain's only world champion (1843–5).

ROBERT GROSSETESTE, BISHOP OF LINCOLN

Robert Grosseteste (1175–1253) was an English theologian and scholar. He was amongst the first to reintroduce Greek learning to Europe by publishing Latin translations of Greek and Arabic works on philosophy and science. A disciple of Aristotle and Augustine of Hippo, Grosseteste pursued rational, divine and natural explanations for creation. Born into a modest Anglo-Norman family in Suffolk, he was educated at Oxford University. From 1215–21 he was Chancellor of Oxford and lecturer in theology to the Franciscan order. He was Bishop of Lincoln from 1235 until his death. He promoted a belief in "cure of souls": which emphasised the hierarchical structure of the Church and reinforced its authority over any other in the land, including the crown.

Cure of souls (*cura animarum*), or "care of souls", is the instruction through sermons and the administration of the sacraments given by a priest to his congregation.

He strongly opposed the practice of granting ecclesiastical livings, intended for the spiritual duty of cure of souls, to lay servants of the crown. Grosseteste died in 1253, regarded as a saintly man – but three attempts to have him canonised, the last in 1307, failed. A greater claim to fame may be that he has been described as "the real founder of the tradition of scientific thought in mediæval Oxford .... and of the modern English intellectual tradition".

NICHOLAS BREAKSPEAR, THE ONLY ENGLISH POPE

Adrian IV (*c.*1100–59) is the only Englishman ever to have occupied the papal throne. He was born Nicholas Breakspear in Abbots Langley in Hertfordshire. He attended the Abbey school in St Albans; but was not allowed to enter the Church until he had completed his education. Frustrated, Nicholas left for Arles in France to become a monk. He was soon promoted Prior; and in 1137 was elected Abbot. Notwithstanding his reforming tendencies, Nicholas's gift for administration so impressed his superiors that he came to the notice of Pope Eugenius III, who appointed him Cardinal Bishop of Albano in 1149. Eugenius sent Nicholas to Scandinavia as papal legate: where, over the next two years, he was so successful that he was called "the Apostle of the North". Eugenius died in 1153 and was succeeded briefly as pope by Anastasias IV. Just before he died in 1154, Anastasias recommended Nicholas as his successor. On 4 December 1154 Nicholas was duly elected pope, becoming Adrian IV.

Adrian may have pleased the King of England: but he outraged Frederick Barbarossa (1123–90) by contending that his title of Holy Roman Emperor was a gift of the pope. The point was tactlessly rammed home by a personal letter from Adrian, delivered by papal legates to Frederick at the Diet of Besançon in October 1157. The legates were lucky to escape with their lives. Frederick avoided excommunication for his defiance only because of Adrian's death at Agnani on 1 September 1159.

Cardinal Reginald Pole (1500–58), the last Roman Catholic Archbishop of Canterbury, is the only other Englishman ever to come close to being elected pope. He lost – by a single vote in 1549.

In 1155 Adrian was visited by John of Salisbury, secretary to the Archbishop of Canterbury. Through John, Adrian granted Henry II the dominion of Ireland, authorised by the issue of the papal bull *Laudabiliter*. The bull made Ireland a feudal possession of the English king, under the nominal suzerainty of the pope.

Henry did not activate *Laudabiliter* immediately; but from 1167 Ireland was overwhelmed by English, Welsh and Norman adventurers responding to a call for help from Dermott MacMurough, King of Leinster – who had been deposed by Rory O'Connor, High King of Ireland and King of Connaught. To prevent the freebooters from establishing a rival kingdom, Henry authorised Richard de Clare's expedition in 1169. He himself invaded Ireland in 1171, using *Laudabiliter* as justification. In 1174 Henry was confirmed as his overlord by O'Connor in the Treaty of Windsor.

AARON OF LINCOLN

Aaron, a Jewish financier, was born in Lincoln around 1125 and died in 1186. He is first mentioned in the pipe-roll of 1166 as a creditor of King Henry II, for sums owing in nine English counties. He conducted his business through a network of agents; building up a great banking association that covered the country. He made a speciality of lending money to build abbeys, cathedrals and monasteries. Among those built were the Abbey of St Albans, Lincoln and Peterborough Cathedrals and no less than nine Cistercian abbeys – all founded between 1140 and 1152.

Aaron not only advanced money on land, but also on wheat, armour and houses. In this way he acquired an interest in properties scattered through the eastern and southern counties of England. When he died in 1186, Henry II seized his property as the escheat of a Jewish usurer: and the English crown became "universal heir" to his estate. The actual cash treasure accumulated by Aaron was sent over to France to assist Henry in his war with Philip II Augustus, but the ship carrying it sank on the voyage from Shoreham to Dieppe. However money owed by some four hundred and thirty barons and knights remained to be claimed by the king.

He left an estate worth about £28 billion today: so large that a separate division of the Exchequer was constituted, called "Aaron's Exchequer". It was still trying to recover outstanding debts in 1201. On Aaron's death however, interest ceased to accrue – the king, as a Christian, could not practise usury. Aaron's house in Lincoln still stands – possibly the oldest private dwelling in England which can be dated with accuracy. Originally the house had no ground floor windows, to make it easier to defend.

Aaron's career illustrates the effective, trusted and self-supporting network mediæval Jewish communities were able to establish throughout the country. Without Aaron and his associates, England would today be immeasurably the poorer. His contribution to the Exchequer also exposes the hypocritical reality: that the state stood to benefit from money-lending more than any individual.

When Richard de Clare invaded Ireland in 1169, it was principally to make enough money from looting to repay his enormous debts to Aaron of Lincoln.

Peter Johns, a British silversmith, invented Argentium in 1996. An alloy of silver and germanium, it is purer and stronger than sterling silver and does not tarnish.

ORIGINS OF THE POUND STERLING, 'STERLING SILVER' AND HALLMARKING

Sterling silver is an alloy of 92.5% pure silver and 7.5% other metals, usually copper. Fine silver (99.9% pure) is generally too soft to make durable decorative pieces.

The Old English *steorling* (coin with a star) is an unlikely origin of the word 'sterling', although small stars occur on some Norman pennies. Around 1300 Walter de Pinchebek stated that Sterling Silver was known first as "Easterling Silver". The term referred to the hard 92.5% grade of silver used for the local currency in the Easterling, five north German towns that banded together in the 12th century as the Hanseatic League, a major trading partner of England. Henry II adopted the alloy as the standard for

In the 8th century King Offa of Mercia decreed that the English 'pound', an old Anglo-Saxon unit of currency, should be coined from a pound weight of silver into 240 pennies (100 pence since decimalisation on 15 February 1971). 'Easterling Silver', later abbreviated to 'Sterling Silver', gave rise to the expression 'pound sterling'. The pound (or £, from the L of *Libra*, the Latin for pound) has been the currency of England for over 1,200 years.

Silver Hallmark

English currency, employing refiners from the Easterling. Coins made before 1158 are called "Tealby Pennies", after a hoard was found at Tealby in Lincolnshire.

A sterling silver object to be sold in the United Kingdom or Ireland must first be tested for purity by an Assay office. The item is stamped with a hallmark, usually using a hammer and punch, and polished.

England and Wales, Scotland and Ireland have very precise hallmarks (the assay took place in a guildhall). Dating in England from a statute enacted by Edward I in 1300, it was an early form of consumer protection.

Hallmarks include a stamp to confirm the purity of the metal, usually a Lion *Passant*, and a symbol to show the city of manufacture. For example, a certain style of crown indicates Sheffield, a castle indicates Edinburgh and a crown above a harp, Dublin.

WALES IN 1093

A POWERFUL WELSH PRINCE, THE LORD RHYS (1132–97)

Rhys ap Gruffydd is usually known as The Lord Rhys. In his lifetime he was called variously: Prince of Deheubarth, Prince of South Wales, Prince of Wales or Prince of the Welsh. On the death of Owain ap Gruffydd, King of Gwynedd, in 1170 Rhys became the principal ruler in Wales.

Although he had paid homage to Henry II of England in 1158, Henry invaded Deheubarth in 1163, sequestered all Rhys's lands and took him prisoner. After payment of a ransom, Rhys was released and a small part of his territory returned. Rhys then allied himself to Owain ap Gruffydd: and together, aided by torrential rains, foiled another invasion by Henry in 1165. Rhys regained most of his lands; but Henry, in a fit of Plantagenet rage, had Rhys's son Marredud, one of his hostages, blinded.

In 1171 Rhys made peace with Henry and was appointed Justiciar of South Wales. He maintained good relations with Henry, even assisting as a loyal ally in his conquest of Ireland, until Henry died in 1189. Sensing weakness, due to King Richard I's absence first on crusade and then in France, Rhys rebelled and seized a number of Marcher castles. In the last years of his life he was troubled by his feuding sons, Maelgwyn and Gruffydd; and in 1194 was defeated in battle by them. Rhys was incarcerated in Nevern Castle, until released by a younger son Hywel, acting without his brothers' authority. In 1196 Rhys began his last campaign against the Plantagenets, defeating an army led by Roger Mortimer. He died suddenly in 1197; and was buried in St David's Cathedral.

In 1163 Henry II stripped Rhys of all Deheubarth except Cantref Mawr. Rhys later regained all but parts of Pembroke (Dyfed) and the Gower peninsula green

William was given the appellation "the Lion" because of his flag or banner, a red lion rampant on a yellow background. This (with the addition of a 'double tressure fleury counter-fleury') became the **Royal Arms of Scotland**, still used today but quartered with those of England and of Ireland. William was first referred to as "the Lion" by the chronicler John of Fordun (died c.1384), who called him the "Lion of Justice".

Anglo-Norman dynastic relationships on both sides of the border in the late 12th century were very close. Of William's daughters, Margaret (1193–1259) married Hubert de Burgh, 1st Earl of Kent; Isabella (1195–1253) married Roger Bigod, 4th Earl of Norfolk; and Marjorie (1200–44) married Gilbert Marshal, 4th Earl of Pembroke. His son, Alexander (1198–1249) married Joan (1210–38), eldest legitimate daughter of King John of England. Ermengarde died on 12 February 1234 and was buried at Balmerino Abbey in Fife.

Arbroath Abbey

The Lord Rhys rebuilt Cardigan Castle in stone c.1170, where he held the first national *eisteddfod* in 1176.

KING WILLIAM I ("THE LION") OF SCOTLAND (REIGNED 1165–1214)

The reign of William I (*Uilleam mac Eanraig* in Gaelic), "the Lion" or *Garbh* ("the Rough"), was the second longest in Scottish history before the Act of Union with England in 1707 – James VI's fifty-seven years, from 1567–1625 (from 1603 he was King of England too), was the longest. He was born c.1143, the second son of Henry, Earl of Northumberland, whose title he inherited in 1152. He was obliged to surrender his earldom to Henry II of England as overlord in 1157, before succeeding his older brother Malcolm IV as King of Scotland on 9 December 1165. In contrast to his deeply religious and frail brother, William was powerfully built, redheaded and headstrong.

William certainly did not earn his sobriquet "Lion" for any military success. In 1173 he joined Henry II's sons in a rebellion against their father, hoping to regain Northumberland from England. A year later, at the Battle of Alnwick, William recklessly charged the English troops, shouting: "Now we shall see which of us are good knights!". He swiftly found out: he was unhorsed and captured by Henry's troops, led by Ranulf de Glanvill, and taken in chains to Newcastle, then Northampton, and finally to Falaise in Normandy. Henry sent an army to Scotland and seized Edinburgh. As a ransom, and to regain his kingdom, William was compelled to acknowledge Henry as his feudal overlord and to pay an exorbitant amount for the cost of the English occupation. Under duress, he agreed to these terms in the Treaty of Falaise. Only then was he allowed to return to Scotland. In 1175 he again swore fealty to Henry at York.

The Treaty remained in force for the next fifteen years. In 1189 Richard "the Lionheart" released William from his homage in return for 10,000 silver marks (£80 million today), to finance the Third Crusade. Under compulsion by King John in the Treaty of Norham in 1209 however, William finally relinquished his claim to Northumberland.

The Treaty of Falaise awarded Henry the right to choose William's bride. He disparaged William by choosing a child, Ermengarde de Beaumont, whose grandmother was Constance FitzRoy, an illegitimate daughter of King Henry I of England. William married her at Woodstock Palace in Oxfordshire on 5 September 1186. Edinburgh Castle was returned as her dowry. It was twelve years before Ermengarde bore him an heir.

William was more successful in dealing with domestic issues. In 1192, despite a quarrel over a Church appointment, he persuaded Pope Celestine III, in a bull titled *Cum Universi*, to rule that the Scottish Church owed obedience, not to Canterbury or York, but only to Rome. He strengthened and extended royal authority by creating an efficient administration and issuing charters to major Scottish burghs. In 1178 William founded Arbroath Abbey. By the time of his death in 1214 Arbroath had become the richest abbey in Scotland. He was succeeded by his red-haired son, Alexander II.

William founded Arbroath Abbey for Tironensian monks from Kelso. The Abbey was consecrated in 1197 with a dedication to St Thomas Becket, whom William had met at the English court. It was William's only personal foundation and he was buried before the high altar. The Abbey is celebrated for its association with the Declaration of Arbroath in 1320. Neglect led to its ruin during the Reformation.

On Christmas Day 1950 the Stone of Destiny was stolen from Westminster Abbey. It was found on the site of Arbroath Abbey's altar on 11 April 1951.

OWNERSHIP OF THE HEBRIDES AND ISLE OF MAN IN THE MIDDLE AGES

Somerled, the "Summer Viking" (*c.*1113–64), was King of the Hebrides (*Ri Innse Gall* in Gaelic) and the first, free from Norse domination, to be called Lord of the Isles (*Dominus Insularum* in Latin). Supposedly descended from Irish kings who had inhabited the Hebrides since the 7th century, Somerled probably owed more to Norse than Gaelic ancestry. His lasting achievement was to wrest the Hebrides and Kintyre, in modern Argyllshire, from the Viking kings of Man.

In 1140 Somerled married as his second wife Ragnhild, daughter of the King of Man, Olaf "the Red". They had three sons: Dugald, Ranald (or Reginald) and Angus. After Somerled's death, his Kingdom of the Isles was divided among them. Dugald founded Clan MacDougall and Ranald, the MacDonald Lords of the Isles and Clan MacRory.

Somerled's relationships with the kings of Scotland were fickle. He supported David I when he invaded England in 1138; but backed an abortive rebellion in 1153 against Malcolm IV. In 1164 Somerled again rebelled against Malcolm. Landing 15,000 men from 164 galleys at Greenock, north-west of Glasgow, in an attempt to capture Renfrew, he was assassinated by a treacherous kinsman in the pay of Malcolm.

The Isle of Man was bought from Norway by Scotland in 1266 and ceded to England in 1346. Given by Henry IV in 1405 to Sir John Stanley (a descendant became Earl of Derby in 1485), the British Crown (not Britain) took back control in 1765. The Inner Hebrides were forfeited by Clan Macdonald to the Scottish crown in 1493. The Outer Isles remained lawless until 1540, when King James V led a fleet to subdue them.

KING RICHARD I OF ENGLAND, "COEUR DE LION" (REIGNED 1189–99)

Richard I was born on 8 September 1157 at Beaumont Palace in Oxford, the third son born to Henry II and Eleanor of Aquitaine. The Angevins did titles rather well: he became variously Duke of Aquitaine in 1168, Duke of Poitiers in 1172 and King of England, Duke of Normandy and Duke of Anjou in 1189. He inherited Aquitaine from his mother, who always regarded him as her favourite son and in whose arms he died. Richard had three sisters and four brothers, the first of which died young. Of the remainder, in 1170 the fifteen year-old Henry (the "Young

> Somerled's ships were fitted with rudders, rather than a steering oar: giving him an important tactical advantage over less manoeuvrable enemies.

> In 2005 a study by Bryan Sykes, Professor of Human Genetics at Oxford, concluded that Somerled has possibly 500,000 descendants living today – making him, as far as is known, the world's second most shared ancestor after Genghis Khan.

Bronze equestrian statue of Richard I by Carlo Marochetti (Palace of Westminster)

King") was named heir to the throne of England and crowned during his father's lifetime – an odd practice adopted from the French Capetian dynasty.

Whilst Richard would be given his mother's huge duchy of Aquitaine and Geoffrey was to inherit Brittany from his father, John, the youngest, was not in line to inherit any territory at all – which earned him the humiliating nickname "Lackland". From the age of twelve Richard owed homage to the French king for his possessions in France.

In 1183 Henry the Young King died, leaving Richard heir to the English throne. Richard reacted violently when Henry II made it clear that he now expected him to surrender Aquitaine to John. He was most reluctant to hand over his mother's inheritance to a younger brother. Moreover, as Henry believed that any devolution of power to his sons might be used against him, he had continued to withhold any real authority from them. On an earlier occasion, in 1173 Richard, supported by his mother and his brothers, had rebelled unsuccessfully. Henry had responded then by imprisoning Eleanor: and she was not released until his death in July 1189. This occurred soon after Richard's second, and this time successful, rebellion – in which he received valuable assistance from the astute French king, Philip II Augustus. Having driven his father to his grave, in September 1189 Richard was crowned King of England in Westminster Abbey.

At the moment of his coronation, news came from the Holy Land that a Kurdish warrior, Saladin had destroyed the Crusader army at Hattin and taken Jerusalem. Richard immediately took the Cross and began raising money to fund a third Crusade.

Salâh ad-Din (meaning "Righteousness of the Faith") Yusuf ibn Ayyub, better known in Europe as Saladin (c.1137–93), was born in Tikrit in Mesopotamia (modern Iraq) – the birthplace 800 years later of Saddam Hussein. Having inclined towards religious scholarship, Saladin began his military career c.1160 under the tutelage of his uncle Asad al-Din Shirkuh, a general of the Sunni dynasty which ruled Syria and Mesopotamia. Through success on the battlefield and clever timing, he was appointed vizier (prime minister) of Fatimid Egypt in March 1169. By 1174 he had schemed and fought his way to supplant the Fatimids, the only Shi'a caliphate in the history of Islam, with a Sunni dynasty of his own. As the first Ayyubid Sultan (Saladin was the son of Ayyub), he united modern Egypt, Syria, Iraq, Israel, Yemen and the Red Sea coast of Saudi Arabia (the Hejaz). His dynasty ruled Egypt until 1517, though in name only after 1250.

In 1185 the Crusader states broke their truce with their Moslem neighbours. Saladin had long awaited such an opportunity and declared a *Jihad* (Holy War). On 4 July 1187 he annihilated the Crusader army in the Battle of the Horns of Hattin and, on 2 October took Jerusalem. Whilst the Crusader conquests of the Holy Land had been marked by brutality, Saladin showed only courtesy to his adversaries.

For Moslems, the effect of Saladin's unforeseen victory at Hattin was astounding. It had destroyed almost the entire Christian military presence in *Outremer*, the Crusader kingdoms in the Holy Land, sending a shock-wave throughout Christendom. By the end of 1187 only the towns of Antioch, Tyre and the county of Tripoli, occupying just a thin, nine-mile coastal strip, remained. Nearly one hundred years of Christian presence in the Holy Land had been virtually extinguished.

The Fatimids (909–1171) were Ismaili Shi'as. Expanding rapidly throughout north Africa and Sicily in the 9th century the Fatimids originally ruled from Tunisia; but later conquered Egypt and made Cairo their capital. They maintained their power through an elaborate network of spies and assassins.

The Assassins (or Nizariyyah) were an Ismaili sect which flourished in Persia and Syria from the 11th to the 13th centuries. They took their name from hashish (*hashashim*), used for hallucinations of heavenly ecstasy before facing a martyr's death. The 49th Imam of the Nizari Ismailis is His Highness Prince Karim Aga Khan (born 1936): who, rather than murder, is devoted to philanthropy and horse racing.

Some time before the Battle of Hattin, Guy de Lusignan, King of Jerusalem had sent Archbishop Josius of Tyre to Europe: to alert Christendom to the threat from Islam posed by Saladin. Christian kings responded immediately. Archbishop Josius persuaded the French King Philip II Augustus and King Richard I to take up the cross together, despite being at loggerheads over the interests of their adjacent kingdoms. On 4 July 1190, three years to the day after the Battle of Hattin, Richard and Philip met at Vézelay, north-west of Dijon, formally to start the Third Crusade.

Having agreed to rendezvous with Richard at Messina in Sicily. Philip embarked first and arrived off Acre on 20 April 1191. Richard's fleet, scattered by storms, put into Cyprus, then ruled by the Greek-Byzantine Prince Isaac Comnenus. Shortly before, Richard's sister Joan and his fiancée Berengaria had been shipwrecked and held captive by Prince Isaac. Foolishly, Isaac attacked Richard's forces but was trounced and captured; and his island was occupied by Richard's army.

Before leaving Cyprus, Richard married Berengaria on 12 May in Limasssol Cathedral. She was the daughter of King Sancho VI of Navarrre, a state which Richard was anxious to secure as an ally, lying on the southern border of Aquitaine. Berengaria accompanied Richard to the Levant, but thereafter saw very little of him because he spent most of his life fighting. She was inconsolable when he died and never remarried. There is no evidence that Richard was homosexual, whereas there are many references to his taking full advantage of a normal, lively Angevin libido.

Richard's capture of Cyprus was the most enduring outcome of the Third Crusade. The island became an invaluable supply base and headquarters to the Knights Templar.

Richard arrived off Acre on 8 June 1191, lending an immediate impetus to the flagging Crusader siege. By July Philip's massive siege engines, Richard's outstanding leadership, and a failure by Saladin to relieve the city, forced Acre to surrender – in spite of an order from Saladin to fight to the death. Surrender terms spared the lives of the Moslem garrison, in exchange for the return of the true cross relic that had been lost at Hattin and a payment of 200,000 dinars. The failure by Saladin to make the first instalment caused Richard to fly into a rage and behead his prisoners – in full view of Saladin's lines. In response Saladin murdered his Christian hostages. Meanwhile, Richard squabbled with Duke Leopold V of Austria over the kingship of Jerusalem – and Philip made a feeble excuse of ill-health to return home.

Richard, like his father, was energetic and courageous to the point of recklessness. He struggled to contain a vile temper and often literally foamed at the mouth. He was capable of quite ferocious cruelty. While Richard would honour any Moslem leader who fell into his hands, the rank and file could expect no quarter. Richard was more sophisticated than his brothers, well educated and an accomplished amateur minstrel. He was more religious than his brothers too, hearing mass every day. An inspirational military leader and a naturally gifted politician, he was capable of generating fierce loyalty. Some historians wrongly suggest that Richard was homosexual and that he had an affair with his page Blondel.

Jean de Nesle (1155–1202), nicknamed Blondel for his golden locks, was a French troubadour. He is known today for the myth of his discovery of Richard I when incarcerated by the Duke of Austria. His wanderings through central Europe, singing outside castles until Richard recognised his melodies and sang back, was the theme of a mediæval French poem, *Les Recits d'un menestrel de Reims.*

The Templars were a religious order of knighthood founded in 1119, after the victorious First Crusade. The first members were nine French knights who pledged themselves to protect Christians on pilgrimage to Jerusalem. Taking vows of poverty, chastity and obedience, the order appealed greatly to the knightly families of Europe. In 1127 Bernard of Clairvaux wrote their rule-book.

By 1307 the Templars had grown in number to a membership of 20,000. While forbidden individually to acquire assets the order itself, exempt from all taxation, became prodigiously rich from gifts and legacies. By the early 14th century the Templars had assembled a vast international estate including their own castles, army and fleet. They were also the leading financial institution in Europe, with the influence almost of an independent state.

On Friday 13 October 1307, with an eye to the Templars' assets and to whom he owed enormous sums, the French King Philip IV, endorsed by a cowed Pope Clement V, arrested scores of Templars on trumped up charges of sodomy and heresy. Their last leader, Jacques de Molay was burned at the stake in March 1314.

The date of the arrests is a source of the superstition attached to Friday the 13th.

Richard, now in sole command, met Saladin at Arsuf on 7 September 1191: the only pitched battle of the crusade. Richard inflicted heavy losses on Saladin, at little cost to himself. Swiftly he captured Jaffa, retook Askalon and marched on Jerusalem.

Twice repulsed at the walls of the city, Richard realised that the Crusaders could not hope to occupy Jerusalem for any length of time without control of the whole Levant: and that the key to victory lay in destroying Saladin's power base, the bread-basket of Egypt. He failed however, to convince his allies. At the same time, Richard received disturbing reports from France, that Philip was preying on English territory.

It is clear that Saladin and Richard held each other in high mutual esteem. Anxious to return to France, to meet the threat from Philip, Richard agreed to a peace treaty on 2 September 1192. The terms guaranteed the Crusaders occupation of a coastal strip between Tyre and Jaffa.

On 9 October Richard left *Outremer*. Although Jerusalem remained in Moslem hands, he had avenged Hattin and gained right of access to Jerusalem for Christian pilgrims.

As Philip was now the enemy and France a hostile nation, Richard planned his journey home through the Adriatic. He sailed with four attendants, disguised as Knights Templar: but his ship was wrecked at Aquila, near Venice. Richard and his party had no choice but to attempt the hazardous land route through central Europe. Their first destination was Saxony, where Richard's brother-in-law Henry ("the Lion") was Duke. Just before Christmas 1192 Richard was identified and arrested, falling into the hands of Duke Leopold V of Austria – whom he had last seen on the worst of terms outside Jerusalem. Leopold accused Richard of conniving at the murder of his cousin Conrad of Montferrat, who had just been stabbed to death by the Assassins.

Richard and his party had been travelling disguised as pilgrims. It is said that they were recognised when Richard insisted on eating roast chicken, an aristocratic delicacy. Leopold took his revenge on Richard by imprisoning him in Durnstein Castle on the Danube. Threatened by the pope with excommunication for detaining a crusader, Leopold passed him on to the Holy Roman Emperor Henry VI . Refusing an offer of 80,000 marks to hand him over to Philip II Augustus and his brother John, Henry offered Richard to his mother Eleanor of Aquitaine for a ransom of 150,000 marks (£1.2 billion today) – amounting to thirty tons of silver and nearly three times the annual tax revenues of England. The money was raised and on 4 February 1194 Richard was released. Philip sent a message to John: "Look to yourself; the devil is loose".

On 17 April 1194 Richard was crowned a second time, to assert his kingship after his long absence. It was only two months however, before he set sail to Normandy – never to return. The last five years of his life were spent fighting Philip II Augustus. He left England in the capable hands of Hubert Walter, his great Archbishop of Canterbury.

Krac des Chevaliers, the greatest Crusader castle, is 40 miles west of Homs in Syria

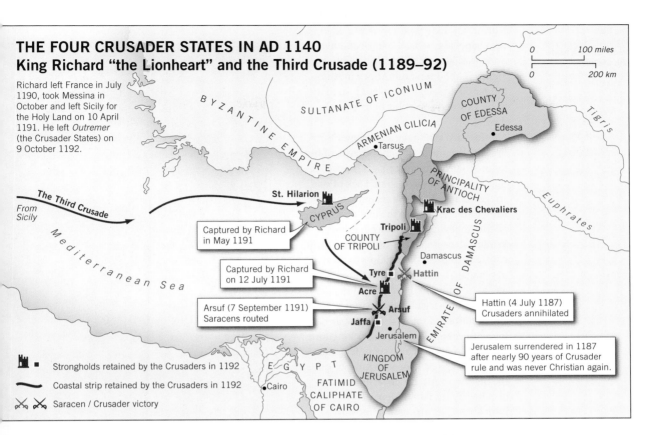

THE FOUR CRUSADER STATES IN AD 1140
King Richard "the Lionheart" and the Third Crusade (1189–92)

Richard left France in July 1190, took Messina in October and left Sicily for the Holy Land on 10 April 1191. He left *Outremer* (the Crusader States) on 9 October 1192.

The Third Crusade

From Sicily

Mediterranean Sea

BYZANTINE EMPIRE

SULTANATE OF ICONIUM

ARMENIAN CILICIA
Tarsus

COUNTY OF EDESSA
Edessa

PRINCIPALITY OF ANTIOCH

Tigris

Euphrates

St. Hilarion
CYPRUS

Krac des Chevaliers

Captured by Richard in May 1191

Tripoli
COUNTY OF TRIPOLI

Damascus

EMIRATE OF DAMASCUS

Captured by Richard on 12 July 1191

Tyre — Hattin
Acre

Arsuf (7 September 1191) Saracens routed

Arsuf
Jaffa

Jerusalem

Hattin (4 July 1187) Crusaders annihilated

Jerusalem surrendered in 1187 after nearly 90 years of Crusader rule and was never Christian again.

KINGDOM OF JERUSALEM

E G Y P T
Cairo
FATIMID CALIPHATE OF CAIRO

Strongholds retained by the Crusaders in 1192

Coastal strip retained by the Crusaders in 1192

Saracen / Crusader victory

Richard strengthened the defences of his French dominions and turned the tables on Philip. When Philip boasted to Richard, during the siege of Richard's fortress Château Gaillard, "If these walls were iron, yet I would take it": and Richard replied, "If these walls were butter, yet I would hold them", it was no exaggeration. Richard was incomparably the better soldier and invariably bested Philip.

In March 1199 Richard was in the Limousin, besieging Château Châlus-Chabrol, the seat of Count Aymar V of Limoges. The castle was poorly defended and Richard conducted the investment too casually. He was inspecting his lines, unprotected by chain-mail, when a bolt from a crossbow fired from the castle ramparts hit him high in the shoulder, near his neck. Crude surgery mangled his arm and the wound became gangrenous. Richard prepared for death, bequeathing his kingdom to John and his jewels to his nephew Otto of Poitou (later Emperor Otto IV of Germany).

As a last act of mercy Richard forgave the crossbow-man who had fired the fatal bolt – and gave him 100 shillings, saying: "Live on and by my bounty behold the light of day". In cruel vengeance, the boy was arrested after Richard's death by Mercadier, captain of his mercenary guard, who had him flayed alive and then hanged.

Richard's mother was by his bedside when he died on 6 April 1199. His brain was buried in Charroux Abbey in Poitou, his heart was interred in Rouen Cathedral in

Map of the Crusader States in "Outremer" (1189–92)

At Gisors in Picardy in 1198, it is said that Richard coined the phrase *Dieu et mon droit* ("God and my right"), as a password of the day. It became his motto; and was first blazoned on the Royal coat of arms in the 15th century by King Henry VI.

Normandy, his entrails were placed in the chapel at Châlus-Chabrol and his body was laid to rest beside his father Henry II at Fontevrault Abbey in Anjou. England had seen too little of him in life to be awarded any of his body parts in death.

Richard's military achievements in France all came to nought because of his failure to produce an heir – it is possible that Berengaria was barren. Lack of one triggered a chain of events that, under King John, resulted in the loss of almost all the Angevin possessions in France. While succeeding kings of England would continue to press their claims to these, never again would they own the territories inherited by Richard I.

Richard's legacy was Cyprus, Christendom's foothold in the Near East for a hundred years. He left his kingdom of England, in which he spent less than six months, to develop and prosper under the highly competent government installed by his father Henry II – although John abused its processes almost to breaking point. Finally Richard, as *Coeur de Lion*, has left an indelible imprint on romantic legend extending to the present day. Let the greatest chronicler of the Crusades, Sir Steven Runciman have the last word on him: "He was a bad son, a bad husband and a bad king, but a gallant and splendid soldier".

The right Valiant Prince RICHARD surnamed Cœur-de-lion King of England and Hierusalem, Duke of Normandy and Aquitane, & of Poiters and Aniou, Lo: of Ireland. &c. He died at the age of yeares An. 1199. after he had raigned 9 yeares, 9 months, and 22 dayes. and lieth buried at Fonteverard in Normandy.

1st State of the plate

KING JOHN OF ENGLAND (REIGNED 1199–1216)

John, known as "Lackland" and in France as *Jean Sans Terre,* was King of England from 1199–1216. Described as a "priapic satyr", he is remembered for two events: the loss of Normandy, Aquitaine and Gascony to King Philip II Augustus of France; and *Magna Carta* , the provisions of which he was forced to seal in 1215.

John, the youngest son of Henry II and Eleanor of Aquitaine, was born at Beaumont Palace in Oxford on Christmas Eve 1167. Though Henry's favourite, he was the youngest of four surviving sons. In 1173 Henry tried to marry John, a "Lackland" who had no expectations, to Alicia, heiress of Humbert III of Savoy who had no son. This ideal solution however, had to be abandoned when John's brothers took exception to the size of the territories Henry proposed to give John and rebelled – and more to the point, because Alicia died.

In 1176 Henry granted John the succession to the earldom of Gloucester instead. In 1177 he also conferred on him the lordship of Ireland, where he lived for eight months in 1185 – acquiring an evil reputation. Nevertheless John remained the apple of Henry's eye, provoking his brother Richard once again to rebel against their father in 1189. Perhaps anticipating Henry's impending death, John joined Richard's campaign.

When Richard succeeded Henry II on 6 July 1189, he created John Count of Mortain, confirmed him as Lord of Ireland, granted him English estates worth £6,000 a year (£70 million today) and arranged his marriage to Isabel, heiress of the Earl of Gloucester. Before embarking on the Third Crusade in March 1190, in exchange for his generosity, Richard extracted a promise from John not to visit England while he was away.

In 1189 Isabel of Gloucester was married to John at Marlborough Castle. He assumed her title in his own right. Shortly after his accession to the throne in 1199, John had the childless marriage annulled by Pope Boniface VIII, on the grounds of consanguinity: as descendants of Henry I, they were second cousins. John offered Isabel no respect as a Queen or as his wife – preoccupying himself with fathering at least twelve bastards.

John's ambitions received a jolt in 1191. Richard recognised their three year-old nephew Arthur, Duke of Brittany (1187–1203), the posthumous son of their brother Geoffrey who had been killed jousting in a tournament in 1186, as his heir to the crown of England. When Richard died, John was not immediately accepted as king – Arthur had a better claim and enjoyed the support of King Philip II Augustus of France.

John reacted to Arthur's preferment by breaking his oath and returning to England – where he tried to undermine the authority of Richard's designated justiciars. Not content with disobedience and disloyalty, when he heard in 1193 that Richard had been imprisoned by Duke Leopold of Austria, John turned to treachery. He made common cause with King Philip II Augustus of France, to invade England and take the throne for himself. In January 1194 Richard returned, to banish John and confiscate his lands. Five months later however, miraculously John gulled Richard into believing his good faith: and received back some of his forfeited estates, including Mortain in Normandy – and Ireland.

On 6 April 1199 Richard died, having bequeathed his kingdom to his brother. John was crowned in Westminster Abbey on 27 May. A week earlier, on 20 May John and Philip II had signed the Treaty of Le Goulet. It was unwise of John to negotiate with Philip, who was twice as wily and as devious as himself – and a brilliant strategist too. John's attempts to outsmart him ended with the destruction of the Angevin Empire.

Scarcely had the ink dried on the parchment of Le Goulet before John abused the feudal obligations the treaty had imposed on him, in an act of mindless lust and staggering stupidity that demonstrated his unfitness to rule. While mediating in a feud between the leading Poitou families of Lusignan and Angoulême in western France, he became strongly attracted to Isabella of Angoulême – and kidnapped her. Aged only twelve, spirited and beautiful, Isabella was married to John at Bordeaux on 24 August 1200, a year after the annulment of his first marriage to Isabel of Gloucester.

John's lechery was legendary. Roger of Wendover describes John's lust for Margaret, the wife of Eustace de Vesci. Eustace substituted a prostitute before the king visited Margaret in the night. The next morning John congratulated Vesci on how good his wife was in bed. Insanely, Vesci revealed the truth to John – and fled.

The conflict of interest between Arthur and John was to have fatal consequences. During the Anglo-French war of 1203–5, Arthur was captured by John's forces. Hubert de Burgh, the officer commanding the Rouen fortress, claimed to have delivered Arthur at Easter 1203 to agents of the King sent to castrate him: and that the boy had died of shock. de Burgh later retracted his statement, but Arthur was never seen again. It was assumed that he had been murdered on John's orders.

Before her abduction however, Isabella had been betrothed to Hugh "le Brun" de Lusignan, son of the Count of La Marche. In fury, the patrician Lusignan turned to John's new overlord, King Philip II Augustus, for redress. Philip ordered John to appear before his court, as he was bound to under the terms of his vassalage sworn at Le Goulet. John played into Philip's hands by ignoring his summons.

John now had little choice but to retire to England: where he prosecuted an unforgiving tax regime on his unfortunate subjects. He also conducted a vicious pogrom against the Jews, seizing their assets without compensation.

Richard's great Justiciar, Archbishop Hubert Walter, had reluctantly supported John's bid for the crown. His death, on 13 July 1205, set John on a collision course with Pope Innocent III. Innocent wished John to appoint Stephen Langton (*c.*1156–1228) as Archbishop, a prelate known to be as incorruptible and forthright as Walter. These were not characteristics that commended him to John, who refused. Only after Innocent had excommunicated him and then threatened a crusade against England, led by the French King Philip II of all people, did John submit.

In 1213 John joined with Emperor Otto V and the Count of Flanders in a war on France. John's campaign culminated in ruinous defeat at the Battle of Bouvines on 27 July 1214, which forced him to accept humiliating terms from Philip – the final straw for his barons, many of whom had already deserted him after his excommunication. On 15 June 1215 John reluctantly met their delegation at Runnymede, to seal *Magna Carta*.

True to form, John immediately reneged on his promise: claiming that he could not be bound by *Magna Carta*, as he had signed it only under duress – a view supported by his new friend, the Pope. John's obduracy led to the First Barons' War (1215–17) and an invitation to Philip II's son Prince Louis of France, to assume the crown of England.

John retreated from the subsequent French invasion by seeking refuge in the northeast of England. Fleeing East Anglia, already in rebel hands, John's escort skirted the marshy area of the Wash. His baggage train, with the crown jewels, crossed the sands instead: and, miscalculating the tides, was lost. John was distraught and succumbed to dysentery – rather than the popular,

---

Magna Carta (the "Great Charter"), also called *Magna Carta Liberatum* was a document guaranteeing English political and civil liberties. It was signed by King John in a meadow by the Thames on 15 June 1215. His barons, infuriated by John's inequitable taxation and aware of his fading authority, were encouraged by the Archbishop of Canterbury Stephen Langton to insist on a solemn declaration of their rights: including a guarantee of an independent Church; restraint in the conduct of royal agents; and reform of the law, explicitly to offer some protection to the common people. Importantly, the Charter introduced the writ of *habeas corpus* – allowing appeal against unlawful imprisonment.

Magna Carta was represented in refined format in 1216, 1217, 1225 and 1297 – the version which remains on the statute books of England and Wales. In December 2007 US businessman David Rubenstein bought the only copy of *Magna Carta* in private hands, for more than £10 million. Dated 1297 and described as "the most important document in the world", the copy that was sold at Sotheby's in New York is one of only seventeen in existence.

The fifth amendment of the US Constitution, signed on 4 July 1776 only by John Hancock (the other 55 delegates signed on 2 August), states that: "No person shall …. be deprived of life, liberty, or property, without due process of law". The sixth states that " …. the accused shall enjoy the right to a speedy and public trial, by an impartial jury".

Magna Carta declares that: "No freeman shall be taken, imprisoned …. or in any other way destroyed …. except by the lawful judgment of his peers, or by the law of the land. To no one will we sell, to none will we deny or delay, right or justice".

probably fictitious, accounts circulated soon after his death: that he had been killed by poisoned ale, poisoned plums or a "surfeit of peaches". He died on 18 October 1216 at Newark Castle in Nottinghamshire. He was buried in Worcester Cathedral, where his inscrutable effigy can still be seen.

Queen Isabella was at Gloucester when news of John's death reached her. She returned to France and married the still unwed Hugh "le Brun" de Lusignan. She bore him five sons and four daughters – having already born John two sons and a daughter. Isabella died in 1246 and was buried at Fontevrault.

John's nine year-old eldest son succeeded him as King Henry III. Prince Louis persisted in his claim to the English throne: but the barons switched their allegiance to their new king. With his army beaten at Lincoln and his navy, commanded by Eustace the Monk, defeated off the coast of Kent, Prince Louis was forced to sue for peace. The principal provisions of the treaty were an amnesty for English rebels, territories to be returned to the *status quo ante*, the Channel Islands to be returned to the English crown (not to England) – and an undertaking by Louis never to attack England again.

John was treacherous, lecherous and cruel, possessing an explosive Angevin temper. Like his father and brothers, he had a restless energy which he expended on hunting, travelling and fornicating ceaselessly around his realm. He almost certainly connived at Arthur of Brittany's murder; and he allowed Matilda de Braose and her son to rot and die unattended in a dungeon in 1210, after he fell out with her husband.

John was not without some merit. He could read and maintained a large library of over 300 books. He endowed the churches of Reading, Coventry and Worcester. He took an intelligent interest in law reform and especially, taxation. During his reign the administration of the Exchequer was overhauled.

He drove an ambitious programme of naval construction and fortified Portsmouth as the headquarters and dockyard of his navy. By the end of 1204 it comprised 45 large galleys, increased by an average of four new ships every year and supervised by an Admiralty of four admirals. Major improvements in ship design were commissioned, including the addition of sails and removable forecastles. The cliché that John was the founder of the Royal Navy is based on the naval Pipe Rolls, annual records of the Exchequer which began in his reign.

Winston Churchill summarised the legacy of John's reign: "When the long tally is added, it will be seen that the British nation and the English-speaking world owe far more to the vices of John than to the labours of virtuous sovereigns". In a recent scholarly article, John was compared to US President Richard Nixon: clever and good at administrative detail; but, as a liar himself, suspicious of others; unscrupulous and deeply distrusted. Many however, would consider this judgement unfair to Nixon.

As a Christian name, "John" lost favour within the royal families of England. No future king was ever again given the name. One royal prince called John though, was the youngest son of King George V and Queen Mary. Born in 1905, the Prince had epilepsy and was largely hidden from the public eye. He had a happy life and was much loved by his parents but died in 1919, aged thirteen.

When the bodies were recovered, it was said that the wretched Matilda had gnawed the flesh off her, presumably dead, son's cheeks in a desperate bid to survive.

WILLIAM THE MARSHAL, "THE GREATEST KNIGHT THAT EVER LIVED"

William Marshal *(Guillaume le Maréchal)*, 1st Earl of Pembroke (1146–1219) was described as "the greatest knight that ever lived" by Stephen Langton, Archbishop of Canterbury. Before him, the hereditary title of "Lord Marshal" designated a sort of head of household security for

Tomb effigy of William the Marshal, in the Temple Church, London

the King of England; by the time he died, when people in Europe (not just England) said "the Marshal", they meant William.

His father, John Marshal switched sides from King Stephen to Empress Matilda when William was about six years old. Stephen took the boy as a hostage, to ensure that John kept his word that he would surrender Newbury Castle. John broke his word – and Stephen ordered John to surrender, or watch him hang William. John replied that he could always make another son, and a better one too. Stephen could not bring himself to hang the boy.

As a younger son of a minor noble without much to leave him, William learned to make his own way: he was knighted in 1167 and made a good living out of winning tournaments – which at that time were bloody, hand-to-hand combat, not the jousting contests that would come later. He fought in 500 such mock battles in his life and never lost once. As a young knight he served in the household of his uncle Patrick, 1st Earl of Salisbury. In 1168 his uncle was killed in an ambush. William was injured and captured in the same affray, but was ransomed by Eleanor of Aquitaine.

In 1170 William was appointed as the fifteen year-old Henry the Young King's tutor in chivalry. He stood by him in his rebellion against his father in 1173 and knighted the boy. However in 1182 William was accused of undue familiarity with Marguerite of France, the Young King's wife, and exiled from court. He went to the court of King Henry II that Christmas to ask for trial by combat in order to prove his innocence, but was refused. A few months later the Young King died. On his deathbed he asked William to fulfil his vow to go on Crusade. William honoured his promise, crusading in the Holy Land from 1183–86: where he swore that he would be buried as a Knight Templar. On his return in 1186, William rejoined the court of King Henry II.

William served five kings of England with unswerving fidelity for forty-nine years: Henry II, Henry the Young King, Richard I, John and for three years, Henry III. William once came face to face with Richard in battle (in rebellion against his father) and could have killed him. To make that point clear, he killed Richard's horse instead. He supported King John when he became king in 1199, but they fell out when William paid homage to King Philip II Augustus of France for his lands in Normandy. He left for Leinster in 1207 and stayed in Ireland until 1212, when he was summoned to fight in the Welsh wars. He witnessed the sealing of *Magna Carta* in 1215.

For his service to them, in 1189 the Plantagenets gave him as his bride (he was forty three and she seventeen) the second-richest heiress in England, Isabel de Clare, who had inherited vast estates in England, Wales and Ireland. Her father, "Strongbow" had been Earl of Pembroke: and his title was granted to William. Their five sons and five daughters all survived into adulthood. The eldest son, another William married Eleanor, the nine year-old sister of Henry III in April 1224 – on his death in 1231, Eleanor married Simon de Montfort, 6th Earl of Leicester.

It was William whom King John trusted on his deathbed to ensure his nine year-old son Henry would inherit the throne. It was William, on 15 June 1215 at Runnymede, who negotiated with the barons who forced John to seal *Magna Carta;* and it was William who treated with the Kings of France, Louis VII and Philip II Augustus. While they would not take the English king's word, they would and did, take William's.

On 11 November 1216 William was named by the King's Council, the leading barons who had remained loyal to John in the First Barons' War, to serve as both Guardian of King Henry III and Regent of England. William's first act after being appointed regent was to reissue *Magna Carta*. He sealed the document, as one of the witnessing barons.

William's sons died without issue. The title of "Marshal" went to the husband of the oldest daughter: Hugh Bigod, 3rd Earl of Norfolk. It passed to the Mowbray Dukes of Norfolk; and then to the Howard Dukes of Norfolk, who still hold the ceremonial rank of "Earl Marshal" today – nearly 800 years later.

William's health began to fail him in February 1219: and in March, he realised that he was dying. He summoned his eldest son and his household knights to his estate at Caversham, near Reading – where he called a meeting of the barons, the boy-King Henry III, the papal legate, Hubert de Burgh (the royal justiciar), and Peter des Roches, Bishop of Winchester (King Henry's guardian). William rejected the Bishop's claim to the regency and entrusted it to the care of the papal legate – it was clear that he did not trust the Bishop or any of the other magnates. He was invested as a Knight Templar before he died, on 14 May 1219, and was buried as he had wished: in the Temple Church in London. William Marshall had led a charmed but exemplary life of outstanding valour, loyalty and achievement – as was Sir Galahad in the Arthurian legend, truly a "perfect knight".

MEDIÆVAL ETIQUETTE AT THE TIME OF MAGNA CARTA

Book of the Civilised Man by Daniel of Beccles is believed to be the first English courtesy book or book of manners. It dates from around 1215, the year of *Magna Carta*.

Civilised Man is a 3,000-line poem in Latin (*Urbanus Magnus Danielis Becclesiensis*) that gives genteel advice on a wide range of situations that a mediæval bourgeois might meet in daily life. Only the second of these examples would be wholly out of place today:

"If you wish to belch, remember to look up to the ceiling"
"Do not attack your enemy while he is squatting to defecate"
"If there is something you do not want people to know, do not tell it to your wife"
"Say thank you to your host"
"Don't mount your horse in the hall"
"If visitors have already eaten, give them drink anyway"
"Loosen your reins when riding over a bridge"
"Receive gifts from great men with gratitude"
"If you are a judge, be just"
"Eating at the table of the rich, speak little"

Daniel may have been a member of Henry II's court. There is a reference to a Daniel of Beccles in the "Seventh Regnal Year of King John" (*c.*1206), who was given the living of Endgate in Beccles in Suffolk by the Abbot of Bury St Edmunds.

There are three important themes in the poem: social distinction, self-control and sexual morality. The first emphasises class differences: and how to behave among those of higher or lower status than oneself – lords and servants.

The second theme concerns itself with self-control, when speaking and eating: and how to disguise bodily emissions. He suggests it is better to keep your thoughts to yourself: "be careful to whom, what, why and when you speak".

He recommends small bites, not to overeat, not to play with your food and not to use fingers to clean bowls. Bodily emissions are discussed with disarming candour: "if you clean out your nose in your hand, do not show people the results".

The third hilarious theme concerns sexual morality. *Civilised Man* was clearly written for men. It offers advice on prostitutes: "If you are overcome with erotic desire when you are young and your penis drives you to go to a prostitute, do not go to a common whore: empty your testicles quickly and depart quickly". He offers advice on how to pick a wife, suggesting an

Daniel states reassuringly, that while guests and servants should not urinate in the dining hall, the host may.

appraisal of her property value and personal traits. Daniel displays an age-old prejudice against women: characterising them as lustful and untrustworthy. The poem describes a woman lying in bed with her husband, with her thoughts on her secret lover: "the lascivious woman throws herself around the neck of her lover, her fingers give him those secret touches that she denies to her husband in bed; one wicked act with her lover pleases the lascivious adulteress more than a hundred with her husband; women's minds always burn for the forbidden". He says she is always ready to fornicate, "with a cook or a half-wit, a peasant or a ploughman, or a chaplain .... what she longs for is a thick, leaping, robust piece of equipment, long, smooth and stiff .... such are the things that charm and delight women". Daniel suffered from a near pathological view of the promiscuity of women; but despite this he says, "whatever your wife does, do not damage your marriage".

He goes on to say: "If you are jealous, do not whisper a word about it .... when you are jealous, learn to look up at the ceiling". The message is clear and repeated throughout the poem: exercise self-control and avoid embarrassment at all costs – though he must have suffered from a severe crick in the neck.

Daniel's advice comes to a climax in what is perhaps the most difficult situation of all: when the wife of one's lord makes a sexual proposition. It represents a combination of all three problems: class relationships, control of bodily emissions and sexual morality. Daniel's solution? Pretend to be ill.

LLWELYN THE GREAT (REIGNED 1194–1240)

Llwelyn ap Iorwerth, known as *Llwelyn Fawr* or Llwelyn the Great (*c.*1172–1240), was one of only two Welsh princes honoured by the word "Great" – the other being his ancestor Rhodri (*c.*820–878). The greatest mediæval native ruler, independent and cultured, he was the grandson of Owain ap Gruffydd, King of Gwynedd. Possibly born in Dolwyddelan Castle in Merioneth,

Cerflun Llwelyn Fawr yn nhref Conwy (statue of Llwelyn the Great at Conwy)

he was exiled from Gwynedd as a young man. He returned in 1194, to depose his uncle Dafydd ap Owain as Prince of North Wales, most of which he controlled by 1202.

In 1205 he married Joan, an illegitimate daughter of King John: but this did not prevent John invading north Wales in 1211, when he considered Llwelyn had become too powerful. Llwelyn outmanoeuvred John and recovered most of his lost territory, by shrewdly allying himself to those barons who would force John to sign *Magna Carta* a few years later. In 1218 Llwelyn clashed with William Marshal, Earl of Pembroke, who occupied Montgomeryshire.

Later that year, Llwelyn signed the Treaty of Worcester: in which

WALES c1217

- Ruled by Llwelyn "the Great"
- Llwelyn's vassals
- Anglo–Norman lordships

Chester
Criccieth
GWYNEDD
POWYS FADOG
POWYS WENWYNWYN
Shrewsbury
Offa's Dyke
Ceredigion
DEHEUBARTH
BRECON
Hereford
YSTRAD TYWL
PEMBROKE
GOWER
GLAMORGAN
Bristol

0   50 miles
0   50 km

John's son and successor, Henry III acknowledged Llwelyn's rule over most of Wales. He proceeded to build the first sophisticated stone castles in Wales to defend his borders: Criccieth, the most famous, still stands today. In 1228 Llwelyn fought a campaign against Hubert de Burgh, Justiciar of England, and captured his most important Welsh ally, William de Braose, Lord of Abergavenny. Llwelyn ransomed de Braose for £2,000 (£25 million today), which he used to buy back his lost Montgomeryshire lands.

De Braose later allied himself with Llwelyn: but in 1230, during an Easter visit to his new lord, he was "hanged by the lord Llwelyn in Gwynedd after he had been caught in Llwelyn's chamber with the King of England's daughter, Llwelyn's wife". Joan was more fortunate than Braose's wife and was only confined for a year, before being restored to her position.

Llwelyn had used the title *Princeps Norwalliae* (Leader or Prince of North Wales), but in 1230 he changed it to Prince of Aberffraw and Lord of Snowdon, to underline his authority over the other Welsh princes. For the next ten years, Llwelyn was engaged in almost ceaseless conflict with the Marcher lords.

The "Peace of Middle", signed on 21 June 1234, effectively marked the end of his soldiering. At the insistence of Pope Honorius, Llwelyn abolished the "detestable" custom of treating all sons equally, whether legitimate or not. This ensured the succession of his only legitimate son Dafydd. Llwelyn then withdrew to Gwynedd – where he died of a stroke at the Cistercian Abbey of Aberconwy, which he had founded.

ROBIN HOOD

Robin Hood was a legendary late 12th or early 13th century outlaw hero, the subject of countless ballads dating from the 14th century. No mediæval writer made any attempt to identify Robin Hood as a person. John Mair, in his 1521 *Historia majoris Brittanniae*, dates Robin Hood and Little John to the years of Richard I's imprisonment in Germany (1193–4). The earliest reference to a real figure is to be found in the records of York Assizes in 1225: when a fugitive, Robert Hod failed to appear before the justices and forfeited his chattels. An official at the court of Exchequer, the King's Remembrancer's roll of Easter 1262 records a William Robehod, a fugitive in Berkshire. Robin Hood must have lived well before these dates in order to have given time for the legend to grow.

Robin Hood memorial statue in Nottingham

The ballads vaunt Robin as a rebel who robbed and killed landowners, government functionaries and wealthy churchmen: handing his takings to the poor. He treated women and common folk with kindness and courtesy. He lived in Sherwood Forest on the Nottingham and Yorkshire border, where he and his "Merry Men" lived cheerfully off the King's deer and game – at that time, anyone caught poaching in a royal forest faced execution. Robin's implacable enemy was the Sheriff of Nottingham.

The allegorical narrative poem *The Vision of Piers Plowman* by William Langland (1325–90), born in Ledbury, Herefordshire, makes the first mention of Robin Hood, *c*.1377. Sloth, a lazy priest, confesses: "I kan [know] not parfitly [perfectly] my Pater noster [Lord's prayer] as the preest it singeth. But I kan rymes of Robyn Hood".

The ballads appeared during the years of agricultural depression and social unrest which culminated in the Peasants' Revolt of 1381. *The Gest of Robyn Hode*, a chronicle of 456 four-line verses assembled soon after 1450, is a minstrel's ballad to be sung in serial form. It is the largest and most important of these ballads and provides a common source for scholars seeking to identify real historical figures of the time. Post mediæval, and particularly Victorian embellishments (such as Sir Walter Scott's *Ivanhoe*), give Robin an aristocratic background (as Robin of Locksley, or even as a dispossessed Earl of Huntingdon) and a female love interest, Maid Marian.

These representations domesticated and softened the Robin Hood legend, making it more acceptable to authority. The legend of King Arthur is similar: in that it too evolved from a dangerous, elitist, male-oriented story to a more chivalrous romance that could be retold for royal entertainment by troubadours. From the 16th century, the legend of Robin Hood is often used in support of an hereditary ruling class, romance and religion. The rogue with a heart-of-gold is synthesised to amuse rather than to challenge the establishment. Robin mutated from a yeoman bandit to a national hero of epic stature: who not only defends the poor by taking from the rich, but finally defends the very throne of England itself from corrupt and unscrupulous officials.

The Radcliffe Camera designed by James Gibbs and built 1737–49

"UNIVERSITIES CHALLENGE"

Oxford University is the oldest university in the English speaking world. It is also one of the world's leading academic institutions, consistently sharing with Cambridge second and third place in global ranking, after Harvard. Oxford has 38 colleges and is famous for the Ashmolean (opened 1683), Britain's oldest museum; the Bodleian Library (opened 1602), one of the greatest collections in the world; Christopher Wren's Sheldonian Theatre (completed in 1668); the Radcliffe Camera, which houses part of the Bodleian Library; and the publications of its University Press, which include the English Dictionary and the Dictionary of National Biography.

When foreigners were expelled from the University of Paris in 1167, within a few years of its foundation, many English scholars settled in Oxford, a centre of learning since 1096. The historian Gerald of Wales is known to have lectured there in 1188. Among the earliest benefactors to establish colleges were John I de Balliol (died 1268), father of the future King of Scotland; and Walter de Merton (*c.*1205–77), Chancellor of England and Bishop of Rochester. 50 Nobel laureates, 25 prime ministers and many world leaders (including US President Bill Clinton) went to Oxford.

In 1209 two Oxford scholars were hanged, without proper evidence, for murder by the town authorities. In protest, some of their community decamped to Cambridge and established a rival university. Peterhouse, the oldest formally established Cambridge college that still exists, was founded in 1284; and there are 31 colleges today. The university is renowned for the Cavendish Laboratory, King's College Chapel and a superb Library. 88 Nobel laureates (not including five who taught or researched there) went to Cambridge – 31 more than the whole of France; 3 more than Chicago University, which comes second; and 45 more than Harvard, which comes seventh, two places after Oxford. Trinity College alone educated 32.

After the establishment of Oxford and Cambridge, no universities were founded in England for over 600 years. London University, founded in 1826 and King's College, founded in 1829 combined to receive a Royal Charter in 1836, as the University of London. It now has 19

John Radcliffe M.P. (1650–1714), King William III and Queen Mary II's doctor, was born in Wakefield in Yorkshire. An alumnus of University College, Oxford, he bequeathed his property to charitable causes. His name is remembered in the world-class Radcliffe Infirmary and Radcliffe Observatory, as well as in the Camera.

St Andrews, established by the Augustine priory of St Andrews Cathedral in 1410, is the third oldest university in the English-speaking world. The University of Glasgow (1451) is the fourth; Aberdeen (1495) is fifth; and Edinburgh (1582) is sixth. The historical emphasis once placed on education in Scotland is clear – but today, despite tuition being free for Scottish students, less than half of Edinburgh's 17,000 undergraduates and 7,000 postgraduates are actually Scots.

Queen Elizabeth I founded Trinity College, Dublin as the "mother of a university" in 1592. It is seventh oldest of the seven "Ancient Universities" of Britain and Ireland.

King's College, Cambridge (founded 1441). The late Gothic Chapel was built between 1446–1531 and features the world's largest fan vault.

institutions and 12 research institutes: and, with over 135,000 students, is by far the largest university in Britain. Imperial College became independent of the University of London in 2007, a hundred years after it was founded: focusing on science, engineering, medicine and business, it was placed fifth in the world overall (2008) and is home to 14 Nobel Laureates and 66 Fellows of the Royal Society. The institutions that combined in 2004 to establish the University of Manchester, a world-leading centre for nuclear physics and computer sciences, have together won 23 Nobel prizes, coming third in the United Kingdom after Oxford: Lord Rutherford was first to split the atom in 1917 and the world's first stored-programme computer was built at the university in 1948. With more than 40,000 students and over 10,000 staff, it is the largest single-site university in Britain. There are more applications for entry to Manchester than for any other university in the country – in 2007 it had 120,000 applicants, of whom only 4,000 were accepted.

After Oxford, Cambridge and London, Durham, which dates from 1832 (Royal Charter in 1839) is the next oldest university. The University of Cumbria, which brought together three institutions, is the youngest (founded on 1 August 2007). The first so-called 'red brick' university was Birmingham, founded in 1900: these universities had often started life as medical schools or scientific institutions fifty or more years earlier. There are well over 100 university institutions in Great Britain today.

Both Oxford and Cambridge, often described as 'Oxbridge', have a little over 12,000 undergraduates. Oxford has almost 7,500 postgraduates and Cambridge nearly 6,500. There is a long history of competition between each other – perhaps nowhere more visibly than in the annual Oxford (wearing dark blue) and Cambridge (light blue) Boat Race – first held in 1829 and viewed by over 100 million people worldwide today.

Cambridge is known for mathematics and science; Oxford for classics and literature.

KING HENRY III OF ENGLAND (REIGNED 1216–72)

Henry III (Henry of Winchester) was born at Winchester on the 1 October 1207, the first boy king of England since Æthelred "the Unready". He was the son of King John "Lackland" and Queen Isabella of Angoulême. His 56-year reign was the third longest by a king in British history (George III reigned for 59 years and James VI of Scotland, for 57).

King John died during a confrontation with his barons, who had invited Prince Louis of France (later King Louis VIII "the Lion") to take the English crown. The Archbishop of Canterbury supported the barons, so the nine year-old Henry was hurriedly crowned in Gloucester Cathedral by the Bishop of Gloucester. On 17 May 1220 Henry was crowned a second time, at the insistence of Pope Honorius III, at Westminster Abbey.

A Council of Regency presided over by the venerable William Marshal, 1st Earl of Pembroke, was established to rule during Henry's minority. By 1217 the rebel barons had been defeated and Louis forced to withdraw from England. The regents immediately declared their intention to rule by *Magna Carta*, which was republished the same year. Henry's regency lasted until 1227, when he reached twenty. Although educated, cultured and benevolent, he quickly showed himself to be a hopeless king.

Although Henry was extravagant, and his tax demands were resented, his accounts show a list of many charitable donations and payments for building works, including the rebuilding of Westminster Abbey. Henry appointed French architects from Reims to renovate the abbey in the Gothic style. Work began, at great expense in 1245. The focus of Henry's new abbey was a shrine to Edward the Confessor, where the saint's relics were interred on completion in 1269.

Henry began to ape the Confessor's simple habits. He had a mural of the Confessor painted in his bedroom and named his eldest son Edward. He established Westminster as the seat of government – Westminster Hall was the largest ceremonial chamber in England.

On 20 January 1236 Henry married Eleanor, the daughter of Count Raymond Berengar IV of Provence, in Canterbury Cathedral. The influence exercised by his new French relations however, together with his arrogance and naïvety in addressing diplomatic affairs and his military incompetence, quickly drove Henry's barons to anger. Worse, he governed for long periods through ministers who were accountable to no one. The marriage arranged in 1238 between Henry's sister, Eleanor and his gifted French favourite, Simon de Montfort, especially antagonised his critics – until they realised that Henry had not sanctioned it.

In May 1230 Henry had invaded France, with the purpose of regaining the lost Angevin province of Poitou in south-west France. By October he was back in England, having achieved nothing. In 1242 Henry's Lusignan half-brothers involved him in another disastrous military adventure in France. On 21 June Henry was humiliated at the Battle of Taillebourg – becoming the only English king ever to be defeated by a French one.

Infuriated by his ineptitude, Henry's barons demanded a voice in choosing his advisors; but Henry stubbornly refused. Finally, in 1254 Henry made a serious error: he promised Pope Innocent IV that he would finance a papal campaign in Sicily if the pope made his infant son Edmund, King of Sicily. Four years later Henry was obliged to raise the money owed from his barons – who agreed, provided he introduced fundamental reforms, which were eventually confirmed under oath in the Provisions of Oxford.

The Provisions of Oxford were sent to sheriffs throughout England. Copies were written in Latin, French and importantly, in English – the first administrative document to be published in English since the Norman Conquest. In 1259 they were superseded by the Provisions of Westminster – rescinded by Henry in 1261. The pope absolved Henry from his oath, sparking the Second Barons' War, which Henry won. In 1266 the Provisions were annulled by the Dictum of Kenilworth.

Henry was extremely pious and his journeys were often delayed whilst he heard Mass several times a day. He once took so long to reach the French court that his brother-in-law, King Louis IX of France, banned priests from attending him. He was also anti-semitic and forced Jews to wear a yellow felt "badge of shame".

Simon de Montfort, 6th Earl of Leicester (1208–65) became the leader of baronial opposition to Henry. de Montfort had been one of Henry's favourites, until he married Henry's sister Eleanor without permission. After the Barons' War of 1264–67, de Montfort became *de facto* ruler of England – summoning the first elected Parliament in mediæval Europe in 1265. He is considered the "father of parliamentary democracy".

The Provisions of Oxford were sealed in October 1258 between Henry III and the barons led by Simon de Montfort. The Provisions, the first written constitution in England, forced Henry to accept a council of fifteen members: to supervise ministerial appointments and local administration; and to take responsibility for the "upkeep" (control) of royal castles. They stipulated that Parliament should meet thrice yearly, to monitor council proceedings. The significance of the Provisions was that, for the first time, the King of England had to acknowledge Parliament.

Henry had accepted the Provisions of Oxford, but never had any intention of abiding by them. The barons who had drafted the Provisions held differing views about how far they should be taken. Simon de Montfort took an extreme position: believing that the Council of Fifteen should be able to override the King's wishes if it disagreed with him. Henry's son Edward (later King Edward I), believed that the council should only act in an advisory capacity.

The Second Barons' War began in April 1264, the Royalists being led by Prince Edward. On 14 May in Sussex, de Montfort defeated and captured the King and his son at the Battle of Lewes. In the fifteen months that Henry and Edward were held under house arrest, de Montfort broadened representation in Parliament, to include each county and the burghers of every large town. It was the moment when England came closest to abolishing the monarchy until the Cromwellian Commonwealth of 1649–60.

De Montfort ruled England in Henry's name until Prince Edward escaped his custody, having been freed by his cousin Roger Mortimer. With the help of Mortimer and other Welsh Marcher barons, Edward defeated and killed de Montfort at Evesham in August 1265, inflicting severe reprisals on the rebels. Royal authority was restored by the Statute of Marlborough in 1267, in which Henry promised to uphold *Magna Carta* and most of the Provisions of Westminster – four of the twenty-nine chapters in the Statute constitute the oldest fragments of legislation still in force in the United Kingdom.

Henry, now weak and senile, handed over government to Prince Edward. He died in London on 16 November 1272. While his sarcophagus was being constructed in Westminster Abbey, Henry was interred in the tomb of St Edward the Confessor.

Henry's feckless reign demonstrated the need for a settled legal system and a formalised relationship between sovereign and barons. By 1240 the Great Council had become known as Parliament. Over four centuries of confrontation between it and the monarch lay ahead, before Simon de Montfort's dream of a constitutional democracy was realised: following the "Glorious Revolution" of 1688.

The US House of Representatives

The tomb of King Henry III in Westminster Abbey

ROGER BACON, "DOCTOR MIRABILIS"

Roger Bacon (*c.*1214–92), one of the earliest experimental scientists in the world, was born in Ilchester into a rich Somerset family. He was educated at Oxford and the University of Paris, where he taught Aristotelian philosophy. In 1247 he returned to Oxford where he met Robert Grosseteste, who introduced Greek learning to the embryo university. He immersed himself in the study of optics, language and alchemy – and joined the Franciscan order. He poured money and energy into scientific experiments, although he used a Frenchman, Master Peter de Maricourt to perform them.

Between 1247–67 Bacon mastered most of the Islamic texts on optics, which led to his invention of spectacles; and he established the principles of reflection, refraction and spherical

aberration. He used a *camera obscura* to observe eclipses of the sun. In 1257 he was one of the first in Europe to describe how to make gunpowder. He also anticipated the invention of microscopes, telescopes, flying machines, hydraulics and steam ships. As imaginative as Leonardo da Vinci, but 250 years earlier, he was the first known European scientific polymath.

From 1267 a Franciscan statute forbade any friar from publishing his findings. Bacon circumvented this through his

Statue of Roger Bacon, Oxford University Museum

friendship, from his years in Paris, with Cardinal Guy le Gros de Foulques: who became Pope Clement IV in 1265. Clement "ordered" Bacon to write him a treatise on the place of philosophy within theology. Bacon sent the pope his *Opus Majus*, which presented his views on how Aristotle's principles and new scientific advances could be incorporated into a new theology. Bacon also sent his *Opus Minus* and *De multiplicatione specierum*. As a philosopher, he was a disciple of Aristotle and was critical of the purely theoretical works of his contemporary philosopher-theologians, such as Albertus Magnus and Thomas Aquinas. Bacon argued that a proper understanding of the natural world would confirm the Christian faith.

In 1277 attacks on his contemporary theologians and scholars persuaded the Franciscans to imprison Bacon for "suspected novelties" (heresies). However he continued to write on mathematics and logic. His last work, *Secretum secretorum* was a Latin translation of an Arabic text *(Sirr-al-asrar)* on the education of a prince, which Bacon believed had been written by Aristotle for Alexander the Great. He died at Oxford in 1292.

WESTERN EUROPE OWED MUCH TO ISLAMIC PHILOSOPHERS AND SCIENTISTS

Daniel of Morley (died 1210), born in Flitcham, near Holkham in Norfolk, was a translator and scientist. He studied the Moorish *doctrina Araborum* at Toledo and published *Philosophia*, addressed to the Bishop of Norwich, sometime before 1200. Another translator, who introduced important Arabic scientific works of astrology, astronomy, philosophy and mathematics into England, was the scientist Adelard of Bath, who died *c.*1152. Adelard was among the first to introduce the Arabic numbering system, which had originated in India, to Europe.

They were perhaps the best known of a group of scholars who helped to bring the genius of Arab science, and translations of Greek philosophy from Arabic, to England at the time of the crusades. Along with their enlightenment, England imported a larger number of Arabic words into English than most people are aware of. Indeed many words beginning with "al" are derived from Arabic ("al" simply means "the"): al-gebra, al-kali, al-chemy, al-embic, al-gorithm and al-cove (from *al-qobbah*, meaning a vault, by way of the Spanish for a recessed sleeping area). One notable exception is Alzheimer, the name of the German psychiatrist Alois Alzheimer, who first diagnosed the dreadful, degenerative and terminal illness in 1906.

Less obvious words taken indirectly from Arabic include: admiral, artichoke, azimuth, cipher (*sifr*, which also provides us with zero), elixir, lemon, syrup and zenith. Zero, a paradox to the Greeks, for "how can something be nothing?", again comes from India (*sunya* in Sanskrit). Perhaps the most surprising contribution from Islam is al-cohol. Europeans might find it difficult to swallow, but they owe a great deal to the Arabs.

An analysis of King Edward I's bloodline shows that Edward was: 50% French, 25% Spanish, 6.25% Italian, 6.25% Hungarian, 6.25% Dutch and 6.25% English. He was considered 100% English however, and was one of England's greatest kings.

KING EDWARD I OF ENGLAND (REIGNED 1272–1307)

King Edward I ruled for 35 years. A tall man, he was popularly known as "Longshanks". He advanced Parliament as an important institution of government in support of the crown. He conquered the Welsh, creating the title of Prince of Wales for his heir. His bid to conquer Scotland failed, but he was described on his tombstone as *Scotorum malleus* ("Hammer of the Scots"). His reforms of the common law and government administration earned him other nicknames: "Lawgiver" and "the English Justinian". Edward was born on the 17 June 1239, at the Palace of Westminster, the eldest son of King Henry III and Eleanor of Provence.

Although Edward was granted Gascony in 1249, his father Henry III had made Simon de Montfort, 6th Earl of Leicester, governor of the province in 1247: as a result he derived from this inheritance neither income nor authority. On 1 November 1254 Edward married Eleanor of Castile at the monastery of Las Huelgas, near Burgos in Spain.

Eleanor was married at the age of thirteen to the fifteen year-old Edward. She came to England when she was eighteen and the couple became inseparable. Eleanor even accompanied Edward on the Eighth Crusade – and produced sixteen children in a long and happy marriage. Late in 1290, while she was travelling north to meet the infant Queen of Scotland, Margaret (the "Maid of Norway"), she became ill near Lincoln.

Edward rushed to her side but she died on 28 November, aged forty-nine. Since Edward wished his queen to be interred in Westminster Abbey, the funeral *cortège* set out by way of Lincoln, Grantham, Stamford, Geddington, Hardingstone, Stony Stratford, Woburn, Dunstable, St Albans, Waltham Cross, Westcheap (Cheapside) and Charing Cross. At each of these twelve places, Edward erected a large cross. Today, only three of the original crosses remain: at Geddington, Hardingstone and Waltham Cross.

Nine years later, in 1299 Edward married Margaret, daughter of Philip III of France, by whom he had three more children: bringing the total of his progeny to nineteen.

In 1255 Edward fought his first military campaign, against the Welsh chieftain Llwelyn ap Gruffydd who had rebelled against the imposition of English land measures. Receiving no help from his father or the Marcher Lords, Edward suffered an humiliating defeat, obliging him to turn to Simon de Montfort, his uncle by marriage and the leader of a faction of barons determined to cap the powers of his father.

Over the two years 1258–60, Edward see-sawed in his support between de Montfort and his father. In 1263 Edward visited Gascony; before returning to England to stand alongside his father against a coalition of rebel barons and Londoners.

Simon de Montfort, 6th Earl of Leicester was the second son of Simon de Montfort (1165–1218), the 5th Earl who had led a murderous crusade against the Cathars. He was killed while besieging Toulouse.

De Montfort gifted his French estates to his brothers and quit France for England: successfully claiming for himself his father's earldom of Leicester. In 1228 de Montfort married Princess Eleanor, Henry III's sister – but without Henry's permission. The barons too, protested that they had not been consulted. De Montfort prudently went on crusade to the Holy Land (1240–2). In 1248 he was appointed governor of the rebellious Duchy of Gascony, but was recalled because of heavy handed behaviour. In 1254, after an insincere reconciliation with Henry, de Montfort led a number of barons in opposition to increased royal subsidies, resulting in the Provisions of Oxford. In 1261 Henry revoked the Provisions; and de Montfort left the country. In 1263, at the invitation of the same group of barons, he returned. He defeated Henry

Margaret, Maid of Norway (born 1283), Queen of Scotland (1286–90), was the last of the line of King Malcolm III Canmore of Scotland; and daughter of King Erik II of Norway. Margaret had been pledged as a bride to Edward I's son Edward, Prince of Wales, later King Edward II, but she died in Orkney on the voyage to Scotland (on which she never set foot) from Norway. Edward I immediately declared himself King of Scotland, selecting John de Balliol as his surrogate.

Charing is wrongly assumed to be a bastardisation of *chère reine* (dear queen). It probably comes in fact, from the Anglo-Saxon *cerring* (a "bend"), as Charing Cross stands on a 90° bend in the River Thames.

Cathars or Albigensians were an heretical Christian sect that blossomed in southwestern Europe during the 13th century. Cathars followed a dualist belief that the material world is evil and that humans must renounce it to free their spirits – which, inherently good, long for union with God. Their priests were known as *Parfaits* (Perfect Men), who were expected to uphold the highest moral standards. In 1200 Pope Innocent III declared a crusade, in which the Cathars were massacred. The heresy was subsequently extinguished by the Inquisition.

Adult males in county constituencies were enfranchised – provided they owned land with a minimum rental value of 40 shillings a year (£23,000 today). Parliament met on 20 January 1265 but was dissolved on 15 February.

The Mamluks were an army of slaves who had won control of Saladin's Ayyubid sultanate by 1250. Mamluk generals ruled Egypt and the Eastern Mediterranean from Cairo as sultans themselves, until the Ottoman Turks overthrew them in 1517. Baybars, a Kipchak Turk born in 1223 on the northern shore of the Black Sea and sold into slavery by the Mongols in 1242, seized the throne in 1260 and turned back the Mongol horde near Nablus in Palestine. He died in Damascus in 1277, after drinking a cup of poison intended for another.

Edward narrowly escaped death, when Baybars sent assassins disguised as Christian converts into his camp. Edward was stabbed with a poisoned dagger: and, it is said, was saved by his wife Eleanor, who swiftly sucked out the poison.

By 1290, the population of England had doubled over 200 years from 2 million to 4 million. In the same period, the population of Scotland had also doubled: from 500,000 to 1 million. The population of Wales in 1290 was between 300,000 and 400,000. France's population in 1290 was about 20 million – of which many were governed by the King of England.

and captured his son Edward at the Battle of Lewes on 14 May 1264. de Montfort immediately summoned the "de Montfort Parliament" – when, on his insistence and for the first time in English history, all representatives were elected.

De Montfort ignored the Parliament he had summoned and proceeded to rule England as a dictator for the next eleven months, at the same time attempting to reach agreement and win support amongst the knights of the shires to offset his lack of baronial support. His conduct caused his chief ally, the Earl of Gloucester to defect to the King and release Prince Edward, who was imprisoned in Hereford castle. Edward now displayed exceptional military skill. On 1 August 1265 he ambushed a large army at Kenilworth marching to relieve de Montfort. On 4 August Simon de Montfort, accompanied by only a few followers, was cornered at Evesham and killed.

Although styled a battle, Evesham was a massacre. De Montfort, proclaiming, "Now is the time to die", was killed. His corpse was dismembered and distributed amongst Henry's barons as a warning of the fate which attended rebellion. Roger de Mortimer, 1st Baron Wigmore, received de Montfort's head and sent it on as a gift to his wife Maud – as an unusual token of love or as a warning, is not recorded.

In 1266, all but senile, Henry III finally handed over power to his son. Edward relentlessly hunted down the rebels until reconciliation was reached in the Dictum of Kenilworth on 31 October. In 1268 Edward undertook to join the French king, Louis IX on the Eighth Crusade; but was unable to set out until 1270 through lack of funds.

He arrived in Tunis with his wife Eleanor, just after Louis's death from dysentery. He reached Acre in May 1271, to unite with an army led by Charles of Anjou. The aim was to reinforce Bohemund IV, Prince of Antioch and relieve the town of Tripoli, then under siege by the Mamluk general, Baybars. Edward and Anjou, deploying from Cyprus, attacked Baybars and broke the siege.

In November 1272 Edward learnt of the death of his father and immediately set out for England. Edward had left his kingdom in the capable hands of Roger Mortimer, Walter Giffard, Archbishop of York (the son of his former tutor, Hugh Giffard) and Robert Burnell, Bishop of Bath and Wells. He felt sufficiently confident in their abilities to return at a leisurely pace, spending several months in Gascony. He did not arrive back in England until shortly before his coronation at Westminster on 19 August 1274.

From 1275, until the end of his reign, Edward summoned regular parliaments. The composition varied greatly: the largest was the Model Parliament of 1295. By Edward's death in 1307 the semblance of a modern parliament was in place in England, albeit irregularly summoned and lacking any real authority. Edward brought together for the first time the important estates of the realm: barons, knights, burgesses (townsfolk) and the clergy. The Parliament of 1304 even included Scottish representatives.

Edward was the first King of England to understand that royal authority would be enhanced if consultation and cooperation with his subjects was combined with the counsel of his advisors. He used parliaments and other councils to arouse an emergent nationalism in the country; and, with the support of his most trusted mentor Robert Burnell (1239–92), to introduce far-reaching legislation.

Edward's statutes, the legacy of his reign, started with the Statute of Gloucester in 1278 and were enacted regularly until *Quo Warranto* in 1290. His legislation did much to formalise the chaotic state of existing monopolies and tenancies and prevented the fraudulent assumption of new ones. The Statute of Mortmain in 1279 enabled the crown to control acquisition of land by the Church. The Statute of Winchester in 1285 laid down basic processes for the maintenance of public order. The Statutes of Acton Burnell in 1283 and the Statute of Acton in 1285 regulated mercantile and trade practices. The Court of Common Pleas was created specifically to deal with property disputes. Edward disliked the idea of estates being broken up. He was a strong supporter of primogeniture and opposed the granting of assignable tenancies. The courts of Exchequer and the King's Bench also date from Edward's reign.

In 1277 Edward decided that the time had come to bring the troublesome Welsh chieftain Llwelyn ap Gruffydd to heel. Llwelyn had taken advantage of Edward's absence in France to expand his kingdom, by incorporating into it all the Marcher territories that had been defined as England's in the 1267 Treaty of Shrewsbury. Ten years later Llwelyn failed yet again to pay Edward homage. With this as a convenient pretext, Edward assembled an army of 15,000 men, the largest ever mustered by an English king, and invaded Wales. To outflank Llwelyn, Edward transported his troops to Anglesey by sea, where they brought in the harvest to deprive the Welsh of food over the winter.

Edward advanced into Wales with three columns across a broad front. He bottled-up Llwelyn in Snowdonia, starved him into submission and consolidated his victory by building a ring of nine fortresses – costing over £80,000 (£864 million today). Conwy and Caernarvon were the first to be incorporated into major towns.

Edward divided Wales into English units of shires and hundreds: legislation which provoked another rebellion five years later. Edward once again systematically reconquered Wales – this time killing both Llwelyn in 1282 and his brother Dafydd in 1283. At Rhuddlan, one of Edward's "ring of iron" castles in North Wales, in a statute proclaimed on 3 March 1284, Wales was subsumed into England. In 1295 Edward brutally suppressed a third rebellion, finally extinguishing all Welsh dissent.

The pacification of Wales had not only emptied Edward's treasury, it had distracted him while Kings Philip III and Philip IV of France surreptitiously eroded his lands in Gascony. Edward's problems escalated when he lost his two best advisors, his wife Eleanor in 1290 and Robert Burnell in 1292. Outbursts of an ungovernable temper, evident in every Plantagenet king, became more frequent and he quarrelled violently with his barons and clergy. In 1290 Edward carried

Llwelyn ap Gruffydd, or Llwelyn "the Last" (*c.*1226–82), proclaimed himself Prince of Wales in 1258. His 'Principality' embraced Powys, Gwynedd, Deheubarth and the Marches. Llwelyn supported Simon de Montfort and married his daughter Eleanor, who died in childbed in 1282. After de Montfort's death in 1265 however, he came to terms with King Henry III. Ill-advisedly, he rebelled against Edward in 1277 by refusing to pay homage. He was killed in a skirmish at Builth in 1282.

Master James of St George or Jacques de Saint-Georges d'Esperanche (died *c.*1309), a military architect and master mason from Savoy, built many of Edward's "ring of iron" Welsh castles: including Conwy, Harlech and Caernarvon in 1283 and Beaumaris in Anglesey in 1295. In 1285 he was appointed Master of the Royal Works in Wales and paid 3 shillings a day (£1,500 today).
• **Caernarvon Castle**

THE ROYAL LINE OF SCOTLAND FOR 332 YEARS (1058–1390)

Malcolm III
Canmore or "Bighead" (1058–93)
son of Duncan I (1034–40); *Malcolm III killed Macbeth (1057) and deposed Macbeth's son Lulach (1058);* m. Margaret, great-niece of Edward "the Confessor", King of England

Donald III
the Fair (1093–94)
Malcolm III's brother; *deposed by Malcolm's eldest son Duncan II (1094); restored and ruled (1094–97)*

Edgar
the Valiant (1097–1107)
fourth son of Malcolm III

Alexander I
the Fierce (1107–24)
fifth son of Malcolm III

David I
the Saint (1124–53)
sixth son of Malcolm III (b. c.1085); m. (c.1113) Matilda (d.1131), dau. of the Earl of Huntingdon *[David's sister Matilda married Henry I, King of England]*

CANMORE

Henry, Earl of Huntingdon
(1114–52)
died before his father; m. (1139) Ada de Warenne (d. 1178) dau. of Earl of Surrey

Malcolm IV
(1153–65)

Alexander II
(1214–49)

Alexander III
(1249–86)
m. (1251) Margaret, dau. of Henry III of England

William I
the Lion (1165–1214)
m. his cousin Ermengarde, granddau. of Henry I of England

David
(1152–1219)
Earl of Huntingdon; m. Matilda, dau. of Earl of Chester

Margaret
(d.1283); m. Erik II of Norway; *she died before her father*

Margaret
m. Alan, Lord of Galloway (d.1234)

Isobel
(d.1251); m. Robert IV de Brus, Lord of Annandale (c.1195–c.1226)

Margaret "Maid of Norway"
(1286–90)
never crowned (end of the Canmore line); the "Great Cause" (competition for the crown 1290–92)

Dervorguilla of Galloway
m. (1233) John de Balliol (d.1268)

Robert V de Brus
(c.1220–95)
m. (1240) Isabel de Clare (d.1264); *a contender (1290–2)*

Robert VI de Brus. Lord of Annadale
(1243–1304)
m. (1271) Marjory, Countess of Carrick (d.1292)

BALLIOL

John de Balliol
(c.1249–1314)
King of Scotland (1292–96); *chosen (1292) but deposed by Edward I. Who ruled 1296–1306;* his son Edward de Balliol (c.1282–1364), **the Claimant**: no ch. *(end of the Balliol line)*

Eleanor
m. John Comyn *the Black* (d.1302); *a contender (1290–2)*

John Comyn
the Red murdered by Robert I (1306)

Robert I   BRUCE
the Bruce
(b.1274) King of Scotland (1306–29) m. (1) Isabella; (2) Elizabeth

Walter Fizalan
(1293–1326)
m. (1315) Marjorie (1296–1316) 6th High Steward of Scotland; *known as "Stewart"*

David II
(1329–71)
(b.1324); no ch. *(end of the Bruce line)*

STEWART

Robert II
(1371–90)
the first Stewart King of Scotland (b.1316)

out a pogrom against the Jews, seizing their possessions and expelling them from England. They were not permitted to return for 365 years, until Oliver Cromwell lifted the ban in 1655.

In 1297 Edward invaded France but was forced immediately to return to England, to tackle a rebellion in Scotland raised by William Wallace.

The wars in Wales and Scotland, and constant attacks on his Gascon territories by the French King Philip IV, placed Edward under great financial strain. Struggling to find sources of revenue, principally by heavy taxation on the export of wool, he clashed with his barons, clerics and inevitably, Popes Boniface VIII and Clement V.

Despite these difficulties Edward renewed his campaign against Scotland. He took Stirling castle in 1304 and sent William Wallace to London, to suffer a barbaric execution for treason the following year. When at last Edward might have congratulated himself on finally pacifying Scotland, Robert the Bruce emerged from the Irish mists: to be crowned King of Scotland and revive rebellion against him. Once again, although in poor health, Edward marched north to meet this new threat: only to collapse and die of dysentery at Burgh-by-Sands, near Carlisle on 7 July 1307.

Edward had willed that his remains were to be buried in Scotland and his heart in the Holy Land. He was buried instead in Westminster Abbey, in a black marble tomb with a plain slab of marble above: on which is engraved *Edwardus Primus Scottorum malleus hic est, pactum serva* ("Here is Edward I, Hammer of the Scots. Keep Troth"). For one hundred years the Exchequer funded candles to be lit permanently by his tomb.

Statue of King Robert I ("the Bruce") at Stirling Castle

KING ROBERT I ("THE BRUCE") OF SCOTLAND (REIGNED 1306–29)

Robert I (1274–1329), Scotland's greatest king and most famous warrior, known to the English as Robert the Bruce, was King of Scotland for twenty-three years. His father's family, originally from Brieux in Normandy, settled in Scotland in the early 12th century and married into the Scottish royal family. His mother Margaret, Countess of Carrick's family was Gael. She was a formidable woman, said to have kept his father Robert, 6th Lord of Annandale captive until he agreed to marry her. Bruce was born at Writtle, near Chelmsford in Essex on 11 July 1274 – not, as is often suggested, at Turnberry Castle in Ayrshire. Bruce's grandfather Robert, 5th Lord of Annandale, who died in 1295, was one of the three principal claimants to the throne when it fell vacant in 1290.

King Edward I of England asserted his feudal sovereignty over Scotland and placed John de Balliol on the throne. Edward thought that de Balliol had the better claim: more importantly, he thought that de Balliol would be an amenable vassal.

During the Scottish rebellions between 1296–1304, though Bruce sympathised with William Wallace's uprising, he acted with circumspection: attracting neither the unwelcome attention of King Edward nor the forfeiture of his estates after Wallace was defeated. In 1298 he became a Guardian of Scotland – with John Comyn, de Balliol's nephew and Bruce's strongest rival for the throne. On 10 February 1306 John Comyn (known as "the Red") was stabbed to death by Bruce, Roger de Kirkpatrick and John Lindsay, before the high altar of Greyfriars Church in Dumfries. Bruce was excommunicated. This was followed by the excommunication of the entire country.

John II de Balliol (c.1249–1314) was King of Scotland (1292–96). Edward I supported his claim which, by strict primogeniture, was stronger than any of the thirteen rivals. De Balliol paid homage to Edward I: but refused to supply troops for service in Gascony, signing a treaty with the French instead. When Edward occupied Gascony in 1296, the Scots raided northern England. In retaliation, Edward I invaded Scotland, beginning the "Wars of Scottish Independence". The Scots were defeated at Dunbar and the English seized Dunbar Castle on 27 April 1296. De Balliol abdicated. The arms of Scotland were formally torn from his surcoat, earning him the derisive name of "Toom Tabard": meaning "Empty Coat".

De Balliol's father, John I (died 1268) founded Balliol College, Oxford in 1263.

John III Comyn, Lord of Badenoch was also known simply as the "Red Comyn". His father, John II Comyn, known as the "Black Comyn", was one of the claimants to the Scottish crown. His mother was Eleanor, eldest daughter of John I de Balliol. The Red Comyn was therefore descended from both Celtic and Norman royal lines. His murder removed an important obstacle to Bruce's political ambitions.

Sir James Douglas (1286–1330), known as "Black Douglas", was Lord of the Douglas family and Bruce's lieutenant. After the Battle of Methven in June 1306, James and Bruce survived together as fugitives. In 1307 they separated, Sir James returning to the south of Scotland where many successful raids on the English earned him his nickname. In 1313 he captured Roxburgh Castle, disguising his men as oxen. After the Battle of Bannockburn on 24 June 1314, in which he commanded the left-wing with Walter the Steward. Douglas was knighted.

In August 1327, shortly before peace was finally made, he nearly captured Edward III in a daring night attack on the English camp in Weardale. Before his death in 1329, Bruce asked Sir James to carry his heart to the Holy Land in redemption of an unfulfilled vow to go on a crusade. Sir James set out in 1330, carrying the embalmed heart in a silver casket. He was killed fighting the Moors in Spain.

Stirling Castle dates from the early 12th century, but was mostly built in the 15th century

Unlike Edward I, both Robert and Edward Bruce allowed garrisons which surrendered safe passage. Many Scotsmen felt that retribution for past atrocities was called for: but this chivalrous policy paid dividends, especially in this instance.

Bruce, with blood on his hands, was crowned King Robert I of Scotland at Scone, near Perth, on 25 March 1306 by Isabella MacDuff, Countess of Buchan – who was alleged by the English to be his mistress. Her family, the Macduff Earls of Fife, claimed the right to crown Scottish kings. Although he was now King, Bruce did not yet have a kingdom: and his efforts to obtain one had to await the death of King Edward I.

Edward I now regarded Bruce as a traitor and murderer, to be hunted down and executed. Edward had garrisoned Scotland in strength: and during 1306, bested Bruce's forces in a number of decisive actions. His wife was captured and three of his brothers caught and executed. Bruce fled Scotland, finding refuge on Rathlin Island, north of Antrim in Ireland – where it is said, he drew inspiration from a spider weaving its web.

Returning to Scotland early in 1307, Bruce linked up with his only surviving brother Edward and recruited an army. In July Edward I died and was succeeded by his son, King Edward II – incompetent and weak, but by no means a coward. The English grip on Scotland loosened. Bruce's able lieutenants, James Douglas and Thomas Randolph, later Earl of Moray had begun independently successful campaigns against the English occupation, regaining significant tracts of Scottish territory.

In 1313 Bruce captured Perth, ejecting the English garrison, before moving south to take Edinburgh. On 24 June 1314 a large English army under Edward II, attempting to relieve the besieged garrison at Stirling, was routed at Bannockburn (*Blàr Allt a' Bhonnaich* in Gaelic) by Bruce – a victory which expelled the English from Scotland, secured Scottish independence and confirmed Bruce as undisputed king.

In the late spring of 1314 agreement had been reached between Edward Bruce and Philip de Mowbray, Governor of Scotland's strategically most important fortress, Stirling Castle: that if it were not relieved by mid-summer's day, it would be surrendered. A huge English army of almost 20,000 men, led by Edward II himself, attempted to fight through to Stirling. Robert, with 7,000 men, chose his defensive positions with care at the Bannockburn: making use of bogs, a gorge and sloping terrain. The English could not deploy properly on the narrow front and Bruce's spearmen held firm. As the day progressed the English began to lose the struggle. Edward II reached Stirling castle with a bodyguard of 500 knights. De Mowbray stuck to his oath saying that the battle was lost, that he was about to surrender and banned Edward's entry.

Although England's power within Scotland had been destroyed at Bannockburn, fighting continued throughout Robert's reign. Berwick was captured in 1318 and the north of England was repeatedly ravaged. It was not until Edward II had been deposed that peace was finally made, confirmed by the Treaty of Northampton on 10 July 1328, and all English claims to Scotland were dropped.

Robert had to recreate a royal government, as all administration had been defunct since 1296. By the end of his reign Robert had restored the Exchequer, established his Seal and come to terms with Pope John XXII. Following the Declaration of Arbroath in 1320, the pope lifted the excommunication orders against Robert and his kingdom. Four years later, Robert received papal recognition as King of an independent Scotland.

Robert the Bruce died on 7 June 1329, at the Manor of Cardross in Dunbartonshire. He had suffered for some years from what contemporary sources described as an "unclean ailment". Most probably he died of leprosy.

Robert's body was interred in Dunfermline Abbey. His heart was to be taken by Sir James Douglas on crusade to the Holy Land: Douglas was killed on the way however, in the Battle of Teba – fighting the Moors in Granada. The heart was saved and brought back for burial at Melrose Abbey. In 1921, and again in 1996, a cone-shaped casket containing a heart was unearthed: but nothing was found to link it to Robert.

In March 1295 Robert married Isabella, daughter of Donald, 6th Earl of Mar, by whom he had an only daughter, Marjorie. She died in childbirth in 1316. Her young son, Robert Stewart, was appointed as his grandfather's heir. In March 1324 however, Bruce's second wife Elizabeth, daughter of the powerful Richard de Burgh, 3rd Earl of Ulster, finally produced a son. He was christened David after Robert's great-great-grandfather, King David I.

Leprosy (Hansens disease) was carried by Crusaders to Europe from the Levant. It is a chronic disease of the skin and underlying nerves, spread by the bacterium *mycobacterium leprae*, causing horrible disfigurement as body parts rot away. Without treatment death soon follows. Isolation is the only way of containing leprosy. In the Middle Ages lepers had to announce their presence by ringing a bell.

The Declaration of Arbroath, upholding Scotland's status as an independent state, is enshrined in a letter to Pope John XXII, dated 6 April 1320. It was sealed by fifty-one barons. Of the three drafted at the time, the only surviving copy is held by the National Archives of Scotland in Edinburgh.

The stirring rhetoric of the *Declaration* has resounded around the world. It has been suggested that the wording influenced the drafting of the United States *Declaration of Independence*. Controversy surrounds the contemporary relevance of the document. Doubters consider the *Declaration* to have been a cynical example of royal propaganda and special pleading (Robert and Scotland were still under excommunication), crafted by Robert's able chief minister, Abbot Bernard de Linton (died 1331). Nationalists believe it represents the proto-democratic right of the people to choose their king. The *Declaration* remains a potent symbol of national identity.

KING EDWARD II OF ENGLAND (REIGNED 1307–27)

Edward II (1284–1327) was the youngest of sixteen children, and the only surviving son, from Edward I's first marriage to Eleanor of Castile. He was born at Caernarvon Castle – where he was created the first Prince of Wales in 1301. Though well-built and personally brave, he was effeminate and proved to be a foolish king. He infuriated his barons by his extravagant display of favour towards an arrogant Frenchman, Piers Gaveston (c.1284–1312). Following Gaveston's murder on the orders of the Earl of Lancaster, Edward transferred his affections to Hugh le Despenser and his villainous son, another Hugh. In 1314 Robert the Bruce defeated Edward at Bannockburn.

In 1324 the French king occupied Edward's duchy of Aquitaine. Edward sent his wife Isabella to treat with her brother; but she eloped with his principal enemy, the exiled Roger Mortimer. Both returned in 1326 with an invasion army. They executed the Despensers, deposed Edward and crowned his fourteen year-old son as Edward III.

On 23 September 1327, to ensure there was no outward sign of violent death, Edward himself is said (though this is disputed) to have been murdered, at Berkeley Castle in Gloucestershire, by the anal insertion of a sawn-off cow's horn: then through it, a red-hot poker – literally a gut-wrenching penalty for failure.

It was recorded that the manner of the younger Despenser's death was designed to keep him alive as long as possible. Still choking from slow hanging, the executioner sliced off his genitals, which were burnt before him – while he groaned, "Not more yet". His entrails were then cut out and thrown on the fire before his eyes – and finally, his heart. Just before he died, it is said that he let out a "ghastly inhuman howl", much to the merriment of the spectators. He was then beheaded.

King Edward III
by unknown artist
(late 16th Century)
National Portrait Gallery, London

KING EDWARD III OF ENGLAND (REIGNED 1327–77)

Edward III, otherwise known as Edward of Windsor, was born on 13 November 1312 at Windsor Castle. He was King of England for 50 years, from 1327–77. His mother, Queen Isabella (c.1295–1358), known as the "She-Wolf of France", was the daughter of King Philip IV. She married the bisexual King Edward II on 25 January 1308. Despite her youth and beauty, Edward paid little attention to Isabella and gave all her wedding presents to his favourite, Piers Gaveston. In 1324, when her brother, King Charles IV seized Edward's possessions in France, Edward sent Isabella to negotiate a peace treaty with him.

Her presence in France however, attracted many English barons opposed to Edward's regime to her side. Together with Roger Mortimer, 1st Earl of March (1270–1330), a Marcher baron who had become her lover, Isabella assembled an army, invaded England and arrested her husband.

Map of the most important battles in the Anglo-Scottish Wars: England was dominant in the 250 years of the wars (1297–1547), but failed to subdue the Scots. In 1603 the two countries were ruled by the same king for the first time, James I of England and VI of Scotland. Full union was finally achieved on 1 May 1707.

THE ANGLO – SCOTTISH WARS (1297–1547)

Scotland

England

Counties recovered by Henry II from Malcolm IV of Scotland (1157)

Occupied by the Vikings (9/10th century)

Battle of Largs (ended Viking control of the Western Isles)

The most important battles in the Anglo–Scottish Wars

Scottish victories

English victories

Castle

Orkney and Shetland were annexed by the Scottish Crown in 1472.

SHETLAND

ORKNEY

0   25 miles
0   50 km

WESTERN ISLES

King James V subdued the Western Isles in 1540.

SCOTLAND

Inverness

Aberdeen

Dupplin Moor 1332
(the first battle to demonstrate the terrible power of the English longbow)

Stirling Bridge 1297
(Wallace defeated Surrey)

Perth

Stirling

Pinkie 1547
(the last major Anglo–Scots battle)

Bannockburn 1314
(secured Scottish independence)

Falkirk 1298
(Wallace captured)

Edinburgh

Largs 1263

Halidon Hill 1333
(10,000 Scots dead)

Flodden 1513
(Scots nobility decimated)

Ancrum Moor 1545

Homildon Hill 1402
(Hotspur's revenge)

Otterburn 1388
(Hotspur captured)

Solway Moss 1542

Carlisle

Neville's Cross 1346
(King David II of Scotland was captured)

The Isle of Man was:
– sold by Norway to Scotland (1266)
– taken by England (1346)
– became a Crown Possession (1765)
It is not part of the UK or the EU.

IRELAND

ISLE OF MAN

ENGLAND

Richmond

York

On 29 January 1327 Isabella arranged Edward's coronation. For nearly four years, with Roger Mortimer, she ruled as his regent – and forced him to sign the Treaty of Northampton in July 1328, guaranteeing the independence of Scotland. Five days earlier Edward had married Philippa of Hainault at York.

Long resentful of his regents, on the night of 19 October 1330 Edward entered Nottingham Castle, where Mortimer was holding a Council, with a few companions by an underground passage. After a brief struggle, Edward arrested Mortimer and proclaimed himself King. He was not yet eighteen years old.

Charged with high treason, Mortimer was condemned without trial and hanged at Tyburn in London on 29 November – despite Isabella's cries of "Fair son, have pity on gentle Mortimer". His large estates became forfeit to the crown. Mortimer's widow, Joan was pardoned in 1336; and lived until 1356. Isabella too, enjoyed a comfortable retirement: becoming a Poor Clare nun. She died on 22 August 1358 and was buried in the Franciscan church at Newgate in London – inappropriately, in her wedding dress.

The Treaty of Northampton still rankled. Edward took advantage of the death of Robert I (the Bruce) in 1329 and the accession of his young son, David II. He defeated the Scots at Halidon Hill on 19 July 1333, forcing David to flee to France: and installed his puppet Edward (*c*.1282–1364), son of John de Balliol, on the Scottish throne.

Berwick-on-Tweed was under siege by Edward III, in support of Edward de Balliol, when a relief force, under the regent for the young King David, encountered the English army drawn-up on a ridge at Halidon Hill. Obliged to attack uphill across marshy ground, the Scots were enfiladed by volleys of arrows. The Scots fled and Berwick surrendered the next day. Although this battle achieved little in the long history of the Scottish wars, and de Balliol was deposed when David returned from France in 1336, the English were to repeat the manoeuvre that had triumphed at Halidon Hill at Crécy, Poitiers and Agincourt. In this sense the battle was decisive.

A dispute over the possession of Gascony, drove Edward to revive his claim to the French throne. In 1339 and 1340 he launched unsuccessful invasions of France which reduced him to near bankruptcy. Nonetheless, in 1340 he declared himself King of France, a title claimed successively by every English sovereign until 1801, and inflicted a crushing naval defeat on the French fleet at Sluys off the coast of Holland.

The Battle of Sluys, fought on 24 June 1340, was the first important English victory in the Hundred Years' War. The destruction of the French fleet removed the threat of invasion, ensuring that the war to come would be fought in France. Through lack of money however, Edward was unable to capitalise on his naval victory for six years.

On St George's Day, 23 April 1344 King Edward III instituted the Order of the Garter.

In July 1346 Edward III again invaded France, with 4,000 infantry and 10,000 archers. At first the campaign lacked any strategic aim, other than a general pillage towards Paris. On 26 August Philip VI, attempting to cut off Edward's line of retreat to Calais, met the English army at Crécy-en-Ponthieu and suffered a crushing defeat.

The Most Noble Order of the Garter was created supposedly after an incident at a court ball when Edward's dancing partner and future daughter-in-law Joan, the "Fair Maid of Kent", lost her garter. Before a tittering audience, Edward picked up the garter and put it on his own leg, chiding his courtiers with the words: *Honi soit qui mal y pense*: "Evil is he, who evil thinks". There is only one rank, Knight Companion. It is the most distinguished and exclusive order of knighthood.

Members however, have sometimes forfeited their rank. 36 Knights of the Garter have been beheaded, with Henry VIII accounting for six. During World War II, the crests and swords of two Supernumerary Knights, Emperor Hirohito of Japan and King Victor Emmanuel III of Italy, were removed from the Order's chapel. The honour has also been declined. In 1945, having lost the general election, Winston Churchill turned down the honour, saying privately: "I can hardly accept the Order of the Garter from the King after the people have given me the Order of the Boot". He relented in 1953. Membership is composed of the Sovereign and the Prince of Wales, with no more than 24 Knight Companions. The Supernumerary Knights and Ladies are members of the Royal Family and foreign monarchs.

Prince Edward so admired the bravery of King John, that he assumed the ostrich feathers on his helmet and the dead king's motto *Ich Dien* ("I serve" in German) for a new badge of his own. It has been used by all Princes of Wales ever since.

"Black Prince" was never used as a sobriquet in Edward's lifetime. It was first mentioned in Richard Grafton's *Chronicle of England* in 1568. It may have derived from an ornate black cuirass presented to the prince by his father after Crécy.

Edward had taken up a defensive position on the top of a slope at Crécy, a small village in the Somme valley near Abbeville. He placed his infantry in the centre and archers on each flank. Prince Edward, later called the "Black Prince", a boy of sixteen, led a force of dismounted men-at-arms on the right. King Edward, wishing his son to "win his spurs", then gave him the command of the van, with the counsel and assistance of the Earl of Warwick and Sir John Chandos (died 1370) – a wise and chivalrous knight.

The French opened the attack with Italian mercenary cross-bowmen – who were swiftly overwhelmed by the rate of fire of the long bow. A series of futile French cavalry charges on sodden ground up the centre of the slope failed to make any impression on the English men-at-arms. The French knights were subsequently enfiladed and cut down by English, in fact mainly Welsh, archers firing volleys from the flanks. At least 1,500 French knights were killed: as were Philip VI's brother Charles II of Alençon, the blind King John of Bohemia and the Count of Flanders.

The French knights' armour provided some protection against high-velocity bodkin arrows, with hardened steel tapered tips, but their horses were barely protected at all. Such was the slaughter, that Crécy is considered the battle which ended the age of chivalry. It was also the first in which cannon *(ribaldi)* were deployed.

Edward of Woodstock (1330–76), known as the "Black Prince", the eldest son of King Edward III and Philippa of Hainault, died the year before his father. The throne passed to the Prince's only surviving son, who was crowned King Richard II aged ten.

Prince Edward was born on 15 June 1330 at Woodstock Palace in Oxfordshire. He was created Earl of Chester in 1333 and Duke of Cornwall in 1337, the first creation of an English duke. He was invested as Prince of Wales in 1343. While Edward III was on campaign between 1339–42, Prince Edward served as regent. He married his cousin Joan, the "Fair Maid of Kent", after the death of her first husband, on 10 October 1361.

The badge of the Prince of Wales
National Army Museum, London

Joan of Kent (1328–85) was the daughter of Edmund, Earl of Kent, Edward I's youngest son by his second wife. She was celebrated for her beauty and charm. On the death of her brother in 1352, Joan became *suo jure* Countess of Kent (in her own right). In 1330 her father had been judged guilty of treason by Mortimer and Isabella for having supported his half-brother, King Edward II: such was public hostility to his execution, that "he had to wait five hours for an executioner, because no one wanted to do it". Finally, a convicted murderer offered his services in return for a full pardon. It was this act of judicial murder that provoked Edward III to charge Mortimer with treason.

On 19 September 1356 the Black Prince won a decisive victory at Poitiers. In the run-up to the battle he sent a 7,000 strong English-Gascon army, led by Chandos and the Captal de Buch, on a *chevauchée* (cavalry raid) from Bordeaux into central France.

Contact with the French army led by King Jean II, who had succeeded Philip VI in 1350, was made on 17 September. A truce agreed for the following day, a Sunday, allowed the English to position themselves in a strong position on an old Roman road south of Poitiers. Dense thickets and marshy ground surrounded the confluence of the nearby Moisson and Clain rivers. Forgetting the lessons of Crécy, the French launched a series of frontal assaults over waterlogged ground. Their knights became quickly mired and presented easy targets for the English archers firing armour-piercing bodkin arrows. Jean led the last charge and was captured, together with many of his knights.

The ransom was guaranteed by the Valois royal family. Jean's second son Louis I, Duc d'Anjou took Jean's place in England while he returned to France to raise it. As a royal hostage, Louis was allowed complete freedom and, once Jean had left for France in 1362, he absconded. Jean, known as the "Good", appalled that his word had been broken, immediately returned to England. Warmly welcomed, he remained a respected prisoner until his death in April 1364. Even by 14th century standards of chivalry, his principled behaviour was excessive – it is more than possible that the frail and artistic Jean was simply tired of being king.

Jean signed a truce with Edward, bringing about the virtual collapse of the French government. Jean's ransom was initially set at two million écus. Jean however, believed he was worth much more and honourably insisted that it be raised to four million. On 8 May 1358 a ransom agreement, the Treaty of London, was signed.

The Second Treaty of London was signed between England and France on 24 March 1359. Normandy, Brittany, Anjou, Maine and all the coastline from Flanders to Spain were ceded to England, fully restoring the former Angevin Empire. Surrender of such huge tracts of territory caused the French Estates-General (Parliament) to repudiate the treaty, resulting in another English invasion, at Calais on 28 October. The treaty, renegotiated at Brétigny, near Chartres, was finally signed on 8 May 1360.

Brétigny represented the high watermark of English supremacy in France and ended the first phase of the Hundred Years' War. The treaty did not lead to lasting peace but did ensure a nine-year lull. In order to raise even a reduced ransom for King Jean II (over £3 billion today), France tripled taxes on salt and wine and introduced a hearth tax.

From 1362–72 the Black Prince served as his father's representative as Prince of Aquitaine, where he and Joan maintained a brilliant and extravagant court. It attracted the exiled Kings James of Majorca and Pedro (the "Cruel") of Castile – who had been ousted by his illegitimate brother, Enrique of Trastamara in 1367. Pedro offered Prince Edward the lordship of Biscay in

The Battle of Nájera (or Navarrete) was fought on 3 April 1367 between English and Franco-Castilian forces, in the province of La Rioja in Castile. It was the first battle of the Hundred Years' War in which the English attacked dismounted French troops. Used for the first time in Spain, the English longbow again proved lethal.

return for his help in recovering his throne: which Edward won back for him at Nájera. Edward demanded and was given the "Black Prince's Ruby", now in the front of the Imperial State Crown of Britain, after the battle.

By 1365 the Black Prince's rule in Gascony had become autocratic and burdensome. Exorbitant taxation led leading Gascons to appeal to Charles V, Jean II's son who had succeeded him the year before. Having never personally renounced his sovereignty over Gascony, Charles launched a guerilla war against the English. By 1374 the rapid decline in the health of the Black Prince enabled Charles to recover all of France except Calais and Aquitaine, effectively vitiating the Treaty of Brétigny.

The Black Prince returned to England in January 1373 – to die from a long, wasting illness that may have been cancer, three years later. His name and impressive tomb in Canterbury Cathedral has led a surprising number of modern day tourists to ask if England had an African population in the Middle Ages.

The Burghers of Calais in Victoria Tower Gardens, London, was completed by Auguste Rodin (1840–1917) in 1888. It was purchased by the British Government in 1911

After the Battle of Crécy on 26 August 1346, Edward III laid siege to Calais. Philip VI of France ordered the town to hold out at all costs; but in August 1347 starvation forced the city to parley for surrender. Edward offered to spare the town if six of its leading citizens surrendered to him. Edward demanded that they walk out almost naked, with nooses around their necks and carrying the keys to the town and castle. One of the richest, Eustache de Saint Pierre, volunteered first and five other burghers soon followed suit. Edward's queen, Philippa of Hainault, persuaded her husband to spare them, arguing that his clemency would be a good omen for her unborn child.

King Edward defeated a Scottish army at Neville's Cross near Durham on 17 October 1346.

English occupation of Calais ended on 1 January 1558. Francis, 2nd Duke of Guise, successfully attacked a weakened garrison manning decayed fortifications. When the dying Queen Mary I of England heard the news she said: "If my heart is opened there will be found graven upon it the word Calais".

The Welsh painter Gwen John (1876–1939), Augustus John's more gifted sister, became Rodin's model and mistress aged twenty-seven. He was sixty-three.

The Scots, in response to a plea for help from the French, had thought the north of England would be undefended because of the war in France. It was a disastrous miscalculation. King David II of Scotland was captured; the English occupied most of his kingdom south of the Forth and the Clyde; and took possession of the Isle of Man.

The bubonic plague known as the Black Death arrived in England in 1348: and over the next two years it killed a third of the population. Nevertheless Edward persisted in small scale skirmishing in France, beginning in 1355 with an unsuccessful expedition from Calais but ending with victory at Poitiers in 1356. He harried the Scots in a scorched-earth campaign known as the Burned

Candlemas in the same year. In 1357, under the terms of the Treaty of Berwick, Edward took the formal surrender of Scotland and released King David. He had been a captive in England for eleven years. Edward's military successes were won despite continuing outbreaks of the plague – but by the early 1350s it had already caused over a million deaths out of a population of about five. The ensuing shortage of labour caused great economic and social distress. Crude attempts were made by Parliament to control prices by legislation.

In 1332 Parliament was divided into Lords and Commons and established at Westminster. Thirty years later all its business was conducted in English. By 1360 Justices of the Peace had become formally known by that name. As the wars in France had depleted his treasury, from 1350 Edward began to cast envious eyes on the wealth of the Church. The Statutes of Provisors in 1351 and Præmunire in 1353 enabled him to extract valuable concessions from the clergy. In 1366 he consolidated these by making it clear that he would brook no interference from the papacy in Rome.

Edward reacted to Charles V's constructive repudiation of the Treaty of Brétigny by once again assuming the title "King of France". A pressing shortage of funds however, Edward's own failing health and a resurgence of French nationalism, all conspired to thwart his attempts to shore up the rapidly deteriorating English position across the Channel. The Black Prince was now an invalid and had returned to England in 1373: leaving his younger brother John of Gaunt to make a last stumbling raid on Bordeaux later that year. Obliged to come to terms in 1375, after all his French exertions Edward was left only with Calais, Bordeaux, Bayonne and Brest – and even Brest was lost in 1397.

With the death of Queen Philippa on 15 August 1369, the fifty-six year-old Edward fell under the influence of his grasping twenty-one year-old mistress Alice Perrers.

By 1374 John of Gaunt had returned from campaigning in France and King Edward found himself drifting between the competing influences of his two youngest sons. With the help of Alice Perrers, Gaunt's party became ascendant: but so corrupt was his administration that it provoked the "Good" Parliament of 1376. Led by the Speaker of the House of Commons Peter de la Mare, a knight representing Hereford, members banished Alice Perrers and impeached several of Gaunt's followers – the first impeachments ever recorded in Parliament. By the time of King Edward's death however, at Sheen Palace on 21 June 1377, Gaunt was firmly back in power.

Edward III was a likeable, glamorous king of extraordinary vigour and a brave soldier. More of a gallant knight than a skilful general, Edward's campaigns lacked cohesion and many of his victories were wasted. His unceasing requirement for resources to sustain his wars imbued Parliament with a growing confidence and influence. Unfortunately, Edward's superficiality and extravagance outweighed his ambition and talents, resulting in a reign that must ultimately be judged a failure.

SIR JOHN HAWKWOOD

Hawkwood, the second son of a tanner in Sible Hedingham in Essex, was an English *condottieri* (mercenary). From 1363–90 he hired out his "White Company" to several Italian states – and the pope. Little is known of his early life or even the date of his birth, but it is likely that he fought in the early campaigns of the Hundred Years' War: and that either King Edward III or the Black Prince knighted him. In 1360, although the Treaty of Brétigny had ended hostilities, Hawkwood decided to remain in France, seeking mercenary employment. By 1364 he was captain-general of the White Company, an English mercenary force in the service of Pisa. The White Company was a disciplined and mobile infantry unit of veteran, lightly armoured long-bowmen. Hawkwood prospered by switching sides when it suited. Italian city states preferred to spend their money on trade and did not maintain standing armies, employing mercenaries when the need arose. Hawkwood became a master of the double cross, playing off one set of employers against another.

In 1369 Hawkwood fought for Perugia against the Papal States. In 1372 he was retained by Bernabò Visconti, Lord of Milan in his war against the Marquis of Monferrato and his allies Pisa and Florence. Shortly afterwards, Hawkwood transferred his loyalties to the pope. In 1368 he had attended the second marriage of Edward III's son Lionel of Antwerp to the daughter of Galeazzo II Visconti in Milan, which was attended by the literati of the age: Petrarch, Jean Froissart and Geoffrey Chaucer.

Hawkwood married Visconti's illegitimate daughter Donnina in 1377. The following year he became captain-general of Florence, only fighting for other clients when his services were not needed by the Florentine republic. In 1381 King Richard II of England appointed him

Funerary Monument to Sir John Hawkwood, a fresco by Paolo Uccello
Duomo, Florence

ambassador to the Vatican. In 1382 however, he bought estates near Florence and lived instead as an honorary, pensioned Florentine citizen. By all accounts, Hawkwood was sharp but almost illiterate, leaving his wife to attend to his commercial and private business.

He was known as Giovanni Acuto by the Italians and Jean Haccoude by the French. Hawkwood, intending to retire to England, died suddenly on 16 March 1394. He was buried in the Duomo at Florence with full state honours. In 1436 the Florentines commissioned Paolo Uccello to paint a monochrome fresco of Hawkwood, which is still in place in the Duomo. In Sible Hedingham his name is commemorated by a memorial chapel and a Hawkwood Road. He was a remarkable man of his times.

KING RICHARD II OF ENGLAND (REIGNED 1377–99)

King Richard II by unknown artist (late 16th century)
National Portrait Gallery, London

Richard of Bordeaux, later King Richard II of England, was born in Bordeaux on 6 January 1367. He was the surviving son of Edward, the Black Prince and Joan of Kent. His grandfather was Edward III. His father died in 1376, followed a year later by his grandfather, leaving Richard to inherit the crown at the age of ten. Until he was sixteen his uncle, John of Gaunt, 2nd Duke of Lancaster, ruled as his *de facto* regent. Gaunt's administrative incompetence, the costly prosecution of the Hundred Years' War with France, another unpopular poll tax and the economic consequences of the Black Death, culminated in the Peasants' Revolt of 1381.

The Peasants' Revolt was the first popular uprising in England. It was ignited by ill-considered and arbitrary efforts to raise a third poll tax. Poll taxes, levied on every man alike, had fuelled a long simmering resentment since the Statute of Labourers in 1351. This legislation attempted to limit wage claims inflated by severe labour shortages caused by the Black Death. The revolt flared in May 1381, originating in south-east England. On 13 June, led by Wat Tyler, Jack Straw and John Ball, a horde of peasants and malcontents from many walks of life, converged on London.

John Ball was a populist "hedge priest", without a parish, who practised the Lollard doctrines of John Wycliffe and called for social justice. After the rebels had dispersed, Ball was captured in Coventry. On 15 July 1381 he was hanged, drawn and quartered at St Albans, in the presence of Richard II.

Ball had been released from Maidstone prison by Kentish rebels when the uprising began – he then preached an open-air sermon at Blackheath to them, that famously included: "When Adam delved and Eve span, who was then the gentleman?".

On 14 June the rebels burned the Savoy Palace, home of the hated John of Gaunt, and stormed the Tower of London. They killed the two officials hiding there who were responsible for the poll tax: the Lord Chancellor and Simon of Sudbury, Archbishop of Canterbury, as well as the Lord Treasurer, Robert de Hales. It was at this point that the fourteen year-old King Richard met Wat Tyler at Mile End and promised to abolish the poll tax and end serfdom. He agreed to meet the rebels at Smithfield the next day.

Richard arrived with his entourage at the appointed hour. Wat Tyler unwisely left his peasant army, to meet the king alone. Tyler rode up on a little horse, dismounted and, half bending, shook the king's hand heartily, saying: "Brother, be of good comfort and joyful, for you shall have, in the fortnight to come, forty thousand more commons than you have at present, and we shall be good comrades". The royal party took offence at his presumption and for not taking his hat off. Surrounded, Tyler was stabbed by the Lord Mayor of London, the Fishmonger Sir William Walworth (died 1385) – and then run through the stomach fatally, by Ralph de Standish, a royal attendant.

Richard II is said to have invented the pocket handkerchief. "Little pieces [of cloth] for the lord King to wipe and clean his nose", appear in his Household Rolls or accounts, which is the first documented mention of them.

Richard showed great courage by riding out to confront the peasant army, shouting: "You shall have no Captain but me". Richard lied that he had knighted Tyler, who would meet them at St John's Fields with all their terms satisfied. Richard broke this promise too and his barons met the rebels with a hastily assembled militia, capturing John Ball and Jack Straw, who were tried and executed. The poll tax was reinstated.

On 20 January 1382 Richard married Anne of Bohemia (1366–94) at St Stephen's Chapel, Westminster. She was the daughter of the Holy Roman Emperor, Charles IV. Anne brought no dowry: quite the reverse. Richard had to pay her brother Wenceslas 20,000 florins for her hand and the union produced no diplomatic or trade benefits – or children. The narcissistic Richard grew to love Anne though: on her death from plague on 7 June 1394 at Sheen Palace, Richard had it burned to the ground.

In the late 1380s, Richard began to surround himself with a clique of ambitious young friends and counsellors, who were resentful and jealous of the power wielded by John of Gaunt. In 1386 Gaunt sailed for Spain with a large fleet to pursue his claim to the kingdom of Castile – which exposed England to the threat of an imminent French invasion. Richard's chancellor, Sir Michael de la Pole found himself obliged to ask Parliament for unaffordable sums of money to fortify the south coast.

Robert de Vere (1362–92) was Richard's lover. Originally the 9th Earl of Oxford, Richard created de Vere Marquess of Dublin and Duke of Ireland. He was the first English marquess and the first English duke not of royal birth. De Vere was loathed by the barons: and Richard's questionable relationship with him was one of the reasons the Lords Appellant emerged to oppose the king. De Vere was exiled by Parliament in 1388 and his lands were confiscated. In 1392 he was seriously injured by a wild boar while hunting in Flanders and died of his wounds. In 1395 Richard had his embalmed body brought back to England for burial. During the funeral, the coffin was opened to allow Richard to kiss the corpse.

England has had five kings who were homosexual: William II, Edward II, Richard II, James I and William III. Edward and James fulfilled their dynastic duties however, and had children. Other kings of England were promiscuous to the point of incontinence. Only in the last hundred years has such self-gratification become unacceptable.

Such was the outrage that greeted this unprecedented demand that Parliament called for de la Pole's resignation. Richard refused to cooperate and won the support of the Royal Courts whose judges confirmed his sovereign powers. A civil war in all but name ensued, with an ignominious outcome for Richard: after which his opponents, calling themselves the Lords Appellant, won control of London and Parliament.

On 19 December 1387 Richard's unpopular favourite Robert de Vere, Earl of Oxford, was defeated at Radcot Bridge in Oxfordshire by the Lords Appellant under the command of Henry of Bolingbroke (later King Henry IV).

A so called "Merciless" Parliament purged the Royal Courts, dismissing and executing several of Richard's allies. By 1389 however, the Appellant tide had turned and Richard regained his authority, on the promise of better governance and fewer taxes.

With his pride deeply wounded by his clash with the Lords Appellant, Richard sought to recover his stature by instigating an exaggerated cult of kingship. He demanded subservient forms of address and insisted that his supporters wear a badge from his coat of arms displaying a white hart. He also conducted elaborate ceremonies in a reconstructed Westminster Hall, designed to invest his monarchy with a mystical, almost religious aura.

In 1394–95 Richard took an army to Ireland where he confirmed his autocratic reputation by demanding both tribute and homage from the Irish High-Kings (chieftains). Bolstered by his apparent success in achieving Irish subjugation, Richard now tried to apply the same brand of high-handed royal authority to England.

In July 1397 Richard took his revenge on the Lords Appellant by executing or exiling their leaders. In February 1399 John of Gaunt died: Richard seized his vast estates and exiled his son Henry of Bolingbroke. Richard then returned to Ireland to put down a new rebellion. He was still in Ireland in July, when Bolingbroke landed in Yorkshire.

Winning over the Earl of Northumberland, Bolingbroke began a triumphal progress across England, attracting immediate acclaim from barons outraged by Richard's behaviour and angered by his attempts to curb their powers. Meanwhile, Richard had delayed too long in Ireland: and by the time he returned to England in early August 1399, all support for him had evaporated. On the 15 August, at Conwy Castle in Wales, Richard had no choice but to surrender to the Earl of Northumberland – who passed him quickly into the custody of Bolingbroke, his first cousin once removed. Imprisoned in the Tower of London, on 29 September 1399 Richard abdicated. The following day a formal statement was approved by Parliament and an act of deposition was passed. Richard was taken from the Tower and imprisoned in Pontefract Castle. Bolingbroke immediately assumed the throne as King Henry IV.

In January 1400 the Earls of Huntingdon, Kent and Salisbury, all now stripped of their rank, rebelled in the Epiphany Rising: an attempt to restore Richard to his throne by killing Henry IV and his sons. Forewarned of the plot, which had received little support, Henry had the conspirators seized and executed. Richard alive, was clearly a liability: and by 14 February he was dead. There is some evidence to show that he was starved, or starved himself to death. In his will, Richard had expressed a wish to be buried in a tomb at Westminster which he had designed himself in 1395. Henry had him buried in a Dominican priory at Kings Langley instead. In early December 1413, to make Henry IV's usurpation more palatable, his son King Henry V ordered Richard to be reburied at Westminster – next to the tomb of his loving friend, Queen Anne.

Richard was said to be tall, fair, handsome and widely read: patronising the early English poets, Geoffrey Chaucer (*c.*1340–1400) and John Gower (*c.*1330–1408).

PUB TALK

In 1393 King Richard II legislated to enforce public houses to erect signs indicating their status as alehouses. Claimants to the title of oldest pub in England include *Ye Olde Trip to Jerusalem* in Nottingham (1189); *Ye Old Fighting Cocks* in St Albans, where the foundations date back to 793; and *The Bell Inn* at Finedon in Northamptonshire – there has been an inn on the site, which is not quite the same thing, since 1042.

The village of Colnbrook however, should be more agreeably remembered as the birthplace of brewer and amateur horticulturist Richard Cox: who crossed a Blenheim Orange and a Ribston Pippin *c.*1825 to create his wonderful Cox's Orange Pippin eating apple – the only apple with pips that rattle.

The Ostrich at Colnbrook in Berkshire claims to be the third oldest pub in England. King John is said to have stayed here on his way to seal *Magna Carta* at Runnymede in 1215. It has another, gruesome reason to be remembered: for its 17th century landlord, Thomas Jarman. He and his wife designed a bed in their best guest room, which was nailed to a trap door above the kitchen. Whenever a rich enough traveller stayed the night and had gone to sleep, Jarman tipped him into a cauldron of boiling water placed below the trap door; and disposed of the corpse in the nearby river. Their last victim, of perhaps sixty, was Thomas Cole: whose valuable horse was found wandering loose, without any sign of its owner. The river subsequently became known as the Colnbrook – and the Jarmans were hanged.

Richard's personal emblem, a White Hart (from heorot, Old English for "stag") became so universal as an inn sign in his reign that it became virtually interchangeable with "inn" itself – as in "biro" or "hoover" today. In a recent CAMRA list of the most popular pub names in Britain: 704 were named Crown, 688 Red Lion (from the coat of arms of King James I of England and VI of Scotland), 541 Royal Oak (the tree the future King Charles II hid in after the Battle of Worcester in 1651), 451 Swan – and, in fifth place with 431, White Hart.

• **The Wilton Diptych (Reverse)** (*c.*1395–99)
National Portrait Gallery, London

The Cock and *The Bull* are two ancient inns in Stony Stratford in Buckinghamshire. Tipsy 18th century guests are said to have swapped such unlikely travellers tales that such embellishments entered the English language as "Cock and Bull stories".

THE MEDIÆVAL MACHINE GUN: THE ENGLISH LONGBOW

The earliest longbow found in England is dated to 2665 BC; but there are no surviving mediæval longbows that can be dated with certainty to the period when the longbow was dominant (1330–1450). It was in the nature of bows to become weaker, break and be replaced, rather than be handed down through generations. However over 3,500 arrows and 137 longbows were recovered from the *Mary Rose*, pride of Henry VIII's navy that sank at Portsmouth in 1545. It is an important source for the history of the longbow, as the bows, archery implements and the skeletons of archers have been preserved. Skeletons of longbow archers are recognisably deformed, with enlarged left arms and often bone spurs on left wrists, left shoulders and right fingers.

Mediæval bows range in length from 4 feet 1 inch to 6 feet 11 inches. They were made from yew if it could be obtained, although ash and other woods were also used. The original draw forces of examples from the *Mary Rose* were estimated at 160–180 lbf (pounds of draw force). A modern longbow's draw is typically 60 lbf or less – much the same as 14th century hunting bows, which is enough for all but the largest game. There are few modern long-bowmen capable of using 180 lbf bows accurately. In its day, the longbow was amazingly accurate, firing arrows at up to 150 mph. An archer could kill a person at 250 yards and even birds on the wing. Equally, it could be used as an 'area' weapon, like a machine gun, for a flight of arrows would always hit an army.

A Welsh or English military archer during the 14th and 15th centuries was expected to shoot at least ten 'aimed shots' per minute, an experienced one up to twenty. He would be provided with between 60 and 72 arrows, which would last from three to six minutes at full rate. Young boys were often employed to run additional arrows to archers while on the battlefield.

An English longbow made of yew, 6 ft 6 in long, with a 105 lbf draw force

This rate was much higher than the crossbow. It was also much higher than early firearms. Though their construction took up to four years, longbows would last a long time if protected with a water-resistant coating of "wax, resin and fine tallow". Bow strings were made of hemp, flax or silk.

On the battlefield, English archers stabbed their arrows upright into the ground at their feet, reducing the time it took to notch, draw and loose (as drawing from a quiver is slower). An additional effect of this practice was that the point of an arrow would be more likely to cause infection. Hardened steel long bodkin arrow heads, with four cutting edges, were capable of piercing chain mail. Short bodkins, used for piercing armour plate, were not so effective, but did terrible damage to less well-protected horses.

31-inch "cloth-yard" shafts were used (one yard of cloth). The only way to remove such an arrow cleanly was to tie a piece of linen, soaked in boiling water or another sterilising substance, to the end of it and push it back through the wound – which was extremely painful. Specialised tools were used when bone prevented the arrow being pushed through.

In much the same way that 18th century Royal Navy stripped England of most of her oak trees, the trade in English yew wood for longbows depleted stocks over huge areas. In 1470 hazel, ash, and laburnum were allowed for practice bows.

The Statute of Westminster in 1472 required every ship arriving at an English port to carry four bowstaves per tun: Richard III increased this to ten. This stimulated supplies, mostly from Spain but also Saxony, Bavaria and Austria. By the late 16th century it seems that no more mature trees were to be had – but by then bows were being replaced by guns.

During the Anglo-Norman invasions of Wales, Welsh bowmen took a heavy toll of the invaders. The English were quick to realise the longbow's effectiveness and, as soon as the campaign was won, Welsh conscripts were incorporated into English armies. Edward I banned all sports but archery on Sundays. The most decisive battles won by English bowmen were Dupplin Moor in 1332 and Halidon Hill the following year during the Scottish wars; and Crécy in 1346, Poitiers in 1356 and Agincourt in 1415 – all in the Hundred Years' War. For over 120 years, the longbow was the most effective and intimidating weapon of war in Western Europe.

There is a long-held belief that the "two-fingers salute" or "V sign" derives from the Battle of Agincourt in 1415, when it is said that the French cut off the two shooting fingers on the right hand of captured English archers – and that the gesture was a sign of defiance from those who were not mutilated.

This however, is unlikely – the first known reference to the "V-sign" is to be found in the works of Rabelais, the 16th century French satirist. Furthermore, archers were commoners and usually executed when captured. When offering the Churchillian "V for Victory" sign, it is important to do so with the palm of the hand reversed.

COINS IN CIRCULATION IN MEDIÆVAL ENGLAND

In the 15th century, one sixth of £1 (three old shillings and fourpence) was called a crown; one third of £1 (six shillings and eightpence) was called a noble; two thirds (thirteen shillings and fourpence) was called a mark; and a groat was fourpence.

First issued in 1279, the farthing (one quarter of an old penny) was demonetised in 1960. The lowest denomination coin ever issued was the copper quarter farthing. It seems extraordinary that a coin worth 3,840 to the £ could have been much needed: but they were minted from 1839–53, chiefly for use in Ceylon (modern Sri Lanka).

The Office of National Statistics gives these price comparisons: £1 in 1264 was worth £525 in 2008, using the Retail Price Index (RPI) as the determinant. In startling contrast, the same £ would have been worth £11,800, using "average earnings". The only investments through the ages that could ever have matched this increase in value are land and property.

THE BLACK DEATH WAS THE MOST DEADLY PANDEMIC IN HUMAN HISTORY

Originating in Central Asia, the plague known as the "Black Death" spread to Europe from the Crimea in the late 1340s. The total number of deaths worldwide is estimated at 75 million: 20 to 30 million in Europe alone, up to 40% of the population.

The plague returned to Europe every generation, with varying degrees of virulence until the late 1700s. During this period, more than a hundred outbreaks swept across the continent. On its return to England in 1603, it killed 38,000 Londoners; and in the Great Plague of 1665, over 100,000. There is controversy over the cause and precise identity of the disease: most commentators are still convinced that it was carried by rats infested with fleas, which transmitted the bacillus to humans; and that it was spread on the breath of infected victims. However it seems to have disappeared from Europe after the 1771 outbreak in Moscow.

The terrible loss of life had a drastic effect, irrevocably changing Britain's social structure. Unable to explain its origins, the Church was blamed for failing to control it; and Jews, foreigners, beggars and lepers for spreading it. The uncertainty of daily survival created a general mood of morbidity influencing people to "live for the moment", as illustrated by Giovanni Boccaccio in 1353, in *The Decameron*.

The Black Death is said to have inspired the nursery rhyme "Ring a-Ring o' Roses, a pocket full of posies, A-tishoo a-tishoo, we all fall down". However, there is no written record of the rhyme before 1881: and if it refers to the plague at all, it is likely to be the Great Plague of London in 1665.

The plague was first reported in the Black Sea trading cities of Constantinople and Trebizond in 1347. In 1346, the same year as Crécy, Caffa (now Feodisya), a Genoese commercial enclave on the Crimean peninsula, had been invested by a Mongol army and their Venetian allies. After a protracted siege, during which the their army was reportedly decimated by the disease, the Mongols used the bodies of their dead as a biological weapon. The corpses were catapulted over the city walls, infecting the inhabitants. It is said that so many died in Caffa that the bodies were stacked like cords of firewood against the city walls. The Genoese traders took to their ships without further ado, accompanied by the rats and fleas that carried the disease.

In October 1347 the Genoese fleet fleeing from Caffa reached Messina in Sicily. All the crew members were either infected or dead. Some ships were found grounded on beaches, with no one aboard alive. Looting also spread the disease. From Sicily the plague reached Genoa, Venice and Marseilles by the end of 1347. The disease spread north-west across Europe, striking France, Spain, Portugal and England by June 1348, then turned and spread east through Germany and Scandinavia from 1348 to 1350.

Finally it spread to Russia in 1351. For some reason the plague largely spared Milan, the Kingdom of Poland and parts of Navarre and the Low Countries.

There was no effective response to the crisis anywhere in Europe. In 1348 the plague spread so rapidly that, before physicians or governments had time to react, about a third of the population had already perished. In crowded cities it was not uncommon for as much as fifty percent of the population to die. Rural populations in isolated areas suffered less: but

The Mongol Empire (1206–1405) was the largest contiguous empire in world history. By 1279 it covered nearly 12.75 million square miles (22% of Earth's total land area); and ruled over 100 million people. Chinggis (or Genghis) Khan's great general, Subutai (1176–1248) penetrated deep into Europe, overrunning Hungary and Poland. It was only the death of Ögedei, the third son of Chinggis Khan who had succeeded his father, that prevented Subutai from reaching Germany and France in 1241. All Mongol commanders had to return home to bury their leader.

A little-known Englishman, a one-time priest, Templar and a linguist, known only as Robert "de London" (*c.*1188–1242) is said to have been a key agent of the Mongols. He was executed – for reasons that are as shadowy as details of his life.

THE ADVANCE OF
THE BLACK DEATH
ACROSS EUROPE (1346–51)

1346–47

1348

1349–50

1351

No cases

The Peasants' revolt (1381) and other 14th century uprisings in Europe

by ship from Gascony (midsummer 1348)

English Gascony

Crimea (1346)

by ship from the Crimea (October 1347)

Edinburgh
Dublin
London
Melcombe Regis
Bruges
Lübeck
Brunswick
Magdeburg
Warsaw
Frankfurt
Prague
Paris
Vienna
Lyons
Milan
Venice
Bucharest
Genoa
Constantinople
Marseilles
Barcelona
Rome
Toledo
Naples
Athens
Cordoba
Messina
Algiers
Tunis

0   300 miles

0   300 km

THE 'BLACK DEATH' ENTERED ENGLAND IN 1348 THROUGH THIS PORT.

IT KILLED 30–50% OF THE COUNTRY'S TOTAL POPULATION

Plaque in Melcombe Regis (now Weymouth) recording the arrival of the Black Death

monasteries and priests were especially hard hit, since they cared for the victims. Because 14th century healers were at a loss in explaining the plague, Europeans turned to astrological forces, earthquakes, and the poisoning of wells by Jews as possible reasons for its emergence. No one even considered rat control: instead people came to believe that only God's wrath could inflict such a disaster.

Disease and famine, due to the inability to sow and harvest crops or tend livestock, left England prostrate. The country had been at war first with Scotland, depleting the treasuries of both nations, and

In 1998 the *Washington Post* carried a report that a scientific team, studying an unusual genetic mutation, had concluded that 14th century survivors of the Black Death might have bequeathed resistance to HIV to their descendants. Genetic mutations emerge strictly by chance and are typically carried by no more than 1% of a population at any given time. A team at the National Cancer Institute discovered a mutation in immune system macrophages. Individuals who inherit this mutant gene from both parents are effectively devoid of the receptor and are immune to HIV. Those with one mutant and one normal version of the gene may be infected with HIV, but are more likely to have a shorter course of the disease than individuals lacking the mutation. It is possible that up to 10% of the white European population carries one or more of these mutant genes; the greatest concentration exists in Sweden, where 14% of the population carry them. Mutant genes become rarer moving south and east from northern Europe; and is nonexistent among East Asians, Africans, and American Indians. Results of the study were featured in the *American Journal of Human Genetics* (1998).

then with France for ten years since 1337, normally an exporter of grain to England. Shipments from elsewhere were difficult to obtain.

It can be argued that the Black Death was a blessing in disguise. The plague did more than just devastate the mediæval population. The Church had been unable to alleviate the symptoms of the disease or care for the dying, leaving it vulnerable to reform. England had been overpopulated before the plague: but an initial reduction of 30% to 50% was followed by further population declines until 1420. To limit inflationary wage increases and the mobility of workers, the *Ordinance of Labourers* in 1349 and the *Statute of Labourers* in 1351 were enacted. 7,556 people in Essex were fined for ignoring the latter in 1352. These measures were extremely unpopular and led directly to the Peasants' Revolt in 1381.

The law of supply and demand however, inevitably drove landlords to compete for workers through wages and freedoms – a competition which watered the roots of a capitalist economy.

The reason so many churches are today a mile or so from villages in parts of England, especially the East Midlands, is that after the plague the few survivors burned their houses to the ground, to avoid reinfection, and rebuilt them elsewhere.

In gaining more bargaining power, workers were able to exchange annual contracts in favour of temporary work that offered higher wages.

The Black Death may also account for Western Europe's 250-year lead in scientific, political and social development over the East. Sparsely populated Russia and her neighbours were less affected; and social mobility did not increase as it did in the West. Moves to liberalise society and government, by restricting the power of the monarch and aristocracy, did not occur. England had ended serfdom well before 1500, while moving towards representative government. Russia did not abolish serfdom until 1861.

The vast areas of farmland that were left untended became available for pasture, increasing wool, meat, milk and cheese production. Middle class food on the table however, did not mean that proletarian aspirations to better themselves became acceptable. Sumptuary laws were introduced across western Europe to regulate what people could wear, and even eat, to ensure that peasants did not try to ape their superiors.

Social mobility as a result of the Black Death has been postulated as a cause of the "Great Vowel Shift", which spread out from London; and which is the principal reason why modern English pronunciation no longer reflects its spelling. In Middle English the "a" in date was pronounced as in modern dart; the "e" in feet was pronounced as in modern fate; the "i" in wipe was pronounced as in modern weep; the double "o" in boot was pronounced as in modern boat; and the "ou" in house was pronounced as in modern whose.

Danse Macabre, an allegory on the universality of death, was inspired by the Black Death. This book illustration was by Michael Wolgemut in 1493

JOHN "OF GAUNT"

John of Gaunt, Duke of Lancaster (1340–99),
the third surviving son of King Edward III and
Philippa of Hainault, was born in Ghent (then
pronounced Gaunt) in Flanders. Fabulously
rich from his first wife's Lancaster inheritance,
Gaunt exercised enormous influence during
the minority of his nephew, Richard II: but
ever cautious, he was careful not to associate
openly with opponents of the King. He is
relevant to English history only for the number
of ambitious children he sired. All British
monarchs, following the accession of Henry
VII in 1485, descend from Gaunt: through
Henry's daughter Margaret Tudor, the great-
grandmother of James VI of Scotland who
became James I of England.

Gaunt's legitimate heirs were from his first
marriage to Blanche (c.1346–68), heiress to the
vast estates of Henry, 1st Duke of Lancaster,
descending through their eldest son who
usurped the throne of Richard II to become
King Henry IV in 1399. This line ended with
the death of Edward, Prince of Wales, the only
son of Henry VI, at Tewkesbury on 4 May 1471.

Gaunt's illegitimate descendants, from his
mistress Katherine Swynford, included his
great-granddaughter Margaret Beaufort (1443-
–1509). She married Edmund Tudor, 1st Earl of
Pembroke in 1455 and her son, who killed
Richard III at Bosworth Field to usurp the
throne, became King Henry VII in 1485.

Gaunt's legitimate children included
Philippa, wife of King John I of Portugal, from
Blanche of Lancaster; and Katherine, daughter
of his second wife Constance (1354–94).
Constance was the daughter of Pedro of
Castile. Katherine's marriage to Henry II of
Castile ended a dynastic conflict within the
royal house of Castile and her son became
King John II. Until Katherine married Henry,
Gaunt had pursued a claim of his own *jure
uxoris* (by the right of his wife) to the throne of
Castile. Despite his lack of success, he insisted
thereafter that he was addressed as "my lord of
Spain".

The most renowned Gaunt D of Lancaster Leicester. Lincolne tenant of Aquitaine Prince John of Earle of Richmont and Darbye. Liuetenant of Aquitaine He died 1399.

Katherine Swynford, *née* de Roet (1350–1403),
was the daughter of Paen de Roet, a Flemish
herald who came to England in the service of
Philippa of Hainault, wife of King Edward III. In
c.1366 Katherine married Hugh Swynford, a
Lincolnshire knight who died in 1372. She bore
him a son and two daughters.

In 1370 Katherine joined John of Gaunt's
household as governess to his two motherless
daughters, the sisters of the future King Henry
IV. By 1373 she was Gaunt's mistress, becoming
his third wife in 1396. Their three sons and a
daughter were given the surname Beaufort.
Though the Beauforts were legitimised by
Richard II in 1397, they were barred from
inheriting the throne by their half-brother Henry
IV. Henry VII however, a Beaufort descendant,
ignored this stipulation.

Katherine Swynford's sister Philippa
married Geoffrey Chaucer, whose poem *The Book
of the Duchess*, was written after Blanche of
Lancaster's death in 1369.

Gaunt was vain and had poor judgement. He was also a timid and unsuccessful soldier. When he died in 1399 his estates were confiscated by the crown, since Richard II had exiled Gaunt's less diplomatic heir, Henry of Bolingbroke the year before. Bolingbroke returned and deposed Richard, to reign as King Henry IV from 1399–1413, the first of Gaunt's descendants to usurp the throne of England.

GEOFFREY CHAUCER

Geoffrey Chaucer was the most important English poet before Shakespeare. He served three kings as a trusted soldier, courtier, diplomat and civil servant. Born in 1342 into a prosperous middle class family in London, he first appears in the household rolls of Elizabeth de Burgh, first wife of Lionel of Antwerp, second surviving son of King Edward III. In 1360, during the siege of Rheims, Chaucer was captured and King Edward contributed to his ransom. In 1366 he was sent on a diplomatic mission to the King of Navarre, the first of many to the courts of Europe. In 1367 he married Philippa de Roet, lady in waiting to Queen Philippa, King Edward's wife. Nine years later he was a senior customs controller in London.

Chaucer's first significant work, *The Book of the Duchess*, was a 1,300 line elegy written for Blanche of Lancaster who had died of the plague It was based on *Roman de la Rose*, the classic 12th century French poem extolling courtly love. By 1375 he had written *Hous of Fame*. Influenced by Dante, Petrarch and Bocaccio, met while Chaucer was on an embassy to Italy, the work was incomplete. In 1385 he became Justice of the Peace for Kent; and in 1386 he was returned to Parliament as knight-of-the-shire.

Chaucer avoided being caught up in the intrigue and political upheaval of the 1380s when his patrons, King Richard II and John of Gaunt were confronted by a group of hostile barons calling themselves the Lords Appellant. It was during this difficult period that he composed *The Parlement of Foules*, *The Dream of Scipio*, *Troilus and Criseyde* and *The Legend of Good Women*. He prospered at court throughout the 1390s, receiving generous royal privileges. He had the foresight to befriend Gaunt's son, Henry of Bolingbroke, later Henry IV. On usurping the throne in 1399, Henry confirmed Chaucer in his royal perquisites.

It was during these last ten years of his life that Chaucer wrote his best known work, *The Canterbury Tales*. The setting is a pilgrimage to the shrine of St Thomas Becket at Canterbury Cathedral which sets out from the Tabard Inn in Southwark.

The subject is a story-telling contest between a group of pilgrims, drawn from various walks of life: reeve (magistrate), clerk, miller, lawyer, franklin (yeoman landowner), merchant, monk, wife, knight, pardoner (dealer in holy relics) and prioress. Although the work as a whole was incomplete, each tale can be read on its own.

The script, written in both verse and prose, addresses the contrast between the material temptations of this life with the exacting moral behaviour required for redemption in the next – very much a mediæval preoccupation. The narrator is Chaucer himself, somewhat disingenuous but fascinated by the frailty and ultimate tragedy of human existence. The Middle English that he wrote in is difficult to read fluently today: but the naturalism, observant narrative and earthy wit of his poetry helped to shape English literature.

Chaucer had four children: one became Duchess of Suffolk. He died on 25 October 1400 and was buried, as was his right as a resident, in Westminster Abbey. In 1556 his remains were re-interred in a fine tomb in what became known as "Poets' Corner".

Geoffrey Chaucer by unknown artist (after 1400)
National Portrait Gallery, London

The Wilton Diptych
(c.1395–99)
National Gallery, London

THE WILTON DIPTYCH

Portable diptychs were icons, commissioned by rich men as personal instruments of devotion. "The Wilton Diptych" is painted on two panels of Baltic oak, framed in the same wood and joined by two hinges so it may be closed to protect the paintings. When closed, it reveals on one side King Richard II's emblem, a white hart with a golden coronet around its throat; and a golden chain set on a gold field and black ground. On the other is a fictive (invented) coat-of-arms of Edward the Confessor, who died in 1066, impaled with the arms of England.

Although heraldic devices did not exist in the 11th century, Richard's coats-of-arms were in use from 1395 – the approximate date of the work.

The exquisite quality and style of the painting suggests that the artist was probably from Northern France. The diptych was first documented in 1649, in an inventory of King Charles I's art collection. It passed to the Earls of Pembroke who kept it at Wilton House, from which it takes its name, until it was bought by the National Gallery in 1929. That it remained intact is remarkable: very few religious images survived the Puritan iconoclasm of Oliver Cromwell's Commonwealth (1649–60). In this case it is all the more remarkable as the paintings illustrate King Richard's belief in his divine right to rule, as well as the ostentation of his Christian devotion.

A tiny map of England, within an orb over the cross of St George, may have been the inspiration for Shakespeare's reference to "this sceptr'd isle" (*Richard II*, Act 2).

BOTTOMS UP

Sir John Arderne (*c.*1308–92) remained the most celebrated English surgeon for 300 years. He is considered the founding father of Proctology or anal surgery. Said to have been born in Wiltshire, he moved to Newark in Nottinghamshire. By the end of his long life he was the Master Surgeon of the Guild of Surgeons in London. His speciality was an operative procedure to correct *fistula-in-ano* or "Knight's bottom", which afflicted many mediæval knights who spent too long in the saddle.

Many of his techniques are still used today. He adopted a Robin Hood approach to his patients, charging a rich man as much as he could bear while treating the poor for free. Arderne used opium, both as an internal and external anæsthetic, so that the patient "schal slepe so that he schal fele no kuttyng".

Anal fistulae appear between the base of the spine and the anus. They are caused by blocked anal glands forming an abscess which ruptures the skin, creating an alternative opening for evacuation of the bowels. The opening, or tract, formed by this process is called a fistula. If left unattended fistulae can split the *intestinum rectum*. The pilonidal cyst, as it is now described, then seals over, causing an accumulation of pus – which can lead to blood poisoning and death.

In 1376, the year before Edward III died, Arderne developed a procedure for cutting out fistulae, with an eighty percent success rate – and which is still consulted today. Arderne was immensely rich when he died.

Among the more ridiculous claims for the authorship of the music for *God Save the King* is one that the French Marquise de

THE ROYAL LINE OF ENGLAND FOR 333 YEARS (1066–1399)

William I

the Conqueror, King of England (1066–87)

Duke of Normandy; *William killed Harold (1066) and took the throne, ending Anglo-Saxon rule*; m. Matilda of Flanders (1053), having four sons and five daus.

William II

Rufus (1087–1100)

third son of William I; *William I's eldest son Robert "Curthose" was passed over for the throne and his second son Richard was killed by a stag in a hunting accident*

Henry I

Beauclerc (1100–35)

fourth son of William I; m. Matilda, dau. of David I, King of Scotland; *his only legitimate son drowned*

THE NORMANS

Stephen of Blois

(1135–54)

son of Adela, fifth dau. of William I; *to end England's first civil war, he agreed to be succeeded by Matilda's son*

Matilda

(1102–67)

dau. of Henry I; m. (2) Geoffrey, 5th Count of Anjou

Henry II

(1154–89)

m. (her 2) Eleanor of Aquitaine (1122–1204), having five sons and three daus. *(the eldest two sons died young)*

THE PLANTAGENETS (OR ANGEVINS)

Richard I

Coeur de Lion (1189–99)

(b.1157); no ch.

Geoffrey

(1158–86)

Arthur of Brittany

(1187–1203)

John

Lackland (1199–1216)

(b.1166); kidnapped and m. (2) Isabella of Angoulème (four ch.); *he murdered his nephew Arthur*

Henry III

(1216–72)

m. (1236) Eleanor of Provence (*c*.1223–91), two sons

Edward I

Longshanks (1272–1307)

m. (1254) Eleanor of Castile (1241–90), having had sixteen ch.; *he was King of Scotland (1296–1306)*

Edward II

(1307–27)

m. (1308) Isabella of France (1295–1358); two sons and two daus.; *created Prince of Wales (1301); murdered in Berkeley Castle*

Edward III

(1327–77)

m. (1328) Philippa of Hainault (d.1369), having five sons *(Thomas was murdered by Richard II)* and four surv. daus.

Edward

the Black Prince (1330–76)

m. Joan of Kent; *died before his father*

(2) Lionel of Antwerp

(1338–68)

m. (1352) Elizabeth de Burgh

(4) Edmund of Langley, Duke of York

(1341–1402)

m. (1372) Isabella of Castile (1355–92)

(3) John of Gaunt, Duke of Lancaster

(1340–99)

m. (1359) Blanche of Lancaster (*c*.1346–68) *died of the plague*

Richard II

(1377–99)

childless; murdered by Henry IV (1400)

Philippa Plantagenet

(1355–82)

m. (1368) Edmund Mortimer

Roger Mortimer, 4th Earl of March

(1374–98)

m. Eleanor of Kent, niece of Richard II (d.1405)

Anne Mortimer

(1390–1411)

m. (*c*.1406) her cousin Richard, Earl of Cambridge (1375–1415) *executed by King Henry V*

Henry IV

Bolingbroke (1399–1413)

Richard, 3rd Duke of York

(1411–60)

father of **Edward IV** and **Richard III**

Créquy mentions in her book *Souvenirs*: that the tune *Grand Dieu Sauve Le Roi*, was written by Jean-Baptiste Lully to celebrate the healing of Louis XIV's anal fistula. Credit for the melody is usually given to the organist and keyboard composer Doctor John Bull in 1619. No one knows who wrote the words; but as early as 1545 "God Save the King" was a watchword of the Royal Navy, with the response being, "Long to reign over us". Some verses of the modern song had been established by 1745 – after 1746 however, one verse lapsed into disuse:

Lord, grant that Marshal Wade,
*   May by thy mighty aid,*
Victory bring.
*   May he sedition hush and like a torrent rush,*
Rebellious Scots to crush,
*   God save the King.*

The dominance of Scotsmen in the Labour Cabinet in the early 21st century (two Prime Ministers and two Chancellors of the Exchequer in succession, among others) has encouraged some Englishmen to suggest that this verse should be reinstated.

KING HENRY IV ("BOLINGBROKE") OF ENGLAND (REIGNED 1399–1413)

Henry was born at Bolingbroke Castle in Lincolnshire in April 1367, the eldest surviving son of John of Gaunt, Duke of Lancaster by his first wife Blanche. Henry married Mary de Bohun in 1380; and, after her death in childbed, Joan of Navarre in 1403.

His first cousin Richard II, exactly the same age as himself, came to the throne in 1377: but Henry's father, John of Gaunt ruled England in his name until Gaunt sailed to Spain in 1386, to pursue a futile claim to the throne of Castile. The following year Henry supported the rebellion of five barons, known as the Lords Appellant, who defeated Richard's favourite Robert de Vere at Radcot Bridge. They maintained Richard as a figurehead with little real power, but exiled de Vere and dealt severely with most of his court. In 1389 Gaunt returned from Spain and forced a reconciliation between Richard and Henry. In 1390 Henry left England for two years to crusade with the Teutonic Knights against the pagan Lithuanians. In September 1392 he went on a pilgrimage to Jerusalem, returning to England in 1393.

Richard II had nurtured a ten-year grudge against the Lords Appellant: and in 1397 had the leading rebels, the Earls of Arundel, Gloucester and Warwick respectively executed, murdered and imprisoned. Henry was banished for ten years. On 13 October 1398 he sailed for France. Within six months, on 3 February 1399 John of Gaunt died. Richard foolishly provoked Henry by seizing his vast Lancastrian inheritance for himself.

Henry invaded England as the champion of a nobility whose lands were vulnerable to sequestration at royal whim. With the help of France, delighted to promote a civil war which would weaken the English hold on Aquitaine, Henry landed north of the Humber at Ravenspur in early July 1399. Richard had left for Ireland a month earlier, leaving England unprotected. Henry recruited an army from his old Lancastrian estates in north Yorkshire, reinforced by the Earl of Northumberland and many northern magnates. Richard dithered, returning to Milford Haven in late July to find that support for him had drained away. On 16 August Richard surrendered to the Earl of Northumberland at Conwy Castle; by 2 September he was a prisoner in the Tower of London; and, on 29 September, he was forced to abdicate. Henry IV

King Henry IV by unknown artist (late 16th Century)
National Portrait Gallery, London

Mary de Bohun (*c*.1369–94), barely twelve when she married, was the mother of King Henry V. His step-mother, Joan of Navarre (1370–1437) was accused of using witchcraft to poison him. In 1419 she was imprisoned for four years in Pevensey Castle in Sussex. Joan is buried in Canterbury Cathedral next to Henry IV.

was crowned on 13 October 1399 – his coronation address was the first since Harold II's in 1066 to be made in English.

Henry's reign was blighted by plots and revolts. The so-called Epiphany Rising, in January 1400, was betrayed and easily crushed: leading directly to King Richard II's death in Pontefract Castle, by murder or ill-treatment. A few months later Owain Glyn Dwr raised a successful rebellion in Wales, allying himself with Henry Percy, Earl of Northumberland and his son Sir Harry "Hotspur". On 21 July 1403 Henry defeated the Percys at the Battle of Shrewsbury, in which his son, later Henry V, suffered a near fatal wound from an arrow in the face. It was the only battle fought by Henry IV in person. In July 1405 Henry had Thomas Mowbray, heir to the 1st Duke of Norfolk executed, together with the Archbishop of York, Richard Scrope, for conspiring with the Percys to raise another rebellion. That year a French force landed in Wales to assist Owain Glyn Dwr, while the Scots carried out a series of border raids. In 1408 he had to deal with yet another rebellion led by the Percys.

Henry's warrior son, Prince Henry finally wore Glyn Dwr down: but only at a huge cost. With continual threats of French invasion there was no relief from demands on the royal purse. Relying wholly on parliamentary grants, Henry was charged with financial incompetence and soon obliged to yield to fiscal supervision by Parliament – and to surrender control over royal appointments. His frequent need to tap church funds obliged him in return to enact the dreadful *De hereticio comburendo* in 1401. In doing so he became the first English king to allow the burning of heretics, which was used in the suppression of the Lollards. Henry's health finally broke down: the painful symptoms that tormented him included epilepsy, leprosy, eczema and gout. Under the circumstances, it is remarkable that he lived to the age of forty-five.

> In 1406, just after his coronation, King James 1 of Scotland was captured by the English while sailing to France. Henry imprisoned him in the Tower of London: where he remained until in 1424, a ransom of £40,000 (£205 million today) was finally paid. His subsequent reign was harsh and unpopular. On 27 February 1437 he was murdered by Sir Robert Graham, in Perth.

It had long been predicted that Henry would die on crusade: and eerily, on 20 March 1413 he collapsed in the Jerusalem chamber of the Abbot of Westminster's house. He died so much in debt that his executors initially balked at the task of administering his will and his debts were never fully extinguished. Usurping, and keeping, the throne depended on reducing taxes and gifting huge tracts of land, principally to his Lancastrian supporters. This obliged him to fight his campaigns with insufficient funds. His greatest error was to allow Glyn Dwr's rebellion to drag on for so long and at such expense to his treasury. It became a financial cancer which eventually destroyed his ability to govern.

Henry was buried in Canterbury Cathedral, near the tomb of the Black Prince in Becket's chapel – he had been a lifelong devotee of the cult of St Thomas Becket. Queen Joan embellished his tomb with a life-size effigy in alabaster. In 1832 his tomb was opened: his face was said to be perfectly preserved, sporting a matted russet beard.

AGRICULTURE IN ENGLAND WAS TRANSFORMED BY ENCLOSURE

Enclosure was the process of hedging and walling communal land, returning it to exclusively private ownership. Common land was usually owned by one person but, by ancient right, had been traditionally enjoyed by others: to graze livestock, gather wood and mow for hay. Before enclosure, farmland was enjoyed by individual yeomen only during the growing season. After the harvest, the land was used by the community.

In England enclosures began in the 13th century, gathered pace from 1450–1640 and were completed only at the end of the 19th century. Demand from the wool trade gave impetus to enclosures: the looms of the Flemish weavers required high volumes of quality English wool, a market which could only be met by increasing farming efficiency of scale. While enclosures created great wealth, particularly in the wool-producing English counties, as evinced by the magnificent churches evident in every great wool town and county, poverty caused by the destruction of subsistence farming and the mass eviction of villagers, was a cause of real concern to the Crown. Enclosure led inevitably to the deterioration of manorial responsibility and reduced royal revenues; while at the same time creating a dispossessed pool of potential rebels and vagabonds. In the words of an anonymous 17th century ditty:

> They hang the man and flog the woman
>> That steals the goose from off the common;
> But let the greater villain loose,
>> That steals the common from the goose.

From 1348 enclosures were boosted by the devastation caused by the Black Death, which wiped out over a third of the English population: fewer peasants made enclosures both easier – and inevitable. From the reign of Henry VII until Cromwell's Commonwealth, there were eleven Acts of Parliament limiting enclosure; and eight Commissions of Enquiry, all largely ineffective. As the 16th century progressed, increased coinage to fund Henry VIII's extravagance, albeit debased, together with the flow of bullion from the New World, dramatically increased the national money supply: causing rampant inflation. Many landowners could only survive this squeeze on their margins by enclosing their lands – which then rose considerably in value.

In the 1660s wars in Flanders sharply reduced demand for English wool. Farm income slowly recovered over the next two hundred years, but only through the introduction of agricultural machines. The first of these, in 1701 was Jethro Tull's seed drill, made out of pieces of an old pipe organ: his horse-drawn drill could seed three rows at once.

Born in the same year as Tull (1674–1741), Charles, 2nd Viscount ("Turnip") Townsend (1674–1738) devised new methods of crop rotation and introduced root crops on his Norfolk estates. These obviated the need each autumn to slaughter livestock, which previously could not be fed through the winter, and allowed cattle to fertilise the land whilst it lay fallow. Taken together, these innovations transformed the profitability of large-scale farming – an evolutionary process that continues to the present day.

Enclosures peaked between 1760–1820: creating a landless working class in time to provide the labour required by the new coal, cotton and manufacturing industries opening up in the north of England. While many landowners became immensely rich, at the cost of misery suffered by farm workers suddenly deprived of their basic security, enclosure did put an end to the unceasing grind and poverty of subsistence farming – and contributed considerably to the prosperity of the nation as a whole.

THE SHEEP WAS ONCE AS VALUABLE TO ENGLAND AS OIL IS TO OPEC

The domestic sheep *(Ovis aries)* is descended from the wild *mouflon* of Europe and *urial* of central Asia: there are now about a billion, spread across the globe. Of the sixty-five distinct sheep breeds in Britain today, the oldest is the Soay – a descendant of animals introduced by the earliest Neolithic incomers. A remnant population still lives on the St Kilda islands off the Outer Hebrides. Initially reared for its meat, by the Bronze Age it had become apparent that the sheep's greatest value lay in its coat – when stripped of lanolin (grease), by "fulling" in cow's urine or a similar astringent, combed and spun, wool is a source of one of the two most valuable natural fibres known to man (the other is cotton). Wool is composed of the animal protein keratin, as is the rhinoceros horn and human hair and nails.

Nowadays it is easy to think of sheep as four-legged mowing machines, reared to attract EU subsidies and to provide rather fatty joints to roast on Sundays. Over a hundred years ago Britain ceded its near-monopoly control of the raw wool trade: the main producers of wool are now Australia, New Zealand and Kazakhstan.

It would be difficult however, to exaggerate the role of sheep in the economic and social history of mediæval England. An inscription carved on a monument in a wool church, "I thank God and ever shall, it was the sheep that payed for all", reflects the economic impact of an enormous trade surplus generated by wool exported to the rich clothmaking towns of Bruges, Ghent and Ypres in Flanders. It is said that it is impossible to be out of sight of a beautiful six or seven hundred year-old church anywhere in Norfolk. Enclosures altered the natural landscape from unkempt scrubland, mossy hillsides and boggy marshes into neat pastures with dry-stone walls or hawthorn hedges.

It is a sad truth though, that wherever they were introduced in great numbers, from the south of England in the 14th century to the hills of Sutherland in the 18th, sheep dispossessed people. In England, surplus farm hands were reduced to begging or died in the Black Death. In Scotland, during a dark period known as the "Highland Clearances", uprooted crofters in desperation migrated to the east coasts of Canada and the US. The trend from a 95% rural society in 1500, to an 80% urban population within a manufacturing economy in 2000, became inexorable – long before the mechanization of agriculture. Great landowners and Cistercian abbeys became richer, middlemen broking raw wool to Flemish and Italian buyers from Antwerp or Genoa created a prosperous middle class – and a capitalist economy was born.

By AD 50, during the Roman occupation, there was a large wool-processing factory at Winchester. By the year 1000 England and Spain were the two most important producers of wool in the Western world (the word "sheep", singular and plural, is a derivation of the Old English *sceap*) – large flocks were recorded in the Domesday Book. High quality Spanish fleeces were still imported in the 12th century; but by 1300, with about 15 million sheep, England held a unique position in Europe as a source of fine wool, with no effective competition. The finest, worth twice as much as wool from the salt marshes of East Anglia, Sussex and Kent, came from the Lincolnshire wolds and the limestone hills of the Welsh borders – especially Herefordshire and Gloucestershire (*Cotswold* means "sheep-hills" in Old English).

13th century Flemish dominance was undermined by the superior financial resources of Italians from Lombardy. Able to lend to English wool producers on the security of the wool clip, they cornered the market with unbeatable prices – before the sheep were even

For 200 years from the late 13th century the wool trade in England was described as "the jewel in the realm" – made plain by the "woolsack", which has been used for centuries as the Lord Chancellor's seat in the House of Lords.

sheared. A letter of 1285 lists 20 monasteries committed to the Riccomanni family, in contracts from two to eleven years. Italian financiers established early banking businesses in a part of the City of London still called Lombard Street.

The Crown and Church were swift to take their cuts too: to pay for magnificent courts, to build castles and cathedrals and to finance foreign wars. In the east of England, the Staple towns (those licensed to export wool) of Norwich, Boston, Lynn, Yarmouth and Ipswich, were amongst the richest in the land – indeed Norwich was second in size only to London for centuries.

The wool trade was so important to England that Edward III, responding to appeals for help against French oppression by the burghers of the rich Flemish cloth-towns, went to war to defend it. The Hundred Years' War (1337–1453), changed England from being a supplier of raw wool into the world's unchallenged producer of woolen cloth – in the same way that some oil producing countries moved downstream into value-added production of chemicals and aromatics in the late 20th century. King Edward's Flemish wife, Philippa of Hainault (1314–69), for whom Queen's College in Oxford was founded, brought over large numbers of Flemish weavers to England, in an early instance of technology-transfer. Crippling taxation imposed on wool, but not levied on finished cloth, to pay for the war, accelerated this trend. In the reign of Queen Elizabeth all English commoners were required to wear a woollen cap to church on Sundays, in support of the cloth industry.

Many Flemings settled in Norfolk and Suffolk. Others chose the West Country, the Cotswolds, the Yorkshire Dales and Cumberland, where weaving flourished – a specialisation mirrored in towns like Hawick in the Scottish borders 400 years later, still known for the manufacture of cashmere and fine lambs wool knitwear.

By the 15th century a large surplus of cloth was available for export. Weavers in little cottages transformed raw wool into textiles for the markets of Bristol, Gloucester, Kendal and Norwich ("worsted" for example, was first woven in Worstead, in Norfolk) – then onwards to the rest of the world. Landowners and farmers in Wales and Scotland were also quick to recognise the profits that could be made from the back of a sheep.

The West Riding of Yorkshire became the centre of a cloth-making industrial revolution. Bradford is said to have been built on wool. From modest beginnings in the 16th century, the industry expanded a hundred-fold through mechanization in the 19th. The Bradford to Liverpool canal, and later the railways, connected Leeds with ports to export huge volumes of high quality finished cloth.

The mighty Bradford mills, the largest the world had seen, eventually required more wool than could be produced in Britain alone, allowing imports from Australia and New Zealand to gain a growing share of the market –

Hainault, in the London borough of Redbridge, has no connection with Queen Philippa or Flanders. It was recorded in 1239 and means "monastic woodland".

Robert Bakewell (1725–95), of Dishley in Leicestershire, a stockbreeder of horses and cattle, bred a new Leicester sheep, which gained weight quickly and grew a heavy fleece. It was one of the first pure sheep breeds introduced in Australia in 1826 – along with Saxon Merinos, a German cross-breed descended from the original Spanish sheep that grew the finest fleeces of all.

The Scottish surname Fleming dates back to knights from Flanders who took part in the Norman invasion in 1066. Other Scots families descended from Flemish knights include Douglas, Innes and Sutherland.

until the late 1960s, when the mills fell silent as cheaper finished cloth from Italy and the Far East flooded into Britain.

Reminders of the skill once employed by British weavers can still be glimpsed in Harris Tweed, cloth that has been hand-woven by the islanders of Lewis, Harris, Uist and Barra – in their homes, using pure virgin wool, dyed and spun in the Outer Hebrides. That even this cloth is still made owes much to Catherine, Countess of Dunmore (1814–86), who greatly improved its quality and marketing after the 1846 potato famine. The Aran Islands, off the west coast of Ireland, and Fair Isle, lying between Orkney and Shetland, are also still known for their hand-knitted woollens.

THE ROSSLYN CHAPEL

Rosslyn Chapel, properly named the Collegiate Church of St Matthew, was built for Sir William Sinclair, 1st Earl of Caithness. It stands on a small hill above Roslin Glen, seven miles south of Edinburgh. Work started in 1446 and took nearly forty years to complete. A century or so later, in the Scottish reformation, Roman Catholic services ceased. Today it is under the direction of the Church of Scotland. Known, with good reason, as a "tapestry in stone", it is one of the most beautiful and atmospheric churches in Britain. Its most famous feature perhaps, is the stunning "Apprentice Pillar".

By 1592 the altar had been destroyed by iconoclasts; and in 1650 Cromwell's Puritan soldiers used the chapel as a stable, whilst investing Roslin Castle. In 1688 the chapel, still viewed as openly Catholic, was ransacked by an Edinburgh mob. It gradually became a ruin, until James Sinclair re-flagged the floor and repaired the roof in 1736.

It is claimed that some carvings in the chapel reflect Masonic imagery. One, much eroded, does appear to show a blindfolded man being led by a noose round his neck, in the way a candidate is prepared for initiation into Freemasonry. However William Schaw (1550–1602), the Scotsman who is considered to have founded modern Freemasonry in Britain, did not do so until 1598. Disappointingly, the carvings were almost certainly added by David Bryce, the finest Scottish architect in the Victorian era and a prominent mason, when he restored the chapel in 1861.

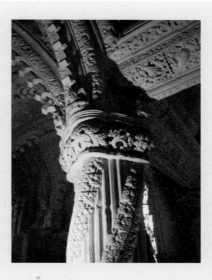

An Account of the Chapel of Roslin, published in 1774, states that: ".... the master mason would by no means consent to work of such a pillar *[sic]* till he should go to Rome .... to take the exact inspection of the pillar from which the model had been taken .... in his absence .... an Apprentice finished the pillar as it now stands .... and the master, upon his return, seeing the pillar so exquisitely well finished made an inquiry as to who had done it, and being stung with envy, slew the apprentice". The apprentice, with a gash in his head, and the master mason who killed him now stare bleakly at each other across the nave – for eternity.

• **Rosslyn Chapel, the "Apprentice Pillar"**

In 2003 Rosslyn Chapel featured extensively in *The Da Vinci Code*, a novel by a well-known American author. Although the book, and a 2006 film made from it, have drawn tourists in great numbers from all over the world, it is clear that he never visited the chapel. He states that, "The Knights Templar had designed Rosslyn Chapel as an exact architectural blueprint of Solomon's Temple in Jerusalem": the chapel however, is an exact copy of St Giles Cathedral in Edinburgh. Another inconvenient fact is that the Templars had been outlawed and hunted down in Scotland by 1312. The six-pointed Star of David on the floor of the chapel that he mentions, does not exist either. Finally, the novel's hypothesis that Rosslyn is derived from "Rose Line", some sort of occult ley-line running from Saint-Sulpice in Paris, is nonsense. *Ros* is Celtic for "promontory" and *Lin* means "a rock pool".

THE WELSH MARCHES

Welsh castles built by Edward I (1277–95)

Offa's Dyke

Chester
Earl of Chester

Shrewsbury
Earl of Shrewsbury

Wales was incorporated into England in 1284, after the death of Llwelyn ap Gruffydd.

Orewin Bridge 1282 (Llwelyn ap Gruffydd killed)

Earl of Hereford

Hereford

Monmouth

Chepstow

Cardiff

Bristol

0   50 miles

0   50 km

Wales was incorporated into England in 1284, after the death of Llwelyn ap Gruffydd

Adding to the mystery of Rosslyn, there are over 110 carvings of Green men in and around the Chapel: symbols of rebirth and fertility – and pre-Christian in origin.

THE ANGLO-SCOTTISH AND ANGLO-WELSH BORDERS

The border between England and Scotland is one of the oldest in the world.

Much of the border had been settled for over two hundred years: when in 1237, most of the rest was agreed by the Treaty of York, signed between King Alexander II of Scotland and King Henry III of England. However two areas were still disputed: the "Debatable Lands", a lawless but small territory in the west, which was settled in 1552; and Berwick-upon-Tweed, which changed hands around 14 times before finally becoming part of England in 1482.

When the Act of Union was passed, which united England and Wales with Scotland on 1 May 1707, the border ceased to be an international frontier.

The Anglo-Welsh border had been disputed since the Iron Age and the arrival of the Romans. They established forts at Chester, Gloucester and Caerleon to contain incursions by Welsh tribes. King Offa of Mercia built a ditch and earthwork barrier along the border at the end of the 8th century, known as Offa's Dyke. Finally, the Normans consolidated the "Marches" into local administration.

"March" is derived from the Anglo-Saxon *mearc* ("boundary"). William the Conqueror was the first King of England to try to subdue the borderlands. He created the Marcher Lordships, granting virtual independence to over 150 of his most trusted supporters.

Their lands were collectively known as the Welsh Marches (*Marchia Wallia*). Marcher lords "possessed all of the royal perquisites", to build castles, make laws, wage wars, establish towns and maintain "the customs of the March". Inhabitants of Wales Proper (*Wallia pura*) were subject to "the laws of Hywel Dda".

Major military depots were established in the three largest cities near the border: Chester, Shrewsbury and Hereford, administered by powerful earls. Twenty-six castles, from the Bristol Channel in the south to the Dee in the north, dominated the March itself. Keeping the peace between England and Wales was an expensive business.

The ancient county of Monmouthshire (*Sir Fynwy* in Welsh) was formed from the Welsh Marches by the 1535 Laws in Wales Act. Historically there was ambiguity as to whether the county was part of Wales or England. Since 1974, as the ceremonial county of Gwent, it has been placed definitively in Wales – though in 1997, 68% of the just over 50% who voted at all, did so against a Welsh Assembly.

THE SHERBORNE MISSAL

The Sherborne Missal is the finest example of English book production in the 15th century. It has no equal in size, originality, artistic imagination or beauty.

The Missal weighs nearly 45lbs – a missal is needed by every priest to peform the Mass, but hardly one as heavy as this. It has 347 leaves, which include some exquisite and careful illustrations of birds: including "Ganett", "More hen", "Cormerant", "Waysteter" (wagtail), "Wodewale" (woodpecker) and "Roddoke" (robin), among many others. There are also seventy or so sets of heraldic arms painted in the Missal, including those of the future King Henry V – which help date it to *c.*1400.

Most mediæval art is anonymous, but this missal contains portraits of the patron, main scribe and main artist; and inscriptions naming them. The patron was apparently Robert Bruyning, the Abbot of Sherborne: on eight occasions he is shown with Richard Mitford, the Bishop of Salisbury, his religious superior. John Whas, a monk at Sherborne Abbey who wrote the script and musical notations, commented that he: "laboured on the writing of this book, and his body was much debilitated by early rising". He is depicted seven times. There are also six portraits of the chief illuminator, John Siferwas.

The early-15th century Sherborne Missal
First page of the feast of Trinity Sunday.
British Library

KING HENRY V OF ENGLAND (REIGNED 1413–22)

King Henry V of England, Duke of Aquitaine and Duke of Lancaster, was the eldest son of Henry of Bolingbroke. His sixteen year-old mother Mary de Bohun gave birth to him in Monmouth Castle on 16 September 1387. He is often referred to as "Monmouth Harry" or Prince Hal. Despite exiling his father in 1398, King Richard II took him into his household and had the boy well educated by his uncle Henry Beaufort, Bishop of Winchester – Henry would become the first king who could read and write in English. His father seized Richard's throne and was crowned King Henry IV on 13 October 1399.

As Prince of Wales, Henry reduced the rebel Welsh chieftain Owain Glyn Dwr (anglicised by Shakespeare as Owen Glendower) to obscurity. He was nearly killed by an arrow, which struck him in his face while fighting Glyn Dwr and Harry Hotspur at the Battle of Shrewsbury in 1403. He was then aged fifteen but already well over six feet tall.

Owain Glyn Dwr (1354–*c.*1415), self-proclaimed Prince of Wales, was born into a prosperous, land-owning Anglo-Welsh family. He studied law in London and served as a soldier with Henry of Bolingbroke in France and Scotland. On returning to Wales in 1400, an altercation with his neighbour, the Marcher Lord Grey of Ruthven, quickly escalated into a full-scale rebellion. At first successful, Glyn Dwr found himself in control of most of Wales, even establishing a Welsh parliament. In 1403 an alliance with the Percys collapsed at the Battle of Shrewsbury. The relentless campaign waged against him by the future Henry V, reduced Glyn

King Henry V by unknown artist (late 16th Century/early 17th Century). As a result of the wound in his face, he is the only king ever painted in profile
National Portrait Gallery, London

Dwr to the status of guerrilla leader. Little is known of him after 1412 and his end is shrouded in myth. Glyn Dwr's rebellion was the last coordinated Welsh attempt to secede from England.

Sir Henry Percy (c.1364–1403), also called Harry "Hotspur", because of his fiery nature, was the eldest son of Henry Percy, 1st Earl of Northumberland. His mother was Margaret Neville of Raby and he was born at Alnwick Castle. In his youth Hotspur acquired a reputation as a brave but impetuous soldier, fighting in Scotland and France. He was captured by the Scots led by James, 2nd Earl of Douglas, at the "Midnight Battle" of Otterburn in August 1388. Douglas was killed.

The Bishop of Durham was blamed unfairly for the English defeat, for moving too slowly to join the battle. The fault lay with Hotspur, for engaging the Scots too rashly.

Having been ransomed by King Richard II and Parliament, he served as Governor of Bordeaux between 1393–95, returning from France to help depose King Richard II in favour of

There are two versions of the 15th century *Ballad of Chevy Chase*, one Scots and one English. Both tell the same tale, in much the same way, and both are based on the Battle of Otterburn. The details of the battle are inaccurate however, and may relate to border skirmishes up to fifty years later. The story describes a large hunting party in the Cheviot Hills ("Chevy Chase"), led by Percy over the border with Scotland. Douglas had forbidden the hunt and assumes it to be an invasion. In the bloody battle that followed, only 110 survived. The Scots version begins:

It fell about the Lammas tide,
    When the muir-men win their hay,
The doughty Douglas bound him to ride
    Into England, to drive a prey.

The nineteenth stanza, perhaps the most memorable, sends a shiver up the spine:

    But I have dream'd a dreary dream,
Beyond the Isle of Skye;
    I saw a dead man win a fight,
And I think that man was I.

The Elizabethan dramatist Ben Johnson (1572–1637) said that he would rather have been the author of *Chevy Chase* than all of his own works. No one knows who wrote it.

Henry of Bolingbroke. In 1403 however, with his paternal uncle, Thomas Percy, Earl of Worcester and the Welsh rebel Owain Glyn Dwr, Hotspur led a rebellion against Bolingbroke. Before they could unite, Hotspur was defeated at the Battle of Shrewsbury on 21 July 1403. On lifting his visor, he was hit in the mouth by an arrow and died instantly. Curiously his adversary, Prince Henry suffered the same fate in the same battle and survived, after dangerous surgery on his face. Hotspur was buried in Whitchurch in Shropshire but was later exhumed, to quash rumours that he was still alive. His body was displayed in Shrewsbury, skewered on a spear, before being quartered and distributed around England. His head was impaled on the gates of York.

Henry succeeded his father on 21 March 1413. Within a year he was faced with both a Lollard uprising and a conspiracy led by Richard, 2nd Duke of York. Warned by spies of the latter, Henry dealt ruthlessly with both. The Lollards might have been more successful had they confined their activities to religious dissent. Under their leader, the Herefordshire knight Sir

John Oldcastle, Lollardy crossed the line into political, hence treasonable protest – which attracted hideous penalties.

Sir John Oldcastle, of Almeley in Herefordshire, a Lollard leader, was prosecuted for heresy against the Church; but escaped from the Tower of London. Subsequently accused of plotting against Henry V, an old friend with whom he had fought in France, he was recaptured and executed on 14 December 1417 – by being hanged over a slow fire, before being drawn and quartered. Though Shakespeare's character Falstaff was named Oldcastle in early versions of *Henry IV*, Sir John Fastolf was his inspiration. In portraying Falstaff as a cowardly buffoon, Shakespeare was unfair to both.

Neither of these domestic incidents distracted Henry long from pursuing his claim to the French throne – and righting the wrongs which he passionately believed had been inflicted by France on England. The province of Aquitaine had been ceded to England under the Treaty of Calais in 1360, but never transferred. Henry not only pressed his claim to Aquitaine: but also to Normandy, Touraine, Maine and Anjou, the old Angevin territories, and even to other parts of France never occupied by England. Henry's timing was opportunistic: France was riven by faction and their king, Charles VI suffered from bouts of lunacy. Nonetheless, Henry was convinced of the justice of his cause and planned, in meticulous detail, a full scale invasion of France.

First, Henry ensured that France was isolated, diplomatically and militarily. He secured not only the neutrality of her most powerful magnate, John "the Fearless", Duke of Burgundy, but also command of the English Channel. Next, he turned to Parliament for money: which, roused to nationalist fervour by Henry's patriotic appeal, responded generously. In contrast to the ill-considered and disorganised military campaigning in France a century earlier, Henry's stratagem favoured the piecemeal reduction and garrisoning of key French towns. By this means he would dominate the countryside, enabling him to administer and tax the conquered territories to pay for his war.

Henry launched his invasion against France in August 1415 with a force of about 11,000 men. By 22 September he had captured Harfleur: the scene of Shakespeare's immortal speech by Henry, "Once more unto the breach dear friends, once more .... the fewer men, the greater share of honour". He lost half his army however, as much to disease as from enemy action. Henry decided to retreat north-east to Calais, then an English enclave, to evacuate his shattered army. But at the small village of Agincourt, he and his exhausted troops found their path blocked by a well-fed and magnificently caparisoned French army. The Constable of France, Charles d'Albret's 25,000 men, including heavy cavalry, outnumbered Henry's by a factor of at least five to one.

"Lollard" was derived from the Dutch word *lollaert*, meaning a mutterer or mumbler, probably coined from the Lollard practice of reading the scriptures aloud. By the late Middle Ages, the expanding power of the Church, artificially maintained by tax exemption and privilege, was a source of great resentment. The Lollards led the first but very limited reform movement. At one time or another, they enjoyed the support of the Black Prince, John of Gaunt and a number of knights who attended Richard II: reflecting an aristocratic jealousy of the Church's huge estates and dislike of the clergy. Lollards taught that piety was the true source of spiritual authority and not the Church hierarchy, so a pious layman could perform the sacraments in place of a priest: while also advocating poverty and the taxation of Church assets. Critically, they believed in consubstantiation: that the consecrated bread and wine (the substance of the Eucharist) are no more than symbols of the body and blood of Christ. Transubstantiation, a fundamental Catholic doctrine, in which the Eucharist is supposed to be physically transformed, was regarded as primitive – and abominated.

The Valois King Charles VI of France (1368–1422), known as "the Beloved" or "the Mad", was crowned at the age of eleven. The country was ruled by his uncles until 1388. In 1392 Charles began to go mad: and royal power oscillated between the rival Dukes of Burgundy and Orléans. Defeat at Agincourt obliged Charles to marry his daughter Catherine to Henry V – and declare Henry both his heir and regent.

On 25 October 1415, St Crispin's Day, after a night of heavy rain, the French imprudently chose to fight on a 1,000 yard front of sodden plough flanked by two woods. Their army was drawn up in a single file of two infantry divisions, with cavalry held back in the rear. Henry arranged his 5,000 archers and 1,000 infantry carefully, into three battalions – with most of the archers concentrated forward of his flanks. They advanced to within arrow-shot of the French, each equipped with a pointed wooden stake. They drove the stakes into the ground and loosed off volleys of arrows. These fusillades, fired at a rate of eight flights a minute, provoked the French into cavalry charges, which foundered in the heavy plough or broke upon the lines of stakes. The French then sent forward detachments of dismounted knights. The English yielded but quickly recovered, as more French knights joined the battle – to struggle in the crush and sink into the mud. At this point Henry ordered forward his lightly-clad men-at-arms to dispatch the helpless, heavily-armoured French. The Constable, twelve members of the royal family, 1,500 knights and at least 4,500 foot-soldiers perished at Agincourt, with thousands taken prisoner. The English lost fewer than 450 men.

A chisel hammered up into the throat through the vulnerable neck coupling of a suit of armour, or into an eye after lifting the visor, enabled English soldiers swiftly to slaughter hundreds of defenceless French knights lying powerless in the mud.

The first dividend from Henry's victory at Agincourt was a visit early in 1416 by the Holy Roman Emperor Sigismund. Henry entertained him lavishly and made him a member of the Garter. On 15 August he and Sigismund signed the Treaty of Canterbury. The terms validated Henry's claims on France and put an end to the schism in the Church that had existed since 1378: of there being two popes at the same time, one in Rome and one in Avignon. Most importantly, a maritime treaty between Genoa and France was annulled. Henry, now in control of Biscay and the Channel, was free to return to the long grind of siege warfare. Over the next few years he gradually reduced Normandy: its capital, Rouen surrendered in 1419. In September that year, Duke John "the Fearless" of Burgundy was assassinated on the Dauphin's order, which gifted Henry his outraged countrymen as allies. These developments brought Henry to the gates of Paris – to confront a French king bereft of anything left to bargain with.

By the Treaty of Troyes on 21 May 1420, Charles recognised Henry as heir to the French throne and Regent of France. The treaty was sealed on 2 June by his marriage to Catherine of Valois, Charles's daughter. Despite France's prostration, Henry continued to invest disobedient French towns. In a devastating reversal of fortune however, when besieging Melun, he contracted dysentery. He died at the Château de Vincennes on 31 August 1422, aged thirty-five. Too late, Charles died on 21 October: "Monmouth Harry" had failed in his ambition to be crowned King of France – by just two months.

In nine years Henry had taken a weak and drifting England and turned her briefly into the most powerful country in Europe. It was perhaps regrettable that Henry chose to devote his outstanding leadership and administrative skills to the prosecution of a morally dubious war. His sudden death deprived England of ultimate victory over the French however – and inflicted on the nation a long period of minority rule.

The Battle of Balaclava and the "Charge of the Light Brigade" in 1854, during the Crimean War, also took place on St Crispin's Day. St Crispin, one of twins martyred c.286, is the patron saint of of cobblers and leather workers.

The misericorde was a long, narrow knife, used to deliver the death stroke (from the Latin *misericordia*, for "mercy") to a seriously wounded or incapacitated knight.

Samuel Pepys kissed the corpse of Catherine of Valois, Henry V's widow, Henry VI's mother and grandmother of Henry VII, in Westminster Abbey: "On Shrove Tuesday 1669, I to the Abbey went, and by favour did see the body of Queen Catherine of Valois, and had the upper part of the body in my hands, and I did kiss her mouth, reflecting upon it I did kiss a Queen: and this my birthday and I thirty-six years old and I did kiss a Queen". She was the same age as Pepys when she died – but 237 years old when he kissed her. His libido was remarkable.

THE NORMANS AND THE PLANTAGENETS 1066–1485

Map showing English possessions in France (1435)

WALES

ENGLAND

London

Thames

Sluys (1340) ⚔

English Channel

FLANDERS
(to Burgundy)

Calais

Agincourt (1415) ⚔

Crécy (1346) ⚔

Cambrai

Somme

Amiens

Calais was an English
possession for over 200
years from 1347-1558.

The Channel Islands have
been Crown possessions
since 1066. They are not
part of the UK or EU.

Harfleur
(1415) ⚔

Rouen

Reims ✝

Seine

Occupied by England (1415-53)

Paris ✝

Marne

Meuse

Troyes

Seine

H O L Y

BRITTANY

Allied to England

Rennes

Le Mans

Orléans

B U R G U N D Y

Dijon

R O M A N

Angers

Loire

Tours

Nantes

Bourges

Saône

FRANCE 1435

Regions controlled by
King Henry VI of England
(1421-71) and the
Anglo-Burgundian alliance

⚔ Poitiers (1356)

Poitiers

Limoges

Clermont

Lyons

Geneva

SAVOY

E M P I R E

Rhône

DAUPHINÉ

Duchy of the King of England
for 300 years (1152-1453)

Henry was crowned King of France,
but only in Paris (1431)

⚔ Castillon (1453)

The first battle in Europe to be
decided by cannon. England lost
all of France, except Calais.

Regions loyal to King Charles VII
of France (1403-61)

Bordeaux

Loire

It was crucial to Charles's authority
that he was crowned in Reims (1429)

T O U L O U S E

Avignon

Albi

PROVENCE

⚔ Battlefield - English victories

⚔ Battlefield - French victory

✝ Cathedral

Retaken by England
(1415-53)

Garonne

Bèziers

Marseilles

Toulouse

NAVARRE

Territory acquired (1209-55)
by the King of France, under
the pretext of the Albigensian
Crusade (see the Dedication
to this book).

CASTILE

Ebro

ARAGON

0   100 miles

0   100 km

15TH CENTURY BATTLEFIELD SURGERY

The arrow which struck the face of the 15 year-old Prince Hal, later King Henry V, penetrated his cheek on the left of his nose, just below the eye. The shaft was quickly removed but the head had broken off in the "furthermost part of the bone of the skull to the depth of six inches". The King's surgeon, John Bradmore, a convicted (but pardoned) forger, was summoned. He made a small set of hollow tongs, the same width as the arrow head with screw threads at the base of each calliper and a screw along the centre. Bradmore had to widen the wound before he could insert the tongs. He achieved this by using probes made from pith of elder wrapped in rose honey-soaked linen. When he found the bottom of the wound, Bradmore inserted the tongs, eventually enclosing the arrow-head in the callipers. By gently jiggling the tongs, "with the help of God", he managed to extract the arrow-head: cleansing the wound with a "squirtillo" (douche) of white wine, before inserting flax pads infused with a mixture of honey, bread soaked in flour and water, barley and turpentine oil.

For three weeks Bradmore continued this treatment: "I always anointed him on the neck every day in the morning and evening, with an ointment to soothe the muscles and placed a hot plaster on top, on account of fear of spasm which was my greatest fear. And, thus thanks to God, he was perfectly cured". With the appalling risks of septicæmia, gas-gangrene and tetanus, let alone the high likelihood of paralysis and disfigurement caused by damage to a facial nerve, Bradmore achieved a near miraculous result. Henry himself acknowledged the skill of his extraordinary physician by granting Bradmore an annual pension of £10 (£49,000 today), paid by the royal household until he died in 1412. The only extant portrait of Henry, made after his coronation in 1413, is painted in left profile. The inference is obvious.

The pain the young prince must have endured during this procedure, is unimaginable. Basic anæsthesia provided by opium, laudanum and henbane was certainly understood and practised in the Middle Ages but was inevitably an extremely uncertain process. The remarkable, antiseptic qualities of honey are being investigated again today.

KING HENRY VI OF ENGLAND (REIGNED 1422–61 AND 1470–71)

In the Middle Ages, when it mattered greatly, and unlike Scotland, England was blessed with a long history of mostly strong and effective monarchs – some of whom were outstandingly able. John was the only king who can be described as irredeemably evil, as even Richard III had some good qualities. Stephen was by all accounts a decent man, but weak; Edward II was seriously flawed but not intrinsically malign; poor Richard II was unlucky and a sad disappointment; Richard I, a hero to Christendom, was absent most of his reign; Henry III was incompetent but artistic; and young Edward V never reigned at all.

King Henry VI by unknown artist (c.1540)
National Portrait Gallery, London

Between the reigns of three remarkable kings, Henry V, Edward IV and Henry VII however, occurred one of tragic uselessness: the reign of the wretched puppet-King Henry VI. Henry's personal role during this excruciating forty-year hiatus takes very few words to describe. The bloodshed it caused however, takes longer to explain.

Henry VI, born on 6 December 1421 at Windsor, was King of England from 1422–61 and from 1470–71. The only child of Henry V and Catherine of Valois (1401–37), he was the antithesis of his iron-willed father. Henry VI was a shy, studious youth whose reluctance later to take up the reins of government was the major cause of the Wars of the Roses.

On 30 May 1431 a nineteen year-old peasant girl, born in Lorraine, was burned at the stake. Having had visions of God, directing her to save France from English oppression, she was sent by the uncrowned King, Charles VII to lift the siege of Orléans – which, overcoming the scoffing of veteran commanders, she did in nine days, on 8 May 1429. This 'miracle', and her leadership in several other victories, led to Charles's coronation at Reims on 17 July 1429 (Henry VI's coronation took place inauspiciously in Paris rather than Reims, the traditional site of the crowning of the kings of France). She was captured in a skirmish by the Burgundians, sold to their English allies and tried in Rouen for heresy by an ecclesiastical court – composed entirely of Frenchmen.

Asked if she knew she was in God's grace, she answered: "If I am not, may God put me there; and if I am, may God so keep me". The question was a trap. Church doctrine held that no one could be certain of being in God's grace. If she had answered "yes", she would have convicted herself of heresy. If she had answered "no", she would have confessed to her own guilt. Notary Boisguillaume later testified that when the court heard her reply, "Those who were interrogating her were stupefied".

George Bernard Shaw's 1923 play *Saint Joan* contains literal translations of the trial record.

When the flames of her pyre subsided, the executioner raked back the ashes to expose her charred body to public view; and burned it twice more to prevent any collection of relics. Her remains were thrown into the Seine. Geoffroy Therage, her executioner said later that he ".... greatly feared to be damned". Despite the ambivalence towards her shown by most Frenchmen at the time, on the initiative of Charles VII (who did not wish to be seen as having been brought to power with the aid of a condemned heretic), she was declared innocent after a posthumous retrial on 7 July 1456 – in which she was described as a martyr. She was beatified in 1909 and canonised in 1920. In 1922, rather late in the day, Joan d'Arc became one of Frances's patron saints.

• **Saint Joan d'Arc (c.1485) by Rossetti**

Aged only one, Henry succeeded his father on 1 September 1422. On 21 October his maternal grandfather, King Charles VI of France whose insanity he had inherited, died. Henry was proclaimed King of France under the terms of the 1420 Treaty of Troyes.

One of his father's brothers John, Duke of Bedford was appointed Regent of France; and another, Humphrey, Duke of Gloucester was made Regent of England. Henry was crowned King of England at Westminster Abbey on 6 November 1429, a month before his eighth birthday, and King of France at Notre Dame in Paris on 16 December 1431.

Henry's minority was never formally concluded: but, on reaching his sixteenth birthday in 1437, he was expected to assume his royal duties – to which, it was clear, he was most unsuited. As a result of an apparently difficult and troubled adolescence, Henry appeared to be interested only in fastidious spiritual observance and his plans for two religious and educational foundations, Eton College and King's College, Cambridge.

The competing ambitions of his chief ministers, drawn from the Houses of York and Lancaster who governed England on his behalf, swirled around Henry's court. The latter included his father's youngest brother Humphrey, Duke of Gloucester (1390–1447); his clever

Eton College is the largest public school or more accurately, independent secondary school, in England. It is located 20 miles west of London, on the Buckinghamshire bank of the Thames, opposite Windsor. It was founded by Henry VI in 1440. Seventy King's scholarships are still awarded each year on a public, competitive basis.

King's College, Cambridge was founded in 1441, also by Henry VI. The original design was unpretentious: but, by 1445 King's College had become a showpiece of royal patronage. Henry planned for a college with a Provost and seventy scholars; and richly endowed it with feudal privileges. King's College was founded specifically to complete the education of boys from Eton; and the connection remained strong for centuries. It was not until 1865 that the first undergraduates from other schools were accepted by King's. The first fellow not to have been at Eton was elected in 1873.

• **The world's largest fan vault (King's College Chapel, Cambridge)**

but avaricious great-uncle, John of Gaunt's illegitimate son Henry, Cardinal Beaufort (*c.*1375–1447); and William de la Pole, Duke of Suffolk (nicknamed "Jack Napes"). Suffolk was dismissed in 1449, to be replaced by two even more determined magnates, who were also implacable enemies: Edmund Beaufort, Ist Duke of Somerset (1406–55), grandson of John of Gaunt; and his cousin Richard, 3rd Duke of York.

Richard of York (1411–60) possessed a more valid claim to the throne than Henry himself. They were both descended from Edward III. The recital of these great names gives a clue to the problems that followed: all of them the result of Edward III having too many surviving sons, some of whose descendants nursed powerful aspirations to the throne themselves. The vacuum caused by Henry V's untimely death, leaving as his heir an infant who grew to be a pitiable milksop, was an open invitation to a greedy wolf-pack of cousins to fight each other. This they did, in what became known as the Wars of the Roses (at the time called the Cousins' War), a war of succession which left many of them and their noble allies dead.

The factions who competed for Henry's throne coalesced into only two: those known as Lancastrians, who were descended, as was Henry from John of Gaunt, Duke of Lancaster, the third son of Edward III; and the Yorkists, who supported Richard, 3rd Duke of York. For thirty years, loyalty to Henry V, a strong regency and a period of grace afforded to the young king on attaining his majority, had kept the disputants apart – at least until his uncle Humphrey and Cardinal Beaufort both died in 1447.

Meanwhile, through neglect and poor leadership, the English position in France was fast deteriorating. A truce and Henry's marriage to Margaret of Anjou in April 1445 had done nothing to prevent the loss of Normandy and Maine in 1449–50, due to the crass conduct of Edmund Beaufort, Duke of Somerset: to be followed, after defeat at the Battle of Castillon in 1453, by the whole of Aquitaine and south-west France.

In 1451 the French seized Bordeaux – to bring, they thought, the Hundred Years' War to an end. But after 300 years of occupation, the Bordelais regarded themselves as English citizens. Taking exception to the prospect of being ruled by France and wishing to protect their wine exports, they appealed to Henry VI. On 17 October 1452 John Talbot, Ist Earl of Shrewsbury (*c.*1387–1453) landed near Bordeaux with 3,000 men. The English were welcomed, Gascony joined them and the French garrison was ejected.

That winter, Charles VII of France assembled three armies for a combined assault on Bordeaux in the spring of 1453. Shrewsbury was reinforced by a further 3,000 men but remained perilously outnumbered. The French laid siege to Castillon, ten miles from Bordeaux, in June. Jean Bureau, Charles VII's master of artillery, ordered his 10,000 soldiers to surround their camp with a ditch and palisade, deploying 300 cannon along the parapet. On 17 July Shrewsbury, mistaking a dust cloud created by camp followers for a French retreat, advanced on the French position: to find the parapets defended by thousands of cross-bowmen and hundreds of cannon. The brave but foolhardy Shrewsbury attacked, only for his army to be cut down by devastating crossbow and artillery fire. After an hour, Breton cavalry charged the English right, turning the battle into a rout. A cannon ball killed Shrewsbury's horse and he fell trapped beneath it. A French archer recognised the old warrior and dispatched him with an axe.

Henry VI's half-brothers, Edmund and Jasper, the sons of his widowed mother Catherine's marriage to Owen Tudor (1400–61), were given earldoms. Edmund Tudor was the father of Henry Tudor, later to usurp the throne as Henry VII.

The Battle of Castillon, on 17 July 1453, was the last battle fought between the French and the English during the Hundred Years' War. It was also the first battle in European history to be decided by artillery.

On 29 May 1453 the Ottoman Turks finally overran Byzantium. The Ottoman Empire now had a toe-hold in Europe, threatening Christian kingdoms to the north and west and destabilizing the eastern Mediterranean. It led however, to an exodus of Greek scholars, mostly to Italy, who helped accelerate the Renaissance. Many historians regard this event to mark the end of the Middle Ages in Europe.

Castillon finally extinguished all English claims to the French throne and made final the loss of Aquitaine. Only the enclave of Calais remained in English hands. In the same month, distraught at his losses in France, Henry VI went mad – being unaware even of the birth of his son, Prince Edward. This prompted the popular Duke of York, who had been Lieutenant of Ireland since 1447, to return to reclaim his place on the council. York was also owed £40,000 by the crown (over £200 million today).

On Christmas Day 1454 Henry recovered his wits: but too late. It has been said that "If Henry's insanity was a tragedy, his recovery was a national disaster". York had been appointed Protector of the Realm by Parliament in March, excluding the Queen completely. York imprisoned her most important ally, the Duke of Somerset in the Tower of London, encouraging his supporters to spread rumours that her son Prince Edward was Somerset's. In May 1455 Queen Margaret and York took up arms against each other – the latter backed by Richard Neville, 16th Earl of Warwick and 6th of Salisbury (1428–71), the most influential magnate in the land and richer than York himself.

York defeated the Lancastrians at the first Battle of St Albans on 22 May 1455, but the indefatigable Margaret toppled him the following year. When hostilities again broke out in 1459, Margaret made matters worse by outlawing the Yorkist leaders –who captured the King at Northampton on 19 July 1460. In response, her supporters ambushed and killed York at Wakefield in Yorkshire on 30 December: and freed King Henry from captivity after the second Battle of St Albans in February 1461. On 4 March Edward of York, Richard's son, seized the throne as Edward IV. He massacred Margaret's army at Towton in Yorkshire on 29 March, forcing her to flee to Scotland with her husband and son. She returned in 1464 to support an ultimately unsuccessful Lancastrian uprising. Henry was recaptured at Clitheroe in July 1465 however, and again imprisoned in the Tower.

In 1470 Margaret, now in France, became reconciled with her former Yorkist enemy, the Earl of Warwick. Warwick, earning himself the sobriquet the "King-maker", restored Henry briefly to the throne in October. However Margaret did not return to England until 14 April 1471, the very day that Warwick was killed at Barnet.

On 4 May 1471 Margaret was defeated by Edward IV at Tewkesbury. Her son, Prince Edward was killed. Between 21–24 May her husband, King Henry VI was murdered, supposedly while he knelt in prayer, in the Tower of London. Margaret remained in custody until 1475 when she was ransomed by the French King Louis XI.

Though England's prosperity was unaffected by the dynastic mayhem of the Wars of the Roses, the country yearned for a sane, strong king who could keep the peace. With the pathetic, scarcely known and unmourned Henry VI finally disposed of, the welcome given to the return of Edward IV was one of heartfelt relief.

Sir Thomas Malory died in 1471, having just completed *Le Morte d'Arthur*, the first novel written in English. William Caxton printed it in 1485.

Margaret of Anjou, Queen of England (1430–82), beautiful and passionate, was queen-consort to Henry VI. Margaret was niece of Henry VI's rival King of France, Charles VII. Her marriage to the mentally disturbed Henry in April 1445, was arranged as part of a truce in the Hundred Years' War between France and England. She fought to secure the crown for her son Edward, Prince of Wales (1453–71). Broken in spirit after his death and impoverished, she returned to France – and died seven years later in Anjou.

THE WARS OF THE ROSES

"The Wars of the Roses" (1455–87) were an intermittent series of dynastic conflicts fought between the houses of Lancaster and York, both of which claimed the throne of England through descent from Edward III. Their roots lay in the seizure of the English throne by Henry IV in 1399, the first Lancastrian king. The label "Wars of the Roses" would have been unfamiliar to contemporaries. It was in fact, the "Cousins' War".

The labels "Lancastrian" and "Yorkist" are a convenient shorthand, referring only to the titles of the chief protagonists. Their supporters, nobles and their retainers, came from all over England and Wales – with a bias towards the north because the great estates of the leaders, as their titles suggest, were concentrated there.

The term "Wars of the Roses" is misleading too. It was coined much later, possibly by Sir Walter Scott in his novel *Ivanhoe* as late as 1820. It derived from Shakespeare's play *Henry VI, Part I*: where he depicts followers of the Duke of York and the Lancastrian Duke of Somerset plucking roses in the Temple Garden in London to denote which faction they supported. The white rose was only one of several badges displayed by the House of York. There is no evidence that the House of Lancaster ever used the red rose at this time either. Henry VI was descended from John of Gaunt, 1st Duke of Lancaster, the third son of Edward III. The House of York was descended from Edmund of Langley, 1st Duke of York, Edward III's fourth son; and, on the maternal side, from Lionel of Antwerp, Edward III's second surviving son. Hostilities only concerned the nobility and took a heavy toll of those with royal or blue blood. In no sense were the Wars a civil war – they were simply an aristocratic contest for the throne of an inadequate king.

John, 9th Baron Clifford (*c.*1435–61) was ruthless with his fellow peers. Known as "the Butcher", he killed the Earl of Rutland, Richard of York's young son, with his bare hands at Wakefield in 1460. He also cut the head off York's dead body (not the origin of the word "dead-heading") and presented it with a paper crown to Queen Margaret. He was slain at Ferrybridge in 1461 and his barony was attainted.

For the most part the rank and file were spared, no castles were besieged, no laying waste of the countryside took place and no towns were pillaged. The common soldier was usually a tenant farmer or farmhand, recruited under the terms of his feudal service by his master for a month or two every few years, who was allowed to go home to bring in the harvest when the battle was won or lost – he had no stake in the result and cared little for the outcome, as long as he kept his life and freedom.

Success relied on quick campaigns and victory on the battlefield, not territorial gain. Apart from anything else, no one on either side had any idea of how to keep an army in the field for more than a few weeks. Indeed, in thirty-two years of sporadic war, there was less than fifteen months of campaigning and twelve weeks of actual combat. Apart from the madness of Towton, no more than a few thousand common soldiers were killed. The nobles were less fortunate: but then, they started it.

The Wars began in 1455, when Richard, Duke of York and the Earl of Warwick first took up arms in the Yorkist cause and defeated Henry VI at the Battle of St Albans – in which the Duke of Somerset, Henry's most important supporter, was killed. The Wars had apparently ended with the death of Richard III in 1485, but there was one battle left: Stoke Field in 1487, in which Henry VII defeated the remaining Yorkist claimants to the throne. Over a period of years Henry saw to it that there were none left alive to challenge him.

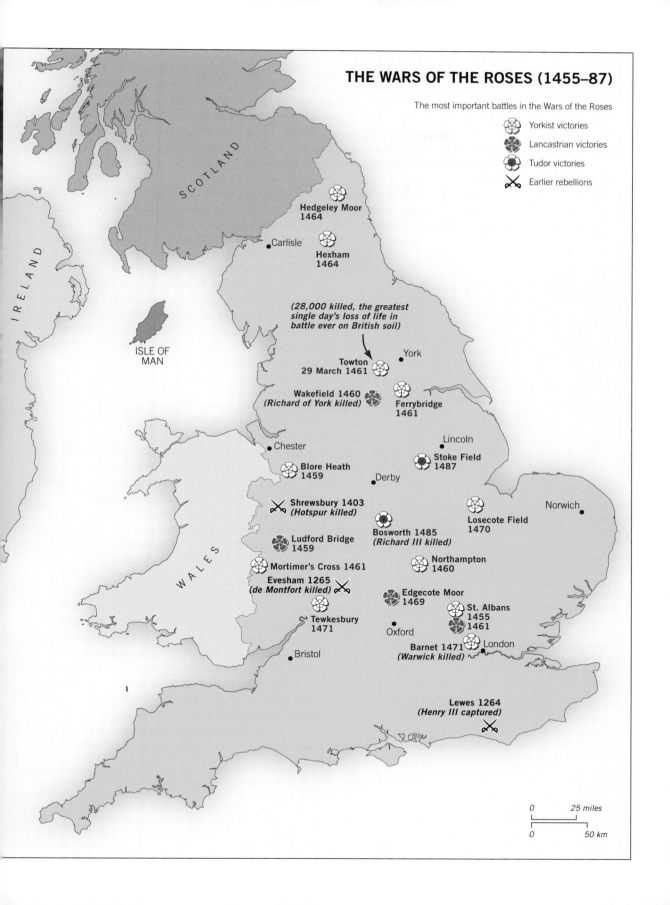

THE WARS OF THE ROSES (1455–87)

The most important battles in the Wars of the Roses

⚜ Yorkist victories

⚜ Lancastrian victories

⚜ Tudor victories

✕ Earlier rebellions

SCOTLAND

IRELAND

WALES

ISLE OF MAN

Carlisle

York

Chester

Lincoln

Derby

Norwich

Oxford

London

Bristol

Hedgeley Moor 1464

Hexham 1464

(28,000 killed, the greatest single day's loss of life in battle ever on British soil)

Towton 29 March 1461

Wakefield 1460 (Richard of York killed)

Ferrybridge 1461

Stoke Field 1487

Blore Heath 1459

Shrewsbury 1403 (Hotspur killed)

Losecote Field 1470

Ludford Bridge 1459

Bosworth 1485 (Richard III killed)

Mortimer's Cross 1461

Evesham 1265 (de Montfort killed)

Edgecote Moor 1469

Northampton 1460

St. Albans 1455 1461

Tewkesbury 1471

Barnet 1471 (Warwick killed)

Lewes 1264 (Henry III captured)

0   25 miles

0   50 km

THE BATTLE OF TOWTON

The Battle of Towton in the Wars of the Roses was the largest and bloodiest ever fought on British soil, with a death toll said by some contemporaries (William Paston and the Bishop of Elpin were two) to have been as high as 28,000. If that were the case, well over one in every hundred Englishmen of that time died at Towton, compared with one in every 500 on the first day of the Somme in 1916. Even though half this figure is more likely, the carnage was still terrible. The battle took place on a snowy Palm Sunday, 29 March 1461, on a plateau between Towton and Saxton in Yorkshire – about 12 miles south-west of York and 2 miles south of Tadcaster.

Some 30,000 on both sides took part – including 28 Lords, almost half the peerage, mostly on the Lancastrian side. It has been suggested that one of the reasons so many died is that, in the parley before the battle, both sides agreed that no quarter would be sought or given – in stark contrast to other battles in the Wars. It was hoped that this would lead to a decisive outcome, which might serve to end a bloody, futile and long-drawn out contest.

Early in the morning, the Yorkist army crossed the River Aire at Ferrybridge, which had been repaired after a brief but deadly encounter the day before. Edward IV led the Yorkist centre, Warwick the right and his uncle, Lord Fauconberg the left. The Duke of Norfolk, with a contingent from the Eastern counties, had yet to reach the battlefield.

The Lancastrian army occupied the high ground, the right flank covered by a stream, the Cock Beck. It was led by the 3rd Duke of Somerset (whose father had been killed at St Albans in 1455), commanding the centre. The Earl of Northumberland commanded the right and the Duke of Exeter the left. Although the Lancastrians occupied a strong position with good fields of fire for their archers, and the Yorkists had to advance uphill to attack, they had not bargained on the foul weather. The Yorkist archers had the wind behind them and out-ranged the Lancastrians, who were blinded by the snow. Yorkists archers loosed volleys into the enemy ranks, falling back out of range when the Lancastrian archers tried to reply. They advanced again and gathered up the enemy arrows which had fallen short, before repeating the manoeuvre. In several places Lancastrian men-at-arms unwisely rushed forward to seek hand-to-hand combat rather than endure the showers of arrows, losing the advantage of the high ground. Cannons were present at Towton, but no shots were fired due to the weather.

The armies closed in on each other and intense close-quarter fighting began, with neither side gaining any decisive advantage. In the early afternoon Norfolk arrived, to extend the Yorkist right flank – in much the same way that the arrival of von Blücher's Prussians saved the day for Wellington at Waterloo in 1815. The Lancastrian left was outnumbered and outflanked; and the rout began here. Some Lancastrians tried to flee north to Tadcaster, but most were pushed into the Cock Beck.

This view however, does not make sense of the order given by King Edward before the battle: "Kill the nobles, leave the commoners!". This was not conventional. Throughout the Middle Ages noble prisoners were highly prized for the ransom that could be extracted to secure their release – death might occur, but it would not be deliberate. In the "Cousin's War" however, each faction regarded itself as legitimate and the other as traitors: nobles on the losing side therefore, would be attainted for treason and their estates confiscated. Without property rights, no ransom could be paid on their behalf – and it made good sense to kill them.

Far more men died in the rout than in the battle. Bridges over nearby rivers collapsed under the weight of armed men, plunging them into freezing water. Those stranded on the wrong side were cornered by their pursuers and killed. The worst slaughter occurred in "Bloody Meadow": where it is said, men crossed the Cock Beck over the bodies of the fallen. All the way from Towton to Tadcaster the fields were filled with dead bodies. Yorkist horsemen and foot soldiers killed many fleeing Lancastrians who had discarded their weapons and helmets as they ran. At Tadcaster some Lancastrians made an unsuccessful stand and were cut down. A total of 20,000 Lancastrians may have been killed, along with 8,000 Yorkists.

The rout lasted all night and into the morning, when remnants of the panic stricken Lancastrian army stumbled into York. Queen Margaret, King Henry VI and Somerset fled north to Scotland, while those Lancastrian lords who were not killed or dispossessed were forced to come to terms with Edward IV. Lord Dacre and the Earl of Northumberland were the most important nobles killed during the battle.

In August 1996 workmen disturbed a mass grave near the Towton battlefield. A team of osteoarchæologists and archæologists formed the 'Towton Mass Grave Project'; and excavated the burial pit, recovering the remains of 43 bodies. Far from the chivalrous conflict associated with the Middle Ages, there was evidence of a brutality more often encountered in the wars of the 20th century.

Many had multiple *perimortem* (time of death) injuries far greater than was needed to kill. Cuts indicated the removal of noses and ears from defenceless victims – the Soviet murder of 22,000 Polish officers in the Katyn Forest on 5 March 1940 comes to mind.

From their misshapen build and long-healed injuries, many of the bodies were clearly those of professional soldiers and archers – recruited perhaps, from those who had returned from the wars in France.

Trained men were not usually present in such numbers in other battles during the Wars of the Roses – which gives rise to the suggestion that the real reason for the terrible bloodshed was that the leaders of both sides were content to rid the country of unemployed and possibly dangerous men.

Sharp force trauma across the face

Sharp force trauma to the back of the skull

SALIC LAW

The Wars of the Roses were a disaster for the noble families of England. Those captured in battle were usually killed immediately. By 1485, after the Battle of Bosworth Field, almost half the lords of the sixty noble families had died. This made it possible for Henry VII to build a new nation state. Once he had disposed of the few remaining contenders to the throne, he could govern as he wished. The titles that became extinct were those that could pass only through a male to a male – as is still generally the case.

The rule excluding females from inheriting a title (or a throne), known as "agnate succession", is one of the best known tenets of Salic Law – which was codified in the 6th century for the Salian Franks in what is now Belgium. Features of it are still in use in many European countries today. The Queen of the Netherlands is formally known as "King", even though her title may be Queen. To Channel Islanders HM Queen Elizabeth II is the Duke, not Duchess of Normandy – and the loyal toast is to "The Queen, our Duke". She is also styled Duke of Lancaster and the Duchy of Lancaster continues to exist as a separate entity from the Crown Estate.

If Hanover had not observed Salic Law in 1839, on the death of King William IV, Queen Victoria would have also become King of Hanover – and King George V would have faced a serious problem in WWI. As it was, he felt obliged to change the Royal surname from Saxe-Coburg and Gotha to Windsor in 1917.

Salic Law is often given as the reason that the British throne is inherited by a prince in preference to a princess, irrespective of which is the older: in fact it has nothing to do with this peculiarly British example of sexism. It is entirely due to the 1701 Act of Settlement, which contained some far-sighted provisions – which is why the present titular Prince of Hanover is not the King of Great Britain.

There are a few exceptions, mostly Scottish. One English Barony however, that can be held by a woman is de Ros (pronounced "Roose") – the most ancient baronial title in the Peerage of England, created by writ in 1264. The reason it is still extant is that it has passed through the female line six times so far.

KING EDWARD IV OF ENGLAND (REIGNED 1461–70 AND 1471–83)

Edward IV (1442–83), 4th Duke of York, was King of England from 4 March 1461 until October 1470 and again from April 1471 until his death in 1483. He was a brilliant soldier, never defeated in battle, who played a pivotal role in the Wars of the Roses.

Edward was the eldest surviving son of Richard, 3rd Duke of York by Cicely (1415–95), daughter of Ralph Neville, Earl of Westmorland. His father was the grandson of Edmund of Langley, fourth son of Edward III. After his father was killed at Wakefield on 30 December 1460, Edward assembled an army in Wales and routed the Lancastrians at Towton. Henry VI fled to Scotland and Edward was crowned at Westminster on 28 June 1461.

Though his father Richard of York had been trusted and respected, the nineteen year old Edward did not at first appear a promising kingly prospect. He had become king entirely due to the efforts of his cousin Richard Neville, Earl of Warwick, the most powerful man in England. Over the next two years, Warwick conducted all royal business, suppressing a Lancastrian rebellion in Northumberland and assuming complete responsibility for foreign affairs. However Edward, six feet four inches tall, charming and good looking, rapidly won support in his own right, especially in London.

Edward began to strain against the Warwick leash. On 1 May 1464 he secretly married Elizabeth Woodville (c.1437–92), a young middle-rank widow he had fallen in love with – deeply upsetting Warwick, who had intended him for a French princess. Edward responded by promoting middle-ranking nobles, loading his newly-acquired stepson with honours, advancing Elizabeth's father and finding husbands for her sisters. In this way, he bought himself strong support from magnates who could balance the Neville clique. Warwick saw his influence at court begin to crumble. This was brought home humiliatingly, when he discovered in 1467 that Edward had already concluded an alliance with Charles "the Bold", Duke of Burgundy – while Warwick was conducting negotiations with Burgundy's enemy, King Louis XI of France (1423–83). Worse, without consulting Warwick, Edward had arranged an elaborate marriage for his sister Margaret to Charles of Burgundy, to take place in July 1468. To cap it all, he learnt that the new brothers-in-law were planning an allied invasion of France.

Seriously alarmed and encouraged by Louis XI, in July 1469 Warwick had Edward arrested and imprisoned. Edward however, had by now won too much support, particularly in London, for Warwick to hold him for long. Edward was released in October and Warwick was forced to flee to France. There he made common cause with Louis XI and the Lancastrians, invading England in September 1470.

Taken off-guard, Edward escaped to Holland in October, to seek help from his brother-in-law Charles of Burgundy. He returned to England in March 1471; and, having taken London, he defeated and killed Warwick at the Battle of Barnet on 14 April. On the same day Queen Margaret, Henry VI's wife, belatedly landed in Dorset from France with her seventeen year-old only son Edward of Westminster, Prince of Wales. Margaret hoped to raise support from Lancastrian Wales – and so began a pell-mell race between Margaret and her son to reach Wales before Edward could intercept her.

King Edward IV by unknown artist (c.1540)
National Portrait Gallery, London

On 4 May Edward caught and defeated Margaret at Tewkesbury in Gloucestershire. The Prince of Wales and most of the Lancastrian leaders were killed or executed after the battle. By 21 May Edward was back in London. Within the next few days Henry VI, a prisoner in the Tower, was murdered. Edward had made his throne secure.

Edward now turned his attention back to France. In 1474, having obtained substantial funds from Parliament, he laid meticulous preparations for an invasion. In 1475 he sailed at the head of a larger English army than had ever before landed in France. Although the Duke of Burgundy failed to come to his assistance, the French clearly indicated that they would rather pay Edward to go home than fight him. This attractive offer would make Edward independent of Parliament – and he happily accepted the bribe.

Finally at peace, England prospered for the remainder of Edward's reign. He displayed remarkable financial acumen and was the first English king since Henry II in 1189 to die solvent. He established order in the traditionally unstable regions of the Welsh marches with the artifice of a Council: to rule through royal prerogative, but to operate from his Welsh estates notionally in the name of his son, the Prince of Wales.

A capable and daring soldier, Edward had a considerable, almost Renaissance cultural and artistic taste, unusual in a late mediæval monarch. He rebuilt St George's Chapel in Windsor and became a patron of William Caxton – who in 1476, established the first printing press in England. His collection of some of Caxton's earliest publications formed the first volumes of the Old Royal Library, later to be incorporated into the British Library. He was also a discerning collector of illuminated Flemish manuscripts.

In 1478 Edward finally lost his patience with his brother George, Duke of Clarence and executed him 'privately', for treason. He had treated George with angry circumspection ever since he had sided with Warwick "the King-maker". The territory of the Duchy of Burgundy having been annexed by France five years earlier, in 1482 Louis XI felt able to repudiate the Treaty of Picguigny and stopped Edward's payments. Edward's immediate response was to launch another invasion: but before he could plan such an enterprise, he fell ill and died on 9 April 1483 at Westminster Palace, three weeks short of his forty-first birthday.

Edward and Elizabeth Woodville had seven children. His two sons, Edward (briefly Edward V) and Richard were murdered in the Tower of London in August 1483. Of his five daughters, the eldest, Elizabeth married Henry VII, founder of the Tudor dynasty.

The precise cause of Edward's death has never been satisfactorily explained. Pneumonia, typhoid and even poison have been suggested. Edward however, was a sexual and culinary glutton: overindulgence in either of these appetites may have proved fatal.

The Treaty of Picquigny was negotiated on 29 August 1475 between England and France. Louis XI paid Edward IV to return to England rather than pursue his claim to the French throne. Edward received an immediate down-payment of 75,000 crowns and a yearly pension for life of 50,000 crowns. Louis also agreed to ransom Queen Margaret of Anjou for 50,000 crowns; and to pay pensions to many of Edward's nobles. A notable exception was his brother Richard, Duke of Gloucester (later Richard III), who opposed the treaty and refused the pension.

Of Edward's many mistresses, the best known was Elizabeth, known as "Jane" Shore. Thomas More said of her: "Where the king took displeasure she would mitigate and appease his mind, where men were out of favour she would bring them to his grace. For many that had highly offended she obtained pardon ....".

CLARENCE, THE UNLUCKIEST ROYAL DUKEDOM

The first dukedom of Clarence ended after only six years with the death of Lionel of Antwerp, second surviving son of Edward III, in 1368 – aged twenty-nine, without a son. The title was next conferred on Thomas (1387–1421), second son of Henry IV, in 1412. He was killed in a reckless skirmish in France – again without a legitimate heir.

William Caxton's personal printing device (1476), the equivalent of a modern "logo"

George, brother of Edward IV, was created Duke of Clarence in 1461. A perpetual irritant to his brother, forever scheming to depose him, George was executed in the Tower of London in 1478 – Shakespeare had him drowned in a butt of Malmsey wine (Madeira), a death he is said to have chosen for himself as it would not mark his body. He had a son, the Earl of Warwick, who did not inherit the dukedom because of the attainder; and was himself executed for treason by Henry VII in 1499.

The title was not used again until it was conferred on William, third son of George III in 1789. He succeeded to the throne as William IV in 1830: though he had eight natural children by Mrs Jordan, an actress, he left no legitimate heir. The last creation of the Clarence dukedom was for Albert Victor, the eldest son of the future King Edward VII, in 1890. Thought by some fanciful conspiracy theorists to have been Jack "the Ripper", he died two years later – also without an heir (he may have been homosexual).

Despite being created five times, the dukedom of Clarence has never been inherited.

WILLIAM CAXTON

Born in Kent, in 1476 William Caxton (*c.*1422–92) established a printing press in Westminster, twenty-one years after the German Johannes Gutenberg invented moveable type in Mainz. He was a prosperous textile importer, working for the Mercers' Company, who enjoyed translating French texts. He studied printing techniques; and in 1474, assembled a press at Bruges in Flanders. Caxton's translation of *Recuyell of the Histories of Troye* was produced by 1475, the first book ever to be printed in English.

Over nearly twenty years Caxton produced more than 100 histories and romances; and in 1481, an encyclopædia. German printers introduced printing to Italy and France – England's first printer was English.

THE PASTON LETTERS

One of the estimates of those killed at Towton was mentioned by William Paston, in a letter to his eldest brother John. *The Paston Letters*, a collection of 1,088 letters and papers, are the correspondence of the ambitious Paston family, which took its name from a village 20 miles north of Norwich, and others connected to them. They are indispensable to historians of the period between 1422–1509.

The first of the family to feature in the letters was Clement Paston, a shrewd peasant who acquired a farm of 100 acres. He educated his son William, who read law: a profession which offered opportunities of advancement for clever men – then, as now. William Paston (1378–1444), described as a "right cunning man", grasped every occasion to advance himself. He bought land; and improved his social standing by marrying the daughter and heiress of Sir Edmund Berry, a landowner in Hertfordshire.

William left a considerable estate to John, the eldest of his five sons. It is during the lifetimes of John Paston (1421–66) and his eldest son, another John, that the letters are most numerous and valuable – not only for family matters, but also for the political and social history of England. A lawyer like his father, Paston spent most of his time in London, leaving his wife to look after his private business in Norfolk.

John Paston was an intimate friend of a rich knight, Sir John Fastolf, probably a relation of his wife, who took took legal advice from Paston on a number of occasions. In 1459 Fastolf died without children. He left his lands in Norfolk and Suffolk, including Caister Castle, to Paston, who died a few years later himself – by which time his eldest son, another John, had been knighted.

Sir John Paston (1442–79) frequently attended Edward IV's court – but changed sides and fought for Henry VI at the Battle of Barnet. The letters reveal the conflicts of loyalty and anxieties that troubled many leading families during the Wars of the Roses. Sir John, a cultured man, left his estate to his brother, yet another John (1444–1504).

After John's death, the letters diminish in regularity and interest, but the family continued to flourish. A descendant, Robert Paston (1631–83), became a Member of Parliament and was created Earl of Yarmouth. Robert's son William (1652–1732), who married a natural daughter of King Charles II, was the 2nd Earl. When he died in 1732, he left no son and his titles became extinct. Though the rise of the Paston family had finally come to a halt, the letters that they preserved are a fascinating and factual commentary on the chronic instability of England during the 15th century.

The bulk of the letters are preserved in the British Museum. Others are in the Bodleian or Magdalen College libraries in Oxford; and a few are at Pembroke College, Cambridge.

In the late 15th century in London there were at least three respectable public baths for women and two for men, in addition to the stews that were mainly in Southwark. Gentlefolk usually owned a tub, covered by a tent on a frame. The tent was often lined and the tub cushioned with sponges. Even those of moderate means might list bath-tubs amongst their possessions. There was also a laundry system – and people of consequence were expected to appear in clean clothes.

Cook-shops ("takeaways" today) were common in London and other cities: partly due to the difficulty of keeping meat fresh, but mainly because only the largest houses had kitchens. Cook-shops prepared a wide range of pies, puddings and baked meats. A customer could either buy a hot dish ready for eating, or he could send his own joint to be cooked.

Fastolf, whose name he took for Falstaff, was misrepresented by Shakespeare as a fat, pompous poltroon. A comic character in three other plays, his death is mentioned in *Henry V*. Fastolf was a brave soldier in the Hundred Years' War.

Another real-life knight, valiant and loyal to King Henry V, Dafydd ap Llewellyn ap Hywel (born in Brecknockshire *c.*1380), was killed at Agincourt. Mentioned, under his nickname "Davy Gam", as being amongst the fallen in Shakespeare's *Henry V*, he may have been the model for Fluellen, an archetypal Welshman. In fact he was a nobleman of ancient lineage – and a prominent opponent of Owain Glyn Dwr.

• Charles Kemble as Falstaff in Henry IV by Richard James Lane: after Alfred Edward Chalon, published May 1890
National Portrait Gallery, London

The Princes in the Tower by Samuel Cousins after Sir John Everett Millais
National Portrait Gallery, London

KING EDWARD V OF ENGLAND (UNCROWNED)

Edward IV died in 1483 and his thirteen year-old son Edward V became King. Edward reigned only 77 days before his uncle and guardian Richard, Duke of Gloucester usurped the throne. Richard arrested senior members of the influential Woodvilles, the family of the young king's mother, Queen Elizabeth, whom he loathed. Richard killed Edward's uncle Earl Rivers, frightening Elizabeth into seeking sanctuary in Westminster Abbey. Having imprisoned Edward and his younger brother Richard, Duke of York in the Tower of London, he declared both boys illegitimate and persuaded Parliament to proclaim him king – the day after the boy-king Edward V should have been crowned himself.

"The Princes in the Tower" were never seen again. Two small skeletons were found in 1674, almost certainly theirs. The boys were probably killed by agents of Richard III. Much later, Sir James Tyrell (1455–1502) is said to have confessed to their murder, "sorrowfully". He was executed by Henry VII for treason.

KING RICHARD III OF ENGLAND (REIGNED 1483–85)

Richard, Duke of Gloucester (1452–85), later Richard III, was known as Richard "Crookback" or "Old Dick". In the Wars of the Roses Richard had assisted his brother Edward IV efficiently, earning him a royal dukedom in 1461. He married into the Neville family, acquiring their immense estates. When Edward died in 1483, Richard became Protector of the Realm. Having done his brutal best to secure his shaky claim to the throne by murdering his nephews, Richard had to crush a revolt by his disaffected right-hand man Henry Stafford, 2nd Duke of Buckingham – who lost his head. William Collingbourne famously lampooned Richard's next three chief supporters in 1484:

"the Catte, the Ratte and Lovell our dogge
rulyth all Englande under a hogge"

King Richard III by unknown artist (late 16th Century)
National Portrait Gallery, London

The cat was Sir William Catesby, the rat Sir Richard Ratcliffe, the dog Lord Lovell, who had a dog on his crest. Hog refers to the emblem of Richard III himself, a wild boar. His wit cost Collingbourne, who was probably a Tudor secret agent, his life.

Opposition from barons resentful of Richard's seizure of the throne led to his defeat and death, aged thirty-three, at Bosworth Field. Tudor publicity depicted him as a deformed and depraved villain, a line understandably adopted by Shakespeare in the reign of a Tudor queen. Richard, like Kaiser Wilhelm II (1859–1941), did have a withered arm, Shakespeare's "blasted sapling", due to his mother's difficult confinement. Ruthless and cynical, Richard was an able administrator and competent general: with considerable support in the north of England.

As Duke of Gloucester, Richard captured Berwick-upon-Tweed in 1482. After changing ownership between England and Scotland at

Elizabeth, known as "Jane" Shore, née Lambert (c.1445–1527), was one of the many mistresses of Richard's brother King Edward IV: three of whom Edward described as "the merriest, the wiliest, and the holiest harlots in his realm". After Edward's death, Richard made Jane do penance at Paul's Cross for her promiscuous behaviour. She was forced to walk barefoot through the streets of London in her shift one Sunday, with a lighted taper in her hand – attracting much admiring male attention along the way.

Richard III was found not guilty in a mock trial presided over by three justices of the US Supreme Court in 1997. Chief Justice William H. Rehnquist and Associate Justices Ruth Bader Ginsberg and Stephen G. Breyer, in a 3–0 decision, ruled that the prosecution had not proved that, "it was more likely than not" the Princes had been murdered; that the bones found in 1674 in the Tower were those of the princes; or that Richard III had ordered or was complicit in their deaths.

least fourteen times, this was the last. Though it became irrelevant after the Union with Scotland in 1707, Berwick has never formally been annexed to England.

One legend has it that Richard consulted a seer in Leicester before Bosworth Field, who told him that, "where your spur should strike on the ride into battle, your head shall be broken on the return". Riding into battle his spur struck a stone on the corner of Bow Bridge: and, as his corpse was carried from the battle over the back of a horse, his head was said to have struck the same stone and fractured. Richard III and Harold II are the only kings of England to have died in battle.

Arthur Mee, a travel writer and children's historian in the early 20th century, wrote an account of *The Very Strange Story of Richard Plantagenet* in Kent, part of *The King's England, County by County* (pub. 1936). Mee states: "… Sir Thomas Moyle (died 1560), building his great house here, was much struck by a white-bearded stonemason his mates called Richard. There was a mystery about him. In the rest hour, whilst the others talked and threw dice, this old man would go apart and read a book. There were few working men who could read in 1545; and Sir Thomas did not rest till he had won the confidence of the man …".

Laurence Olivier played Richard III on the stage of the Old Vic in London in 1944 and on film in 1955.

• Laurence Olivier as Richard III. Publicity poster. Collection of Paul Trevor.

It is said the book Richard was reading was in Latin, a language understood only by the educated classes. The mason told Sir Thomas that he had been brought up by a schoolmaster. "From time to time, a gentleman came who paid for his food and school, and asked many questions to discover if he were well cared for," wrote Mee. Richard went on to describe being taken to Bosworth Field and meeting King Richard III. The king said: "I am your father, and if I prevail in tomorrow's battle, I will provide for you as befits your blood. But it may be that …. I shall not see you again … Tell no one who you are unless I am victorious". When the battle was lost, Richard chose a simple trade in which to lose his identity and had found work at Eastwell Manor (which is a luxury hotel today). According to Mee: "Sir Thomas Moyle determined that the last Plantagenet should not want in his old age. He had a little house built for him in the Park and instructed his steward to provide for him every day".

If there is any truth in this story, the last male Plantagenet was not the simple minded Edward, Earl of Warwick who "could not tell a goose from a capon" and was executed by Henry VII in 1499, but Richard III's bastard son Richard, who died in 1550 – nearly 400 years after the accession to the throne of the first, King Henry II in 1154.

The Tudor dynasty, which replaced the Plantagenets, ruled England for 118 years: a short period in historical terms but one in which England became Anglican, turned herself into a powerful nation state and took the first steps towards the creation of an Empire. The mediæval period in England was finally at an end.

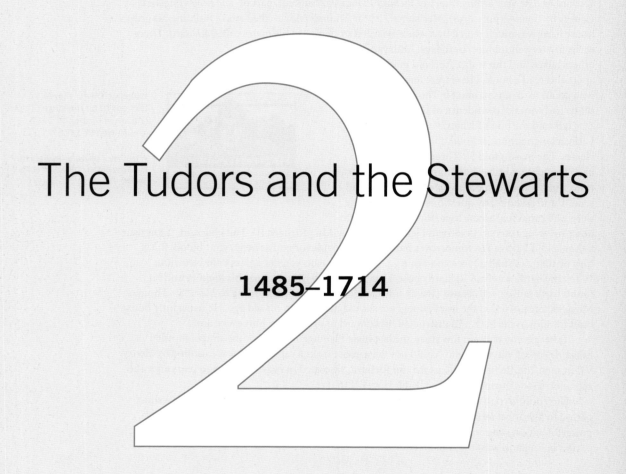

The Tudors and the Stewarts

1485–1714

Henry VII,
King of England

THE TUDORS AND STEWARTS

King Henry VII by unknown artist (1505) attributed to Michel Sittow (c.1469–1525)
National Portrait Gallery, London

KING HENRY VII OF ENGLAND (REIGNED 1485–1509)

Henry Tudor, Earl of Richmond brought to an end the Wars of the Roses. As King Henry VII, he founded the Tudor dynasty and through sound financial management, ensured its survival for over one hundred years.

Henry was born at Pembroke Castle on 28 January 1457, the only son of Lady Margaret Beaufort, a great-granddaughter of John of Gaunt and Katherine Swynford, his mistress and third wife. His father, Edmund Tudor died of the plague three months before he was born and his uncle Jasper, later 1st Duke of Bedford (c.1431–95) brought him up. When the Yorkist Edward IV regained the throne in 1471 Henry was forced to flee to Brittany, where he spent the next fourteen years.

Edward IV died in 1483. His sons were most probably murdered by his brother Richard who promptly crowned himself King. Encouraged by his mother to support a rebellion raised by the Lancastrian Duke of Buckingham and provided with a fleet and supplies by Duke Francis II of Brittany, Henry prepared to invade England. Storms scattered his ships, Buckingham's revolt collapsed and Richard tried to extradite Henry from Brittany. He escaped arrest at Saint-Malo and slipped into France: where the young king Charles VIII's regents offered to equip him for a second invasion. Ever cautious, Henry first won the support of the powerful Woodville family by promising to marry Elizabeth of York, Edward IV's eldest daughter by Elizabeth Woodville. She was the sister of Earl Rivers whom Richard had ambushed and executed in 1483.

Richard never overcame the revulsion caused by the murder of his nephews and by early 1485 opposition to him was so great that Henry decided to risk a second invasion. On 1 August he sailed from the mouth of the Seine with 400 English exiles and over 1,000 French and Scottish troops. Two days later the fleet arrived off Milford Haven in Pembrokeshire. Accompanied by his uncle Jasper Tudor, Earl of Pembroke and John de Vere, 13th Earl of Oxford (1442–1513), both seasoned soldiers, Henry marched north-east, recruiting over 5,000 men on the way. Aware that Richard had massed an army of 8,000 between Nottingham and Leicester,

Although Bosworth Field was not the last battle in the Wars of the Roses, it was the decisive one. Outnumbered, Henry was helped by the defection of the Earl of Northumberland, Sir William Stanley and his brother Thomas, 2nd Baron Stanley. The latter, lord of the Isle of Man and created Earl of Derby after the battle, was Henry's stepfather. Richard had made a grave mistake in relying on his support. Richard's army was routed, he famously lost his horse, became stranded in a bog and, if we believe Shakespeare, was killed ingloriously. His broken, naked corpse was paraded through the streets of Leicester, slung over the back of a horse. His grave most likely now lies under a municipal car park.

he decided to attack before Richard could manoeuvre against him. On the 22 August, Henry caught up with Richard at Bosworth Field, 12 miles west of Leicester.

Henry, though the victor in battle, was still politically far from secure. Astutely he dated his kingship from the day before the battle: if need be enabling him to charge those who opposed him with treason. He also had himself crowned in Westminster Abbey a week before Parliament met to ensure that it could never contend that it had granted him the throne. His claim was tenuous, dependent on an illegitimate line of succession, through a female, from King Edward III. His mother's family, the Beauforts, though later legitimised by King Richard II, had been barred from inheriting the throne – by none other than their legitimate half-brother, King Henry IV.

Henry dealt with this disqualification speciously, arguing that it did not apply to an already crowned king. Many Yorkists declined to accept either this interpretation, or that defeat at Bosworth was final. Their support was strong in the north of England and Ireland. They also had a powerful ally in Margaret of Burgundy, sister of Richard III. On the Continent, most countries were happy to shelter rivals to the English throne.

The first of many conspiracies that threatened Henry throughout his reign was fomented in 1486 by Richard III's chamberlain, Lord Lovell. It quickly petered out, giving way to the more serious threat from the pretenders, Lambert Simnel and Perkin Warbeck.

Lambert Simnel (1476–c.1534) was the pawn of John de la Pole, Earl of Lincoln. Richard III's nephew and designated heir, Lincoln had been spared by Henry after Bosworth. Henry had reason to regret his forbearance when Lincoln rebelled in 1487. With strong support from Margaret of Burgundy who had coached Simnel in an impersonation of her nephew, the Earl of Warwick (1475–99), the last surviving male member of the House of York, Lincoln attempted to instal his pretender on the throne but was killed on 16 June 1487 at Stoke, near Newark, in the hard-fought battle that ended the Wars of the Roses. The plan was doomed from the start, as young Warwick was alive and in Henry's custody. Henry displayed unexpected kindness, by accepting that Simnel was a stooge and found him a position in the royal kitchens. He rose to become royal falconer and died aged fifty, a rare survivor of treason against a Tudor king.

Perkin Warbeck (c.1474–99), the son of a poor Flemish burgess, was a royal servant in Yorkist Ireland. Dressed up in his master's finery, he was once mistaken for a prince of the blood and persuaded to impersonate Richard, Duke of York, the younger of the two princes presumed to have been murdered by Richard III in the Tower of London. The Yorkists, encouraged by the Holy Roman Emperor Maximilian I and James IV of Scotland amongst other European monarchs, assembled forces on the Continent for an invasion of England. Warbeck landed in Cornwall in 1497 but was captured at Beaulieu in Hampshire. Less fortunate than Simnel, he was hanged in 1499.

On Christmas day 1483 Henry Tudor had sworn to marry King Edward IV's daughter, Elizabeth of York (1465–1503) should he become king. On 18 January 1486 he fulfilled his pledge. Henry adopted the Tudor Rose as his badge, combining the white rose of York with the red rose of Lancaster, in the hope that its symbolism would help to unite the factions of the Plantagenet dynasty whose throne he had usurped.

The marriage turned out to be a happy one, producing seven children of whom four survived childhood. By all accounts, Elizabeth was beautiful, generous and kind, fond of dancing, music, gambling and hunting. She kept greyhounds and practised archery. She died in childbed, on her thirty-seventh birthday. Elizabeth is said to be the model of the Queen in a pack of playing cards.

Henry secured his crown by reducing the power of his nobles, principally by requiring substantial financial guarantees of good behaviour. He prohibited "maintenance" (the keeping of private armies) and forbade the use of "livery" (uniforms), to prevent them ever again from "flaunting your adherents by giving them badges and emblems". Aware that many of the most powerful barons at Bosworth had either switched sides or stood aloof until the outcome was clear, he imposed swingeing fines on any by whom he felt menaced. Some great magnates believed that their wealth and position entitled them to behave quite outside the control of the crown. Henry's favoured mechanism for

The Tudor Rose is the emblem of England – along with the thistle of Scotland, the leek of Wales and the shamrock of Ireland. It is the badge of the Yeomen Warders at the Tower of London and of the Yeomen of the Guard. It features on the British 20 pence coin and on the Royal Coat of Arms. In heraldry, the rose is depicted as white on red, if set against a field of gold – but silver or red on white, if placed on a field of another colour, according to the heraldic "rule of tincture".

The Court of the Star Chamber was named for the stars painted on the ceiling of the room in Westminster Palace where it held its meetings. Composed of Privy Counsellors and common-law judges, the court was established by Henry VII in 1487. It was effective in prosecuting those barons so powerful that no jury would ever convict them, especially where corruption and undue influence were apparent. Sessions were held in secret, with no indictments, no rights of appeal, no juries and no witnesses. Evidence was presented in writing.

Under the later Tudors it met in public and could not impose a death sentence. King Charles I however, convened the court in secret and used it to circumvent Parliament – which duly abolished it in 1641. It is a by-word today for oppressive government.

restraining them was his skilful use of the Star Chamber as a personal and prerogative court.

Henry also extended the writ of Justices of the Peace into all the corners of his realm. Appointed in every shire, serving for one year at a time, JPs were responsible for maintaining law and order, enforcing acts of parliament and verifying weights and measures. JPs were unpaid but the office was prestigious. Henry controlled them in the same way that he controlled the nobility, by exacting financial penalties for failure. They provided local governance, a free police service and were effective in combatting corruption.

Henry's determination to live within his means sprang from his firm belief that a king should avoid dependence on Parliament. In

Margaret Tudor, Queen of Scotland,
great-grandmother of King James VI and I by Daniel Mytens (c.1620–38)
The Royal Collection, London

1492, when pressed to join an alliance with Maximilian I, the Holy Roman Emperor and the King of Spain to resist French annexation of Brittany, he declined: pleading poverty. Henry understood that war was not an option for an impecunious king whose legitimacy to the throne was uncertain. He maintained cordial relations with France instead, on terms that brought him not only a substantial pension but more importantly, French recognition of his dynasty.

Henry overcame centuries of Scottish hostility to England with a treaty in 1499, followed by another in 1502 which provided for the marriage of Henry's daughter Margaret (1489–1541) to James IV of Scotland in 1503. The Scottish 'makar' (mediæval poet), William Dunbar (*c.*1460–*c.*1520) celebrated the rapprochement:

Sweet lusty lovesome lady clear
  Most mighty Kinges daughter dear,
Born of a Princess most serene,
  Welcome to Scotland to be Queen.

John (Giovanni) Cabot (*c.*1450–1499) was a Genoese navigator and explorer who learnt his trade on Venetian merchant ships plying the eastern Mediterranean. In 1490 he moved to Bristol, then the most important commercial port in England. In 1497, financed by city merchants and underwritten by the King, Cabot led an expedition across the Atlantic to find a western trade route to Asia. He made landfall either in Labrador or Cape Breton Island, claimed the land for Henry VII and made a cursory survey of the coastline. Although he disappeared on a second voyage, presumed lost at sea, his expeditions laid the basis for a later British claim to Canada.

John Cabot, not Christopher Columbus (another Genoese), made the first 15th century European landfall in North America. Columbus only reached the Bahamas and Cuba in 1492. In none of his subsequent voyages did he ever approach the mainland, though he did set foot in South America. The Vikings, who left traces of a settlement at L'Anse aux Meadows in Newfoundland *c.*1003, have a far better claim than either to have been the first Europeans to discover North America.

Amerigo Vespucci, an Italian cartographer, is commonly supposed to have given his name to America. Many believe however, that the word "America" was derived from the name of a Welsh-born Bristol tax collector, Richard Ameryke (or ap Meryke), who had helped to finance Cabot's first voyage.

In 1501 Henry arranged the marriage of his eldest son Arthur to Catherine of Aragon. Spain was emerging as a powerful nation, recently united under the crowns of King Ferdinand II of Aragon and Queen Isabella of Castile. Arthur died in 1502 but Henry, already in possession of half of Catherine's dowry as well as Catherine herself, won papal dispensation for her marriage instead to his second son Henry, later King Henry VIII.

Henry's greatest diplomatic triumph however, was the betrothal in December 1508 of his daughter Mary to Charles of Ghent, Catherine of Aragon's nephew who later became the Holy Roman Emperor, Charles V.

Without the impediment of waging war on his neighbours, Henry could increase excise duty on exports, principally wool, and his Navigation Acts ensured that English goods were carried only in English ships. He sanctioned the voyages of John Cabot and his son Sebastian and built the world's first dry-dock in Portsmouth.

In his relentless pursuit of income, Henry targeted rich nobles and the prosperous middle class. His principal tax gatherer and debt collector was his Archbishop of Canterbury John Morton, ably assisted by Sir Richard Empson (*c.*1450–1510) and Edmund Dudley (*c.*1462–1510). The grasping and venal Empson and Dudley, usually referred to almost as a single person, paid for the resentment generated by their ruthless efficiency with their lives. King Henry VIII won himself immediate popularity by executing both of them, for "constructive treason", as one of the first acts of his reign.

John Morton (*c.*1420–1500) was born in Dorset and educated at Balliol College, Oxford. In 1477 Edward IV appointed him ambassador to France and two years later, Bishop of Ely. A great survivor, in 1486 Henry VII promoted him to Canterbury – where the young Thomas More served in his household as a page. More later gave Morton a mention in *Utopia*. Morton is remembered for his 'catch-22' approach to taxation, known as "Morton's fork". When sizing-up a tax prospect, Morton advised: "If the subject is seen to live frugally tell him, because he is clearly a money saver of great ability, he can afford to give generously to the King. If however, the subject lives a life of great extravagance tell him, he too can afford to give largely, the proof of his opulence being in his expenditure". Morton's sense of humour extended to the grave. On his tomb in Canterbury Cathedral, amongst all the heraldic clutter, is carved an image of tun barrels, over-inscribed with the initials MOR: a pun on his name Mor-ton.

On Saturday 21 April 1509 Henry died, his end hastened by the pain of arthritis and gout. His attendants kept his death secret for two days to ensure a seamless succession by the young King Henry VIII. Empson and Dudley were arrested early the next morning.

Henry VII had inherited a bankrupt kingdom with an annual income of barely £42,000 (£200 million today). In the course of twenty-four years, he tripled crown revenues without recourse to Parliament. Indeed, only seven parliaments were summoned during his entire reign, sitting for a total of little more than forty-two weeks.

Henry's portraits reveal a shabby, careworn man with small blue eyes, poor teeth and thinning grey hair. Despite this image, he liked gambling, played real tennis, was a competent harpist, maintained an exotic zoo and enjoyed good food. His early experiences had made him wary and patient, also inscrutable and unpredictable. Throughout his reign, all Henry sought was financial security and international recognition for his Tudor dynasty. In pursuit of these two goals he was spectacularly successful.

Fortuitous and unintentional though it may have been, it can be argued that Henry's pragmatism in avoiding futile interventions in Europe, turning outwards instead to new horizons across the Atlantic, altered the blinkered mindset of his subjects and laid the foundations of Britain's future prosperity. Furthermore, in marrying his daughter to the King of Scotland, he made possible the creation of Great Britain, albeit 200 years later. As an English sovereign, his far-sighted wisdom would be matched in the future only by the caution and thoughtfulness of his granddaughter, Queen Elizabeth I. The reign of his very different son Henry VIII however, had to be endured first.

He was interred in his own memorial Henry VII Lady Chapel at Westminster Abbey. In 1512 his executors commissioned Pietro Torrigiano to build a magnificent tomb. Completed in 1518 and embellished with Florentine flourishes of putti, saints and angels, it is regarded as one of the first great monuments of Renaissance art in England.

The Yeomen of the Guard, or *The Merryman and His Maid*, opened on 3 October 1888 at the Savoy Theatre and ran for 423 performances. It is the darkest of the Gilbert and Sullivan operas, dealing with despair, love and sacrifice. Many consider the score to be Sullivan's finest. Sullivan wrote the music for the hymn *Onward Christian Soldiers* in 1871.

THE YEOMEN OF THE GUARD

The Queen's Bodyguard of the Yeomen of the Guard, not be confused with the yeomen warders of the Tower of London (often called "Beefeaters"), is the world's oldest military corps. Created by Henry VII on 22 August 1485, after the battle of Bosworth Field, there are today 79 Yeomen of the Guard: recruited from retired members of all the British armed services other than the Royal Navy. Members must be aged between 42 and 55, have been awarded good conduct medals and have retired after at least 22 years service, in the rank of senior noncommissioned or warrant officer. The Captain of the Bodyguard is a political appointment, traditionally a government whip in the House of Lords.

Today the Yeomen of the Guard perform only ceremonial functions: the most famous of which is to search the cellars before the State Opening of Parliament, a tradition dating from the Gunpowder Plot of November 1605. Yeomen still wear the original red and gold Tudor uniform.

Yeomen of the Guard

KING HENRY VIII OF ENGLAND (REIGNED 1509–47)

Henry VIII was born at Greenwich Palace in London on 28 June 1491. He was the second son of Henry VII and grandson of Edward IV, the first Yorkist king. Henry's elder brother Prince Arthur died in 1502, the year after his marriage to Catherine of Aragon. Henry VII applied to Pope Alexander VI for a special dispensation to enable his second son to marry his brother's widow which would secure the alliance he had previously negotiated with Spain. The Pope was amenable and in 1503 Henry was betrothed to Catherine, though the marriage was not solemnised until 11 June 1509.

The young Henry who inherited the throne in 1509 was not the gross and cruel Henry VIII of popular imagination. At seventeen, this "great boy" as Henry VII referred to him, was six feet 3 inches tall, scholarly and attractive. He had also received a £1.5 million inheritance from his thrifty father (£7.4 billion today). His grandmother, Lady Margaret [Beaufort] acted as regent until he came of age. As a second son he had had little preparation for kingship and had to rely on his counsellors in the early years of his reign. He applied himself to study under his tutor, the Norfolk-born poet John Skelton (c.1450–1529), as well as to hunting and jousting. At the age of ten he could play the fife, harp, viola and drums.

Henry was beguiled by the glory of war and eagerly sought excuses for military adventure. The most important issue in Europe was the Franco-Spanish territorial dispute in northern Italy. In 1512 Henry eagerly took his first opportunity to establish his status as an influential European monarch and reputation as a soldier, by joining with his father-in-law Ferdinand II of Spain and the Holy Roman Emperor, Maximilian I against the traditional enemy, France. French troops had also threatened the Pope himself, with whom the devout Henry had formed an almost servile relationship.

Throughout the early years of his reign, Henry remained on excellent terms with the Holy See. Pope Julius II awarded him the Golden Rose in 1510 and in 1514 Leo X bestowed on him an honorific cap and sword, presented with great solemnity in St Paul's Cathedral. In 1520 Henry wrote *Assertio Septem Sacramentorum*, a vigorous denunciation of Martin Luther and the Reformation. Pope Leo X repaid his loyalty by bestowing on Henry the title "Defender of the Faith" *(Fidei Defensor)*, retained by

Catherine of Aragon (1485–1536) was the youngest daughter of King Ferdinand II of Aragon and Isabella I, Queen of Castile whose marriage on 19 October 1469 led to the creation of the Kingdom of Spain. Catherine was betrothed to Henry within fourteen months of Prince Arthur's death, as Henry VII wished to retain her dowry. She produced six children but only a daughter, later Queen Mary I, survived infancy. Pressed for a legitimate male heir, Henry appealed to Pope Clement VII for an annulment. The Pope refused, causing the rift that led directly to the English Reformation. In 1533 Thomas Cranmer, Archbishop of Canterbury, annulled the marriage.

Catherine's rank of Queen was replaced with that of Princess Dowager of Wales, a title she refused to accept. She lived out the rest of her life, separated from her daughter, in a series of gloomy castles. She never complained, spending her days in prayer, eventually to die in Kimbolton Castle in Cambridgeshire. She was interred in Peterborough Abbey: neither splendidly as a former Queen of England nor as a Princess of Spain but simply as a Princess Dowager. Had Henry waited three more years, her death would have removed the obstacle that led to his break from the Church in Rome and England might still be a Catholic country.

There was much sympathy for Catherine and Mary, when Henry stripped Catherine of her title of Queen and declared Mary illegitimate. Severe measures were taken against anyone who openly declared their disapproval. The "Holy Maid of Kent", Elizabeth Barton, claimed to have had revelations of God's displeasure at Catherine's treatment and strongly opposed the Henrician Reformation. In 1532 she prophesied that if the King was to remarry, he would soon die. Barton was arraigned for unlawful sexual congress with her priests, tortured and forced to confess to having fabricated her revelations. She was hanged at Tyburn for treason in 1534.

- **Catherine of Aragon by unknown artist (early 18th century)**
National Portrait Gallery, London

the British monarch to this day. Henry however, observing the more tangible rewards received by his European counterparts, regarded the paucity of the acknowledgement as a snub.

The first year of Henry's French war was marked by a series of failures, brought about by Ferdinand's treachery, the reluctance of his own council to break with his father's tradition of avoiding war and an embarrassing lack of allies. In 1513 however, Henry led an army into Flanders and won a cavalry skirmish, capturing Tournai and Thérouanne in the so-called Battle of the Spurs. Quite unjustifiably, Henry acquired a reputation for military prowess that endured the rest of his life. Meanwhile the Earl of Surrey had annihilated the Scots at Flodden Field, in a much more significant encounter.

Flodden Field was fought on the 9 September 1513, near Branxton in Northumberland. Early in 1513, as Henry invaded France, King Louis XII had appealed to King James IV of Scotland to carry out a diversionary attack on England. James, respecting the "auld alliance"

18 year-old Henry VIII by unknown artist (1513)
Denver Art Museum

Flodden was the last great battle fought in Britain principally with bill and pike. It was also the first in which artillery was decisive. The famous piper's lament, *The Flowers of the Forest* was composed to commemorate the Scottish dead in the battle – in which every noble family in Scotland lost at least one member.

The "Auld Alliance" dated from a defensive treaty against Edward I of England, signed by John Balliol and Philip IV of France in 1295. During the 14th and 15th centuries, the treaty was invoked to combine against England six times. Protestant Scotland formally abrogated the alliance with Catholic France in 1560.

between Scotland and France, invaded England with an army of 30,000 men. Although outnumbered three to two, Thomas Howard, Earl of Surrey and later 3rd Duke of Norfolk, routed the Scots and killed their king.

In 1514 Maximilian deserted Henry. Under pressure from the Pope, Henry was obliged to sue for peace. He married his sister Mary to the unsavoury French king, Louis XII who died childless less than three months later, supposedly exhausted by his exertions in the bedchamber. The war saw the emergence of Thomas Wolsey as an able and energetic minister in the King's Council. Wolsey, who had administered Henry's campaign in France, opened up the attractive

Thomas Wolsey (1475–1530), the son of an Ipswich butcher, served first in a modest role as chaplain to both Henry VII and Henry VIII. In return for his formidable efficiency in relieving him from the tedium of administration, Henry prevailed upon the Pope to make Wolsey Archbishop of York in 1514, Cardinal the following year and finally Papal Legate in 1518. In 1515 Henry appointed him Lord Chancellor, giving him the chance of self-enrichment, an opportunity which Wolsey seized avidly. Wolsey attempted to act as peace-broker to Europe but having allied England with the

Holy Roman Emperor, Charles V against France, he became immensely unpopular by raising taxes to fight the war.

In 1529 Wolsey failed to obtain from the Pope an annulment of Henry's marriage to Catherine of Aragon. Further, his lavish construction and appointment of Hampton Court roused the King's envy and suspicion. Wolsey fell from favour and was stripped by Henry of all his offices. He was finally arrested for treason, having conducted secret negotiations with the French court. Fortunately for Wolsey he died, possibly from complications caused by diabetes, in Leicester on his way south to plead his case before the King. His last words were: "I se the matter ayenst me howe it is framed, But if I had served god as dylygently as I have don the kyng he wold not have geven me over in my grey heares".

• **Cardinal Woolsey (an archaic spelling) by unknown artist (*c*.1520)**
National Portrait Gallery, London

The Field Of The Cloth Of Gold: a coloured print made by James Basire in 1774

From a 16th century oil painting in the Royal Collection, London

possibility to the King of governing through a principal minister, rather than in person through the cumbersome mechanism of the Council.

The "Field of the Cloth of Gold" was the the historic meeting-place, arranged by Cardinal Wolsey, near Calais where Henry VIII met Francis I of France in 1520.

The meeting was designed to foster friendship between the two young kings, following the Anglo-French Treaty of London in 1518. The Treaty was a non-aggression pact between the major European states, to confront the serious threat of a Muslim invasion into south-eastern Europe by the Ottoman Turks. Henry and Francis were the same age and each regarded himself as a model renaissance prince, influenced by Machiavelli who believed that peace was best negotiated from a position of overwhelming strength.

Cardinal Wolsey maintained a rigorous equality between the two camps. He arranged for the first meeting between the two kings to take place on the border of France and the English enclave of Calais. He even arranged landscaped contours to ensure that each royal retinue met at an equal altitude. The two kings met on 7 June and the following weeks were filled with tournaments, banquets and entertainments of every kind, including demonstrations of archery and Breton wrestling. Each king entertained the other's queen. The Field of the Cloth of Gold made a great impression at the time but the political dividend was negligible. By the end of the year relations between the two countries had deteriorated when Wolsey allied England to the Holy Roman Empire – which now included Hapsburg Spain and the Low Countries, as well as Austria. Shortly afterwards, Emperor Charles V declared war on France.

The Field of the Cloth of Gold was orchestrated to display the magnificence of each court and to establish a mutual basis of respect between two traditional enemies. The meeting took place from 7–24 June 1520, in luxurious but completely prefabricated housing. Splendid, temporary palaces and pavilions were built respectively for Henry at Guines and Francis at Ardres. Both Henry and Francis strove to outdo each other in displays of opulent entertainment and elaborate accommodation for themselves and their large retinues. Henry's temporary palace was laid-out with walls made of timber, covered by tarpaulins painted to resemble brick and stone. Slanting canvas roofs faked slate and lead with an extravagant use of glass. Gilt fountains spouted a choice of red and spiced wines. 2,200 sheep and cattle were slaughtered to feed the English camp alone. The French Royal Chapel boasted the finest choir in Europe.

From 1515–27, against a backdrop of Hapsburg dominion, Wolsey dithered and reversed old alliances which damaged England's lucrative wool trade in Flanders and undermined her position in Europe. His attempts to raise taxes without the endorsement of Parliament made him extremely unpopular: so much so that, in 1523 he was obliged to summon one. In 1527, amidst his other troubles, Wolsey was confronted by the insoluble complication of "The King's Great Matter".

"The King's Great Matter" arose from Henry's urgent need to divorce Catherine of Aragon, so that he could find another queen and beget a son. Speciously, Henry argued that his soul was in mortal danger because he had married his brother's wife: even though Prince Arthur's marriage to Catherine had not been consummated. Henry's timing was unfortunate. From 1527–28 Pope Clement VII was the prisoner of Charles V, Catherine's nephew. Furthermore Henry, through Wolsey, wished Clement to declare invalid an earlier papal dispensation to Henry VII which had permitted Catherine's marriage to Henry VIII in the first place. In 1529 Wolsey conducted a hearing of the "King's Great Matter" with Cardinal Campeggio, the papal legate sent by Clement under orders to frustrate the King's application. Failure, to achieve what he should have realised from the outset was impossible, destroyed Wolsey.

Henry appointed Sir Thomas More as Lord Chancellor in Wolsey's place. It was an unpropitious choice, as More had made it clear to Henry that he disapproved of divorce and wished only to contest the Lutheran reformation. "If a Lion knew his strength, it would be hard for any man to hold him", More said of his king.

Henry was desperate for a son and heir but all Catherine's babies from their marriage, "blighted in the eyes of God",

Sir (later Saint) Thomas More (1477–1535) was a statesman and philosopher. Born in the City of London and educated at Oxford, he became a lawyer in 1501. He served as a magistrate in London from 1510–18, winning popularity and distinction as a fair and honest judge. In 1515 More published his great satire *Utopia*, highly praised by the celebrated Dutch humanist, Erasmus and in print ever since.

In 1517 More was appointed to the King's Council, becoming Henry's private secretary. In 1523 he was elected Speaker to the House of Commons. In 1529, following Wolsey's disgrace, More was appointed Lord Chancellor. He resigned in 1532, unwilling to connive at Henry's divorce from Catherine of Aragon. In 1534 he refused to sign the Act of Supremacy. Charged with high treason, he was imprisoned in the Tower of London where he wrote *A Dialogue of Comfort Against Tribulation*.

In 1535 he was tried and sentenced to death by hanging, a punishment reserved for common criminals. Henry relented and he was beheaded on Tower Hill on 6 July 1536.

• **Sir Thomas More by Hans Holbein the Younger (1527)**
National Portrait Gallery, London

Anne Boleyn (1507–36) had attended the French Queen Claude as a young girl, spoke French fluently and had a taste for French music, poetry and clothes. She was rumoured to have been born with a sixth finger and birthmarks, those on her neck being hidden by a large 'B' pendant suspended from a pearl necklace. She had dark eyes, olive skin and thick brown hair. Henry wrote her a series of passionate love letters in spite of his dislike of writing them: ".... to wish myself, specially an evening, in my sweetheart's arms whose pretty ducks (breasts) I trust shortly to kiss". Curiously, seventeen of these letters are preserved in the Vatican Library.

• **Anne Boleyn by unknown artist (*c.*1533–1536)**
National Portrait Gallery, London

Thomas Cromwell by Hans Holbein the Younger (1532/3)

National Portrait Gallery, London

were stillborn or died in early infancy, except Mary who was born in 1516. Henry's disappointment with his wife's physical failings encouraged an infatuation with Anne Boleyn, the sister of one of his earlier mistresses. Anne had spent her youth at the French court and was no stranger to intrigue. Just twenty when Henry's eye first alighted on her, she was also aware that Henry would have to marry her before she could bear him a legitimate heir.

Wolsey had died in disgrace and his replacement, Thomas More was not prepared to help Henry find a solution to his "Great Matter". In April 1532 Henry turned to Thomas Cromwell, a leading member of the King's Council: with the ambition and ruthlessness required to conceive and execute the King's business.

In 1533 Cranmer advised Henry on the introduction of the Buggery Act, the first legislation against homosexuals. The Act made 'buggery' punishable by death, a penalty not lifted until 1861. Frighteningly, in 2010 sodomy was still a capital offence in seven countries, albeit seldom exacted. All of them are Islamic states.

Cranmer became a close advisor to Henry's son Edward VI, entrenching England's Protestantism and composing the 42 Articles of the Anglican creed – from which is derived the beautiful language of the 39 articles of the Book of Common Prayer.

Putney-born Cromwell, later Earl of Essex (1485–1540) had been a close associate of Cardinal Wolsey, before becoming a Member of Parliament in 1529 and entering Henry's service the following year. His gift for administration swiftly won him control of the government. He contrived the instruments of policy that led to the creation of the Church of England and oversaw the dissolution of the monasteries.

Cromwell constructed a legal artifice to separate the English Church from Rome, contending disingenuously that it was an independent branch under the rule of the king. Henry said: "We are, by the sufferance of God, King of England; and Kings of England in times past never had any superior but God". The Act of Supremacy in 1534 recognised Henry VIII as The Supreme Head of the Church of England. The act also required an oath of allegiance from every English subject, also acknowledging the King's marriage to Anne Boleyn. The Act was repealed by Queen Mary in 1555 but reinstated in 1559 by Queen Elizabeth. Thomas More had been executed for refusing to sign it.

Henry found in Thomas Cranmer an archbishop who was prepared to accommodate this fiction. Cranmer also presided over the 'trial' to annul Henry's marriage to Catherine of Aragon which decided unsurprisingly that the marriage was indeed void.

Thomas Cranmer (1489–1556) was the first Protestant Archbishop of Canterbury. Born in Nottinghamshire, he was educated at Cambridge and ordained in 1523. He was Henry's spiritual advisor in 1533 when Henry finally broke with the Church of Rome. Cranmer officiated at Henry's marriage to Anne Boleyn and also structured his subsequent divorce from her.

On the accession of Mary to the throne in 1553, Cranmer was charged and convicted of heresy. To save his life, he repudiated all Protestant theology, fully accepted Catholic doctrine and stated that there was no salvation outside the Catholic Church.

Cranmer's recantation convinced no one and he was burned at the stake in Oxford, on 21 March 1556. He renounced his recantations and swore that the hand that had written or signed them would be punished by being burnt first. He said: "And as for the pope, I refuse him, as

Thomas Cranmer, Archbishop of Canterbury by unknown artist (after 1547) – his beard signified his rejection of the old Church

Lambeth Palace, London

When the executioner held up Anne's head, it is said that her eyes moved rapidly and her lips worked, as if trying to speak, for nearly 30 seconds. It is true that a gruesome motive for holding the head up high was so that it might both see its own decapitated body and hear the roars of the crowd. It is considered unlikely however, that a severed head could remain conscious for more than thirteen seconds: before lack of oxygen caused unconsciousness and death.

In 1076 Waltheof, Earl of Northumberland was beheaded whilst reciting *The Lord's Prayer*. To the crowd's amazement, the severed head continued as if nothing had happened, mouthing the words, "But deliver us from Evil. Amen".

Jane Seymour (1509–37), the third wife of Henry VIII, had been lady-in-waiting to his first wife, Catherine of Aragon and later to Anne Boleyn. Coming to the King's attention in 1536, Jane refused to become his mistress: a factor which certainly hastened Anne Boleyn's execution. Married privately, Jane produced Henry's only son, Edward. Jane made both Henry's daughters Mary and Elizabeth godmothers.

Henry was profoundly affected by Jane's death and had her buried in a vault at St George's Chapel in Windsor Castle, a tomb that he had built for himself. Jane was the only one of Henry's wives to be buried with him. He remained single for over two years after her death. Jane never received a coronation.

• **Jane Seymour, by Hans Holbein the Younger (1536/7)**
Kunsthistorisches Museum, Vienna

Christ's enemy, and Antichrist with all his false doctrine". As the flames grew around him, he kept his word by placing his right hand into the heart of the fire. His dying words were, "Lord Jesus, receive my spirit .... I see the heavens open and Jesus standing at the right hand of God".

By mid-1532 Cromwell's solution to Henry's "Great Matter" was in place and in January 1533, Henry married Anne Boleyn. On 7 September she gave birth to a daughter, later Queen Elizabeth I. However, the six-year interval between his initial infatuation and marriage to Anne had allowed Henry's ardour to cool. Within two years Henry had grown tired of her and failure to produce an heir sealed her fate. Henry had her charged with treasonable adultery, along with members of her family and his court. Anne was terrified by the thought of her impending execution. In an act of 'mercy', possibly to assuage his feelings of guilt, Henry brought over a skilled headsman from Calais who struck off her head in a single stroke, in the French fashion with a sword, at the Tower of London on 19 May 1536.

Henry married Jane Seymour ten days later. She bore him a son, later King Edward VI, on 12 October 1537. She died of septicæmia, less than a fortnight later.

In 1536 Parliament passed the Act of Union, confirming the 1284 Statute of Rhuddlan, which finally incorporated Wales into England. Five years later in 1541, Henry was proclaimed King of Ireland by the Irish Parliament. Only Scotland remained outwith the English Crown, a prize that Henry came within a hair's breadth of achieving.

Cromwell desperately sought to find Henry a new wife. In 1539 he chose Anne of Cleves, more as a pawn in his game of creating a north European alliance against France and the Holy Roman Emperor than a wife to delight his monarch. Having never seen her himself, he misled the King with a too-flattering portrait of her. Henry, unable to contemplate bedding her, was appalled: "You have sent me a Flanders mare", he said. The brief marriage destroyed Cromwell. His enemies persuaded Henry to charge Cromwell with heresy and treason. He was summarily executed without trial.

Anne of Cleves (1515–57) was the fourth wife of Henry VIII, foisted upon him by Thomas Cromwell. Her brother was William, Duke of Cleves, an important German Protestant leader. Cromwell believed that England needed allies to fend off a potential attack by France and the Holy Roman Emperor. When that threat disappeared, Henry's marriage to the stout and homely Anne became unendurable. In 1540 their marriage was annulled by Archbishop Cranmer. Anne did not complain and was given the title "King's Sister" and accepted her fate without comment. She spent the rest of her life at Hever Castle in Kent (ironically once the home of Anne Boleyn), a gift from Henry. She attended the coronation of her step-daughter Mary and died in 1557.

• **Henry was shown this picture of Anne of Cleves**

Catherine Howard (1520–42) was Henry VIII's fifth wife, described as: "a rose without a thorn, the very jewel of womanhood". She was a grand-daughter of the 2nd Duke of Norfolk and maid of honour to Henry's fourth wife, Anne of Cleves. Henry married Catherine in 1540. A year later however, he discovered that not only had Catherine enjoyed a number of sexual liaisons before their marriage but that she was still actively, if unwisely promiscuous – even taking her private secretary as a lover.

Cuckolded and enraged, Henry required Parliament to pass a bill making it treasonable for a sullied woman to marry the King. Two days later, on 13 February 1542, Catherine was executed at the Tower of London.

• **Miniature of Catherine Howard, after Hans Holbein the Younger**
National Portrait Gallery, London

Catherine Parr (1512–48) was born in Kendal Castle, the daughter of Sir Thomas Parr, an officer of the Royal Household. Catherine had been twice widowed when she married Henry in 1543. Her calming influence did much to soothe Henry's unreasonable behaviour and she went to great pains to befriend his children.

After Henry's death in 1547, Catherine married her old love whom she had had to abandon when Henry set his heart on her, Thomas Seymour. He was the brother of Edward, Duke of Somerset and the young Edward VI's Lord Protector. She died soon afterwards, another victim of puerperal fever having given birth to a daughter.

• **Catherine Parr by unknown artist (c.1545)**
National Portrait Gallery, London

Chester's racecourse, the Roodee (from *Rood Eye*, meaning "Island of the Cross") is Britain's oldest functioning sporting venue. Horse races have been held there since 1540. It and York are the only racecourses in Britain that lie entirely within a city.

By 1540 Henry was the longest-reigning monarch in Europe. He had grown immensely fat and his health was deteriorating. He suffered from an ulcerated thigh, the result of a jousting accident. He had also started to exhibit alarming and irrational behaviour. Paranoia, brought on by long periods of depression, had made him secretive and dangerously unpredictable.

Henry was forty-nine, lonely and probably impotent when he was beguiled by Catherine Howard – thirty years his junior but with a sexual history that was literally to be the death of her. Unaware of her flightiness, Henry appeared to dote on Catherine: even though she was described as short and graceful rather than beautiful.

In 1543 Henry married his sixth and last wife, the wise and gentle Catherine Parr.

In June 1542 war broke out between Charles V and the French King Francis I, presenting Henry with his first chance to meddle in Continental politics since the 1520s. He allied himself with Charles who was poised to invade France and in February 1543 sent 5,000 men across the channel in support. In 1544 Henry landed in France with 40,000 men and invested Montreuil and Boulogne. He captured Boulogne on 14 September, four days before Charles and Francis made peace at Crépy. Henry fought on regardless, beating off counter-attacks on Boulogne throughout 1545. In June 1546 however, unable to pay his soldiers and facing encirclement from a reinforcement of French troops in Scotland, he was forced to sue for peace with France at Ardres.

Henry's excursions in France were prompted by his desire for military and dynastic glory. His engagement with Scotland however, was driven by a far more serious consideration. After his son Prince Edward, James V of Scotland (Henry's nephew) was the next legitimate heir to the English crown. Henry's concern that James was forging strong links with Catholic France was genuine. Having brought Ireland and Wales under the English Crown, the replacement of James by Mary, Queen of Scots had created an opportunity to secure Scotland: through marriage to his son Edward.

Attempts were made by Henry and, after his death even greater efforts by Protector Edward Seymour, Duke of Somerset, to force the Scots to honour the terms of the 1543 Treaty of Greenwich to betroth their infant queen to Prince Edward. These efforts, which proved fruitless, became known as the "Rough Wooing" – a phrase coined by Sir Walter Scott to describe the Anglo-Scottish war fought intermittently from 1544–51. The defiant Scots betrothed their queen to the French *dauphin* instead. Her Regent, the Earl of Arran, smuggled her out of the country to France, despite having suffered a catastrophic defeat by Somerset's army at Pinkie Cleugh, on the coast of East Lothian, on 10 September 1547. In Scotland the battle is known as "Black Saturday".

Henry ultimately failed in both his French and Scottish endeavours, by falling between two stools. His invasion of France yielded Boulogne for eight years: but deprived him of the resources he needed to compel the Scots to accept a marriage with Prince Edward. Furthermore, in 1545 the French attacked England's south-coast, invading the Isle of Wight. This resulted in the loss of his beloved flagship, *Mary Rose*.

1545 marks the emergence of the Royal Navy. *Mary Rose* was already out of date, with too many types of armament and too big a crew. Earlier that year Henry had laid down three new warships, carrying only heavy cannon and far more manoeuvrable: the progenitors of the ships which, forty years later, defeated the Spanish Armada.

King Henry VIII after Hans Holbein the Younger (c.1536)
National Portrait Gallery, London

Henry VIII, by Hans Holbein
the Younger

The last few years of Henry's reign were dismal. His dreams of a Scottish marriage and unification had evaporated, to be replaced by the nightmare of French occupation of Scotland. Virtually bankrupt, he was forced to sell his sequestered monastic lands, further depriving him of a substantial income. To raise more funds, Henry debased the coinage, triggering uncontrolled inflation. Most importantly, he had made no provision for a regency during his sickly son's minority.

In the midst of all these futile foreign adventures, in 1546 Henry founded Trinity College, Cambridge. When Thomas Cromwell dissolved the monasteries, as part of the English reformation, Oxford and Cambridge had expected to be plundered too, as they were both religious institutions. The universities pleaded with Henry's sixth wife Catherine Parr who persuaded him to create a new college rather than close down the universities. Reluctant to spend royal funds, Henry combined two colleges, King's Hall and Michaelhouse, to which he gifted lands confiscated from the church. This endowment forms the bulk of Trinity's immense estate today: which includes the port of Felixtowe and Cambridge Science Park.

> The stairlift was not invented, as is commonly supposed, by an American in 1930: 400 years earlier Henry's servants had used a block and tackle to shift his enormous bulk upstairs – described as "a chair .... that goeth up and down". He was also manoeuvred about his palaces in three thrones on wheels. At his death Henry weighed nearly thirty stone. It took sixteen strong men to carry his coffin.

Conscious to the end, Henry died at Whitehall Palace in the early hours of 28 January 1547, aged fifty-five. His embalmed body lay in state until the 14 February. Two days later Henry was interred in the vault of St George's Chapel in Windsor Castle, next to his third and probably most loved wife, Jane Seymour.

Henry's reformation created dangerous national and religious differences which surfaced in the series of plots and conspiracies that plagued the reign of his daughter Elizabeth. Henry squandered the wealth seized from the monasteries on pointless wars with France and Scotland. The resulting sale of monastic lands to the aristocracy and professional classes caused a shift of economic power from the King, encouraging the fierce factions that blighted the next hundred and fifty years.

Finally, in spite of his prodigious efforts to secure an heir, Henry's six marriages produced only one delicate son and the insecure succession of two childless princesses, whom he had bastardised. But whatever his failings as king, lover, husband, father, diplomat and warrior, Henry, in the words of William Shakespeare, was undeniably "a man of an unbounded stomach".

Rievaulx Abbey

THE DISSOLUTION OF THE MONASTERIES

The Dissolution of the Monasteries (1536–1541) was the largest, legal transfer of property in the British Isles since the Norman Conquest. The Act of Supremacy in 1534, the First Act of Suppression in 1536 and a second in 1539 vested in Henry VIII the power to sequester every abbey, monastery, friary and nunnery in the land, expel their residents and appropriate their income. 825 religious communities were subsequently dissolved by Thomas Cromwell and his draconian Court of Augmentation.

By 1536 however, monastic life in England had long been in decline and the religious houses attached to most principal English towns were rarely even half-occupied. Henry was not alone in preying upon ecclesiastical wealth. European princes also found the temptation to confiscate church property and to tax the clergy irresistible. Catholic princes though, had first to seek approval from the Pope: which, for a share of the proceeds, was readily given.

The Pilgrimage of Grace, a popular uprising centered on Yorkshire in 1536–37, in protest at Henry VIII's break with Rome and the dissolution of the monasteries, was put down by the Duke of Norfolk. After 216 lords and knights, abbots, monks and parish priests had been executed, martial law was imposed – ending the rebellion. The leader, Robert Aske was hung in chains from the walls of York Castle.

Cromwell's wanton destruction of so many superb ecclesiastical buildings left England much the poorer in comparison with France. Such was the thickness of the walls and pillars (eighteen of which were 14 feet thick) of the church of Lewes Priory, dating from 1078, that in 1537 it required the services of Sir John (Giovanni) Portinari, a highly-skilled military engineer from Florence, to demolish them.

In 1539 a shocking incident occurred during the process of dissolution. Glastonbury Abbey was burned and looted by the King's men and seventy-eight year-old Abbot Richard Whiting was hanged from the top of Glastonbury Tor

• **The ruins of Lewes Abbey**

As a result of the dissolution, crown revenues were increased by about £150,000 per year (over £700 million today) but a third of this was committed to pay for monastic pensions. Although Cromwell had intended to use the windfall to finance the administration of government, Henry's need for money to fund his military ambitions in France and Scotland was unrelenting. By 1547 he had realised £1.4 million (over £6.5 billion today) from selling monastic property, usually at the market rate of twenty years' income. Sadly, most of it was wasted.

GREENSLEEVES

It is often said that Henry VIII, an accomplished musician who played a number of instruments, composed the music for *Greensleeves* to woo his mistress Anne Boleyn. The words "cast me off discourteously" are thought to reflect an unrequited passion. This may well be the case but the passion was not Henry's. *A New Courtly Sonnet of the Lady Green Sleeves*, was first registered, at the London Stationer's Company, in 1584. Henry died in 1547, nearly forty years earlier.

My Lady Greensleeves by Dante Gabriel Rossetti (1863)

Greensleeves is written in a style that became popular throughout Europe in the late 16th century as an accompaniment for dance. Rather than an instance of courtly seduction, the words seem to imply that the "lady" was a promiscuous young woman, possibly even a prostitute. The colour green was associated with "the oldest profession", possibly because casual sex was often conducted hastily in the long grass, leaving stains on the sleeves of the lady's dress. Alternatively, the ungallant lover might have simply assumed that because she was wearing green, the object of his desire was a whore – and that she had spurned him out of pique. Whoever she was, she inspired one of the most lovely English melodies of all time.

Christopher Wren's south
front, built for King William
III and Queen Mary II

HAMPTON COURT

Hampton Court Palace, on the banks of the Thames at Richmond-upon-Thames in Surrey, has not been lived in by the British royal family since the 18th century. It was originally built for Cardinal Wolsey between 1514–25, at a cost of 200,000 gold crowns. It was a mistake to incur the King's envy. Wolsey was quick to offer the palace as a gift to Henry VIII in 1528, in a vain attempt to stave off his ruin.

Between 1529–35 Henry added the mediæval Great Hall (the last to be built in England), the Royal Tennis Court and quadrupled the size of the kitchens, to feed 1,000 people. In January 1604 the palace hosted the Hampton Court Conference which led directly to James I commissioning the glorious *Authorised Version of the Bible.*

At the end of the 17th century William III commissioned Sir Christopher Wren to enlarge Wolsey's structure, to rival Versailles. Work was halted on Queen Mary's death in 1694, leaving the palace built in two distinct, and very different, architectural styles: Tudor perpendicular Gothic and repetitive Baroque. A remarkable harmony exists between the two, due to the use of pink bricks in both styles. Antonio Verrio (frescos), Jean Tijou (ironwork), Grinling Gibbons (woodcarvings) and Daniel Marot (furnishings) are among the famous artists who decorated the palace.

William III fell off his horse at Hampton Court in 1702 but died in Kensington Palace. George II was the last monarch to use the palace as a residence. It and St James's Palace are the only two of the many palaces owned by Henry VIII to survive.

Hans Holbein, self-portrait
(*c*.1542–43)
Uffizi, Florence

HANS HOLBEIN, THE YOUNGER

Hans Holbein the Younger (*c*.1497–1543) was a German artist and printmaker who worked in a Northern Renaissance style. He was one of the greatest portraitists of the 16th century. He is called "the Younger" to distinguish him from his father, an accomplished painter of the Late Gothic school. Born in Augsburg in Bavaria, Holbein worked in Basel in Switzerland as a young artist.

Holbein made his international mark with portraits of the humanist Desiderius Erasmus of Rotterdam who recommended him to Thomas More in 1526. He established himself in England, before returning to Basel for four years. He returned to England in 1532, to execute commissions to paint Anne Boleyn and Thomas Cromwell. In 1535 Henry VIII appointed him his King's Painter. He also designed jewellery.

Holbein was forty-five when he died, in Aldgate in the City of London. The site of his grave is unknown. His portraits are a vivid record of a brilliant court, at a time of great religious, social and political upheaval.

THE REIVERS

To "reive" is an early English word for to "rob". The Reivers or Reavers (nicknamed the "Steel Bonnets") were close-knit families from both sides of the Anglo-Scottish border who, for over three hundred years, survived by cattle rustling and raiding. They were most active during the 16th century. The area especially affected was known as the "Debatable Lands", extending little more than ten miles east of the Solway Firth and three miles either side of the border.

Nobleman or commoner, all were equally involved: raiding by night on hardy and sure-footed ponies. The Armstrongs alone were said to be able to put 3,000 men in the field.

Even in peace time the region existed in a state of near anarchy – not helped by the local tradition of "gavelkind", whereby land was divided equally among sons, so that there was never enough for anyone. The border lands were also mostly hill and moor, unsuitable for arable farming but ideal for sheep and cattle grazing. Cattle and sheep were an easy prey to mounted reivers with an intimate knowledge of the terrain. As soldiers, the Border Reivers were considered among the finest light cavalry in Europe.

Reiver families bore no particular allegiance either to England or Scotland, acting only in their family or clan self interest. As one commentator at the time put it: "They are people that will be Scottish when they will and English at their pleasure". Many Reivers had relations on each side of the border. At Ancrum Moor in 1545, Borderers changed sides in mid-battle. During the Battle of Pinkie Cleugh in 1547, Scottish and English Borderers were seen talking to each other in the middle of the battle. When spotted, they made a farcical pretence of fighting.

In 1603 Reiver influence was sharply curtailed when James I united the thrones of Scotland and England. He proclaimed the borders to be "the heart of the country": and that "no supply should be given to all rebels and disorderly persons, their wives or their bairnes and that they be prosecuted with fire and the sword".

James imposed severe measures to restore law and order. Suspects were summarily executed and Borderers were forbidden to carry weapons or own a horse worth more than 50 shillings. They were dispossessed of their lands and their homes burnt. The more alert reiver families swiftly offered their services to the King. Enthusiastically betraying old friends, they were rewarded by confirmation of their estates. Many were exiled to the bogs of Connaught and Roscommon in Ireland while others migrated to England or North America. Reiver descendants include Prime Minister Sir Alec Douglas Home, US President Richard Nixon and the first man on the moon, Neil Armstrong.

Preston pele tower, Northumberland

Elizabeth I, Queen of England

ENGLAND'S GREATEST QUEEN

KING HENRY VIII'S CHILDREN RULED ENGLAND FROM 1547–1603

Elizabeth was born at Greenwich Palace on 7 September 1533. She was the daughter of Henry VIII and his second wife Anne Boleyn. Henry's first wife Catherine of Aragon, whom he had married in 1509, had already borne him a daughter. It was with bitter disappointment that he greeted the arrival of another. By the time Elizabeth was three her mother was dead, beheaded by Henry on trumped-up charges of adultery and treason. Henry also demanded an Act of Parliament to declare his marriage to Anne Boleyn invalid which bastardised the young princess. Her half-sister Mary had suffered the same ignominy earlier that year.

Sequestered in a separate household at Hatfield, Elizabeth was a precocious but serious child, with a gravitas remarkable for her age. She was not however, neglected by her father and she received the classic education of a renaissance prince from the distinguished Cambridge professor Roger Ascham (1515–68). Ascham described his charge with the unabashed sexism of the age: "Her mind has no womanly weakness and her perseverance is equal to that of a man". Elizabeth studied the classics, becoming proficient in Latin, French and Italian, as well as receiving a thorough grounding in history, theology and moral philosophy.

In 1547 Henry VIII died and his delicate ten year-old son Edward inherited the throne. Elizabeth's position became suddenly most precarious. Her step-mother, Henry's widow Catharine Parr wasted little time grieving, before she married the Lord High Admiral Thomas Seymour – an arrogant and scheming man, intent on replacing his older brother Edward as Lord Protector (Regent) during King Edward's minority. Shortly after Catherine's death from puerperal fever, in September 1548, Thomas was arrested and accused of plotting to marry Elizabeth and rule England. Thomas had undoubtedly made the most intimate overtures to the young princess when she was

King Edward VI (reigned 1547–53) after William Scrots (c.1547)
National Portrait Gallery, London

Portrait of Elizabeth to commemorate the defeat of the Spanish Armada attributed to George Gower (1588)
National Portrait Gallery, London

living in his household but, under a humiliating interrogation by Sir Robert Tyrwhitt, she maintained her dignity and emerged unscathed. Her stubbornness exasperated Tyrwhitt who reported, "I do see it in her face that she is guilty". Elizabeth's vulnerability increased when her Protestant half-brother Edward VI died in 1553, from tuberculosis, scrofula and possibly, though very unlikely, syphilis inherited from his father. Edward's short reign left little mark on English history, other than the introduction of Cranmer's glorious *Book of Common Prayer* in 1549.

Elizabeth's half-sister Mary, intent on returning England to the Catholic Church, now became Queen. On 25 July 1554 she fuelled the flames of Protestant anxiety by marrying Philip II of Spain, the most Catholic of all Europe's monarchs. Not only had Elizabeth to adhere openly to the ordinances of the old religion but her person became the focus of Protestant rebellion, placing her life in extreme danger. In January 1554 Sir Thomas Wyatt, a country gentleman from Kent and son of the distinguished poet and courtier of Henry VIII, marched on London with 100 men in a pathetic undertaking with no clear purpose, known as Wyatt's Rebellion. Given short shrift, he was hanged, drawn and quartered in April.

**Lady Jane Grey
by unknown artist**
National Portrait Gallery, London

Edward VI had wished to disinherit the Catholic Mary, in order to protect his Protestant reforms but was advised that he would have to disinherit the Protestant Elizabeth as well. The vacuum that would be left by his intestacy was opportunistically filled by the sisters' sixteen year-old cousin, Henry VIII's Protestant great-niece, Lady Jane Grey. A girl of exceptional academic ability, Jane became the puppet of the ambitious John Dudley, 1st Duke of Northumberland who had replaced Edward Seymour as the young King Edward VI's regent in 1549. Northumberland married his son Guildford Dudley to Jane in May 1553 and persuaded Edward to name her as his heir. Edward died on 6 July 1553. Four days later, Lady Jane Grey was proclaimed Queen.

Edward's sister Mary evaded Northumberland's efforts to capture her. Within nine days Mary had managed to find sufficient support to ride into London in a triumphal procession on 19 July. Northumberland was executed on 21 August. Jane and her husband were tried in November. They were sentenced to death: she to be burnt alive, the traditional punishment for women found guilty of treason. Her life was spared – until Wyatt's Rebellion, of which she knew nothing, made her too dangerous a threat to Mary to be allowed to live.

Poor Jane, who had suffered a miserable childhood at the hands of her domineering mother Frances, the daughter of Charles Brandon, Duke of Suffolk, now faced a tragic and undeserved death. On 12 February 1554 Jane viewed her husband's body being removed from Tower Green, before being beheaded herself. She died bravely, in private, by special dispensation from her cousin, the now unchallenged Queen Mary.

**Queen Mary I by
Hans Eworth (1554)**
National Portrait Gallery, London

Elizabeth, under grave suspicion herself, was imprisoned in the Tower of London and questioned closely. Two months later she was placed under virtual house arrest in Woodstock Manor near Oxford. Over the next five years, Mary's calamitous reign (1553–58) was characterised by the burning of Protestants and humiliating military reverses. The loss of Calais in January 1558 was the worst. Mary died of cancer on 17 November, still grieving the loss of

THE ROYAL LINE OF ENGLAND FOR 204 YEARS (1399–1603)

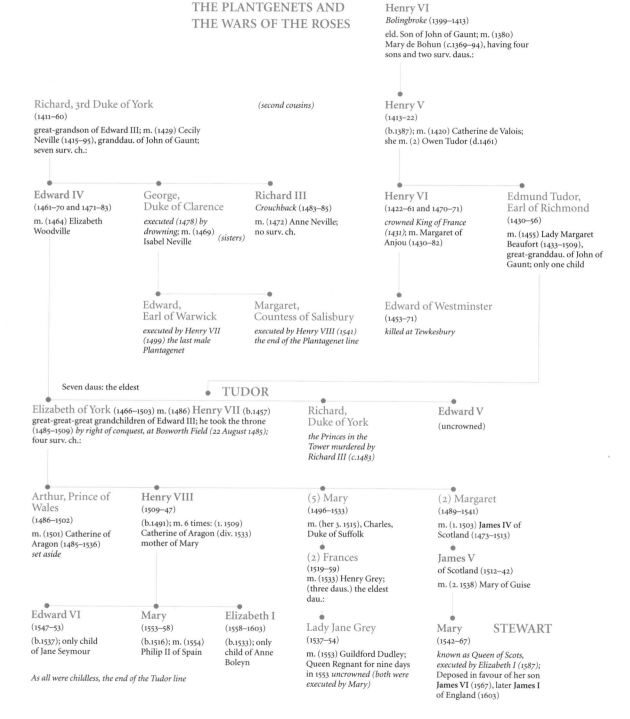

THE PLANTGENETS AND THE WARS OF THE ROSES

Henry VI
Bolingbroke (1399–1413)

eld. Son of John of Gaunt; m. (1380) Mary de Bohun (*c.*1369–94), having four sons and two surv. daus.:

Richard, 3rd Duke of York
(1411–60)

great-grandson of Edward III; m. (1429) Cecily Neville (1415–95), granddau. of John of Gaunt; seven surv. ch.:

(second cousins)

Henry V
(1413–22)

(b.1387); m. (1420) Catherine de Valois; she m. (2) Owen Tudor (d.1461)

Edward IV
(1461–70 and 1471–83)

m. (1464) Elizabeth Woodville

George, Duke of Clarence

executed (1478) by drowning; m. (1469) Isabel Neville *(sisters)*

Richard III
Crouchback (1483–85)

m. (1472) Anne Neville; no surv. ch.

Henry VI
(1422–61 and 1470–71)

crowned King of France (1431); m. Margaret of Anjou (1430–82)

Edmund Tudor, Earl of Richmond
(1430–56)

m. (1455) Lady Margaret Beaufort (1433–1509), great-granddau. of John of Gaunt; only one child

Edward, Earl of Warwick

executed by Henry VII (1499) the last male Plantagenet

Margaret, Countess of Salisbury

executed by Henry VIII (1541) the end of the Plantagenet line

Edward of Westminster
(1453–71)

killed at Tewkesbury

Seven daus: the eldest

TUDOR

Elizabeth of York (1466–1503) m. (1486) **Henry VII** (b.1457) great-great-great grandchildren of Edward III; he took the throne (1485–1509) *by right of conquest, at Bosworth Field (22 August 1485);* four surv. ch.:

Richard, Duke of York

the Princes in the Tower murdered by Richard III (c.1483)

Edward V
(uncrowned)

Arthur, Prince of Wales
(1486–1502)

m. (1501) Catherine of Aragon (1485–1536) *set aside*

Henry VIII
(1509–47)

(b.1491); m. 6 times: (1. 1509) Catherine of Aragon (div. 1533) mother of Mary

(5) Mary
(1496–1533)

m. (her 3. 1515), Charles, Duke of Suffolk

(2) Frances
(1519–59)

m. (1533) Henry Grey; (three daus.) the eldest dau.:

(2) Margaret
(1489–1541)

m. (1. 1503) **James IV** of Scotland (1473–1513)

James V
of Scotland (1512–42)

m. (2. 1538) Mary of Guise

Edward VI
(1547–53)

(b.1537); only child of Jane Seymour

Mary
(1553–58)

(b.1516); m. (1554) Philip II of Spain

Elizabeth I
(1558–1603)

(b.1533); only child of Anne Boleyn

As all were childless, the end of the Tudor line

Lady Jane Grey
(1537–54)

m. (1553) Guildford Dudley; Queen Regnant for nine days in 1553 *uncrowned (both were executed by Mary)*

Mary   STEWART
(1542–67)

known as Queen of Scots, executed by Elizabeth I (1587); Deposed in favour of her son **James VI** (1567), later **James I** of England (1603)

England's last possession in France. As she lay dying she said: "If my heart is opened there will be found graven upon it the word Calais".

Elizabeth ascended the throne, knowing that the country yearned for religious stability after the savage reprisals of Mary's reign. By a number of small but avidly noted symbolic gestures, Elizabeth made clear that she had consigned the Old Religion to the past. When the Abbot and monks of Westminster Abbey came out to greet their new sovereign holding lighted candles in the middle of the day, Elizabeth commanded them sharply: "Away with those torches, we can see well enough".

Elizabeth made haste to form her government. She purged the Privy Council of Catholics and reduced its number. The royal household was cut back too. Most importantly, she assembled a small and trusted band of personal advisors: including William Cecil, Francis Walsingham, Nicholas Bacon (1510–79) and Nicholas Throckmorton (c.1515–71).

The most immediate challenge which Elizabeth faced was that of her sex. The mid-16th century was uncompromisingly a man's world. After the disastrous reign of Mary, the principal concern of all who advised Elizabeth was to underpin this dangerous feminine instability, as it was then perceived, with the sensible guiding hand of a man.

William Cecil, 1st Lord Burghley (1520–98) was appointed by Elizabeth to be her Principal Secretary of State on the day she came to the throne. He had served Edward VI as advisor and secretary. Cecil was created Baron Burghley in 1571 and Lord High Treasurer in 1572, a post which he held until he died. He was implacable in securing the execution of Mary Queen of Scots, in order to safeguard the Protestant succession. He was also responsible for preparing the country to meet the threat of the Spanish Armada. Though he tried on a number of occasions, he never persuaded Elizabeth to marry – he excluded himself.

• **William Cecil, 1st Baron Burghley by unknown artist (c. 1585)**
National Portrait Gallery, London

John Knox (1514–72), a leading light of the Scottish Reformation, founded Presbyterianism in Scotland. He studied Divinity at the University of St Andrews, being ordained in 1540. In 1547 Knox was barricaded, with a band of Protestants, in St Andrews castle, by the French forces occupying Edinburgh. The French maintained a strong presence in Scotland because the young Mary Stuart had married King François II of France.

Knox was taken prisoner and sent to the French galleys where he suffered appallingly. He was released in 1549 and preached in England, until the accession of Queen Mary in 1553. He fled to preach in Frankfurt and later Geneva, returning to Scotland in 1559. Queen Mary of Scotland found him unbearable.

• **John Knox statue at Reformation Wall in Geneva**

John Knox, a Calvinist preacher published *The First Blast of the Trumpet Against the Monstrous Regiment of Women* in 1558, in which he wrote: "God hath revealed to some in this our age that it is more than a monster in nature that a woman should reign and bear empire above a man". It was an opinion shared by most people at the time.

Elizabeth's crown lawyers devised a legal fiction to deflect concern about rule by a woman. They postulated the wonderful theory of "The King's two bodies": two separate bodies which bound the Queen's physical, corruptible being with an immortal, perfect Body Politic, thus making gender irrelevant. Quite apart from the effect of two consecutive queens of England, the urgent matter of the succession had to be addressed. Elizabeth was the last of her Protestant line. If she died her cousin, Mary Queen of Scots would inherit her throne and the country

Robert Dudley (1532–88) was a younger son of the Duke of Northumberland, executed in 1553 for his part in the attempt to put Lady Jane Grey on the throne. Dudley was held briefly in the Tower of London, at the same time as his childhood friend, Princess Elizabeth. By this time he was already married to Amy Robsart.

On Elizabeth's accession, Dudley was appointed Master of the Horse. Rumours of a relationship with the Queen were rife. When Dudley's wife Amy died in 1560, after falling down a flight of stairs in mysterious circumstances, it was widely believed that Dudley had arranged her murder in order to marry the Queen. In 1563 however, Elizabeth proposed Dudley for marriage to the widowed Mary, Queen of Scots whose threat she hoped to counter by marrying her to a Protestant. The State Papers record how she hinted that this was to be a reward to Dudley, "whom, if it might lie in our power, we would make owner or heir of our own kingdom", for his loyal service. Mary was insulted by the idea of accepting Elizabeth's former lover and sharply rejected him.

In 1564 Elizabeth raised him to the earldom of Leicester. On 21 September 1578 Dudley married the beautiful Lettice Knollys, widow of Walter Devereux, 1st Earl of Essex and a maternal cousin of Queen Elizabeth – who was distraught.

Eventually restored to Elizabeth's favour, Dudley was placed in command of the Dutch campaign of 1585, culminating in the Battle of Zutphen the following year. In 1588, despite an undistinguished showing as a military leader, Dudley was put in command of the English land forces opposing the Spanish Armada. He died soon after at his home near Oxford. By the time of his death, his stepson Robert Devereux, 2nd Earl of Essex was already taking his place as Elizabeth's favourite.

- **Robert Dudley, Earl of Leicester by unknown artist**

would again be plunged into the horror of religious turmoil.

There was no shortage of royal suitors for Elizabeth's hand, Catholic and Protestant, from Spain, France, Austria and Sweden. At home, Elizabeth was ardently courted by her handsome Master of Horse and Privy Councillor, Robert Dudley, 1st Earl of Leicester. There is little doubt that Leicester was the great love of Elizabeth's life.

It is unclear what thoughts Elizabeth really entertained on this pressing matter. Significantly, her sister Mary Tudor had died barren, despite the most strenuous attempts to conceive by her husband King Philip II of Spain. Elizabeth was a highly intelligent woman who would have realised that it was more than possible that she also might be infertile. The prospect of making a disastrous marriage with the added humiliation of being childless was unthinkable.

Elizabeth played a game of dither and delay. So skilfully did she prolong it that the window of her child-bearing years melted away imperceptibly, yielding to the myth of the Virgin Queen, married only to her realm. In 1560 she contracted small pox and for many days her life and the nation's fate hung by a thread. More important than any ill health that she might have inherited from her father was his imperiousness, a loathing to compromise a power so hardly won and dangerously come by: "I will have here but one mistress and no master", she once upbraided Leicester. Not once in her long reign did she ever concede her power to take decisions. It was never a good idea to offer her gratuitous advice: a pamphleteer, John Stubbs and his publisher learned this lesson at the cost of their right hands, for writing a tract in 1579 denouncing the possibility of marriage by Elizabeth to the Catholic Duc d'Alençon.

Burghley House in Lincolnshire, built by William Cecil (1587)

From the start of her reign Elizabeth moved cautiously but firmly to anchor Protestantism in England. In 1559 Parliament passed the Act of Supremacy which declared the Queen Supreme Governor of the church; while the Act of Uniformity established Cranmer's prayer book as the official order of worship. Elizabeth required full conformity to the new statutes as a prerequisite to any state office. Priests, officials and all holders of university degrees were obliged to swear an oath of allegiance or forfeit their positions. This ensured that all key government appointments were held by staunch Protestants.

It is a tribute to the greatness of Elizabeth that she resisted this clamour. Her sole concern was to provide the roots of a lasting religious and political order. "I care not what lieth in a man's heart", she said: but she insisted he attended church on Sunday.

"There is only one Christ Jesus, one faith" she exclaimed later in her reign, "all else is a dispute over trifles", adding that she had "no desire to make windows into men's souls".

Mary Stewart was born on 8 December 1542 at Linlithgow Palace near Edinburgh. She became Queen of Scotland when her father, James V died within a week of her birth. Her mother, Mary of Guise brought her up at the French court of King Henri II. In 1558 she was married to his son François II. He died however, after barely a year on the throne. Attractive and 5 feet 11 inches tall, she returned to Scotland in 1561. In 1565 she married her cousin Henry Stewart, Lord Darnley. The murky intrigues of the Scottish court that she immediately became immersed in were exacerbated by her Catholicism. Her faithful secretary David Rizzio was murdered before her eyes at the instigation of her husband. Her son, who became James VI of Scotland and then James I of England in 1603, was born in 1566.

In 1567 Darnley was assassinated. Mary promptly but imprudently married James Hepburn, Earl of Bothwell (1535–78), who had almost certainly been implicated in her husband's murder. The Scottish nobles forced Mary to abdicate in favour of her son in 1567, obliging her to seek sanctuary in England from her cousin Elizabeth I. At first Mary enjoyed a considerable amount of freedom and independence: until her ever deepening involvement in Catholic plots, the most significant being those led by Ridolfi in 1570 and Babington in 1586, finally exhausted Elizabeth's patience and brought her to the headsman's block.

- **Mary, Queen of Scots by unknown artist (*c.*1560–1592)**
National Portrait Gallery, London

Compromises tend to inflame argument at the extremes of opinion. Militant Protestants who had fled the bloodshed of Mary's reign returned from Calvinist Geneva and Lutheran Frankfurt and Holland, to find Elizabeth's settlement weak and disappointing. They demanded that every remnant of the liturgy and ritual of the old religion be purged; and pressed for the persecution of every non-compliant Catholic.

Elizabeth detested evangelical excess and dismissed her Archbishop of Canterbury Edmund Grindal in 1576 when he refused to suppress the growing Puritan practice of Propheseyings. Grindal was replaced by the uncompromising Archbishop John Whitgift (*c.*1530–1604) who gave short shrift to reformers of any persuasion.

Elizabeth's fledgling, moderate church was menaced not only by Puritan zealots but also by a more insidious and dangerous threat from the Counter-Reformation. In 1569 Mary Queen of Scots was driven from Scotland to seek refuge in England, where she was regarded by the Catholic Church as the lawful Queen. For the next eighteen years Mary remained a prisoner, perilously indulging her taste for intrigue and making herself the focus of every frustrated Catholic in the land.

Elizabeth ignored pressure from Parliament to execute her cousin. She thought that to execute a queen, even a deposed one, would set a precedent from which she shrank.

In 1570 Pope Pius V excommunicated Elizabeth, absolving her Catholic subjects from any oath of allegiance they had taken. This further endangered the already precarious position of English recusants (those who refused to convert to the Church of England). On St Bartholomew's Day, 24 August 1572, 3,000 Huguenots (French Protestants) were massacred in Paris. In spite of a royal command to cease the slaughter, the killing quickly spread to the provinces where over the next two months at least another 7,000, possibly as many as 30,000 Huguenots perished.

Such a violent manifestation of Catholic resurgence deeply alarmed the English government. This fear was reinforced by the clandestine appearance of English Jesuit priests, trained in the special seminaries of Douai and St Omer: to stiffen Catholic resolve in England, to incite treason and if necessary, to accept martyrdom.

Despite her unwillingness to support insurrection and aversion to pointless expenditure on war, Elizabeth's Privy Councillors pressurised her relentlessly to support the Protestant struggle in Europe, especially in the Netherlands, which was occupied by Spain. Elizabeth first contributed small sums to the Dutch resistance. In December 1585 she despatched an expeditionary force under the inept command of the Earl of Leicester. The campaign ended in humiliating defeat at Zutphen on 22 September 1586.

In 1580 Pope Gregory XIII announced that anyone who managed to assassinate Elizabeth would be forgiven, as murder in this exceptional circumstance would not be regarded as a sin. A few years later, in 1584 William of Orange, Europe's other major Protestant leader, was murdered in Delft. The anxiety of Elizabeth's Privy Council led to an intensified hunt for clandestine Jesuit priests who, on discovery in their priest holes and cellars, could expect only the most hideous interrogation by racking, followed by a dreadful death.

Following the execution in 1584 of Sir Nicholas Throckmorton's nephew Francis, for plotting to murder Elizabeth and replace her with Mary Stewart, Elizabeth's Privy Council drew up a Bond of Association. The signatories bound themselves to execute any claimant to the throne in whose name treason had been committed. Clearly it was Mary whom they had in mind, for Francis Walsingham had by now uncovered her complicity in a tangle of plots and intrigue.

A plan to murder Elizabeth, concocted in 1570 by Roberto Ridolfi, a Florentine banker with business interests in England, in anticipation of an invasion by the Spanish Duke of Alba to put Mary on the throne, was exposed by Walsingham before it came to fruition. The Duke of Norfolk, who wished to marry Mary, was executed. In 1586 Walsingham uncovered another plot to assassinate Elizabeth, this time by Anthony Babington (1561–86). By devious means, finally he was able to prove an incriminating link between Mary and her conspirators. From this moment Mary's fate was sealed.

The plot implicated many English Roman Catholics and was supported by Philip II of Spain. It was foiled when Walsingham, through a well-placed Catholic double agent Gilbert Gifford, intercepted messages passed between Mary Queen of Scots and the plotters concealed in beer barrels. The code was cracked by Thomas Phelippes (c.1556–1625), a master cryptographer and forger, also in Walsingham's employ.

Nicholas Owen, canonised in 1970, was a lay preacher only slightly bigger than a dwarf. He was a master carpenter who specialised in building secret hiding places for itinerant Jesuit missionaries, called "priest holes". One of his finest can be seen today in Oxburgh Hall, the home of a then devoted Catholic family. Oxburgh was built c.1482 by Sir Edmund Bedingfield and is still occupied by his descendants. Saint Nicholas Owen died under torture in 1606.

The Rack consisted of an oblong wood or metal frame, slightly raised from the ground, with a roller at each end. At one end was a fixed bar to which the legs were fastened and at the other a moveable one to which the hands were tied. The victim's feet were manacled and the wrists were chained. As the interrogation progressed, a handle and ratchet attached to the top roller were turned, very gradually increasing the tension on the chains inducing excruciating pain while the victim's joints slowly dislocated. The rack's mechanically precise operation made it particularly suited for hard interrogation and the extraction of confessions. A gruesome feature of the body being stretched too far on the rack was the loud popping of snapping cartilage, ligaments and bones. Eventually, if the application of the rack was continued, the victim's limbs were ripped off.

Forcing a prisoner to watch an associate being racked was particularly effective.

• **Oxburgh Hall, Norfolk**

In July 1586 Phelippes (or Philipps) forged a postscript to a letter from Mary to Babington, requesting details of the other conspirators. In reply, Babington readily revealed every detail of the plot. Walsingham had known that the only way he could persuade Elizabeth to execute her cousin was to present her with irrefutable evidence that Mary was actively involved in a plot to murder her. "You have planned in divers ways and manners to take my life and to ruin my

England's first spymaster, Sir Francis Walsingham (1532–90) was born in Kent. Between 1550–53 he studied at King's College, Cambridge and Gray's Inn. On the accession of Queen Mary he fled to Padua, to continue his legal studies. When Elizabeth came to the throne, supported by Sir William Cecil, he was elected to Parliament. In 1569 Cecil assigned him to investigate the Ridolfi plot, his first government task. In 1570 he succeeded Sir Henry Norris as ambassador to France. He was instructed to promote an alliance with Charles IX, the Huguenots and the Dutch Protestants, in support of the revolt in the Spanish Netherlands. Catholic opposition to this alliance resulted in the St Bartholomew's Day Massacre.

Walsingham was appointed joint Principal Secretary of State in 1570. Elizabeth called him her "Moor" because of his small, dark frame and preference for dark clothes. She knighted him in 1577. Walsingham greatly admired Sir Francis Drake and was a shareholder in his circumnavigation of the world. He died on 6 April 1590.
• **Francis Walsingham attributed to John De Critz (Serjeant Painter to the king from 1603) the Elder (c.1585)**
National Portrait Gallery, London

In October 1586 Mary had said to her gaoler, Sir Amyas Paulet, "As a sinner I am truly conscious of having often offended my Creator and I beg Him to forgive me, but as a Queen and Sovereign, I am aware of no fault or offence for which I have to render account to anyone here below".

kingdom", wrote Elizabeth to Mary on 12 October 1586. On 20 September 1586 Babington and his associate John Ballard had been publicly executed in a particularly disgusting and savage manner.

Mary Stewart, since her time in France spelled "Stuart" (as the letter "W" is awkward in French), was executed on the 8 February 1587 at Fotheringay Castle – in spite of three month's hand-wringing and prevarication by Elizabeth. When Elizabeth heard that the deed had been carried out she displayed great grief and imprisoned the luckless messenger who had delivered the death warrant that she herself had signed.

Tensions were rising between England and Spain. One threat, dispelled so finally by the execution of Mary Queen of Scots, was replaced by the immediate menace of King Philip's "Great Enterprise of England", the Spanish Armada. Elizabeth, notoriously parsimonious when invited to finance and equip military expeditions, had nonetheless maintained a navy of small, fast and well-designed ships which could be quickly reinforced by vessels from the merchant fleet. Moreover they were commanded by seamen of exceptional courage and experience. Her overall Lord High Admiral, Lord Howard of Effingham assembled under him the freebooting privateer captains Sir Francis Drake and Sir John Hawkins.

Sir Francis Drake (1540–96), the greatest seaman of the Elizabethan age, was born in Tavistock in Devon. His father Edmund was a Protestant tenant farmer. When he was thirteen Drake found a berth on a small merchant ship plying the North Sea, becoming master at the age of twenty. In 1563 Drake first sailed to the Spanish Main on a slave ship owned by his cousin, John Hawkins. Surprised by a large Spanish fleet while sheltering in the port of St Juan de Uloa, Drake escaped capture by being able to swim, a rare ability amongst seamen of the time.

Miniature of Sir Francis Drake by Nicholas Hilliard (1581)
National Portrait Gallery, London

Sir John Hawkins (1532–95) was born in Plymouth He was the first Englishman to involve himself in the West African slave trade, buying natives from local chiefs and Arab traders to transport them to the West Indies, to work in the sugar plantations. The trade became known as the "Golden Triangle": linking Bristol, Benin and Barbados. Hawkins was appointed Treasurer to the Navy in 1577 and Comptroller in 1589. He advocated the design of smaller and faster warships which outmanoeuvred the clumsy galleons of the Armada. He was also the first to use the tactic of "blockade", by lying off Spanish ports in the New World to intercept treasure ships leaving for Spain. Hawkins consolidated the foundations of the Royal Navy laid by Henry VIII.

- **Sir John Hawkins by unknown artist (1581)**
National Maritime Museum, Greenwich, London

In July 1575 Drake was in command of a detachment of troops on Rathlin Island, part of the English plantation in Ulster, when 600 men, women and children of Clan MacDonnell were massacred after surrendering to the Earl of Essex.

Pelican was renamed by Drake for his patron Sir Christopher Hatton (1540–91), a courtier much favoured by Queen Elizabeth – his heraldic device was a golden hind. The vessel was a three-mast, 300 foot galleon manned by a crew of 85.

In July 1572, while raiding in the waters off Panama, Drake looted Nombre de Diós. Although he seized a hoard of treasure, he was unable to carry it away. In early 1573 however, he returned to Panama and captured a mule train of gold and silver. Climbing a tree in the interior of the Isthmus of Panama, he became the first Englishman to glimpse the Pacific Ocean. Drake returned to Plymouth on 9 August 1573. He had made himself a rich man but only one in ten of his original crew had survived.

On 13 December 1577 Drake was commissioned as a privateer by Queen Elizabeth, to lead an expedition to South America and on into the Pacific. He sailed from Plymouth in *Pelican*, with four other ships and over 150 men. After two ships had to be abandoned off modern Guyana, the three remaining departed for the southern tip of the continent. Drake crossed from the Atlantic to the Pacific through the Magellan Strait, after which a storm blew *Pelican* so far south that he realised that Tierra del Fuego was not part of a southern continent, as was believed at the time. Although a route south of Tierra del Fuego around Cape Horn is known as "Drake's Passage", it is misleading. It was discovered by a Dutchman – but not until 1616. Drake became the world's first Antarctic explorer when he reached a latitude of 55° south, a feat unsurpassed until Captain James Cook's survey in 1773.

Even before Drake reached the Pacific violent storms had sunk another of his ships while yet a further one became separated and returned to England. He sailed on alone in his flagship, which he renamed *Golden Hind*.

Drake sailed northward along the Pacific coast of South America. He captured two Spanish caravels on the way – and made good use of their more accurate charts. On 17 June 1579 Drake landed on the west coast of the North American continent where he discovered an excellent anchorage, probably the site of San Francisco today. Having repaired and restocked his vessels, Drake claimed the land for the English Crown as Nova Albion. Drake now headed westward across the Pacific and Indian Oceans, rounding the Cape of Good Hope, to reach Sierra Leone by 22 July 1580. On 26 September the *Golden Hind* sailed into Plymouth. Although only Drake and 59 crew had survived, he returned with a rich cargo of spices and Spanish gold. The Queen's half-share of the cargo surpassed the rest of the crown's income for that entire year.

Hailed as the first ship's captain to circumnavigate the world, as Magellan had himself been killed in the Philippines, Drake was knighted by Queen Elizabeth aboard *Golden Hind* on 4 April 1581. He later became Mayor of Plymouth and a Member of Parliament. In 1585 Drake sailed to the New World and sacked the ports of Santo Domingo and Cartagena. On the return leg of the voyage, he sacked the Spanish fort of San Augustíne in Florida. Drake's barely legal privateering exploits played a major part in prompting King Philip II of Spain to plan an invasion of England.

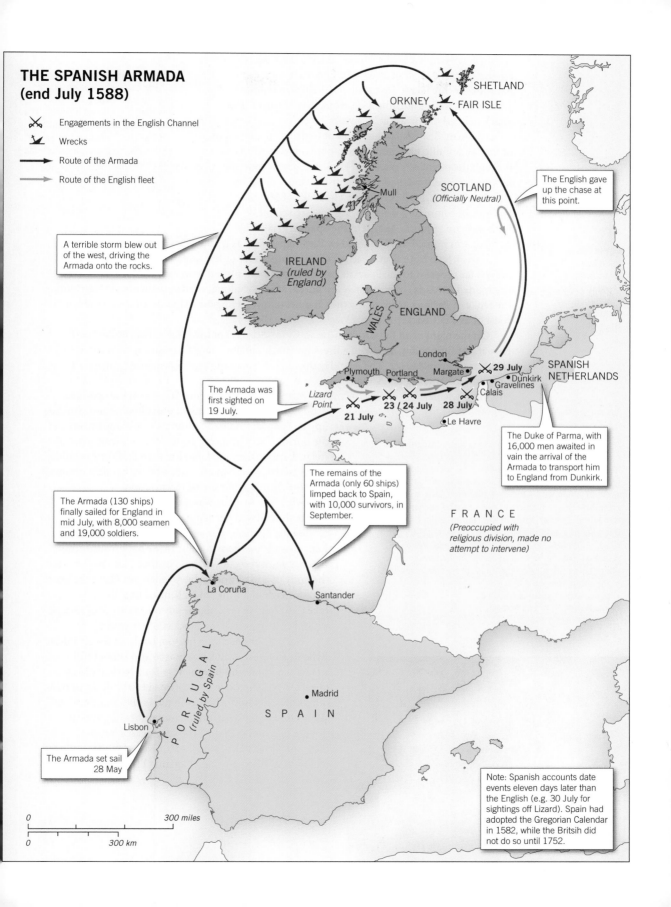

THE SPANISH ARMADA
(end July 1588)

⚔ Engagements in the English Channel

⚓ Wrecks

➡ Route of the Armada

➡ Route of the English fleet

SHETLAND

ORKNEY • FAIR ISLE

The English gave up the chase at this point.

SCOTLAND
(Officially Neutral)

Mull

A terrible storm blew out of the west, driving the Armada onto the rocks.

IRELAND
(ruled by England)

WALES ENGLAND

London

Plymouth   Portland   Margate   29 July   SPANISH NETHERLANDS

The Armada was first sighted on 19 July.

Lizard Point   Dunkirk   Gravelines   Calais

21 July   23 | 24 July   28 July

Le Havre

The Duke of Parma, with 16,000 men awaited in vain the arrival of the Armada to transport him to England from Dunkirk.

The Armada (130 ships) finally sailed for England in mid July, with 8,000 seamen and 19,000 soldiers.

The remains of the Armada (only 60 ships) limped back to Spain, with 10,000 survivors, in September.

F R A N C E
(Preoccupied with religious division, made no attempt to intervene)

La Coruña   Santander

PORTUGAL
(ruled by Spain)

Madrid

S P A I N

Lisbon

The Armada set sail 28 May

0 ————————— 300 miles

0 ————————— 300 km

Note: Spanish accounts date events eleven days later than the English (e.g. 30 July for sightings off Lizard). Spain had adopted the Gregorian Calendar in 1582, while the Britsih did not do so until 1752.

In a pre-emptive strike, Drake "singeid the King of Spain's beard", by sailing into Cádiz and occupying the harbour for three days. He captured six ships and destroyed 31 others, as well as burning a large quantity of stores. The attack delayed the invasion by a year.

The Armada began to assemble at Cádiz for the invasion of England. Philip had been driven to this extreme measure through the plight of persecuted English Catholics and the serious depredations made on Spanish possessions in the New World by English privateers. The Duke of Medina Sidonia, in command of some 130 ships, arrived off Plymouth on 21 July (1 August to the Spanish) 1588. The Armada was immediately engaged by the English fleet as it sailed up the channel.

A week later both fleets reached Calais roads, more or less undamaged. English gunnery proved far superior to the Spanish: but had nonetheless failed to make much impact on the disciplined Armada convoy. Safely anchored, Medina Sidonia's orders were now to transport the Duke of Parma's army across the Channel to invade England, landing either on the Kent coast or as a fall-back, the Isle of Wight.

On the night of 28 July Drake, who was Vice-Admiral of the English fleet under Lord Howard of Effingham, mounted a fire-ship attack: forcing many Spanish captains to cut their cables and run out to sea. The next day the English attacked their disorganized enemy off Gravelines, scattering the Armada.

The Armada, now unable to embark Parma's army, turned north towards the open sea. Although it eventually escaped pursuit when a storm blew up, the Spanish fleet had to find its way home by way of the north of Scotland and the treacherous west coast of Ireland. 17,000 men died and less than half the Armada returned to Cádiz. Not one ship from either fleet however, was sunk through gunfire or naval action.

While the Armada was sailing up the channel Elizabeth reviewed her army, drawn up at Tilbury ready to repulse the Spanish who were expected to land on the Kent coast. It was here that she made her great address, that has since rung down the centuries: "I know that I have the body of a weak and feeble woman but I have the heart and stomach of a King, and a King of England too, and take foul scorn that Parma or any other Prince of Europe should dare to invade the borders of my realm".

Walsingham had died in 1590, Drake at sea off Puerto Bello in Panama on 27 January 1596 and her faithful statesman and friend Burghley, in 1598. Now in old age, Elizabeth was increasingly depressed by the death of many others of her closest advisors in the Privy Council, whom she refused to replace, and the indignities of physical decline. She had to endure the spectacle of her last favourite Robert Devereux, Earl of Essex being humiliated in Ireland by the wily clan chieftain O'Neill. She lost him

Elizabeth was a model of hygiene for her day – she was known to "take a bath once a month, whether she needed it or no". Her godson, Sir John Harington (1561–1612), known as "Saucy" for his *risqué* poetry, invented the first flushing lavatory in 1596 – the US euphemism "john" derives from his name.

Drake was called *El Draque* ("the Dragon"), pronounced "Drake", by the Spanish.

As the English chased the Armada up the Channel in closing darkness, Drake put his duty and the strategic necessity to pursue the Spanish fleet second to his greed for plunder: by capturing the Spanish galleon *Rosario*, along with Admiral Pedro de Valdés and his crew. The Spanish ship was known to be carrying bullion to pay the Spanish Army in the Netherlands. Drake had been leading a flotilla of warships following the light of his stern lantern, in pursuit of the Armada. When he attacked *Rosario* he extinguished the lantern: abandoning his supporting ships, to be swallowed by the night and dispersed.
• **Defeat of the Spanish Armada by Phillippe-Jacques de Loutherbourg (1796)**
National Maritime Museum, London

altogether when he attempted a farcical coup: she was offered no alternative but to send him to the Tower and then to the block, on a charge of high treason.

There is a perception that the final years of Elizabeth's reign represented a golden age, with the Spanish defeated, the Protestant religion established, the country prosperous and "a nest of singing birds" of culture and literature.

Although the Elizabethan Age is celebrated for the flowering of literature, especially poetry and drama, indeed the final coming of age of the English language itself, the truth was a stark reality of war-weariness, inflation brought about by the influx of gold and silver from the New World, recurring plague, rotten harvests and high taxation. Wages were at their lowest since the last century, crime was rising and vagrancy rampant. In response, Elizabeth's government closed ranks, becoming ever more intolerant of any sign of disorder. Qualified sovereignty was shifting abruptly towards despotism. Factions and corruption in government were fast replacing an earlier devotion to public service, with clever men nakedly on the make: such as Elizabeth's last Lord High Chancellor, Thomas Egerton (1540–1617). Egerton was born Catholic and illegitimate but died as Lord Ellesmere, Viscount Brackley. His son became Earl of Bridgewater – and a descendant was created Duke of Sutherland in 1833. The Elizabethan age was possibly the most meritocratic in England's history.

Though Philip II of Spain had died in 1598, a beaten man and no longer a threat to her, the declining years of Elizabeth's life were marked instead by the brutal suppression of Ireland at the hands of Essex's successor Charles Blount, Lord Mountjoy (1563–1606). He finally brought about Tyrone's surrender, at an appalling cost in cruelty and blood – poisoning Anglo-Irish relations for the next four hundred years. At home Parliament's antagonism to the increasingly unjust and scandalous award of monopolies was only at the last moment mollified by Elizabeth's "golden" speech: ".... though you have had and may have many mightier and wiser princes sitting in this seate, yet you never had nor shall have any that will love you bettere".

Elizabeth had always been prey to depression. By December 1602 it had completely overwhelmed her, possibly triggered by the death of her great friend and companion Katherine Howard, Countess of Nottingham but more likely by the public concern

Robert Devereux, 2nd Earl of Essex (1567–1601) was the son of Lettice Knollys, a cousin of Elizabeth I, and stepson of her great love, Leicester. As a young man he became the favourite of the ageing Queen. It was a tempestuous relationship. In 1591 he commanded the English expeditionary force to reinforce the French Protestant pretender Henri of Navarre in his struggle against French Catholics. In 1596 he was present at a spectacular but indecisive attack on Cádiz. In 1597 however, he failed to intercept a Spanish treasure fleet off the Azores. In 1599 Elizabeth sent him to Ireland as Lord-Lieutenant, where his hopeless campaign ended in a shameful truce. Essex promptly deserted his post, to put his case privately to the Queen.

Importuned by a disturbed and mud-spattered Essex in the middle of the night, Elizabeth stripped him of his offices and perquisites. On 8 February 1601, with only 200 followers, Essex rushed into a foolhardy attempt to raise London in rebellion against the Queen. He was prosecuted before his peers by his former friend, Francis Bacon, and was executed on 25 February 1601.

• **Robert Devereux, 2nd Earl of Essex after Marcus Gheeraerts the Younger**
National Portrait Gallery, London

Edward de Vere, 17th Earl of Oxford, suggested by some to have been the author of a number of Shakespeare's plays, exiled himself from court after he was embarrassed when bowing deeply in front of Elizabeth. On his return she rebuked him for his absence with the words, "My Lord, we had quite forgot the fart".

The second Anglican Archbishop of Canterbury and the first to be married, Matthew Parker (1504–75), had a prominent nose and an inquisitive nature. Queen Elizabeth dubbed him "Nosy" Parker.

The greatest trading company the world has ever seen, the *Governor and Company of Merchants of London Trading into the East Indies*, was granted a Royal Charter by Elizabeth I on 31 December 1600. Known as the Honourable East India Company, or colloquially "John Company", it grew from modest origins to conquer and control the whole of the Indian Subcontinent. It was dissolved in 1873, having surrendered its powers to the British Government after the Mutiny in 1858.

John Dee (1527–1609), born in the City of London, was a mathematician, astronomer, and magician. A friend and advisor to Elizabeth I, he was the first to record in print the term 'British Empire'. He published *Propædeumata Aphoristica* in 1568.

over the unresolved succession. Elizabeth had never named a successor: and though it was clear that the front runner was James VI of Scotland, there were other contenders, including James's first cousin Arabella Stuart. No one knows whether Elizabeth ever, by word or gesture, sanctioned James as her successor. Refusing food and unable to sleep other than by standing up leaning against a pile of cushions, she died of pneumonia at Richmond Palace on 24 March 1603. The last rites were administered by "her little black husband" Archbishop Whitgift. Within minutes of Elizabeth drawing her last breath, Sir Robert Carey had saddled his horse to ride north. He arrived sixty hours later in Edinburgh, to announce to a delighted Scottish court that James VI of Scotland was now also James I, King of England.

WILLIAM GILBERT

William Gilbert, personal physician to both Elizabeth and for a few months, King James I, died on 30 November in the same year as his Queen. Born in Colchester in Essex in 1544, he was one of the greatest 16th century experimental scientists: regarded by many as the "father of electrical engineering, electricity and magnetism". Gilbert's great work, *De Magnete, Magneticisque Corporibus, et de Magno Magnete Tellure* ("On the Magnet, Magnetic bodies and the Great Magnet of the Earth") was published in 1600. He was the first to realise that a compass needle dips while pointing north because the Earth is a bar-magnet, rightly surmising that iron must lie at its core. Gilbert introduced the terms "electric force" (derived from the Greek *elektron* for the amber that he rubbed to produce static electricity) and "magnetic pole". Twenty years before Galileo's telescope, he discovered fixed stars at varying distances from the Earth. He died of bubonic plague.

Doctor William Gilbert by R. Clamp (published 1796)
National Portrait Gallery, London

In 1495 the first accounts of syphilis described pustules covering the body from head to knees, causing flesh to fall from the face, leading to death within a few months. Syphilis is a sexually transmitted disease caused by the spirochete *Treponema pallidum*. It is contracted by direct sexual contact with the infectious lesions found on the genitalia of a carrier. The disease progresses to the secondary and tertiary stages, initially becoming visible within 21 days in the form of a chancre (a painless ulcer). The lesion persists for a few weeks and then heals spontaneously. Patients, often show no signs of the disease during this incubation period but remain highly infectious. Secondary symptoms occur within 6–8 weeks of the primary infection, including rashes and moist, mucous patches *(condylomata lata)* on the genitalia and in the mouth. This is the most contagious period: attended by weight loss, fever and enlarged lymph nodes. Tertiary syphilis, occurring in those still alive within 1–10 years of the initial infection, is characterised by soft, tumour-like balls known as *granulomas* or *gummas*. *Gummas* can occur on the skin and mucous membranes but can also attach to any organ of the body, including the skeleton.

SYPHILIS – DID IT KILL THE TUDORS?

It is widely held that Henry VIII, his son Edward and his daughters Mary and Elizabeth, were all to a lesser or greater extent victims of the "new" and dread disease, syphilis. From descriptions by Hippocrates there is some evidence that syphilis was present in ancient Greece. In Renaissance Europe the first recorded outbreak of syphilitic symptoms occurred amongst French troops besieging Naples in 1494. French soldiers may have contracted the disease from Spanish mercenaries serving the French King Charles VIII. They may have caught it through sailors infected by Carib Indian women, returning in 1492 from Columbus's voyage to the West Indies.

Edward Teach, or Thatch (c.1680–1718), better known as "Blackbeard", was born in Bristol. Though he terrorised the North American coast between 1717–18, there are no accounts of him ever having killed any of his captives.

To begin with, there were no effective treatments for syphilis. Mercury was found to have a palliative effect in the 17th century, though acutely painful in its applications – giving rise to the quip: "a night in the arms of Venus leads to a lifetime on Mercury". Today, diagnosed early, syphilis is cured by one dose of penicillin. Amongst the artefacts discovered in Blackbeard's pirate ship, discovered off North Carolina in 2006, was a pewter penis-syringe, designed to deliver mercury directly into the urethra.

A detailed analysis of the well-recorded ailments which so afflicted Henry VIII in later life, does not support the popular thesis that he and his children died of syphilis. His paranoia and a suppurating ulcer that would not heal, are often cited as *prima facie* evidence of syphilis. Complicating any physical symptom in the 16th century was the primitive medicine and appalling sanitation. "Pox", the usual name for syphilis, also covered smallpox, chickenpox, diabetic ulcers and infected sores, all common afflictions of the period. Equally, any condition, particularly cancer and type-1 diabetes that caused wasting or emaciation was described as consumption. This gave rise to the conclusion that Henry's son Edward VI died of tuberculosis.

Henry VIII's leg ulcer was the result of a jousting injury. The wound apparently healed normally, only to re-open a few years later when ulcers appeared in both Henry's legs and feet. His toes turned black as they became infected with gangrene, a symptom more associated with diabetes than syphilis. The excruciating treatments to which his continually re-infected ulcers were submitted included lancing, cauterisation, leeching and poultices of ground pearls and lead. As he aged, Henry's deteriorating mental health is presumed to be symptomomatic of syphilitic progression – the spirochete, having attacked the nasal linings, usually advances to the brain. Henry suffered several strokes, suggesting the presence of arteriosclerosis and late stage diabetes. Poor blood circulation can cause degenerative mental impairment, leading to Alzheimer's disease. Henry's sister Margaret, Queen of Scotland also suffered from mental problems and strokes in later life. Further evidence that circulatory problems lay at the root of Henry's degeneration is his affliction with dropsy (an oedema or swelling), a malady caused by poor circulation, resulting in swollen fingers and an inability to hold objects (hence the name "dropsy"), as well as affecting the whole body.

In 1553 Henry's son Edward died aged fifteen from a wasting condition, commonly assumed to be tuberculosis, having contracted either measles or smallpox the previous year. Congenital diabetes however, may offer a more plausible explanation, exacerbated by an adolescent growth surge. Medicines of the day often contained arsenic. Edward is recorded as having lost both his hair and his nails before death, as well as suffering from an outbreak of ulcers and breath smelling strongly of garlic: all are possible clinical consequences of arsenic poisoning

Henry's daughter Mary, who succeeded Edward as Queen, had suffered from poor health since childhood. Records reveal serious menstrual aberration, migraine and dental problems. The severe stress suffered by Mary following the declaration of her illegitimacy might well have triggered a variety of psychosomatic disorders, including two phantom pregnancies while married to Philip II of Spain. The probable cause of Mary's menstrual cessation, nausea and swollen abdomen was ovarian or uterine cancer.

There is also little evidence to suggest that Elizabeth I suffered from congenital syphilis. Indeed, and to the contrary, Elizabeth enjoyed robust health and remarkable energy throughout

Cerne Abbas (or rude) Giant, Dorset

her long reign. She danced, played tennis, hunted and walked, displaying a liking for physical exercise unusual in a 16th century woman of rank. Her teeth certainly decayed in old age, from an over-fondness of sugar imported from the New World, and she suffered like her father increasingly from depression – though she never showed any sign of degenerative deterioration, the hallmark of congenital syphilis.

A CHALK FIGURE THAT DOES NOT APPEAR TO HAVE SYPHILIS

The Cerne Abbas, or Rude Giant is cut into a hillside north of Dorchester in Dorset. It is 180 feet high and 167 feet wide. The carving comprises a trench a foot wide and a foot deep, cut through grass to the underlying chalk. In his right hand the giant holds a knobbed club 120 ft long. It is believed to be less than 400 years old, perhaps made by servants of the Lord of the Manor Denzil Holles, during the Civil War, possibly as a parody of Oliver Cromwell.

Bess of Hardwick by unknown artist (c.1590)
National Portrait Gallery, London

BESS OF HARDWICK

Elizabeth Talbot, Countess of Shrewsbury (1527–1608), known as Bess of Hardwick, was the third surviving daughter of John Hardwick of Hardwick Hall in Derbyshire. When she was twelve years old, she was sent to live in London. In 1541 she married Robert Barlow, a rich but delicate boy of fourteen. Elizabeth was too young and Robert too frail to consummate the marriage. On his death a year later however, she inherited a third of his estate. Five years later in 1547, she married Sir William Cavendish (1505–57), Treasurer of the King's Chamber who had been widowed twice. At forty-five, he was more than twice her age.

In 1549 Bess persuaded Sir William, who had made a fortune from the Dissolution of the Monasteries, to buy the Chatsworth estate near her family home in Derbyshire. She had eight children by Sir William, of whom three boys and three girls survived. Through them she became an ancestress of the Dukes of Devonshire, Newcastle, Norfolk and Rutland, as well as the Earls of Pembroke and Shrewsbury.

In 1559, two years after William Cavendish died, Bess married again. Her third husband was the Captain of Queen Elizabeth's Guard and chief Butler of England, Sir William St Loe who owned substantial estates in Somerset and Gloucestershire. In 1565 Sir William died, probably murdered by his brother. Having no male heir, he left his whole estate to Bess. With a fortune in excess of £60,000 (£165 million today), she was now the richest and most influential woman in England after the Queen, to whom she had daily access as Lady of the Bedchamber. In 1568, aged forty-one, the indomitable Bess married her fourth husband, George Talbot, 6th Earl of Shrewsbury (1528–90). He had seven children from his first marriage. She rose to the challenge, by simultaneously marrying one of her own sons and a daughter to two of Shrewsbury's children.

In a final flourish, in 1574 Bess arranged for her daughter Elizabeth to marry Charles Stuart, 1st Earl of Lennox, the younger brother of Lord Darnley, the second husband of Mary, Queen of Scots whose only son was James VI of Scotland and the future King

Hardwick Hall (built 1590–97)

It is thought that Devonshire, rather than Derbyshire, was mistakenly inscribed in the original letters patent for the earldom.

THE RELATIONSHIP BETWEEN KING JAMES VI AND ARABELLA STUART

James IV
(1488–1513)

(b. 17 March 1473); *killed at Flodden 9 Sep 1513*; m. (8 Aug 1503, at Holyrood Abbey) Margaret Tudor (1489–1541), eldest dau. of Henry VII of England; having six legitimate children; the only surv. son:

James V
(1513–42)

(b.1512); m. (his and her 2. 1538) Mary of Guise (1515–60), having one child surv:

Mary
(1542–87)

(b.1542); *known as Queen of Scots*; m. (her 2. 1565) Henry Stewart, Lord Darnley

James VI
(1567–1625)

(b.1566); who became James I of England in 1603

1st cousins

Margaret Tudor

m. (2. 1514) Archibald Douglas, 6th Earl of Angus (1490–1557), div. 1528; their only child:

Margaret Douglas
(1515–78)

m. (1544) Matthew Stewart, 4th Earl of Lennox (1516–71); their younger son:

Charles Stewart
(1556–76)

Earl of Lennox *younger brother of Henry, Lord Darnley*; m. Elizabeth Cavendish (1555–82), **she was the daughter of Bess of Hardwick**

Arabella Stuart
(1575–1615)

m. (1610) William Seymour, 2nd Duke of Somerset (1588–1660); no ch.

Chatsworth House across the River Derwent

James I of England. Bess's granddaughter from this marriage, Arabella (or Arbella) Stuart, 2nd Countess of Lennox married William Seymour, 2nd Duke of Somerset. As Queen Elizabeth's first cousin twice removed and King James's first cousin, Arabella was considered one of the natural candidates for succession to the English crown. In 1592 however, Queen Elizabeth's advisor, Lord Burghley and his son Sir Robert Cecil, created Earl of Salisbury in 1605 by King James, decided against her. Three queens in a row was at least one too many. Nonetheless, Arabella Stuart's claim (never pursued by her it has to be said) was Bess's not-quite-crowning glory. It confirmed her as the arch manipulator of the late 16th century.

Bess's power was illustrated most clearly in the marriage negotiations between Charles Stuart and her daughter, in which her husband Shrewsbury wisely played no part. Since royal assent had not been obtained and as the Lennox family had a claim to the throne, the marriage was considered potentially treasonable. The Countess of Lennox, Charles's mother, was imprisoned in the Tower of London and not pardoned until 1577, after her son's death. Bess simply ignored Elizabeth's summons to London.

For fifteen years, from 1569–84, Bess and Shrewsbury fulfilled the duty of 'guardians' to Mary, Queen of Scots. She was a prisoner in one or other of their various houses, until handed over to the decidedly unamiable Sir Amyas Paulet, her last custodian.

Arabella Stuart married William Seymour, thirteen years her junior, in secret on 22 June 1610 at Greenwich Palace. For marrying without his permission, King James confined the couple to house arrest. Arabella, dressed as a man, escaped to Lee in Kent but Seymour failed to rendezvous with her before their ship sailed to France. He embarked on the next vessel to Flanders instead. Arabella's ship was overtaken by the King's men before it reached Calais and she was imprisoned in the Tower of London, never to see her husband again. She died in the Tower in 1615.

Bess was an accomplished needlewoman. While Mary Queen of Scots was held at Chatsworth House in 1569–71, they worked together on the Oxburgh Hangings. In 1601 Bess made an inventory of all her furnishings and tapestries. She willed them to her heirs, to be preserved in perpetuity. The 400 year-old collection, now known as the Hardwick Hall Textiles, is the largest collection of tapestry, embroidery and canvas-work conserved by a private family.

In 1590 Shrewsbury died. He and Bess had separated ten years before, after she suspected him of having an affair with Mary Queen of Scots. As Dowager Countess of Shrewsbury, she devoted herself to two major building projects, Chatsworth and Hardwick – known as "Hardwick Hall: more glass than wall", due to its size and number of windows. She died aged eighty, in 1608 and is buried in Derby Cathedral.

Bess is the only woman of consequence in English history who can compare with Eleanor of Aquitaine, King Henry II's consort, for longevity, strength of character and the exercise of power (Eleanor had ten children, Bess had eight). Perhaps Bess is the more remarkable, in that she came from a much more modest background.

THE SURPRISING ORIGINS OF SOME WELL-KNOWN ENGLISH NURSERY RHYMES

English nursery rhymes usually refer accurately to specific incidents; more often than not with a grisly theme, disconcertingly disguised by rustic jolliness:

Baa, Baa, Black Sheep, have you any wool? Yes sir, yes sir, three bags full.
One for the master, one for the dame,
and one for the little boy who lives down the lane.

In oral tradition, this inoffensive rhyme refers to King Edward I's wool tax, imposed in 1272 to fund his conquest of Wales and his subsequent castle building programme. A third of the price of wool went to the king (the "master"), a third to the monasteries (the "dame") and a third to the shepherds (the "little boy, who lives down the lane").

Jack and Jill went up the hill to fetch a pail of water.
Jack fell down and broke his crown and Jill came tumbling after.

The most ingenious origin often given for this rhyme is that in the 1630s, when he tried to raise revenues from sales of alcohol, King Charles I was blocked by Parliament. In retaliation, he decreed that the volume of a Jack (1/2 pint) was to be reduced but the tax was to remain the same. This ploy outmanoeuvred Parliament and Charles won his tax increase. Thus "Jack fell down and broke his crown" (many UK pint glasses still have a line marking the 1/2 pint level with a crown above it); "and Jill came tumbling after" refers to the gill (1/4 pint) which was also decreased in volume. "Fetch a pail of water" might be an observation that beer had also been watered down.

Half a pound of tuppenny rice, Half a pound of treacle.
That's the way the money goes, Pop! goes the weasel.

This rhyme is thought to refer, with sardonic Cockney humour, to the 19th century cycle of despair among poor textile workers in the East End of London. The spinner's "weasel" was a spoked wheel with a ratchet that clicked every two revolutions and made a "pop" sound after a chosen length of yarn had been measured. The first three lines of each verse describe some essential goods to be bought with meagre wages, followed always by a reminder that "pop goes the weasel" meant a return to tedious and repetitive work.

Georgie Porgie, Puddin' and Pie, Kissed the girls and made them cry,
When the boys came out to play, Georgie Porgie ran away.

This is an early reference to sexual harassment. "Georgie" was almost certainly George Villiers, Duke of Buckingham (1592–1628), a favourite and lover of King James I.

A handsome bisexual, he also had affairs with many ladies at court: "ran away" is scornful shorthand for his ability to avoid retaliation from their husbands through the King's protection. Buckingham was finally murdered and his tomb in Westminster Abbey bears a Latin inscription translated as: "The Enigma of the World".

The grand old Duke of York, he had ten thousand men.
He marched them up to the top of the hill and he marched them down again.

The most likely candidate for the "Duke of York" was Prince Frederick, Duke of York and Albany (1763–1827), the second son of King George III and Commander-in-Chief of the British Army during the Napoleonic Wars. He won a small victory over the French at Beaumont in April 1794 but was heavily defeated at Tourcoing in May. The precise location of the "hill" in the rhyme is presumed to be the town of Cassel, built on a hill rising nearly 600 feet above the flat lands of Flanders.

Little Bo Peep has lost her sheep and can't tell where to find them.
Leave them alone and they'll come home, wagging their tails behind them.

In Sussex, people claim that this rhyme is an encoded smuggling tale from the town of St Leonards-on-Sea, near Hastings. One of the Martello Towers (built in the Napoleonic Wars to deter a French invasion), known informally as "Bo Peep", was used by excise or customs men, sometimes to imprison smugglers. The Bo Peep public house (still in existence) is also said to have been used by smugglers.

Little Jack Horner sat in the corner, eating his Christmas pie.
He put in his thumb and pulled out a plum and said "What a good boy am I!"

This rhyme accuses Jack Horner, steward to Richard Whiting (the last abbot of Glastonbury Abbey before the dissolution of the monasteries by King Henry VIII), of treachery and theft. Before the abbey was seized and destroyed, the abbot sent Horner to London with a huge Christmas pie. The pie contained the deeds of a dozen manors hidden within it, to fool the highwaymen who swarmed over Hounslow Heath, as a 'present' to the King – or more likely to Thomas Cromwell, his Chief Minister. During the journey Horner opened the pie and extracted the deeds of the manor of Mells in Somerset. The manor properties included iron and lead mines in the Mendip Hills: hence "pulled out a plum", from the Latin *plumbum* for lead.

That "good boy" Horner became the owner of Mells Manor is well recorded. His descendants, despite having lived there from 1543–1975, still maintain that the legend is untrue. In their defence, it is true that

In 1592, the year of Buckingham's birth, Lord Macfarlane, was caught enjoying the favours of Lady Colquhoun of Luss, wife of Sir Humphrey, the neighbouring clan chief.

Macfarlane fled to one of his castles; but was smoked out, wounded by an arrow shot by his treacherous brother and beheaded. His testicles were cut off, cooked and served up in a rich sauce to Lady Colquhoun for dinner.

James (Jem) Hadfield (1772–1841) was severely wounded at the Battle of Tourcoing. Before being captured by the French, he was struck eight times on the head with a sabre, the scars remaining horribly visible for the rest of his life. On 15 May 1800, owing King George III no personal malice but believing that the Second Coming of Jesus Christ would be advanced if he himself was killed by the British government, he fired a pistol at the King. He made no attempt to escape, addressing the King with the words, "God bless your Royal Highness; I like you very well; you are a good fellow".

All who knew him spoke highly of him at his trial and he was found unfit to plead, by reason of insanity. He was however, the first lunatic to be detained rather than being released back into society. Parliament hastily passed the Criminal Lunatics Act of 1800, to provide for the indefinite detention of insane defendants.

The Abbot's kitchen at Glastonbury Abbey

their ancestor was called Thomas ('Jack' can of course, be a nickname) and that the records also show that he 'bought' the manor for £1,831 9/3d – and, in a nice touch, 3 farthings (just over £9 million today). Whatever the truth, wretched seventy-eight year-old Abbot Whiting (1461–1539) was hanged, drawn and quartered on Glastonbury Tor, for trying to bribe the King.

His head was nailed over the gate of his ruined abbey and his limbs were displayed at Wells. The lyric of the rhyme does not appear to have been published until 1725.

Goosey Goosey Gander, whither shall I wander?
Upstairs and downstairs and in my Lady's chamber.
There I met an old man who wouldn't say his prayers,
So I took him by his left leg and threw him down the stairs.

This rhyme is the earliest known reference to Roman Catholics as "left-footers" and probably dates back to Oliver Cromwell and the mid-17th century. The first line is a reference to "goose-stepping" Roundheads, searching houses for Royalists and nonconformists. Anyone who refused to accept the sovereignty of Parliament or Puritanism was severely dealt with (thrown "down the stairs").

Humpty Dumpty sat on a wall. Humpty Dumpty had a great fall.
All the King's horses and all the King's men couldn't put Humpty together again.

This mocking little rhyme is a 17th century example of political propaganda. Humpty Dumpty did not start off life as an egg, a pleasantry introduced by Lewis Carroll in *Alice through the Looking Glass* and memorably illustrated by Sir John Tenniel in 1871, but as an enormous cannon. It was used by Royalist forces under Sir Charles Lucas to defend Colchester when the town was besieged by Parliamentarians for eleven weeks in 1648. The gun was mounted on the church tower of St Martin-at-the-Walls. Both gun and gunner were toppled into the Essex mud on 14 July when the Roundheads scored a direct hit on the tower. "Humpty Dumpty" could not be recovered or "put together again" by "all the King's horses and all the King's men". The remains of the gun are still buried near the castle.

Mary, Mary, quite contrary, how does your garden grow?
With silver bells and cockle shells and pretty maids all in a row.

There are several sources quoted for this apparently rather charming little rhyme, all of them dating from the reign of "Bloody" Queen Mary (1553–58). The most believable, also the grimmest, is that when her bloodthirsty Lord Chancellor Stephen Gardiner (*c.*1497–1555) tended her "garden" (a sly little pun on his name) by persecuting Protestants, the "silver bells and cockle shells" were euphemisms for instruments of torture. If true, "maids" may be a reference to 'maidens', early Yorkshire and Scottish devices similar to the guillotine, used in executions. "Contrary" in this context might mean cruel – somewhat of an understatement.

The burning of Latimer and Ridley in Foxe's Book of Martyrs (1563)

Three blind mice. Three blind mice. See how they run. See how they run.
They all ran after the farmer's wife. She cut off their tails with a carving knife.
Did you ever see such a thing in your life as three blind mice.

The supposed origin of this rhyme really was unpleasant. It refers to the burning at the stake of the "Oxford Martyrs" for heresy, on the orders of "Bloody" Queen Mary. The three martyrs were the Protestant bishops Hugh Latimer and Nicholas Ridley, who burned slowly and suffered dreadfully, and the Archbishop of Canterbury, Thomas Cranmer. The executions took place in Oxford, just outside the city walls. Latimer and Ridley died on 16 October 1555; Cranmer five months later, on 21 March 1556.

The "mice" in the rhyme were the martyrs, who were rumoured (incorrectly) to have been blinded before execution. The "farmer's wife" was Queen Mary herself.

Ring a-ring o' roses, a pocketful of posies. A-tishoo!, a-tishoo! We all fall down.

Variations of this rhyme were common across Western Europe following the first visitation of the bubonic plague *Yersinia pestis*, known as the Black Death, in 1347. This version in English however, first recorded in Kate Greenaway's 1881 edition of *Mother Goose*, is said to describe the sequence of events that ended in death during the Great Plague of London in 1665 – which killed "only" 100,000 people. A roseate rash was indeed a symptom of the plague. Posies of herbs were carried, both for protection and to disguise the smell of rotting corpses. Sneezing was a final, fatal symptom and "we all fall down" was the inevitable conclusion. A reason for saying "God bless you" today when someone sneezes may be that, at the height of the plague, there was no time for a priest to give the last rites before death overtook the victim. Laymen had to bless their neighbours – quickly.

Latimer is quoted by the martyrologist John Foxe, in his grisly *Book of Martyrs*: "Be of good comfort, Master Ridley, and play the man; we shall this day light such a candle, by God's grace, in England, as I trust shall never be put out".

TOBACCO AND THE POTATO

In 1559 Jean Nicot de Villemain, the French ambassador to Portugal, sent a consignment of tobacco to the court of Queen Catherine de Medici in France, claiming it was a cure-all for a range of ailments. He gave his name to the genus *nicotiana* (and nicotine). In one form or another, tobacco has been used in the Americas for at least 3,000 years. Sir Walter Raleigh is usually credited with being the first Englishman to introduce tobacco to England *c.*1586. Sir John Hawkins and his crew however, are thought to have caught the habit in 1564, twenty years earlier. Sir Francis Drake is also believed to have bought a consignment back to England in 1573.

The first known addict was Thomas Harriot, the clever scientist sent to Roanoke Island, Raleigh's settlement in Virginia that failed in mysterious circumstances. Harriot wrote *A Brief and True Account of the New Found Land of Virginia* in 1588, in which he said: "There is a herb which is sowed apart by itself and is called by the inhabitants *Uppowoc*. In the West Indies it hath diverse names, according to the several places and countries where it groweth and is used: the Spaniards generally call it *Tabacco*". It was widely available in England by 1604 when James I, a staunch anti-smoker, wrote *A Counterblaste to Tobacco*, a prescient treatise and very relevant today.

Harriot is also thought to have brought back the potato. He certainly described it: "The second part of suche commodities as Virginia is knowne to yeelde for victuall and sustenance of mans life, vsually fed vpon by the naturall inhabitants: as also by vs during the time of our abroad. And first of such as are sowed and husbanded. *Openauk* are a kind of roots of round forme, some of the bignes of walnuts, some far greater, which are found in moist & marish (swampy) grounds growing many together one by another in ropes, or as thogh they were fastnened with a string. Being boiled or sodden they are very good meate". In about 1589 Raleigh grew potatoes, Harriot's *Openauk*, in his garden at Myrtle Grove in Youghal near Cork. It is thought to have been the first crop to be planted in the British Isles.

It is a terrible irony that, while the potato fed an enormous growth in the population of Ireland for 250 years, it was the failure of the potato crop that caused the dreadful famines and starvation of the 1840s.

Thomas Harriot (*c.*1560–1621) was born in Oxford. An astronomer, mathematician, ethnographer, and translator, he was the first person to make a drawing of the Moon through a telescope, on 26 July 1609, over four months before Galileo.

THREE IMPORTANT ELIZABETHAN EXPLORERS

Richard Chancellor (*c.*1515–56) was an English seaman whose visit to Moscow (1553–54) first established English trade with Russia. In 1553 he was appointed pilot-general to Sir Hugh Willoughby's expedition, to find a North-East passage to China. Scattered by storms, Chancellor's ship *Edward Bonaventure* was the only one to reach modern day Archangel in the White Sea.

From Archangel Chancellor made the 700 mile journey overland to Moscow. He was welcomed by Tsar Ivan IV who granted England privileged trading terms. Chancellor returned to England in the summer of 1554. The following year the Muscovy Company was granted a charter and a monopoly of Russian trade. In July 1556 Chancellor was drowned when his ship foundered off the coast of Scotland, on his way back to Russia.

Humphrey Gilbert (*c.*1539–83) was an English adventurer, M.P., soldier and navigator. He was born near Dartmouth in Devon and was Sir Walter Raleigh's half-brother. He was educated at Eton and Oxford. In 1566 he presented Queen Elizabeth with a proposal for *A discoverie for a new Passage to Cataia* (Cathay, the mediæval name for China), believing that he would discover a North-West route. Queen Elizabeth refused to sponsor his expedition and sent him instead to Ireland from 1567–70 to suppress a rebellion. Having accomplished this, with merciless brutality, Gilbert was rewarded with a knighthood. In 1578 he commanded a fleet of seven ships to establish a colony in North America. The expedition failed due to his poor leadership. Some of his ships returned to England; the rest turned to piracy.

In 1583 he set out again for North America with a fleet of five ships, reaching St John's in Newfoundland. He took possession of the island and surrounding territory for the English crown on 5 August. On 9 September, on the return voyage, Gilbert's ship *Squirrel* foundered in a storm. He and his crew were drowned. Gilbert's annexation of Newfoundland in 1583 was recognised internationally in 1610. His letters patent of 1578 were reissued to Walter Raleigh, who launched his own expedition to Roanoke in 1584. It was the first English attempt to found a settlement in North America.

Henry Hudson (*c.*1550–1611) was an English explorer and navigator. In 1607 the Muscovy Company of London commissioned Hudson to renew the quest for a North-East passage to China. Hudson sailed within 577 miles of the north pole. He was almost certainly the first man to discover Jan Mayen Island. On the return journey he was also the first Englishman to visit Spitzbergen. The following year Hudson attempted to sail the length of Russia's northern coast; but had to turn back at Novaya Zemlya.

In the employ of the Dutch East India Company, Hudson sailed to the eastern seaboard of North America in *Halve Maen* (Half Moon) and explored Chesapeake Bay. He sailed up the Hudson river, to which he gave his name, from modern New York to Albany, before realising there was no South-West passage this far north. His voyage established the Dutch in America, with New Amsterdam (later New York) as the capital of New Netherlands. In 1610 he set out in *Discovery*, funded by the Virginia Company and the British East India Company, to find a North-West passage to the Pacific.

> Between August 1941 and May 1945, 85 merchant vessels and 16 Royal Navy escorts were lost and many British seamen drowned, in the seas off Norway's North Cape. They were on the same route to the ice-free port of Murmansk, supplying Russia with vital munitions. German naval losses were even higher.
>
> Murmansk is near the border between Russia and Norway. *Murman* derives from the Old Russian word for Norwegians which has the same root as the English "Norman" or "Norseman".

By 25 June he had reached the Hudson Strait, at the northern tip of Labrador, and entered Hudson Bay, the huge inland sea which was named for him. He spent the summer mapping the eastern shore but in November, he was trapped in the winter ice. When he disembarked, intending to continue in 1611, his crew mutinied, wanting to return home. They set Hudson, together with his teenage son and a few loyal or sick crew members, adrift in an open boat. He was never seen again. Only eight out of the remaining crew of thirteen managed to reach England. Although they were arrested, the men were never held to account. It is believed that their knowledge of the New World was reckoned too valuable to lose. Hudson's discoveries laid the basis for future English claims to large tracts of Canada.

NICHOLAS HILLIARD

Nicholas Hilliard (*c.*1547–1619) was the first English Renaissance painter. He specialised in miniature portraits and was appointed miniaturist (limner) to both Queen Elizabeth I and King James I. He was born in Exeter, the son of a goldsmith.

At thirteen he was employed in the household of a prominent Exeter protestant, John Bodley, the father of Thomas Bodley the founder of the Bodleian library in Oxford. During the reign of Mary I, Hilliard followed the Bodleys into exile in Geneva. Returning to London, he was apprenticed to Queen Elizabeth's jeweller, Robert Brandon. In 1571 he painted a "book of portraitures" for the Earl of Leicester, the Queen's favourite. From 1570 he frequently painted the Queen and her court, including Sir Francis Drake and Sir Walter Raleigh. After the Queen's death, he was retained by King James I who granted him a monopoly of engraved portraits. The largest collections of his work are in the Victoria and Albert Museum and the National Gallery. He published *The Art of Limning* in 1600 which is in the Bodleian Library. Hilliard died on 3 January 1619 and was buried in St Martin-in-the-Fields.

Hilliard's most famous miniature, Young Man Among Roses (*c.*1585) – probably a portrait of Robert Devereux 2nd Earl of Essex (1567–1601)

THE FLIGHT OF THE EARLS

The Flight of the Earls *(Teitheadh na nIarlaí* in Irish Gaelic) is the romantic name given to the self-imposed exile of Hugh O'Neill, 2nd Earl of Tyrone and Rory O'Donnell, 1st Earl of Tyrconnell on 14 September 1607. They left Ireland in a French ship from the village of Rathmullan, on Lough Swilly in County Donegal, with ninety loyal followers. They intended to seek support from Spain to reopen their rebellion, having failed to realise that, after the accession of King James I in 1603, a peace treaty had been signed by Spain with England in 1604. They left their wives and families behind in Ulster – never to return. Tyrconnell died in July 1608, aged thirty-three, and Tyrone on 20 July 1616, aged about sixty-six, both of them in Rome.

The Earls had no real reason to flee. Having being defeated at Kinsale in 1601, they were pardoned by King James: but found it difficult to accept that their rebellion, which had devastated Munster, had failed. They could have lived easily within the benign settlement proposed by King James. O'Neill chose to reject his family's 1,300-year history, his duty to his countrymen and the earldom that his grandfather had been glad enough to accept from Henry VIII fifty years earlier.

Tyrone's pretensions and strategic mistake cost Ulster dearly, resulting in new plantations of settlers from England, Wales and Scotland – sponsored in part by City of London merchants, who renamed Derry as Londonderry. This displaced the poorer Gaelic speaking population of Ulster and changed the course of Irish history.

KING JAMES VI OF SCOTLAND (REIGNED 1567–1625) AND I OF ENGLAND AND IRELAND (REIGNED 1603–25)

James inherited the Scottish crown when he was only a year old, becoming King James VI. In 1603, as King James I, he was the first Stuart to accede to the English throne and the first monarch of "Great Britain". After centuries of warfare and attempts by English kings to seize the Scottish throne, it is ironic that it was a Scottish king who oversaw the transition to a dual monarchy. His stubborn belief in the Divine Right of Kings and severe financial difficulties brought him into conflict with Parliament, setting the scene for the English Civil Wars and the execution of his son Charles I.

In 1603 England's new "God", James I was thirty-seven. Wearing thickly padded clothes and in constant fear of an assassin's dagger, he was ugly and uncouth. He was also a pedantic bigot. He harangued his court and Parliament ceaselessly in an impenetrable Scots accent, rarely

Henry Stewart, 1st Duke of Albany, usually known as **Lord Darnley** (1545–67), was the son of Matthew Stewart, 4th Earl of Lennox, a pretender to the Scottish throne. Darnley, a great-grandson of Henry VII through his grandmother Margaret Tudor, married his cousin Mary against the wishes of both Queen Elizabeth I of England and the Scots Protestants. Darnley instigated the murder, in her presence, of Mary's secretary, David Rizzio before he himself was murdered, at the age of twenty-one. Though handsome, Darnley was immature, mean, violent and a drunk. It is more than likely that Mary was complicit in his death.

Henri IV of France clearly no admirer of James, teasingly referring to him as the "Modern Solomon" – a pun implying that he was "the son of David", meaning Rizzio.

- **Henry Stuart, Lord Darnley probably Reginold Elstrack (published c.1610–1627)**
National Portrait Gallery, London

"The state of the monarchy is the supremest thing on earth; for kings are not only God's lieutenants upon earth and sit upon God's throne but even by God himself they are called gods", James asserted to Parliament on 21 March 1610.

Morton introduced the 'Maiden', a primitive guillotine, from Halifax in Yorkshire, having been "impressed by its clean work". His own death was testament to that.

attending to any view but his own. He rejoiced in court revels, had a weakness for drink and a passion for hunting. His head was disastrously turned by handsome young men with well-turned calves and sculpted buttocks. He was highly educated and a considerable scholar in his own right. James's arrogance and lack of common sense however, led Henri IV of France to dub him, "The wisest fool in Christendom". This was the cynical, Protestant Henri who had said that Paris *"vaut bien une messe"* ("Paris is well worth a mass").

James was the only son of Mary Queen of Scots and her second husband Henry Stewart, Lord Darnley. Born on 19 June 1566 at Edinburgh Castle, James was only eight months old when his father was blown-up by a mine. His suspected murderer, James Hepburn, 4th Earl of Bothwell then married his mother. She abdicated the throne a few months later. Effectively an orphan, the baby James became King of Scotland.

James grew up alone but received a superb classical and religious education: beaten into him by his tutors, principally George Buchanan. He had a life-long fear of violence, suffered from irritable bowel syndrome and was

LATE MEDIÆVAL IRELAND (1169–1641)

- Anglo–Norman lands in 1300
- Native Irish lands in 1300
- By 1450 only the "Pale" around Dublin was still governed by England
- Still settled by Anglo–Irish in 1450
- — Northern Ireland (1922)

By 1641 80,000 English and Scots had been settled in Ulster.

SCOTLAND

U
L
S
T
E
R

O'Neill

Londonderry (settled 1613 besieged 1688–9)

Ireland was ruled by England until 1707 and then by Great Britain until 1921.

OFFALY and LAOIS (settled 1556)

The Aran Islands

Drogheda (1649)

Boyne (1690)

Dublin

Irish Sea

Richard de Clare ("Strongbow") landed 1 May 1169.

MUNSTER (settled 1586)

Waterford

Wexford

WALES

Henry II landed 18 October 1171 determined to restrain the independence of his knights.

0 25 miles
0 50 km

Map of Ireland 1169–1641: In his bull Laudabiliter, Adrian IV (the only English Pope) granted Ireland to Henry II in 1155. In 1169 Dermot MacMurrough, King of Leinster, sought Henry's help to regain his kingdom. In fact the first Norman, Richard fitz Godbert de Roche, had landed in Ireland in 1167. By 1172 most of Ireland was under Anglo-Norman control. For 369 years, distracted by the Third Crusade, wars in France and the Wars of the Roses, England took little interest in Ireland. But in 1541 Henry VII changed the status of Ireland from a lordship to a kingdom and re-conquered the country. By 1588 all Ireland had been subdued and the Elizabethan Protestant plantations were largely complete. Ulster was settled principally by Prebyterians from Lowland Scotland (1609–41). The scene was set for the terrible visitation of Oliver Cromwell. In a recent analysis of the DNA of the Irish population however, even in the last stronghold of Erse-speakers, the Aran Islands, some people were shown to be descendants of 17th century Cromwellian soldiers from England. Ireland and Britain share close ties not only of history, culture, language and literature – but also of blood.

tediously long-winded (in speech). In 1578 James's Regent, the Earl of Morton was removed: leaving him at the mercy of various intriguing court factions. One, led by William Ruthven, 1st Earl of Gowrie even kidnapped him. James's four successive regents died violently. The Earls of Moray, Lennox and Mar were assassinated and Morton was executed in 1581, fourteen years after the event, for his guilty association with Darnley's murderers.

At this point, a French cousin of James's father, Esmé Stuart, Sieur d'Aubigny, arrived in Scotland. He became a Protestant and swiftly established himself as James's favourite, by "drawing the King into carnal lust". James made him Duke of Lennox, the only Duke in Scotland at that time. Loathed by the Scottish nobility, Lennox was forced to leave Scotland, leaving James with a marked sexual predilection for men.

James was astute enough to realise that his future security depended upon the childless Elizabeth I of England. From 1587 she paid him a handsome subsidy. He was careful never to do anything to anger her, limiting his protest at his mother's death to a formality: remarking only that he thought it "a preposterous and strange procedure".

In 1589 James risked her disapproval however, to secure his dynasty: by marrying the fourteen year-old Protestant Princess Anne of Denmark. In August, after a proxy marriage, Anne (1574–1619) sailed to Scotland but was driven by storms to take shelter in Norway. On an impulse and quite out of character, in "the one romantic episode of his life", James sailed from Leith to Oslo with a retinue of 300 and married Anne in the Old Bishop's Palace on 23 November 1589, returning to Scotland in May 1590. They had three children: Henry who died of typhoid in 1612; Elizabeth who became Queen of Bohemia; and Charles who was doomed to become King of England, Scotland and Ireland.

For the next thirteen years, James's reign in Scotland was successful. In a careful balancing act, he included both Lowland Protestants and Highland Catholics in a General Assembly. He ruled through commissioners known as the Octavians, managing his jealous court and religious factions by the simple device of divide and rule. By 1584 he had made himself head of the Presbyterian Church, with the power to appoint bishops.

By 1601 it was clear to the English Privy Council and particularly to Elizabeth's chief minister, Robert Cecil, 1st Earl of Salisbury (1563–1612), that James was the only credible heir to the throne. Cecil established a secret correspondence with James, aimed at securing a smooth succession. In the early hours of 24 March 1603 Elizabeth died and James was proclaimed King. Within minutes of her death Sir Robert Carey (1560–1639), anxious to ingratiate himself with his new king but disobeying the orders of the council, galloped out of Richmond Palace, bound for Edinburgh. He rode 332 miles in 60 hours: and was immediately appointed a Gentleman of the Bedchamber.

James lost no time in hurrying south to seize the prize he had anticipated for so long. All England flocked to catch a glimpse of him and cheer him on his way, deeply relieved that the succession had been achieved without bloodshed or a change of religion.

James started his reign auspiciously, if undemocratically, by announcing: "I will govern according to the common weal but not according to the common will". He was faced with some pressing issues: the war with Spain, religion and union with Scotland. He addressed these by summoning, in a remarkably modern style, two major conferences. In January 1604 the first took place at Hampton Court. Its ambitious purpose was to establish a religious settlement acceptable to all. The more extreme Protestants, derisively nicknamed Puritans, were raucous in their demands to purify the Anglican Church of every last vestige of "Popery" retained by the old Queen. They were supremely confident that James, with his impeccable Presbyterian provenance, would be a natural ally. It was an error. Particularly to the fore in James's memories of his unpleasant childhood was the ceaseless bullying he had suffered from his harsh Presbyterian tutors: who fiercely derided kingship, maintaining that "all kings are devil's children" and referring to James contemptuously as "God's silly vassal".

In contrast, the Elizabethan settlement was very much to James's liking. The Royal Supremacy of the Anglican Church elevated him high above the preachers who had so tormented him in his youth. To intense Puritan disappointment, James plumped decisively for the established church, refusing to consider for a moment exchanging bishops for Presbyterian assemblies which he regarded as potential hothouses for disaffection. James summed up his view succinctly: "No bishop, no king". He appeased the Puritans however, by agreeing to their demands for a new translation of the Bible. He hated the existing Geneva Bible of his youth, as it was full of annotations denigrating kings. The result was the King James Bible.

"The scholars who produced this masterpiece are mostly unknown and unremembered but they forged an enduring

MONARCHS OF SCOTLAND (1390–1685) AND ENGLAND (1603–85)

Robert II
(1371–90)

(b.1316); the first STEWART King of Scotland; he succeeded his younger half-brother David, the last Bruce king, aged 55; m. (1) Elizabeth (d. c.1355), dau. of Sir Adam Mure of Rowallan, having ten children (five children by his second wife, eight illegitimate):

Robert III
(1390–1406)

(b. c.1340); *his birth name was John*; m. (1367) Anabella (c.1350–1402), dau. of Sir John Drummond of Stobhall:

James I
(1406–37)

(b.1394); eldest surv. son; *imprisoned by Henry IV of England for 18 years, released (1424), assassinated*; m. (1423) Joan Beaufort (c.1404–45), granddau. of John of Gaunt; only one surv. son:

James II
Fiery Face (1437–60)

(b.1430); *killed in an accident*; m. (1449) Mary of Guelders (1434–63), having seven children; the eldest:

James III
(1460–88)

(b. c.1430); *killed at the Battle of Sauchieburn*; m. (1469) Margaret of Denmark (1456–86), having three sons only:

James IV
(1488–1513)

(b. 17 March 1473); *the most successful Stewart king, subdued the Western Isles (1489), but killed at Flodden*; m. (1503) Maragret Tudor (1489–1541), eldest dau. of **Henry VII** of England, having six legitimate children; the only surv. son:

James V
(1513–42)

(b.1512); m. (his and her 2. 1538) Mary of Guise (1515–60), having one surv. child:

Queen Margaret
m. (2. 1514) Archibald Douglas, 6th Earl of Lennox (1490–1557), div. 1528; their only child:

Margaret Douglas
(1516–71)

m. (1544) Matthew Stewart, 4th Earl of Lennox (1516–71); their eldest son:

Mary
(1542–87)

(b.1542); *known as Queen of Scots*; crowned 1543; m. (2. 1565) her first cousin **Henry Stewart**; their only child was: *executed by Elizabeth (1587)*

Henry
(1546–67)

Duke of Albany *known as Lord Darnley (murdered 1567)*

STUART

James VI
(1567–1625)

(b.1566); *Stewart now spelled Stuart in the French manner*; crowned 1567; succeeded **Elizabeth I** as **James I** of England in 1603; m. (1589) Anne of Denmark (1574–1619); three surv. ch.:

Henry
(1594–1612)

Charles I
(1625–1649)

(b.1600); m. (1625) Henrietta Maria of France (1609–69); six ch. surv. *executed* [**Commonwealth**] *(1649)*

Elizabeth of Bohemia
(1596–1662)

m. (1613) Frederick V, Elector Palatine

HANOVER

Charles II
(1630–85) *Restoration (1660)*

King of Scotland 1651, King of England 1661; m. (1662) Catherine of Bragança (1638–1705): no issue; but at least thirteen illegitimate ch.

James II
(1685–8)

Sophia
(1630–1714)

m. (1658) Ernst Augustus, Elector of Hanover (1629–98); *sister of Prince Rupert and mother of King George 1*

George
(1660–1727)

King of Hanover; **George I**, King of Great Britain and Ireland (1 August 1714)

Guy Fawkes, recruited by Robert Catesby for his expertise in explosives, was a Roman Catholic soldier who for many years had fought as a mercenary for Spain. He took a small house near the Palace of Westminster and the conspirators began to dig a tunnel which they intended to use to mine Parliament. The tunnel was abandoned when it was discovered that a vault below the House of Lords could be rented. 36 barrels of gunpowder were installed and hidden under a woodpile ready for the opening of Parliament on 5 November 1605. One of the plotters however, warned his brother-in-law Lord Monteagle not to attend Parliament and the alarm was raised. On the night of the 4 November a search was made of the premises and Guy Fawkes, booted and spurred, was discovered lurking there with a slow match. Under torture, Fawkes revealed the names of the conspirators who were either killed resisting arrest or were executed. Fawkes himself avoided being hanged, drawn and quartered by jumping from the scaffold and breaking his neck. The government encouraged Londoners to light bonfires in celebration of their deliverance, a custom that has endured ever since.

Feeling against the Scots ran deep. The English courtier Sir Anthony Weldon (1583–1648) wrote of them: "Their flesh naturally abhors cleanness. Their breath commonly stinks of pottage .... to be chained in marriage with one of them, were to be tied to a dead carcass and cast into a stinking ditch". Weldon was dismissed.

A quip in 1611 by the diplomat Sir Henry Wotton (1568–1639) was later turned against him: "An Ambassador is an honest man sent abroad to lie for his country".

Robert Cecil, 1st Earl of Salisbury by John De Critz the Elder (1602)

link, literary and religious between the English speaking world", is how it was described by Winston Churchill.

The second of James's great conferences was held at Somerset House between May and July 1604. It was called to negotiate an end to nineteen years of pointless war with Spain. Under James's skilful direction, and guided by his declared conviction that "unity [is] the perfection of all things", peace was concluded on terms that were satisfactory to most of his subjects: but not all. Abandoned by their powerful ally, in the autumn of 1605 a fanatical group of Catholic gentlemen led by Robert Catesby, conspired to blow up Parliament in what is now known as The Gunpowder Plot.

In that unforgiving and brutal age, it was a great tribute to James that he managed to contain the repercussions which could have torn the country apart. Catholic reprisals were avoided, Protestants desisted from privateering and the peace with Spain held.

In March 1604, in a speech from the throne to his first Parliament, James revealed his plans for union between England and Scotland. He argued that it would be easier for one head to rule two bodies which already shared a common language, religion and culture. Not only would it be politically irresponsible to resist union but also blasphemous to keep apart two kingdoms that God himself intended should unite: under James suggested, the name of "Great Britain".

Parliament however, refused to grasp the concept. Dislike of the Scots was coupled to a very real fear that a new kingdom would reduce Parliament to the status of a parish council. By wiping the slate clean of both English and Scottish laws, James could rule unrestrained as a freshly-minted monarch of Great Britain. Had not James himself described this in his treatise, *The Trew Law of Free Monarchies*?

James assumed the title "King of Great Britain" by proclamation. He redesigned the royal coat of arms, combining the Scottish unicorn with the lion of England, and a new national flag which was to become known as the Union Jack.

The only official link between England and Scotland was the King himself – until the Act of Union in 1707 finally tied the knot between the two countries.

Soon after his accession James, if only briefly, calmed the naturally turbulent state of Ireland by encouraging thousands of Scots Protestants to settle in Ulster, on land seized from Irish Catholics in the aftermath of "the Flight of the Earls".

The first five years of James's reign were deftly managed by his chief minister Robert Cecil, Ist Earl of Salisbury, ensuring a period of great prosperity for both England and Scotland. James's experience in Scotland had made him skilled in the art of steering a middle course. He soon offended Parliament however, by

The Plantation of Ulster was a planned settlement by English and Scottish Protestants. Over the preceding century Ulster had been the most violent of the Irish provinces. The plantation was financed by the sale of baronetcies, an honour introduced to bridge the gap between a knighthood and a peerage. On 22 May 1611 James offered the dignity to 200 gentlemen of good birth, for £1,095 (£2 million today) – a sum equivalent to three years' pay for 30 soldiers, at 8d (£64 today) per day per man. The idea came from the Earl of Salisbury. He thought that: "The Honour will do the Gentry very little harm", while doing the Exchequer a great deal of good. Lloyd George would have agreed.

introducing himself as "an old and experienced king", before proceeding to lecture the members of both Houses on his dogmatic views of divine kingship.

Very soon James's extravagant life style and philosophy, "for a king not to be bountiful is a fault", obliged him to ask Parliament for further funds. Rejected, James imposed new customs dues which he proclaimed by law. Vainly did Robert Cecil attempt to persuade Parliament by a "Great

Hatfield House, Hertfordshire was built for Robert Cecil (1611)

Contract" to exchange the Crown's feudal dues for an annuity. The Commons refused to comply and was promptly dissolved by James. The following year, in 1612 Cecil died, depriving him of his most experienced and able minister.

In 1614 James tried again to raise funds from the "Addled Parliament", so called because, refusing to co-operate, it was dissolved after only eight weeks. From 1612–22, James survived without recourse to Parliament. He resorted to the profoundly unpopular expedient of raising money by direct taxation. At the same time he fell under the spell of the comely but hopelessly incompetent Robert Carr. He was thought, scurrilously by some at the time, to have fellated the King in 1603 all the way from Edinburgh to London down the Great North Road (now the A1).

In the last six years of his reign, James's acuity dulled and he began to pursue a foreign policy influenced by Diego Sarmiento de Acuna, Conde de Gondomar, the Spanish ambassador to London from 1613–22, which was quite at odds with public opinion.

The Thirty Years' War (1618–48) was sparked by James's Protestant son-in-law Frederick, Elector of the Palatine's unwise acceptance of the

Robert Carr (or Ker), Ist Earl of Somerset (c.1587–1630) was the younger son of Sir Thomas Carr, a Scottish knight. In 1603 he accompanied James I as a page to England before being educated in France. Returning to England, he was just seventeen when he broke his arm at a joust attended by King James. James fell in love with Carr, showering him with gifts and preferences: until they quarrelled in 1614 and he was replaced by George Villiers. James wrote Carr a letter that year, complaining that Carr had withdrawn himself from his chamber despite the King's "soliciting to the contrary". The reason was simple. Carr had married and not unreasonably preferred to spend the night with his pretty young wife rather than the drunken and drooling old King.

George Villiers, Ist Duke of Buckingham (1592–1628) succeeded Robert Carr as royal favourite in 1614. Infatuated, James referred to him as, "my sweetheart, my sweet child and wife" – and himself as, "your dear dad and husband". Villiers quickly dominated the King and controlled access to him. Within four years, between 1615–19, James raised him from Gentleman of the Bedchamber to Duke of Buckingham. Resentment of Buckingham sprang not from his homosexual relationship with James but his crass involvement in domestic, and particularly foreign policy decisions.

• **Robert Carr, Earl of Somerset after John Hoskins (c.1625–1630)**
National Portrait Gallery, London

throne of Bohemia, enraging the Catholic Hapsburg dynasty. The war was essentially a power struggle between the Hapsburg-Spanish Holy Roman Empire and Protestant principalities clustered east of the Netherlands, together with Sweden. Most of the battles were fought in modern day Germany which was devastated by ceaseless plundering armies. The Peace of Westphalia in 1648 left France as the dominant power in an exhausted Europe.

Anne of Denmark attributed to Marcus Gheeraerts the Younger (*c*.1612)
National Portrait Gallery, London

It became only too clear that there was no agreed English foreign policy. Buckingham and a vociferous Parliament clamoured for war against Spain whereas James and most of his advisors shrank from the prospect. In 1621 James called a Parliament, to raise funds to promote his schemes for Anglo-Spanish cooperation. He was rudely refused by outraged members who not only demanded an all-out war with Spain but also that James's son Charles should marry a Protestant. James in a rage, tore the page of the record from the Commons journal and dissolved Parliament.

James was a prolific author. He wrote poems, political philosophies, bible commentaries, translated *The Book of Psalms* and wrote two treatises on kingship. In the first, *The Trew Law of Free Monarchies*, he argued the case for the Divine Right of Kings. In the second, *Basilikon Doron*, he laid down his perception of the duties of a king.

James wrote *Basilikon Doron* "(Kingly Gift")" for the private instruction of Henry, the Prince of Wales, should James not survive to teach him himself. James was frequently ill and survived several assassination attempts. The printer, Robert Waldegrave was bound to secrecy and ordered to print only seven copies. Inevitably it reached a wider audience and attracted such demand that James had to publish it to prevent pirated and inaccurate versions. For the next 50 years it was published in English, French, Welsh, Latin, Swedish and German. On a king's duty to his queen, James exhorts his son: to "Keep your body clean and unpolluted while you give it to your wife, to whom it only belongs".

In 1604, James wrote an astonishingly prescient warning about the dangers of smoking tobacco: "a custom loathsome to the eye, hateful to the nose, harmful to the brain and dangerous to the lungs". He was keenly interested in scientific development and was patron to various inventors, including Cornelius Drebbel.

James was also patron of Shakespeare's troop of actors who became known as "The King's Men". Indeed, James had a special relationship with Shakespeare who wrote Macbeth for him: cleverly appealing to James's interest in witchcraft, on which he had written a treatise, *Dæmonologie*.

The last four years of James's reign were miserable. Abroad, the aggravation of a hostile Spain and an exiled son-in-law combined with the intractability of the Puritans at home, baying to purge the Liturgy of all Catholic influence. Amongst the extreme Puritan sects who refused all communion with the established Church of England, and despairing of toleration, were the Pilgrim Fathers – "Separatists" who found their differences with the Church of England to be irreconcilable.

Unlike the Puritans, the Pilgrims left England seeking a complete physical separation. They derived from a Nottinghamshire congregation which fled to Holland to escape persecution. They arranged with English investors to establish a colony in Virginia. The colonists had to overcome bureaucracy, impatient investors, internal conflicts, sabotage, storms and disease. 102 Colonists and 35 crew left Plymouth on 11 September on board *Mayflower* and arrived in America on 21 November 1620 (Gregorian calendar). Blown violently off course, they landed on Cape Cod in Massachusetts. The colonists faced a harsh New England winter and uncertain relations with the local American Indian tribes. They were woefully unprepared. One had

Cornelius Drebbel (1572–1633) invented the first twin-lens microscope. In 1620, while contracted to the English navy and working from a 1578 design by William Bourne of Gravesend, he built the first navigable submarine with a leather-covered wooden hull. Between 1620–24, Drebbel successfully built and tested two more submarines, each one larger than the last. The final model had six oars and could carry sixteen passengers. Drebbel demonstrated this version to King James I in person and several thousand Londoners. The submarine stayed submerged for three hours and completed a return voyage from Westminster to Greenwich, cruising at a depth of 12–15 feet. Drebbel even took James for a test dive beneath the Thames, making him the first monarch to travel underwater. The submarine failed to attract Admiralty attention and was never used in combat.

King James I of England and VI of Scotland after John De Critz the Elder (c.1606)
National Portrait Gallery, London

King James I of England and VI of Scotland by Daniel Mytens (1621)
National Portrait Gallery, London

brought seventeen pairs of boots and none had so much as a single fishing line By the end of the first year, half their number had died.

Plymouth Colony became the second successful English settlement in what was to become the United States of America. The first was Jamestown in Virginia, founded by the London Company, later the Virginia Company, on 14 May 1607.

Impeachment of James's astute Lord Treasurer, the Earl of Middlesex in 1622 was followed by clamour for the removal of that "grievance of grievances" – his embattled favourite "Steenie", the Duke of Buckingham. Steenie's pernicious influence, directing all James's political and foreign policy decisions, together with mounting royal debt, caused the French ambassador to remark gloomily: "the end of all is in the bottle".

An alcoholic, in excruciating pain from bladder stones and a face covered in ulcerated sores, James was crippled by arthritis. He also suffered from indigestion, diarrhoea and insomnia, none of them life-threatening but

On 16 March 1621 Samoset (1590–1653), an Abenaki who spoke broken English, was the first native to contact the Pilgrims. He introduced Squanto, or Tisquantum (c.1580–1622) who was a Pawtuxet. Captured by Captain Thomas Hunt during an expedition to New England in 1614, Squanto was taken to Malaga in Spain to be sold into slavery. He escaped by converting to Christianity.

Arriving in London in 1617 he was housed by John Slany, treasurer to the Newfoundland Company. He returned to North America in 1618, to find the Pawtuxet decimated by European diseases. He became envoy to Governor William Bradford (1590–1657) of Plymouth colony and interpreter for Edward Winslow (1595–1655), a spokesman for the Pilgrims. Concluding a peace between the Pilgrims and the Wampanoag tribe, Squanto spent the winter of 1621–22 teaching the Pilgrims to fish and plant corn seed mixed with fish meal as fertiliser. Probably poisoned by a disenchanted Wampanoag, he lies in Burial Hill Cemetery at Plymouth.

Governor Bradford celebrated the survival of the Pilgrims by inviting the local Indians to a three-day festival, in gratitude for the abundant harvest. Since 1957 Thanksgiving Day, a US national holiday, has been celebrated on the fourth Thursday in November – by eating a meal of turkey, cranberry sauce and pumpkin pie.

In the same year the moderate Calvinist Dubliner, James Ussher (1581–1656) was appointed Archbishop of Armagh. He dated creation of the Universe (not just planet Earth) precisely to 23 October 4004BC. Modern geophysicists believe "Big Bang" occurred around 13.73 billion years ago.

all contributing to an acute melancholy (depression). In September 1624 his kidneys began to fail. On 27 March 1625 he died from a massive stroke at his favourite residence, Theobalds in Hertfordshire. He was buried on 5 May 1625 in the Henry VII chapel in Westminster Abbey.

An entry in the *Gay Guide to Westminster Abbey* is a reminder of James's abiding passion: "If we make our solemn way thence to the Great Nave, we will come upon the effigy of one of the gayest of monarchs, King James I (1566–1625), whose tomb was lost and not rediscovered until 1869. On His Majesty's left is the magnificent tomb of his lover George Villiers, 1st Duke of Buckingham (1592–1628); and on his right is the tomb (with huge bronze figures representing Hope, Truth, Charity and Faith) of his other boyfriend, Ludovic Stuart, Duke of Richmond and Lennox (1574–1624), Oh, to be so happily flanked for eternity".

This peccadillo aside, James's reign, in Scotland the longest of any monarch ever, represents a milestone towards the unification of the two countries and a consensual government of both. Sadly, his heir King Charles I set back James's moves towards achieving either for another two generations.

FRANCIS BACON, 1ST VISCOUNT ST ALBANS

Francis Bacon (1561–1626) was an English statesman and natural philosopher. He founded the modern scientific method of observation and experiment (empiricism) to verify conclusions. He was educated at Cambridge and studied law at Gray's Inn.

Bacon was appointed Solicitor-General in 1607, Attorney-General in 1613 and Lord Chancellor in 1618. He was accused by Lord Justice Edward Coke of accepting bribes from litigants in his court, convicted and imprisoned. He was sacked from all his public offices in 1621 and died deeply in debt.

In 1620 his work, *Novum Organum* laid down the principles of his scientific methodology. He also published *The Advancement of Learning* in 1605 and contributed several significant legal and constitutional volumes. He was considered by some as a pederast and mystifyingly, by others as having written some of Shakespeare's plays. Alexander Pope described Bacon as the "Brightest, wisest and meanest of mankind".

Sir Francis Bacon, Viscount St Albans by unknown artist after 1731 (*c*.1618)
National Portrait Gallery, London

Holkham Hall was built by Thomas Coke's great-uncle, another Thomas Coke (1697–1759), 1st Earl of Leicester (5th creation)

SIR EDWARD COKE

Sir Edward Coke (1552–1634), pronounced "Cook", was a celebrated English jurist and M.P. He was renowned for his defence of the Common Law against encroachment by the King. He was the originator of the legal axiom: "For a man's house is his castle". His *Reports* (1600–05) was the first modern compendium of English common law.

Coke, born in Norfolk, was educated at Norwich Grammar school and Trinity College, Cambridge. He entered the Inner Temple in 1572 and was called to the bar in 1578. In 1589 he was elected M.P. for Aldeburgh. In 1592 he was appointed Solicitor-General and in 1594 promoted to Attorney-General, frustrating his formidable rival

Francis Bacon. Coke prosecuted the 2nd Earl of Essex in 1601, Sir Walter Raleigh in 1605 and the Gunpowder Plot conspirators, also in 1605. In 1606 Coke became Chief Justice of the Common Pleas. In 1610 he enraged James I by insisting that he could not change the common law by royal proclamation. He also infuriated the bishops by limiting the jurisdiction of ecclesiastical courts. Coke purchased the Holkham estate in north Norfolk in 1609.

In 1613 James made a last attempt to suborn Coke by making him, on Bacon's advice, a Privy Councillor and Chief Justice of the King's Bench. He was the first judge to be called Lord Chief Justice of England. James hoped that Coke would become more amenable but Coke continued to defy royal injunctions, until he was dismissed in 1616. In 1620 he re-entered Parliament and again challenged royal interference with Parliament's privileges. He opposed Prince Charles's proposed marriage to the Spanish infanta, accused Lord Chancellor Bacon of taking bribes and charged the government with corruption. Exasperated, James imprisoned Coke in the Tower of London for nine months. He was released because no incriminating evidence could be found. Coke's greatest hour in Parliament arrived in 1628, when he prepared the Petition of Right. This was a charter of parliamentary liberties and a defence of the Common Law, both of which were threatened by the royal prerogative. The Petition of Right is regarded as one of the corner stones of the English constitution.

A descendant of Sir Edward Coke, Thomas William Coke (1754–1842), 1st Earl of Leicester (7th creation) was one of the great innovators of the British Agricultural Revolution. Known as "Coke of Norfolk", he introduced improvements in cattle, sheep and pig breeding and husbandry. People flocked to annual three-day gatherings, the forerunners of today's agricultural shows, called the Holkham Clippings, at sheep-shearing time. Starting in 1776, Coke created the Holkham estate from marshland and saltings.

Sir Edward Coke died at Stoke Poges in Buckinghamshire on 3 September 1634. King Charles I immediately seized all his private papers.

Sir Edward Coke (1551–1633) Lord Chief Justice (1551–1633) by Marcus Gheeraerts
Holkham Hall, Norfolk

The bowler hat, also known as a Coke hat, or "derby" in the US, was created in 1849 for Edward Coke, the younger brother of the 2nd Earl of Leicester.

SIR WALTER RALEIGH

Sir Walter Raleigh (1552–1618) was an English adventurer, soldier, sailor, explorer, M.P., author, poet and courtier. Born in Hayes Barton in Devon and educated at Oriel College, Oxford, he joined his half-brother, Humphrey Gilbert on a buccaneering expedition against the Spanish in 1578. Between 1579–83 he fought Irish rebels in Munster; and was present at an infamous massacre of Italian and Spanish soldiers at Smerwick. He was granted 40,000 acres of land confiscated from the Irish – where he is credited, though this is disputed, with planting the first potatoes in Ireland. It was the strength of his opinion of the Irish that first caught the attention of Queen Elizabeth I. Tall, bold, handsome, firmly Protestant and a poet, he soon became one of her favourites.

Sir Walter Ralegh by Nicholas Hilliard (c.1585)
National Portrait Gallery, London

In 1584 he financed an expedition to the east coast of North America which he named Virginia for his Queen. Raleigh's voyages were funded by himself and his friends: but with never enough capital to maintain his main ambition, a colony in North America.

Roanoke Island in North Carolina was the first English colony established in North America. The colonists landed during the summer of 1585. When a supply ship finally arrived in 1591 they had all vanished, including little Virginia, without trace.

In 1585 Virginia Dare became the first English child to be born in North America.

Raleigh was knighted in 1585 and appointed warden of the "stannaries" (tin mines) in Cornwall and Devon, Lord Lieutenant of Cornwall and vice-admiral of the two counties. In both 1585 and 1586, he sat in Parliament as the member for Devonshire. In 1594, out of favour at court, he led a futile expedition to a "City of Gold" – which was thought to exist on Lake Parime far up the Orinoco River in the Guyana Highlands.

After Elizabeth's death, he was accused of plotting against King James I. Imprisoned in the Tower of London for twelve years, where he wrote the first volume of his *Historie of the World*, he was released in 1616. Another unsuccessful expedition to Guyana, where his crew burnt down the Spanish settlement of San Thomé but his son Walter was killed, proved his final downfall. On his return to England, at the insistence of the Spanish ambassador Count Gondomar, Raleigh was again charged with treason and executed on 29 October 1618. Allowed to see the axe that would behead him, he remarked: "This is a sharp Medicine, but it is a Physician for all diseases and miseries". His final words were to his executioner: "Strike man, strike!".

His execution was seen by many, both at the time and since, as unnecessary and unjust. One of his judges later said of his show trial: "the justice of England has never been so degraded and injured as by the condemnation of the honourable Sir Walter Raleigh". He left a small tobacco box in his cell. Engraved on it was a Latin inscription: *Comes meus fuit illo miserrimo tempo* ("It was my comfort in those miserable times").

Sir Walter spelled his name "Rawleigh", "Ralegh" and "Rawley", pronounced "rawleye" – but never it is said, in the modern way as "Raleigh", pronounced "Rally".

THE CHEAPSIDE HOARD

In June 1912 a workman, demolishing some old houses in Cheapside in the City of London, drove a pickaxe through a rotten floor and uncovered a decayed wooden box containing 500 pieces of neatly trayed jewellery. The box had belonged to a jeweller, in business around 1650, whose customers were clearly neither royal nor aristocratic but almost certainly prosperous local merchants and their wives.

The Hoard is the finest collection of Elizabethan and Jacobean jewellery in the world. All the jewels are genuine: Columbian emeralds, topaz and amazonite from Brazil, lapis lazuli and turquoise from Persia, iolites, spinel and chrysoberyl from Ceylon, rubies from India, Red Sea peridots, as well as Hungarian opals, garnets and amethysts. Polished but not faceted gems (cabochons) abound together with rose and star cut stones first seen in portraits of Cardinal Mazarin of France (*c*.1640). Enamelled gold, once popular amongst the mercantile classes is there in profusion. The most important piece is a gold verge watch set in a massive hexagonal Columbian emerald, with a dial of translucent green enamel. Most remarkable is a small hat pin: a large pearl worked to the shape of a ship, with a delicate gold mast and rigging complete with rotating pennant, recalls the huge distances travelled by these jewels. Parts of the Hoard can be viewed today at the Victoria and Albert Museum, the British Museum and the Guildhall Museum, with the bulk being displayed in the Museum of London.

Scottish clans (from the Gaelic clann, meaning "children") identify shared descent. A structure of Clan Chiefs, together with their heraldic devices, is registered with the Court of the Lord Lyon, King of Arms in Edinburgh.

THE PRINCIPAL SCOTTISH CLANS

Highland clans

Lowlands (the clan system did not apply)

Orkney and Shetland were Norwegian until 1472
(never adopted the clan system)

– – – Highland "boundary"

ORKNEY

SHETLAND

WESTERN ISLES

MORRISON
MACAULAY
MACLEOD (of Lewis)
MACIVER
MACLEOD (of Harris)

MACDONALD

MACDONALD (of Clan Ranald)

MACNEIL

MACDONALD

MACLEOD
MACDONNELL (of Glengarry)
MACLEOD (North)
MACLEOD (of Harris)
MATHIESON
MACRAE
MACDONNELL (of Glengarry)

MACKAY

SUTHERLAND

GUNN

SINCLAIR

MACLEOD
MACNICOL

ROSS

MACKENZIE

MUNRO
URQUHART

FRASER
ROSE
Inverness

INNES   KEITH

HAY

LESLIE

Aberdeen

CHISHOLM
GRANT
FRASER
MACKINTOSH
CLAN CHATTAN
MACPHERSON
MACDONNELL (of Keppoch)

GRANT

SHAW
GORDON
STEWART & FORBES
FARQUHARSON

FORBES

BARCLAY

11
12

CLAN RANALD

MACLEAN
MACLEAN
MACDONALD
MACLEAN

CAMERON

STEWART   2

MACINTYRE

MENZIES

MENZIES

ROBERTSON

STEWART

LINDSAY

OGILVY

DUNCAN

MACLEAN
CAMPBELL
MACQUARIE
MACLEAN
MACDOUGALL

STEWART

MACNAB
MACGREGOR
GRAHAM
BUCHANAN
COLQUHOUN

MURRAY
3
6
5
4

HAY
Perth

LINDSAY
MACDUFF

CAMPBELL

7

DUFFIE or MACFIE

MACLEAN

MACDONALD (South)

10

9
8

NAPIER

ERSKINE
Stirling

BRUCE

LIVINGSTONE

STEWART
ERSKINE
Glasgow
MONTGOMERY
CUNNINGHAM

Edinburgh
RAMSAY
HAMILTON
BAIRD

HAY
LINDSAY
NESBITT
SWINTON

MELVILLE

MACNEIL

HAMILTON
HUNTER

WALLACE
Ayr
KENNEDY
DOUGLAS

SCOTT

ELLIOT
KERR

BRUCE
JOHNSTON

ARMSTRONG

FERGUSSON

Carlisle

IRELAND

ENGLAND

1. MACGILLIVRAY
2. MACDONALD
3. MACLAREN
4. STEWART and DRUMMOND
5. MACFARLANE
6. MACNAUGHTON
7. MACLAUGHLAN
8. STEWART
9. LAMONT
10. MACMILLAN
11. MACKINNON
12. MACLEOD

0   25 miles

0   50 km

Charles I signature

CHARLES I, KING OF ENGLAND, SCOTLAND AND IRELAND (REIGNED 1625–49)

Charles, the younger son of James VI of Scotland and Anne of Denmark, was born on 19 November 1600 in Dunfermline Palace in Fife. He had rickety legs and was so puny that in 1603, he was left behind when his father acceded to the English throne. He was not expected to survive the journey to London. He was brought up by Sir Robert and Lady Carey. In 1605 he was baptised as Duke of Albany and created Duke of York. Devoted to his brother Henry and adored by his sister Elizabeth, he was devastated when Henry died of typhoid fever aged eighteen in 1612 and Elizabeth married Frederick, Elector of the Rhine Palatinate the following year.

Charles grew up stammering and, at a little over 5 feet 3 inches tall, small and shy. He was even tempered, polite and without vice but lived an insulated life, rarely moving out of his palaces to meet ordinary people. His tutor, Thomas Murray was a Scots Presbyterian who later became provost of Eton. Charles was a serious student who excelled in his father's chosen subjects: divinity, rhetoric and languages. He also resolutely overcame his physical defects to become an accomplished horseman and a fanatical huntsman. His taste for beauty led him to become a discerning, if extravagant connoisseur of the arts. He assembled the most remarkable private collection of paintings and tapestries of any British monarch, nearly bankrupting himself in the process.

Charles I had an natural eye for fine paintings and his expertise developed with experience – Peter Paul Rubens considered him a connoisseur. Charles personally helped to invent the technique of painting enamelled miniatures on gold. He

The Prince of Wales's death was a tragedy for the nation. Witty and outgoing, he was much more popular than his father. An "obdurate Protestant", he disapproved of King James's court, disliked Robert Carr and thought highly of Sir Walter Raleigh.

"Few heirs to the English throne have been as widely and deeply mourned as Prince Henry". His body lay in state for four weeks in St James's Palace while the King raised money for an extravagant funeral. His father, who hated funerals, refused to attend. Many places in Virginia were named in honour of Prince Henry.

Triple portrait of Charles I by Sir Anthony Van Dyck (1599–1641) in 1635–36
The Royal Collection, London

collected widely and intelligently, preferring Italian paintings above all others. Although his purchases included over a dozen paintings by Titian and several wonderful works by Raphael, his most important acquisition was the superb Gonzaga, Dukes of Mantua, collection in 1628.

He constructed a private gallery at Whitehall which also contained portraits of English kings starting with Edward III and many of their European relations. He also created a cabinet room to hold his rare books and manuscripts, classical sculptures, curiosities and huge quantity of antique medals.

Rubens (1577–1640) was paid £3,000 (£5.75 million today), given a heavy gold chain and awarded a knighthood for the Banqueting House ceiling.

Charles commissioned Rubens to paint the ceiling in the Banqueting House at Whitehall and established Sir Anthony Van Dyck (1599–1641) as his court painter.

He patronised the great sculptors of the day, including Hubert Le Sueur (1580–1658) who created the equestrian monument to Charles in Trafalgar Square. Charles commissioned a bust from Bernini, for which Van Dyck painted the King in triple view. Having approved the design, Charles paid for the new west portico of St Paul's Cathedral. He also planned to rebuild his palace at Whitehall on a grand scale. Selected pieces from his collection were on display to foreign ambassadors and dignitaries. The reception room in the Banqueting House was designed to impress visitors.

The ceiling of the Banqueting House in Whitehall (1629–30) by Sir Peter Paul Rubens

Sadly, Charles's unique collection was broken up and sold during the Commonwealth.

Charles was deeply religious. His devotions and natural asceticism immediately transformed the coarse and drink sodden court of his father James. Unfortunately, Charles inherited from his father the same mulish belief in the Divine Right of Kings which led him into immediate conflict with an unruly House of Commons.

As a young man Charles fell under the pernicious influence of his father's favourite and lover, the foolhardy and venal George Villiers, 1st Duke of Buckingham (1592–1628). In 1623, two years before his father died, Buckingham persuaded Charles to join in a feckless venture to secure a marriage treaty with the Spanish infanta, the daughter of King Philip III. Inevitably, this ended in fiasco: entirely due to Buckingham's insensitivity and arrogance. Charles then rushed into an injudicious marriage to Henrietta Maria, another Catholic and the sister of the French King Louis XIII.

On the death of James I in March, Charles's relationship with his first

Two other great royal collectors were George III and George IV. The former commissioned silver, porcelain, ceramics, furniture, innovative time-keeping devices and complex scientific instruments. George III also bought Continental paintings and historic drawings. Above all he acquired books. At the heart of the British Library in London, a tall glass tower houses his library, one of the greatest collections of books in the world. It comprises 65,000 volumes of printed books and 19,000 pamphlets printed mainly in Britain, Europe and North America, from the mid-15th to the early-19th centuries. George III's other greatest act of artistic patronage was to support and help pay for the foundation of the Royal Academy in 1768.

George V's Royal Philatelic Collection, housed in St James's Palace, is the world's largest collection of postage stamps devoted to Great Britain and the Commonwealth.

• King George III (c.1809), studio of Sir William Beechey (1753–1839)
National Portrait Gallery, London

Parliament summoned in June 1625, swiftly descended into acrimony. The Spanish war which he and Buckingham had provoked was a disaster. Denied any proper explanation of the war's purpose, direction and cost, Parliament refused to vote Charles the right to levy tunnage and poundage, customs duties that for centuries had been granted to the king.

Before summoning his second Parliament in February 1626, Charles resorted to the first of a long series of political deceits, by infiltrating Parliament with his supporters. To this end, he

Henrietta Maria (1609–69) was the daughter of Henri IV of France and Marie de Medici. She married Charles by proxy on 11 May 1625, shortly after his accession to the throne. The marriage was solemnised in Canterbury a month later. However, as a Roman Catholic, she could not be crowned with Charles in an Anglican service. Her enormous retinue of Catholic priests and noblemen caused great public resentment and Charles soon expelled them. To begin with, their relationship was awkward but they grew to fall genuinely in love. Charles greatly valued her advice and remained faithful to her all his life.

Sir Jeffrey Hudson (1619–82) was born in Oakham in Rutland: perfectly proportioned but only 3 feet 9 inches tall. Known as "Lord Minimus", he was considered one of the "wonders of the age". He was a Captain of Horse in the Civil War and fled with Henrietta Maria to France in 1644; where he killed a man in a duel and was expelled from her court. He was captured by Barbary pirates and spent 25 years as a slave in North Africa, before being ransomed back to England. He died in poverty.

• **Queen Henrietta Maria by Sir Anthony Van Dyck (c.1632–1635)**

appointed the most strident of his opponents to the posts of county sheriffs which were incompatible with attending Parliament. The ruse bought Charles little respite as Parliament now demanded the impeachment of Buckingham. In June Charles was obliged to dissolve Parliament to save his friend from charges of treason. Once again, through Buckingham's political ineptitude, England found herself at war with both France and Spain. Pressed for funds, Charles imposed a loan on the country which his judges declared unlawful. Charles sacked the Lord Chief Justice, arresting nearly 80 knights and gentry who refused to pay

By the time Charles summoned his third Parliament in March 1628, Buckingham had led yet another abysmally unsuccessful expedition to relieve the French Huguenots at La Rochelle. Moreover, the burden of arbitrary taxation had become unendurable. Parliament, in no mood to truck with the King, now presented Charles with a Petition of Right, demanding four fundamental liberties: no taxation without parliamentary consent, no arbitrary imprisonment, no billeting of troops on the civil population and no martial law when the country was at peace. Grudgingly, Charles gave his formal consent before he dissolved Parliament.

Charles was obliged to summon his fourth Parliament in January 1629. Though Buckingham had been assassinated by John Felton, a disaffected Puritan army officer, the year before, a still seething Parliament vehemently opposed the enforcement of the high church party's "popish practices"; and also forbade the king's officers from levying customs duties without parliamentary consent. On 2 March Charles dissolved Parliament again. Before the Speaker was able to obey the royal command, members held him down in his chair while the House passed resolutions deploring the king's conduct.

George Villiers, Duke of Buckingham (1625) by Peter Paul Rubens
Pitti Palace, Florence

King Charles I by Anthony van Dyck
The Louvre, Paris

Charles, recognising the futility of any further relations with his Commons, dissolved Parliament and ruled England for the next eleven years as an absolute monarch.

Charles reduced his expenditure, made peace with France and Spain and shrank his royal households. He continued to collect customs duties as part of his royal prerogative and extended the reach of Ship Money, a tax levied on seaports to pay for the Royal Navy, to include inland towns. Although extremely unpopular, on this occasion the royal judges concluded that the tax was lawful. Charles was just able to make ends meet. Indeed, the so called "eleven years' tyranny" was a period of prosperity for both Charles and his realm. Peace and expanding trade increased his revenues, enabling him to add considerably to the royal collection.

This period of relative peace and plenty came to an abrupt end in 1637 when Charles made his first of several irredeemably stupid decisions. He tried to impose the English *Book of Common Prayer* on the Scots who immediately signed a National Covenant to defend Presbyterianism. Foolishly, Charles turned from intimidation to force of arms. He quickly found himself outmanoeuvred by a well-trained Covenanter army. On the 18 June 1639 Charles signed a truce with the Scots at Berwick-on-Tweed.

William Laud, Archbishop of Canterbury, after Sir Anthony Van Dyck (c.1636)
National Portrait Gallery, London

When he heard that Charles had signed his death warrant at Parliament's insistence, Strafford quoted Machiavelli with weary resignation: "Put not your trust in princes".

Charles's principal advisors, William Laud (1573–1645), his Archbishop of Canterbury, and Thomas Wentworth, Earl of Strafford (1593–1641), a highly competent Lord Deputy of Ireland from 1632–39, advised him to call a parliament as the only way to raise money to fight the Scots. The so called "Short Parliament" was summoned in April 1640 but soon proved so intractable to the king's cause that it was prorogued a bare month later. The Scots army invaded England, defeating a royalist army at Newburn in August. In November 1640 a despondent Charles was forced to convene another Parliament.

The "Long Parliament" proved just as unmanageable as its "Short" predecessor. A bill was quickly drawn up to impeach Strafford, ostensibly for treason, as well as a Triennial Act, requiring the King to summon a parliament every three years. Crushed and helpless, Charles was unable to save Strafford who was executed on 12 May 1641. Further, he had to agree to Parliament dissolving itself only by its own consent.

In August Charles travelled surreptitiously to Scotland to enlist support. His proposals to establish the Presbyterian Church in Scotland and to permit the Scottish Parliament (the "Three Estates") to appoint royal officials were rejected.

On 22 November 1641 Parliament reassembled in London and drew up a Grand Remonstrance, an exhaustive complaint of Charles's conduct since his accession. Added to his woes came the news of an Irish rebellion. Fearing that a royal army might be used against them, the Commons coerced Charles to agree to a Militia Bill to prevent this eventuality. "By God not for an hour", came the King's bitter response. Alerted to the threat that Parliament might try to impeach his wife, Charles made his second irretrievably foolish decision: to arrest one member of the House of Lords and five Members of Parliament. At the head of 400 soldiers, Charles attempted to seize the men in person but they were forewarned. Charles arrived too late, eliciting his famous if forlorn remark: "I see the birds have flown". The fugitive members sought refuge in the City of London, now firmly committed to the parliamentary cause.

The enormity of Charles's assault on the rights of Parliament swung public opinion decisively against him. On 10 January 1642 Charles left London for York. A month later Queen Henrietta Maria left for Holland to pawn the crown jewels. On 22 August 1642 Charles raised his standard in Nottingham. In the words of Sir William Waller, Parliamentary general but a moderate: "this war without an enemy" had begun.

The first serious engagement of the Civil War, the Battle of Edgehill on 21 October 1642, revealed that both armies were poorly trained and evenly matched.

Thomas Wentworth, 1st Earl of Strafford, after Sir Anthony Van Dyck (c.1633)
National Portrait Gallery, London

Jacob Astley, 1st Baron Astley of Reading (1579–1652), was a Major-General in the royalist army. His characteristic battle-prayer at the Battle of Edgehill has rung down the centuries: "O Lord, Thou knowest how busy I must be this day. If I forget Thee, do not forget me". He followed this promptly with the order, "March on, boys!"

The Queen's House at Greenwich, commissioned by Anne of Denmark (King Charles I's mother), was designed by Inigo Jones (1573–1652) and built 1614–17

The north, west and south-west of England remained loyal to Charles. Parliament retained London, East Anglia and the south-east. Interspersed, were pockets of resistance from isolated garrisons to large cities. Ironically, after all the years of being maintained by the controversial Ship Money, the Royal Navy sided with Parliament. This effectively cut off the Royalists from continental or mercenary help.

From 1644 Parliamentary forces predominated, largely because of the professionalism of the New Model Army. In 1643 M.P.'s were forbidden to take up army commands. This passed control to professional soldiers like Sir Thomas Fairfax and Oliver Cromwell. By employing a more rigorous strategy and disciplined troops, Parliament won the decisive battles of Marston Moor in 1644 and Naseby in 1645 – where the capture and decoding of the King's secret correspondence revealed the extent to which he had been trying to seek help from the Irish and the French.

In May 1646 Charles placed himself "under the protection" of the Scots. They handed him over to Parliament nine months later, in return for settling their army's arrears of pay.

Parliament held Charles first at Hampton Court and then, from November 1647, at Carisbrooke Castle on the Isle of Wight. Rather than treat with Parliament in good faith, Charles continued on his lunatic path of self-destruction by opening negotiations with the Scots. He agreed that if the Scots would restore him to the throne, he would establish the Presbyterian church in England. This inevitably led to a brief resumption of the war in 1648, sometimes referred to as the "Second" Civil War. It was decided by Oliver Cromwell's crushing defeat of the Scots at Preston in August that year.

The New Model Army was now all-powerful. Cromwell, realising that there could be no peace while Charles lived, determined to bring him to trial and execution. In December 1648 Cromwell purged Parliament of elements not loyal to the army. In January 1649 the "Rump Parliament" established a High Court of Justice to try the King. On 20 January 1649 Charles was charged with "High Treason against the Realm of England".

Charles chose not to plead on the powerful but futile grounds that a "High Court" created by a parliament, purged of dissent and without the House of Lords, was manifestly unlawful. Ten days later, on 30 January 1649, Charles was beheaded on a scaffold erected outside Inigo Jones's beautiful Banqueting House (completed in 1622) in Whitehall.

On the morning of his execution, Charles put on two shirts: "The season is so sharp as probably may make me shake which some observers

Inigo Jones (1573–1652), by William Hogarth (1697–1764) in 1757–58

National Maritime Museum, London

"God's meanest servants must not be afraid to oppose the mighty". Lord Clarendon described the lukewarmth of most royalists from this point: "as long as they did nothing against the King they were supporting him, whereas those who fought for Parliament were totally committed".

The identity of Charles's masked executioner is uncertain. He was probably Richard Brandon, the Common Hangman of London. He died, it is said of remorse, within the year. An Irishman called Gunning is an unlikely alternative, despite later boasting a plaque in the King's Head public house in Galway. In 1813 an examination of Charles's remains indicated that his execution had been the work of a professional.

may imagine proceeds from fear. I would have no such imputation". On the scaffold he repeated his case, concluding: "If I would have given way to an Arbitrary way, for to have all laws changed according to the power of the sword, I needed not to have come here; and therefore I tell you …. That I am the Martyr of the People". His last words, before his head was taken off with a single skilled stroke, were: "I go from a corruptible to an incorruptible Crown where no disturbance can be, no disturbance in the World".

After an execution it was the custom for the executioner to hold up the head to the crowd, shouting: "Behold the head of a traitor". Charles head was displayed but the words were not used. Instead of the usual cheers, all that could be heard was a terrible groan. Cromwell's unease over the execution of his King was such that he allowed Charles's head to be sewn back on the body before his family paid their respects.

To avoid public disturbance, Charles's body was hurried to Windsor Castle and buried at night on 7 February, in the Henry VIII vault within St George's Chapel.

Charles's failure to compromise, first with the Scots and then with the English Parliament, over evolving religious and political issues, had led to civil war, his own execution and the abolition of the monarchy for eleven years: a sad end for a brave but foolish man.

JAMES GRAHAM, 1ST MARQUESS OF MONTROSE (1612–50)

In 1641 Charles I had sacrificed his loyal deputy, the Earl of Strafford to appease Parliament. A few years later his son, the future Charles II showed an equal lack of scruple when he abandoned the Marquess of Montrose to the merciless Covenanters.

James Graham was the chief of Clan Graham. He was educated at St Andrews University and at military academies in France and Italy. In 1638 he joined the Covenanters in the Wars of the Three Kingdoms but, from 1644–46, he supported Charles I in the last days of the first English Civil War. Montrose proved himself to be one of the greatest soldiers of the war, culminating with his rout of the Covenanters at the Battle of Kilsyth on 15 August 1645. On 12 September however, deserted by his Highlanders and guarded only by a little group of followers, he was defeated by David Leslie, later Lord Newark, at Philiphaugh. In despair, Montrose exiled himself to Norway. In June 1649 he was restored by the exiled Charles II to the now nominal lieutenancy of Scotland and, from 1650, he fought a civil war of his own on Charles's behalf. On 27 April 1650 Montrose was surprised and routed at the Battle of Carbisdale in Ross-shire. He was surrendered by Neil MacLeod of Assynt, into whose protection he had entrusted himself, and brought to Edinburgh. He was hanged on 21 May.

Charles had abandoned his noblest supporter in order to become King: on terms dictated by Archibald Campbell, 1st Marquess of Argyll, the self-appointed representative of the Presbyterian and national party. Shortly after Montrose's death the Argyll Government switched sides and became Royalists. After formally accepting the Solemn Oath and Covenant, Charles was crowned King of Scotland on 1 January 1651 by Argyll, who was himself beheaded in 1661.

The National Covenant of February 1638 was based upon the Confession of Faith signed by James VI in 1581. It called for adherence to doctrines already enshrined by Acts of Parliament and for a rejection of untried "innovations" in religion. Although it emphasised Scotland's loyalty to the King, the Covenant also implied that any moves towards Catholicism would not be tolerated.

Its sister document, the 1643 Solemn League and Covenant, was a treaty between the Covenanters and the English Parliament. It highlighted the Covenanters' lack of religious tolerance and led to confrontation with Oliver Cromwell, defeat at the Battle of Dunbar on 3 September 1650 and their gradual disbandment.

James Graham, 5th Earl and 1st Marquess of Montrose, known as the "Great Montrose" after Gerrit van Honthorst (1649)

National Portrait Gallery, London

In January 1661 Montrose's mangled torso was disinterred, his head was removed from the Tolbooth and his limbs were recovered from the towns to which they had been sent. His body, reassembled in a magnificent coffin, lay in state at Holyrood for a few days, before a splendid funeral in St Giles's Cathedral. By then Montrose was beyond caring.

Montrose was also a considerable poet. He wrote at least thirteen poems, including one composed with amazing calmness the night before his execution:

Let them bestow on ev'ry airt a limb;
    Open all my veins, that I may swim
To Thee, my Saviour, in that crimson lake;
    Then place my parboil'd head upon a stake,
Scatter my ashes, throw them in the air:
    Lord (since Thou know'st where all these atoms are)
I'm hopeful once Thou'lt recollect my dust,
    And confident Thou'lt raise me with the just.

In his desire to make atonement in some way, Charles II had indeed recollected Montrose's "dust". Montrose was less well-served by William Topaz McGonagall (1825–1902). Deaf to poetic metaphor and unable to scan or spell, he is without doubt Britain's worst ever poet. A verse near the beginning of his awful poem describes a jolly little conversation between Montrose and the Clerk Register:

When he told him he shouldn't be so particular with his head,
    For in a few hours he would be dead;
But Montrose replied, While my head is my own I'll dress it at my ease,
    And to-morrow, when it becomes yours, treat it as you please.

He concludes his factually correct account of Montrose's life with a final flourish:

    Thus died, at the age of thirty-eight, James Graham, Marquis of Montrose,
Who was brought to a premature grave by his bitter foes;
    A commander who had acquired great military glory
In a short space of time, which cannot be equalled in story.

General Bernard Montgomery, on the eve of D-Day in June 1944, quoted Montrose: "He either fears his fate too much, or his deserts are small that puts it not unto the touch to win or lose it all".

Oliver Cromwell

BRITAINS ONLY DICTATOR LORD PROTECTOR OF THE COMMONWEALTH OF ENGLAND, SCOTLAND AND IRELAND

Oliver Cromwell, a farmer, soldier and statesman, commanded the New Model Army raised by Parliament to defeat King Charles I in the English Civil Wars. He conquered Ireland and Scotland, creating a republic known as the Commonwealth of which he became Lord Protector. Cromwell also restored England to a ranking European power.

He was born on 25 April 1599 in Huntingdon. His father Robert was descended from Thomas Cromwell, chief minister to Henry VIII who supervised the suppression of the monasteries. His family acquired substantial monastic lands, of which a modest holding passed down to Oliver: "I was by birth a gentleman, living neither in considerable height, nor yet in obscurity".

Oliver Cromwell by Sir Peter Lely (1653–54)
Birmingham Museums & Art Gallery

Cromwell's house in Ely

Robert had been an M.P. and JP in Queen Elizabeth's reign but died when Cromwell was eighteen. His mother Elizabeth (*née* Steward) lived until she was eighty-nine. Cromwell was educated at the local grammar school before enrolling in Lincoln's Inn. In 1620 he married Elizabeth, the daughter of Sir James Bourchier, a London merchant. In the 1630s Cromwell experienced an intense spiritual agony. He emerged from this convinced that he was one of God's chosen.

By 1631 Cromwell's fortunes were in decline. He was forced to sell most of his Huntingdon property and for the next five years became a tenant farmer at St Ives. In 1636 his fortunes improved when his childless uncle Sir Thomas Steward died, leaving him a substantial inheritance. It included a house next to St Mary's Church in Ely and the position of local tax-collector for the two Ely parishes of St Mary's and Holy Trinity. Cromwell's improved place in society and his strong connections with local Puritans earned his nomination as a freeman of the borough of Cambridge, for which he was returned as M.P. in the Short and the Long Parliaments of 1640.

THE CIVIL WARS (1639–1746), "The War of the Three Kingdoms" and Rebellions

The last battle on British soil ended the "Jacobite" rebellion.

✗ The Civil Wars (1642–51) and the War of the Three Kingdoms (1639–51)

Rebellions –

✗ Duke of Monmouth (1685) and James II's attempted comeback in Ireland (1689–90)

✗ First "Jacobite" uprising (1715)

✗ Second "Jacobite" uprising (1745–6)

Inverness ●

Culloden 16 April 1746

Inverurie 1745

Aberdeen ●

Glenfinnan 19 August 1745

SCOTLAND

Bonnie Prince Charlie landed from France.

Perth ●

Sheriffmuir 1715

Dunbar 1650 (Cromwell defeated the Scots, who were loyal to Charles II)

Falkirk 1746

Edinburgh ●

Prestonpans 1745

Philiphaugh 1645 (Montrose defeated)

Carlisle (taken in 1745)

IRELAND

ISLE OF MAN

Marston Moor 1644 (Prince Rupert defeated)

Preston 1648

York ●

Adwalton Moor 1643

Boyne 1690

Drogheda 1649

Preston 1715

Chester ●

Lincoln ●

Rathmines 1649

WALES

ENGLAND

Derby (December 1745)

The farthest point south reached by Bonnie Prince Charlie.

Norwich ●

Naseby 1645 (Charles I captured)

Wexford (besieged 1649)

Colby Moor 1645

Worcester 1651 (Charles II escaped capture)

Edgehill 1642

Colchester (besieged 1648)

Roundaway Down 1643

Oxford ●

London ●

Bristol ●

Newbury 1643 / 1644

Sedgemoor 1685 (Monmouth captured)

Langport 1645

| 0 | | 50 miles |
| 0 | | 100 km |

When King Charles I and Archbishop William Laud tried to impose elaborate, high-church practice and ritual on the Church of England Cromwell, now M.P. for nearby St Ives, though badly dressed and clumsy proved himself to be a passionate speaker. He supported the idea of a state church, as long as it contained no bishops and did not follow the canons laid down in *The Book of Common Prayer*.

Cromwell's unforgiving beliefs brought him into direct conflict with royal authority. In 1641 he wholeheartedly supported the Grand Remonstrance, a list of 200 grievances, presented by John Pym (1584–1643), which included harsh criticism of the bishops and clergy. Charles rejected the Remonstrance and by-passed Parliament's authority, using an ancient system known as Commission of Array. Permitted to recruit local men directly in specific counties, the King raised his standard at Nottingham and the First Civil War began.

In 1642 Cromwell left Parliament to raise a troop of cavalry from Huntingdon. That August, with 200 volunteers, he prevented a royalist attempt to seize the silver plate from Cambridge colleges, capturing the magazine at Cambridge Castle. On 22 October 1642 he fought his first battle at Edgehill. By 1643 Cromwell had become a competent military instructor and a formidable leader of men. Promoted to colonel, he began to recruit and train a cavalry regiment composed only of men of good character on whom he imposed strict discipline. Cromwell's control of his cavalry units proved an essential factor in achieving victory for Parliament. By the end of 1643 he and Sir Thomas Fairfax had secured most of East Anglia and had taken the key town of Newark on the River Trent in Nottinghamshire.

Early the following year Cromwell was made second-in-command to Edward Montagu, 2nd Earl of Manchester in the "Eastern Association" army, with the rank of lieutenant-general. He accused Manchester of lethargy and demanded that a new army under Sir Thomas Fairfax should be formed. A Self-Denying Ordinance, to prevent M.P's holding command in the army or navy, was carried on 3 April 1645. It made for an independent and efficient New Model Army.

The New Model Army was recruited to provide a well-trained national force instead of one cobbled together from local militias. It also replaced private armies raised by individual generals which lacked cohesion and a unified command.

In July 1644 a Royalist army under Prince Rupert had raised the siege of York and chased the Parliamentary army to Long Marston. An unexpected counter-attack by Cromwell however, inflicting heavy casualties on the Royalist army, resulted in Charles's

Thomas Fairfax, 3rd Baron Fairfax of Cameron (1612–71), born near Otley in Yorkshire, was appointed Commander-in-Chief of the Parliamentary army in 1645. He and his father were both professional soldiers who had fought several campaigns in Holland. Fairfax, though badly wounded, was instrumental in winning the key Battle of Marston Moor on 2 July 1644, the first serious defeat inflicted on the Royalists by Cromwell's New Model Army. He was succeeded by Cromwell as Commander-in-Chief in 1650.

Fairfax refused to sit on the commission that condemned Charles I to death. In 1658 he helped General George Monck restore Parliamentary rule after Cromwell died and was a member of the Parliament that invited Charles II to return to England in 1660.

• **Thomas Fairfax, 3rd Baron Fairfax of Cameron by Wenceslaus Hollar; after Robert Walker (1648)**
National Portrait Gallery, London

Prince Rupert "of the Rhine" (1619–82), the most important Royalist army commander, was the son of the Elector Palatine and his wife Elizabeth, daughter of James I of England. After arriving in England in 1642, Rupert became a great favourite of his uncle Charles I. He was given command of the Royalist cavalry and distinguished himself in early encounters by his daring, if reckless, cavalry charges. In 1645 he was sacked after losing Bristol to Parliament and expelled from England. He returned with Charles II in 1660 to command a fleet in the subsequent wars against the Dutch. He was founder and first governor of the Hudson's Bay Company. A Fellow of the Royal Society and a keen amateur scientist, he is credited with the invention of the mezzo-tint.

• **Prince Rupert, Count Palatine (1619–82) after Sir Peter Lely (c.1665–1670)**
National Portrait Gallery, London

loss of York and the northern counties. Cromwell became the leading Parliamentary general under Fairfax.

In 1645 Fairfax insisted on Cromwell becoming his second-in-command and together they fought the decisive battles of Naseby in June and Langport in July.

The Battle of Naseby, fought near Leicester on 14 June 1645, was the decisive Parliamentary victory. The armies formed up and occupied parallel ridges. Charles's cavalry, commanded by Prince Rupert, charged and broke the left wing of the Parliamentary cavalry. Failing to pull up and circle back up to attack the enemy infantry in the rear however, he continued in pointless pursuit. Cromwell's more disciplined troops regrouped and counter-attacked, routing the Royalists and taking 4,000 prisoners. With his army destroyed, Charles had lost the war.

Parliament wished to disband the army as quickly as possible. A Scots army was hired when the army refused to disperse. In June 1647 Cromwell, appalled by Parliament's disgraceful treatment of his soldiers, took up their cause as mediator, eliciting the dry comment from Sir Arthur Haselrig: "If you prove not an honest man, I will never trust a fellow with a great nose for your sake". While trying to appease the General Council of the Army and the soldiers' representatives, known as Agitators or Adjutators (who wanted no more dealings with the King), Cromwell was also concerned that abolition of the monarchy and the House of Lords would lead to anarchy.

On 11 November 1647 King Charles escaped from Hampton Court where he had been held under loose house arrest. He fled to the Isle of Wight and opened negotiations with the Scots to restore him to the throne, on their condition that he would impose Presbyterianism on England. These negotiations, and Cromwell's failure to unite the army, encouraged the Royalists to begin what is known as the Second Civil War.

Early in 1648 Fairfax sent Cromwell into Wales. He quickly suppressed a Royalist uprising led by Colonel Poyer who had refused to hand over Pembroke Castle. At the same time Fairfax crushed other insurrections in Kent and Essex, before despatching Cromwell north in June 1648 to confront a Scots army that had invaded England. Between 17–19 August 1648, in a brisk Lancashire campaign, Cromwell defeated the Duke of Hamilton's 10,000 Scottish "Engagers" (Covenanters who had "engaged" in negotiations with the King) and 3,000 northern Royalists at the Battle of Preston.

At the same time Cromwell's son-in-law, Henry Ireton (1611–51) and other army officers had petitioned Parliament with a remonstrance condemning the negotiations with the King in the Isle of Wight. It also demanded that he be put on trial as "a man of blood". Ireton had proposed a formula for a constitutional monarchy which was rejected out of hand by Charles.

In a coup called "Pride's Purge", Ireton followed up his remonstrance by sending Colonel Thomas Pride to expel all those Members of Parliament who still favoured negotiations with the King. The remaining members became known as the "Rump Parliament". Cromwell, who had been ordered back to London, hesitated until Christmas 1648 before reluctantly agreeing to put Charles on trial and signing his death warrant. After the King's execution, Cromwell is said to have looked down on Charles's corpse, murmuring, "cruel necessity".

After the execution of King Charles, Parliament declared the British Isles a republic, called the Commonwealth – with Cromwell serving as first Chairman of the Council of State, the executive arm of a single

Parliament rewarded Cromwell handsomely with cash and land, a generosity he vainly petitioned the Speaker of the House of Commons to extend to his soldiers.

Prince Rupert is said to have coined the name "Ironside" for Cromwell, which became popular with the army and was extended to his troopers.

Ireton was one of the commissioners who signed Charles's death warrant. He took over as Lord Deputy and Commander-in-Chief in Ireland when Cromwell left to fight the Scots, prosecuting a grim war of attrition against Irish rebels and Royalists. He died of dysentery a few days after the surrender of Limerick in 1651. His loss "struck a great sadness into Cromwell". After the Restoration, as a regicide, Ireton's corpse was dug up and hanged in chains from Tyburn gallows.

chamber parliament. There was to be no rest for Cromwell during the first three years of the Commonwealth. First, he had to extinguish a mutiny of extreme Puritan army officers known as the Levellers, before moving to Ireland where he put down a Royalist rebellion with brutality.

In September 1649 Cromwell ordered the slaughter of the garrisons of Drogheda and Wexford, conducted with a ferocity that ignited the intense sectarian hatred that has blighted Anglo-Irish relations ever since. On returning to England in May 1650, Cromwell was sent to Scotland where the Scots had declared Charles II to be their king. On 25 June he was appointed Captain-General and began a difficult campaign against a numerically superior Scottish army which he crushed at Dunbar on 3 September 1650. On the same day the following year, 3 September 1651 he routed Charles II, in personal command of yet another Scots army, at the Battle of Worcester.

Commonwealth Coat of Arms (1649–60)

Worcester brought an end to the English Civil Wars. He now had every expectation of a period of peace in which to create a new constitution. But peace for Cromwell was to be denied. Despite a general amnesty, called the Act of Oblivion, his army and the Rump Parliament began a bitter dispute, in which he vainly tried to mediate. Finally losing patience and suspecting the Rump might be planning to perpetuate itself, on 23 April 1653, at bayonet point Cromwell purged Parliament of its members, replacing them with a Nominated Assembly of his choosing. This came to be known as the "Barebones" or "Little Parliament", also as the "Assembly of Saints". Although he made no personal attempt to seize power, the first of his unsuccessful experiments in republican government had begun.

Expected to bring "righteous, godly government" to the Commonwealth, the Nominated Assembly collapsed when the Saints, failing to heed or consult Cromwell, threatened to pass intemperate and radical legislation. He ordered Major-General John Lambert to arrange a coup, to expel the Saints and deliver power into his own hands.

Reluctantly, Cromwell decided that as Parliament had appointed him Commander-in-Chief, he was now the only constitutional authority left in the land. It was a clear sign from God that he should take supreme power. Under the *Instrument of Government*, drawn up by Lambert and the army, Cromwell adopted the title Lord Protector. He now ruled a Commonwealth of England, Scotland and Ireland. It was to be advised by a Council of State and a parliament, elected every three years. In April 1654 he moved into Whitehall Palace, the former residence of King Charles.

Cromwell called his first Protectorate Parliament (1654–56) on 3 September 1654. He had already passed decrees through the Council of State, establishing a Puritan church and overhauling the school system, together with administrative and legal reforms. This Parliament contained for the first time members from Scotland and Ireland.

Of the two great European powers, France and Spain, Cromwell believed a French alliance would bring most benefit to England. In 1655 his navy captured

Cromwell's speech to Parliament in 1653 bears quoting in full, in the light of allegations of wholesale parliamentary corruption made in 2009: "It is high time for me to put an end to your sitting in this place, which you have dishonored by your contempt of all virtue, and defiled by your practice of every vice; ye are a factious crew, and enemies to all good government; ye are a pack of mercenary wretches, and would like Esau sell your country for a mess of pottage, and like Judas betray your God for a few pieces of money. Is there a single virtue now remaining amongst you? Is there one vice you do not possess? Ye have no more religion than my horse; gold is your God; which of you have not barter'd your conscience for bribes? Is there a man amongst you that has the least care for the good of the Commonwealth? Ye sordid prostitutes have you not defil'd this sacred place, and turn'd the Lord's temple into a den of thieves, by your immoral principles and wicked practices? Ye are grown intolerably odious to the whole nation; you were deputed here by the people to get grievances redress'd, are yourselves gone! So! Take away that shining bauble there, and lock up the doors. In the name of God, go!".

John Lambert (1619–84) was the author of the *Instrument of Government* in 1653, the first written constitution in the world to codify sovereign powers. This was replaced in May 1657 by England's second and last attempt at a written constitution, the *Humble Petition and Advice*.

Committees called "Triers and Ejectors" were created to supervise and discipline clergy and schoolmasters. Cromwell became Chancellor of Oxford University. He increased the number of Grammar Schools, elevating them to unprecedented standards of excellence.

Jamaica in the Spanish West Indies in a combined operation. This was followed by the acquisition of the port of Dunkirk from France, in return for the despatch of an English expeditionary force to assist the French in Spanish Flanders. At home, he abolished the unpopular monopoly system used by Elizabeth I to reward favourite courtiers. Yet in 1657 he granted the East India Company a charter, in exchange for a substantial lump sum. In common with his royal predecessors, Cromwell was always short of money.

From the outset Cromwell's first Protectorate Parliament, called to "heal and settle" the nation, was disturbed by the agitations and disruptions of the Levellers, Fifth Monarchy Men and extreme republicans. They were all far more interested in questioning the underlying basis of the Commonwealth and destroying the last vestiges of the Anglican Church, than passing the ordinances of good government.

Cromwell strove in vain to impress upon his truculent Parliament four principles of good government: one supreme head of state, or Protector; regular summoning of limited-life parliaments; liberty of conscience; and control of the armed forces to be split between Protector and Parliament. To this end Cromwell insisted on a signed agreement from Members to uphold these principles, as a condition of holding their seats. A hundred Members refused. On 22 January 1655 Cromwell dissolved Parliament.

Penruddock's Royalist rebellion in March 1655 convinced Cromwell that he should tighten his grip on the provinces. In the most unpopular act of his rule, Cromwell sent his Major-Generals, answerable only to him, to control all of England and Wales. They were supported by militias raised from New Model Army veterans, paid-for by fines and confiscations levied on convicted Royalists. The Major-Generals were charged with ensuring public order and enforcing a moral "reformation of manners".

The second Protectorate Parliament (1656–58) met a year early, summoned by Cromwell to raise money for the war against Spain. It brought an end to the Major-Generals but attacked Cromwell's toleration of nonconformists, particularly the Quakers and the Jews – having permitted the latter to return to England in 1655.

By 1656 Cromwell had begun to adopt the trappings of royalty. He liked to be addressed as "Your Highness" and granted knighthoods. In March 1657 Parliament, tired of ever-changing experiments with forms of radical government, presented a new constitution called the *Humble Petition and Advice*. As the concept of sovereignty was fundamental to the laws of England, Cromwell was offered the Crown. He brooded but, faced with strong opposition from the army and committed republican Members, refused. On 8 May, he announced: "I will not build Jericho again". He restored many of the features of monarchy however, including the House of Lords.

The Petition was amended to allow him to name a successor but removed all reference to a royal title. On 26 June 1657 Cromwell was re-installed as Lord Protector. The ceremony was a crypto-coronation with Cromwell decked out in a purple, velvet and ermine-lined robe, bearing a golden sceptre. He was now King in all but name.

In February 1658 Cromwell dissolved his last Parliament. He was likened to Pharaoh, in imposing a second Egyptian bondage. Cromwell maintained a nice sense of humour however, observing: "No one rises so high as he who knows not whither he is going".

Cromwell's Major-Generals were an eerie harbinger of Hitler's Gauleiters. For fifteen months, independent of Parliament, they enjoyed a similarly detested authority.

Oliver Cromwell by Hamo Thornycroft

The last few months of Cromwell's life were made miserable by the death of his beloved daughter Elizabeth, from a hideous cancer, and his own contraction of malaria. Preparing for death, he nominated his eldest son Richard to succeed him.

Cromwell died from septicæmia, caused by a urinary infection, on 3 September 1658.

A violent storm wracked England on the night of Cromwell's death: believed by his enemies to be the Devil carrying away his soul. He was buried in Westminster Abbey with a funeral service based on that of King James I, the last king with the good fortune to die in his own bed.

CROMWELL LOST HIS HEAD TOO

Cromwell's body was embalmed: but the work was botched and his putrefying corpse was hastily and secretly buried. However the Lords of the Council ordered a lavish state-funeral to be conducted with a wax effigy, complete with mace and crown. Eleven weeks after Cromwell's death a seven-hour funeral *cortège,* costing £60,000, delivered a magnificent, empty coffin for burial in the Henry VII chapel in Westminster Abbey.

On 6 December 1660 the" Convention" Parliament ordered the corpses of Cromwell, his son-in-law Henry Ireton and John Bradshaw, all of whom had signed Charles I's death warrant, to be disinterred, dragged on hurdles and hanged from Tyburn gallows. This was duly done on 30 January 1661, the anniversary of King Charles' execution. The bodies were exposed for a day before being cut down, decapitated and flung into a pit below the scaffold. The heads were then stuck on poles and placed on the roof of Westminster Hall – where Samuel Pepys recorded seeing them in February.

In March 1684 a storm blew down Cromwell's head. It landed at the feet of a night watchman who took it home and hid it in his chimney. He only revealed its presence to his family on his deathbed. On 1 July 1710 a German tourist, Zacharias Conrad von Uffenbach, visited a Museum of Curiosities where he saw Cromwell's head jammed on the end of broken wooden shaft.

It is next recorded as the property of Samuel Russell, who sold it on to one James Cox, a London jeweller, for £118 (£143,000 today) on 30 April 1787 (the receipt is in the possession of

Sidney Sussex College, Cambridge). Cox then sold the head for £230 to three brothers called Hughes. They exhibited it in 1799 at Mead Court off Old Bond Street, London at a charge of 2s/6d (£100 today). A daughter of one the brothers sold it to Josiah Wilkinson of Kent. He showed it to the Victorian novelist Maria Edgecombe who recorded her impressions in a letter of 9 March 1822: "there is the mark of a famous wart of Oliver's just above the left eyebrow on the skull precisely as in the cast".

In 1898 Canon Horace Wilkinson inherited both the head and a portrait. He kept the head in a wooden box. Prior to a famous pathological examination by Pearson and Morant in 1911, who declared the head authentic, Wilkinson had allowed it to be examined by the Royal Archaeological Institute. However he refused the BBC permission to film it in 1954. On Wilkinsons's death, the head was stored in a bank vault in Woodbridge.

After 300 years Cromwell's head was finally laid to rest in an unmarked plot near the door of Sidney Sussex Chapel. A plaque in the ante-chapel is inscribed: "Near to this place was buried on 25 March 1960 the head of Oliver Cromwell, Lord Protector of the Commonwealth of England, Scotland and Ireland, Fellow Commoner of this College 1616–17".

Unfinished miniature of Oliver Cromwell (1649) by Samuel Cooper (1609–72)
National Portrait Gallery, London

THE QUAKERS

Mid-17th century England was a religious laboratory with a remarkable number of mad scientists conducting experiments to see just how far they could stretch the limits of credulity and the patience of the government. All Christian sects, usually Protestant but including Catholics, that did not "conform" to the established Anglican church were referred to as nonconformist. Until Charles II's Declaration of Breda on 4 April 1660, guaranteeing "a free parliament by which, upon the word of a king, we will be advised" and religious toleration as a condition of his Restoration, nonconformists were liable to suffer imprisonment, savage persecution and, in extreme cases, death.

In 1673 Parliament repudiated the Declaration of Breda and passed the Test Act, followed by another in 1678. These required holders of public office to take the Oath of Supremacy, recognising the sovereign as supreme governor of the Church of England.

The Toleration Act of 1689 mitigated the religious, but none of the political, disabilities of some of the nonconformists – while ignoring Catholics, Jews, Unitarians and atheists. Nonconformists could not attend universities, live within a city which had a corporation charter, sit on juries, hold municipal, judicial or public office, or become Members of Parliament or the armed forces. These restrictions were not lifted until the Test Acts were repealed in 1828. Oxford and Cambridge continued to disqualify nonconformists until 1871. As it happened, many nonconformists were also pacifists and would not have wished to become soldiers or sailors under any circumstances.

Fifth Monarchy Men, the Diggers, the Ranters, the Adamites, the Behmenists, the Familists, the Grindletonians, the Muggletonians, the Sabbatarians and the Seekers were among the many bizarre dissenting creeds that sprang up briefly between 1645–65. There was however, one remarkable sect that has stood the test of time – the Quakers.

The Religious Society of Friends, whose members are known as Quakers or Friends, was founded by an itinerant preacher, George Fox (1624–91) from Fenny Drayton in Leicestershire, who began to preach publicly in 1647. In 1667 one of his most celebrated converts was Robert Barclay of Urie in Kincardineshire (1648–90) known as "the Apologist", son of a distinguished soldier in the Thirty Years' War. Another was William Penn (1644–1718), the world's largest private landowner, with over 45,000 square miles granted in his sole name by Charles II to found Pennsylvania in 1681.

The name Quaker was first used derisively in 1650, because followers "trembled at the word of God". Though represented in many countries, the total number of Quakers is barely 350,000 world wide. The greatest concentration is in Pennsylvania. Unlike other Christian groups, the Religious Society of Friends has shied away from creeds and hierarchical structure. The various branches have widely divergent beliefs and practices, the central concept being the "Inner Light" – allowing each member to develop a personal creed from his own conscience. Quakers spoke plainly, dressed soberly, were committed to pacifism and opposed to slavery. Long devotion to philanthropy, together with a distinguished record of aiding refugees and victims of natural disaster, resulted in the the US and British Friends sharing the 1947 Nobel Peace Prize.

Quakers avoided professions where oath-taking was required, believing it set a double standard of integrity, and turned instead to industry, banking and commerce. Many were at the forefront of the Industrial Revolution and some founded companies that are still in business today. The principal commodity traded by Quakers was trust and the trades they pursued had to be "innocent", not contributing to war or its preparations.

Ethical conduct is still a Quaker business practice today, though most of the companies founded by Friends have passed out of Quaker hands. Quaker families include the chocolate manufacturing Frys, Rowntrees and Cadburys. The importation of cocoa beans from West Africa led to their leading role in the abolition of slavery.

Abraham Darby (c.1678–1717), another Quaker, was the first man in the world successfully to smelt iron with coke. His grandson, Abraham Darby III (1750–91) built the first iron bridge in the world over the River Severn which opened in 1781. The Stockton and Darlington Railway, the world's first to carry passengers, was founded by Quaker Edward Pease and others in 1821.

Wedgwood (fine china), Clark (shoes), Albright and Wilson (chemicals), Huntley & Palmer (biscuits) and Jacobs (more biscuits), Bryant and May (matches), Reckitt (household goods), Truman, Hanbury and Buxton (brewers), Allen and Hanbury (pharmaceuticals, now owned by Glaxo), Friends Provident (life assurance), Waterford (glass) and famously, both Barclays and Lloyds Banks, were all businesses founded by Quakers. Perhaps the most unexpected of all is Sony (formerly Tokyo Tsushin Kogyo): TTK's founding chairman was Tamon Maeda, a Japanese Quaker.

Leading Quakers include the scientist John Dalton (1766–1844) who formulated the Atomic Theory; Elizabeth Fry, *née* Gurney (1780–1845), the prison reformer; Herbert Hoover (1874–1964), 31st US President; Joseph, Lord Lister (1827–1912), the bacteriologist; Richard Nixon (1913–94), 37th US President; Arthur Cooper (1833–92), the chartered accountant; James Taylor (1791–1844) who founded the *Manchester Guardian* in 1831; Benjamin West (1738–1820), the historical artist and James Wilson (1805–60) who founded the *Economist* in 1843 and the Chartered Bank in 1853.

Contemporary celebrities who were born Quakers include the actors Jim Broadbent (born 1949), Sir Ben Kingsley (born 1943) and Paul Eddington (1927–95); the actresses Dame Judi Dench (born 1934), Billie Whitelaw (born

One US business that was *not* founded by Quakers is Quaker Oats.

Elizabeth Fry after Charles Robert Leslie (died 1859)
National Portrait Gallery, London

1932) and the comedienne Victoria Wood (born 1953); the historian
David Starkey (born 1945) and the novelist sisters, A.S. Byatt (born
1936) and Margaret Drabble (born 1939). Surprisingly, the US film
star James Dean (1931–55) was a Quaker too.

Organisations founded by Friends, or by Friends working with
others, include Amnesty International, Greenpeace, Oxfam, Peace
Action and WILPF. Many conscientious objectors were Quakers.
There are far more practising Quakers in the US today, where
religious observance is still strong, than there are in an increasingly
secular Britain.

THE RETURN OF THE JEWS AFTER MORE THAN 350 YEARS

In 1653 the leader of the Dutch-Jewish community, Rabbi Menasseh Ben Israel (1604–57), born
Manoel Dias Soeiro on the Portuguese island of Madeira, contacted Oliver Cromwell to explore
the possibility of allowing Jews to return to England. No Jews had been permitted to live in
England since their expulsion by King Edward I in 1290. Although there is no record of any Jews
in England before the Norman Conquest, Jewish metal traders are known to have visited
England to buy tin in the 1st century AD and Gallo-Roman Jewish slave-traders were active
throughout the Roman occupation.

William I invited a group of Jewish merchants from Rouen to England in 1070 to benefit
from their skills and capital. They were not permitted to own land nor to participate in any
trade other than as doctors; or money lenders, as Christianity held that usury was a sin. It was
extremely dangerous however, for a Jew to be owed too much money. He risked violence from
his customers in place of repayment.

"I had rather", Cromwell said, "that Mahometanism were permitted amongst us than that
one of God's children should be persecuted". In December 1655 he decided that the ban on Jews
would no longer be enforced. By 1690 several hundred Sephardic Jews, from Spain, Portugal,
Morocco and Italy, were living in England. In the 1745 Jacobite rising, when London was
threatened, the Jewish community behaved with such loyalty that in 1753 Parliament passed the
Jewish Naturalisation Act. Following the 1829 Catholic Emancipation Act, support for similar
treatment of the Jews increased.

By 1837 Queen Victoria had dubbed the first Jewish knight, Moses Montefiore. In 1841 Isaac
Goldsmid became the first Jew to receive an hereditary title. The year 1855 saw the first Jewish
Lord Mayor of London, Sir David Salomons. Full Jewish emancipation followed in 1858. In July
that year Lionel de Rothschild became the first Jewish M.P. – although Benjamin Disraeli, a
baptised Christian, was already sitting. In 1884 Nathan
Mayer, 1st Baron Rothschild sat as the first Jewish
member of the House of Lords. By 1882 46,000 Jews had
settled in Britain, mostly Ashkenazim from Russia and
Poland; and by 1890 Jewish emancipation was complete.
Since 1858 Parliament has never been without Jewish
members and many have served in the Cabinet,

Approximately 40,000 Jews from Austria and
Germany settled in Britain before World War II, to
escape the Nazis, in addition to 50,000 from Italy and
Eastern Europe.

The loss of so many great scientists amongst these emigrés quite possibly cost Hitler the war. It is more than likely that the Nazis would otherwise have developed an atomic bomb before the allies – with unimaginable consequences. Several immigrant Jewish scientists went on to win Nobel prizes; while others have enhanced artistic and literary life in Britain immeasurably.

Culturally and intellectually, the Jewish contribution to Britain is out of all proportion to the size of their community. Lucien Freud (1922–2011), one of Britain's greatest 20th century artists, came to Britain from Berlin in 1934. There are about 285,000 Jews in Britain today, of whom two-thirds live in London.

Around 50,000 Jews served in the British armed forces during WWI. Some 10,000 were killed and five won the Victoria Cross. 60,000 also joined up in World War II, including 30,000 from Palestine which was then under British administration.

ROBERT BLAKE

Robert Blake (1599–1657), often referred to as "Father of the Royal Navy," was an English admiral and commander of the navy under Oliver Cromwell's Commonwealth. He was the author of "Fighting Instructions" and "Sailing Instructions", engagement handbooks for naval officers which required attacks to be made "in-line-ahead," a tactic successfully practised by the Royal Navy throughout the next century. He also created and introduced the Articles of War, the foundation of naval discipline, and increased the navy from barely a score of ships to over a hundred. He was the first naval commander to winter a fleet at sea.

One of thirteen children born to a prosperous merchant in Bridgwater in Somerset, he attended Wadham College, Oxford in 1625. Only 5 feet 6 inches tall and ambitious, he was elected to the Short Parliament in 1640: where, as a stalwart Puritan, he immediately embraced the Parliamentary cause. In 1644, despite having no military experience, he won great acclaim as the general commanding the defence of Lyme Regis in Dorset. From July 1644 to July 1645 he withstood another siege, at Taunton in Somerset, declaring: "I will eat three of my four pairs of boots before I surrender".

In January 1649 Cromwell appointed Blake one of his three "Generals-at-sea" and ordered him to pursue a small Royalist fleet under Prince Rupert which had been preying on Parliamentary shipping in the Channel. Rupert was chased to Lisbon where he took shelter. Blake forced him out by seizing several Portuguese ships to bargain with and then harried the Royalist fleet into the Mediterranean. In November 1650 he scattered their ships off the south-eastern coast of Spain at Cartagena. A few months later he captured the Isles of Scilly, a Royalist stronghold, before he was appointed to serve on Cromwell's Council-of-State.

During the Dutch war of 1652–54, Blake commanded the Channel squadron and fought a number of successful engagements against the Dutch admiral, Maarten Tromp. Assigned to the Mediterranean, in April 1655 he destroyed a fleet of Barbary pirates in the Bay of Tunis. It was the first naval engagement in which shore batteries were neutralised without landing parties. During the 1656–58 war with Spain, in April 1657 he captured a Spanish treasure fleet in the Canary Islands. He seized £2 million (£3 billion today) in bullion without the loss of a single ship.

Mortally ill, Blake sailed for England. He died just an hour before his fleet reached Plymouth. Cromwell attended his funeral in Westminster Abbey. Charles II however, ordered his corpse to be exhumed and thrown into a lime pit with other Commonwealth leaders. In Blake's case, this was mean spirited.

Robert Blake miniature by Samuel Cooper (early 1650s)
National Maritime Museum, London

CHARLES II, KING OF ENGLAND, SCOTLAND AND IRELAND (REIGNED 1660–85)

Described by the diarist John Evelyn as "a prince of many virtues and many great imperfections, debonair, easy of access, not bloody or cruel," Charles Stuart, the eldest son of King Charles I and Henrietta Maria, was born in St James's Palace on 29 May 1630. He was brought up by the Protestant Countess of Dorset. At the age of eight Charles was given his own household at Richmond under the Earl of Newcastle.

Louis XIV, born in 1638, was glamorized as *le Roi Soleil* (the "Sun King") due to the brilliance of his court. He succeeded his father Louis XIII at the age of four. When his chief minister, Cardinal Mazarin died in 1661 Louis, a believer in the divine right and absolute power of kings, assumed control of France. He ruled until his death at the age of seventy-seven, the longest reign in European history. His influence on Charles was unhelpful throughout his reign, entangling him with Catholicism and a web of secret alliances. The appalling treatment of the Huguenots that he permitted in his name should be an eternal stain upon it.

On Sunday 23 October 1642, aged twelve, Prince Charles was present with his father at Edgehill, the first formal battle of the "First" English Civil War. In 1645 he was made titular commander of the English forces in the West Country. By early 1646 it was clear that the Royalists had lost the war. Charles left England, eventually arriving in France by way of the Scilly Islands and Jersey. His mother Henrietta had already fled there. His eight year-old first cousin, Louis XIV was now King of France, under the regency of his mother Anne of Austria, having inherited the throne in 1643.

In 1648, during the "Second" English Civil War, Charles moved to The Hague to canvass support from his sister Mary and his brother-in-law William II, Prince of Orange. William appeared a better prospect for Charles's cause than his mother's French family.

Charles had a brief affair with Lucy Walter (*c.*1630–58). The diarist John Evelyn described her as a "brown, beautiful, bold but insipid creature". Charles recognised the son she bore in 1649, later creating him Duke of Monmouth and Duke of Buccleuch. Their affair ended in 1651. Lucy died in penury in Paris, aged twenty-eight. It is unlikely that she ever underwent a ceremony of marriage with Charles, as was later asserted by Protestant supporters of Monmouth's claim to the throne.

Charles I was beheaded on 30 January 1649 and England became a republic. On 5 February, the Scottish Parliament declared Charles II King of Scots, on the condition that he agreed to the Solemn League and Covenant – and that Presbyterianism would become the official religion of England. On 23 June 1650 Charles reluctantly signed the Covenant, aware that it would lose him English support. On 3 September 1650 the Covenanters were defeated at the Battle of Dunbar by a much smaller force led by Oliver Cromwell. Charles was crowned King of Scotland at Scone on 1 January 1651. The Scots invaded

Charles II attributed to Thomas Hawker (c.1680)
National Portrait Gallery, London

England but were soundly beaten on 3 September, at Worcester. In a series of disguises, despite a bounty of £1,000 on his head and being tall and swarthy, Charles had some narrow escapes over the following six weeks, once by hiding in an oak tree. Eventually, on 16 October he landed in Normandy.

Impoverished and friendless, Charles found little cheer on the Continent. His cause was ignored by the princely houses of Europe and his overtures of marriage to their daughters were scorned. Even Cromwell's death in 1658 seemed unlikely to restore his fortunes. It was General George Monck (1608–70), one of Cromwell's most competent

"The Royal Oak", the tree in which Charles II hid after the Battle of Worcester, stood in the park of Boscobel House in Staffordshire, the home of John Gifford, a Catholic landowner. Charles told Samuel Pepys in 1680 that, while he was hiding in the tree, a Parliamentary soldier passed directly below him. After the Restoration, Thomas Toft, a Staffordshire potter, made large dishes decorated with the Boscobel Oak, supported by the Lion and Unicorn, with the King's face peering through the branches. 29 May, Charles's birthday, is known as Oak-apple day.

The tree standing on the site today is not the original Royal Oak which was destroyed over time by souvenir hunters. It is a 300 year-old descendant of the original, known as "Son of Royal Oak". In 2000, Son of Royal Oak suffered severe storm damage and was nearly destroyed. In 2001 another oak sapling was planted near the site of the original Royal Oak by Prince Charles. It had been grown from one of the Son's acorns and is a grandson of the original tree. The Royal Oak is the third most common pub name in Britain. The King's Head is the tenth.

On 23 August 1650 Monck raised the Coldstream Guards, the oldest Corps in the British Army in unbroken service. The Regiment fought with distinction at Dunbar on 3 September. In 1652 and again in 1664 soldiers from the Regiment served at sea against the Dutch, giving weight to the Regiment's claim to be the parent of the Royal Marines. The seniority of the Regiment dates from 14 February 1661 when it laid down its arms as part of the New Model Army and took them up again in the service of the Crown.

generals who was the unlikely catalyst for Charles's restoration to the English throne. The inadequacy of Richard Cromwell, the Lord Protector's heir, was so apparent that Monck realised the country could well be destroyed by another civil war. He perceived that Englishmen above all else yearned for a lawful and secure monarchy. In 1660, as *de facto* ruler of England, he used his command of the New Model Army to create a climate favourable to Charles's return.

On 4 April 1660, with the help of Edward Hyde, his principal advisor, Charles made his Declaration of Breda, in which he promised a general amnesty, liberty of conscience, fair resolution of property disputes and payment of all arrears of pay to the army. Parliament agreed to settle the details and Charles was proclaimed King. On 29 May 1660, his thirtieth birthday, he arrived in London to a rapturous reception.

The Parliament elected in 1661 must have surprised and delighted Charles with its determination to stamp an uncompromising Anglican and royalist mark on government. Charles was given unrivalled powers to maintain a standing army by the Militia Act of 1661. By the Corporation Act, in the same year, he could dismiss any subversive local government official. Furthermore, the nation was to be circumscribed by strict press and public assembly laws. Charles's improvident career, with his morals tailored to survival, had made him tolerant of all religions. In 1663 however, his attempts to indulge nonconformists and Catholics were quickly quashed by Parliament.

On 14 May 1662 Charles married the Portuguese Infanta, Princess Catherine of Braganza (1638–1705). It was not a popular marriage. As a Roman Catholic, she could not be crowned in an Anglican service. Her substantial dowry however, brought Tangiers and, importantly for the

George Monck, 1st Duke of Albemarle, studio of Sir Peter Lely (1665–66)
National Portrait Gallery, London

Ilustration of the Coldstream Guards

Edward Hyde, 1st Earl of Clarendon (1609–74) was a lawyer, statesman and the first historian of the English Civil Wars. He was grandfather to two British monarchs, Mary II and Queen Anne. During the Civil War, Hyde served on the King's Council as Chancellor of the Exchequer. By 1645, although his moderation had alienated him from Charles I, he was made guardian to the Prince of Wales, with whom he fled to Jersey in 1646. Prince Charles appointed Hyde Lord Chancellor in 1658. On the restoration of the monarchy in 1660, he returned to England. His daughter Anne married Charles's brother James, Duke of York, later King James II.

Hyde dominated the early years of Charles II's reign but his criticism of the King's morals ruined their friendship. Parliament blamed him for the disastrous Anglo-Dutch War of 1665. He was dismissed in 1667 and died an exile in France.

• Edward Hyde, 1st Earl of Claredon after Adriaen Hanneman (c.1648–1655)

National Portrait Gallery, London

future British Empire, Bombay. Catherine frequently miscarried but had to endure the birth of at least thirteen bastards by her husband's mistresses. Despite her inability to have children, Charles respected her greatly and refused Parliament's entreaties to divorce her for a Protestant bride. Catherine introduced the custom of tea drinking to England.

The first decade of Charles's reign was bleak. The Anglo-Dutch War of 1665–67 ended on the Medway in the ignominious defeat of his navy. His flagship, HMS *Royal Charles* was captured and towed to Holland. Although Parliament had voted him a generous allowance, Charles was a profligate spender and was soon floundering in debt. To make things even worse, London was ravaged by plague in 1665 and the Great Fire in 1666.

On 2 September 1666 a bakery in Pudding Lane caught fire. Most London houses were built of wood. The fire spread swiftly, destroying 13,000 buildings and 87 churches. Molten lead streamed down Ludgate Hill from St Paul's Cathedral. The Lord Mayor Sir Thomas Bloodsworth, who had at first dismissed the fire as something "a woman might piss out", was unable to cope. Both Charles and his brother James distinguished themselves by taking charge of soldiers to create firebreaks. Remarkably, only nine people perished. The devastation gave Sir Christopher Wren the opportunity to redesign and rebuild the old, mostly still mediæval city.

In 1668 England formed the Protestant Triple Alliance with the Netherlands and Sweden, to oppose Louis XIV's territorial ambitions in Europe. In May 1670 however, in a startling volte-face, necessitated by his dire financial position, Charles signed the Treaty of Dover.

The Great Plague of London killed at least 100,000 people, nearly a fifth of the population. Although propagandists tried to blame the French, it probably spread from Dutch East India merchant ships docked in the Port of London.

The terms of the treaty required Charles to support French policy in Europe, in return for an annual subsidy from Louis XIV of £160,000 (£236 million today). This freed Charles from financial dependence on Parliament – but, in a secret clause, he was required to convert to Catholicism. Charles had placed himself in an extremely dangerous position. Had this promise become known, it would swiftly have lost him the confidence of the nation which would have detested any alliance with Catholic France.

A large carved stone pineapple in the corner of the Great Hall in Dorney Court in Buckinghamshire, commemorates the first pineapple to be grown in England. It is said that the top of a pineapple, imported from Barbados, was sliced off at a dinner in the City of London and given to the Earl of Castlemaine's gardener to plant at Dorney Court, one of the finest Tudor manor houses in England. The pineapple thrived and was presented to Charles II by his royal gardener, John Rose (1619–77) in 1661.

It is more likely however, that the first pineapple raised in England was grown at Hampton Court in 1690.

MONARCHS OF SCOTLAND, ENGLAND, BRITAIN (1685–1760)

Charles II
(1630–85)

the two surv. sons of Charles I

crowned King of Scotland (1651) crowned King of England (1661); m. (1662) Catherine of Bragança (1638–1705); no issue; but he had at least thirteen illegitimate ch.:

by Lucy Walter (c.1630–58):

● James Crofts, later Scott
(1649–85)

Duke of Monmouth and Duke of Buccleuch
executed by James II for rebellion

by Elizabeth Killigrew (1622–80):

● Charlotte
(1650–84)

Lady Yarmouth

by Catherine Pegge (b. c.1635):

● Charles FitzCharles
(1657–80)

Earl of Plymouth; and Catherine FitzCharles (b.1658)

by Barbara Villiers (1641–1709), Lady Castlemaine and Duchess of Cleveland:

● Anne
(1661–1722)

Countess of Sussex *possibly Lord Castlemaine's child*

● Charles Fitzroy
(1661–1730)

Duke of Southampton;

● Henry Fitzroy
(1663–90)

Duke of Grafton

● Charlotte
(1664–1717)

Lady Lichfield

● George Fitzroy
(1665–1716)

Duke of Northumberland

by Nell Gwyn (1650–87):

● Charles Beauclerk
(1670–1726)

Duke of St Albans

● James, Lord Beauclerk
(1671–80)

by Louise de Kéroualle (1649–1734), Duchess of Portsmouth:

● Charles Lennox
(1672–1723)

Duke of Richmond and Duke of Lennox

by Mary (*Moll*) Davis (c.1651–1708):

● Lady Mary Tudor
(1673–1726)

Charles II had no legitimate heir and was succeeded by his brother **James II**

James II
(1633–1701)

Catholic succeeded his brother (1685) but deposed by his son-in-law (1688);

m. (1. 1660) Anne (d.1671), dau. of Edward Hyde; six ch. died, only two daus. survived:

Mary II
(1662–1694)

m. (1677) her first cousin William of Orange, son of Mary Stuart, eldest dau. of King Charles I; *her husband deposed her father*

William III
(1650–1702)

reigned jointly (1688–94), then alone until his own death, without issue: *William was suc. by Mary's sister*

Anne
(1665–1714)

m. (1683) Prince George of Denmark (1653–1708); eighteen ch., *none survived. Queen of Great Britain (1707)*

Anne was suc. by her *Protestant* second cousin, great-grandson of **James I** *the end of the Stuart line*

m. (2. 1673) Mary of Modena (1658–1718); one surv. son:

James Francis Edward Stuart
the Old Pretender; a Catholic
(1688–1766)

m. (1719) Maria Klementyna Sobieska (1703–35)

Charles Edward Stuart
the Young Pretender (1720–88)

known as Bonnie Prince Charlie neither he nor his brother Cardinal Henry Stuart (1725–1807) had any legitimate children; Henry was the last male Stuart

HANOVER (GUELPH)

Georg Ludwig (1660–1727) Elector of Hanover (1689);

George I

King of Great Britain and Ireland (1 August 1714); m. (1682), Sophia Dorothea of Celle (1666–1726); the eldest son:

Georg August, King of Hanover (1683–1760)

George II

King of Great Britain and Ireland (1714–60); m. (1705), the Princess Caroline of Brandenburg-Ansbach and had issue: *great-great-great-great-great-great-great-great-grandparents of* **Elizabeth II**

Titus Oates (1647–1705), the fabricator of the Popish Plot (1678–81), was the son of an Anabaptist preacher in Rutland. He was ordained in the Church of England but defrocked for buggery while serving as a chaplain in the Navy. He was subsequently expelled from two Jesuit seminaries for indecency. Oates spread the story that he had uncovered a Catholic plot to murder Charles and place his brother on the throne. Charles was not convinced but in the religious frenzy that sought to bar his brother from the succession, he very nearly lost control. Thirty-five innocent men were executed before Oates was unmasked in 1681, having lived in a grace-and-favour Whitehall house on a government annuity of £1,200. In 1685 James II ensured that Oates was flogged, pilloried, fined and imprisoned.

In 1673 this unhappy situation was compounded by the marriage of Charles's Catholic brother James, Duke of York to the Catholic Mary of Modena. It prompted the 1673 and 1678 Test Acts, which excluded Roman Catholics from both respective parliaments. Over the next few years an increasing public apprehension of a Catholic succession fomented, before erupting into the xenophobic hysteria of the Popish Plot.

From 1681 national fear of anarchy outweighed distrust of the Duke of York and Charles enjoyed an upsurge of loyalty unseen since his accession. With his finances restored by another secret treaty with France, he dismissed his fractious Parliament and ruled as an absolute monarch in peaceful affluence.

Charles suffered a stroke on 2 February 1685, at Whitehall Palace. Taking four days to die, he apologised to his courtiers: "I am sorry Gentlemen, for a most unconscionable time a-dying". The night before he died he was received into the Roman Catholic Church, though how conscious or committed he was is unclear. His last words, to his brother, were: "Let not poor Nellie starve".

Medal struck in 1667 by John Roettier after the Second Dutch War, showing all Charles II's titles

Charles once said that he believed "God would not make a man miserable only for taking a little pleasure out of the way". His idea of "little" was an understatement. Bishop Burnet commented of him: "He has a strange command of himself. He can pass from business to pleasure and from pleasure to business in so easy a manner that all seems alike to him". His main vice was not promiscuity but laziness. Physically strong, he had a low boredom threshold and an even shorter attention span. He had at least thirteen illegitimate children. "Restless he rolls from whore to whore, A merrie monarch, scandalous and poor", wrote the Earl of Rochester.

Charles had a remarkable constitution: long nights of debauchery left him invigorated. Rising at dawn, he liked to sally out into St James Park for brisk walks, his spaniels at his heels. He was a keen rower and loved to swim in his own private canal.

"It was always very merry in good King Charles's golden days" *(anon)*. The Restoration was a rackety age of stark contrasts. In reaction to the grim Puritans of the Commonwealth, the joyful licence of Charles's court created the climate for a flowering of literature and drama. It also fostered a free-thinking approach to science that had never before been possible without fear of religious censure at best and

Nell (Eleanor) Gwyn (1650–87) was born in Hereford. She became an usherette in her teens, selling spiced oranges at the Drury Lane Theatre in London. The leading actor, Charles Hart trained her for the stage and, despite being illiterate, she became a prominent actress in the King's Company (1666–69). As "Pretty, witty Nell", she was loved for her salacious prologues and epilogues. In 1669 Charles took her as his mistress, a relationship which lasted until his death. Saucy and fun, she was popular with Londoners. When her carriage was once mobbed by a hostile crowd, mistaking it for that of the haughty Catholic and French Louise de Kéroualle, Nell leaned out and shouted: "Pray good people be silent. I am the Protestant whore".

• **Nell Gwyn (c.1675) studio of Sir Peter Lely (c.1675)**
National Portrait Gallery, London

Charles II gave his mistresses (especially Nell Gwyn) an ancient slimming remedy to keep them in the shape he liked. The heath pea (*lathyrus linifolius*), or bitter vetch was used in the Middle Ages as an appetite suppressant when crops failed. It is being reconsidered today to fight the nation's weight crisis. The tubers, which have a leathery liquorice taste, are supposed to make people forget to eat.

persecution at worst. Yet it was also an age of black farce, mirroring the bawdy Restoration comedies that filled the theatres of London. In what other age would it have been possible for a man to be rewarded by the King for botching an attempt to steal the Crown Jewels?

Colonel Thomas Blood (1618–80), born in County Meath, was the son of a prosperous blacksmith. During the English Civil Wars, Blood first fought for the King but changed sides when he realised the Royalists were losing. Cromwell rewarded him with land for his services. Blood was an adventurer of great ingenuity and style: not many would try to storm Dublin Castle by throwing bread over the walls, to distract the guards, in an attempt to kidnap the Lord Lieutenant of Ireland, James Butler, 1st Duke of Ormonde. The plot failed and Blood fled to the Netherlands where he joined George Villiers, 2nd Duke of Buckingham, who also hated Ormonde.

Despite being a wanted man and in a plan bordering on the lunatic, on 6 December 1670 Blood ambushed Ormonde in Piccadilly and rode off with him to Tyburn, near Marble Arch, to hang him from the public gallows. Though Ormonde escaped, Blood was not suspected, as Ormonde's son Thomas openly accused the Duke of Buckingham of the attack. Five months later in May 1671, Blood attempted to steal the Crown Jewels.

The Crown Jewels were kept in a dungeon at the Tower of London behind a large metal grille. Talbot Edwards, the Keeper of the Crown Jewels, lived in rooms directly above. Blood, disguised as a parson and masquerading as a tourist, visited the Crown Jewels, befriended Edwards and asked if he could return with his wife. On leaving after her visit, Mrs Blood was "taken ill" – only to recover in the Edwards' apartment. Blood returned a few days later with a present of white gloves for Mrs Edwards. The Edwards family and Blood then became friends and began to meet regularly. Edwards had a daughter and was delighted when Blood suggested she meet his wealthy nephew.

On 9th May 1671 Blood arrived at 07:00 with his "nephew" and two accomplices. While the nephew met Edwards's daughter, Edwards offered to show the Crown Jewels to the rest of the party. The moment Edwards had unlocked the grille, Blood knocked him out with a mallet and stabbed him. The gang then seized the crown, orb and sceptre: flattening the crown with the mallet and stuffing it into a bag. Blood crammed the orb into his breeches. The sceptre was too long to go into the bag, so Blood tried to break it in half. Edwards then regained consciousness and raised the alarm. The gang dropped the sceptre and ran off. Having taken a shot at one of the guards, Blood was arrested as he tried to leave the Tower by the Iron Gate. In custody, Blood refused to answer questions and insisted on answering "to none but the King himself".

Blood knew that the King had a soft spot for likeable rogues and hoped to charm his way out of trouble. He was brought before Charles who was indeed tickled by Blood's effrontery: particularly when he told him that the Crown Jewels were not worth their valuation of £100,000 but only £6,000. The King asked Blood: "What if I should give you your life?". Blood replied humbly, "I would endeavour to deserve it, Sire!".

Blood is said to have flattered the King with his revelation of an earlier plot to kill him, whilst he was bathing in the Thames, but that he had changed his mind because of his "awe of majesty". It is likely though, that at some point in Blood's career as variously soldier, assassin, priest, Quaker and physician he had been employed by Charles as a secret agent. Whatever the reason, Blood was not only pardoned but granted an Irish estate worth £500 a year. He enjoyed his notoriety in London, frequently appearing at Court. Talbot Edwards was rewarded with a pension and lived to a great age.

In 1679 Blood quarrelled with his old patron the Duke of Buckingham, fell ill and died. Such was Blood's reputation for trickery that the authorities had his body exhumed.

Racing at Newmarket has been dated to 1174, when English knights returning from the Crusades with swift Arab horses made the Suffolk town the earliest known racing venue of post-classical times. King James I greatly increased the popularity of horse racing near the town in the early 17th century and King Charles I followed his father, by inaugurating the first cup race in 1634.

James Weatherby, a lawyer born in Northumberland c.1733, was appointed to trace the pedigree of every racehorse in England. In 1791 he published the results of his research as the *Introduction to the General Stud Book*. From 1793 to today members of the Weatherby family have recorded the pedigree of every descendant of the racehorses he researched, in subsequent volumes of the *General Stud Book*. By the early 1800s the only horses allowed to race were those descended from the horses listed in the *General Stud Book*. These horses were called "Thoroughbreds". Every thoroughbred can be traced back to one of three stallions, called the "foundation sires". These stallions were the Byerley Turk (foaled c.1679), the Darley Arabian (foaled 1700) and the Godolphin Arabian (foaled c.1724).

Charles II was nicknamed Old Rowley after a stallion of the same name, unattractive but remarkable for siring fine colts. Old Rowley was a great favourite of the King.

"WHEN DID YOU LAST SEE YOUR FATHER?"

Charles II became King on 30 January 1649 *de jure*, the day of his father's execution. The monarchy was replaced by a republic governed by Oliver Cromwell, the Lord Protector. Scotland and Ireland however, were under military occupation. On 29 May 1660 the monarchy was reinstated and the crown was restored to Charles II *de facto*. He became known as the "Merry Monarch".

The famous picture by W.F. Yeames of a child being interrogated by Parliamentarians begs a question of the teenage future Charles II: not *where* was his father, but *who* was his father?

King Charles I's life was one of blameless personal morality and he is the only person to be canonised by the Church of England since the Reformation. He had fine aquiline features but was less than 5 feet 4 inches tall, the reason he was usually painted on horseback. He married the 4 feet 10 inches tall Henrietta Maria (1609–69), daughter of King Henri IV of France in 1625 when he was twenty-four and she was fifteen. They had never met and were married by proxy. By 1630 they had fallen in love and went on to have nine children, with three sons and three daughters surviving infancy.

Henrietta Maria was brought to England by an embassy sent to collect her. This included the 20 year-old Henry Jermyn (1605–84), later to become Earl of St Albans, after whom Jermyn Street in London's West End was named. He was tall, well built and red haired, from an unremarkable landed family living at Rushbrook in Suffolk. They were distantly related to the Suckling ancestors of Lord Nelson.

Henrietta Maria (whose name was taken for the colony of Maryland) underwent two pregnancies before she was happy in her marriage. Until then she was "far closer" to Jermyn than her husband. Frequently the two were described as having been found "in great familiarities". It is more than likely that Jermyn turned the head of the homesick princess for they remained close for the rest of her life. Throughout her twenty years of widowhood, Jermyn's excessive influence with the queen was a continual embarrassment at court. They were assumed by many to have been lovers. There were even rumours that they had secretly married.

Henry Jermyn was described in old age, memorably but severely, by Sir Henry Craik, in his 19th century *Life of Clarendon* as: "An adventurer of a base type, who managed by over-weening self-confidence, a specious address and unbounded powers of dissimulation, to gain some credit for a manliness which he did not possess, and a certain clumsy cajolery supplied him in place of wit .... at once a bully and a coward, a hypocrite and a bungler; a gamester who haunted the card-table when his palsied hands could scarcely grasp the cards .... a glutton .... a spendthrift loaded with ill-gotten gains, and yet with all the avarice of a miser – a byeword even to the gallants of Charles II's court as a loathsome monument of a decayed debauchery".

But in his youth, with a fleshy-lipped countenance, good physique and the charm of a courtier, Jermyn had much of the appearance, genial loucheness and above all height, of the young Charles II. Unlike the diminutive Charles I, Jermyn was 6 feet 2 inches tall. No one will ever know the truth, but it is "a wise man who knows his own father".

King Charles II after Sir Peter Lely (c.1675)
National Portrait Gallery, London

SAMUEL PEPYS

Samuel Pepys (1633–1703), pronounced "Peeps", was born in Fleet Street in the City of London. His father was a tailor and his mother a butcher's daughter. Despite his modest calling, Pepys's father had many well-placed relations who helped to advance Samuel's career. He was educated at St Paul's School in London and at Cambridge, where his uncle John Pepys was a fellow. On graduating in 1655, he was employed as his secretary by a cousin, Sir Edward Montagu (1625–72), a councillor of state in Cromwell's Protectorate.

Since adolescence Pepys had suffered excruciating pain from kidney stones and blood in his urinary tract, an inherited affliction. In 1657, following his marriage to a fourteen year-old Huguenot girl, Elisabeth de St Michel, Pepys's condition was so severe that he was forced to take the appalling risk of surgery. The procedure was successful but an incision in his bladder later split, probably leaving him sterile. In spite of manful efforts, he never had children.

In 1658 he was working as a teller in the Exchequer under Sir George Downing, 1st Bt. (1623–84), an Anglo-Irish soldier, diplomat and ruthless political operator.

Pepys began his famous diary on 1 January 1660, daily recording details of his private life, often with excruciating frankness. He abandoned it in 1669 because of failing eyesight. The diary was written in a contemporary shorthand called tachygraphy. When describing intimate or scatalogical details, he reverts to a mixture of French, Spanish and Latin. He describes himself, when caught by his wife *in flagrante delicto* with her paid companion, "Coming up suddenly, [his wife] did find me imbracing the girl con my hand sub su coats and endeed I was with my main in her cunny. I was at a wonderful loss upon it and the girl also". The diary is a unique record of the Plague of 1665 and the Great Fire of London which followed it. Although Pepys did not set out to write for posterity, the care with which he bound and preserved the volumes of his diary suggests he was aware of its likely interest to future generations.

In 1660 he accompanied a fleet commanded by Montagu to bring back Prince Charles from exile in the Netherlands. On his restoration, Charles II created Montagu 1st Earl of Sandwich. He also appointed Pepys as Clerk of the Acts to the Navy Board, a post which attracted a salary of £350 and numerous benefits, including

Downing's mother, was a sister of the Massachusetts Bay Governor, John Winthrop (1588–1649). His family joined Winthrop in America in 1638, settling in Salem. Downing became Harvard's second-ever graduate. He was reckoned to be the richest man in England. Downing Street is named after him and Downing College, Cambridge after his grandson: Sir George Downing, 3rd Bt. (1685–1749).

Harvard University was established in 1636 and named in 1639 for John Harvard (1607–38), a clergyman born in Southwark in London, who was its first benefactor.

**Samuel Pepys (1666)
by John Hales (1600–79)**
National Portrait Gallery, London

Tangier, a Portuguese colony since 1471, was part of the dowry of Catherine of Braganza, Charles II's wife. It was returned, without regret, to Morocco in 1684.

bribes. Pepys excelled in his job, learning arithmetic from a private tutor and improving his knowledge of ships from scale models. In September 1660 he was made a Justice of the Peace. A few months later

When Pepys joined the admiralty in 1660, the English line of battle consisted of 30 battleships, totalling 25,000 tons and carrying 1,730 guns. On retirement in 1689, he left a battle line of 59 ships totalling 66,000 tons and carrying 4,492 guns.

he was admitted as a Younger Brother of Trinity House, becoming Master in 1676. In 1662, through Sandwich's influence, he joined the Tangier Committee and in 1665 became its Treasurer.

The Second Dutch War began in 1665. Pepys introduced a centralised system to supply the navy which was so successful that he was made Surveyor-General of victualling with a £300 salary increase. The war ended in disaster. The Dutch raided Chatham on the Medway and towed away the flagship HMS *Royal Charles*, pride of the English fleet. Pepys and the Navy Board came under great scrutiny. In spite of evidence of corrupt dealings, Pepys emerged unscathed. In 1672 he was promoted Secretary to the Admiralty Commission; and elected M.P. for Castle Rising in Norfolk, followed by Harwich in Suffolk. In 1673 he was one of the founders of the Royal Mathematical School at Christ's Hospital.

1679 was not a good year for Pepys. He was accused by his political enemies, led by Anthony Ashley-Cooper, 2nd Earl of Shaftesbury, of both leaking naval intelligence to the French and being a closet Roman Catholic. He was imprisoned briefly in the Tower of London but all charges were dropped in 1680. Back in favour, he was sent to Tangier to arrange the evacuation of the colony. He returned to become King's Secretary for the affairs of the Admiralty, a post he held from 1684 until James II's abdication in 1688. In this office Pepys was one of the most powerful men in England, heading the largest spending department of state. With extraordinary energy and competence, he rebuilt the navy from a corrupt shambles into an efficient fighting force.

Pepys created a navy which dominated the seas for 300 years and endowed it with a discipline and tradition of service it has never lost. In 1689 and 1690 he was again briefly imprisoned, this time as a suspected Jacobite, but no charges were brought. In 1701, aged fifty-seven, Pepys retired to Clapham. He died there on 26 May 1703: still cared for by Will Hewer, a former *protégé* of his early years at the Admiralty.

JOHN MILTON (1608–74)

Milton was born in London, the son of a prosperous scrivener (legal draughtsman). Poet, historian and pamphleteer, he is considered by some the most important English poet after Shakespeare. Recurrent themes in his writings are a dislike of an absolute monarchy and organised religion. He believed in both the absolute integrity of the Bible and in religious toleration.

He was educated at St Paul's School and Christ's College, Cambridge, earning the nickname "Lady of Christ's College" because of his pale complexion and long fair hair. He wrote the masque, *Comus* in 1637 and his great pastoral elegy *Lycidas* in 1638. He then spent fifteen months in Italy where he met Galileo.

At the outbreak of the English Civil War Milton supported the Puritan cause. From 1641–58 he was Oliver Cromwell's pamphleteer and Secretary of "foreign tongues".

He dealt with the Commonwealth's international correspondence, also acting as the regime's chief propagandist. In 1644 he wrote his famous tract on freedom of the press, *Areopagitica*. In 1651 however, a victim of glaucoma, he lost his sight.

During the Restoration in 1660, as a staunch Puritan and loyal servant of the Commonwealth, Milton was briefly imprisoned and came close to being executed. He was saved by his brother Christopher and his great friend, the poet Andrew Marvell (1621–78), who was a Member of Parliament. From 1658–64 he dictated his sublime magnum opus *Paradise Lost* which was published in 1667. This monumental work on the "Fall of Man", written in blank verse, reflects his despair at the failure of the Commonwealth. It also affirmed his ultimate faith in humanity. In 1671 he again expressed his trust in God and the infinite power of the human spirit, by composing *Paradise Regained* in which Christ resists Satan, the tempter. This poem proclaimed Milton's belief that the loss of national salvation did not imply a loss of individual freedom. In the same year, he wrote *Samson Agonistes* in which the Old Testament character overcomes an obsessive personal despair to become God's crusader.

Milton died of kidney failure on 8 November 1674. His funeral at St Giles Cripplegate was attended by "his .... great friends, not without a friendly concourse of the Vulgar".

> Galileo is the only contemporary person mentioned by name in *Paradise Lost*.

John Milton by unknown artist (*c.*1629)
National Portrait Gallery, London

> In 1642, Milton was deserted by his sixteen year-old wife Mary Powell, prompting a series of startling pamphlets, *The Doctrine and Discipline of Divorce* (1643–4), in which he argued for the desirability of divorce. He came close to being imprisoned for these heretical tracts – which provoked him into writing *Areopagitica*, his celebrated attack on censorship. In 1656, blind and a widower, he married Katherine Woodcock. She died in childbed fifteen months later. Elizabeth Minshull, whom he married in 1663, with the help of his daughters from previous marriages, acted as his amanuensis and secretary. She recorded the great poems of his last years.

JOHN BUNYAN (1628–88)

John Bunyan (1628–88) was born in Elstow in Bedfordshire. He was exposed to extreme left-wing politics while serving in Oliver Cromwell's New Model Army during the English Civil Wars. Having experienced a cathartic spiritual revelation, Bunyan became a preacher. After the Restoration, he was imprisoned for twelve years in Bedford gaol for preaching without a licence. Whilst in prison, he wrote the best known allegorical tale in the English language, *The Pilgrim's Progress* (1678–84).

The narrative reveals Bunyan's strong Puritan beliefs, expressed through the encounters of the protagonist Christian on his journey to the Celestial City. It also exhibits Bunyan's hatred of Catholicism: "Now I saw in my dream .... blood, bones, ashes, and mangled bodies .... their names were Pope and Pagan .... I have since learned that the Pagan has been dead a long time. As for the other one [the Pope], though he is still alive".

The Pilgrim's Progress is probably the most widely read book in the English language and has been translated into more languages than any book except the Bible. A passage from Part

Two, beginning: "Who would true Valour see", was changed by Percy Dearmer in *The English Hymnal* (1906) into "He who would valiant be 'gainst all disaster", in the much-loved hymn *To be a Pilgrim*. The rousing music was written by Ralph Vaughan Williams OM (1872–1958).

The eminent Victorian poet and historian, Thomas Babington Macaulay (1800–59) opined: "In England during the latter half of the 17th century there were only two minds which possessed the imaginative faculty in a very eminent degree. One of these minds produced *Paradise Lost*, the other *The Pilgrim's Progress*".

THE ROYAL SOCIETY

The Royal Society was conceived *c.*1645 when a number of scientists first held regular meetings. Their aim was to acquire knowledge by experimental investigation, embodying the principles first set out thirty years earlier by Sir Francis Bacon. They included the scientist Robert Boyle, the diarist John Evelyn (1620–1706), the architect Christopher Wren and the economist, philosopher and inventor, Sir William Petty (1623–87).

In 1912 J. Pierpont Morgan bought Bunyan's signed copy of *Foxe's Book of Martyrs* from the Bedford General Library, for $10,000 (£750,000 today).

The Royal Society of London for the Improvement of Natural Knowledge, known simply as The Royal Society, was founded in 1660, shortly after the Restoration of King Charles II. The Royal Society received its first Royal Charter in 1662 and is considered to be the oldest such society still in existence. Although a voluntary body, it serves as the academy of sciences of the United Kingdom, receiving £40 million annually from the UK Government. Past Presidents of the Royal Society (PRS) include some of Britain's most celebrated scientists and thinkers:

Sir Christopher Wren 1680–82 ● **Samuel Pepys** 1684–86 ● **Sir Isaac Newton** 1703–27 ● **Joseph Banks** 1778–1820 ● **Sir Humphry Davy** 1820–27 ● **Sir Joseph Dalton Hooker** 1873–78 ● **Thomas Henry Huxley** 1883–85 ● **William Thomson, 1st Baron Kelvin** 1890–95 ● **Joseph Lister, 1st Baron Lister** 1895–1900 ● **John William Strutt, 3rd Baron Rayleigh** 1905–08 *Nobel Laureate* ● **Sir Joseph John Thomson** 1915–20 *Nobel Laureate* ● **Sir Ernest Rutherford** 1925–30 *Nobel Laureate* ● **Sir William Henry Bragg** 1935–40 *Nobel Laureate* ● **Sir Henry Hallett Dale** 1940–45 *Nobel Laureate* ● **Martin Rees, Baron Rees of Ludlow** (2005) *Nobel Laureate*

The Fellowship of the Royal Society comprises 1,300 of the most distinguished scientists from the United Kingdom, the British Commonwealth and the Republic of Ireland. There are currently 21 Nobel prize winners among the Fellows as well as many holders of equally prestigious awards. The Royal Society also has 127 Foreign Members, a further 48 Nobel prize winners amongst them.

In 1904 Hertha Ayrton was the first woman to lecture the Royal Society. It was not until 1945 however, that the first two women were elected: the crystallographer, Dame Kathleen Lonsdale (1903–71) and the biochemist, Marjory Stephenson (1885–1948).

The Royal Society has occupied Carlton House Terrace in London since 1967. *Philosophical Transactions of the Royal Society,* first published in March 1665, is the world's oldest scientific journal. Fellows are elected for life and are entitled to use the letters FRS after their names. The Society's motto is *Nullius in verba*, implying "take nobody's word for it" – as experimental scientists, its members never had to.

WILLIAM HARVEY

William Harvey (1578–1657) was an English physician who discovered the exact nature of the heart, as a pumping mechanism and its role in the circulation of blood. He was born in Folkestone in Kent, the eldest of nine children of a prosperous merchant. He attended Cambridge University and spent two years studying at the University of Padua, then the leading medical school in Europe, under the celebrated anatomist, Hieronymous Fabricius. On return to England, he became a fellow of the College of Physicians before being appointed to St Bartholomew's Hospital in 1609. He was appointed one of James I's physicians – and gave evidence after the King's death when James's favourite, the Duke of Buckingham was suspected of having poisoned him.

Harvey relied on his own clinical observations and reasoning in working out the function of the heart and circulation of the blood. In his *Anatomical Exercise Concerning the Motion of the Heart and Blood in Animals*, published in 1628, Harvey revealed the mechanism of the heart's valves; proved that blood did not pass through the septum (the partition separating the chambers of the heart) and explained the purpose of valves in the veins. He showed that pulmonary circulation involves blood being pumped from the atria into the ventricles and thence into the rest of the circulatory system. He also proved that the pulse simply reflects the contractions of the heart.

During the First Civil War, Harvey attended King Charles I and his children. During the Commonwealth he was regarded as politically unsound, through his long association with the King, and confined to house arrest. All his papers were destroyed in the Great Fire of London in 1666, although his lecture notes have survived. He died of a stroke and was buried in the Harvey Chapel, at Hempstead in Essex.

SIR ISAAC NEWTON

Isaac Newton PRS (1643–1727) was an English mathematician, physicist, astronomer, alchemist and natural philosopher. He is one of only a handful of true "geniuses", in the sense that their achievements or discoveries defy comprehension or explanation. Britain has been blessed with at least four: William Shakespeare, Isaac Newton himself, Thomas Young and Alan Turing. Genius is separated from lunacy by a hair's breadth and, though some have been homosexual, none can be categorised in any way.

Newton was born on 4 January 1643 (under Julian calendar prevailing at the time, on Christmas Day 1642) to Hannah Newton, *née* Ayscough, at the Manor House, Woolsthorpe, near Grantham in Lincolnshire. A sickly child, not expected to live, it was said that his tiny body could have fitted into a quart mug.

His family were farmers but his illiterate father Isaac died three months before Newton was born. Two years later Hannah married Barnabas Smith, the vicar of North Witham, a neighbouring village, leaving the young Isaac at Woolsthorpe Manor with her parents Margery and James Ayscough. The Reverend Smith refused to accomodate Isaac and he had an unhappy and lonely childhood as a virtual orphan. Smith died when Newton was ten, leaving him nothing in his will.

Robert Boyle after Johann Kerseboom (c.1689–1690)

National Portrait Gallery, London

Boyle's Law states that at a constant temperature, the pressure of a gas varies inversely with its volume.

From a later shorthand entry in Newton's diary, it appears that he heartily disliked his mother and stepfather: "threatening my father and mother Smith to burn them and the house over them". When he was twelve Newton was sent to lodge with William Clark, an apothecary at Grantham, to attend the Free Grammar School. He apparently showed little promise in his studies and his school reports are unenthusiastic, describing him as idle and inattentive. At this point, as his mother's eldest son, he was taken away from school to learn how to manage the substantial family farm. The experiment was not a success. Newton showed no aptitude or interest in farming.

His uncle, William Ayscough decided to return Newton to the Grammar school in Grantham to complete his education, before entering university. He lodged with Stokes, the headmaster. From a confidence in his diary ("setting my heart on money, learning and pleasure more than thee"), it is clear that this time Newton had adopted the right attitude. Headmaster Stokes wrote of him: "In everything he undertakes, he discovers an application equal to the pregnancy of his parts and exceeds even the most sanguine expectations I have conceived of him". Little is known about his academic achievements, save that he displayed a noticeable mechanical and model-making ability. In June 1661 he entered Trinity College, Cambridge to study law as a "sizar", a class of poor student who was paid a stipend by the college to act as servant to the wealthier students, in spite of his mother's evident affluence. Although Aristotle still dominated university courses at this time, Newton would soon have come into contact with the thinking of the new philosophers: Robert Boyle, John Wallis, the German astronomer Johannes Kepler (1571–1630) and the French mathematician and scientist René Descartes (1596–1650). Descartes is celebrated for his dictum, *cogito ergo sum* ("I think, therefore I am"). This distinguishes between the mind which is cognitive and inert matter which, existing in only three dimensions, is clearly not.

Robert Boyle (1627–91), the fourteenth child of the 1st Earl of Cork, was born at Lismore Castle in County Waterford. A chemist and natural philosopher, he experimented with gases, assisted by Robert Hooke. He was the first to analyse the properties of air. He demonstrated its function in respiration, combustion and the transmission of sound – refuting Aristotle's four-element theory of fire, earth, air and water. His particle-based explanation of matter anticipated the discovery of chemical elements. He published *The Sceptical Chymist* in 1661 and was a founder of the Royal Society.

John Wallis (1616–1703), born in Ashford in Kent, was the most influential English mathematician before Newton. When Savilian professor of Geometry at Oxford, Wallis invented the symbol ∞ for infinity. He also laid the basis of calculus, later developed by Newton, by addressing the problem of finding a square that has an equal area to that of a given circle. He was an active contributor to the meetings that led to the establishment of the Royal Society. Like so many outstanding scientists of his day, Wallis quarrelled bitterly with his contemporaries. The philosopher Thomas Hobbes (1588–1679), born in Malmesbury in Wiltshire, who published *Leviathan* in 1651, described Wallis's *Arithmetica* as "a scab of symbols".

In 1664 Newton wrote *Quæstiones Quædam Philosophicæ*, recording his views on the scientific world: "Plato is my friend, Aristotle is my friend, but my best friend is truth". It is said that Newton's interest in mathematics was fired in 1663 by the purchase of a book on astrology at a

The husband of Newton's niece, John Conduitt, recorded that Newton was entirely self-taught in mathematics: "He bought Descartes's Geometry & read it by himself…. when he was got over 2 or 3 pages he could understand no farther than he began again & got 3 or 4 pages farther till he came to another difficult place, than he began again & advanced farther & continued so doing till he made himself Master of the whole without having the least light or instruction from any body".

Cambridge fair: which led him to read, among many other works on algebra and geometry, *Arithmetica Infinitorum* by John Wallis. Newton wrote: "Thus Wallis doth it, but it may be done thus ....", in which Newton refers to his first piece of original work.

Newton received a Bachelor's degree in April 1665, with his mathematical genius still not apparent. A few months later the plague reached Cambridge and the university closed. Newton retired to Woolsthorpe Manor and immersed himself in mathematical study over the next two years. This led to his ground-breaking advances in astronomy, physics and optics.

It was at Woolsthorpe in 1666 that the true concept of gravity first occurred to Newton. It was a result, he said later, of observing the way an apple always fell towards the centre of the earth. He realised that this would still be the case however far the apple were to fall and conjectured whether gravity might also be the force holding the moon to its orbit.

He discovered the Binomial Theory, allowing him to develop the principles of differential and integral calculus six years before the great German mathematician and inventor, Freiherr Gotfried Wilhelm von Leibniz (1646–1716), proposed his own version.

Sir Isaac Newton by Sir Godfrey Kneller (1702)
National Portrait Gallery, London

Leibniz published *De arte combinatoria* in 1666 which proposed a universal mathematical, logical language based on binary numbers. Unaware of Newton's work, he published a theorem of calculus. The bitter feud with Newton which followed degraded English mathematics for a generation. Leibniz's superior version was eventually adopted. In both optics and mechanics Leibniz made important contributions.

Newton's greatest gift to science was his theory of gravitation. In 1666 he sketched out his three laws of motion. He also proposed a law, to calculate the centrifugal force on a body moving at a constant speed around a circular path, although he never mastered completely the mechanics of circular motion. In the same year Newton realised that the earth's gravity affected the moon, counter-balancing its centrifugal force. From his own law of centrifugal force and, borrowing from Kepler's third law of planetary motion, Newton proved the law of the inverse-square.

In 1667 Cambridge reopened. Newton applied for a fellowship and was granted a minor one at Trinity College in October. When he was awarded his Master's degree, he was elected a major fellow. In 1669 Newton succeeded Isaac Barrow as Lucasian professor of mathematics. His first work was devoted to optics and the nature of light. From the time of Aristotle it had been assumed that light was white but Newton, noticing the chromatic aberration in a telescope lens, passed a beam of light through a prism.

The resulting spectrum of colour confirmed his intuition that white light was comprised of several colours, refracted through the glass at slightly different angles. As a result of this discovery, he invented and built a reflecting telescope to eradicate chromatic aberration in 1668, saying: "If I had stayed for other people to make my tools and things for me, I had never made anything". Newton's first telescope, capable of magnifying forty times, was a remarkable achievement.

A replica of the reflecting telescope that Newton presented to the Royal Society in 1672

Newton's Principia, with his hand-written corrections

In 1672, after donating a copy of his telescope to the Royal Society, Newton was elected a member; and published his first treatise on light and colour in the Society's journal.

Robert Hooke FRS (1635–1703), born in Freshwater on the Isle of Wight, was a remarkable man: albeit given to bearing grudges and making a nuisance of himself. Like Leibniz, he was a true polymath: a chemist, physicist, astronomer, inventor and Oxford don. He was educated at Westminster School and Christ Church, Oxford. In 1662 Hooke became Curator of Experiments to the Royal Society and Secretary in 1677.

In 1660 he formulated Hooke's law, on the extension and compression of elastic bodies. He anticipated the invention of the steam engine and experimented with clock pendulums and watch balance springs. The quadrant, a marine barometer, the Gregorian reflecting telescope, microscope and universal joint were largely his inventions. He suggested that Jupiter rotated on its axis and his detailed sketches of Mars helped astronomers to calculate its rotation rate in the 19th century. He attempted to show that the earth and moon followed an elliptical path around the sun and that the force of gravity could be measured by the motion of a pendulum.

Hooke proposed the inverse-square law, to describe planetary motion, which Newton later proved in a modified form. Hooke's complaint that he had not received sufficient recognition led to an acrimonious row with Newton. In 1665 Hooke published *Micrographia* (small drawings), in which he drew illustrations of the structure of snowflakes and first used the word "cell" to describe the honeycomb cavities in cork. He became one of the first proponents of a theory of evolution, having studied microscopic fossils and fleas. Hooke was the first to state that all matter expands when heated; and that air is made up of particles separated by relatively large distances. He proposed a wave theory of light to explain diffraction, the behaviour of a light beam passing through a small aperture and spreading out on the other side.

Hooke, a hunchback, slept only with his servants, avoiding women of his own class. In his diary, he uses the symbol ¥ to signify an orgasm. No known likeness of him exists.

Newton's reaction to his difference of opinion with Hooke was ambivalent. Although he yearned for fame and recognition, he was also hypersensitive to criticism. His anxiety often persuaded him not to publish his work. In pursuing Hooke and Leibniz with unrelenting acrimony, Newton gave his first indications of irrational behaviour.

In 1675 his feud with Hooke plummeted to a new depth when Hooke accused Newton of purloining some of his optical experiments. Newton avoided the Royal Society and delayed full publication of his *Opticks* until Hooke died. In 1678 he appears to have suffered a nervous breakdown. Following the death of his mother in 1679, he withdrew from society and revisited his early interest in alchemy, then indistinguishable from science. In his *Hypothesis of Light* Newton posited the existence of ether to transmit forces between particles: but as a keen student of Hermetic writings he replaced the ether with occult forces. "Newton was not the first of the age of reason, he was the last of the great magicians", observed John Maynard Keynes.

In 1684 Newton published the results of his work on gravitation in *De motu Corporum*, proposing the laws of motion which would be fully developed in his *Philosophiae Naturalis Principia Mathematica*. In 1686 he had recovered his composure sufficiently to respond to Edmond Halley's suggestion of writing a full treatise on his physical discoveries and their application to astronomy.

Hermetic writings were occult texts on philosophical or theological subjects. Written in the form of dialogues, they synthesised near-eastern religions: Platonism, Stoicism and also early Roman views on astrology, alchemy and magic.

Halley was instrumental in the publication in 1687 of the *Principia*, probably the most famous scientific book ever published. In it he clarified a number of hitherto inexplicable phenomena: including the motion of the moon as it is affected by the sun, equinoxes, the variation of tidal flow and the eccentric orbits described by comets. In the same work, based on Boyle's Law, Newton presented the first analysis of the speed of sound in air.

This seminal work propelled Newton to the top of the European scientific community. Amongst his many admirers was the young Swiss-born mathematician Nicolas Fatio de Duillier (1664–1753) with whom Newton formed an intense, most probably homosexual attachment. He had his second nervous breakdown when the friendship suddenly and inexplicably ended in 1693. He may also have been suffering from mercury poisoning.

In the 1690s Newton wrote many tracts based on a literal interpretation of the Bible, his private passion. He corresponded with the philosopher John Locke (1632–1704), the "father of English empiricism", on the existence of the Trinity. Newton believed that the original text had been corrupted. He was deeply religious and saw God alone as the creator – "in the absence of any other proof, the thumb alone would convince me of God's existence".

In 1699 the notorious confidence trickster and coiner, William Chaloner begged Newton for his life: "I shall be murdered the worst of all murders that is in the face of justice unless I am rescued by your mercifull hands". He was hanged – having prepared a dying statement too libellous for a printer to risk publication.

Two years after the *Principia* was published, Newton moved to London, having been elected M.P. for Cambridge. He did not seek re-election in 1690 but stayed in London, finally meeting John Locke and, amongst others, the gifted physicist and inventor, Christian Huygens (1629–95).

In 1695, through the influence of his friend Charles Montagu, later Earl of Halifax, the Chancellor of the Exchequer, Newton was appointed Warden of the Mint. He became Master in 1699, with an enormous salary of £2,000 (over £3 million today). Although a sinecure he took his duties seriously, pursuing and severely punishing counterfeiters. Ten were executed.

Newton revised the coinage of the realm. In 1717 he introduced a golden guinea, worth 21 silver shillings and effectively put Britain onto a gold standard when he established a fixed price in sterling for one troy ounce of 22 carat gold. This maintained a constant purchasing value of the pound for over 200 years, until 1926.

Newton was elected President of the Royal Society in 1703, an office he held until his death. In 1705 Queen Anne knighted him in Cambridge, the first scientist ever to be so honoured. Disgracefully, he abused his office as President by bullying the Astronomer Royal, John Flamsteed (1646–1719) into surrendering his valuable but incomplete records, to assist his own and Edmond Halley's researches.

During his last years, looked after by his niece Catherine Conduitt, he dozed through meetings of the Royal Society and commissioned many portraits of himself. After years of ill health, he died on the 31 March 1727 at his house in Jermyn Street. He was buried with great pomp in Westminster Abbey.

Newton was born into an age when science amounted to little more than a string of unrelated and isolated observations, offering few explanations and fewer predictions. By the time of his death his two seminal works, *Opticks* and the *Principia*, had left science with a unified body of laws that could not only be applied across a wide range of physical phenomena but could be used to make precise calculations. He was capable of modesty: "If I have been able to see farther, it was only because I stood on the shoulders of giants", he wrote in a letter to

Robert Hooke in 1675. It has been suggested that his irrational reaction to criticism and capacity for harbouring resentment and bearing grudges might have been the result of an autistic condition, Asperger's syndrome. This often causes adult sufferers to appear indifferent or averse to affection and physical contact. He never married, the only real passion in his life being Fatio de Duillier. Newton is rightly regarded as the founding father of modern science.

Newton stated: "I do not know what I may appear to the world but to myself I seem to have been only like a boy playing on the sea shore and diverting myself in now and then finding a smoother pebble or a prettier shell than ordinary, whilst the great ocean of truth lay all undiscovered before me". Alexander Pope put it differently: "Nature and Nature's laws lay hid in night – God said 'Let Newton be!' and all was light".

Newton's creativity extended from discovering the laws of gravity to inventing the cat-flap, enabling him to conduct his experiments uninterrupted by his pet.

AN AFFECTING TALE OF ALTRUISM

Throughout the 17th century bubonic plague was a regular and deadly visitor to every corner of England: especially in 1665, the year of the Great Plague in London. In August George Vicars, a tailor in the tiny Derbyshire village of Eyam, just off the A623 today, received a parcel of cloth from London. Sodden from the journey, Vicars hung the damp material in front of his fire to dry: in the process releasing a host of plague-infected fleas. On 7 September he died a horrible death. The plague then raced through the village, killing many of the inhabitants.

The parson, twenty-eight year-old William Mompesson took immediate charge of the effort to contain the disease. He held open-air church services at Cucklett Delf and persuaded his congregation to stay within the confines of the village. He arranged with the local magnate the Earl of Devonshire, whose Chatsworth estate was not far away, to provide parcels of food and medicine. These were left outside the village boundary, along with other essential supplies provided by nearby villages. Money to pay for these was left in specially constructed holes filled with vinegar or purified under running water from the village well, since then named for Mompesson.

The plague killed Farmer Hancock before claiming the lives of his six children. In the capricious way of the disease, his wife Elizabeth, who had to bury her family, was spared – although she had almost certainly infected them all after burying a neighbour. On 25 August 1666 Catherine Mompesson, the parson's wife died. Mompesson himself, despite exposure to the disease throughout twelve months of nursing and burying victims, miraculously lived until 1709.

Mompesson's well

By 1 November 1666 the plague had run its course. Although it never again returned to Britain, in its final appearance had killed 259 villagers out of Eyam's original population of 290, a toll of nearly ninety percent. That the plague had not broken out of Eyam into the surrounding countryside was entirely due to the inspired leadership of Mompesson and the strong, selfless Christian faith of his flock.

In Eyam today a service of remembrance is held at Cucklett Delf every last Sunday in August. In 2001 another plague, in the form of Foot and Mouth disease, blighted the north of England and the plague-Sunday service had to be held once again in Eyam churchyard. Most farmland in the area had been quarantined.

"THE KING'S MONKEY"

John Wilmot, 2nd Earl of Rochester (1647–80) was born near Ditchley in Oxfordshire. His father Henry, Viscount Wilmot, a hard-drinking Anglo-Irish Royalist, had been created Earl of Rochester in 1652 for services to Charles II during his exile. He died abroad in 1658. His mother Anne St John was a Royalist and a staunch Anglican.

Rochester graduated from Wadham College at Oxford, where he "grew debauched", aged twelve. He was awarded an MA *filius nobilis* on 9 September 1661 by Edward Hyde, Earl of Clarendon – who was Chancellor of the University and Rochester's uncle. After a Grand Tour of France and Italy, Rochester returned to illuminate the Restoration court.

His courage in the bloody Four-Days' sea-battle against the Dutch in June 1666 made him a hero. He was a patron of the arts and an astoundingly energetic and abandoned libertine.

He died aged thirty-three, from a cocktail of venereal diseases and alcoholism which made an early death inevitable.

A friend of Charles II, he is celebrated for an impromptu exchange with the King:

God bless our good and gracious King,
Whose promise none relies on;
Who never said a foolish thing,
Nor ever did a wise one.

John Wilmot, 2nd Earl
of Rochester (1647–80)
by unknown artist
(*c.*1665–1670)
National Portrait Gallery, London

The King replied: "That is true; for my words are my own, but my actions are those of my ministers". Rochester's calculated sycophancy earned him the sobriquet "the King's Monkey" from jealous admirers but his lifestyle exacted a terrible price.

A notable member of a "mob of gentlemen who wrote with ease", he is also known for his fine poetry, some of which is scatological and unprintable.

KINGS (AND A QUEEN) OF THE ROAD

John, *aka* William, Nevison (1639–84) started life as an exciseman at Barnsley, 30 miles from York, before becoming one of England's most notorious highwaymen. A gentleman-rogue, his exploits caught the fancy of Charles II who nicknamed him "Swift Nick", after a remarkable 200 mile gallop from Kent to York. Nevison made his epic ride to give himself an alibi for a robbery he had committed that day. The feat is often wrongly attributed to Dick Turpin, a less likeable highwayman fifty years later. The ride took place in the summer of 1676, after Nevison had robbed a sailor in Rochester who recognised him. Nevison escaped using the Tilbury ferry, before galloping by way of Chelmsford, Cambridge and Huntingdon to arrive at York before sunset, in time to play a game of bowls with the Lord Mayor. His alibi was accepted and he was acquitted by the court. A few months later Nevison was again arrested, found guilty of theft and transported to Tangier, which had come to the crown as part of the dowry of Charles II's Portuguese queen, Catherine of Braganza. Having returned to a life of crime in 1681, he was arrested near Wakefield in 1684 for the murder of Darcy Fletcher, a nightwatchman, while resisting arrest. He was hanged at York Castle in May 1684 and buried in an unmarked grave in St Mary's Church in Castlegate.

Richard (Dick) Turpin (1705–39) became legendary as a charismatic highwayman. The son of an innkeeper, aged sixteen he was apprenticed to a butcher. On setting up his own business,

Turpin increased his margins by stealing his meat on the hoof. Coming under suspicion for cattle rustling, he joined the notorious Gregory gang of Essex deer stealers and smugglers. In 1735 the gang was broken up and Turpin went into partnership with "Captain" Tom King, a well-known "gentleman" highwayman. He had first encountered King when he tried to rob him on the highway: "What is this, dog eat dog?", asked King. Turpin accidentally killed him while firing at a constable who was trying to arrest them. Turpin established himself in Yorkshire as a horse dealer, calling himself John Palmer. In 1739, through an intercepted letter, he was finally convicted at York assizes of horse stealing, at that time considered a more heinous crime than murder, and hanged. He was buried in St George's Church in York but was dug up by body-snatchers working for anatomists. His corpse was recovered and buried a second time in quicklime. In 1834 Harrison Ainsworth published *Rookwood*, a celebrated romance, giving a highly coloured account of a ride by Dick Turpin on his mare Black Bess from London to York. The incident is purely imaginary, almost certainly confused with John Nevison's amazing feat fifty years earlier.

Lady Katherine Fanshawe, dubbed "The Wicked Lady" (1634–60), was born into the Ferrers family who owned a large estate at Markyate Cell in Hertfordshire. Her father and grandfather died before she was six. Her mother Catherine died two years later, having just married Simon Fanshawe.

When Katherine was fourteen, Fanshawe betrothed her to his nephew Thomas Fanshawe, whose lands marched with the Ferrers's. During the Civil War, both estates were devastated and Katherine turned to highway robbery in desperation. She is said to have preyed on travellers crossing Nomansland Common, near Wheathampstead. She may have teamed up, or even cohabited with Ralph Chaplin, a notorious highwayman who was later caught in Finchley, some 20 miles away, and hanged. Katherine was wounded during a robbery but was carried home by her servants to die. There are no parish records to substantiate the tale due to the Civil Wars – but Katherine is said still to haunt the house and park today. A rhyme is sung by local children: "In the Cell there be a well, by the well there be a tree, under the tree the treasure be".

The unrelated Northumberland mouthful of a surname, Featherstonehaugh (meaning "the meadow near the feather-shaped stone") is usually pronounced Fanshawe.

THE CABAL

In 1654, with the publication of *Cabala*, a strange collection of obscure and largely incomprehensible letters and scribbles, a new word entered the English language: "cabal". Cabal is derived from *Kabbalah*, the mystical interpretation of Hebrew scripture, with a cult following today, meaning something occult or secret. Cabal is now used however, to describe a furtive group of self-promoting people united for a common purpose. It usually implies intrigue and conspiracy.

The word took on its present meaning in the years following 1 June 1670, when a group of Charles II's ministers signed the Treaty of Dover, a military alliance between England and France against the Dutch Republic. Although most of its terms were made public, the treaty contained some secret provisions – which were not revealed until 1830. These included a promise by Charles, always short of money, to convert to Catholicism in return for a large annual subsidy from King Louis XIV. The initial letters of these ministers conveniently spelled out CABAL: Sir Thomas (later Lord) **C**lifford, Lord (later the Earl of) **A**rlington, the Duke of **B**uckingham, Lord **A**shley (later the Earl of Shaftesbury) and the Earl (later Duke) of **L**auderdale.

SIR CHRISTOPHER WREN

Christopher Wren (1632–1723) was a polymath, best remembered as the architect of St Paul's Cathedral. He was also an astronomer, anatomist, mathematician, physicist, geometer, designer and inventor. He was a founder of the Royal Society.

Wren was born at East Knoyle in Wiltshire, the only son of the rector who later became Dean of Windsor. As a child he played with the future King Charles II. When the deanery was pillaged in the Civil War, the Wrens went to live with William Holder, the dean's son-in-law in Oxfordshire. Holder tutored the young Wren, with an especial emphasis on astronomy. In 1647 the fifteen year-old Wren was employed by the anatomist Sir Charles Scarburgh (1615–94) to prepare experiments and to make models of muscles and tendons. His surviving anatomical diagrams show that he was an extremely talented draughtsman. In 1649 he attended Wadham College, Oxford, graduating in 1651. He was elected a Fellow of All Souls in 1653.

In 1661, less than thirty years old, Wren became Savilian professor of astronomy at Oxford. Still overwhelmed by his abundance of talent, he found it difficult to settle into a steady career. His chance came in 1663 however, when he was invited by the Archbishop of Canterbury, Gilbert Sheldon (1598–1677), to design a theatre in Oxford as a gift to his old university. Since the death of Inigo Jones in 1652, the formal study of architecture in England had been neglected. The physicist and mathematician Wren was also an accomplished model maker; and was well qualified to re-establish architecture as a discipline worthy of Royal Society attention.

In 1665, when Sheldon proposed to involve him in the plans to modernise St Paul's Cathedral, Wren realized that he needed urgently to immerse himself in European architectural developments. He joined an embassy to Paris, where Louis XIV was completing an immense programme of classical building works. He met Gian Lorenzo Bernini (1598–1680), the pre-eminent sculptor and architect who was building the vast palace complex at Versailles and completing the Louvre. Paris was filled with classical, domed churches which Wren later shamelessly copied.

By March 1666 Wren had presented his first designs for a dome for St Paul's. They were accepted in August but made redundant almost immediately by the Great Fire of London, which blazed from 2–5 September, destroying two thirds of the City. Within a week he had submitted to Charles II a magnificent urban plan of splendid buildings and broad avenues. Unfortunately, the difficulties posed by surveying each house, compensating the owners and allocating sites proved insuperable. His grand design was whittled down to some street widening and a few public buildings.

In 1669 Wren was appointed Surveyor of Works by Charles II, his childhood friend, a post which he held until 1718. In 1670 the coal tax was increased, paying not only for St Paul's Cathedral but also fifty-two of the eighty-seven churches destroyed by the fire. He was responsible for co-ordinating their design and reconstruction. As a mark of the King's esteem, he was knighted in 1673.

The Warden and College of the Souls of all Faithful People deceased in the University of Oxford, known as All Souls, is unique. All its members are elected as Fellows and it has no undergraduates. It is also one of the richest colleges in Oxford.

Christopher Wren by Sir Godfrey Kneller (1711)
National Portrait Gallery, London

The Great West Door of St Paul's Cathedral

By 1673 Wren had produced two models for the total reconstruction of St Paul's, the second of which was spectacular. Both were rejected in favour of a third, much more prosaic Classical-Gothic compromise, known as the Warrant design, submitted in 1679. Fortunately, as the new cathedral emerged from its foundations, a beautiful, structured version arose, bearing little resemblance to the plans. Wren had simply ignored them.

After many years of painstaking construction, he was put on half-pay until the cathedral was completed in 1711. Wren was seventy-nine when he finally received his arrears.

In 1681 he rebuilt the main gateway of Christ Church, Oxford. A year later he was asked by Charles II to draw up plans for the Royal Hospital at Chelsea, inspired by the Hôtel des Invalides in Paris, to house pensioners from his standing army. The hospital was finished in 1690. With the accession in 1689 of William and Mary who both hated Whitehall Palace which was destroyed by fire in 1698, Wren found himself rebuilding both Kensington and Hampton Court Palaces simultaneously. In 1696, at the instigation of Queen Mary II, he designed the Greenwich Hospital for Seamen.

Wren's first wife died of smallpox in 1675 and his second wife in 1679. He was married for only nine of his ninety years of life. Dying peacefully in his sleep on 23 February 1723, his tomb in St Paul's Cathedral was marked by the simple inscription: *Lector, si monumentum requires, circumspice* ("Reader, if you seek a monument, look around").

JAMES II, KING OF ENGLAND, SCOTLAND AND IRELAND (REIGNED 1685–88)

James II was both the last Stuart and last Catholic King of Great Britain and Ireland. He was also the last British monarch to wield absolute power. James's second marriage to a Catholic princess and his conversion to Catholicism were imprudent. The unexpected birth of a Catholic heir was disastrous. This event, together with James's insistence on promoting Catholics to senior posts in government and the armed forces, led to the Glorious Revolution of 1688. James was deposed and replaced by his daughter, Queen Mary II and her Dutch husband, the Protestant Prince of Orange who became King William III. Parliament was established as the sovereign power of England.

James, the second son of Charles I and Henrietta Maria, was born at St James's Palace in London on 14 October 1633. The following year his father created him Duke of York. In June

King James II by Sir Godfrey Kneller (1684)
National Portrait Gallery, London

1646, during the "First" Civil War, he was captured by Parliamentary forces and held under house arrest at St James's Palace. In April 1648, while playing a game of hide-and-seek, James escaped. Dressed as a girl, he was smuggled onto a boat to Holland. He joined his mother in France the following year. In 1652 James was commissioned into the French army in which he served with great courage during four campaigns under Louis XIV's great general, Marshal Turenne.

In the opinion of the venal Earl of Lauderdale, "This good prince has all the weakness of his father without his strength. He is as very papist as the Pope himself which will be his ruin".

In 1655 Oliver Cromwell, the Lord Protector, made an alliance with Louis XIV, compelling James's elder brother Charles to ally himself to Philip IV of Spain. In 1656 Charles established himself in Bruges and, despite the Spanish providing only five regiments, James was obliged reluctantly to change sides.

On 14 June 1658, at the Battle of the Dunes near Dunkirk, he commanded the right wing of the Spanish army against his former commander, Turenne. Unsurprisingly, the Spanish were routed.

On Charles's restoration to the English throne, James was made Lord High Admiral and created Duke of Albany to please Charles's Scottish subjects. He oversaw a series of critical naval reforms carried out by his able Secretary to the Admiralty, Samuel Pepys and supervised the fortification of the south coast of England. James also supported a number of colonial ventures. He became Governor of the Hudson's Bay Company and President of the Royal African Company which traded slaves to the sugar plantations of the West Indies. In 1664 Colonel Robert Nicholls captured the Dutch province of New Netherland which was renamed New York in James's honour. Fort Orange became Albany. In the Second (1665–7) and Third (1672–4) Dutch Wars, James commanded the navy at sea.

In 1668 James converted to Catholicism, though Charles still required him to take the Anglican sacraments and to bring up his daughters as Protestants. James continued to maintain close links with the Anglican Church and Anglican members of Parliament with whom he shared firm, royalist views.

In September 1660 James married Anne Hyde, the daughter of Charles II's chief minister Edward Hyde, 1st Earl of Clarendon.

It was his failure to produce a Protestant heir that now exerted pressure on James. His conversion to Rome provoked public concern that the clock would be turned back to the dark days of "Bloody" Mary – with memories of stake, block and gallows. In 1673 a jittery Parliament passed the Test Act, denying Catholics any position in the church, state or armed forces. James immediately resigned all his offices rather than swear to the anti-Catholic conditions of the Act, dangerously advertising his Catholicism. His wife Anne had died in 1672 and now, with an insensitivity bordering on insanity, James married a fifteen year-old, Italian Catholic princess, Mary of Modena.

The marriage raised serious dynastic and political issues. James had two Protestant daughters, Mary and Anne, from his first marriage to Anne Hyde. A son by Mary of Modena would become a Roman Catholic King of England. Though Mary was pretty and delightful, the stigma of her religion set the country against her. Rumours were put about that Mary was an agent of the pope, Clement X. During the surreal nightmare of the Popish Plot in 1678, in which her secretary was involved, Mary and James discreetly went abroad. They took refuge first in Brusssels, then in Edinburgh.

From 1679–81 three Parliaments, all dismissed by an outraged Charles II, attempted to exclude James from the succession by statute. By 1681 however, the old fear of republicanism, most keenly felt by the high-Anglican gentry, had returned. From their perspective, the security

Anne Hyde (1638–72) was seduced by James when in exile in 1659. She was Maid of Honour to Mary, Princess of Orange, Charles II's and James's sister. Charles insisted on James marrying the intelligent and witty Anne, believing that her strong character would be a steadying influence on his licentious brother. James's libido exceeded even his brother's gargantuan lust. He kept scores of mistresses, the most famous being Arabella Churchill and Catherine Sedley, Countess of Dorchester. James was reckoned to be "the most unguarded ogler of his time". Although Samuel Pepys described Anne Hyde as being downright plain, she produced eight children.

Only two daughters, Mary and Anne survived, both later Queens of England. Their mother converted to Catholicism, to the horror of her firmly Protestant family. In 1672 she died of breast cancer, just after the birth of her last child. She was buried in Westminster Abbey. Anne was the last Englishwoman to marry the heir to the British throne until Lady Diana Spencer married Charles, Prince of Wales in 1981.

• **Anne Hyde by Sir Peter Lely (1660s)**
National Portrait Gallery, London

James, Duke of Monmouth was the eldest illegitimate son of Charles II, by his mistress Lucy Walter. He was born in 1649 in Rotterdam, during Charles's exile. Some saw him as the Protestant heir to his Catholic uncle, James II. Monmouth had already been implicated in the ill-planned Rye House Plot to murder Charles II. Although on that occasion, Charles's affection for his bastard son saved him from charges of treason, on his accession James immediately exiled him to Holland. Monmouth allowed himself to be persuaded to lead a rebellion and claim the throne. In June 1685 his pathetically small invasion force of three ships landed at Torbay in Devon where he tried to raise support. On 6 July a ragged army of peasants was destroyed at Sedgemoor.

Monmouth was captured and taken to London to be executed. He made an abject appeal to James for mercy. Appalled at his nephew's cowardice, James refused. In spite of being heavily bribed, the executioner Jack Ketch, botched his job. In the words of a witness: after the first stroke the Duke "lookt up, & after the third he putt his Leggs a Cross, & the Hangman flung away his Axe, but being chidd took it againe & gave him tother two strokes; and severed not his head from his body till he cut it off with his Knife".

After his execution, it was realised that there was no official portrait of Monmouth, the son of a king and a pretender to the throne. His corpse was exhumed and the head carefully stitched back onto the body. The cadaver then sat for its portrait.

- **James, Duke of Monmouth and Buccleuch possibly after William Wissing (c.1683)**
National Portrait Gallery, London

offered by James's absolutist views, Catholic or not, seemed infinitely preferable. In 1682 James returned to England and resumed his place as the Anglicans' rightful representative.

In 1683, the Rye House Plot was uncovered. The conspirators planned to murder both Charles and James, sparking a republican revolution. Its discovery provoked such a wave of royalist sympathy that, when Charles died in 1685, James's succession was seamless. At the head of the Anglican Church, his future as an absolutist British monarch seemed assured.

The Parliament summoned by James on his accession responded warmly to his declaration, that "the best way to engage me to meet you often is always to use me well", by voting him an annual income of £2 million (£3 billion today) and an army of 20,000 men. The country was at peace and there was no reason to doubt that given time and tact, a certain measure of toleration for Catholics could be achieved. Six months after his smooth succession however, James's reign was interrupted by two rebellions: the Duke of Argyll's in Scotland and the Duke of Monmouth's in England.

In October 1685 King Louis XIV revoked the Edict of Nantes, ending Huguenot toleration. James hated religious persecution and protested discreetly but to no avail. Any attempt to integrate Catholics into English political life was now doomed.

The Monmouth and Argyll rebellions were swiftly and brutally extinguished, giving James an excuse to raise five more regiments, all commanded by Roman Catholics and foreign service veterans whom he could trust. Parliament reacted so vociferously to this development that James promptly dissolved it, never to call another one. In 1687 he concocted a legal ruse, using one of his most trusted Catholic army officers, Sir Edward Hales, to force the issue of the King's prerogative to invalidate the Test Act. James's *Declaration of Indulgence* in April that year gave freedom of conscience to Catholics and nonconformists alike. James received no credit for this liberal measure. Instead it was interpreted as a plot to return England by stealth to the "old" religion.

The Edict of Nantes was issued on 13 April 1598 by Henri IV of France, granting Huguenots religious toleration. In October 1685 his grandson Louis XIV, renounced the Edict and declared Protestantism illegal.

On 21 May 1688 Alexander Pope was born in Lombard Street in London. Master of satire and the heroic couplet, he is the third most quoted poet in *The Oxford Dictionary of Quotations* after Shakespeare and Tennyson. He lived in Twickenham (planting the first weeping willow in England from sprigs of a basket of figs, made of willow from Turkey) and died in 1744. Some of his best known lines:

"Hope springs eternal in the human breast"
"Damn with faint praise"
"For fools rush in where angels fear to tread"
"A little learning is a dangerous thing"
"To err is human, to forgive divine"

In April 1688 James re-issued the *Declaration of Indulgence*, requiring all Anglican clergymen to proclaim it from their pulpits. When the Archbishop of Canterbury, William Sancroft and six bishops presented a petition requesting that he reconsider his religious policies, they were arrested and tried for seditious libel.

On 10 June 1688 came the dramatic news that Mary of Modena had been delivered of a healthy boy. Mary's gynæcological history to this point had been a sorry series of miscarriages and still-births. In the prevailing religious climate, the rumour that the new heir must be a changeling, smuggled into Mary's bed in a warming pan, took hold of the public imagination. With the sudden arrival of a Catholic heir to the throne, several prominent statesmen known as the "Immortal Seven", including William Compton, Bishop of London, the Earls of Devonshire and Shrewsbury and Henry Sydney who wrote the invitation, offered the throne to William of Orange, precipitating the Glorious Revolution and the Bill of Rights.

Hilaire Belloc (1870–1953) regarded James as honourable in pursuing religious toleration for his realm. Belloc believed that "men in the small clique of great fortunes" were responsible for destroying the "ancient monarchy of the English".

The Revolution saw both the last successful invasion of England and the last abdication of a British monarch until 1936. Most importantly it saw the birth of a constitutional monarchy and modern parliamentary democracy. Never again would a British monarch hold absolute power. The ejection of James II removed the possibility of Catholicism re-rooting in England for centuries. The Revolution meant limited toleration for nonconformist Protestants but for English Catholics, it spelt social and political disaster. The Protestant succession was secured.

The 1689 Bill of Rights, incorporating the *Declaration of Rights*, anchored the British Constitution. By declaring the royal prerogative illegal, the Bill represented the culmination of the long struggle between the Stuart kings and the English Parliament. The Crown was henceforth dependent on the will of Parliament, ensuring freedom from arbitrary government.

William of Orange had been preparing for an invasion of England ever since the spring of 1688, waiting only for the right "Protestant Wind". On the 5 November, with 500 ships and 21,000 men, including a portable bridge and a smithy, William sailed into Tor Bay, landing at Brixham. On mounting the quay, he announced to the watching crowd: "I come to do you goot. I am here for all your goots". He advanced cautiously on London, while gauging the mood of the country.

When the gentry, senior army officers, including John Churchill, later Duke of Marlborough and even his own daughter Anne deserted him, James sent Mary of Modena, disguised as a washerwoman and their son to France. James soon followed, throwing his Great Seal of Office into the Thames. At Faversham, on the Kent coast he was recognised by fishermen and embarrassed into returning to London. Cheering crowds momentarily raised a flutter of hope, swiftly dashed by the arrival of a detachment of Dutch troops requiring James to accompany them to Rochester. On 23 December he was put on a boat for France. A convenient fiction was encouraged: that, in jettisoning the Great Seal, James had abdicated, vacating the throne for his daughter Mary and her husband William.

James arrived at the court of Louis XIV on Christmas Day 1688. He was accommodated comfortably with his family in the vast château of St Germain-en-Laye, near Versailles. On 12

February 1689 a Convention Parliament, so-called as it had not been summoned by the King, declared that James had abdicated. On 13 February Parliament offered the crown to William and Mary. The Scottish Parliament followed suit in May.

James, now suffering the early stages of dementia, would have been perfectly content to pass his time in hunting and compulsive praying to atone for his lubricious life. Louis XIV would have none of it. He told James brusquely that he had a holy, bounden duty to regain his throne. In the spring of 1689 he sent him off to loyal, Catholic Ireland with 6,000 French troops, to raise rebellion as a first step towards his restoration.

The Catholic gentry in Ireland had lost almost all their lands during Cromwell's Commonwealth, along with the right to hold public office, practise their religion or sit in the Irish Parliament. James's arrival represented an opportunity to recover the governance of Ireland from the English Parliament. Richard Talbot, 1st Earl of Tyrconnel had raised an army to restore James to his throne after the Glorious Revolution. By 1690 Catholic Irishmen controlled all of Ireland except Ulster,

In March 1689 James had landed at Kinsale where he was immediately acknowledged as King by the Irish Parliament. At James's urging, it went on to pass an Act of Liberty of Conscience, granting religious freedom to all Catholics and Protestants in Ireland. In June James's usurper, now King William III, arrived in Ireland to crush the Jacobite threat with a powerful army stiffened by his elite, Dutch Blue Guards. A month later he defeated James's French-Irish army at the battle of the Boyne.

The Battle of the Boyne took place on 12 July 1690 near the town of Drogheda, the scene of a massacre by Cromwellian troops in 1649. The armies, unusually with both their respective monarchs present, faced each other across the River Boyne. William's forces outnumbered and easily defeated the poorly armed and ill-trained Jacobite army. The symbolic importance of this battle has made it one of the best-known in Anglo-Irish history, enshrined in Irish Protestant legend. The anniversary is still commemorated enthusiastically each year by the Orange Order.

With a small escort, James hurried directly from the battlefield to Duncannon and returned to France. His ineptitude and hasty flight betrayed his Irish supporters who fought on until the Treaty of Limerick in 1691. For abandoning Ireland, James lives on in Irish folk lore as *Seamus a' chaca* ("James the shit").

James returned to St Germain-en-Laye. Over the next ten years, living the austere life of a penitent, his dementia took an ever stronger hold. In 1696 a Jacobite plot to assassinate William made his cause deeply unpopular in England. In 1697 Louis XIV offered James the Polish crown which he refused. In the same year Louis recognized William in the Treaty of Rijswijk and James's hopes of restoration finally died.

On 16 September 1701 James collapsed with the stroke that killed him. He was buried in the Chapel of the Scots College in Paris. In 1734 there was a move to canonise him but it came to nothing. James's tomb was desecrated during the French Revolution and his remains were scattered.

An intriguing question-mark hangs over any study of the life of James II. Was he just a foolish, conceited despot, careless of the religious views of his English and Scottish subjects: or was he rather a far-sighted, even enlightened ruler, way ahead of his time?

THE MASSACRE OF GLENCOE

In 1689 the English and Scottish thrones were assumed by the Protestant Prince of Orange who became William III. He replaced the Stuart King James II who had abdicated in 1688. In August 1691 the government offered an indemnity to the clan chiefs in the Highlands of Scotland who had previously sworn allegiance to King James, on condition that they swore an oath of allegiance to King William before 1 January 1692.

It was widely anticipated that some chiefs would refuse to take the oath. William prepared for this by signing "Letters of fire and the sword", which would authorize the slaughter of any potentially rebellious clans who failed to comply.

Glencoe, in winter

In the event, all clan chiefs obeyed, with the exception of Alexander MacDonald ("The MacIain") of Glencoe. He had postponed his submission until 31 December when, at the last minute, he received release from his previous oath by King James II, now in exile in France. Although he went to Fort William to swear his new oath, there was no magistrate able to accept it. In technical default, the royal authorisation was activated.

Over a hundred soldiers who had been billeted on the MacDonalds were secretly ordered to attack their hosts. Thirty-eight men, including the chief, two women and two children were killed. The perpetrator of this massacre was the secretary of state, John Dalrymple, Master of Stair. Dalrymple was a Lowlander and a Protestant, who strongly disliked Catholic highlanders in general and the MacDonalds in particular. Deliberately he had refused to accept Alexander MacDonald's late-delivered oath, unavoidably delayed by heavy snow, when it arrived in Edinburgh. With grim satisfaction, he issued the order to cut off the MacDonald clan "root and branch".

Orders were issued to three local commanders to carry out the massacre. Two of these detachments, aghast at their orders, disobeyed and blamed the appalling weather.

It was the commander of the third detachment, Captain Robert Campbell of Glen Lyon who carried out Dalrymples's order to "put all to the sword under seventy". Campbell was a desperate man who had just gambled away the last of his family fortune. On the night of 13 February a blizzard was raging through Glencoe when the soldiers received their orders to attack their sleeping hosts. It is clear that many of the clansmen were given enough warning by their guests to escape into the hills, including the chief's wife, though she subsequently died of exposure. The Scottish Parliament eventually held an enquiry and declared the incident an act of murder. Although Dalrymple resigned, the affair was quickly forgotten by the government in London.

It is worth pointing out that the massacre, known as *Mort Ghlinne Comhann* in Gaelic, or "Murder of Glen Coe", was an act of official policy devised by a Scottish Secretary of State, ordered by a Scottish Commander-in-Chief and executed by a Scottish regiment. The unfortunate English, who played no part in the crime, as usual still get the blame.

The nine of diamonds playing card is often referred to as the "Curse of Scotland". There are a number of reasons given for this connection. The most commonly quoted is that it was the playing card used by Sir John Dalrymple, Master (later 1st Earl) of Stair, cryptically to authorise the Glencoe Massacre. The Dalrymple coat of arms has nine diamond-shaped lozenges on its saltire.

Two lieutenants, Francis Farquhar and Gilbert Kennedy broke their swords rather than carry out their orders. They were imprisoned: but were exonerated, released and later gave evidence for the prosecution against their superior officers.

Two Macdonald brothers escaped to Ireland and changed their name to McKern. A descendant emigrated to Australia in about 1850 from whom Leo McKern (1920–2002), the actor who played Horace Rumpole in John Mortimer's *Rumpole of the Bailey* on Thames Television (1978–92), claimed ancestry.

The Clachaig Inn in Glencoe has a sign on its door: "No Hawkers or Campbells".

**Statue of William III by
John Michael Rysbrack
erected in Queen Square,
Bristol in 1736**

THE LAST STUART MONARCHS (REIGNED 1688–1714)

William III (1650–1702) was the son of William II, Prince of
Orange and Mary Stuart, daughter of Charles I of England. His
father died of smallpox eight days before his birth. In 1672 he
became Stadtholder (Head of State) of the United Provinces of the
Netherlands. He defended his country ably against an alliance of
Louis XIV and his own uncle, Charles II. In 1677 he married his
first cousin Mary Stuart, daughter of James, Duke of York, later
James II. In 1688, after the birth of a Catholic son to James II,
English nobles offered the throne to both William and Mary. In
1689 they were proclaimed joint rulers of England and Scotland.

Later that year the deposed James II, backed by Louis XIV,
landed in Ireland. In 1690 he was defeated by William at the Battle of the
Boyne. At the same time, a Jacobite rising in Scotland was crushed at the
Battle of Killiecrankie. After Mary's death in 1694 William, now the
Protestant champion of Europe, led an alliance against the expanding
power of Louis XIV. A small, frail, asthmatic man, William was a
competent soldier and diplomat. He was never popular with the English,
in spite of his commitment to religious toleration and parliamentary
reform. His support for the Act of Settlement in 1701 made Parliament
independent of the judiciary. The Act also prevented a Jacobite
restoration, by settling the succession on the Electress Sophia of Hanover,
grand-daughter of James I. William and Mary produced no children.

In 1695 Sir John Trevor M.P.
(c.1637–1717) of Bryncunallt in
Denbighshire became the only Speaker
of the House of Commons to be expelled
for taking bribes. He was so cross-eyed
that members of the House were
frequently uncertain which of them had
"caught the Speaker's eye" and would
inadvertently speak out of turn. No
Speaker was ever subsequently
dismissed until Michael Martin in 2009.

William was bisexual. His special favourites were two Dutch
courtiers whom he raised to the peerage: Hans Willem Bentinck became
Earl of Portland and Arnold Joost van Keppel was created Earl of
Albemarle. William died on 8 March 1702 after a fall from his horse
which had put its foot in a molehill. Complications set in and he died from pneumonia sixteen
days later. Frustrated Jacobite supporters toasted the "little gentleman in black velvet". William's
reign marked the start of a slow but irreversible transition to constitutional governance under
Parliament.

Born in 1662, Mary II was Queen of England and Scotland from 1689–94. The daughter of
James II, she was brought up as a Protestant, though her father later became a Catholic. In 1677
she married her cousin William of Orange. Despite their difference in size (William was small
and Mary substantial), having no children and William's preference for men, the marriage was a
great success. A popular queen, Mary always insisted that William was King, rather than her
equal or consort and deputized for him competently when he was abroad. She showed little
sympathy for her father whose throne she had usurped.

**Queen Mary II by
Sir Peter Lely (1677)**
National Portrait Gallery, London

Mary chose to live at Kensington Palace and Hampton Court, which was renovated for her
by Christopher Wren. Her delight in Dutch design influenced English pottery, landscape
gardening and interior decoration. When she died of smallpox in 1694, William was so
overwhelmed with grief that there were fears for his sanity and his life. Queen Mary was buried
in Westminster Abbey.

Anne (1665–1714) inherited the throne of Great Britain and Ireland, as the last Stuart
sovereign (1702–14), from her brother-in-law King William III when he died on 8 March 1702. A
large, friendly woman of no great intelligence but devoted to duty and her country, she married
the equally amiable but dim-witted George (1653–1708), Prince of Denmark, son of King

THE TUDORS AND THE STEWARTS   1485–1714

Frederick III. Their tragedy was that they were unable to provide an heir, despite her eighteen confinements. Five reached full-term, only to die in infancy – including William, Duke of Gloucester, who died when he was eleven.

Anne's reign was marked by the Union with Scotland on 1 May 1707, making her the first sovereign of the United Kingdom of Great Britain and Ireland. The Scots lost their Parliament but kept their Presbyterian religion and legal system. Her strong preference for the Whigs sparked a a bitter rivalry with the Tories. Anne formed two intense female relationships. The first was with Sarah Churchill, whose husband John, 1st Duke of Marlborough enriched Anne's reign with his great victories over the French; and later with Abigail Masham.

Her health was wretched, exacerbated by gout and a disorder which made her enormously fat. Frequently she could only be moved about in wheeled chairs hauled by ropes and pulleys. She died aged forty-nine and was buried in a huge square coffin in Westminster Abbey. The crown passed to George, Elector of Hanover, a great-grandson of James I whose daughter Elizabeth had married Frederick V of Bohemia, the "Winter King".

Queen Anne studio of John Closterman (1702)
National Portrait Gallery, London

WILLIAM PATERSON, THE BANK OF ENGLAND AND THE DARIEN SCHEME

William Paterson (1658–1719) was born in Skipmyre in Dumfriesshire. When he was seventeen he emigrated to the Bahamas: where he first had the idea of creating a colony on the Darien Isthmus of Panama, to facilitate trade with Asia. Returning to England, he tried unsuccessfully to persuade James II's ministers to underwrite his scheme. By 1686, having settled in London, Paterson had made a fortune in trade with the West Indies. In 1692 he suggested that the English national debt could be transferred to a bank. With Charles Montagu, Lord of the Treasury, he proposed a Bank of England which was approved by Parliament and incorporated by Royal Charter on 27 July 1694. Paterson raised £1.2 million (£1.8 billion today) from private subscription, as a loan to the Crown in return for privileges and fees for managing the nation's debt. He returned to Edinburgh and was instrumental in founding the Bank of Scotland. Buoyed with success, he turned to his dream of colonising the Darien Isthmus.

Paterson and five ships carrying 1,500 settlers sailed from Leith in July 1698. He had originally raised half the capital from English and Dutch subscribers: but England was at war with France and King William III did not wish to offend Spain, which claimed Darien as part of New Granada. The Scottish public however, raised £500,000, amounting to half of all Scottish cash deposits. The Scots also backed the scheme with people, many of them highland clansmen.

The enthusiastic settlers found a swamp and jungle infested with mosquitoes. Nevertheless, they christened their new colony Caledonia and founded New Edinburgh and New St Andrews. Paterson's wife and child died, followed by 400 settlers who succumbed to malaria and yellow fever. Survival was only made possible by the charity of the local natives who befriended the starving colonists. King William had forbidden English colonies in North America to supply the settlement or help it defend itself against Spanish retaliation. The colony was joined by five more ships before Darien was abandoned in July 1699. News of the first disastrous expedition did not reach Scotland in time to prevent a second fleet from arriving on St Andrew's Day, 30 November 1699. 2,000 settlers died and barely 500 survived. Only one ship returned to Scotland and the Scheme's entire capital was lost, devastating the Scottish economy.

> The Bank of Scotland was founded on 17 July 1695, solely as a commercial bank and prohibited from lending to the Scottish government without Parliamentary approval. It was the first bank in Europe to print its own banknotes, which it still does. On 19 January 2009 it became a subsidiary of the Lloyds Banking Group.

The Darien disaster led directly to the Act of Union in 1707, which was strongly supported by Paterson. He knew that Scotland needed to share the benefits of English international trade and Article 14 of the Act granted £398,085 and 10 shillings to the Scots. Paterson died in Westminster in January 1719. The site of his grave is unknown.

THE "OLD PRETENDER" (1688–1766) AND THE 1715 REBELLION

Prince James Edward Stuart, known as the "Old Pretender", was the only son of James II and his second wife, Mary of Modena. After his father's abdication of the English throne in December 1688, he was brought up as a Catholic exile in France. On James II's death in 1701, he was proclaimed King of Great Britain by his cousin Louis XIV of France. The British Parliament responded by passing a bill of Attainder for treason against him in 1702, declaring that all his royal titles were forfeit. In 1708 he tried to land in Scotland but was chased off by a fleet led by Admiral Sir George Byng.

On 22 December 1715 James belatedly landed in Scotland. A rising in the north of England in his name had already been crushed at Preston on 14 November. Another, led by the Earl of Mar, was halted by the Duke of Argyll at Sheriffmuir in Perthshire the day before he disembarked.

Admiral of the Fleet Sir George Byng, later Ist Viscount Torrington (1668–1733), had fifteen children. His fourth son, Admiral John Byng was court-martialled and shot at the outbreak of the Seven Years' War, for losing Minorca to the French at the Battle of Mahon on 28 June 1756. The French philosopher Voltaire remarked, "From time to time, the English shoot an Admiral in order to encourage the others". The victorious French admiral, the Duc de Richelieu ordered his cook to create a dish worthy of his victory. He invented a sauce named after Mahon: Mayonnaise.

Depressed at the lack of support for his planned coronation at Scone, James returned to France. He found that Louis XIV had died and he was now a political embarrassment. Happily, Pope Clement XI offered him refuge and a substantial pension in Rome. In 1719 he married Maria Sobieska (1702–35), grand-daughter of the Polish king, John III Sobieski. They had two sons. The eldest, Charles Edward became the "Young Pretender", known as Bonnie Prince Charlie. The younger son, Henry Benedict (1725–1807), probably homosexual, rose to become a cardinal. James died in Rome on 1 January 1766 and was buried in the Vatican. A fortnight later the Papacy recognised the Hanoverian dynasty as the legitimate kings of Britain and Ireland.

Prince James Francis Edward Stuart the "Old Pretender" studio of Alexis Simon Belle (c.1712)
National Portrait Gallery, London

Bonnie Prince Charlie studio of Antonio David (c.1732)
National Portrait Gallery, London

THE "YOUNG PRETENDER" (1720–88) AND THE 1745 REBELLION

Prince Charles Edward Stuart, "Bonnie Prince Charlie", or the "Young Pretender", was the son of the "Old Pretender", James Edward Stuart and grandson of King James II, who had abdicated the thrones of England and Scotland in 1688.

On 23 July 1745, with French assistance and cutting an attractive, youthful figure, the Prince landed at Eriskay in the Outer Hebrides but with just seven men. He raised his standard at Glenfinnan on 19 August. With 2,500 Highlanders, he captured Edinburgh and defeated a slightly smaller force of Lowlanders at Prestonpans on 21 September.

He took Carlisle and marched on Derby, only 130 miles from London which, unknown to the Jacobites, was virtually defenceless. But with their lines of communication hopelessly extended, the morale of the clansmen collapsed and they retreated back to Scotland.

In January 1746 a French brig carrying £13,000 in gold (£19 million today) was intercepted on the north coast of Sutherland, by HMS *Sheerness*. The rebel clansmen on board fled to Kinloch, at the head of the Kyle of Tongue, but were ambushed by Lord Reay, chief of the loyal Hanoverian Clan Mackay. The Jacobite army went unpaid and elements of it melted away before the Battle of Culloden.

On 16 April 1746 Charles's little army was crushed at Culloden by Prince William Augustus, Duke of Cumberland (1721–65), and his highly trained Hanoverian infantry. A fugitive in the Western Isles, he narrowly escaped capture. He was helped by Flora Macdonald (1722–90), who disguised him as her maid. He subsequently wandered Europe in futile attempts to revive his cause but his drunken, debauched behaviour made him an unattractive prospect. He settled in Rome where he died an alcoholic.

Bonnie Prince Charlie has been the subject of countless legends and ballads. The most haunting dates from about 1884, ironically with words written by an Englishman, Sir Harold Boulton who was the editor of *Songs of the North*. The first half of the tune is an old sea shanty. The other half is attributed to Annie MacLeod, later Lady Wilson, after she heard the first part in 1879 while being rowed from Torrin to Loch Coruisk in Skye. The words describe a moment in the wanderings of Bonnie Prince Charlie, when a storm was rising and his pursuers chose not to follow:

Speed bonnie boat, like a bird on the wing,
*   Onward, the sailors cry*
Carry the lad that's born to be king
*   Over the sea to Skye*

Fort George was completed, after 21 years, in 1769. A decade late, it was also well over budget. The estimate for construction had been £92,673 19s 1d. The final cost was over £200,000 (£268 million today), more than the GNP of Scotland in 1750.

FORT GEORGE IS THE FINEST ARTILLERY FORTIFICATION IN EUROPE

Following the defeat of Bonnie Prince Charlie and his Jacobite army at Culloden in 1746, Fort George was built as an impregnable defence against any further unrest. It was conceived by William Skinner, the King's Military Engineer for North Britain.

Built on a barren spit of land jutting into the Moray Firth at Ardersier, north-east of Inverness, Fort George's elaborate 18th century bastioned defences and garrison buildings survive intact. Almost a mile around, the fort encloses an area of 42 acres. The garrison chapel was probably designed by Robert Adam (1728–92), whose family construction company built the fort. Though the magazine held 2,672 barrels of gunpowder, the fort never fired a shot in anger.

Fort George

John Churchill, 1st Duke of Marlborough

BRITAIN'S MOST SUCCESSFUL GENERAL

John Churchill, 1st Duke of Marlborough possibly by John Closters (*c.*1685–90) (after John Riley)
National Portrait Gallery, London

John Churchill was born on 26 May 1650 at Ashe House, in Devon to Sir Winston Churchill and his wife Elizabeth, *née* Drake. Winston and Elizabeth were living with her mother Lady Eleanor, because the Royalist Captain Winston had been fined the vast sum of £4,400 (£6.7 million today) for being caught on the wrong side of the English Civil war. The Churchills had twelve children of whom only five survived.

It was in every sense an uncomfortable household into which to be born. Although Lady Eleanor had supported Parliament in the recent conflict, she too was living in genteel impecuniousness. It was in these straitened circumstances that John Churchill may have developed his considerable diplomatic skills, fear of poverty and legendary avarice.

Following the restoration of King Charles II in 1660, Winston Churchill's fortunes improved. He was offered first a position in Ireland as Commissioner for Land Claims; and then as Junior Clerk Comptroller to the King's household in Whitehall. Winston's eldest child Arabella was appointed Maid of Honour to the Duchess of York. A year later, John became page to her husband, the Duke of York, the future King James II.

John Churchill attended St Paul's School in London, where he was an inattentive student (as was his descendant, Winston Churchill), who never learnt to spell correctly. James, Duke of York exposed him to the military world from an early age. At seventeen he enlisted as an ensign in the King's Company of the 1st Guards (after the Battle of Waterloo, the 1st Guards became the Grenadier Guards). In 1668 he embarked with the fleet to garrison Tangier in North Africa, a Portuguese possession which had been handed to England as part of King Charles's wife, Catarina de Bragança, or Catherine of Braganza's dowry. He received valuable training and tactical experience in clashes with the Moors over the next three years. Returning to London in 1671, Churchill began a heady liaison with the King's mistress Barbara Villiers, Duchess of Cleveland. Caught by the King *in flagrante delicto*, he was lucky to receive only a royal reprimand, "You are a rascal but I forgive you because you do it to get your bread".

In June 1672 Churchill saw action against the Dutch on board the Duke of York's warship *Royal Prince* at the Battle of Solebay, off the Suffolk coast, where he won praise for his courage. He was promoted captain and served in the Lord High Admiral's Regiment.

In 1673, during the war fought by the First Grand Alliance against the Dutch, he was present at the siege of Maastricht (where Dumas's real-life hero d'Artagnan, captain of Musketeers, was killed) – again distinguishing himself, by leading a successful attack on the fortress. He is also said to have saved the life of the ill-starred Duke of Monmouth. Churchill was commended for valour by King Louis XIV.

Although England withdrew from the Franco-Dutch conflict in 1674, several British regiments remained in the Netherlands as mercenaries in the service of the French. Churchill took command of one of these regiments: and was present in 1675 at the close-fought battles of Sinzheim and Entzheim serving under the renowned Marshal-General Turenne.

Churchill courted Sarah Jennings, to whom he had been introduced by his sister Arabella (now the Duke of York's mistress). Sarah was a Maid of Honour at the court of the Duchess of York and, like Churchill, her family of minor gentry had been impoverished by debt. Although it was a love match, it meant that Churchill would have to rely on the Crown for employment – a stringency which would have deepened his unattractive acquisitiveness. Churchill married Sarah on 1 October 1678.

Churchill's career began to accelerate. He was made Gentleman of the Bedchamber and Master of the Robes. At the same time he was asked to negotiate an alliance between the Dutch and Spanish against the French: which King Charles quietly sabotaged – he was being financed secretly by Louis XIV. Churchill returned to England with Sidney Godolphin: having much impressed his Dutch interlocutor William, Prince of Orange with his sound common sense and instinctive negotiating skills.

The pernicious effects of the "Popish Plot" which led to the Catholic James, Duke of York's exile for three years, reduced Churchill's options. He was obliged to attend the Duke in Scotland: where in 1682, he was ennobled as Baron Churchill of Eyemouth in the peerage of Scotland. He was also given command of the King's Own Royal Regiment of Dragoons. When Princess Anne married Prince George of Denmark she invited her childhood confidante, Sarah Churchill to join her household.

Alexandre Dumas, born Dumas Davy de la Pailleterie (1802–70) was the grandson of a Haitian slave. He once remarked to a man who insulted him about his mixed race background: "My father was a mulatto, my grandfather was a Negro, and my great-grandfather a monkey. You see Sir, my family starts where yours ends".

Turenne (1611–75) often gave orders to his generals seated on a *chaise percée*, "evacuating mightily". Napoleon, who judged him to be the greatest of all French marshals (before himself), moved Turenne's body from St Denis to the Invalides.

Sarah Jennings was born in Holywell in Hertfordshire on 5 June 1660, the daughter of Richard Jennings and his wife Frances Thornhurst. Sarah's friendship with Princess, later Queen Anne began in 1673 when she joined the household of Anne's father James, Duke of York. They called each other pet names, Sarah being "Mrs Freeman" and Anne "Mrs Morley". From the moment of Anne's accession to the throne on St George's day 1702, Sarah was made Mistress of the Robes and Keeper of the Privy Purse. For seven years she exercised great personal and political influence over Queen Anne – until reluctantly obliged to support the Whig faction in parliament to keep her husband in the field.

The Queen, who strongly disliked the Whigs, found a new favourite: Sarah's own cousin and devious rival, Abigail Masham. By 1711 the politically astute Abigail had entirely replaced Sarah in the Queen's affections. Sarah died on 18 October 1744, over twenty years after her husband, aged eighty-four.

• **Sarah, Duchess of Marlborough after Sir Godfrey Kneller, Bt (*c.*1700)**
National Portrait Gallery, London

In 1685 King Charles II died and his brother James, Duke of York came to the throne. James's accession prompted a rising led by the Duke of Monmouth. Although Major-General Churchill played a significant part in crushing the rebellion, the savage retribution wreaked on the rebels by Judge Jeffreys (1645–89) was very likely an important factor in Churchill's decision to abandon King James three years later.

James II had already begun to dig his political grave by appointing Catholics to key positions in the armed forces and government institutions. This unwise and unpopular policy led directly to the "Glorious Revolution" in 1688. A petition was signed by leading Protestants (but not by Churchill), inviting William of Orange to invade England to ensure the Protestant succession. On 5 November 1688 William landed at Torbay. Most of James's army deserted and Churchill crossed over to William's lines at Axminster with 400 officers and men. In April 1689 William created Churchill Earl of Marlborough, giving rise to allegations that his defection was motivated more by a desire for personal gain rather than by patriotic conviction.

The Grand Alliance comprised (at various times) Austria, Bavaria, Brandenburg, England, the Holy Roman Empire, the Palatinate of the Rhine, Portugal, Savoy, Saxony, Spain, Sweden, and the United Provinces (Holland). Founded in 1686 as the League of Augsburg by the Holy Roman Emperor Leopold I and advised by the Dutch Stadtholder William of Orange (later King William III of England), it was known as the "Grand Alliance" after England joined the League in 1689.

John Churchill, 1st Duke of Marlborough by Sir Godfrey Kneller (1646–1723)

National Portrait Gallery, London

The Grand Alliance was a coalition formed to contain the expansionist policies of King Louis XIV of France. The "War of the Grand Alliance" lasted nine years. Marlborough took part for only three and only in subordinate commands. Although he was appointed Commander-in-Chief on his return to England, he was mistrusted by William and his wife Queen Mary who, as James II's eldest daughter, was joint sovereign.

William was suspicious of any defector from King James's court, while Mary both disliked Marlborough and resented the influence his wife Sarah exercised over her sister, Princess Anne. She wrote of him, "I can neither trust or esteem him".

Meanwhile, on 11 July 1690 William had defeated James's army in the Battle of the Boyne in Ireland, a victory still enthusiastically celebrated by Ulstermen as "King Billy's Day". Having reduced the ports of Kinsale and Cork, Marlborough joined up with William. William however, found him "very assuming" and no appointment or promotion expected by Marlborough was forthcoming.

To this slight was added Marlborough's profound dislike of William's habit of preferring Dutch over English officers in his army. In January 1691 he contacted the exiled King James in France, seeking a pardon for having deserted him in his hour of need – an understandable precaution in the event of James ever regaining his throne. William however, was well aware of his duplicity. On 20 January 1692 Marlborough was suddenly and without warning stripped of all his offices of state, both civil and military and expelled from Court. Shortly afterwards he was arrested and imprisoned in the Tower of London, accused of being a signatory to a letter to James welcoming his restoration. The letter was discredited and Marlborough was released after a month. In the meantime his youngest son had died.

Whispers of treachery continued to pursue him. In 1692 he was suspected of betraying a British attack on the French port of Brest. Although this was untrue, Marlborough was still conducting a questionable correspondence with James which further undermined his reputation. Queen Mary died in January 1695, leaving her sister Anne heir to her husband's throne. Marlborough was permitted to return to Court, though no offer of employment followed. In 1700 the death of the childless Charles II of Spain posed the alarming possibility that the crowns of Spain and France would be united under the French House of Bourbon. This was unacceptable to England, Holland and Austria.

Meanwhile William's health was deteriorating. He realised that he had not much longer to live. This reality persuaded him to overcome his personal dislike of Marlborough, in the greater interest of his kingdom. He knew that both Marlborough and his wife exercised marked influence over his successor, Princess Anne. He sent Marlborough as his representative to the Hague. There, as commander of all British forces, he was instructed to forge a coalition against France and Spain. On 7 September 1701 the Treaty of the Second Grand Alliance was signed by England, Holland and Austria. A few months later, on 8 March 1702 William died, as a result of a riding accident.

The Marlboroughs' circumstances took an immediate turn for the better. The Polish Ambassador Count Wratislaw reported that, "Marlborough .... by reason of his credit with the Queen [Anne] can do everything". Marlborough was quick to translate this "credit" to his advantage. Within months he was appointed Master-General of the Ordnance, Knight of the Garter and Captain-General of all British forces, both at home and abroad. Sarah was similarly favoured: swiftly acquiring the offices of Groom of the Stole, Mistress of the Robes and Keeper of the Privy Purse. The Marlboroughs now enjoyed a joint annual income of £60,000 (about £90 million today).

Meanwhile, on 15 May 1702 England (union with Scotland did not take place until 1707) declared war on France. Marlborough was given command of the army of the Second Grand Alliance, which included Holland, Austria, Savoy and a force of German

THE DUKE OF MARLBOROUGH'S CAMPAIGNS (1702–11) IN THE WAR OF THE SPANISH SUCCESSION

- ♜ Fortress (date of capture)
- ♜ Earlier siege (date)
- ⚔ Marlborough's battles
- ⚔ Later battles

The Battle of Blenheim, on 13 August 1704, was the most famous of Marlborough's many victories in the War of the Spanish Succession. English and Austrian armies, the latter commanded by Prince Eugène, surprised a French-Bavarian army at Blenheim (correctly, Blindheim), on the banks of the Danube, taking 13,000 prisoners. A further 18,000 were killed, wounded or drowned – the commander, Marshal Tallard was captured and taken back to England. It was worst defeat the French suffered for centuries and Bavaria was knocked out of the war.

François-Eugène, Prince of Savoy-Carignan (1663–1736), was arguably the greatest general ever to serve the Habsburg Emperors of Austria. He was born in Paris, possibly a bastard son of Louis XIV and his mistress Olympia Mancini, the niece of Cardinal Mazarin. Eugène was destined for the church but his choice was the army. When Louis XIV refused to grant him a commission, he left for Austria and joined the Imperial army. After Blenheim he fought a campaign in southern France and Italy, where in 1706 he inflicted a decisive defeat on the French at the Battle of Turin. He then rejoined Marlborough in Flanders, where they won the battles of Oudenarde and Malplaquet. Eugène is buried in St Stephen's Cathedral in Vienna.

mercenaries, in what became known as the War of the Spanish Succession. As with most coalitions, what was to become the most glorious phase of his military career opened with serious problems. The Dutch contingent would only come under his direct command when manoeuvring for battle: and once engaged, its enthusiasm was questionable. By the end of 1702 however, largely due to Marlborough's intuitive command of strategy and remarkable powers of persuasion, the unwieldy Alliance had proved its worth. His grateful Queen acknowledged this by creating him a Duke.

By early 1703 Marlborough had married off his daughters most satisfactorily. He had lost his only surviving son John, while an undergraduate at Cambridge, to smallpox: but his dukedom was allowed, by a special Act of Parliament, to pass to a daughter *suo jure* (in her own right). It is from a younger daughter Anne, who married Charles Spencer, 3rd Earl of Sunderland (1674–1722), that the Dukes of Marlborough descend.

Although grief stricken by his son John's death, Marlborough returned to Flanders to resume his campaign against the French – whose previous theatre commander had been replaced by the far more effective Marshal Villeroy. Although Marlborough swiftly won a few skirmishes and captured several important fortresses, most importantly Liège, his campaign soon stalled through Dutch reluctance to engage the enemy and dissent in England over the strategic aims of the war. For the first time, he was required by Parliament to justify the cost of the war in the light of its limited achievements: complaints which were temporarily silenced by his great victory at Blenheim in 1704.

Blenheim was followed by a number of successful encounters on the Moselle. By the end of 1704 Marlborough had become the most distinguished soldier of his age.

The year 1705 was a disappointment for the Grand Alliance. Hampered by his timid and lethargic Dutch allies, Marlborough was frustrated in every attempt at a major offensive: "I find so little zeal for the common cause that it is enough to break a better heart than mine".

1706 was a much more successful year for the Allies. On 23 May in Flanders, near the village of Ramillies, Marlborough inflicted on a French army commanded by Villeroy, "the most shameful, humiliating and disastrous of routs". The Spanish Netherlands (modern Belgium) was now directly under the control of the Alliance.

In 1708 Marlborough was for a time able to win back the strategic initiative. On 11 July he defeated the Duc de Vendôme at the Battle of Oudenarde. In April 1709 attempts to make peace were frustrated by excessive Whig demands for French reparations. Marlborough's influence over Queen Anne having been lost, Sarah was abruptly informed by the Queen that, "it is impossible for you to recover my former kindness". On 11 September Marlborough and Marshal Villars fought the Battle of Malplaquet. It was a pyrrhic victory for the Alliance, which suffered twice as many casualties as the French. By the end of 1710 diminishing Whig support for the war forced Marlborough's loyal friend Godolphin from office.

Marlborough, persuaded from resignation only by the entreaties of Prince Eugène and, though out of office, Lord Godolphin, returned to England in early 1711. He found the political landscape greatly changed. Sarah had been dismissed by the Queen and obliged to surrender her Gold Key of Office. Yet, in spite of the upheaval in his domestic and political life, he returned to his Headquarters in the Hague, to prepare for his last campaign. In September 1711 Marlborough, in poor health, once again opposed Marshal Villars. By dint of a skilful night march, covering 40 miles in 18 hours, he penetrated Villars's supposedly impregnable lines and invested the fortress of Bouchain. Villars, totally outmanoeuvred, was forced to surrender. These remarkable feats were of limited consequence. Secret negotiations between London and Versailles, from which Marlborough had been pointedly excluded, culminated in October 1711, when the preliminaries of peace were signed in London.

Although favourable terms had been negotiated by Henry St John (later Viscount Bolingbroke), Marlborough, the King of Prussia, the Elector of Hanover (heir to the British throne) and the Princes of the Grand Alliance were all opposed to a separate peace treaty between England and France. Nonetheless Great Britain (no longer just England) and the Netherlands ceased fighting France when the Treaty of Utrecht was concluded in 1713. For Marlborough though, time had run out nearly two years earlier.

A report by the Public Accounts Commissioners published on 1 January 1712 accused the Duke of embezzling public monies. On the 11 January the Queen dismissed him from all his offices. A charge that he had received a percentage from Dutch military contractors was refuted, on the grounds that it had long been accepted practice in the Netherlands for army contractors to pay a perquisite to the

"Whig" was originally a name for a Scottish Presbyterian. It came to describe a political faction, originating in the mid-17th century which, although opposed to the succession of the Catholic James, Duke of York to the throne, espoused religious toleration. Whigs represented the interests of the aristocracy and the prosperous middle classes, maintaining power through a network of parliamentary connections and patronage. Whigs became a coherent political party in 1784 when Charles James Fox united industrialists and religious dissenters seeking parliamentary reform. In the mid-19th century the Whigs evolved into the Liberal Party.

Opposing the Whigs were the Tories. "Tory" was Irish slang for an outlaw. It was used as a term of abuse for those who supported the hereditary right of the Duke of York (King James II) to succeed to the throne. By the mid-18th century the Tories had trimmed their belief in divine-right absolutism and had come to represent the country gentry who opposed religious toleration and foreign alliances or intervention. In 1764 William Pitt, "the Elder", was the first leader of a new Tory party, largely representing the gentry, merchants and civil servants. After the Napoleonic wars the Tories evolved into the Conservative Party.

A mnemonic, useful when Britain's schoolchildren were still taught history, to remember Marlborough's victories was a pre-STD telephone number: BROM 4689 – Blenheim (1704), Ramillies (1706), Oudenarde (1708) and Malplaquet (1709).

William Cadogan, 1st Earl Cadogan (1675–1726) born in Liscarton, County Meath, was Marlborough's Quartermaster General and de facto Chief of Staff. He fought in all the Duke's battles, playing an especially important part at Oudenarde in 1708. The fortune Cadogan made during the War of the Spanish Succession was used to buy and develop much of Chelsea – which is still owned by his descendants.

Commander-in-Chief. In regard to a second charge of syphoning off sums from foreign soldiers' pay, Marlborough was able to produce a Royal warrant authorising him to draw down these funds to finance an intelligence network. Nevertheless, impeachment proceedings were only halted when it was discovered that the Duke of Ormonde, his successor had been authorised to do exactly the same.

Vilified and isolated, Marlborough decided to leave England; and for two years he and Sarah enjoyed a royal progress through Europe. He was welcomed everywhere; and fêted in the European courts, where his reputation as a great marshal and his rank of Prince of the Holy Roman Empire were deeply respected. Sarah though, did not enjoy their self imposed exile, writing home, "It is much better to be dead than to live out of England". Her depression was compounded in 1714 by the death of their daughter Elizabeth, Countess Bridgewater from the smallpox which had killed their son.

Marlborough returned to England in 1714, the day after Queen Anne died, to a warm welcome from his old friend Prince George of Hanover, now King George I – who greeted him with the words, "My Lord Duke, I hope your troubles are now all over".

Sir John Vanbrugh (1664–1726) is best known as the designer of Blenheim Palace and Castle Howard, creating what became known as English Baroque.

He also wrote two outspoken, in their defence of women's rights in marriage, and sexually explicit Restoration comedies: *The Relapse* in 1696 and *The Provoked Wife* in 1697. They have become enduring stage favourites but were considered highly controversial at the time. As a young man, the dangerously radical Vanbrugh had spent time as a political prisoner in the Bastille fortress in Paris.

As indeed they were. Marlborough was reinstated as Master-General of the Ordnance and Captain-General of the army. Sadly the old Duke's health now began to fail and his executive duties were increasingly discharged by Robert Walpole (1676–1745), who was later to become Britain's first Prime Minister. Marlborough was only nominally in command during the Jacobite rebellion of 1715; and after the death of yet another of his children, Anne (Countess of Sunderland) early in 1716, he suffered a debilitating stroke. In 1719 the Marlboroughs were at last able to move into the east wing of the still unfinished Blenheim Palace; where of sound mind, but speechless he was able to watch the completion of his great memorial edifice.

On the night of 27 June 1722, just after Blenheim Palace had at last been completed, while staying at Windsor Lodge, the great Duke finally suffered a this time fatal stroke.

John Churchill ranks amongst the greatest military commanders in history. He was a handsome man of rare courage, endowed with enormous mental and physical strengths. Perhaps he missed true greatness: flawed as he was in his loyalties, his eye to the main chance and his undoubted appetite for office and perquisites.

In the words of Marlborough's even greater descendant, Sir Winston Churchill: "He commanded his armies of Europe against France for ten campaigns. He fought four great battles and many important actions. He never fought a battle that he did not win, nor besieged a fortress that he did not take. He quitted war invincible and no sooner was his guiding hand withdrawn than disaster overtook the armies he had led. Successive generations have not ceased to name him with Hannibal and Caesar".

Blenheim Palace was created a World Heritage site in 1987. It was the birthplace of Sir Winston Churchill in 1874.

One of England's greatest houses, Blenheim Palace was built between 1705–22 on the site of the old royal manor of Woodstock in Oxfordshire. It is the only non-episcopal country house in England to be called a "palace". Marlborough's exile and his Duchess's disgrace however, severely damaged the reputation of the architect, Sir John Vanbrugh.

Although it was intended to be a gift to Marlborough from a grateful nation, he actually paid for most of its £270,000 cost himself (some £400 million today).

Sir Robert Walpole, studio of Jean- Baptiste van Loo (1740)

National Portrait Gallery, London

SIR ROBERT WALPOLE, BRITAIN'S FIRST PRIME MINISTER, DIED IN 1745

Sir Robert Walpole (1676–1745), created Earl of Orford in 1742, was born at Houghton Hall in Norfolk. A King's Scholar at Eton, he graduated from King's College, Cambridge in 1698. In 1701 he was elected to Parliament in the Whig interest, serving as Secretary at War (1708–10) and Treasurer of the Navy (1710–11). He was a close advisor to John Churchill, 1st Duke of Marlborough and dominated the Cabinet in the war of the Spanish Succession which ended in 1713.

In 1712, loathed by the Tories, charges of corruption were brought against him. He was impeached, briefly imprisoned in the Tower of London and expelled from the Commons. In 1714 George I (1714–27), deeply suspicious of the Tories for their opposition to his succession, restored Walpole to office. He became Chancellor of the Exchequer in 1715 and First Lord of the Treasury in 1721. Walpole was implicated in the disastrous South Sea Bubble speculation in 1720; but survived to serve George II (1727–60). He used royal patronage to secure his economic policies, particularly the establishment of a Sinking Fund to reduce the national debt. The political fixer of all time, Walpole observed that "All men have their price".

As First Lord of the Treasury Walpole was effectively Britain's first prime minister. He continued in office from 1721–42, making his administration the longest in British history. His influence on British politics was enormous, although he relied on the support of the King rather than the House of Commons. He avoided foreign entanglements in the pursuit of peace,

Number 10,
Downing Street

The South Sea Bubble was a wave of manic speculation inadvertently triggered by the British government. It exchanged lucrative bonds in the South Sea Company, trading in cloth, agricultural goods and slaves, for Britain's national debt. Walpole was himself an investor but, on the advice of his banker Robert Jacomb, sold his shares before their collapse. It was a disaster which degraded market efficiency for generations. Walpole used his profits to rebuild Houghton.

• Houghton Hall, built for Sir Robert Walpole between 1722–35

Walpole's youngest son Horatio (1717–97), 4th Earl of Orford, known as Horace, was a man of letters, antiquarian and gossip. After an indifferent career in Parliament, he acquired a small house in Twickenham. He transformed it into a pseudo-Gothic temple he called Strawberry Hill, kindling an English Gothic revival. He also wrote the first English Gothic novel, *The Castle of Otranto* in 1765. His correspondence with a diplomat, Sir Horace Mann provides an elegant window on the mores of 18th century England. Walpole was effeminate, once called an "hermaphrodite horse", and never married – possibly the reason he coined the word "serendipity".

The Exemplification of the Act of Union, ratified by the Scottish Parliament in 1707

National Archives of Scotland

coining the phrase "the balance of power". He told Queen Caroline in 1734, "Madam, there are fifty thousand men slain this year in Europe – and not one an Englishman". Britain prospered and the Hanoverian dynasty was secured.

As an expression of gratitude, George II offered Walpole Number 10, Downing Street as a personal gift in 1732. He accepted the property, built by Sir George Downing in 1684, but only as a residence for the First Lord of the Treasury. It has been the official residence of the prime minister ever since.

He died aged sixty-nine and was buried at Houghton. The nursery rhyme, "Who Killed Cock Robin?" is said to refer to his fall from office, after misjudging the outcome of a vote of no confidence.

In 1779 Robert Walpole's superlative art collection was sold by his grandson to Empress Catherine II of Russia and it is now exhibited in the Hermitage museum in St Petersburg.

King George I by Sir Godfrey Kneller (c.1714)
National Portrait Gallery, London

THE HANOVERIAN SUCCESSION TO THE THRONES OF GREAT BRITAIN AND IRELAND (1714)

On 1 August 1714 George Louis (*Georg Ludwig* in German), Elector of Hanover, Queen Anne's second cousin, succeeded to the throne. Although over fifty people were closer in blood to Anne, the 1701 Act of Settlement barred Catholics from the throne. George (1660–1727) was her closest Protestant relation.

The "Glorious Revolution" had turned Britain and Ireland from an absolute into a constitutional monarchy: and British history was no longer closely intertwined with the reign of any monarch. Our history now turns to the people of these islands who shaped the modern world.

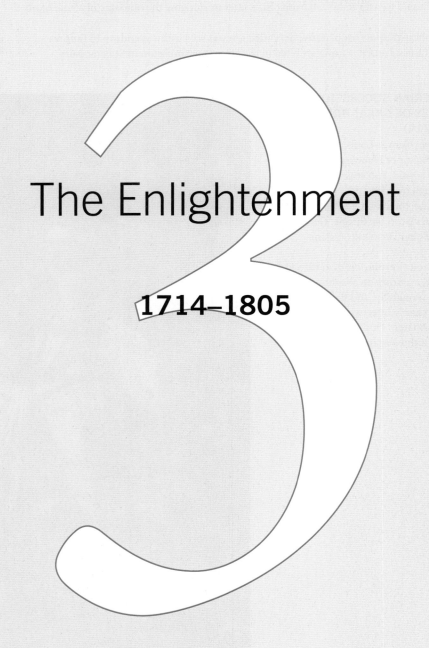

The Enlightenment

1714–1805

Horatio, Viscount Nelson

BRITAIN'S BRAVEST, MOST FAMOUS SAILOR

Horatio, Viscount Nelson by Sir William Beechey (1800)
National Portrait Gallery, London

Vice-Admiral Horatio, Viscount Nelson; Knight of the Bath; Baron Nelson of the Nile and of Burnham Thorpe; Baron Nelson of the Nile and Hilborough; Duke of Bronte, in the kingdom of Naples

Horatio Nelson was born at the rectory in Burnham Thorpe, Norfolk on 29 September 1758. He was the sixth of eleven children to Edmund and his wife Catherine, daughter of the Reverend Maurice Suckling. His father was the rector and the family was respectable and refined, but poor. Catherine was the great-niece of Robert Walpole, 1st Earl of Orford (1676–1745), Britain's first Prime minister.

Nelson, who preferred as a boy to be called Horace, was educated at schools in Norwich and North Walsham, before joining the Royal Navy in 1770. His mother died when he was nine but her brother Captain Maurice Suckling, who rose to become Comptroller of the Navy, offered to sponsor the young Nelson. This was a crucial connection: in the armed forces of the Crown during the 18th century, preferment was almost impossible without patronage.

Captain Suckling ensured that Nelson's early years were spent gainfully, first on his own ship, the 64-gun *Raisonnable* at Chatham and then in the West Indies attached to a merchantman. This was followed by an unsuccessful scientific expedition to the Arctic in 1773 – where he provoked an alarming confrontation with a polar bear (both were unhurt). He then went out to the East Indies and saw his first action; before he was struck down by a fever in 1776, almost certainly malaria, and invalided home.

As a consequence, Nelson suffered badly from depression and partial paralysis. The latter affected him intermittently for the rest of his life and exacerbated his incurable sea-sickness. Despite these chronic disorders, Nelson passed his lieutenant's exam in 1777. His uncle was President of the examining board.

Newly promoted, Nelson sailed to the West Indies as a lieutenant in the frigate *Lowestoffe*. The Caribbean had become a major theatre of war in the wake of France's support for the American colonists' Declaration of Independence in 1776. In 1779 he transferred to the frigate *Hinchingbrooke* and was promoted Captain at the precocious age of twenty. In January 1780, serving under Admirals Robert Digby and Samuel Hood (1724–1816), Nelson took command of a naval expedition against Spanish colonies in Nicaragua – now also an enemy, since Spain had sided with France and the American Revolutionaries. Nelson led a successful but ultimately pyrrhic attack against the capital San Juan. Yellow fever, rife in the West Indies, killed most of the British force.

Nelson himself was lucky to survive. His health broke down and, once again, he had to be invalided home.

In 1784 Nelson was offered command of the frigate *Boreas*, to impose the Navigation Act in the West Indies. The Act barred the newly independent American colonies from trading with British settlements. Nelson's zeal in enforcing it brought him swiftly into conflict with British traders, the Governor of the Leeward Islands and his Commander-in-Chief. Attempts made by the latter to court-martial him were deflected when Nelson petitioned both the Admiralty and King George III over his head. It was during 1787, a lonely and uncomfortable year spent on the island of Nevis, that he met and married the widow of the local doctor, Frances (known as Fanny) Nisbet. Fanny (1761–1831) brought with her a five year-old son Josiah, whom Nelson later sponsored into the Navy.

Now began Nelson's five years in the wilderness (1787–92), when he was obliged to linger unemployed on half pay at Burnham Thorpe. His officious application of the Navigation Act had embarrassed the Admiralty; and an exuberant association with the raffish midshipman, Prince William Henry (a lifelong friend, later King William IV) had upset King George. "I am aware of a prejudice at the Admiralty, evidently against me, which I can neither guess at, nor in the least account for", he wrote to a friend.

Nelson's frustrating exile was brought to an end by the execution of King Louis XVI of France and the start of the French Revolutionary Wars (1792–1801). In 1793 he was given command of the 64-gun *Agamemnon* and sailed with Lord Hood to the Mediterranean; where he was ordered to seek out and engage the French. He wrote from *Agamemnon*, ".... you must consider every man your enemy who speaks ill of your king .... and you must hate a Frenchman as you hate the devil". His first task was to assist in the defence of Toulon which was invested by the French Revolutionary army: included in its ranks was a twenty-four year-old artillery officer, Napoleon Buonaparte.

Reinforcements were urgently required and Nelson was sent to Naples to raise them: a city which Nelson, with some feeling, was later to describe as being "full of fiddlers and poets, whores and scoundrels". Nelson was given considerable help by Sir William Hamilton, who had been British Minister in Naples for thirty years – and his glamorous young wife Emma.

When Toulon finally fell to the Revolutionary army Lord Hood planned to move his operational headquarters to Corsica, having first captured the key ports of Bastia and Calvi, and to install Elliot as Viceroy. Nelson, while leading his ship's company in the attack on Calvi, was blinded in the right eye by stone splinters caused by a shell bursting on a parapet wall. Despite this debilitating injury, Nelson was on duty the following day. Though Nelson could only distinguish light from darkness thereafter, the eye appeared undamaged. Certainly he did not need, and never wore, an eye-patch.

In 1796 Admiral Sir John Jervis, later created Earl of St Vincent (1735–1823), was appointed Commander-in-Chief of the British Mediterranean Fleet.

A series of victories by the French army forced the British fleet to abandon its Mediterranean bases and withdraw to Gibraltar, ultimately to Lisbon. On 14 February 1797 the Spanish fleet, in the belief that Jervis had reached Lisbon when he was in fact just over the horizon, ventured out of Cádiz. Despite a superiority of twenty-seven ships over the British fifteen, Jervis savaged the Spaniards off Cape St Vincent, at the south-westernmost tip of Europe. The Spanish were sailing in two divisions. It was clear that the British ships could not be brought into action before the enemy closed up. Nelson, in the 74-gun *Captain* and entirely on his own initiative, instantly saw the danger this represented and hauled out of the line, to attack the second Spanish division head-on. For over an hour Nelson, with the help of his friend Cuthbert, later Vice-Admiral Lord Collingwood heroically kept the two Spanish squadrons apart, at one time engaging seven of their ships on his own.

During the battle Nelson took two valuable prizes. He rammed *San Nicolas* and then, by leading an attack across her decks, captured *San Josef* entangled on the other side. For this feat of arms Nelson was awarded a knighthood and the Cross of the Bath. In July 1797 he was promoted Rear Admiral. In his first command of a major independent force, he was sent to Santa Cruz in the Cape Verde Islands, to capture a Spanish treasure ship. The British force lost all elements of surprise and was severely mauled. Nelson was hit in the elbow by grapeshot, resulting in the amputation of his right arm.

By the spring of 1798 Nelson was fit enough to rejoin the Earl of St Vincent in the Mediterranean, where his small force was engaged in observing a French fleet embarking an expeditionary army. Never a great seaman, Nelson was suddenly struck by a violent north-westerly storm: his flagship, *Vanguard* lost her mast and his squadron was scattered. By the time

It was the Earl of St Vincent who said, when Britain had good cause to fear invasion in 1803, "I do not say the French cannot come. I only say they cannot come by sea".

Emma was born plain Amy Lyon at Nesse in the Wirral in Cheshire on 26 April 1765, the daughter of a blacksmith. After her father's early death she changed her name to Hart and moved to London. Her wild beauty and uninhibited reputation soon secured her a string of wealthy and aristocratic lovers. To two of them, one a naval captain and the other a baronet, she bore a child. Her colourful career as a fêted beauty included appearances in the salacious "Temple of Hygiea and Hymen", established by the notorious Scottish quack-doctor James Graham – a popular venue much visited by London society, including the Duchess of Devonshire and the Prince of Wales. Still only seventeen, she was solicited by the Hon. Charles Greville who established Emma as his mistress and her mother as his housekeeper.

George Romney (1734–1802) painted a dozen studies of Emma – making his reputation with depictions of her posing as the "Divine Lady".

• **Emma Hamilton as Circe by George Romney** (*c.*1782–86)
Tate, London

Orient was the flagship of Vice-Admiral François-Paul de Brueys, commander of the French fleet at the Battle of the Nile (1–2 August 1798). At 22:00, nearly three hours after his brave death, she blew up. Her captain, Luc-Julien-Joseph Casabianca may have detonated her powder magazine to avoid capture. Felicia Hemans's poem *Casabianca* ("The boy stood on the burning deck") was written about his twelve year old son Giocante. He remained at his post, despite all the guns being abandoned, and perished in the explosion.

Nelson's coffin was carved out of *Orient's* mainmast.

• **Battle of the Nile (1834) by Thomas Luny (1759–1837)**

Sir William Hamilton (1730–1803), grandson of the 3rd Duke of Hamilton, was a professional diplomat and gifted antiquary. He had been British minister in Naples (the second largest city in Europe after Paris) since 1764. Knighted in 1772, his wife had died childless in 1782. He was introduced to Emma by his nephew Charles Greville in 1784. The meeting was timely for all concerned and a convenient bargain was struck swiftly. Greville, wishing to marry an heiress, required both money and instant respectability. He offered Emma to his uncle who, in exchange, settled his estate on his nephew.

Emma, oblivious to this tidy arrangement, was only twenty-one when she arrived in Naples, in the expectation that Greville would shortly come out to fetch her. She soon realised that this was not going to happen; but Hamilton was a decent and humane man and Emma settled happily enough into the richly diverse Neopolitan life which swirled around the British Embassy. Sir William adored his young and vivacious mistress; but was unable to present her at court as a single woman. In 1791 they married. As Sir William was sixty-one and Emma twenty-six, Sir William was aware from the start of the high risk of being cuckolded – famously summed up by the contemporary satirist John Wolcott:

Knight of Naples, is it come to pass,
  That thou hast left the Gods of stone and brass
To wed a deity of flesh and blood?
    O lock the temple with thy strongest key,
For fear thy deity, a comely She,
    Should one day ramble, in a frolic mood!

---

he was able to reassemble his ships, having first carried out repairs at San Pietro in Sardinia, the French fleet was well on its way to Egypt. After a fruitless search Nelson put into Syracuse in Sicily in June, where at last he discovered the enemy's destination. On 1 August he found his quarry at anchor in Abu Qir Bay, near Alexandria. Immediately he ordered an audacious night attack saying, "Before this time tomorrow, I shall have gained a peerage or Westminster Abbey".

Nelson's fleet was inferior in numbers but, by attacking unexpectedly through shoals at the weather end of a breeze blowing down the line of the French fleet, fires started by his initial assault engulfed many of the other French ships. In the morning, after eight hours of heavy fighting in which the great French flagship *Orient* blew up, the enemy lay virtually annihilated. Only two of their thirteen warships managed to cut their cables and escape.

The significance of this remarkable victory was immeasurable. Napoleon's army of Egypt was now cut off from France and no longer a threat to British India.

Nelson had received a nasty head wound in the battle and repaired to Naples, the nearest convenient port to refit. He was given a rapturous welcome from King Ferdinand, Queen Caroline, Sir William Hamilton and most significantly, his wife Emma.

Queen Caroline (Maria Carolina), whom Napoleon once described "as the only man in Naples", was a sister of the executed Queen Marie Antoinette of France. Both were Habsburg princesses married to Bourbons. Her brother Leopold was Emperor of Austria. Emma Hamilton had become the close confidante of Caroline and found herself at the centre of the political dramas engulfing the Kingdom of the Two Sicilies.

Nelson was raised to the peerage, as Baron Nelson of the Nile and Burnham Thorpe and appointed Military Adviser to the court of Ferdinand I, King of the Two Sicilies. Parliament voted him £2,000 a year

(£1.7 million today), the East India Company gave him £10,000 and Ferdinand made him Duke of Bronte (a district west of Mount Etna in Sicily). In spite of this, Nelson's sojourn in Naples was now marked by both military disaster and personal controversy.

Nelson advised Ferdinand to recapture Rome from the French. The result was a humiliating defeat for the shaky Neapolitan army led by the obese Austrian Karl Mack (1752–1828), to whom Nelson took an instant dislike: "General Mack cannot move without five carriages". A brusque counter-attack by the French led to the occupation of Naples; and King Ferdinand fled to Palermo in Sicily. In 1799 however, with the assistance of Nelson's fleet, Naples was recaptured.

At this point Nelson suddenly displayed the ugly side to his nature that had previously manifested itself on *Boreas* in 1774. A short lived, French-incited Jacobin rebellion had been extinguished by the monarchist Cardinal Ruffo, who favoured lenient treatment of the rebels. Queen Caroline and Nelson took the view that the rebels should be severely punished. The defeated rebels believed they were protected by a truce when they began to evacuate Naples by sea. Nelson's sailors captured them and, on Nelson's orders, 99 were hanged – including Prince Caracciolo, previously Commodore of the Neapolitan navy. He had fled with King Ferdinand to Palermo but subsequently returned to Naples to join the rebel cause. Nelson tried him by drumhead court martial. The prince was allowed neither defence counsel nor to call witnesses. Turning down his request to be shot as an officer and gentleman, Nelson hanged him from the yardarm of a man-of-war – refusing him even a priest. This little publicised act earned Nelson censure from the House of Commons, for committing an unnecessary and degrading act of vengeance. At the same time Nelson began a very public relationship with Emma Hamilton, exposing himself to jibe and criticism at home, much to the displeasure of the Admiralty.

Napoleon escaped from Egypt on 8 August 1799. Admiral George Elphinstone, soon to become Viscount Keith (1746–1823), had replaced the Earl of St Vincent as Commander-in-Chief in the Mediterranean. He became convinced that the French, who still occupied Malta, would make an attempt on Minorca and ordered Nelson to proceed there immediately with all his ships to thwart them. But Nelson, a peevish subordinate, refused: arguing that the real threat was directed at Naples. Events later proved him right; but such a brazen refusal to obey orders, and strong disapproval of his acceptance of the Dukedom of Bronte, provoked an exasperated Admiralty into recalling him. Nelson chose to return to Britain overland, with the Hamiltons. "It is melancholy", noted Sir John Moore who met the party at Leghorn, "to see a brave and good man, who has deserved well of his country, cutting so pitiful a figure".

Unwisely but perhaps understandably, in the adulation and aftermath of battle, with Emma bathing his head wound and feeding him asses' milk, Nelson wrote home to his wife Fanny, "She is one of the very best women in the world .... she is an honour to her sex and a proof that even reputation can be regained, but I own it requires a great soul". At this time it is well recorded that Emma liked to wear around the Embassy thin muslin skirts unfettered by stays, petticoats or knickers. Despite continuous close contact following the battle of the Nile, recent research has revealed that it was fully eighteen months, much later than previously suspected, before Nelson and Emma became lovers.

Nelson's letters of this period (Emma kept them all, despite an agreement with Nelson to destroy them) show a strong and explicit physical undercurrent: "In one of my dreams, I thought I was at a large table .... sitting between a Princess whom I detest and another. They both tried to seduce me and the first wanted to take those liberties with me which no woman in this world but yourself ever did". Later in the same dream he imagined that Emma wispered [sic] "I kissed you fervently and we enjoyed the height of love. No love is like mine toward you". Again, "What must be my sensations at the idea of sleeping with you! It setts [sic] me on fire, even the thoughts much more the reality. I am sure my love and desires are all to you, and if any woman naked were to come to me, even as I am at this moment from thinking of you, I hope it might rott [sic] off if I would touch her even with my hand". In another letter he says he could be " trusted with fifty virgins in a dark room".

Horatia married the Reverend Philip Ward and had nine children: the eldest was named Horatio Nelson. She died in 1881. As Nelson had no legitimate heir, the Viscountcy and 1798 Barony of the Nile and Burnham Thorpe became extinct. The 1801 Barony of the Nile and Hilborough however, passed by special remainder to his brother, the Reverend William Nelson. He was also created Earl Nelson and awarded £99,000 (£68 million today) with a £5,000 annual pension (£3.4 million) in recognition of his brother's services. This title is still extant. Nelson's wife Fanny, received a pension of £2,000 a year (£1.4 million). Emma and Horatia were ignored.

In 1801 Nelson instructed Emma to buy Merton Place, a fine house near London. Emma purchased it for £9,000 (£6.9 million today); and moved into it with Nelson and her ever compliant husband, shortly before Sir William's death. She and Nelson were both at his bedside when he died on 6 April 1803.

The day before Nelson left Emma for the last time, they exchanged rings in a form of marriage service – and took communion together in the church at Merton.

Sir Gilbert Elliot, now Lord Minto remembered his meeting Emma and Nelson in March 1802 (Life and Letters): "The whole establishment and way of life is such as to make me angry .... nothing shall ever induce me to give the smallest countenance to Lady Hamilton .... she is high in looks, but more immense than ever. She goes on cramming Nelson with trowelfuls of flattery, which he goes on taking as quietly as a child does pap. The love she makes to him is not only ridiculous, but disgusting".

Nelson was widely criticised for supporting the notoriously corrupt Bourbons. It was thought that he was putting his own interests, his relationships with the Bourbons and Emma Hamilton, before his duty to Britain's longer-term policy in the region. The Admiralty however, now had to handle Nelson, the nation's hero, with care.

When this odd little *ménage à trois* finally reached England in November 1800 it was clear that the British public regarded Nelson as a hero. His progress to London was triumphal. Shortly after, Nelson met his wife Fanny for the last time.

Unconscious of any irony, in the light of his subsequent partying in Naples, he had earlier written to her: "Duty is the great business of a sea officer; all private considerations must give way to it, however painful it may be". There can be no doubt of his sincerity.

In January 1801 the Admiralty swallowed its pride and promoted Nelson to Vice-Admiral. He was appointed second-in-command to Admiral Sir Hyde Parker (aged sixty-one and newly married to an eighteen year-old girl), who was fitting out an expedition to compel the Danes, now allied to France, to re-open the Baltic to British trade. Sweden was a vital source of timber, tar and other naval stores. Just before his departure Emma Hamilton gave birth to his daughter Horatia. In March Nelson wrote to her, "Now my own dear wife, for such you are in my eyes and in the face of heaven".

On arrival off Copenhagen, Nelson's advice was not sought; but once battle was engaged and Danish resistance stiffened he was able to write, "Now we are sure of fighting, I am sent for". Nelson's strategy was brilliant: to avoid the shore batteries protecting the northern approaches to Copenhagen, he used the ships in his fleet with the shallowest draught to navigate a difficult channel. The next day, 1 April 1801 his squadron attacked the Danish fleet which put up a fierce resistance. In the middle of the engagement Sir Hyde Parker signalled Nelson to retire, believing him to be outgunned. Famously, Nelson raised his telescope to his blind eye, declaring that he had seen nothing, "I have only one eye, I have a right to be blind sometimes .... I really do not see the signal". An hour later the Danish fleet surrendered, having suffered 6,000 casualties at a cost of only a few hundred British lives. An armistice followed which, on the murder of Tsar Paul of Russia, was upgraded into a permanent peace.

When he returned to Britain Nelson was created a Viscount, succeeded Hyde Parker as Commander-in-Chief and was given a home command: responsible for defending the channel coast against an invasion by the army that Napoleon was assembling at Boulogne. On 10 October 1801 however, Britain and France signed an armistice.

In May 1803 the Treaty of Amiens was abandoned. War with France was renewed – and a little later, with Spain. Nelson was given command in the Mediterranean and raised his standard in the 104-gun ship HMS *Victory*. At the end of the year Emma had another daughter, who died soon after – Nelson did not hear of this for some months.

For eighteen months Nelson blockaded Toulon and bottled up a large French fleet commanded by Admiral Pierre Villeneuve. The aim was to prevent the French from joining the Spanish fleet in Cádiz and Cartagena – and especially to prevent it from then combining with the rest of the French navy in Brest. Villeneuve however, planned first to draw the British fleet over to the West Indies: to attack it there, return across the Atlantic and then turn on the pursuing British off the western approaches. He hoped that this would enable Napoleon's invasion army of 350,000 men to cross the Channel unmolested, to invade Britain.

In March 1805 Villeneuve slipped out of Toulon, evaded the British and crossed the Atlantic to Martinique – where he hoped to be joined by the French fleet from Brest. Nelson, ignorant of Villeneuve's plans, took six weeks to discover where he had gone, but made up half that delay in swift pursuit. Villeneuve however, unnerved by news of Nelson's impending arrival, had already decided to return to Europe. On the homeward leg Nelson, unaware that he had overtaken Villeneuve and fearing that the two French fleets would combine off Brest, strongly reinforced the western approaches. He also took the opportunity briefly to come ashore. It was the last time he saw Britain.

Two weeks later word came that Villeneuve, demoralised after an inconclusive engagement against Sir Robert Calder on 22 July, off Ferrol in northern Spain, had retired to Cádiz. In September Nelson resumed his command: to move against the fleet of thirty-four French and Spanish battleships that were blockaded in Cádiz harbour by a squadron under the command of his great friend Cuthbert Collingwood (1748–1810). Collingwood used false signals to disguise just how small his squadron was.

"I believe my arrival was most welcome, not only to the commander of the Fleet but almost to every individual in it; and when I came to explain the "Nelson touch", it was like an electric shock. Some shed tears, all approved – it was new, it was singular, it was simple", wrote Nelson on rejoining Collingwood, one of his "Band of Brothers".

On 29 September (his forty-seventh birthday) Nelson dined with fifteen of his captains on his flagship *Victory*. He unveiled his plan to bring about a "pell-mell battle", in which superior Royal Navy gunnery and aggression

It remains a mystery why Napoleon, so determined to avenge "six centuries of shame and insult" from England, failed to take advantage of a new technology that had been demonstrated to him. He had heard of Symington's steamboat *Charlotte Dundas* from the American Robert Fulton who built one of his own to exhibit on the Seine. On 9 August 1803 this boat navigated the Seine successfully, at over 3 mph against the current, in front of a large crowd of Parisians. Steam-powered tugs had been developed by Symington since 1788; and Fulton knew him well.

It seems extraordinary that Napoleon did not order fifty steam tugs, to tow the invasion barges that had already been built and were waiting in Boulogne for an opportunity to cross the Channel without interception by the Royal Navy. On a few calm days without a wind, the soldiers of *L'Armée de Bretagne* might have been transported to Britain, whilst sailing ships would have been literally powerless to intervene.

When Fulton suggested this to Napoleon, he was rebuffed with the words, "What Sir, would you make a ship sail against the wind and currents by lighting a bonfire under its deck? I pray you excuse me, I have no time to listen to such nonsense".

In fact Napoleon did not wait for Villeneuve to outmanoeuvre Nelson. As soon as he heard that Villeneuve had run for Cádiz after the action off Ferrol in July, he started to move his Army away from Boulogne. He marched 200,000 men from the army he had assembled to invade Britain across the Rhine on 25 September; and forced the Austrian General Mack (Nelson's *bête noire*) to capitulate at Ulm on 20 October – just one day before Trafalgar.

In August Lord Minto "met Nelson today in a mob in Piccadilly .... it is really quite affecting to see the wonder and admiration, love and respect of the whole world; and the genuine expression of all those sentiments at once, from gentle and simple, the moment he is seen. It is beyond anything represented in a play or a poem of fame".

Collingwood left Britain in 1803. His health, already poor prior to Trafalgar, seemed afterwards entirely to fail and he repeatedly requested to be relieved of his command in the Mediterranean. However the government requested him to remain, stating that his country could not dispense with his services. He died of cancer aged fifty-nine, off Port Mahon on 7 March 1810, having never once returned home.

would be decisive. Nelson would advance on the Franco-Spanish fleet at right angles in two divisions, break their line into three, rendering the leading third unable to turn-about or intervene in the battle. He intended to destroy each half of the rest of the enemy fleet separately – in a rejection of the rigid 18th century tradition of engaging an enemy fleet in an extended, parallel line of battle. While the British ships approached the allied fleet however, they would be exposed to the full fire of the enemy, with no means of firing back.

The payback would come when the British warships passed broadside-on to the vulnerable enemy transoms, able to rake the flanks of their ships from stern to bow with murderous fire. This would be far more effective than laying ships beam to beam and slugging it out broadside for broadside.

With his fleet continuously at sea for years on end, Nelson sent ships regularly to Gibraltar for repair and provisioning. His captains however, fearful of missing action, were reluctant to go. Six ships-of-the-line left for Gibraltar in mid-October reducing the British fleet to twenty-two. Villeneuve, now with thirty-three ships, believed the odds had swung in his favour: and, aware that his own replacement had already left Madrid, he decided on the 20 October to run for the Straits of Gibraltar and back to Toulon.

Happily, Nelson had been reinforced by five ships which had been watering on the Moroccan coast: raising the number in his fleet to twenty-seven. Resisting the temptation immediately to engage the enemy, as urged by Collingwood, Nelson decided to use the whole of the next day to fight the battle. That night, dining with his midshipmen he said, "Tomorrow I will do that which will give you younger gentlemen something to talk about for the rest of your lives. But I shall not live to know about it myself".

The next day, 21 October 1805, off Cape Trafalgar Nelson hoisted the most famous naval signal in history, "England expects *that* every man *will* do his duty".

The British fleet, sailing at barely three knots, slowly bore down on the enemy, taking at great cost the full brunt of fire they could not return. Strenuous attempts were made by Nelson's officers to reduce their Admiral's exposure to danger. Nelson however, refused to transfer his flag to another ship or to haul back *Victory* from point position.

On crossing the French line *Victory* was soon engaged by three French ships, her decks raked with broadsides and with sharpshooters firing directly down from the enemy mastheads. Nelson's secretary, John Scott was pulped by a cannon ball and heaved over the side. A file of eight marines was cut down by another ball; and the buckle was torn from Captain Hardy's shoe by a huge splinter as he paced the quarter-deck with his admiral. Nelson wore a shabby 'undress' uniform, with sequined facsimile medals. In the murk and smoke of battle, he did not present an especially clear or obvious target: but at 13:15 he was hit by a musket ball fired from the mizzen-top of *Redoubtable.* It pierced his collarbone, shattered his spine and lodged in his lung.

Sergeant Secker of the Royal Marines and two seamen took Nelson below, where he was attended by

Rear-Admiral Sir Horatio Nelson by Lemuel Abbott (1760–1802)
National Maritime Museum, London

Gibraltar is still a British crown colony, with a population of nearly 30,000 in 2010. It is a 2.5 square mile narrow, rocky peninsula extending into the Mediterranean Sea from south-east Spain. Most of the peninsula comprises the Rock of Gibraltar, one of the "Pillars of Hercules", which guards the north-eastern end of the Strait of Gibraltar, linking the Mediterranean with the Atlantic, and provides a safe, enclosed harbour of 440 acres. The rock is honeycombed with roads, defence works and arsenals, which are largely concealed. A tunnel bisects the rock from east to west.

The name Gibraltar derives from the Arabic *Jabal-al-Tarik* (mount of Tarik), dating from the capture of the peninsula by the Moorish general Tarik in 711. The Spanish held the peninsula from 1309–33, but did not secure it until 1462. The British captured it in 1704 and have maintained possession ever since, despite continual Spanish claims. The British post was besieged unsuccessfully by the Spanish and French in 1704; by the Spanish in 1726; and again by the Spanish (who sided with the American colonists in order to recover it) and French in 1779–83.

Gibraltar has been a naval base of immense strategic value to Britain for 305 years, 63 years longer than it was ever owned by Spain. It has never been of more critical importance than in the Napoleonic Wars, when it guarded the door to the Mediterranean and its dockyard provisioned and maintained the Royal Navy.

The Battle of Trafalgar by Joseph Mallord William Turner (1822–24)
National Maritime Museum, Greenwich

A map of the Battle: the British are coloured red: the enemy, blue and yellow

Surgeon William Beatty. Nelson covered his face with a handkerchief so that the men should not see that he was dying.

Mortally wounded, Nelson continued to command his fleet while lying against a massive timber, deep down on the orlop (lowest) deck. He realised from the rising swell that a storm was fast approaching and he sent orders to his second-in-command, Collingwood to anchor the fleet so that the prizes could be secured. At about 15:30, Hardy was able to report to his admiral that fifteen of the enemy had struck their colours.

Hardy visited him several times and Nelson asked that he should not be thrown overboard. Shortly before he died he said, "Kiss me Hardy" and a moment later, "Now I am satisfied. Thank God I have done my duty .... God bless you Hardy". He reminded Hardy that he was leaving Lady Hamilton and his daughter Horatia as a legacy to his country; and repeated, "Thank God I have done my duty". Hot and thirsty, while his chaplain massaged his chest to ease the pain, his last words were to his steward: "Drink, drink. Fan, fan. Rub, rub". He died, fully aware of the scale of his victory, at 16:30.

The leading enemy ships had sailed out of the battle and on to Cádiz. Four of these were subsequently captured in the Bay of Biscay by Admiral Strachan. Seventeen of the remainder were taken and one was burned. British (30% of the seamen and five of the twenty-seven captains were Scots) casualties in the battle were 449 dead and 1,241 wounded. The French and Spanish lost 4,408 dead and 2,545 wounded. Regrettably, Collingwood never received the order to anchor the fleet. By the time the implications of the worsening weather were obvious, all but four prizes were lost.

The bullet that killed Nelson is permanently on display in Windsor Castle. The uniform that he wore during the battle, with the fatal bullet hole still visible, can be seen at the National Maritime Museum in Greenwich. A lock of Nelson's hair was given to the Imperial Japanese Navy by the Royal Navy after the Russo-Japanese war, to commemorate the Battle of Tsushima in 1905. It is exhibited at Kyouiku Sankoukan, a public museum maintained by the Japan Self-Defence Forces.

The victorious Japanese Admiral, Count Heihachiro Togo so admired the Royal Navy and Nelson that he delayed his fleet's return home after Tsushima until he could do so on the hundredth anniversary of the Battle of Trafalgar, 21 October 1905.

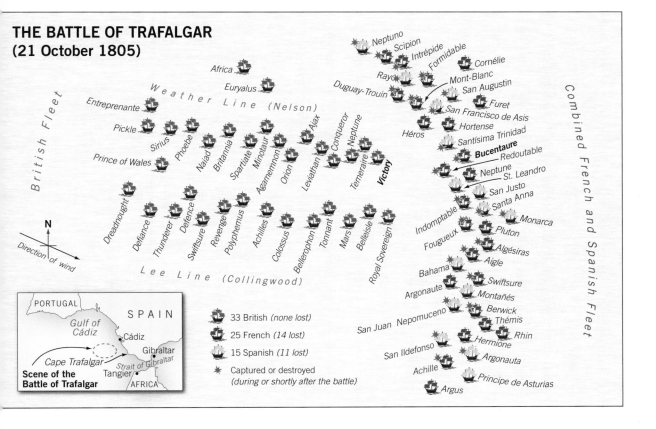

THE BATTLE OF TRAFALGAR
(21 October 1805)

Weather Line (Nelson)

Lee Line (Collingwood)

British Fleet

Combined French and Spanish Fleet

Direction of wind

N

Africa
Euryalus
Entreprenante
Pickle
Sirius
Phoebe
Naiad
Britannia
Spartiate
Minotaur
Agamemnon
Orion
Leviathan
Ajax
Conqueror
Neptune
Temeraire
Victory
Prince of Wales
Dreadnought
Defiance
Thunderer
Defence
Swiftsure
Revenge
Polyphemus
Achilles
Colossus
Bellerophon
Tonnant
Mars
Belleisle
Royal Sovereign

Neptuno
Scipion
Intrépide
Formidable
Cornélie
Rayo
Mont-Blanc
Duguay-Trouin
San Augustin
San Francisco de Asis
Furet
Hortense
Héros
Santísima Trinidad
Bucentaure
Redoutable
Neptune
St. Leandro
San Justo
Santa Anna
Indomptable
Monarca
Fougueux
Pluton
Algésiras
Aigle
Bahama
Swiftsure
Argonaute
Montañés
Berwick
Thémis
San Juan Nepomuceno
Rhin
Hermione
San Ildefonso
Argonauta
Achille
Principe de Asturias
Argus

PORTUGAL
Gulf of Cádiz
SPAIN
Cádiz
Gibraltar
Cape Trafalgar
Strait of Gibraltar
Tangier
AFRICA
Scene of the Battle of Trafalgar

🚢 33 British (none lost)

🚢 25 French (14 lost)

🚢 15 Spanish (11 lost)

✳ Captured or destroyed (during or shortly after the battle)

The death of their admiral hit the fleet hard. Captain Fremantle wrote of the effect on Collingwood, "the poor man does not own his mind five minutes together"; and Nelson's chaplain Doctor Alexander Scott, "was stupid with grief for what I have lost". A boatswain's mate was unable to pipe the men to quarters: "hang me, I can't do it. To lose him now! I wouldn't have cared if it had been my old father, or my brothers or sisters if there were fifty of them – but I can't think of parting with Nelson".

"A seaman's friend and father of the fleet", wrote one of his junior officers. A literate seaman from *Royal Sovereign* recorded, "We have paid pretty sharply for licking them. I never set eyes on him, for which I am both sorry and glad – for to be sure, I should have liked to have seen him. But then, all the men in our ships who have seen him are such soft toads, they have done nothing but blast their eyes and cry ever since he was killed".

Grief for the loss of their hero far exceeded any feelings of elation for the great victory which had secured Britain against the long threat of invasion. The public response was sombre. The King was made speechless and people wept openly in the streets.

IN MEMORIAM

Nelson was an uncomplicated, extremely religious man. He was energetic, shrewd, innovative, flexible and brave beyond imagination. He was also insecure, anxious to please, naive, generous and loving. From every account of Nelson's life, events seem to point to the inevitability of an heroic death at the climax of victory.

However reckless his behaviour though, there is little to suggest that he ever sought martyrdom. He strove only for glory. "A glorious death is to be envied", he had written on 10 March 1795: it would earn the approbation of those he served – and even more, of his fellow officers and the seamen under his command. But he was a realist and knew the risks he ran: and they were calculated. He had an actor's awareness of image, drama, timing and good lines. His behaviour in Naples was abhorrent, but out of character. Perhaps his judgement was skewed by love, his loins or his head wound.

There is however, a line to be drawn between Nelson's private life and his public service. His cruel parting from Fanny and the public display of his affair with Emma disgusted the King and Establishment: who, even in those lax times, wholeheartedly condemned and rejected his behaviour. Despite a once-close friendship, the Earl of St Vincent and 18 other admirals refused to attend his funeral. Emma was left to squander her inheritance and to die forgotten in cheap Calais lodgings, a hopeless and penniless alcoholic; and Horatia was pointedly ignored. In contrast, the public service which Nelson rendered his country is commemorated still: as the quintessential example of a British hero whose courage and leadership have resounded for over 200 years.

It is a dark thought to contemplate Nelson's future and reputation had he not triumphed at Trafalgar; and had he not been picked off in his finest moment by a mizzen-top marksman in the shrouds of *Redoutable* – securing him the immortality he craved.

Fragments of Nelson's last letter from Victory to Lady Hamilton, on 19 October 1805. It was written with his left hand – unpunctuated and vivid, as though he was speaking.

NELSON WAS BURIED IN ST PAUL'S CATHEDRAL
ON 9 JANUARY 1806

Victory anchored off Portsmouth on 4 December 1805, with Nelson's body on board. She then sailed to the Nore at the mouth of the Thames; where the corpse was placed in an iron coffin to be taken to Greenwich Hospital. From the moment the news of Nelson's death reached Britain, "Men started at the intelligence and turned pale as if they had heard of the death of a dear friend", said the poet Robert Southey. Elaborate arrangements, under the auspices of the Garter King at Arms, Sir Isaac Heard were set in hand for the first state funeral ever accorded to a commoner.

A mahogany coffin had been fashioned from the mainmast of the French battleship *Orient*. Together with its elaborate outer shell, it measured 6 feet 8 inches by 26 inches, weighed one ton

Winston Churchill believed that Alexander Korda's 1942 film *Lady Hamilton* was worth four divisions to the nation's morale in the gloomy days of WWII.

Six other commoners have had full *state* (as opposed to *ceremonial*) funerals: the Duke of Wellington, Lord Palmerston, W.E. Gladstone, Lord Roberts VC, Earl Haig and and Sir Winston Churchill.

and was made by a Mr Chittenden at a cost of £800 (£546,000 today). The undertakers, France and Banting (still conducting business as Albert France & Son, today in Monmouth Street) displayed the empty outer coffin at their premises in Pall Mall. Motif panels emblazoned on the exterior surfaces commemorated each of Nelson's campaigns.

Great pains were taken to ensure that Nelson's severe wounds were hidden from the eyes of family mourners because, in the understated words of Thomas Banting, "Lord Nelson had really suffered for his country".

A public outcry fanned by the Press broke out when it was discovered that no plans had been made to include the sailors of *Victory* in the funeral arrangements. At the same time the Prince of Wales had a furious row with his father King George III, who refused to let his son attend the funeral in his official capacity. The Prince eventually paid his respects as a private citizen. Neither Lady Nelson nor Lady Hamilton were expected at the service, which was the custom of the day.

Nelson's body lay in state from 5–7 January 1806 in the Painted Hall at Greenwich Hospital, surrounded by the trophies and captured colours of his many naval encounters. The first mourner was the Prince of Wales, who spent an hour alone by Nelson's catafalque before the doors were thrown open to the thousands thronging outside to pay their respects. On 8 January Nelson's body was conveyed in a grand river procession up the Thames to Whitehall Stairs and thence to the Admiralty where it passed the night in the Captain's Room. City of London Livery companies

The Death of Nelson at the Battle of Trafalgar. From the Original wall painting in the Palace of Westminster by Charles William Sharpe after Daniel Maclise (published 1874)
National Portrait Gallery, London

Nelson's body was preserved first in a cask of French brandy, said to have been taken from a prize at Trafalgar. This was changed to spirits of wine at Gibraltar. The cask was lashed to the mainmast and guarded day and night by a marine sentry, as his cabin had been. Sailors are supposed to have used straws of macaroni, inserted through holes drilled in the barrel, to syphon off the liquor – the origin of the expression "tapping the Admiral", i.e: stealing drink. However, since the spirits had been mixed with camphor and myrrh it seems unlikely, in this instance at least.

supplied a flotilla of magnificently gilded barges. The richly decorated barge bearing Nelson, originally made for Charles II, was covered in black velvet while his body had been placed upon a platform in the stern, under a canopy of black ostrich plumes.

On 9 January Nelson set out on his last journey, conveyed in an ornate funeral car (a replica of *Victory*) and attended by 31 admirals and 100 captains. It was hung with his trophies and escorted by Greenwich pensioners, Nelson's brother officers and members of *Victory*'s crew. Forty-eight sailors from *Victory* carried her ensign. So long was the procession that by the time the head of the *cortège* had reached St Paul's Cathedral Nelson's hearse had not left Whitehall. Nelson's remains reached St Paul's at 16:00 and it was nearly dark. A giant chandelier of over 130 lanterns was suspended inside Sir Christopher Wren's great dome, together with the standards and colours of captured French and Spanish warships. Nelson was borne up the nave to the high altar followed by his closest male relations, including his nephew George Matcham who remarked, "It was the most aweful *[sic]* sight I ever saw".

A service of evensong followed, with a specially composed Grand Dirge. The coffin then sank slowly into a sarcophagus, carved originally for Cardinal Wolsey nearly 300 years earlier, in the crypt below. The Chief Herald read out Nelson's full list of titles followed by the declaration, "the hero who in the moment of victory, fell covered with immortal glory". The officers of Nelson's household then broke their staves which were placed in the crypt. At this point the sailors from *Victory* were expected to fold up her ensign and place it on a table before it too was interred with Nelson. Without warning, the sailors tore it up and distributed the pieces amongst themselves, each to place a fragment inside his shirt – a simple and spontaneous gesture of homage.

Nelson's magnificent tomb dominates the crypt directly beneath the dome of St Paul's. Many other sailors have since joined him close by – including his old friend, comrade in arms and second-in-command at Trafalgar, Vice-Admiral Cuthbert Collingwood. Every year a special service is held at St Paul's on the Sunday nearest Trafalgar Day.

HMS VICTORY

On 13 December 1758, precisely 75 days after Nelson's birth, the Board of Admiralty ordered the construction of 12 line-of-battle warships, including one 100-gun 'first-rate'. The Royal Navy commissioned only ten ships of this size in the whole of the 18th century. She was designed by Sir Thomas Slade (1704–71), Surveyor of the Royal Navy. Later named *Victory*, to commemorate *Annus Mirabilis* or the Year of Victories, her keel was laid at No. 2 Dock, Chatham Dockyard on 23 July 1759 and launched on 7 May 1765, at a cost of £63,176 and 3 shillings (£90 million today).

HMS Victory

Victory was 227 feet long, 51 feet 10 inches wide with a draught averaging 24 feet. Her masthead was 220 feet above the sea. She used 27 miles of cordage, had a sail area of 4 acres and carried 38 tons of iron ballast to the port side, to stabilise her trim. Her hull was 2 feet thick at the waterline; she displaced 3,500 tons; had a complement of around 850 (at Trafalgar it was 663 men and officers, the youngest aged ten); and, due to her excellent underwater lines, could exceed 9 knots in perfect conditions.

As Britain was then at peace, *Victory* was placed 'in ordinary' (without masts and roofed over) and moored in the River Medway for thirteen years – until France joined the American Revolution in 1778. She was then completed and fitted out with 100 guns. Later she would carry two carronades, firing 68 pound round shot (known as 'ship smashers'), and two 12-pounders on her forecastle.

In March 1780 her hull was sheathed with 3,923 sheets of copper to protect it against shipworm. In 1796 she became the flagship of Admiral Sir John Jervis. She was in her first decisive action at Cape St Vincent the following year. After the battle she was moored in the river Medway as a hospital ship for wounded prisoners of war.

From 1800–03 *Victory* underwent substantial rebuilding at Chatham Dockyard, at a cost of £70,993 (nothing much changes – the original estimate was £23,500), a further £55 million today. Extra gun ports were added, taking her from 100 guns to 104.

Nelson hoisted his ensign in *Victory* on 16 May 1803, to assume command in the Mediterranean. In July his new flag-captain, Thomas Masterman Hardy came aboard.

After Trafalgar *Victory* took part in two campaigns in the Baltic, before ending her active career on 7 November 1812. She was then moored in Portsmouth Harbour, as a depot ship; and finally a signal school, until 1906.

It is said that, when he was First Sea Lord, on returning home Thomas Hardy (1769–1839) told his wife that he had just signed an order for *Victory* to be broken up. She burst into tears and sent him straight back to his office to rescind the order. True or not, the page of the duty log containing his orders for that day has been torn out.

Having slowly deteriorated at her moorings, a campaign to save her was successful: on 12 January 1922 *Victory* was moved into the oldest dry-dock in the world, No. 2 Dock at Portsmouth. In 1928 King George V unveiled a tablet celebrating completion of the work. She underwent further restoration to mark the bicentenary of the battle of Trafalgar in 2005.

HMS *Victory* is the world's only existing 18th century ship-of-the-line and is the oldest warship still in service. She is the flagship of the Second Sea Lord, Commander-in- Chief Naval Home Command – and attracts around 350,000 visitors each year.

An oak had to have usable cuts 80 feet long and at least 20 inches thick to build a large ship. The sternpost of a ship-of-the-line was 40 feet long and 28 inches thick. Tall, forest-grown oaks, plentiful in Sweden, were required for shell-built Viking boats, which were 90% planks and only 10% frame timber. Ships-of-the-line were skeleton-built: 75% frame timber, 15% thick-stuff to stabilise the frame and only 10% planking, to cover the sides and the frame. Huge oaks, with branches up to ninety feet long at right angles to the trunk, grown in the open were

---

2,000 oaks (60 acres of century-old trees), comprising over 3,000 loads, were felled to build *Victory*; with elm used for her keel and decks and pine for her masts. 20 miles was the furthest a load could be hauled by oxen and horses, to the nearest waterway for final delivery to the dockyard by sea – the origin of the phrase "in for the long haul".

The Carron Ironworks, which developed the carronade for the Royal Navy, was established in Falkirk by two Englishmen in 1759. William Symington (1764–1831), the company's chief engineer, built the world's first practical steamboat, the *Charlotte Dundas* at Grangemouth in 1803. On 28 March she towed two barges of 80 and 50 tons for 18 miles into Glasgow, in just over 9 hours. Carron Ironworks traded profitably for 223 years, until it was closed in 1982.

Portsmouth is home to another two of the most famous ships ever built: Henry VIII's *Mary Rose*, which sank in 1545 and was raised in 1982 to a worldwide audience of over 60 million; and HMS *Warrior*, built in 1860, as the world's first iron-hulled armoured battleship, propelled by sail and steam.

HM Prison Dartmoor, at Princetown in Devonshire, was built between 1806–09 to hold prisoners of the Napoleonic Wars, mostly French seamen. 4,799 were brought back to Britain while many others were simply dumped in neutral ports.

In 1914 Kaiser Wilhelm II signed the order to mobilise the German army on a table made of oak from *Victory*, with a stand for stationery flying Nelson's famous signal.

now needed; and only their girth limited the size of the ships that could be built. Oak was never bent or stressed: all joints and knuckles had to be cut in conformity with the shape of the living tree.

The English had taken a lead in shipbuilding before the defeat of the Spanish Armada in 1588; and the British held on to it for most of the next 350 years. The "wooden walls of England", made from *Quercus Robur* (the 'English Oak'), were never breached.

THE MODERN UNION FLAG WAS FIRST FLOWN IN BATTLE AT TRAFALGAR

James VI of Scotland inherited the throne of England as James I of England in 1603. On 12 April 1606 a new flag to represent this personal union of the two crowns was specified in a royal decree – in which the flag of England and the flag of Scotland, known as the Saltire, would be "joyned together according to the forme made by our heralds and sent by Us to our Admerall to be published to our Subjects".

In 1800 the Act of Union merged the Kingdoms of Ireland and Great Britain. The present Union Flag, incorporating St Patrick's Cross, dates from 1 January 1801. It was borne in the top left corner of the White Ensign flown by Nelson at Trafalgar.

No law has ever been passed making the Union Flag the national flag of the United Kingdom. Its first recorded recognition as a national flag came in 1908, when it was stated in Parliament that, "the Union Jack should be regarded as the National flag".

"Jack" may have been an abbreviation of *Jacobus*, the Latin for James, in honour of the King. Such was the importance of the Royal Navy to Britain, it is also possible that it is derived from the 'Jack Staff' – the flagpole found at the bow of a ship.
• **Union Jack flag with bullet holes resulting from the battle of Trafalgar**

DID A FRENCHMAN BRING THE NEWS OF TRAFALGAR TO THE ADMIRALTY?

Less than eleven days after he left the British fleet in the schooner HMS *Pickle* with Vice-Admiral Collingwood's despatches, Lieutenant Lapenotière reached the Admiralty.

Despite high winds and heavy seas, Lapenotière made the voyage of more than a thousand miles in just over eight days, reaching Falmouth on the morning of 4 November. From there he took 36 hours, in twenty-one stages, to cover the 271 miles to Whitehall. The cost of his journey was £46 19s 1d (over £32,000 today) – almost half his annual salary. Lapenotière arrived at 01:00 on Wednesday 6 November 1805. He handed the despatches to William Marsden, Secretary to the Board, who was on his way to bed, and said: "Sir, we have gained a great victory. But we have lost Lord Nelson".

He went on to have breakfast with King George III at Windsor; and soon became a national celebrity. As was customary, Lapenotière was rewarded for being the bearer of news of victory: with promotion to the rank of commander and a reward of £500 (£344,000 today). He was also presented with a sword valued at 100 guineas by the Patriotic Fund at Lloyd's. His feat is honoured every year by the Royal Navy with "Pickle Night" dinners; and by a special service in the church at Madron, near Penzance.

John Richards Lapenotière was born in 1770 at Ilfracombe in Devonshire. He was descended from Huguenot refugees who came to England with King William III in 1688 and settled in Ireland. His great-grandfather, Frederick La Penotière served in the Royal Irish Regiment with the Duke of Malborough at the Battle of Blenheim in 1704; his father Frederick served in the Royal Navy. Lapenotière was promoted to captain in 1811, but retired shortly afterwards to Roseland in Cornwall. He died in 1834.

THE HUGUENOTS IN THE BRITISH ISLES

The origin of the word is obscure, but it was the name given in the 16th century to the Protestants in France, especially by their enemies.

The impact of the Protestant Reformation was felt throughout Europe in the early 16th century. Its greatest preachers were the German Martin Luther and the Frenchman Jean Calvin, who moved to Switzerland. In France Calvinism permeated all ranks of society, especially literate craftsmen in the towns and the nobility. There were eight civil wars in France between 1562–98, known as the Wars of Religion. The single worst atrocity was the massacre of Huguenots on St Bartholemew's Day in 1572, following which the first to flee France came to England and settled in Canterbury.

In 1589 the Protestant King of Navarre, inherited the French throne as Henri IV. In 1593, famously saying "Paris is worth a Mass", Henri (later known as the "Good") converted to Catholicism. Five years later, to end the civil wars, Henri issued the Edict of Nantes: which gave the Huguenots, his former co-religionists and comrades in arms, considerable privileges – including religious liberty within certain areas of France.

Their position became increasingly insecure however, as his grandson King Louis XIV was persuaded that this sizeable religious minority (some 2 million, 10% of the population) threatened the absolute authority of the monarch. Gradually Huguenot privileges were eroded. Finally, in 1685 Louis revoked the Edict of Nantes, exiling all Protestant pastors but forbidding the laity to leave the country. Men who were caught trying to escape were sent as galley slaves to the French fleet in the Mediterranean – a virtual death sentence. Women were imprisoned and their children sent to convents, to be brought up as Catholics. The cruel treatment meted out by Catholic Frenchmen on their fellow citizens has uncomfortable parallels with the Holocaust in the 20th century. Louis XIV, the *soi disant* "Sun King", deserves vilification for encouraging it.

Over 200,000 Huguenots fled France, settling in non-Catholic Europe – the Low Countries, Germany (especially Prussia), Switzerland, Sweden and Russia. The Dutch East India Company sent a few hundred to the Cape to develop vineyards in southern Africa: where an early settlement was at Franschhoek ("French Corner"). A small number found their way to British North America. More than 50,000 came to England: of which some 10,000 moved on to Ireland, where they founded the linen industry.

The Huguenots made their presence felt in banking, commerce, manufacturing industry (especially textiles and paper making), the book trade, the arts and the army, on the stage and in teaching. Although many retained their Calvinist organisation and worship, by about 1760 they had ceased to stand out as foreign: indeed, most became Anglicans.

The loss of so many skills and highly educated natural leaders contributed, despite its much larger population, to France's military and naval humiliations at the hands of the British for a hundred and thirty years – and a total eclipse by Britain in science, enterprise, industrialisation and commerce thereafter.

TWENTY-FIVE WELL-KNOWN PEOPLE OF HUGUENOT DESCENT:

Sir Francis Beaufort Hydrographer of the Royal Navy ● **Warren Buffet** US investor and richest man in the world in 2008 ● **Philip Cazenove** founder of the British stockbroker Cazenove & Co. ● **John Courage** founder of a British brewer ● **Samuel Courtauld** founder of the British textile company Courtaulds ● **Joan Crawford** US actress ● **Davy Crockett** US folk hero ● **Sir Peter de la Billière** British Military Commander in the First Gulf War ● **Johnny Depp** US film star ● **Daphne du Maurier** British novelist ● **Éleuthère Irénée du Pont** founder of the US chemical company du Pont ● **Peter Carl Fabergé** Russian jeweller ● **David Garrick** English dramatist, actor and theatre manager ● **Albert Gore Jr.** Vice-President of the United States ● **Sir John Houblon** First Governor of the Bank of England *see the 1994 £50 note* ● **Eddie Izard** British comedian and actor ● **Simon Le Bon** British musician ● **Henry Wadsworth Longfellow** US poet ● **Laurence, Lord Olivier** British actor ● **Charles, 1st Viscount Portal** British Chief of the Air Staff 1940–45 ● **John Davison Rockefeller** founder of Standard Oil ● **Peter Mark Roget FRS** British physician and lexicographer ● **Franklin Delano Roosevelt** 32nd President of the United States ● **Jean-Jacques Rousseau** Swiss writer and philosopher ● **Alexander von Humboldt** German naturalist

THE DUKE OF WELLINGTON MET LORD NELSON ONLY ONCE

Wellington and Nelson met by chance, on 10 September 1805. The Duke later recalled, "I went to the Colonial Office in [No. 12] Downing Street and there I was shown into the little waiting-room on the right hand, where I found, also waiting to see the Secretary of State, a gentleman whom, from his likeness to his pictures and the loss of an arm, I immediately recognised as Lord Nelson. He could not know who I was, but he entered at once into conversation with me, if I can call it a conversation, for it was almost all on his side and all about himself, and in, really, a style so vain and so silly as to surprise and almost disgust me. I suppose something that I happened to say may have made him guess that I was *somebody*, and he went out of the room for a moment, I have no doubt to ask the office-keeper who I was, for when he came back he was altogether a different man, both in manner and matter. All that I had thought a charlaton [sic] style had vanished, and he talked of the state of this country, and of the aspect and probabilities of affairs on the Continent with a good sense, and a knowledge of subjects both at home and abroad that surprised me ....in fact he talked like an officer and a statesman. The Secretary of State kept us long waiting, and certainly, for the last half or three-quarters of an hour, I don't know that I ever had a conversation that interested me more. Now, if the Secretary of State had been punctual, and admitted Lord Nelson in the first quarter of an hour I should have had the same impression of a light and trivial character that other people have had".

Another connection between Nelson and Wellington is the Hilborough estate, near Swaffham in Norfolk, where Nelson's father once had the living. It was later given to the Duke by a grateful nation after the Battle of Waterloo.

1759 WAS *ANNUS MIRABILIS* OR THE "YEAR OF VICTORIES"

The Seven Years' War (1756–63) might be described as the "First World War". The principal antagonists were an unlikely combination of France, Austria, Russia and (from January 1762) Spain: pitted against the man who provoked it, Frederick the Great of Prussia. He was financed by Britain: which, unable to field a large army on the Continent, chose to fight the war elsewhere overseas. Since these operations were conducted in the Mediterranean, Atlantic,

Canada, the West Indies, India, the Philippines and Europe, the conflict was indeed global. It ended in ignominy for France, the aggrandisement of Prussia and the triumphant establishment of the British Empire.

The year 1759, the most astoundingly successful in British history, decided the outcome of the war. A spectacular run of victories began on 1 May, when Colonel John Barrington of the Coldstream Guards captured Guadeloupe. On 1 August British and Hanoverian troops led by John Manners, Marquess of Granby (1721–70) contributed decisively to the French defeat at Minden in North Germany. Eighteen days later, the Cornishman Admiral Edward Boscawen (1711–61) captured three and sank two French ships off Lagos, on the southern coast of Portugal. The main French fleet was itself destroyed in November by Admiral Edward Hawke (1705–81) at Quiberon Bay in Brittany.

But by far the most significant loss to France, her claims to the territory between the Ohio and Mississippi rivers and all her settlements in Canada, was precipitated by the capture of Quebec on 18 September. That waspish man of letters, Nelson's cousin Horace Walpole, 4th Earl of Orford (1717–97) languidly remarked, "We are forced to ask every morning what victory there has been, for fear of missing one".

Robert Clive, through his victory at Plassey on 23 June 1757, secured with only 3,000 men against 50,000, had already secured Bengal for the East India Company – ending France's pretensions in India. The capture of Havana and Manila in 1762 led to the cession of Florida by Spain (returned in 1781) at the Treaty of Paris the following year. Included in the terms of the treaty, Britain also regained Minorca (Admiral Byng had been executed in 1757 for its loss on 20 May 1756); and, except for New Orleans, gained all of North America, including Canada, that she did not already control; India; the Senegal River; and swapped some islands in the West Indies.

The Death of General Wolfe by Benjamin West (1738–1820)
National Maritime Museum, London

Major-General James Wolfe (1727–59) began the siege of Quebec on 25 June 1759. Its "impregnable" position high above the St Lawrence river, with a resolute garrison of 15,000, defied him for three months. The city finally surrendered five days after Wolfe had been killed leading a surprise attack across the Plains of Abraham with only 4,500 men in the early hours of 13 September. The French commander, the Marquis de Montcalm, was also mortally wounded and died the following day.

Captain James Cook's accurate survey of the St Lawrence enabled Wolfe to land his troops and scale the cliffs where least expected. The 78th Fraser Highlanders took the highest number of casualties in the battle.

At the Battle of Culloden in 1746 Wolfe had been ordered by General "Hangman" Hawley or the Duke of Cumberland to shoot "that Highland scoundrel who dares to look upon us with so insolent a stare", pointing to the fatally wounded Charles Fraser of Inverallochy. Wolfe indignantly replied that, "he never would consent to become an executioner". Although Fraser was shot by someone less fastidious, his act of decency was repaid by the warmth with which the Fraser Regiment greeted Wolfe when he arrived in North America in 1758: and by the bravery with which it fought for him.

Robert Clive

THE AMATEUR SOLDIER WHOSE CONQUEST OF BENGAL LED TO BRITISH RULE THROUGHOUT INDIA (THE RAJ)

Robert, 1st Baron Clive, studio of Sir Nathaniel Dance, Bt. (c.1773)
National Portrait Gallery, London

Robert Clive was born at Styche Hall, Market Drayton, in Shropshire on 29 September 1725. He was the eldest of thirteen children fathered by Richard Clive, a lawyer and Member of Parliament. His mother Rebecca, *née* Gaskell, came from Manchester. An average scholar with an unruly, truculent nature, Robert became involved in many daring escapades: which included scaling his local church tower. After two years at Merchant Taylor's school in London, his father secured an appointment for him as a clerk in the East India Company. Robert sailed for India in March 1743.

The East India Company, which later achieved the unique distinction of ruling an entire country, was founded by a Royal Charter granted by Queen Elizabeth I on 31 December 1600: for the purpose of engaging in the spice trade with India and south-east Asia. Gradually the Company eclipsed the earlier established Portuguese merchants and rapidly established trading posts at Bombay, Madras and Calcutta: broadening its commerce to silks, cottons, indigo, tea, jute and other commodities. In 1717, as a reward for a successful operation performed by a British surgeon on the Moghul emperor Farrukhsiyar, the Company was granted a *firman* (royal dictat), exempting the Company from all customs duties levied in Bengal. By 1801 the Company's turnover exceeded £7.5 million (£6 billion today). The Company became the principal instrument of British imperial policy, exercising considerable influence throughout the sub-continent and beyond. Opium, produced in Bengal but banned in China where it was sold, financed the Company's tea trade – and led to the morally indefensible Opium wars of 1839–42. The British overwhelmed antiquated Chinese forces and Hong Kong was ceded to Britain. The Company was wound up in 1858, following the Indian Mutiny.

By the time of Clive's arrival in India in 1745, the East India Company had established three coastal trading posts at Bombay, Madras and Calcutta. Activity was entirely commercial, with a small private army dedicated to the protection of the Company's forts and warehouses. Clive settled into the dull routine of a clerk in Madras. A year later he was transferred to more interesting work in the commercial office: astutely, he also took advantage of the well-furnished Fort library to improve his education.

In September 1746 Madras was captured by the French. Clive escaped to Fort St David, south of Madras: and volunteered with such vigour in helping with the construction of the hastily flung-up fortifications that he attracted the attention of Major Stringer Lawrence, who was responsible for the Fort's protection.

In 1748, under the terms of the Treaty of Aix-la-Chapelle which ended the war of the Austrian Succession, Madras was returned to the British; and by the end of 1749 Clive had been discharged from the Company army. His patron, Stringer Lawrence secured him the contract to supply Company troops: a lucrative position which enabled Clive to lay the basis of his fortune, due to the large commissions paid. In 1750 he left Madras for Calcutta, to recover from a nervous breakdown – a disability which returned regularly throughout his life. A year later, in 1751 hostilities broke out between the French and the Company, in support of rival claimants for control of the Carnatic region of south-east India. Clive was summoned back to Madras with the rank of captain. His conduct, seizing Arcot and besieging Trichinopoly, earned him a hero's reputation – but again his health broke down and he decided to return to Britain. On 18 February 1753 he married Margaret, the sister of his friend Nevil Maskeleyne (later the Astronomer Royal) and a seventeen year-old beauty, before leaving India in March.

In October 1753 Clive arrived in Britain to receive a warm welcome, wide public acclaim and a fortune amounting to £40,000 (£60 million today). With more than enough money to support his social and political ambitions, he looked for a seat in parliament. His efforts were unsuccessful. In early 1755 Clive was offered a royal commission and the post of second-in-command of an expedition to be launched from Bombay against the French-sponsored Nizam of Hyderabad. He was also invited to take up the governorship of Fort St David at Madras. Clive, not yet thirty and disappointed in his parliamentary ambitions, accepted both offers. In April he sailed for India.

In June 1756, just as Clive returned to Madras to take up his position, Siraj-ud-Daula, the Nawab of Bengal, seized Calcutta and the Company's headquarters, Fort William.

Following the capture of Calcutta by Siraj-ud-Daula, there took place the notorious incident called the "Black Hole of Calcutta. On 20 June 1756, 123 British residents were crushed and stifled to death after 146 of them had been locked overnight in a small room. The only contemporary account of the event comes from a survivor, one Zephaniah Holwell (1711–98). Modern Indian

Stringer Lawrence (1697–1773), credited as "the father of the Indian army", was born in Hereford. He resigned his army commission in 1746 for the better pay and promotion to major in the East India Company army. In command at Madras, rapidly he turned men who had been no more than garrison security guards into a small and effective army. In 1761 Lawrence was promoted to Major-General. In 1766 he left India, but on arrival in Britain found that his welfare had been ignored: "He saved his Country yet is not worth a Groat, whilst Clive for one or two trifling Affairs has got half a million". Clive did however give Lawrence an annuity of £500 from his own pocket (over £700,000 today). Lawrence had shown that a well trained, integrated force of Indians and Europeans, with high morale and good leadership, was the equal of much larger armies.

Siraj-ud-Daula (1729–57) succeeded his grandfather as Nawab of Bengal in April 1757. British propaganda of the day projected him as an arrogant despot: yet weak and indecisive, with an uncontrollable temper. Soon after succeeding to his throne, Siraj-ud-Daula objected to the British construction of fortifications at Fort William in Calcutta: which were of course, designed to be used against him. His protests ignored, the Nawab took the city. Clive recaptured Calcutta and defeated Siraj-ud-Daula at the Battle of Plassey in June 1757. His body was found a few days later floating in the river. Responsibility for the notorious incident known as "The Black Hole of Calcutta" has long been laid at Siraj-ud-Daula's door.

Robert Clive meeting Mir Jafar after Plassey by Francis Hayman (c.1760)
National Portrait Gallery, London

historians are understandably inclined to believe that Holwell may well have grossly exaggerated his story as a convenient piece of British propaganda – while others question whether the incident ever happened at all.

The date often taken for the start of British Rule in India is 23 June 1757 when, at the small mango grove village of Plassey between Calcutta and Murshidabad, Robert Clive defeated Siraj-ud-Daula's army. To dignify the occasion with the name "battle" is an exaggeration: since the outcome had been decided long before the armies clashed. The aspirant to the Nawab's throne, his uncle Mir Jafar, was secretly in league with the British and plotting to overthrow him. Many of the Nawab's army were disaffected; and a number had been bribed to surrender prematurely and even turn their weapons on their own army.

The two sides appeared to be staggeringly mismatched: 50,000 Indians against 950 Europeans and 2,100 sepoys, with almost no artillery – but only twenty British soldiers were killed. There are some grounds for justifying Jawaharlal Nehru's, admittedly biased, comment in his 1946 book *The Discovery of India*, that Clive won "by promoting treason and forgery"; and that British Rule in India "had an unsavoury beginning and something of that bitter taste has clung to it ever since". Victory at Plassey however, made the British masters of Bengal. Whatever else, Clive was a master of intrigue.

Clive's first Bengal administration lasted until February 1760. As was usual at the time, the transfer of British backed authority to Mir Jafar was marked by generous "presents" of money from the new Nawab, amounting to some £1.2 million: to be shared among those senior officers in the Company and its army who had brought about the successful coup. In 1757 Clive personally received the stupendous sum of £234,000 (£350 million today) from a grateful Mir Jafar. Two years later in 1759, having repulsed at Patna an invasion of Bengal by the son of the Moghul emperor, and having despatched Colonel Francis Forde to destroy an attempt by the Dutch to reinforce their colony at Chinsura, Mir Jafar gave Clive a *jagir*: a grant of land worth nearly £30,000 (£43 million today) a year. Clive's acquisition of such fabulous wealth of course, set a terrible example to junior Company servants as well as attracting the attention of the British government: which was dismayed by the corruption of grasping Company officials or "nabobs" – and aware of the envy and division it caused.

Clive was confirmed as Governor of Bengal in November 1759. He realised that, having established his authority over the Nawab and eliminated French and Dutch competition, the vast hinterland of India lay open to Company trade. Clive wrote to the Prime Minister William Pitt in 1759, *Annus Mirabilis*: "so large a sovereignty may possibly be an object too extensive for a mercantile company". He suggested that the government should now take responsibility for ruling India. The government was however, reluctant to take on such a huge commitment – since its interests were so effectively being maintained by the East India Company.

Clive's management of Company affairs failed to match his perceptive vision of India. His dealings with regular army officers, such as Eyre Coote, became strained and bitter. More importantly, exemptions from internal duties on Company goods traded by Company servants on their private account, were strangling Bengal's economy and threatened the Company with bankruptcy. In seizing India's richest province however,

> Nabob was the name given to a Muslim official or governor in the Moghul Empire. It became a term extended to cover any rich or important person.

> Sir Eyre Coote (1726–83) was the sixth son of an Irish Protestant clergyman, born near Limerick. He first saw active service with the British army in the 1745 Jacobite uprising. He then obtained a captaincy in the 39th Foot, the first regiment to be sent to India. In 1756, while quartered in Madras, Coote was ordered to join Clive on his campaign to recapture Calcutta. He was rewarded handsomely by the Company and became Member of Parliament for Leicester. As Commander-in-Chief in 1781 he defeated, with great difficulty, Prince Hyder Ali of Mysore at Porto Novo. This battle saved the whole of southern India for the British.

THE BRITISH IN INDIA (1612–1804)

Battlefields

Cities
*(dates of arrival
or foundation)*

British Dominions

Protectorates

Independent States

Portuguese / French

AFGHANISTAN

BALUCHISTAN

KASHMIR

Indus

PUNJAB

Lahore

Sutlej

C H I N E S E   E M P I R E

SIND

Indus

RAJPUTANA

Delhi

**Laswari
(1803)**

Agra

Gwalior

Jamuna

OUDH

Lucknow

N E P A L

BHUTAN

Brahmaputra

M A L W A H
Dominions of Holkar and Sindhia

Benares

Patna

Ganges

B E N G A L

**Buxar
(1764)**

**Plassey
(1757)**

Dacca

Calcutta
(1690)

Hoogli

Chittagong

GUJERAT

Nerbudda

B   E   R   A   R

Mahanadi

Surat
(1612)

**Assaye
(1803)**

CUTTACK

BURMA

Irrawaddy

Bombay
(1668)

Poona

Godavari

CIRCARS

Bay
of
Bengal

Malabar

Hyderabad

Krishna

Coast

Masulipatam (1759)

GOA
(Portuguese)

Porto Novo (1781)

Arcot (1751)

Coromandel Coast

ANDAMAN
ISLANDS

LACADIVE
ISLANDS

MYSORE

**Seringapatam
(1799)**

C   A   R   N   A   T   I   C

Madras
(1639)

PONDICHERRY
(French)

**Wandiwash
(1760)**

NICOBAR
ISLANDS

Cauvery

Coast

Arabian   Sea

Cape
Comorin

CEYLON
(1796)

Colombo

I n d i a n   O c e a n

0   300 miles

0   300 km

Clive had done his country great service. In February 1760 he returned to Britain.

Once again, he arrived home to a hero's welcome, with a fortune of £300,000 (£426 million today) together with the income from his *jagir*. Though William Pitt had described him as a "Heaven born general" and he received many official honours, he was disappointed not to secure an English peerage: receiving only an Irish title, as Baron Clive of Plassey, in March 1762. Clive became Member of Parliament for Shrewsbury, bought several estates and began to use his vast wealth to build a political career.

In 1764 however, the Company once again turned to Clive for leadership and direction. Mir Jaffa had been deposed by Mir Kassim in 1763; the Moghul emperor had attacked Bengal; and the Company itself was in grave danger. Clive was appointed Governor with powers to override the local council. He was charged with regulating Bengal's foreign policy: and in Clives's own words, with "cleansing the Augean stable" of Company internal affairs. This was a bitter irony, which further fuelled the hatred of his many enemies, as it was Clive himself who had enabled that stable to exist.

Clive sailed on 4 June 1764 but, long delayed at Rio de Janeiro, he only arrived in Bengal on 3 May 1765: to find the political situation transformed. On 22 October 1764 a Company army under Hector Munro had defeated the combined armies of Shuja-ud-Daula, the Nawab Wazir of Oudh, Mir Kassim the Nawab of Bengal and Shah Alam II the Moghul emperor at Buxar so decisively that the whole of India from Bengal to Delhi now lay at the Company's feet.

Sensibly, Clive now turned from any further expansion, preferring to consolidate and entrench the Company's political and commercial control of Bengal. His statesmanship, in settling the political and economic affairs of the province, was masterful.

On 29 January 1767, aged forty-one and on the verge of another nervous breakdown, Clive left India for the last time. His return to Britain was again marked with honours and expressions of official gratitude – his fortune was now probably in excess of £400,000 (£560 million today). Envy of his huge wealth and criticism of his Bengal administration however, soon forced him on to the defensive. Further, a lobby led by the Earl of Chatham (William Pitt "the Elder") voiced concern over the effect of nabob wealth on British public morals. In 1772 the East India Company was obliged to appeal to the government to save it from bankruptcy, allowing two committees to expose the levels of corruption amongst Company officials – for which Clive was blamed. Clive however, despite recurring attacks of ill-health, strongly defended himself in Parliament. On one occasion he complained of being treated by the Commons "like a sheep stealer"; and on another, he famously remarked: "Mr Chairman, at this moment I stand astonished at my own moderation". In May 1773 he made a dramatic appeal to the House: "Leave me my honour, take away my fortune". The debate that followed resolved that

Clive had not behaved improperly. A further motion was then immediately pressed by Clive's supporters: that "Robert Clive did at the same time render great and meritorious service to his country". Shortly after these proceedings the East India Company was reformed by Lord North's Regulating Act of 1773.

After several months of recuperation, spent buying works of art in Italy, Clive arrived at his house at 45, Berkeley Square (next door to the night club Annabels today); and, in great distress, resorted to large doses of opium. Shortly afterwards, on the evening of 22 November 1774, he excused himself while playing cards with friends. He was found in the lavatory, having cut his throat with an ivory-handled razor. Clive's abilities were exceptional. His behaviour was no more unethical than many of his contemporaries. Although envy and criticism of his fabulous wealth robbed him of the possibility of becoming a national statesman and a place in the ranks of the truly great, were he never to have lived, the words combining "British" and "Empire" would have been a laughable conceit.

Clive left six children. His grandson, the 2nd Earl of Powis, was accidentally shot dead by one of his own sons – who was thereafter known as "Baghdad".

WILLIAM PITT ("THE ELDER"), 1ST EARL OF CHATHAM

William Pitt (1708–78) was known as the "Great Commoner" because of his extraordinary national following. His finest hour was as Secretary of State during the Seven Years' War. His dynamic leadership galvanised the armed forces to win the many victories that resulted in Britain emerging as the first world power. Pitt is known deservedly, as "the Father of the British Empire".

Pitt's father Robert Pitt of Boconnoc in Cornwall, was an unremarkable Member of Parliament. Pitt was born on 15 November 1708 in Westminster and educated at Eton and Trinity College, Oxford; but congenital gout obliged him to leave without a degree. A younger son with little money, Pitt was befriended by Lord Cobham who sent him on the Grand Tour; and in 1731, bought him a commission in the Dragoons. In 1735 he was elected to Parliament for the 'rotten borough' of Old Sarum.

With a coterie of Cobham supporters, Pitt opposed the long and increasingly unpopular ministry of Sir Robert Walpole, Britain's first prime minister.

William Pitt (c.1754) by William Hoare (c.1707–92)
National Portrait Gallery, London

In a brilliant maiden speech, Pitt so discomfited Walpole that he was deprived of his military commission. The Prince of Wales however, also disliked Walpole and gave Pitt a salaried position in his household. Pitt was the first British statesman to give a voice to public opinion and to those commercial and colonial interests which, despite great wealth, had no representation in parliament. In 1744 the Duchess of Marlborough died leaving Pitt £10,000 (£14.3 million today), making him financially secure for the rest of his life. On 16 November 1754, disappointed in office, he married Lady Hester Grenville. He was devoted to her and they had five children.

The outbreak of the Seven Year's War in 1756 presented Pitt with his first real opportunity. In November he formed his first ministry. Like Henry V and Winston Churchill, Pitt united the whole country behind him, enabling Britain to fight a truly national war. He identified America and India as the key objectives of the conflict (Pittsburgh was named for him in 1758), sending expeditions to secure Canada while relying on Robert Clive, a "heaven born general" to defeat the French in India. He financed Frederick the Great of Prussia while sending the Royal Navy to harass France's mainland ports and her colonies in the West Indies. 1759 was Britain's *Annus Mirabilis*: "Our bells are quite worn threadbare with ringing for victories", wrote Horace Walpole.

By 1763 the French had had enough. In the Treaty of Paris, France ceded more than even Pitt had dreamed of. In 1760 however, George III had came to the throne, leading to Pitt's resignation the following year: when he failed to persuade his king and cabinet to declare a pre-emptive war on Spain. Pitt became increasingly incapacitated by gout; but went on to defend the cause of the American colonists, particularly in their resistance to the 1765 Stamp Act. He formed another ministry in 1766: in which he served, due to infirmity, in second place as Lord Privy Seal. He was created Earl of Chatham, as a champion of both imperialism and constitutional freedom. He died on 11 May 1778, having suffered a seizure in the House of Commons while speaking on behalf of the American revolutionaries. He was buried in Westminster Abbey, with the magnificent pomp befitting a national hero.

The British Museum

THE BRITISH MUSEUM OPENED TO THE PUBLIC IN 1759

One of the world's greatest museums of human history and culture, with more than 7 million objects, the British Museum was based on the collections of the Ulster-Scot physician and scientist from County Down, Sir Hans Sloane, 1st Bt. (1660–1753). He was President of the Royal Society, invented drinking chocolate and bought the manor of Chelsea in 1712. Sloane bequeathed his collection to the nation in return for a modest £20,000 to be paid to his executors (£29 million today).

The museum opened to the public in Montagu House in Bloomsbury on 15 January 1759. The present building was designed by Sir Robert Smirke (1781–1867) and built between 1823–31. The museum's natural history collection was transferred to South Kensington in 1887; and the new British Library acquired its books and manuscripts, including George III's magnificent collection, in 1997.

THE FIRST VOLUMES OF TRISTRAM SHANDY WERE PUBLISHED IN 1759

The Reverend Laurence Sterne was born in 1713 in Clonmel, County Tipperary where his father, an ensign in the army, was stationed. Six months later the family returned to Yorkshire. Sterne was sent to school near Halifax when he was ten – and never saw his father again. He attended Jesus College, Cambridge in July 1733. He was ordained in 1738 and given the living of Sutton-on-the-Forest in Yorkshire. He married Elizabeth Lumley in 1741. Both suffered from consumption: which, after great suffering on his part, killed them both – Sterne in 1768 , Elizabeth in 1773.

Sterne wrote *A Sentimental Journey Through France and Italy*; but it is for his satirical masterpiece, *The Life and Opinions of Tristram Shandy, Gentleman*, published in nine volumes between 1759 and his death that he is remembered.

The novel is ostensibly the story of Tristram's life. The most important characters are his irascible and cynical father Walter, his mother, his gentle and unworldly Uncle Toby, Toby's servant Trim – and the minor characters, Doctor Slop and Parson Yorick. The tale rambles between domestic crises and comical differences of opinion, interspersed with Tristram's views on just about everything: sex and obstetrics, snobbery, warfare and philosophy.

Nothing is straightforward (the circumstances of his birth are not even mentioned until Volume III), but Tristram's journey is colourful and wonderfully described.

Laurence Sterne by Sir Joshua Reynolds (1760)
National Portrait Gallery, London

JOHN LAW, THE FIRST PAPER MONEY AND THE MISSISSIPPI SCHEME

John Law, who had brokered the sale of Thomas Pitt's diamond to Philippe, Duc d'Orléans in 1717, led an extraordinary life. He was a philanderer, accused of murder after a duel – and an early Scottish economist whose theories, though they ultimately failed, were 300 years ahead of their time. He put them to the test in France: where he was appointed *Contrôleur Général des Finances*; instituted some important and long-needed reforms (industry increased 60% in two years); founded the Bank of France; introduced paper money; and promoted a number of large, but wildly speculative companies trading overseas. The collapse of these nearly bankrupted the French economy.

John Law by Casimir Balthazar

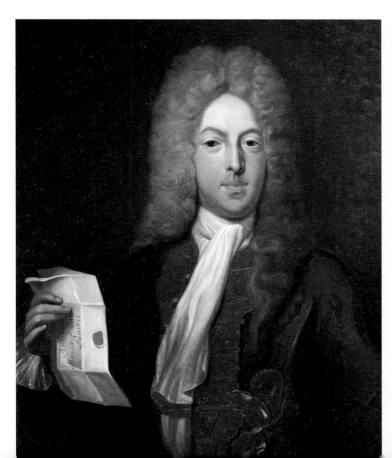

Law argued that money, backed by property or gold, was only a means of exchange: and did not constitute wealth in itself. National prosperity depended entirely on trade, which could most easily be facilitated and financed, but not measured, by money or monetary instruments. Law was also a brilliant gambler. He lived for years on his winnings, due to his amazing ability to calculate odds at lightning speed.

Law was born in 1671, the son of a successful banker and goldsmith from Fife who had purchased Lauriston on the Firth of Forth, now a suburb of Edinburgh. From the age of fourteen Law was trained as a banker in the family business. When his father, William Law died in 1688 he left Scotland for London to continue his education.

Whilst trying to keep himself by gambling he caught the eye of Elizabeth Villiers (later Countess of Orkney) who was more than ten years his senior, the mistress of King William III and much admired by hot-blooded young thrusters. On 9 April 1694 he was challenged for her affections in a duel with Edward "Beau" Wilson and killed him. Law was found guilty of murder and sentenced to death. This was commuted to a fine for manslaughter, but Wilson's brother appealed and Law was imprisoned. He managed to escape and fled to Amsterdam where he completed his education.

In 1705 he returned to Scotland and wrote *Money and Trade, Consider'd with a Proposal for Supplying the Nation with Money*. He suggested to the Scottish Parliament that it establish a national bank. Following the disaster of the Darien Scheme in 1698 however, his idea was turned down. This was especially galling as the author of the Scheme, William Paterson had founded the Bank of England in 1694 and influenced the establishment of the commercial Bank of Scotland the following year.

After Union with England in 1707, to avoid imprisonment, Law left Scotland again for the Continent. In 1715 he settled in France and came to the attention of the Regent, the Duc d'Orléans. From this lucky happenstance his rise was meteoric. After Louis XIV's death the country was in a dire economic position, from ruinously expensive wars, and receptive to Law's salesmanship and financial wizardry.

On 20 May 1716 Law was granted a licence to establish a *Banque Générale*. The initial capital of six million livres (some £500 million today) was divided into 1,200 shares, each of 5,000. The shares were payable in four instalments: 25% in cash and, although it was a private bank, 75% in government bills called *billets d'etat*. Law was authorised to issue notes payable on demand to the cash value of the money denominated. On 10 April 1717 it was decreed that Law's notes would be accepted in payment of taxes. These notes were the first proper paper money issued in Europe.

In August 1717 Law founded the *Compagnie de la Louisiane ou d'Occident*, which was granted extensive powers to exploit the catchment area of the Mississippi and its tributaries. The Mississippi basin included the Missouri and the Ohio Rivers, a vast area which overlapped with territory also claimed by the British. In 1718 Law purchased the tobacco monopoly for the region. His proposal to exploit its apparently limitless resources, known as the Mississippi Scheme, caused a tremendous wave of interest – not just in France. It encouraged the development across Europe of several other overseas companies; and speeded expansion of the South Sea Company in Britain, founded in 1711, and a number of smaller companies in the Dutch Republic.

In December 1718 Law's *Banque Générale* was converted into the *Banque Royale*, with Law as a director. More importantly, the bank's new notes were guaranteed by the Crown. In 1719 the *Compagnie de la Louisiane* took over the *Compagnies des Indes Orientales et de la Chine*. The new company was called the *Compagnie des Indes*. At this time Law's reputation was of the highest order. When he undertook to repay the national debt, in return for control of national revenues (and the French mint for nine years), the share price of the *Compagnie* soared dramatically. By now the mania, or 'bubble' was in full swing – but to be fair, this was not entirely Law's fault.

Shares in the *Compagnie* were originally issued at 500 livres: they rose to 10,000 livres in the course of 1719. When the *Compagnie* issued a 40% dividend in 1720, the share price rocketed to 18,000 livres, far-outstripping the capital base of the *Compagnie*. At this point, the frenzy subsided and speculators tried to take their profits. The share price dropped as fast as it had risen. As panic set in depositors clamoured to redeem their promissory notes – but the *Compagnie* ran out of money and went bankrupt.

The effects were felt throughout Europe. Many investors from outside France were ruined. Moreover confidence in similar European companies was also destroyed, including the South Sea Company in Britain. These in turn went bankrupt. At the end of 1720 with reluctance, Orléans dismissed Law who left France immediately.

He fled first to Brussels, then to Rome, Copenhagen and Venice; but his skill at cards had deserted him and he lived in genteel obscurity. Even when Orléans died in 1723 Law knew he could never return to France. Having at long last received a British pardon in 1719, he moved to London for four years: but ever restless, he returned to Venice. He died there, poor and unremarked, from pneumonia on 21 March 1729. He left two children from a permanent liaison

with Katherine Knollys, but had never married. Undoubtedly a financial genius, Law was a victim of his own inflated claims and became carried away by a success that had been dazzling in its speed and extent.

THREE 17TH CENTURY CITY COFFEE HOUSES SOLD MORE THAN COFFEE

Nathaniel Conopius, a student from Crete (then part of the Ottoman Empire) at Balliol College, Oxford is the first man who is known to have brewed coffee in England. It was witnessed and mentioned by the diarist John Evelyn in 1637. Over the following 150 years, coffee houses sprang up in towns all over the country. Three in the City of London were to become world famous, but not for selling coffee.

The new Lloyd's Building by Richard Rogers, opened by HM The Queen in 1986

The first was established by Thomas Garraway (died 1692) in Change Alley, near the Bank of England. Customers of Garraway's, which flourished until 1897, traded shares in newly floated businesses. Another, also in Change Alley, known simply as "Jonathan's", was founded by Jonathan Miles around 1680: where, from 1698 a broker named John Castaing also posted prices of stocks and commodities. Jonathan's is considered to be the birthplace of the London Stock Exchange – which formally established itself in 1801. By 1695 there were at least 140 joint-stock companies with daily price quotations. In 1697 a law was passed to "restrain the number and ill-practice of brokers and stockjobbers", following incidents of insider trading. Brokers had to be licensed and to take an oath promising to behave honourably – *plus ça change.*

In 1691 Edward Lloyd (*c*.1648–1713) moved his recently established coffee house from Tower Street to Lombard Street. Lloyd's clientèle used his premises to underwrite each other's commercial risks. Their association evolved into the insurance behemoth, Lloyds of London.

Lloyd was a man of considerable intelligence and enterprise. His reliable (and free) weekly news sheet listing shipping movements, first circulated sometime around 1692, was well respected by 1696.

Formally established in 1734, it is now published as Lloyd's List. Known as "The List", it is one of the world's oldest daily newspapers: with issue number 60,000 in 2010. By 1700 two lines of doggerel showed that Edward Lloyd had made his mark:

"Then to Lloyd's Coffee House he never fails
To read the letters and attend the sales".

In 1771 a group of Lloyd's old customers formed their own association of underwriters and took rooms in the Royal Exchange. After a fire in 1838 Lloyd's moved to South Sea House. In 1871 The Society of Lloyd's was incorporated by Parliament for the "promotion of marine insurance and the diffusion of shipping intelligence". The Corporation moved to Leadenhall Street in 1928 and to Lime Street in 1958. It remains the world's largest market place for syndicates of insurance underwriters.

The Babylonian Code of Hammurabi, *c*.1750 BC records that if a merchant received a loan to fund his shipment, he could pay the lender an additional sum for the lender's guarantee to cancel the loan should the shipment be lost. Nearly 3,100 years later, the earliest authenticated shipping insurance contract was on the *Santa Clara*, dated 1347 in Genoa.

Nicholas Barbon M.P. (1640–98), an economist, physician and financial speculator, was one of the first proponents of free markets – and is also credited as the first to establish a fire insurance company in England. The Great Fire of London in 1666 destroyed 13,200 houses: and in 1667, he opened "The Fire Office". In 1680 he offered to insure 5,000 homes – and founded the first London fire brigade. Barbon was one of the most important financiers involved in the rebuilding of the City.

He was the son of the wonderfully named Praisegod Barbon (*c*.1598–1680), for whom the short-lived Commonwealth parliament in 1653 was nicknamed "Barebone's Parliament". His writings on *laissez-faire* economics were generations ahead of his time – and he proposed paper money twenty years before John Law.

Captain James Cook RN FRS

BRITAIN'S GREATEST NAVAL EXPLORER AND THE WORLD'S FINEST HYDROGRAPHER

J ames Cook was born on 27 October 1728 in the north Yorkshire village of Marton. One of five children, he was the son of James Cook (1694–1765), a farm foreman from Roxburghshire and his wife Grace, *née* Pace (1701–65). He was educated at Great Ayton school at the expense of his father's employer until he was thirteen; leaving to work with his father. At sixteen he was apprenticed to William Sanderson, an haberdasher in the nearby fishing village of Staithes. After eighteen unsettled months Cook answered the call of the sea. Sanderson obligingly introduced him to the Quaker brothers John and Henry Walker, owners of a small fleet of coal ships. They accepted Cook as an apprentice; and for the next few years he served on a number of their colliers journeying between Tyneside and London.

Captain James Cook RN by Sir Nathaniel Dance, R.A. (1775–76)
National Maritime Museum, London

During the worst of the winter weather the apprentices were responsible for laying up the colliers. At night Cook studied mathematics and navigation. The Whitby 'Barks', working the North Sea off poorly marked and dangerous lee shores, furnished Cook with a thorough grounding in practical seamanship.

His apprenticeship completed, Cook transferred to ships working the Baltic routes. By 1752 he had qualified as Mate (navigator) on the collier-brig *Friendship*. Three years later he turned down an offer of command and joined the Royal Navy. Britain was mobilising for the Seven Years' War (1756–63) – and the young Cook rightly sensed wider and more interesting opportunities for advancement.

On 17 June 1755 Cook joined HMS *Eagle* as an able seaman, under the command of Captain Hugh Palliser. Within a short time he was promoted to Master's Mate; and two years later passed his Master's examination. Cook was now fully competent to navigate any ship in the Royal Navy.

During the Seven Years' War Cook spent most of his time off the eastern coast of Canada. In 1758, aged twenty-nine he was appointed Master of the 60-gun HMS *Pembroke*; and was present on 26 July at the capture of Louisbourg, an important fortress in Nova Scotia which protected the mouth of the St Lawrence river. After the surrender Cook met an army surveyor, Major Samuel Holland, who was drawing up a plan of the fort with a sophisticated surveying instrument known as a plane-table.

This chance acquaintance fired Cook with an interest in hydrography; and a few months later he charted the Gulf of Gaspé in the St Lawrence estuary. Over the next three years Cook, assisted by Holland, went on to survey the St Lawrence itself; and in particular, the hazardous shifting shoals called the Traverse. In the most skilful combined operation of the war, Cook and Holland's accurate charts enabled the British fleet, carrying Major-General Wolfe and his army, to navigate the river safely and capture Quebec. In 1760 the charts were printed and published in London.

After the capture of Quebec, Cook was appointed Master of the 70-gun HMS *Northumberland* commanded by Captain Lord Alexander Colville, 7th Viscount Culross (1717–70). From this ship-of-the-line Cook spent the next three years surveying Halifax harbour and Newfoundland, drawing up a comprehensive set of sailing directions for the whole of the Gulf of St Lawrence. In July 1762 *Northumberland* was present at the recapture of the port of St John's from the French; and Cook took this opportunity to undertake the first survey of the Newfoundland coast. His work attracted high praise from both his captain and the Governor of Newfoundland, Thomas Graves. By November 1762 Cook was back in London.

On 21 December 1762 he married Elizabeth Batts (1740–1835). Her father was the proprietor of The Bell Inn, at Execution Dock in Wapping. Elizabeth died aged ninety five, having had six children – three died in infancy and the others died without issue.

In April 1763 Cook returned to Newfoundland at the request of Thomas Graves to conduct a survey of two offshore islands, St Pierre and Miquelon, before they were restored to France under the terms of the 1763 Treaty of Paris. In command of the schooner HMS *Grenville*, Cook continued to survey the waters off Newfoundland until the end of the year; when he returned to England to prepare his charts for printing. In early 1764 his former Commodore Sir Hugh Palliser, now the new Governor of Newfoundland, asked Cook to complete his survey – and by the spring Cook, commanding the schooner HMS *Antelope*, was hard at work off the Newfoundland coast.

Over the next four years, Cook settled into a routine of surveying in the spring and summer; sailing *Antelope* back to England in the autumn, to prepare his charts for the printers and to refit his vessel. Cook was well aware that his charts were only accurately graduated for latitude, because there was no precise method of measuring longitude. On 5 August 1766 however, Cook observed an eclipse of the sun: from which he was able

A plane table is a device used for direct plotting in the field. It has a circular drawing board and a pivoted sighting device (an alidade) for measuring angles.

Cook's chart of Newfoundland remained in use for 150 years

The most important instrument for establishing latitude, by sighting the sun at noon, is the **sextant**. Sir Isaac Newton FRS invented the principle of a doubly reflecting navigation device, but never explained how to make one. John Hadley FRS (1682–1744), a mathematician born in London, invented the octant c.1731; from which Vice-Admiral John Campbell FRS (c.1720–90), born in Kirkbean in Dumfriesshire, developed the sextant in 1757.

John Paul (1747–92) was also born near Kirkbean. He went to sea in 1760 and rose rapidly to the rank of Master. When one of his crew died after a vicious flogging and he killed another in a dispute about wages he fled to Virginia where he added Jones to his surname. In the American Revolution his privateering voyages off the British coasts gave rise to his sobriquet "Father of the US Navy". In one famous exchange with a Royal Navy captain, when invited to surrender, he quipped "I have not yet begun to fight!".

to calculate longitude in the area of his survey. This enabled him to construct the first naval chart ever to include a matrix graded for longitude.

By November 1767 Cook had at last completed the task of charting the waters and mapping the islands off Newfoundland. His return to England coincided with plans for a Royal Society expedition to the South Pacific to observe the transit of Venus across the face of the sun – so that the distance between the earth and the sun could be precisely determined. A suitable ship would be provided by the Admiralty, which not unreasonably required the vessel to be commanded by a naval officer. On 18 May 1768 Lieutenant Cook was given command of HM Bark *Endeavour*, a renamed 98-foot Whitby collier, displacing 336 tons. *Endeavour* was later to give her name to the late-20th century US space shuttle.

The complement of scientists included the astronomer Charles Green (1734–71), who had been tasked by the Royal Society to make the observation, and Joseph Banks, a rich amateur botanist with two Swedish assistants, Daniel Solander and Herman Sporing. Alexander Buchan, a landscape painter and the Edinburgh-born Sydney Parkinson (1745–71), who specialised in botanical drawings, were charged with recording what they found. Tahiti, in the south Pacific had been chosen because the island's longitude had recently been established by astronomical observation.

Endeavour sailed from Plymouth on 25 August 1768, touching at Madeira and Rio de Janeiro before making the passage around Cape Horn and across the Pacific; to drop anchor in Matavai Bay, Tahiti on 13 April 1769. Cook was carrying sealed orders from the Admiralty which he opened as soon as the Transit of Venus observation on 3 June had been completed. He was instructed now to sail due south as far as latitude 40° to find *Terra Australis Incognita* ("Unknown Southern Land" in Latin), a great southern continent: which geographers and philosophers had long believed to exist, for no better reason than to balance the land masses in the northern hemisphere.

Encountering nothing but the boundless southern ocean, Cook sailed west to search for the land last seen by the Dutchman Abel Janszoon Tasman (1603–59) in 1642. On 6 October 1769 he sighted the east coast of New Zealand (Zeeland means "Sea-land" in Dutch). Over the next six months Cook surveyed both North and South islands, proving that they were not part of a great southern continent. He was helped by a Tahitian called Tupaia, a reliable guide for the

The Whitby collier was not only the ship with which Cook was most familiar, having spent nine years on them, but was also a most sensible choice. The vessel's large capacity, great strength and shallow draught made the collier ideal for extended voyages amid the coral reefs scattered throughout the southern oceans.

First Lieutenant Cook mapped the entire New Zealand coastline, making some minor errors: such as thinking that Banks Peninsula was an island and Stewart Island (Rakiura) was part of South Island. He also discovered Cook Strait, which separates North Island from South Island. Tasman never saw this. Cook claimed New Zealand for Britain on 15 November 1769. Jules Crozet, unaware of Cook's prior claim, claimed the islands for France on 12 July 1772. Although Crozet's claim was abandoned, he had provisionally named the islands Austral-France.

- **James Cook's first map of New Zealand (1775)**

Determining longitude by moon sighting was a skilled and complex calculation. With the assistance of his astronomer Charles Green, the recently published *Nautical Almanac Tables* and by measuring the angular distance from the moon to either the sun during daytime or one of the brightest stars at night, Cook was able to determine the time at the Royal Observatory at Greenwich. Then, by comparing that time to his local time, reckoned by measuring the angle of declination of the sun, moon or stars, he was able to arrive at the longitude of his position.

Botany Bay was the second name chosen by Cook, because of the "great quantity of plants found in this place by Mr Joseph Banks and Dr Solander". Originally Cook had named it Stingray Bay. It was selected in 1787 as the site for a penal settlement: and on 18 January 1788 Captain Arthur Phillip (1738–1814) arrived with a fleet of convicts. Finding the soil infertile Phillip moved to a site further north which he named Port Jackson – later renamed Sydney, the surname of the Home Secretary who had issued the charter authorising Phillip to establish a colony.

Humans and guinea pigs are the only animals that are unable to synthesise vitamin C.

Scurvy is a nutritional disorder caused by a deficiency of vitamin C. Even though the body only requires minute amounts of vitamin C to stay healthy, below this minimum level it suffers severe tissue damage. The symptoms are swollen, bleeding gums, loose teeth, sore stiff legs and bleeding under the skin and in deep tissue. Other symptoms include anæmia and the reluctance of wounds to heal. The condition used to decimate crews on long voyages. Cook not only ensured that his crew's quarters were properly cleaned and ventilated; but also insisted on a diet which included cress, sauerkraut and an orange extract drink. The health of his ships' companies became legendary throughout the Royal Navy.

Accurate local time is required to calculate longitude – to establish the time difference between points on the surface of the earth. This converts to 15 degrees every hour; and therefore 1 degree every 4 minutes. Thus longitude corresponds to time.

A chronometer is a particularly accurate marine clock or watch. Early pendulum clocks could not be used at sea because of the ship's motion. Temperature extremes also caused the metal in the mechanism to expand and contract, preventing the clock from keeping precise time. A Yorkshireman, John Harrison (1693–1776) built the first chronometer in 1735. He overcame the problems of temperature variation by bonding metals of differing expansion coefficients which stabilised the mechanisms to the point where a marine clock was accurate to 0.3 seconds in 24 hours.

The difficulty in making a chronometer to this degree of accuracy was so intractable that in 1714 Parliament offered an award of £20,000 (£31 million today) for a solution. Harrison was treated shabbily when he claimed his prize. In an audience with George III, the King tested Harrison's 'H5' chronometer himself. After it had lost only three seconds in ten days the King exclaimed, "By God Harrison, I'll see you righted!". The King told Harrison to petition Parliament, threatening to appear in person on his behalf. In 1773, aged eighty he finally received £8,750, but not the official prize (which was never awarded). In fact Harrison, a good Yorkshireman, had been paid a total of £23,065 over the years – despite the fuss he made.

The crew's encounters with the Aboriginal people were mainly peaceable. From a group encountered at Botany Bay the name 'kangaroo' entered into the English language: it came from a local Guugu Yimidhirr word, *gangurru*. The first name of the singer Kylie Minogue (born 1968), means "boomerang" in the same language.

south Pacific. Despite the lack of a chronometer, Cook was able to determine longitude by moon sightings.

Cook then sailed Endeavour west and surveyed the quite unknown east coast of Australia, including Botany Bay and a 1,616 mile-long reef – which was later named the Great Barrier Reef by Matthew Flinders (1774–1814).

After a near fatal mishap caused by grounding *Endeavour* on submerged rocks, which he named Endeavour Reef, Cook was forced to spend six weeks on the Endeavour River repairing her hull. He then sailed north to Batavia (now Jakarta) in the Dutch East Indies, via the Torres straight – last penetrated by Luis Vaez de Torres in 1606. Before departure, Cook claimed the whole east coast of Australia in the name of King George III, naming it South Wales – which later he amended to New South Wales.

By way of Table Bay in Capetown and revictualling at St Helena, Cook arrived back in England on 29 August 1771. Thirty of his crew had died during the voyage, including the artist Sydney Parkinson, the astronomer Charles Green and the Tahitian pilot Tupaia – nearly all of them from malaria and dysentery contracted while ashore in Batavia. Cook though, had not lost a single man to scurvy.

Promoted Commander and having been presented to King George III, Cook was invited by the Royal Society to make another search for the elusive *Terra Australis*. Two Whitby-built ships were purchased and named HMS *Resolution* and HMS *Adventure*. Cook commanded *Resolution* and Tobias Furneaux (1735–81) was given command of *Adventure*. Science was represented by a German naturalist, Johann Reinhold Forster (1729–98), assisted by his son Georg; and the expedition artist was William Hodges.

Importantly, four newly-perfected chronometers were taken for extended trials. The Board of Longitude appointed two astronomers, William Bayly and William

Wales, to be responsible for testing their accuracy and robustness.

On 13 July 1772 once again Cook sailed from Plymouth, directly to Table Bay; and thence into the southern ocean. On encountering scattered formations of large icebergs, he began to sail east along the edge of the ice pack – becoming on 17 January 1773, the first person to cross the Antarctic Circle. After a month searching fruitlessly for the land sighted by Kerguelen the previous year, and having been parted from the *Adventure* in fog, Cook continued on to New Zealand. He reached Dusky Sound on South Island in mid-March 1773, having sighted no land for four months.

Cook met up with Furneaux in *Adventure* at their fall-back rendezvous in Queen Charlotte Sound (the easternmost of the main Marlborough Sounds, running from the top of South Island into the Cook Strait); and by 7 June was back in Tahiti. Returning to New Zealand after quartering the Society islands, Cook once again lost contact with *Adventure* in a severe storm. Having failed to find Furneaux in Queen Charlotte Sound, he continued on his cruise around the ice-pack, twice crossing the Antarctic circle – the third time to 71° 10', thereby narrowly missing the discovery of the continent of Antarctica. Cook decided to spend another winter in the south Pacific, so that he could explore the southern Atlantic the following year, and set sail for Tahiti. He arrived there, by way of Easter Island and the Marquesas islands, on 22 April 1774.

After several weeks surveying the Society Islands, where he recruited an islander called Omai to replace Tupaia, he returned to Queen Charlotte Sound – to learn that he had missed Furneaux in *Adventure* by just a few days. Having lost some men in a fight with Maoris, Furneaux decided to sail back to Britain – taking Omai with him. Cook had found that his knowledge of south Pacific waters was virtually nonexistent.

On 11 November 1774 Cook returned to the south Atlantic for his third cruise along the ice-pack. He discovered South Georgia on 14 January 1775 and the South Sandwich Islands a week later. In March 1775 Cook was once again in Table Bay with *Resolution*. He reached Spithead on 30 July, after a voyage **of three years and three weeks. Remarkably, he had lost only** four men – but again, not one from scurvy.

Cook was immediately promoted to Captain and given honorary retirement from the Royal Navy, as an officer of

Resolution and Adventure in Matavia Bay, Tahiti by William Hodges R.A. (1744–97)

National Maritime Museum, London

On 12 February 1772 the Breton navigator Yves-Joseph de Kerguelen-Tremarec (1734–97) discovered an archipelago in the southern Indian ocean. The largest, Kerguelen (or Desolation) Island is surrounded by over 300 islets, covering 2,400 square miles. The glacial island is 100 miles long, with a mountain range rising to 6,455 feet.

Aside from other British navigators, several Frenchmen were busy criss-crossing the southern oceans at the same time as Cook. The best known was Louis-Antoine de Bougainville (1729–1811), who gave his name to islands, mountains and plants – including bougainvillea. Another was Julien-Marie (Jules) Crozet (1728–82).

Omai arrived at Portsmouth on 14 July 1774 as a twenty-one year-old crew-member on board HMS *Adventure*, captained by Tobias Furneaux. Taken immediately to meet Lord Sandwich, he was presented to King George III and Queen Charlotte at Kew on 17 July. He was placed in the care of Sir Joseph Banks until he returned home with Cook, arriving in November 1777. During his two years in England Omai had provided polite society with a living example of the "noble savage". He died around 1780.

Sir Joshua Reynolds P.R.A. (1723–92) painted this fine portrait of Omai in 1776. It was sold by Castle Howard for over £10 million in 2001.

• **Omai (1776) by Sir Joshua Reynolds**

Geenwich Hospital. In March 1776 the Royal Society made him a Fellow and awarded him the Copley Gold Medal for his success in combating scurvy. Shortly afterwards, Cook emerged from retirement to command yet another expedition to the Pacific: but this time with the purpose of discovering a northern passage by sea from the Pacific to the Atlantic Ocean.

In his second and last voyage in *Resolution*, Cook was accompanied by a newly purchased collier, HMS *Discovery*, commanded by Captain Charles Clerke. They set sail from Plymouth on 12 July 1776. The two ships were soon separated but met up in Table Bay on 18 October; and then sailed east across the Indian Ocean. Cook was able to fix precisely the position of Prince Edward Island and the Marion Islands by using the K1 chronometer, a replica of Harrison's H4 made by Larcum Kendall (1719–90) the size of a large pocket watch, 15 inches in diameter. H4 had proved itself to be the first to keep accurate time at sea on HMS *Deptford*, en route to Jamaica in 1761–62.

The Copley Medal is a scientific award for work in any field of science and is the highest award granted by the Royal Society. It is also its oldest medal, first awarded in 1731. The Award was created in honour of Sir Godfrey Copley, 2nd Bt. (1653–1709), who bequeathed £100 in 1709 (£152,000 today) to the Royal Society. He was a substantial landowner from Sprotbrough near Doncaster in Yorkshire, who was elected a Fellow in 1691. Today the winner of the award is presented with a silver-gilt medal and a cheque for £5,000.

The "sandwich" is named after the 4th Earl of Sandwich. Contemporary accounts refer to it with a capital 'S' and date the invention to around 1762. It was a popular myth that bread and meat sustained Lord Sandwich while gambling.

Able and efficient, Sandwich was also famously corrupt. Often in conflict with John Wilkes (1727–97), a radical demagogue, in one celebrated exchange he shouted, "Upon my soul, Wilkes, I don't know whether you'll die upon the gallows or of the pox". Wilkes replied, "That depends my Lord, on whether I first embrace your Lordship's principles, or your mistress". Wilkes was once told by a constituent that he would rather vote for the devil. Wilkes replied, "Naturally": adding, "If your friend decides against standing, can I count on your vote?".
• **John Montagu, 4th Earl of Sandwich by Thomas Gainsborough (1783)**
National Maritime Museum, London

Pausing briefly at Adventure Bay in Tasmania, then once again in Queen Charlotte Sound, he was forced by contrary winds to sail to Tonga instead of Tahiti, before heading north-west across the Pacific. He made his first major discovery of the voyage on 18 January 1778, when he sighted the islands of Oahu (Hawaii) and Kauai, at the western end of the Hawaiian archipelago. Cook named them the Sandwich Islands after John Montagu, 4th Earl of Sandwich (1718–92), the First Lord of the Admiralty.

In early March Cook reached the west coast of North America. He spent seven months conducting a running survey of the coast from California to the Bering Strait, on the way naming Cook inlet in Alaska, a distance of some 4,000 miles. At this point he was forced back by a solid wall of ice. He then tried to sail along the north coast of Siberia but soon encountered the same unyielding ice-pack. Perhaps due to the frustration and discomfort of this dispiriting voyage, Cook became increasingly irritable: exacerbated by a stomach complaint that had troubled him for some time. One manifestation of this was his attempt to force his crew to eat walrus meat. They found it inedible.

Cook returned to north-west America, becoming the first European to enter Nootka sound on the west coast of what was later named Vancouver island. He took astronomical observations and cut timber from the abundant forests for emergency masts and spars.

Before making another attempt on a north-east passage through the Arctic Ocean the following year, Cook decided to return to the Hawaiian Islands to sit out the winter of 1778–79.

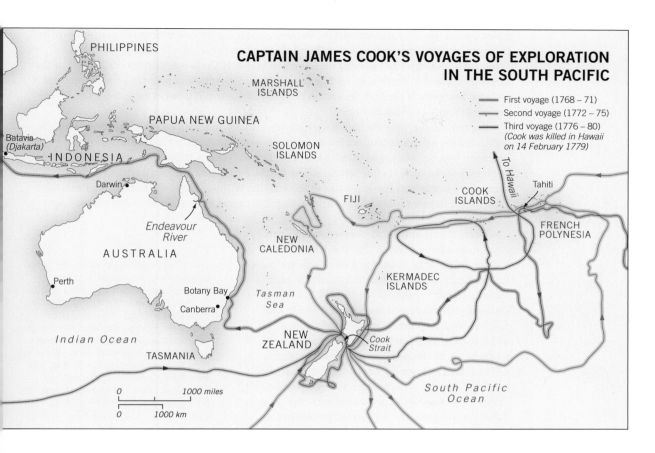

CAPTAIN JAMES COOK'S VOYAGES OF EXPLORATION IN THE SOUTH PACIFIC

First voyage (1768 – 71)
Second voyage (1772 – 75)
Third voyage (1776 – 80)
(Cook was killed in Hawaii on 14 February 1779)

On 17 January 1779, having surveyed the eastern end of the archipelago, Cook anchored in Kealakekua Bay off the main island of Hawaii.

Cook's arrival coincided with *Makahiki,* the most important Hawaiian New Year festival to honour the Polynesian god *Lono.* At first the natives were friendly, possibly believing him to be a visitation of *Lono* himself – a belief oddly reinforced by the similarity of the shape of Cook's ships to devotional objects associated with the god. Another coincidence was that Cook's clockwise progress around the islands during his survey resembled the religious processions that took place at the time of the festival.

On 4 February 1779 Cook hoisted sail to continue his survey of the island chain; but was forced to return to Kealakekua Bay a week later to carry out repairs to *Resolution*'s foremast, which had snapped in a fierce storm. It was immediately apparent that the expedition was not welcome. Relationships rapidly deteriorated when the islanders stole *Resolution*'s cutter.

On 14 February Cook, displaying less than his usual good judgement, went ashore with a light detachment of marines: with the intention of luring one of the local chiefs back to *Resolution,* where he would be held hostage against the return of the cutter. Cook apparently delayed casting off from the beach to retrieve a

South Pacific routes of Captain James Cook's voyages His first voyage is shown in red: second voyage in green: third voyage in blue

Hawaii (formerly the Sandwich Islands) became the 50th US state in 1959. The *Ka Hae Hawaii,* the official **State flag of Hawaii,** was designed at the request of King Kamehameha I (the "Great") in 1816. The Union Flag of Great Britain is emblazoned in the upper left corner, to honour Hawaii's friendship with the British.

stolen pair of tongs. This infuriated the natives, who attacked Cook's party. His marines fired at the crowd, but their musket balls largely failed to penetrate the native's thick grass shields. While his back was turned to assist the launch of his boats, Cook was clubbed on the back of the head and speared to death as he lay face down in the surf. Following their tradition, the natives stripped his bones of the flesh which was ceremonially burnt. The bones were distributed amongst the tribe's chiefs and elders.

Captain Clerke, who was suffering from tuberculosis, took command of the expedition. He persuaded the natives to return a few of the bones which were placed in a coffin and on 21 February 1779, he committed them to the deep. Two days later Clerke put to sea and completed the survey of the island before setting course for the Bering Strait, through which he intended yet again to attempt an Arctic passage to the Atlantic. Within sight of the Kamchatka Peninsula, Clerke died. Responsibility for the entire expedition passed to Virginia-born Lieutenant John Gore (1729–90).

Three junior officers who served under Cook went on to notable careers. The first, Cornishman William Bligh (1754–1817), was Cook's sailing master. In command of HMS *Bounty* in 1787, he sailed to Tahiti to obtain breadfruit plants. Bligh is best known for the mutiny of his crew in 1789. He and fourteen loyal crewmen were set adrift in an overloaded launch: but in an amazing act of seamanship, he reached Timor in 47 days – after a 3,618 nautical mile voyage across the Pacific. He later became Governor of New South Wales, where he suffered the indignity of another mutiny, the "Rum Rebellion" in 1808 – the only armed takeover of a colonial government in Australia. Much maligned and a brilliant seaman, Bligh ended his career as a Rear Admiral.

Captain Charles Clerke (1741–79) sailed on four voyages of exploration. He accompanied Captain John Byron in 1764 on HMS *Dolphin* to the Pacific. *Dolphin* completed a record circumnavigation in twenty-two months. His last three voyages were with Captain Cook. Between Cook's voyages he volunteered to serve time in the Fleet Debtors' prison for his brother, Sir John Clerke, where he contracted the tuberculosis which killed him. He was buried on the Kamchatka Peninsula.

The second, George Vancouver (1757–98), one of Cook's midshipmen, was born in King's Lynn in Norfolk. He led a remarkable voyage of exploration to the Pacific Coast of North America (1791–94). Vancouver Island in British Columbia and the city of Vancouver in Washington State are named after him. He died in obscurity, aged forty.

The third, George Dixon (1748–95), was born in Kirkoswald in Ayrshire – where Robert Burns went to school. He sailed under Cook on his third expedition. He left the navy and led an expedition to British Columbia and Hawaii in *Queen Charlotte* (1786–87).

Captain Cook left no descendants. His legacy lies in his remarkable contributions to exploration, science and the Royal Navy. He disproved the existence of a great southern continent, completed littoral surveys of eastern Canada, eastern Australia and New Zealand, charted the Society Islands, the New Hebrides, New Caledonia and the Hawaiian islands. Further, he accurately surveyed the north-west coast of America. Cook encouraged scientific research in natural history and ethnology; and the many drawings by his expedition artists were of outstanding merit. Having sailed the breadth of the Pacific from the Philippines to the Society Islands, he was the first European correctly to conclude that there was an ethnic connection between all the peoples of Oceania, despite living on islands thousands of miles apart. Finally, Cook's contribution to the future health of British sailors on long journeys was seminal.

There are many statues of Cook and monuments to his achievements around the world. The most exceptional however, was erected by his old captain Admiral Sir Hugh Palliser, in the grounds of his estate at Chalfont St Giles in Buckinghamshire. On each of the memorial's four sides is carved the legend: *To the memory of Captain James Cook, the ablest and most renowned Navigator this or any country hath produced.*

To Australians and New Zealanders especially, this was nothing less than the truth.

WHY THE PRIME MERIDIAN (0°) IS AT GREENWICH

The Prime Meridian, also known as the International Meridian or Greenwich Meridian, is the line of longitude passing through the Royal Greenwich Observatory in Greenwich. It is the meridian at which longitude is defined to be zero degrees. The prime meridian, and the opposite 180th meridian (at 180° longitude), which the International Date Line generally follows, separate the Eastern and Western Hemispheres. The Prime Meridian and the 180th meridian encircle the Earth like a longitudinal equator.

Unlike the parallels of latitude, which are defined by the rotational axis of the Earth (the poles being 90° and the Equator 0°), the prime meridian is arbitrary. Multiple variations have been used throughout history as the prime meridians of different mapmaking systems. The Greenwich Meridian, established by the Astronomer Royal, Sir George Airy (1801–92) in 1851, was agreed as the international standard in October 1884. At the behest of US President Chester Alan Arthur, 41 delegates from 25 nations met in Washington DC for the International Meridian Conference. France abstained when the vote was taken: and French maps continued to use the Paris Meridian for many years. The abbreviation GMT, for Greenwich mean time, has been replaced with UTC, for coordinated universal time.

Britain, to the *chagrin* (an appropriate word) of the French, has benefited greatly from London's position. By straddling the time differences across global markets, the City is the world's financial centre: earning £43 billion overseas in 2007 – perhaps it was to 0° that Nancy Mitford was referring in her 1949 novel, *Love in a Cold Climate.*

Louth in Lincolnshire is the most northerly town in the world situated on the Prime Meridian. At 295 feet, Louth also has the tallest church steeple in England. The most southerly point of land on the meridian before Antarctica is on the coast of Ghana.

In August 2007 the Tolai tribe in New Britain (Papua New Guinea) apologised for killing and eating four missionaries from Fiji, led by the Reverend George Brown of Durham, in 1878. Brown was aware of cannibalistic traditions in the region and once described a visit to a village in which he counted 35 smoke-blackened human jaw bones dangling from the rafters of a hut. "A human hand, smoke-dried, was hanging in the same house. And outside I counted 76 notches in a coconut tree, each notch of which, the natives told us, represented a human body which had been cooked and eaten there", he told the Royal Geographical Society.

ONE FOR DINNER

John Williams was born near London in 1796, the same year as William Banting and William Marsden – and the year of Robert Burns's death. Trained as a foundry worker and mechanic, in 1816 he was recruited by the London Missionary Society.

In 1817 Williams sailed to the Society Islands, establishing a mission on Raiatea, the second largest island after Tahiti. He returned to Britain in 1834 to have his translation of the New Testament into the Raratongan language printed. He also published a *Narrative of Missionary Enterprises in the South Sea Islands.*

Williams returned to the South Pacific in 1837. Most of his missionary work was very successful. In November 1839 however, he visited the New Hebrides (now Vanuatu)– and was killed and eaten by cannibals on the Melanesian island of Erromango.

JAMES LIND DISCOVERED THE CURE FOR SCURVY

James Lind (1716–94) was born in Edinburgh. Apprenticed to a surgeon in 1731, he joined the Royal Navy in 1739. In 1744 the catastrophic result of Anson's circumnavigation attracted much attention in Europe: out of 1900 men, 1400 had died, most of them from scurvy – the cause of many more deaths in the British fleets than in battle.

In 1747, while serving in the Channel, Lind conducted an experiment to find a cure for scurvy. He picked twelve men with the same symptoms and divided them into six pairs. He gave each pair different supplements to their basic diet. One pair received a quart of cider daily and another an unspecified elixir three times a day. The third pair drank seawater and the fourth, vinegar. The fifth pair was fed a mixture of garlic, mustard and horseradish; and the last two men ate two oranges and a lemon every day.

Four out of the six groups reported no change. Those given cider reported only a slight improvement – but the two seamen fed citrus fruits experienced a remarkable recovery. While there was nothing new about his discovery (the benefits of lime juice had been known for centuries), Lind had established the superiority of citrus fruits above all other quack remedies. In 1754 he published *A Treatise of the Scurvy* which came to the notice of Lord Anson. Anson helped to secure Lind's appointment as Physician to the Naval Hospital at Haslar, near Portsmouth in 1758 – the year of Nelson's birth.

Admiral George Anson, 1st Baron Anson M.P. (1697–1762) was born at Colwich in Staffordshire. He is chiefly remembered for his remarkable circumnavigation of the world during the War of the Austrian Succession (1740–48). As a Commander he was sent, with a squadron of six warships and two store ships, to harass Spanish possessions in South America. He left Britain on 18 September 1740; and, after a nightmare voyage of repeated disasters, overcome by heroism and stoical endurance, and the loss of three-quarters of his men, mostly through scurvy, returned in triumph in June 1744. Anson's greatest success was in capturing *Nuestra Señora de Covadonga*, a Spanish galleon sailing from Manila in the Philippines to Mexico, on 20 June 1743.

The treasure ship was carrying 1,313,843 pieces of eight and 35,682 ounces of pure silver: three-eighths of the value of which was claimed by Anson in prize money – worth £91,000 (£129 million today). Despite his immense fortune, Anson remained a sailor and at his post until his death: haunted by his terrible losses from scurvy, which made him especially attentive to Lind's proof of how to prevent it.

- **Admiral George Anson attributed to Thomas Hudson (before 1748)**

National Maritime Museum, London

Lind also proposed a simple method of supplying ships with fresh water. While it was already known that distilling sea water removed the salt, the process left a disagreeable taste. Lind demonstrated that the burnt taste quickly disappeared on exposure to air, dispensing with the need to alter the distillation process. Although the importance of Lind's findings on scurvy were recognised quickly, it was only 40 years later that an Admiralty Order was issued on the supply of lemon or lime juice to ships. The effect was almost immediate and scurvy disappeared from the fleets. American sailors began to call their British counterparts "limeys" shortly afterwards.

YANKEES ARE OKAY

In 1758 Major-General James Wolfe referred to New England soldiers under his command as Yankees: as in, "I can afford you two companies of Yankees". It is possible that the expression derives from the Cherokee *eankke*, meaning coward when referring to New Englanders.

As the letter "J" is pronounced "Y" in Dutch however, it is much more likely that the expression comes from a combination of two Dutch first names Jan and Kees (an abbreviation of Cornelius), still common Dutch first names and nicknames. Jan-Kees is also often used as a single first name in the Netherlands.

'Yankee' was used first by the British as a term of derision to describe Dutch-speaking colonists and later by the Royal Navy as a derogatory response to being called 'limeys'.

The curious expression 'Okay', now used worldwide, first appeared in the US during the mid-19th century. Its origin is unknown but continues to invite speculation. Among the more fanciful suggestions for its derivation are: the Scots "och aye", the Greek *ola kala* ("it is good"), the Choctaw Indian *oke* or *okeh* ("it is so"), the French *au quai* ("to the quay", as supposedly used by French-speaking dockers); or the initials of Obadiah Kelly, a railway freight agent, who stamped them on his loading documents.

The oldest written references to 'OK' follow its adoption as a slogan by Democrats during the US Presidential election in 1840. The party's candidate, President Martin Van Buren, was nicknamed "Old Kinderhook" (after his birthplace in New York State) and his supporters formed the "OK Club". This popularised the term but did not get Van Buren re-elected. Earlier, in the late 1830s, there was a craze in the US for humorous misspellings and "orl korrekt" was one of them. The theory that this led to the initials 'OK' appears in many dictionaries.

WILLIAM HOGARTH WAS BORN IN THE SAME YEAR AS ADMIRAL ANSON

William Hogarth was one of England's greatest, most interesting and original painters. His pictures satirised early 18th century life in London and provide a unique commentary on the double standards and corruption that were common in public life at that time. He was born at Bartholomew Close in London on 10 November 1697, the son of Richard Hogarth, a Latin teacher and author of school textbooks, and Anne Gibbons. Richard spent five years in the Fleet prison for debt: and, though he never referred to it, his father's shabby treatment greatly influenced Hogarth's views on the society, its morals (or lack of them) and hypocrisy that had ruined him. Hogarth was intelligent but stubborn, a proud libertarian, natural rebel and patriotic Englishman.

An Election Entertainment by William Hogarth (1755)
Sir John Soane's Museum

He trained as an engraver, but by 1720 had established his own business printing posters, book illustrations and funeral notices. In his spare time he learnt to paint, first at St Martin's Lane Academy; and then under Sir James Thornhill (1675–1734), whose daughter Jane he married in 1729. Hogarth made a name for himself with small family groups and conversation pieces. He also touted himself as a portrait painter. In 1731 he painted his first morality pictures, a genre which he invented. *A Harlot's Progress* was followed by *A Rake's Progress* in 1735 and *Marriage à-la-Mode* in about 1743.

The engravings of the first series were so popular that they were pirated – Hogarth's angry reaction led directly to the 1735 Copyright Act. Unfortunately, he found it difficult to sell the original paintings. Hogarth thought of his satires as pictorial theatre. In the wings were

**William Hogarth
self-portrait (1745)**
Tate, London

**The Shrimp Girl by
William Hogarth**
Tate, London

hilarious caricatures of petty larceny, venality and social affectation: whilst centre stage was used to highlight and lampoon serious criminals or debauched libertines and their vices.

His pictures are marvellously observant, meticulously detailed, richly coloured and beautifully painted: his little figures especially, sparkle like jewellery.

He targeted French and Italian artistic arrogance with venom. His mild xenophobia became extreme after a trip to Calais in 1748, at the end of the War of the Austrian Succession, when he was arrested as a spy for drawing the fortifications. His painting, *O the Roast Beef of Old England* was a statement of the pride he had in his country.

His ability as a painter is best observed in a small number of sympathetic and sensitive portraits. His compositions are masterly, his brushwork is fluent and bold. His obstinacy and prickliness precluded flattery and he painted what he saw as the truth. It is significant that his finest portraits, the carefree *Shrimp Girl* and the tender *Artist's Servants* (both in the Tate Gallery), were not commissioned; while the most celebrated of all, *Captain Coram* was that of a friend. They were all painted between 1735–40. From 1735–55 he ran his own academy in St Martin's Lane. It anticipated the Royal Academy, which was founded in 1768, a few years after his death.

Hogarth, a generous and public-spirited artist, did more than anyone to establish English painting as important in its own right; and as a more natural alternative to the lofty and self-regarding continental schools. His work for charity was unostentatious and unstinting. In the late 1730s he and a group of friends donated their history paintings to Thomas Coram's Foundation. An exhibition of theses pictures was very successful.

In 1753 he published *The Analysis of Beauty*, written in the belief that artists understand art better than their critics. Hogarth argued that beauty of line in all art and nature is of curves that adjust from one incline to another – not straight, parallel or right-angled intersecting lines which he thought were rigid and untrue to life. He called this "line of beauty" the 'S' line – which he claimed is the secret of all great art. In a self-portrait painted in 1745, *Painter and his Pug*, the 'S' line can be seen on his palette. The picture is now in the Tate Gallery.

In 1757 Hogarth was appointed Serjeant Painter to King George II. He died on 26 October 1764 and was buried in St. Nicholas's Churchyard, Chiswick Mall, in London. His friend, the actor David Garrick wrote the inscription on his tombstone:

Farewell, great painter of mankind!
*   Who reach'd the noblest point of art;*
Whose pictur'd morals charm the mind,
*   And through the eye correct the heart.*
If genius fire thee, reader, stay;
*   If nature touch thee, drop a tear;*
If neither move thee, turn away,
*   For Hogarth's honour'd dust lies here.*

Hogarth's House in Chiswick is now a museum: it is near one of London's best known and busiest road junctions – the "Hogarth Roundabout".

Sir John Soane's Museum in London's Lincoln's Inn Fields houses 30,000 architectural drawings, sculpture, books and paintings: including the eight canvases of Hogarth's *A Rake's Progress* and four of his *Humours of an Election*. Soane (1753–1837), born John Swan in Goring-on-Thames, was a neo-classical architect.

THE PHILANTHROPIST CAPTAIN CORAM WAS A FRIEND OF HOGARTH

The philanthropist Thomas Coram (*c.*1668–1751) established the London Foundling Hospital in Lamb's Conduit Street in Bloomsbury. It was the world's first incorporated charity – and a precursor of the homes for destitute children opened in London by the Dublin-born son of a Jewish immigrant from Prussia, Thomas Barnardo (1845–1905) in 1870.

Coram was born in Lyme Regis in Dorset. He spent his early life at sea and in the American colonies. From 1694–1705 he owned a dockyard at Taunton in Massachusetts. Returning to Britain, he became a successful merchant in London. He was appointed a trustee of Oglethorpe's Georgia colony in 1732 – and in 1735 he sponsored a colony in Nova Scotia for unemployed artisans.

Coram was appalled by the abandoned, homeless children living in the streets of London. On 17 October 1739 he was granted a Royal Charter by King George II: to set up a "hospital for the maintenance and education of deserted young children". Georg Frederic Handel donated the proceeds of a performance of *Messiah* and presented the manuscript of the *Halleluja Chorus* to the hospital. He also composed the *Foundling Hospital Anthem*.

Thomas Coram by William Hogarth (1740)
Foundling Hospital

SIR JOSEPH BANKS, BT. PRS

Joseph Banks was born on 13 February 1743 in London, the son of William Banks M.P., a rich Lincolnshire landowner, and Sarah, daughter of William Bate.

Banks was given a baronetcy in 1781, three years after being elected president of the Royal Society – a position he held for a record forty-two years. In charge of the Royal Botanic Gardens, Banks sent explorers and botanists across the globe: through his foresight Kew became the pre-eminent botanical gardens in the world. The name Banks dots the map of the Pacific: Banks Peninsula on South Island, New Zealand; the Banks Islands in modern-day Vanuatu; and Banks Island in the Northwest Territories in Canada. The suburbs of Banks in Canberra and Bankstown in Sydney are named for him. Banks is credited with the introduction to Europe of eucalyptus, acacia, mimosa and the genus named after him, Banksia. He died on 19 June 1820.

Sir Joseph Banks, Bt. PRS by Sir Joshua Reynolds (*c.*1773)
National Portrait Gallery, London

THE PLANT COLLECTORS

At the end of the last ice age only four important tree species had survived in Britain: the Oak, Juniper, Pine and Yew. Recolonisation through introductions by the Romans and Normans recreated a North European landscape; but it is entirely due to the exertions of British plant collectors over four hundred years that the British Isles have become host to the most varied ornamental and economic plants in the world. There are too many of these intrepid, usually unsung heroes (often Scotsmen) to list but a few:

John Tradescant "the Elder" (*c.*1570–1638), the first great English plant collector, was born in Suffolk. In 1610, as head gardener to the Earl of Salisbury, he was sent to the Netherlands to bring back fruit trees for Hatfield House. In 1618 the royal favourite, George Villiers, Ist Duke of Buckingham sent him on expeditions to the Nikolo-Korelsky Monastery in Arctic Russia and to the Levant. In 1620 he accompanied a punitive expedition to Algiers against the Barbary pirates, to collect seeds and bulbs. He also gathered specimens from American colonists. The genus *Tradescantia* is named after him.

John Tradescant "the Younger" (1608–62), born in Meopham in Kent, was the son of "the Elder". In 1628 he travelled to Virginia where he spent nine years collecting thousands of plant specimens. He brought back to England magnolias, bald cypress, tulip trees, phlox and aster plants. In 1638 he became head gardener to Charles I and created the gardens at the Queen's House in Greenwich.

Alexander Garden FRS (1730–91), born at Birse in Aberdeenshire, trained as a doctor in Edinburgh and served in the Royal Navy before following his father to Charleston in South Carolina. He sent many new plants, including several magnolias and the *Gordonia*, back to the Royal Society in London. The Swedish ecologist and taxonomist Carl Linnaeus named the genus *Gardenia* for him.

Francis Masson (1741–1805), born in Aberdeen, was the first collector to be employed by Sir Joseph Banks for Kew Gardens. He sailed with Captain James Cook on HMS *Resolution* to South Africa in October 1772. By 1775 he had discovered geraniums (*Geraniacae*) and sent back to England over 500 plant species. Masson's only book, *Stapeliae Novae*, on the South African succulents, was published in 1796. He discovered over 1,700 species: including Arum lily, Agapanthus, Belladonna lily, Bird of Paradise flower and Red Hot Poker.

This Eastern Cape giant cycad, a survivor from the Jurassic period, was sent to Kew Gardens as a seed from South Africa by Francis Masson in 1775. It needed to be repotted in 2009.

John Fraser (1750–1811) was born in Tomnacross in Inverness-shire. He discovered many American plants and trees including *Magnolia fraseri*. In 1780 he established an American nursery at Sloane Square in London. In 1798 he was appointed Plant collector to the Czar of Russia. He was amongst the first to issue nursery catalogues.

John Murray, 4th Duke of Atholl (1755–1830), known as "Planter John", was urged in a poem by Robert Burns to transform his Perthshire estates. After Burn's death in 1796, Murray began an ambitious scheme to plant native Scots pine and larch from the Austrian Tyrol, a species introduced by Robert More FRS M.P. (1703–80) in 1740. On one occasion, following a suggestion made by Alexander Nasmyth (1758–1840) who was known as the "father of Scottish landscape painting", he used a small cannon to fire canisters of seeds at an inaccessible hillside. This unusual method of propagation was extremely successful. He planted over 15 million trees, before he drowned in the river Tay.

John Reeves (1774–1856), plantsman and artist, was born in Essex. He joined the East India Company and in 1812, was sent to China. At the request of Sir Joseph Banks, he collected plants and sent back to England several hundred new species: including azaleas, chrysanthemums and wistaria. He also gave his name to a pheasant and a muntjac, a small Asian deer – now a pest in southern England.

David Douglas (1799–1834), born near Perth and trained at the Botanical Gardens in Glasgow, was sent by the director Sir William Jackson Hooker on a plant-hunting expedition to the Pacific north-west in 1824. There he discovered the 'Douglas' fir, which he introduced into the British Isles in 1827, along with many other conifer, spruce and pine species: transforming the landscape of Britain and revolutionizing the timber industry. He died mysteriously aged thirty-five in Hawaii, when he fell into a bull pit and was crushed to death by a bull which tumbled in after him.

William Lobb (1809–64), known as the "messenger of the big tree", was born at Perranarworthal in Cornwall. He was sent to South America and the west coast of North America by John Veitch, the celebrated Exeter horticulturist. Among a large number of his successful introductions are *Araucaria araucana* ("Monkey-Puzzle" tree) in 1843, *Nothofagus obliqua* (the Antarctic Beech), *Pinus radiata* (the Monterey Pine) and, most famously,

Sequoiadendron giganteum ("Wellingtonia") in 1853 – the year after "that giant among men", the 1st Duke's death. Lobb died, probably of syphilis, in San Francisco.

In the early 1800s it was noticed that the people of Assam, in north-east India, drank a tea made from a local, unidentifiable plant. In 1823 Major Robert Alexander Bruce (*c.*1789–1824) sent samples to the East India Company's Botanical Gardens in Calcutta: which could not confirm their identity as tea plants. In 1831 Lieutenant Charlton, on service in Assam, sent plants to the Agricultural and Horticultural Society in Calcutta, noting that the leaves were drunk as an infusion in Assam; and when dried, tasted of Chinese tea. Charlton's plants also defied identification. Official recognition did not come until Christmas Eve 1834, when Charles Alexander Bruce, Robert Bruce's brother, sent more samples to Calcutta – and the true identity of the plant was finally confirmed as *Camellia sinensis* var. *assamica* or the Assam tea plant. This discovery laid the foundation of the Indian tea industry.

Invented by an English doctor, Nathaniel Bagshawe Ward (1791–1868) the Wardian case was a portable greenhouse for growing and transporting plants.

Robert Fortune (1812–80), born in Kelloe in Berwickshire, was trained at the Royal Horticultural Society in Chiswick. In 1842 he was sent to China to collect plants, following the Treaty of Nanking which ceded Hong Kong to the British. In 1848, at the behest of the East India Company, he smuggled tea plants from China to India in Wardian cases. Although the penalty for tea smuggling was decapitation, Fortune, disguised as a Manchu courtier, managed to acquire cuttings of the famed silver-tipped tea, which came from the White Cloud Monastery in the Drum mountains of Fujian province in south-east China. Silver-tip tea (or *Yinkzhen*) had been the favourite of the Song dynasty Emperor Huizong (1082–1135) – said to have lost his empire through his obsession with brewing the perfect cup of tea.

Fortune propagated 20,000 tea plants in the Royal Horticultural Society's greenhouses, before sending them to Darjeeling in north-east India. Fortune's illicit expedition destroyed China's tea monopoly and undermined a staple of the country's economy. He also introduced the cumquat to Britain, along with many trees and flowers: including varieties of tree peonies, azaleas and chrysanthemum.

Sir Joseph Dalton Hooker OM PRS by William Hawker

Sir Joseph Dalton Hooker OM PRS (1817–1911) was born in Suffolk. One of the greatest British botanists and explorers of the 19th century, Hooker was an early exponent of geographical botany and Charles Darwin's closest friend. He was Director of the Royal Botanical Gardens in Kew for twenty years in succession to his father, William Jackson Hooker, and was awarded the highest honours of British science. In December 1859 Hooker published *Introductory Essay to the Flora Tasmaniæ*, describing botanical discoveries on his Antarctic voyage (1839–43). It was the last scientific expedition to be conducted under sail.

It was in this essay, which appeared just one month after the publication of Charles Darwin's *On the Origin of Species*, that Hooker announced his support for the theory of evolution by natural selection – the first respected scientist publicly to support Darwin. He started the series *Flora Indica* in 1855 with Thomas Thompson, having published the *Rhododendrons of Sikkim-Himalaya* between 1849–51.

Hooker's greatest botanical work was the *Flora of British India*, published in seven volumes, starting in 1872. Hooker was offered interment in Westminster Abbey, close to Charles Darwin, provided he was cremated. His wife Hyacinth refused. He died aged ninety-four and was buried beside his father in the churchyard of St Anne's, Kew – within sight of the Gardens to which both had devoted their lives.

Richard Spruce (1817–93), born in Malton in Yorkshire, was one of the greatest Victorian botanical explorers. He spent fifteen years exploring the Amazon basin from the Andes to the sea, collecting over 30,000 plant specimens. He learned from natives the anti-malarial properties of the cinchona tree's bitter bark – quinine.

Charles Ledger (1818–1906) was born in London. In 1836 he became a dealer in alpaca wool, an animal which he tried unsuccessfully to introduce into Australia. In 1863 he discovered a variety of the cinchona tree, to which he gave his name *Cinchona calisaya ledgeriana*. Attempting to smuggle a parcel of cinchona seeds out of Bolivia, his servant was beaten to death. A small portion was bought by the Dutch government and some reached British India. Ledger died in poverty, after losing all his money in the Australian bank failures of the early 1890s. From 1897, in belated recognition that the millions of cinchona trees grown in India and Java, which provided over two thirds of the world's supply, had originated from his seeds, the Dutch government paid Ledger an annuity of £100 (£45,000 today).

Sir Henry Alexander Wickham FRS (1846–1928), born in Hampstead, was responsible in 1876 for smuggling 70,000 seeds of the rubber tree *Hevea brasiliensis* from the Santarem region of Brazil to the Royal Botanic Gardens at Kew. After propagation, the seedlings were sent to British colonies in Africa and the Far East – where they thrived. Wickham's 'bio-piracy' not only broke the Brazilian monopoly of rubber production, but established the commercial Asian rubber estates in Malaya which provided most of the world's rubber for a hundred years.

Sir Henry Nicholas Ridley FRS (1855–1956), born at West Harling Hall in Norfolk, trained as a botanist at Oxford. He worked at the British Museum and travelled to South America, before he was sent to Singapore in 1888 to take charge of the Botanic Gardens and the forestry department of the Straits Settlements. His experiments with rubber trees (*Hevea brasiliensis*) led him to realise the economic potential of rubber as a plantation crop. After developing an efficient way of tapping latex, he campaigned single-handedly to establish the rubber industry. He met with considerable opposition but persisted doggedly, until by 1896 he had established his first commercial plantations. From this faltering start the rubber industry became the economic staple of the Malay States. He died aged 100.

George Forrest (1873–1932) was born in Falkirk in Stirlingshire and trained as an apothecary. After working in the Royal Botanic Gardens in Edinburgh, he was sent to China to find seeds. He obtained the cooperation of the Chinese by using his medical skills to treat them. He died in Yunnan province, having discovered varieties of adenophera aster, acer, iris, primula and *Rhododendron forrestii*.

Ernest Henry "Chinese" Wilson (1876–1930) was born in Chipping Camden in Gloucestershire. In 1897 James Veitch & Son commissioned him to find the Dove or Pocket-handkerchief tree *Davidia involucrata*. Wilson spent two years in the remote mountain valleys of China's Hupeh province searching for it. In 1902, six months after his return to England, Veitch & Co sent him back to China to find the yellow Chinese poppy *Meconopsis betonicifolia*. Then in 1903, in spite of suffering a crushed leg in an avalanche, he discovered the Regal lily (*Lilium regale*) in Szechuan province. In 1930 he and his wife were killed in a car crash in Worcester, Massachusetts. Sixty Chinese plant species are named after him.

Francis Kingdon-Ward (1885–1958) was born in Manchester. From his 25 expeditions to Tibet, China, Burma and Assam, he introduced the Himalayan blue poppy (*meconpsis betonificolia*) and the Giant cowslip (*Primula florindae*), as well as the yellow-flowering rhododendron (*Rhododendron wardii*). During WWII he set up a Jungle Survival School to teach soldiers how to recognise edible plants.

THE CONNECTION BETWEEN NELSON'S DUKEDOM AND THE BRONTË SISTERS

In 1802 a clever Ulsterman of humble birth from Drumballyroney in County Down, reading theology at Cambridge, so admired Nelson that he changed his name from Prunty, or Brunty, to Bronte (the district of Sicily near the volcano Mount Etna, so named from the Greek word for "thunder") – in a genuflection towards the dukedom given to Nelson by King Ferdinand. He added a diacritic, to turn it into Brontë in 1811.

Charlotte Brontë (1850) by George Richmond R.A. (1809–96)
National Portrait Gallery, London

The Reverend Patrick Prunty (1777–1861) married Maria Branwell, a twenty-nine year-old Cornish girl from Penzance, in 1812. While vicar of Thornton, near Bradford in Yorkshire the couple had the four youngest of their six children. Tragically, Maria died in 1821 aged only thirty-eight, of chronic pelvic sepsis as a result of childbearing. The children were brought up by her selfless sister Elizabeth.

Patrick wrote poetry and novels, one titled *The Cottage in the Wood* in 1815. He gave his children an excellent education, with a particular emphasis on literature. It is the novels written by his three youngest daughters which the world chiefly remembers now. Haworth, a bleak moorland village in the West Riding, where Patrick had the living from 1820, was a powerful influence on all three girls.

Charlotte was born in 1816 and married her father's curate Arthur Bell Nicholls (1819–1906) in 1854. She wrote poetry under the pseudonym Currer Bell. Weakened by morning sickness, she caught a chill and died on 31 March 1855 aged thirty-eight, less than a year after she was married. She had published *Jane Eyre*, arguably the best known of the sisters' novels, in 1847.

Emily Brontë by Patrick Branwell Brontë (c.1833)
National Portrait Gallery, London

Her powerful story, probably autobiographical, projects the intellect, self-sufficiency and sexuality of her heroine. *Jane Eyre* has been filmed and televised many times. It is an inspiration to proud, passionate and independent women.

Emily Jane was born in 1818 and never married. She published her poetry under the pseudonym Ellis Bell. Her only novel, *Wuthering Heights* was also published in 1847. She died of tuberculosis in 1848 aged thirty, three months after the sisters' only brother Branwell, who had suffered from the same disease, aggravated by *delirium tremens*, had died aged thirty-one. Her tale of brooding, passionate, self-destructive love has been staged and filmed many times and remains a much-loved classic.

The youngest and prettiest child, Anne was born in 1820. In 1846 she and her sisters had a volume of their poems printed privately, under their supposedly male pseudonyms (Anne's was Acton Bell), but only two copies were sold. The sisters finally found a publisher for their novels the following year. Charlotte's *Jane Eyre*, Emily's *Wuthering Heights* and Anne's *Agnes Grey* all became best-sellers.

Anne Brontë (left), from a group portrait by Patrick Branwell Brontë (c.1834)
National Portrait Gallery, London

Anne wrote several more books, the best remembered being *The Tenant of Wildfell Hall*, published in 1848. She died unmarried, also of pulmonary tuberculosis, at Scarborough in May 1849 aged twenty-nine.

Patrick Brontë died on 7 June 1861, aged eighty-four, and was interred in the family vault at Haworth church. He had lived and preached in the parish for forty-one years, outliving all his children.

THE INVENTOR OF THE WORLD'S FIRST IRON GUNBOAT WAS BORN IN 1805

John Laird was born in Greenock in Renfrewshire on 14 June 1805, the eldest son of William Laird and Agnes Macgregor. In 1824 William and Daniel Horton established the Birkenhead Iron Works to manufacture boilers, near Wallasey Pool in Cheshire. John Lairg joined his father in 1828 and the company was renamed William Laird & Son.

John Laird saw that the techniques of bending iron plates and riveting them together to build ships were much the same as those used to make boilers. His first vessel, *The Wye* was a 60-foot prefabricated iron lighter of 60 tons, built in 1829. In 1834 he built a paddle-steamer *John Randolph* for the town of Savannah in Georgia, the first iron ship in the US. In 1839 he built HEICS *Nemesis* for the Honourable East India Company, the first iron gunboat. John Laird died in Birkenhead on 29 October 1874.

By 1840 Laird had built another four gunboats for the East India Company's antipiracy patrols in Borneo and the South China Sea. Perhaps Laird's most famous vessel was the Confederate raider CSS *Alabama* in the US civil war (1860–65).

The business merged with Johnson Cammell to form Cammell Laird in 1903. It was nationalised along with the rest of the British shipbuilding industry, as British Shipbuilders in 1977. In 1986 it returned to the private sector as part of VSEL (Vickers Shipbuilding and Engineering Ltd). VSEL and Cammell Laird were the only British shipyards capable of making nuclear submarines. In 1993 it delivered HMS *Unicorn* (now the Canadian HMCS *Windsor*), the last ship of any sort to be completed at its yard before the company was declared insolvent in 2001, after 172 years in business.

HMS *Birkenhead*, one of the first iron-hulled RN frigates, was converted to a troopship before commissioning. She was built by John Laird in 1845. On 26 February 1852, while transporting the 73rd Regiment of Foot, she was wrecked at Gansbaai near Cape Town. There were not enough lifeboats on board for all the passengers. The soldiers stood firm however, allowing women and children to board the boats safely. Only 193 of the 643 passengers survived. The soldiers' chivalry led to the "women and children first" protocol when abandoning ship; and Kipling's "Birkenhead Drill" became the description of courage in hopeless circumstances.

Although carrying fewer cannon than even a corvette in the Royal Navy, *Nemesis* proved admirably suited to navigating the river mouths of China which were impassable to ships-of-the-line, because of mud flats and sand bars. She first saw action on 7 January 1841 when, having landed a force of 600 Indian Army sepoys near the Chuenpi forts, *Nemesis* bombarded the city's watchtower while three 74-gun wooden warships remained on station off Boat Island. While Chinese gunnery proved inaccurate, every round from *Nemesis* found its mark and the fortress fell shortly afterward. After serving as Britain's secret weapon in the First Opium War, *Nemesis* was last on patrol in Burmese waters in the early 1850s. Her finest hour was in late May 1841 at the top of the Macao Passage when her manoeuvrability, steam power and pivot-guns made her invincible against Chinese fire-boats and shore batteries. Her master found a safe place upriver from Canton to land a force led by General Gough (1779–1869) and he took the city.

The Wreck of the Birkenhead by Thomas M. Hemy

James Brooke by Sir Francis Grant (1847)
National Portrait Gallery, London

JAMES BROOKE, THE "WHITE RAJA", ERADICATED PIRACY FROM BORNEO

James Brooke (1803–68) was born in Benares in British India. He was a soldier, trader and explorer who arrived in Singapore in May 1839, on his way to survey Borneo. Just before his arrival, some British seamen had been shipwrecked and had been treated kindly by a relation of the Sultan of Brunei, Raja Muda Hussin. Governor Bonham of the Straits

Settlements and some British merchants asked Brooke to take the Raja letters of thanks and gifts but the Raja had been sent to put down a rebellion in Sarawak, which was then ruled by Brunei. The Sultan asked Brooke to go to his assistance. Brooke soon put an end to the rebellion with the aid of John Laird's gun boats.

In gratitude the Sultan of Brunei made Brooke Raja of Sarawak, almost the size of England, in September 1841. Raja Brooke worked hard to stamp out piracy and bring law and order to the coasts of North Borneo. As a result the population doubled within a few years. When coal was discovered on the island of Labuan, Raja Brooke advised the British Government to annexe it from the Sultan of Brunei, so that it could be used as a coaling station by steam ships voyaging in the South China Sea.

In 1847 James Brooke was knighted, appointed Governor of Labuan and British Consul-General in North Borneo. He retired from Borneo in 1863; and when he died in 1868, his nephew succeeded him as Raja. In 1888 Sarawak was made a British Protectorate. The Brooke dynasty ruled Sarawak for a hundred years, from 1841 until the Japanese occupied Malaya in 1941. Sarawak was ceded to Great Britain by Sir Charles Vyner Brooke (1874–1963) on 1 July 1946 and it became a crown colony. As part of the new state of Malaysia, Sarawak was granted independence on 16 September 1963.

James Brooke was buried in Sheepstor, near Plymouth.

Angela Burdett-Coutts (1814–1906) was the daughter of the radical politician Francis Burdett and grand-daughter of the enormously rich Edinburgh banker, Thomas Coutts (1735–1822). She had planned to marry Raja Brooke. He broke off the "engagement" however, using the excuse that he had been emasculated by a musket-ball in 1825, while storming Rangpur in Burma. A closet homosexual with an eye for pretty boys, he had actually been hit in the lung.

Denied marriage, Angela poured her energies into good works; and established church schools in Australia, Canada and South Africa. She also supported widely diverse projects: ranging from soup kitchens, dog fountains, bee-keeping, the first archaeological survey, the NSPCC, to that great Victorian favourite – the Temperance movement.

At the age of sixty-seven Angela married her American secretary, who was twenty-seven years her junior. In 1871 she was raised to the peerage as Baroness Burdett-Coutts of Highcliffe. She was buried in Westminster Abbey. By the time she died in 1906, Angela Burdett-Coutts had given away nearly £3,000,000 (£1.2 billion today). Raja Brooke, whatever his proclivities, must have been off his head to spurn her.

- **Angela Burdett-Coutts by unknown artist (c.1840)**
National Portrait Gallery, London

SIR STAMFORD RAFFLES

Stamford Raffles (1817) by George Francis Joseph
National Portrait Gallery, London

Thomas Stamford Bingley Raffles (1781–1826) was born off Jamaica aboard the West Indiaman *Ann*. His father was the Master, a Yorkshireman who died young. Raffles had to leave school at fourteen to support his mother and four sisters. Family influence secured him a clerkship at the East India Company's London office. In spite of long hours, Raffles determined to compensate for his inadequate education by studying hard in his own time. In March 1805 the secretary to the court of directors, William Ramsay, recommended him for the post of assistant secretary to the Company's recent settlement at Penang in north Malaya. Raffles sailed in April, having first married Olivia Fancourt (1771–1814) – the beautiful Irish-Indian widow of a Madras surgeon and ten years his senior. On the voyage Raffles learnt Malay, beginning a life-long study of Malayan history and botany.

On arrival in September 1805, he assumed the extra duties of Malay interpreter and court registrar. In 1807, on sick leave in Malaccca, Raffles frustrated the East India Company's intention to raze the town and transfer its population to Penang. In 1810 he sent a report, followed up by a visit to Calcutta. He impressed the Governor-General, Lord Minto by offering to use his intimate knowledge of local language and customs to suborn the rulers of Java and turn them against Dutch occupation in preparation for a British invasion. In September 1811 the Dutch administration surrendered and Minto appointed Raffles lieutenant-governor, with wide ranging powers. Unlike his East India Company directors, who were only concerned with profit, Raffles regarded the British occupation of Java as an unrivalled opportunity to extend British influence – and to change the rule of the road to driving on the left.

Commanding the northern approach to the strategic Malacca Straits, between West Malaysia and Sumatra, Penang is off the north-west coast of the Malay peninsula. The East India Company established a colony there in 1786. In 1826 Penang joined Malacca and Singapore to form the Straits Settlements.

Raffles replaced Dutch colonial practices with British law and improved the conditions of the native population. He introduced the jury system, abolished forced labour, dismantled monopolies and installed British residents at the courts of local rajas. He promoted an ambitious plan to appoint British agents in all the Malay archipelago's leading ports: in Borneo, Bali, Siam, Sumatra, Cambodia and Cochin China. Raffles's good intentions foundered when his radical reforms led to a slump in government and East India Company revenues. In December 1813 charges were brought against him in the Governor-General's court in Calcutta which he vigorously and successfully rebutted. However his patron, Minto died in March 1814; and his beloved wife died in November. Depressed and ill, Raffles left for Britain in March 1816.

The Governor of St Helena, Sir Hudson Lowe (1769–1844), an Anglo-Irish soldier, was born in Galway in the same year as Wellington and Napoleon. As Napoleon's "gaoler", from 1815 until his death in 1821, Lowe obeyed his instructions to the letter; but, widely criticised for his unnecessarily harsh regime, received little thanks from his government. Wellington thought little of him too; and said, "he was a very bad choice; he was a man wanting in education and judgement. He was a stupid man, he knew nothing at all of the world, and like all men who knew nothing of the world, he was suspicious and jealous".

Throughout his career Raffles put together an astonishing botanical collection, much of which he sent to Sir Joseph Banks, a founder of Kew Gardens. His name was immortalised when his botanist, Joseph Arnold discovered the largest flower in the world, *Rafflesia arnoldi*: and Raffles himself found a brilliantly coloured pitcher plant, the carnivorous *Nepenthes rafflesiana*.

On his way back to Britain, Raffles stopped at the island of St Helena and visited Napoleon who had been exiled there after the Battle of Waterloo. Much to his disappointment, he found the Emperor dull and unpleasant.

Though unpopular with the directors of the East India Company, Raffles was lionized in London, particularly by the Prince Regent's daughter Charlotte. Written in seven months, he published an outstanding work: *The History of Java*. In 1817 he was knighted and elected a fellow of the Royal Society. In October that year he was appointed Governor-General of Bencoolen in Sumatra, having just married his second wife: Sophia Hull (1786–1858), a plain but brave thirty year-old woman. In spite of his grand title, Raffles's authority had been severely reduced. Bencoolen was a fever-ridden port on the west coast of Sumatra, whose only activity was the export of pepper.

At the end of the Napoleonic wars, the British government was everywhere cutting costs. To Raffles's dismay, Java and other former Dutch possessions were returned to Holland. Raffles however, won limited approval to protect the Malacca trade route to the China seas. On 29 January 1819 he signed a treaty with the local *temenggong* (raja): allowing the East India Company to establish a trading-post on the Singapore river.

By October 1822 Raffles and his wife were both emotionally shattered and physically ill. Three of his four children had died – and he described himself at this time as, "a little old man, all yellow and shrivelled". Nevertheless, before retiring to Britain, and in spite of blinding headaches, harbinger of the brain tumour that was to kill him, he decided to pay Singapore, "this, my almost only child", a last visit.

Raffles's model for Singapore was based on the absolute principal that it should be a free port, "open to ships and vessels of every nation" – incorporating the highest notions of personal freedom, education, judicial equality, penal reform and slave emancipation. His dearest project was the foundation of the Singapore Institute, reflecting not only his strong belief in education but also a forward-thinking determination to meld Asian cultural values with the best Western traditions.

In March 1824 the Dutch formally relinquished their previous claims to Singapore. Raffles and his wife arrived back in Britain in August; and bought an estate near Hendon. In 1825, with the support of Sir Humphrey Davy, the President of the Royal Society, he proposed a London Zoo: to promote the science of zoology. In February 1826 he became its first president. In the same year he lost much of his remaining fortune in a failed bank. He was only forty-five when he died of a fit induced by a brain tumour, on 5 July 1826. He was buried in St Mary's church in Hendon.

A more selfless and far-sighted man, yet one so sadly treated by life, would be hard to find. His name will forever be linked to the prosperous and civilised nation he founded.

On 2 February 1824 Raffles and his wife with all their worldly possessions left for Britain on the East Indiaman *Fame*. That night *Fame* caught fire and her entire cargo was destroyed: including all of Raffles's lifetime collection of plants, animals, manuscripts, drawings, historical notes and scientific papers.

Raffles's grave remained unmarked until April 1914, when his coffin was accidentally discovered during building works. The vicar of St Mary's, whose family owned plantations in the West Indies, had disliked Raffles's support for the abolition of slavery – and had refused even to erect a tombstone in his memory.

THE YANGTZE INCIDENT – THE LAST HURRAH FOR 'GUNBOAT DIPLOMACY'

On 20 April 1949 HM sloop *Amethyst* was on her way from Shanghai on the Yangtze River to replace the destroyer HMS *Consort* as guard ship to the British Embassy in Nanjing (Nanking) during the civil war between the Kuomintang Nationalists (KMT) and the Chinese Communists, the People's Liberation Army (PLA).

At about 09:30, as *Amethyst* approached Kiangyin, a shell hit the wheelhouse and the injured coxswain grounded the ship on Rose Island. Another shell mortally wounded Lieutenant Commander Skinner. By the time the shelling stopped at about 11:00, 22 men had been killed and 31 wounded. The ship managed to send off a signal to all ships in the area, "Under heavy fire, am aground, large number of casualties"; before further shelling wrecked the power room below decks, disabling the gyrocompass, wireless and electrically-controlled firing circuits. *Amethyst* was now a helpless target. About 65 men were ordered to abandon ship and attempt to escape to KMT controlled territory. Some were shot in the water but the survivors made it back to Shanghai. Remaining on board were about 62 men, twelve of them wounded. The shelling had stopped but no one could move without attracting sniper fire.

Amethyst had received over 50 hits. Holes below the waterline were plugged with hammocks and bedding. During this time HMS *Consort* was sighted, flying 7 White Ensigns and 3 Union Jack flags, steaming down from Nanking at 29 knots. *Consort* came under fire which she returned with her 4.5 inch guns, destroying the enemy shore batteries, before attempting to take *Amethyst* in tow. *Consort* turned about with all guns targeting the north bank batteries, destroying one of them. However, *Consort* came under further heavy fire and the attempt was abandoned, with ten men killed.

Lieutenant Geoffrey Weston refloated *Amethyst* on 22 April but, fortunately out of range of the PLA's artillery, she ran onto a mud bank. The British Naval Attaché, Lieutenant Commander John Kerans joined the ship the same day and assumed command. On 24 April *Amethyst* was refloated a second time and moved up river to anchor off Fu Te Wei. Later that day a signal was received: "HM ships *London* and *Black Swan* are moving up river to escort the *Amethyst* down stream. Be ready to move". The cruiser *London* and the sloop *Black Swan* were heavily shelled as they attempted to help *Amethyst* and withdrew. Three British sailors had been killed, with a further fourteen wounded, as well as 250 PLA soldiers in artillery exchanges.

Amethyst remained under menace from the PLA for ten weeks, with vital supplies withheld from the ship. Negotiations were unsuccessful as Kerans would not accept Major Kung's demand that the British admit that they had wrongly "invaded" Chinese national waters and had fired upon the PLA first.

On 30 July *Amethyst* slipped her chain and headed down river in the dark, running the gauntlet of Communist guns on both banks of the river for 104 miles. She followed a merchant ship through the shoals, which confused the PLA. At 05:00 on 31 July *Amethyst* approached the PLA forts at Woosung and Par Shan with their searchlights sweeping the river. At full speed ahead, she broke through the boom at the mouth of the river, making the signal "Have rejoined the fleet off Woosung .... God save the King".

Amethyst re-enacted her role in the 1957 film *Yangtse Incident*. Richard Todd (1919–2010), a Dubliner, starred as John Kerans. Sadly, the flashy and aggressive Kerans (1915–85), another Anglo-Irishman, born in County Offaly "then Kings' County", and later a Conservative M.P., was an officer not greatly liked by his contemporaries or admired by his superiors. He died an embittered alcoholic.

NURSE MARY SEACOLE WAS BORN IN THE YEAR OF TRAFALGAR

Mary Jane Seacole was born in 1805 in Jamaica. She was a mixed-race British nurse who operated boarding houses and treated the sick in Panama. Seacole had been taught herbal remedies and folk medicine by her mother. A nomad and a patriot, on hearing of the terrible conditions faced by the sick and wounded in the Crimean War and sure that her knowledge of tropical medicine would be of use, she travelled to London and volunteered as a nurse. Although experienced in dealing with cholera, her application to join Florence Nightingale (1820–1910) was rejected. She borrowed the money to make the 4,000 mile journey to the Crimea alone.

On arrival Mary Seacole attended to the wounded on the battlefield. On many occasions she treated wounded soldiers, from both sides, while under fire: Florence Nightingale and her nurses were based in a hospital several miles from the front.

Mary Jane Seacole by Albert Charles Challen (1869)
National Portrait Gallery, London

Florence Nightingale (1820–1910), known as "The Lady with the Lamp", was a hospital reformer and fine statistician. She suffered from depression and spent most of her last 40 years in bed. The best known woman in Britain after Queen Victoria, she was the first woman (in 1907) to be made a member of the Order of Merit by King Edward VII.

In 1856, at the end of the war, Mary Seacole found herself stranded in the Crimea and almost destitute. She was saved from penury by Lord Rokeby (1798–1883), who organised a benefit for her. She died of "apoplexy" (a seizure) in Paddington in London in 1881.

Mary Seacole was lauded in her lifetime but then forgotten. Today she is remembered not only for her bravery, but as "a woman who succeeded despite the racial prejudice of influential sections of Victorian society". Her 1857 autobiography, *Wonderful Adventures of Mrs Seacole in Many Lands*, a vivid account of her life and experiences, is one of the first autobiographies by a black woman.

INCOME TAX WAS INTRODUCED TO PAY FOR THE NAPOLEONIC WARS

There were 140,000 men in the Royal Navy in 1809. In 1803 Britain possessed 202 ships-of-the-line and over 500 'cruisers', more than half the world's warships. France had only 39 ships-of-the-line but, in combination with the Dutch and Spanish, controlled a total of 118. This was the only time in modern history that one nation has been so dominant at sea. The 1801 census of Great Britain and Ireland recorded a total population of less than 16 million: of which, by 1810 some 500,000 were serving in the army or navy – perhaps one able-bodied man in every twelve, a staggering percentage. With a population of over 29 million, France was far less strained.

The Prime Minister, William Pitt ("the Younger"), introduced income tax for the first time in his December 1798 budget, to fund the enormous cost of the wars with France. It was levied in 1799 at 2d in the £ (0.833%) on annual incomes over £60, increasing to a maximum of 2s (10%) on incomes of over £200.

The population of Great Britain and Ireland in 1801 was (in millions): England 8.5, Wales 0.54, Scotland 1.6 and Ireland 5.2. Ireland's population continued to rise sharply, but unsustainably, to 8,175,124 in 1841. It had plummeted to 6.9 million by 1851, as a result of the Potato Famine in 1845 and emigration, especially to the United States. In contrast, and also despite considerable emigration, by 1851 the population of Great Britain had doubled to 21 million.

WHY THE TAX YEAR BEGINS ON 6 APRIL

There is often confusion about dates before the introduction of the Gregorian calendar to Britain in 1752. A modification of the Julian calendar (named after Julius Caesar, who introduced it in 45 BC), it was decreed by Pope Gregory XIII on 24 February 1582.

The Gregorian Calendar was devised because the mean year in the Julian was slightly too long. The vernal equinox had drifted slowly backwards in the calendar year and the lunar calendar, used to compute the date of Easter, was out of alignment too. The Gregorian system dealt with both problems by dropping some days to bring the calendar back into synchronisation with the seasons; then slightly shortening the average number of days in a calendar year, by omitting three Julian leap-days every 400 years.

The British Empire did not adopt the Gregorian calendar until 1752. It was then necessary to adjust the date by eleven days (Wednesday 2 September being followed by Thursday 14 September 1752). It included an extra day for 29 February 1700 (Julian).

The British name for the Christian festival of the Annunciation of the Virgin Mary (25 March) is Lady Day: until 1752 it was the beginning of the legal year in England. From 1753 until 1799, the tax year in Great Britain began on 5 April – the 'old style' (O.S.) new year of 25 March. A 12th Julian leap-day skipped in 1800 changed its start to 6 April. It was not changed when a 13th Julian leap day was skipped in 1900, so the start of the tax year in Britain stayed on 6 April – and has done so ever since.

William Pitt "the Younger"
attributed to Thomas
Gainsborough

WILLIAM PITT ("THE YOUNGER") WAS BORN IN 1759, *ANNUS MIRABILIS*

William Pitt, "the Younger" (1759–1806), was Britain's youngest and second longest serving prime minister – only Robert Walpole has ever served longer. Pitt's two ministries, from December 1783 to February 1801 and May 1804 to January 1806, totalled nineteen years. He defined and consolidated the duties of prime minister by his dextrous administration of key government departments, while maintaining the confidence of the King. His conduct of the wars with France were of critical importance to Britain's ultimate victory – which he never lived to see.

Pitt, the second son of William Pitt ("the Elder"), 1st Earl of Chatham, was born at Hayes Place in Kent; and educated privately, due to his frail constitution. A precocious child, he was only fourteen in 1773 when he attended Pembroke Hall (now College), Cambridge. In 1776 ill health obliged him to leave without taking a degree. He was permitted to graduate however, taking advantage of a privilege only granted to the sons of noblemen. In 1778, the year of his father's death, he was called to the Bar by Lincoln's Inn. In 1780 he failed to be elected as a Member of Parliament for Cambridge; but in January 1781 he was returned for Appleby in Westmorland. Appleby was a "rotten borough", as was Old Sarum, the constituency that had elected his father nearly half a century before.

Once in the House of Commons however, he turned on the hand that had fed him: strongly arguing against the existence of rotten boroughs. He aligned himself with the leading Whig libertarian, Charles James Fox; and proposed, as his father had done, that Britain should make peace with the American rebels. In supporting Fox's determination to end the slave trade, Pitt renewed an old university friendship with William Wilberforce, the most prominent abolitionist. His self-confidence and new-found debating skills were astounding in one so young and previously unassuming.

In 1782 Pitt was appointed Chancellor of the Exchequer in Lord Shelburne's administration. Fox refused to serve under Shelburne. His refusal brought down Shelburne's ministry and led to a lifelong political enmity with Pitt.

Rather than see Fox take office, the King invited Pitt to form a ministry. Knowing he would not secure a majority, Pitt wisely refused – but shot Fox's fox by raising the question of parliamentary reform with the coalition government that had been formed by Fox with Lord North. Fox's reformist supporters now looked to Pitt as their natural leader. In December 1783, after the loss of the American colonies, Fox introduced an East India Bill, which was defeated. George III once again invited Pitt to form a government: and entirely through the influence of the crown, Pitt became Prime Minister two months before his twenty-fifth birthday. A popular ditty observed that it was "a sight to make all nations stand and stare: a kingdom trusted to a schoolboy's care".

In 1784 Pitt enacted his own East India Bill: creating a Board of Control, which gave the government authority over the East India

Charles James Fox (1749–1806) was a brilliant orator and a champion of liberty. He entered Parliament in 1768 and rose to become leader of the Whig party. He vehemently defended the rights of the American colonists, a stance which was principled but unpopular. Nearly always in political opposition, he conducted a campaign against George III.

The King disliked his gambling and colourful private life, believing that Fox had debauched his eldest son, the appalling future King George IV. Fox served as Britain's first foreign secretary on three brief occasions. In his championship of the French revolutionaries however, Fox became increasingly isolated as the Reign of Terror revealed its horrors. He died nine months after Pitt.

• **Charles James Fox by Karl Anton Hickel (1794)**

National Portrait Gallery, London

Company and the right to appoint Governors-General as supreme head of the administration of India. In 1791 he secured the future of Canada, by passing the Constitutional Act, dividing the colony into French and English-speaking provinces. In 1786 Pitt addressed the problem of the huge national debt of £250 million (£310 billion today), incurred during the American Revolution. He created a sinking fund and reorganised excise revenues.

The French Revolution (1789–93) encouraged radicals but frightened Pitt's ministry into passing repressive legislation. *Habeas Corpus* was suspended for seven years from 1794–1801; and, in 1792 the Seditious Meetings Act forbade the founding of any movement for political reform. France also fomented revolution in Ireland: which Pitt tried to counter by uniting Ireland with England in the Act of Union of 1800. George III however, baulked at Pitt's supplementary proposal for full Catholic emancipation, believing it would be a violation of his coronation oath. In February 1801 Pitt resigned.

In 1792 George III had offered Pitt a Knighthood of the Garter. Pitt snubbed the King when he proposed instead that the honour be given to his elder brother, the 2nd Earl of Chatham. When the King became temporarily insane in 1801, though the cause was later identified as porphyria, he blamed Pitt for his condition.

The next administration, formed by Pitt's friend Henry Addington, soon began to disintegrate: and in 1804 the King had to ask Pitt to form a second ministry. In spite of Nelson's victory at Trafalgar in 1805, after the defeat of the Austrians at Austerlitz two months later Pitt had to cope with the collapse of the Third Coalition which he had assembled against Napoleon. Gazing at a map of Europe, he said "Roll up that map; it will not be wanted these ten years". It was an amazingly accurate prediction.

In 1789 Andrew Pears (1767–1845) from Mevagissey in Cornwall, opened a barber's shop in Soho. After years of experimentation, in 1807 he invented a gentle soap for delicate complexions.

It is still known for its oval shape and translucent amber colour. Each bar is aged for three months, until it reaches a pure transparency – a process still followed today. By commissioning Sir John Millais, Bt. R.A. (1829–96) to paint *Bubbles* (a portrait of the artist's grandson), Pears Soap blurred the line between advertising and art.

• **Bubbles by Sir John Everett Millais**

Pitt's health, always fragile and exacerbated by an addiction to port, now broke down. On 23 January 1806 he died. His last words were much later said by a kinsman to have been, "Oh, my country! How I love my country": but by others nearer the time, "I think I could eat one of Bellamy's veal pies". On 22 February he was buried in Westminster Abbey. There was never a possibility of a Pitt "the Youngest", if rumours of his homosexuality were true. He is certainly never known to have touched a woman in a suggestive manner and he never married. It is most likely that he was a capon: like Doctor Johnson, but a great deal better looking.

In 1805 Pitt made the remark, in response to the Lord Mayor's toast, for which he is best remembered: ".... Europe [will] not be saved by any single man. England has saved herself by her exertions, and will, I trust, save Europe by her example".

Though Pitt was unquestionably an outstanding parliamentarian, he was in truth, the nominee of the King. His personal support in the Commons never exceeded fifty. To his great disappointment, he failed to pass bills to abolish the slave trade, reform parliament or emancipate Catholics: because George III, a good man in many ways and devoted to his people, had little interest in change of any sort – the principal reason the American colonies had been lost in 1781, the year Pitt had first entered Parliament.

BEAU BRUMMELL

The decade between 1811, when King George III was deemed unfit to rule and his son, the Prince of Wales, ruled as Prince Regent until his father died in 1820 is known as the Regency. During that period George Bryan ("Beau") Brummell (1778–1840) was the supreme dandy and arbiter of London fashion. He abandoned knee-breeches and pioneered the wearing of dark, well tailored, full length "pantaloons". His style of menswear, consisting of plain but immaculately fitting clothes and elaborate cravats, evolved into the modern suit and tie.

Brummell was born in London, the son of the private secretary to the Prime Minister, Lord North. Educated at Eton and briefly at Oriel College, Oxford, he was from a prosperous but far from aristocratic background. When he joined the 10th Light Dragoons he met and joined the circle of the Prince of Wales (1762–1830), known as "Prinny". Brummell was not a serious soldier and resigned his commission when his regiment was posted to Manchester.

In an age insensitive to personal hygiene, Brummell was extraordinary in following a fastidious daily routine of bathing, shaving and cleaning his teeth. He refused to wear a wig and had his hair cut "à la Brutus", in the fashion of ancient Rome. His elegant dress, insistence on impeccably starched linen and elaborate cravats soon set a fashion enforced by his sharp wit and quick tongue.

At first Prince George had imitated the Beau's exquisite style; but his self-indulgence and obesity soon precluded dandyism, making him a focus of Brummell's sardonic humour.

Walking in St James's with Lord Moira, Brummell ran into the Prince: who greeted Moira warmly but pointedly ignored Brummell. "Pray who is your fat friend?", asked Brummell of Moira as they resumed their walk – in a voice calculated to be heard. The Prince never addressed another word to Brummell.

In 1799 Brummell inherited £30,000 (over £31 million today) from his father which he squandered, going bankrupt in 1816. He escaped his creditors by fleeing to Calais where he lived off the charity of his friends. In 1830 he was appointed Consul at Caen but was dismissed in 1832. In 1839, after years of surviving on handouts from shopkeepers, he suffered a series of strokes and was committed to the local asylum of Bon Saveur. On 30 March 1840 he died there, aged sixty-two, and was buried in Caen's Protestant cemetery.

Beau Brummell by Richard Dighton (1805)

The Royal Pavilion at Brighton was redesigned between 1815–22 by John Nash (1752–1835) for the Prince Regent, later George IV

Brummell's valet dressed him in public and once had to throw away 27 cravats to satisfy the Beau. He insisted on his boots being polished with champagne.

Sixty years later, history repeated itself when Edward, Prince of Wales was playing billiards with his old friend Sir Frederick Johnstone (1849–1913) at the Marlborough House Club – which the Prince had established after being forbidden to smoke in White's Club. When Johnstone miscued, Edward rebuked him saying "Freddie, Freddie, you are too drunk". Johnstone replied, pointing to Edward's considerable girth, "Tum-Tum, you are very fat". Johnstone was immediately asked to leave and was never spoken to by the Prince again.

TOM CRIBB WON HIS FIRST PUBLIC PRIZE FIGHT IN THE YEAR OF TRAFALGAR

Tom Cribb (1781–1848), born in Hanham in Gloucestershire, was one of England's most celebrated bare-knuckle champions, known as "The Black Diamond". He won his first public contest, against George Maddox, at Wood Green on 7 January 1805. The fight lasted seventy-six rounds, taking two hours and 10 minutes.

The modern boxing code was devised in 1867 by a young journalist from Carmarthenshire, John Graham Chambers (1843–83). "The Queensberry rules for the sport of boxing" are so named because the 9th Marquess of Queensberry publicly endorsed them. The rules required the use of boxing gloves, a count of ten and three-minute rounds. They were designed to persuade boxers that, "you must not fight simply to win: no holds barred is not the way; you must win by the rules". There were twelve.

Cribb held the title throughout the years of the sport's peak in popularity. On his retirement in 1822, he was awarded a lion-skin championship belt, the first ever "title belt". After retirement Cribb kept a pub, The Union Arms in Piccadilly, until 1839.

Tom Cribb Staffordshire portrait figure by unknown artist (*c.*1810–1815)
National Portrait Gallery, London

KING GEORGE III'S 'BOLT-HOLE' IN THE EVENT OF INVASION

Weedon, in Northamptonshire is in the very heart of England. An Act of Parliament was passed in 1803 for the purchase of 53 acres there, "for erecting buildings thereon for the service of His Majesty's Ordnance": subsequent purchases increased the estate to about 150 acres. In order to move goods quickly into the depot, a canal was cut to the nearby Grand Junction Canal, which formed the eastern boundary of the estate. Three spacious white brick buildings, later known as the Pavilion, were also built. They were to be used as a residence for King George III and the royal family, who would have been sent there by canal, should the invasion threatened by Napoleon occur.

Rich and athletic young dandies or "bloods", who attended "Gentleman" John Jackson's boxing academy in Bond Street, were known as "Corinthians". Jackson (1769–1845) became Champion of England on 15 April 1795. Lord Byron mentions that he received instruction from Jackson.

THE IMPRESS SERVICE, KNOWN AS THE 'PRESS GANG'

The organisation employed to crew the Royal Navy was known as the Impress Service. The Impress Service was supposed to seize only men aged between 18 and 55 who were already "seamen": a description given a broad interpretation. The word "press" was a corruption of the old French *prest* for a "loan". A man paid the King's shilling to enlist, became an "imprest" or a pressed man: i.e. given an "advance" of pay.

The Impress Service covered the country. The senior officer in each major port was known as the Regulating Officer and his headquarters were called the Rendezvous. Having chosen his Rendezvous, the Regulating Officer would hire some of the local hard men as "gangers", to form the Press Gang. On land the press gang was rarely formed by sailors, who might simply abscond themselves: conversely, being a ganger was perhaps the only certain way of not being pressed. The Gang was sent out to roam the surrounding countryside in search of suitable recruits. They were paid money for travel (3d per mile for officers, 1d for men) and money per man pressed – anything up to 10 shillings. The scope for corruption was large and many would bribe their way out of the Gang's clutches. For a prosperous man, a £10 bribe (£10,000 today) to the press gang was a small price for keeping his liberty.

The press had existed in one form or another for centuries; and certain rules had evolved about the taking of men for service at sea. Merchant ships were obvious targets for the press gang and a Royal Navy captain could board a merchant ship to take off any men he might want: officers and apprentices were exempt. Many merchant captains built hideaways for particularly valuable men to hide in if the press gang came aboard. The rule was that the captain must be left with enough men on board to "navigate the ship", again a tradition that was often disputed – occasionally with force.

THE BEAUFORT SCALE WAS INVENTED IN THE YEAR OF TRAFALGAR

Rear Admiral Sir Francis Beaufort (1774–1857) was of Huguenot extraction and born in Navan, County Meath. He introduced a scale in 1805, to help sailors gauge wind speeds through observation of the state of the sea. It was adopted by the Royal Navy in 1838 and became mandatory for all ships' log entries. It is still in use today.

The scale runs from force 0 (dead calm) to force 12 (hurricane). Gale warnings are issued when winds of force 8 or greater are forecast. In 1955 forces 13 to 17 were added by the US Weather Bureau, for use in tropical cyclones, typhoons or hurricanes of exceptional ferocity. The scale was adapted for use on land in the 1850s.

NELSON'S COLUMN

Nelson's Column was built between 1840–43. The 18-foot statue of Nelson stands on top of a 151-foot granite column, facing south: towards the Admiralty and down Whitehall. The column is usually said to be 185 feet tall; but when it was steam-cleaned in 2006, it was found to be only a touch over 169 feet from the bottom of the first step to the tip of Nelson's hat.

The top of the Corinthian column is decorated with bronze acanthus leaves cast from British cannons. The square pedestal is decorated with four bronze panels, cast from captured French guns, depicting Nelson's four great victories.

The monument was designed by architect William Railton (1801–77) in 1838. His 1:22-scale stone model is in the National Maritime Museum at Greenwich. Sir Edwin Landseer's four lions, guarding the pedestal of the column, were an afterthought, added in 1867. The entire edifice cost £47,500 (£36 million today).

At the base of the column, Nelson's famous signal before Trafalgar is misquoted. In place of: "England Expects *That* Every Man *Will* Do His Duty", is: "England Expects Every Man *To* Do His Duty". The latter version had appeared wrongly in the logs of several ships after the battle: and it has proved persistent ever since.

Thomas Gainsborough self-portrait (*c*.1758–59)
National Portrait Gallery, London

THOMAS GAINSBOROUGH WAS TAUGHT BY WILLIAM HOGARTH

Thomas Gainsborough R.A. (1727–88) was born in Sudbury in Suffolk, the fifth son and ninth child of a clothier. While J.M.W. Turner and John Constable (1776–1837) are more celebrated as landscape painters and Joshua Reynolds (1723–92) and possibly a few others were finer portraitists, no other English painter has been as successful in both genres as Gainsborough – not even William Hogarth who taught him.

In 1740 Gainsborough's father John, impressed by his son's gift for drawing, sent him aged thirteen to London to study art. He was taught portraiture in the studios of Francis Hayman and William Hogarth. He also helped decorate Thomas Coram's Foundling Hospital.

In 1746 Gainsborough impregnated and then married Margaret Burr (*c*.1728–98), an illegitimate daughter of the 3rd Duke of Beaufort: who settled an annuity of £200 (£287,000 today) on the couple. This comfortable affluence did not last – by the 1750s, as a *bon viveur* with two surviving daughters and expensive tastes, he began seriously to paint for a living. His best known double portrait of *Mr and Mrs Andrews* dates from this period. In his early thirties he moved from Ipswich to Bath, to attract the wealthy clientèle who thronged the fashionable spa town. By this time Gainsborough's pictures reflected the style of the great Court painter from Antwerp – Anthony Van Dyck, whose techniques he copied in his famous 1770 portrait *The Blue Boy*.

In 1774 Gainsborough moved to London; where he delighted the royal family who preferred him to the official court painter, Joshua Reynolds. Gainsborough's output was enormous. He was the only important English portrait painter to devote time to landscapes: as well as seascapes, pastoral themes and children. He was a founder of the Royal Academy, with whom he fell out over the hanging of his work. In 1836 his pictures moved Constable to exclaim, "On looking at them, we find tears in our eyes and know not what brings them". But in 1784, tired of altercation, Gainsborough said of his remaining ambition: "I am sick of portraits and very much wish to .... walk off to some sweet village, where I can paint landskips *[sic]* and enjoy the fag end of life in quietness and ease". He died of cancer on 2 August 1788 and is buried in Kew churchyard.

The Rev. John Chaly Playing the Violoncello in a landscape by Thomas Gainsborough (*c.*1750–52)
Tate, London

ANOTHER SUFFOLK MAN WAS CAPTAIN SIR PHILIP, "BRAVE" BROKE

Philip Bowes Vere Broke was born in 1776 at Broke Hall, overlooking the River Orwell, near Ipswich. The eldest son of Philip Bowes Broke, he went to school in Ipswich and joined the Royal Navy in 1788. He went to sea as a midshipman on HMS *Bulldog* in 1792; served as a Lieutenant on the frigate HMS *Southampton* in the Battle of Cape St Vincent in February 1797; was promoted to Commander in 1799 and Captain in 1801. Broke took command of HMS *Shannon* on 31 August 1806.

HMS *Shannon* was a 38-gun frigate. Since the 1750s the term frigate had described the smaller, faster types of warship used for commerce protection, raiding or scouting for the main fleet. They had two decks, with the main armament carried on the upper deck. Completed in 1806, the year after Trafalgar, *Shannon* was a Fifth Rate 'Leda' class frigate, mounting twenty-eight 18-pounder guns on her upper deck – the Royal Navy's largest type of frigate during the Napoleonic Wars.

To meet all its commitments the Admiralty decided to make a larger number of frigates rather than fewer, more powerful ones. Nevertheless, British admirals frequently complained that they did not have enough. While searching for the French fleet before the Battle of the Nile in 1798, Horatio Nelson wrote to Sir William Hamilton, "All my ill-fortune hitherto, has proceeded from want of frigates".

In the 1790s the US built some large 44-gun frigates. When war broke out between Great Britain and the US in 1812, these won a series of single-ship actions: USS *Constitution* captured HMS *Guerriere* and HMS *Java*, whilst USS *United States* overwhelmed HMS *Macedonian*. The British public, accustomed to naval victories regardless of the odds, was incensed. However, as the best British ships and crews were in European waters, the defeats were unsurprising.

The British retaliated by instituting a close blockade of US Atlantic ports. During his seven years in command of HMS *Shannon*, Captain Broke had worked up his ship to a peak of fighting efficiency, with the best gunnery drill of any vessel in the Royal Navy. His gun crews were trained to fire into the hull of the enemy ship, to kill the crew instead of shooting down the masts. Throughout his career Broke had prepared for a single-ship action. He even refused to

Sir Philip Broke

capture US merchant ships, as this would require him to put crews on board and reduce *Shannon*'s efficiency.

After a long patrol off Boston, Broke was rewarded on 1 June 1813, when the 38-gun USS *Chesapeake* came out to challenge him. The ensuing battle was the finest single-ship action in the age of sail. Captain James Lawrence, the new commander of *Chesapeake* had confidence in his veteran crew: but he had reckoned without Broke and *Shannon*.

As *Chesapeake* approached, *Shannon* fired her first devastating broadside at a range of about 35 yards. Lawrence was wounded: but ordered *Chesapeake* to tack, to enable her to return fire. However, the US gunners did not have time to adjust their aim as the carronades of the British ship swept *Chesapeake*'s quarterdeck. On her upper deck two-thirds of the gun crews were already casualties.

At a crucial moment *Chesapeake*'s wheel was destroyed by a 9-pounder that Broke had installed on *Shannon*'s quarterdeck for that purpose. Out of control, the vulnerable stern of the US ship was exposed to devastating British fire. In desperation Lawrence ordered his men to board, as *Chesapeake* drifted stern first towards *Shannon*.

Instead it was Broke who seized the moment, leading his own boarding party onto *Chesapeake*. Despite a final appeal from Captain Lawrence, "Don't give up the ship!", the battle was effectively over. In its last moments however, three US sailors attacked Broke. He killed the first, but the second clubbed him with a musket and the third sliced open his skull before being overwhelmed. The entire action lasted only eleven minutes: but its ferocity left 148 US and 83 British sailors killed or wounded. All *Chesapeake*'s officers were casualties and Lawrence died of his wounds three days later.

Broke recovered and returned to England where he received a hero's welcome, for restoring the pride of the Royal Navy. He was made a baronet on 2 November 1813. Later in his career, as a Rear Admiral he made a decisive contribution towards the establishment of professional standards of gunnery at HMS *Excellent*. HMS *Shannon* was placed in reserve in 1831 and broken up in 1859. But her name and Sir Philip, "Brave" Broke's will forever be linked with her devastating victory. He died in 1841.

He had married Sarah Middleton on 25 November 1802. They had eleven children.

A YOUNG HERO IN THE TRADITION OF GIOCANTE CASABIANCA

John ("Jack", or "Boy") Travers Cornwell was born on 8 January 1900, the third child of a working-class family in Leyton, Essex. He joined the Royal Navy in October 1915.

Jack Cornwell VC

On 31 May 1916 HMS *Chester* was scouting ahead of the 3rd Battlecruiser Squadron at the Battle of Jutland, when she turned to investigate gunfire in the distance. *Chester* soon came under intense fire from four Kaiserliche Marine cruisers, each her own size, which had suddenly emerged out of the haze and funnel smoke of the battle. The shielded 5.5-inch gun mounting, where Cornwell was serving as a sight-setter, was blasted by at least four near misses.

Although severely wounded, Cornwell remained at his post until *Chester* retired from the action, with only one main gun still working. *Chester* had received a total of 18 hits; but partial hull armour meant the interior of the ship had suffered little serious damage and the ship was never in peril. The situation on deck however, was a bloody shambles. Many of the gun crews had lost legs due to splinters passing under the gun shields. The crews of British ships reported passing *Chester* to cheers from limbless gunners laid out on her deck, smoking cigarettes – only to hear that these same men had died a few hours later from loss of blood or shock.

After the action Cornwell was found to be the sole survivor at his gun, shards of steel in his chest, looking through the gun sights and still waiting for orders. Incapable of further action, *Chester* was ordered to Immingham, a port on the River Humber. Cornwell was transferred to Grimsby General Hospital nearby: where he died on 2 June, before his mother could get there.

Admiral Beatty wrote of " .... the devotion to duty by Boy (1st Class) John Travers Cornwell who was mortally wounded early in the action, but nevertheless remained standing alone at a most exposed post, quietly awaiting orders till the end of the action, with the gun's crew dead and wounded around him. He was under sixteen and a half years old. I regret that he has since died, but I recommend his case for special recognition in justice to his memory ....". The epitaph on Jack's grave monument reads:

*"It is not wealth or ancestry
    but honourable conduct and a noble disposition
that maketh men great".*

On 16 November 1916 Jack Cornwell's mother received her son's Victoria Cross from King George V at Buckingham Palace.

On 10 December 2006 Kenneth Cummins, a Merchant Navy captain who saw active service in both world wars, died aged 106. He was born in Richmond in Surrey on 3 March 1900; and joined the P & O shipping company as a cadet in 1915. An almost exact contemporary of Jack Cornwell, he had a long and exemplary career at sea: but unlike Jack, he was fortunate to enjoy a further 90 years of life.

THE VICTORIA CROSS

The Victoria Cross is the highest recognition for valour "in the face of the enemy" that can be awarded to members of the British and Commonwealth armed forces, of any rank in any service; and civilians under military command. It is also the highest military award in the British Honours system.

Victoria Cross
National Army Museum, London

The bronze decoration is, in heraldry: a cross pattée (one that has arms which are narrow at the centre and broader at the perimeter), moulded with a crown surmounted by a lion, and the inscription "FOR VALOUR". This was originally to have been "FOR BRAVERY", until it was changed by Queen Victoria: who thought it implied that only the recipients of the VC were brave in battle. The recipient's name, rank, number and unit are engraved on the back of the suspension bar; and, on the reverse of the cross, the date of the act for which it was awarded. The ribbon is crimson, 1.5 inches wide. Awards of the Victoria Cross are announced in *The London Gazette*.

The VC was created on 29 January 1856, backdated to 1854, to recognise acts of valour during the Crimean War of 1854–55. The first award ceremony was on 26 June 1857. The corresponding honour for acts of valour that do not qualify as "in the face of the enemy" is the George Cross, which ranks alongside the VC.

All VCs are cast from two cannon of Chinese origin captured from the Russians at the siege of Sevastopol (except during WWI, when metal from guns captured from the Chinese during the Boxer Rebellion was also used). The remaining 358 ounces, enough for only another 80 or so medals, is stored at a Logistic Corps headquarters at Donnington, near Telford. It can only be removed under armed guard. A firm of jewellers, Hancocks & Co. of Burlington Arcade in London, has made every VC awarded since the medal's inception.

A total of 1,357 Victoria Crosses have been awarded since 1856 (the last posthumously to Corporal Bryan Budd of the Parachute Regiment

Dublin born William Manley (1831–1901), who ended his career in the British Army as Surgeon-General, is the only man to have been awarded a Victoria Cross and an Iron Cross. He won his VC, as an assistant surgeon in the Royal Artillery, on 29 April 1864 near Tauranga in New Zealand, for saving lives during the storming of the rebel Maori Gate Pah (fort); and the Iron Cross (2nd class), whilst serving with the British Ambulance Corps, for tending the wounded during the Franco-Prussian War of 1870–71. He was also awarded the French Red Cross medal – and a further seventeen decorations as well. He politely refused a knighthood from Queen Victoria, as he could not afford the change in his lifestyle that it would entail.

Charles Upham was posted to Egypt in early 1940, as a sergeant in the 20th Canterbury–Otago Battalion. His first VC was won in Crete at the end of May 1941. The citation states that he displayed outstanding gallantry in close-quarter fighting, twice hit by mortar fire and badly wounded. In spite of this, and a severe attack of dysentery, he refused hospital treatment and carried a badly wounded man to safety when forced to retire. Eight days later he fended off an attack at Sphakia, killing 22 Germans. Evacuated to Egypt and promoted from second lieutenant to captain, when told of his award he said only: "It's meant for the men".

He received the bar for his actions in mid-July 1942. When leading his company in an attack on an enemy-held ridge overlooking El Alamein, he was wounded twice; but took the objective after fierce fighting. He destroyed a German tank, several guns and vehicles with grenades. A machine-gun bullet shattered Upham's arm; but he continued to a forward position and brought back some of his men who had become isolated.

Upham's South Island community raised £10,000 to buy him a farm. A man of extraordinary modesty, he gave the money to charity and took out a loan instead.

- **Charles Hazlitt Upham VC and Bar**
Alexander Turnbull Library, New Zealand

in December 2006). 1,353 have been awarded to individuals, three with bars (a second award); and one in 1921 to the US Unknown Soldier of the First World War *[described in the dedication to this book]*.

Since the end of WWII the VC has been awarded only thirteen times. Four were awarded during the Korean War, one in the Indonesia-Malaysia confrontation in 1965, four to Australians in the Vietnam War, two during the Falklands War in 1982, one in the Second Gulf War in 2004 and one in Afghanistan in December 2006.

Only three men have been awarded the Victoria Cross twice: Noel Chavasse (1884–1917), who won his bar posthumously, and Arthur Martin-Leake (1874–1953), both members of the Royal Army Medical Corps in WWI; and in WWII, an insouciant New Zealander – Charles ("Pug") Upham (1908–94), of Christchurch.

Captain Umrao Singh, the last surviving Indian holder of the VC, died in November 2005. By December 2010 only six holders of the VC were still alive: three Britons, one Australian and two Gurkhas – two of them for exploits in WWII.

Until the 1920s the rules relating to the Victoria Cross allowed for the expulsion of a VC recipient from the list of honour if they committed "discreditable acts". King George V insisted on changing this, saying that: should a VC recipient later in his life be convicted for a capital crime, he should be permitted to wear it on the gallows.

The Ugandan Dicator Idi Amin awarded himself the VC. Businessman Michael Ashcroft has acquired 168 VCs, the largest private or public collection (2011). In November 2009 the VC awarded to Flight Lieutenant Bill Reid in 1943, was sold for £348,000.

The little town of Carluke, in the heart of Lanarkshire, with a population of only 7,000, has a remarkable distinction: three recipients of the Victoria Cross were born there. Lance-Corporal William Angus (1888–1959), of the Highland Light Infantry, won his VC on 12 June 1915 at Givenchy, in France. He rescued a wounded officer lying near the enemy's position. Angus received about 40 wounds, some serious.

On 31 October 1918 near Audenarde in Belgium, Sergeant Thomas Caldwell (1894–1969) of the Royal Scots Fusiliers, captured a farmhouse and 18 prisoners single-handedly, despite very heavy fire – greatly facilitating his battalion's advance.

On 22 September 1943 at Kåfjord on the Altafjord in North Norway, Lieutenant Donald Cameron RN (1916–61), commanding Midget Submarine X.6 (and Lieutenant Basil Place RN VC, commanding X.7) carried out a daring and successful attack on the German battleship

Tirpitz. The submarines were towed for at least 1,000 miles from base, then had to negotiate a minefield, nets, gun defences and listening posts. Having overcome these hazards, they placed the charges underneath the ship. They detonated an hour later and *Tirpitz* was out of action for months.

Carluke was also the birthplace of Major-General William Roy FRS (1726–90), a mapmaking genius whose work effectively established the Ordnance Survey in 1791.

HALLEY'S COMET WAS SEEN IN THE YEAR OF LORD NELSON'S BIRTH

Halley's Comet, named after Edmond Halley (1656–1742), can be seen every 75 to 76 years. It is the most famous of all periodic comets. Although many long-period comets are more spectacular, Halley is the only short-period comet that is visible to the naked eye; and is also certain to return within an average human life time.

Halley, the first person to recognise the comet as 'periodic', observed that the characteristics of the comet of 1682 were similar to those of the two which had appeared in 1531 and 1607: and concluded that all three were the same comet returning every 75 or 76 years. Allowing for the gravitational pull of the planets, he predicted correctly its return in 1757 – although it was not seen until 25 December 1758, three months after Lord Nelson was born and sixteen years after Halley himself had died. Its appearance over the centuries coincided with many important events in history.

The appearance of the comet is noted in the Anglo-Saxon Chronicle. Having first seen it as a child in 989, Eilmer of Malmesbury (985–1067) declared prophetically in 1066: "You have come, have you?....You have come, you source of tears to many mothers. It is long since I saw you; but as I see you now you are much more terrible, for I see you brandishing the downfall of my country". In about 1005 Eilmer, known as "the Flying Monk", had "flown" 600 feet from a church tower at Malmesbury in a primitive glider – breaking both legs.

Halley's Comet last appeared in 1986 and will next appear in mid-2061.

Halley's calculations identified earlier appearances found in historical records. The comet's appearance in 12 BC might explain the Biblical story of the Star of Bethlehem.

The comet was seen in England in 1066 and thought to be a bad omen: on 14 October King Harold was killed at the Battle of Hastings. Halley's Comet can be seen in the top right-hand corner of the Bayeux Tapestry, which was completed *c*.1077.
- **Edmond Halley attributed to Isaac Wood (*c*.1720)**
National Portrait Gallery, London

American satirist and writer Mark Twain was born on 30 November 1835, exactly two weeks after the comet's perihelion (when it is closest to the sun) in that year. He wrote in his autobiography, "I came in with Halley's comet in 1835. It's coming again next year and I expect to go out with it. The Almighty has said no doubt, "Now here are these two unaccountable freaks; they came in together, they must go out together". Twain died on 21 April, the day after the comet's perihelion in 1910.

ANOTHER NORFOLK-BORN HERO TRAINED AND INSPIRED BY NELSON

Captain William Hoste, 1st Bt. RN (1780–1828) was born at Ingoldisthorpe in Norfolk, the son of the Reverend Dixon Hoste. He was educated at Kings Lynn and later at Paston school in North Walsham – which Horatio Nelson had also attended. In 1793 war broke out with France and Dixon Hoste approached his landlord, Thomas Coke, 1st Earl of Leicester about placing his thirteen year-old son in the Royal Navy. The Earl introduced him to Horatio Nelson, then living close by in Burnham Thorpe, who had just been appointed Captain of the 64-gun, third-rate HMS *Agamemnon*.

William joined Nelson as his servant in April 1793, when *Agamemnon* joined Lord Hood's squadron in the Mediterranean. For five years he followed Nelson from *Agamemnon* to *Captain*, *Irresistible* and *Theseus*. In 1794 Nelson promoted him to midshipman saying, "without exception one of the finest boys I have ever met with. His gallantry can never be exceeded and …. each day rivets him stronger to my heart". In 1796 Hoste accompanied Nelson aboard *Captain* and fought with him at the Battle of Cape St Vincent and later at Tenerife, where Nelson lost his arm. Nelson promoted Hoste to Lieutenant in February 1798, aged eighteen, and he was present at the Battle of the Nile on *Thetis*. He took over command of the brig *Mutine* from Thomas Capel, when Capel landed at Naples in order to carry Nelson's despatches overland to London.

Hoste commanded *Mutine* for the next three years, until he was promoted by Lord St Vincent to Post Captain in January 1802. In the same year Hoste contracted malaria while serving in Alexandria, followed by a lung infection – maladies which undermined his health for the rest of his life. In September 1805 Nelson gave Hoste command of the 36-gun frigate *Amphion*; and sent him on a diplomatic mission to Algiers. He returned in November, having missed the battle of Trafalgar. "Not to have been in it is enough to make one mad, but to have lost such a friend as well is really sufficient to almost overwhelm me", he wrote to a friend.

His audacious attack on the armed French store ship *Baleine* beneath three strong batteries in the Bay of Rosas, on the north-east coast of Spain, persuaded Admiral Collingwood to send Hoste in *Amphion* to the Adriatic, with orders to patrol aggressively. He did this with such success that, by the close of 1809, he had accounted for over 200 enemy ships captured or sunk. In 1810 Hoste was reinforced by the 36-gun *Active* and the 32-gun *Cerberus* – and destroyed another 46 ships. On 13 March 1811 Hoste's four frigates (with 124 guns and 900 men) were attacked by an eleven ship Franco-Venetian fleet (with 276 guns and 2,000 men), commanded by a feared frigate commander, Commodore Bernard Dubourdieu, near the island of Lissa (now Vis in Croatia). Hoisting the signal "Remember Nelson", Hoste drove a French frigate ashore and captured two Venetian vessels, losing only 50 men killed. *Amphion* was so badly damaged that she was obliged to return to Britain. Hoste was given immediate command of the 38-gun *Bacchante* and returned to the Adriatic in 1812. In 1814 he captured the mountain fortress of Cattaro (now Kotor in Montenegro), by hauling guns from his ships by block-and-tackle to positions overlooking the fort. He repeated the same tactic successfully at Ragusa (now Dubrovnik) a year later.

In 1814 poor health obliged Hoste to return to Britain, where he was made a baronet. In 1817 he married Lady Harriet Walpole, a distant relation of Nelson, by whom he had six children. In 1825 he was appointed commander of the Royal Yacht. In January 1828 he caught 'flu, which affected his already damaged lungs and developed into tuberculosis. He died in London on 6 December 1828.

C.S. Forester and Patrick O'Brian modelled *Hornblower* and *Jack Aubrey* on the lives and careers of William Hoste and Thomas Cochrane. One can see why.

THE GREAT LEXICOGRAPHER, DOCTOR SAMUEL JOHNSON

Samuel Johnson, usually referred to simply as Doctor Johnson, was one of the finest critics of English literature. A poet, essayist, biographer and above all lexicographer, he was also a great wit and observer of life, whose *bons mots* are frequently quoted.

Born on 18 September 1709, the son of a poor bookseller in Lichfield in Staffordshire, Johnson was educated at Lichfield Grammar School and Pembroke College, Oxford. Poverty drove him to leave Oxford without taking a degree and he became a teacher at Stourbridge in Worcestershire. He married Elizabeth ("Tetty") Porter, a widow of forty-six, when he was twenty-five.

Johnson's first book was published in 1735. The following year he opened an academy near Lichfield: where an early pupil was David Garrick (1717–79), the greatest actor-manager of the 18th century and a life-long friend. He left for London, accompanied by Garrick in 1737.

Samuel Johnson by Sir Joshua Reynolds (1772)
National Portrait Gallery, London

Johnson wrote his only novel *Rasselas* in January 1759, *Annus Mirabilis*, in only one week, to pay for his mother's funeral and to settle her debts. Published as *The History of Rasselas, Prince of Abissinia*, it is in a similar vein to Voltaire's *Candide*, also published in 1759; but written with a lighter, less sardonic and more humorous touch. It is not a satire either – depressed by his mother's illness and death, the philosophical question *Rasselas* poses is whether or not mankind can ever attain true happiness.

For the next 30 years he wrote biographies, poems, essays and parliamentary reports for *The Gentleman's Magazine*. He made insufficient money to live off from this; but was able to supplement his income by publishing poems and biographies privately. Between 1747–55, Johnson wrote his marvellous, idiosyncratic *A Dictionary of the English Language*.

Instead of the three years for which his publisher had paid him £1,575 (£2.27 million today) to complete it, the enormity of the project kept him busy for over eight. It was by no means the first English dictionary to be published, but it was certainly the most comprehensive: witty, meticulously researched and carefully written. A huge book, containing 42,773 words, its retail price was the equivalent of some £600 today.

Johnson was fortunate in his friends, some of whom petitioned King George III for a pension on his behalf. Granted in 1762, it was this £300 (£420,000 today) he received each year that sustained him until his death: though he made a good living from his dictionary, he made little from anything else that he wrote.

In 1763 Johnson formed "The Club", a group of his younger friends: Joshua Reynolds (1723–92), Edmund Burke, David Garrick, the poet Oliver Goldsmith (1730–74) and a new

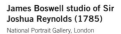

David Garrick by Thomas Gainsborough (1770)
National Portrait Gallery, London

James Boswell studio of Sir Joshua Reynolds (1785)
National Portrait Gallery, London

Sir Joshua Reynolds P.R.A. self-portrait

acquaintance, James Boswell. Johnson was by now a celebrity – he received an honorary doctorate from Trinity College, Dublin in 1765, having received one from Oxford the year before.

Much of Johnson's fame is due to the Scotsman James Boswell (1740–95), whose *Life of Johnson*, published in 1791 is perhaps the most celebrated biography in the English language. Boswell however, having met Johnson after he had become well-known and prosperous, portrayed Johnson as more of a crusty but endearing society figure than as the impoverished writer that he was for much of his life.

Boswell, who made a memorable tour of the Scottish Highlands and the Hebrides with him in 1773, deeply admired Johnson and made much of his character – and characteristics. Although Johnson was a scrofulous, untidy and fat old capon, he was revered by his following of young literati who hung on his every word. It is entirely thanks to Boswell that Johnson's wisdom and so many of his aphorisms and witticisms became appreciated and well-known after his death. The best are still familiar; but there is such an abundance that the following is no more than a representative selection:

Boswell noted that Johnson used to shake his head in a tremulous manner whilst talking, often rubbing his knee and making unexpected, often odd outbursts: "In the intervals of articulating he made various sounds with his mouth; sometimes giving a half whistle, sometimes making his tongue play backwards from the roof of his mouth, as if clucking like a hen, and sometimes protruding it against his upper gums in front". Neurologists have linked Johnson's extraordinary bursts of mental energy and creativity to Tourette's syndrome.

"A cucumber should be well-sliced, dressed with pepper and vinegar, and then thrown out".

"Curiosity is one of the permanent and certain characteristics of a vigorous mind".
"Do not accustom yourself to use big words for little matters".

"Hope is itself a species of happiness, and, perhaps, the chief happiness which this world affords".
"If a man does not make new acquaintances as he advances through life, he will soon find himself alone. A man should keep his friendships in constant repair".
"It is better to live rich than to die rich".
"It is better to suffer wrong than to do it, and happier to be sometimes cheated than not to trust".
"Love is the wisdom of the fool and the folly of the wise".
"Of all noises, I think music is the least disagreeable".
"People need to be reminded more often than they need to be instructed".
"Praise, like gold and diamonds, owes its value only to its scarcity".
"Silence propagates itself, and the longer talk has been suspended, the more difficult it is to find anything to say".
"The world is not yet exhausted; let me see something tomorrow which I never saw before".
"We are inclined to believe those whom we do not know because they have never deceived us".
"What is written without effort is in general read without pleasure".
"A man of genius has been seldom ruined but by himself".
"Wine makes a man more pleased with himself; I do not say that it makes him more pleasing to others. A man may be so much of everything that he is nothing of anything".
"Your manuscript is both good and original, but the part that is good is not original and the part that is original is not good".
"The true measure of a man is how he treats someone who can do him absolutely no good".
"It matters not how a man dies, but how he lives. The act of dying is not of importance, it lasts so short a time".
"Read over your compositions, and wherever you meet with a passage which you think is particularly fine, strike it out".
"Every man thinks meanly of himself for not having been a soldier, or not having been at sea".
[On sex] *"The expense is damnable, the position is ridiculous and the pleasure fleeting".*
[A second marriage is] *"the triumph of hope over experience".*
"A woman preaching is like a dog walking on its hind legs. It is not done well; but you are surprised to find it done at all".
"Sir, let me tell you, the noblest prospect which a Scotchman ever sees, is the high road that leads him to England". [This remark was made to tease Boswell.]
[Oats is] *"a food given in England to horses and in Scotland to men".*
[Self-interest cloaked as] *"patriotism is the last refuge of a scoundrel".*

Johnson's last work of importance was *Lives of the English Poets*, commissioned by a consortium of London booksellers and published in 1781. He died three years later, on 13 December 1784 and was buried in Westminster Abbey.

THE ORATOR EDMUND BURKE WAS A CLOSE FRIEND OF DOCTOR JOHNSON

Edmund Burke was born on 12 January 1729, of Munster Roman Catholic stock. The son of a Dublin solicitor who converted to the Protestant Church of Ireland, he was an Anglo-Irish statesman, author, orator, political theorist, and philosopher.

Burke represented Wendover in Buckinghamshire for many years in the House of Commons, as a member of the Whig party. He is chiefly remembered for his support of the colonists in their dispute with Britain, that led to the American Revolution, and for his strong opposition to the French Revolution. The latter made Burke one of the leading figures within the conservative faction of the Whig party (which he dubbed the "Old Whigs"), in opposition to the pro-revolutionary "New Whigs", led by Charles James Fox. In 1758 Burke founded the *Annual Register*, a chronicle of British and world history, published annually. He is often called "the father of Anglo-American conservatism".

Burke died in Beaconsfield, where he was buried, on 9 July 1797.

> Perhaps Burke's most famous saying: "The only thing necessary for the triumph of evil is for good men to do nothing", does not appear in any of his works or recorded speeches and has also been attributed to the 4th century Saint Jerome.

Edmund Burke studio of Sir Joshua Reynolds (1767–69)
National Portrait Gallery, London

DOCTOR JOHNSON COULD REACT UNGRACIOUSLY TO COMPETITION

Philip Dormer Stanhope, 4th Earl of Chesterfield (1694–1773) was a politician and diplomat. His literary fame rests entirely upon his letters to his illegitimate son, Philip Stanhope, written between 1746–59 and published after his death, and his letters to his godson. For some reason these were not published until 1890. He also invented the metal printing press. Until then books were printed on wooden presses, little changed since Gutenberg's original press.

Chesterfield's Letters to his son were famously described by Johnson as exhibiting

"the morals of a whore and the manners of a dancing master".

Despite this acid remark, some extracts certainly stand comparison with Johnson's own wit and common sense:

"Whatever is worth doing at all, is worth doing well".
"An injury is much sooner forgotten than an insult".
".... lies are always detected, sooner or later".
"Do as you would be done by, is the surest method of pleasing".
"Advice is seldom welcome; and those who want it the most always like it the least".
"The characteristic of a well-bred man is, to converse with his inferiors without insolence, and with his superiors with respect and with ease".
"Manners must adorn knowledge, and smooth its way through the world".
"I wish to God that you had as much pleasure in following my advice, as I have in giving it to you".
"Let blockheads read what blockheads write".
"The reputation of generosity is to be purchased pretty cheap; it does not depend so much upon a man's general expense, as it does upon his giving handsomely where it is proper to give at all. A man, for instance, who should give a servant four shillings, would pass for covetous, while he who gave him a crown, would be reckoned generous; so that the difference of those two opposite characters, turns upon one shilling".
"Let this be one invariable rule of your conduct: always smile, where you cannot strike".

James Watt by Carl Frederik von Breda (1792)
National Portrait Gallery, London

Matthew Boulton by Lemuel Francis Abbott (1801–03)
Birmingham Museums and Art Gallery

THE LUNAR SOCIETY

The Lunar Society (1765–1813) was an informal dining club and learned society founded in Birmingham in 1765 by a number of leading industrialists, natural philosophers and intellectuals. They met regularly in each other's houses until 1813: when most of them had died. First called the Lunar Circle, by 1775 it was formally known as the Lunar Society: so called because members met during the full moon to ensure the late night journey home was better lit. Founder members included both of Charles Darwin's grandfathers: the doctor, poet and inventor, Erasmus Darwin (1731–1802) and Josiah Wedgwood (1730–95), the potter who patented "Queen's Ware" in 1763. Fellow members referred to each other as the "lunaticks".

The Society attracted many of the most influential men in Britain: including Sir Richard Arkwright (1733–92), who is credited with inventing the spinning frame; Joseph Priestley (1733–1804), who discovered oxygen; as well as James Watt (1736–1819) and Matthew Boulton (1728–1809), inventors of the steam engine. The French chemist Antoine Lavoisier, the "father of modern chemistry", who was guillotined in 1794, was a correspondent; and Benjamin Franklin was a regular visitor. William Withering (1741–99), born in Wellington in Shropshire, who in 1785 was the first doctor to use *digitalis* (common foxglove) to regulate heart contractions, was also a member. The Society met at Matthew Boulton's home, Soho House in Birmingham.

The Lunar Society is commemorated today in a museum at Soho House.

Bayer did not invent 'Aspirin', though the German company patented it in 1899. The Reverend Edward Stone (1702–68), of Princes Risborough in Buckinghamshire, first used dried willow bark (acetylsalicylic acid) to treat fevers in 1763.

THE FIRST ENTREPRENEUR

Matthew Boulton (1728–1809) was one of those rarest of men, more often found today in the US than Britain: an inventor and entrepreneur who took his designs from patent to marketplace. He was a self-taught engineer, who manufactured steam-engines, steam presses and pioneered the production line; a silversmith, who made exquisite, but affordable, plated cutlery, tableware and household ormolu (a gold-coloured alloy of copper, zinc and tin) ornaments; and finally, the minter of Britain's coinage. One of his greatest achievements was to empower women of a rapidly expanding middle class to equip and embellish their houses.

A founder of the Lunar Society, Fellow of the Royal Society and High Sheriff of Staffordshire, he was compassionate and fair. His partner, James Watt described him as an "amiable character .... a most affectionate friend and patron".

Boulton was born in Birmingham, the son of a toymaker (a manufacturer of small metal items such as buckles, buttons, snuffboxes and sword hilts). He was educated at a local private academy, until joining his father in business aged fifteen. At twenty-one he married Mary Robinson, daughter of a prosperous Lichfield mercer. When his wife and father died in 1759, *Annus Mirabilis*, Boulton, in partnership with John Fothergill (1712–82), began to manufacture Sheffield plate (a layered combination of silver and copper) household articles and ormolu. They were among the first to make superbly crafted and beautiful jewellery from highly burnished steel: "The love of fame has been for him a greater stimulus than the love of gain", said James Watt.

In 1760 Boulton married his late wife's sister, Ann Robinson. The following year he built a showcase factory at Soho, two miles from the centre of Birmingham. It quickly became an international tourist attraction: "Last week we had Prince Poniatowski, nephew of the King of

Poland, and the French, Danish, Sardinian and Dutch ambassadors; this week we have had Count Orloff and the five celebrated brothers who are such favourites with the Empress of Russia; and only yesterday I had the Viceroy of Ireland who dined with me. Scarcely a day passes without a visit from some distinguished personage", he boasted in 1767. Far ahead of its time, the Soho factory was clean, well lit, properly ventilated and centrally heated; with all manufacturing processes under one roof. He introduced, for the first time ever, the highly efficient practice of making interchangeable components. Employing only the finest craftsmen, he pioneered social insurance schemes and refused to engage young children.

In 1774 Boulton began a long association with James Watt, who installed a steam-powered engine to pump water back up to the Soho factory's millpond to increase the flow in the summer. Joined by the brilliant Ayrshire-born engineer William Murdock (1754–1839), who invented gas lighting in 1802, they established the world's first steam-engine industry: building pumping engines to drain the Cornish tin mines.

Boulton & Watt diversified into making engines for mills, breweries and factories: in twenty-five years they installed over 500 in Britain and abroad, enabling British industry to expand at an accelerated pace. When James Boswell visited Soho, Boulton told him: "I sell here Sir, what the whole world desires to have – POWER".

In 1786 Boulton recognised and seized an opportunity to mint coins. The national coinage had long been a shambles: two-thirds of the coins in circulation were counterfeit. The Royal Mint, unable to prevent forgers (known as "shavers") from shaving the rims of coins, closed down; and struck no copper coins for nearly fifty years (1773–1821).

By 1788 Boulton had incorporated the Soho Mint. He installed eight steam-driven presses, capable of striking 700 coins a minute, and employed expert international engravers. He introduced diagonally reeded, lettered and milled edges to the coin rims, making shaving instantly detectable; and raised lettering around the coin's border to improve its wear. The weight of his copper coins was proportional to their value: two pence weighed two ounces and one penny weighed one ounce. This enabled a bag of coins to be valued by weight.

Failing to obtain a government licence to strike coins, Boulton won contracts from the East India Company, the US, Russia and .... Sierra Leone. In 1790 he exported over 20 million high quality blanks to the US Mint at Philadelphia, to be made into cents and half-cents. The Director pronounced them to be "perfect and beautifully polished".

In 1796 Boulton was invited by Catherine the Great (1729–96) to equip the new Russian Mint in St Petersburg, that had been

James Watt (1736–1819), born in Greenock, Renfrewshire, did not invent the steam engine. That honour had gone half a century before to the Devonshireman Thomas Newcomen (1663–1729). In 1769 however, Watt had greatly increased the efficiency of Newcomen's crude model, by adding a separate condenser to reduce the loss of latent heat. In 1774, with his patents about to expire, Watt approached Boulton; and their partnership was the most important of the Industrial Revolution.

The "Terracotta Army" (c.210 BC), some 8,000 life-sized ceramic soldiers and horses commissioned by the first Chinese Emperor Qin Shi Huang, had their body parts made by separate workshops to be assembled and completed elsewhere. In the 16th century, the Venetian Arsenal employed 16,000 men in an assembly line to produce, with standardised parts, nearly one new galley every day: each fitted out, armed, provisioned and ready to be launched. The first known assembly-lines of the Industrial Revolution were the Portsmouth Block Mills (1801–03), built by Marc Isambard Brunel, to make the blocks used by the Royal Navy. Such was its efficiency, the factory remained in use until the 1960s.

Elizabeth Garrett Anderson (1836–1917), Richard Garrett I's great-granddaughter, was born in Whitechapel, in London's East End. In 1865 she was the first woman to win a medical qualification in Britain – and in 1908, became the first female mayor in England (of Aldeburgh). Her younger sister Millicent Fawcett (1847–1929) was a leading suffragist, who co-founded Newnham College, Cambridge in 1871.

Elizabeth Blackwell (1821–1910), a devout Quaker born in Bristol, emigrated with her family to the US in 1832. She became the first female doctor in the US, winning her degree in 1849. She returned to Britain in 1857; and, under a clause in the Medical Act 1858 that permitted doctors with foreign degrees to practise in Britain, on 1 January 1859 she became the first woman entered in the General Medical Council's register.

In a report commissioned for the NHS in 2009, by 2017 the majority of doctors in Britain will be female.

designed by the Birmingham architect William Hollins (1763–1843). To fulfil this contract, Boulton pioneered the production line: strips of metal fed into the presses emerged as coins the other end.

In 1797 the British government finally commissioned Boulton to produce 45 million new twopenny and penny pieces, known as George III "cartwheel pennies" because of their raised border. Coin sizes and weights set by Boulton remained constant until decimalisation over 173 years later (1971).

The following year, Boulton was invited to refurbish the Royal Mint in London; but bureaucratic delays postponed completion until well after his death.

Having long endured painful kidney stones, Boulton died on 17 August 1809. He left a son and a daughter by his second marriage; and £150,000 (over £100 million today). He is buried with James Watt and William Murdock, in St Mary's Church in Handsworth, Birmingham. In 2009, the Bank of England announced that Boulton and Watt would feature on a new £50 note.

Leiston, near Aldeburgh on the Suffolk coast, was the unlikely site of Britain's first proper assembly line. Richard Garrett & Sons, founded by Richard Garrett I (1755–1839) in 1788, manufactured steam tractors, portable steam engines and agricultural machinery. The business was family owned until 1932 and finally closed in 1981. In its heyday the "Leiston Works" employed 2,500 men.

Richard Garrett III (1807–66), grandson of the founder, introduced flow line assembly in 1852, having observed US developments in manufacturing at the Great Exhibition the previous year. He built "The Long Shop" at Leiston: to process the manufacture of a machine from a block of cast iron at one end of the building, with parts made on upper levels lowered at the appropriate stage, to final completion at the other. 90% of the firm's production was exported: mainly to Italy, France, Germany and Austria.

Long Shop Museum from
the Long Shop Gallery
(2004)

"CAPABILITY" BROWN CHANGED THE LANDSCAPE OF ENGLAND

Lancelot Brown was Britain's greatest landscape gardener. Immortalised by his naturalistic designs, he acquired his nickname from his habit of telling his clients that their estates had "great capabilities". He was born on 30 August 1716 at Kirkharle in Northumberland; the fifth of six children to William Brown, a yeoman farmer.

Despite rumours of his illegitimacy, nothing is known of his mother. It was for the excellent education he received in the local school at Cambo at the expense of Sir

William Loraine, a local magnate, and because he was taken on as a trainee gardener on Loraine's Kirkharle Hall estate, that gossips suggested that he might have been Loraine's natural son. Although this is most unlikely, Brown certainly had a privileged start in life. His plans for remodelling Loraine's extensive gardens, which were laid out in the formal Anglo-Dutch style previously fashionable, survive; but they may relate to plans he drew up later.

Having left Kirkharle in 1739, Brown's employment in 1741 by Lord Cobham at Stowe, in Buckinghamshire, proved critical to his career. At the age of twenty-five he was made responsible for implementing the architectural and landscaping designs of the celebrated Yorkshireman, William Kent (1685–1748) and Aberdonian, James Gibbs (1682–1754). The work involved building temples, excavating lakes and valleys; and planting vast quantities of trees. When Cobham died in 1749, Brown left Stowe and set himself up in London. By 1753 the patronage of Cobham's patrician friends had won him a reputation of being the pre-eminent "improver of grounds" in England. He had captured the market for creating the idealised landscapes of the Italian painters that his clients had admired as young men, on their "Grand Tours" of Europe.

Brown's technique was simple. He razed and replaced his clients' existing gardens, often employing the simple but clever device of the ha-ha to deceive the eye, with broad, undulating parks, featuring sepentine belts and groups of trees. These opened up to reveal harmonious vistas of irregularly shaped lakes, waterfalls, classical temples, Palladian bridges, grottoes, monuments and *exedra* (arcades with seats where people could converse). His meticulous, but informal, Arcadian set-pieces emphasised the beauty of nature unadadorned – the complete antithesis of the great French landscape gardener André Le Nôtre (1613–1700), designer of the formal gardens at Versailles.

His prodigious output was made possible by combining his skills with those of others, including Robert Adam and Sanderson Miller (1716–80). Many of Brown's foremen were exceptionally talented and traded on their own account, enabling him to undertake commissions on a vast scale: landscaping over 170 of the greatest estates in England, from Alnwick Castle, Blenheim Place and Longleat, to Woburn Abbey. Every landscape gardener in the developed world since Brown, has been influenced by him.

Brown's marriage was happy. He and his wife Bridget had two daughters and three sons: one served as an MP and another rose to the rank of an admiral of the blue. Often derided by rivals for his humble origins and lack of education, Brown climbed higher than many of his clients: becoming high sheriff of Huntingdon in 1772, enjoying the friendship of several prime ministers, including William Pitt ("the Elder"), and the ear of King George III – although he was never employed to remodel Windsor Great Park.

He died in London on 6 February 1783: of overwork aggravated by asthma, constant travel and financial worries brough about by casual billing. He is buried at Fenstanton, an estate in Huntingdonshire which he had bought in 1767.

THOMAS MALTHUS

The Reverend Thomas Robert Malthus FRS (1766–1834) was born a year after the Lunar Society was founded. He was brought up in comfortable circumstances near Guildford in Surrey and was elected a Fellow of Jesus College, Cambridge in 1793. He is regarded as the "father of demographics". In *An Essay on the Principle of Population*, published in 1798, he was the first economist to draw attention to the dangers of population growth: "The power of population is infinitely greater than the power in the earth to produce subsistence for man".

Thomas Malthus probably by Amable Nicolas Fournier (before 1861)
National Portrait Gallery, London

Georg Friederich Händel attributed to Balthasar Denner (1726–1728)
National Portrait Gallery, London

Malthus argued that populations always outrun the available food supply: unless checked by famine, plague or war. His conclusion was that charity was pointless and should be reduced to the minimum, since it encouraged the poor to breed excessively. His views led directly to the inhuman Poor Laws of the 1830s and 1840s which condemned sick paupers and the unemployed to the Workhouse – graphically described by Charles Dickens in his second novel *Oliver Twist*, published in 1838.

Malthus became hugely influential (and controversial) in economic, political, social and scientific thought. Many evolutionary biologists found Malthusianism a stepping-stone to the concept of the survival of the fittest: notably Charles Darwin and Alfred Russel Wallace. Malthus's views also influenced Karl Marx, John Maynard Keynes and Mao Zedong. He was a thinker of great significance.

Ironically, Malthus had a hare-lip and cleft palate. If he had been born a few thousand years earlier, he would probably not have survived at all.

> Darwin developed his own ideas of natural selection and the "survival of the fittest", caused by competition for scarce resources such as food, habitat and mates.

GEORG FRIEDRICH HÄNDEL DIED IN 1759, ANNUS MIRABILIS

Georg Friedrich Händel, supreme master of Baroque music, was born on 23 February 1685 in Halle, a large town in the state of Brandenburg in north-east Germany. His father, a barber surgeon, died before Händel was eleven; but he left his family sufficiently provided for to enable Händel to study law at the University of Halle in 1702. From an early age however, Händel had shown a remarkable gift for music: and he chose to become a pupil of the Halle composer Friedrich Zachow who taught him the musical disciplines of keyboard and composition. In 1703 he abandoned the law to join the Hamburg opera orchestra. In 1705, aged twenty Händel composed his first opera, *Almira*.

Händel was deeply influenced by Italian music, particularly opera; and later by the Baroque composers Jean-Baptiste de Lully and Henry Purcell (1659–95). In 1710 he was appointed Kapellmeister to the Elector Georg Louis of Hanover. 1711 saw Händel in London for the opening of his opera *Rinaldo* which was a great success. The next year Händel returned to London to promote two further operas; and in 1713 he attracted the attention of Queen Anne with his *Ode* for the Queen's birthday and the *Utrecht Te Deum* and *Jubilate*, to celebrate the end of the ten-year war of the Spanish Succession. As a result Anne rewarded Händel with an annuity of £200 (£327,000 today) – and his career was launched. In 1714 Anne died and his patron, Elector Georg became King George I of Great Britain.

In 1718 Händel was made Director of Music to the Duke of Chandos. He wrote the 12 *Chandos Anthems* and the masque, *Acis and Galatea* shortly afterwards.

The majestic *Chandos Anthems* represent Händel's finest body of church music. Although conceived on a grand scale, the works require only a small number of singers and instrumentalists. *Acis and Galatea*, possibly his finest secular choral work, is based on a story from Greek mythology. Shortly afterwards Händel produced another masque, *Haman and*

Mordecai, which in essence was the first oratorio in English. Though he continued to write (over 40) operas until 1741, in 1733 Händel was quick to take advantage of the oratorio's new popularity with *Deborah* and *Athalia*.

Händel settled in Britain, became a British subject in 1726 and was appointed composer to the Chapel Royal. He wrote four *Coronation Anthems* for George II in 1727 – one of which, *Zadok the Priest* has been played at every British coronation since. He also wrote the *Funeral Anthem* for Queen Caroline in 1737.

In 1737 the Royal Academy of Music went bankrupt and Händel suffered either a mild stroke or a nervous breakdown. By 1739 he had recovered, after recuperating in Aix-la-Chapelle (Aachen today), where he wrote two of his most famous oratorios: *Saul* and *Israel in Egypt*. To celebrate his return to good health, and with the revenue provided by twelve *Concerto Grossi* (Opus 6), Händel helped to create a Fund for the Support of Decayed Musicians, which later became the Royal Society of Musicians. With the concertos of Bach, Händel's *Concerto Grossi (*grand concertos) represent the high point in baroque orchestral music.

By 1741 Händel was at the height of his powers. *Messiah*, first performed in Dublin on 13 April 1742, was closely followed by the equally inspired *Samson* in 1743, a secular work *Semele* and a *Te Deum* to celebrate the British victory at the Battle of Dettingen in the same year. Yet more oratorios followed: *Joseph and his Brethren* in 1744, *Belshazzar* and *Hercules*, both in 1745.

Händel's baroque music perfectly caught the mood and tastes of the emerging and increasingly prosperous British middle classes. They had come to regard the contortions of Italian opera with distaste and were more than ready to be both entertained and morally uplifted by tales from the Bible set to noble, stately music with words sung in English. The *Music for the Royal Fireworks* and *Water Music*, written in 1749 to celebrate the Treaty of Aix-la-Chapelle, brilliantly reflected this change in public interest.

In 1750 Händel began to lose his sight. Only with the greatest difficulty was he able to complete the last of his great oratorios, *Jeptha* in 1752. Though alert and interested in all musical activities until his death on 14 April 1759, blindness prevented any further compositions. Having never married, he left his estate of £20,000 (£28 million today) to his relations in Germany and his servants.

Händel's statue, carved by Louis François Roubiliac (1702–62) in 1738 and erected in the Vauxhall Gardens but now in the V & A, was the first full effigy in Britain of a commoner. He was buried in Poet's Corner in Westminster Abbey.

"Masque", which peaked in popularity at the end of the 17th century, was a short dramatic play by masked actors. Usually following an allegorical theme and using song, speech and dance, masque was performed in elaborate costumes on a dazzling stage-set. By the early 18th century masque had evolved into opera.

Händel's oratorios were non-liturgical, moral and musical presentations in English, rather than Latin. An oratorio is a sacred composition on a grand scale: using orchestra, solo voices and chorus, without acting or scenery. The first oratorio, effectively a religious opera, was performed in Italy in 1600. Händel, perhaps the most famous oratorio composer of all, was inspired by J.S. Bach's *Passions* to write his wonderful *Messiah* in 1742. In the 20th century the outstanding composers of oratorio were Stravinsky and Sir Edward Elgar.

The Battle of Dettingen took place on 16 June 1743 in Bavaria, during the War of the Austrian Succession. It was the last time that a British monarch, George II, personally led his troops into battle. In alliance with the 35,000 strong "Pragmatic Army" of Hanover and Hesse, British forces defeated an army of 26,000 Frenchmen commanded by the Duc de Noailles.

Baroque is a period as well as a style. It used exaggerated motion and easily interpreted detail to produce exuberance and grandeur in architecture, sculpture, painting, literature, dance and music. The style started around 1600 in Rome.

ROBERT BURNS WAS BORN IN 1759, *ANNUS MIRABILIS*

Robert Burns was born in Alloway, near Ayr on 25 January 1759. He was the eldest son of William Burnes of Kincardineshire, then a nurseryman on the banks of the River Doon.

Always extremely poor, William tried to give his children a good education; and Robert was sent to several schools in the neighbourhood. But it was to his father himself, and to his own reading, that he owed most of his education. He had a good grounding in English grammar, could read French and was familiar with the best of English literature, from Shakespeare to his own day. He was also influenced by the tales and ballads of Betty Davidson, an old woman who lived with the family.

In 1766 William Burnes borrowed money to rent the farm of Mount Oliphant; and in helping to make this a success, Robert seems seriously to have over-strained his physique. In 1777 the family moved to Lochlea and Burns went to the nearby town of Irvine to learn flax-dressing. The only outcome of this venture however, was a friendship with a dissipated sailor – whom he was to blame, rather pathetically, as the instigator of his early debauchery. His father died in 1784, worn out and bankrupt. Burns's later cynicism and outspoken dislike of any form of religion or politics that could condone inhumanity stems from experiencing his father's ruin.

With his brother Gilbert, Burns rented the farm of Mossgiel; but this again was unsuccessful. His first illegitimate child, by Elizabeth Paton, whom he abandoned, had been born in 1785; but by this time he was living with Jean Armour (1767–1834), for which he was censured by the Kirk Session. As a result of his failure as a farmer and the attempts of his father-in-law to set aside his irregular arrangement with Jean, who was now pregnant (with twins), he decided in 1786 to emigrate.

To raise money for the passage, on 31 July 1786 he published *Kilmarnock*, a volume of poems which he had written over some years. It was unexpectedly successful and, instead of sailing for Jamaica, he went up to Edinburgh. Over the winter he was the literary celebrity of the season. An enlarged edition of his poems in 1787 sold so well that was able to help his brother at Mossgiel; and rent and stock Ellisland farm in Dumfriesshire for himself. His fame as a poet had won over the Armours. Having married Jean in 1788 she bore him nine children, three of whom survived into adulthood.

He abandoned Ellisland in 1791 and moved to Dumfries, where he had obtained a position in the Excise. With his reputation damaged by his intemperate radicalism, his muse had vanished and work had become drudgery. Depression led him into a downward spiral of licentiousness, fuelled by alcohol, and his health finally collapsed. He died in Dumfries, where he was buried, on 21 July 1796. He was only thirty-seven.

Despite his short life Burns has made an enormous impact in the 200 years since his death on the national pride and literary confidence of Scotland. It has been said that: "Lowland Scotland as a distinct nationality came in with two warriors, William Wallace and Robert the Bruce, and went out with two bards, Burns and Sir Walter Scott. The first two made the history, the last two told the story and sang the song".

Almost single-handedly Burns rescued Scots folk music tradition from obscurity and preserved its Lallans (Lowland Scots) vernacular. His later life was spent collecting or writing songs for traditional Scottish airs. He contributed about a hundred to George Thomson's *Select Collection of Original Scottish Airs* in 1792. In all he wrote 368 – regarding his work as a service to Scotland and refusing all payment.

Burns was clever, restless and fiery: a skilful letter writer and a brilliant speaker who could hold his own in any company. But it is for his songs that he is best known around the world. Burns is the greatest songwriter Britain, not just Scotland has ever produced.

Burns's most celebrated song is *Auld Lang Syne* (1788). It is sung to usher in the New Year in many parts of the globe, with linked arms but doubtful comprehension among most of its singers. The Scots themselves sing it on 25 January, wherever they are on Burns Night, to celebrate the poet's birth: understanding and loving every word.

Burns's humanitarian deism is illustrated in this celebrated extract from *To a louse*:

> *"O wad some Pow'r the giftie gie us*
> *To see oursels as others see us!*
> *It wad frae many a blunder free us,*
> *And foolish notion."*

and in the Selkirk Grace which, though disputed, was almost certainly written by him:

> *"Some hae meat, and canna eat,*
> *And some wad eat that want it;*
> *But we hae meat and we can eat,*
> *And sae the Lord be thankit".*

SAWNEY BEAN LIVED 20 MILES SOUTH OF ALLOWAY, WHERE BURNS WAS BORN

Alexander "Sawney" Bean was a cannibal and mass-murderer. Born in the late 14th century in East Lothian, son of a ditcher and hedger, Bean was work-shy and dishonest and he married a woman of similar character. The couple, having been driven away by their disgusted neighbours, settled in a deep cave on the sea at Bennane Head, near Ballantrae, now in Ayrshire but then in Galloway, on the other side of Scotland. They lived here for the next 25 years; but, as they had never visited the nearby villages, their existence was unknown. They had many children and through incest, their family grew into a gang of forty-eight.

Travellers in the area began to go missing. The authorities accused and even executed several innkeepers and vagrants; but eventually up to 1,000 people had disappeared. Having robbed and killed their victims, the Beans would drag them back to their cave where they were eaten or their flesh was smoked to preserve it for future consumption. The local villagers became suspicious when body parts washed up on beaches nearby. The Beans had apparently thrown the remains of the carcasses into the sea.

Finally a victim escaped and reported the attack to the authorities in Glasgow. A full-scale search for the killers was instigated. The reports were so horrific that King James I (1394–1437) himself led a troop of 400 soldiers, with several bloodhounds, to conduct a systematic search. The cave was discovered, with money, stolen possessions and human remains. The Beans, who had become utterly accustomed to their life of cannibalism, the children having known nothing else, could not see the error of their ways. The entire family were taken to Edinburgh in chains, where they were kept in the Tolbooth jail, before being taken to Leith to be executed. Their execution was particularly gruesome: the men had their limbs amputated and were left to bleed to death. The women and children were burned at the stake.

SIR ALEXANDER FLEMING WAS BORN 15 MILES EAST OF ALLOWAY

Sir Alexander Fleming (1881–1955), known as Alec, was the bacteriologist whose discovery of penicillin in 1928 transformed medicine – and has saved many millions of lives.

He was born near Darvel in Ayrshire, the seventh son of a hill farmer who died when Fleming was seven. He was educated at Kilmarnock Academy, until his brothers sent him to London to attend the Polytechnic Institute in 1895. He spent four wasted years, working as a clerk in a shipping office and playing rugby, before pulling himself together and enrolling at St Mary's Hospital medical school in 1901. In 1908, as its prize student, Fleming won the University of London's gold medal.

With this commendation, he was hired by the Inoculation Department of St Mary's Hospital in Paddington, under the renowned bacteriologist and immunologist, Sir Almroth Wright (1861–1947): who was conducting ground-breaking experiments in the field of vaccine therapy. By 1914 Fleming had established a prosperous private practice specialising in venereal diseases. During WWI, Wright and Fleming treated wounded soldiers in a makeshift hospital set up in Boulogne casino. Fleming proved that using powerful antiseptics merely exacerbated wounds: by suppressing the body's immune system more effectively than they eliminated the invading bacteria. He simply kept wounds clean, using a weak saline solution. After the Armistice Fleming returned to St Mary's Hospital: the inoculation department is now the Wright-Fleming Institute.

On 28 September 1928 Fleming noticed that a petri dish containing a bacteria culture, *Staphylococcus aureus*, had become contaminated with a fungus – which he identified as *Penicillium notatum*. By observing, with his sharp eye for inconsistency, that the bacteria culture had been killed, Fleming had accidentally discovered antibiotics.

In November 1921 Fleming isolated an enzyme he called Lysozyme, the first of his important discoveries. While suffering from a heavy cold, a droplet of his nasal mucus fell into a culture dish of bacteria. Several days later, he noticed that the bacteria had dissolved. Fleming always considered that his work on lysozyme was his most important, for it taught him how the body fights infection.

Fleming named his "mould juice" penicillin: but, working with just two assistants, he was unable to isolate, stabilise or purify it. He realised immediately however, its huge clinical and therapeutic potential. It took dedicated pharmacologists from Oxford, to isolate and purify penicillin sufficiently to make it safe for public use. The team was led by an Australian, born in Adelaide, Howard (later Lord) Florey OM PRS (1898–1968) and Ernst Chain FRS (1906–79), who was born in Berlin, came to Britain in 1933 and was knighted in 1969. Although all three shared the Nobel prize in 1945, there was contention over the credit due to each of them.

Funded by the British and US governments, refined penicillin was mass-produced after the bombing of Pearl Harbour. By D-Day, there was enough to treat every wounded allied soldier.

Fleming married Sarah McElroy in 1915 and left one child. He was knighted in 1944 and died of a heart attack in 1955. His ashes are interred in St Paul's Cathedral.

THE ABOLITIONIST WILLIAM WILBERFORCE WAS ANOTHER BORN IN 1759

William Wilberforce (1759–1833) was an evangelical British politician who devoted his career to parliamentary reform, Catholic emancipation and the abolition of slavery. For twenty-six years he led a campaign in Parliament against British participation in the slave trade.

Sir Alexander Fleming by Helen McDougall Campbell (1944)

National Portrait Gallery, London

He was born into a prosperous family in Kingston-upon-Hull in Yorkshire but was only eight years-old when his father died. His mother sent him to live in Wimbledon with his aunt Hannah, a committed Methodist. He met George Whitefield (1714–70) a famous Methodist preacher; and the Reverend John Newton (1725–1807), once a slave trader but now an evangelist – who persuaded Wilberforce to commit his life to God.

He completed a rather chaotic private education at St John's College, Cambridge, where he was an indifferent student but enjoyed undergraduate life to the full. In 1780, aged twenty-one and at an unbelievable cost of £9,000 (over £11 million today) spent in securing the necessary votes, he entered parliament as an independent member for Hull. He soon attached himself to William Pitt ("the Younger"), an old Cambridge friend, becoming one of his close advisors.

William Wilberforce by Sir Thomas Lawrence (1828)
National Portrait Gallery, London

While on holiday on the Continent in 1784 Wilberforce read *The Rise and Progress of Religion in the Soul*, by the Nonconformist writer and hymnist Philip Doddridge (1702–51). This powerful book started him on his spiritual journey: and the following year he converted to evangelical Christianity. Wilberforce made his first important speech in Parliament in 1789. He condemned the slave trade as morally repugnant and contrary to natural justice. In 1791 he introduced his first Parliamentary Bill to abolish the trade. It was defeated by 163 votes to 88. He tried again five times between 1792–97. Despite his eloquence, he made no headway.

After eighteen years of untiring persistence the Slave Trade Act, abolishing the slave trade in the British West Indies, became law on 25 March 1807. Wilberforce spent the rest of his life agitating for the universal emancipation of slaves.

Wilberforce, deeply conservative, was not without his detractors. In 1795 he had opposed giving workers the right to form trade unions, describing them as a "general disease in our society" and voting for the Combination Acts which forbade them. The radical writer William Cobbett (1763–1835) attacked his apparent hypocrisy in campaigning to abolish the slave trade while ignoring the horrifying conditions of British workers at home. "Never have you done one single act in favour of the labourers of this country", Cobbett told him. Later in life, Wilberforce did in fact involve himself deeply in improving the hellish lot of child chimney-sweeps.

Wilberforce's other religious and philanthropic concerns included Indian missionary societies and the Society for Suppression of Vice. He was also cofounder of the British and Foreign Bible Society; as well as the Society for the Prevention of Cruelty to Animals, later the RSPCA. He was a leading light in the foundation of Sierra Leone.

In 1792 Wilberforce and other philanthropists formed the Sierra Leone Company. They founded Freetown as a private enterprise to

Newton, a curate at Olney in Buckinghamshire, published the *Olney Hymns* in 1779. His best known are "Glorious things of thee are spoken", "How sweet the name of Jesus sounds!" and, best-loved of all, "Amazing Grace".

James Boswell listened to one of Wilberforce's speeches in the House of Commons and wrote: "I saw what seemed a mere shrimp mount upon the table; but as I listened, he grew and grew until the shrimp had become a whale".

It is often overlooked that it was not until Lord Exmouth's Anglo-Dutch fleet pounded Algiers into submission in 1816 that the corsairs of the Barbary Coast ceased raiding the coasts of Europe, as far as southern England and the west of Ireland, to seize slaves. It is estimated that from the 16th to the 19th centuries over a million white Christians had been sold into slavery by North African traders.

provide a haven for freed and runaway slaves. The dream, into which Wilberforce personally injected a huge amount of capital, was to attract both black and white settlers. They were to be drawn from Britain, Nova Scotia and Jamaica as well as native Africans: to create an ideal society in which diverse races would live in harmony. The reality proved very different.

Racial tension, crop failure, disease, death and desertion forced the British Government to assume responsibility for the settlement. In 1808 it was declared a Crown colony: the whole region became a British Protectorate in 1896.

Aged thirty-seven Wilberforce was smitten by twenty year-old Barbara Ann Spooner (1777–1847). Following a romance which lasted all of eight days, they married in Bath in Somerset on 30 May 1797. They had six children in less than ten years: Wilberforce was a wonderful father to them all. He retired in 1826, due to failing health. His place as the principal sponsor of anti-slavery legislation was taken on by Sir Thomas Buxton, 1st Bt. (1786–1845), who became known as "the Liberator". Wilberforce died a contented man on 29 July 1833 – three days after Parliament had passed The Slavery Abolition Act, emancipating slaves throughout the British Empire.

It took another 32 years and a bloody civil war costing 624,000 lives, before the US followed suit and freed her own slaves.

Wilberforce was buried in Westminster Abbey, near William Pitt, and a statue of him by Samuel Joseph was erected in 1840. During his funeral both Houses of Parliament suspended their sittings as a mark of respect. In Hull, the public funded a 100-foot Doric column, topped by a statue of Wilberforce in 1834. In 1903 Wilberforce House, his old family home, was opened as Britain's first museum dedicated to slavery.

MARY WOLLSTONECRAFT, AN EARLY FEMINIST, WAS ALSO BORN IN 1759

Mary Wollstonecraft (1759–97) was one of the first English feminist writers. She was born in Spitalfields in London. Her father was a handkerchief-maker. In 1784 she and her sister Eliza opened a school in Hackney: where Mary made a friend of Richard Price (1723–91), a Welsh nonconformist minister who wrote the influential *Review of the Principal Questions of Morals* in 1759. Price introduced her to Joseph Priestley, with whom he had formed The Religious Dissenters, condemned by many as atheistic.

Through Price and Priestley, Mary met many leading radicals including the publisher Joseph Johnson (1738–1809) to whom she confided her unprecedented ideas on the education of women. He commissioned her to write a book on the subject which he published under the title *Thoughts on the Education of Girls* in 1786. In 1788 Mary helped Johnson found a journal, *The Analytical Review*.

Her next book, *A Vindication of the Rights of Man* was written in support of the radical Tom Paine's great work, in which he defended man's right to liberty and equality. Mary attacked the evils of society: which she perceived principally to be the slave trade, unjust game laws and neglect of the poor.

Joseph Priestley (1733–1804) was a theologian, political theorist and chemist. His 1767 *History and Present State of Electricity* became a seminal work. In 1768 his *Essay on Government* led him and Price to form the Unitarian Society which pointed the way to Utilitarianism – a philosophy promoted by Jeremy Bentham (1748–1832) and John Stewart Mill. He discovered nitrogen, carbon monoxide, ammonia and in 1774, most important of all, oxygen. In 1770 Priestley coined the word "rubber". In 1794 his obnoxious heretical opinions, and support for the French Revolution, forced him to emigrate to the US.

In 1793 she published her most important work, *A Vindication of the Rights of Women*. She attacked society's failure to educate women, as an immoral means of keeping women "docile and attentive to their looks to the exclusion of all else". She regarded marriage as "legal prostitution" which both "degraded the master and the abject dependent". She argued that the abolition of the monarchy, the church and the military was necessary to achieve an equal society: views that alarmed even hardened radicals.

Mary's revolutionary beliefs earned her the derogation "a hyena in petticoats". In 1793 she moved to France and became the mistress of the American speculator, diplomat and writer Gilbert Imlay: and a year later her first daughter Fanny was born.

In March 1797 Mary married William Godwin, a Presbyterian minister who had lost his faith. On 10 September 1797 Mary died from blood poisoning caused by a retained placenta, soon after giving birth to their daughter Mary. She was only thirty-eight.

Mary Godwin (1797–1851) eloped in 1814 with the poet Percy Bysshe Shelley (1792–1822) and, after his first wife Harriet drowned herself, married him in 1816. She became so frustrated by Shelley's narcissistic behaviour that she turned to writing Gothic novels. The most famous was *Frankenstein*, written in 1816 and published in 1818. The classic horror story, often emulated but never surpassed, tells of the dreadful consequences of a scientist creating an artificial human being. Her other outstanding novel is *The Last Man*, published in 1826, a fantasy about the elimination of the human race through the plague.

Mary Wollstonecraft by John Opie R.A. (1761–1807)
National Portrait Gallery, London

Mary Shelley by Richard Rothwell (1840)
National Portrait Gallery, London

SURGEON WILLIAM MARSDEN WAS BORN IN 1796, THE YEAR BURNS DIED

William Marsden was born in Sheffield in August 1796. He moved to London in 1816 and was apprenticed to a surgeon practising in Holborn. He trained at Joshua Brookes's Anatomical School in Blenheim Street and at St Bartholomew's Hospital, under John Abernethy (1764–1831) who had founded the hospital's medical school.

In 1820 he married Elizabeth-Ann Bishop. In 1827 he was elected a member of the Royal College of Surgeons. His inability later that year to obtain hospital treatment for an eighteen year-old girl whom he found on the steps of St Andrew's Church in Holborn, almost dead of disease and starvation, appalled him and he turned his attention to hospital relief. At that time treatment was given only to patients with a governor's letter. To circumvent this he set up a small dispensary in Hatton Garden, the London General Institution for the Gratuitous Cure of Malignant Diseases, in 1828. Although the Institution met initially with great opposition, its value became widely recognized during an outbreak of cholera in 1832. It was the only London hospital prepared to care for affected patients. After the epidemic the in-patient beds were retained and the hospital changed its name to the London Free Hospital. In 1842 it moved to the Light Horse Volunteers' barracks in Gray's Inn Road. Marsden was the senior surgeon, having obtained a degree in medicine from the University of Erlangen in 1838.

In 1846 Marsden's wife died of cancer. Deeply affected, he opened a centre in Cannon Row for cancer patients in 1851. Within ten years it moved to the Fulham Road – where it remains to this day. It was called the Cancer Hospital: with Marsden as its senior surgeon. Later in 1846 he married Elizabeth, daughter of Frances Abbott. William Marsden died of bronchitis on 16 January 1867. He had one surviving son, Alexander.

In 1954 his hospital, the world's first dedicated to the treatment of cancer, was renamed The Royal Marsden, in recognition of the vision and commitment of its founder.

EDWARD GIBBON WAKEFIELD WAS ALSO BORN IN 1796

Wakefield (1796–1862) was the most influential promoter of colonisation in South Australia and New Zealand. He also played a key role in the Durham report that led to the union of Upper and Lower Canada. His early life was scandalous.

From a respected Quaker family, originally from Kendal in Westmorland (now Cumbria), he was born in London. His father, also Edward (1774–1854), was a philanthropist, economist and land agent. After a patchy education, Wakefield was employed as a diplomatic messenger during the last years of the Napoleonic wars. In 1816, aged twenty, with bright blue eyes and enormous charm, he eloped with a sixteen year-old heiress, Eliza Pattle (1799–1820). Her father, a rich merchant, had just died in Macau. He married her in Edinburgh: but she died after giving birth to their second child.

Wakefield, though now well-off, considered he still had insufficient funds to purchase an estate and enter Parliament. In 1826 he abducted a fifteen year-old heiress, Ellen Turner, from her school near Liverpool. Wakefield drove directly to Gretna Green in Dumfriesshire and married her – with the intention of acquiring her fortune.

Before the Married Women's Property Acts, a woman's fortune passed on marriage to her husband. Victorian fathers, trying to protect their daughters from fortune hunters, would later lobby to change Trust law – efforts that finally bore fruit in 1868. Gretna's famous runaway marriages date from 1753: when Lord Hardwicke's Marriage Act was passed. It stated that if both parties to a marriage were not at least twenty-one years-old, consent to the marriage had to be given by the parents. This Act did not apply in Scotland, where it was possible for boys to get married at fourteen and girls at twelve – with or without parental consent.

The couple were overtaken by Ellen's outraged family at Calais, en route for Paris. Although the marriage had not been consummated Wakefield and his brother, who had helped him, were sentenced to three years imprisonment. It required an Act of Parliament to annul the marriage – which in Scotland had been entirely legal. The case attracted huge publicity and it seemed that the Wakefield brothers must be irretrievably ruined.

Serving his sentence in Newgate gaol, Wakefield became deeply interested in the theory and economics of colonisation. In 1829 he wrote a *Letter from Sydney*, in which he proposed the sale by the government of small landholdings to law-abiding British citizens. In 1831 he promoted the colonisation of South Australia by this method. Wakefield believed that most of the ills afflicting contemporary Britain were the result of uncontrolled population growth and overcrowding. While in prison, he had drawn up a blueprint to show how a colony could be sustained from the outset: not by convicts but by a balance of artisans, professionals and capital.

Wakefield was the initial, driving force behind the scheme to colonise South Australia, the only state in Australia that was never a convict settlement: but he found himself marginalised because of his criminal record.

Wakefield was unfairly accused by Karl Marx (1818–83), in *Das Kapital* (published in 1867), of wishing to replicate the aristocratic society of Britain in the colonies. In fact Wakefield was a radical and greatly admired the meritocratic US.

Edward Gibbon Wakefield by unknown artist (*c.*1820)

National Portrait Gallery, London

Far from losing his interest in colonisation as a tool for social engineering, Wakefield turned his attention to New Zealand. Together with John George Lambton, Ist Earl of Durham (1792–1840), he became a leading light in the New Zealand Association: which had been given a charter to promote a settlement in 1837. The scheme came to nothing, because the Colonial Office imposed conditions that the Association found intolerable. That same year, rebellion had broken out in Lower Canada. Lord Melbourne, the Prime Minister invited Lord Durham to go to Canada as Governor-General, to stabilise the colony. Durham had become very close to Wakefield while working on the New Zealand Association and was convinced by his theories. Durham was determined to have Wakefield by his side in Canada: but both understood that Wakefield would be unacceptable to the British government in any official capacity.

In 1838 Wakefield sailed secretly for Canada: where Durham retained him as his unofficial advisor and negotiator. Almost immediately Durham fell ill and most of his work was conducted, highly competently, by Wakefield and a fellow advisor, Charles Buller (1806–48). The mission was a complete success. A dangerous situation had been defused and, most importantly, union between English-speaking Upper and French-speaking Lower Canada had been achieved. On his return to Britain, with the help of Wakefield and Buller, Durham wrote a report for Parliament. It immediately became the prescription for British Colonial policy.

In March 1839 Wakefield was invited to become a director of the New Zealand Company, a recreation of the defunct New Zealand Association. On 12 May the first settlers sailed for New Zealand, under the leadership of Wakefield's faithful brother William. By the end of the year Wakefield had despatched eight more ships and, in 1841 recruited another brother, Arthur to settle the north of South Island.

In 1840 Wakefield was invited by the North American Colonial Association of Ireland (NACAI) to advise them, for a fee of £20,000 (£15 million today), on the purchase of a large tract of land near Montreal. In 1842 he sailed to Canada as their representative: and was elected to the Canadian Parliament, although he never took his seat.

In 1848 Wakefield was asked to become a founder member of a New Zealand settlement association: which, in 1850 became the Canterbury Association. It was sponsored by the Church of England. The Association was founded in London and incorporated by Royal Charter on 13

Many considered Durham an odd choice. One of the most splendid dandies of the age, he once made the useful comment that anyone should be able "to jog along on 40,000 pounds a year" (£32 million today). Despite his enormous wealth from coal mines in the north-east, he was a true liberal, known as "Radical Jack".

The 1839 *Report on the Affairs of British North America*, commonly known as Lord Durham's Report is a key document in the history of Canada and the British Empire. Durham appointed a new executive council to placate the rebellious French Canadians, for which he was heavily criticised in Parliament. In the Report, Durham strongly urged the union of Lower and Upper Canada, together with increased self-government, to preserve Canada for Britain.

Captain Arthur Wakefield (1799–1843), passed over for promotion, left the Royal Navy in 1841. He joined William in New Zealand the following year. Arthur was killed, with twenty-three others, in the "Wairu Massacre" – caused entirely by the headstrong action of Henry Thompson, the Chief Magistrate of the township of Nelson in attempting to expropriate Maori land illegally. The Maoris were exonerated in a subsequent government enquiry. Wairu is only a few miles from the township of Wakefield.

John George Lambton, 1st Earl of Durham by Thomas Phillips
National Portrait Gallery, London

November 1849. The promoters were Wakefield and John Robert Godley (1814–61). Wakefield's New Zealand Company had already established four other colonies. The President of the Association's Committee of Management was the Archbishop of Canterbury. The Committee also included several other bishops and clergy, as well as members of both Houses of Parliament. The settlement was to be called Canterbury, for the Archbishop of Canterbury: and the seat of the settlement Christchurch, after Godley's old Oxford College.

In 1852 the New Zealand Constitution Act was passed, empowering New Zealand as a self-governing colony: a goal towards which Wakefield had worked since 1847. In September 1852 Wakefield sailed for New Zealand – never to return. He was immediately elected to both the Provincial Council and General Assembly: where he clashed with Sir George Grey (1812–98), New Zealand's twice-serving Governor, on land sale policy. It was one of Wakefield's fundamental tenets that land sales should be kept high, to finance the settlement's growth. Grey wished to keep prices low, to encourage a continual flow of settlers. In December 1855 Wakefield, who had already suffered a series of strokes, collapsed and was forced to retire. He lingered as a semi-invalid for another seven years, before dying on 16 May 1862 in Wellington.

Wakefield altered completely the style and tempo of the British Empire. He provided a spark of genius: combining a vision of systematic colonisation with an almost messianic belief in the merits of colonial self-government. His obituary, written by Thornton Hunt in the *Daily Telegraph* eulogised Edward Gibbon's achievements: "Administrative and constructive reform [in the Empire] can scarcely be traced to the single hand of any other man".

This was the man who had once kidnapped a teenage bride to line his own pockets but had changed his ways – small wonder that the Anglican church found him so appealing.

MEN YOU COULD BANK ON

David Barclay (1682–1769) was the second son of Robert Barclay of Urie in Kincardineshire, who published an *Apologia of the Principles and Doctrines of the People called Quakers* in 1675. An highly influential work, it was translated into seven languages. It even found favour at court at a time when Quakers were persecuted. He was also a co-founder, with George Fox and William Penn, of Philadelphia (the Greek for "brotherly love"), capital of the Quaker state of Pennsylvania.

Sampson Lloyd (2nd)
replica by unknown artist

David started out as a draper in London, before building a prosperous business trading in the West Indies. Through his second wife Priscilla, daughter of John Freame (1665–1745), a Quaker goldsmith who had established a bank in 1690, he turned to banking; and acquired premises at 54, Lombard Street – which in 1728, was the original site of what became Barclays Bank. David was a strict Quaker: on obtaining a West Indian estate, he freed his slaves and taught them skills and trades. He was a friend of King George III: who permitted him not to kneel before his monarch, as self-abasement was against Quaker belief. He refused both a knighthood for himself and preferment for his son at court. Far better, he explained, to bring up his boys in "honest trade".

One of those boys, another David married Rachel Lloyd as his second wife in 1767: her father Sampson Lloyd III (1699–1779), also a Quaker, had co-founded a bank in Birmingham in 1765. If David and Rachel had had a son, the two great 21st century international banks might now be linked – which, in the 2008–09 banking crisis, would have given the Government and City regulators a fit. To look on the bright side though, no one in authority had anyone remotely as imaginative as John Law to deal with.

MUNGO PARK DISCOVERED THE RIVER NIGER IN 1796

Mungo Park (1771–1806) was a Scots explorer of the Niger Basin in West Africa and the first European to view the Niger River upstream from its delta. He was born near Selkirk where his father was a prosperous tenant farmer of the Duke of Buccleuch. Apprenticed at fourteen to a local surgeon Thomas Anderson, he attended Edinburgh University: where he studied medicine and botany. His brother-in-law James Dickson, a renowned botanist, had a seed business in Covent Garden in London. On field trips to the Highlands, he developed Park's interest in botany into a consuming passion.

Dickson was a friend of Sir Joseph Banks and together, in 1788 they had founded the Linnean Society. Park passed his medical exams in 1793 and, through the influence of Banks, secured the post of assistant surgeon on the East Indiaman *Worcester*, bound for Sumatra. On his return Park addressed the Linnean Society on his discovery of eight new Sumatran plants – which he presented to Banks.

In 1794 the African Society was lobbied successfully by Banks to send Park to discover the course of the Niger River. On 21 June 1795 he set out from the mouth of the Gambia River and headed upstream. On 2 December, with two local Mandinka (Gambian) guides, he set out for the unknown territory of the upper Senegal River basin. He reached Ludamar: where he was imprisoned by the local Moorish chief, Ali who made him share a hut with a pig. Four months later Park managed to escape. Though Ali had deprived him of most of his possessions, he retained a horse, a compass and a beaver hat, in which he kept his journal. He reached Segou three weeks later on 21 July, to become the first European to look upon the upper Niger River: "Then, at last I saw with infinite pleasure the great object of my mission; the long sought for majestic Niger, glittering to the morning sun, as broad as the Thames at Westminster and flowing slowly to the *eastward*".

Park followed the river downstream for 80 miles to Silla where, "worn down by sickness, exhausted by hunger and fatigue, half naked without any article of value", he decided to turn

Mungo Park after Henry Edridge (c.1797)
National Portrait Gallery, London

Map of the course of the River Niger

The Niger is the principal river of western Africa, about 2,600 miles long. Its source is in the highlands of south-eastern Guinea. It runs in a crescent through Mali, Niger and Nigeria: discharging through a massive delta into the Gulf of Guinea. The Niger is the third-longest river in Africa, exceeded only by the Nile and the Congo. It is a relatively clear river, carrying only a tenth as much sediment as the Nile: the Niger's headlands are in ancient rocks that provide little silt.

The Niger takes one of the most unexpected routes of any major river, a boomerang shape that baffled European geographers for 500 years. Its source is just 150 miles inland from the Atlantic Ocean. The river runs north-east, away from the sea into the Sahara Desert; then takes a 90° right turn near Timbuktu and heads south-east to the Gulf of Guinea.

This strange geography is because the Niger is two ancient rivers joined together. The upper Niger, from the source past the trading city of Timbuktu to the bend in the current river, once emptied into an ancient lake, while the lower Niger started in nearby hills and flowed south into the Gulf of Guinea. As the Sahara dried up in 4000–1000 BC, the two rivers altered their courses and joined up.

back. He followed the Niger for 300 miles to Bamako (now in Mali). Heavy rains had set in, he had nothing to eat and he had to swim countless swollen torrents, pushing his horse ahead of him. His journal notes though, remained safely stowed in his beaver hat. Park struggled on, until he reached Kamalia where he collapsed. Emaciated by malaria and various tropical diseases, his life was saved by a kindly Muslim slave trader, Karfa Taura. For seven months Taura nursed him back to health and returned him to Gambia in the company of a slave caravan, to embark on an American slave ship. The surgeon had died and Park secured his passage as a replacement. He tended the ship's cargo of slaves during the voyage to Antigua; from where he returned to Britain, having been away for two years and seven months. In 1799 he published *Travels in the Interior Districts of Africa*, which became an immediate best-seller. It was translated into French, German and later, several other languages.

Park found it very difficult to settle down. Reluctantly he practised as a physician in Peebleshire, having married Alison Anderson, the daughter of the surgeon to whom he had first been apprenticed. In 1804 his patience was rewarded. Park was offered £5,000 (£3.7 million today) by the British government to lead another expedition: to follow the Niger, "to the utmost possible distance to which it can be traced". His instructions were to land at Goree, an island recently captured from the French, and assemble enough soldiers from the garrison to accompany the expedition. On 31 January Park, now a captain in the British army, sailed for the Gambia from Portsmouth. The expedition included forty soldiers and two seamen.

On 6 April 1805 the party left for the Gambia: where Park recruited a Mandinko trader, Isaaco as their guide, before heading into the interior to Bamako on the Niger. Progress for such a large party was slow and by June the expedition had been overtaken by torrential rain. By the time they reached Bamako thirty-one soldiers and an officer had perished. Park himself was suffering from dysentery – which he cured with mercury, an excruciatingly painful remedy. The survivors then proceeded downstream to Sansanding, where they sold off their excess baggage to convert two canoes into a flat-bottomed sailing boat, drawing only one foot of water: which Park christened HMS *Joliba* (the Niger). He recruited a slave trader, Amadi Fatouma as a guide to take them on into Hausa country in present-day Nigeria. At the end of January 1806 a resolute Park with his eight survivors headed downstream to the Gulf of Guinea.

Park wrote in his last despatch to London, "I shall set sail for the east with the fixed resolution to discover the termination of the Niger or perish in the attempt. Though all the Europeans who are with me should die, and though I were myself half-dead, I would still persevere and if I could not succeed in the object of my journey, I would at least die on the Niger".

Park had food and ammunition on board and planned to make a dash for the coast without stopping or landing anywhere on the way. He ordered that anyone who approached *Joliba* should be fired upon. This was a foolhardy decision, which inflicted heavy and unnecessary casualties on the local natives, suggesting that Park's sound judgement had become affected by stress. The course of the Niger had at last turned south when *Joliba* arrived at Yelwa. They had sailed over 1,500 miles from Sansanding; and, although unaware of it, were a bare 500 miles from the mouth of the river. At Yelwa, Amadi left the party as had been agreed. A few miles downstream *Joliba* was ambushed, while attempting to negotiate fast-flowing rapids at Bussa, and swamped. Park and his companions were lost, presumably drowned.

In 1810 Amadi and his assistant, Isaaco produced a journal written in Arabic. In 1816, together with Park's own diary, they were translated and published in London. Park's wife was paid £4,000 (£2.7 million today) by the British Government in compensation. In 1827 Park's son Thomas, an officer in the Royal Navy, set off from the Gold Coast to discover his father's fate – but died of fever in the attempt.

Statues and memorials of Mungo Park abound in Scotland, Gambia and Nigeria. In 1971 two commemorative chairs were installed in St Giles' Cathedral in Edinburgh, in celebration of the bicentenary of his birth.

In the 19th century, the river steamer proved itself the most suitable vessel to access the vast interior of West Africa. The Laird shipyard built the first in 1832. Macgregor Laird (1808–61), the younger son of William and Agnes Laird, designed an iron paddle-steamer SS *Alburkah*, the first ever ocean-going iron ship. It was capable of making its own way to the Gulf of Guinea, where Laird hoped to trade, and he led the expedition. *Alburkah* steamed south from Milford Haven in July 1832 with a crew of 48, reaching the mouth of the Niger three months later.

After navigating one of the many tributaries of the Niger, *Alburkah* made her way upstream as far as Lokoja, to the confluence with the Benue River. The steamer's performance was a triumph. The expedition demonstrated that the Niger offered a highway into the continent for ocean vessels. In 1834, when *Alburkah* returned to Liverpool, only nine of the original crew survived: including a skeletal Macgregor Laird.

THE WORD "VACCINATION" ENTERED THE ENGLISH LANGUAGE IN 1796

Edward Anthony Jenner (1749–1823), after training in London and a period as an army surgeon, spent his entire career as a country doctor in his native county of Gloucestershire. His research into smallpox was based on careful case studies and clinical observation, more than a hundred years before scientists could identify the viruses themselves. His "vaccination" was so successful that by 1840 the British government had banned all alternative preventive treatments for smallpox. Vaccination, the word Jenner coined for his treatment (from the Latin *vacca*, a cow), was adopted by the great French chemist and biologist, Louis Pasteur for immunisation against other diseases.

Lady Mary Wortley Montagu, *née* Pierrepoint (1689–1762), was an amateur physician and writer. She introduced inoculation (using smallpox itself rather than cowpox) to Britain from Turkey, where she had accompanied her diplomat husband, as early as 1721 – when she saved her daughter's life. The practice, although taken up for a time by many in fashionable society, was regarded as dangerous and unnatural.

Edward Jenner by William Say after James Northcote (published 20 August 1804)
National Portrait Gallery, London

In the 18th century smallpox was a killer disease. The majority of its victims were children. In 1980, as a result of Jenner's discovery, the World Health Organisation officially declared "the world and its peoples" free from endemic smallpox.

WILLIAM BANTING, THE "FATHER OF THE LOW CARBOHYDRATE DIET"

William Banting was born in Westminster in December 1796, the year Robert Burns died and Mungo Park first reached the Niger. Banting was a funeral director in Pall Mall: and is one of only a handful of people whose names have entered the English language as both a verb and a noun – others include Captain Boycott, a despised land agent in Ireland; Hoover, the manufacturer of vacuum cleaners; and the French chemist Louis Pasteur. Mackintosh, Watt, Diesel and many more are used only as nouns.

His father, Thomas Banting, by trade a cabinetmaker and upholsterer, had made such a spectacular success in conducting Lord Nelson's that King George III appointed him to undertake all future royal funerals. By 1834 his son William was indispensable: he directed the Duke of Wellington's funeral in 1852 and Prince Albert's in 1861. The family retained the royal warrant for four generations, from 1811–1928: Queen Victoria's funeral in 1901 cost £594 8s 3d (£247,000 today). The hallmark of Banting funerals was grandeur and finery, "the pomp of death".

William Banting was only 5 feet 5 inches tall and became extremely fat. By the time he was sixty he was unable to tie his shoe laces, "or attend to the little offices which humanity requires without considerable pain and difficulty". He could only go downstairs backwards and "puffed and blowed [sic] in a way that was very unseemly and disagreeable". His doctors urged him to take exercise but it only increased his appetite and added to his weight. On 26 August 1862, aged sixty-five, Banting weighed 202 lbs. A body mass index of 30 or more defines clinical obesity: Banting's was 33.6.

After trying a course of fifty Turkish baths and "gallons of physic" without success, he consulted an ENT specialist, William Harvey for an increasing problem of deafness.

Harvey believed that obesity was the source of this. He suggested that Banting should avoid bread, pastry, butter (thought to contain starch), milk, sugar, soup, potatoes, and beans: and in their place adopt a diet of any meat *except* pork (for some curious reason, also thought to contain starch), any fish except salmon, and dry toast. Good claret (several glasses a day), sherry, Madeira, gin, whisky and brandy were all permitted; champagne, port and especially beer, were not. In a matter of weeks Banting felt better than he had for twenty years. Within a year he had lost 46 lbs and twelve inches from his waistline – and had recovered his hearing.

Banting published a booklet entitled *A Letter on Corpulence, Addressed to the Public* in 1863. He identified sugar and fats as the main causes of obesity. Written in plain, sensible language, it became an overnight success. By 1869 it had been translated into French and German and had run to four editions. To "bant", or "banting", became fashionable words for slimming and continued in use well into the 20th century. It is still the preferred word in Swedish. Thousands followed the Banting diet, worrying doctors over the right balance of the "carbonaceous and nitrogenous qualities of food". They were especially anxious to include milk: although humans are the only animals that drink milk after weaning, let alone that of another species.

Not all humans can drink milk. In Southern Europe and Africa lactose intolerance can affect up to 90% of the population. In East Asia, where milk consumption is low, breast cancer

Oliver Percy Lane was born in St Ives in Cornwall in 1878, the year William Banting died. In 1893 he passed first in the Civil Service Examination out of 449 candidates but was rejected by the Medical Board. In 1893 he became instead an assistant librarian with Camberwell Borough Council in London. In 1901 he was transferred to the Town Hall where he remained until his retirement. He was a founding member of the Camberwell Division of the British Red Cross and its honorary secretary in 1910.

In October 1921 he received a telephone call from nearby King's College Hospital, urgently seeking a blood donor. Lane chose Sister Linstead, one of his Red Cross workers, to be the first volunteer. With the help of his wife, Lane went on to found what later became the National Blood Transfusion Service. He died in 1944.

is unusual. Cancer deaths among women aged between thirty-five and sixty-four in the US are nearly five times more frequent than in China.

Considerable research was undertaken in food chemistry in the late 19th century and far greater attention was paid to nutrition and diet after Banting published his little book. He gave the proceeds from it to charity before he died in 1878, aged eighty-one.

A distant relation, born in Canada and killed in a WWII plane crash, Sir Frederick Banting (1891–1941) shared the 1923 Nobel Prize for medicine with John Macleod (1876–1935), born in Perthshire, which was awarded for the isolation of insulin. Despite the obvious association with type-2 diabetes, often caused by obesity, the word "banting" precedes his discovery by nearly sixty years.

ALMOST EVERY INTERNATIONAL SPORT WAS INVENTED BY THE BRITISH

More games and competitive sports played in international fixtures today, were invented or popularised by the British, than by the rest of the world put together: notably cricket, soccer, rugby union and rugby league, golf and lawn tennis.

Many others should also be mentioned: badminton, rackets, squash, table tennis, bowls, croquet, curling, boxing, clay pigeon and game bird shooting, cycling and motor cycling, darts, fives, beagling, coursing and fox hunting, greyhound and horse racing, steeplechasing and three-day eventing, hockey, ice hockey and lacrosse (both taken up and refined by British Army officers in Canada), hurling and shinty, mountaineering, billiards, snooker, downhill and slalom skiing, 'head first' sledding and water polo. Furthermore baseball derives from rounders (and was first played in England); rugby spawned American football; and basketball was invented in 1891 by a Canadian of Scottish ancestry, James Naismith.

France has a longer association with motor racing than Britain: but the first officially sanctioned Formula One championship was held at Silverstone in May 1950. Although polo was invented in Iran 2,000 years ago, it was only after the Calcutta Polo Club was founded in 1862 that the sport spread around the world – pig-sticking however, though also much loved by British Army officers in India, failed to travel very far.

Just as the Boat Race, quintessentially English, was the origin of all modern rowing events, so the excitement generated by the America's Cup encouraged round-the-world yacht races and in-shore sailing competitions have become a popular sport.

The Much Wenlock international athletics competition, introducing many new field and track events and pioneered in Shropshire by Dr William Penny (1809–95), was held between 1850–90. It led directly to, the first modern Olympic Games in 1896.

The Victorian era of muscular Christianity and enthusiastic amateurism in Britain bequeathed an obsession with sport to the modern world. Though now often played by professionals and ruthlessly promoted, international sporting contests must rank amongst the greatest influences for good that ever came from these islands.

The Boat Race, watched by an estimated 120 million people in 2009, was first held in 1829 as a result of a challenge by Charles Merivale, a student at St John's College, Cambridge to his old friend at Harrow, Charles Wordsworth who was at Oxford. Oxford won: and to date have won 75 times against 80 for Cambridge. In 1877 the race was declared a dead heat. Oxford claimed that the judge, "Honest John" Phelps was asleep under a bush as the crews passed him: he announced that the result was a "dead heat to Oxford by four feet".

The America's Cup, originally the Royal Yacht Squadron Cup, was named in honour of the first yacht to win the 53 mile race round the Isle of Wight: the 100-foot schooner America, on 22 August 1851. Donated to the New York Yacht Club in 1857, the trophy remained there until won by Australia II in 1983. Known affectionately as the "Auld Mug", it is the oldest trophy in international sport.

America beat fifteen British yachts, winning by 8 minutes. Queen Victoria asked who had come second: the answer was, "Ah, Your Majesty, there is no second".

CRICKET

Cricket was the first 'major' sport to develop into a modern game. The best known reference to it in poetry was written by Sir Henry Newbolt (1862–1938) in 1897:

There's a breathless hush in the Close to-night
Ten to make and the match to win
A bumping pitch and a blinding light,
An hour to play, and the last man in.
And it's not for the sake of a ribboned coat,
Or the selfish hope of a season's fame,
But his captain's hand on his shoulder smote
"Play up! Play up! And play the game!"

The earliest official reference to cricket appears in a 1598 court record. In dispute over a plot of land, The Royal Grammar School in Guildford established a *prima facie* claim when John Derrick, a 59 year-old Queen's coroner, testified that he and his friends had played "creckett" on the site fifty years earlier. By the 14th century, many Middle Dutch words had found their way into the English language as a result of the wool trade with Flanders. "Cricket" is probably derived from a cross between the Dutch *krick*, meaning a stick; and the old English *cryce*, denoting a staff or crutch.

The first mention of cricket played as an adult sport appeared in 1611: when two Sussex men were prosecuted for missing church and playing on a Sunday. After the Restoration in 1660, cricket became popular – due principally to the opportunity it offered for betting. Early 18th century reports delight in the size of the stakes, rather than the intricacies of the game. From 1725 aristocratic patrons intent on reinforcing their bets with skilled players, attracted comment from a press still celebrating its freedom from the censor in 1696. Cricket rapidly spread throughout the Empire. It was introduced to the West Indies by sugar planters; by the East India Company servants and soldiers to India; and to Australia by the officers of the penal settlements from the moment colonisation began in 1788.

The laws of cricket were first drawn up in 1744; and were amended in 1774 by the Star and Garter Club, later the Marylebone Cricket Club (the MCC). They introduced a middle stump, the leg-before-wicket rule and a maximum bat width. In the 1820s the ball began to be thrown: developing into an art form of its own through the bowler's judgment of pace, length and pitch. Pitched bowling resulted in the straight bat.

The most famous of the early clubs was Hambledon in Hampshire, founded in 1757. Until the formation of the MCC and the opening of Lord's cricket ground in 1787, Hambledon was the hub and the boisterous home of English cricket. It grew from a parish team known as Squire Land's Club into a private club patronised by nobility and gentry. A few chose to play, but players were usually professional.

By the last quarter of the 18th century, cricket had become very popular in London. In 1786 The Earl of Winchilsea and Colonel Charles Lennox, later 4th Duke of Richmond, approached a young Yorkshireman from

Before the 19th century, bowlers rolled the ball along the ground to a batsman wielding a bat shaped like a hockey stick. Today, the cricket bat is made from the "cricket-bat" willow *(Salix alba var. caerulea)*, which grows especially well in southern England (and Kashmir). The bat is treated with raw (unboiled) linseed oil. Willow is tough, light and does not splinter. The modern handle dates from an 1880 design by an engineer pupil of Isambard Kingdom Brunel, Charles Richardson. The oldest existing bat dates from 1729 and is displayed in the Sandham Room at the Oval cricket ground in south London.

Thirsk, Thomas Lord (1755–1832) who was an attendant at the White Conduit Club in Islington. They invited him to find a suitable cricket ground close to the West End of London and guaranteed to underwrite his costs. Lord first leased land in Marylebone, in today's Dorset Square, where the first match was played on 31 May 1787 – the date the MCC takes for its foundation. Within a few years, the MCC had replaced Hambledon as the home of cricket.

In 1810 the Dorset Square lease expired and Lord found a temporary location in St John's Wood, before moving to the present-day Lord's Cricket Ground in 1814. Known simply as Lord's, it is owned by the MCC; and regarded as the home of cricket. It also houses the oldest sporting museum in the world. The earliest recorded match played at Lord's was on 22 June 1814, between the MCC and Hertfordshire.

Lord's Cricket Ground

Thomas Lord is buried at St John's Church at West Meon in Hampshire – close by the traitor and Soviet spy, Guy Burgess (1910–63).

Sussex, the first county club, was founded in 1839. The rapidly expanding railway system enabled both teams and spectators to travel far greater distances, increasing both the number of fixtures played and the size of crowds. On 31 August 1846 William Clarke (1798–1855) of Nottingham, a one-eyed, underarm spin bowler who established the Trent Bridge ground, formed and captained a travelling All England Eleven. Although a commercial venture, his team popularised the game in parts of England that had never before been visited by first-class cricketers.

In 1864 Wisden's Cricketers' Almanack was first published. It was founded by a fast bowler from Brighton, John Wisden (1826–84). "The little marvel" has been published without interruption until the present day. It is the longest surviving sports annual in history. In the same year over-arm bowling was legalised; and in 1865 W.G Grace made his debut. His feats made cricket a major attraction.

William Gilbert Grace (1848–1915), known familiarly by his sobriquet "WG", was Victorian England's most famous cricketer. Born at Downend near Bristol, he became a doctor like his father but devoted his life to cricket. A natural all-rounder, he bowled, batted and fielded with equal success. Barely out of his teens, he developed modern batting techniques: on primitive, unprepared pitches. During his career in first-class cricket (1865–1908), "W.G." scored 54,896 runs, including 126 centuries. Between 1866–80, he achieved the highest first-class annual batting average twelve times; and remained at the top of the game until well into his fifties. In 1880 he played in the first home Test match against Australia.

W.G. Grace attributed to Archibald James Stuart Wortley (1890)
National Portrait Gallery, London

From the 1880s cricket was played by county sides: but organisation of games remained haphazard until 1894, when the MCC was invited to draw up a system of

In the winter of 1883–84, the Hon. Ivo Bligh (later Earl of Darnley) led a demoralised English side to Australia declaring, with some presumption, that he would "recover the ashes". On arrival, Florence Murphy and her girl friends presented Bligh with a small urn of ashes. The myth that the ashes were the remains of a stump and bail is not true: her daughter revealed much later that the ashes were from Florence's wedding veil. There was a doubly happy outcome: England defeated Australia 2:1 in the series – and Bligh married Florence a year later. The "Ashes" remains the most fiercely contested trophy in modern cricket, but the trophy is surprisingly small.

• **The urn containing "the Ashes" (1882)**

On 30 September 1930 Oliver Locker-Lampson M.P., an ardent admirer of Adolf Hitler, wrote a piece in the *Daily Mirror* describing a game of cricket played in WWI between British army officers, who were prisoners of war, and a side assembled by Lance Corporal Hitler who was recovering from his wounds in a nearby hospital. Though his team lost, Hitler is said to have found the game intriguing enough to "study it as a possible medium for the training of troops"; but declared that it was "unmanly". Hitler "advocated the withdrawal of the use of pads and .... recommended a bigger and harder ball". Locker-Lampson founded the Sentinels of Empire, a group of right-wingers dedicated to fighting Bolshevism: supported by, amongst others, Lord Rothermere – the owner of the *Daily Mail.*

classification. The MCC decreed that: "Cricketing counties shall be considered as belonging to the first class or not. There is no necessity for further subdivision". The MCC itself would decide which counties qualified, on the basis of playing an agreed number of three-day games, at home or away. As a result fifteen counties were declared first-class. Imperfect though it was, there was now an official County Championship.

In 1844 the first international game of cricket had taken place in New York, between the USA and Canada. In 1859 a professional English team toured North America on the first ever overseas tour. In 1868 the first Australian team to travel abroad consisted of a side composed entirely of Aborigines. The first Test match took place in Melbourne in March 1877: when James Lillywhite's professional touring team was defeated. On 29 August 1882 disaster struck, when a strong Australian visiting side beat England, all out for 77 runs, at the Oval. This dismal result was made immortal when the *Sporting Times* published an "obituary" the next day: "In Affectionate Remembrance Of English Cricket which died at the Oval on 29 August 1882. Deeply lamented by a large circle of sorrowing friends and acquaintances, RIP. *NB* the body will be cremated and the ashes taken to Australia".

In 1909 the Imperial Cricket Conference (ICC) was created to arrange fixtures between the three Test match countries: England, Australia and South Africa. They were joined later by India, the West Indies, New Zealand, Pakistan, Ceylon (now Sri Lanka), Rhodesia (Zimbabwe) and East Pakistan (Bangladesh) – all former member states of the British Empire or the Commonwealth. The Netherlands, Ireland and Scotland are now cricketing nations too.

Sir Donald Bradman

Of the many memorable contests for the Ashes, the England touring side in 1932–33 is still especially resented in Australia. The England captain, Douglas Jardine (1900–58), a merciless Scotsman born in Bombay, planned the series meticulously with only one aim – how to overcome possibly the finest batsman of all time, Don Bradman (1908–2001). When Jardine was appointed captain, his old housemaster at Winchester was asked to comment on his chances of success. The reply was uncannily prescient: "He might well win us the Ashes, but he might lose us a Dominion".

Having watched hours of film clips from the 1930 series, Jardine convinced himself that Bradman was "yellow", after he saw him struggle against "bouncers" at the Oval. He decided to pack his squad with five fast bowlers. In particular, Jardine picked the accurate and terrifyingly fast Harold Larwood (1904–95) from Nottingham, to pursue the "fast leg theory". Larwood and Bill Voce (1909–1984), another Nottinghamshire player, repeatedly struck Australian batsmen with fast balls: seriously injuring two of them. The tourists won the "Bodyline" series and regained the Ashes: but only by employing intimidating tactics.

The MCC was jubilant, until it realised how badly relations between the two countries had been damaged. Larwood was asked to sign a Letter of Apology to the Australian Cricket Board & Players. He refused: explaining that, as a professional cricketer, he was obliged to follow the directions of his captain. Larwood never played cricket for England again; and emigrated to Australia in 1950, with his honour intact – unlike the MCC, which changed the rules but was guilty of hypocrisy; and Jardine, who retired from first class cricket the following year. Poetic justice is an overworked term: but Bradman died aged ninety-two and Larwood was ninety – Jardine died of cancer, aged only fifty-seven.

> Cricketing expressions have been adopted to describe some of the joys and vexations of everyday life: when life is going well, you are "on the front foot". When things are going badly, you are "on the back foot" or "on a sticky wicket". When perplexed or confused, you are "stumped"; and if you make an error, you are "caught out". When a calamity occurs, you are "hit for six". If you disregard or bend the rules, your behaviour is described as "just not cricket". Finally, if you are a lawyer, you can require a contract to be signed "by the close of play".

BRITAIN AND HER AMERICAN COLONIES NEED NEVER HAVE GONE TO WAR

In 1776 Britain's American colonists enjoyed the highest standard of living and the least oppressive government in the world. Nonetheless a powerful minority, goaded by the resentful venom of Samuel Adams (1722–1803) in Boston; the anarchic idealism of the Norfolk-born Quaker pamphleteer, Tom Paine (1737–1809); the expansionism of Scotch-Irish frontiersmen, who wished to abrogate British-Native American treaties and expand to the west; and the greedy opportunism of slave-owning magnates, keen to exploit their fiefdoms without moral supervision and to repudiate their debts, combined to trump up spurious pretexts to seek independence from Britain.

Thomas Paine by Auguste Millière (c.1876 (1792))
National Portrait Gallery, London

Most of these would have been easy to correct, for Britain had already conceded almost every demand made by the colonists, except sovereignty, and was reluctant to take up arms against fellow British citizens. Indeed a a third or more of the colonists remained loyal to Britain throughout the war, many of whom later preferred life in Canada under the Crown, and much of the fighting that took place was between irregulars on both sides. Only French intervention in 1778 turned stalemate eventually into British defeat and withdrawal. Most contemporary American accounts of the run-up to war and the conflict itself amount to little more than self-serving propaganda.

Distance from, rather than representation in Parliament, a New World rather than an European perspective and the continuance of slavery were all deeper and more valid concerns, that would have made a rupture of some sort inevitable at a later date, were never at issue. With more time and caution to think and talk, bloodshed could easily have been avoided. One of the considerations that might have

George Washington (1732–99) by Gilbert Stuart (1796). First US President (1789–97)
National Portrait Galley, London

Scotch-Irish is a term used to describe Scottish immigrants from Ulster, who formed distinctive communities with social characteristics very different from the mostly prosperous, middle-class settlers of English descent. Their loyalty to kin, mistrust of authority and a propensity to bear arms helped shape the the US identity and extend the colonial frontiers hundreds of miles to the west.

More than 250,000 Presbyterian Scots, only a few generations after implantation in Ulster, migrated to Britain's North American colonies between 1717–70. They were not welcomed by the genteel, less fervently Protestant colonial government; and quickly left for the western mountains where they could live without interference, carving their own world out of the wilderness. Early frontier life was extremely challenging and dangerous, but poverty and hardship were familiar to them. The word "hillbilly" had its origins in Ireland itself ("billy" referred to King William III) and was often used disparagingly. The Scotch-Irish at first called themselves Irish and were called Irish by everyone else. It was not until the mass immigration of Catholic, indigenous Irish in the 1840s, due to the Potato Famine, that the earlier Irish-Americans called themselves Scotch-Irish: to distinguish themselves from those they had generally despised in Ireland and had emigrated to avoid.

The Scotch-Irish, perhaps 15% of the 2.8 million colonists in 1780 (itself over 40% of the then population of Britain), became the most important social and ethnic group in the creation of the modern US. No less than 47% of all US Presidents since 1789 have been of some Scotch-Irish descent, fourteen (33%) strongly so – including Richard Nixon, Ronald Reagan and Bill Clinton.

cooled intemperate hastiness in the colonists, would have been the continuation of a powerful French presence threatening them from the north, in Canada. When Britain removed that threat in 1763, rabble-rousing demagogues were able to exploit any minor errors of judgment or policy from London – and sadly, there were plenty of both.

In one of the successful "side shows" of 1759, *Annus Mirabilis*, Colonel Barrington captured the French island of Guadeloupe in the Caribbean. He offered the plantation owners and colonists extraordinarily generous terms: and they accepted the transfer of power with an equanimity bordering on gratitude. As a major exporter of sugar, Guadeloupe generated an income four times as great as the vast expanse of Canada which at that time was virtually a subsistence economy. Things are rather different today: but at the 1763 Treaty of Paris, the French were anxious to regain Guadeloupe to repair their finances, which had been mauled by a world-wide war.

When tentative negotiations to end the Seven Years' War began in 1762, Pitt was urged by influential traders and Royal Navy strategists to retain the island, together with Martinique and almost every other prewar French possession in the West Indies, other than Hispaniola; and to return Canada and Minorca to France instead. It can be argued that with little left to defend, there would have been no reason for France to maintain a naval presence in the Caribbean – releasing warships to patrol the seas off North America. This might have acted as another strong incentive to the colonists to avoid any provocation that would prejudice Royal Navy protection.

It was a covert promise of French support made to the colonists before the war that gave the rebels the confidence to start it; and it was French military and naval action that decided its conclusion. It is ironic that many Americans seem to have forgotten this.

Great Seal of the United States (1782)

FREEMASONRY WAS THE MIDWIFE OF THE UNITED STATES

Many of the founding fathers of the US were Freemasons. George Washington, Benjamin Franklin FRS, Samuel Adams, John Hancock and James Madison certainly were; Thomas Jefferson and Alexander Hamilton probably were. Indeed nineteen of the fifty-six signatories of the Declaration of Independence were Masons or sympathetic to Freemasonry, as were half of the delegates who signed the US Constitution in 1787. Furthermore, thirty-three generals in the Continental Army, out of seventy-four, were Freemasons. John Paul Jones, the "founder of the US navy", Paul Revere (famed for his "midnight ride") and even the Marquis de Lafayette, the French general whose assistance to the colonists proved crucial, were all Masons – so was the British orator Edmund Burke, who strongly supported the colonists.

Fifteen out of the forty-two US Presidents were active Freemasons, the last being Gerald Ford. Several others, including Abraham Lincoln and Lyndon Johnson, had prepared for initiation. Even Ronald Reagan, though not a Mason, was an honorary member of the Imperial Council of the Shrine; Bill Clinton joined a Masonic youth group; and Vice President Albert ("Al") Gore, who starred in the controversial documentary film *An Inconvenient Truth*, is said to be a "33 degree" Freemason.

It is unsurprising to find that the reverse side of the Great Seal of the United States is "A pyramid unfinished. In the zenith an eye in a triangle, surrounded by a glory, proper". The Eye of Providence is important in the iconography of Freemasonry. Here it represents the all-seeing eye of God, a reminder that a Mason's deeds are always observed by God, who is referred to in Masonry as the Great Architect of the Universe. Since 1935 this symbol has appeared on every US$1 bill.

Modern Freemasonry is of Scottish origin and dates from 1598. William Schaw (1550–1602), who was born in Stirlingshire and buried in Dunfermline Abbey, is regarded as its founder. The first recorded initiation, on 8 June 1600, was that of the Ayrshireman John Boswell of Auchenleck.

The earliest documented admission of a Freemason in England was in 1646, when the antiquarian and astrologist Elias Ashmole (1617–92), of Lichfield in Staffordshire, entered the event in his diary on 16 October. Ashmole was the founder of the world's first public museum, the Ashmolean in Oxford, in 1683.

The first known Freemason in North America was a Scot, John Skene, who immigrated around 1680. The Lodge of St Andrew in Boston is the oldest in the US.

THE US – CANADIAN BORDER

The undefended international border between Canada and the United States is the longest in the world. It stretches for 5,525 miles, including 1,538 miles between Canada and Alaska. Canada is by far the largest country in the world to have only one land border. Native Americans called it the "Medicine Line", because of its mysterious significance for the white people who crossed it.

The present border originated with the Treaty of Paris in 1783 which ended the civil war between Great Britain and the fledgling United States. Expansion of both British North America and the US saw the boundary extended west along the 49th parallel, agreed by the Anglo-American Convention of 1818. Disputes over the border between Maine and New Brunswick led to the bloodless Aroostook War and the Webster-Ashburton Treaty in 1842. An 1844 boundary dispute led to a call for the northern boundary of the US west of the Rockies to be latitude 54° 40' north, the southern boundary of Russia's Alaska Territory. The British however, wanted a border that followed the Columbia River to the Pacific Ocean. The dispute was resolved in the Oregon Treaty of 1846. This confirmed the 49th parallel as the boundary through the Rockies. After the "Pig War" in 1859 (the only casualty was a pig), arbitration in 1872 determined the border between Vancouver Island and Oregon. Finally, in 1903 a joint UK-Canada-US tribunal established the boundary with Alaska.

"THE GREATEST LAND GEOGRAPHER WHO EVER LIVED"

The surname Thompson is the 16th most common in Great Britain, especially to be found in West Yorkshire and Lancashire but spread across the British Isles from Cornwall to Morayshire. When spelled Thomson it is more likely to be of Scottish origin. Both are patronymics, derived from the Aramaic *Tôm*, meaning "twin". There are perhaps more Thompsons or Thomsons of exceptional abilities or distinction – more than for any other group sharing the same name, except Smith.

The list includes two great explorers with only a "p" between them. The first, Joseph Thomson (1858–95) from Dumfriesshire, was the first European to reach Lake Nyasa in Malawi in 1878 and Lake Baringo and Mount Elgon in Kenya. A gazelle affectionately called the "Tommy", found in great quantities all over East Africa, is named for him. The second, a Canadian fur trader and explorer, was "the greatest land geographer who ever lived". He literally put Canada on the map.

David Thompson (1770–1857) was born in Westminster in London to poor Welsh migrants. His father, Dafydd ap Thomas died when he was two and he was placed in Grey Coat Hospital, an institution for the disadvantaged children of Westminster. He thrived at the school, excelling in mathematics and learning basic navigation skills, the basis of his future career as a surveyor.

At the age of fourteen Thompson was apprenticed to the Hudson's Bay Company (HBC). He sailed to Canada on 28 May 1784, never to return to Britain. He spent the first few years of his seven-year apprenticeship working as a clerk at various trading posts in northern and western Canada. He used a long period of convalescence after breaking his leg to study mathematics, astronomy and surveying under the HBC's chief surveyor Philip Turner.

In 1792, now employed as a fur trader, Thompson was asked to undertake his first important survey: to map a route to Lake Athabasca on the Alberta-Saskatchewan border. In 1797, frustrated in his career prospects, he left the HBC without notice and trekked over 80 miles in midwinter to join the rival North West Company of Montreal. The NWC encouraged his exploring ambitions and, over the next few years, he surveyed the lands around the headwaters of the Mississippi River. In 1798 he discovered one of its sources, Turtle Lake. He was made a full partner in the NWC in 1804.

In 1806, prompted by British concerns over the success of the US backed Lewis and Clark expedition, Thompson was sent west to survey a route over the Rocky Mountains to the Pacific Ocean: aimed at opening up the rich fur trading potential of the Pacific Northwest.

In 1807 Thompson crossed the Rocky Mountains via the Howse Pass and built the first trading post on the Columbia River. In 1811, while carrying out a survey of north-west Montana, he was the first European to navigate the full course of the Columbia River.

In 1790, on completing his apprenticeship, Thompson asked for the customary gift of clothing normally made to graduates to be waived in favour of a set of surveying tools. So impressed were his superiors that he received both clothes and tools.

In 1799 Thompson married Charlotte Small, the daughter of a Scots fur trader and a Cree Indian mother. Their marriage was formally recognised at the Presbyterian Church in Montreal on 30 October 1812. The marriage lasted fifty-eight years, the longest in pre-Confederation Canada's history and produced thirteen children.

The Lewis and Clark Expedition (1804–06) was the first to be completed overland to the US Pacific coast. Initiated by President Thomas Jefferson (1743–1826), it was led by his personal secretary, Meriwether Lewis (1774–1809) and an army officer, William Clark (1770–1838). All three had been born British citizens.

Leaving St Louis in 1804, the 40-man expedition travelled up the Missouri River into present day North Dakota to winter amongst the Sioux Indians. The next spring they rode westward through Montana over the continental divide to the headwaters of the Clearwater River. Travelling in a fleet of canoes down the Snake River they reached the mouth of the Columbia River on the Pacific coast. After building a fort (later Astoria in Oregon) in which to spend the winter, the expedition split before returning to a rapturous reception at St Louis, having lost only one man.

That year, near present-day Jasper in Alberta, Thompson recorded a set of giant, unidentifiable footprints with a small nail at the end of each toe. It was possibly the first real clue to the existence of the Sasquatch or "Bigfoot", a hairy humanoid creature occasionally reported in isolated areas of the Pacific north-western US and Canada. Some footprints, discounting obvious hoaxes, measured up to 24 inches long. No actual sighting of "Bigfoot" however, has ever been confirmed.

DAVID THOMPSON'S TRAVELS

David Thompson's travels
in the employment of:-

— Hudson's Bay Company
— North West Company
■ Trading post

Thompson retired from NWC service in 1812 on a generous company pension, settling in Terrebonne near Montreal, to devote himself to his greatest achievement: a map including all his surveys from Lake Superior to the Pacific coast. Published in 1814, Thompson's map was so precise that a century later it was still in use by the Canadian government.

From 1818–26 Thompson was employed surveying the border between the US and Canada as determined by the Treaty of Paris in 1783; and confirmed in the Treaty of Ghent in 1814 which terminated the Anglo-American war of 1812.

In 1831 Thompson once again retired to the life of a land-owner but, overwhelmed by debt, he slid slowly into poverty. He began an autobiography based on his twenty-eight years in the fur trade, drawn from his 77 field notebooks in 1845; but had to abandon it when his sight failed. He died on 10 February 1857, forgotten and unrecognised. He was buried in an unmarked grave in Montreal's Mount Royal Cemetery.

In 1957, one hundred years after his death, the Canadian Government honoured Thompson's memory by printing his image on a 5 cent postage stamp and naming the main road through Alberta, the David Thompson Highway. In the course of his lifetime, Thompson mapped 2.4 million square miles or one-sixth of North America.

The two greatest trading companies in world history were both British, the Honourable East India Company and the Hudson's Bay Company (HBC). The HBC was incorporated in England on 2 May 1670 by Royal Charter as: "The Governor and Company of Adventurers of

England trading into Hudson's Bay". Its purpose was to find a Northwest Passage to the Pacific Ocean, to occupy lands lying adjacent to Hudson Bay and to trade with Indian and Eskimo tribes. The territory was named Rupert's Land, after Prince Rupert (1619–82), first cousin of King Charles II, the founder and first governor of the company. Covering an area of over 1.5 million square miles, its range extended from the west coast of Labrador to the Rocky Mountains, making the HBC the largest private landowner in the world.

From York Factory on the south-west shore of Hudson's Bay, the HBC established trading posts to trade in furs. From 1686 most of these posts were captured by the French until restored to the HBC by the Treaty of Utrecht in 1713. In 1783 a rival North West Company of Montreal was founded (NWC). Both companies existed in a state of armed conflict until the British government brought about a merger in 1821.

The HBC enjoyed exclusive fur trading rights until 1858 when its monopoly expired. In 1870 the company sold its land holdings to the Canadian government for £300,000 (£177 million today) while retaining the mineral rights surrounding its many trading posts, together with a fertile stretch of western Canada. The HBC was governed entirely from Britain until 1931. A Canadian board was then given exclusive authority in Canada but was still accountable to the Governor and Committee in London.

Throughout the 20th century the HBC remained one of the principal fur trading and marketing operations in the world. In the 1970's however, with international aversion to the fur trade increasing, the company began a diversification programme into department stores, financial services and oil exploration. In 1991 the HBC closed down its fur trading activities. It remains today one of Canada's most important businesses.

The honorific term United Empire Loyalists was given to the 70,000 Americans, around 3% of the total population, who left the fledgling US during the Revolution or the newly created Republic in 1783, rather than forfeit their British identity.

During the war, at least a third of the colonists had supported the Crown. Many chose or were forced to flee the new republic. 62,000 were white and 8,000 were black: 46,000 went to British North America (Canada), 7,000 to Britain and 17,000 to British islands in the Caribbean. An unwillingness to rebel against the Crown was the principal reason; but a belief in peaceful evolutionary independence was almost as important. As Daniel Bliss of Concord in Massachusetts, who later became a Chief Justice of New Brunswick, stated: "Better to live under one tyrant a thousand miles away, than a thousand tyrants one mile away".

Sir Alexander Mackenzie (1764–1822) made the first recorded transcontinental crossing of the North American continent north of Mexico. He also discovered the Mackenzie River in north-west Canada.

He was born in Stornoway, on the Isle of Lewis in the Outer Hebrides. In 1774 his family emigrated to New York State. In 1776, during the American Revolution, as "United Empire Loyalists" they moved to Montreal in Canada.

Mackenzie applied for a position with the NWC. In 1788 he was sent to Lake Athabasca on the Alberta-Saskatchewan border to found a trading post, Fort Chipewyan. Hearing from the local Indians that the rivers of the region all flowed to the north-west, he set out to confirm this information. On 10 July 1789 he discovered an unknown river and followed it from Great Slave Lake to its mouth, hoping to find the fabled north-west passage to the Pacific Ocean. When he discovered it flowed into the Arctic Ocean, rather than into Cook Inlet in Alaska, he named it Disappointment River. It was later renamed Mackenzie River in his honour.

In 1791 he sailed to Britain to study the new method of measuring longitude. He returned to Canada in 1792, to make another attempt to find an overland route to the Pacific. He ascended the Peace River and crossed the continental divide before finding the upper reaches of the (later to be named) Fraser River. He then ascended the West Road River and crossed the Coast Mountains. On 20 July 1793 he descended the Bella Coola River, in present-day British Columbia, to reach Vancouver Sound. He missed George Vancouver by less than two months.

Mackenzie was prevented by hostile Heiltsuk Indians from reaching the open Pacific. On 22 July he reached the westernmost point of his journey at Dean Channel where he inscribed on a rock, in a mixture of vermilion and bear grease: "Alexander Mackenzie from Canada by land, 22d July, 1793". His words, preserved by later surveyors, are still there – secure in the Sir Alexander Mackenzie National Park.

Sir Alexander Mackenzie by Thomas Lawrence (*c*.1800)

Mackenzie was knighted in 1802 and served in the Legislature of Lower Canada from 1804–08. In 1812 he married and returned to Scotland. He died ten years later, from kidney failure (Bright's disease), aged fifty-six. He is buried at Avoch on the Black Isle in Ross and Cromarty.

Simon Fraser was born in New York State on 20 May 1776, during the American Revolution, the tenth and youngest child of a British army captain who was taken prisoner by the American forces at Saratoga. He died in custody and, after the war ended, Fraser's mother moved the family to Canada.

Fraser became a clerk in 1791, then a partner in 1801 in the North West Company of Montreal (NWC). In 1805 he was dispatched west to discover trade routes for the fur traffic. He found the Fraser River, which he assumed was the Columbia, only realising his mistake after following its course for more than a year. On 2 July 1808 he reached the sea, on the Gulf of Georgia.

In 1816 he was head of the NWC's Red River Valley District and was arrested for his participation in the Seven Oaks Massacre.

While Alexander Mackenzie had conducted only reconnaissance trips, Fraser was the first to establish trading posts and routes to open up Northwest Canada. These links were used successfully in 1859 to claim British Columbia for Canada: where his achievements are honoured today in the name of the Simon Fraser University.

In 1818, after a career of hazardous exploration, confronting hostile Indian tribes and mutinies amongst his men, Fraser retired and settled in Ontario. In 1837 he was offered a knighthood, which he declined on grounds of poverty.

He died on 18 August 1862. His wife died the next day and they were buried together in the Roman Catholic cemetery at St Andrews in Ontario.

The Seven Oaks Massacre occurred when a Scottish settlement, sponsored by the HBC, in the fertile Red River basin near present-day Winnipeg was destroyed by half-breed allies of the NWC. They were intercepted by Robert Semple, Governor of the colony and 25 soldiers. A fight broke out and the governor and 20 soldiers were killed. The remaining settlers were forced to abandon the colony on threat of massacre. Fraser and five other partners were all acquitted; and in 1817 the colonists regained possession of their settlement.

Simon Fraser, 11th Baron Lovat after William Hogarth (1746)
National Portrait Gallery, London

WHY THE INDUSTRIAL REVOLUTION TOOK PLACE IN BRITAIN

The earliest example of a mediæval industrial process is said to be the assembly-line used to build galleys in the Venetian Arsenal. The first use of mass production in England was the the printing press, brought by William Caxton from Germany in 1476. This might be taken as the first stirring of the Industrial Revolution in Britain. The English Civil Wars (1642–51) finally extinguished the remnants of feudalism – and that is perhaps a more telling development from which to date its beginning.

By the end of the 17th century, the spread of diseases, especially the plague, had decreased. The percentage of children surviving beyond infancy had increased significantly – providing a large pool of labour and an ever-expanding domestic market for the cheap manufactured goods of early industrial processes. Enclosures and a revolution in British agriculture had made food production less labour-intensive. Farm hands who became surplus to agricultural production found work in cottage industries, such as weaving: and later would man the factories of early industrialisation. 17th century colonial expansion provided unlimited worldwide outlets for British goods, particularly in India and the Far East, and created booming capital markets. These generated an enormous accumulation of savings to finance new industries at low rates of interest. From the mid-17th century there was also a steady stream of scientific discoveries and technological advances in which to invest.

The double-acting steam engine that powered the Industrial Revolution in Britain. It was invented and developed by James Watt FRS (1736–1819) and his partner, Matthew Boulton FRS (1728–1809)

From c.1760 enormous advances in agriculture, manufacturing, mining, canals and roads had a huge impact on the cultural and economic topography of Britain. Innovation and social economics were the principal drivers of change. New foundry processes transformed iron and later, steel production. Steam engines, fuelled by abundant supplies of coal, replaced men with mechanical power. From c.1840, sometimes called the Second Industrial Revolution, the pace of invention gathered speed. The harnessing of electricity, petroleum and the internal combustion engine accelerated the trend set by steam: of increasing production while reducing capital and labour costs.

Powered machinery had to be housed in factories. This entailed the division of labour into specialised tasks, making manufacture ever more efficient and cheaper. Rapid advances in transport and communications, first by the steam locomotive, followed by the steamship, motor cars, aeroplanes, the telegraph and telephone, wireless, television and recently the internet, all demonstrate the critical link between science and industry. In their turn, these technological advances were stimulated by newly discovered natural resources and an increasing choice of mass-produced consumer goods.

The transition started in Britain towards the end of the 18th century. An economy based entirely on human and animal muscles, supplemented by wind and water mills, began to move towards steam-powered manufacturing in the textile industry and the mechanization of hand looms. Rapid and bulk movement of every sort of manufactured product to expanding domestic markets was enabled by the introduction of canals, road surfaces improved by John "Tar" McAdam (1756–1826) and above all, the railways. All-metal machine-tools manufactured yet more machines for use in other industries – one of the most important and beneficial developments in human history.

Why did it begin in Britain? In short, it was through the unique combination of the best educated and most innovative upper and middle classes in the world, energetic, inquisitive and adventurous; a scientific and engineering ethos; sophisticated City of London institutions to finance invention and production; an abundance of easily extracted coal, limestone and iron ore near to hand; a pool of cheap labour; the Empire as a market, with trade routes protected by the Royal Navy; and the support of a constitutional government in favour of free and international trade. Nor should it be forgotten that this miracle of opportunity, and the ability to grasp it, was only possible in a country where democratic freedoms and property rights, under the protection of fair and effective law, had evolved over centuries: in contrast with the absolutism and repression that was the norm in every other country in Europe except Holland – a small country that Britain had first copied and then left far behind, a century or more before.

THE BRITISH HAVE NEVER KEPT THEIR INVENTIONS SECRET FOR LONG

Three Englishmen in particular will always be remembered for the transfer of British technology abroad in the 18th century. John Holker (1719–86) is the most interesting: a brave Jacobite soldier, born in the Manchester suburb of Stretford, he fled to France after the failure of Bonnie Prince Charlie's rebellion in 1746. A brilliant, self-taught engineer, he took vital technology and skills from the Lancashire cotton mills with him – and became a French citizen in 1766. He provided the first proper stimulus to industrialisation in France. Samuel Slater (1768–1835), from Belper in Derbyshire, was quite simply a thief: he emigrated to the infant United States in 1789, but returned in 1794 to filch blueprints and techniques that gave such an advantage to his country of adoption that he was dubbed "the father of the US industrial revolution". The last of the three, another Lancashireman, born in Haslington, William Cockerill (1759–1832) did nothing underhand: he merely crossed the Channel and set up an engineering and steel-making business. In doing so he introduced the Industrial Revolution to Belgium.

Air Commodore Sir Frank Whittle OM FRS (1907–96) by Elliott & Fry (30 Nov. 1950). "The father of jet propulsion", he invented the jet engine in 1932
National Portrait Gallery, London

Once the "genie was out of the bottle", examples of how individual Britons helped other countries to industrialise in the 19th and early 20th centuries are legion: three in particular, gave enormous assistance to Japan. Thomas Blake Glover (1838–1911), from Fraserburgh in Aberdeenshire and known as "the Scottish Samurai", established Mitsubishi Heavy Industries in 1870 (the manufacturer of the deadly Zero fighter in WWII) and Kirin Brewery in 1885. William Burton (1856–99), born in Edinburgh, built water and sewage systems in most large Japanese cities between 1887–99. Albert Penniall was seconded by Wolseley to Japan in 1920, to introduce British methods of manufacturing motor cars. In the late 20th century Japan returned Britain the favour: Honda, Nissan and Toyota are now the largest car makers in Britain – a telling confirmation of the irritating axiom, that "what goes up comes down".

The most heinous of all technology thefts from Britain was the systematic betrayal of the enormous advances made by British scientists in the field of nuclear physics. Four traitors did the most damage, but only one was born in Britain: Alan Nunn May (1911–2003). The other three, Berti Broda (1910–83), Klaus Fuchs (1911–88) and Melita Norwood (1912–2005), should have been detected by the security services. The failure to do so gave the Soviet Union the atomic and then the hydrogen bomb. No one knows who enabled the Russians to fly a supersonic airliner before Concorde itself ever flew – but as "Concordski" proved a disaster, it was a case of the "biter bit".

While the Russians have had to steal from Britain, the US only had to ask. Sadly, this has seldom been reciprocated – and then only at a price. During WWII the UK willingly gave the secrets of the magnetron, which is also the key component of microwave ovens, and radar to the US. The legendary Mustang P51 fighter had a marvellous airframe, but an underpowered engine: until Britain provided the Rolls Royce Merlin, which raised its "ceiling" from 16,000 to 32,000 feet. If that was no enough, General Electric was given the blueprints of the jet engine in mid-1942. GE is Rolls Royce's major competitor to this day.

The "Manhattan Project" would not have succeeded in making an atom bomb, in time to drop two of them on Japan, without the vital contributions made by seconded British physicists and metallurgists: who alone knew how much uranium would be needed. The list of British inventions shared with the US goes on and on, almost to the present day (Chobham armour from 1965–73 is a case in point): but the exchange has nearly always been one way. Whether this was due to subservience or naivety, it is a pity.

It took Britain until 2008 to repay the last instalment of her wartime debt to the US.

ADAM SMITH PUBLISHED THE WEALTH OF NATIONS IN 1776, THE YEAR OF THE AMERICAN REVOLUTION

Adam Smith (1723–90) was a moral philosopher and political economist. Regarded as the father of modern economics, he was also a leading light of the Scottish Enlightenment. His most famous works are *The Theory of Moral Sentiments* (1759) and *An Inquiry into the Nature and Causes of the Wealth of Nations* (1776). The latter is the first modern treatise on economics. He was born in Kirkcaldy, the son of a lawyer and later a civil servant. He was educated at Glasgow University and won a scholarship to Oxford – where he found the teaching inferior to Glasgow. He left in 1746, suffering from nervous fits, before his scholarship expired.

Adam Smith by John Kay (1790)

National Portrait Gallery, London

In 1748 Smith embarked upon a series of lectures in Edinburgh which attracted first the attention and then the lifelong friendship of the philosopher David Hume (1711–76). In 1751 he was appointed to the faculty of Glasgow University, taking over in 1752 the Chair of Moral Philosophy. From 1763–66 Smith was employed by a politician, Charles Townshend to tutor his stepson, the young Duke of Buccleuch. Travelling through France and Switzerland, Smith met many of the great thinkers of the day: including Voltaire, Benjamin Franklin and Helvetius.

In 1776, after nine years of writing, Smith published *The Wealth of Nations*: in which he stated his theory that an economic system driven by individual self-interest would lead, as if by "an invisible hand", to the greatest universal good. He also suggested that a careful division of the skills required to manufacture an item would result in the greatest increase in production. "The real price of everything …. is the toil and trouble of acquiring it". His theories quickly supplanted the current belief in Mercantilism: which posited that trade primarily generates a wealth

Smith is often taken as the model of the absent-minded professor. He held conversations with imaginary colleagues, developed a curious gait and once, having buttered a piece of bread, placed it in a teapot and having swallowed the contents, declared it to be the worst cup of tea he had ever drunk.

Kirkcaldy (pronounced "Kurcoddy" by Fifers) is a seaside town in the Kingdom of Fife (so called because it was once a Pictish kingdom), with a population of only 48,000. The Battle of Raith took place 4 miles to the west in 596, where the Angles fought an alliance of Scots, Picts and Britons led by King Áedán mac Gabráin of Dál Riata. Gordon Brown (born 1951), who was brought up in the manse, spent most of his premiership reliving the battle. For its size Kirkcaldy has been the birthplace of an amazing number of famous people, aside of Adam Smith. Among these are: Robert Adam (1728–92), the celebrated architect; Sir Thomas Elder (1818–97), who emigrated to Australia in 1854 to become the world's largest wool merchant; and Sir Sandford Fleming (1827–1915), who built the Canadian Pacific railway and invented time zones.

that governments had a duty to stimulate by imposing protectionist measures, such as tariff barriers. Smith's *magnum opus* immortalised his reputation and became perhaps the most influential work on economics ever published. Although popularised as the Bible of Capitalism, *The Wealth of Nations* is severely critical of promoting unrestrained free enterprise *(laissez-faire)* and monopolies. Smith presented his ideal economic man *(homo economicus)* as a moral being. He opposed slavery, colonialism and the expansion of empire, vigorously supporting high wages for the poor and the belief that "a common street porter was not intellectually inferior to a philosopher".

He died in Edinburgh on 17 July 1790, aged sixty-seven; and is buried in Canongate Kirkyard. In March 2007 Adam Smith's likeness appeared on the £20 notes issued by the Bank of England, the first Scotsman ever to be portrayed on an English banknote.

WHY BRITAIN DRIVES ON THE LEFT AND FRANCE DRIVES ON THE RIGHT

In 1300 Pope Boniface VIII decided that pilgrims should keep to the left of the road, freeing their sword arms for protection. It became the rule throughout Christendom.

In the late 18th century however, large farm wagons in America and France had no driver's seat: and were controlled by drivers sitting on the left-rear horse of the team hauling them, allowing the driver to use his right arm to whip the horses. It was easier to see oncoming traffic by driving on the right-hand side of the road. After the French Revolution, an anti-clerical France extended this practice to all road users. It was enforced by Napoleon everywhere under his control in Continental Europe, notably in the states of Germany and Italy. His conscripted armies were drawn from countries, even communities that did not necessarily like each other – and, by making it harder to draw their swords, it reduced aggression between troops marching in different directions along the same road.

Britain is a small island and had no regular need for big wagons, so drivers sat on a seat in the front. Most people are right-handed and drivers sat on the right to ensure that the whip would not snarl up with the reins when used to lash the horses. This practice was confirmed in law in 1756, to govern traffic on London Bridge. The British Empire duly followed

The world's first traffic lights were installed in Bridge Street, Westminster in 1868.

Britain's first motor car fatality occured in 1896. Bridget Driscoll was "struck at a tremendous speed" (4 mph) by Arthur Edsall near Crystal Palace in London.

The 30 mph speed limit was introduced in 1934 – when, with 2.5 million vehicles on the roads, there were 7,343 deaths. In 2008 the figures were 33 million and 2,538.

Walter Arnold received the first speeding conviction in the UK, also in 1896. He was caught doing 8 mph in a 2 mph zone and was fined 1s (5p) – £23 today.

In 1897 George Smith, a London taxi driver, was the first to be convicted of driving whilst under the influence of drink and was fined £1 (£500 today). He drove into the glass-plated front corridor of 165, Bond Street.

The first number plate in Britain was A1. It was issued to Earl Russell for his 12-hp Napier, in 1903. On 1 June 1935 the UK driving test became compulsory. A licence cost 7s 6d (38p) – nearly £71 today.

suit: notably in India, parts of Africa and the Middle East. Motorists in Indonesia, which was governed briefly by Sir Stamford Raffles in the early 19th century and Japan, where the British established the car industry, also drive on the left.

The US, the last of the four important countries to pioneer motoring (the others being the UK, France and Germany), continued the colonial habit of driving on the right. Countries which bought US cars chose to do so too: in particular China, Canada and Latin America. Francophone countries naturally followed France – as did the rest of Europe, except for Sweden which subsequently changed its mind, expensively, in 1967.

In a few out of the way places, where the only law is survival of the fittest, it is disconcerting but customary to occupy the middle of the road. A blaring horn is only marginally less menacing than a drawn sword.

THE LAST TIME THE ROYAL NAVY DESTROYED A FRENCH FLEET

In 1940, following the armistice between France and Nazi Germany, the future of the French navy became a vital concern to Britain. Despite French assurances to the contrary, the British government feared that the Germans might seize the ships. Winston Churchill ordered that the French navy should either fight alongside the Royal Navy or be neutralised – the plan to achieve this was called *Operation Catapult*.

The most powerful concentration of French warships at the time was the squadron located at Mers-el-Kébir, near Oran in French Algeria. Admiral James Somerville (1882–1949) commander of Force H based in Gibraltar, was ordered to deliver an ultimatum to the French. It demanded the surrender or internment of the squadron, offering a number of options: including sailing it to neutrality in the US. Failing acceptance, force would be used to prevent the ships from falling into German hands.

It is debatable whether this ultimatum was fully understood by Admiral Marcel-Bruno Gensoul, who took offence at the junior rank of the British officer sent with Somerville's terms. He certainly ignored or forgot a directive from Admiral Darlan, head of the French Navy, that in such a situation he should opt to sail to the US. Negotiations were terminated. On 3 July 1940 the battle cruiser HMS *Hood*, the battleships HMS *Valiant* and HMS *Resolution* and the aircraft carrier HMS *Ark Royal*, with an escort of cruisers and destroyers, crippled the French squadron which was bottled-up in the harbour. 1,297 French sailors were killed and about 350 were wounded. Although relations between Britain and the Vichy French government were severely strained, the action made a great impression in the US. Reluctant to prepare US public opinion for war, "Oran" was hailed by the US government as a clear sign of Britain's determination to fight to the bitter end.

On 9 November 1942, in an attempt to seize the remnants of the French navy in Toulon, the ships were scuttled on Darlan's orders, as the Germans drove into the base.

Christopher Merret (1614–95), born in Winchcombe in Gloucestershire, was a physician, scientist and a founder of the Royal Society. His prime interest was glass-making. In 1662 he developed a bottle strong enough to withstand the pressures of a deliberately induced secondary fermentation. By adding sugar, he became the first to produce sparkling wine.

The French monk Dom Pérignon (1638–1715), who is said to have exclaimed "I am seeing the stars" when he stumbled upon his *méthode champenoise*, must have been unaware that an Englishman had seen the same stars nearly forty years earlier.

Miles Kington (1941–2008), born in Downpatrick in County Down, was a journalist, musician and broadcaster. Kington spent fifteen years as a columnist for the satirical magazine *Punch*. In the late 1970s he introduced a sketch entitled "Let's Parler Franglais!", written in an amusing mixture of English and French. He coined perhaps the funniest Franglais pun ever when he claimed that the French navy had adopted a new slogan to inspire matelots to glory: "To the water! The hour has come!". In French this might be rendered: "A l'eau! C'est l'heure!".

Thomas, Lord Cochrane
10th Earl of Dundonald

BRITAIN'S FINEST SEAMAN, WHO BROUGHT INDEPENDENCE TO CHILE, PERU, BRAZIL AND GREECE

Thomas Alexander Cochrane, styled Lord Cochrane between 1778–1831, was a politician and naval adventurer. He was the most daring and successful captain of the Napoleonic Wars, nicknamed *"le loup des mers"* ("the sea wolf") by the French. Later he led the navies of Chile, Peru, Brazil and Greece in their struggles for independence. His career inspired a number of writers of nautical fiction.

Frederick Marryat (1792–1848) joined the Royal Navy at fourteen, served under Cochrane on HMS *Imperieuse* and retired as a Captain in 1830. He devoted his retirement to writing adventure novels: *The King's Own* (1830), *Peter Simple* (1834), and *Poor Jack* (1840) – all based on his time at sea. *Children of the New Forest* (1847) is a classic children's tale of the English Civil War. His character *Mr Midshipman Easy*, published in 1836, was based on Cochrane.

The *Horatio Hornblower* stories, written by C.S. Forester (1899–1966) and published from 1937–67, and the *Jack Aubrey* novels in the *Aubrey-Maturin* series by Patrick O'Brian (1914–2000) which were published between 1969–2004, borrowed heavily from the life and exploits of Thomas Cochrane.

Lord Thomas Cochrane, 10th Earl of Dundonald by James Ramsay (1786–1854)

The death of Nelson at Trafalgar towered over all the 19th century naval careers that followed. Other than the vitally important reforms and technical advances introduced by 'Jackie' Fisher in the years before WWI, which enabled Jellicoe to win an uncertain 'victory' at Jutland in 1916, little is now remembered of British naval history between 1805–1914 – other than in the fields of exploration and gun-boat diplomacy.

There is, however, one remarkable exception that illuminates the otherwise little noticed years of Royal Naval history so completely eclipsed by Nelson's resounding triumph, namely Thomas Cochrane, 10th Earl of Dundonald.

Thomas Cochrane was born at Annesfield, near Hamilton in Lanarkshire on 14 December 1775, the eldest son of Archibald Cochrane, 9th Earl of Dundonald (1748–1831) and his first wife Anne Gilchrist (1755–84), second daughter of Captain James Gilchrist RN. As was the practice of the time, through the influence of an uncle

Admiral of the Fleet Sir John Arbuthnot Fisher, 1st Baron Fisher of Kilverstone OM (1841–1920) was born in Ceylon (now Sri Lanka). He is arguably the most important figure in the history of the Royal Navy after Nelson. As First Sea Lord from 1904 to 1910, Fisher reduced naval budgets and reformed the navy for a modern war. Amidst massive public controversy, he sold off 90 obsolete and small ships and put a further 64 into reserve – describing all these vessels as "too weak to fight and too slow to run away"; and "a miser's hoard of useless junk". This freed up crews and money to increase the number of large modern ships in home waters. His motto was *Si vis pacem, para bellum* ("If you wish for peace, prepare for war").

He chaired the Committee which approved the outline design for the first modern battleship, *Dreadnought* in 1906. His committee also produced a new type of cruiser in a similar style to *Dreadnought* with a high speed achieved at the expense of armour protection, the battle cruiser – the first being *Invincible*. Fisher's attitude to Dreadnoughts has often been misunderstood: it was not a class of ship that he favoured. When Admiral of the Mediterranean fleet he had seen the vulnerability of slow big-gun ships to mines, torpedoes and submarines. He wanted battle cruisers to defend Britain's colonies and a large fleet of small ships to defend the British Isles. He also encouraged the introduction of submarines into the Royal Navy and drove the conversion of all its ships from coal to oil.

- **Captain Fisher by Sir Hubert von Herkomer (1911)**
National Portrait Gallery, London

his father purchased for him, while Thomas was only a boy, a commission in the 104th regiment. At the same time another uncle, Captain Alexander Cochrane placed his name on the books of his warship. Thomas was sent to Chauvet's military academy in London aged thirteen, where six months later he expressed a strong wish to join the Royal Navy.

Having lost the family fortune through too large an investment in a new chemical process which failed to live up to its expectations, his reluctant father agreed. In 1793 the Dundonald family seat was sold to cover debts.

Thomas joined his uncle's ship HMS *Hind* in the Baltic on 27 June 1793 aged seventeen. He proved to be a willing and enthusiastic apprentice. His mentor was *Hind*'s first lieutenant Jack Larmour, an excellent seaman who had risen from the ranks. This sound training ensured that Thomas became a highly competent sailor. In January 1795 Captain Cochrane took his nephew (now an acting lieutenant) and Lieutenant Larmour with him to HMS *Thetis*, under orders for the North American station. In May 1796 Thomas was confirmed lieutenant; and was posted to the successive flagships of Admiral Sir George Elphinstone (later Lord Keith) – where he was court-martialled following an argument with the first lieutenant of *Barfleur* whom he had challenged to a duel. Keith acquitted Thomas, but reprimanded him for flippancy. This incident was a significant straw in the wind, a glimpse of his Achilles' heel.

In February 1800 Cochrane, as prize master, commanded the captured French warship *Genereux*. In heavy weather, with only a skeleton crew, Cochrane distinguished himself by safely delivering the seriously damaged ship to Port Mahon in Minorca. In March 1800 Admiral Keith appointed Cochrane commander of the 158 ton, 14-gun sloop HMS *Speedy* with orders to patrol the Spanish coast.

On encountering a much larger Spanish frigate, Cochrane resorted to the first of the many ruses he used to escape from a more powerful enemy. He had disguised *Speedy* as a Danish freighter, (a forerunner of the 'Q' ships, disguised merchantmen used in WW1) and under threat of being boarded, broke out the yellow plague flag. Later he escaped during the night from a Spanish frigate by extinguishing all his ship's lights and floating off a candle attached to a barrel – which the enemy obligingly followed.

Returning to his patrol station, not greatly admired for this ploy, Cochrane wasted no time in attacking a much larger 600-ton Spanish xebec (slightly smaller than a frigate), *El Gamo*. Flying the US flag Cochrane's brilliant tactic was to place his much smaller vessel as close to *Gamo* as possible, below the maximum depression angle of the enemy cannon. As the Spanish crew assembled to board, Cochrane pulled away and scythed them down with chain-shot. At a loss of four men killed he captured *Gamo*, sailing her back to Port Mahon with her entire crew crammed into the hold, covered by cannon filled to the brim with musket balls. Again, Cochrane was accused of being unsporting and never received a proper reward for his daring initiative. The First Lord of the Admiralty, Lord St Vincent made it clear that he did not believe in rewarding an officer who had just been reprimanded.

In Malta in February 1801 Cochrane arrived at a fancy dress party tricked out as a common sailor; and was mistaken for one by a Royalist French officer. Ever prickly, Cochrane overreacted and challenged him to a duel.

Cochrane paid for a poster in 1806: "Wanted – Stout, able bodied men who can run a mile without stopping with a sackful of Spanish dollars on their backs".

In July Cochrane was surrounded by three French battleships, to which he surrendered after a fierce fight. So courageous was Cochrane's resistance that the French admiral allowed him to keep his sword. Shortly after, Cochrane was exchanged for a French captain at Gibraltar. He was court-martialled for the loss of *Speedy* but was honourably acquitted, having captured over 50 enemy ships and 500 prisoners in thirteen months. On 8 August 1801 aged twenty-six, Cochrane was promoted Post-Captain.

After the Peace of Amiens in 1802 Cochrane was unemployed. He enrolled as an undergraduate at Edinburgh University to read political economy. On the resumption of hostilities in 1803 Lord St Vincent gave him command of *Arab*, a run-down 20-gun French prize – an indication of the old Admiral's regard for cheeky, disrespectful "Scotchmen". Cochrane was loud in complaints about his sluggish ship, which was barely seaworthy. His persistence was rewarded by being ordered to patrol the Orkney Islands on fishery protection duties, where he spent the next fifteen long months.

In 1804 Cochrane's luck changed with the outbreak of war with Spain, the appointment of a fellow Scot, Lord Melville, as First Lord of the Admiralty and the retirement of Lord St Vincent. Cochrane was given command of the 32-gun frigate *Pallas* and ordered to patrol the Azores. Between February and April 1805 Cochrane captured many lucrative Spanish prizes as well as escaping from a powerful French squadron by again floating off a barrel with a lamp attached.

After a brief period escorting a convoy to Canada, Cochrane joined Admiral Thornborough's squadron in the Bay of Biscay. Between February and May 1806, while on detached service he captured and destroyed a large number of enemy merchantmen. In action on the Garonne estuary near Bordeaux, Cochrane destroyed three French corvettes, but once again this heavily lop-sided action went unrecognized and unrewarded due to the still baleful influence of Lord St Vincent.

In July 1806 Cochrane stood for Parliament in the constituency of Honiton in Devon, where corruption was particularly rife. After his defeat in the by-election he paid his supporters 10 guineas each, so that when the general election was called a year later he attracted all the

William Cobbett (1763–1835) joined the army in 1785 and served in Canada until 1791. Having attacked the military corruption that he observed there, he moved to the US. He became a journalist and a fierce advocate of parliamentary reform, earning himself the nickname of Peter Porcupine.

In 1800 he returned to Britain; and in 1802 founded the *Political Register* which he published until his death. Cobbett recognised the menacing implications of the emerging Industrial revolution.

Uncompromising, he argued for the upkeep of traditional rural values while railing against low wages, harsh laws and corruption. His famous book *Rural Rides* was published in 1830. From 1832 until his death from influenza he represented Oldham in Parliament.

- **William Cobbett possibly by George Cooke (*c*.1831)**
National Portrait Gallery, London

voters who had previously voted against him. He paid them nothing– and formed an association with the radical journalist William Cobbett.

In May 1807 Cochrane took sick leave from his ship which was blockading San Sebastian, on the north-east coast of Spain; and in April stood (in the interest of Parliamentary Reform – which eventually culminated in the Reform Bill of 1832) for the large constituency of Westminster, to which he was returned with the support of William Cobbett and other radicals. On taking up his seat he vociferously attacked abuses and corruption in the Navy, particularly citing Lord St Vincent whom he accused of bartering naval commissions. His strident calls for discovery of the key documents supporting these allegations were ignored. In September 1807 Cochrane was back at sea – having made yet more powerful enemies in government and the Admiralty.

During the next two years Cochrane served in *Imperieuse* under Admiral Lord Collingwood whose fleet was blockading Toulon. Collingwood sensibly put Cochrane on detached duties, free to "harass the French and Spanish coast as opportunity served". Between January 1808 and November 1809 Cochrane rampaged up and down the coasts of France, Catalonia and Spain. In an uncanny forerunner to the commando raids of WWII, he conducted a series of devastating combined operations against small coastal shipping, isolated harbours, warehouses, bridges, lighthouses, signal stations and shore batteries. It was the tip-and-run warfare to which he was uniquely suited.

At the beginning of 1809 Cochrane returned to Britain, once again on sick leave; but on arrival in Plymouth he was immediately summoned to the Admiralty to assist in the planning of an attack on a powerful French squadron which was assembling in the Basque Roads. Cochrane came up with a plan drawn directly from tactics once used against the Armada: the use of mined fire-ships which would drive the anchored and battery-protected French warships ashore, there to be destroyed by the Channel fleet in close support. Lord Mulgrave, the First Sea Lord seized upon this bold stratagem and authorised Cochrane to prosecute the attack, despite the objections raised by James, Lord Gambier (1756–1833), the Admiral in command.

Cochrane's appointment by the Admiralty board over the heads of the Channel fleet commanders caused considerable resentment, even jealousy but nevertheless the fire ships were prepared. On the night of 11 April Cochrane led the attack and quickly destroyed the French protective boom. Predictably, the French cut their cables and drifted onto the shore in spite of many of the fire-ships being blown off course. The advantage was lost because the Channel fleet was still inexplicably over fourteen miles away. Cochrane in HMS *Imperieuse* alone followed up and attacked the hapless French. Admiral Gambier approached within three miles and lent Cochrane limited assistance – but having destroyed four French warships he withdrew, allowing the French fleet to re-float their beached vessels and seek the protection of the shore batteries.

Cochrane was made a Knight Commander of the Bath later in 1809, but was still simmering with resentment at the failure of Gambier to support his attack. He made it clear that he would oppose any attempt by Parliament to move a vote of thanks to Gambier by insisting that he had manifestly failed to destroy the French Fleet when he had the opportunity to do so. The naval establishment then closed ranks. Gambier, assured of a friendly tribunal, asked to be court-martialled. Inevitably he was acquitted, "most honourably", leaving Cochrane isolated with his naval career in tatters.

Cochrane, refused permission to rejoin his ship, devoted his time to Parliament. He exposed naval abuses in a series of uncomfortable speeches, which perversely resulted in him being ordered back to the Mediterranean fleet. Cochrane refused to oblige, went on half pay and continued his relentless campaign to expose naval corruption. Unfortunately, although his complaints were completely justified and largely addressed by the time of his death in 1860, Cochrane was far too abrasive, tactless and uncompromising. His acrimonious, sometimes violent and vindictive language alienated and angered not only the government and Admiralty but even those with whom he had much in common and should have been his natural allies.

In 1810 the radical Sir Francis Burdett (father of the celebrated philanthropist, Baroness Burdett-Coutts), an M.P. and political ally, had barricaded himself into his house in Piccadilly, resisting arrest by the House of Commons for breach of privilege. Cochrane went to assist Burdett's defence of the house. His approach to this however, was essentially similar to the approach he had taken in defending forts that he had captured; would have led to numerous deaths amongst the arresting officers; and at least partial destruction of Burdett's house, along with much of Piccadilly. On realizing what Cochrane planned, Burdett and his allies took steps to end the siege.

Cochrane's enduring sense of injustice was reinforced by an inventive and imaginative mind. Quite apart from addressing the corrupt practices of the Admiralty and the Malta Prize Court, campaigning for pensions for wounded seamen, arguing for a naval rather than a costly military solution for maintaining the despotic, corrupt regimes of Sicily and Portugal, he was the first strategist to advocate the use of poison gas. In an exotic plan designed to destroy the French fleet, scattered as it was behind secure defences throughout the harbours of France, he proposed bombarding these ports from barge-mounted mortars firing sulphur-filled shells. Cochrane's plans were scrutinised by the Prince Regent and pronounced workable by a committee chaired by the Duke of York – and served by Admiral Lord Keith, the rocket inventor Sir William Congreve and Admiral Edward Pellew, Lord Exmouth (1757–1833). The plans were finally rejected because the committee was reluctant to be the first to endorse such a barbaric weapon, fearing that Britain would be declared an international pariah: and also because gas might later be used against Britain herself – the German army ignored this risk to its cost when it introduced the use of mustard gas in WWI. The plans were kept secret until 1895.

Sir William Congreve, 2nd Baronet (1772–1828) was an Artillery officer. He invented the military rocket, inspired by the wildly unpredictable paper rockets used by Tipu Sahib at the battle of Seringapatam in 1799. In 1805 he built a rocket 3 foot 6 inches long with a 16-foot stabilisation stick. The range was 2,000 yards. They were used to bombard Napoleon's invasion fleet at Boulogne and later at the siege of Copenhagen and Danzig (the only British force present at the Battle of Leipzig in 1814 was a rocket troop). In 1806 Congreve replaced his original paper-clad rockets with iron. Later in the century rockets found a more practical use as ship rescue flares.

On 8th August 1812 Cochrane married Katherine "Kate" Barnes, a beautiful girl of Anglo-Spanish parentage more than twenty years his junior. They had eloped and were married in a civil ceremony in Annan. Although Cochrane's rich uncle Basil had opposed the marriage and now disinherited him, he and Kate went through two further marriage ceremonies: in an Anglican church in 1818 and in the Church of Scotland in 1825. The confusion of multiple ceremonies led to the suspicion that their son Thomas Barnes Cochrane (1814–85) was illegitimate, delaying his accession to the earldom.

In the autumn of 1813, with the Anglo-US war at its height, his uncle Admiral Sir Alexander Cochrane was appointed commander of the North American station and Cochrane was nominated his flag captain. These cheerful arrangements were suddenly thrown into acute disarray by the great 'Stock Exchange Fraud' of 1814. An exiled French officer and undischarged bankrupt, Captain Random de Berenger spread a rumour that Napoleon was dead and that the Allies were about to occupy Paris. Government stock rose sharply: and before the hoax was revealed a number of people, including Cochrane's uncle Andrew Cochrane-Johnstone had netted a large profit. Captain de Berenger had used Cochrane's London house to change clothes before making his escape.

Cochrane alerted the authorities as soon as he 'discovered' the fraud; and claimed that he had been duped. Despite this he was arrested, together with his uncle and de Berenger – the circumstantial evidence was overwhelming. The guilt of his uncle; his association with de Berenger; a large portfolio of government stock of his own and a well known obsession with money, served to convict him of fraud before a court presided over by a malevolent Lord Ellenborough. Cochrane was sentenced to an hour in the pillory (abandoned for fear that it would provoke public disorder), a year in prison and a fine of £1,000. He was expelled from the Navy and the House of Commons – and in a degradation ceremony, he was deprived of his knighthood. Within a few days Cochrane was returned by the outraged electors of Westminster, who also raised the money to settle his fine by public subscription.

Cochrane was imprisoned in The King's Bench, from which he absconded. On being recaptured his conditions were made particularly harsh. He was finally released, still vigorously protesting his innocence on 15 July 1815. He returned to the House of

The Fall of Valdivia
Chilean Naval Museum

Ambrosio O'Higgins, Marquis of Osorno, Marquis of Vallenar, Baron of Ballynary was born Ambrose O'Higgins (Ambróis Ó hUigínn) c.1720 in Ballnary, County Sligo. He established himself in Spain in 1751 as an employee of the Butler Trading House; and, as an Irishman and a Catholic, he was able to emigrate legally to Spanish America in 1756. A very capable and energetic man, he served the Spanish Empire as Captain General (military governor) of Chile from 1788–96.

In 1796, O'Higgins was appointed Viceroy of Peru – then comprising presentday Peru, Chile, Bolivia, north-west Argentina and parts of western Brazil. Peru was the richest colony in the Spanish Empire; and the Viceroyalty was the most prominent post in Spanish America. He occupied it until his death in 1801. Chilean independence leader Bernardo O'Higgins (1778–1842) was his illegitimate son.

O'Higgins derives from the Gaelic *uigan*, for Viking. It dates in Sligo from c.1100.

Although Cochrane and Kate appeared a happy couple, indeed she remained devoted to him until his death and was fiercely loyal to his memory thereafter, Kate conducted a passionate affair with Lord Auckland whilst Cochrane was in Brazil.

Commons, where for two years he harried the government – voting against increasing the pension of the Duke of Cumberland and enthusiastically supporting reform. He was charged with prison breaking, a year after his release – a charge entirely motivated by the malice of his political opponents. For this he suffered the indignity of sixteen days in prison and a fine of £100, which again was paid by public subscription.

In May 1817 rumours circulated that Cochrane was involved in a bizarre and treasonable plot to release Napoleon from St Helena and take him to South America to unify the Spanish colonies in their war of independence. This, and a timely invitation from the Chilean revolutionary government to reorganise and command their navy, persuaded him to become a mercenary. Before embarking for Valparaiso he steered a bill through Parliament commissioning the construction of *Janus,* the world's first steam warship. The Chilean fleet Cochrane inherited amounted to seven motley vessels, including condemned Royal Navy warships and a handful of old merchantmen. The pride of the Chilean navy was a captured 50-gun Spanish frigate, renamed *O'Higgins.*

Cochrane set about recruiting British and US crews, to form the backbone of the Chilean navy (the Spanish government had realised the potential threat and tried to employ him itself before he had even left Britain). In January 1819 Cochrane embarked upon a repeat of his commando-style raids along the coast of Chile – attacking bottled-up Spanish ships, capturing coastal vessels and landing companies of soldiers to storm forts and strong points. He carried out a spectacular but meticulously planned attack on the fort of Valdivia, Spain's most important base in Chile, which he captured – killing over a hundred of the defenders while losing only seven of his own men.

Cochrane returned to Valparaiso – and, true to form, promptly disputed his share of the prize money from Valdivia. He was placated temporarily by being asked to support an invasion force to liberate Peru, led by General Jose de San Martin – who in August 1820 embarked an army of 4,000 men from Valparaiso. Impatient at the lack of direct action taken by San Martin, Cochrane decided to attack Callao, where *Esmeralda* was anchored, the last effective Spanish frigate in the region.

On 5 November, in an operation more akin to a raid by the Special Boat Service over 150 years later, Cochrane's cutters crept in by night under the batteries of Port Callao and boarded *Esmeralda* – which surrendered after a fierce fight, in which Cochrane was badly wounded. The shore batteries suddenly began indiscriminately to open fire. Cochrane noticed that the other foreign ships had begun to hoist a pattern of lights high into their rigging. Correctly realising that this was a prearranged identification code he did the same on *Esmeralda* – and though damaged, he was able to limp out to sea and escape. Despite his injury, by destroying all the other Spanish ships in Callao, Cochrane had crippled Spain's military machine in Peru. Her army was isolated and deprived of all movement by sea. He persuaded San Martin to lend him a force of 600 soldiers, which he landed near Lima; forcing the capitulation of the colonial government on 6 July 1821.

San Martin proclaimed himself Protector of Peru and refused to pay Cochrane's fleet its prize money and wages until Cochrane swore loyalty to the new Republic. Cochrane refused and sailed back to Valparaiso to an enthusiastic welcome, but found the government on the point of collapse. This was the last straw for Cochrane and he took leave of absence. He wished to consider invitations from Mexico, Greece and Brazil, countries all anxious to secure his services to help them achieve independence.

In March 1823 Cochrane took up service with Emperor Pedro I of Brazil and spent the next 18 months reorganising the Brazilian navy. He recruited British and US crews and fended off attempts by the Portuguese to regain control. Through intrigue and by fomenting rebellion, Cochrane dislodged the Portuguese army from the important northern city of Maranhao. Pedro created him Marques de Maranhao, but once again, Cochrane's relations with his employer deteriorated into bickering over money and corruption. In early 1825 Cochrane sailed the flagship of the Brazilian navy *Pedro Primeiro* to Spithead for a thorough refit. When the Brazilian minister in London refused to pay, Cochrane resigned his commission.

Cochrane turned next to the liberation of Greece from Turkey – a cause passionately supported by his radical friends Cobbett, Burdett, Hobhouse, Hume and "Orator" Hunt, all of whom encouraged him to support the Greeks.

The Battle of Navarino was the last major battle between wooden sailing ships. A combined British, French and Russian fleet sank three-quarters of a much larger Egyptian-Turkish fleet commanded by Tahir Pasha, found anchored in Navarino Bay in the Greek Peloponnese. It was the decisive action in the Greek War of Independence against Turkey. Within ten months the Turks had evacuated Greece, which led directly to the creation of an independent Kingdom of Greece in 1832.

Bruised by his South American dealings, Cochrane accepted a contract only on a strict prepayment basis. He spent the next eighteen months supervising the construction of six war steamers, ideally suited to island warfare and which would have easily destroyed the wooden Turkish fleet, but he was frustrated in his efforts by design faults and poor construction. He failed to enlist British and US sailors due to erratic Greek funding (still the case in the early 21st century); and found Greek sailors to be unpatriotic and venal. Greek independence was assured however, when Vice-Admiral Sir Edward Codrington destroyed the Turko-Egyptian fleet at Navarino on 27 October 1827.

The accession of the "Sailor King" William IV in 1831 and a change of government brought happier times for Cochrane. In 1832 he was pardoned for his fraud conviction, restored to his rank in the Royal Navy as a Rear-Admiral and was received again at Court – but his GCB was not returned until 1847. Frederick Marryat's novel *Mr Midshipman Easy*, based on his own remarkable experiences under Cochrane's command, was published in 1836. It did much to help to accelerate his return to favour.

Cochrane had made his last speech in parliament, in favour of parliamentary reform, in 1818. In 1830 he was invited to stand again for parliament by the progressive government of Lord Brougham. Having initially expressed interest, Cochrane declined as Lord Brougham's brother had decided to run for the seat. He also thought it would look bad publicly to support a government from which he sought a pardon for his fraud conviction.

In 1831 his father died and Cochrane became the 10th Earl Dundonald. As such he was eligible to sit in the House of Lords – but no longer in the House of Commons. Without this platform, he could contribute little to the passage of the 'Great Reform Bill' in 1832, a measure that he supported passionately.

Cochrane busied himself instead with the development of steam warships, culminating in the launch of HMS *Janus* in 1848. In that year his old friend Lord Auckland became First Lord of the Admiralty and appointed him to his last sea-going command, as Commander-in-Chief in the West Indies – an appointment he held until 1851, when he was aged seventy-six. He was the first to introduce asphalt, using bitumen he had found in Trinidad, to the streets of Westminster. Raised to full Admiral in 1851, he again dusted off his poison gas plans as a means of attacking the fortresses of Sevastopol and Kronstadt in the Crimean War (1855). Initially turned down by Michael Faraday, advisor to the naval committee, the operation was authorised by Lord Palmerston. Perhaps it was just as well that Sevastopol fell before the gas could be used.

Cochrane was the most dazzling naval officer in the fifty years after the death of Nelson and the only one to achieve worldwide fame. As a highly successful sea guerrilla, his reputation was made by conducting lightning raids: first on the coasts of Spain and France and then, with well trained and experienced British and US crews, to great effect in South America. However, unlike Nelson, Cochrane never commanded a squadron or a fleet against a well-equipped or seasoned enemy. His opponents were often demoralised and isolated. But he was the first proponent of using naval power as a cost-effective way of exerting diplomatic and military influence on land.

Cochrane was also far ahead of his time in realising the potential of steam ships, held back only by the material imperfections of an emerging technology. He attempted to take a steamship from Britain to Chile; but its construction took too long and it arrived as the war was ending. In the 1830s he developed a rotary engine and a propeller. In 1851 Cochrane was awarded a patent for powering steamships with bitumen.

The audacity, vision and leadership which made him such an outstanding naval raider were manifestly lacking in his political career. Cochrane's aggression, tactlessness and hatred of corruption made enemies where he might have found friends. His conviction for fraud in 1814 may have been engineered by those who had been embarrassed and harried by his sharp tongue: but he had clearly manipulated the market. As in his approach to war, he had employed morally dubious tactics and his defence was specious. He believed that the end justified the means and always saw things in the starkest black and white.

In old age Cochrane wrote an autobiography, devoting too much time in picking over the coals of his career. It was his father's insolvency that lay at the root of Cochrane's financial insecurity. It plagued him throughout his long and heroic life, unhappily obscuring his true greatness.

Convoys were guided by ships following the lamps of those ahead. In 1805 Cochrane entered a Royal Navy competition for the design of a superior convoy lamp. Knowing that the judges would be biased against him, he asked a friend to enter on his behalf. When his design won Cochrane revealed his identity. As he had expected, the Navy never bought any of the lamps.

Cochrane's remarkable qualities however, transcended all other considerations. To the end he lived secure in the affection and trust of all those officers and men who had served under him, including his raucous Westminster constituents. He concluded the Nelson era with an unrivalled display of naval tenacity, daring and romance: which finds more than an echo in the Royal Marine commandos of the modern Royal Navy.

Cochrane died suddenly, aged eighty-five, in London on 31 October 1860. His banner was finally returned to Westminster Abbey – just in time for his funeral on 14 November.

LORD BYRON DIED FIGHTING FOR GREEK INDEPENDENCE

George Noel Gordon Byron, 6th Baron Byron was born (with a club foot) on 22 January 1788. He was a Romantic poet famous overnight at twenty-four and, like Sir Walter Scott, famous throughout Europe. Lord Byron's best-known works are the narrative poems *Childe Harold's Pilgrimage* (1812–18) and the unfinished satire *Don Juan* (1819).

On January 1815 Lord Byron married Anne Isabella Milbanke (1792–1860), the only child of Sir Ralph Milbanke, 6th Bt. Byron's fame however, rests not only on his writings but also on the extravagance of his life: which featured love affairs, debts, separation and allegations of incest and sodomy. He cut a sexual swathe that still astonishes by its sheer brazenness and multiplicity, bragging that he had sex with 250 women in Venice over the course of a single year. Furthermore, he was all-inclusive – boys, siblings, women of all classes. He was described by

Lady Caroline Lamb, after a noisy and public affair with him, as "mad, bad, and dangerous to know".

Byron loved animals, most famously a Newfoundland dog named Boatswain. When Boatswain contracted rabies, Byron nursed him without any fear of being bitten and infected.

Boatswain was buried at Newstead Abbey, with a monument larger than his master's. Its inscription, "Epitaph to a dog", has become one of Byron's best-known works:

Near this Spot
*   are deposited the Remains of one*
who possessed Beauty without Vanity,
*   Strength without Insolence*
Courage without Ferosity,
*   and all the Virtues of Man without his Vices.*
This praise, which would be unmeaning Flattery
*   if inscribed over human Ashes,*
is but a just tribute to the Memory of
*   BOATSWAIN, a DOG,*
who was born in Newfoundland May 1803,
*   and died at Newstead Nov.r 18th, 1808.*

Byron lived abroad to escape the censure of British society, where men could be forgiven for sexual misbehaviour only up to a point – one which Byron far surpassed. He served as a regional leader in Italy's revolutionary organisation, the Carbonari in its struggle against Austria; and fought the Turks in the Greek War of Independence. The Greeks fêted him as a hero when he died from fever at Missolonghi, in western Greece on 19 April 1824 – aged, as his daughter after him, only thirty-six.

Byron's only legitimate daughter Ada King, Countess of Lovelace (1815–52), was a superb mathematician. She financed and assisted Charles Babbage FRS (1791–1871), a genius who invented an "analytical Engine" – an early computer. The computer language of the US Department of Defense is called 'Ada' after her.

Ada died aged thirty-six, on 27 November 1852, from uterine cancer and bloodletting by her physicians, survived by her three children. She was buried next to the father she never knew at the Church of St. Mary Magdalene, at Hucknall in Nottinghamshire.

• **The London Science Museum's Difference Engine no. 2, built from Babbage's design**

"HEART OF OAK"

It is the official march of the Royal Navy and of the Canadian Navy too. The music was composed by Doctor William Boyce (1711–79) and the words were written by the 18th century actor David Garrick. The "wonderful year" is of course, 1759.

Come, cheer up, my lads, 'tis to glory we steer,
To add something more to this wonderful year;
To honour we call you, as freemen not slaves,
For who are as free as the sons of the waves?

"RULE BRITANNIA"

Rule, Britannia! was written by the Scottish poet James Thomson (1700–48) and set to music by Thomas Arne (1710–78) in 1740. The words "Britannia, rule the waves" were changed to "Britannia rules the waves" in the Victorian era. The Victorians also changed "will" to "shall" in the line "Britons never shall be slaves":

When Britain first, at heaven's command,
Aro-o-o-ose from out the a-a-a-zure main,
Arose, arose, arose from out the a-azure main,
This was the charter, the charter of the land,
And guardian A-a-angels sang this strain:
Rule Britannia!
Britannia rules the waves
Britons never, never, never shall be slaves.
Rule Britannia!
Britannia rules the waves.
Britons never, never, never shall be slaves.
The nations, no-o-o-o-ot so blest as thee,
Must i-i-i-i-in their turn, to ty-y-yrants fall,
Must in, must in, must in their turn, to ty-y-rants fall,
While thou shalt flourish, shalt flourish great and free,
The dread and e-e-e-e-nvy of them all.
Rule Britannia!
Britannia rules the waves.
Britons never, never, never shall be slaves.
Rule Britannia!
Britannia rules the waves.
Britons never, never, never shall be slaves.

The song never fails to stiffen the back and quicken the pulse of all who hear it sung at the last night of the Promenade Concerts each year.

Britain remained the supreme world maritime power in the 19th century and the Royal Navy did indeed "rule the waves". The expansion of the British Empire however, would now depend on the British army and be paid for by the colossal wealth generated through overwhelming industrial supremacy – the position the US and China occupies today.

The Victorians

1805–1874

Arthur Wellesley, 1st Duke of Wellington

BRITAIN'S GREATEST SOLDIER

Arthur Wellesley, 1st Duke of Wellington by Robert Home (1804)
National Portrait Gallery, London

FIELD MARSHAL ARTHUR WELLESLEY, 1ST DUKE OF WELLINGTON KG FRS

Baron Douro, of Wellington in the County of Somerset 4 September 1809 ● **Viscount Wellington**, of Talavera and of Wellington 4 September 1809 ● **Earl of Wellington** 28 February 1812 ● **Marquess of Wellington** 3 October 1812 ● **Marquess Douro** 11 May 1814 ● **Duke of Wellington** 11 May 1814 ● **Knight of the Bath** 1804 ● **Privy Councillor of Great Britain** 8 April 1807 ● **Privy Councillor of Ireland** 28 April 1807 ● **Knight of the Garter** 4 March 1813 ● **Knight Grand Cross of the Order of the Bath** 1815 ● **Lord Lieutenant of Hampshire** 1820 ● **Lord Warden of the Cinque Ports** 1829 ● **Peninsular Cross medal with nine bars for all campaigns** *the only one issued* ● **Fellow of the Royal Society** 1847 ● **Chancellor of Oxford University** 1834–1852 ● **Conde de Vimeiro** 18 October 1811, Portugal ● **Duque de Ciudad Rodrigo** January 1812, Spain ● **Grandee of the First Class** January 1812, Spain ● **Marquês de Torres Vedras** August 1812, Portugal ● **Duque da Vitória** (Duke of the Victory) 18 December 1812, Portugal ● **Knight of the Golden Fleece** 1812, Spain ● **Prins van Waterloo** 18 July 1815, The Netherlands ● **Knight Grand Cross of the Order of Hanover** 1816, Hanover ● **Field Marshal batons from 12 countries** *these can be seen at Apsley House.*

Arthur Wesley (he changed his name to Wellesley in 1798) was born on 1 May 1769 either at Dungan Castle, County Meath or, more likely, at No. 6, Merrion Street in Dublin. He was the fifth, but third surviving son of the 1st Earl of Mornington and Anne, eldest daughter of Arthur Hill, 1st Viscount Duncannon. The Wesleys originally hailed from Somerset: from the second half of the 14th century however, they had lived entirely in Ireland. The first recorded Wesley accompanied Henry II as Standard-Bearer during his invasion of Ireland in 1171.

The Wesley name died out with the childless Garret Wesley in 1728. Fortuitously, Garret left his fortune to Richard Colley, a distant Wesley cousin, who became Arthur's grandfather. Richard (1690–1758) immediately changed his name, by adoption to Wesley – and to Mornington in 1746, by ennoblement to a barony.

As a member of the Protestant Anglo-Irish ascendancy which ruled Ireland, Wesley was touchy about his Irish origins. When towards the end of his life, as Duke of Wellington, someone congratulated him on being a famous Irishman, he tartly replied that, "being born in a stable does not make one a horse".

Richard Wellesley, 1st Marquess Wellesley by John Philip Davis ('Pope' Davis) (c.1835–1860)
National Portrait Gallery, London

Arthur was an introverted and difficult boy, though he had inherited a love of music from his gifted father Garret (1735–81), a violin-playing composer who was created Earl of Mornington in 1760. By 1785, callow and aggressive after three years at Eton, Arthur had been surpassed by his older and younger brothers. His widowed mother, Lady Mornington had moved for economy to Brussels. In desperation, she decided to send her awkward son to a military academy at Angers in the Loire valley of France – a robust and clever lady, she regarded Arthur as only, "fit food for powder". Angers was an inspired move. On returning home at the end of 1786, Arthur's manners and deportment had markedly improved. He was also fluent in formal 18th century French.

In 1787 his eldest brother, Lord Mornington secured Arthur a commission: and then an appointment as *aide-de-camp* to the Lord-Lieutenant of Ireland, Lord Buckingham. His elder brother William became a M.P. at Westminster; and Arthur replaced him in the Irish parliament in 1790, sitting for the family borough of Trim in County Meath. In 1793 the long revolutionary war with France began: and Arthur was promoted major in the 33rd Foot, his sixth regiment in five years. He proposed marriage to Lady Catherine Packenham, sister of the young Lord Longford, whom Arthur had been assiduously courting for the past year. His proposal was refused on her behalf by her brother, on the practical grounds of Arthur's inability to support her. He responded to this unexpected blow to his pride by turning in on himself. He abandoned music, symbolically burnt his violin and devoted himself to studying his military profession. He asked his brother to help him obtain a posting to one of the formations being assembled for overseas service. By the end of 1793 Arthur had been advanced to lieutenant-colonel, commanding the 33rd Foot. His brother's influence had taken him seamlessly this far: but to climb further up the military ladder, he had to seek active service. The chance came when his regiment was sent to the Netherlands under Lord Moira, in support of the Duke of York's army.

The expedition was a disaster. The small British expeditionary force, deserted by its Austrian and Prussian allies, was obliged to withdraw, starving and demoralised to Hanover. The emaciated soldiers were eventually evacuated to Britain in April 1795. Arthur however, benefited considerably from the experience. On his own initiative, while in command of three battalions, he arrived in Antwerp by sea well ahead of the main British land forces. He went on to earn an official commendation for having disrupted the advance of a French column. The regiments had behaved well, but the staff work had been lamentable: teaching him a lesson which the future Field Marshal took to heart. Many years later, as Duke of Wellington, he recalled that he had learnt, "what one ought not to do and that is always something".

Meanwhile, the 33rd Foot had been posted to India. In June 1796 Arthur sailed from Portsmouth, taking with him hundreds of instructive volumes, to study India's history, language and customs – as well as military history and the art of war. He arrived in Calcutta in February 1797, soon after his brother Lord Mornington had been offered the post of governor-general and Commander-in-Chief of India. Arthur was sent to Madras where the Sultan of Mysore, Tipu Sahib was believed to be conspiring with the French to expel the British from southern India. Colonel Wellesley, as Arthur Wesley now spelled his name, prepared his force for action: while advising on how best to extricate the friendly Nizam of Hyderabad from the

After the Battle of Waterloo, Wellington and Blücher met at the appropriately named inn, La Belle Alliance – Napoleon's command post, to the rear of the French lines at the start of the battle. The only language they shared was French. Having shaken hands most cordially, Blücher's opening remark to Wellington was *"Quelle Affaire!"* ("What a business!"). Regrettably, Wellington's reply is unrecorded.

influence of his French officers. War broke out in February 1799. Wellesley, at the request of the Nizam's Prime Minister, was given command of the Hyderabad army – stiffened with elements of his own regiment.

On 27 March 1799 the 33rd Foot clashed with Tipu's French-trained army – before proceeding to attack Seringapatam on 3 May. Wellesley, suffering from dysentery, attempted a disastrous night attack: although he took the fortress the next day, killing Tipu in the process. Wellesley had learnt another valuable lesson: never to attack a prepared position, which had not been properly reconnoitred, by night. Wellesley was made governor and received £4,000 (£3.4 million today) in prize money. He spent the following year restoring law and order in Mysore. He hunted down Dhundia Wagh, a formidable guerrilla leader, eventually cornering and killing him in Hyderabad. Dhundia's four year old son was discovered hidden in his mule train. Generously, Wellesley made himself responsible for the boy's upbringing and education.

In April 1802 Wellesley was promoted to Major-General in the Indian list: and was charged with restoring the Peshwa (hereditary ruler) of Poona to his throne – from which he had been removed by the Maratha chiefs of the Deccan. He achieved this without difficulty: before moving to pacify the Deccan, by declaring war on the two principal Maratha states of Sindhia and Berar. Having seized, in a surprise attack, the massive fortress of Ahmednagar. Wellesley advanced 120 miles: to find himself unexpectedly facing a Maratha army of 50,000, with over 100 cannon, drawn up under French officers behind the river Kaitna. His own force numbered barely 9,000 mixed troops, with only 17 cannon. Advancing boldly, Wellesley forded the river on the Maratha left flank and took up a position between the Kaitna and its tributary, the Juah – which protected his flanks and rear, but cut off all prospect of retreat. In the ensuing battle of Assaye, on 23 September 1803, he lost over 1,500 of his men and had his horse shot from under him. Nonetheless he routed the Maratha army. Wellesley's courage and opportunism had won the day; but he had taken an appalling risk against a well-trained and numerically superior enemy. Much later Wellesley recalled Assaye as, "the finest thing he had ever done in the fighting line". He had also broken the Maratha fighting spirit. In the winter of 1803 he routed the remaining Maratha forces and captured their fortress of Gawilgargh. Peace was restored to Sindhia and Berar.

His brother Richard having been recalled to Britain, Wellesley now wished to return home too. Apart from frequent bouts of minor tropical

Tipu Sahib (1749–99), known as the "Tiger of Mysore" was the son of Haider Ali, a soldier of furtune who had siezed control of Mysore and called himself Sultan. Tipu was trained by French officers retained by his father. In 1782, he defeated Colonel John Braithwaite at the Colereen River: before succeeding his father in December. Nursing a strong grievance against the British, misguidedly he began negotiations with Revolutionary France. Lord Mornington promptly declared war on Tipu and launched the fourth Mysore war. On 4 May 1799 he died bravely at the head of his troops, defending a breach in the walls of his fortress at Seringapatam.

"Tipu's Tiger", in the Victoria and Albert Museum, is life-sized and made of carved and painted wood, in the act of eating a prostrate European soldier. Inside the tiger and the man are bellows with pipes attached. Turning the handle pumps the bellows to simulate the growls of the tiger and cries of the victim, which vary with the movement of the hand towards the mouth and away, as the left arm (the only moving part) is raised and lowered.

Tipu's great-great granddaughter, Noor-un-Nissa Inayat Khan (1914–44), an half-American SOE wireless operator (code named "Madeleine"), was betrayed in occupied France and murdered by the Nazis in Dachau. She was awarded the George Cross for her refusal to betray her comrades, despite being tortured.

Thomas Daniell (1749–1840) and his nephew William (1769–1837), both born in Kingston-upon-Thames and both R.A., worked in India from 1786–94. Their 6-volume collection of 144 *Oriental Scenery* aquatints (1795–1815), engraved and hand-coloured to look like the water colour originals, a new and complex technique, is the finest nonphotographic representation of Indian scenes ever published. Thomas died aged ninety-one.
• **The Water-Fall at Puppanassum in Tamil Nadu by Thomas and William Daniell (1807)**

Arthur Wellesley, 1st Duke of Wellington by James Bruce (c.1830)

National Portrait Gallery, London

diseases, Wellesley had amassed £42,000 (£30 million today) in prize money; and he correctly perceived that Europe offered far better prospects for the advancement of his career than India. He also rightly considered that he had completed his professional education: in his own words, "understanding as much of military matters as I have ever done since".

In 1806 Wellesley arrived in London, to find that the reason for his brother's recall was government dissatisfaction with his treatment of the Marathas. While waiting in an anteroom of the old War and Colonial office in Downing Street to lobby the government on Richard's behalf, Wellesley had his only meeting with Horatio Nelson – beside whom he would be buried 46 years later in St Paul's Cathedral.

For the first time Wellesley met the great politicians of the day, including William Pitt and Viscount Castlereagh – who were both impressed by his grip of both Indian politics and European strategy. His promotion in 1802 to Major-General was confirmed; and in January 1806 he was appointed colonel of the 33rd Foot (now the Duke of Wellington's Regiment). He spent six wasted weeks commanding a brigade near Hanover, returning to write a series of critical memoranda on how best to assist the awakening independence movements in the Spanish colonies in Latin America. In April 1806, with the support of the Prime Minister Lord Grenville, he was elected M.P. for Rye – enabling him better to defend his brother, against motions in the House of Commons of fraud and maladministration in India.

His first sight of the 34 year-old Kitty after so many years, chaperoned by her maiden aunt Lady Elizabeth Pakenham, was a shock to Wellesley: "She has grown ugly, by Jove", he whispered to his clergyman brother who was about to marry them.

On 10 April 1806 Wellesley married Catherine "Kitty" Packenham – whom he had neither seen nor written to for twelve years. It was an extraordinary decision, unfathomable in a man who had learnt to plan his life to a nicety. Kitty had suffered a nervous breakdown in 1802, when a previous engagement was broken off, and her youthful looks were now ruined, her charm and confidence lost.

On 3 February 1807 Kitty gave birth to a son, Arthur: followed by Charles less than a year later. Why Wellesley made such a marriage cannot be divined: sadly, it proved to be long and unhappy for them both. Kitty died, abandoned and miserable in 1831.

Throughout his life, Wellington enjoyed the company of women: and because of his stature, means and influence, was never short of offers from society beauties, rich *grande dames* and ladies of the stage. When he was ambassador to Paris he probably consummated affairs with two of Napoleon's mistresses. The first was the singer Giusepinna Grassini, who had performed in 1800 at La Scala to great acclaim: subsequently charming Napoleon, becoming *La chanteuse de l'Empereur*. Wellington supposedly carried a miniature of her portrait. The second was the actress Mademoiselle Georges (Marguerite Wiemar): in 1802 she had made her début in Paris, catching the Emperor's eye.

Returning to England at the end of the wars, Wellington formed an enduring and affectionate relationship with Harriet Arbuthnot, almost certainly Platonic – which allowed her to introduce Wellington to the young Princess Victoria. Throughout his years in politics Harriet provided Wellington with true friendship, becoming his social secretary and confidante. Her husband Charles was Treasury Secretary. Charles became such a friend of Wellington that, on Harriet's death in 1834, he lived with him at Apsley House: dying there in 1850 aged eighty-three. Wellington also enjoyed a relationship with the heiress and philanthropist Angela Georgina Burdett-Coutts. Wellington's famous exclamation, "Publish and be damned" is attributed to the occasion when a courtesan, Harriet Wilson threatened to publish her memoirs and his letters, if he did not accede to her financial demands.

In March 1807 Wellesley was offered the post of chief secretary of Ireland: which he accepted on the condition that it would not interfere with his military career. He also changed his parliamentary seat for the safer one of Newport, on the Isle of Wight. In June, on learning that Lord Cathcart was assembling an expedition to impound the Danish Fleet at Copenhagen, he applied successfully for command of a division; and sailed at the end of July. During the subsequent siege, he thwarted a Danish feint at Kjoge. This success reinforced his excellent relationships with government ministers and earned him the thanks of the House of Commons. He returned to finish his memoranda on the future of Spain's colonies; and to address the mundane tasks required of an Irish chief secretary. Wellesley was confident ("I have got pretty high up on the tree") that he was now well-placed for appointment to a senior command in any planned European intervention.

In May 1808 he was promoted lieutenant-general at the moment when the Spanish rebelled in protest at French occupation of their country. Wellesley abandoned his halfhearted dialogue with General Miranda, envoy of the South American revolutionary party; and, in tune with public opinion, advised the government to view the event as "a crisis in which a great effort might be made with advantage". In June Wellesley was asked to lead a combined fleet and army, already assembling in Ireland, to the Iberian Peninsula. The British purpose was to support the Portuguese and Spanish armies.

The expeditionary force of 9,000 soldiers sailed from Cork on 12 July 1808. Cavalry numbers were light, but the British infantry was perhaps the best trained in the world. Wellesley, sailing ahead in a fast sloop, conferred with the Spanish in La Coruña, the Portugese in Oporto and the British Naval commander of the Tagus squadron, well before the fleet arrived. The news he received on 30 July was disquieting. Marshal Andoche Junot, Duc d'Abrantes (1771–1813) was revealed to be occupying Lisbon with a much larger army than expected. It was decided to reinforce Wellesley with another 15,000 men under Sir Hew Dalrymple, the Governor of Gibraltar. Dalrymple was also to be joined by Generals Burrard and Sir John Moore. The thought that his precious command would be taken from him galvanized Wellesley into seeking battle with Junot before these senior officers arrived on the scene. Fortunately, he had just received a reinforcement of 5,000 men from Cádiz under General Spencer.

In the first week of August Wellesley disembarked his main force at Mondego Bay, 100 miles north of Lisbon; and then advanced south along the coastal road. On 17 August the British column encountered the first French troops at Rolica, under General Delaborde. Outnumbered, the French were able to retreat without pursuit because the British lacked cavalry. Wellesley advanced south to Vimeiro to protect the disembarkation of two more brigades from England. On the 20 August General Burrard arrived and, to Wellesley's intense frustration, forbade any further advance until General Moore, who was disembarking at Mondego Bay, had joined them. Junot happily resolved this impasse by attacking Vimeiro the next day, while Wellesley was still in command. Junot, outnumbered by 5,000 men, now found himself fighting the first of Wellesley's classic defensive battles. Disciplined musketry volleys followed by fierce bayonet charges, protected by enfilading fire from well-placed detachments on the flanks, caused Junot to fall back. Again, it was the British deficiency in cavalry that saved the French from humiliating defeat. The next day Junot proposed an armistice to Dalrymple, who had just arrived: under its terms, the British would repatriate Junot's army to France, provided the French surrender Lisbon and the strategic frontier fortresses of Almeida and Elvas. On 31 August 1808 these conditions, regarded by Wellesley as shameful, were ratified by the Cintra Convention.

At Dalrymple's insistence Wellesley, most reluctantly, signed the treaty – immediately making sure that his disappointment, that so little advantage had been taken of his victory, was known in London. Strongly recommending that Sir John Moore should take over the Portugal command, Wellesley returned to England – where an outraged public had also taken the view that a rare victory over the French had been squandered. A court of enquiry was inconclusive: but it gave Wellesley, called as a witness, a chance to speak out. Dalrymple and Burrard were never given important commands again.

Events soon moved in Wellesley's favour. In January 1809 the British army in Spain was safely taken off at La Coruña in a brilliant rearguard action conducted by General Moore. A few weeks earlier Britain had committed to an alliance with the Spanish provisional government. Much account had been taken of Wellesley's advice: that Portugal's coastline and narrow topography offered both a secure naval supply line and short land distances from which to attack the French. In April 1809 he was given command of a second expeditionary force to the Peninsula. His brief from the government on this occasion was confined simply to the defence of Portugal.

Wellesley landed at Lisbon on 2 April 1809. He ordered the 20,000 British garrison to be brigaded with Portuguese regiments immediately; and advanced rapidly north to Oporto, where he surprised Marshal Nicolas-Jean de Dieu Soult, Duke of Dalmatia (1769–1851) who was preparing to evacuate the city. Wellesley's forces managed to cross the broad and swiftly-flowing river Douro. On 12 May he drove Soult and his army pell-mell down the road to Spain – with the loss of nearly a quarter of his men and all his guns. Wellesley linked up with the Spanish General Cuesta and began an advance on Madrid along the Tagus valley, on the understanding that the Spanish would supply his army.

He had placed General William Beresford, 1st Viscount (1768–1856), commanding a Portuguese force, on his northern flank – having been assured of cover for his southern flank from the Spanish General Venegas. This protective screen never materialised: and Wellesley only just managed to avoid a repeat of the disaster that had overtaken Sir John Moore the year before. The Spanish had provided the British with only ten day's provisions and no transport; Soult had reorganised much faster than expected; Beresford's northern force proved inadequate; and Venegas never appeared at all. An ideal moment to attack the French was lost, when Cuesta refused to move. The British advantages of momentum and strength, when battle was eventually joined at Talavera a few days later, had evaporated.

Talavera, on 27 July 1809, was the second great defensive, and hardest fought, battle fought by Wellesley

Lieutenant-General Sir John Moore (1761–1809) led the retreat to La Coruña (January 1809) during the Peninsular campaign. The son of a doctor in Glasgow and the step-son of the Duke of Argyll, Moore joined the British army in 1793. He served in Corsica, the West Indies, Ireland, the Netherlands and Egypt. While serving as a corps commander at Shorncliffe Camp in Kent (1803–06), Moore's training methods earned him a reputation as the finest instructor of light infantry and the description, "the Founding Father of the Rifles". He was knighted in 1804, subsequently serving in Sweden and the Mediterranean.

Sent to Portugal in 1808, he took over command from Wellesley in September: with orders to assist the Spanish in driving the French army from Spain. Realising that the Spanish forces were disintegrating, Moore decided to retreat to Portugal. On the way he was prevailed upon to attack Marshal Soult's corps to the west of Burgos: but, hearing that Napoleon had cut the road to Portugal, he led his army 250 miles over snow-clad mountains to a beach-head at La Coruña. In the subsequent battle of "Corunna" (16 January 1809) Moore died of his wounds, having held the pursuing French army at bay. "I hope my country will do me justice", he said: but his hope was not fulfilled – and he was widely criticised for retreating. He had in fact won a strategic victory, by delaying the French conquest of Spain for a year. Despite his intention to do so, Napoleon never again intervened personally in the Peninsular theatre. Wellesley was Moore's greatest supporter.

Moore's funeral was celebrated in the only poem written by the Reverend Charles Wolfe (1791–1823) worth remembering – the first and last verses especially:

Not a drum was heard, not a funeral note,
*   As his corse to the rampart we hurried;*
Not a soldier discharged his farewell shot
*   O'er the grave where our hero we buried.*
Slowly and sadly we laid him down,
*   From the field of his fame fresh and gory;*
We carved not a line, and we raised not a stone,
*   But we left him alone with his glory.*

• **Sir John Moore by Sir Thomas Lawrence (c.1800–1804)**
National Portrait Gallery, London

before Waterloo. His flanks were protected by the river Tagus on the right and a high ridge on the left. His centre lay behind a ravine, a small stream and a thick olive grove: where he placed the unreliable Spanish contingent. Wellesley mustered an allied army of 52,000 against a French force of 46,000 commanded by General Jourdan and General Victor – under the nominal command of Napoleon's brother Joseph, King of Spain. After an abortive French night-attack, fierce fighting continued over two days before the French broke off the action: leaving 7,000, mostly British casualties on the field. Wellesley then learnt that Soult was advancing rapidly down the road from Salamanca with a large army. He had not a moment to lose. He abandoned his wounded and crossed the Tagus: to seek the shelter of the Portuguese border fortress of Badajoz for his famished and exhausted soldiers.

Wellesley had escaped Soult's trap by less than a day; and though victory at Talavera had been impossible to exploit, in the eyes of both the British government and public, the battle did

The principal battlefields in Portugal and Spain (1808–14)

THE PRINCIPAL BATTLEFIELDS OF PORTUGAL AND SPAIN (1808–14)

much to expunge the defeat at La Coruña. Furthermore the Spanish had seen at first hand the resolution of their British allies – a fact that brought little comfort to Wellesley when he wrote to Castlereagh: "I can only tell you that I feel no inclination to join in cooperation with them again". On 4 September Wellesley was raised to the peerage as Viscount Wellington and given a pension.

In July 1809 Napoleon defeated Austria at the battle of Wagram, enabling him to give substance to his declared intention, made in December 1808, of personally leading 140,000 veteran soldiers to the Peninsula – to sweep the British into the sea. By January 1810 the new administration of Lord Liverpool was seriously concerned for the safety of Wellington's small force in Portugal: which amounted to Britain's only army, the loss of which would have been catastrophic. Wellington however, had not been idle in the months following Talavera. He had already surveyed the Torres Vedras region to the east of Lisbon: whose contours he adapted to form three lines of defensive fortifications. Having been made Marshal-General of Portugal the previous year, he conscripted the entire Portuguese male population of military age; and exhorted all the inhabitants who lived along the expected French line of advance to burn their fields and drive their livestock to the rear of the "Lines of Torres Vedras".

In the spring of 1810 Napoleon, distracted by his divorce from the Creole beauty Josephine and his forthcoming marriage to Marie-Louise of Austria, delegated command of his army in Spain to the ablest of his marshals, the Jewish Jean-André Masséna, Duke of Rivoli and Prince of Essling (1758–1817). Wellington, occupying a defensive position in the north of Portugal, refused to dilute his forces by reinforcing his Spanish allies. In July the Spanish fortress of Cuidad Rodrigo surrendered to Masséna, followed by the capitulation of the Portuguese frontier fortress at Almeida. Falling back before Masséna, Wellington appealed to the local residents to leave nothing for the invader – to which he received an indifferent response. Morale within his army was low and panic was rising in Lisbon as refugees poured into the city. But by a happy chance, Masséna mistakenly directed his army along the worst road to Lisbon.

On 21 September 1810 Wellington decided to stand and fight on the ridge at Busaco: and on 27 September the French army attacked. He was chronically short of artillery and cavalry; and was defending a ridge five miles long. He won the day by skilful use of reverse slopes and a lateral path behind them, which he had widened, enabling him rapidly to reinforce any threatened point of his line. Inflicting 4,500 French casualties at a cost of 1,200 of his own, Wellington had won a decisive victory: but had not halted the French – who had unexpectedly outflanked him and continued their advance. Wellington was therefore obliged to press on with his own retreat south. When Masséna arrived before the lines of Torres Vedras in October however, he realised that he could never breach them. Within a month, his supplies severely depleted, he retreated. By spring 1811 he had returned to Spain.

Wellington resolved to prevent any further attacks on Portugal by capturing the frontier fortresses of Cuidad Rodrigo and, 130 miles to the south, Badajoz. The citadels straddled the two main roads into Portugal. Leaving Beresford to invest Badajoz, on 5 May 1811 Wellington attacked Almeida – and found himself engaged in his most perilous battle ever, Fuentes d'Oñoro. Surprised by Masséna's strength and resolve, Wellington was outnumbered and fighting with inexperienced troops – who, freshly arrived from England, buckled under the weight of the French cavalry. His rapid but risky response of pulling back his line was rewarded by the insubordination of Masséna's generals, which caused the French marshal to break off the engagement. Wellington later wrote that: "If Boney had been there, we should have been beaten". Almeida fell two days later, but the French garrison escaped.

On 16 May Beresford defeated Soult's relief column at the battle of Albuera – but at an hideous cost of 4,000 casualties out of his 7,600 strong force. Wellington wrote to his brother William, "another such battle could ruin us". He then laid siege to Badajoz, making two unsuccessful attacks in June before retreating to Cuidad Rodrigo in the face of an approaching French force, commanded by Marshal Auguste Frederic-Louis Viesse de Marmont, Duke of Ragusa (1754–1852), who had replaced Masséna. Wellington's army, riddled with disease, was too weak to attack. During the course of the winter of 1811–12, Marmont was able to reinforce the garrison – and to detach a large part of his army to reinforce the French campaign against a Spanish army in Valencia. In January 1812 Wellington, with rested troops and a new siege train, successfully stormed Cuidad Rodrigo. In April he renewed the attack on Badajoz – threatened by Soult, who was only three days march away. In the assault on Badajoz the storming parties, simultaneously attacking three breaches, suffered over 5,000 casualties. The next day Wellington, surveying the piled heaps of British dead, broke down and wept. He was comforted with an earldom.

The French had finally been thrown out of Portugal. By the summer of 1812 Wellington, reinforced with fresh drafts from England, confronted a French army depleted by withdrawals for Napoleon's invasion of Russia. Nonetheless the French still had 280,000 men in Spain – though under constant harassment from Spanish guerrillas, separated by mountains and rivers and split by the antagonisms of their generals. As Wellington marched into Spain to confront Marmont, the more lightly equipped French at first outmanoeuvred the British and refused to fight. Wellington then noticed that a gap had opened up between the enemy vanguard and main body. Swiftly exploiting this opportunity, he attacked and trounced Marmont (who was wounded) at Salamanca on 22 July 1812 – in what is regarded as Wellington's greatest and most skilful Peninsular victory. That October he was made a marquess, to add to his recent earldom.

Rather than pursuing the French army, now commanded by General Count Bertrand Clausel (1772–1842), Wellington chose a triumphal entry into Madrid to rest his army. He also needed to provide the precarious British government (Prime Minister Perceval had just been assassinated) with a tangible result. The French took full advantage of this respite to reform behind the river Ebro.

As a result Wellington had to assault the town of Burgos five times in filthy weather, losing over 2,000 men – before being forced into a disorderly retreat down the road to Cuidad Rodrigo, pursued by superior French forces. The lessons of Talavera,

French Imperial "Eagles", the equivalent of British Regimental Colours, were captured on four occasions: twice in the Peninsula and twice at Waterloo. At Barrosa in 1811, Sergeant Patrick Masterson of the 87th Prince of Wales's Irish won an immediate battlefield commission ("By Jaysus, boys, I have the Cuckoo!"); and Ensign Pratt of the 44th foot captured his at Salamanca in 1812. Alexander Kennedy (later Lieutenant-General Sir Alexander Clark-Kennedy) of the 1st Royal Dragoons and Sergeant Charles Ewart of the Royal North British Dragoons (more commonly known as the Scots Greys) both captured theirs at Waterloo, the latter being commissioned immediately afterwards.

• An Imperial French Eagle

Wellington's despatch from Spain to Whitehall in August 1812:
Gentlemen,
Whilst marching from Portugal to a position which commands the approach to Madrid and the French forces, my officers have been diligently complying with your requests, which have been sent by H.M. Ship from London to Lisbon and thence by despatch rider to our headquarters.

We have enumerated our saddles, bridles, tents and tent poles, and all manner of sundry items for which His Majesty's Government holds me accountable. I have dispatched reports on the character, wit, and spleen of every officer. Each item and every farthing has been Accounted for, with two regrettable exceptions for which I beg your indulgence.

Unfortunately the sum of one shilling and ninepence remains unaccounted for in one infantry battalion's petty cash and there has been a hideous confusion as to the number of jars of raspberry jam issued to one cavalry regiment during a sandstorm in Western Spain. This reprehensible carelessness may be related to the pressure of circumstances, since we are at war with France, a fact which may come as a bit of a surprise to you gentlemen in Whitehall.

This brings me to my present purpose, which is to request elucidation of my instructions from His Majesty's Government, so that I may better understand why I am dragging an army over these barren plains. I construe that perforce it must be one of two alternative duties, as given below. I shall pursue either one with my best ability, but I cannot do both: 1. To train an army of uniformed British clerks in Spain for the benefit of the accountants and copy-boys in London, or, perchance: 2. To see to it that the forces of Napoleon are driven out of Spain.

Your most obedient servant, WELLINGTON

Salamanca and now Burgos established that combined French armies were always able to prevent the small British army from exploiting local victories, no matter how dazzling.

In May 1813, nominally in command of the Spanish army, Wellington launched another advance into Spain: bringing the French to battle at Vitoria on 21 June. He routed their army and seized its baggage train, including a war chest of over £1 million (£655 million today).

The main body of the French army though, escaped into the Pyrenees while the British plundered their prize: causing a furious Wellington to describe them as: "the scum of the earth, the mere scum of the earth" – but victory at Vitoria had given the coalition against Napoleon a much needed boost. After being temporarily halted by a skilful campaign fought by Soult in the Pyrenees, Wellington, overcoming prodigious difficulties of lengthening supply lines, awkward terrain, an ever extending front and exasperating Spanish allies, finally reduced the fortresses of San Sebastian on 8 September and Pamplona on 27 October. Having waited until the dry weather, in February 1814 Wellington invaded France: defeating Soult at Orthez – his army already fragmented by desertion and troop withdrawals, following Napoleon's defeat at Leipzig on 16–19 October 1813. The high road to France now lay open: and on 14 April 1814, after a brief skirmish, Wellington marched into Toulouse – by which time Napoleon had abdicated. On 19 April Wellington signed a treaty with Soult and Marshal Louis Gabriel Suchet, Duke d'Albufera da Valencia (1770–1826), ending hostilities and requiring the removal of all French forces from Spain. The Peninsular war was over.

The question is often asked: how did Wellington manage to sustain his small army against French forces ten times his number, over five arduous years of continuous fighting? Spain had the reputation of being a country where small armies were defeated and large armies starved. Wellington avoided both, by maintaining his army in the field quite differently to the French. Whereas the French lived off the land, seizing whatever they could from a hapless population, earning its abiding enmity, Wellington did the opposite. He rarely used his powers of requisition: preferring to pay for his supplies foraged from local merchants and contractors, which were distributed evenly amongst his troops. Whenever possible, Wellington imported supplies from Britain (and until July 1813, vast amounts of US grain

In 1800 the Board of Ordnance chose London master gunsmith Ezekiel Baker's third design for the first standard-issue British-made rifle. It was issued to elite units, especially skirmishers and snipers, though it weighed nearly 9 pounds and was 45 inches long, not including the bayonet. It did not replace the faster reloading and cheaper Brown Bess musket, but for accuracy it was a revelation.

With a series of ridges and grooves down the barrel, spinning the bullet to ensure stability in the air, the rifle's accuracy proved precise at long range. It also had a tool bag in the butt; and a browned barrel to prevent glare revealing the shooter's position. Both features were considered ingenious at the time. During the retreat to Corunna in 1809, rifleman Thomas Plunkett amazed his superiors, by killing the French General Colbert at a distance estimated at 800 yards with his Baker Rifle – and then picked off his aide, to show that it was not just a lucky shot. Throughout four decades of international warfare (1800–38), during the Napoleonic and Indian wars and even the Texas Revolution, where it was used by the Mexican army at the Alamo in 1836, the Baker Rifle was the weapon of choice. The Nepalese Army released some from their stores in 2004 – sadly, no longer fit for use.

– paid for, as in both World Wars, in cash), established depots on his lines of march and paid for cohorts of civilian wagoners, muleteers and draught animals to supply his army on the march. Looting, theft, rape, violence and drunkenness were inevitable consequences of war, particularly among British troops at Cuidad Rodrigo, Badajoz, Vitoria and San Sebastian: where exceptionally fierce resistance had been encountered. Wellington exercised strict discipline over his soldiers and regularly hanged them for pillaging, rape and desecration of religious sites. To help curb these excesses, he created a corps of provosts (military police). Drawing upon his Indian experiences, Wellington did everything possible to respect the religion, sensibilities and properties of the Portuguese and Spanish. He adapted to the demands imposed by a mountainous, often impassable landscape by organising divisional transport to accompany his forward troops. He collected a rich dividend from his consideration of the civilian populace: generating a stream of intelligence about the movements and dispositions of the French armies.

Above all Wellington took the greatest care of his soldiers: interesting himself in every aspect of their welfare down to the issue of kettles, blankets and tents. By 1814 his imposition of uniformity and discipline had produced a staff without equal in any army in Europe – save possibly the Prussians. The bill for Wellington's disbursements was colossal: but his continual demands for bullion were met, with few exceptions, by fully supportive and uncomplaining ministers. Luckily Britain, by far the richest trading nation in the world, could afford it – ironically, in 1812 boots manufactured in Northampton shod the feet of Napoleon's *Grande Armée* when it marched to Moscow. Yet, without the unfailing support of the British government, particularly when his campaign faltered, Wellington would have foundered – and suffered the same fate as Sir John Moore in 1809.

Wellington also created a secret intelligence staff, a map-making section under the direction of his remarkable quartermaster, George Scovell; and a corps of guides to direct his divisions through intractable country.

The French usually encrypted communications in simple ciphers known as *petits chiffres*. These were designed to be written and deciphered in haste on the battlefield and were generally short, based on 50 numbers. In the spring of 1811 they began to use a more sophisticated code, based on a combination of 150 numbers – known as the Army of Portugal Code. George Scovell cracked it within two days.

At the end of 1811 new cipher tables were sent from Paris to all army commanders. Based on 1,400 numbers and derived from a mid-18th century diplomatic code, the tables were sent with advice on subterfuges, such as adding meaningless figures to the end of letters – code breakers often try to tackle the end of a letter first, looking for the standard phrases which close formal correspondence.

Scovell pored over intercepted documents for a year – making gradual progress by using letters that contained unencoded words or phrases, so that the meaning of coded sections could be inferred from the context. Knowledge of troop movements, gathered by Scovell's Army

Sir George Scovell (1774–1861) was born in London. He was commissioned into the 4th Queen's Own Dragoon Guards in 1798. He transferred to the 57th Foot in 1807. Posted to the Peninsula in 1808, he worked in the Quartermaster General's department and was delegated to decipher coded enemy messages.

He commanded the newly formed corps of guides and the army postal service until 1813: when he was given command of the cavalry staff corps. He served in every Peninsular campaign; and, as Assistant Quartermaster General, was present at Waterloo.

He died in 1861: having commanded the Royal Wagon Train in 1820, served as Lieutenant-Governor of the RMC Sandhurst from 1829–37 and as Colonel of his old regiment, the 4th Dragoons in 1847. He left £70,000 (£45 million today) – but the haughty Duke of Wellington never once asked him to dinner.

• **Sir George Scovell by Thomas Heaphy (1813–1814)**
National Portrait Gallery, London

The Great Paris Cipher (*c*.1812)
The National Archives, UK

Arthur Wellesley, First Duke of Wellington by Sir Thomas Lawrence (1769–1830)
Apsley House, London

Guides, was crucial in making informed guesses about the identity of a person or place mentioned in coded letters, solving one more piece of the puzzle.

When a letter from his brother Joseph to Napoleon was intercepted in December 1812, Scovell had cracked enough of the code to decipher most of his explicit account of French operations and plans. This information allowed Wellington to prepare for the final battle for control in Spain, Vitoria in June 1813. That night British troops seized Joseph Bonaparte's coaches and discovered his copy of the Great Paris Cipher table. The code was broken and French letters were never secure again.

On 21 April 1814 Wellington was appointed British ambassador to the restored Bourbon court of Louis XVIII – an obese monarch, "who had learned nothing and forgotten nothing". The Foreign Secretary, Castlereagh wanted Britain to take the lead in the subsequent peace negotiations in Paris: and Wellington's presence there would lend gravitas to the British diplomatic effort. "His military name would give him and us the greatest ascendancy", he advised the Prime Minister Lord Liverpool. Wellington agreed: for he now genuinely saw himself as the personal embodiment of Britain.

On 3 May Wellington was made a duke – in time for his arrival in Paris the following day. His first task was to persuade the French government to abolish France's involvement in the slave-trade. He was then diverted to pay a quick visit to the Spanish King Ferdinand VII, in an attempt to coerce him and his government to introduce liberal reforms. Unsurprisingly, both these endeavours proved futile. On his return to Paris, Wellington was greeted by Bourbon jealousy and assassination threats from thwarted Bonapartists. On 3 February 1815, having taken his seat in the House of Lords and been voted £400,000 (£278 million today) for the purchase of Stratfield Saye in Hampshire, he made his appearance at the Congress of Vienna.

Barely had the delegates begun their deliberations before the news that Napoleon had escaped from his confinement on the island of Elba disrupted the proceedings. On 1 March 1815 the Emperor had landed in France to begin his "hundred days" of freedom. Immediately the allied sovereigns asked Wellington to take command of all forces in the Netherlands. The Coalition itself began to plan for an invasion of France, to be launched in July. Wellington realised that it was unlikely that the allies' elaborate manoeuvring would be successful before Napoleon had completed his preparations. Meanwhile, the Netherlands had to be protected against a probable French attack.

"I have got an infamous army", was Wellington's comment on reviewing the hotchpotch forces under his command. Over the next month assiduously he improved their quality, by summoning many

His brother William chose his title Wellington for its loose similarity to Wellesley. The surname itself derives from the village of Wellesley, which is near Wellington, in Somerset. The Duke is said to have visited the town only once – in 1819.

of his Peninsular generals and staff officers – and on 17 June he received a welcome injection of 2,000 of his veteran Peninsular infantry. Of the 95,000 troops assembled under his direct command: 33,000 were British (over 48,000 British soldiers were still in North America, having fought in the war of 1812–14), of which only 7,000 had served in Spain; 8,000 men of the elite King's German Legion; 27,000 Hanoverian, Dutch, Nassau and Brunswick troops of widely differing quality – with another 6,000 Belgians, recently loyal to Napoleon and rightly presumed unreliable. Commanding an army speaking four languages and having no common training or equipment presented difficulties enough: and sharing command to some extent with the 73 year-old Prussian Field-Marshal Gebhard von Blucher only compounded them.

Napoleon's European enemies reacted to his unexpected return to power by forming the Seventh Coalition and proclaiming a general mobilisation. The first to assemble were the armies of Britain and Prussia. It was Napoleon's plan to attack them before they could be joined by the other more ponderous and less threatening members of the Coalition – whose stated intention was to invade France in overwhelming force

Wellington expected that Napoleon would plan his strategy as he would have done himself: to cut him off from his base at Ostend, by advancing through Mons to the south-west of Brussels. Although Napoleon had rejected this option, because of his concern that it would push Wellington's army closer to the Prussians, by sowing disinformation he duped Wellington into detaching 17,000 soldiers that he could ill spare, as a precaution. Napoleon divided his army into three: his left was commanded by Marshal Michel Ney, Duke of Elchingen (1769–1815), his right by Marshal Emmanuel, Marquis de Grouchy (1766–1847) and a reserve – which he commanded himself. All three formations were able to support each other.

In the early hours of 15 June Napoleon crossed the frontier at Charleroi and began rapidly to occupy the central ground separating Wellington from Blucher. Ney was ordered to secure the cross-roads at Quatre Bras. It was only very late on the night of the 15 June, while attending the Duchess of Richmond's ball in Brussels, that Wellington realised Napoleon's true intention. A galloper had arrived from the Prince of Orange who was covering the cross-roads at Quatre Bras, with the news that Dutch pickets were being engaged by the French. Meanwhile Napoleon used his reserves and right wing to attack and push back Blucher's centre at Ligny: but in failing to follow-up, he allowed the Prussians to reform at Wavre – only about 8 miles to the east.

The disciplined Prussian commander, General August Wilhelm Antonius, Graf Neidhardt von Gneisenau (1760–1831), resisted the temptation to retreat along his own lines of communication. Instead he fell back north, always within reach of Wellington – and always maintaining communications with him.

Wellington, having reinforced Quatre Bras and driven back the French, was now himself obliged to retreat: due to the Prussian withdrawal to Wavre. The French pursued him but after a brief skirmish at Genappe, a torrential downpour forced them to break off the engagement. Napoleon now ordered Grouchy, commander of the right wing, to pursue

The Prussian army was far from the formidable fighting machine that it was to become fifty years later. Napoleon's reappearance had caught the Prussians in the throes of reorganisation. *Landwehr* (militia) regiments were in the process of being absorbed into the regular army: and many who had just arrived in Belgium were untrained and ill-equipped. The Prussian cavalry and artillery were in a similar state of disarray – the artillery units were to perform especially poorly at Waterloo. These deficiencies however, were offset by the excellence of the Prussian General Staff – which ensured, the day before defeat at Ligny, that most of the Prussian army would still be able to retire, reform and intervene decisively in support of Wellington. By 18:00 on 18 June, 48,000 Prussians were engaging the French at Waterloo.

• **Field-Marshal Gebhard Leberecht von Blucher, Furst von Wahlstatt** the Prussians with a force of 33,000 men. Uncertain of the direction the retreating Prussians had taken, Grouchy was too late to prevent the Prussians reaching Wavre: but still continued to carry out his orders to press the Prussians to the letter ("with your sword at his back"): despite being urged by his subordinate General Gerard the next day, to "march to the sound of the guns". Failing to use his initiative, Grouchy proceeded to fight the subsequent Battle of Wavre – effectively depriving Napoleon of his 33,000 men at a crucial point in the forthcoming battle. This was the first in a series of blunders, which would destroy Napoleon's army.

Meanwhile Wellington had taken up a strong defensive position on the long, low ridge of Mont St Jean, at right angles to and bisected by the main road to Brussels, 12 miles away. He had reconnoitred the ground two days before: and in many ways, the dispositions he made were a repeat of his first, classic defensive battle at Vimeiro in 1808. Along the top of the ridge lay a sunken road to Ohain. Near the Brussels crossroads was a large elm, which marked the approximate centre of Wellington's line and was to serve as his command post for much of the day. Along the reverse slope of the Ohain road Wellington placed his infantry, as he had done at Busaco, to be invisible to Napoleon – save for a screen of skirmishers and artillery on the forward slope. Wellington's front was less than 3 miles wide, enabling him to concentrate his forces on his right and in the centre, in the expectation that the Prussians would reinforce his left wing later in the day. Before the ridge stood three features which Wellington fortified heavily. On his extreme right lay the substantial country house and orchard of Hougoumont. Conveniently, the house faced along the Ohain road, or "hollow way" as it came to be known, enabling the outpost to be supplied and reinforced. To the far left was the tiny hamlet of Papelotte, commanding the road to Wavre which Blücher would have to use to join the battle. At the centre of Wellington's line, to the west of the Brussel's road, was the farmhouse and orchard of La Haye Sainte: which Wellington garrisoned with 400 light infantry of the King's German Legion. On the opposite side of the road was a disused sand quarry, where the 95th Rifles were posted as sharpshooters – taken together, it was a strong and intimidating defence.

On the morning of the 18 June the French began to form up on the forward slope of a ridge to the south of Mont St Jean: and, as Napoleon could not see Wellington's army, he arranged his forces equally around the Brussels road. His right wing was commanded by Marshal Count Jean-Baptiste Drouet d'Erlon: whose 1 Corps included 16,000 infantry, 1,500 cavalry and a reserve of 4,700 men. The centre was taken up by Georges Mouton, Count de Lobau's VI Corps: with 6,000 in line regiments, 13,000 infantry of the Imperial Guard and a cavalry reserve of

The King's German Legion (George III was also King of Hanover) was founded on 19 December 1803. In the thirteen years of its existence, the Legion grew to over 14,000 men; and was renowned for its excellent fighting ability.

THE BATTLE OF WATERLOO (18 June 1815)

To Brussels (12 miles)

Bois de Ohain

von Ziethen I

Le Mesnil

Mont St. Jean

Uxbridge

Braine-l'Alleud

Merbraine

Beau-Chêne

Picton

La Haye

von Bülow IV

Clinton

Fichermont

Bois de Paris

DUTCH

Alten

Papelotte

Cooke

La Haye Sainte

Uxbridge

0   1 mile

0   1/2 km

Hougoumont

Ney

Kellerman

D'Erlon

Reille

La Belle Alliance

Lobau

Lobau

NETHERLANDS

Waterloo

BELGIUM

FRANCE

Plancenoit

Rossomme

▬	Anglo–Dutch infantry
◹	Anglo–Dutch cavalry
⚬	Anglo–Dutch artillery
■	French infantry
▮	Imperial Guard
◹	French cavalry
⚬	French artillery
▢	Prussian corps
∨	Defended positions
▱	Roads / settlements

2,000. The French left wing consisted of II Corps, commanded by Marshal Honore Charles-Michel-Joseph Reille: with 13,000 infantry, 1,300 cavalry and 4,600 in reserve.

Wellington rose at 03:00 on 18 June, when he received a reassuring message from Blücher that he would send him at least three Corps. Napoleon had a restless night made hideous by piles: which prevented him from attending the forthcoming battle on his favourite charger, Marengo – only fourteen hands tall, Marengo's skeleton is in the National Army Museum. Napoleon fought Waterloo from the dangerously distant comfort of his carriage instead.

Napoleon breakfasted with Marshal Soult, his chief-of-staff: who suggested strongly that Grouchy be recalled immediately to take part in the forthcoming battle. This sensible idea provoked a revealing and hubristic reply from his Emperor: "Just because you have all been beaten by Wellington, you think he is a good general. I tell you he is a bad general, the English are bad troops and this affair is nothing more than eating breakfast". Napoleon compounded this error of judgement, by choosing to ignore intelligence from his brother Jerome, passed by a waiter serving British officers at the King of Spain inn at Genappe, of the Prussian intent to march from Wavre to Waterloo.

At 11:00, having delayed his attack to allow the ground to dry after the heavy downpour of the previous night, Napoleon issued his orders. This delay was the second disastrous mistake made by Napoleon. It bought Blücher's Prussians the time they needed to reach Waterloo and support Wellington.

Napoleon's plan was simple: and Hougoumont was to be the pivot on which it depended for success. He believed that its capture, threatening Wellington's line of retreat to the Channel, would draw in and exhaust the British reserves. At 13:00, his artillery would be redirected to pound Wellington's centre, followed by an attack by d'Erlon on his left wing: which would roll up the British front from east to west. Napoleon's aim was to separate Wellington from the Prussians – and drive his army to the sea.

Extraordinarily, there is no certainty of when the battle actually began: but by 11:30 Hougoumont had come under attack. Its garrison remained in action until the end of the battle, drawing in large numbers of Frenchmen – the reverse of what Napoleon had intended. The house was completely destroyed: but was held, due to the heroism of the light companies of the three regiments of Foot Guards, under the overall command of Sir James Macdonnell.

Both Napoleon and Wellington knew that Hougoumont was the key to the battle. Napoleon expended 33 battalions totalling over 14,000 men, and Wellington 21 battalions of 12,000, in contesting the supply line provided by the "hollow way". Wellington was also forced to divert valuable artillery batteries from his hard-pressed centre.

Unusually, Napoleon's artillery battery of eighty guns was not deployed efficiently. His *Grande Batterie*, set too far back, had to sweep the entire span of the British front: and could not see the enemy, concealed behind the reverse slope of the ridge of Mont St Jean. The sodden ground also absorbed the impact of cannon shot. Although impressive in its sound and thunder, which Napoleon hoped would "astonish the enemy and shake his morale", his artillery did relatively little damage. When the *Grande Batterie* opened up, Wellington remarked to his staff: "Hard pounding this, gentlemen. Let's see who will pound the longest".

Soon after 13:30 d'Erlon began his advance towards La Haye Sainte. He was a veteran of the Peninsula and was acutely aware of Wellington's tactic of using close-range, concentrated musket-fire against massed French columns. This time, his infantry battalions supported by two brigades of Cuirassiers advanced in line-of-file and quickly isolated the farmhouse. Having wiped out an entire relief regiment of the King's German Legion, the French attack rolled on to the crest of the ridge. When General Sir Thomas Picton and his 5th Division infantry stood up to open fire, Picton was picked on and instantly shot through the head – and the British line began to break up.

Lord Uxbridge, commander of the two brigades of British heavy cavalry, drawn up undetected behind the ridge, now ordered a charge to relieve the reeling infantry.

Sir James Macdonnell of Glengarry (1773–1857) entered the army as an ensign in 1793. He was a battalion commander under Sir John Moore, before seeing varied service in the Mediterranean and Egypt. In 1811 he exchanged into the Coldstream Guards, serving in the Peninsula from 1812–14. During a critical moment in the attack on Hougoumont, the gates of the courtyard were opened to receive an ammunition wagon, allowing the French to force their way in.

Macdonnell, although seriously wounded, together with another Coldstreamer Sergeant Graham, managed to close the gates and save the day. Subsequently voted the bravest British soldier at Waterloo, in a competition bequeathed by a well-to-do clergyman, Macdonnell was awarded the £500 prize (£350,000 today) by Wellington himself. Macdonnell immediately gave half to Sergeant Graham.

Pembrokeshireman Sir Thomas Picton (1758–1815) was the Lieutenant-General commanding the 5th Division at Waterloo. A veteran of the Peninsula, he was the highest ranking British casualty. Since his baggage had not caught up with him, he fought the battle wearing civilian clothes and a top hat.

Walter Paget, 2nd Earl of Uxbridge (1768–1854), was riding beside Wellington when his leg was shattered by grapeshot fired from a cannon in one of the last shots of the battle, giving rise to a famous exchange. "By God Sir, I have lost my leg!", exclaimed Uxbridge: to which Wellington replied, "By God Sir, so you have". The leg was amputated below the knee and buried in the garden of a house on the outskirts of Waterloo village.

Napoleon's campaigns in Europe and Russia had drained the continent of good horses, leaving the finest to be found in Britain. This, taken with an unrivalled training in equitation, might explain the overconfidence of the British cavalry regiments at Waterloo.

Each side of a 500-man battalion square would have been only 60 feet long.

Vulnerable to artillery, particularly when firing grape and chain-shot, and infantry attack, disciplined squares that held firm were fatal to cavalry. They could not be outflanked, nor would horses charge onto a bank of bayonets. Close horse-artillery support was the best instrument to break squares, allowing cavalry to slaughter the survivors. At Waterloo fortunately, cooperation between the French cavalry and artillery was poor: with the artillery sited too far away. After perhaps twelve futile charges up the slope of Mont St Jean, Ney's cavalry was spent.

The 79th Cameron Highlanders fought at Quatre Bras and Waterloo – out of the original 675 men they sustained 456 casualties, of whom 103 were killed. In the early afternoon of 18 June the battalion beat off a determined French cavalry attack, by forming a "Defensive Square". Piper Kenneth Mackay, from Tongue in Sutherland, showing no fear, moved out of the protection of the square and marched round it, playing the traditional rallying tune *Cogadh ná Sith* ("War or Peace – The True Gathering of the Clans"). Mackay was presented with a set of silver mounted pipes by the King for his individual bravery in the battle.

- **Piper Kenneth Mackay**
Highlanders Museum, Scotland

With Uxbridge leading, and leaving no reserves, the two brigades of 2,000 men plunged down off the ridge – sweeping the dispersed Cuirassiers into the Ohain sunken road. Disregarding every attempt to recall them, the Union (which included the Scots Greys) and Household Cavalry Brigades charged headlong down the slope only to pull up on blown horses well beyond La Haye Sainte, at the bottom of the hill: to face a French brigade formed up into squares under Colonel Anton Schmitz – a survivor of the German contingent that had marched to Moscow with Napoleon in 1812.

Napoleon immediately ordered a counter-attack which decimated the British heavy cavalry, but at great cost to the French – particularly in time. By now the Prussians were beginning to appear on the French right flank. Uxbridge, having failed to rally his command, spent the rest of the battle leading a series of charges by light cavalry regiments and had nine horses shot from under him. "Our officers of cavalry have acquired a trick of galloping at everything. They never consider the situation, never think of manoeuvring before an enemy and never keep back or hold a reserve", Wellington said later.

At about 16:00 a third, strong French attack was launched: after Ney had noticed an apparent gap in Wellington's centre. Ney had no infantry reserves left, since most of them had been committed to Hougoumont on his left and to fending off the increasing number of Prussians beginning to appear on his right. Imprudently, he chose this moment to try to break the British centre, using cavalry alone. Ney mounted 67 squadrons (9,000 men) of cavalry, including Marshal Francois Christophe de Kellerman's heavy cavalry corps and the heavy cavalry of the Imperial Guard, commanded by Major-General Claude Etienne Guyot. Wellington responded by directing his infantry to form hollow-box infantry squares, four ranks deep.

Henry William Paget, 1st Marquess of Anglesey by Henry Edridge (1808)
National Portrait Gallery, London

Ney eventually realised the stupidity of his unsupported cavalry attacks. Belatedly, he tried instead to organise a combined arms assault on the centre right of Wellington's line with 6,500 infantry from Reille's II Corps and such of his cavalry still able to fight. Ney's initiative rallied scattered elements of d'Erlon's I Corps, which renewed the attack on La Haye Sainte. This time the farmhouse was taken – but only because the defenders had run out of ammunition. Ney, as he should have much earlier, then moved up horse-artillery towards Wellington's centre: and began to pour canister rounds at short range into the British squares, to terrible effect. The 27th Inniskilling Regiment was virtually wiped out; and the 30th and 73rd Regiments were so depleted that the survivors were combined to form a single square.

Around 16:30, when the cavalry attack on the British squares was at its height, the first Prussian elements of General Friedrich Wilhelm von Bülow's IV corps were arriving in increasing numbers on the battlefield. Under the plan agreed the day before, between Wellington and Blücher, should Bülow low find Wellington's centre under attack he would occupy the hamlet of Frichermont, on the French right. Bülow however, saw that there was a gap which might take him through to Plancenoit village, behind the French line. Napoleon immediately sent Lobau's Corps to intercept Bülow: whose 15th Brigade drove Lobau from Frichermont back to Plancenoit – threatening the *Grande Armée*'s only line of retreat. Napoleon had no choice but to commit eight battalions of the Young Guard: who secured Plancenoit after fierce fighting, but were themselves then counter-attacked and driven out. In response, Napoleon committed two battalions of the Old Guard: who recaptured the village at bayonet point. The dogged Bülow however, counter-attacked Plancenoit yet again, with 30,000 troops of his IV and II Corps – by then tying up 20,000 French defenders.

The Imperial Guard was under the direct command of Napoleon. It acted as his bodyguard and tactical reserve: and was never squandered in battle. In 1804 the Guard fielded 8,000 men: by the time of Napoleon's invasion of Russia in 1812 it had expanded to 100,000. The Old Guard had served Napoleon since his earliest campaigns; the Middle Guard dated from 1805; whilst the Young Guard was recruited from the best of the annual conscript draft. The Guard had its own artillery, infantry and cavalry. Despite being better paid and equipped, with guardsmen graded one rank higher than in the regular army, they became known as *Les Grognards* ("the Grumblers"). They were also referred to as "the Immortals".

The critical hour had arrived. Wellington's squares could not have survived any further French attacks. Fortunately Ney's frantic request for infantry was refused – because Napoleon was fully committed to beating off Bülow's attack on his right flank. Only after 19:00 did Napoleon release two battalions of the Imperial Guard to Ney, but it was too little too late. The respite had given Wellington the chance to reorganise his defences, by which time Field Marshal Hans Ernst Karl, Graf von Ziethen's I Corps had arrived to reinforce his centre. The Prussians then advanced towards the Brussels-Charleroi road, cutting the only line of retreat left open to the French.

At 19:00, with Wellington's centre still apparently exposed by the capture of La Haye Sainte and the Plancenoit defence stabilised, Napoleon committed his Imperial Guard to an attack on the British centre: with the aim of rolling up his front, away from the advancing Prussians. It proved to be his last roll of the dice.

Five battalions (3,000 men), probably of the Middle Guard, advanced through a storm of canister and sharpshooter fire to the west of La Haye Sainte. Two Grenadier battalions demolished Wellington's first line of defence, manned by British, Brunswick and Nassau

The Battle of Waterloo by William Sadler

The Battle of Waterloo (18 June 1815), by William Sadler (1782–1839) "A damned nice thing – the nearest run thing you ever saw in your life".

infantry, before being cut down by Baron David de Chasse's Netherlands Division: which fired its artillery into the Grenadiers' flank. Further west, two battalions of Imperial Guard Chasseurs advanced: until they encountered 1,500 British Foot Guards, commanded by Major-General Peregrine Maitland, lying down in the face of an intense artillery bombardment. To a man, the Foot Guards rose and delivered a series of withering volleys at point-blank range, followed by a bayonet-charge.

The Chasseurs wavered, then recoiled. A third battalion of Chasseurs arrived in support, pushing back the guardsmen: until the 52nd (Oxfordshire) Light Infantry, commanded by Colonel John Colborne appeared on their flank to empty devastating volleys into their ranks – and they too broke into headlong retreat. "*La Garde recule. Sauve qui peut!*" ("The Guard is retreating. Everyone for himself"): the cry sent waves of panic through the French lines. Wellington now stood up in the stirrups of his charger Copenhagen and raised his hat, in the signal for a general advance. The battle was won.

Napoleon lost 25,000 men killed and wounded and 9,000 taken prisoner. Wellington lost 15,000 and Blücher 8,000. "Nothing except a battle lost can be half so melancholy as a battle won", was Wellington's grim comment as he surveyed the carnage.

In 1819 Wellington was appointed Master-General of the Ordnance in the Tory government of Lord Liverpool, who had supported him throughout his Peninsular campaigns. In this office he was not considered subordinate to the Commander-in-Chief.

Wellington denied that he ever cried: "Up Guards and at 'em!". Maitland himself only recalled: "Now Maitland, now's your time!". In his novel *Les Misérables*, Victor Hugo credits Maitland with asking for the surrender of the Imperial Guard – and receiving from General Cambronne (1790–1842) the reply: *"Merde!"* ("Shit!").

News of the victory was rushed to London by Harry Percy (1786–1825), Wellington's only unwounded *aide-de-camp*. He carried the despatch in a velvet handkerchief sachet an admirer had thrust into his hand as he hurried from the Duchess of Richmond's Brussels ball on the eve of battle. He had no sleep that night, nor the five nights following, and had to row himself ashore after crossing the Channel. His scarlet and gold tunic was still torn and blood-stained when he burst into a St James's ballroom, a captured French standard in each hand, and dropped to one knee before the Prince Regent. It was pure Shakespeare.

During his ten year stint as its effective head, Wellington saw no reason to change the organisation or equipment of an army which had beaten Napoleon. His mind had not always been so closed to innovation. As a general in the Peninsula, he had been the first to use shrapnel shells; and was excited by Congreve's spectacular but unreliable rocket batteries. Thirty years later though, he regarded the Brown Bess musket as the most dependable infantry weapon ever produced. Reluctantly, he allowed the introduction of the new Minié rifle in 1851 – but insisted on modifying its percussion so that stocks of smooth-bore musket ammunition could still be used. Wellington opposed sensible attempts by Earl Grey in 1847 to reduce the minimum period of army service to ten years; and to amalgamate the Ordnance office with that of the Chief-of-Staff. He defended the retention of flogging as a necessary disciplinary measure to the last.

Heir to an enormous cotton-spinning fortune and with a strong Lancastrian accent, Sir Robert Peel Bt., 2nd Baronet (1788–1850) was twice Prime Minister – and the real founder of the Conservative party. As Chief Secretary for Ireland (1812–18) he had resisted Catholic emancipation and admittance to Parliament. As Home Secretary, he modernised England's criminal code and founded London's first disciplined police force, staffed by uniformed constables known as "Bobbies" or "Peelers". Peel led the Conservative party to a land-slide victory in 1841.

He regularised income tax, reformed the Bank of England and, late in the day, attempted to address Irish grievances. To ease poverty, he repealed tariffs on imports, including the Corn Laws– a significant step towards free trade, but which brought down his government. Continuing to support free trade in Parliament, he laid the foundations of mid-Victorian prosperity. Peel was one of Britain's greatest Prime Ministers.

- **Sir Robert Peel, 2nd Bt by Henry William Pickersgill**
National Portrait Gallery, London

In 1827 he was appointed Commander-in-Chief of the British Army: and, with Robert Peel, became identified as one of the leading lights of the Tory Party.

In 1828 Wellington became Prime Minister, maintaining his inflexible conservatism: "You must build your House of Parliament upon the river so that the populace cannot exact their demands by sitting down around you", he advised, obsessed that England had not heeded the lesson of the French Revolution – and reflecting his loathing for "the mob" (a

Wellington's nickname, "Iron Duke" was earned after he had protected the windows of Apsley House with iron shutters, at the height of his unpopularity. Officers under his command called him "The Beau", due to his immaculate dress. To his soldiers he was "Old Hookey" or "Old Nosey", on account of his prominent, beaky nose. His distaste for the niceties of democratic government was revealed, only half in jest, in a letter to a friend after his first Cabinet meeting: "A most extraordinary affair! I gave them their orders – and they wanted to stay to discuss them".

contraction of the Latin *mobile vulgus*). His premiership though, was distinguished by the repeal of the Test Act in 1828 and the 1829 Catholic Relief Act. In 1830 Wellington was targeted by rioters who smashed all his windows at Apsley House in Hyde Park (his address was: No. 1, London), obliging him to fit iron shutters.

The cause of the riots was Wellington's uncompromising refusal to entertain a Reform Bill or to extend the franchise. On 15 November 1830 his government fell.

The Whigs took over government on the Reform Bill ticket. Largely due to the intransigence orchestrated by Wellington however, the Bill was defeated in the Lords. An election returned the Whigs with an even larger majority: but a second Reform Bill met the same fate as the first – and insurrection swept the country. At the opening of the Liverpool to Manchester Railway in 1830, Wellington had to face down a hostile crowd: and on the fall of the Whig government found he was unable to form a government. Only when William IV (the "Sailor king") threatened to swamp the House of Lords with newly created Whig peers was the Bill finally passed. On entering the

The 1832 Reform Bill extended the right to vote from small rural boroughs controlled by the upper classes to the heavily populated industrial towns.

William Huskisson M.P. (1770–1830) accompanied Wellington to the opening of the Liverpool to Manchester Railway. He was run over by George Stephenson's locomotive *Rocket*, becoming the world's first railway fatality.

Commons after the election that followed, Wellington remarked: "I never saw so many shocking bad hats in my life".

When the Whig government fell in 1834, Wellington refused to be prime minister again. Peel accepted in his place and Wellington became Foreign Secretary. In Peel's second administration (1841–46), Wellington became Minister without Portfolio and Leader of the House of Lords. In 1846 he retired from politics, though he remained Commander-in-Chief of the army – in which capacity he advised on the protection of London in 1848, when revolution swept through most of Europe.

St Paul's

Wellington died on 15 September 1852, following a stroke, in his camp bed at Walmer Castle, his official residence as Lord Warden of the Cinque Ports. Despite having disliked trains intensely, his body was conveyed to London by rail – to lie in state at Chelsea Hospital, before a state funeral at St Paul's Cathedral on 18 November. Only six other commoners have been so honoured: Admiral Nelson, Lord Palmerston, Lord Roberts of Kandahar VC, William Gladstone, Earl Haig and Sir Winston Churchill.

His funeral was the most spectacular in Queen Victoria's 63-year reign. The procession, from Horse Guards via Constitution Hill to St Paul's, was watched by more than a million and a half people. So dense were the crowds that the lamplighters could not reach the street lights to extinguish them. Wellington's huge, 18-ton funeral carriage (described as a "Triumphal Car") reputedly designed by the Prince Consort, had been fashioned from the bronze of melted-down French cannon captured at Waterloo.

When the carriage arrived at St Paul's, there was an hour's delay while the bearers worked out how to lift the coffin 15 feet to the level of the waiting bier above them. Hundreds of mourners, seated in specially built stands in the nave, suffered as a freezing wind swept in through the open west door. Both Houses of Parliament attended in full. The Dean of St Paul's Henry Milman, had arranged for the service to take place under the Dome of the Cathedral rather than the Quire. A dramatic lighting arrangement to bar daylight, by using swathes of black crêpe, and provide only artificial light from 6,000 newly-installed gaslights, suspended from the Whispering Gallery, was spoiled when the sun came out. Dean Milman later described the sound of the 2,600-capacity congregation reciting the Lord's Prayer as "the roar of many waters"; and the rustle of so many people turning their service sheets, "such as a sudden gust causes in a forest in autumn". The Duke's coffin was lowered into the crypt, where it was placed into a sarcophagus made of Cornish porphyry, next to the tomb of Admiral Nelson.

Wellington's undertaker was William Banting, whose father, Thomas Banting had performed the same service for Lord Nelson on 4 December 1805.

IN MEMORIAM

The influence of his family, especially the patronage and financial support given by his brother Richard, undoubtedly gave Wellington a vital start to his career. The use he made of those advantages was however, the result of an outstanding character and determination. He enjoyed astonishing luck in avoiding death or injury during so many desperate battles and hazardous engagements. He was the quintessential example of the adage that "Lady Luck rewards those who set out to look for her". He was more than brave: he was immune to fear and indifferent of danger – to himself, but not to his soldiers. No historian would argue that Wellington had the dash and brilliance of Napoleon, or his great predecessor Marlborough. However he more than compensated for a lack of *élan*, by becoming a master of his trade.

Luck certainly smiled upon him but he never relied on it, planning his battles meticulously to reduce the element of chance to the minimum. A lesser man might well have emerged from such extraordinary success, arrogant and conceited. He was remarkable in that his modesty, humour, integrity and attention to detail enabled him to assume an important career in politics – though it was a duty to which he was manifestly unsuited. His premiership, perhaps the worst of the 19th century was redeemed by his one outstanding achievement: Catholic emancipation. In the House of Lords he maintained the fledgeling Conservative Party in the 1830s and underpinned Peel's ministry in the 1840s.

Wellington was of course human and had his frailties. He could be secretive and prejudiced in many of his views, self-centred and insensitive – particularly in his later years. He was nonetheless very kind to children, generous to his friends, concerned for his soldiers and fair-minded when not challenged or confronted. He was personally modest, uninterested in creature comforts and as austere in his personal habits as he was in his evaluation and treatment of those he commanded. Impatient with failure, unforgiving of defects in character, snobbish and reactionary he may have become – but he richly deserves his place in the pantheon of British history.

Arthur Wellesley, 1st Duke of Wellington by Alfred, Count D'Orsay (1845)
National Portrait Gallery, London

Queen Victoria's seventh child and favourite son was named Arthur (1850–1942) after the Duke, who was his godfather – and he became a soldier too. Arthur in turn, stood as godfather to HM Queen Elizabeth II in 1926.

"THE WATERLOO DESPATCH" WAS FLAWED BY TWO GLARING OMISSIONS

The most authentic record of the battle is "The Waterloo Despatch", Wellington's official report of the battle. The Duke began writing it on the morning after Waterloo before completing it later that day at his Headquarters in the Rue Royale in Brussels. The despatch was then handed to Harry Percy, who arrived in London on 21 June. It was published in *The Times* the next day.

John Colborne, 1st Baron Seaton (1778–1863), born in Hampshire, entered the army as an ensign in 1794. Unusually, he gained all his subsequent promotions without purchase. He served with distinction throughout the Peninsular campaign. Commanding the 52nd at Waterloo, the regiment had fallen back to the cross-roads on the ridge to the north-west of Hougoumont. At about 19:00 the Imperial Guard attacked the British centre. Colborne, anticipating Wellington's orders (the only tactful way of describing his timely initiative), threw the 52nd forward, wheeled it to the left – and poured fire into the French flank, driving them back in disorder. Colborne's prescient action is deemed by many as the blow that finally broke the spirit of the French at Waterloo. The Duke made no mention of Colborne in his Waterloo despatch. This inexplicable omission was controversial at the time – but Colborne wisely refused to comment.

His subsequent career did not suffer as a result. In 1839 he was raised to the peerage as Baron Seaton; attaining Field-Marshal rank in 1860 – a fitting reward for silence.

William Siborne (1797–1849), a young officer serving with the administration of Ireland at Dublin Castle, was known as a skilled surveyor and cartographer. In 1822 he had published *Instructions for Civil and Military Surveyors in Topographical Plan-Drawing*. In 1830 he was

commissioned by the Commander-in-Chief, Lord Rowland ("Daddy")
Hill (1772–1842) to make a model of the Battle of Waterloo. He spent eight
months researching the positions of all the formations engaged in the
battle. Siborne obtained permission from Lord Fitzroy Somerset, to
circulate a printed map of the battlefield: asking each recipient to mark the
position of his unit at exactly 19:00 on 18 June.

19:00 was the precise moment of crisis in the battle, when Napoleon
ordered his Imperial Guard to attack Wellington's weakening centre. The
subsequent defeat of the hitherto invincible Guard was considered the
climax of the battle and the greatest military feat in Wellington's glorious
career. There was however, a problem. Siborne's meticulous research over
many years, including interviews and correspondence with combatants
from the British, French and Prussian armies, had revealed the inescapable
fact that by 19:00 that evening 48,000 Prussian soldiers had arrived on the
battlefield. Von Bülow, the first to arrive, followed his orders to the letter: if
Wellington's weak left-wing and centre were in danger, he should
immediately attack the French right-wing, anchored on the village of
Plancenoit. Wellington had started the day with 68,000 troops but by the
evening, he had lost nearly 15,000 of them and was hard pressed. The
Prussian army had reached the battlefield just in time to save the day. It
must be remembered though, that Wellington only gave battle on 18 June at all, on the clear
promise of Prussian support – the whole day was spent anxiously awaiting their arrival.

John Colborne,
1st Baron Seaton

When Wellington was first shown the model's dispositions, he agreed with them:
remarking in a memo, found after his death, that he could not really remember – and that he
was, "disgusted and ashamed by all I have seen of the Battle of Waterloo". He also pointed out
that: "No Drawing or representation as a Model can represent more than one moment of an
Action. But this model tends to represent the whole action .... I don't want to injure the man ....
The fact is, a battle is like a ball (everyone sees *something*, nobody sees *everything*) – they keep
footing it all the day through".

It was drawn to Wellington's attention however, that Siborne's scrupulously accurate
positions conflicted with his account of the Prussian role in the Waterloo Despatch. Siborne
was summoned to London for a conference with the Duke to discuss the misunderstanding.
Unfortunately, Siborne never attended probably because he could not afford the passage from
Dublin to London. Official funding had been withdrawn and all his resources had been devoted
to completing his model. Siborne's promised promotion to Captain mysteriously failed to
materialise and unpleasant rumours began to circulate. It was put about that Siborne had been
working at his model in army time and that his unpatriotic portrayal of the Prussians was
because of his German ancestry.

In 1838, at a cost of £3,000
(£2.4 million today), the model
was exhibited. It was a great
success, with over 100,000
visitors: but Siborne was left
out of pocket, probably
swindled by the exhibitors.
Siborne became desperate. In a
belated act of contrition, he

Siborne's model is a 400 square foot
canvas, accurate in every detail of
topography and contour, with a scale
of 9 feet:1 mile. There are 75,000
Allied and French soldiers (one for
every two on the battlefield). Each
tiny alloy, 3/8ths of an inch tall figure
was hand-painted with exact
regimental detail – but not one of the
48,000 Prussians is present.
• Siborne's model of Waterloo (photograph)
National Army Museum, London

removed 8,000 Prussian lead soldiers from his model's canvas in the hope that funds would flow, but to no avail. The Duke of Wellington had been embarrassed before his peers and there would be no redemption – too late had poor Siborne realised that historical exactitude was not the issue. Financial hardship broke his health: which led to his premature death in 1849.

Having interviewed many veterans and survivors of the battle and campaign, Siborne had published in 1844 a two-volume *History of the War in France and Belgium in 1815*. It was the standard reference for 150 years and is still in print today. His model was stored originally at the Royal United Service Institute before being put on display in the National Army Museum in London, where it can be seen today.

A HORSE AND CARRIAGE

Copenhagen, the Duke of Wellington's charger at the battle of Waterloo was born in 1808. He was a chestnut stallion of 15 hands, sired by Meteor – who came second in the 1786 Derby. Copenhagen was not good enough to race, winning only once at Newmarket in thirteen attempts. He was drafted to the Peninsular army and was bought by Wellington in 1813. Copenhagen carried the Duke safely throughout the Battle of Waterloo: but tried to kick him when he finally dismounted late that evening.

Copenhagen was sent back to Wellington's seat at Stratfield Saye in Hampshire, a gift from a grateful nation, where he died in 1836, aged twenty-eight. He was given a military funeral, with all honours – his grave is marked by a splendid turkey oak, planted by Mrs Apostles, the Duke's housekeeper. Only one of Copenhagen's hooves was removed (by Wellington's groom, to Wellington's fury) and turned into an ink-well. Several more have been claimed – perhaps this was the secret of his speed.

Napoleon's carriage was a "dormouse" (sleeper) built by Goeting of Paris in April 1815 – to a remarkable specification. The dark blue doors, emblazoned with the Imperial Arms, were bullet proof; as were louvred steel shutters protecting the windows. A large, folding steel bed was contained in a compartment under the boot. Another compartment, accessed from the outside, enabled the removal of chamber pots without disturbing the occupant. The interior could be adapted for use as kitchen, bathroom, dressing room, office or dining room. Storage included a retractable desk, with secret drawers and compartments for maps and telescopes. Built-in holsters contained doublebarrelled, rifled pistols: complete with repair and charging tools. Major von Keller of the Prussian 15th Fusilier Regiment captured the carriage, which was abandoned after the battle. A bag of diamonds found inside were despatched to the Prussian King Friedrich-Wilhelm, to be included in his crown jewels. Major Keller received the *Pour le Mérite* (called in WWI the "Blue Max"), Prussia's highest order of gallantry.

WATERLOO TEETH

By the mid-18th century, highly organised slave labour working the sugar plantations of the French and British West Indian colonies exported increasing quantities of sugar to Europe. It was expensive and could only be afforded by the rich – who suffered tooth decay as a result. This led to an increase in the number of specialist dentists manufacturing dentures: but the problem lay in identifying a material for false teeth that could match real ones. Bone and ivory had proved unsatisfactory; and porcelain teeth, invented in 1774, apart from being eerily white, had a tendency to chip and crack. The usual sources of human teeth were suspect, deriving from unidentified paupers, executed criminals, mortuaries, graveyards and from the utterly

Wellington astride Copenhagen, in Matthew Wyatt's statue on Round Hill, Aldershot destitute. Teeth from such origins were most unlikely to be pristine. In the Napoleonic wars there was a sudden abundance of teeth which were plundered from the battlefields of Europe.

Some 50,000 young men, with sound teeth, fell at Waterloo. Most of these found their way back to Britain, the richest country in Europe: and best able to afford the new dentures, known as "Waterloo Teeth". They were worn with great pride and continued to be in great demand until manufactured false-teeth became available in the 1840s. The US Civil War (1861–65) gave a final boost to the grisly trade in battlefield teeth.

TRUMP

The Reverend John ("Jack") Russell (1795–1883), known as the "Sporting Parson", was born at Dartmouth in Devonshire. In 1815, the year of Waterloo, while at Oxford he is said to have seen a little white terrier bitch called "Trump" owned by a milkman: with tan spots over her eyes and a tan tip to her tail. Russell immediately bought her – and she became the foundation bitch of a line of celebrated fox terriers known as Jack Russells.

Charles Cruft (1852–1938) was born in Bloomsbury in London in the year that the Duke of Wellington died. The general manager of James Spratt, a dog biscuit manufacturer, he introduced his eponymous "dog show" in Islington in 1891.

Ironically, although the Parson was a founding member of the Kennel Club of Great Britain, on 4 April 1873, Jack Russells were not recognised as a breed until 1991. The Parson would never show his own Jack Russells: maintaining that comparing his dogs with show dogs was like contrasting wild with cultivated flowers. A painting of Trump was commissioned by the Prince of Wales, forty years after her death.

The Parson died at Swimbridge, a few miles from Barnstaple, on the north Devon coast. The local public house was named after him – and it stands there to this day.

"THE YEAR WITHOUT A SUMMER"

Mount Tambora is an active stratovolcano on Sumbawa, an island south-east of Borneo. On 10 April 1815 it was 14,000 feet high – before a massive eruption, the world's largest since the explosion which created Lake Taupo in New Zealand in about AD180, reduced its summit to 9,354 feet. The explosion was heard in Sumatra over 1,200 miles away. The subsequent pyroclastic rains, lava flows and tsunamis killed 10,000 people. A half-inch layer of ash covered an area of nearly 200,000 square miles – some 80,000 more died from thirst, starvation and disease. An opaque cloud of ash, pumice and colloidal suspensions (aerosols) was carried around the world by the jet stream: darkening the skies for months, preventing sunlight from reaching the earth's surface and reducing the mean global temperature by 3° centigrade. A year later European countries and North America were devastated by heavy falls of snow and sub-zero frosts throughout the summer months: resulting in crop failure, dead livestock and famine. 1816, the year after Waterloo, became known as "The year without a summer", "the Poverty Year" and "Eighteen Hundred and Froze to Death".

1816 was the year in which Mary Shelley wrote her gothic novel *Frankenstein* (published in 1818) whilst holidaying on Lake Geneva with her husband and Lord Byron. Tambora has been known as "Frankenstein's Volcano" ever since.

China suffered catastrophic floods in the Yangtze Valley in 1816 – as did the Ganges plain in India. Mount Tambora, though a global disaster, might offer a clue to the amelioration of "global warming" in the 21st century.

SIR WALTER SCOTT

Sir Walter Scott, 1st Baronet (1771–1832) invented the historical novel. He influenced Pushkin, Tolstoy, George Eliot, Dickens and many other 19th century writers. His output was prodigious.

Born in Edinburgh, from his earliest years Scott learnt from his mother and Aunt Jenny the ballads, legends and tales of the Scottish Borders. He was a voracious reader and had a photographic memory, astounding family and friends with his recitations. He roamed the Borders, appreciating the rich local history and its outstanding beauty. In 1783 he attended Edinburgh University: where he was fascinated by German romanticism and Gothic novels.

His father was a Writer to the Signet (Solicitor) in Edinburgh, to whom he was apprenticed in 1786. Scott was appointed deputy Sheriff of Selkirk and Clerk to the Session of Edinburgh. In 1797 he married Charlotte Charpentier, a French royalist émigrée. They lived happily together until her death in 1826. They had five children.

Scott's love of Scottish ballads led him to publish a 3-volume anthology, *The Minstrelsy of the Scottish Border* in 1803. In 1805 Scott founded a printing press – and soon after published a narrative poem, *The Lay of the Last Minstrel*, which made his name. The very successful *The Lady of the Lake* followed in 1810; then *Rokeby* in 1813; and the *Lord of the Isles* in 1815. He also found time to publish an 18-volume collection of the works of John Dryden in 1808; and in 1814, 19 volumes of Jonathan Swift.

He wrote a volume of poetry *Marmion* in 1808, which contains the often misquoted lines: "Oh! What a tangled web we weave, When first we practice [sic] to deceive".

In 1813 Scott had to save his printing press venture from bankruptcy, by virtually mortgaging his future literary output to his creditors. Scott wrote remorselessly to pay off this debt – and the over-spend on his magnificent house Abbotsford, which he had built near Melrose and filled with antiquarian objects. In 1814, with remarkable speed, he produced *Waverley*: a story of the 1745 Jacobite rebellion – such was its success that Edinburgh Railway station was named after it.

Sir Walter Scott, 1st Bt. by Sir Edwin Henry Landseer (c.1824)
National Portrait Gallery, London

Scott capitalised on *Waverley* with a series of 25 more adventures: all set in Scotland and all written anonymously under the *nom de plume* "Wizard of the North". Known as the *Waverley* novels, the first were *Guy Mannering* in 1815 and *The Antiquary* in 1816. He wrote *Rob Roy* in 1817 and *The Heart of Midlothian* in 1818. *The Bride of Lammermoor* (which inspired Donizetti's 1835 opera *Lucia di Lammermoor*) and *A Legend of Montrose* appeared in 1819.

Having whetted an insatiable public appetite for fictionalised history and exhausted his Scottish theme, Scott now turned to England and elsewhere for inspiration: the best being *Ivanhoe* in 1819, still one of his most popular books, set in the 12th century. The best of his last novels are *Redgauntlet*, in an 1824 return to the Borders; and *The Talisman* in 1825, set in the Holy Land in the time of the crusades. In 1827 Scott, who never punctuated his books (leaving it to the printers), acknowledged that he was the author of the *Waverley* novels. It had been an open secret for some time.

In 1822 Scott was awarded a baronetcy and charged with welcoming King George IV to Scotland. He organised an elaborate pageantry in Edinburgh, in which he represented the obese monarch as a highland chief. The farce was accepted in good heart and the event was a huge success – above all, it propelled tartans and kilts into high fashion as new, potent symbols of Scottish national identity.

His publisher, Archibald Constable's bankruptcy nearly brought him down again. Scott bravely assumed his debt; but the strain of maintaining his flow of novels eventually affected not only his health but eventually the quality of his work. After *Redgauntlet*, Scott produced little of note. His *Provincial Antiquities and Picturesque Scenery of Scotland*, illustrated by J.M.W. Turner, between 1819–26 was a commercial failure. His biography of Napoleon Bonaparte in 1831 however, showed that the rapidity and fluency of his writing remained unimpaired – as was his popularity. His creditors were sympathetic; and Scott's reputation as the grand old man of Scottish, and indeed English, letters was unimpeachable. In 1831 his health broke down and, after a sad attempt to recuperate in Naples, he died at Abbotsford on 21 September 1832. He was buried in Dryburgh Abbey – next to a statue of William Wallace, another of Scotland's great national heroes.

Sales of Scott's novels were unaffected by his death: and he finally settled his colossal debts from beyond the grave. Scott was a lowlander: and his portrayal of Highlanders and their clansmen was sentimental. But he did more than any other to redeem the misrepresentation of their culture from the contempt and distrust which had been engendered by the 1745 rebellion and the cruel aftermath of Culloden.

The world's first colour photograph (1861)

The English word tartan comes from the French *tiretain*, in reference to woven, rather than knitted cloth. It is a pattern of diagonal, horizontal and vertical stripes (setts) in multiple colours, unmistakably associated with Scotland. All Scottish kilts have a tartan weave. "Plaid" is simply a cloth worn over the shoulder or a blanket.

Until the middle of the 19th century, highland tartans were normally associated with regional weavers rather than individual clans: because tartan designs were dictated by local conditions, tastes and the dyes available. There is a myth that tartans were designed for Hunting (green for camouflage), for Battle (red to conceal blood) and for Dress (blue and yellow, to symbolise water and crops). The earliest, known as "Falkirk", piece of tartan dates from the 3rd century, close to the Antonine Wall between the rivers Clyde and Forth. It is a fragment of cloth in a check design of natural light and dark wools, used to stopper an earthenware pot containing a trove of Roman coins. These simple tartan designs almost certainly predate the Roman occupation of Britain.

Coloured, patterned tartans did not exist in Scotland before the 16th century: and it was not until the late 17th century that any kind of uniformity emerged. Indeed it was common for highlanders to wear a variety of tartans simultaneously. In battle clansmen relied on coloured ribbons tied to their bonnets to distinguish friend from foe. From 1725 locally raised militia, the Highland Independent Companies, adopted a deliberately standardised tartan to avoid association with any individual clan: becoming in 1739, the Black Watch Regiment.

Highland Scottish clans were the principal supporters of the Jacobite rebellion of 1745: which, ending in defeat, led to the Dress Act of 1746 banning the wearing of any tartan except by the army and the gentry. By the early 19th century *Ossian* the fake epic translation of poems from the Gaelic (Napoleon carried a copy on campaign) by James Macpherson (1736–96) and the novels of Sir Walter Scott had encouraged a Highland romantic revival. In 1815 The Highland Society of London (founded 1778) resolved to identify and register official clan tartans. These beginnings were given a huge boost when King George IV visited Edinburgh in 1822, the first reigning monarch to visit Scotland in 171 years. Sir Water Scott, who had founded the Celtic Society in 1820, was the impresario – the event was lampooned as "Sir Walter's Celtified Pageantry". The royal visit sparked a rush of tartan directories and the fashion became a craze.

A Quaker from Chorley in Lancashire, Thomas Rawlinson has now been accepted, to the indignation of many Scots, as the originator of the *feilidh-beag* (philabeg), or short kilt. A producer of charcoal, he designed it in 1725 – to protect his foresters in Glengarry from injury when their long plaids caught in machinery.

In 1848 Queen Victoria and Prince Albert bought Balmoral Castle; and used a combination of Hunting, Royal and Dress Stewart tartans for soft furnishings. Prince Albert designed his own "Balmoral" tartan. Today the Scottish Tartans Society, founded in 1963, keeps a register of 1,300 known tartans. The world's first colour photograph that did not fade, created by the Scottish scientist James Clerk Maxwell in 1861, was of a tartan ribbon.

JANE AUSTEN

Jane Austen (1775–1817) was the first novelist to write in a distinctly modern style. She described ordinary people in a realistic context: although her characters were drawn from the placid, protected world of the English minor landed gentry and the vicarage. She was born into a large and happy, literate family in Steventon in Hampshire: the younger daughter of the village rector. She also had five older brothers and one younger. The family could not afford to educate two daughters properly: but she did go to school for a time – and then made good use of her father's extensive library. She lived briefly in Bath but "never again lived anywhere beyond the bounds of her immediate family environment". She received one marriage proposal: from the younger, oddly named Harris Bigg-Wither in 1802. She accepted; but refused him the following day.

Jane began to write fiction in 1789; but took nearly ten years properly to get into her stride. Her early works are parodies of the sentimental romances then fashionable. In 1811 she published the first of the six novels for which she is remembered, *Sense and Sensibility*. *Pride and Prejudice* followed in 1813, *Mansfield Park* in 1814, *Emma* in 1815, *Persuasion* in 1817 and *Northanger Abbey*: which was also published in 1817 but had in fact, first been written in 1798. She accurately reflected the mores and mannerisms of the "Regency". The Prince Regent himself, later King George IV had a set of all her works in each of his residences. Her novels have been adapted for film and television more than those by any other female author.

Watercolour and pencil sketch of Jane Austen, possibly by her sister Cassandra (*c.*1810)
National Portrait Gallery, London

They are remarkable for their lack of sentimentality; but also for their humour, understanding and compassion. They were published anonymously, with two of them appearing only after her death – most likely from Addison's disease (a rare disorder of the adrenal glands), or possibly tuberculosis. She never married. Her most cherished companion was her elder sister Cassandra (1773–1845), who also never married; and jealously guarded Jane's privacy – after her death Cassandra censored or destroyed all her correspondence. Jane Austen set a standard that few novelists since have been able to match.

CHARLES DICKENS

Charles John Huffam Dickens FRSA (1812–70) was the greatest and most popular British novelist of the 19th century. He created the richest diversity of memorable characters in English literature. His compassion for the poor in Victorian society, and concern over the appalling conditions they endured, are recurring themes of his novels. He became the most influential voice of conscience of his age. Dickens's works have never been out of print; and today he enjoys ever greater critical acclaim.

He was born in Portsmouth in Hampshire, the second child and eldest son of John Dickens, a clerk in the Navy pay office. Dickens was privately educated until the age of twelve, when his father was imprisoned for debt. The boy was forced to work a ten-hour day, in a rat infested blacking factory, on the Thames embankment in central London. This hideous

A key event in Dickens's life occurred when he met Maria Beadnall, the daughter of a rich banker. Rejected because of his unfavourable prospects, his disappointment instilled in him an implacable will to succeed.

Dickens kept a pet raven called "Grip". When it died in 1841, he had it stuffed. It now resides in the Free Library of Philadelphia.

In 1929 Dickens's beautiful artist daughter Katey was dismissed as "mad" when she claimed that her father had sired a secret love child with his sister-in-law.

experience deeply affected the sensitive young Dickens.

In 1827, after two years of resumed schooling in north London, the fifteen year-old Dickens began work as a junior clerk in the offices of a firm of solicitors in Holborn, where he remained for a year. He left to become a freelance reporter. He had used his time wisely and become fluent at shorthand. Before becoming a parliamentary and newspaper reporter, for the next four years Dickens reported interminable law cases, an experience which coloured his subsequent novels, *Nicholas Nickleby*, *Dombey & Son* and particularly, *Bleak House*.

After considering an acting career, in 1833 Dickens began to write short journalistic pieces, reprinted as *Sketches by Boz*. This led to the serialisation of his first comic novel *The Pickwick Papers* in 1837. Dickens had showed a remarkable ability to spin a story in an appealing, compulsive "page turning" style which soon made him the most widely read author of his time. *The Pickwick Papers* has become one of the best known novels in the world. Dickens's characters owed are well served by his original illustrators, George Cruikshank in *Sketches by Boz* and "Phiz" (Hablot K. Browne) in *Oliver Twist*.

In April 1836 Dickens married Catherine Hogarth (1816–79) the daughter of the editor of the *Evening Chronicle*. They settled in Bloomsbury and produced ten children.

Catherine's 17 year-old sister Mary moved in with them, a not unusual arrangement at the time; and to whom Dickens became devoted. Having died in his arms barely a year later, he relived her death in Little Nell (*The Old Curiosity Shop*). Oscar Wilde remarked sardonically fifty years later: "You would need to have a heart of stone not to laugh at the death of Little Nell". G.K. Chesterton however, complained: "It is not the death of Little Nell, but the life of Little Nell, that I object to".

The serialisation of *Oliver Twist* in 1838, *The Old Curiosity Shop* and *Barnaby Rudge* in 1841, came next. In Oliver Twist, Dickens's description of poverty and crime in a London "rookery" (dense slum housing) in Bermondsey, known as Jacob's Island, deeply shocked his readers, forcing the authorities to clear it.

In 1842 Dickens and his wife visited the US and Canada on a lecture tour. He was well received, in spite of his support for the abolition of slavery, and met President John Tyler at the White House – as well as the poets Henry Wadsworth Longfellow (1807–82) and Ralph Waldo Emerson (1803–82).

His father was released a year later when an inheritance enabled him to settle his debts. Dickens's mother however, kept Charles at the blacking factory. Resentment of his mother's treatment may have contributed towards his demanding relationships with women. Dickens portrayed much of his father's exuberance and ineptitude through the character of Mr Micawber, in the partly autobiographical *David Copperfield*. Dickens himself became a "control freak" later in life, displaying many of the symptoms of obsessive compulsive disorder – which was also reflected in the behaviour of some of his characters.

Charles Dickens by Ary Scheffer (1855)
National Portrait Gallery, London

In 1842 Georgina Hogarth, another sister-in-law, replaced her sister Mary in the Dickens household, to care for their young family while they were away in the US. She remained Dickens's housekeeper until his death in 1870. In 1858 she survived the humiliation of a virginity test which Dickens forced her to take: to still salacious gossip and to protect his public image as a guardian of Victorian family values. There were however, persistent rumours of an illegitimate child, Hector Charles Dickens. In his will, Dickens lovingly described Georgina as his most trusted friend: and left her most of his jewellery and £8,000 (£4.7 million today) in cash – far more than he left to his estranged wife or mistress.

On his return from the US in 1843 Dickens wrote *A Christmas Carol* in a few weeks. He spent 1844 in Italy and 1846 in Switzerland, before returning to write the equally successful *Dombey & Son* in 1848 and *David Copperfield* in 1850. Dickens's novels now began to reveal a disquieting unease over the social evils spawned by Victorian industrial society: which intensified in *Bleak House* in 1853, *Little Dorritt* in 1857 and *Great Expectations* in 1861. In 1858, aged forty-six, Dickens left his wife – soon after an eighteen year-old actress Ellen "Nelly" Ternan had caught his eye.

Dickens's adulterous affair with Nelly Ternan (1839–1914) ended with his death, twelve years later. He kept their affair secret by resorting to extreme Machiavellian intrigue, placing his reputation as a stern upholder of domestic probity in grave jeopardy. He excised Nelly's name from reports of the Staplehurst train crash in which they were both involved while returning from Paris. He always approached the house in which he kept her indirectly through muddy fields and burnt all their correspondence. Their only child, a son, died in infancy. There is little doubt that the immense strain of maintaining a complex double-life hastened Dickens's death.

The Staplehurst crash occurred on 9 June 1865. The first seven carriages plunged off a cast iron bridge under repair. The only carriage to remain on the track was the first class car in which Dickens and Nelly were travelling. Although uninjured, Dickens was badly shaken by the sight of the mangled dead – and his attempts to revive the injured with a bottle of brandy. He never got over the experience.

In November 1867 Dickens embarked upon an exhausting second reading tour of the US; before returning home in 1868 to give a series of strenuous "Farewell" readings across the British Isles. In April 1869 he collapsed after a mild stroke. Recovering, he started his last, unfinished novel, *The Mystery of Edwin Drood*. On 8 June 1870 he suffered another stroke, at his house at Gad's Hill in Kent.

He never regained consciousness and died the following day. He had long expressed a wish to be buried in a small graveyard under Rochester Castle wall: but, by national demand, he was interred in Poet's Corner in Westminster Abbey. The ceremony was held in strict privacy. He was 58 years old.

Charles Dickens featured on £10 bank notes issued by the Bank of England between 1992–2003.

It was strongly rumoured at the time, that Dickens suffered his stroke while visiting Nelly in Peckham. She delivered him unconscious in a closed cab to Gad's Hill, where Georgina took him in.

A Tale of Two Cities, an enthralling story set principally in France during the French Revolution, has sold well over 200 million copies since it was first published in 1859. It is said to be the best-selling English language novel of all time.

THE CRUEL TREATMENT OF CHILD LABOUR IN EARLY VICTORIAN BRITAIN

By the middle of the 19th century, the rapidly expanding urban population had created a huge demand for chimney sweeps. The trade employed very small lads known as "climbing boys", who were able to squeeze into the narrowest chimneys and clean them from the inside. The work was filthy and dangerous. The children were frequently exploited and abused by cruel and vicious employers: who forced their charges up chimneys, by applying lighted straws and pins to their naked feet. Climbing boys suffered grievously. Quite apart from twisted spines, deformed joints, eye inflammations, burns and infected cuts and bruises, there was a high incidence of testicular cancer caused by the carcinogenic chemicals in the soot. Suffocation through inhaled soot and respiratory illness were an everyday hazard; and falls maimed and killed countless tiny sweeps. It was also a short-lived apprenticeship, limited only to the very young.

In 1788 Parliament passed an Act for the Better Regulation of Chimney Sweepers, which limited a sweeper to six apprentices of not less than eight years-old: but the Act was rarely enforced. In 1840 another attempt was made to regulate the employment of young boys, by making it illegal for anyone below the age of 21 to clean chimneys: but again the legislation was largely ignored. In 1864 Lord Shaftesbury proposed the Chimney Sweepers Regulation Act which was further reinforced by the Chimney Sweepers Act of 1875, that required anyone setting up in practice as a chimney sweep to be licensed by the local police.

Anthony Ashley Cooper, 7th Earl of Shaftesbury (1801–85) was a politician and social reformer. Though he opposed the Reform Bill of 1832, from 1833 he was the prime mover in factory legislation: and was chiefly responsible for the successful passage of the Mines Act in 1842, followed by the Ten Hours Act in 1847 – which limited the working hours in the newly industrialised, steam-powered textile mills. He was president (1843–83) of the Ragged Schools Union, which arranged for the free education of distressed children. Apart from being one of the most competent Victorian social reformers, Shaftesbury was also a leading light of the Evangelical Movement within the Church of England – and a generous supporter of missionary societies.

The Shaftesbury Memorial Fountain in Piccadilly Circus, with its aluminium statue of Eros by Sir Alfred Gilbert R.A. (1854–1934), was erected in 1893 in his memory.

CLEANING LONDON'S WATER (1856–75)

Since Roman times, the River Thames has provided London's sewer. By 1851 a population of 2,362,236 was still dumping its sewage into the river: and public health began to collapse, with an increasing incidence of cholera epidemics.

By the end of August 1854 London was gripped by a particularly severe outbreak, which killed 400 people in three days. The prevailing medical theory was that cholera was carried in a "miasma" of foul air. Dr John Snow (1813–58), who had long suspected that cholera was water-borne, analysed where the victims had lived. He realised that each fatality had used a water pump on Broad Street, in Soho. Snow convinced the authorities that this well had caused the outbreak: and forthwith the pump handle was removed. The effect was dramatic, with not one new cholera case being reported.

Cholera is a severe bacterial infection caused by the bacteria *Vibrio cholerae* – resulting in violent and severe diarrhoea, dehydration and the rapid depletion of body fluids and mineral salts. Cholera usually spreads in epidemics, through water or food contaminated by faeces. The symptoms also include severe muscle cramps, vomiting and intense thirst, before the victim succumbs to coma and death through shock. The infection passes within a week if fluids and minerals are replaced, more quickly if antibiotics are taken immediately. Prevention mandates good sanitation and clean drinking water.

In 1848 an misguided attempt by the Metropolitan Commission of Sewers to prevent the use of cesspits resulted in a cholera epidemic the following year, in which over 14,000 Londoners died. Proposals to build a sewage system had been postponed in 1856, through lack of funds: but two years later the Thames reached sewage saturation-point, in the "Great Stink" of 1858. Parliament at last recognised the urgency of the problem: and appointed Joseph Bazalgette (1819–91), Chief Engineer of the Metropolitan Board of Works, to undertake the work.

Snow, a Yorkshireman known as the "father of epidemiology", had administered an anaesthetic to Queen Victoria for the birth of Prince Leopold, in 1853.

Bazalgette designed a vast system of underground channels which directed sewage into the Thames estuary, well downstream from London. Three main sewers were constructed (with remarkable foresight, Bazalgette doubled then redoubled the planned diameter) north of London, with one under the Thames embankment. The statistics of the enterprise are impressive. Between 1859–65 100 miles of six principal underground sewers were built which connected to 450 miles of feeder sewers – in turn linking into 13,000 miles of street sewers: using nearly 350 million bricks, a million cubic yards of cement and the excavation of 31/2 million tons of earth. It is a testament to the prescience and quality of the work that the same brick sewers are still in place today. London contours enabled the natural gravity flow of sewage eastwards: but in low lying areas such as Chelsea, Deptford and Abbey Mills, pumping stations had to be built to lift and accelerate the flow. The system was opened by the Prince of Wales on 4 April 1865: it was not completed however, for another ten years.

MICHAEL FARADAY FRS

Michael Faraday by Thomas Phillips (c.1841–42)
National Portrait Gallery, London

Michael Faraday (1791–1867) was a chemist and physicist. He discovered electromagnetic induction, diamagnetism and the laws of electrolysis. He established that magnetism could affect rays of light: and that there was an underlying relationship between the two phenomena. His inventions provided the basis of electric motor technology; and it was largely due to him that electric power became viable. As a chemist: Faraday discovered benzene, investigated the clathrate hydrate of chlorine, invented an early form of the bunsen burner and the system of oxidation numbers; and popularised words such as anode, cathode, electrode and ion – which he asked the Reverend William Whewell (1794–1866) to coin from the Greek for him. His contributions to science literally transformed the world.

Albert Einstein kept a photograph of Faraday on his study wall, alongside pictures of Isaac Newton and James Clerk Maxwell.

Faraday was the first and foremost Fullerian Professor of Chemistry at the Royal Institution of Great Britain, a position to which he was appointed for life.

Although Faraday received little formal education and his knowledge of higher mathematics such as calculus was superficial, he was one of the most influential scientists of all time. Indeed, some historians of science refer to him as the best experimentalist in its history. The SI unit of capacitance, the "farad", is named for him; as is the Faraday constant, the charge on a mole of electrons (about 96,485 coulombs). Faraday's law of induction states that a magnetic field changing in time creates a proportional electromotive force – reader and author alike, there will be few who understand any of this.

Faraday was a member of the Sandemanian Church, a Christian sect founded in 1730, which demanded total faith and commitment. Biographers have noted that "a strong sense of the unity of God and nature pervaded Faraday's life and work". From 1991–2001 Faraday's portrait featured on the reverse of £20 English bank notes.

Faraday was born in Newington Butts, now part of the London Borough of Southwark – but then a suburban part of Surrey, a mile south of London Bridge. His family was not well off. His father James, born in Yorkshire, was a Sandemanian who had come to London in 1788 from Outhgill in Westmorland, where he was the village blacksmith. Michael, one of four children, having only the most basic of school educations, had largely to educate himself. At fourteen he was apprenticed to a local bookbinder and bookseller, George Riebau. During his seven-year apprenticeship he read voraciously. *The Improvement of the Mind* by the Reverend Isaac Watts (1674–1748), which emphasized the need for the rational testing of ideas, especially influenced him.

He was also inspired by *Conversations in Chemistry*, a book written for children by Jane Marcet (1769–1858) in 1805. His interest in science, particular in electricity and chemistry dates from this time – clearly, selling books was less interesting than reading them.

In 1812 Faraday attended lectures by the eminent chemist Sir Humphry Davy, of the Royal Institution and President of the Royal Society; and by John Tatum, founder of the City Philosophical Society. Faraday sent Davy a 300-page book of his notes taken during the lectures. Davy's reply was immediate and favourable – after Davy damaged his eyesight in an accident with nitrogen trichloride, he employed Faraday as a secretary. When John Payne, one of the Royal Institution's assistants, was sacked, Davy was asked to find a replacement. He appointed Faraday as Chemical Assistant at the Royal Institution on 1 March 1813.

In the class-based English society of the time, Faraday was not considered a gentleman. When Davy went on a long tour to the continent in 1813–15, his manservant did not wish to accompany him. As Faraday was going as his scientific assistant, Davy asked him to be his valet until a replacement could be found in Paris. Faraday was forced to fill both roles throughout the trip. Worse, Davy's wife, Jane Apreece refused to treat Faraday as an equal – making him travel outside the coach and eat with the servants. She made Faraday so miserable that he contemplated returning to Britain alone – and giving up science altogether. The trip did however, give him access to the European scientific elite and a host of stimulating ideas.

Faraday rejected a knighthood: and twice refused to become President of the Royal Society. He was one of eight foreign members elected to the French Academy of Sciences in 1844. In 1848, as a result of representations by the Prince Consort, he was awarded a grace and favour house in Hampton Court, free of all expenses or upkeep. In 1858 Faraday retired to live there.

Michael Faraday

Sir Humphry Davy, 1st Baronet PRS (1778–1829), a Cornishman born in Penzance, is probably best remembered today for his discoveries of several alkali and alkaline earth metals, as well as contributions to the discoveries of the elemental nature of chlorine and iodine. He invented the Davy lamp, which allowed miners to enter gassy workings and saved countless lives.

Berzelius called Davy's 1806 Bakerian Lecture *On Some Chemical Agencies of Electricity*, "one of the best memoirs which has ever enriched the theory of chemistry". This paper was central to all chemical affinity theories in the first half of the 19th century. He died, and is buried, in Geneva.
• **Sir Humphry Davy, Bt. after Sir Thomas Lawrence (c.1821)**
National Portrait Gallery, London

Faraday died at Hampton Court on 25 August 1867. He had previously refused to be buried in Westminster Abbey – instead there is a memorial plaque, near Isaac Newton's tomb. Faraday was interred in the Sandemanian plot in Highgate Cemetery. Faraday married Sarah Barnard (1800–79) on 2 June 1821: but they had no children.

When asked by the British government to advise on the production of chemical weapons for use in the Crimean War (1853–56), Faraday refused to participate – citing ethical reasons. Thomas, Lord Cochrane had no such reservations and enthusiastically promoted the use of poison gas.

JOSEPH MALLORD WILLIAM TURNER R.A,

J.M.W. Turner was born on 23 April (St George's Day) 1775 at 26, Maiden Lane, Covent Garden in London, where his father, a Devonshire man, was a barber. Turner's schooling was rudimentary. His father taught him to read; but all his life he remained virtually illiterate. By thirteen William, as he was known, already showed a precocious talent for drawing and water colouring. He began to display his work, which was sold to customers, in the window of his father's shop. In 1789, aged fourteen Turner was accepted into the Royal Academy schools: from where he soon began to exhibit his watercolours. At fifteen Turner exhibited one of his paintings at the Royal Academy, an extraordinary accomplishment for one so young. He spent the next few years travelling and making architectural drawings throughout England and Wales.

Joseph Mallord William Turner (aged 24) self-portrait
Tate Britain, London

He was befriended by Tom Girtin (1775–1802), with whom he began a fruitful liaison. Girtin drew the outlines of the paintings while Turner washed in the colours. Their cooperation greatly enhanced the beauty, charm and delicacy of current watercolour painting. Girtin died aged twenty-six – later Turner remarked that, "had Girtin lived, I would have starved". During these early years Turner concentrated on purely topographical subjects, painted in the best techniques and traditions of the period.

He also caught the attention of several engravers, who employed him in designing for *en gravure* magazines; and finished several uncompleted drawings by the landscape painter John Robert Cozens (1752–97). He was also introduced to the work of another popular landscape artist, Richard Wilson (1714–82), a Welshman who had cofounded the Royal Academy: and the influence of these two great artists inspired Turner to create landscapes – that soon went far beyond an accurate rendition of what he saw, enhancing them with a wonderful luminous imagination.

Rochester, on the River Medway by Joseph Mallord William Turner (1822)
Tate, London

From 1792–99, when at the age of twenty-four he was elected an Associate member of the Royal Academy, Turner increasingly moved from his comfortable niche as a topographical watercolourist to painting in oils: a fine example is *Millbank at Moonlight*, painted in 1797. The first of his oils to be shown at the Royal Academy was *Fishermen at Sea* in 1796, which won high critical acclaim; and in 1802 Turner became a full Academician. At this point he started to paint in the style of the 17th century Old Masters, much influenced by the works of Nicolas Poussin, Willem Van der Welde, Claude Lorrain and Albert Cuyp. Turner also travelled widely, first of all to Scotland, Wales, Yorkshire and the Lake District; before crossing the Channel, to put together a collection of over 400 drawings in France and Switzerland. A visit in the same year to the Louvre, recently filled with Napoleon's booty, introduced him to the great Italian painters, especially Titian. Nonetheless, Turner went on to develop his own romantic individualism, exemplified in *Calais Pier* in 1803.

In 1800 Turner began living with a widow, Sarah Danby by whom he probably had two children. That year his mother died in an asylum. His father then joined Turner's household where he remained until his death in 1830, acting as Turner's principal studio assistant and agent. Turner started to display signs of the reclusive eccentricity which pursued him into old age. He was reticent, odd and unsociable, preferring to paint and travel alone. As he grew older Turner became ever more disinclined to sell his paintings. A sale depressed him for days.

The Fighting Temeraire by Joseph Mallord William Turner (1839)
National Gallery, London

In 1804, with more commissions than he could satisfy, Turner opened a gallery at 64, Harley Street. He provoked huge controversy amongst the critics. They were sharply divided by his delicate gradations of light on theatrically drawn mountains, waves, shipwrecks and fantastical architecture, which induced powerful and climactic feelings, all shot through with vivid colour. *Frosty Morning* in 1813 and *Crossing the Brook* in 1815 (the year of the Battle of Waterloo) are representative of this period.

Turner's great 17th century hero Claude Lorrain had drawn copies of all his own paintings into a six-volume compendium he called *Liber Veritatis* ("the Book of Truth"). In 1807 Turner, partly to rebut his critics, began a similar series of engravings, which he called *Liber Studiorum* ("the Book of Studies"). His purpose was to illustrate and record his own interpretation of the complete spectrum of landscape painting. In 1819 however, after producing some 71 plates, his grossly underpaid employees lost interest and he abandoned the project.

From 1814 Turner began a series of historic and allegorical Carthaginian paintings. He associated them with quotations from Shakespeare, Milton, Pope, Byron, *Seasons* by James Thomson, who wrote *Rule, Britannia!* – and his own uncompleted poem, *Fallacies of Hope*. In 1819 Turner paid his first visit to Italy – his obsession with classical influences was apparent in *Ulysses deriding Polyphemus*, painted in 1829, considered to be amongst his masterpieces. His achievements as a watercolourist peaked with his illustrations for a *History of Richmondshire* in 1823, *Rivers of England* in 1824, *The Provincial Antiquities of Scotland* by Sir Walter Scott, between 1819–26, and the *Rivers of France* in 1834.

During the 1820s Turner travelled between England, Scotland and the continent, assembling some 1500 drawings from which he painted a series of outstanding oils. His style had become purer, with more varied colours.

In 1829 Turner visited Italy again, initiating his last artistic period: which embraces his famous Venice collection; *The Fighting Temeraire* in 1838; and *Rain, Steam and Speed* in 1844 – the latter highlighting Turner's intense interest in the emerging industrial age. He also explored in dramatic fashion the components of steam, fire and water: in *Burning of the House of Lords and Commons* and *A Fire at Sea*, both in 1835, and *Rockets and Blue Lights* in 1840.

In the last twenty years of his life Turner slipped into a strange existence. As his wealth grew, he became secretive and introverted, preferring to live alone in a series of taverns in the east end of London. His public involvement with the Royal Academy diminished: and in 1836 he resigned his Professorship of Perspective, which he had held since 1807. In 1846 he bought a house in Chelsea, shared with Sarah Booth, a widow whose name he adopted. He travelled frequently to the continent; where he amassed a collection of 20,000 drawings made in Italy, Switzerland, Germany and France.

By the 1840s Turner had become obsessed with the effects of light – mass and form were increasingly blurred and unimportant. He created a revolution in painting techniques: dominated by fluidity, light, space and colour. In this he anticipated, and indeed inspired, the French Impressionists. He won the support of the influential art critic John Ruskin (1819–1900), which was reflected in the first volume of his *Modern Painters* in 1843.

Turner exhibited for the last time in 1850. The next year he disappeared: and it was many months before his housekeeper finally tracked him down to a lodging house in Chelsea, where he had been living under his assumed name of Booth – confused and probably mad. He died the following day, 19 December 1851 (the year before the Duke of Wellington), and was buried, at his own request, in St. Paul's Cathedral.

Turner left a fortune of over £ 140,000 (£ 108 million today), to be applied to the welfare of "decayed artists". He left all his works, some 400 paintings and 20,000 drawings to the National Gallery, as the "Turner Bequest". Sadly his relations, though distant, successfully contested his will: leaving little for his charity. Turner's works are to be seen in two extensions of Tate Britain: the Sir John Duveen Gallery, built in 1908, and the Clore, designed by James Stirling in 1987; most of his drawings are in the British Museum; and a few oil paintings are in the National Gallery.

It has been suggested that Turner was slightly colour-blind: and that this particularly affected his perception of red and blue. It is also very likely that, late in life, the centre of his field of vision was blurred by cataracts: which would explain the shimmering light effects at the edges of his paintings, and their slightly foggy centres.

One evening when Turner was painting a sunset from a Thames bridge, an old lady approached him and said: "Oh Mr Turner, I don't think I have ever seen a sunset like one of them before", to which Turner replied "Don't you wish you had?".

Turner was unusual in that he remained profoundly successful throughout his life, in spite of spanning an artistic period of extraordinary change. Grounded in the formal disciplines of the 18th century, which he effortlessly and brilliantly reproduced in the remarkably accurate work of his early years, Turner went on to knock on the very door of Impressionism. His earlier works were mostly settings for the human form, whereas his latter years were concerned with expressing the unharnessed forces of nature. Such an astonishing breadth of subject matter marks Turner out as the most innovative painter of his century.

THE HOPE DIAMOND

Thomas Hope (1769–1831), an art collector who invented the Battenburg cake, was born in Amsterdam on 30 August 1769, the same year as the Duke of Wellington. He was the eldest of the three sons of John Hope (1737–1784) and his wife, the daughter of Rotterdam's burgomaster. John Hope was a member of an immensely rich family of Amsterdam merchants descended from Sir Thomas Hope, lord advocate, and the Earls of Hopetoun. He was a partner in Europe's

The Smithsonian Institute, the world's largest museum complex and research organisation is in Washington D.C. It includes 19 museums, a zoo and nine research centres. It has over 136 million items in its collections. It was founded in 1846, for the "increase and diffusion" of knowledge, from a bequest of 104,960 gold sovereigns (£78 million today) by the British mineralogist and chemist, James Smithson FRS (1765–1829) – who had never even visited the US. Smithson was the natural, but unacknowledged son of Sir Hugh Smithson, 4th Bt – who changed his name to Hugh Percy, and became the 1st Duke of Northumberland. Smithson was a brilliant scientist and a shrewd investor. The motive for the bequest is unknown: perhaps it was to found an institution that would outlast his father's dynasty.

then most powerful merchant bank, Hope & Co. – which raised huge sums for US and European governments.

Thomas's eldest son, Henry Thomas Hope (1808–62), an art patron and M.P., was persuaded by Isambard Brunel to chair the Eastern Steam Navigation Co., principally to raise funds to build the SS *Great Eastern*. His daughter, Henrietta named the ship in November 1857.

Henry Hope acquired the Hope Diamond from his uncle, who had bought it in London. It was put on display in the 1851 Great Exhibition of London. After many changes in ownership, in 1958 New York diamond merchant Harry Winston gave it to the Smithsonian Institute, sending it through the US Mail in a plain brown paper bag.

The Hope Diamond

The Hope Diamond is a 45.52 carat, deep blue diamond, cut from the Tavernier Blue, which was mined at Kollur in Golconda in India: and was originally a crudely cut triangle of 115 carats. French merchant-traveller Jean-Baptiste Tavernier purchased it in about 1660. According to legend, the Tavernier Blue had been stolen from an eye of a sculpted idol of the goddess Sita. In 1668 Tavernier sold it to King Louis XIV of France. His court jeweller cut it to a little over 67 carats. Louis XVI gave the diamond to Marie Antoinette. In September 1792, during the French Revolution, it was stolen. It reappeared, without explanation, ten or so years later in London. Most of the stories attributing ill fortune and early deaths to its owners are false. Whilst under the care of the Smithsonian there have been no untoward incidents – so far.

THOMAS TELFORD'S GREAT BRIDGE OVER THE MENAI STRAITS

Before the Menai Suspension Bridge, the only way to and from Anglesey and the mainland was by ferry or hazardously, by foot at low tide. The Act of Union with Ireland in 1800 increased the flow of traffic between Dublin and the port of Holyhead on Anglesey. Thomas Telford was given the task of improving the road between London and Holyhead and constructing a bridge over the Menai Straits.

Vessels with 100-foot masts had to be able to pass beneath it at high water, necessitating a suspension bridge. Tower construction began in 1819 and was completed in 1824. Next came sixteen huge chain cables, supporting a 580-foot span. To prevent rusting, the cables were treated with a thick coating of warm linseed oil – not as the White Knight said to Alice, in *Through the Looking Glass* by Lewis Carroll:

"I heard him then, for I had just
    completed my design,
To keep the Menai bridge from rust
    By boiling it in wine?"

Thomas Telford (1757–1834) was born in Dumfriesshire. A civil engineer, architect and stonemason, who specialised in road, bridge and canal construction, he built the Ellesmere, Caledonian and Gota canals (the last between Gothenburg and Stockholm in Sweden) – as well as St Katherine's docks in London. He was a pioneer in the use of cast iron for large scale structures. His most notable achievement was the design and construction of the great Menai Suspension Bridge (Pont Grog y Borth). Altogether, he built 1,200 bridges and over 1,000 miles of road. He was the first president of the Institution of Civil Engineers, founded in 1818. The Poet Laureate, Robert Southey (1774–1843) gave Telford a punning nickname "Colossus of Roads". He was buried in Westminster Abbey.

Thomas Telford's
Menai Bridge

The bridge opened on 26 January 1826, reducing the journey from London from 36 to 27 hours. In 1893 the wooden roadway was replaced with steel decking. In 1938 the wrought iron chains were replaced with steel ones – while the bridge remained open. In 2005 the bridge was featured on British one pound coins.

Thomas Telford's Menai Bridge

VICTORIA, QUEEN OF GREAT BRITAIN AND IRELAND (1819–1901), EMPRESS OF INDIA (1876–1901)

Alexandrina Victoria was born on 24 May 1819 at Kensington Palace in London. Her ancestry was entirely German. She was the only legitimate child of Edward, Duke of Kent (1767–1820), the fourth son of King George III. Her mother was Princess Victoire of Saxe-Coburg-Saalfeld: whose brother Ernst, Duke of Saxe-Coburg-Saalfeld, was the father of Albert, who became Victoria's husband; and Leopold, who became King of the Belgians. On 23 January 1820 the Duke of Kent caught a chill and died, only a week before his father. Victoria, now fourth in line for the throne, was left with her mother as her only guardian. The Duchess of Kent herself was under the influence of the unscrupulous Sir John Conroy, comptroller of her household. An Irish soldier and adventurer, he was rumoured to be the Duchess's lover.

Victoria spent her childhood in shabby Kensington Palace. She had little company of her own age but found compensation in her dolls and small dogs. "Dash", a King Charles spaniel and a gift from Conroy, was the first of a long line of cherished pets. With her last breath, she called for her little Pomeranian dog. She coped with a deprived childhood, through her strength of character and the support of her governess, Baroness Lehzen.

With memories of her obese and extravagant uncle, the previous Prince Regent, who became King George IV in 1820 and died in 1830, only too fresh in the nation's mind, Victoria reached her eighteenth birthday – relieving the country of the dire possibility of another regency, under her mother. In the early hours of 20 June 1837, Victoria's second uncle, King William IV died: and Victoria ascended the throne.

On 28 June 1837 she was crowned amid great public acclaim. Her first prime minister, the suave and elegant Whig Lord Melbourne,

> Sir John Conroy, 1st Baronet (1767–1854) saw an opportunity to use Victoria to acquire influence and wealth. With the co-operation of Victoria's mother, he instituted the "Kensington system": to bend her will to their purpose, by isolating her from her "wicked uncles" and contemporaries. They hoped that this ploy would ensure that Victoria would look only to them for advice when she became queen.

> Louise Lehzen (1784–1870), daughter of a Hanoverian Lutheran pastor, was the most important formative influence on Victoria. Taking Queen Elizabeth I as the role model for her charge, Lehzen instilled in the spirited, but haughty and stubborn princess a deep sense of duty and a work ethic which lasted all her life.

Queen Victoria by Sir George Hayter (1838)
National Portrait Gallery, London

played an avuncular, almost romantic role in the fatherless young queen's life. Victoria became so susceptible to his charm that she was referred to by contemporary wits as "Mrs Melbourne".

Melbourne's influence was not entirely beneficial. He hid from Victoria the true nature of the nation's appalling social problems. He considered Lord Shaftesbury's efforts to improve the working conditions of children in mines unnecessary – and he encouraged the impressionable Victoria to favour his Whig party, uncritically and inappropriately. In 1839 her political partiality led to the first two crises of her reign.

The first concerned her lady-in-waiting, Lady Flora Hastings: whose family were committed Tories. When it was noticed that her stomach was swelling, Victoria ordered a pregnancy examination – in spite of Flora's vehement denials of indiscretion. A few months later Flora died in great pain from liver cancer, undetected by the incompetent Doctor Clark, who had also misdiagnosed her pregnancy. Victoria was hissed at the theatre and at Ascot as a result. The second, "bedchamber" crisis broke in May, when Melbourne resigned in favour of Sir Robert Peel. According to convention, the queen was expected to change her household attendants – in line with the change of political parties. On this occasion, egged on by Melbourne, she refused to do so: Peel refused to form an administration as a result and Melbourne made a rather undignified and unpopular return.

On 15 October 1839 Victoria proposed to her cousin Albert (1819–61): in full his name was Franz Albrecht August Karl Emanuel, Prince von Sachsen-Coburg-Gotha. They were married on 10 February 1840. Children followed in quick succession.

Her first child Victoria, the Princess Royal, was born in 1840. In 1858 she married the crown prince Frederick of Prussia and became the mother of the future Kaiser Wilhelm II. Outliving her mother by six months, she died of spine cancer in 1901. The Prince of Wales (later King Edward VII) was born in 1841. Victoria had an iron constitution. During nine pregnancies, she suffered no miscarriages or stillbirths and all her children reached adulthood. By the standards of even aristocratic Victorian families, this was remarkable. In 1853 Victoria became the first queen to have an anaesthetic, while giving birth to her eighth child, Prince Leopold. She was also the first monarch to be photographed; and in 1878, to take a private telephone call.

Her last child, Princess Beatrice, was born in 1857. In 1859 Victoria was presented with her first grandchild; and twenty years later, her first great-grandchild – by the time she died she had been blessed with another thirty-six. It was little wonder that she was known as the "Grandmother of Europe".

Victoria's fecundity came at a price. She suffered from severe post-natal depressions and intensely disliked the whole business of

Prince Albert of Saxe-Coburg-Gotha replica by Franz Xaver Winterhalter (1859)

National Portrait Gallery, London

Victoria passed hæmophilia on to several of her children, a condition where blood lacks the ability to clot: severe cases suffer, and can even die from uncontrolled bleeding, caused by the smallest cut. It subsequently afflicted most of the royal families of Europe. Haemophilia is more likely to occur in the children of older fathers: Victoria's father was fifty-six when she was born. Her great-grandson Alexei, Tsarevitch of Russia, was severely affected. He was attended by two devoted Cossacks, whose 24-hour task was to prevent accidental bruising and bleeding which might have killed the boy. In 1918, along with the rest of his family, he was murdered by the less considerate Bolsheviks instead, aged thirteen.

Albert is credited with introducing the Christmas card and Christmas tree to Britain. Although early cards have a strong Germanic influence (15th century Germans sent *Andachtsbilder*, greeting cards with devotional pictures), it had been an English tradition dating from the early 1400s to send New Year greetings. John Horsley R.A. (1817–1903), Isambard Brunel's brother-in-law, made the first known commercial Christmas card, a hand-coloured lithograph, in 1843.

In 1846 Victoria and Albert were portrayed standing with their children around a Christmas Tree in the *Illustrated London News*. The triangular shape of the fir tree, to represent the Holy Trinity of God the Father, Son and Holy Spirit, had been revered as "God's Tree" in Germany for centuries. It quickly became fashionable.

The Crystal Palace at the Great Exhibition in 1851

child-bearing ("much more of our being like a cow or a dog"), which she referred to as the "shadow side of marriage". Neither was she taken with "frog-like" babies and small children: whom she lumped with pets, as being "a constant source of worry and vexation". She had scant regard for her children's happiness when it came to choosing their husbands or wives: dynastic imperatives overruled all other considerations – and they were cowed into obedience. Beatrice was allowed to marry only if she promised to continue living with and caring for her mother. Victoria was dutiful but selfish, not at all a kind or sympathetic parent.

Initially Victoria excluded Albert from any share in government, a position which Melbourne persuaded her to soften, by allowing him to read state papers. Albert responded so punctiliously and efficiently that, within six months, he had a key to all the despatch boxes. A succession of uncomfortable, sometimes wretched pregnancies meant that Albert gradually assumed Victoria's workload, to the point where: "It is obvious that while she has the title, he is really discharging the functions of the Sovereign", in the words of the diarist Charles Greville.

With the departure to Germany in 1842 of Baroness Lehzen, Albert assumed total control of the queen's life. He became her private secretary and manager of her private estate, considerably increasing her revenues: to such an extent that he was able to persuade his wife to acquire Osborne House on the Isle of Wight and Balmoral on Deeside, in Aberdeenshire. Osborne was bought as a summer holiday retreat. Albert built a Swiss cottage for their children, the first "Wendy House", complete with a garden in which the children were taught how to grow vegetables – and the principles of commerce, by then selling them to their father for the royal kitchen.

In 1848 Victoria leased the Balmoral estate; and bought it in 1852 from the trustees of Sir Robert Gordon for £30,000 (£23 million today). Albert designed the "Scottish baronial" Castle himself, which is still used every summer by the royal family. Although festooned with tartan, the interior was not very cosy. Ministers hauling up from London hated staying there; and the Tsar of Russia remarked that even Siberia was warmer. Victoria's *Highland Journals* of 1867 and 1883 were instant best-sellers.

Albert's greatest moment arrived in 1851 with the Great Exhibition: an international trade fair of huge proportions, displaying Britain's astonishing wealth and the latest technology – all

housed in the glass-walled Crystal Palace,
erected in Hyde Park.

The Great Exhibition of the Works of
Industry of all Nations, was organised by Prince
Albert, Henry Cole, Francis Henry, Charles
Dilke and other members of the Royal Society
for the Encouragement of Arts, Manufactures
and Commerce, as a celebration of modern
industrial technology and design. Isambard
Brunel was on the committee.

The Crystal Palace was designed by Joseph
Paxton and constructed from cast iron frame

components and glass. The huge structure
was 1,848 feet long, 408 feet wide and 108 feet
high; and took, from blueprint to grand
opening, 2,000 men nine months to build. It
enclosed not only trees, but hundreds of
sparrows. In despair at their droppings, the
committee turned to the old Duke of
Wellington, who suggested introducing
sparrow-hawks. The building was later
moved and re-erected at Sydenham in south
London, an area which was renamed Crystal
Palace. It was destroyed by fire in 1934.

Six million people, nearly a third of the
entire population at the time, visited the
Exhibition. Profits of £186,000 (£144 million
today) were used to found the Victoria and
Albert , Science and Natural History
Museums: all built in the area to the south of
the exhibition, which was nicknamed
"Albertopolis". George Jennings designed the
first public conveniences in the Retiring
Rooms of the Crystal Palace, for which he
charged one penny (£3–22p today) – hence
the expression, "To spend a penny".

Sir Joseph Paxton was born in 1803,
the seventh son of a farming family,
at Milton Bryan in Bedfordshire. In
1823, whilst employed as a garden
boy at the Horticultural Society's
Chiswick Gardens, he caught the eye
of William Cavendish, 6th Duke of
Devonshire – who took him on as
Head Gardener at Chatsworth aged
20, one of the finest gardens in
Britain. Among several other large
projects at Chatsworth, such as the
Rock Garden, the Emperor Fountain
(twice the height of Nelson's
Column) and the rebuilding of
Edensor village, he is best
remembered for his glass houses.

In 1850 he designed Mentmore
Towers in Buckinghamshire for Baron Mayer de Rothschild. He was
knighted after the Exhibition, made a fortune from speculating in the
railways and was Liberal M.P. for Coventry from 1854 until his death in
1865.

- **Sir Joseph Paxton by Octavius Oakley (*c.*1850)**
National Portrait Gallery, London

Albert and Victoria took a keen interest in foreign affairs. They had unrivalled contacts
with the European royal houses, soon to be reinforced by their own children's marriages.
Victoria was the first reigning British sovereign to visit France since Henry VIII in 1520. Albert
expected to be consulted on British Foreign policy – however this brought him into conflict
with Lord Palmerston, the Foreign Secretary.

With the strong disapproval of both Albert and Victoria, Palmerston blithely encouraged
Italian nationalist movements that threatened the Austrian Empire. In 1848 he went too far.
Having endorsed the *coup d'état* which brought Louis Napoleon to the French throne without

Henry John Temple, 3rd Viscount Palmerston (1784–1865) was Foreign Secretary three times and Prime Minister twice, between 1855–65. He entered parliament as a Tory in 1807 and, without a seat in the cabinet, was Secretary at War for nearly twenty years. In 1830 he joined the Whig Party. As Foreign Secretary, he strongly supported British interests abroad – using "gunboat diplomacy" whenever it suited.

Between 1830–31 Palmerston was largely responsible for winning independence for Belgium in 1831 and Greece in 1832; and he strongly supported the creation of the Kingdom of Italy. In 1856 he concluded the Crimean War and refused to embroil Britain in the American Civil war in late 1862. Known as "Pam", he was a symbol of Britain abroad – and the country's most popular politician. In 1864, when it was gleefully reported to his opponent Disraeli that the eighty year-old Palmerston had ruined his electoral chances by fathering a bastard, Disraeli is said to have replied, "Nonsense, he will sweep the country".

Palmerston's last words were: "Die, my dear doctor, that is the last thing I shall do".

- **Henry John Temple, 3rd Viscount Palmerston by Francis Cruikshank (c.1855)**
National Portrait Gallery, London

Florence Nightingale OM (1820–1910), born into a rich English family, was named after her birthplace in Italy. She went to Turkey during the Crimean war as a volunteer nurse. In charge of filthy, rat infested, waterless wards, she bought the necessary materials out of her own resources. She was immortalised as the "Lady with the Lamp", because of her nightly rounds of the wards. Despite suffering from depression and being almost bedridden for over fifty years, she was a fine statistician and hospital administrator. Her vision led to the establishment of an Army Medical School and a Sanitary Department in India. She established the first nursing school, as well as ensuring proper training for midwives and Poorhouse nurses. In 1907 she was the first woman to receive the Order of Merit.

- **Florence Nightingale by Sir George Scharf (28 December 1857)**
National Portrait Gallery, London

informing his Queen, the prime minister, Lord John Russell had little choice but to sack him. Hugely popular, Palmerston was soon returned to office as Home Secretary. After Albert's death Victoria came round to Palmerston. She liked his conservative domestic policies and warmed to his protection of British interests.

The Crimean War (October 1853 to February 1856) was fought principally in the Crimean peninsula of the Ukraine: with Turkey (the Ottoman Empire), Britain, France and Sardinia-Piedmont allied against the Russians. It was the first media war and was well reported and photographed, highlighting the appalling consequences of poor equipment and medical care. Over 250,000 casualties were suffered in total by both sides, mostly from disease and malnutrition. The war was sparked by Russian demands to protect Orthodox subjects of the Turkish sultan and was bungled by both sides. Two bloody battles, Balaclava and Inkerman, were fought along the Alma River, before the siege and capture of the port of Sevastopol by the allies. Russia eventually accepted peace terms, ratified by the Congress of Paris on 30 March 1856 – with very little having been achieved by either side.

Victoria however, fought a good war: by responding to disasters with sympathy and drive. She placed herself at the head of committees of ladies arranging relief for the troops; and supported Florence Nightingale by visiting military hospitals and decorating wounded soldiers. She also instituted the Victoria Cross.

No sooner had the country recovered from the Crimean War

FitzRoy James Henry Somerset (1788–1855), was the youngest son of the 5th Duke of Beaufort. Educated at Westminster School, he entered the army in 1804 and, in 1807, joined Wellesley's staff. Severely wounded at Busaco, he showed outstanding courage storming the breaches at both Ciudad Rodrigo and Badajoz. Somerset was Wellington's right-hand man: first as his *aide-de-camp* and then his military secretary – until he lost his own right arm at Waterloo.

He became an M.P., but resumed his service as Wellington's military secretary in 1827, until the Duke died in 1852: when he was created Baron Raglan. In 1854, having never directed any large formation in the field, he was unaccountably promoted to full General in command of the British army sent to the Crimea.

He was brave and obedient, but this was a promotion too far. If the disasters of the Crimean War had a single cause, it was the incompetence of Lord Raglan. Appalling logistical support from Britain hardly helped: but he refused to buy wood from Turkey, to make floors for the tents, or to allow the troops even to light fires, despite a bitter and damp winter. Before the Siege of Sevastopol, his army had only 9,000 out of nearly 35,000 soldiers fit for duty.

At the battles of Balaclava and Inkerman he repeatedly sent greatly outnumbered detachments to their deaths. Only the stoicism and bravery of his soldiers prevented the total destruction of his army – remembered to this day whenever "the thin red line" is mentioned. Modern items of warm woollen clothing reflect on the weather they had to endure: Balaclava, Cardigan and the Raglan overcoat, which has sleeves continuing in one piece up to the neck – very practical for a man with only one arm.

Raglan's inability to give sensible or timely commands on the battlefield, and his failure to observe the undisguised animosity between the Earl of Lucan and his brother-in-law the Earl of Cardigan, led directly to the disastrous Charge of the Light Brigade during the Battle of Balaclava, on 25 October 1854.

• **Charge of the Light Brigade by Richard Caton Woodville (1825–55)**

National Army Museum, London

Lucan, commanding the Heavy Brigade, misunderstood Raglan's hopelessly unclear orders: and, without questioning them, instructed Cardigan to lead 673 troopers of the Light Brigade straight into the "Valley of Death", as it was described by the poet Tennyson. Twenty battalions of Russian infantry supported by over fifty guns were deployed on both sides and at the opposite end of the valley. Lucan himself was to follow with the Heavy Brigade – unsurprisingly, Lucan changed his mind.

The brigade lost 118 men killed and 127 wounded. Only 195 men still had horses. The reckless bravery exhibited in this futile action prompted the French Marshal, Pierre Bosquet to say: *"C'est magnifique, mais ce n'est pas la guerre"* ("It is magnificent, but it is not war"). To begin with, the Russians thought that the British were drunk.

Cardigan had led the charge from the front and never looked back. He reached the Russian guns, fought bravely and then trotted back alone up the valley – to eat a champagne dinner on his yacht in Balaclava harbour.

Raglan remained in command for a further nine months, now as a Field Marshal – presumably to fool the British public into believing that the conduct of the war was safe in his hand. He died of dysentery on 29 June 1855 – ten days after yet another assault on Sevastopol had failed. He was buried at Badminton, the Duke of Beaufort's great house in Gloucestershire.

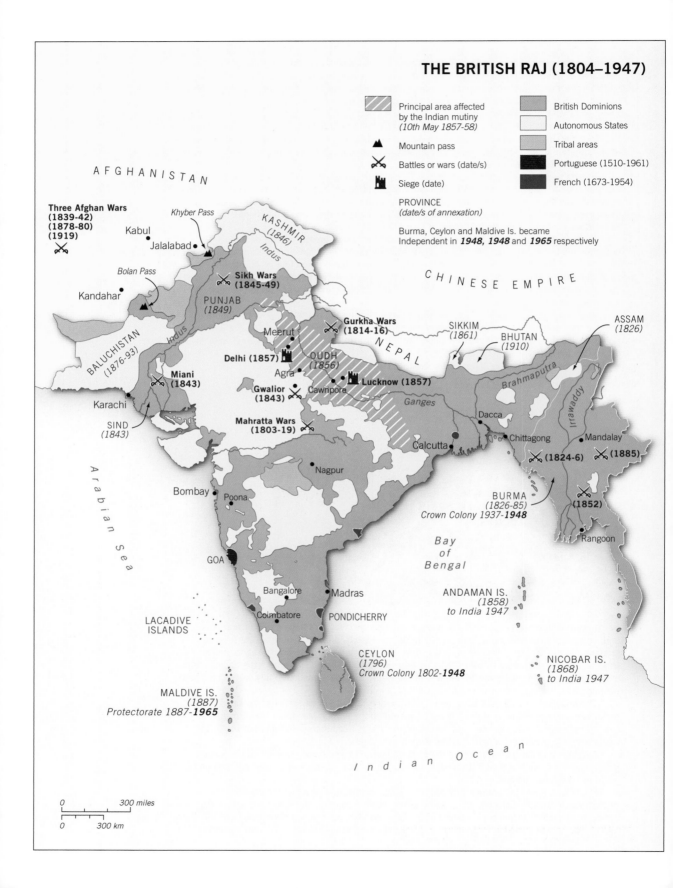

THE BRITISH RAJ (1804–1947)

Principal area affected
by the Indian mutiny
(10th May 1857-58)

▲ Mountain pass

⚔ Battles or wars (date/s)

🏰 Siege (date)

PROVINCE
(date/s of annexation)

Burma, Ceylon and Maldive Is. became
Independent in *1948, 1948* and *1965* respectively

British Dominions

Autonomous States

Tribal areas

Portuguese (1510-1961)

French (1673-1954)

AFGHANISTAN

**Three Afghan Wars
(1839-42)
(1878-80)
(1919)**
⚔

Kabul

Jalalabad ●

Khyber Pass

KASHMIR
(1846)

Indus

CHINESE EMPIRE

Bolan Pass

⚔ **Sikh Wars
(1845-49)**

PUNJAB
(1849)

Kandahar ●

BALUCHISTAN
(1876-93)

Indus

Meerut ●

**Gurkha Wars
(1814-16)** ⚔

SIKKIM
(1861)

ASSAM
(1826)

BHUTAN
(1910)

Delhi (1857) 🏰

Agra ●

OUDH
(1856)

N E P A L

Brahmaputra

⚔ **Miani
(1843)**

Karachi ●

SIND
(1843)

**Gwalior
(1843)** ⚔

Cawnpore ●

🏰 **Lucknow (1857)**

Ganges

Dacca ●

Chittagong ●

Irrawaddy

Mandalay ●

**Mahratta Wars
(1803-19)** ⚔

Calcutta ●

⚔ **(1824-6)**

⚔ **(1885)**

● Nagpur

A
r
a
b
i
a
n

S
e
a

Bombay ●
Poona ●

*B a y
o f
B e n g a l*

⚔ **(1852)**

**BURMA
(1826-85)**
*Crown Colony 1937-**1948***

GOA

Bangalore ●

Madras ●

**ANDAMAN IS.
(1858)**
to India 1947

Rangoon ●

Coimbatore ●

PONDICHERRY

LACADIVE
ISLANDS

**NICOBAR IS.
(1868)**
to India 1947

CEYLON
(1796)
*Crown Colony 1802-**1948***

I n d i a n   O c e a n

MALDIVE IS.
(1887)
*Protectorate 1887-**1965***

0			300 miles

0			300 km

Until the day she died, Albert's clothes were laid out on his bed every evening at Windsor; and every morning his shaving bowl was filled with hot water. Victoria slept below a head-and-shoulders photograph of his corpse hung on the wall.

than alarming news of insurrection and massacres by sepoys (native troops), serving with the army of the East India Company, reached Britain. The Mutiny, or India's First War of Independence as it is sometimes called today, lasted from May 1857 to June 1858. It was suppressed with ruthless severity: but it was the end of the 258 year-old Company's rule of the subcontinent. From 1858–1947 India was ruled directly by the British Government.

On 14 December 1861 Prince Albert died of typhoid fever, contracted from the insanitary water supply at Windsor Castle – bringing to an abrupt end the "Albertine" monarchy. Albert's health had been poor in the years leading up to his death. Modern diagnosis suggests that he was suffering from bowel cancer. Albert's influence on Victoria endured throughout her long life. She maintained his methodical, disciplined approach to state business. By the time of his death, Albert had transformed Victoria's fragile prerogative on her accession into a formidable, if informal authority over her prime ministers.

Victoria was plunged into a deep depression, refusing all ceremonial duties. She spent over four months each year secluded at Balmoral and Osborne, causing severe inconvenience to her ministers.

Keeping faith with Albert, Victoria throughout her self-imposed retreat continued to read state papers meticulously and maintained a keen interest in cabinet appointments. She insisted on wearing her widow's weeds long after the time required by the already prolonged mourning conventions of the day. The people, at first sympathetic, became irritated by their sovereign's excessive seclusion – exacerbated by her refusal to involve the Prince of Wales in even insignificant official duties. Indeed, she resented and was jealous of the Prince and Princess of Wales's increasing popularity.

It was her prime minister Benjamin Disraeli, novelist and subtle observer of character, who roused Victoria from her depression. The greatest political rivalry of 19th century British politics was conducted between the conservative Disraeli and the liberal William Ewart Gladstone. Victoria knew that Albert had regarded Disraeli with grave suspicion, as "insufficiently a gentleman" and "an adventurer and unprincipled rogue"; but had approved of the priggish Gladstone. In 1868, at the start of his first administration, it was Disraeli who coaxed

During the long periods Victoria spent at Balmoral after Albert's death, she formed a deep attachment to John Brown (1826–83), one of the ghillies on the estate. Although no hard evidence to support the rumour has ever surfaced, at the time speculation of a romantic liaison, even a secret marriage began to circulate: to the extent that courtiers referred to Victoria, behind their hands, as "Mrs Brown". Victoria's body was laid in her coffin with Albert's dressing gown by her side – but in her left hand was placed a lock of Brown's hair and his portrait. It was recently revealed that Victoria's doctor, Sir James Reid had also secretly slipped Brown's mother's wedding ring on her finger.
• **John Brown by (Cornelius) Jabez Hughes**
National Portrait Gallery, London

Victoria blamed the Prince of Wales for causing Albert's death. Albert had fallen ill after a visit to Cambridge, to upbraid his son for having entertained a prostitute during a night of regimental revels in Ireland. His fellow officers had smuggled the girl, Nellie Clifden into his bed before the merry Edward retired. Most shocking, when the news came out, was that Edward had clearly enjoyed the experience.

The 2nd Sikh War (1849) completed the conquest of India. British complacency was shattered by the Mutiny (1857–58), which ended the charade of the East India Company rule. All of Burma had been annexed by 1885, leaving only the North-West Frontier as a sore to fester into the 1920s.

Benjamin Disraeli, 1st Earl of Beaconsfield (1804–81) was prime minister twice, in 1868 and from 1874–80. He was of Italian-Jewish descent but was baptised a Christian. This enabled him to enter politics because until the Jews were emancipated in 1858, they were excluded from parliament. In 1837 he was elected to parliament as a Conservative. To Prince Albert's intense annoyance, he brilliantly opposed Sir Robert Peel's decision to repeal the Corn Laws – and replaced him as leader of the Conservative Party. He was three times Chancellor of the Exchequer. He played a key role in the passing of the 1867 Reform Bill – an important step towards making Great Britain a full democracy.

During his second ministry, exercising an opportunistic foreign policy, he bought a controlling interest in the Suez Canal from the bankrupt Egyptian Khedive. He cemented his friendship with the Queen by conferring on her by Act of Parliament, the title "Empress of India" in 1876 (proclaimed in India on 1 January 1877).

By his attendance at the Congress of Berlin in 1878, he became the first British prime minister to practise shuttle diplomacy (by ship and train) – to great effect. He reduced Russian influence in the Balkans and secured British control of the strategically important island of Cyprus. Disraeli's imperialism generated two small wars, the Zulu war in 1878 and the second Afghan war between 1878–80, irrevocably committing Britain to the expansion of her empire. In the words of one historian, "There was not a single year in Queen Victoria's long reign in which somewhere in the world her soldiers were not fighting for her and her empire".

• **Benjamin Disraeli, Earl of Beaconsfield by Sir John Everett Millais, 1st Bt (1881)**
National Portrait Gallery, London

William Ewart Gladstone (1809–98) was four times prime minister between 1868 and 1894. He started his political career as a Tory, twice becoming Chancellor of the Exchequer; but by 1866 was Liberal Party leader. His first premiership achieved both educational and electoral reforms; as well as the disestablishment of the Irish Protestant Church in 1869. His second term saw the passing of the Reform Bill in 1884, which enfranchised six million voters. He sanctioned, reluctantly, the occupation of Egypt in 1882 – but his subsequent failure to rescue General Charles Gordon, besieged in Khartoum, enraged the Queen and brought down his government.

He spent the rest of his career failing to secure Home Rule for Ireland. He was buried in Westminster Abbey. Gladstone had a taste for self-flagellation and an obsession with trees – and saw nothing odd in inviting prostitutes back to No 10 Downing Street for tea.

• **William Ewart Gladstone by Eveleen Myers (*née* Tennant) (25 April 1890)**
National Portrait Gallery, London

the "widow of Windsor" from her long seclusion and charmed her. Disraeli was quite frank in his advice on using unbridled flattery in handling sovereigns, recommending that "you should lay it on with a trowel". He revealed his secret in queen-management: "I never deny, I never contradict, I sometimes forget". He shared her grief, restored her self-confidence and pandered to her love of gossip, securing her partisan support for his Conservative Party, to the great discomfort of his rival Gladstone.

Gladstone used to address Victoria, "like a public meeting". She regarded his moralistic approach as hypocritical and sanctimonious, calling him an "incomprehensible old fanatic" and a "half-mad firebrand". One of the few things that they agreed upon however, was an implacable opposition to the growing movement for women's suffrage. Gladstone's mission in life was Irish Home Rule, a cause with which Victoria, like most of her subjects, had little sympathy. She was intensely irritated by his frequent exhortations for her to resume her ceremonial duties. Disraeli lost no time in turning Victoria's increasing distaste for Gladstone and his "radical politics" into strong support for the Conservative Party. Victoria showed little interest in Disraeli's domestic reforms but was captivated by his adroit handling of the Suez Canal share purchase in 1875.

Victoria was convinced that Gladstone's Liberal Party was dominated by dangerous radicals. Unchecked, she believed they would undermine the country: even setting it on course for republicanism – a process which had been tumbling royal houses throughout Europe since 1848, the "year of revolutions". Under the administration of Lord Salisbury (1895–1902), Victoria's last years were much more congenial.

On 22 September 1896 Victoria became the longest reigning monarch in British history. She asked that the celebrations be delayed until 1897, the year of her Diamond Jubilee. Joseph Chamberlain (1836–1914), the Colonial Secretary planned the event as an Imperial festival. The Prime Ministers of every dominion and colony were invited; and the procession was composed of troops from every corner of the British Empire. A service of thanksgiving was held outside St Paul's Cathedral, with Victoria seated in her carriage throughout. Amongst many memorial tree plantings, 60 oak trees were planted at Henley-on-Thames in the shape of a Victoria Cross.

On 22 January 1901, in the sixty-fourth year of her reign, at 18:30 Victoria suffered a stroke and died. "We all feel a bit motherless today. Mysterious little Victoria is dead and fat, vulgar Edward is King", wrote the novelist Henry James (1843–1916).

Her deathbed was attended by Edward, Prince of Wales (King Edward VII) and her eldest grandson, the German Emperor Wilhelm II – with whom Britain, thirteen years later, would be at war. Her unembalmed (it was her wish) body crossed the Solent from Cowes on the Isle of Wight, on board the royal yacht *Alberta* flanked by two rows of warships: thirty from the Royal Navy, the remainder from the navies of Germany, France, Portugal and Japan. Minute guns were fired to mark her passing.

The Queen's body was encased in triple coffins of lead and oak, weighing over half a ton, dressed in white and wearing her wedding veil. After two days lying in state, while London was draped in purple and white (despite wearing it for so many years, she hated black), and a short service at St George's Chapel in Windsor Castle, on 4 February Victoria was buried beside Prince Albert in the mausoleum at Frogmore in Windsor Great Park. While her tomb was being sealed, it began to snow.

At her death few of Victoria's subjects could remember a time when she had not been on the throne. The population of Great Britain had doubled from 25 to 42 million. Railways and steamships crossed the world: the London Underground in 1863, the internal combustion engine and the motor car had arrived. High explosives, the machine gun and barbed wire

Robert Arthur Talbot Gascoyne-Cecil, 3rd Marquess of Salisbury (1830–1903), was educated at Eton College and Christchurch, Oxford. Over thirteen years between 1885–1902, he was three times prime minister – Victoria's tenth and last. As Foreign Secretary he played a leading part in convening the Congress of Berlin in 1878. He led the Conservative opposition in the House of Lords: disliking alliances, promoting only national interests and overseeing Imperial expansion in Africa. He once declared that if he could know what the Queen thought about an issue, he would know at once what the middle-classes thought too.
• **Robert Arthur Talbot Gascoyne-Cecil, 3rd Marquess of Salisbury by George Frederic Watts (1882)**
National Portrait Gallery, London

With advancing years Victoria became ever more detached from the world around her. She remained deeply suspicious of democracy. There were more women than men in 19th century Britain: due to a higher mortality rate in boys, emigration to the colonies and wastage in the armed forces. Men's rights far exceeded those of women. On marriage, a woman's property and income became her husband's. Children belonged to their father.

A man could divorce a woman for infidelity but not vice versa. However, as the century advanced small improvements in women's rights were made. The 1882 Married Women's Property Act allowed women to hold property after a divorce.

introduced new horrors to warfare; while in medicine, anaesthetics, disinfectants and X-rays were bringing increasing relief to a suffering humanity. Electric light brought safety to the streets of London and comfort to private homes. Trades Unions had begun to empower the working classes.

Victoria however, is chiefly remembered for the significance of the age in which she lived and to which she gave her name.

COURAGE UNDER FIRE

In 1834 the philosopher and economist, John Stuart Mill (1806–73) signed a contract with his publisher to write a history of the French Revolution. Realising that he had taken on too many commitments, he asked his friend the essayist and historian, Thomas Carlyle (1795–1881) to write it for him. Carlyle was hard up and accepted the commission with alacrity, believing it would make his literary reputation. Throughout the rest of that year, Carlyle wrote furiously for 18 hours a day. In March 1835 he delivered his completed Volume One to Mill for review. A few days later Mill arrived at Carlyle's house, at Ecclefechan in Dumfriesshire (just off the A74(M) motorway), in great distress. Mill had left the manuscript with his mistress, Harriet Taylor – and her illiterate maid had used it to light the fire. All that remained were a few charred leaves.

It was a household catastrophe. The Carlyles had no money; he had thrown away his notes – and he knew he could never write that volume again. He wrote despairingly: "I can remember still less of it than anything I ever wrote with such toil. It is gone". He would have to abandon the project. That night however, he dreamed that his dead father and brother implored him not to give up. The next day Carlyle started writing again. He wrote Volumes Two and Three before recreating Volume 1, writing the entire manuscript from memory, "directly and flamingly from the heart".

The heroic three-volume work, a colossal undertaking, describing the French Revolution from 1789–95 was published in 1837. It has never since been out of print. Carlyle kept the blackened remains of his original Volume One in his study for the rest of his life.

Thomas Carlyle by Sir John Everett Millais, 1st Bt (1877)

National Portrait Gallery, London

ALFRED, LORD TENNYSON

Alfred Tennyson, 1st Baron Tennyson of Aldworth and Freshwater (1809–92), was Poet Laureate (1850–92) – and one of the most popular and enduring poets of the Victorian age. He was born into a large family at Somersby in Lincolnshire, where his mentally unstable father was the rector. In 1827, after the local grammar school, he attended Trinity College, Cambridge: where he won the Chancellor's Gold Medal for a precocious poem, *Timbuctoo*. He also formed a deep, possibly homosexual attachment to Arthur Hallam, the son of the distinguished historian.

While still at Cambridge, in 1830 Tennyson published the much acclaimed *Poems, Chiefly Lyrical*: but on the death of his father, was forced to leave before taking his degree. At this time Arthur Hallam became engaged to his sister Emilia. In 1833 Tennyson published his second book of poetry, including his famous *The Lady of Shalott*: but the critical reviews were so harsh that he published nothing more for ten years – until Hallam suddenly died of a cerebral haemorrhage in Vienna in 1833. His death had a profound effect on Tennyson, inspiring his 1850 poem *In Memoriam A.H.H.*

Impoverished by an unwise investment in an ecclesiastical wood-carving business, Tennyson was living modestly in London when, in 1842 he published two volumes of poetry including *Locksley Hall*, *Morte d'Arthur*, *Tithonus* and *Ulysses*, which met with immediate success. In 1850 Tennyson reached the peak of his career: he was appointed Poet Laureate, succeeding William Wordsworth (1770–1850); he

Alfred, Lord Tennyson by Samuel Laurence, and Sir Edward Coley Burne-Jones, 1st Bt (c.1840)
National Portrait Gallery, London

finally published *In Memoriam A.H.H.*; and he married his childhood sweetheart, Emily Sellwood. They had two sons: one of whom, Hallam became Governor-General of Australia. In 1855 Tennyson published his immortal *Charge of the Light Brigade*; in 1859 *Idylls of the King*, a treatment of the Arthurian legend; and *Enoch Arden* in 1864. Queen Victoria was an avid reader of his work and asked to meet him. In 1884 she created him Baron Tennyson – the only 19th century English writer to be raised to the peerage other than Thomas Babington Macaulay (1800–59). He continued writing until he died, aged eighty-three. He was buried in Westminster Abbey.

Tennyson's popularity reflected the Victorian concern for order; and a tendency to moralise and indulge in melancholy. His religious beliefs were unconventional. In *In Memoriam*, he wrote: "There lives more faith in honest doubt, believe me than in half the creeds". Like so many of his contemporaries, he was troubled by the conflict of religious faith and expanding scientific knowledge.

Tennyson wrote lines that have become part of the English language: "Nature, red in tooth and claw"; "Better to have loved and lost than never to have loved at all"; "Theirs not to reason why"; and "Men may come and men may go, but I go on forever".

Tennyson took seventeen years to write his requiem – regarded as one of the greatest 19th century poems. Queen Victoria found it a great consolation after Prince Albert's death in 1861, saying: "Next to the Bible, *In Memoriam* is my comfort".

IT TOOK NEARLY 100 YEARS (1832–1928) TO GIVE EVERYONE THE VOTE

Reform Bills were Acts of Parliament to extend the franchise from rural constituencies and "rotten" or "pocket boroughs" (Old Sarum was a blatant example, where seven voters sent two members to parliament), controlled by the land owning nobility and gentry, to the largely unrepresented, rapidly expanding industrial towns. Before 1832 not even one adult male in ten had the vote: and though reform had been proposed in the 18th century by John Wilkes and William Pitt, "the Younger", there was strong national opposition to voting reform – following the carnage of the French Revolution. In 1792 France was the first country to adopt universal male suffrage. Perversely, French women were not given the vote until 1944.

The first Reform Bill was proposed in 1832 by the Whig Prime Minister Charles, 2nd Earl Grey (1764–1845), and introduced to Parliament by John, 1st Earl Russell (1792–1878) – the courage this required should not be underestimated. The Bill was passed in the House of

House of Commons (1833–43): This painting by Sir George Hayter (1792–1871) depicts the first session of the reformed House of Commons on 5 February 1833: held in St Stephen's Chapel, which was destroyed by fire in 1834. The picture includes some 375 out of the 658 Members and reflects the relative sizes of the parties. In the foreground are grouped figures from the Lords: Earl Grey, Viscount Melbourne and the Whigs on the left; and the Duke of Wellington with the Tories on the right. It took ten years to complete and another fifteen to sell. Ironically, it was the Tories who agreed to purchase it in 1858, for the recently founded National Portrait Gallery, London.

Commons three times; but on each occasion was rejected by the House of Lords. Grey, believing the country to be on the point of revolution if electoral reform was not introduced, threatened to ask King William IV to create enough Liberal peers to carry the bill. Under this threat, it was passed. The Act redistributed seats in the Commons – and reduced the franchise qualifications to include householders owning property worth £10 (£8,245 today). This added 217,000 voters to an electoral roll, not including Ireland, of only 435,000 (out of a population of over 16 million).

The second Reform Bill, introduced by the Tory Prime Minister Benjamin Disraeli in 1867, enfranchised a further one million voters, doubling the English and Welsh electorate to nearly two million (out of a population of over 20 million) – in the cynical hope that this would expand his popular support. The third Reform Bill, in 1884, enfranchised agricultural labourers; and, together with the Redistribution Act in 1885, created constituencies with an electoral roll of 50,000. These two acts tripled the electorate and laid the basis for universal male suffrage.

Women's suffrage was achieved largely through the efforts of the suffragettes. The name was coined by the *Daily Mail* for women in the late 19th 20th century who organised, under the leadership of Emmeline Pankhurst (1858–1928) and her daughter Christabel (1880–1958), a campaign of militant demonstrations for the right of women to vote. In 1889 Emmeline founded the Women's Franchise League: which in 1894 won the right of married women to vote in local elections. In 1903 she founded the Womens' Social and Political Union. By 1912 she was encouraging extreme militancy, usually in the form of arson attacks. She was arrested twelve times in one year. She died in 1928, just a few weeks before the Act was passed enfranchising women. In 1913 the suffragettes acquired a martyr in Emily Davison, who threw herself under King George V's horse Anmer in the Derby Stakes at Epsom Down.

Alexander Fraser Tytler, Lord Woodhouselee (1747–1813), a lawyer and writer born in Edinburgh, famously commented in 1787 on the new US constitution: "A democracy is always temporary in nature: it simply cannot exist as a permanent form of government. A democracy will continue to exist [only] until the voters discover that they can vote themselves generous gifts from the public treasury. From that moment on, the majority will always vote for the candidates who promise the most benefits from the public treasury, with the result that every democracy will finally collapse due to loose fiscal policy, [which is] always followed by a dictatorship. The average age of the world's greatest civilizations from the beginning of history has been about 200 years. During those 200 years, these nations always progressed through the following sequence: From bondage to spiritual faith; From spiritual faith to great courage; From courage to liberty; From liberty to abundance; From abundance to complacency; From complacency to apathy; From apathy to dependence; From dependence back into bondage".

Tytler made his observations after studying the causes of the fall of the Athenian Republic over 2,000 year earlier: but some may consider them relevant today.

Earl Grey, China tea flavoured with the rind of the bergamot orange, was named by Jacksons of Piccadilly for the 2nd Earl in 1830. The firm retains the original recipe.

In 1918 all men over twenty-one were given the vote: and for the first time, women over thirty. The Equal Franchise Act in 1928 finally put women on the same footing as men – and universal suffrage was at last achieved.

MRS BEETON

Isabella Mary Beeton, *née* Mayson was the author of the world famous cookery book, Mrs Beeton's *Book of Household Management*, in 1861. It was also the first "domestic science" manual. She was born on 12 March 1836 in Milk Street, off Cheapside in the City of London. On the early death of her father, her mother married the Clerk to Epsom Racecourse: where she was brought up, as the eldest of twenty-one children. Having been given a privileged education at Heidelberg in Germany, she was an accomplished pianist and fluent in both French and German. She also became a capable pastry cook and started work in Barnards, an Epsom confectioner. Her family thought this unseemly for a genteel young lady.

On 10 July 1856 Isabella married Samuel Beeton (1831–77), a publisher of popular books and magazines – who had spotted the appeal of Harriet Beecher Stowe's *Uncle Tom's Cabin* in 1852 and published the first English edition. The newly-wedded couple went to live at Hatch End in Harrow – where her neighbour was Horatia Ward (*née* Nelson), the daughter of Admiral Lord Nelson and Emma Hamilton.

Isabella Beeton (aged about 26) by Maull & Polyblank (1857)
National Portrait Gallery, London

In spite of difficult pregnancies and losing her first son, from 1859 for two years Isabella wrote monthly articles on cooking and household management for her husband's magazine: *The Englishwoman's Domestic Magazine*, which he had started in 1852. By 1856, selling for 2 pence (£5–50 today), it had a circulation of 50,000. Like many of her new class of suburban young women living away from home, Isabella had no mother to turn to. She was the first to identify and fill the need for a book of instructions.

Her articles were published in a single volume in 1861. The collection embraced every aspect of Victorian middle-class life: and, apart from cookery, offered advice on managing servants, child care, pets, sanitation, medicines, poisons and the law.

Isabella's *Book of Household Management* contained over 2,000 recipes, illustrated with coloured engravings and laid out in a format still used today. Her recipes were arranged alphabetically, in sections: with directions, ingredients, weights, prices, oven times and servings, all neatly and logically accessible. There were 100 recipes for soup, 200 for sauces and 128 for fish. Their appeal combined good living with economy. A compiler rather than an originator, Isabella's book provided a reliable domestic benchmark for an ambitious, prosperous and growing British middle-class.

Isabella also became a journalist, an occupation regarded then as quite shocking for a woman. From 1860 she shuttled back and forth to Paris, reporting on the latest fashions. These

Sam Beeton may have given Isabella syphilis on their honeymoon. It was a common enough hazard for even the most respectable Victorian young lady. In 1860 it was reckoned that there were at least 80,000 prostitutes on the streets of London alone.

were incorporated into her husband's magazine, using high quality fashion plates and the offer of a pattern service to readers: so that they could make their own clothes at home. It was a revolutionary development at the time.

On 6 February 1865 Isabella died from puerperal fever, probably caused by the failure of the attending physician to wash his hands, and peritonitis – eight days after the birth of her fourth child. She was only twenty-eight. Her first son had died of croup in 1857; and her second of scarlet fever in 1864. The ability of the Victorians to cope calmly with such disasters is astounding – and the contrast with today's "caring and counselling", "health and safety" society, is humbling.

Charles Frederick Worth, born in Bourne in Lincolnshire in 1825, was the *"father of haute couture"*. Apprenticed to two textile merchants in London, he joined Gagelin-Opigez, a well-known fashion house in Paris, in 1846. He opened his own dressmaking establishment in 1858; and within weeks was patronised by the Empress Eugénie, the ladies of her court – and the actress Sarah Bernhardt. He reinterpreted female fashion, avoiding fussy ruffles and frills, using rich fabrics in simple but flattering styles and paying great attention to fit. He was the first designer to put labels into his clothes: the "House of Worth". He died near Paris, on 10 March 1895.

ISAMBARD KINGDOM BRUNEL FRS

Isambard Kingdom Brunel FRS (1806–59) was the greatest 19th century British civil and mechanical engineer. He was born the first son and third child of Marc and Sophie (*née* Kingdom) Brunel at Portsea in Hampshire, on 9 April 1806. The young Brunel demonstrated from an early age that he had inherited his father's remarkable mechanical and architectural talents. Marc Isambard (he preferred Isambard, but history knows him as Marc) Brunel FRS was a French royalist *émigré*, engineer and inventor. After an education at a seminary in Rouen, he spent six years in the French navy. In 1793, during the French Revolution, he fled to the US. Having taken US citizenship, he settled in New York and quickly became the city's chief engineer. His design for the new Capitol, to be built in Washington D.C., was rejected only on grounds of expense.

Isambard Kingdom Brunel
by Robert Howlett (1857)
National Portrait Gallery, London

In 1799, having perfected a production-line method of making ships' blocks (pulleys), until then laboriously assembled by hand, he sailed to Britain and sold the system to the Admiralty – which needed 10,000 blocks a year. He also invented mechanical ways of making army boots, milling timber, knitting stockings and printing. Peace with France in 1815, and the cancellation of a large boot contract, pushed him into bankruptcy – and, for 88 days, a debtors prison. The government however, realising his value to the nation, settled his debts. His last great undertaking was the first Thames tunnel. Brunel was knighted in 1841 and elected to the Royal Society. Having been born in the same year as Wellington, he died on 12 December 1849 in London.

In 1820, after early schooling in Chelsea and Hove, the fourteen year-old Isambard was sent to Paris for two years to complete his education. In 1822 he returned to London and was apprenticed to his father, always his best tutor, who was planning the first tunnel under

Eventually hailed as the eighth wonder of the world, the first tunnel under the Thames was attempted in 1806 by Richard Trevithick (1771–1833), the brilliant Cornish inventor and engineer: but quickly abandoned because there was no way at that time of tunnelling through waterlogged strata. Brunel began a new tunnel (between Rotherhithe and Wapping) in 1825. It was to be the first tunnel built under any river – and the only project on which both Marc and Isambard cooperated. It took so long to build, because of accidents and floods, that the company ran out of money. As a result it was limited to a foot tunnel 35 feet wide and 1,300 feet long. The tunnel shield, used in every similar tunnel thereafter, was patented in 1818 by Marc Brunel and Thomas, Lord Cochrane.

The Clifton suspension bridge

the Thames, using an ingenious but untried device: a tunnel shield.

An important innovation was the use of compressed air to prevent the workface from flooding. The dangers of compression and decompression however, were not understood: and workmen began to die from the "bends", as well as from inhaling methane and hydrogen sulphide fumes; and from drowning in floods. The tunnel was finally opened on 25 March 1843: but was not a commercial success, soon acquiring an unsavoury reputation as a sheltered place of business for prostitutes. In 1869, after being operated unprofitably as a foot tunnel, the East London Railway Co. converted it to rail – still in use today, 188 years after work started.

While recovering in Clifton, a prosperous residential suburb of Bristol, from serious injuries incurred during a flood in the Thames tunnel, Isambard Brunel was invited to submit a design in a competition to bridge the 250-feet gorge above the river Avon.

An inconclusive competition was held in 1829. The Bristol Society of Merchant Venturers, held another in 1830: which twenty-four year-old Brunel won. He was appointed project engineer, his first major commission, to start work the following year. Dogged by political and financial problems, only the two towers had been completed by 1843 when the project was abandoned.

Through an influential circle of Bristol merchants Brunel secured his second commission: to advise the Bristol Docks Co. on a proposed railway line from London to Bristol. In March 1833, aged twenty-seven, Brunel was appointed chief engineer to the Great Western Railway. For the next fifteen years Brunel surveyed and supervised "the finest work in England": a line from Paddington in London to Temple Meads in Bristol. So skilful and gradual were his gradients that the Great Western line (GWR) became known as "Brunel's billiard table". The GWR was the first in the world to provide high speed passenger transport: along a series of superbly

The bridge was eventually completed in 1864, as a memorial to Brunel: with iron chains taken from his Hungerford suspension bridge in London. Designed in the early 19th century, for light horse-drawn traffic, it carries 12,000 cars every day.

The two railway arches over the Thames at Maidenhead support the widest and flattest bridge ever built of brick. Each span is 128 feet, with a rise of only 24 feet. the lowest-ratio span of any large non-suspension bridge. It was built to carry trains weighing not more than 100 tons: but today regularly carries trains of over 600. Box Tunnel is 1.8 miles long and descends a 1:100 gradient from east to west. It took over four years to build (1836–41) and cost the lives of over 100 navigators ("navvies"). When the tunnellers, digging from both directions, finally met, the alignment was out by less than two inches. On opening, it was the longest railway tunnel in the world. It is part of the Brunel legend that it is so angled that the sun shines straight through it only on 9 April, his birthday.

engineered viaducts (Hanwell and Chippenham); tunnels (Box); and both brick (Maidenhead) and later, iron bridges (Chepstow and Saltash).

Brunel designed a broad, 7-foot gauge to ensure safety and smoothness for his highspeed line. In 1846 however, an Act of Parliament standardised the 4 foot 8½ inch gauge. Regardless of the engineering merits, it was cheaper and easier to lay closer rails within the wide-gauge track, than to widen thousands of miles of track already operating throughout the country. The GWR gauge was not changed however, until 1892.

Brunel's mind, as ever leaping ahead to the next challenge, had barely begun work on the GWR when he suggested to his directors that he continue the line westwards: by offering a steamship mail and passenger service between Bristol and New York. These far-sighted men immediately formed the Great Western Steamship Co. and appointed Brunel chief engineer: charged with designing and constructing the world's largest steamship, to be named the SS *Great Western*.

By midnight on Friday 20 May 1892 every locomotive and carriage on the entire GWR system had been located to Swindon; and replacements with wheels set closer together were ready. The following day the GWR converted from broad to the narrow gauge standard. 177 miles of track were lifted and relaid in two days. At 04:04 on Monday 23 May the mail train left Penzance, arriving on time at Paddington.
• **Paddington Station, London terminus of the Great Western Railway**

Financed by the GWR and launched in 1837, the wooden-hulled, paddle-driven SS *Great Western*, was the first regular transatlantic steamer. She displaced 1,321 tons, was 212 feet long and carried 148 passengers. She was capable of sailing at nine knots, driven by two engines, with four small masts. Her maiden voyage on 8 April 1838, from Bristol to New York, took fifteen days – halving the time normally taken by sailing ships. She was broken up in London in 1856, having completed 74 Atlantic crossings and having been used as a troopship to the Crimea. The *Great Western* proved Brunel's calculation: that, while the power needed to drive a ship increases only by the square of her dimensions, the carrying capacity increases by the cube – so she was able to carry the extra bunkering. On her maiden voyage, she arrived with coal to spare.

Once a transatlantic steam crossing had proved successful, Brunel designed a sister ship to take advantage of the lucrative mail and passenger market. He was frustrated however, by a Nova Scotian, Samuel Cunard (1787–1865): who began operating his British and North American Royal Mail Steam Packet Co. (the Cunard Line) out of Liverpool in 1839. Cunard won the mail contract well before the SS *Great Britain* was completed, five years later.

SS *Great Britain* was launched in July 1843. Originally designed to be driven by paddle-wheels, she was the world's first large, iron-hulled, six-bladed screw-propelled ship. Brunel's propellers have been tested against modern computerised models: the latter have been found to be less than 10% more economical than those he had designed by instinct. The *Great Britain* displaced 3,270 tons, was 322 feet long with six masts. She carried 250 passengers, 130 crew and 1,200 tons of cargo.

SS *Great Britain* made her maiden voyage from Liverpool to New York in 1845. After early transatlantic runs and acting as a troopship to the Crimea, she passed most of her working life

SS Great Eastern (1859)

sailing to and from Australia. In 1884 she struck a rock rounding Cape Horn: and, until she was scuttled in 1937, she remained as a storage hulk in the Falkland Islands. She was towed back to Bristol in 1970, restored and put on display in the same dry-dock in which she had been constructed.

In 1851, having been diagnosed with a potentially fatal kidney disease, Brunel started to design an enormous steamship as a memorial to his career– the SS *Great Eastern*. This leviathan would be twice the length and five times the tonnage of the greatest ship then afloat. She would be the largest moveable object ever made by man: with a double hull made of wrought iron; and six funnels more than 100 feet high.

The ship was ordered by the Eastern Steamship Navigation Co. and launched in 1858. She displaced 32,160 tons: and at 692 feet long, was the largest vessel built in the 19th century – the forerunner of the great 20th century ocean liners. She had a double iron hull and was driven by three engines generating over 3,600 hp. Rigged with six masts of sails, named "Monday" to "Saturday", she was capable of 14 1/2 knots.

SS *Titanic*, built over fifty years later, and SS *Great Eastern* are often compared. *Titanic* struck an iceberg at full speed and sank, with great loss of life: the *Great Eastern* struck a rock at full speed, ripped open her hull, causing enormous damage and was repaired in New York. The passengers scarcely noticed the bump.

She was designed to carry cargo and 4,000 passengers between Britain and India; but was too large for the Suez Canal. Her first years were spent on the New York trade route operated by the Great Ship Co.: her huge holds however, were never filled and she ran at a loss, unable to compete with smaller, faster steamships. From 1864–74 she was used as a cable-layer: her first task, to lay the first transatlantic 5,000-ton telegraph cable, was completed on I September 1866. She carried US tourists to France, including Jules Verne: who wrote a novel based on his experience called *The Floating City*. SS *Great Eastern* was broken up in 1889: having spent her last years ignominiously, as a billboard on a Mersey beach.

John Scott Russell FRS (1808–82) was a civil engineer and naval architect. Born in Parkhead near Glasgow, Russell became professor of natural philosophy at Edinburgh University in 1832. Having noticed that the bow wave created by a barge being towed continued after the barge had hit a bridge pier, he became absorbed in the study of the impact of wave patterns on ships' hulls (the Soliton theory).

In 1860 Russell built HMS *Warrior*, the first iron warship in the world, at his shipyard at Millwall on the Thames.

Brunel liked to exercise complete control over his projects from concept to completion: but in this instance, he joined forces with John Scott Russell. It was not a happy association.

The two men held each other in high esteem. Unfortunately their respective roles were never clearly defined: which led to serious disagreements, exacerbated by contention over who should take the credit for Brunel's "Great Babe". The press also questioned the viability of such a colossal ship. The ship required three million hand-driven rivets, each an inch thick, applied by 200 rivet gangs each consisting of five men. Two riveters were assisted by one "holder-on" and two "bash boys", one of whom heated the rivets while the other inserted. During construction of the outer hull, half the gang were occupied for months between the two hulls in hellish conditions of virtual darkness, deafened by the pounding of several hundred rivet hammers. Health and safety precautions were primitive and scores of workers fell to their deaths: to be impaled on standing iron bars or crushed by pile-drivers.

Thousands flocked to Millwall for the launch on 4 November 1857. In the words of The Times the crowds were drawn by: ".... a splendid chance .... of a fearful catastrophe". Sadly that chance presented itself: the multiplying winch controlling the launch spun out of control, killing or injuring several of the crew. The £750,000 hull (£494 million today) moved just three feet, before the rails jammed. On 31 January 1858, after unremitting effort with hydraulic rams and at a cost of £120,000, finally the hull floated off on a high tide.

After eighteen months fitting out, on 8 September 1859 the *Great Eastern* sailed down the Thames to the English Channel. Four days later disaster struck again. An explosion destroyed a forward funnel and scalding steam killed five stokers, injuring many more. *The Times* reported on 15 September that: "a man blown up by gunpowder is a mere figure of raw flesh which seldom moves after the explosion. Not so with men blown up by steam who for a few minutes are able to walk about, apparently almost unhurt, though in fact mortally injured beyond all hope of recovery .... where not grimed by the smoke and ashes, the peculiar bright white softness of the face, hands or breast, told at once that the skin, though unbroken, had been boiled by steam". A court of enquiry found that the explosion had been caused by a stopcock being closed in error during the testing of the engines.

Brunel had collapsed from a stroke on the deck of the Great Eastern just before she left London on her maiden trip; and now lay speechless and unable to move in Duke Street. When he heard of the tragedy, he turned his face to the wall and died three days later, on 15 September 1859. He was buried in Kensal Green cemetery. Brunel designed and built twenty-five railway lines, five suspension bridges, 125 conventional bridges, eight pier and dock systems and three ocean liners. He constructed an observatory and the water towers for the Great Exhibition's Crystal Palace in 1851. He also built an armoured floating battery, used at Kronstadt in the Baltic, and a prefabricated hospital erected at Renkoi during the Crimean War (1853–56).

Brunel had two sons and a daughter. One of his sons, Henry Marc (1842–1903) followed in the footsteps of his grandfather and father and became a successful civil engineer. Most of Isambard's short career however, was spent supervising too many huge projects to enjoy much of a personal life. He also had to attend and give evidence to numerous committees and oversee firms from whom he had commissioned work. He had made a fortune; but on his death left only £90,000 (£60.5 million today) – having spent over £120,000 personally on finally launching the *Great Eastern*. His greatest friends were Robert Stephenson (1803–59), the

Renkoi hospital was designed to care for 1,500 patients, built and shipped over 1,000 miles to the Dardanelles in Turkey: all within five months. In February 1855 Brunel had been commissioned to design a prefabricated hospital; and within a fortnight submitted the first drawings. On 7 May 1855 the hospital was unloaded in Turkey and the first patients arrived on 2 October. By March the accommodation had been extended to 2,200, although only 642 patients were admitted before the Crimean War ended in January 1856. Of the 1,331 patients who eventually passed though Renkoi only 50 died, a 4% fatality rate – which compared well with the 42% death rate at Scutari, admittedly a much larger hospital. Brunel designed every aspect of the hospital including structure, finish, ventilation, water supply and drainage systems. His design showed how infection could be reduced by competent staff in a properly run, well-designed hospital with good sanitation.

locomotive and railway engineer, and John Horsley R.A., his artist brother-in-law. He laid out the grounds and gardens of a grand estate at Watcombe near Torquay, which were never finished.

Brunel was fortunate to have been born in a century of unprecedented commercial expansion, where his genius was able to find unlimited scope. He had the perception and enterprise to exploit Victorian vision and capital to a greater extent than any other engineer of his time. In doing so, he made an important contribution to British national and imperial ambition.

Sir Richard Burton (c.1872–75) by Frederic, Lord Leighton PRA (1830–96)
National Portrait Gallery, London

A shrine to wives of the Maharajas of Jodhpur who had committed suttee

SIR RICHARD BURTON

Richard Francis Burton (1821–90) was an extraordinarily gifted linguist, scholar, explorer, travel writer and orientalist, who played a major part in identifying the source of the White Nile. He was born in Torquay, the eldest of three children. In 1820 his father, Colonel Joseph Burton had been placed on half pay, as a result of having refused to testify against Queen Caroline during a divorce action brought by her husband, King George IV. It was claimed that Caroline had committed adultery with a low-born foreigner, Bartolomeo Pergami. The trial before Parliament caused a sensation, as scandalous details of Caroline's life with Pergami were disclosed.

In reduced circumstances, the Colonel moved his family to the Continent, where Richard was brought up. With an almost comical lack of prescience, in the light of what followed, the Colonel believed his son best suited to the church, sending him to Trinity College, Oxford. Richard's behaviour at Oxford was so outlandish that he was sent down in 1842, before he could take his degree. His father bought him a commission in the Bombay army, where he spent the next two years in the recently annexed state of Sindh – and revealed a remarkable gift for languages.

Burton qualified in seven languages in India, later acquiring mastery in more than forty tongues and dialects. He became extraordinarily adept in absorbing cultures and adopting disguises. His favourite character was that of Mirza Abdullah, an Arab-Iranian quack doctor. Burton was so successful in playing out this role that he acquired a thriving medical practice amongst the native population.

Sir Charles Napier (1782–1853), the governor of Sindh soon recognised Burton's extraordinary talents and employed him as an undercover agent, in his attempts to bring order to an unruly province. Operating in deep disguise, Burton was able to provide Napier with the evidence he needed to tackle the endemic problems of *Suttee*, infanticide and male prostitution: while Napier established British law in the region.

The proliferation of male brothels in Sindh was an abomination to British rule. Burton penetrated these establishments: and

Suttee was a barbaric Hindu funeral practice in which a widow would immolate herself on her husband's funeral pyre. *Suttee* was supposed to be voluntary, but in many cases it was not. There are many accounts of widows being physically forced to their deaths. Napier is said to have summarised the British attitude to *Suttee*: "You say that it is your custom to burn widows. Very well. We also have a custom: when men burn a woman alive, we tie a rope around their necks and we hang them. Build your funeral pyre; beside it, my carpenters will build a gallows. You may follow your custom. Then we will follow ours".

A cartoon of his annexation of Sindh in Punch magazine in 1844 was simply captioned *Peccavi* (Latin for "I have sinned"). Napier never said it himself.

Burton made little from his huge literary output. Ironically, many of his books have recently been reprinted: selling in numbers much greater than in his lifetime.

Burton came close to discovery when a young camel boy saw him late at night urinating in the European manner, rather than squatting like an Arab.

Burton was struck in the face by a spear which penetrated both cheeks: resulting in a horrific scar which can be clearly seen in all of his subsequent portraits.

provided the evidence Napier required to suppress them. Unfortunately, after Napier's departure, Burton's secret report was circulated amongst jealous officers bent on his ruin: who spread the rumour that Burton had himself been a patron. He narrowly avoided a court martial; but his career was blighted.

In 1849 Burton contracted cholera. He was granted sick leave and returned home: where in 1851, he wrote the first of nearly 40 travel books, *Goa and the Blue Mountains*.

In 1852 the Royal Geographical Society agreed that he make the *hajj* to Mecca.

Burton made the *hajj* alone and in disguise, an extremely dangerous undertaking. Only one European, the Swiss explorer Jacob Ludwig Burckhardt (1784–1817), had previously visited Mecca and survived. Discovery, as an infidel in Islam's most holy place, would have spelt instant death.

Returning to Egypt, between 1855–56 he wrote the three-volume *A Personal Narrative of a Pilgrimage to Al-Madinah and Meccah*. The book not only made his name but became a travel classic. Back in Bombay, Burton planned a trip to the forbidden city of Harar, in Somalia: a notorious centre of the slave trade, which no European had ever visited. In 1855, sponsored by the Bombay government, he set off – initially disguised as a Turkish trader. Soon rumbled, he forged letters of accreditation and boldly presented himself to the Amir of Harar as a British diplomat. The ruse worked. His report was published in 1856: *First Footsteps in East Africa*. His taste for further African exploration now thoroughly whetted, Burton applied for further leave: to search for the source of the White Nile – the most intriguing geographical mystery of the day. His expedition had not travelled far however, before it was attacked. One member was killed and he himself was severely wounded, resulting in his return to Britain.

In July 1855 Burton volunteered for the Crimea, where Britain was at war with Russia. He trained *Bashi-Bazouks* (Turkish irregular troops) in the Dardanelles; but hostilities ended before he could see action. Between 1857–58 he organised a second Nile expedition: with John Hanning Speke (1827–64), an Indian army officer who had been badly wounded on Burton's first Nile expedition. Suffering untold miseries, robbed and deserted by their servants, blinded and crippled by malaria, for months they lay prostrate by the shores of Lake Tanganyika. Speke recovered first; and pushed on alone to the north-east: where he discovered Lake Victoria, which he named for his queen. He was convinced, correctly as it turned out, that he had discovered the source of the Nile. Speke swiftly returned to London and, claiming all credit, was hailed as a hero. Burton slipped unnoticed back into Britain a few months later. Ill and cheated, he was largely ignored. In retaliation, he published *Lake Regions of Central Africa* in 1860, attacking Speke's extravagant claims.

The *hajj* is the pilgrimage to Mecca that Muslims are supposed to make at least once in their lifetime. The freshly bathed pilgrim, clothed entirely in white, circles the *Ka'aba* (a cube of grey stone and marble near the centre of the Great Mosque) and touches the Black Stone, at its eastern corner (probably a meteorite), which dates from pre-Islamic times.

In 630 the Prophet Muhammad destroyed the pagan idols in Mecca and dedicated the shrine to Islam.

• **Pilgrims circumambulating the Ka'aba (Arabic for "cube") during the *Hajj***

Later that year Burton left suddenly for the US: where he visited Salt Lake City in Utah. He met the Mormon leader Brigham Young, later writing a balanced account of the Church's practice of polygamy. Returning in 1861, he married in secret Isabel Arundell (1831–96), a member of an aristocratic Catholic family which disapproved of him, who had been in love with him since she was a schoolgirl. He also joined the Foreign Office, becoming consul in the fever-ridden Spanish island of Fernando Po, off the west coast of Africa. He filled his three-year tour by making short trips into the interior: which he drew on later to fill five volumes describing, in gruesome detail, tribal practices of fetishism, ritual murder, cannibalism and bizarre sexual rites.

In 1864 Burton was invited to debate the source of the Nile with Speke, at a meeting of the British Association for the Advancement of Science. Following the opening session at Bristol on 15 September, Speke was found dead from a wound from his own shotgun – while walking up game on a cousin's estate, at Neston Park in Wiltshire. The coroner's court ruled that Speke's death was an accident. Burton wrote to a friend: "The charitable say that he shot himself, the uncharitable say that I shot him".

Burton was then posted to Santos in Brazil: where he passed the next four years writing and exploring the central highlands of the country. He was unhappy and took to drink. In 1869, through the influence of his wife, he was appointed consul to a much more suitable post: Damascus, in Syria. After an encouraging start however, the missionary zeal of his Catholic wife caused deep resentment: and in 1871 he was recalled. In 1872 Burton reluctantly accepted the consulate at Trieste. Despite his initial reservations, he lived there contentedly until his death – turning out a stream of lurid erotica, which he had printed secretly. *The Kama Sutra of Vatsayana* in 1883, *Ananga Ranga* in 1885 and *The Perfumed Garden of Cheikh Nefzouai, a Manual of Arabian Erotology* 1886, were followed by 16 volumes of *The Arabian Nights* between 1885–88.

In February 1886 Burton's long service to the British crown was finally acknowledged, when he was knighted. On the night of 20 October 1890 he died after a heart attack: while putting the finishing touches to a translation from the original Arabic of his last, massive erotic work, *The Scented Garden*. He considered it his crowning achievement.

In 1891 Burton was interred in a concrete mausoleum, designed by Lady Burton, in the shape of a Bedouin tent, in the cemetery of St Mary Magdelene at Mortlake in Surrey. After his death, despite an offer of £6,000 (nearly £3 million today) for them, to spare his reputation Lady Burton burned virtually all of Burton's vast accumulation of papers – including the manuscript of his prized *The Scented Garden*.

Title page of Rambles and Recollections of an Indian Official by William Sleeman

SIR WILLIAM SLEEMAN AND SUPPRESSION OF THE THUGS

William Henry Sleeman (1788–1856) was born in Stratton in Cornwall, the son of a exciseman. In 1809 he joined the Bengal army of the East India Co. and served in the Gurkha War of 1814–16. He contracted jungle fever so severely that he was transferred to the civil administration: though retaining his military rank and right to promotion – rising from captain in 1825, colonel in 1843 to major-general in 1854. He married the daughter of a French nobleman, who owned estates in Mauritius, in 1829: and had one son and three daughters.

From 1825–35 Sleeman served as magistrate and district officer in what became the Central Provinces (now Madhya Pradesh); and went on to be resident (the Governor-General's representative) at Gwalior from 1843–49 and at Lucknow from 1849–56. He submitted reports disagreeing with the annexation of Oudh by Lord Dalhousie (one of the causes of the Mutiny in 1857), but his advice was not accepted.

In December 1851 an attempt was made to assassinate Sleeman. Despite failing health, he stayed at his post for another five years, until he was ordered home to Britain. On Dalhousie's recommendation he was knighted – four days before he died on board the *Monarch*, off Ceylon, on 10 February 1856. He was buried at sea the same day. The village of Sleemanabad in Madhya Pradesh was named in his honour.

In 1828 Sleeman found remains of dinosaurs in the Nerbudda valley, the first ever to be identified and recovered anywhere in Asia. He was efficient, determined, honest and fair. He spoke four Indian languages and was immersed in the culture and history of the country – typical of British administrators at that time in India. Little would now be remembered of his career, save for what he achieved between 1830–41 – the suppression of a secret society called *Thuggee*.

No organised gangs of killers have ever murdered as many people as the *Thugs*. In the 1830s they strangled over 30,000 travellers, some say many more (the *Guinness Book of Records* puts the figure as high as two million) – as a sacrifice to the goddess *Kali*, the "Dark Mother", the Hindu Triple Goddess of creation, preservation, and destruction. The name *Thuggee* comes from the Sanskrit *sthaga*, "deceiver" and is the origin of the English word, "thug". Though *Kali* was a Hindu deity, her devotees were just as likely to be Moslem, even Sikh. The cult probably originated in the 16th century.

Thuggee was hereditary. From early childhood members of the cult were taught how to strangle their victims, quickly and quietly, with a strong cloth noose called a *rumal*, weighted in one corner with a silver rupee, which was worn about the waist. *Thugs* disguised themselves as traders, pilgrims, even as soldiers marching to or from their cantonments. Each band, led by a *jamadar*, had scouts who loitered around hotels and market places to gain information about travellers and their likely wealth: and agents pretending to be headed in the same direction as their intended victims. They would inveigle themselves into the confidence of their prey, under the pretext of safety in numbers. During an evening of gaiety and song, and on a given secret signal, the killings began: though the shedding of blood was not permitted, scouts were posted to make sure that no one ever escaped. The victims were considered sacrifices to *Kali*: and a large share of the booty was set aside for her.

British administrators became increasingly alarmed by the unexplained disappearance of so many travellers. Finally, the bodies of fifty victims were found in wells near the Ganges. Rumour bred fear: and grew to the point where the problem could no longer be ignored. In 1835 Sleeman was charged by the Governor-General, Lord William Bentinck (1774–1839) to look into it; and formally appointed commissioner for the suppression of *Thuggee and Dacoity* in 1839. He knew how difficult his task would be. *Thugs* were indistinguishable from any other of the many bands of outlaws who infested the roads – and identical to the travellers and merchants who were their victims. They were indeed, master deceivers.

Sleeman realised that success would depend upon informers – who would be vulnerable to the vengeance of their previous associates. He built a special prison at Jubbulpore for their protection. Meticulously, he

Victims were often buried under crossroads, which would disguise footprints, with their bellies slashed open to prevent the build up of gasses which might push up the broken soil; and the area was sprinkled with Asafoetida grass (also known as "devil's dung" or "stinking gum") to deter jackals and other scavengers.

Elderly thugs at Jubbulpore (*c*.1863)

mapped the sites and analysed the frequency of each reported disappearance: until he could predict when the next murders would occur.

Using his agents and informers to identify known *Thuggees* operating in these areas, he sent hand-picked police officers, disguised as merchants, to entice and then ambush them. Between 1830–41, Sleeman's police captured over 3,700 *Thuggees*. Although vigilance was maintained until the 1870s, by then the cult had become extinct.

Fifty were pardoned for turning their coats: 500 were hanged. The remainder were imprisoned for life or exiled from British India. Without exception, *Thuggees* died with the same lack of emotion with which they had murdered their victims – often their only request was that they be allowed to place the noose around their own neck.

Thuggee trials exposed some grisly details. One band of twenty confessed that they had perpetrated 5,200 murders: among the group was an individual named Bahram, a strangler for 40 years, who boasted the highest lifetime score – 931. When asked if he had ever felt remorse or guilt, he replied sharply that no one should feel any regret for following his trade; and that it had given him great satisfaction to do his job so well – in much the same way, he explained, that a *shikari* (hunter) would feel content after tracking down and shooting a cattle or man-eating tiger.

Thuggee has been the subject of a number of films: *Gunga Din* in 1939 with Cary Grant and Douglas Fairbanks, Jr.; *Stranglers of Bombay* in 1960; Steven Spielberg's *Indiana Jones and the Temple of Doom* in 1984, with Harrison Ford and Kate Capshaw; and, most accurately in 1988, in Merchant Ivory's *The Deceivers*, starring Shashi Kapoor, Pierce Brosnan, Saeed Jaffrey and Dalip Tahil. The most enjoyable written account is perhaps *The Deceivers*, a 1952 novel by John ("Jack") Masters (1914–83).

> The British entered India as traders: early in their rule they were largely indifferent to local practices. The suppression of *suttee* and *thuggee* however, are among the early achievements often quoted to justify the *Raj*.

> Eleanor Roosevelt, the leftist wife of the US WWII President, once subjected Winston Churchill to a rant about British imperialism. "The Indians have suffered for years under British oppression", she declared.
>
> "Are we talking about the brown-skinned Indians in India who have multiplied under benevolent British rule", Churchill replied, "or are we speaking about the red-skinned Indians in America who, I understand, are now almost extinct?".

In July 2007 the populations of the countries that once made up the British Indian Empire were: India – 1,129,866,154 (including some 150 million Muslims or 13.4% of the population); Pakistan – 164,741,924; Bangladesh – 150,448,389. The total is a mind-numbing 1.445 billion, 22% of all the people in the world.

To the figure of 1.445 billion should be added the populations of Sri Lanka – almost 20 million; and Burma – over 42 million: for a total of 1.507 billion. This amounts to 185 million more than the estimated population of China in the same year.

VALENTINE BAKER, A MAN OF HONOUR OR A LECHER

Valentine Baker (1827–87), also known as "Baker Pasha", was born in Gloucestershire. He was the third son of Sir Samuel Baker, a rich West Indian plantation owner and successful local

Sir Samuel White Baker FRS (1821–93) was an explorer, army officer, naturalist, engineer, author and anti-slavery abolitionist. He discovered Lake Albert, into and out of which the White Nile flows, in 1864. In 1858 Baker was on a hunting trip to Hungary with Maharaja Duleep Singh when he fell in love with Florence, a sixteen year-old slave girl, kidnapped as a child during the Hungarian revolution in 1848, who was being groomed for the harem of the Ottoman Pasha of Vidin in Bulgaria by an Armenian slave trader. Outbid by the Pasha, Baker bribed her attendants and escaped with her in a closed carriage. She became Lady Baker (1841–1916) and accompanied her husband on all his exotic and dangerous explorations.

Lieutenant-General Sir Harry Smith (1787–1860), a brave soldier in the Peninsular Wars, whose great achievement was to rout the Sikhs at Aliwal in 1846, was another who acquired a young wife who devoted her life to his. In 1812 the fourteen year-old Juana Maria de los Dolores de Leon, born into an old Spanish noble family, was orphaned when Badajoz was besieged for the fourth time. After a bloody storming by the British, she married the then Brigade-Major Harry Smith of the 95th Rifles. She spent the rest of the war with the baggage train, sleeping in the open and suffering all the hardships of campaigning.

Her beauty, courage, calmness and charm endeared her to officers and soldiers alike. The Duke of Wellington called her Juanita. With the exception of his service during the British-American War in 1814, she accompanied her husband throughout his career – most notably in two postings in South Africa, where Sir Harry served as Governor of Cape Colony and High Commissioner. Juana gave her name to Ladysmith, a town in KwaZulu-Natal, which was besieged by the Boers in the Second Boer War for 118 days – from November 1899 to February 1900.

• **Sir Harry Smith, Bt by D.J. Pound, after a photograph by John Eastham**
National Portrait Gallery, London

Duleep Singh, Maharaja of Lahore (1838–93), was the last Maharaja of the Sikh Empire. He was the youngest son of the legendary "Lion of the Punjab", Maharaja Ranjit Singh and the "Messalina of the Punjab", Maharani Jind Kaur. His kingdom was annexed by Britain in 1849; and in 1854 he was exiled to Britain, having converted to Christianity.

Befriended by Queen Victoria, he gave her the *Koh-i-Noor*, which became part of the Crown Jewels when Prime Minister Benjamin Disraeli proclaimed her as Empress of India on 1 January 1877. The India Office bought a 17,000 acre estate at Elveden in Suffolk for Duleep in 1863. He converted the house into a quasi-oriental palace and lived as a British aristocrat. He joined the Carlton Club and became a freemason.

Duleep married twice: first to an Arabic-speaking German whose mother was an Ethiopian slave girl; and then to his mistress, a chambermaid called Ada Douglas Wetherill. None of his eight children had issue. Duleep died after an epileptic fit aged fifty-five and was buried in Elveden Church – beside his first wife Maharani Bamba and his third son, Prince Edward Albert Duleep Singh.

• **Maharaja Duleep Singh by Franz Xaver Winterhalter (1854)**
The Royal Collection, London

The *Koh-i-Noor*, "Mountain of Light" in Persian, is a 105 carat diamond. Mined c.1323 at Golconda in India (the only source until diamonds were discovered in Brazil in 1730), it was owned by the rulers of the Delhi sultanate: and then by Babur, the first Moghul emperor, in 1526 who held it in his hand and calculated how many people in the world it would feed and for how long. It was carried off to Persia in 1739; and eventually given by Shah Shuja of Afghanistan to Ranjit Singh, as a reward for having won back his kingdom for him, in 1830. Legend has it that whoever owns the *Kohi-Noor* rules the world. That claim looks a little thin today.

• **The Koh-i-Noor Diamond**

Valentine Baker in Turkish uniform

Uzbekistan was a dangerous place. In June 1842 two British intelligence officers, Charles Stoddart and Arthur Conolly (who coined the phrase "the Great Game", to describe the struggle between the British and Russian Empires for domination over Central Asia) had been beheaded by the Emir of Bukhara. Their lives would have been spared if they had been willing to convert to Islam.

businessman. After schooling in Gloucester, Baker accompanied his elder brother Samuel to Ceylon (Sri Lanka), where Samuel had bought land: intending to found a British colony and indulge his passion for big game hunting.

In 1848 Baker enlisted as an ensign in the Ceylon Rifles; before transferring in 1851 to the 10th Hussars, who were stationed in India. In 1852 he volunteered for the 12th Lancers, so that he could participate in the Basuto War in South Africa – where he distinguished himself with conspicuous gallantry. In 1855, still serving with the 12th Lancers in India, he accompanied the regiment to the Crimea: where he fought at the battle of Chernaya and was present at the fall of Sevastopol. Returning to India in 1856, he purchased a captaincy in the 10th Hussars; a majority in 1859; and command of the regiment in 1860 – a post he held until 1873.

In 1858 he published *British Cavalry*, a seminal work aimed at improving training, tactics, horse blood-lines, equipment and uniforms. In 1860 he published *Our National Defences*, to meet the perceived menace from French militarism. He recommended the establishment of a national guard, linked to front-line regiments: the precursor of the Territorial Army. In 1869 he wrote *Army Reform*, recommending an overhaul of military education and administration. He reinforced his expertise by observing first hand the Prussian Wars with Austria in 1866 and France in 1870.

In 1863 the Prince of Wales (later King Edward VII) was appointed colonel-in-chief of the 10th Hussars. The Prince became a close friend of Baker and arranged his membership of the exclusive Marlborough Club. In 1865 Baker married Fanny Wormald, the daughter of a rich Yorkshire landowner. In April 1873 Baker and two companions, in the guise of a hunting party, set off to reach the Khanate of Khiva in Central Asia (present day Uzbekistan). It was really an unofficial attempt to monitor the spread of Russian influence, which was beginning to threaten the north-west frontier of India.

In 1876 Baker published *Clouds in the East*, an account of his travels, in which he advocated a robust British stance towards Russia.

In September 1874 Baker was appointed Assistant Quarter-Master-General at Aldershot. On 17 June 1875 he caught a train to London, where he was to dine with the Duke of Cambridge, the Commander-in-Chief of the British army. Sitting alone with him in his first class carriage was a Miss Kate Dickinson, the young sister of an officer in the Royal Engineers. On arrival in London, Baker was arrested for attempted rape.

On 30 July Baker appeared before Mr Justice Brett (later 1st Viscount Esher, Master of the Rolls) at Croydon assizes. On 2 August he was acquitted of attempted rape; but convicted on a lesser charge of indecent assault. He was fined £500 (£260,000 today) and sent to prison for one year. He did not utter a single word in his own defence. On the insistence of Queen Victoria, Baker was cashiered from the army. However his wife, family and friends, including the Prince of Wales, his old regiment and most of the army staunchly stood by him: refusing to believe that he had received a fair trial.

On his release from prison in September 1876, through the intervention of the Prince of Wales, Baker took up an appointment with the Turkish government: to reorganise their gendarmerie (a paramilitary police force) and reinforce the defences of Constantinople. When war broke out between Turkey and Russia in April 1877, Baker was transferred to the Turkish general-staff. He was soon given command of an infantry division.

He was joined at his headquarters at Shumla in Bulgaria by a polyglot assortment of observers: newspaper reporters, English members of Parliament and army officers: including Baker's great friends Frederick Burnaby and Herbert Kitchener – later Field Marshal, Earl Kitchener of Khartoum (1850–1916), a great supporter of Baker.

On 31 December 1877, commanding Sultan Suleiman's rearguard and vastly outnumbered by the Russians, for ten blood-soaked hours Baker held the vital pass of Tashkesan. Suleiman immediately promoted him to *Ferik* (Lieutenant-General) in the field. Bitterly disappointed however, by the craven terms of the subsequent peace treaty of San Stefano, Baker returned to Britain.

Acclaimed a hero, his defence of Tashkesan was hailed as the greatest rearguard action since Leonidas and 300 Spartans died to the last man in 480 BC, defending the pass at Thermopylae against a huge Persian army. As a result of Tashkesan, Baker was re-elected to the Marlborough Club in 1878; and the Army and Navy Club in 1881.

Frederick Gustavus (Fred) Burnaby (1842–84), by James Jacques Tissot. It is a superb caricature of an arrogant poseur – but he was also a brave soldier
National Portrait Gallery, London

Nicolas Chauvin was a Frenchman, whose distinguished record of service and devotion to Napoleon gave rise to the term "chauvinism". The word "jingoism", which means much the same, was coined from a song aired during the Russo-Turkish war of 1877–78 ("by jingo" was an old "minced oath", meaning "by Jesus"):

"We don't want to fight but by Jingo if we do
We've got the ships, we've got the men, we've got the money too
We've fought the Bear before, and while we're Britons true
The Russians shall not have Constantinople".

Mahdism was a movement founded by the Sudanese prophet Osman Digna (1844–85) who called himself *al-Mahdi*, meaning the "divinely guided one". In 1881 he fomented an uprising against Sudan's Egyptian ruling class who, he was convinced, had abandoned the Muslim faith. Within four years he had conquered virtually all the territory occupied by Egypt – culminating in the capture of Khartoum and the death of General Charles ("Chinese") Gordon in 1885.

In 1882 Baker was invited by the Khedive of Egypt to take command of a newly created Egyptian army in Cairo – however Queen Victoria refused to ratify his appointment. He was offered a dismal alternative; command of the gendarmerie, a ramshackle force with low morale and even less discipline. In 1882 a Sudanese warlord, known as "the Mahdi", rebelled against Egyptian rule and besieged the Egyptian fort at Tokar.

On 4 February 1884 a relief force of 4,000 gendarmes led by Baker was ambushed at El Teb and destroyed. The British government belatedly sent an expedition, including the 10th Hussars under Major-General Sir

Gerald Graham, to join a fleet of five warships, under Admiral Sir William Hewett VC, at Suakin on the Red Sea. Baker, acting as guide and intelligence officer, led the relief force back to El Teb: where, on 29 February, the Mahdists were defeated. Baker was badly wounded in the face. In spite of receiving General Graham's highest commendations for bravery, appeals for reinstatement to his Egyptian army command failed. The Queen remained implacable.

Baker returned to Cairo to continue as Inspector General of the Gendarmerie. In January 1885 he suffered a series of personal losses. His best friend, Fred Burnaby died in a skirmish at Abu Klea; he lost his eldest daughter Hermione, who was only eighteen; followed by his wife a month later – both died of typhoid.

In June 1887, the year of her golden jubilee, Queen Victoria finally relented: and wrote to the Prince of Wales proposing Baker's reinstatement. Administrative incompetence however, delayed the news reaching Cairo. On 17 November he died, after a heart attack aboard the steam pinnace *Vigilant* on the Sweetwater Canal near Tel el Kebir. A telegram from the Duke of Cambridge arrived shortly afterwards, instructing the authorities to bury Baker with full military honours. On 18 November *The Times* declared: "His career .... might have been amongst the most brilliant in our service.... but for the error which deprived his country of his services".

Sir Hector Macdonald by John Singer Sargent (1906)
National Portrait Gallery, London

THE HERO OF OMDURMAN'S LIFE ENDED IN TRAGEDY

Major-General Sir Hector Archibald Macdonald (1853–1903) was born near Dingwall in Ross-shire, the youngest of five sons of a crofter and stone-mason. His family were all Gaelic speakers. At fifteen he was apprenticed to a tweed mill in Inverness: he was soon bored however, and joined the Inverness Highland Rifle Volunteers. In 1871 he enlisted in the 92nd (later Gordon) Highlanders at Fort George. Five feet nine inches tall and broadshouldered, he was described by Sir Arthur Conan Doyle as "a bony, craggy Scotsman, with a square fighting head and a bulldog jaw".

Frederick Sleigh ("Bobs") Roberts VC OM, later Field Marshal 1st Earl Roberts of Kandahar (1832–1914), was the second son of General Sir Abraham Roberts of Waterford, born in Cawnpore in British India. He was educated at Eton, Sandhurst and Addiscombe Military Academy, before entering the East India Company Army as a Second Lieutenant with the Bengal Artillery on 12 December 1851. He fought in the rebellion often described as the Indian Mutiny: and was present at both the capture of Delhi and the relief of Lucknow. He was awarded the Victoria Cross for actions on 2 January 1858 at Khudaganj. He married Nora Bews on 17 May 1859.

Both his sons predeceased him, including Frederick Hugh Sherston Roberts VC who was killed in action at the Battle of Colenso during the Second Boer War. Roberts and his son are one of only three pairs of father and son to be awarded the VC.

Aside of the 1867–68 Abyssinian campaign, his service was entirely in India: culminating in his capture of Kabul in 1879 – following which the Emir of Afghanistan, Mohammad Yaqub Khan (1849–1923) ceded control of Afghanistan's foreign affairs to the British Empire.

In 1885 Roberts became Commander-in-Chief in India and was appointed Field Marshal in 1895. In command of the British forces in the Second Boer War, he relieved Kimberley and captured Pretoria on 29 May 1900; before being succeeded by Lord Kitchener. He died of pneumonia, as Commander-in-Chief of the British Army, at St Omer in France, while visiting Indian troops in WWI.

On 19 November 1914 he was the only commoner to be given a state funeral in the 20th century, other than Winston Churchill. He was interred in St Paul's Cathedral. Charming, careful, subtle but quite able to be ruthless, Roberts was Britain's most effective army commander since Wellington.

• **Frederick Sleigh Roberts, 1st Earl Roberts by John Singer Sargent (1906)**
National Portrait Gallery, London

Macdonald rose rapidly through the noncommissioned ranks. As a colour-sergeant during the Second Afghan War (1878–80), he so distinguished himself by exemplary conduct and outstanding courage, that on 7 January 1880 Major-General Roberts commissioned him in the field from the ranks – an extremely rare promotion.

Returning to Britain by way of South Africa, Macdonald's regiment saw action in the First Boer War (1880–81); and was present at Majuba Hill, the most important battle of the war, on 27 February 1881. It ended in a crushing British defeat. The 92nd Gordon Highlanders had occupied the summit of Majuba Hill in Natal under the command of Major-General Sir George Pomeroy Colley. Believing that his position was impregnable, Colley had neither brought up artillery nor ordered his men to entrench. The Boers stormed the hill, by using "fire and movement" (*vuur en beweeg*), an infantry tactic years ahead of its time. The British broke; and fled down the hill. Out of a force of 405 soldiers and sailors, the British sustained 280 casualties, killed, wounded and taken prisoner.

In 1883 Macdonald arrived in Egypt to serve under Sir Evelyn Wood VC (1838–1919), later Field Marshal, in the reorganisation of the Egyptian army. Lacking the private means required by a British army officer, Macdonald accompanied the Nile expedition in 1885 as a member of the Egyptian gendarmerie. In 1888 he transferred to the Egyptian army, to train Sudanese troops. During the Sudanese campaign (1888–91) he displayed a brilliant talent for command, receiving a DSO at the battle of Toski in 1889. When General Herbert Kitchener (1850–1916) embarked on the re-conquest of Sudan from the Mahdists in 1896, he gave Macdonald command of an Egyptian Brigade. At Omdurman Macdonald's skilful handling of his brigade, at a critical moment in the battle, saved Kitchener's columns from being outflanked.

Macdonald, now known as "Fighting Mac", returned home to a hero's welcome. Feted and lionised everywhere, he was promoted colonel in the British army, appointed *aide-de-camp* to Queen Victoria and received the thanks of both Houses of Parliament – together with a lump sum. In Scotland, he was given a victory lunch by the Edinburgh City Council, where he was introduced as the "Hero of Omdurman".

Macdonald commanded the Punjab district in India for a short period, before embarking for South Africa at the beginning of the Second Boer War – where he was promoted Major-General. Commanded by Field Marshal Lord Roberts, with Kitchener as his chief-of-staff, Macdonald's Highland Brigade participated in the 1900 Boer defeats at Paardeburg and Brandwater. In April 1901 however, rumours of buggery with a Boer prisoner forced Kitchener to send Macdonald home. Despite questions in Parliament over his "sacking", on 14 May 1901 Macdonald was knighted – and posted back to India.

For a few months he commanded Belgaum district in southern India, before transferring to a more senior and remunerative post in Ceylon (now Sri Lanka). Far from active service and underemployed, Macdonald did not thrive on the island. He offended the tea-planter officered

Macdonald, serving as a newly commissioned subaltern, was captured. General Piet Joubert (1834–1900), the Boer commander, was so impressed by his display of leadership and courage that, after his release, he returned his sword.

On 2 September 1898, advancing in two columns, Kitchener's rear flank was exposed to a force of 15,000 Mahdists, hidden behind a ridge. The Mahdists made a two-pronged attack. To face them, Macdonald had to wheel his Sudanese troops through a half-circle, while maintaining a concentrated rate of fire. This complex manoeuvre, the result of Macdonald's obsession with drill and discipline, saved the day. At the end of the battle, his soldiers had barely two rounds left per man. 10,000 Mahdists were killed, 13,000 wounded and 5,000 taken prisoner. Kitchener's army lost 48 men killed and 382 wounded, mostly from Macdonald's brigade.

volunteer militia, by treating them like native levies. He also made it clear that he preferred Eurasian to official and planter society. In retaliation anonymous and unsubstantiated rumours began to circulate, that Macdonald had engaged in homosexual activity with Sinhalese school boys and had even seduced the governor's son. Finally, a tea-planter reported to the governor Sir Joseph West Ridgway, that he had "seen" Macdonald in a railway carriage with four boys. Ridgway, who disliked him, immediately sent Macdonald home on leave: cabling the Colonial Office that it was "essential to save a grave public scandal".

Lord Roberts, now Chief of the Imperial General Staff, advised Macdonald that his only option was to return to Ceylon and clear his name before a court martial – even though sodomy was not a criminal offence on the island. On 20 March he left London for Ceylon, by way of Paris and Marseilles. Three days later he checked into Room 105 at the Regina Hotel on the fashionable Rue de Rivoli. On the morning of the 25 March, while at breakfast, he read in a copy of the *New York Times* that "opprobrious charges" had been laid against him in Ceylon. He went directly up to his room and shot himself with his service revolver. His brother William said, "It was the act of a proud and sensitive man" – it certainly saved the army, and his wife, from scandal.

Macdonald's body was returned to Scotland, destined for a funeral with full military honours. But on 30 March a distraught Lady Macdonald (1869–1911) had him buried quickly and privately in Dean Cemetery in Edinburgh. All over Scotland there was an outpouring of grief. On the first Sunday after his burial over 30,000 people visited his grave, bringing so many flowers that the superintendent had to turn them away. His name endures in a memorial tower, built at Dingwall by public subscription.

Conspiracy theories abounded, claiming Macdonald to have been a victim of English jealousy and class prejudice. Many refused to accept that he had died at all. He was rumoured still to be alive: first in Russia, fighting the Japanese; then, as WWI approached, in France – serving as an officer with the French High Command. During the war itself, in a rare attempt at humour, the Germans encouraged speculation that Macdonald was actually their General Von Mackensen (1849–1945).

> Kitchener was himself suspected of closet homosexuality – giving rise to a street boys' rhyme: "boy soldiers for war if you fancy, all for Kitchener 'cos he's a nancy".

> In Scotland the public was shocked by the death of their hero – and worse, by the revelation that Macdonald had a wife and son. In January 1884 he had secretly married a girl of fifteen: Christina Duncan, the daughter of a Leith schoolmaster.
>
> He had kept his marriage secret as Lord Kitchener did not allow his officers to marry. They had seen each other only four times in nineteen years. Their only child, Hector Duncan Macdonald (1887–1951), educated at Dulwich College and trained as an engineer, was described as "warped, a bitter man, latterly a recluse".

Thomas Cook

THOMAS COOK, THE WORLD'S FIRST TOUR OPERATOR

Thomas Cook (1808–92) was born in Melbourne in Derbyshire, the only son of a labourer. He left school when he was ten. In 1828, after a series of odd jobs, he became a Baptist missionary. Appalled by the evil effects of drink, he devoted himself to the Temperance Movement: for which he arranged outings and picnics, as wholesome alternatives to the pub. In the process he founded the first travel agency – and became the first tour operator.

On 5 July 1841 Cook organised an outing for 500 temperance enthusiasts on the new railway service from Leicester to Loughborough. The fare was a shilling each (£38–50 today). It was the world's first publicly advertised excursion by train.

Cook arranged more ambitious trips to Snowdonia and Scotland and prepared handbook guides for his customers. In 1851 he organised 150,000 people to visit London for the Great Exhibition. Increasingly confident, he ran train tours to all the famous towns, resorts and beauty spots of Great Britain. He planned the routes, provided maps and guides and chaperoned unaccompanied women. In 1862 the Scottish Railway companies refused to provide Cook with cheap tickets, so he switched his destinations to Europe. By 1863, from an office in London, he was conducting over 2,000 tourists to France and 500 to Switzerland each year. For these holidays, Cook provided the first complete package deal: by issuing coupons covering transport and hotel accommodation. The joy for the traveller was that on a Cook's tour he did not have to worry about language or being cheated by venal hoteliers. Having paid in advance, a Cook's tourist could ignore the vexations of dealing with "Johnnie Foreigner".

1866 saw the first Cook's tours to the US; and by 1869 he was taking tourists to the Holy Land and Egypt. In 1872 he arranged the first organised tour around the world– for 200 guineas (£114,000 today), over 222 days. In 1879 his son John Mason Cook (1834–99) took over the business. In 1878 John started a foreign banking department and money exchange, issuing the first travellers' cheques. In the 1880s the British government contracted Thomas Cook & Son to provide military transport and a postal service to Egypt. By 1888 the company had established offices around the world. By 1890 the company had sold over 3.25 million tickets.

John Cook went on to develop the exclusive tourist market. He made the lavish arrangements for conducting Indian Maharajas to Queen Victoria's golden and diamond jubilees. He also bought the Mount Vesuvius funicular railway. In 1884 the government contracted the firm to transport the expedition to Khartoum to relieve General Gordon. A dispute over the final bill denied John Cook the knighthood he craved.

In 1898 he planned and accompanied Kaiser Wilhelm II on a tour of the Holy Land. He contracted dysentery however and died a few months later on 4 March 1899. The company passed to Cook's grandsons, remaining in the family until February 1928 – when unexpectedly it was sold for £3.5 million, to the Compagnie Internationale des Wagons Lits of Belgium (nearly £700 million today).

FOOTBALL

The Ancient Greeks played a game called *episkyros*, developed by the Romans into *harpastum*, which required a marked rectangular field and involved two teams: the aim was to carry a ball over the other team's base line using both hands and feet. The Romans introduced it to England; and by the ninth century references to boys playing ball games are recorded in *Historia Brittonum* (the "History of the Britons"). The Normans may have brought with them a ball game called *La Choule* in 1066.

Mediæval Englishmen, particularly on Shrove Tuesday, enjoyed a form of mob football played between neighbouring towns and villages. Unlimited numbers of players on both sides strove by any means to move a ball or inflated pig's bladder to a predesignated "goal", often several miles away, such as an opponent's church. These games caused riots and were hugely destructive of property. The first official reference to football in England was recorded in 1314, during the reign of King Edward II, when the Lord Mayor of London, Nicholas de Farndone forbade "hustling over large foot balls".

In 1363 Edward III banned football; as well as cock fighting, hockey and coursing. He was concerned that these were diverting young men from the compulsory archery practice considered essential to the defence of the realm. A pair of football boots was ordered by King Henry VIII in 1526: and the first reference to ladies playing football was made in 1580, by Sir Philip Sydney in a poem: "When she, with skirts tuckt up very hy, with girles at football playes". In 1581 the headmaster of Eton College, Richard Mulcaster wrote about the rules of the game as it was played at Eton. In 1608 William Shakespeare, in *King Lear*, comments disapprovingly: "Nor tripped neither, you base football player". King James I however, in his 1618 *Book of Sports*, an edict to resolve a conflict with the Puritans in Lancashire on the subject of Sunday recreations, instructs Christian men to play football every Sunday afternoon after church.

Between 1649–1830 football declined, for a number of reasons: during the Commonwealth the Puritans forbade any leisure activity on Sundays, the only day when working-men had time off; subsequent land enclosures, growing industrialisation and more effective town policing made it difficult to find fields on which to play; and the opposition of an increasing, and increasingly prosperous, urban middle class, which disliked any form of civil disorder. But, in the early 19th century, there was one place where football could, and did, thrive – the English public school. Each had its own unique set of rules, defined by geography and the space available in which to play.

By the 1830s the public schools were themselves changing: as parents, newly enriched by the profits of industrialisation, required a more modern, disciplined and focused curriculum – for sons destined to be soldiers, merchants, doctors, lawyers, administrators and engineers, equipped to run the British Empire. Led by Dr Thomas Arnold (1795–1842), headmaster of Rugby School, a new sense of discipline was injected into every aspect of public school life, including sports. The Victorians believed that disciplined team sports developed character: by fostering team work, self-reliance, endurance and above all courage – healthy exhaustion also discouraged masturbation, a uniquely Victorian moral hazard ("muscular Christianity" never risked leaving matters in teenage boys' hands). Team spirit was the very essence of what was required to rule an Empire: and competitive team games required codified rules – as, in due course did individual sports, like boxing, golf and tennis. From the 1840s the public schools began to introduce them to football: Eton and Harrow agreed teams of eleven; and Eton suggested a referee. These small beginnings led to the "Cambridge Rules".

The Cambridge Rules of football were drawn up at Trinity College, Cambridge in 1848 by representatives from Britain's leading public schools: one of whom, the Reverend John (J.C.) Thring (1824–1909), was headmaster of Uppingham from 1853–87. They laid the basis for codes of conduct in the future, the most important being the code of Association Football. Other football codes were written at this time, notably by the Sheffield Football Association in 1857. In 1862 J.C. Thring wrote a simpler set of rules, the "Uppingham Rules". A combination of his original and newer rules, they were adopted by the Football Association in 1863 – if anyone should be considered the "father" of the modern game, it would be Thring.

Oliver Cromwell became a noted footballer at Sydney Sussex College, Cambridge – it was only by good fortune that his skull was not used as a football when it landed after a storm, at the feet of a night watchman in 1684.

Charterhouse used the site of an old Carthusian monastery in the City of London, where paving stones discouraged tackling and a dribbling game developed. Westminster, Eton, Harrow, Winchester and Shrewsbury all favoured dribbling too, but forbade running with a ball in hand: the one exception being Rugby, which did.

The Football Association was formed on 26 October 1863 (the year before over-arm bowling was permitted in cricket), at the Freemasons Tavern in Great Queen Street in London. Five meetings later, the first set of comprehensive rules were produced. But, led by Blackheath, several dissenting football clubs, which objected to the rule disallowing handling and running with the ball, withdrew – and founded the Rugby Football Union in 1871. The eleven remaining clubs, under Ebenezer (E.C.) Morley (1831–1924), ratified the thirteen original laws of the game. The rules had now been clarified, for what is now the most popular sport in the world – soccer.

In 1870 an old Harrovian, and committee member since 1866, Charles William Alcock (1842–1907), became the Honorary Secretary of the Football Association. He led the development of both international football and cricket: and was the creator of the FA Cup – first contested in 1872. Fifty clubs were eligible to participate, but only fifteen entered. The Cup was won by the Wanderers, a mostly Harrovian side, who beat the Royal Engineers at the Oval. The Wanderer's Captain was, of course – Charles Alcock.

The Old Etonians won the FA Cup twice, in 1879 and 1882, and were six times runners-up before the professional game developed. They were the last amateur team to win the Cup; and the last public school ever to reach the final.

Charles Wreford-Brown (1866–1951) captained the England national football team, was also a county cricketer and went on to act as a sports legislator in the 20th century. Despite a lack of supporting evidence, Wreford-Brown is credited with inventing the term "socca" as an abbreviation for as[soc]iation football, around 1889. Referred to as "socker" in 1891, by 1895 it had become soccer ("-er" was a colloquial Cambridge word-ending, as in "brekker", or indeed "rugger").

On 2 May 1982 the nuclear submarine HMS *Conqueror*, commanded by Commander Christopher Wreford-Brown sank ARA *General Belgrano* during the Falklands War.

In the decades following the founding of the Football Association in 1863, football had progressed out of all recognition. It had started as a confused medley of games played to different rules by a small number of public school boys. Fifty years later 120,000 spectators attended the 1913 Cup Final. The game's popularity was mirrored abroad. Football is today followed by nearly 3 billion people – many more Chinese watched England lose to Portugal in the quarter-final of the 2006 FIFA World Cup than viewers in England itself. The final was watched by an audience of over 715 million worldwide. In 2008 there were 204 countries affiliated to FIFA – in all history, there has never been a sport to compare with it.

In November 1872 Alcock organised the first formal international: between England and Scotland (playing as Queen's Park Football Club). It took place in Glasgow, before a crowd of 4,000 – and although a draw, it was a landmark in the history of the game.

In 1888, in Birmingham, William McGregor (1846–1911), a director of Aston Villa, persuaded eleven other clubs to establish the first national Football League in England.

A league was founded in Ireland in 1890 and in Scotland in 1891 – the year that the English League expanded to fourteen clubs. In 1892 a second Division, of another fourteen, consisting entirely of Northern and Midlands clubs was formed. It was not until 1894, when they formed their own league, that Southern clubs were able to compete. It took until 1901 for one of them, Tottenham Hotspur to win the FA Cup. By 1905 the Football League had expanded to forty clubs, in two divisions. In 1904 the French had established the Fédération Internationale de Football Association (FIFA) in Paris – declaring however, that FIFA would abide by the Laws of the Game of the Football Association. In 1913 FIFA members were admitted to the Board of the International Football Association (IFAB), which had been established in England in 1886. The laws of Football are still made by IFAB.

At the end of the 19th century the British ruled, traded, opened banks, built and managed railways and operated mines across the globe. Wherever they went, the British formed football

Sir Stanley Matthews (1915–2000), nicknamed "the wizard of dribble" and "the Magician", was born in Hanley, Staffordshire. As an outside-right, he played for Stoke City from 1932–47 and again from 1961–66. He was capped for England 54 times. He is the only player to have been knighted while still playing.

A vegetarian teetotaller, at the age of fifty Matthews was the oldest player ever to play in the First Division – and is England's best-loved footballer of all time.

• **Sir Stanley Matthews**

In December 1915 British soldiers of the Royal Welch Fusiliers heard German soldiers in their trenches on the other side of No Man's Land singing *Silent Night*: and replied with *Good King Wenceslas*. On Christmas Day, spontaneously both sides emerged from their trenches and advanced towards each other: someone produced a football; and a kick-around, with up to fifty players on each side, took place for thirty minutes – until a British officer reminded them that, "they were there to kill the Hun not to make friends with him". British artillery opened up shortly afterwards and seasonal goodwill ended abruptly – never to be repeated in WWI.

clubs: AC Milan was founded in 1899 by Alfred Edwards and Herbert Kilpin – which is why the name is not *AC Milano* and the cross of St George forms part of its badge. Expatriate sporting clubs often attracted the local "smart set", with ambitions to educate their own sons in the admired imperial traditions at British boarding schools. Back home they repeated the British experience: first the clubs, then a knockout challenge – finally local and national leagues with professional players.

Athletic Bilbao, the first football club in Spain, was founded in 1889 by British mining engineers extracting copper in Andalucia. The first football club in France was established in Paris in 1863 by English expatriates. A newspaper article announced: "A number of English gentlemen living in Paris have lately organised a football club …. the football contests take place in the Bois de Boulogne, by permission of the authorities and surprise the French amazingly". In 1887 Clement Charnock, the Lancastrian owner of a Russian textile mill, founded *Morozovtsi Orekhovo-Zuevo Moskva* for his employees, in an attempt to curb drunkenness. It became *OKS Moskva* in 1906, now possibly the most famous Russian football club of all: Dynamo Moscow.

In 1894 Charles William Miller (1874–1953) turned soccer into a sensation in São Paulo, the game having first been introduced to Brazil by an Englishman running the railway in Jundiaí in 1882. The first game under FA rules took place in Buenos Aires in 1867, home then to 40,000 British expatriates. By 1891 The Argentine had founded its own league (the first officially recognised outside the British Isles), run by Alexander Watson Hutton (1853–1936), a Scottish school teacher, now regarded as the "father of Argentine football". Virtually everywhere in South America before WWI it was the same: first the local gentry took up the game, then it became the consuming passion of the working-classes. This gave rise to the snide quip, that soccer "is a gentleman's game played by yobs; whilst rugby is a yob's game played by gentlemen".

As with cricket, the influence of football extends to the vernacular. In starting a meeting, you might "kick off" or "get the ball rolling". If you are in agreement, you are "on side". When reflecting on an idea, you might "kick it around": before you either "kick it into touch" or "give it your best shot". If we make a mess of it, we can be said to have "scored an own goal" – or we can excuse ourselves by claiming that "the goal posts have been moved". A fair contest of any description can be described as taking place "on a level playing field". Finally, we ought to be reminded of the dangers of "playing away from home".

RUGBY FOOTBALL

Rugby Football is divided into two variants, Rugby Union and Rugby League. The game originated at Rugby School in Warwickshire in 1823. It is said that William Webb Ellis (1806–72), "with a fine disregard for the rules as played in his time, first took the ball in his arms and ran with it". Certainly the H-style goal posts and the requirement to kick the ball over the cross bar were unique to Rugby School; and an oval ball was in use at Rugby by the 1830s. By 1845 these features had been included in the first written rules. It was only the issue of hacking, the deliberate kicking of opponent players on the shins, that caused F.W. Campbell, Captain of Blackheath Club, to lead 15 clubs out of the fifth meeting of the Football Association in 1863.

Rugby School went its own way, with a growing number of other clubs developing their own versions of the game. In 1870 the crowds attracted by a properly regulated Football Association game, and increasing public concern over the infliction of serious rugby injuries persuaded the two Old Rugbeian secretaries of the Richmond and Blackheath Clubs to write to *The Times*. They advocated the urgent need for a codified set of rules for all "rugby" clubs: and invited a response from any club that might be interested. On 26 January 1871 representatives from 21 clubs met at the Pall Mall Restaurant. Within two hours it was agreed to form "The Rugby Football Union" (RFU). On 24 June 1871 fifty-four new rules were passed – the most important being the one that forbade the practice of "hacking, hacking-over and tripping".

The Scots created their own rugby union in 1873, the Irish in 1879 and the Welsh in 1881 – where it was so popular that within ten years, virtually every substantial town boasted its own club. The game also flourished in the north of England. The northern counties, led by Yorkshire, started their own competition in 1877, nicknaming their cup "T'owd tin pot". In 1885 it was decided that the rules were to be enforced by referees equipped with whistles; and that the existing umpires would be replaced by flag-carrying touch judges. By 1893 various experiments in point-winning were set aside in favour of the system used at Cheltenham College – very similar to today's.

Two attempts were made, in 1876 and 1881, to introduce a Rugby Union Challenge Cup to compete with the hugely successful FA cup: but the RFU committee was unwilling to open a "Pandora's Box" of evils – principally betting. The committee also believed that "competition" was contrary to the game's amateur status. When the first challenge cup, the Calcutta Cup, was presented to the RFU, the committee decided that it would be contested only by England and Scotland.

By 1893 the issue of professionalism had reached a head. The northern clubs were attracting increasingly large crowds, a trend that could only be sustained by fielding the best players available – and this meant paying them. In 1885 the Football Association had avoided a split by making their game professional. Rugby players however, particularly in the south, considering themselves gentlemen, disliked and banned professional status. Four northern clubs were suspended for trying to sidestep the ruling. Later that year all the Yorkshire clubs protested: and on 29 August 1895 twenty-two northern clubs met in the George Hotel in Huddersfield to form the Northern Rugby Football Union: and then resigned from the RFU. Mass defections followed. In 1893 there had been 481 clubs in the RFU: but by 1903 only 244 remained. Professionalism in rugby football meant that the sides were now composed of the best players drawn from all over the British Isles. The new union became the Rugby Football League in 1922.

The main reason for the split in 1895 was the RFU's decision to enforce the amateur principle, disallowing "broken time payments" to players who had taken time off work. Northern teams had fewer players who could afford to play without compensation than those in the south. New South Wales, the industrial heartland of Australia, experienced a similar division: and rugby league swiftly became the more popular sport.

Since 1906 the laws of rugby league have evolved to eschew most struggles for possession; while rugby union still contests the ball – after a tackle, or on the ground in scrums, rucks and line-outs. There are fewer rules in the league game and less stoppages, with the ball typically in play for 50 out of the 80 minutes, against less than 40 in rugby union. Additionally, with only thirteen players, rugby league is more exhausting. It is probably the most physically demanding of any team sport in the world.

In 1905 the first All Blacks side arrived in Britain. They won all 27 of their matches, including internationals against England and Ireland – scoring a total of 801 points against a paltry 22 scored by all their opponents combined.

The Rugby Union season revolved around the Home Nations Championship: which became the Five Nations in 1910, when the French were invited to join. France was expelled in 1932 for fielding professionals and did not rejoin until 1947. In 2000 it became the Six Nations, when Italy was admitted. Like football, rugby was gaining popularity all over the world. By 1874 Sydney had fourteen clubs: but it was not until 1949 that the Australian RFU was formed. The first game of rugby was played in New Zealand in 1870. Socially inclusive, it was also played by native Maoris; and in 1892 The New Zealand RFU was founded. It is now New Zealand's national game.

South Africa had been playing a bastardised form of rugby, called Gog's football since 1862, but switched to Rugby Union in 1878. Gog's Football, played by Winchester School, was introduced by an old Wykehamist, Canon G. Ogilvie. The name arose from the only legible part of his signature.

The British and Irish Lions, known as the "British Isles" from 1888–1950 and the "British Lions" from 1950–2001, is a touring team made up of players from all four home countries. Test series are held every four years, usually against Australia, New Zealand and South Africa. The last amateur tour was in 1993. The World Cup was first held in 1987, confirming Rugby's status as a major international sport.

The South African Rugby Football Board was established in Kimberly in 1889. In 1906 the Springboks toured Britain, losing only two matches: and returned in 1912 to defeat all four home nations. In 1908 the Australian Wallabies lost only five out of 25 matches. Rugby also spread to South America, particularly Argentina and Uruguay – where it was adopted by the expatriate British cricket clubs as a winter game. Rugby became instantly popular in Fiji too, when it was first played there in 1884.

International matches generated a thriving income, encouraging the RFU to buy a site at Twickenham as a home for England games. "Twickers" is the largest rugby stadium in the UK, seating 82,000. In 1907 RFU Committee member Billy Williams bought a 10.25 acre market-garden for £5,572 12s 6d (£2.2 million today) – the reason for the ground's nickname, the "Cabbage Patch". The first game, between Harlequins and Richmond, was played on 2 October 1909; and the first international, England against Wales, on 15 January 1910 – when the stadium held a maximum capacity of 20,000.

On 26 January 1995, three days short of the centenary of Rugby Football's great schism, the International Rugby Board voted to accept professionalism. Pretence at amateur status had long evaporated; and star players, although strictly not paid a salary, had lived perfectly well off a stream of perks and sponsorship.

The RFU, anxious to rid the sport of hypocrisy, accepted the decision – but change was difficult and some British clubs went bankrupt. They now compete in the Heineken Cup, the major European competition. The first four World Cups were won by southern hemisphere sides: a record broken by England in Sydney in 2003 and nearly again in 2007.

THE MAP THAT CHANGED THE WORLD

William Smith was born in 1769, the same year as Wellington and Napoleon, in Gloucestershire. He invented the science of Stratigraphy; and in 1815, made the world's first national geological map. Many of the names he gave to strata (layers or a series of layers of rock) are still used today.

The son of a respectable farmer who died when he was a child, Smith was brought up by his uncle. Although he attended only the village school, he was an avid reader who taught himself the basics of surveying from books he bought himself.

While working as a surveyor in Somerset, Smith noticed that many layers of rock (strata) were arranged in a predictable pattern each with its own identifiable fossils. He was inspired to discover whether these patterns and characteristics were repeated throughout the country. Smith mapped the strata and drew pictures of the fossils he uncovered in canals, road and rail cuttings, quarries, cliffs and escarpments.

He assembled a huge collection of fossils: and in 1799, published his findings in his first large scale geological map of the area around Bath, in Somerset. Whilst unemployed, he travelled throughout the country developing his technique of illustrating soils, rocks and strata in different coloured inks. In 1801 he produced his completed "Map that changed the world".

By 1800 Smith had acquired a sound reputation as a geological engineer and had established a busy practice: not only with gentleman farmers but also government funded reclamation, colliery and canal projects. He also helped restore the hot springs at Bath. Smith travelled over 10,000 miles a year, made possible by road surfaces improved by John "Tar" McAdam; and a swift, national mail coach service.

Sir Herbert Beerbohm Tree
in Pygmalion (1852–1917)

In 1815, the year of Waterloo, he published the first geological map of Britain: followed in the same year by his *Delineation of the Strata of England and Wales*, in which he showed how stratified fossils could be used to match rocks across Britain. In 1817 he published a remarkable geological section map from Snowdon to London. Unfortunately, Smith's humble origins and lack of social connections prevented him from being welcomed into learned society. Consequently his work, unprotected by copyright, was plagiarised and undercut. He fell into debt, was declared bankrupt and spent ten weeks in the filthy King's Bench debtors' prison. On his release in 1819, he found that his London house at 15 Buckingham Street, in which he kept his unique fossil collection, had been seized; and his fossils sold to the British Museum.

Near destitute, for several years Smith eked out a living as an itinerant surveyor: until Sir John Johnstone, 2nd Baronet (1799–1869) of Scarborough in Yorkshire, one of his employers and himself a keen amateur geologist, realised the extent of Smith's extraordinary achievements. He took Smith in and set about establishing his deserved reputation – easing Smith's life considerably. From 1824–26 he was employed building the Scarborough Rotunda, a geological museum dedicated to the Yorkshire coast.

On 9 May 2008 the Rotunda was reopened as "The William Smith Museum of Geology", a project strongly supported by The Prince of Wales.

In 1831 Smith at long last, received his due recognition: when the Geological Society of London presented him with its first Wollaston Medal. This was capped in 1832 by the award of an annual pension from the crown. At his medal presentation the President, Adam Sedgwick referred to Smith as "The Father of English Geology". In 1835 Smith was invited to accompany the Society to Dublin: where to his delight he received an honorary Doctorate from Trinity College. In 1838 he was appointed one of the commissioners to select the stone for the new Palace of Westminster.

Smith died in Northampton on 28 August 1839. His contribution to geology was both so original and yet so logical, that his techniques are still in use. The modern geological map of Britain is very similar to Smith's – which is on display at the Geological Society in London.

THE PERFORMING ARTS

Sir Herbert Draper Beerbohm Tree (1852–1917) was born in Kensington in the year that the Duke of Wellington died. His father, Julius Ewald Edward Beerbohm, of Dutch, German and Lithuanian extraction, was a corn merchant who came to Britain *c.*1830. He married Constantia Draper and had four children by her.

Educated both in England and in Germany, Herbert joined his father's business – but spent his spare time performing with amateur dramatic groups. In 1878 he turned professional, taking the stage name of Beerbohm Tree. His half-brother, the author and caricaturist Max Beerbohm (1872–1956), joked that Herbert worried that audiences would find "Beerbohm" awkward when calling for encores (*bohm* means "tree" in Low German). As Tree, he was to become the greatest actor-manager of the Edwardian age.

Sir Henry Irving (1838–1905), born John Henry Brodribb to a working-class family in Keinton Mandeville in Somerset, was Tree's great Victorian predecessor. Irving was perhaps the finest tragedian of all time – and utterly dedicated to his profession. When his pregnant wife criticised him on the way to an opening night at the theatre: "Are you going on making a fool of yourself like this all your life?", Irving got out of their carriage, walked off into the night and never saw her again. He only grew close to his children late in life. In the 1981 musical Cats, Gus the theatre cat sings, "He has acted with Irving, he's acted with Tree".

Tree had a natural talent for romantic roles and was a genius in comedy. In 1884 he won great acclaim in Charles Hawtrey's adaptation of *The Private Secretary*, acting the part of a curate, Robert Spalding. His next success was as a raffish spy, Paolo Marcari in Hugh Conway's *Called Back*. These contrasting roles demonstrated Tree's versatility – though, with a rather reedy little voice, he never quite mastered tragedy.

In 1887 Tree leased the Haymarket Theatre, staging and directing lavish Shakespearean productions, as well as acting in a wide range of plays and parts. Ten years later he moved to Her Majesty's Theatre (in 1901 it became "His Majesty's" with the accession of Edward VII): which he re-designed in a Louis XV style. Tree's characterization of Fagin in Charles Dickens's *Oliver Twist* was considered brilliant. Unlike many managers of his time, Tree recognised the importance of promoting new playwrights and staging modern dramas, with artistic rather than just commercial merit: such as *The Intruder* by Maurice Maeterlinck in 1895; and, both in 1893, *A Woman of No Importance* by Oscar Wilde and *An Enemy of the People* by Henrik Ibsen.

From 1897 until his death Tree mounted over 60 richly diverse productions, mingling classical, including *The School for Scandal* by Sheridan in 1909, and popular plays: such as his contemporary, Shaw's *Pygmalion* in 1914. Poetic drama also interested him: he produced *Ulysses* in 1902, *Nero* in 1906 and *Faust* by Stephen Phillips in 1908. He introduced stage versions of the works of 19th century novelists (Thackeray, Dumas and Tolstoy) and stage adaptations of foreign plays (*Beethoven* by Louis Parker): as well as a lively mix of melodramas, farces and romantic comedies, such as *The Perfect Gentleman* by Somerset Maugham in 1913.

Over 20 years at His Majesty's Theatre, always hiring the best actors available, Tree staged sixteen Shakespeare plays – proving how appealingly the Bard's works could be presented to the public. His *Julius Caesar* in 1898 continued for 165 performances, attracting an audience of 242,000. In 1900 his *King John* was watched by 170,000 and *Midsummer Night's Dream*, which used battery-operated lights to illuminate the fairies, by 220,000. In 1910 his *Henry VIII* ran for 254 consecutive performances. A rare mistake was a well-meaning attempt in 1908 to challenge prevailing anti-Semitism in his *Merchant of Venice*, criticised for histrionic and scenic excess.

Tree's career was among the most important in providing a continuum for one of Britain's greatest contributions to the modern world (and now a valuable source of foreign earnings): taking a 400 year-old tradition of make-believe from the theatre, first to the cinema and, long after his death, to television.

From Charlie Chaplin (1889–1977) and Stan Laurel (1890–1965) as comics, Ronald Coleman (1891–1958) and Cary Grant (1904–86) as *matinée* idols, to Laurence Olivier (1907–89) and a host of famous Shakespeareans in tragedy; from Alfred Hitchcock (1899–1980) and David Lean (1908–91) as just two of the many great British film directors, to all the makers of popular programmes, "sitcoms", dramas and comedies, documentaries and natural history series – the sweep of British culture is as well known across the globe as the English language itself. The employment of so many

Sir Henry Irving by Jules Bastien-Lepage (1880)
National Portrait Gallery, London

The first of Tree's two greatest contributions to British theatre was his international popularisation of the plays of William Shakespeare, anticipating the Royal Shakespeare Company. The second was in 1904, when he founded the Royal Academy of Dramatic Art (RADA), the most prestigious acting school in the world.

Sir Charles Spencer "Charlie" Chaplin took the music hall tradition to the cinema

Marie Lloyd by Schloss (1890). Born Matilda Alice Victoria Wood, she was a celebrated music hall singer (1870–1922)
National Portrait Gallery, London

Cary Grant (born Archibald Leach)

Laurence, Lord Olivier OM, Britain's greatest 20th century actor

gifted scriptwriters, animators, set designers and cameramen, to mention but a few of the skills and techniques supported by the media, and to ignore the world of advertising and news dissemination, is vital to the nation. The BBC itself is rightly considered one of the greatest international brand names, a byword for impartiality and quality.

Tree created spectacular stage-sets, treating his Edwardian audiences to realistic backdrops such as a shepherd's cottage complete with babbling brook in *The Winter's Tale* in 1906. He was the first to have Shakespeare filmed (in four one-minute scenes) – *King John* in 1899. He made an expensive film of *Henry VIII*, with himself as Cardinal Wolsey, at Will Barker's Ealing Studios in 1911: and, in 1916, played the title role in *Macbeth*, filmed by D.W. Griffith in California. Unlike his brother Max, a theatre critic who was disparaging, Tree greeted the arrival of film with enthusiasm.

Tree married an actress, Helen Maud Holt (1863–1937), who often appeared opposite him, and they had three daughters. Tree was president of the Theatrical Manager's Association and a lifelong supporter of the Actors' Benevolent Fund. He toured the US with Shakespeare revivals and even accepted an invitation from Kaiser Wilhelm II in 1907, to perform Shakespeare in Berlin. He was knighted in 1909.

Tree was almost last in the line of great actor managers which had begun with Geoffrey de Gorham (*c*.1098–1146), who produced the first "mystery" play in England, at Dunstable Priory around 1118. It continued through Edward Alleyn (1566–1626), who founded Dulwich College in 1619; David Garrick (1717–79); Edward Kean (1787–1833); and Henry Irving, who with Dame Ellen Terry (1848–1928) dominated English and US theatre from 1878–1902. Only Sir Donald Wolfit (1902–68), a noted Shakespearean who founded his own company in 1937, and Bernard, Lord Miles (1907–91), a character actor and Shakespearean who established the Mermaid Theatre in 1951, were to follow him.

The world of theatre and the "silver screen" is now split between impresarios, producers, directors and actors – all of whom know their place.

Tree died suddenly on 2 July 1917, from a pulmonary blood clot after an operation on a broken leg. He was cremated and his ashes were interred in Hampstead cemetery. He fathered six illegitimate children by his mistress May Pinney, later Reed: including the film producer Sir Carol Reed (1906–76), who made *The Third Man* in 1949 and won the 1968 Academy Award for Best Director for *Oliver!*; and Peter Reed, the father of the boisterous actor and heavy-drinker, Oliver Reed (1938–99).

THREE GUERNSEY TO WELLINGTON CONNECTIONS

Major-General Sir Isaac Brock (1769–1812) successfully defended Upper Canada (now Ontario) against invasion during the Anglo-US War of 1812. He was born, in the same year as the Duke of Wellington, at St Peter Port on Guernsey, in the Channel Islands.

In 1810 he was appointed commander of all British forces in Upper Canada, taking over the civil administration of the province in 1811. When war broke out between Britain and the US the following year, Major-General Brock organised the defences of Upper Canada swiftly and effectively. He had only four regular British regiments, a total of 1,450 men, augmented with native Indians from the Shawnee tribe, whose chief Tecumseh he had befriended, to defend a 1,000 mile frontier.

On 15 August 1812, although vastly outnumbered, with a motley force of 300 British regular troops, 600 local Canadian militia and 400 untrained American Indians, Brock attacked and seized Detroit from the US commander, General Hull. On 13 October his small army defeated

US forces decisively at Queenston Heights, overlooking Niagara on the Canadian frontier. He was killed, together with his *aide-de-camp* Colonel McDonell, leading an uphill charge against a captured British 18-pounder gun.

There is a statue commemorating Brock in the south transept of St Paul's Cathedral. On 13 October 1824 Brock and McDonell were reburied on Queenston Heights.

Sir Rowland Hill FRS (1795–1879), later the Secretary of the General Post Office, and his Western District Surveyor, Anthony Trollope are credited with the introduction of the pillar box. Hill invented the postage stamp in 1837 and introduced the world's first uniform penny postal service in 1840.

In 1852 Hill sent Anthony Trollope to the Channel Islands to reorganise mail collections, often disrupted by weather and tides. Trollope had recently noticed "letter receiving pillars" in Paris: and recommended them to Hill. A cast iron, 4 foot 6 inches high octagonal cylinder was designed and painted olive green – later changed to "pillar box red" for visibility and recognition. Vaudin & Son, a Jersey foundry, was commissioned to build four which were erected around St Helier. They were officially introduced on 23 November 1852, less than nine weeks after the death of the Duke of Wellington. On 8 February 1853 Guernsey received its first three pillar boxes – one of which, marked "VR" (for *Victoria Regina*), is still in use.

Anthony Trollope was born in 1815, the year of Waterloo. For 33 years he worked for the post office in England and Ireland. From 1844 he published 47 novels, which he wrote early in the morning at a rate of 1,000 words an hour, and dozens of short stories. His best loved are the Chronicles of Barsetshire, the first serial fiction in English literature: beginning with *The Warden* in 1855 and ending with the *Last Chronicle of Barset* in 1867. *Can You Forgive Her?* in 1865 was the first of a series centred round Plantaganet Palliser, later Duke of Omnium – the most popular was a sharp satire, *The Eustace Diamonds* in 1872.

Trollope's father was a barrister and small landowner: clever but so bad-tempered that he lost his clients and failed as a farmer. Though Trollope attended Harrow as a day-boy and Winchester as a boarder, it was as an impoverished outsider and he was miserable. An older brother, a prefect, beat him every day – aged twelve he even contemplated suicide.

In 1834 Trollope found work as a clerk in the General Post Office, a poorly paid but respectable post. In 1842 however, he was sent to Ireland. His superior was indolent, allowing the efficient and indefatigable Trollope to earn a considerable reputation. He rode to hounds

with a passion, came to know Ireland and the Irish intimately; and in 1843, having become engaged to an English girl, Rose Heseltine (died 1917), began to write. They settled happily at Clonmel in Tipperary, where their two sons were born. In 1859, Trollope moved back to London; and in 1867 resigned from the Post Office – to stand, unsuccessfully, for Parliament as a Liberal candidate in 1868. In 1871 and again in 1875, the Trollopes travelled

As a result of the 1812–14 war between Britain and the US, and concern that Britain might intervene in the US Civil War (1861–65) in support of the Confederate States, Anglophobia strongly influenced US foreign policy until 1940. In 1935 secret plans to launch surprise attacks on Canada, including bombing Halifax, Montreal and Quebec City, were inadvertently published by the US Government Printing Office and reported by the *New York Times* and *Toronto Globe*.

As it was the first country to introduce them, the UK remains the only country not to identify itself by name on its stamps.
The adhesive stamp was invented by a bookseller from Arbroath, James Chalmers (1782–1853), in 1838.

An 1853 "VR" pillar box

Anthony Trollope by Samuel Laurence (*c.*1864)
National Portrait Gallery, London

While writing *The Last Chronicle*, Trollope overheard two clergymen at the Athenaeum Club complaining that his characters, including Mrs Proudie, reappeared too often. He rose and introduced himself, saying: "As to Mrs Proudie, I will go home and kill her before the week is over" – and he did.

to Australia to visit their younger son Frederic, who was a sheep farmer in New South Wales.

In 1869 he wrote *He Knew He Was Right*, an exquisite account of a rich man's jealousy of his blameless wife. This, and *The Way We Live Now* in 1875, a fascinating portrayal of Melmotte, a villainous financier, display extraordinary psychological insight and a sardonic understanding of the Victorian upper classes. In his autobiography, Trollope wrote that the novelist's task is, "to make his readers so intimately acquainted with his characters that the creation of his brain should be to them speaking, moving, living, human creatures". He died after a stroke in London in 1882 and was buried in Kensal Green cemetery. The novelist William "Wilkie" Collins (1824–89) (*The Moonstone*, *The Woman in White*) lies nearby.

Flourishing Trollope Societies exist today in both Britain and the US. W.H. Auden (1907–73) wrote of him: "Of all novelists in any country, Trollope best understands the role of money. Compared with him even Balzac is a romantic".

Joanna Trollope (born 1943), the best-selling author of what are described by envious critics, as "Aga sagas", and who also dreaded her schooldays, is a distant relation.

Another Harrovian, the playwright and novelist John Galsworthy OM (1867–1933), who wrote *The Forsyte Saga* (1906–21), a series comparable in vein and style with the best of Trollope, won the Nobel Prize for Literature in 1932.

THE NATION'S DARLING

Grace Darling, another born in 1815, was the epitome of a Victorian heroine, created by a dramatic sea rescue. She was born in Bamburgh in Northumberland. Her father, William Darling was a lighthouse keeper. In the early hours of 7 September 1838, Grace looked out from the Longstone Lighthouse on the Farne Islands and saw a ship wrecked on the rocks and a few huddled survivors. The 270-ton paddle-steamer SS *Forfarshire*, carrying 63 passengers and crew from Hull to Dundee, had foundered the previous night on Big Harcar, a low-lying rocky island. Her father, perhaps hoping to secure salvage rights by being first on the scene, and realising that the weather was too bad to call out the lifeboat from the mainland, launched the lighthouse rowing boat: a four-man, 21-foot Northumberland coble.

Keeping in the lee shore of Big Harcar, Grace and her father rowed a mile in terrifying seas; and carried to safety four men and a woman. William and two of the survivors, set out again for Big Harcar to rescue four remaining survivors. In all, William rescued nine people.

"Grace's deed" brought a frenzy of attention to the "girl with the windswept hair", from a national press enabled by the recent inventions of telegraph and railway to distribute such popular copy swiftly to every corner of the land. Grace became a heroine: and she and her father, were presented with silver medals by the National Institution for the Preservation of Life from Shipwreck, forerunner to the Royal National Lifeboat Institute (RNLI) – which has saved over 137,000 lives at sea since 1824.

The government awarded Grace £50 (nearly £40,000 today); and a further £1,000 (£785,000 today) in trust was raised through public subscription for her and her father. She sold locks of her hair and cut up her dress to satisfy public demand for souvenirs. Summer visitors swarmed to view her and the shipwreck site. A circus proprietor tried to engage her as a travelling curiosity.

Grace died of tuberculosis on 20 October 1842 and was buried in St Aidan's churchyard in Bamburgh, under an elaborate monument. Her father

Grace Darling by Henry Perlee Parker (1838)
National Portrait Gallery, London

Forfarshire was renamed County Angus in 1928. Hugh Watson (1780–1865) was a stockbreeder whose bull "Jock" was No. 1 in the herd book of the Aberdeen Angus breed of black, polled cattle in 1842. Introduced in 1873, Black Angus is the most popular breed of beef cattle in the US: with 324,266 registered in 2005.

William died in 1865. The poets William Wordsworth (1771–1855) and Algernon Swinburne (1837–1909) commemorated "Grace's deed" – both, regrettably, in rather indifferent verse.

SIR JAMES MATTHEW (J.M.) BARRIE WAS BORN IN FORFAR

James, known usually as J.M. Barrie (1860–1937) is best known for creating the character loved by all children, *Peter Pan*.

Peter Pan was inspired by a chance meeting with Sylvia Llewelyn-Davies and her children while walking his St Bernard dog, "Porthos" in Kensington Gardens in 1897. He relived his childhood by telling them *Peter Pan* stories. Barrie had many friendships with children, inevitably leading to conjecture that he was a pædophile. The rumour was always strongly denied by the youngest Llewelyn-Davies child, Nicholas (1903–80): "He was innocent – that is why he could write Peter Pan".

Barrie was born in Kirriemuir in Forfar, now Angus, the son of a Calvinist weaver. The family's favourite son died in a skating accident when Barrie was six years old. The traumatic effect of this tragedy possibly induced in the young Barrie psychogenic dwarfism (he grew to be only 5 foot 3 inches) and an undeveloped sexuality. He learned how to divert and comfort his mother by telling her stories. He was educated at Dumfries Academy, then at Edinburgh University. Destined for the Ministry, Barrie wrote for the University newspaper; before working first as a journalist in Nottingham, then moving to London as a freelance writer. A London editor was so much taken by his stories that he commissioned a series of novels: *Auld Licht Idylls* in 1888, *A Widow in Thrums* in 1890 and *The Little Minister* in 1891. Although overly sentimental and far removed from the harsh reality of the age, the novels sold well. Turning to drama, Barrie wrote a number of successful plays: *Ibsen's Ghost* in 1891, *Quality Street* and the critically acclaimed *The Admirable Crichton* in 1902.

Peter Pan first appeared in a serialised novel, *Little White Bird* also in 1902; and as a play in 1904. To capitalise on its success, Barrie published *Peter and Wendy* in 1911.

Peter Pan, the boy who refused to grow up, was described by George Bernard Shaw as "ostensibly a holiday entertainment for children but really a play for grown-ups". Barrie gave the copyright to the Great Ormonde Street Hospital for Sick Children in 1929. *Peter Pan* was followed over the years by a string of successes: *The Twelve Pound Look* in 1910, *Dear Brutus* in 1917 and *The Boy David* in 1936.

In 1894 Barrie married an actress, Mary Ansell: but divorced her in 1910 – after discovering he had been cuckolded by one of his literary associates, Gilbert Cannan. The marriage was almost certainly not consummated. The fairyland of Barrie's second boyhood, as portrayed through *Peter Pan*, ended in tragedy. Four months after his divorce, the widowed Sylvia Llewelyn-Davies died. Barrie became guardian to her two sons: one drowned with his homosexual lover and the other was killed in WWI.

J.M. Barrie by George Charles Beresford (1902)
National Portrait Gallery, London

The Admirable Crichton is a comedy, parodying the ridiculous values of a deferential society. There was however, a real "Admirable" Crichton in Scottish history: James Crichton of Clunie (1560–82), an extraordinarily gifted 16th century figure.

Educated at St. Andrews University, James was taught by the celebrated scholar and historian George Buchanan (1506–82), who described him as a prodigy, with a gift for perfect recall. By the age of twenty, he could discourse, in both prose and verse, in Hebrew, Syriac, Arabic, Greek, Latin, Spanish, French, Italian, English, Dutch and Slavonic. He was also an accomplished horseman, fencer, singer, musician, orator and debater. Noted for his good looks as well as his refined social graces, some consider him close to the ideal of the complete man. He was murdered in Mantua, aged only twenty-one.

Barrie was created a baronet in 1913; awarded the Order of Merit in 1922; elected president of the Society of Authors in 1928; and Chancellor of Edinburgh University in 1930. He died on 19 June 1937 and is buried in Kirriemuir. His birthplace at 4, Brechin Road is now a museum. He left his estate to his secretary, Cynthia Asquith. "May God blast anyone who writes a biography of me", was his stated wish – in a curse scrawled across the pages of one of his last notebooks.

Barrie based the character he named "Wendy" (which became fashionable) on Margaret Henley, from the only way that she could pronounce her surname.

DAVID LIVINGSTONE

David Livingstone (1813–73) was a missionary and one of the greatest European explorers in Africa of his time. Lost for several years, his meeting with H.M. Stanley in 1871 provoked the immortal greeting, "Doctor Livingstone, I presume?". He was born at Blantyre near Glasgow into a poor family. By the age of thirteen, he was working in a local cotton mill and attending night school where he developed a deep interest in science and nature. In 1836 he began studying medicine and theology at Anderson's College in Glasgow, with the intent of becoming a missionary doctor. In 1841 he was sent by the London Missionary Society to Kurumi on the edge of the Kalahari Desert: where in 1845 he married Mary Moffat, the daughter of a fellow missionary. In 1844, while setting up a new mission station, he was mauled by a lion.

David Livingston by Frederick Havill
National Portrait Gallery, London

His left arm caused him considerable pain for the rest of his life. Livingstone was frustrated by his failure to win converts; and planned to explore more deeply into the African interior. On 17 November 1855 he discovered the Victoria Falls, which he named for his Queen. He was also one of the first Europeans to cross from the Atlantic to the Indian ocean: a near suicidal expedition, due to the presence of malaria, sleeping sickness (preventing the use of draught animals) and dysentery – quite apart from hostile tribes. Livingstone travelled light with few bearers or weapons, bartering for supplies along the way. He preached Christianity but did not promote it unless he was encouraged to do so. He understood tribal mentality and took care never to present a threat. He believed the best conduit for Christian conversion was trade – at the base of his statue at Victoria Falls is carved the legend "Christianity, Commerce and Civilization". He was convinced that the key to this lay in the navigation of the Zambezi River.

He returned to Britain in 1856 to raise support for his ideas. He published *Missionary Travels and Researches in South Africa* the following year, which established him as a national hero. Also in 1857, believing it God's will, he resigned from any further missionary work: to devote himself to exploration.

With government support for a Zambezi expedition, Livingstone left for Africa in 1858, to carry out an official exploration of eastern and central Africa. Recalled home in 1864 by a government impatient for results, the expedition was castigated in the press as an ignominious failure. Livingstone had been unable to organise such an ambitious project; the Zambezi had proved unnavigable due to cataracts; and his wife had died of malaria.

Undismayed, Livingstone publicised his first-hand experiences of the horrors of the slave trade, which secured funding for another African expedition: with the aim of discovering the source of the Nile and reporting further on the slave trade, a subject which held Victorian Society spellbound.

H.M. Stanley by Eveleen Myers (*née* Tennant) (1890)
National Portrait Gallery, London

In 1866 Livingstone left on his last expedition – and disappeared. In 1869, after three years of silence, H.M. Stanley was sent by the *New York Herald* to find him.

Henry Morton Stanley (1841–1904) was born John Rowlands in Denbigh, north Wales. His mother, Elizabeth Parry was nineteen: his father, also John Rowlands was an alcoholic. They were unmarried and his birth certificate recorded him as a bastard: a stigma he fought to overcome for the rest of his life. He was brought up by his grandfather until he was five. Shortly after he died, Stanley was sent to St. Asaph Union Workhouse for the poor, where lack of supervision resulted in frequent abuse by older boys who "took part in every possible vice". When he was ten, his mother and two siblings were committed to the same workhouse, without Stanley realising who they were. Aged fifteen, after completing his elementary education, he was employed as a pupil teacher in a National School. In December 1858 he emigrated to the US as a cabin boy, in search of a new life. He absconded from his ship when it docked in New Orleans. He met a rich but childless British migrant called Henry Hope Stanley, who first gave him a job and then effectively adopted him. The boy changed his name, became a US citizen and fought for both sides in the Civil War: before turning to journalism. In 1867 he was hired by James Gordon Bennett (1795–1872), founder of the *New York Herald*, who sent him to cover the British expedition to Abyssinia.

In 1869 the silver-tongued Stanley persuaded James Gordon Bennett, Jr. (1841–1918) to commission him to find Livingstone. When he asked how much he could spend, he was told: "Draw £1,000 now (£600,000 today), and when you have gone through that, draw another £1,000, and when that is spent, draw another £1,000, and when you have finished that, draw another £1,000, and so on .... BUT FIND LIVINGSTONE!".

Having found Livingstone, Stanley joined him to explore the region, establishing for certain that there was no connection between Lake Tanganyika and the River Nile. On his return, he wrote *How I Found Livingstone; travels, adventures, and discoveries in Central Africa*. This brought him to the attention of the British public – and King Leopold of the Belgians. Leopold commissioned him to explore the Congo, ostensibly for philanthropic purposes. In fact the King wished to map and exploit his new colony.

Stanley married in 1890, became an M.P. and was knighted in 1899. He died in London.

On 10 November 1871 Stanley found Livingstone at Ujiji, on the shore of Lake Tanganyika. Resupplied by Stanley,

King Leopold II of the Belgians (1835–1909) succeeded his father in 1865. He was Queen Victoria's first cousin. He is chiefly remembered as the founder and sole owner of the Congo Free State. He used Henry Morton Stanley to help him lay claim to over 900,000 square miles of what is now the mineral-rich Democratic Republic of the Congo (which has a current population of nearly 70 million).

Leopold employed mercenaries to plunder the Congo, as his personal fiefdom. His profits were enormous and his regime was brutal. A 1904 report by the British Consul Roger Casement led to the prosecution of white officials for murder (including one Belgian national for killing 120 people in cold blood). In 1908 the Belgian state was embarrassed into assuming responsibility for the colony.

Stanley recounted an incident in *The Times* on 8 November 1890, that illustrated only too graphically the horrors that awaited European explorers in Africa – as recently as the end of the 19th century. It was witnessed by James Jameson (1856–88), a member of the Irish whiskey distilling family and a relation of Gugliemo Marconi's mother Annie. He joined the Emin Pasha Relief Expedition led by Stanley in 1887. Jameson gave six handkerchiefs to a local chief at Riba-Riba in the Congo: who, by way of thanks, promptly produced a ten-year old girl who was killed, dismembered and eaten in front of him. Aghast and sickened Jameson may have been – but he still managed to sketch and document the incident.

Livingstone doggedly continued to search for the source of the Nile. In April 1873 his health, already ruined by disease, finally broke down: and he died on 1 May. His body, borne over a thousand miles by his faithful bearers Chuma and Susi, was returned to Britain – where he was interred in Westminster Abbey. His heart was buried where he died, under a mvula tree near Lake Bangweulu in Zambia. It is now the site of the Livingstone Memorial.

LINKED BY DESIGN

William Morris (1834–96), one of the greatest cultural figures of Victorian Britain and founder of the Arts and Crafts movement, was a painter, designer, craftsman, poet and social reformer. He was born in Walthamstow in north London. His father was a prosperous City bill broker. A precocious child, by the age of four he had read all Sir Walter Scott's *Waverley* novels. He attended Marlborough College, before studying mediæval architecture at Exeter College, Oxford. In 1856 he was apprenticed to the Gothic revival architect, G.E. Street (1824–81), who designed the Royal Courts of Justice in the Strand: but took up painting instead. In 1861, with the "Pre-Raphaelites" Dante Gabriel Rossetti, Edward Burne-Jones and Ford Madox Brown, he founded Morris, Marshall, Faulkner & Co., an association of skilled craftsmen – inspired by, and based on the mediæval guild.

Most famous for Morris's innovative, nature-inspired wallpapers and textiles, the company designed and produced furniture, tapestry, carving, metal work, stained-glass, chintzes and carpets. Morris rejected cheap, manufactured household decorations: his aim was to raise craftsmen to the status of artists and to create hand-made, affordable works of art.
• **A William Morris design**

In 1858 Morris married his model: the beautiful but humbly-born Jane Burden (1839–1914), who posed for his painting *La Belle Iseult* – often misnamed as *Guinevere*. It hangs today in London's Tate Britain. Mixing rather too freely with the Pre-Raphaelites, she had a long-standing affair with Rossetti (1828–82), who was besotted by her.

In 1877 Morris founded the Society for the Protection of Ancient Buildings – the world's first conservation group, it led to the foundation of the National Trust in 1895. Morris wrote volumes of prose and poetry, which were very popular. The best known include the epic *Sigurd the Volsung*, reflecting Morris's fascination with the Icelandic sagas; *The Defence of Guinevere and Other Poems* in 1858; and *The Earthly Paradise* between 1868–70. On the death of Lord Tennyson in 1892, Morris was discreetly approached to be his successor as Poet Laureate: but he

William Morris (1870) by George Frederic Watts OM R.A. (1817–1904) – Watts was known ironically as "England's Michelangelo"
National Portrait Gallery, London

Art Nouveau was a decorative style that blossomed in Western Europe from 1890–1910. The name derived in 1895 from a Parisian art gallery called *L'Art Nouveau*. The style's hallmark, based on plant forms and expressed in sinuous, asymmetric lines, was used in architecture, interior design, graphic art, jewellery and glass. Other important disciples of Art Nouveau were Aubrey Beardsley, Louis Comfort Tiffany in the US and Antonio Gaudi in Spain.

Charles Macintosh (1766–1843), who invented waterproofing by dissolving rubber in 1818, spelled his name differently – the raincoat however, is spelled with a "k".

The Apple Inc. series of laptop computers, first introduced in 1984, were named Macintosh by the designer Jef Raskin, after the variety of North American apple of that name.

declined. In 1884, a committed utopian, he founded the Socialist League.

In 1891 Morris founded the Kelmscott Press, named after his Manor house in the Cotswolds: which published 53 titles in 66 volumes, including the *Works of Geoffrey Chaucer* – one of the pinnacles of book-printing.

Morris died on 3 October 1896 and is buried in Kelmscott churchyard – under a tombstone designed by the architect Philip Webb (1831–1915).

Charles Rennie Mackintosh (1868–1928) was an architect, designer and water colourist. He was a leading light in the Arts and Crafts movement as well as the British champion of Art Nouveau. He exerted a major influence on European design – and still does.

Mackintosh was born in Glasgow to William McIntosh *[sic]* and Margaret Rennie, the fourth of eleven children. Apprenticed to a local architect at sixteen, he attended night classes in the city's School of Art – where he met his wife and collaborator, Margaret MacDonald. His first notable building was for the *Glasgow Herald* in 1893; followed by the Willow tearooms in Sauchiehall Street, between 1896–1904. The architectural project that clinched his international reputation was the Glasgow School of Art (1897–1909). In 1913 he moved to London to concentrate on painting and textile design – derived, in its restrained and economic style, to a great extent from his fascination with Japan.

He admired simple forms and natural materials – in stark contrast to the ostentatious and overstuffed designs of the Edwardian period. Japanese art and minimalist furniture projected simplicity and calm. Mackintosh was also a pioneer of the European Modernist movement which flourished in the years following WWI.

In 1923 poverty drove Mackintosh to settle in Port Vendres, in the South of France, where he created a striking portfolio of architectural and landscape watercolours. He died in London, from cancer of the throat and tongue, on 10 December 1928.

In 2009 the Clydesdale Bank featured Mackintosh on its £100 bank notes: notes which are unique in Britain to Scotland – as of course, was Mackintosh.

Charles Rennie Mackintosh by James Craig Annan (1893)
National Portrait Gallery, London

Mackintosh Chair for the Ingram Street Tea Rooms

TWELVE USEFUL BRITISH INVENTIONS MADE IN WELLINGTONS'S LIFETIME

Steam engine	James Watt FRS (1769)
Tin can (for preserving food)	Peter Durand (1810)
Railway locomotive ("Puffing Billy")	William Hedley (1813)
Tarmacadam (for road surfaces)	John Loudon McAdam (1816)
Portland cement	Joseph Aspidin (1824)
Blood transfusion	James Blundell (1828)
Lawn mower	Edwin Budding (1830)
Screw propeller	Sir Francis Smith (1835)
Bicycle	Kirkpatrick Macmillan (1840)
Artificial fertilizer	Sir John Lawes FRS (1842)
Passenger lift	Michael Loam (1842)
Vulcanized rubber	Thomas Hancock (1843)

THE ESSENCE OF BRITISH TASTE

In 1834 John Wheeley Lea (1791–1874) and William Henry Perrins (1793–1867), apothecaries at Broad Street in Worcester, invented Lea & Perrins Worcestershire sauce. Designed to enhance meat and fish dishes, it was composed of malt and spirit vinegar, molasses, sugar, salt, anchovies, garlic, spices and flavourings. The pair were requested to make up a sauce based on a recipe brought back from India, allegedly by a returning governor of Bengal. They advertised the origin of their sauce discreetly, as derived from "the recipe of a nobleman in the county". The partners prepared a few jars for themselves; but finding the brew unpalatable, left them in the cellar. Some months later they tasted the concoction and, to their astonishment, found it appetising. By 1837, the year of Queen Victoria's accession, the sauce was sold widely. Ironically, John Wheeley Lea died of acute dyspepsia.

Marmite was the creation of a Swiss, Frederick Wissler, a German, Georg Huth and an Englishman, Alexander Vale. The Marmite Food Extract Company began manufacture at Burton-on-Trent in 1902. Marmite is a B vitamin-enriched, savoury spread made from spent brewer's yeast. In 1865 Baron Justus von Liebig (1803–73), a German chemist, had discovered how to concentrate yeast into a vegetarian foodstuff. Marmite was included in soldiers' ration packs in both world wars.

Bovril was invented by John Lawson Johnston (1839–1900), a food chemist born near Edinburgh. In 1874 he won a contract to supply the French army with canned beef emergency rations. He developed an extract he called Johnston's Fluid Beef, establishing the brand name Bovril in 1889 – derived from *bos*, the Latin for ox and *vril*, a contemporary "sci-fi" energy fluid. It became an essential part of the rations supplied to the army during the Boer and subsequent wars. Bovril powered Lawson Johnston to father thirteen children, to whom he left £850,197 (£371 million today).

Bovril beef tea was the only warm drink that Ernest Shackleton's men had to drink when they were marooned on Elephant Island in 1916.

Charles Darwin FRS

THE SCIENTIST WHO FIRST PROPOSED THE "ORIGIN OF SPECIES"

Charles Robert Darwin was born on 12 February 1809 at Shrewsbury in Shropshire. He was the second son of a rich and fashionable doctor, Robert Waring Darwin and Susannah, *née* Wedgwood. His grandfather Josiah Wedgwood, a prominent member of the Unitarian church (which denies the divinity of Jesus Christ and the concept of the Trinity, holding that God exists only as one being), had founded the famous pottery business; while his paternal grandfather, Dr Erasmus Darwin was the respected author of *Zoonomia and the Laws of Organic Life*, published in 1796.

**Charles Darwin (1881)
by John Maler Collier
(1850–1934)**
National Portrait Gallery, London

Darwin was brought up by his three sisters, as their mother had died when he was only eight. He attended Shrewsbury school as a boarder – he hated having to learn by rote but showed a great interest in chemical experiments, earning the nickname "Gas".

In 1825, after a stint assisting his father on his rounds in Shropshire, Darwin was sent to Edinburgh University to study medicine. The brutality of contemporary surgery revolted him, particularly after attending the amputation of a young child's limb.

Neglecting his medical studies, Darwin turned to the gentler science of biology. He fell under the spell of Edmund Grant FRS (1793–1874): who was developing the theories of Jean-Baptiste Lamarck (1744–1829), said to have coined the word "biologist" and the first to relate fossils to living organisms, and Darwin's own grandfather Erasmus.

Darwin took part in Grant's experiments in marine biology along the shores of the Firth of Forth: which pointed towards the novel possibility that

Body-snatching was the furtive disinterment of recently buried corpses from churchyards to sell for dissection or anatomy lectures in medical schools. Those who practised body-snatching or grave robbing were called "resurrectionists".

Two men in Edinburgh became notorious for not waiting for people to die. Between November 1827 and the following October two Ulstermen, William Burke (1792–1829) and William Hare, murdered seventeen people – and sold their bodies to Doctor Robert Knox (1791–1862), a lecturer at Edinburgh University Medical School, who paid them £17 10/- (over £14,000 today) for each victim. Their accomplices were Burke's mistress, Helen MacDougall and Hare's wife, Margaret.

The case against them, based largely on hearsay, was weak. Hare turned King's evidence however, and was last seen in Carlisle; but Burke was hanged and publicly dissected (his skeleton, death mask and a wallet made from his skin are on display in the School's museum). Despite public outrage, neither Knox nor either of the women was ever charged – for lack of evidence. Knox continued to employ Edinburgh body-snatchers, while lecturing on anatomy, until the Anatomy Act was passed in 1832. He moved to the Cancer Hospital in London and died in 1862.

Alexander Humboldt (1769–1859) was a German polymath, naturalist and explorer. In 1792 he started work in the Prussian department of mines, where he invented a safety lamp and founded a technical school. From 1799–1804 he explored in South America travelling extensively throughout the Amazon basin and the Andean ranges; where he realised that altitude sickness was caused by lack of oxygen. He discovered the nexus between the Orinoco and Amazon River systems, as well as the cold current flowing off the Peruvian coast named after him. On returning to Europe, Humboldt's researches predated the science of climatology and addressed the composition of the earth's crust.

Robert Fitzroy (1805–65) was Captain of *Beagle* during her voyage around the world with Charles Darwin. He was a meteorologist and hydrographer. One of his uncles was the Foreign Secretary, Lord Castlereagh and another was the Duke of Grafton. He joined the Royal Navy aged fourteen in 1819. His early service was spent off South America and in the Mediterranean. In 1828 he was appointed Captain of *Beagle* and ordered to survey the coastline of Patagonia and Tierra del Fuego, returning to Britain in 1830. He was elected a member of Parliament in 1841 and appointed Governor of New Zealand in 1843. He was recalled in 1845 because he championed the territorial rights of the indigenous Maoris.

He retired from the Navy in 1850 to devote himself to meteorology, inventing both a barometer and a storm warning scale. In 1863 he published the *Weather Book*. Fitzroy established in Whitehall the first government-sponsored telegraphic storm warning system in the world, only to see it dismantled shortly afterwards because of pressure from fishing-fleet owners who believed the warning system encouraged their captains to stay in port. At the same time the US adopted Fitzroy's system, generously funding their own meteorological office. Captain Maury of the US Weather Forecasting Department took the credit and was awarded the French *Legion d'Honneur*. Fitzroy committed suicide in a fit of depression in 1865. Within ten years, as a result of a public outcry, Fitzroy's classification of 31 sea areas was reinstated. It is reassuringly with us still, in the nightly shipping forecasts: "Cromarty", "Dogger", "German Bight", "Dover," "Wight", "Rockall" and so on – one of which, "Finisterre" has recently been renamed "Fitzroy".

• **Vice-Admiral Robert Fitzroy RN by London Stereoscopic & Photographic Company (early-mid 1860s)**
National Portrait Gallery, London

all animals share similar organs, differing only in complexity. He attended Robert Jameson's natural history courses, learning geology and how to classify plants. A freed South American slave, John Edmonstone taught him basic taxidermy, particularly the skill of stuffing birds.

In 1827 his father sensibly sent Darwin to Cambridge, with a view to becoming a clergyman. This was an astute move. At this time the Church of England not only provided their parsons with a comfortable living but encouraged them to explore the wonders of a divine universe. His cousin, William Darwin Fox not only introduced him to the current craze of competitive beetle-collecting; but more importantly, to the naturalist the Reverend John Stevens Henslow (1796–1861). Darwin joined Henslow's natural history course, rapidly becoming his favourite pupil and known as "the man who walks with Henslow". Henslow was able to lure Darwin away from his obsession with hunting, shooting and drinking and introduce him to *Evidences of Christianity* by the Reverend William Paley (1743–1805) – and the concept of a "divine designer".

After reading the *Personal Narrative* of Alexander Humboldt, Darwin was inspired to visit the Cape Verde Islands, to carry out post-graduate study.

To prepare himself, he joined a geological field expedition to Wales led by the Reverend Adam Sedgwick, also a strong supporter of "divine design." On his return he received a letter from Henslow, who had recommended Darwin as an unpaid companion to Robert Fitzroy: in command of HMS *Beagle*, a 240-ton brig, and about to set off on a survey of the South American coastline – which was expected to take two years.

In fact *Beagle*'s voyage lasted five years (1831–36); although Darwin spent two-thirds of this time ashore collecting a vast range of plant, fossil and geological specimens, many of them unknown to science. From his extraordinary experiences Darwin began to develop his theories about how a widely diverse number of different organisms and species are all part of an integrated community (biocenosis). He was much influenced by Charles Lyell's *Principles of Geology*, included in *Beagle*'s library, which suggested that geological features had been formed over hundreds of millions of years.

After an earthquake in Chile, Darwin saw how mussel beds had been raised above the high tide mark. He also noted the presence of sea shells in the rocks of the high Andes. He worked out correctly that coral reefs are formed on the rims of sinking volcanoes.

On a voyage to Patagonia in 1828 Fitzroy had brought back to Britain three Patagonian Indians, who had been bizarrely named by *Beagle*'s crew: Fuega Basket, Jemmy Button and York Minster. During their stay in Britain they had become "civilised" and, before sailing home on *Beagle*, had taken tea with King William IV and Queen Adelaide. Darwin was appalled by the naked savagery of their Patagonian tribe, describing them as "little above animals". Within a year the three emigrants had reverted to the primitive level of their tribe and showed no inclination to return to "civilization". This experience, together with his observation of slavery in Brazil and the ill-treatment of the aborigines by British settlers in Tasmania, caused Darwin to reflect that mankind was not as far removed from the animals as polite society at home believed.

In the nineteenth century, and in dangerous ignorance, arsenic was often used as a non-specific palliative. Darwin started taking it to treat eczema while at university: and it was very likely to have been a source of his lifelong dyspepsia.

Sir Charles Lyell, 1st Bt. FRS (1797–1875) was born in Forfar. He was the first to propose that there was a natural rather than a miraculous explanation for all geological phenomena. Initially reluctant to accept Darwin's theory of evolution, he was the first correctly to propose that the same physical, chemical and biological processes have been active on and within the earth for hundreds of millions of years: indicating that the present is the key to the past. This counter-intuitive principle, called "uniformitarianism", still underwrites the whole science of geology.

Life aboard *Beagle* was uncomfortable. For much of the voyage Darwin was exhausted by acute sea-sickness. Shortly after *Beagle*'s return to Britain on 2 December 1836, he began to suffer from miserable ill-health. Heart palpitations, nausea, stomach cramps, flatulence, severe vomiting after almost every meal, boils and migraines tortured him into old age. Darwin's suffering, defying all contemporary attempts at diagnosis and cure, was exacerbated by his sampling of every known treatment, both formal and eccentric. His symptoms became particularly severe at moments of stress, which he experienced when arguing his controversial evolutionary "transmutationist" theories.

Darwin returned to Britain a celebrity, due to the attentions of Henslow: who had already circulated Darwin's geological writings to selected naturalists and given them access to his geological and fossil specimens. Darwin met Charles Lyell who introduced him to (later Sir) Richard Owen (1804–92), a rising anatomist who identified, to much public excitement, several of Darwin's fossils as giant, extinct rats and sloths. He then read a paper to the Geological Society showing that the South American landmass was rising. Staying with his free-thinking brother Erasmus, he was lionised by London intellectual society, many of whom were moving away from the notion of a miraculous creation, towards entertaining dangerous, even blasphemous theories of species transmutation. These opinions became associated with the radical "Chartist" unrest then sweeping the country which aimed to overthrow society. In the prevailing climate Darwin was careful to confide his thoughts only to his secret "B" notebook.

His brother Erasmus introduced Darwin to his close lady friend Harriet Martineau (1802–76), the first female journalist in Britain, novelist and propagandist for the harsh Whig poor laws which were based on the popular if baleful writings of the Reverend Thomas Malthus. She had even sent her pamphlets to Darwin on *Beagle*. Borrowing from Malthus's theories, Darwin went on to develop his own ideas of natural selection and the "survival of the fittest", an expression later coined by the sociologist Herbert Spencer (1820–1903), caused by competition for food, habitat and mates. His researches, uncovering the random cruelty of natural selection, eventually led him initially to struggle with and then reject the concept of a benign deity.

On 9 January 1839 Darwin married his first cousin Emma Wedgwood: and, after living for three years at Gower Street in London, moved in 1842 to Down House near Orpington in Kent. Over the next seventeen years they had ten children, three of whom died early. Several suffered from sickness and one from cretinism which convinced Darwin that he and Emma should never have married. This strong belief emerged in a number of his subsequent writings on the ill effects of inbreeding. The young Darwins were rich from Emma's dowry and the shrewd investments made by Darwin's father in farmland in Lincolnshire, railways and canals. By the time *Origin of Species* was published, Darwin's fortune exceeded £250,000 (£168 million today).

On 29 January 1839 Darwin was elected Fellow of the Royal Society; and in May published his *Journal and Remarks*, together with Robert Fitzroy's account of the expedition, *Voyage of the Beagle* – which became a best-seller.

Still acutely aware of the sensitivity of his natural selection theory, Darwin, between 1842–44, expanded his ideas from a "pencil sketch" to a 240-page essay. He confided the content in the young Kew Gardens botanist Sir Joseph Dalton Hooker OM PRS (1817–1911): who in 1847 provided Darwin with the dispassionate critique he needed to build his case. He was also secretly supported in his views by the freethinking naturalist Thomas Huxley (1825–95). In 1853 he was awarded the Royal Society's Royal Medal for his monumental study on barnacles, which established his reputation as a leading biologist.

In 1851 Darwin's beloved daughter Annie caught typhoid. She was placed in the care of Dr Gully at Malvern, from whose bizarre ministrations Darwin believed she would derive some comfort. The sick child had to submit to a crank cold water regime – and, in hideous distress, she died in 1851. From this time Darwin lost all faith in an omnipotent and benevolent God. When pressed about his beliefs, Darwin described himself as "agnostic", a word coined by Huxley in 1860 – from the Greek agnosis, meaning "without knowledge". His parish priest and friend, the Reverend John Brodie Innes recalled Darwin saying to him: "you are a Theologian, I am a Naturalist, the lines are separate. I endeavour to discover facts without

Alfred Russel Wallace OM FRS, naturalist, geographer, humanist and spiritualist, was born in 1823. He formulated a theory of evolution by natural selection before Charles Darwin. Brought up in penury, Wallace attended the one-room Hertford Grammar school; then, aged fourteen, a mechanical institute in London. Living with his brother John, an apprentice carpenter, Wallace became involved with the Robert Owens, father and son, and their efforts to improve the education of working men. His dislike of organised religion turned him towards natural history and evolution.

In 1848, with Henry Bates who had introduced him to entomology, Wallace travelled to Brazil as self-employed specimen collector. The Royal Geographical Society funded his next expedition to Malaya, which lasted eight years and resulted in two remarkable articles, pointing towards natural evolution, published in 1855.

Three years later he sent a more rounded paper to Darwin. Startled, Darwin published a joint article in the proceedings of the Linnean Society: *Perpetuation of Varieties and Species by Natural Means of Selection.* Wallace had unwittingly provided vital evidence for Darwin's evolutionary theories by identifying the "Wallace Line", an unexplained boundary separating the fauna and flora of Australia and Asia. By the time Wallace died in 1913, loaded with honours (including the Royal Society's Copley Medal), he had published 21 books and over 700 articles and papers. In 1881 Darwin was instrumental in saving the improvident Wallace from penury.

• **Alfred Russel Wallace by Thomas Sims** (*c*.1863–1866)
National Portrait Gallery, London

considering what is said in the Book of Genesis. I do not attack Moses and I think Moses can take care of himself".

In March 1856 Lyell read a paper by Alfred Russel Wallace, a naturalist working in Borneo, entitled *On the Law Which has Regulated the Introduction of Species* – which clearly preceded Darwin's own theories on natural selection.

Encouraged by Lyell, Darwin embarked upon a three-volume book to be titled *Natural Selection*. In December 1857 Wallace wrote to Darwin enquiring whether he would address the origins of human beings. "I think I shall avoid the whole subject", replied Darwin, "as so surrounded with prejudices, though I fully admit that it is the highest and most interesting problem for a naturalist".

On 1 July 1858, under the awkward title *On the Tendency of Species to form Varieties: and on the Perpetuation of Varieties and Species by Natural Means of Selection*, Darwin published his theory of evolution. The presentation made little initial impact, seemingly indiscernible from the many circulating varieties of evolutionary thought.

In spite of the death of his son and suffering from severe bouts of his many debilitating illnesses, Darwin struggled over the next thirteen months to produce his great book on "Species". On the 22 November 1859 it was finally published by John Murray, under the title *On the Origin of Species by Means of Natural Selection*. The initial run of 1,250 copies was oversubscribed. In spite of Darwin's scrupulous attempts to avoid the evocative word "evolution", with all its connotations of creation without divine intervention, the book sparked a public "men from monkeys" controversy.

Darwin was too ill to be able to defend his theories in person and could only do so through a lively correspondence. He was supported by a devoted circle of friends Lyell, Hooker, Huxley and Asa Gray: which culminated in 1864 with Darwin winning the Royal Society's Copley Medal. Meanwhile *On the Origin of Species* was translated into many languages, becoming a standard, if controversial scientific textbook.

Darwin went on to publish in 1871 two volumes: *The Descent of Man and Selection in relation to Sex*, in which he explained the evolution of mankind, with particular regard to developing morality and civilization. These proposals or "social Darwinism", a term coined by Richard Hofstadter in 1944, led on to the popular but increasingly sinister study of Eugenics, a term first used by Darwin's cousin Francis Galton. This flawed pseudo-science led, over the next fifty years, to

A famous confrontation occurred at Oxford, between Thomas Huxley and the Bishop of Oxford, "Soapy Sam" Wilberforce. Wilberforce mocked Huxley, asking him from which side of his family was he descended from monkeys. Huxley replied that he "would rather be descended from an ape than from a cultivated man who used his gifts of culture and eloquence in the service of prejudice and falsehood". That Huxley would prefer to be an ape than a Bishop entertained the country.

Born into a Quaker family and a child prodigy, Sir Francis Galton FRS (1822–1911) was a polymath: an anthropologist, explorer, criminologist, statistician, meteorologist and the inventor of "Eugenics". Galton read medicine at Cambridge but left without taking his degree, after suffering a nervous breakdown. His father left Galton with sufficient means to indulge his craving for travel. After tours of southern Europe, Palestine and Egypt, Galton explored south-west Africa (Namibia). As a result of his findings around Lake Ngami he was elected a fellow of the Royal Geographical Society and the Royal Society, whose Copley Medal he won in 1910.

Galton was a pioneer of forensic finger-printing and an authority on applied statistics, criminality, the incidence of twins, blood transfusion and the precision of measurements. In his last years he studied Eugenics, a term he used to describe the science of improving the mental faculties of human beings by selective breeding. He enshrined these thoughts in *Hereditary Genius*, published in 1869.

- **Sir Francis Galton FRS (1822–1911) by Gustav Graef (1882)**

National Portrait Gallery, London

reproduction control programmes in the US and Europe, in an attempt to breed out undesirable physical and genetic traits.

Eugenic experiments culminated horrifyingly in Nazi Germany, with sterilisation laws and mobile gas chambers carrying this twisted version of "social Darwinism" to extreme and dreadful limits.

In 1872 Darwin published *The Expression of the Emotions in Man and Animals*, refuting the notion that human facial muscles had been designed by God to reflect uniquely human thoughts and ideas. Ten years later, in 1881 Darwin published his final volume, prosaically entitled *The Formation of Vegetable Mould through the Action of Worms*.

In March 1882 Darwin had a heart attack while walking in the Lake District. He died on 19 April, aged seventy-three. He had wished to be buried in the churchyard at Downe ("the sweetest place on earth"), where his brother Erasmus had been buried the year before. The free-thinking Huxley however, perhaps the agnostic Darwin's greatest champion, together with Darwin's many friends and supporters from the scientific elite, surprisingly managed to persuade a canon of Westminster Abbey to accept his body for burial. On the 26 April Darwin was interred, close to Isaac Newton.

EMIGRATION FROM THE BRITISH ISLES IN THE 19TH CENTURY

The people of the British Isles are natural migrants: and since the late 16th century they have spread to the four corners of the earth. Over 11 million from Britain and a further 7 million from Ireland, together accounting for 35% of the 52 million from Europe in total, emigrated between 1815–1930. The majority of those from the British Isles went to the US; most of the remainder to Australia, Canada, New Zealand and South Africa. Reflecting (generally, but by no means universally) huge improvements in sanitation, water quality, medical care and increasing supplies of affordable food, the population of Britain doubled from 10.5 to 21 million between 1801–51 – and double again to 42 million between 1851–1901.

Family sizes of over 20 children were not uncommon, whereas today they are on average, less than two. Across the globe and amongst all classes, rising affluence decreases the need, and desire, to breed. In the last few decades this has proved to be the case throughout Western Europe, Japan and South Korea. The great exception is the US: now the third most populous country in the world. The US population reached 300 million at 11:46 GMT on 17 October 2006. By April 2011 it had exceeded 311 million.

In mid-19th century Britain, life-expectancy was around forty years – but it depended greatly on where you lived. In 1851 a boy in Liverpool could expect to live only to twenty-six: in Okehampton in Devon, to fifty-seven.

From small beginnings, there was a net emigration of about 6,000 people each year from Britain and Ulster between 1630–1800, about 25% of the natural increase: all of it to British North America. By the late 1800s this had risen to some 90,000 from the British Isles – especially from Ireland, following the potato famine years in the 1840s. The peak was reached in about 1900, by which time a large percentage had been diverted to Britain's overseas dominions. Up to a third returned, particularly from the US during the depression. Other than in the 1930s, more people left each year than arrived – until the last two decades of the 20th century brought large inflows of immigrants to Britain, the majority from the third world.

After WWII, emigration was encouraged by British and Commonwealth "assisted passage" schemes until the 1960s. After 1966, annual emigration to the US never exceeded about 13,000,

In 1865 a "little Wales beyond Wales" was established in the far south of Argentina, in Patagonia. It thrives to this day as a community of about 20,000, up to a quarter of which is Welsh-speaking – and still maintains a connection with Wales.

but the net loss to Australia, Canada and New Zealand was as high as 104,000 as recently as 1974.

The number of people today claiming British and Irish ancestry in the following countries is impressive: in the US, 35.5 and 30.6 million respectively; in Canada (total population 33.2 million in 2008), 22.6 million British (of which over 5 million are Scots) and 4.6 million Irish; in Australia (total population 21.8 million in 2009) it is harder to analyse, as 7.7 million referred to themselves in the census questionnaire only as "Australian" – even so 6.6 million said they were of English descent; 1.9 million said Irish; 1.6 million said Scottish; and 119,000 said Welsh. Of New Zealand's 2009 population of 4.3 million: 3.04 million (70%) were of British or Irish descent; and in the Republic of South Africa (despite 1 million departures since 1994), the rough figure is 1.5 million. In addition, 300,000 Argentinians (out of 40.1 million) and 700,000 Chileans (out of 16 million) also claim British ancestry.

A recent phenomenon has been migration by around 1 million retired or rich Britons, seeking the sun and lower taxation but often retaining houses and close links with Britain, within Europe itself: principally to France, Italy and Spain. Including these, between 110 and 120 million people living overseas today can trace their ancestry to the British Isles: yet the 2009 population of the UK still managed to reach over 60 million – and, on the present trend of net immigration, is set to climb inexorably higher still.

THE ARMOURERS

The Vickers company was established in Sheffield as a steel foundry in 1828: by a miller, Edward Vickers and his father-in-law George Naylor. In 1854 Edward's sons Thomas and Albert Vickers joined the firm. Thomas, a founder of the volunteer Hallamshire Rifles and known as "Colonel Tom" (1833–1915), was chairman of the company from 1873–1909. Having completed his training as an engineer in Germany, Tom focused on technical innovation: while Albert, having worked in the US, was responsible for sales and planning. Tom's first act was to acquire a series of German patents, which made Vickers pre-eminent in the manufacture of castings and steel tyres – by 1861 it was second only to Krupp of Essen.

Sir Hiram Maxim

After a downturn in business, Vickers entered the armaments industry in 1888. Tom acquired the rights to the Maxim machine-gun when he bought Barrow Shipbuilding in 1897 – by which time the company was manufacturing battleships complete with armour, engines and guns.

Maxim met an old American acquaintance in Vienna who advised him: "Hang your chemistry and electricity. If you want to make a pile of money, invent something that will enable these Europeans to cut each other's throats with greater facility".

Sir Basil Zaharoff, nicknamed "Zedzed" (1849–1936), was an arms dealer and financier – the first to be called a "merchant of death". He was born Basileios Zacharias in Turkey, of poor Greek parents who were driven into exile in Russia: where they Russified their name. During a tumultuous youth, he occupied himself variously as an arsonist for the Constantinople fire brigade, a brothel tout in Athens, a storekeeper in Cyprus, an embezzler in London and a bigamist in New York. In 1877 he met a Greek diplomat, Stefanos Skouladis.

Impressed by Zaharoff's fluency in eight languages, Skouladis recruited him as an arms salesman. Using bribery and playing off one country against the other, Zaharoff sold primitive submarines to Greece and Turkey; before turning to machine guns. In 1897 he was retained, in the sardonic phrase of the Vickers financial director Sir Vincent Caillard, as "Our General Representative for business abroad". He developed a lucrative naval market for Vickers in Spain – as a result of a liaison with a member of the Spanish royal family, the Duchess of Villafranca whose husband had gone mad. In 1913 he became a French citizen.

In 1915, during WWI Zaharoff was employed by the British government to induce neutral Greece to join the allies; and to bribe Enver Pasha and other Turkish politicians with £10 million in gold, to declare an armistice in 1917. King George V, who loathed him, awarded Zaharoff an honorary knighthood in 1919. The French matched this with the *Légion d'Honneur*. In 1926, Zaharoff retired to Monte Carlo: where he controlled the Casino – although he never gambled. He died on the 27 November 1936.

Sir Hiram Stevens Maxim (1840–1916) was born in Sangerville, Maine in the US. He was the son of a farmer who was also a gifted mechanic. An apprentice coach builder at fourteen, after many different jobs, he moved to Massachusetts, to work as an instrument maker and draughtsman. In the late 1870s, as chief engineer to the US Electric Lighting Co., Maxim claimed to have invented the incandescent light bulb. He became embroiled, and eventually bested in a series of patent disputes with Thomas Edison. In 1881, paid off by Edison, he left the US for Europe, then Britain in 1883.

He established himself in Hatton Garden in London and turned his attention to gun design. In 1884 he invented the world's first machine gun. Ever since firing a rifle as a young man and noticing its kick, Maxim had been intrigued by the possibility of harnessing the power of the recoil gases from a fired cartridge. He designed a watercooled mechanism which, using the recoil both to eject the spent cartridge and reload the chamber, could fire ten rounds a second – this time Maxim patented every piece of the firing mechanism. The Maxim gun was adopted by the British army in 1889 and by the Royal Navy in 1892. In 1896 Maxim's company was absorbed by Vickers Ltd.

Maxim remained a director of Vickers until 1911: for whom he travelled tirelessly throughout Europe, often with the mountebank Basil Zaharoff, promoting and demonstrating to great effect, his new weapon's lethal firepower. In 1900 he was naturalized a British citizen; and in 1901 he was knighted by Queen Victoria.

Maxim was an inventor of extraordinary versatility. He took out hundreds of patents, ranging from inhalers for bronchitis sufferers to an aerial merry-go-round for amusement parks, a steam-powered "aeroplane", lawn-sprinkler system and a mousetrap.

He was also a philanderer and bigamist, who haunted brothels specialising in very young girls – unsurprisingly, his otherwise vivid and mendacious biography *My Life*, published in 1915, failed to mention this. He died of pneumonia in London in 1916.

Over the next fifty years, Maxim's machine guns killed countless millions of men. Many different models were manufactured under licence all over the world, including Germany and Russia. It remained in service with the British army until 1963.

The Vickers facility at Barrow-in-Furness became the "Naval Construction Yard". By 1900 the company could manufacture an enormous range of products: ships of every size, marine equipment and armour plate; and an assortment of battlefield ordnance, including artillery, infantry weapons and later, tanks. In 1901 Britain's first submarine, *Holland 1* was launched in Barrow – today the yard builds nuclear-powered hunter-killer submarines for the Royal Navy; and an even larger class armed with Trident missiles.

In 1902 Vickers took a half-share in the famous Clyde shipyard, John Brown and Co. – which built the *QEII* in 1967. Established in 1847, the last ship of any size to be built at the yard was completed in 1972. In 1902 Vickers also bought a half-share in William Beardmore & Co., an armour plate and warship manufacturer in Glasgow.

Further diversification took place with the purchase of the car manufacturing facilities of the Wolseley Sheep-Shearing Machine Co. in 1901: which became the Wolseley Tool and Motor Car Co. – until it was sold to William Morris, later Lord Nuffield in 1927. It seems odd today that Vickers failed to exploit the potential of the car market.

In 1911 Vickers bought control of the torpedo manufacturer, Whitehead & Co.

Robert Whitehead (1823–1905) was one of a family of eight children born in Bolton in Lancashire. Educated at Bolton grammar school, he was apprenticed to a Manchester engineering company. In 1844 he joined his uncle, the manager of an engineering works, in Marseilles. In 1847 he moved to Milan and set up an engineering business of his own. In 1848 however, the revolutionary Italian government annulled his patents: and he left Italy. He opened an engineering works in Fiume (now in Croatia), then the headquarters of the Austro-Hungarian navy: for which he designed and built warship boilers and engines. By 1866, with the help of his 12 year-old son John, he had secretly conceived and designed a new naval weapon: a self-propelled, compressed air device – the Whitehead torpedo.

Thirty years later his originally unstable torpedo could reach a speed of 29 knots and travel 1,000 yards, driven by a small reciprocating, compressed air engine. Key to its success was a hydrostatic valve and pendulum (balance chamber), which maintained the torpedo at a predetermined depth. In 1898 Whitehead installed a gyroscope: and, in stabilising its course, it was transformed into a lethal weapon – which has hardly changed in design over the last 100 years. By 1900 construction licences had been acquired by every major power across the globe, including the US, China and Japan.

Whitehead was awarded honours and decorations by many European monarchs: but not by Britain – his device sank so many allied merchant ships during both World Wars that the country twice came close to being starved into submission.

In 1920 Albert James Penniall (1872–1949), a Wolseley engineer on secondment to the Tokyo Ishikawajima Shipbuilding and Engineering Company (today it is called Isuzu), introduced British car manufacturing methods to Japan: which is why the Japanese drive on the left side of the road today.

On 9 April 1940, the first day of Hitler's invasion of Norway, *Blucher* (named after Wellington's ally at Waterloo), a 14,000 ton heavy cruiser, was sunk by a Norwegian shore battery firing 40 year-old Whitehead torpedoes – which worked perfectly.

In 1912 Whitehead's granddaughter, Frances launched an Austrian submarine. She fell in love with her captain, Georg von Trapp and married him: their children were the von Trapp singers in the 1965 film, *The Sound of Music*.

Robert Whitehead (right) with test torpedo, Fiume (*c*.1875)

Whitehead died at his home in Shrivenham in Berkshire on 14 November 1905.

In 1911 Vickers expandeded into aircraft manufacture. In 1928 the Aviation Department acquired Supermarine: and renamed it Supermarine Aviation (Vickers) Ltd. By 1914 Vickers was capitalised at £6 million, employed 22,000 men and made annual profits of over £600,000. By 1919 Vickers had become the fourth largest quoted British company, with a market value of £20 million (over £3 billion today).

Tom Vickers died at his home in London on 19 October 1915. In 1927 Vickers allied itself with W.G. Armstrong, to form Vickers Armstrong.

British Aerospace, today Britain's largest manufacturing company and Europe's principal armaments contractor, with a market value of more than £11 billion, is the legacy of Tom Vickers and William Armstrong (1810–1900).

Armstrong is a surname steeped in the history of the Border Reivers. William George Armstrong was born in Newcastle, the son of a corn merchant. After attending the local grammar school he entered the law, becoming a partner in a firm of solicitors in 1835. The senior partner, Armorer Donkin was an amateur engineer. Twelve years later, with Donkin's support, Armstrong resigned: to become an engineer himself.

Cragside

Fascinated by the inefficiency of a waterwheel he came across on a fishing holiday, Armstrong designed an hydraulic engine to replace it. In 1847, employing just 30 men, he began to manufacture hydraulic cranes at Elswick, a mile up-river from Newcastle. By 1863 W.G. Armstrong & Co was manufacturing over 100 cranes a year and employing 4,000 men. In 1846 Armstrong's work as a creative engineer was recognised by his election as a Fellow of the Royal Society.

In 1854, struck by reports from the Crimea of the British army's heavy field guns' lack of manoeuvrability, Armstrong decided to design a much lighter, more mobile gun: with greater range, accuracy and rate of fire. He built a breech-loading gun with a rifled barrel, firing an elongated shell rather than a ball. The barrel was reinforced by a helix of wrought iron, wrapped around a steel inner lining. An 18-pounder model was tested by the army and declared superior to all rivals. Armstrong refused to make a profit from the resulting order and surrendered the patents to the government. In 1859 he was knighted and presented to Queen Victoria. Armstrong subsequently sold his firm's guns to both sides in the the US Civil War.

In 1864 Armstrong turned his attention to building naval guns. In 1868 Armstrong & Co. signed an agreement with the shipbuilders, Charles Mitchell & Co. whereby Mitchell would build warships and Armstrong would furnish the guns. In 1884 the two companies merged.

Launched in 1887, HMS *Victoria* collided with HMS *Camperdown* on 22 June 1893, near Tripoli in Lebanon, during manoeuvres: and sank with 358 crew – including the commander of the Mediterranean Fleet, Vice-Admiral Sir George Tryon. One of the survivors was his second-in-command, John Jellicoe: later in command of the British Grand Fleet at the Battle of Jutland – described by Churchill as "the only man on either side who could lose the war in an afternoon".

Sir Joseph Wilson Swan (1828–1914), born at Bishopwearmouth in Durham, was a physicist and chemist. He patented an incandescent light bulb in 1878, preempting by a few months the application granted to Thomas Alva Edison (1847–1931) in the US – who is usually credited with the invention.

Full warship production was started from a new shipyard at Elswick, which became the first yard in the world capable of building and arming a warship. The first warships from Elswick were the torpedo-cruisers *Panther* and *Leopard* for the Austro-Hungarian navy. The first battleship to be built was HMS *Victoria*.

Initially, Japan was the Elswick yard's most important customer, ordering six cruisers – which participated in the battle of Tsushima in 1905, when the Japanese navy annihilated the Russian Grand Fleet.

By 1863 Armstrong had withdrawn from everyday management of his business, although he retained control and exercised oversight. He acquired land outside Newcastle near Rothbury: and built a house called Cragside. He planted seven million trees, created five artificial lakes and built 31 miles of roads. His guests included the Prince and Princess of Wales, the Shah of Persia, the King of Siam and the Prime Minister of China. Cragside was the first house in the world to be lit by hydroelectricity, using incandescent lamps – invented in 1870 by Armstrong's neighbour, Joseph Swan.

Only in 1871, during a Tyneside strike of engineers aimed at reducing the working week from 57 to 54 hours for the same wage, did Armstrong's leadership falter. He closed down the schools he had established for his workers, to accommodate imported foreign labour; and locked out even those of his engineers who had not joined the strike – irretrievably damaging his paternalistic image. In 1897 W.G. Armstrong & Co. merged with Whitworth's cannon and machine-tool manufacturing business.

In 1887 Armstrong was ennobled, taking the title Baron Armstrong of Cragside. His last great project, which he took on aged eighty-four, was the purchase and restoration of Bamburgh Castle on the Northumberland coast – which is still owned by the Armstrong family. He died on 27 December 1900, leaving £1,400,682 (over £611 million today).

Sir Joseph Whitworth, 1st Baronet (1803–87), born in Stockport in Cheshire, was one of the finest British engineers of all time. He was the first to grind a true plane surface (vital for steam engine valves, printing press tables, lathes and planing machines). He also invented a measuring device that was accurate to one two-millionth of an inch; small arms; and in 1862, a gun that could penetrate armour-plating more than 4 inches thick, six miles away. He was an irascible perfectionist but an endearing optimist – his catch phrase was, "let us try". He was also wonderfully kind to his workers and a generous philanthropist. He married twice but had no children.

- **Sir Joseph Whitworth by C.A. Duval & Co (Charles Allen Du Val) (1860s)**
National Portrait Gallery, London

Armstrong defended the ethics of arms manufacture forcefully: "It is our province as engineers to make the forces of matter obedient to the will of man: those who use the means we supply must be responsible for their application".

THE POINT OF BELGIUM

Straddling the cultural boundary between Germanic and Latin Europe, Belgium has two main linguistic groups: the Flemish, who speak Dutch (59%), and the Walloons, who speak French

(31%) – plus 10% who speak German. From the 16th century so many battles were fought in the area that it was dubbed the" Cockpit of Europe".

The reunification of the Low Countries, as the United Kingdom of the Netherlands, occurred at the dissolution of the First French Empire after the Battle of Waterloo in 1815. A bloodless revolution in 1830 led to the establishment of an independent, Catholic and neutral Belgium: with Leopold I (1790–1865), chosen by the National Congress from a list of noncontroversial minor royal candidates in 1831, as king. Leopold, a distinguished soldier in the Imperial Russian army and the widower of King George IV of Britain's only daughter, was Queen Victoria's uncle.

Lord Palmerston, the British Foreign Secretary determined that a neutral Belgium would be a useful buffer state, between an ever-aggressive France and the German principalities. These were already linked by a *Zollverein* (customs union) with Prussia – as a precursor to the formal unification of Germany after the Franco-Prussian War, announced on 18 January 1871 at Versailles. His conduct of the negotiations between the Netherlands, supported by the northern powers, and France, which wished to annexe the country, was masterly. It is no exaggeration to claim that Belgium's very existence as a sovereign state is due to Palmerston's perception that it was very much in Britain's interest. His prescience in recognising that a territorial division between France and Germany would one day be needed was not matched by his presumption that such a small country could in itself provide one.

In the event, the Belgian province of Flanders was the scene of much of the fighting on the Western Front in WWI; and Germany simply walked through Belgium in WWII. It is unsurprising that the country, riven by internal division to this day, wished to place itself at the heart of a European Union in the 1950s – Belgium's best hope of no longer acting as the main theatre of other countries' wars. From Britain's point of view, Belgium has never quite lived up to Palmerston's vision or expectations.

In 1991 Belgium (a member of NATO) refused to supply the British army with artillery ammunition made on contract, because it disapproved of the Gulf War.

THE EUROPEAN ARMS RACE LED TO THE FIRST WORLD WAR

For a hundred years after Waterloo, Europe largely remained at peace. By 1900 however, technological developments had given the continent's industrialised nations the ability to slaughter each other on an unprecedented scale. Vickers and Armstrong in Britain; Hotchkiss and Schneider in France; Krupp and Mauser in Germany; Skoda and Steyr in Austria-Hungary; and the Putilov and Obukhov works in Russia, all bear great responsibility for the carnage of two World Wars – within 21 years of each other.

The years 1888–1906, known as the "pre-Dreadnought period", were marked by Britain's determination to reassert her naval dominance. This was precipitated by a war scare with France and an escalation of Russian warship construction. The aim was to

HMS Dreadnought, built at Portsmouth and launched on 10 February 1906 make the Royal Navy twice as powerful as the French and Russian fleets combined. This policy, designed to deter these navies from competing with Britain, had the reverse effect. The 1890s saw a scramble to build more and better warships: but by 1900, the contest had been reduced to a naval arms race between Britain and Germany.

In 1883 the Royal Navy possessed 38 battleships: more than twice those of the combined fleets of France and the rest of the world. By 1897 British dominance had been eroded by a frenzy of naval construction – by the United States, France, Germany, Russia and Japan. Increasing improvements to guns, turrets, armour plate, engines and, most lethally to big ships, the torpedo, spurred the competition. In 1906 the arms race reached a new height with the launch of the first British Dreadnought.

Inspired by Admiral Sir John Fisher, HMS *Dreadnought* immediately outdated every existing battleship. Combining the prodigious firepower of ten 12-inch guns, protected by belts of armour plate and capable of 21 knots driven by revolutionary steam turbine engines, *Dreadnought* dramatically raised the strategic stake. The major naval powers raced to build their own Dreadnought fleets – then on a par with the weapons possessed today by members of the nuclear club of nations.

New and terrifying instruments of war were waiting to be used. All it would take to light the touchwood was the apparently inconsequential murder of an Austrian Archduke in Sarajevo on 28 June 1914.

The assassination of Franz Ferdinand of Austria in Bosnia-Herzegovina, then part of the Austro-Hungarian Empire, brought the tensions between Austria-Hungary and Serbia to a head. This triggered a chain of international events that embroiled first Russia and then all the other major European powers. On 4 August 1914 Britain declared war on Germany – by the dreadful conclusion of which, Europe would have been changed forever.

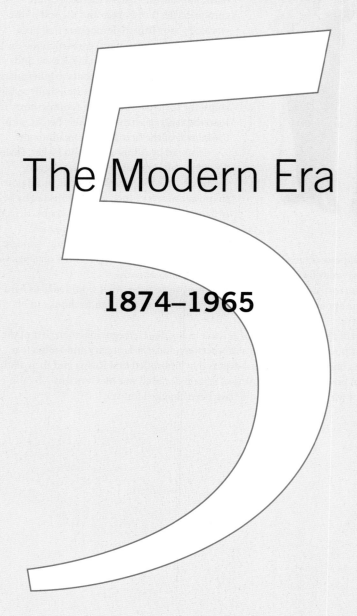

The Modern Era

1874–1965

Winston Spencer Churchill OM

BRITAIN'S BRAVEST STATESMAN

Sir Winston Leonard Spencer Churchill by Walter Stoneman (1941)
National Portrait Gallery, London

Sir Winston Leonard Spencer Churchill KG OM CH FRS was born on 30 November 1874 at Blenheim Palace in Oxfordshire, the elder son of Lord Randolph Churchill (1849–95) and his American wife Jeanette, known as Jenny (1854–1921). A younger son of the 7th Duke of Marlborough, Lord Randolph was a distinguished politician whose career was ruined by scandal; Jenny was the daughter of Leonard Jerome, a flamboyant speculator known as "The King of Wall Street". Suggestions that Jerome had changed his name from Jacobson were false: he came from farming stock in upstate New York and was of Huguenot descent. Later suggestions that Jenny was part Iroquois may also be discounted. Jerome was a keen yachtsman, helped found the American Jockey Club and Manhattan's Academy of Music.

Jenny, *née* Jerome Lady Randolph Churchill

Jenny was beautiful: but an ambitious, often vulgar socialite and a notorious adulteress (King Edward VII, Count Charles Andreas Kinsky and King Milan of Serbia were among her lovers), twice marrying younger men after Lord Randolph's early death. Indeed, Churchill's younger brother Jack (1880–1947) was rumoured to be the son of an Irishman, Colonel John Strange Jocelyn, later 5th Earl of Roden.

Only Jenny's dowry, some $5 million today, secured her hasty marriage on 15 April 1874 – Churchill was born seven and a half months later. All the female love in his early life came from his beloved nanny, Mrs Elizabeth Everest who died in 1895. He nicknamed her "Woom" or "Womany" and kept her picture in his bedroom until the day he died.

Lord Randolph became Chancellor of the Exchequer in 1886 but overestimated his support in the Cabinet and resigned, ending his political career. He died from syphilis (he is said to have told Jenny, "what does an occasional cook or housemaid matter?"), a recluse aged forty-five. He was a loving if remote father; and the brothers, despite the difference in their ages, were close friends.

Lord Randolph Churchill by Edwin Longsden Long, exhibited 1888
National Portrait Gallery, London

Churchill was only 5 feet 7 inches tall; kept at a distance by his mother and a failure at school; insanely brave and blazing with a ruthless, sometimes shameless ambition; an autodidact with a superb memory and

Winston derives from Wynnstan – or "joy-stone" in Old English. It was the name of Churchill's great ancestor, the 1st Duke of Marlborough's father.

Churchill (1895)

command of English, written and spoken. His early life was one of precocious success followed by setbacks and gloom in middle age. Were it not for WWII and winning glory at the age of sixty-five: as the most courageous and effective war leader and orator that Britain and possibly any other country in history has ever had, he would scarcely deserve a footnote in any history of the 20th century. "Cometh the hour, cometh the man", has never been proved more apt.

In 1963, authorised by Congress, President John F. Kennedy named Churchill the first Honorary Citizen of the United States. Churchill was too ill to attend the White House ceremony, so his son and grandson accepted the award for him. In Kennedy's words: "**He mobilised the English language and sent it into battle**".

Churchill was lazy and inattentive at Harrow. He only scraped into RMA Sandhurst in 1893, on his third attempt. Here he excelled, coming eighth out of 102 in his intake. He was commissioned into the 4th Hussars, serving in India and on the North-West Frontier. In 1895 he took leave to go to Cuba as a military observer with the Spanish army in its civil war. He also reported for the Saturday Review. In 1898 he was attached to the 21st Lancers as a war correspondent, joining the Nile Expeditionary Force to the Sudan: taking part in a famous mounted charge during the Battle of Omdurman. 10,000 Dervishes, but only 48 British, were killed – in Hilaire Belloc's words, "Whatever happens, we have got / the Maxim gun: and they have not".

> It was for Balfour that the saying, "Bob's your Uncle" was coined. The helpful uncle was his mother's brother: Robert, 3rd Marquess of Salisbury.

In 1899 he fought a by-election at Oldham in the Conservative interest, unsuccessfully. Arthur Balfour commented, "I thought he was a young man of promise, but it appears he is a young man of promises". Churchill later repaid the compliment: "Balfour is wicked and moral. Asquith is good and immoral". He also said, "If you wanted nothing done, Arthur Balfour was the man for the task. There was no equal to him".

Again a journalist in the Second Boer War (1899–1902), Churchill was captured on an armoured train which was ambushed and derailed. He escaped from prison, making a daring 300 mile journey across Boer territory to Lourenço Marques (now Maputo) in Mozambique. He was present at some of the most famous battles of the campaign, including Spion Kop. He was later recommended for a Victoria Cross which was vetoed by Kitchener – of whom Margot Asquith remarked in WWI, "If he was not a great man, he was at least a great poster".

Churchill fought Oldham again in 1900: and this time he won. In 1904 he fell out with his party, crossing the floor of the House to the Liberal benches. He was appointed Under-Secretary for the Colonies in 1906; and, as President of the Board of Trade two years later, introduced labour exchanges. Promoted to Home Secretary in 1910, he was criticised by the press the following year – characteristically, he had insisted on taking command of the police when they cornered an armed gang in Sidney Street.

Lord Kitchener WWI recruiting poster

He exhilarated in his next job, First Lord of the Admiralty, and worked tirelessly to prepare the Royal Navy for the war with Germany that he knew was inevitable – saying later of the Germans, "The Boche is forever at your feet or at your throat". He also urged the development of the tank. In 1915 however, he took the blame for the disaster at Gallipoli and resigned. Major Churchill joined the 2nd Battalion Grenadier Guards on the Western Front in November: and two weeks later took command

"YOUR COUNTRY NEEDS YOU"

It was poor planning and abysmal leadership that led to the awful bloodshed and defeat at Gallipoli. If the campaign had been successful WWI might have been won in 1916 – by knocking Turkey out of the war, joining up with Serbia to penetrate the soft underbelly of Austria, then linking with the Russians to attack Germany's eastern flank. This would have avoided millions of deaths in Flanders and spared Russia from revolution. Even so, some good came of it: Churchill heeded this terrible lesson in 1944. He resisted Russian pressure to act prematurely, insisting on meticulous planning and intelligence, huge amounts of equipment and supplies, overwhelming numerical superiority and better generals for D-day, on 6 June. Nor did he underestimate the enemy – unlike the widely held belief in 1915 that "Johnny Turk" would be no match for a modern army. In fact the bravery and tenacity of the Anatolian peasant soldiery gave the British Army unpleasant surprises whenever it encountered them.

If Turkey had remained neutral in WWI, albeit no longer an empire nor even Ottoman, the country would today be a powerful rival to Europe and the US – with a population of over 250 million and in control of the vast oil reserves of Iraq, Kuwait, Saudi Arabia and southwest Iran.

of the 6th Battalion Royal Scots Fusiliers. Few politicians are prepared to seek redemption quite so bravely.

Churchill (1900)

Churchill returned to Britain in 1916; and in 1917 took up the post of Minister of Munitions in the Coalition government, now headed by Lloyd George. He was Secretary for War and Air from 1919–21, then Colonial Secretary until he lost his seat in 1922.

After two years out of the House of Commons, the only break in a 64 year Parliamentary career, he changed allegiance in 1924; and was elected to represent Epping as a 'Constitutionalist' with Conservative backing. The following year he formally rejoined the Conservative Party, commenting wryly that, "anyone can rat (change parties), but it takes a certain ingenuity to re-rat". He served as Chancellor of the Exchequer under Baldwin until 1929 and oversaw the United Kingdom's disastrous return to the Gold Standard: which resulted in deflation, unemployment and the miners' strike that led to the General Strike of 1926. This decision prompted the economist John Maynard Keynes to write *The Economic Consequences of Mr. Churchill,* correctly arguing that the return to the gold standard would lead to a world depression. Churchill later regarded this as one of the worst decisions of his life. To be fair, he was not an economist and he acted principally on the advice of the Governor of the Bank of England, Montague Norman – of whom Keynes said: "Always so charming, always so wrong".

There is an uncanny similarity between Nelson's "Wilderness Years" between 1787–92 and Churchill's between 1929–39. Although Churchill was out of office for ten years, it is interesting that Major Desmond Morton, the senior officer in the Secret Intelligence Service charged with monitoring armament developments in Europe, was permitted by

Two decisions made by Churchill as Colonial Secretary have cast a long shadow over the Middle East today: he confirmed Palestine as a Jewish national home (while recognising continuing Arab rights); and he created modern Iraq out of the wreckage of the Ottoman Empire. Unable to fulfill T.E. Lawrence's WWI promise to gift Syria to the Hashemite clan (it was claimed by France), in March 1921 he installed them as an artificial monarchy – in a country that had been cobbled together and was lived in by people who were largely unfriendly to each other. Unsurprisingly, rule by an alien king was tolerated for only 37 years. Sadly, the subsequent 45 years of tyranny were replaced by near civil war following the second Gulf War in 2003.

Chaim Azriel Weizmann, the first President of Israel (1949) was born in Motol, Russia (Belarus today) in 1874, the same year as Churchill. He settled in Manchester in 1904, becoming a British citizen in 1910. A brilliant chemist, at Churchill's request he devised a process to make acetone for munitions. He died in Israel in 1952.

Arthur Neville Chamberlain by Henry Lamb (c.1939)
National Portrait Gallery, London

the three Prime Ministers of the decade (MacDonald, Baldwin and even Chamberlain) to provide Churchill with 'Most Secret Information'. It was as though all three knew that Churchill's time was coming – they were certainly aware of his fierce patriotism. There were many others who, out of despair at Government inertia, helped him too. With accurate insight, increasingly he warned from the backbenches of the dangers of German rearmament, of appeasement of the dictators and of Britain's dire lack of preparedness – referring to the Munich settlement of 29 September 1938 as "a total and unmitigated defeat". Churchill despised Neville Chamberlain: saying of him, "He has a lust for peace"; and, "In the depths of that dusty soul there is nothing but abject surrender". Now he told him bitterly, "You were given the choice between war and dishonour. You chose dishonour and you will have war".

With France committed to a static defence behind the Maginot Line Chamberlain had very little option other than to appease Hitler once again. The damage he (and Baldwin) did through appeasement had already been done. However the year between Munich and the declaration of war was spent well: in completing the development of the Spitfire and Hurricane fighter aircraft and in strengthening the RDF or Radar grid in England – both crucial to victory in the Battle of Britain.

When war came Churchill re-joined the government in the same post, First Lord of the Admiralty, as in 1914. A signal was transmitted round the Fleet: "Winston's back". By early May 1940 most of Norway was in German hands; and the looming threat to the BEF (British Expeditionary Force) from a *blitzkrieg* through Belgium, precipitated a vote of no confidence in the government. On 7 May Leo Amery, once Chamberlain's close friend, concluded his indictment in the Commons of his leadership with Oliver Cromwell's words to the Long Parliament in 1653: "You have sat too long here for any good you have been doing. Depart I say, and let us have done with you. In the name of God, go". Chamberlain won the vote but lost the argument: 40 Conservatives voted against the government – John Profumo was the youngest.

Chamberlain (and the King) wanted the Foreign Secretary, Lord Halifax to replace him. Halifax thought it impossible to lead an administration from the House of Lords: and refused. If Halifax (the "Holy Fox") had agreed to lead a National Government, it is more than possible that he would have sued for peace, with incalculable consequences. On 10 May it was Churchill, with the support of the Labour party, who became Prime Minister.

The Wehrmacht occupied Luxembourg on 9 May and invaded Belgium the following day. Unaccountably, Hitler halted his forces on 24 May at Dunkirk: enabling the Royal Navy, between 26 May-4 June, to evacuate 338,226 Allied soldiers. On 10 June Italy declared war on Britain and France; and on 22 June Marshal Pétain of France signed an armistice with Germany. Britain and her Empire now faced Hitler alone.

Victory in the Battle of Britain saved the nation from invasion and bought the time needed to prepare to fight back. Despite a U-boat campaign that threatened the country with starvation and military disasters in the Mediterranean, Churchill's courage and oratory held the nation steady – until successes at sea and in North Africa, supported by Russia from 22 June and the US on 11 December 1941, began to turn the tide against the Axis powers. The following are extracts from his best known WWII speeches:

"…. I have nothing to offer but blood, toil, tears and sweat". (13 May 1940)

"…. we shall fight on the beaches, we shall fight on the landing grounds, we shall fight in the fields and in the streets, we shall never surrender". (4 June 1940)

"The Battle of France is over. I expect the Battle of Britain is about to begin. Upon this Battle depends the survival of Christian civilisation. Upon it depends our own British life and the long continuity of our institutions and our Empire. The whole fury and might of the enemy must very soon be turned on us. Hitler knows that he will have to break us in this island or lose the war. If we can stand up to him, all Europe may be free, and the life of the world may move forward into broad, sunlit uplands; but if we fail, then the whole world, including the United States, and all that we have known and cared for, will sink into the abyss of a new dark age made more sinister, and perhaps more protracted, by the light of a perverted science. Let us therefore brace ourselves to our duty and so bear ourselves that if the British Empire and its Commonwealth lasts for a thousand years, men will still say, 'This was their finest hour'". (18 June 1940)

American World War II poster depicting Winston Churchill as a British Bulldog (1942)

"Never in the field of human conflict was so much owed by so many to so few". (20 August 1940, referring to the Battle of Britain)

"Give us the tools and we will finish the job". (9 February 1941, Broadcast to US)

"This is not the end. It is not even the beginning of the end. But it is perhaps, the end of the beginning". (10 November 1942, referring to the Battle of Egypt)

Churchill's friendship with President Roosevelt cemented co-operation with the US; and his ability to cajole and stand up to Stalin led to a compact with the Soviet Union that won the war in Europe. By the end of 1942 German defeats in Libya and at Stalingrad, and US victories over the Japanese in the Pacific, marked the watershed. From 1943 Churchill used all his energy and leadership to focus the Allies on total victory. Never before had the British been so united, or organised so ruthlessly behind one man.

But that one man, Churchill did not share in the final triumph. In the July 1945 general election, two months after Germany's unconditional surrender on 8 May, a war-weary nation voted him out of office – it was Clement Attlee (1883–1967), the new Labour prime minister who oversaw the final defeat of Japan on 15 August. Emperor Hirohito declared in a memorable broadcast to his people, after atom bombs had devastated two Japanese cities: "…. the war situation has developed not necessarily to Japan's advantage".

The "Big Three" at Yalta (February 1945)

Clement Richard Attlee, 1st Earl Attlee by Howard Coster (1945)
National Portrait Gallery, London

Churchill liked Attlee, but made fun of him, as: "a sheep in sheep's clothing" and, "He is a modest man who has much to be modest about". Perhaps his best known quip was, "An empty taxi arrived at 10 Downing Street and when the door opened, Mr Attlee got out".

By 1954 Churchill had overcome his bitterness at what he considered to be the ingratitude of the British people sufficiently to say: "I have never accepted what many people have kindly said, namely that I inspired the Nation. It was the Nation and the race dwelling around the globe that had the lion heart. I had the luck to be called upon to give the roar".

As leader of the Opposition Churchill, admired and fêted across the globe to a degree never seen before or since, was still able to hold the Labour government to account. In 1951 he became Prime Minister again – aged seventy-seven. He resigned in 1955, in favour of his faithful amanuensis Anthony Eden. He stayed on as a backbencher until 1964, when he was almost ninety. On 15 January 1965 Churchill suffered a cerebral thrombosis. His last words were, "I'm bored with it all". He died nine days later, on 24 January – 70 years to the day since his father's death. His body lay in State in Westminster Hall for three days, followed by a service in St Paul's Cathedral – the first state funeral for a commoner since that of W.E. Gladstone in 1898.

If de Gaulle was to outlive him, it was Churchill's wish that his funeral procession should pass through Waterloo Station ("We all have our crosses to bear and mine is the Cross of Lorraine"). As his coffin was transported down the Thames, the cranes of London's docklands bowed in salute. He was buried near his ancestors in Saint Martin's Churchyard at Bladon, not far from his birthplace at Blenheim.

Churchill's first love Pamela Plowden, remarked: "The first time you meet Winston you see all his faults, and spend the rest of your life in discovering his virtues". As he once said (clearly thinking of himself), "The characteristic of a great man is his power to leave a lasting impression on people he meets".

He also published volumes of speeches, broadcasts, autobiography – and two biographies, of *Marlborough* (four volumes, 1933–8) and of his father (two volumes, 1906). He acknowledged however, that his one novel, *Savrola* (1900) was unworthy of him, commenting: "I have consistently urged my friends to abstain from reading it". Among his hundreds of articles were some on painting, which were collected in a book, *Painting as a Pastime* (1950). It is said that he published more words than Charles Dickens and Walter Scott put together.

He certainly manipulated and enjoyed controlling other people ("Of course I am an egotist. Where do you get if you are not?"). But Churchill was a fine historian and his prose was as memorable as his oratory. His histories include *The World Crisis* (four volumes, 1923–9), The *Second World War* (six volumes, 1948–54) and *A History of the English-Speaking Peoples* (four volumes, 1956–8).

Churchill took up painting in 1915, later saying: "I know of nothing which, without exhausting the body, more entirely occupies the mind". He preferred to paint outside in the sunshine – usually landscapes, with bold sweeps of bright colours. His near neighbour in London, the talented portraitist Sir John Lavery R.A, (1856–1941) gave him some early lessons and great encouragement: saying, without apparent irony, that, "had he chosen painting instead of statesmanship, I believe he would have been a great master with the brush". Churchill exhibited in the Royal Academy; and his work hangs in the Tate Gallery and the Louvre. Churchill himself was modest and made no pretence of his painting being anything other than a hobby.

THE MODERN ERA 1874–1965

Sir Ernest Swinton (1868–1951) invented the modern tank in 1914: but it was Churchill in January 1915, having seen its potential in an instant, who urged the Prime Minister Herbert Asquith to sponsor immediate production. He suggested that the army should: "…. fit up a number of steam tractors with small armoured shelters, in which men and machine-guns could be placed, which would be bullet-proof. The caterpillar system would enable trenches to be crossed quite easily and the weight of the machine would destroy all wire entanglements".

Churchill was a keen and good polo player in India, still hunted at 70 and was an excellent shot. He owned race horses: one of which, Colonist II won thirteen races in his father's old colours before it was put to stud. When asked if Colonist was still racing he replied: "No, he has given up racing. He is now rogering". He also took great pleasure in bricklaying at Chartwell, his house in Kent, usually wearing a hat and smoking a cigar – he was proud to have been given a membership card by the Amalgamated Union of Building Trade Workers.

Churchill's extraordinary abilities are attributed by some to a bipolar disorder, commonly known as manic depression. Certainly he had fits of depression that he called his 'black dog'. He was not dyslexic, simply uninterested in most subjects at school – although he won the fencing championship. He represented Dundee in Parliament for fourteen years, but lost his seat in 1922, partly because he had appendicitis, writing later that: "I left [Dundee] short of an appendix, seat and party". He had a minor stroke in 1949 and a serious one in 1953, which was kept secret, that paralysed his left side. He may have suffered from Alzheimer's Disease at the end of his life. Overall however, he had a remarkable constitution; which he did his best to undermine.

His self-discipline has been wrongly questioned. He was however, amazingly self-indulgent (he always wore silk underwear); and was spoiled by his research assistants and Private Secretaries – who adored him, despite often being shouted at and taken for granted. He was quite capable of self mockery: "I always manage somehow to adjust to any new level of luxury without whimper or complaint. It is one of my more winning traits".

Churchill could be absurdly soft-hearted and childish. On one occasion, watching a film of *Oliver Twist* at home, he was seen to cover his dog Rufus's eyes when Bill Sikes drowned Bullseye. He used to tell his secretary that she could put a book away because Toby, the budgerigar "had read it". Toby and a cat called Nelson kept him company in his bedroom while he worked in bed – where Rab Butler, his rather spineless Chancellor of the Exchequer once came to go through Budget (Churchill might have referred to them as "budgie") papers with him. Jock Colville, one of Churchill's Private Secretaries, counted fourteen droppings on Butler's bald head afterwards. Butler himself recalled a visit to Chequers in 1943: where he found Churchill in bed as usual, with Nelson the cat curled up on his feet. "This cat", teased Churchill, "does more for the war effort than you do. He acts as a hot-water bottle and saves fuel and power".

Whatever has been said, drink seldom got the better of him. "Always remember Clemmie, that I have taken more out of alcohol than it has taken out of me", he told his wife; and "A single glass of champagne imparts a feeling of exhilaration. The nerves are braced, the imagination is agreeably stirred, the wits become more nimble. A bottle produces the contrary effect". He also said, "I have been brought up and trained to have the utmost contempt for people who get drunk". He stayed in bed most mornings throughout WWII, because it was the most comfortable and peaceful place to write his speeches. His literary output and career shows clearly that he was far from slothful: if anything he was hyper-active, almost manically so in early life.

Churchill's obsession with his illustrious ancestor the 1st Duke of Marlborough was as much a fascination with war as with the man. It is impossible to know which came first – he spent much of his childhood playing with toy soldiers. However his lineal descent from Britain's finest and most successful general was a source of pride and inspiration to him. His colleagues found it irritating. Not everyone shared his opinion of Marlborough either: W.E.

Gladstone wrote that, "There never was a Churchill, from John of Marlborough down, that had either principles or morals".

Churchill's espousal of Zionism won him the support of international Jewry. The help and advice given to him by the American Bernard Baruch, the most successful speculator and financier of the 1920s, is well-known. A more shadowy figure, introduced to Churchill by Brendan Bracken, was a South African of Jewish-Austrian origin who had made a fortune speculating in South African mining ventures, Sir Henry Strakosch. In 1932 he settled his Stock Exchange losses of over £18,000 (£3.5 million today) with his broker Vickers da Costa, where Churchill's brother Jack was a partner. His beloved Chartwell, which had been advertised for sale in *The Times* on 2 April 1932, was saved. Strakosch became a valuable source of information on German rearmament.

Churchill's three closest friends had names that began with a 'B'. They were also disliked by his wife Clemmie; and not much trusted by anyone else. Brendan, later Viscount Bracken (1901–58), born in Tipperary, was editor of the Financial Times then Churchill's Minister of Information; Max Aitken, Lord Beaverbrook (1879–1964) was the Canadian-born owner of the *Daily Express* and Minister of Aircraft Production, whom Churchill once described as "a foul weather friend"; and Frederick Edwin (F.E.) Smith, Lord Birkenhead (1872–1930) who had been Attorney General in Lloyd George's administration – of whom Churchill once said, "He had all the canine virtues in a remarkable degree: courage, fidelity, vigilance, love of chase". Margot Asquith was not so sure: "F.E. Smith is very clever, but sometimes his brains go to his head". Bracken was so close to Churchill that he was rumoured to be his son; curiously neither tried very hard to deny it – and both were red-haired.

Often overlooked but undeniable, Churchill would have been thought a bigot and racist today. He opposed giving the vote to women, fought against independence for India and recommended the use of mustard gas against the Kurds in Iraq.

Comparisons between Churchill and Hitler may be odious, but some are interesting. They both had lonely childhoods; were both brave soldiers; authors; artists (of a sort); orators; small (Churchill was 5'7" and Hitler was 5'8"); lateral thinkers who bullied their generals; ruthless and sentimental, often simultaneously.

Fortunately there were fundamental differences. Churchill was a Freemason from 1901–12: Hitler despised them. Churchill hunted: Hitler abolished hunting in Germany. Churchill cared little for his health, had expensive tastes and enjoyed his food: Hitler was ascetic, obsessive about his health and a near-vegetarian. Churchill was a great wit and had a wonderful sense of humour: Hitler was not remotely funny, in any usual meaning of the word. Churchill had a normal libido, producing five children. Hitler certainly admired family life – but in his case it included incest. Hitler was a racial supremacist: Churchill was a straightforward imperialist with an affection for every country in the Empire. Aside of the obvious differences in class, above all Churchill was an honest, highly moral democrat – Hitler was an obsessive control-freak who turned into a Satanic madman.

Churchill dismissed making speeches as "the art of making deep sounds from the stomach sound like important messages from the brain". He knew that this was silly. His friend Lord Birkenhead's quip, "Winston has devoted the best years of his life to preparing his impromptu speeches", was observant – he also said "Mr Churchill is easily satisfied with the best". Churchill never employed a speechwriter: he worked hard preparing his speeches, usually in bed.

In 1955 he was asked by Adlai Stevenson to whom did he owe his oratorical style. Churchill replied: "America: and Bourke Cockran – who taught me to use every note of the human voice as if playing an organ". Churchill had met Cockran, a New York politician, on his first visit to the United States sixty years before. Churchill said that Cockran, "could play on every emotion and hold thousands of people riveted".

Churchill described how to prepare for a speech: "Before [a speaker] can inspire [his audience] with any emotion, he must be swayed by it himself. When he would rouse their indignation, his heart is filled with anger. Before he can move their tears, his own must flow. To convince them, he must himself believe. His opinions may change as their impressions fade, but every orator means what he says at the moment he says it. He is never consciously insincere". Churchill was very emotional himself and not ashamed of showing his feelings – "I blub an awful lot, you know. You'll have to get used to it", he warned Anthony Montague Browne, his new Private Secretary.

Clemmie Churchill

After proposing unsuccessfully three times to other girls, in 1908 Churchill married Clementine Ogilvy Hozier – "my most brilliant achievement was to persuade my wife to marry me", he was later to say. Born in 1885, her mother was Lady Blanche Henrietta Ogilvy, second wife of Sir Henry Montague Hozier and a daughter of the 7th Earl of Airlie. Lady Blanche was well known for sharing her favours: and was eventually divorced as a result. She maintained that Clementine's father was Captain William George "Bay" Middleton, a noted horseman.

But Clementine's biographer Joan Hardwick believed, due to Hozier's reputed infertility, that all Lady Blanche's children were actually fathered by her sister's husband, Algernon Bertram Freeman-Mitford, better known as a grandfather of the remarkable Mitford sisters. Created a life peer in 1965, Clemmie died in 1977 aged ninety-two.

Stories about Churchill and remarks supposedly made by him abound. He could not resist puns, however inappropriate. When touring Africa in 1907, he was informed by a Colonial Governor that venereal disease was spreading at an alarming rate among the natives. "Ah, Pox Britannica!", Churchill quipped. The playwright George Bernard Shaw sent Churchill a telegram: "Two tickets reserved for you, first night Pygmalion. Bring a friend. If you have one". Churchill replied: "Cannot make first night. Will come to second. If you have one".

"I can well understand the Honourable Member's wish to speak on. He needs the practice badly". Churchill was notoriously unpunctual: "I am a sporting man. I always like to give trains and aeroplanes a fair chance of getting away". Churchill knew his faults: "Eating my words has never given me indigestion". On being told that his fly-buttons were undone, "Dead birds don't fall out of their nests". Another version of this was, "Do not worry, the lion is asleep".

In 1943 Churchill sent Anthony Eden on a mission to bring Turkey into the war. In due course he received a telegram from Eden: "Progress slow. What more can I tell Turkey?" Churchill is said to have replied: "Tell them Christmas is coming!" In 1960 Churchill was asked by a reporter from the Evening Standard what he thought of the prediction that by the year 2000 women would be ruling the world. He replied gloomily, "They still will, will they?"

In Richmond, Virginia where a sculpture of him was being unveiled, a magnificently Rubenesque lady came up to Churchill and cooed enthusiastically: "Mr Churchill, I want you to know I got up at dawn and drove a hundred miles for the unveiling of your bust". Gazing at her spectacular poitrine he answered, "Madam, I want you to know that I would happily reciprocate the honour".

On another occasion, in Canada he was seated next to a very strait-laced Methodist minister at a reception. A pert young waitress came up to them with a tray of glasses of sherry. She went first to Churchill, who took a glass, and then turned to the minister. He was appalled to be offered alcohol: "Young lady", he announced, "I'd rather commit adultery than take an intoxicating beverage". Whereupon Churchill beckoned the girl: "Come back miss, I didn't know we had a choice".

A few months after Chamberlain's return from Munich, waving his famous piece of paper, during a debate on Palestine, Malcolm MacDonald, Secretary of State for the Colonies, had reached the end of a difficult speech and was discoursing lyrically about the country itself: "Bethlehem, where the Prince of Peace was born ...." he intoned, to be interrupted by Churchill's voice: "Bethlehem? I thought Neville was born in Birmingham".

Asked if he had any complaints about the US, Churchill replied, "Lavatory paper too thin, newspapers too thick". "Although prepared for martyrdom, I preferred that it be postponed". "I am just preparing my impromptu remarks".

Churchill once told his Irish counterpart that the situation in Britain was serious but not hopeless. The Irish Premier replied (according to Churchill) that in his country the situation was hopeless but not serious. "I am ready to meet my maker, but whether my maker is prepared for the great ordeal of meeting me is another matter".

When in the lavatory, a discreet knock on the door by his butler woke Churchill from a reverie: "Mr Churchill, sir". "Yes", said Churchill, "what is it?". "The Lord Privy Seal is here to see you", said the butler. Churchill replied, "Tell the Lord Privy Seal that I am sealed in the privy and can only deal with one shit at a time".

In May 1940, while Guderian's panzers were overrunning Belgium and the surrender of France was imminent, Churchill became Prime Minister and started his work to save the nation. With a typically British sense of priorities, amongst the first papers to cross his desk were orders to dispose of equipment no longer needed by the army. British forces had recently been expelled from Narvik in Norway and cases of 10" long, thick rubber sheaths for protecting rifle barrels against snow were on the docks waiting to be condemned. "No", said Churchill, "all that this requires is reclassification. These cases must now be stencilled: 'Condoms, British Soldiers for the use of, size…...medium'. That should make it clear to the Germans who really is the master race".

On hearing that the Greek premier was called Plasteras, he remarked that he hoped that he didn't have feet of clay too.

An American GI accosted him in the lobby of an hotel and asked him rudely where was the 'john'. Churchill replied that it was down the corridor, on the left and marked with a sign saying 'Gentlemen' – "but don't let that put you off".

SOME OF CHURCHILL'S BEST KNOWN APHORISMS

"A nation that forgets its past has no future" *[The theme of this book]*.

"It is a good thing for an uneducated man to read books of quotations".

"You can always count on the Americans to do the right thing – after they have first tried everything else".

"A lie gets halfway around the world before the truth can get its pants on".

"Courage is rightly esteemed the first of human qualities, because it is the quality that guarantees all others".

"Courage is going from failure to failure without losing enthusiasm".

"A prisoner of war is a man who tries to kill you and fails, and then asks you not to kill him". (The Observer, 1952)

"The worst quarrels arise when both sides are equally in the right and in the wrong".

"It is wonderful how well men can keep secrets they have not been told".

"There is no such thing as public opinion. There is only published opinion".

"An appeaser is one who feeds a crocodile, hoping it will eat him last".

"Battles are won by slaughter and manoeuvre. The greater the general, the more he contributes in manoeuvre, the less he demands in slaughter".

"A fanatic is one who can't change his mind and won't change the subject".

"The English never draw a line without blurring it".

A parliamentary candidate is "asked to stand, he wants to sit, he is expected to lie".

"The young sow wild oats. The old grow sage".

"Always remember, a cat looks down on a man, a dog looks up to a man, but a pig will look a man right in the eye and see his equal".

"Some people regard private enterprise as a predatory tiger to be shot. Others look on it as a cow they can milk. Not enough people see it as a healthy horse, pulling a sturdy wagon".

"Too often the strong, silent man is silent only because he does not know what to say; and is reputed strong only because he has remained silent".

"It is more agreeable to have the power to give than to receive".

"Socialism is like a dream. Sooner or later you wake up to reality".

"Nothing is so exhilarating in life as to be shot at with no result".

Towards the end of WWII he forecast, "The next enemy will be the Russians, our next friends will be the Germans".

"You may have to fight when there is no hope of victory, because it is better to perish than live as slaves".

"In War: Resolution; In Defeat: Defiance; In Victory: Magnanimity; In Peace: Good Will".

"Democracy is the best form of the worst type of government".

"The best argument against democracy is a five-minute conversation with the average voter"

Winnie-the-Pooh's first published appearance was in 1926. Alan Alexander (A.A.) Milne (1882–1956) did not name Winnie after Churchill, as some surmise. Winnie was a bear cub, brought to Britain in WWI by a Canadian soldier, Harry Colebourn. He had bought her for $20 from a hunter who had killed the mother. He named her "Winnipeg", or "Winnie" for short, after his home town. When Colebourn's Brigade was posted to France he gave her to London Zoo – where she died, in 1934.

IN MEMORIAM

"Luckily, life is not so easy as all that; otherwise we should get to the end too quickly", Churchill wrote in *My Early Life* (1930). In his ninety-year life he was awarded, among others too numerous to list, these honours: Companion of Honour (1922), Fellow of the Royal Society (1941), Order of Merit (1946) and Knight of the Garter (1953). He also won the Nobel Prize for Literature in 1953. He had occupied every great office of state other than the Foreign Office. It is said that he was offered a dukedom after WWII, as the 1st Duke of London and that he was argued out of it by his son Randolph, who aspired to a career in politics himself: which would have been difficult from the House of Lords. It is also possible that disappointment with his only son was such that Churchill would not accept any title that was hereditary.

No commentary on Churchill however, would be complete without addressing one harsh reality: it is that effectively, he sold out the British Empire to the US to win the war. When assessing the Allies' contributions to defeating Germany in WWII, it can be said that Russia paid in blood and

Churchill loved Randolph, but he did not much like him. He urged Randolph not to get captured during the war, for then "the Gestapo would try to blackmail me by sending me your fingers one by one: a situation I would have to bear with fortitude".

the US in credit and materiel: but Britain, in facing the Nazis alone for two years, bought the time for those great resources to tip the balance. Hitler was insane to declare war on both: but had he not, there would be a very different European Union, itself a Churchillian ideal (not that he ever wished Britain to join it), today – and possibly, no independent Britain. In a 2002 BBC poll to establish the greatest Briton ever, Churchill came **first**.

CHURCHILL'S DAUGHTER-IN-LAW EARNED A REMARKABLE REPUTATION

The Hon. Pamela Beryl Digby, daughter of the 11th Baron Digby of Geashill, was born in Farnborough in Hampshire on 20 March 1920. She was brought up in the family home at Minterne Magna in Dorset. Though a fine horsewoman, she received the education considered appropriate to her class and generation – virtually nil. At seventeen she went to a 'finishing' school in Munich; and was introduced to Hitler by Unity Mitford. When she was nineteen she was invited to dinner by Churchill's son Randolph. She agreed to marry him that night and did so within weeks, on 4 October 1939. Her only child, another Winston was born in 1940. She divorced Randolph, who drank heavily and was abusive, in 1946.

Pamela's great-great aunt was the 19th century adventurer and courtesan Lady Jane Digby (1807–81), a famous traveller, notorious for her sexual exploits. Auburn haired, inclined to plumpness but vital and self-disciplined, it was probably unhappiness that drove Pamela to follow her forebear's example: to become "the 20th century's greatest courtesan". She threw herself into her new career, learning quickly and shamelessly how to please men. She had affairs with Averell Harriman, a US politician and heir to a railway fortune; General Fred Anderson; Jock Whitney, owner of the New York Herald Tribune and US Ambassador to Britain; Bill Paley, the billionaire owner of CBS; and Edward R. Murrow, an influential journalist and broadcaster. Randolph thought that his parents had condoned Pamela's affair with Harriman, which ended when Harriman was posted to Moscow in 1943 – corroding Randolph's already shaky relationship with his father.

Divorced and only twenty-six, Pamela moved to fresh grazing in France. In 1947 she kicked off with Prince Aly Khan, son of the Aga Khan, for two years; then spent five years with Gianni Agnelli, the Fiat heir, who let her down after she had aborted his child in Switzerland and converted to his catholicism in 1950. Spyros Niarchos, a Greek shipping billionaire, came next: until in 1954 she became Baron Elie de Rothschild's *maîtresse en titre*. She married Leland Hayward, a theatrical impresario, in 1960 – but when he died in 1971, now known as "The Widow of Opportunity", she returned to her old flame Harriman.

On 28 September 1971 they married. Although he was seventy-nine and she was fifty-one, the years before his death in 1986 were happy. She became a US citizen in 1971 and, with Harriman's support, entered politics, raising $12 million for the Democrats. Harriman left her $115 million in his will, which was contested by his children, and a respected position in US society. In May 1993 President Clinton appointed her US Ambassador to France. The French admired her looks, which had been surgically enhanced; and her charm did much to foster relationships between the two countries.

Pamela Harriman died at the American Hospital in Neuilly-sur-Seine on 5 February 1997, after suffering a stroke in the swimming pool at the Hôtel Ritz in Paris. President Jacques Chirac of France placed the Grand Cross of the *Légion d'Honneur* on her flag-draped coffin. President Clinton ordered her body to be flown home in 'Air Force One' and spoke movingly at her funeral in Washington, D.C. She had been a wise and surprisingly skilled stateswoman, who served her adopted country well.

"TREASON DOTH NEVER PROSPER – WHAT'S THE REASON? WHY IF IT PROSPER, NONE DARE CALL IT TREASON."

This epigram was written by Sir John Harington (1561–1612), Queen Elizabeth I's "saucy Godson" – who invented a flushing lavatory in 1596. Two cases of treason involved close friends of Churchill.

In 1916 F.E. Smith, later Lord Birkenhead, having succeeded Sir Edward Carson as Attorney General, prosecuted with ferocious eloquence Sir Roger Casement at his trial for treason. Casement, a foolishly deluded Anglo-Irish Protestant but regarded by Irish nationalists as an hero, had his character ruined before the trial by stories that circulated about his homosexual practices with native boys in the Congo, when he was the British Consul at Boma – which were later proved from his diaries in graphic detail to be true. He was hanged at Pentonville on 3 August 1916. In 1965 his remains were given a state funeral in Dublin – an honour perhaps undeserved by an incompetent gun-runner, German stooge (an opinion held by many of the Irish Republican Brotherhood at the time) and pædophile.

John Amery, the son of Churchill's school-friend and cabinet colleague Leo Amery (1873–1955), was born on 14 March 1912. Sir Cyril Norwood, his headmaster at Harrow said of him: "Of all the boys whom I have known, John Amery was the most abnormal .... morally imbecile". Amery went into business but was declared bankrupt in 1936. By this time he had acquired seventy-four convictions for motoring offences.

In October 1936 Amery moved to Spain where he worked as a gun-runner for General Francisco Franco during the Spanish Civil War and served as an intelligence officer with Italian volunteer forces. Amery also met Jacques Doriot the French fascist leader. In 1939 he and Doriot travelled together to Austria, Czechoslovakia, Italy and Germany before going to live in France. In 1941 Amery was recruited by the Nazis: and in November 1942 he began to broadcast in praise of Adolf Hitler, from Berlin.

In April 1943 Amery established the Legion of St. George and tried to persuade British prisoners to fight for Germany against Russia on the Eastern Front. This devastated Leo Amery, secretary of state for India and Burma during WWII. In the final months of the war Amery moved to Italy where he made propaganda speeches on behalf of Benito Mussolini. He also made broadcasts on Italian radio. Amery was captured by Italian partisans in Milan in April 1945 and handed over to the British authorities.

After being interviewed by MI5 Amery was tried for high treason. On 28 November 1945 Amery pleaded guilty to eight counts of treason – perhaps he wished to save his family the pain of a long trial. John Amery was hanged on 19 December 1945. His executioner, Albert Pierrepoint said that Amery was the bravest man he had ever hanged.

It is a sad irony that Leo (Leopold Charles Moritz Stennett) Amery had (and hid) a Jewish mother, whilst his son became a Nazi. Fortunately, Leo had another son, Julian (1919–96), a distinguished Conservative M.P. who was created a life peer in 1992.

In 1241 a new penalty for high treason (or any crime, often and cynically determined by the monarch to be treasonable) was introduced in England. It was last inflicted in full at Portsmouth on 24 August 1782 – on the Scottish spy David Tyrie, for conducting a treasonable correspondence with the French. The appalling procedure, the epitome of "cruel" punishment, was designed to instil horror amongst spectators – the purpose being, by prolonging the agony and degradation of the victim, to discourage emulation. Following sentence to be "hanged, drawn, and quartered", the traitor was dragged on a hurdle (a wooden frame) to the place of execution (drawn). He was then hanged by the neck, but cut down before death (hanged); castrated and disembowelled; and the genitalia and entrails were burned before the still living victim's eyes. Finally, the heart was plucked out and burned, the corpse was beheaded and the body divided into four parts (quartered).

Typically, the resulting five parts (the four quarters and the head) were parboiled to preserve them; and gibbeted (put on public display) in different parts of the city, town or even country. Gibbeting was abolished in England in 1843 – but the ghastly procedure itself remained on the statute book until 1870. It is hard to believe that this was just four years before Churchill was born.

Women found guilty of treason were burned at the stake, a punishment abolished only in 1790.

John ("Jack") Ketch, who died in 1686 was an executioner employed by King Charles II. He was notorious for the incompetent and barbarous way in which he performed his duties. He executed Lord William Russell in Lincoln's Inn Fields on 21 July 1683; and James Scott, 1st Duke of Monmouth on 15 July 1685, after the Monmouth Rebellion. He was either very awkward, drunk or sadistic with his beheading technique; and his victims often suffered dreadfully at their deaths. He managed to bungle hangings too.

The French as ever, did things with more panache. On 5 January 1757 Robert-François Damiens attempted to kill Louis

The execution of Guy Fawkes (Guy Fawkes) by Claes Jansz Visscher (1606)
National Portrait Gallery, London

On 13 October 1660 Samuel Pepys wrote in his diary, "I went out to Charing Cross, to see [the regicide] Major-General Harrison hanged, drawn, and quartered .... he looked as cheerful as any man could do in that condition. He was presently cut down, and his head and heart shown to the people, at which there were great shouts of joy .... Harrison's head has been set up [on a pole] on the other side of Westminster Hall".

XV with a knife. Condemned as a regicide, he was the last to be executed in France by *ecartèlement* ("drawn and quartered").

He was tortured first with red-hot pincers; and the hand that had held the knife was burned with sulphur, molten wax, lead and boiling oil. In the Place de Grève, horses were harnessed to his arms and legs and forced to gallop in four different directions. However Damiens' limbs and ligaments did not separate easily; and after some hours, officials ordered the executioner to cut his joints. Dismemberment followed, to the applause of the crowd; and his torso, apparently still living, was burned at the stake.

Damiens's house was razed to the ground; his brothers and sisters were ordered to change their names; and his father, wife and daughter were banished from France.

Among the observers of Damiens's terrible death was the English fop and wit George Selwyn (1719–91), who spent 44 years in Parliament without making a speech. A necrophiliac, his obsession with executions and corpses was legendary. When he was asked by an aristocrat at the scene if he was an executioner, Selwyn replied: "No monsieur, I have no that honour. I am only an amateur".

When Selwyn visited the dying Henry Fox, 1st Lord Holland, he was refused admission. Having been informed, Fox gave instructions that, "If Mr Selwyn calls again, show him up. If I am alive, I shall be pleased to see him; but if I am dead, he will be pleased to see me". In *The Diaboliad* (1766), a satirical poem by William Combe (1742–1813), the Devil considers Selwyn a natural successor.

IN 1874 A HEADSTONE WAS ERECTED FOR FANNY ADAMS AT ALTON, HAMPSHIRE

Eight year-old Fanny Adams was brutally murdered in Alton, Hampshire on 26 August 1867 by Frederick Baker, a 24 year-old solicitor's clerk. He never gave a reason for his terrible crime, but there was insanity in his family. It was a crime that is all too familiar today.

Her dismembered body was found in a field near the town. It was a sickening scene of carnage. The child's severed head lay on two poles, deeply slashed from mouth to ear and across the left temple. Her right ear had been cut off. Most horribly, both eyes were missing.

Nearby lay a leg and a thigh. A search revealed her dismembered torso: the entire contents of chest and pelvis had been torn out and scattered, with some internal organs even further slashed or mutilated. So savage was the butchery that other parts of her body were recovered only after extensive searches over several days. Her eyes were found in the River Wey.

Baker's father had "shown an inclination to assault, even to kill his children"; a cousin had been in asylums four times; brain fever had caused his sister's death; and he had attempted suicide after a failed love affair. The jury rejected Mr. Justice Mellor's judicial advice that they might consider the prisoner insane, the inevitable verdict today. After only 15 minutes the jury returned a guilty verdict: and Frederick Baker was hanged before a crowd of 5,000, mostly women, in front of Winchester Prison at 08:00 on Christmas Eve 1867.

> The guillotine was not invented by Dr Joseph-Ignace Guillotin, nor in France. Similar devices, such as the Halifax Gibbet and Scottish Maiden, were used for executions in several European countries long before the French Revolution.
> The Nazis executed 40,000 people in Germany with the *Fallbeil* ("falling axe") – more than were beheaded during the 'Reign of Terror' in France (1793–94).

Fanny Adam's headstone

Before his execution Baker wrote to the parents of the murdered child to express deep sorrow over the crime that he had committed, "in an unguarded hour and not with malice aforethought". He earnestly sought their forgiveness – adding that he was "enraged at her crying, but it was done without any pain or struggle". The prisoner denied most emphatically that he had violated the child, or had attempted to do so.

The case was the source of enormous public concern and newspaper reports concentrated on the youth and innocence of the victim. Everyone living in England at the time would have known the name of 'sweet' Fanny Adams. With typically grisly humour, sailors in the Royal Navy came to use the expression to refer to the unpleasant meat rations they were often served – likening them to the dead girl's remains. Walter Downing, an Australian soldier who fought in Europe in WWI, wrote a glossary of soldiers' slang called *Digger Dialects* in 1919. He is the first to record the link between "F.A." (meaning "fuck all") and Fanny Adams.

The last fully public hanging in Britain took place at Newgate on 26 May 1868, when Michael Barrett was executed for the Fenian bombing at Clerkenwell in London, which killed seven people. The last fully public hanging in the British Isles took place on 11 August 1875, when Joseph Phillip Le Brun was executed for murder on Jersey.

> Albert Pierrepoint (1905–92) was by far the most prolific British hangman of the 20th century. In office from 1932–56, he is credited with having executed 433 men and 17 women, including 6 US soldiers at Shepton Mallet – and some 200 Nazis after WWII. In retirement he ran a pub near Manchester called "Help the Poor Struggler" – where he put up a sign saying, "No hanging around the bar".

Peter Allen, at Walton Prison in Liverpool, and Gwynne Evans (real name John Walby), at Strangeways Prison in Manchester, were the last people to be hanged in the British Isles. Their executions took place simultaneously at 08:00 on 13 August 1964.

SIR EDWARD CARSON DESTROYED OSCAR WILDE'S REPUTATION

F.E. Smith's predecessor as Attorney General, Edward Henry Carson was born on 9 February 1854 in Dublin. His father, also Edward Henry was an architect and civil engineer. His mother, Isabella Lambert came from a land-owning family in County Galway. Both parents hailed from staunchly Protestant, Anglo- Irish backgrounds, haughtily known as the "Ascendancy".

Carson was educated in Queen's County (County Laois today) before going up to Trinity College, Dublin in 1871 to read classics. Securing only a moderate pass, he read for the Bar at King's Inns, Dublin and was called to the Irish Bar in 1877.

His first five years were spent mostly in representing poor tenants. He was so successful that, in a remarkable switch of roles, he was appointed senior crown prosecutor in Dublin. His effectiveness in pursuit of Irish nationalists who attacked estates owned by English absentee landlords and in enforcing tenant rent rolls, earned him the nickname "Coercion Carson". He

Oscar Wilde by W. E. D. Downey (28 May 1889, Published 1891)
National Portrait Gallery, London

Sir Edward Carson, 1st Baron Carson by John George Day (1914)
National Portrait Gallery, London

was appointed Solicitor-General for Ireland in 1892, shortly before being elected to the Westminster Parliament. Called to the English Bar in 1893, Carson swiftly established his reputation. In 1895, it was his devastating cross-examination of Oscar Wilde in his case against the Marquess of Queensberry for criminal libel that secured Wilde's conviction in his own trial a few weeks later.

Oscar Fingal O'Flahertie Wills Wilde (1854–1900) was born in Dublin, the son of Sir William Wilde, a renowned ear and eye surgeon. His mother Jane Francesca (*née* Elgee), under the pseudonym "Speranza" was a romantic poet and an Irish Nationalist. Disappointed that Oscar had not been the daughter she longed for, she dressed him as a girl until he was nine. He attended Trinity College, Dublin in 1871, from where he won a demyship in classics to Magdalen College, Oxford in 1874. He graduated with a double first in classical moderations and Greats in 1878.

He was unpopular at Oxford. His fellow undergraduates frequently tossed him into the River Cherwell, trashed his rooms and smashed his blue china. He failed to win election to the Oxford Union; and was humiliated by having a collection of his *Poems* rejected as mere plagiarism by the Union Library in 1881.

On a lecture tour of the US in 1882 to promote the Aesthetic movement, dressed in a velvet jacket, knee breeches and black silk stockings, he met with a mixed reception. Surprisingly, in sophisticated Boston his poetry was criticised as likely to turn men into "effeminate dandies" – while he was warmly welcomed in the rough mining town of Leadville in Colorado. It was in New York that he is said to have announced to a customs officer: "I have nothing to declare except my genius".

He returned to London a year later to lecture on the US. In 1884 he married Constance Lloyd, the daughter of an Irish barrister. They had two sons: Cyril, born in 1885 and Vyvyan, born in 1886. He wrote for the *Pall Mall Gazette* before being appointed editor of *Woman's World* from 1887–89. *The Happy Prince and Other Tales*, published in 1888, demonstrated a remarkable gift for romantic allegory disguised as fairy tales. Wilde wrote his best work during the last ten years of his life. His only novel, a Gothic tale mocking bourgeois morality in 1891, *The Picture of Dorian Gray*, created a storm of criticism and charges of immorality.

Wilde defended himself by arguing that morality was irrelevant to art. His greatest and most popular achievements were plays that mocked high society in a way new to late Victorian theatre. The first, *Lady Windermere's Fan* in 1893, showed how well sharp wit could transform farce. In the same year however, he wrote a macabre play, *Salomé*. Written in French, with scenes of incest, necrophilia, adultery and decapitation, it was halted by the censor during rehearsal, because the play blasphemed biblical characters. In 1894 an English translation appeared, salaciously illustrated by Aubrey Beardsley. His second society comedy, *A Woman of No Importance* in 1893, received high critical acclaim. It was followed in quick succession by *An Ideal Husband* and *The Importance of being Earnest* in 1895.

Though happily married and at the height of his success, Wilde began a homosexual relationship with Lord Alfred Douglas, the young son of the Marquess of Queensberry, whom he called "Bosie".

Furious, Queensberry hounded Wilde in public, presenting him with a bouquet of turnips at the opera; and eventually leaving his card at Wilde's club with the words "For Oscar Wilde posing Somdomite" *[sic]* written on the back. Bosie persuaded Wilde to sue his father for criminal libel.

The trial opened on 3 April 1895, with Edward Carson leading Queensberry's defence. Carson's cross-examination of Wilde started badly. The agile-tongued Wilde effortlessly turned his questions and made Carson look a crude bully. *Hubris* quickly turned to *nemesis* however, when Wilde carelessly gave as his reason for not kissing a boy, that "he was not pretty enough". From that moment, despite Wilde's attempt to withdraw the prosecution, Carson was relentless: and Wilde was revealed as a frequenter of male brothels and an associate of deviants and blackmailers. His case against Queensberry collapsed and he was advised immediately to leave the country, before a warrant for his arrest could be issued. He refused: and was apprehended in the Cadogan Hotel in Knightsbridge.

Marquess of Queensbury card, sent to Oscar Wilde (calling him a "somdomite")

Wilde's unique contribution to the theatre was his witticism, apparently lighthearted but in reality, remorselessly poking fun at Victorian hypocrisy:

"If the lower orders don't set us a good example, what on earth is the use of them?".

"Truth is rarely pure and never simple".

"I can resist anything except temptation".

"All women become like their mothers. That is their tragedy. No man does. That's his".

"What is a cynic? A man who knows the price of everything but the value of nothing".

"I have the simplest tastes. I am always satisfied with the best".

John Sholto Douglas, 9th Marquess of Queensberry (1844–1900) is best known for sponsoring the eponymous code of boxing rules. The code insisted on the wearing of boxing gloves, forbade the use of wrestling holds and required a fallen fighter to be given a free count of ten to recover. The three-minute "round" was established, followed by a one-minute rest period. Seconds were forbidden to enter the ring during a round.

On 25 May Wilde was convicted of "divers acts of gross indecency" and sentenced to two years' hard labour. *The Ballad of Reading Gaol* was written in 1898, in protest at the inhumane conditions he had encountered and the suffering of his fellow prisoners – he made little mention of his own. The following lines describe how he reacted to hearing that the guardsman who "walked the yard, in the suit of shabby grey", with a cricket cap on his head, was "the man who had to swing" (for killing his unfaithful wife).

Dear Christ! The very prison wall
Suddenly seemed to reel
And the sky above my head became
Like a casque of scorching steel;
And though I was a soul in pain
My pain I could not feel.

Wilde was bankrupted, all his possessions were sold and his life was destroyed. His blameless and bewildered family were uprooted and fled to Switzerland: where Constance changed her and her sons' surnames to Holland. She never saw him again.

Carson served as Solicitor General from 1900–05 and was knighted. One of his cases was the Archer-Shee action against the Royal Naval College at Osborne, made famous by the Terence Rattigan play, *The Winslow Boy* in 1946. Carson, a stern and disciplined professional was nonetheless passionate in his pursuit of justice for the "little" man.

In February 1910, sacrificing his chances to lead the Conservative party, Carson became the parliamentary leader of the anti-Home Rule Irish Unionists. The political future of Ulster was precarious. The General Election in January 1910 had left the Liberal government of Herbert Asquith entirely dependent for its majority on the votes of John Redmond and the Irish Nationalists. The Liberals had begun legislation to remove the right of veto from the House of Lords, for bills from the Commons that they did not like. Once enacted, the last constitutional barrier against Irish Home Rule would disappear. Carson strongly disapproved of such cynical horse-trading. He liked even less the price of Irish Nationalist support for pushing through the Lords Bill – a new Home Rule for Ireland Bill which Asquith put before the Commons in April 1912. Carson had always maintained that the lodestar of his political career was the preservation of Ulster: and now that moment was upon him.

His aim was to defeat Home Rule for the whole of Ireland. He did this by pleading Ulster as such a special case, that the Bill would have to be abandoned if Ulster refused to cooperate. In September 1912 the Unionists declared a Solemn League and Covenant, which pledged itself to resist Home Rule. Carson eagerly joined the Covenant, quoting Randolph Churchill: "Ulster

In January 1908 George Archer-Shee, a cadet at Osborne, was accused of stealing a five shilling postal-order from a fellow cadet and expelled. His father Martin, a strict Roman Catholic and an official of the Bank of England, demanded a proper enquiry and engaged Edward Carson to represent his son. In July 1910 the case came to trial. Osborne College was represented by the Solicitor General Sir Rufus Isaacs, later Marquess of Reading, but after four days the case collapsed, with George given an unequivocal and complete exoneration. The Admiralty had decided, on advice, that the post-mistress who had cashed the cheque was so old and myopic that she would be unconvincing as a Crown witness, especially under Carson's forensic cross-examination. A demand for restitution was at first contemptuously dismissed; but by this time members of Parliament had taken up the case. In April 1911, the family received £7,120 in compensation from the Admiralty (£2.8 million today). George continued his education at Stonyhurst College. He was killed in the first Battle of Ypres In October 1914.

will fight and Ulster will be right". He also supported in 1912, the raising and public drilling of the Ulster Volunteer Force. In 1914 he sanctioned the purchase of a large shipment of arms from Germany.

In March 1914, in what became known as the Curragh Mutiny, 58 officers from the Curragh Camp in County Kildare announced they would rather face a court martial than obey any order to fire upon Ulster Unionists. This slap in the government's face presented Carson with the opportunity of presenting an alternative Home Rule Bill which would exclude six of the nine counties of Ulster. He was ignored and tension increased. By May 1914, the Irish Home Rule Bill was awaiting only the Royal Assent. A last ditch attempt to exclude the six counties was made in July at a conference in Buckingham Palace, but to no avail.

On 4 August, the Ulster crisis was averted by the outbreak of WWI. It was agreed by all parties that the Home Rule Bill would be left dormant on the Statute Book until after the war. Even so, this decision was seen by the Unionists as a betrayal.

Carson spent the first months of the Great War as a Unionist backbencher. In May 1915 Asquith decided to include members of the opposition in his cabinet. Carson was appointed Attorney General. Amid a background of mounting disaster and bungling, demonstrated by the needless bloodshed of Gallipoli, the dud British artillery shells at La Neuve Chapelle and the collapse of Serbia, he resigned. Any lingering talk of betrayal of the six counties now evaporated and he became the darling of the Unionists. In June 1916 he chaired their war committee, a "think-tank" dedicated to a more robust and efficient prosecution of the war – it played an important part in replacing the ineffectual Asquith with the silver tongued "Welsh Wizard", David Lloyd George. Lloyd George immediately appointed Carson First Lord of the Admiralty. Carson's skills however, were not suited to administration.

The Easter Rising of April 1916 caused the British government rapidly to reconsider the Home Rule Bill, still lying on the statute book. Asquith gave Lloyd George the urgent task of suturing the tear between the Nationalists and Unionists, so that the war effort would not be endangered by a renewal of the Irish crisis. Lloyd George believed that a failure to solve the problem could lose the war: "then we are all lost". The outcome was that the Ulster Unionist Council accepted the exclusion of the six counties – a settlement which was rejected by Carson's own southern Unionists. In March 1917, with the imminent entry of the US to the war, the Irish question was once again raised to fend off any lurking doubts from that quarter. Forlornly, Carson suggested a federal solution, but the idea was rejected by the Unionist convention. In January 1918, disheartened and disillusioned, Carson resigned from the cabinet.

"I will not vote for Home Rule, although I shall do nothing to prevent this Bill from becoming law". With these words, Carson accepted the inevitability of partition, even though he attacked the concept in a speech of superb invective. He could not however, conceal his bitter disappointment that he had not carried his southern Unionist constituency with him – now to be abandoned to the Irish Free State.

In May 1921, accepting a life peerage as Baron Carson of Duncairn (his Belfast constituency), Carson was appointed a Lord of Appeal, until he retired in 1929. On 22 October 1935 he died in his bed at Cleve Court on the Isle of Thanet. He was buried in St Anne's Cathedral in Belfast; after being accorded a state funeral by the new government of Northern Ireland – the only person ever to be so honoured. Yet sadly, for Carson, "Northern Ireland provided him with a tomb and not a home".

> Irishmen were prominent in the Peninsular war; provided 98% of the British Army in India in 1857; and 50,000 died for Britain in WWI. Irishmen have won 168 VCs.

Released in 1897, but destitute, Wilde sailed directly to France – never to return. Calling himself Sebastian Melmoth, he spent his last three years in Paris living off remittances sent to him by his wife and friends.

He became addicted to absinthe; and was soon joined by Bosie, who described him as, "hand in glove with all the little boys on the Boulevard". He died of cerebral meningitis and absinthe poisoning on 30 November 1900. On his deathbed, he was received into the Roman Catholic Church, which he had once derided as suitable for "Saints and sinners alone – for respectable people, the Anglican Church will do".

> Wilde assumed the names Sebastian from the early Christian martyr who was shot to death with arrows; and Melmoth from the satanic subject of his great-uncle Charles Maturin's gothic novel *Melmoth the Wanderer*. Patrick O'Brian (1914–2000) used the name Maturin for a physician and spy in his "Jack Aubrey" novels.

> Epstein had decorated the tomb with a modernist angel sporting a handsome set of genitals, which were soon removed and used by generations of cemetery keepers as paperweights. In 2000, in a service of dedication, called "The Re-membering of Wilde", the artist Leon Johnson replaced them with a silver prosthesis.

A few days before his death and in excruciating pain, Wilde said to the few close friends attending his bedside: "My wallpaper and I are fighting a duel to the death. One of us has to go". Max Beerbohm recounted that one of these friends, Reggie Turner found him depressed after a nightmare. "I dreamt", Wilde told him, "that I had died and was supping with the dead". "I am sure, Oscar", Turner comforted him, "that you were the life and soul of the party". Wilde was finally laid to rest in the famous Paris cemetery, Père Lachaise. His tomb was designed by the sculptor Sir Jacob Epstein (1880–1959) at the request of his most devoted lover, Robert Ross.

In 1905 Ross published part of a 50,000 word essay Wilde had written to Bosie whilst in prison, entitled *De Profundis*. It was an unsparing and moving analysis of his love and tragedy. The first full publication was not until 1962.

THERE WAS MORE THAN ONE NEVILLE CHAMBERLAIN

Colonel Sir Neville Francis Fitzgerald Chamberlain (1856–1944) is widely regarded and certainly claimed (in the *Field* on 19 March 1938), to have invented snooker – in the officer's mess of the Devonshire Regiment at Jubbulpore, British India in 1875.

He waited a long time before proclaiming himself the "Father" of the game. Despite considerable speculation since it became popular in the 1880s, Chamberlain only revealed in his 84th year that he had created the game of snooker 63 years previously.

There were a number of serious inconsistencies in Chamberlain's version; but he was strongly supported by amongst others, the author Compton Mackenzie (1883–1972). As no one else has ever registered a better claim, his is usually allowed to stand.

His uncle, another Neville, Field Marshal Sir Neville Bowles Chamberlain (1820–1902) was regarded as one of the bravest soldiers ever to have served in the Indian Army.

THE SPANISH LADY

The 1918 category 5 influenza pandemic was caused by an unusually severe and deadly 'A' virus strain of subtype H1N1. By far the most destructive pandemic in history, infecting one third of the world's population, it killed some 50 to 100 million people worldwide in just 18 months – dwarfing the bloodshed of WWI. Many victims were healthy young adults, in contrast to most influenza outbreaks (which predominantly affect juvenile, elderly or otherwise weakened patients). The disease was first observed at Fort Riley in Kansas, US. The WWI Allies called it the 'Spanish Flu', nicknamed "The Spanish Lady", principally because the pandemic was fully reported only in Spain. Spain was not involved in the war and had not imposed wartime censorship.

POMP AND CIRCUMSTANCE

Sir Edward William Elgar, 1st Bt. OM was the son of a piano tuner and music dealer, born on 2 June 1857 in Lower Broadheath, near Worcester. The young Elgar taught himself music; and from studying manuscripts in the countryside for hours on end, he would link his music to nature for the rest of his life: "There is music in the air, music all around us, the world is full of it and you simply take as much as you require".

His years as a young violinist for Worcester's Philharmonic Society were happy; but after his marriage in 1889 (he gave his wife the short violin and piano piece *Salut d'amour* as an engagement present), Elgar moved to London and began to compose. He could not make ends meet however, and had to return to Great Malvern, to earn a living from teaching.

In 1899, the year Churchill fought a by-election in Oldham, he wrote his first major orchestral work, the *Enigma Variations*. It was premiered in London and received with acclaim, establishing Elgar as the pre-eminent British composer of his generation. *The Dream of Gerontius*, which had a disastrous first performance in 1900, is now considered to be one of the finest examples of English choral music.

Elgar is best known for his five *Pomp and Circumstance* marches, composed between 1901 and 1930. He set the trio melody in the first march to words by A.C. Benson (1862–1925) as an *Ode* to mark the coronation of King Edward VII in 1902 – with slightly different words, it was later published as *Land of Hope and Glory*.

**Sir Edward Elgar, Bt.
by Edgar Thomas Holding
(*c*.1905)**
National Portrait Gallery, London

Between 1902–14 Elgar enjoyed phenomenal success. His *Symphony No. 1* (1908) was given one hundred performances in its first year. In 1911, the year after he wrote his *Violin Concerto,* he was appointed to the Order of Merit. Shortly before his wife's death in 1920, he composed the elegiac *Cello Concerto.* He died on 23 February 1934 and is buried in Little Malvern. Within four months, two other notable British composers, Gustav Holst and Frederick Delius (1862–1934), had also died.

SOMERSET MAUGHAM WAS BORN AND DIED IN THE SAME YEARS AS CHURCHILL

William Somerset Maugham was born in the British Embassy in Paris on 25 January 1874. His father was Robert Ormond Maugham, a rich solicitor. Both his parents died before he was ten and he was sent to live with his uncle, the Rev. Henry Maugham in Whitstable, Kent.

After King's School, Canterbury and Heildelberg University in Germany, Maugham became a medical student at St. Thomas's Hospital in London. During his training he worked in the slums of Lambeth. This inspired his first novel, *Liza of Lambeth* in 1897. The book sold well and he abandoned medicine to write. He achieved fame with *Lady Frederick* in 1907, a comedy about money and marriage. By 1908 Maugham had four plays running simultaneously in London.

On the outbreak of WWI, Maugham, aged forty, joined a Red Cross ambulance unit in France. While serving on the Western Front he met a 22 year-old American, Gerald Haxton. The two men became lovers and lived together for the next thirty years. During the war Maugham was recruited by Sir John Wallinger, head of MI6 in France, as a link between MI6 in London and its agents in Europe.

Maugham had affairs with both men and women. In 1915 Syrie Wellcome, the daughter of Dr Thomas Barnardo (a saint to others but a dreadful father to Syrie), bore his child. Her husband, Henry Wellcome, cited Maugham as co-respondent in his divorce. In 1916 Maugham married Syrie but continued to live with Gerald Haxton.

William Somerset Maugham by Graham Vivian Sutherland (1953)
National Portrait Gallery, London

During the war, Maugham's best-known novel, *Of Human Bondage* (1915) was published; followed by *The Moon and Sixpence* (1919). Maugham was a fine short-story writer – *Rain,*

Sir Henry Solomon Wellcome was born in a log cabin in 1853, in Wisconsin. He became a British citizen in 1910 and was knighted in 1932. He was a pharmaceutical entrepreneur; and was the first to sell medicines in pill ('tabloid') form. He died on 25 July 1936 in London, leaving his fortune to the Wellcome Trust – the world's second richest medical charity, with net assets in 2009 of over £14 billion (the richest is the Bill & Melinda Gates Foundation, with nearly £19 billion).

He and Syrie had a son, Henry Mounteney Wellcome, in 1903. He was sent to foster parents aged three. He was considered to be sickly; and his parents spent most of their time travelling. Syrie never contested Sir Henry's custody of the child.

Thomas John Barnardo (1845–1905) was born in Dublin, the fourth child of John Michaelis Barnardo, a Jewish furrier from Prussia (naturalized British in 1860) and his second wife, Abigail O'Brien. Thomas founded a home for destitute children in London in 1868. When he died there were 8,000 children in his residential homes; 4,000 were boarded out; and 18,000 had been sent to Canada and Australia.

which appeared in *The Trembling of a Leaf* (1921), was turned into a successful film. Popular plays written by Maugham include *The Circle* (1921), *East of Suez* (1922), *The Constant Wife* (1926) and the anti-war, *For Services Rendered* (1932).

Maugham moved to Cap Ferat on the French Riviera in 1928 (he described Monaco as "a sunny place for shady people"), where he wrote his autobiography, *Summing Up* (1938) and works of fiction such as *The Razor's Edge* (1945), *Catalina* (1948) and *Quartet* (1949). Somerset Maugham died on 16 December 1965.

THE POET AND AUTHOR, G.K. CHESTERTON WAS ALSO BORN IN 1874

Gilbert Keith ("G.K.") Chesterton was born on 29 May 1874 in Campden Hill, Kensington. Known as the "prince of paradox", he wrote in an off-hand, whimsical prose characterized by lateral thinking. His prolific and diverse output included journalism, poetry, biography, Christian texts, fantasy and detective fiction. He is a rarity, a Christian thinker who is admired and quoted equally by liberal and conservative Christians – indeed by many non-Christians too. Chesterton's political opinions cannot be described as "liberal" or "conservative". He derided both labels saying, "The whole modern world has divided itself into Conservatives and Progressives. The business of Progressives is to go on making mistakes. The business of the Conservatives is to prevent the mistakes from being corrected".

Chesterton's father, Edward was a successful estate agent in London; and he was educated nearby, at St Paul's. A huge man, 6 feet 4 inches inches tall and weighing 21 stone (294lbs), his girth occasioned a famous anecdote. During WWI a lady in London asked why he was not "out at the Front"? He replied, "If you go round to the side, you will see that I am". On another occasion he remarked to his skinny friend George Bernard Shaw (1856–1950), "To look at you, anyone would think there was a famine in England". Shaw retorted, "To look at you, anyone would think you caused it".

G.K. Chesterton

He usually wore a cape and a crumpled hat, with a sword-stick in hand; and had a cigar hanging out of his mouth. Chesterton often forgot where he was supposed to be going and would miss the train to take him there. On several occasions he sent a telegram to his wife from some distant (and incorrect) location, asking: "Am at Market Harborough. Where ought I to be?". To which she would reply, "Home". Chesterton died there, at Beaconsfield in Buckinghamshire on 14 June 1936.

Chesterton wrote some 80 books, several hundred poems, 200 short stories, 4,000 essays and several plays. He was a literary and social critic, historian, playwright, novelist, Catholic Christian theologian and apologist, debater and mystery writer. He was a columnist for the *Daily News*, the *Illustrated London News*, and his own paper, *GK's Weekly*; he also wrote articles for the *Encyclopedia Britannica*. His best known character is the priest-detective *Father Brown*, who appeared only in short stories. *The Man Who Was Thursday* (1908) is his best-known novel. He was a convinced Christian long before he was received into the Catholic church; and Christian themes and symbolism appear in much of his writing.

Few of his poems are known well today. The best written is probably *Lepanto*. The most familiar, *The Rolling English Road* begins:

Before the Roman came to Rye or out to Severn strode,
The rolling English drunkard made the rolling English road.

CHURCHILL ACQUIRED CONTROL OF BP FOR THE BRITISH GOVERNMENT

William Knox D'Arcy (1849–1917) was born in Newton Abbot, Devon and emigrated with his father to Queensland, Australia in 1866. He made a fortune between 1882–89 in the Mount Morgan goldfield. He returned to London: and in 1901, with British Government assistance, obtained a concession to explore for oil in Persia (now Iran). From 1905 the concession was financed by the Burmah Oil Company, whose chairman was Lord Strathcona, and oil was discovered in 1908. The Anglo-Persian Oil Company was incorporated on 14 April 1909 and took over ownership of the concession, remaining a subsidiary of Burmah Oil. Following the conversion of the Royal Navy from coal to fuel oil, Winston Churchill decided to take a strategic (66%) interest in the company for the British Government.

The British Government remained a majority shareholder in the Company until it sold most of its shares on the stock exchange in 1987. The sale was poorly handled and badly timed. The issue was 95% left with the underwriters, as a result of the 19 October Wall Street collapse ("Black Monday") – an opportunistic purchase in the aftermarket of 22% of the company in May 1988 by the Kuwaiti Investment Office caused great embarrassment and was scaled back.

In 1923 the Company discovered oil in Iraq. In 1914 it had become a shareholder in the Turkish Petroleum Company, later renamed the Iraq Petroleum Company; which in 1927, also struck oil in Iraq. In 1934 the Kuwait Oil Company Ltd was incorporated as a jointly-owned venture with Gulf Oil, which discovered oil in Kuwait in 1938.

The Company was renamed the Anglo-Iranian Oil Company in 1935. In 1951 the Iranian Oil industry was nationalised and the Company was expelled from Iran. It changed its name in 1954 to The British Petroleum Company Limited.

During the 1960s and 70s the Company pioneered oil and gas exploration and production in the North Sea and Alaska. To finance the purchases of Standard Oil of Ohio (SOHIO) in May 1987 and Britoil in March 1988, BP Minerals, BP Coal and BP Nutrition were sold. One significant survivor from years of diversification is BP Solar: which is one of the world's largest solar energy companies, with a global market share of over 20%.

On 31 December 1998 the Company merged with the US Amoco Corporation (on a 60/40 basis). Following the acquisition of Atlantic Richfield (ARCO) and Burmah Castrol, on 1 May 2001 the Company was renamed BP plc (the initials stand for nothing).

DONALD SMITH, BARON STRATHCONA WAS THE FIRST CHAIRMAN OF BP

The Grants of Strathspey were once summoned to battle by fires kindled on the mountain tops of Craigellachie and their battle-cry was, *"Stand fast, Craigellachie"*.

In 1885 it was at another Craigellachie, in the heart of the Rocky Mountains, that a distinguished descendant of the Grants drove in the last spike to complete the construction of the first transcontinental railway in Canada. It welded into one mighty nation, provinces and districts stretching for 3,700 miles across a vast continent.

Such was the crowning triumph in the life of one who, forty-seven years previously, had arrived in Canada as a poor but well-educated Scottish lad. He started his career as a clerk-apprentice to the Hudson's Bay Company at a salary of £20 a year and his food. When he died, his estate was valued at over £4,500,000 (£1.62 billion today).

Donald Alexander Smith was born on 6 August 1820, in Forres in Morayshire. After school he worked in the Town Clerk's Office until 1838. His uncle John Stuart, a pioneer fur trader who worked for the Hudson's Bay Company, persuaded Smith to join him in Canada as a clerk for the company, at Hamilton Inlet in Labrador.

Sir John Macdonald, the great Prime Minister of Canada, once wrote that he was convinced beyond any doubt that after the Civil War, the United States Government was resolved to do all it could, short of going to war, to obtain possession of Western Canada. In 1879, to frustrate this Smith persuaded his cousin, George Stephen (later Lord Mountstephen) to join his railway group. The "St Paul, Minneapolis and Manitoba Railway Company" was incorporated with George Stephen as President and Smith as Principal Director. A syndicate was formed in 1880, with the aim of completing a Canadian transcontinental railway. Building commenced on 2 May 1881 at an average of 2.6 miles per day. The railway was completed at 9:30am on 7 November 1885 when Smith hammered home the last spike, at Craigellachie in British Columbia.

In 1897 Smith was created "Baron Strathcona and Mount Royal of Glencoe, Argyllshire and Montreal, Canada". Wishing to help Britain in the Boer War, he raised Lord Strathcona's Horse, a mobile force of 600 Canadian rough riders led by Colonel Steele. Lord Strathcona had been appointed High Commissioner for Canada in 1896; and he died in that office, on 21 January 1914 at 28, Grosvenor Square in London.

Strathcona and Cecil Rhodes, the South African diamond monopolist, were the two greatest imperialists of the last imperial age.

THE ZINOVIEV LETTER

Churchill returned to Parliament in 1924. In October MI5 intercepted a letter written by Grigory Zinoviev, chairman of the Comintern in the Soviet Union. In it Zinoviev urged British communists to commit acts of sedition. Vernon Kell, head of MI5 and Sir Basil Thomson head of Special Branch, were convinced that the letter was genuine. Kell showed the letter to Ramsay MacDonald, the Labour Prime Minister. It was agreed that it should be kept secret, but it was leaked to *The Times* and the *Daily Mail*.

The letter was published four days before the General Election. It contributed to the heavy defeat of MacDonald and the Labour Party (the Conservatives won 419 seats, a majority of 268). After the election it was claimed that two MI5 agents, Sidney Reilly and (Arthur) Maundy Gregory, had forged the letter: and that Major Joseph Ball, a MI5 staffer had leaked it to the press – from 1927 Ball worked for the Conservative Central Office where he pioneered the art of "spin-doctoring". It has been suggested that several MI5 and MI6 officers had attempted to bring down the Labour Government – including Sir Stewart Menzies (1890–1968), a future head of MI6.

Sir Basil Home Thomson (1861–1939) trained as a barrister. He joined the Colonial Office; and for a time held the post of Prime Minister of Tonga. Later, he joined the prison service and became Governor of Dartmoor Prison and Wormwood Scrubs. In 1913 Thomson became Deputy Commissioner of the Metropolitan Police; and five years later was made head of the Special Branch. Basil Thomson's career came to an abrupt end when he was arrested for committing an act of indecency in Hyde Park.

Georgi, or Salomon ("Shlomo") Rosenblum was born in the Jewish Kherson gubernia of Tsarist Russia on 24 March 1874 – the same year as Churchill. Highly intelligent and fluent in seven languages, Rosenblum was recruited by MI6 and given the name Sidney Reilly. He was cold, hard and practical – and got results, whatever the cost. Before WWI Reilly had won Persian oil concessions for the British, disguised as a priest; and spied on Germany and its armaments industry. He was considered to be Britain's most important secret agent – and one of the role models for Ian Fleming's *James Bond* in the 1950s.

On the outbreak of WWI Reilly was sent to Russia to procure arms for Britain's allies. After spending a short time in London in 1917, Reilly was smuggled into Germany to discover how close the country was to defeat. In 1918 MI6 sent him to Russia to assassinate Lenin. Dora Kaplan got to him first however; and, though Lenin survived the attempt, Reilly was recalled to England. In their absence, both he and Robert Bruce Lockhart, Head of Special Mission, were found guilty of espionage and sabotage and were sentenced to be executed by the Russians if caught.

In 1925 Reilly was sent back again to spy on the Leninist government. In November he was entrapped (by Boris Gudz, who died in 2007, aged 104), interrogated and shot.

Sir Ernest Henry Shackleton by Alich P. F. Ritchie (1907 or after)
National Portrait Gallery, London

SIR ERNEST SHACKLETON WAS ANOTHER BORN IN 1874

Sir Ernest Henry Shackleton (1874–1922) was born on 15 February 1874 in County Kildare. He was the eldest son of a family of ten children. His mother Henrietta, was the daughter of Henry John Gavan of Wallstown in County Cork. His father Henry, was a doctor of Yorkshire Quaker descent. They left Ireland in 1884 to settle in south London. Shackleton was educated at Dulwich College: which he left at the age of sixteen to join the merchant navy – gaining his master's certificate in April 1898. He was a third officer in the Union Castle line when he was invited to join the crew of *Discovery*, to convey the Antarctic expedition (1901–4), under Commander Robert Falcon Scott, to the Southern Ocean.

Shackleton was chosen by Scott to accompany him on a major reconnaissance expedition over the Ross Ice Shelf towards the South Pole. Shackleton was put in charge of the dogs, but had to shoot them after they had been fed an unsuitable diet of dried fish – recommended by the renowned Norwegian scientist, Fridtjof Nansen (1861–1930). The party then had to haul their sledges themselves. Shackleton particularly, suffered from pneumonia, frostbite and scurvy. On return to *Discovery*, he was invalided home on the supply ship *Morning* – bearing a warm endorsement from Scott: "It is with great reluctance that I order his return and trust that it will be made evident that I do so solely on account of his health and that his future prospects may not suffer".

In 1907 Shackleton returned to Antarctica, sponsored by William Beardmore (later Lord Invernairn). Over the next two years, he led three sledge expeditions. He reached both the summit of Mount Erebus (12,448 feet), an active volcano on Ross Island, and the magnetic South Pole. The third journey took him within 97 miles (88° 23') of the South Pole itself. He also claimed Victoria Land Plateau for the British Crown. Further progress was halted by the loss of one of the Mongolian ponies which fell into a crevasse, taking most of the party's food with it. Shackleton reluctantly decided to turn back. As he explained in a letter to his wife: "Better a living donkey than a dead lion". Debilitated by dysentery, from eating rotten horse flesh, the expedition eventually reached its supply ship *Nimrod*, which had waited well beyond the appointed date for her departure. On 4 March 1909 *Nimrod* sailed for New Zealand – with every expedition member safely aboard. Deemed an outstanding success and having achieved national acclaim, the British government paid off the expedition debt of £20,000 (nearly £8 million today).

Shackleton spent the next four years conducting lecture tours throughout the British Isles, Europe, Canada and the US. He was knighted and lionised everywhere. Business ventures he promoted however, were all unsuccessful. Meanwhile Roald Amundsen and Robert Scott had reached the South Pole in December 1911; as had Robert Peary, the North Pole on 6 April 1909. There remained only the crossing of the Antarctic continent, the "one great object of Antarctic journeyings" – and this Shackleton resolved to achieve.

In December 1913 the expedition was announced. It was sponsored by Sir James Caird, a Scots jute manufacturer with £24,000, the British government with £10,000 and the Royal Geographical Society with £1,000. The British Trans-Antarctic Expedition sailed from Westminster in *Endurance* on 4 August 1914 – the day Britain declared war on Germany. Shackleton offered his ship and crew to the Admiralty but was ordered to proceed. *Endurance* arrived in Antarctica on 30 December; but two weeks later became trapped in dense pack-ice, making landfall impossible. Nine months later, on 27 October 1915, *Endurance* was crushed and sank: leaving the expedition members marooned on the ice, drifting north and surviving entirely on seals for food and their blubber for fuel. On 9 April 1916 Shackleton's crew escaped in three boats into clear water; and, six days later, landed on barren Elephant Island. On 24 April, with just five men, Shackleton set out to sail 800 miles in the 22–foot open boat, *James Caird* across the world's stormiest seas: to reach on 9 May, after an extraordinary feat of navigation, Cape Rosa on the southern shore of South Georgia. Shackleton knew that there was a whaling station at Stromness on the north side of the island. Not wishing to hazard his boat in hurricane force winds, to get there he had first to cross two formidable, unexplored mountain ranges, the Allardyce and Salvesen.

South Georgia's spine is mountainous, rising to 9,626 feet on Mount Paget. Huge glaciers (Fortuna is the largest) and snowfields cover two-thirds of the island in the southern summer (November to January); in winter, snow blankets the entire island.

Leaving three men with the *James Caird*, Shackleton, Frank Worsley and Tom Crean, equipped with only a short length of rope and a carpenters' adze (a pickaxe with the blade set at right angles to the shaft, used for hollowing out logs), set off into the unknown. Shackleton had given his mittens to the expedition photographer Frank Hurley, who had lost his own during the crossing. Shackleton suffered badly from frostbite as a result. Thirty-six hours later, on 20 May 1916, in a feat of great fortitude, Shackleton's party arrived at Stromness, twenty miles north of Grytviken – to be welcomed by an incredulous manager and his fellow Norwegians. It took Shackleton three months and three failed attempts before he was able to rescue his twenty-two crewmen marooned on Elephant Island, on board the Chilean government tug *Yelcho*. Not a man had been lost: they were, as one of them shouted from the shore, "All safe, All well".

In May 1917 Shackleton arrived back in Britain, suffering from an overstrained heart, compounded by alcoholism. He volunteered for the front; but instead was sent to Buenos Aires on a propaganda mission to persuade the governments of Argentina and Chile to join the Allied cause. Frustrated, he returned home in April 1918. He was commissioned into the army as a major and sent to Murmansk; but returned in March 1919 when the region was overrun by the Bolsheviks. He was awarded an OBE. In 1920, after several months on the lecture circuit, Shackleton decided to make one last expedition. Funded by an old school friend, John Quiller Rowett, plans were made to circumnavigate the Antarctic continent and search for undiscovered islands. On 24 September 1921 the Shackleton-Rowett Expedition left Britain in a

Many of the men who had survived the appalling rigours of the *Endurance* expedition returned to England, joined the Royal Navy and were killed in the Great War.

The church at Grytviken, on South Georgia, where Shackleton is buried

Alice entering Wonderland by Sir John Tenniel

Alice Liddell, by Lewis Carroll (1858)

Norwegian whaler, renamed *Quest*. On 4 January 1922 the party arrived on South Georgia, by way of Buenos Aires. Early in the morning on 5 January Shackleton summoned the ship's doctor Alexander Macklin to his cabin, complaining of chest pain. Macklin suggested that the "Boss" stopped drinking. It was too late – within minutes, at 02:50 Shackleton suffered a fatal heart attack.

Shackleton's body was consigned to Britain; but, while at Montevideo, word came from his wife Emily (1868–1936) that she wished him to be buried in South Georgia. He lies there, in Grytviken cemetery. For fifty years his reputation was eclipsed by that of Robert Falcon Scott, to whom countless statues and memorials were raised. In the 1970's however, perceptions of the two changed. Today Shackleton is the model for many corporate leadership courses – he is also cited as the perfect example of a great leader by the US Navy.

Shackleton left two sons and a daughter. The younger son Edward, Baron Shackleton (1911–94), was a geographer and Labour Party politician.

It was another Briton, Sir Vivian Fuchs (1908–99) who made the first 2,158 mile crossing of Antarctica, from the Weddell Sea to the Ross Sea, via the South Pole – but not until 1957–58. The second crossing of the continent was in 1981, during the Transglobe Expedition led by Sir Ranulph ("Ran") Twisleton-Wykeham-Fiennes, Bt. (born 1944) – another cast in the Shackleton mould.

LEWIS CARROLL BEGAN "THE HUNTING OF THE SNARK" IN 1874

Lewis Carroll, the pseudonym of Charles Lutwidge Dodgson (1832–98), was a clergyman, mathematician, logician, novelist and photographer. He achieved lasting international fame through his childrens' stories: *Alice's Adventures in Wonderland* (1865), its sequel *Through the Looking-Glass* (1871); and his outstanding nonsense poems: *Jabberwocky* (1871) and *The Hunting of the Snark* (1876). He was the eldest son of a family of eleven children born to the vicar of Daresbury in Cheshire.

In 1843 his father became the rector of Croft-on-Tees in North Yorkshire. Brought up in isolated rectories, Dodgson learned early to amuse his younger siblings by telling them stories and compiling a series of "Rectory Magazines". In 1844 he attended Richmond School in Yorkshire followed by Rugby School (1846–50), where he was bullied because of a serious stammer. His health broke down and he became deaf in one ear. In 1850 he entered Christ Church, Oxford where he excelled in classics and mathematics. He was awarded a first class degree, passing out top of his year. He accepted an invitation to lecture in mathematics, a post he held for thirty-one years – though his position depended on remaining unmarried and entering the Church of England. He was made a deacon in 1861: but declined to become a priest (when he could have married), believing himself to be unsuited to parish work. Dodgson enjoyed the company of artists and writers. He met John Ruskin, the influential art critic, in 1857; and moved among the Pre-Raphaelite set, especially William Holman Hunt (1827–1910) and Dante Gabriel Rossetti (1828–82) – who was convinced that *The Hunting of the Snark* was based on him. He was a friend of the popular fairy-tale author George MacDonald (1824–1905), whose children's enjoyment of the draft *Alice* manuscript first encouraged Dodgson to publish his stories.

As a bachelor still living in college, Dodgson made friends with Lorina, Alice (1852–1934) and Edith, the daughters of the dean of Christ Church, Henry George Liddell. He took them on rowing trips and picnics, entertaining them with fantastical stories centred round the middle child, Alice: who implored him to write them down for her. This he did, illustrating the manuscript with his own naïf drawings, expecting that would be the end of the matter. The novelist Henry Kingsley spotted the manuscript in the Christ Church drawing room while visiting the Dean, read them and was entranced. He pressed Mrs Liddell to persuade Dodgson to find a publisher.

Excited by Kingsley's enthusiasm, Dodgson revised and redrafted his original version. The book was illustrated by the popular *Punch* cartoonist John Tenniel, to whom Dodgson had been introduced by his friend and fellow Oxford don, Robinson Duckworth. The book was published as *Alice's Adventures in Wonderland*.

The book initially sold slowly, but within a year was selling so well that Dodgson started work on a sequel: *Through the Looking Glass and What Alice Found There*. Dated 1872 but actually published in 1871, the sequel is regarded as equal, if not superior, to the original. By the end of the 19th century, the two volumes of *Alice* were the most popular children's books in Britain: and by the centenary of Dodgson's birth in 1832, possibly the best known in the world.

In 1856 Dodgson became interested in the new art form of photography, at which he excelled. Over the next twenty-four years, he recorded over 3,000 images – less than 1,000 have survived. He photographed many contemporary celebrities: including John Everett Millais, Ellen Terry, Michael Faraday and Alfred, Lord Tennyson. Inexplicably, he abandoned photography in 1880.

It is unlikely that Dodgson ever interfered with children, though there are indications that he was tempted. His diary, like his correspondence written in purple ink, records desperate pleas to God for help in self-improvement and control – suggesting an uneasy conscience, particularly when they occur after his meetings with young girls.

In spite of wealth and fame, the last twenty years of his life changed little. He taught at Christ Church until 1881, where he lived until his death. His last novel, the two volumes of *Sylvie and Bruno*, published in 1889 and 1893, has been described as, "one of the most interesting failures in English literature".

Henry Kingsley (1830–76) was a novelist and war reporter in the Franco-Prussian war. Far more famous was his brother Charles (1819–75), who was a clergyman, Christian Socialist and novelist. He became chaplain to Queen Victoria, professor of modern history at Cambridge and a canon of Westminster Abbey. A successful historical novelist, publishing *Westward Ho!* in 1855 and *Hereward the Wake* in 1866, he was convinced by Charles Darwin's theory of evolution: which provoked him to write the popular children's book, *The Water Babies* in 1866.

Sir John Tenniel (1820–1914) was the chief illustrator of *Punch* magazine. His best known illustrations are those of *Alice's Adventures in Wonderland* and *Through the Looking-Glass*. They are striking in their delicacy and animation. The original print run of *Alice's Adventures in Wonderland* was botched and had to be withdrawn. The first edition was finally published at Christmas 1865, though dated 1866. Only twenty-five copies survive – as the rarest of Victorian volumes.

Charles Dodgson's chosen pseudonym Lewis Carroll, was a play on his real name. Lewis was the anglicised form of *Ludovicus*, the nearest Latin equivalent of Lutwidge. Carroll was a corruption of *Carolus*, the Latin for Charles.

A high proportion of Dodgson's surviving prints are of young, often naked girls: which, given his many friendships with children and a lack of interest in adult women, have attracted suspicion of pædophiliac tendencies. Victorians however, believed that child nudity was an expression of innocence. Contemporary photographers all used them and child nudes even appeared on Christmas cards.

Dodgson was fascinated by gadgets, puzzles and games. He made a travelling chess board which secured the chessmen on their holed squares with pins; and thought up an early form of the game which became Scrabble. He invented a system to 'justify' the right-hand margin of a typewritten letter; and a gum for sealing envelopes. He also devised ciphers and any number of card games.

On 14 January 1898 Dodgson died at his sister's house, from pneumonia following a bout of influenza, and was buried in the Mount Cemetery at Guildford in Surrey. He had given away most of his money to children's charities (so much so that he was often overdrawn at Barclays Bank); and left only £5,000 (£2.2 million today) – not much of a reward for the magical, creative genius with which he transformed children's stories, from preaching a moral purpose to making them friendly and fun. They still are.

Dodgson invented "portmanteau" words to combine the meanings of two words in one: "'Slithy' means 'lithe and slimy' .... You see it's like a portmanteau – there are two meanings packed up into one word .... 'Mimsy' is 'flimsy and miserable' (there's another portmanteau .... for you)".

BEATRIX POTTER

On 28 July 1866, the year that *Alice's Adventures in Wonderland* were published, (Helen) Beatrix Potter was born in South Kensington in London. Her father, Rupert (1832–1914) was a barrister who had inherited a large fortune. Her mother, Helen was the daughter of a rich cotton manufacturer.

As a child, Beatrix was lonely and often ill. Her welfare and education were supervised by a series of nurses and governesses. She filled her solitary hours painting and drawing, encouraged by her parents who were both gifted amateur artists. Every summer, her parents took Dalguise House in Perthshire and then later, in Lindeth Howe in the English Lake District, where Beatrix illustrated *The Tale of Timmy Tiptoes* and *The Tale of Pigling Bland*. In 1882 the family met the local vicar, Canon Hardwicke Rawnsley whose passion was the protection of the Lake District from the encroachment of industry and tourism. In 1895 Rawnsley was one of the founders of the National Trust.

Most weekends were spent at Beatrix's grand-parents' house in Hertfordshire. She became entranced by the natural world and soon noted the habits of a host of pet animals and birds. She recorded her observations in a code, which was only broken in 1958, and added fossil gathering, photography and the study of fungi (mycology) to her list of interests. In 1897 Beatrix submitted a paper, *On the Germination of Spores of Agaricineae*, to the Linnaean Society which was read by a male member, as women were not admitted.

In 1893, aged twenty-seven, Beatrix began to write stories for a sick child. It was from one of these that *The Tale of Peter Rabbit and Mr McGregor's Garden* was born. In December 1901 Beatrix published the black-and-white illustrated story privately. The book caught the attention of the publishers Frederick Warne & Co who persuaded her to reissue the book with coloured illustrations.

By 1913 Warne & Co had published 22 beautifully illustrated small books featuring, among others: *Benjamin Bunny*, *Squirrel Nutkin*, *Jemima Puddle Duck*, *Mrs Tiggy-Winkle* and *Samuel Whiskers*.

Beatrix was thirty-nine when her editor Norman Warne asked her to marry him. Her parents strongly opposed her engagement to a man engaged in "trade", a problem resolved when Warne died suddenly of blood poisoning.

Devastated, Beatrix sought refuge in the purchase of Hill Top Farm near Sawrey in the Lake District. She spent the rest of her life breeding Herdwick sheep, writing and acquiring, paid for with her substantial royalties, ever more farmland – to conserve the region's natural beauty. In 1913 Beatrix married her solicitor, William Heelis (1871–1945). Due to failing eyesight, she published her last book in 1930: *The Tale of Little Pig Robinson*. She had a heart attack and died on 22 December 1943. She was cremated in Blackpool and her ashes were scattered over Hill Top Farm by her shepherd, Tom Storey. She bequeathed her estate of £211,000 (£22.4 million today) and over 4,000 acres of Lakeland farmland to the National Trust.

The largest collection of her original artwork is in The Victoria & Albert Museum. Her books have been translated into 44 languages, with annual sales of $500 million.

AUBREY BEARDSLEY'S ILLUSTRATIONS WERE QUITE UNLIKE TENNIEL'S

Aubrey Vincent Beardsley (1872–98) was a celebrated illustrator of the 1890s and was second only to Oscar Wilde as the leader of the Aesthetic movement in Britain.

Beardsley was born in Brighton in Sussex, the son of a ne'er-do-well who had inherited and lost a fortune. His mother, the daughter of an Indian Army surgeon-major, brought up Beardsley and his older sister Mabel alone and close to poverty. At the age of seven Beardsley contracted tuberculosis. He attended Brighton grammar school; but left in 1888 to become a clerk in London, as his mother had moved to Pimlico. In 1889 his tuberculosis erupted in the form of lung hæmorrhages and oral bleeding.

In 1890 he became fascinated by the work of the Pre-Raphaelites and decided to become an artist. After a year of teaching himself in the evening, Beardsley showed his work to the Pre-Raphaelite painter, Sir Edward Burne-Jones (1833–98) who recommended him to seek professional tuition. He was accepted by Westminster School of Art in 1892, but left after only a few months. He had begun to experiment with a new "process block", particularly suited to his curvilinear style – using just pitch blacks and icy whites, with no hint of grey in between.

In 1893 he was invited to illustrate a new edition of Sir Thomas Malory's *Le Morte D'Arthur*. A year later he took up the post of art editor and illustrator of an extraordinary new quarterly review, the *Yellow Book*.

The *Yellow Book*, published in London from 1894–97, sold for the enormous sum of 5 shillings (£120 today). It was a leading journal of

Aestheticism was a late 19th century European arts movement founded by James McNeil Whistler, Oscar Wilde and Stephane Mallarme. The movement was inspired by the proposition of the philosopher Immanuel Kant in reaction to the ugliness and utilitarianism of the industrial age. Kant believed that aesthetic standards could be separated from morality, practical need and happiness. Aestheticism was closely associated with French Symbolism and was the harbinger of Art Nouveau.

the 1890s in Britain. Though associated with Aestheticism and Decadence, it contained a broad spectrum of literary and artistic styles as well as reproductions of paintings. Aubrey Beardsley suggested a yellow cover, attracted by the colour's association with French fiction of the period.

He used illustrations by accomplished artists such as John Singer Sargent, Walter Sickert, and Philip Wilson Steer. The literary content was equally distinguished. Subscribing authors included Max Beerbohm, Arnold Bennet, Henry James, H.G. Wells and William Butler Yeats. Though Oscar Wilde never contributed a word, he became linked to the journal because Beardsley had illustrated his play *Salomé* in 1894. Moreover, in Wilde's 1891 play *The Picture of Dorian Gray*, a major corrupting influence on Dorian is "the yellow book", which Lord Henry sends him after the suicide of his first love.

This "yellow book" is thought to be *À rebours* ("Against the Grain" or "Against Nature") by Joris-Karl Huysmans, an example of Parisian decadence that heavily influenced British aesthetes like Beardsley. Such books in Paris were wrapped in yellow paper to alert the reader to their lascivious content. The *Yellow Book* differed from other periodicals in that it was cloth-bound. Critics attacked Beardsley's title page when the first issue went on sale in April 1894. It became the talking point of London: they were shocked because it showed a woman playing a piano out of doors. Beardsley subsequently designed a different cover for each volume. His illustrations in *Salomé* reflected underlying themes of lust, adultery, incest and murder to such effect that he won instant notoriety as a pornographer.

Beardsley melded his curvilinear style with the bold, fluid designs found in Japanese woodcuts in a series of drawings. His critics and the Victorian public alike were disturbed by their unwholesome eroticism, charged by overtly sensual women – emphasised in his licentious illustrations for Aristophanes's play *Lysistrata* in 1896.

In 1895 Oscar Wilde was arrested on ten charges of gross indecency with young men. The revelations of his trials, his conviction and imprisonment provoked a public revulsion against Aestheticism. Although Beardsley was not homosexual, he was tainted by his association with Wilde, and sacked from his post at the *Yellow Book*.

Beardsley was the first illustrator to exploit the metal process block: which could reproduce much finer lines than wood, without blurring in the printing process.

Speculation over Beardsley's true sexuality remains ambivalent. He was probably asexual, given the severity of his chronic tuberculosis and his all-consuming dedication to his work. Rumour circulated at the time of an incestuous connection with his red-haired sister Mabel, the only woman whom he really loved, and a resulting pregnancy which was aborted.

Beardsley once announced: "I have one aim – the grotesque. If I am not grotesque, I am nothing". According to Oscar Wilde, he dyed his hair "grass green". He took enormous pains in his personal dress: favouring dove grey suits, hats and ties, with yellow gloves. When visiting his publisher, he always wore a morning coat and patent leather shoes. His sense of fun and lovable nature made him many friends.

• Beardsley's illustration of Lysistrata (1896)

He was immediately engaged by another new magazine, *The Savoy* and went on to illustrate a number of books, including Alexander Pope's *Rape of the Lock* in 1896.

By 1897 Beardsley's tuberculosis was in its final stage. He became a Roman Catholic and retired to Menton on the French Riviera. He died on 16 March 1898, the same year as Lewis Carroll, aged only twenty-five – having asked his publisher "to destroy all copies of *Lysistrata* and bad drawings .... by all that is holy all obscene drawings". Beardsley was buried in the public cemetery. The lasting impact of his short and painful life is a remarkable testimonial to his originality and skill.

SHERLOCK HOLMES, THE MOST FAMOUS DETECTIVE IN HISTORY

Sir Arthur Ignatius Conan Doyle (1859–1930) was a writer immortalised by his fictional detective Sherlock Holmes. He was born into straitened circumstances in Edinburgh, to an alcoholic Protestant English father of Irish descent and a Roman Catholic Irish mother. Funded by a rich uncle, he was educated at a private Jesuit school, Stonyhurst College, but left in 1875 as an agnostic. In 1876 he attended a school at Feldkirch, in Austria, which gave him a life-long international perspective. In 1881 he graduated as a doctor from Edinburgh University, having already written his first short stories.

After a brief spell as a ship's doctor, he set up a practice at Southsea in Portsmouth: but work was slow in coming. He used his spare time in writing his first important novel, *A Study in Scarlet* (1887) – in which Sherlock Holmes made his first appearance. Holmes was inspired by a physician, Joseph Bell, who had been Conan Doyle's professor at Edinburgh medical school. Bell possessed remarkable powers of deduction in diagnosing his patients' disorders, which Conan Doyle assumed for his detective.

An illustration from one of the Sherlock Holmes stories

Conan Doyle spent 1890 in Vienna studying ophthalmology; returning to London in 1891, to establish another practice. Once again business was slow: and again he turned to writing – in total 56 short stories and four novels featuring Sherlock Holmes.

So successful were the Holmes series that Conan Doyle tried to kill him off. He believed that the public obsession with him was overshadowing his historical output: principally *The White Company* (1891); stories of his fictional Napoleonic War hero, the absurd *Brigadier Gerard*; *The Great Boer War* (1900); and *The Crime of the Congo* (1909), describing Belgian atrocities.

Conan Doyle was a patriotic supporter of the Boer War, having served in South Africa as a doctor in a volunteer hospital in 1900. His *War in South Africa: Its Causes and Conduct* (1902) presented the world with the British argument for the conduct of a controversial war – and earned him a knighthood in 1902. In 1903 Conan Doyle was offered $45,000 to resuscitate Sherlock Holmes by the American *McClures Magazine* – the first of a new series of thirteen stories appeared in 1905.

His crusades against the Belgian slave state in the Congo were the inspiration for several characters in the *Lost World* (1912). He also campaigned for reform of British divorce law; and, by successfully exposing several miscarriages of justice, hastened into being the Court of Criminal Appeal in 1907. He twice unsuccessfully stood for Parliament in the Unionist interest, becoming a champion for Irish Home Rule.

Between 1906–21, Conan Doyle lost his first wife Louisa from tuberculosis; his eldest son Kingsley in Flanders; his brother Innes; two brothers-in-law (one was E.W Hornung, the creator of the gentleman thief *Raffles*) and two nephews. He sank into depression, finding comfort in Spiritualism and a belief in fairies: publishing *The Coming of the Fairies* in 1921. He was convinced that the American magician Harry Houdini (1874– 1926) possessed

> Conan Doyle thought he had disposed of Sherlock Holmes in *The Final Problem* (1893). Holmes plunges to his death at the Riechenbach Falls in Switzerland, during a fatal confrontation with his arch enemy, the evil genius Professor Moriarty. The ploy backfired: such was the national outcry, that Conan Doyle had to bring Holmes back to life – now embedded even more firmly in the public affection.

supernatural powers – much to Houdini's exasperation. His love of cricket proved another distraction (between 1899–1907, he had played 10 first-class matches for the MCC). He was elected captain of his local golf club in 1910.

Conan Doyle died of a heart attack at his home at Windlesham, near Crowborough in Sussex on 7 July 1930. He was buried in his rose garden, before being reburied with his second wife Jean, at Minstead in Hampshire in 1940. She and four of his five children survived him – the last of whom, a daughter died in 1997, aged eighty-five.

Conan Doyle wished to be regarded as a leading Spiritualist and as a serious historical novelist: but it is chiefly for his creation of Professor Challenger, Brigadier Gerard and, by a distance, above all – Sherlock Holmes, that he is remembered.

TWO WHO WOULD NOT HAVE WANTED BEARDSLEY AS AN ILLUSTRATOR

Dame Agatha Mary Clarissa, Lady Mallowan (*née* Miller), best known as Agatha Christie (1890–1976) was a prodigious and innovative writer of crime novels, plays and short stories. She also wrote romantic novels under the name of Mary Westmacott. She is best known for her *Hercule Poirot* and *Miss Jane Marple* detective novels and successful London theatre plays.

Agatha was born in Torquay, in south Devon. Her father, Frederick Miller was an American stockbroker; and her mother Margaret (*née* Boehmer) was the daughter of a British army officer. After a private education, she worked during WWI as a hospital nurse and then in a pharmacy – many of her murders were later to be committed using poison. In December 1914 she married Archibald Christie (1889–1962), an officer in the Royal Flying Corps. She wrote her first novel, *The Mysterious Affair at Styles* in 1920 – in which she introduced Hercule Poirot, a vain and meticulous, retired Belgian police officer. He subsequently appeared in 33 novels and 54 short stories.

In 1926 Archibald Christie left Agatha for his golfing partner, Nancy Neele: Agatha promptly disappeared in mysterious circumstances, triggering a nationwide police hunt, involving bloodhounds and clairvoyants. Christie himself was suspected of her murder. She was eventually discovered in an Harrogate hotel, registered in the name of Nancy Neele. Agatha never explained her behaviour, claiming amnesia. In 1930 she married Max Mallowan (1904–78), an archaeologist fourteen years her junior – to whom she remained happily married until her death in 1976.

The Mousetrap is the longest running play in the world. It opened at the Ambassadors Theatre in London on 25 November 1952. It is still running after more than 23,000 performances.

Her other famous detective character, Miss Jane Marple, a gentle, elderly but highly observant, rather inquisitive spinster, was introduced in 1927: in a short story called *The Tuesday Night Club*. She was based on Agatha Christie's own grandmother.

Most of her novels are "whodunits", centred on English upper-middle class life. The murders are highly original, committed in an atmosphere of taut psychological suspense. Most of her 80 novels such as *Murder on the Orient Express* in 1933, which was filmed in 1978, are still best-sellers. They have been translated into 100 languages and have sold more than a billion copies.

Christie disliked her celebrity status. She refused wireless and television interviews: giving only one strictly controlled recording to the Imperial War Museum, on her experiences as a WWI nurse. She was sensitive about her appearance. In later life she became heavily overweight, due to her love of rich food and a weakness for drinking cream. She lived privately and serenely in her two houses, noted for their beautiful gardens: Winterbrook House, at Wallingford on the banks of the Thames; and Greenway House on the River Dart in south Devon.

On 12 January 1976 Agatha Christie died in the early afternoon at Winterbrook: and was buried in the churchyard of the neighbouring village of Cholsey. Greenway House and gardens are preserved by the National Trust.

> In 1942 Christie wrote a novel *Curtain*, in which Hercule Poirot was finally "killed off". The book was sealed in a bank vault and released only at the end of her writing career. When it was published, just before her death, Hercule Poirot was the first and only fictional character to be given an obituary in the *New York Times*.

Enid Mary Blyton (1897–1968) was a prolific children's writer who published over 600 books, articles and poems. Born in East Dulwich, in south London, the daughter of a cutlery traveling salesman, she was a gifted pianist: but abandoned music to train as a schoolteacher at Ipswich High School. In 1922 she published her first book, *Child Whispers*. She went on to become famous as the creator of *Little Noddy*, *The Famous Five*, *The Secret Seven*, the "Adventure" series, *The Faraway Tree* and *Malory Towers*.

> She also wrote under the name of Mary Pollock, the surname of her first husband, Hugh. After her divorce in 1943 and remarriage to a surgeon, Kenneth Waters she changed her two daughters' surnames to his. They never saw their father again.

Imogen Pollock; Enid Mary Blyton by John Gay (1949)
National Portrait Gallery, London

The best known series features the adventures of *Little Noddy*, *Mr Plod the Policeman*, *Big Ears* and a host of colourful characters who people *Toyland* village. The editions containing coloured illustrations by the Dutch artist Harmsen van der Beek, enjoyed huge acclaim and made her a household name.

Blyton's books were themed in black and white. Good and bad characters peopled exciting plots with an underlying, high moral purpose. She used simple language, readily understandable by very young children. Her elementary vocabulary and prose style has attracted much criticism – particularly because of her supposed snobbery and xenophobia.

The BBC banned her work for 30 years, judging it to be second-rate: "There is rather a lot of the Pinky-winky-Doodle-doodle Dum-dumm type of name in the original tales", said one executive. Her popularity though, continues unabated: with an apparently unlimited appetite for reprints of her books.

After WWII such was the demand for Blyton's books, that public libraries limited, and in many cases banned them in order to achieve a fair spread of authors. In 1973 the renowned children's book critic, Margery Fisher described her work as "slow poison".

She died of dementia in Hampstead on 28 November 1968: and was cremated at Golders Green. Enid Blyton books have sold 400 million copies and have been translated into nearly 90 languages (behind Lenin and Christie, but almost equal to Shakespeare). A set of British postage stamps in 1997 commemorated her most famous series.

Fourteen authors who were born British or Irish, who chose to become British or who were born in the British Isles have won the Nobel prize for literature: Rudyard Kipling (1907), W.B. Yeats (1923), G.B. Shaw (1925), John Galsworthy (1932), T.S. Eliot (1943), Bertrand Russell (1950), Winston Churchill (1953), Samuel Beckett (1969), Patrick White (1973), William Golding (1983),

Seamus Heaney (1993), V.S. Naipaul (2001), Harold Pinter (2005) and Doris Lessing (2007). White, though Australian, was born in London.

Nobel Prizes are awarded annually to people (the Peace Prize has occasionally been awarded to organisations) who have completed outstanding research; invented groundbreaking techniques or equipment; or made an outstanding contribution to society: in physics, chemistry, literature, peace, medicine or physiology and economics. The Prizes were instituted by the Swedish inventor of dynamite Alfred Nobel (1833–96), through his will. They were first awarded in 1901. The prize in economics, instituted by the Bank of Sweden in 1968, was first awarded in 1969 – too late for John Maynard Keynes, who died in 1946. By October 2010, a total of 813 Nobel Prizes had been awarded to individuals (four of these twice), including 41 to women; and 23 to organisations (three of these twice). Individual awards, other than for literature, are often shared. Two winners refused their prizes and four were unable to accept them.

128 Nobel prizes have been won by 127 people who were born British or Irish, who chose to become British or who were born in the British Isles – 16% of all individual awards. The list includes six women: four for Peace, one for Chemistry (Dorothy Hodgkin in 1964) and one for Literature (Doris Lessing in 2007). Frederick Sanger OM (born 1918) is the world's only double laureate for Chemistry (1958 and 1980).

The US has won the most prizes and is increasing its lead with every passing year: US citizens have won over 50% of all prizes awarded since 1970. Britain and Ireland (citizens of Éire did not cease to be British subjects in British law until the coming into force of the British Nationality Act on 1 January 1949) rank second; Germany third (102); then France (57). Sweden (28) and Switzerland (26), lying fifth and sixth, have won most prizes per head of population. Russia lies seventh with 25; Canada and Italy have each won 20; and the Netherlands lies tenth (19). The youngest ever prizewinner (for physics) was Sir Lawrence Bragg CH FRS in 1915, aged twenty-five.

It matters to the reputation and commercial importance of an institution to claim as many Nobel Laureates as possible. That caveat aside, affiliates of Cambridge University have been awarded 88 prizes (not including those who only researched there), more than any other in the world – and 31 more than France. Trinity College alone has won 32 of these and would come fifth if it were a country. The University of Chicago claims 85 (but this includes many more properly associated with other institutions); MIT has won 76; the University of London and Imperial College, 72; Oxford University, 48; UC Berkeley, 47; Harvard University, 43; and the University of Manchester, 25.

It seems perverse however, that such brilliant writers as Joseph Conrad, E.M. Forster, Graham Greene, Thomas Hardy, Henry James, James Joyce, D.H. Lawrence, George Orwell, Evelyn Waugh all went unrecognised by the Swedish Academy.

The Nobel Prize medal for Literature
The Nobel Foundation

David Lloyd George, 1st Earl Lloyd-George of Dwyfor OM

STATESMAN AND PARLIAMENTARY REFORMER

**David Lloyd George,
1st Earl Lloyd-George
of Dwyfor (1927) by
Sir William Orpen**
National Portrait Gallery, London

David Lloyd George, 1st Earl Lloyd-George of Dwyfor was born on 17 January 1863 in Manchester, where his father William George (1820–64) was a schoolteacher. His mother Elizabeth (1828–96) was the daughter of David Lloyd, a cobbler and radical Baptist pastor in Llanystumdwy in Caernarvonshire. Both his parents were Welsh speakers. In 1864 David's father died and his mother returned to her old home in north Wales to live with her unmarried brother Richard, a master cobbler. His formidable uncle "Lloyd" was the most important influence in Lloyd George's life until his death in 1917. He was a self-taught, passionate Liberal of great culture and perception. He directed Lloyd George towards the law; and after a sound education at Llanystumdwy village school, he was articled when he was fifteen, to a firm of solicitors in the nearby town of Portmadoc. In 1884 he qualified with Honours and immediately established his own practice in a back room of his uncle's house. The practice flourished and by 1887 he had established branch-offices in the neighbouring towns – as well as becoming passionately involved in Liberal politics.

In January 1888 he married Margaret Owen, the daughter of a prosperous yeoman farmer. In the same year, with a group of like-minded Welsh Liberals, he founded a monthly periodical called *Udgorn Rhyddid* (*Trumpet of Freedom*). He also won an appeal in the Divisional court of the Queen's Bench, which confirmed the right of Nonconformists to be buried with their own denominational service in parish cemeteries, a right that had been promised in the 1880 Amendment to the Burial Act of 1857. The public exposure he gained from this case and his articles in the *Trumpet* led to his adoption as the Liberal candidate for Caernarvon Boroughs. In April 1890, at a by-election caused by the sudden death of the sitting Conservative member, Lloyd George won the seat by nineteen votes; and became the youngest M.P. in the House of Commons. From this platform he pressed for the disestablishment of the Welsh Church, Home Rule for Wales and Temperance Reform. Lloyd George would remain a Member of Parliament for the next fifty-five years.

As M.Ps were unpaid in the 1890s, Lloyd George had no option but to continue and expand his practice in Criccieth, near Caernarvon; and later in London, where he merged his firm with that of fellow Welshman Arthur Roberts (who later became the Official Solicitor). He devoted his first ten years in Parliament wholly to Welsh affairs, ardently and persistently arguing the case for Welsh Home Rule. His enthusiasm led him and his little group of Welsh Liberal M.Ps to refuse the Liberal Whip – yet, despite abandoning his support for Home Rule, he was blamed in the Welsh press and the principal Liberal organ, the *Manchester Guardian* for losing the 1895 General Election to the Conservatives.

Lloyd George won national prominence through his vigorous opposition to the Boer War. Conservative justification for the war was on the grounds that the "Uitlanders" (mostly British miners working in the Transvaal) were denied the vote.

He argued that as a *casus belli*, this was specious, in that Britain herself did not have universal male suffrage; and that the real reason for the war was the government's concern for British mining interests. He argued that the cost of the war was delaying important social reforms, especially in introducing old-age pensions and building houses for working men. He went on to accuse the army High Command of failing adequately to care for the wounded and exposed the horrifying conditions in the British concentration camps. Finally he embarrassed the Colonial Secretary, Joseph Chamberlain by revealing that his family firm, Kynoch Ltd of Birmingham, had tendered for and unfairly won several substantial War Office contracts. Lloyd George's scathing attacks were considered unpatriotic and nearly split the Liberal Party.

> In 1897, Lloyd George made an ill-advised investment in a Patagonian gold mine. He lost a considerable sum; and as a result, was worried about money for years.

The Education Act of 1898 had imposed a duty on county councils to fund Church Schools, but only if the buildings were in good repair. This disqualified most of the church schools in Wales. Lloyd George confirmed his reputation as an upholder of justice with attacks on the illogical wording of the Act, which he succeeded in amending.

In 1905 Lloyd George was invited to join the Liberal government of Sir Henry Campbell-Bannerman (1836–1908); and was appointed President of the Board of Trade. He was a great success in this office, steering through the Commons a raft of Acts regulating public corporations and private businesses; also nipping in the bud a potentially disastrous railway strike in 1907. However his triumph was soon blighted by the death from appendicitis of his daughter Mair.

On 22 April 1908 Campbell-Bannerman died. He was replaced by Herbert Asquith (1852–1928); who appointed Lloyd George Chancellor of the Exchequer, an office he retained until 1915. As Chancellor, Lloyd George laid the foundations of the welfare state by introducing a series of social measures known as the Liberal Reforms: to "lift the shadow of the workhouse from the homes of the poor". He believed that the best way of achieving this was to guarantee an income to individuals who were too old to work. Based on the ideas of Tom Paine (1737–1809), set out in *Rights of Man* in 1791, Lloyd George's Old Age Pensions Act paid between 1s. and 5s. a week to men over seventy years of age (£98–50p today). His next reform, the most far-reaching until William Beveridge recommended a National Health Service in 1942, was the 1911 National Insurance Act. This provided the working classes with their first contributory system of insurance against illness and unemployment. All wage earners between the ages of sixteen and seventy had to join the health scheme, each paying 4d. a week. The employer added 3d. and the state 2d. In return, free medical attention, including medicine was given.

Unemployed workers who had contributed were also guaranteed 7s. each week for fifteen weeks in any one year.

Lloyd George took great pains to overcome the instinctive reservations of doctors who feared for their incomes; insurance companies who foresaw erosion of their business; and the Trades Unions, concerned about further deductions from the wage packets of the hard-pressed working-man. In April 1912 he averted a national miners' strike, by introducing the principle of a minimum wage.

Lloyd George met a brick wall when he proposed raising the £16 million required to fund this ambitious legislation by increasing income tax: to 1d. in the pound for the lowest paid, to 3d. for those earning an annual salary of over £3,000 and a super-tax of 6d. in the pound for those earning over £5,000 (£2 million today). The Conservative dominated House of Lords was outraged and rejected his proposal. This led directly to the 1911 Parliament Act, which allowed the Lords to return a Bill to the Commons only three times, before it automatically became law. Indeed, so dangerous had the crisis become that Asquith threatened that he would ask King George V to swamp the House of Lords, by creating another 250 Liberal peers.

At this point difficulties in Lloyd George's marriage were made worse when he employed an attractive young woman, Frances Stevenson to teach French to his daughter Megan.

The problems posed by Lloyd George's tangled private life (about which the Press exercised exemplary discretion) were compounded by the Marconi scandal, that came close to destroying his political career. Hilaire Belloc (1870–1953) and G.K. Chesterton, in the political weekly *The Eye-Witness,* accused Lloyd George and some of his cronies of corruption.

It came to light that Lloyd George and the Attorney General, Sir Rufus Isaacs had bought shares in the US Marconi Company from Sir Rufus's brother just before the British Marconi was due to sign an enormous contract with the British government, to build wireless telegraphy stations across the Empire. Lloyd George argued that he had not only lost money but

---

This Act of constitutional imbalance was used to drive through Mike Foster's anti-hunting bill in 2004. The M.P. for Worcester (born in 1963) first introduced his divisive piece of legislation in 1997. Setting aside the rights and wrongs of hunting: bicameral government, with an effective reforming second chamber to prevent prejudiced and ill-informed oppression of a minority, could be said to no longer exist in Britain today.

Lloyd George was sexually incontinent (he was known as the "Welsh Goat"), which Margaret chose to overlook. It was not a happy marriage, although it produced two sons and three daughters. A.J. Sylvester, Lloyd George's principal private secretary, after seeing him get out of his bath, wrote in his diary: "There he stood as naked as when he was born with the biggest organ I have ever seen. It resembles a donkey's more than anything else. It must be a sight for the God's [sic] – or the women – in erection! No wonder they are always after him; and he after them!".

The most important and long lasting of his lovers was Frances Stevenson. She was born in London in 1888 (the year Lloyd George married Margaret) and became a teacher at a boarding school in Wimbledon. In 1911 she was employed by Lloyd George, then Chancellor of the Exchequer, to coach his youngest daughter Megan. They were soon attracted to each other – and in 1913 Frances began an affair with Lloyd George which lasted the rest of his life. Her vitality, loyalty and discretion won her lover's admiration (but not his fidelity – he sired several illegitimate children by other women) and she exercised considerable power in his household. She accompanied Lloyd George to the Paris Peace Conference in 1919. She also chose the location and supervised the building of his house at Churt in Surrey.

After two abortions, in 1929 Frances gave birth to a daughter, Jennifer, who was probably Lloyd George's (Frances had a brief liaison with Thomas Tweed, one of Lloyd George's political advisors, but had ended it some time earlier). During the 1930s she organised Lloyd George's extensive archive to enable the drafting of his war memoirs. In 1943, two years after Margaret's death, Lloyd George married Frances, but died within two years. Frances continued to live at Churt, involved in an array of projects aimed at perpetuating her husband's name. She died in 1972.

Lloyd George once had six mistresses on the go at the same time. When one complained that she was playing second fiddle, Lloyd George told her that she should be grateful to be in the orchestra.

Eye-Witness was a forerunner of the satirical magazine *Private Eye*, which was first published in 1961. Private Eye was first edited by Christopher Booker. Richard Ingrams, who was a struggling actor, did not fully take over until issue no. 40.

Gugliemo Marchese Marconi (1874–1937) was born near Bologna. His mother, Annie Jameson was a grand-daughter of the founder of the Jameson Irish whiskey distillery in Dublin (a Scot from Alloa in Clackmannanshire) and Marconi was fluent in English. Fascinated by electricity but finding little interest in his experiments in Italy, he moved to London with his mother, aged twenty-one. He took out a British patent (No. 12,039) on 2 July 1896; and established British and US companies to exploit his technology.

He won the support of William Preece (1834–1913), Chief Electrical Engineer of the General Post Office; and a series of demonstrations to the British government followed. On 13 May 1897 he transmitted Morse code signals across the Bristol Channel, from Lavernock Point in South Wales to Brean Down, a distance of 8.7 miles. On 12 December 1901, using a 400-foot kite-supported antenna at Signal Hill in Newfoundland, he received signals from his new high-power station at Poldhu in Cornwall. The distance between the two points was about 2,100 miles.

Marconi was awarded the Nobel Prize for Physics in 1909. He was not involved in the 'Marconi Scandal' of 1912 in any way – and when the British Broadcasting Company was formed in 1922, his British Marconi Company was a prominent participant (it later became a subsidiary of GEC, which was renamed Marconi in 1999). Marconi died aged sixty-three and Italy held a state funeral for him. As a tribute, radio stations throughout the world observed a two minutes silence.

that he had in fact invested in the US subsidiary not the British parent company. To the British public however, the transaction bore the hallmark of ministerial corruption. The affair attracted the venom of those Conservatives who had been humiliated so often at the hands of the "little Welsh lawyer"; and the Isaacs brothers predictably suffered especial vilification, made worse by anti-Semitic prejudice. The government accepted the verdict of a select committee, chosen fairly from all parliamentary parties and Lloyd George narrowly escaped a fatal censure.

In 1913 the suffragettes added their protests to the government for treating their members harshly during demonstrations and then cruelly in prison.

Despite his support for the movement in Opposition, Lloyd George's new house at Walton Heath was burned down. March 1914 brought him yet more opprobrium, with his unsuccessful attempt to modify the Irish Home Rule Bill. Civil war loomed: and both sides made arrangements to arm themselves.

It is often thought that Lloyd George, until becoming Prime Minister in December 1916, was interested only in domestic issues. From his speeches during the Boer war and his opposition to the Naval Estimates, many considered him to be a pacifist "Little Englander". This was far from the case. He had visited Germany in 1908, meeting the Kaiser and his Foreign Minster, Bethman Hollweg. He was alarmed by the pace, dictated by the Kaiser, of German naval construction. He served on the committee of Imperial Defence; and would have been fully briefed on the likelihood of a German attack through Belgium on the Channel ports. In 1911 he took an unexpectedly aggressive anti-German stance during the "Agadir Crisis" in Morocco. He also regarded the Turks, as had his old mentor William Ewart Gladstone (1809–98), as "unspeakable" and supported a war in the Balkans to thwart them.

A crisis arose when Germany sent the gunboat *Panther* to the Moroccan port of Agadir, to reinforce her claim for compensation from France for having accepted French colonisation of Morocco. Tensions between Britain and Germany, already high because of increasing naval competition, were exacerbated by the fear that the Germans intended to develop Agadir as a naval base. The French gave way: and the outcome was a restatement of the *Entente Cordiale* – an agreement, signed in 1904, that ended colonial antagonism between Britain and France; and presumed that the two countries would unite in opposition to German aggression. Germany mistakenly, thought itself the winner.

A 40 year-old suffragette, Emily Davison died on 8 June 1913, having thrown herself under the hoofs of Anmer, King George V's horse in the Derby Stakes four days earlier.

On 3 August 1914 Lloyd George was committed to war with Germany. Conflict suited his temperament. Relieved to put behind him the troubles of peacetime, he plunged into the preparations for war. As Chancellor, he and Walter Cunliffe (Governor of the Bank of England from 1913–18) took tight control of the national finances. A moratorium between banks provided guarantees against bad debts on all bills of exchange transacted before 4 August. New £1 and ten shilling (50 pence) notes were issued. On the Home front the Chancellor acted with equal assurance. He restricted the opening hours of public houses (a measure that was not repealed for nearly ninety years) and ordered the strength of beer to be reduced. He persuaded King George V to sign "the (King's) pledge" for the duration of the war – a commitment that must have appealed to Lloyd George's nonconformist temperance. Capitalising on his excellent relationship with organised labour, Lloyd George brokered an agreement between the Treasury and Arthur Henderson (1863–1935) of the Trades Union Council, to suspend strike action for the duration of the war and to accept the inclusion of women in the workplace.

By early 1915 Lloyd George was at odds with the Secretary of State for War Lord Kitchener, over shortages of munitions. He supported Churchill's efforts to break the deadlock of the trenches with "sideshows", attacking Germany's "underbelly" in the east – which ended in the bloody fiasco of Gallipoli. By mid-1915 Asquith's government was in serious trouble and reluctantly considering coalition with the Conservatives. To avoid this, Lloyd George was appointed Minister for Munitions.

Lloyd George realised that to win the war the country had to be transformed into a command economy. He imposed controls on the allocation of raw materials, effectively taking over the coal, steel, chemical and engineering industries. Women were recruited for the arms factories. Relations with the Unions held firm thanks to the agreement made in 1914. When he left the Ministry a year later in July 1916, supplies of shells, ammunition and especially machine guns and artillery were being turned out in prodigious quantities. Manufacturing processes that had taken a year in 1915 had been shortened to three weeks in 1916; and the first tanks were being sent to the front.

1916 was a dreadful year for the Allies. Churchill, discredited and bearing the blame for Gallipoli, resigned from the cabinet and departed in disgrace for the trenches. Lord Kitchener was drowned when the cruiser HMS *Hampshire* carrying him to Russia struck a mine off Orkney. The Loos offensive had won nothing to compensate for a loss of 61,000 casualties; and the French army at Verdun was being bled white, as the Germans fully intended, at an eventual cost of over 370,000 casualties. In April the Easter Rising in Dublin threatened to ignite the unresolved Irish Question.

Meanwhile, on the 31 May off Jutland, Sir John Jellicoe (1859–1935) and the Grand Fleet had received a mauling in an inglorious engagement with the German High Seas Fleet – a betrayal of the "Nelson tradition". "There is something wrong with our bloody ships today", Sir David Beatty remarked famously as three of his battlecruisers sank after

Sir John Rushmore Jellicoe, 1st Earl Jellicoe by Reginald Grenville Eves (1935)
National Portrait Gallery, London

their magazines were ignited by flash fires. To cap this list of disasters, on 1 July came news of 60,000 casualties, of which 20,000 were killed, on the first day of Sir Douglas Haig's futile offensive on the Somme.

In the face of these terrible losses, Lloyd George drew closer to the Conservatives – especially on the issue of conscription: anathema to the Liberals but vital to the Conservatives. In January 1916 Asquith, exhausted and soon to be stricken by personal tragedy (his son Raymond was killed at the Somme in September), finally gave way. All single men, without skills essential to the war effort, between eighteen and forty-one were called up; in June conscription was extended to married men; and eventually to men aged up to fifty-one. On 4 July 1916 Lloyd George accepted Asquith's invitation to become Secretary of State for War.

Allied disasters continued into the last six months of 1916. The British offensive on the Somme petered out with a terrible loss of life. Diversionary campaigns launched by Russia in Poland, and by Italy in the Dolomites against Austria, almost immediately lost momentum. Lloyd George, despite the flow of munitions now reaching the front, was in despair at the incompetence he perceived around him, confiding gloomily to Sir Maurice Hankey: "We are going to lose this war".

Conscription put into uniform virtually every able bodied man in Britain, six million out of the ten million who were eligible. 750,000 conscripts were killed and a further 1,700,000 wounded. Most of the dead were bachelors. Nonetheless, 160,000 wives lost their husbands and 300,000 children lost their fathers.

The shifty manoeuvres of July 1916 had split the Liberal Party: between those who wished to replace Asquith with another Liberal; and those, headed by Lloyd George who supported a coalition with the Conservatives. In December Lloyd George replaced Asquith as Prime Minister. In his first War Cabinet Conservatives occupied the key posts (Churchill rejoined the Cabinet, becoming Minister for Munitions), with Arthur Henderson, who was to win the Nobel Peace Prize in 1934, as the sole Labour Party representative. A ministry of talent, drawn from across the entire political spectrum, made it impossible for Lloyd George, unlike Churchill in 1940, to control military strategy on his own – the need for consensus resulted in some of the most costly blunders of the war. However he was able persuade the Admiralty to adopt the convoy system – saving Britain from starvation.

Nevertheless, Lloyd George's War Cabinet, under the secretaryship of Sir Maurice, later Lord Hankey (1877–1963), functioned with remarkable efficiency. Meeting almost daily, the Cabinet made every important military, political, economic and diplomatic decision – including the imposition of rationing in early 1918.

Herbert Henry Asquith, 1st Earl of Oxford and Asquith by Sir Francis Carruthers Gould ('F. C. G.') (1900s or 1910s)
National Portrait Gallery, London

On Armistice Day, 11 November 1918 Lloyd George enjoyed an unrivalled reputation: "He can be a dictator for life if he wishes", said Andrew Bonar Law (1858–1923) – who was to succeed him as Prime Minister. In the December 1918 General Election his National-Liberal Party won a landslide victory. The Conservatives however, dominated the coalition with over two-thirds of its seats. Asquith

In 1917 Lloyd George supported, but only with great misgivings, two ruinous offensives. First the French assault on the Aisne launched in April by the flamboyant, half-English General Robert Nivelle – an inglorious failure which resulted in serious mutinies within the French army and came close to forcing France out of the war. The second was Passchendaele (Third Battle of Ypres) between July-November, led by Field Marshal Sir Douglas Haig. It foundered in heavy rain and mud, compounded by the German use of mustard gas, against heavily fortified concrete bunkers *(stollen)*. The offensive cost 310,000 British, Canadian, Australian and South African casualties – 90,000 British and Australian bodies were never identified; and 42,000 were never recovered.

• **Douglas Haig, 1st Earl Haig by Graham Smith (1894)**
National Portrait Gallery, London

lost his own in East Fife; and his Liberal contingent won only thirty-three, fewer even than the Labour Party – leaving it where it remains today, stranded in the doldrums.

Lloyd George realised the folly of his proposal to "make Germany pay" on the first day of the Versailles Peace conference. He saw that the French approach to reparations was so harsh that there was not the slightest chance of the prostrate German goose laying any sort of an egg, let alone a golden one, because the French would have long since strangled it. With nearly 1.7 million dead, the French Prime Minister Georges ("Tiger") Clemenceau was neither magnanimous nor realistic. Lloyd George wished to punish Germany politically and economically, but soon saw the futility of utterly destroying her economy. He told Clemenceau that his proposals were too harsh and would "plunge Germany and the greater part of Europe into Bolshevism". Clemenceau replied that Lloyd George's alternative would lead to Bolshevism in France.

In no time, Lloyd George's freedom of action was constrained by the Conservative majority within his administration. The decision to extend conscription to Ireland in 1918 was stupid and disastrous, provoking most Irish M.Ps to declare for independence. He had said earlier, in reference to republican guerrillas, "We have murder by the throat!". However a nasty campaign of oppression ensued, marked by the brutality and ill-discipline of the Auxiliaries (the "Black and Tans") – leading to the Anglo-Irish Treaty and the creation of the Irish Free State in 1922.

By 1921 Lloyd George's coalition had begun to unravel. It could not contain such a broad diversity of opinion and, without the discipline of total war, could not properly function. Fissures began to appear, not only between the Conservative and National Liberal factions, but amongst the Conservatives themselves. Internecine party warfare; the onset of the first post-war depression in May 1920, aggravated by the sleazy traffic in honours; and a tiresomely non-consultative style of premiership, all combined to hustle Lloyd George from power. Bonar Law and Stanley Baldwin (1867–1947), a rising junior Treasury minister, proposed a motion to abandon the coalition to fight the impending election as Conservatives on their own. It was carried by 187 votes to 86 on 22 October 1922.

For the remaining twenty-three years of his life Lloyd George stood on the touchline of British politics. He succeeded Asquith as leader of the Liberal Party in 1926, but a prostate operation prevented him from joining the National government in 1931. During the 1920s he produced several reports on how Britain could be better governed, including: *Coal and Power* (1924), *Towns and the Land* (1925), *Britain's Industrial Future* (1928) and *We Can Conquer Unemployment* (1929). In 1935, in a pale imitation of the US "New Deal", he promoted a radical programme of economic reform, titled *Lloyd George's New Deal*, which attracted little support. In 1936 he visited Hitler at Berchtesgarten. Flattered by Hitler's gift of a signed, silver-mounted photograph, captioned: "To the man who won the war", he hailed the deranged Fuhrer as "the greatest living German". This miscalculation subsequently did him great damage. He made his last outstanding Commons speech on 8 May 1940 at the age of seventy-seven, mounting a devastating assault on Neville Chamberlain – which helped pave the way for Winston Churchill. In January 1945 he was elevated to the peerage as Earl Lloyd-George of Dwyfor (a river and a town in Caernarvonshire) and Viscount Gwynedd. He died two months later, on 26 March, aged eighty-two.

Lloyd George left a legacy still debated today. Although bitterly opposed to Home Rule in Wales later in life, he was the harbinger of devolution. As Chancellor of the Exchequer, he laid the foundations of the welfare state. As Minister for War, he transformed the munitions industry; and as Prime Minister, he led Britain through the darkest months of WWI with an inspiration to compare with Churchill's in WWII.

Lloyd George's record as a peacetime Prime Minister however, is more contentious. His premiership, followed by twenty-five years of political inactivity, remains tarnished. His meddling contributed great pain to the birth of the Irish Free State; and his insouciant approach to the creation of Israel was devastating in its consequences. He lauded the emancipation of women but did nothing to hasten it. He connived at many of the most deplorable clauses of the Versailles Peace Treaty. He was never a creature of his party; and throughout his life his loyalties were shallow, his friendships expedient. He was perhaps dazzled by the concept of a government of national unity but as a result, he was the agent of the Liberal Party's premature eclipse. A pall of moral turpitude will forever hang over Lloyd George. Shady financial dealings, evidenced in his venal behaviour in commercialising the award of honours, together with his licentious approach to sexual mores, have done much to erode his reputation.

Lloyd George was indisputably a colossus amongst 20th century British statesmen: but Winston Churchill was by far the better man.

LLOYD GEORGE AND THE SALE OF HONOURS SCANDAL

Lloyd George had trenchant views on members of the House of Lords, saying that: "A fully-equipped duke costs as much to keep up as two Dreadnoughts. They are just as great a terror and they last longer"; and, on another occasion, stating that they were: "five hundred men chosen at random from the ranks of the unemployed".

From 1916 his Coalition Liberals increasingly needed to replenish party funds – and the easiest method was to sell honours. The 'sales' were handled by Lloyd George's Chief Whip Freddy Guest and his press agent William Sutherland: but the operation was actually run by Maundy Gregory, a former actor and theatrical impresario. Gregory had his own offices in Parliament Square and openly touted the sale of honours on official writing paper, detailing the "exceptional opportunity" on offer. There was even a published tariff: a knighthood cost £10,000, a baronetcy £25,000 (£3.25 million today), a barony £30,000 to £50,000 and a viscountcy £80,000 to £100,000.

Between 1916–22 1,500 knighthoods and baronetcies and 91 peerages were awarded, twice as many as in the previous twenty years. Indeed Gregory, noting that there were men with cash to spare who could not afford a knighthood, invented the Order of the British Empire to fill this gap in the market. As a result 25,000 people were "awarded" the OBE over a period of four years and the 'honour' became devalued so rapidly that it was commonly known as the "Order of the Bad Egg", or "Other Buggers' Efforts".

Not everyone was required to pay: around fifty or so honours were awarded in the direction of Fleet Street. All the leading newspaper owners, such as William Astor (Viscount Astor), Maxwell Aitken (Baron Beaverbrook), Alfred Harmsworth (Viscount Northcliffe) and his brother Harold Sidney Harmsworth (Viscount Rothermere) found themselves raised to the peerage. This cynical protection money ensured that for some time the press turned a blind eye to the whole affair.

The July 1922 honours list included John Drughorn (convicted in 1915 for trading with the enemy), William Vestey (accused of tax evasion) and Joseph Robinson (a South African recently convicted of a share fraud and fined £500,000). This was too much for the King. He wrote to Lloyd George, complaining that "the Robinson case must be regarded as little less than an insult to Crown and to the House of Lords".

Nothing changes in politics. King James I introduced the rank of baronet in 1611. 200 "gentlemen" paid £1,095 (£2 million today) – to finance the plantation of Ulster.

It was also too much for Fleet Street which, despite being early beneficiaries of Lloyd George's largesse, now turned against him. He was forced to concede a parliamentary debate on 17 July 1922. Speaking in the House of Commons he described the selling of honours as a "discreditable system. It ought never to have existed. If it does exist, it ought to be terminated" – and explained that it was the war that was responsible for the high volume of honours awarded under his administration. Although he continued to insist (privately at least) that "the sale of honours is the cleanest way of raising money for a political party", the scale of opposition to the practice in Parliament was such that he was forced to promise reform.

In a time-honoured tradition, Lloyd George appointed a Royal Commission: but cannily ensured that its terms of reference were confined to making recommendations for the future – and excluded any remit to examine previous practice. He managed to avoid any

After Robinson had knocked Gregory's price down from £50,000 to £30,000, the intention to ennoble him was gazetted. When Robinson, in his eighties and stonedeaf, was asked to write a letter to the Prime Minister declining the peerage, he thought he was being asked for more money and pulled out his cheque book. The Chief Whip later asked Gregory what had become of the £30,000: and received the jaunty reply, "Oh, I've spent it". Gregory was imprisoned for two months in 1933. He spent the rest of his life in Paris, on an annual pension of £2,000 provided by the Conservative party, in return for his silence (it is worth remembering that the Conservatives were Lloyd George's coalition partners at the time of the 'sales'). Gregory was arrested by the Germans and died in their unloving care in 1941.

responsibility for the scandal; but this did little to disguise the terminal state of his administration. Lloyd George resigned in October 1922, ending his career in mainstream politics. He is thought to have amassed £1.5 million (£147 million today) personally – which must have comforted him in his disappointment.

THE ROYAL BRITISH LEGION

The British Legion, founded in 1921, was a merger of four organisations. It was granted the "Royal" prefix on 29 May 1971, to mark its

James Buchanan (1849–1935), the Canadian-born entrepreneur behind the success of Black & White blended whisky, was a larger-than-life figure. In 1920 Lloyd George offered him a barony, as Lord Woolavington, in return for a donation of £100,000 to Liberal Party funds. Buchanan was keen to take up his offer, but in keeping with his own business acumen and Lloyd George's reputation, he signed his cheque 'Woolavington' – to cash it Lloyd George had first to honour his promise.

A racehorse owner, Woolavington assembled the largest collection of British sporting art in Europe, which included "Gimcrack" by George Stubbs (1724–1806).

One of the finest animal, especially equine, painters that has ever lived, Stubbs was born in Liverpool; and worked for his father, a currier and leather merchant, until he died in 1741. He then taught himself how to paint; studied human anatomy in York from 1745–51; visited Italy in 1754 ("to convince himself that nature was and is always superior to art whether Greek or Roman"), returning to Britain by way of Morocco; and spent eighteen months first bleeding to death, then preserving and dissecting horses in Lincolnshire. In 1759 he moved to London; and in 1766 published "The Anatomy of the Horse". His attention to detail and accurate likenesses defy belief – famously to be observed in "Whistlejacket" (1762), commissioned by his most discerning patron, the 2nd Marquess of Rockingham. Thirty years later he painted the Prince of Wales on horseback (1791).

Stubbs also painted lions, tigers, cheetahs, moose, red deer, giraffes, kangaroos, monkeys, rhinoceroses and zebras, all studied minutely in private menageries. His depictions of wild horses attacked by a lion were especially vivid. Experimentation with enamel however, was less successful.

Elected to full membership of the Royal Academy in 1781, Stubbs refused to bow to bureaucracy and never became an Academician. Nevertheless, he established an unrivalled reputation among a mostly aristocratic clientele, for a prodigious range and output of individual and group portraits in oils, some life-size, of horses – often with grooms, who could be recognised, or with hounds. He remained active, though increasingly impoverished, until he died aged eighty-one, in London. His son, by his common-law wife Mary Spencer, George Townley Stubbs (1756–1815) became a printmaker and engraver.

- **George Stubbs self-portrait (1781)**
  National Portrait Gallery, London
- **Whistlejacket by George Stubbs (about 1762)**
  National Gallery, London

Field of poppies

fiftieth anniversary. Field Marshal Douglas, 1st Earl Haig OM (1861–1928), the much maligned Commander-in-Chief on the western front from December 1915 until the end of WWI, was instrumental in establishing the British Legion; and remained its president until his death.

A Remembrance Day silence was first mooted by Australian ex-soldier and journalist Edward Honey (1885–1922), writing as Warren Foster, in a letter to the *Evening News* on 8 May 1919.

On 7 November 1919, King George V issued a proclamation asking that: "at the hour when the Armistice comes into force, the 11th hour of the 11th day of the 11th month, there may be for the brief space of two minutes a complete suspension of all our normal activities .... so that in perfect stillness, the thoughts of everyone may be concentrated on reverent remembrance of the glorious dead".

Robert Laurence Binyon (1869–1943), a Quaker born in Lancaster, is remembered for one particular poem – *For the Fallen*. It is used everywhere in Remembrance Sunday services:

They shall grow not old, as we that are left grow old.
Age shall not weary them, nor the years condemn.
At the going down of the sun and in the morning,
We will remember them.

Honey's suggestion was for a five-minute silence; but that was thought too long. One minute was deemed too short.

CASUALTIES IN WWI BY BORDERS AND POPULATIONS IN 1914

	Population (millions)	Deaths (military)	(civilian)	Total	% of population	Wounded
Australia	4.5	61,928		61,928	1.4	
Canada	7.2	64,944	2,000+	66,944	0.93	149,732
Indian Empire	315.1	74,187		69,214	0.02	
New Zealand	1.1	18,050		41,317	1.64	
Newfoundland	0.2	1,204		2,314	0.60	
South Africa	6.0	9,463		12,029	0.16	
GB and Ireland	45.4	885,138	109,000	994,138	2.19	1,663,435
British Empire		1,114,914	111,000	1,225,914		2,090,212
Belgium	7.4	58,637	62,000	120,637	1.63	44,686
French Empire	39.6	1,397,800	300,000	1,697,800	4.29	4,266,000
Greece	4.8	26,000	150,000	176,000	3.67	21,000
Italy	35.6	651,000	589,000	1,240,000	3.48	953,886
Portugal	6.0	7,222	82,000	89,222	1.49	13,751
Romania	7.5	250,000	430,000	680,000	9.07	120,000
Russian Empire	175.1	1,811,000	1,500,000	3,311,000	1.89	4,950,000
Serbia	4.5	275,000	450,000	725,000	16.11	133,148
United States	92.0	116,708	757	117,465	0.13	205,690
Total Allies		5,711,696	3,674,757	9,386,453		12,809,280
Austria-Hungary	51.4	1,100,000	467,000	1,567,000	3.05	3,620,000
Bulgaria	5.5	87,500	100,000	187,500	3.41	152,390
German Empire	64.9	2,050,897	426,000	2,476,897	3.82	4,247,143
Ottoman Empire	21.3	771,844	2,150,000*	2,921,844	13.72	400,000
Central Powers	143.1	4,010,241	3,143,000	7,153,241	5.0	8,419,533
Total (millions)		**9.722**	**6.821**	**16.543**		**21.229**

(including colonial troops and allies too small to mention, also Scandinavian neutrals)
+ Halifax harbour: 6 December 1917 (largest ever man-made accidental explosion)
* including 1,500,000 murdered Armenians – still not acknowledged by Turkey (2010)

The totals of those killed or wounded in WWI are horrifying, but are often misquoted. Though estimates vary between sources, it is interesting to know roughly what they were.

Romania and Serbia suffered the most. Turkey's terrible total of civilian deaths* was self-inflicted and appalling. Of the larger countries, among the Allies the British Empire did not suffer as much as France, which explains why Clemenceau insisted on such brutal terms at Versailles; or, as a percentage, even Italy. Among the Central Powers, there was little to choose between them. Included in the civilian deaths are some that died during the influenza pandemic in 1918. A world total of 16.5 million dead and 21.2 million wounded is hardly imaginable – and makes it all the more extraordinary that President Woodrow Wilson was permitted such an important role at Versailles. The US had certainly not paid for it in blood.

LAWRENCE "OF ARABIA"

Thomas Edward ("T.E.") Lawrence was born on 16 August 1888 at Tremadoc in Caernarvonshire. He was the third of five illegitimate sons of Sir Thomas Chapman, an Anglo-Irish baronet, who had abandoned his wife for his daughter's governess. Intelligent and diligent, in 1907 Lawrence won a history scholarship to Jesus College, Oxford.

In 1914 Lawrence worked for British military intelligence, surveying the Negev desert (in modern Israel) under cover of an archaeological expedition. The Negev was strategically important: it would have to be crossed by a Turkish army attempting an invasion of Egypt, to capture the Suez Canal and threaten imperial communications with India.

Aesthetic, athletic and very tough, he had "ice-blue eyes .... and a long, determined jaw". From all accounts, it appears that he was disinterested in sex: although his strange reaction to being beaten and raped by the pederastic (his word) Turkish governor in Deraa (in modern Syria) in 1916, suggests a strong streak of masochism. A man driven by devils, his single-minded pursuit of physical and mental challenges was tempered by a manic sense of humour and the ability to inspire devotion.

In 1909 Lawrence travelled alone to Syria where in three months he walked over 1,000 miles, researching a thesis on Crusader castles. In 1910, after graduating with a first class degree, he joined an archaeological dig in Syria where he learned Arabic, Turkish and Syriac; while developing a deep sympathy for the Arabs, who had been oppressed for centuries under Turkish rule.

In 1916, with WWI in full swing and Germany allied to Turkey, Lawrence became the agent of a plan conceived by the British Foreign Office's Arab Bureau, to undermine the Turks by fomenting and supporting Arab rebellion. Lawrence became liaison-officer and adviser to Emir Faisal ibn Ali (1885–1939), son of Sharif Hussein of Mecca, the Hashemite leader of the Arab revolt. Lawrence, displaying a natural flair for guerrilla warfare, led a small but highly effective force of Arab irregulars behind the Turkish lines. By tying down the bulk of the enemy forces, Lawrence enabled General Edward Allenby (1861–1936) to capture Jerusalem; before defeating the Turkish army led by the German General Liman von Sanders in 1917. On 1 October 1918 Lawrence, at the head of his Arab guerrillas, joined Allenby's victorious army and entered Damascus. Lawrence's ability to weld together such a loyal yet diverse Arab force was underpinned by his personal promise to secure an independent Arab state. After the fall of Damascus, Lawrence immediately left for London; and then the Paris Peace Conference at Versailles, as a member of Faisal's delegation, to lobby on the Arab behalf. Before the conference had even begun, Lawrence was shocked to discover that in 1916, the French and British had already agreed to carve up the Ottoman Empire into respective spheres of influence.

The Sykes-Picot agreement (16 May 1916) was named after the negotiators, Sir Mark Sykes of Britain (1879–1919) and François Georges-Picot of France. In anticipation of the dismemberment of the Ottoman Empire, it was a secret protocol agreed between Great Britain and France with the assent of Imperial Russia. It led to the division of Syria, Iraq, Jordan, Lebanon and Palestine into French and British mandates. It also led to the "Balfour Declaration".

The declaration was set out on 2 November 1917 in a letter from Arthur Balfour, the British Foreign Secretary, to Walter, 2nd Baron Rothschild. It stated that: "His Majesty's government view with favour the establishment in Palestine of a national home for the Jewish people" – though not at the expense of "the civil and religious rights of existing communities in Palestine". Unwittingly, the British had opened Pandora's box: and lit a fire in the Middle East that rages to this day. On 14 May 1948 the State of Israel was formally established, announced the day before the British mandate was due to expire.

The Sykes-Picot agreement conflicted with simultaneous undertakings made by the British to Sharif Hussein, to secure an independent Arab homeland. This cynical promise, reinforced in good faith by Lawrence, was made just before he launched the Arab revolt. Following the Russian Revolution in October 1917, the Bolsheviks exposed it: "the British were embarrassed, the Arabs dismayed and the Turks delighted".

Humiliated and embittered by his failure to achieve Arab home-rule, Lawrence had become a celebrity, due to his cooperation in 1918 with an American journalist, Lowell Thomas.

In 1919 Lawrence joined the Colonial Office and served as an adviser on Arab affairs to Winston Churchill. In 1922 he changed his name to John Hume Ross and enlisted as an aircraftman in the RAF. Exposed by the *Daily Express* in 1923, he changed his name again, to T.E

Shaw, and joined the Royal Tank Corps – which he disliked. He was permitted to re-enlist in the RAF in 1925, serving two years on a remote airfield in British India. During this time he wrote *The Seven Pillars of Wisdom,* his account of the Arab revolt, *Revolt in the Desert, The Mint* and a translation of Homer's *Odyssey.* In March 1935 Lawrence left the RAF. Two months later at Wareham, near his Dorset cottage Clouds Hill, he was thrown from his beloved Brough Superior SS100 motorbike while swerving to avoid two children on bicycles.

Lawrence remained in a coma for six days, before dying on 19 May 1935.

The author John Buchan, later Governor-General of Canada, said of Lawrence: "I could have followed [him] over the edge of the world"; and described him as, "The only man of genius I have ever known" (this included Churchill and Lloyd George).

Sheikh Hamoudi, a ferocious Arab warrior, reacted to his death with anguish: "Oh! If only he had died in battle! I have lost my son, but do not grieve for him as I grieve for Lawrence .... My heart was iron, but his was steel. A man whose hand was never closed, but open .... Tell them in England what I say. Of manhood, the man, in freedom, free; a mind without equal; I can see no flaw in him".

Lawrence remains enigmatic: visionary, charismatic, ignorant of fear and larger than life. His poisoned legacy is relevant to the continuing troubles in the Middle East today.

SCAPA FLOW

Scapa Flow has been used as an anchorage for well over 1,000 years, first by the Vikings – who settled Shetland, Orkney, the Hebrides and much of northern Scotland, especially Caithness. It is 140 square miles in area, has a sandy bottom and is never deeper than 160 feet. Protected by the Orkney islands of Mainland, Graemsay, Burray, South Ronaldsay, Flotta and Hoy, it is one of the greatest natural harbours in the world.

In 1904, threatened by the build-up of the German Kaiserliche Marine's High Seas Fleet, Scapa Flow was chosen as a northern base for the British Grand Fleet, to control the entrances to the North Sea. It was Great Britain's most important naval base during the First (or Great) and Second World Wars – and was only closed in 1956.

At the end of WWI, seventy-four German ships were interned in Gutter Sound: awaiting a decision on their future in the peace Treaty of Versailles.

At 10:30 a.m. on 21 June 1919 Rear Admiral Ludwig von Reuter, after waiting for the British fleet to leave on exercises, gave the order to scuttle the ships. Only the destroyers HMS *Vespa* and HMS *Vega* remained on guard in Scapa Flow.

Fifty-one ships of 400,000 tonnage sank without loss of life. However nine German sailors were killed by British marines as they tried to scuttle their ship (having surrendered, they were considered mutineers), the last casualties of the Great War.

Thirty-five of the ships were salvaged by engineer Ernest Cox (1883–1959) between 1924 and 1931. The high quality steel recovered from the wrecks is a source of (pre-Hiroshima and Nagasaki) radiation-free metal, vital for some scientific instruments.

SCAPA FLOW

The main Royal Navy base for the Grand Fleet in the First and Second World Wars.

The German Kaiserliche
Marine's Hochseeflotte
(High Seas Fleet)

Britain declared war on Hitler's Germany on 3 September 1939. At 01:29 on 14 October, a moonless night with a high tide, Kapitänleutnant Gunther Prien (1908–41), captain of U-47, sank HMS *Royal Oak* in Scapa. 833 men died, including Rear-Admiral Henry Blagrove. Prien was awarded the Knight's Cross of the Iron Cross for his exploit.

The anchorage had been considered impregnable. However, with the aid of German air reconnaissance, Kriegsmarine Commander of Submarines Karl Dönitz calculated that a daring U-boat commander might be able to sneak through the barrier formed by block-ships sunk at

HMS Royal Oak

The Germans were careful not to disclose that three of the seven torpedoes fired had missed their target – one rose to the surface in 2002 and was destroyed by the Royal Navy.

critical points in Lamb Sound and linked by floating booms – undetected, when the booms were opened to allow the passage of local shipping. Dönitz thought that success would constitute a fitting act of revenge for the ignominious surrender and scuttling of the Hochseeflotte in 1919.

Prien was one of the most successful U-boat aces in WW II, spending 238 days at sea and sinking thirty ships. He was awarded the Oak leaves to the Knight's Cross in 1940, but went missing west of Ireland with his crew on 7 March 1941.

Bermuda flag

BRITAIN'S OLDEST COLONY CELEBRATED ITS 400TH BIRTHDAY IN 2009

Bermuda is named after the Spanish navigator, Juan de Bermudez, who discovered the uninhabited group of islands in 1503. There were no permanent residents until 1609: when the flagship *Sea Venture* of the English Third Supply Fleet to the colony of Virginia foundered in a hurricane with 150 colonists and crew.

The survivors, including the commander, Admiral Sir George Somers (the Somers Isles remains an alternative name for the colony), Sir Thomas Gates, Virginia's first Governor-Designate, and John Rolfe reached Virginia in 1610 – in two vessels they had constructed from native juniper, also called Bermuda cedar, which covered the islands.

The Tempest, by William Shakespeare, was first performed on 1 November 1611. It was written soon after reports of the shipwreck, and the safe arrival of the survivors in Jamestown, were received in London.

Bermuda, 650 miles east-southeast of Cape Hatteras in North Carolina, is the oldest and most populous remaining British overseas territory – settled by England a century before the creation of the United Kingdom of Great Britain itself. Bermuda's first capital, St George's, was founded in 1612. It is the oldest continuously inhabited British town in the Americas. The present capital, and main harbour, is named after Sir Henry Hamilton, governor from 1778–94.

The islands have a total area of 20.6 square miles. Financial services and tourism have brought Bermuda the world's highest GDP per capita. It has a subtropical climate.

John Rolfe, who buried a wife and child in Bermuda, married Princess Pocahontas (c.1595–1617). She was baptised as Rebecca: and her only child Thomas, was the ancestor of many notable Virginians, one of whom was Nancy, wife of President Ronald Reagan. Pocahontas died near Gravesend, on her way home from England.

WILLIAM THOMSON, 1ST BARON KELVIN OM

William Thomson FRS (1824–1907) was an Ulster-born physicist and engineer. A child prodigy, he entered Glasgow University when only ten and had published two papers on electricity and thermodynamics by the time he was seventeen. He graduated from Cambridge aged twenty. In 1846 he was awarded the Chair of Natural Philosophy at Glasgow University: a post which he retained until 1899. In 1848 he proposed the Second Law of Thermodynamics and the "absolute zero" temperature scale to which he gave his name. The zero point of the Kelvin scale marks the theoretical absence of all thermal energy: minus 273.15° centigrade – or zero Kelvin (0 K).

In 1845, while working with Michael Faraday, he discovered the Faraday Effect: which established that light, electricity and magnetism were all related. Kelvin served as consultant to the first transatlantic telegraph cable-laying enterprise: which, after many set-backs, was eventually completed in 1866 by Isambard Kingdom Brunel's leviathan, the SS *Great Eastern*. Kelvin's design of a mirror galvanometer and message transmission key not only transformed the cable's signal strength – it also made him a fortune from the patents he secured.

He went on to supervise the laying of French Atlantic and Brazilian submarine cables between 1869–73. His work on electricity and magnetism led directly to James Clerk Maxwell's Theory of Electro-Magnetism. He also contributed significantly to the study of hydrodynamics and to the exact calculation of the earth's age.

Kelvin's love of the sea prompted him to invent a compass which adjusted to the magnetic variation caused by iron ships; a depth sounder which functioned even when sailing at full speed; a tide-predicting machine; and a set of longitude tables.

He was raised to the peerage in 1892 (the river Kelvin flows near Glasgow university), having published over 600 scientific papers. Brilliant scientist though he was, Kelvin was not always right. He refused an invitation to join the Aeronautical Society: "I have not the smallest molecule of faith in aerial navigation ...."; and in 1900, made his famously crass pronouncement that: "There is nothing new to be discovered in physics now. All that remains is more and more precise measurement". He died aged eighty-three at Largs, in Ayrshire: honoured and very rich.

In simple terms, the Second Law of Thermodynamics states that, over time and ignoring the effects of self-gravity: differences in temperature, pressure, and density tend to even out in a physical system that is isolated from the outside world.

William Thomson, Baron Kelvin by Elizabeth King (*née* Thomson) (1886–1887)
National Portrait Gallery, London

The first successful submarine cable was laid by Samuel Morse in New York harbour in 1842. It was a single copper wire, sheathed in tarred hemp. In 1843 Sir Charles Wheatstone (1802–75) who, with William Coke had invented a telegraph system in 1837, repeated the exercise in Swansea Bay. In 1850 London was connected to Paris; and to Ireland in 1853. In 1870 the *Great Eastern* laid the first cable to link Britain to India, *via* the British Protectorate of Aden.

JAMES CLERK MAXWELL RANKS BEHIND ONLY NEWTON AND EINSTEIN

Another great 19th century Scottish scientist, James Clerk Maxwell FRS (1831–79) was a mathematician and theoretical physicist. His insights and explanations of natural forces led directly to the most important 20th century advances in physics, especially Albert Einstein's *Theory of Special Relativity*, first introduced in 1905. In 1873 he formulated an electro-magnetic theory ("Maxwell's Equations") in *A Treatise on Electricity and Magnetism*: in which, for the first time, all the existing but unconnected observations, experiments and equations on electricity, magnetism and light were pulled together. He showed that all are part of the earth's electro-magnetic field and that electro-magnetic fields spread at the speed of light.

Maxwell was born in Edinburgh, the son of a successful lawyer. Aged fourteen he published a remarkable and precocious scientific paper, *Oval Curves* (describing how to draw mathematical curves with string and the properties of ellipses and curves with more than two foci) which was presented to the Royal Society of Edinburgh. At sixteen he entered Edinburgh University; and later graduated from Cambridge – by which time he had, through private study, discovered photo-elasticity (which reveals stress distributions within physical structures). He went on to win lasting fame with his discovery that light is an electro-magnetic wave. He outlined the concept of electro-magnetic radiation in *On Physical Lines of Force* in 1861.

James Clerk Maxwell after a photograph by unknown photographer (*c*.1870s)
National Portrait Gallery, London

Einstein described Maxwell's work as the "most profound and the most fruitful that physics has experienced since the time of Newton". He kept photographs of Maxwell, Michael Faraday and Isaac Newton in his study.

He carried out important work in the study of colour: producing in 1861 the world's first colour photograph, of a tartan ribbon. He formulated the kinetic theory of gases, known as the "Maxwell Distribution"; and established the composition of Saturn's rings – as individual particles ("brick-bats"), each independently orbiting the planet. The Astronomer Royal, Sir George Biddell Airy FRS observed that: "It is the most remarkable application of mathematics to physics that I have ever seen". Maxwell's theory was confirmed nearly 150 years later by the *Voyager* satellite in the 1980s.

His ideas laid the basis for 20th century research into Quantum Mechanics; and investigations into atomic and molecular structures. In 1871 Maxwell became the first Cavendish Professor of Physics at Cambridge – and supervised the building of the world-famous Cavendish laboratory which opened in 1874.

Maxwell died of stomach cancer, which had also killed his mother, aged only forty-eight. His early death deprived the world of a genius. Despite his scientific brilliance however, he remained a committed Christian all his life: becoming an Evangelist in 1853. He loved poetry: and even wrote some of his own, strongly influenced by Robert Burns. He is buried at Parton Kirk, near Castle Douglas in Dumfriesshire.

LAWN TENNIS WAS PATENTED IN THE YEAR OF CHURCHILL'S BIRTH

Tennis (derived from the French *tenez*, meaning "to hold") probably originated in the cloisters of monasteries in France early in the 13th century. At the end of the 14th century Charles V built a court in the Louvre; and by 1592 Paris boasted 250 courts.

Introduced to England by King Henry V in the 1420s, the English were not far behind the French in their enthusiasm for the game. Though King Henry VIII built a court at Hampton Court Palace in 1530 for himself, common people were forbidden to play: and only those with an annual income of £100 or more (£500,000 today) were allowed to build a court on their property. This led inevitably to tennis, now known as Real (or Royal) Tennis, becoming a minority sport for the leisured classes. In the summer of 1873 however, Real Tennis was suddenly overtaken by a revolutionary variant.

In June 1873 Major Walter Clopton Wingfield (born in Ruabon, Denbighshire in 1833) called on Lord Lansdowne (later Governor General of Canada, Viceroy of India and Foreign Secretary), at his house in Berkeley Square: to ask if he could try out a new game he had invented for four players, on the lawn in front of Lansdowne's house. The first game of lawn tennis took place between Major Wingfield, Lord Lansdowne, Arthur Balfour (later Prime Minister) and Walter Long. The four found the game, called by Wingfield *Sphairistike* (Greek for "skill at playing ball games") but shortened to "Sticky", so enjoyable that they played together throughout the summer. *Sphairisitike* was an impossible name to remember: when Balfour suggested "Lawn Tennis", Wingfield agreed – and patented his game on 23 February 1874.

> A real tennis court *(jeu à dedans)* is larger than a lawn tennis court; enclosed by high walls on all sides, three of which have sloping roofs, and a buttress off which shots may be played. Courts are doubly asymmetric – each end of the court differs in shape from the other, and the left and right sides of the court are also different.

> In 1875 a standardised set of rules for Lawn Tennis was established. J.M. Heathcote, a Real Tennis player, finding the existing rubber balls too unpredictable, asked his wife to sew one up in flannel cloth – creating the tennis ball still used today.

Wingfield withdrew from any further involvement in Lawn Tennis and did not renew his patent in 1877. He never sought or made significant money from his game – though he also invented a "butterfly" folding bicycle and a tobacco mixture called "Wingfield" (still sold today). By the time of his death in 1912, his wife had gone mad and he had lost all three of his young sons. He was buried in Kensal Green Cemetery. After years of neglect, his grave is now maintained by the All England Lawn Tennis and Croquet Club (Wimbledon).

The first Lawn Tennis championship for men was held at Wimbledon in 1877; and for women in 1884. Today, the principal international team tournaments include the Davis Cup for men: and since 1963, the Federation Cup for women. The main tournaments for individual, now professional, players are those which comprise the "Grand Slam": the national championships of Britain (at Wimbledon), the US (at Flushing Meadow), Australia (in Melbourne) and France (the Roland-Garros, named after a WWI pilot). "Wimbledon", the only one played on grass, is still regarded as the most important.

SIR OSWALD MOSLEY

Sir Oswald Ernald Mosley, 6th Bt. was born on 16 November 1896 at 47, Hill Street in London. He was a brilliant but deeply flawed politician, who might have become a great statesman. Impatient with the rejection of his radical ideas for revitalising Britain after WWI, by both Labour and Conservative parties, he founded the British Union of Fascists.

His father, also Sir Oswald (1874–1928) was born in the same year as Winston Churchill. He was judicially separated from his wife Katherine (*née* Edwards-Heathcote of Betton Hall, near Market Drayton in Shropshire) when Oswald, the eldest of his three sons was only five. The boy was brought up by his adoring mother and his indulgent grandfather, the 4th Baronet

**Sir Oswald Mosley, 6th Bt.
by Glyn Warren Philpot
(1925)**

National Portrait Gallery, London

(1848–1915), at his huge neo-Gothic mansion at Rollestonon-Dove, near Newcastle-under-Lyme in Staffordshire. The Mosleys were an old, established Staffordshire landed family.

Katherine had parted from her husband, not only because of his serial infidelity but more importantly, to prevent him from bullying Oswald, whom she confusingly called Tom. Oswald (Tom) was educated at Winchester where he distinguished himself at boxing and fencing, winning the public schools fencing championship with both foil and sabre (he represented England with the épée in 1937, aged forty and despite a war wound). He entered the Royal Military Academy at Sandhurst in January 1914, from which he was rusticated briefly for loutish and drunken behaviour. At the outbreak of war on 4 August 1914 he was commissioned into the 16th Lancers.

Mosley volunteered immediately for the Royal Flying Corps, qualifying as a pilot in 1915. He nearly died in a crash, but survived with a permanent limp. He rejoined his regiment in time to take part in the second battle of Loos, where he was found unconscious at the bottom of a trench. It was discovered that he had collapsed because his leg injuries had not properly healed. He was sent home for further surgery which saved his leg but confined him to desk jobs for the rest of the war.

On returning home after the Armistice Mosley, though only 21, decided to enter politics. His platform, deriving from his trench experiences, was to build "a land fit for heroes" and to prevent another war. In 1918 he stood for the coalition Unionist (Conservative) seat of Harrow. Unexpectedly he won, becoming the youngest member in the House of Commons: where he made an immediate impact as a natural orator. In 1920 Mosley married Lady Cynthia Blanche Curzon (Cimmie). She was the second daughter of George Curzon, 1st Earl of Kedleston – once Viceroy of India, now Foreign Secretary.

Cimmie's mother Mary, *née* Leiter, was an American real estate heiress from Chicago. The Curzons initially regarded Mosley's advances with extreme suspicion – which turned out to be fully justified (he seduced both Cimmie's sister and her step-mother, amongst others). King George V and Queen Mary attended the wedding at the Chapel Royal in St James's, London.

Mosley soon fell out with the Conservatives, largely over the use of the infamous "Black and Tans" (demobilised soldiers) for suppressing Irish insurrection through reprisal. In November 1920, barracked by his party, Mosley crossed the floor of the house. Nonetheless, Mosley managed to hold on to his constituency as an independent in the general elections of 1922 and 1923, albeit with declining majorities. In March 1924 Mosley joined the Labour Party, which had just formed its first government under Ramsay MacDonald. He also joined the Independent Labour Party (ILP), thereby placing himself on the left of the political spectrum. The fledgling Labour government fell in October 1924. In the following general election, Mosley decided to abandon his Harrow seat and take the fight to Neville Chamberlain in Birmingham Ladywood, which he failed to take by only 77 votes.

In the two years Mosley was out of Parliament (1924–26) he set about energetically developing a new economic policy for the ILP, called the *Birmingham Proposals*. Mosley's ideas were brave and well ahead of their time. He suggested the creation of a massive programme of public works to address the increasing problem of unemployment, high import tariffs to protect British Industry from foreign predators and the nationalisation of Britain's principal industries (Hitler launched just such a programme in 1933 to solve Germany's dire inflation).

THE MODERN ERA 1874–1965

During a visit to the slums of Liverpool in 1926 Mosley said, "This is damnable. The re-housing of the working classes ought in itself to find work for the whole of the unemployed for the next ten years".

In the meantime he and Cimmie had travelled to India and the US where he met Franklin Roosevelt. He returned convinced of the dangers threatening the Lancashire cotton industry from cheap Indian labour and the importance of erecting trade barriers.

MAYNARD KEYNES

(John) Maynard Keynes, Baron Keynes of Tilton (1883–1946) was an economist, famous for his theories designed to relieve prolonged unemployment. He is regarded as the father of macroeconomics and the most influential economist of the 20th century.

He was born in Cambridge, the eldest of three children. His father, John Neville Keynes was a lecturer in economics at the University. A King's Scholar at Eton, he went up to King's College, Cambridge to study mathematics. He became active in the Apostles, a quasi-secret debating club, which attracted the most gifted undergraduates. During WWI he worked in the Treasury with such distinction that in 1917 he was appointed Companion of the Order of the Bath. He attended the Versailles Peace Conference in 1919 where he was frustrated in his attempts to prevent the imposition of excessive war reparations on Germany. He realised the dire consequences of the Treaty of Versailles and resigned, returning to teach at Cambridge.

He published his objections in 1919, in *The Economic Consequences of the Peace*. In 1935 he wrote *The General Theory of Employment, Interest and Money* in 1935. It explained some of the most profound economic theories ever published. Keynes rejected *laissez-faire* capitalism, suggesting instead that periods of economic depression could be ameliorated by increased public and private investment, to keep people in work and mitigate the cost of the dole. He argued that subdued economic activity could be invigorated by easing credit restrictions and reducing interest rates.

John Maynard Keynes, Baron Keynes by Gwendolen ('Gwen') Raverat (*née* Darwin) (*c.*1908)
National Portrait Gallery, London

The US was the first nation to put Keynes's ideas into practice – Franklin Roosevelt's "New Deal". During WWII, Keynes was appointed to the Court of the Bank of England; and in 1942 was raised to the peerage. A key participant at the 1944 Bretton Woods conference in the US, which was the cornerstone of European economic unity, he proposed a World Bank and an International Clearing Union (later the International Monetary Fund).

Keynes died on 21 April 1946, worn out by negotiating a US post-war loan to Britain. His celebrated observation, "in the long run we are all dead" came too early for him: if he had lived until 1969, he would have surely won the first Nobel Prize for Economics.

In the 1926 General Strike Mosley toured despairing and starving mining communities throughout Britain, making speeches and generous donations. He became closely associated with the miners' leader Arthur Cook, who secured his election

Keynes had an affair with the painter Duncan Grant (1885–1978). Grant was a lover of the historian and critic (Giles) Lytton Strachey (1880–1932). Strachey invented a new form of biography, in which psychological insight and sympathy are combined with irreverent wit – *Eminent Victorians* was published in 1918.

Strachey was openly homosexual, as were many of the "Bloomsbury Group", and was also a conscientious objector in WWI. When asked by the examining board, to test his conviction, what he would do if a Prussian Uhlan (cavalryman) attempted to rape his sister, he is said to have lisped, "I would interpothe my body".

After WWI Germany was obliged to export free coal to the allies, as part of her war reparations. This, and Winston Churchill's decision, as Chancellor of the Exchequer, to rejoin the gold standard in 1925, made British coal uncompetitive abroad. Colliery owners immediately threatened to impose longer hours for reduced wages to maintain profits. Stanley Baldwin (1867–1947), Conservative Prime Minister (1924–29), responded to the protests of the Miner's Federation by offering a nine-month subsidy and a Royal Commission to report on the coal industry. This respite, known as "Red Friday" and considered a victory for Socialism, was a false dawn: it simply bought the Government time to prepare for industrial turbulence.

The Commission, under Sir Herbert Samuel, reported in March 1926. Rejecting nationalisation, it recommended the withdrawal of the Government subsidy and supported the coal owners. Effectively wages would be reduced by 10–25%. The miners had to accept the new terms by 1 May or they would be locked out.

The Miner's Federation appealed to the Trades Union Council (TUC), which called for a General Strike in support, to begin on 3 May. With memories of the Bolshevik revolution still fresh, the TUC and Labour leaders were terrified that this would be suborned by revolutionary elements within the union movement. The TUC called out only workers in key industries – but the Government had created an Organisation for the Maintenance of Supplies (OMS) and prepared the army, to keep food stocks moving. Thousands of volunteer workers were ready to maintain basic services.

By raising the spectre of revolution ("The General Strike is a challenge to the Parliament and is the road to anarchy"), Baldwin rallied the public. When the army succeeded in transporting food from the docks, it was clear that the Government had regained the initiative. On 12 May Mr Justice Astbury, in a case brought by two trade unions resisting a strike call from the TUC, declared the strike illegal.

No longer covered by the Trades Disputes Act, the Government could sequester union funds. The TUC called off the strike, having gained nothing. The effect on the mining industry was profound. In 1926 1.2 million miners were employed: but by the outbreak of WWII, this number had fallen by a third. Output per man however, was over 300 tons – a level of productivity not seen since the early 1880s.

The Mosley Memorandum represented the high point of his career. In it he argued for a small "war cabinet", advised by an economic general staff headed by Maynard Keynes; Government protection of and investment in British industry; and a £200 million schedule of public works to be financed by borrowing. It is interesting to reflect that Mosley's proposals formed the basis of Franklin Roosevelt's "New Deal" which six years later pulled the US out of its own deep depression.

William Richard Morris, 1st Viscount Nuffield (1877–1963) was born in Worcester, but moved to Oxford aged three. In 1912 he founded the Morris Motor Company to make the 'Bull Nose' Morris car – by 1925 he was making 56,000 of them each year. He established the Nuffield Foundation for medical research in 1943, endowing it with £10 million (£1 billion today); and founded Nuffield College, Oxford. He died without an heir, leaving all his money to charity.

---

to the National Executive of the Labour Party (1927–30). In a by-election on 21 December 1926 Mosley was returned to Parliament for Smethwick, a suburb of Birmingham.

When Labour won the "Flapper" general election in 1929, Mosley was rewarded only with the post of Chancellor of the Duchy of Lancaster, outside the Cabinet and without portfolio. Ramsay MacDonald made him responsible for solving the problem of chronic unemployment: but Mosley found that his proposed, sweeping reforms were not being taken seriously either by his minister, the Lord Privy Seal J.H. Thomas, or by the Cabinet. In January 1930 he presented a wide ranging paper to the Cabinet, *The Mosley Memorandum* which he sent directly to MacDonald. It was immediately rejected.

On 20 May 1930 Mosley resigned. His hour-long resignation speech on 28 May, delivered without notes and with utter sincerity, presented cogently and clearly the case for a British 'New Deal'. He closed with the urgent appeal to the government, "I beg the Government tonight to give the vital forces of this country the chance they await. I beg Parliament to give that lead". Many in the House of Commons that night thought that they were listening to a future Prime Minister. In October 1930 however, when he tried again to get his ideas accepted by the Labour Party conference, he failed.

Despairing of the principal British political parties, Mosley plunged into the organization of a new party of his own, called the New Party, founded on 31 March 1931. Sir William Morris donated £50,000 but only five Labour M.P.s and one Tory joined him.

At first the only effect of the New Party was to split the Liberal-Labour vote in by-elections, enabling the Conservatives to win. Within a year though, Mosley's corporatist, economic policies began to attract attention from rising stars from both left and right of the political spectrum: including Harold Macmillan and Aneurin Bevan. Lord Rothermere (proprietor of the *Daily Mail*) campaigned strongly for Mosley.

Mosley attracted only limited support from either side of the House. 29 Labour M.P.s backed his vote of censure immediately after his resignation speech.

The following two years of frustration and despair quickly eroded the substantial reserves of political capital that Mosley had so carefully accumulated. Three distorted opinions fed his disastrous descent into political oblivion. He was convinced that Britain was about to be engulfed by an economic tsunami; that "the old gangs" were hopelessly ill-equipped to cope; and that only his war generation of disciplined servicemen had the will and understanding to rise to the challenge.

In 1931, before Mosley was able to organise and mobilise his New Party, another General Election was called. Mosley lost his seat and his candidates their deposits. In the dispiriting aftermath Mosley inclined his party more and more to the right, eventually to embrace Fascism; causing most of his original supporters to melt away.

Almost immediately the New Party became involved in street brawling, an activity in which Hitler's "Brown Shirts" *(Sturm Abteilung)* excelled. Labour loyalists and communists who feared the rise of fascism, as evinced by Mussolini in Italy, from the outset tried to break up New Party meetings. In response, Mosley formed a private army of stewards led by a famous boxer called Kid Lewis. The New Party's national platform rapidly became submerged in a general perception of thuggery, street battles and violence.

In the 1931 General Election the New Party came bottom of the polls: while the new National Government formed by the Conservatives, joined by Ramsay Macdonald and his best cabinet ministers, won a huge majority. There was no place for Mosley in the Labour Party (who had expelled him for disloyalty); nor had the Conservatives any need of his services either. At the age of only thirty-five Mosley was alone in the political wilderness, heading for certain destruction.

Only Mosley refused to see it that way, believing that all he had to do was to hang on until the national catastrophe he anticipated carried him to victory on the shoulders of the mob.

In 1933 his wife Cimmie died of peritonitis: leaving Mosley free to marry his mistress Diana, the wife of Bryan Guinness, Lord Moyne. Diana Mitford (1910–2003) was the third and most beautiful of Lord Redesdale's remarkable daughters. She divorced Lord Moyne and married Mosley in October 1936 at a ceremony in Berlin, with Hitler a guest at the reception.

Mosley had by now painted himself into an impossible corner. The BUF (the title was shortened to the British Union), trading on its novelty, had begun with an encouraging flow of recruits. It was soon apparent however that his party no longer had any rationale, save for the empty projections and tin-drum rantings of Mosley himself. For the rougher elements, who were naturally attracted to the prospect of fighting the "Reds" on the streets, the sound of

Harold Nicolson (1886–1968), diplomat, biographer and bisexual husband of Vita Sackville-West, herself famous for a lesbian affair with Violet Trefusis, was a recruit.

Fascism emphasises the supremacy of the nation, unquestioning obedience to its leader and ruthless suppression of dissent. Martial virtues are celebrated and democratic values disparaged. Fascism arose in the 1920s and 1930s as a reaction to the power of the emerging working classes. It differed from the Communism of Joseph Stalin's Russia only in supporting capitalism and the class system. Fascist leaders were presented as the embodiment of the strength needed to lead their nations out of chaos.

Oswald Mosley

marching feet and all the paraphernalia of sinister uniforms, night parades, drums and bands, it did not matter.

Mosley's choreographed, menacing meetings mostly repelled everyone else and frequently ended in violence. On 7 June 1934 Mosley held a huge rally at Olympia where his black-shirted "stewards" brutally expelled a number of hecklers – horrifying the large, mainly middle class audience. The façade of respectable fascism fell away, exposing the psychopaths behind.

By the mid 1930s the British Union had mired itself in a populist, but local to the East End of London, anti-Semitism – which culminated on 4 October 1936 in the Battle of Cable Street. The government was shocked and hastily passed the Public Order Act, banning uniformed political

P.G. Wodehouse (1881–1975) based the unlovable Roderick Spode, 7th Earl of Sidcup, an "amateur Dictator" and the leader of "The Black Shorts", on Mosley.

Harold Macmillan OM (1894–1986), created Earl of Stockton in 1984, Conservative Prime Minister from 1957–63 (nicknamed "Supermac"), was a clever, complex and, above all, lucky character. His grandfather, Daniel MacMillan or *Dòmhnall MacMhaolain* (1813–57), was the son of a crofter from the Isle of Arran, who founded Macmillan Publishers in 1843. Like Churchill's, Macmillan's mother was an American socialite: dominating and artistic. He was the last prime minister to have been born in the reign of Queen Victoria and to have fought in WWI; and, cutting a carefully contrived Edwardian facade to mask his shyness and self-doubt, the last to sport a moustache. To some he was an actor, a feline and careful "Iago": glib, brilliant at self-advancement and a superlative political assassin. Others might remember him more kindly as the last British statesman with the international attention (at least in his mind) accorded to the US president or Russian premier.

Macmillan's standing in Europe was insufficient however, to win British membership of the European Union in 1963: his application was met with a disconcerting "Non!" from the French president Charles de Gaulle – whom he had spent the best part of WWII, mostly in North Africa, trying to befriend. He spoke of the "winds of change" in 1961, a wise enough observation, which led to the dismantling of the British Empire: but thought it through too hastily, leaving many countries in Africa to fend for themselves before they were ready. It may be that he hoped his initiatives overseas would distract attention from the domestic issues he ignored.

Though another of his remarks, that "most of our people have never had it so good" in 1957, was true, especially if contrasted with the years of post-war austerity, in his six-year premiership he achieved little to modernise Britain's economy or protect her financial standing in the world. Indeed, despite Sir Walter Monckton's success in negotiating industrial settlements between 1951–54, Macmillan's failure to confront over-mighty left-wing led trades unions in the early 1960s led to fifteen years of social mayhem, manufacturing decline and soaring inflation.

From his early days as a scholar at Eton, which he left early (his homosexual inclinations as a sensitive young man were widely rumoured), and his experiences as a soldier, which were overblown, Macmillan stands accused of a number of devious sleights of hand and "understatements". With few close friends, his marriage, to a daughter of the 9th Duke of Devonshire, was miserable: she betrayed him sexually for years and belittled him socially. His determination to overcome these setbacks was admirable; but the way he did so is controversial. Those who see the worst in him believe that he should share the blame for returning 50,000 Cossacks to Russia and certain death in 1945, not just the wretched Lord Aldington who bore most of it alone: like T.S. Eliot's mystery cat, "For when they reach the scene of the crime, Macavity's not there". Most serious is the charge that, as Chancellor of the Exchequer, he shook the confidence of Anthony Eden, Prime Minister during the Suez Crisis in 1956, by inflating US disapproval into an implied threat to undermine the international value of sterling. Eden's subsequent nervous breakdown left Macmillan as the only credible candidate to replace him.

When asked what represented the greatest challenge for a statesman, the arch trimmer Macmillan replied with insouciance and practised condescension: "Events, dear boy, events". His resignation in October 1963, having been misdiagnosed with inoperable prostate cancer, was mourned by few; and he died with more credit and honour than he deserved or ever offered his opponents. His legacy was the corruption of many of the public service values and upright behaviour that had made Britain great – and ushered in the slick opportunism and 'spin' of today. Harold Wilson carried on where he left off.

• **Harold Macmillan, 1st Earl of Stockton by Bryan Organ (1980)**

National Portrait Gallery, London

assembly; after which the BU found it difficult to find anyone prepared to rent them premises for their meetings. Mosley had dug his political grave.

When war broke out, Mosley exhorted his followers to do nothing "to injure our country", but persisted in campaigning for peace. On 24 May 1940 Mosley, his wife and senior associates were all arrested under Regulation 18B as security risks. They were held in Brixton and Holloway prisons until 1943, when Home Secretary Herbert Morrison, worried that he might die in prison, released Mosley on medical grounds.

So what were the character defects that so violently blew Mosley off a course of outstanding political achievement? Theories abound: the instincts of a natural bully, fuelled by a privileged, aristocratic background; a spoiling, adoring mother; or a capacity for making unrealistic assessments which drove him to absurd actions – the list is endless. Perhaps the last word should come from Harold Macmillan, who probably came closest to identifying Mosley's fatal flaw, when he described it as an "insane impatience".

Mosley lingered on until dying of Parkinson's disease, at the beautiful home which Diana had created, *Temple de la Gloire* at Orsay, near Paris on 3 December 1980.

BEYOND THE FRINGE

Beyond the Fringe, a British comedy stage revue written and performed by Peter Cook (1937–95), Dudley Moore (1935–2002), Alan Bennett and Jonathan Miller (both born in 1934), played in the West End and on Broadway from 1960. Regarded as seminal to modern satire in Britain, The Establishment, and Harold Macmillan in particular, were attractive targets. This sketch was typical of their irreverent humour:

[Said by Squadron Leader to Flight Officer Perkins:] "I want you to take up a crate, Perkins". " Sah!". "Fly over to Jerry"; "Sah!". "And don't come back". "Sah!". "You are going to lay down your life, Perkins". "Sah!". "We need a futile gesture at this stage. It will raise the whole tone of the war". "Goodbye Sah!, or is it au revoir?" – "No, Perkins, goodbye".

Lady Diana Cooper by Emil Otto ('E.O.') Hoppé (1916)
National Portrait Gallery, London

"UPSTAIRS, DOWNSTAIRS"

Diana Olivia Winifred Maud Cooper, Viscountess Norwich (1892– 1986) was a socialite and actress, best known as Lady Diana Cooper. She married Duff Cooper, later 1st Viscount Norwich (1890–1954) in 1919, to the disappointment of her parents who had even hoped that she might marry the Prince of Wales – but Cooper was almost the last of her friends to have survived WWI. Her husband, a friend and colleague of Churchill, was a diplomat, cabinet minister, biographer and author. Their only son John Julius Norwich, the historian and travel writer, was born in 1929. Born Lady Diana Manners, she was officially the youngest daughter of the 8th Duke of Rutland and his wife, the former Violet Lindsay.

Lady Diana's biological father however, was widely known to be the writer Henry Cust, a very handsome man and a noted philanderer. She was said to be the most beautiful young woman in Britain. Countless profiles, photographs and articles in the press made her the Princess Diana of her era.

Henry (Harry) John Cockayne Cust (1861–1917) was an M.P., journalist and poet. An article by Maurice Chittenden in the 25 October

1998 issue of *The Sunday Times* suggested that in 1887 or 1888, Harry Cust had ravished Phoebe Stephenson, one of the domestic servants at Belton House, his family's estate near Grantham in Lincolnshire. Phoebe gave birth to a daughter Beatrice, in 1888 – supposedly fathered by Cust.

Beatrice Stephenson married Alfred Roberts, a Grantham grocer – and their daughter Margaret, married Denis Thatcher. If this rural gossip has any truth in it, Harry Cust, a cousin of the third Baron Brownlow, would be a grandfather of Margaret Hilda, Baroness Thatcher – the crusading first woman Prime Minister of Britain, from 1979–90.

GUSTAV HOLST WAS BORN IN 1874, THE SAME YEAR AS CHURCHILL

Gustav Theodore Holst was born in Cheltenham, Gloucestershire – of Swedish extraction, by way of Latvia and Russia. He is best remembered for *The Planets*, a seven-movement suite written between 1914–16. Holst died in 1934.

I Vow to Thee, My Country is an Anglican hymn. The lyrics were written by Sir Cecil Spring-Rice (1859–1918) in 1918, just after WWI. In 1921 the music of *Jupiter* from Holst's *Planets* suite was added. In hymnals, the melody is usually referred to as *Thaxted*. A deeply patriotic and moving song, a variation of the tune entitled *The World in Union* was a theme for the 2003 Rugby World Cup – which was won appropriately, by England (Jonny Wilkinson scored 113 points). Namibia did well to come last.

Thomas Hardy OM (1840–1928), novelist and poet, published *Far from the Madding Crowd* in 1874. He was born in Upper Bockhampton in Dorset.

Stan Laurel and Oliver Hardy

BIRTHS, DEATHS AND EVENTS IN 1965, THE YEAR CHURCHILL DIED

Joanne Kathleen (J.K.) Rowling, the author of the *Harry Potter* series, was born in Chipping Sodbury, Gloucestershire; Ian Smith declared UDI (Unilateral Declaration of Independence) for Southern Rhodesia (now Zimbabwe) on 11 November; Stanley Laurel, Oliver Hardy's 'stooge' (born Arthur Stanley Jefferson in Ulverston, Lancashire), died; Elizabeth Hurley, Lennox Lewis and Steve Coogan were born; Sir David Lean's *Doctor Zhivago* was first shown; Arthur Hailey published *Hotel*, Len Deighton published *Funeral in Berlin*, John Fowles published *The Magus*, John Le Carré (born David Cornwell) published *The Looking Glass War;* and Howard Spring (author of *My Son, My son*) died.

"THE MAN WHO BROKE THE BANK AT MONTE CARLO"

Joseph Hobson Jagger (1829–92), born near Halifax in Yorkshire, trained as an engineer in the textile industry. His experience of spinning machines led him to conclude that imperfections in roulette wheels might produce results that were anything but random – and that, with careful observation, these outcomes could be predicted.

In 1874, the year of Churchill's birth, Jagger spent months at the Beaux-Arts Casino in Monte Carlo just watching the play – until he saw that one of the six wheels showed a clear bias in favour of nine numbers. He placed his first bets on 7 July 1875 and proved his point. Over the next three days Jagger won a fortune – and other gamblers started to follow him. The casino rearranged the wheels: and Jagger began losing – until he found his favourite wheel again, which had a tiny scratch, and resumed his winning streak. Jagger and the casino attacked and counter-attacked for another two days, until Jagger gave up and left Monaco, never to return. He had won 2 million francs, then about £65,000 (over £33 million today). He resigned from his job and invested his money in property. He is buried at Bethel Church, Shelf.

In 1892 Fred Gilbert wrote a popular song, *The Man Who Broke the Bank at Monte Carlo*. The song refers in fact, to Charles Wells, another Englishman, who in 1891 also won a huge sum in Monte Carlo.

TEN OF THE BEST KNOWN BRITISH SONGS IN THE 1965 TOP HITS

[I Can't Get No] Satisfaction (The Rolling Stones)

Downtown (Petula Clark)

Help! (The Beatles)

What's New Pussycat? (Tom Jones)

Ticket To Ride (The Beatles)

I'm Telling You Now (Freddie and The Dreamers)

Ferry Cross The Mersey (Gerry and The Pacemakers)

Goldfinger (Shirley Bassey)

It's Not Unusual (Tom Jones)

The Last Time (The Rolling Stones)

Andrew Carnegie

ANDREW CARNEGIE DIED DURING THE VERSAILLES PEACE CONFERENCE

Andrew Carnegie (1835–1919), the leading American industrialist, was the most important philanthropist of his time. He was born in Dunfermline in Fife, the son of a weaver and Chartist agitator. In 1848 the introduction of the steam power loom threw his father out of work. The Carnegies emigrated to the US to settle in Allegheny, Pennsylvania. At twelve Carnegie was employed as a bobbin boy in a cotton factory, where he educated himself by attending night school.

In 1853, aged fourteen he became a messenger in a Telegraph office: where he caught the eye of Thomas Scott, the Superintendent of the Pennsylvania Railroad Company – who made him his private secretary and personal telegraph operator. Six years later Carnegie was made superintendent of the Railroad's Pittsburgh Division. In this position he was able to make a number of shrewd investments, most importantly in the Woodruff Sleeping Car Company: holder of the original Pullman patents which had introduced the first successful sleeping cars to the US railroads.

By the age of thirty, Carnegie was earning over $50,000 a year: with large stakes in The Keystone Bridge Company, The Superior Rail Mill and Blast Furnaces and the Pittsburgh Locomotive works. In 1865 he left the Pennsylvania Railroad to concentrate on steel. He founded the J. Edgar Thomson Steel Works, which soon became the Carnegie Steel Company.

Allan Pinkerton (1819–84), a fellow Scot born in Glasgow, emigrated to the US in 1842. In 1849 he was appointed as the first detective in Chicago.

In the 1850s he and Chicago attorney Edward Rucker founded the North-Western Police Agency, later known as the Pinkerton National Detective Agency – which is still in business. His insignia was a wide open eye with the caption "We never sleep". Pinkerton was the first to introduce two techniques still practised by police today: "shadowing" (surveillance of a suspect) and "assuming a role" (undercover work). Following the outbreak of the Civil War, Pinkerton served as head of the Union Intelligence Service in 1861–62 and is said to have foiled an attempt to assassinate Abraham Lincoln before his inauguration. His agents often worked undercover disguised as Confederate soldiers.

• Antietam, Md. Allan Pinkerton, President Lincoln, and Maj. Gen. John A. McClernand by Alexander Gardner

The Bessemer process was invented in 1856 by an Englishman, Sir Henry Bessemer (1813–98). The process, to turn pig-iron into steel, was first used commercially in 1860. Air blown through liquid pig-iron in a refractory-lined (heat resistant) converter oxidises carbon and silicon in the iron: resulting in the production of large, slag free steel ingots as malleable as wrought or cast iron.

He also invested in oil fields and travelled to Europe to raise bonds for American enterprise. He was the first to introduce the new Bessemer steelmaking process and quickly adopted every new technology that could reduce the cost of steel manufacture.

In 1889 Carnegie's huge holdings, embracing every part of the steel manufacturing process from mines to railroads and shipping, were amalgamated into the Carnegie Steel Company – whose production in 1890 surpassed that of Great Britain. By 1900, Carnegie was receiving annual personal profits of over $25m.

Carnegie bought Skibo Castle, near Dornoch in Sutherland, in 1898 and spent $2 million on rebuilding it

The Carnegie Steel company prospered even during the depression of 1892, marred by the bitter strikes at Carnegie's Homestead Steel plant. This strike lasted 143 days and was the one of the most serious in American labour history. Carnegie had left for Scotland before the crisis broke, leaving the management of the business in the hands of his associate and partner, the formidable "Union basher", Henry Clay Frick. Frick brought in thousands of strike breakers to work the mills, protected by a force of 300 hundred Pinkerton agents – seven strikers and three Pinkerton agents were killed and hundreds injured. Carnegie, who had always professed support for the Union movement, found his reputation permanently damaged. His ensuing devotion to philanthropy may have been an attempt at atonement for this shocking incident.

In 1901 he sold Carnegie Steel to J.P. Morgan's newly created US Steel Corporation for $250 million and retired to devote himself to philanthropy. Carnegie wrote extensively on political and social issues. His best-known article *Wealth* was published in the June 1898 edition of *The North American Review*, often referred to as *The Gospel of Wealth*. Carnegie's principle was that a man who "dies rich, dies disgraced" – in that a rich man has a duty to use his wealth for "the improvement of mankind".

Carnegie practised what he preached. Before he died he gave away $350,695,653 (around $15 billion today) to libraries and universities: founding the Carnegie Mellon University and endowing the Carnegie Institute of Pittsburgh and the Carnegie Corporation of New York, his largest foundation. He did not forget Scotland and gave substantial sums to his birthplace

Dunfermline, as well as Edinburgh, Glasgow and St Andrews Universities. He also installed organs in 3,800 churches and chapels in the UK.

He died on 11 August 1919 at his summerhouse "Shadowbrook" in Lenox, Massachusetts of bronchial pneumonia. He left his last $30,000,000 to foundations, charities and pensioners. He had said famously some time before, that the worst thing he could do for his children was to give them each a million dollars. What his children thought of this is not recorded. He was buried at the Sleepy Hollow Cemetery in North Tarrytown, New York.

Bletchley Park

BLETCHLEY PARK

Bletchley Park, now subsumed by Milton Keynes in Buckinghamshire, also known as Station X, was Britain's main code-breaking establishment in WWII. Codes and ciphers of several Axis countries were decrypted there, most famously the German *Enigma*. The high-level intelligence produced, code-named *Ultra*, shortened the war by months, possibly years. Bletchley Park is now a museum and open to the public.

In 1938 Bletchley Park was nearly sold to develop a housing estate. Admiral Sir Hugh Sinclair, nicknamed "Quex" (1873–1939), Director of Naval Intelligence, head of MI6 and founder of the Government Code and Cipher School (GCCS), intervened and bought it himself – having failed to persuade any government department to pay for it. The cover story for the first intake was "Captain Ridley's shooting party".

The estate was conveniently located on the "Varsity Line" between the Universities of Oxford and Cambridge, which supplied many of the code-breakers, at its junction with the railway line from London to Glasgow; near the A5 trunk road to London; and within easy access to a major telephone exchange.

GCCS (later GCHQ) moved into the mansion in 1939. A wireless room was set up in its water tower and code-named "Station X". Listening stations ("Y" Stations) at Chicksands, in Bedfordshire and Beaumanor Hall, in Leicestershire gathered and recorded coded messages by hand: and sent them to Bletchley on paper or later, by teleprinter. Station X is mainly remembered for decrypting *Enigma*, though its greatest achievement was the breaking of *Fish*, the German High Command teleprinter cipher. This contributed greatly to the Allied success in defeating the U-boats in the Battle of the Atlantic and to the British naval victories at Cape Matapan and the North Cape.

From 1943 a series of digital computers known as *Colossus* were constructed, to break a German teleprinter cipher known as *Tunny*. They were designed by Tommy Flowers (1905–98) and built by the Post Office facility at Dollis Hill, in north-west London.

American cryptographers were posted to Bletchley in 1942. An outpost was established at Kilindini in Kenya, to decipher Japanese codes: with skill and good fortune, it was so successful that 90% of the Japanese merchant marine had been destroyed by August 1945. Churchill described the code-breakers at Bletchley Park as the "geese that laid the golden eggs and never cackled". *Ultra* was kept secret by over 10,000 people for nearly 40 years – a discretion that is difficult to believe could be maintained today.

At its peak in January 1945, some 9,000 people worked at Bletchley Park. Recruits were chosen for various intellectual achievements: chess champions, crossword experts, polyglots and accomplished mathematicians. On one occasion the ability to solve *The Daily Telegraph* crossword in under 12 minutes was used as a test. The newspaper was persuaded to run a competition, after which each successful participant was contacted to see if he or she would be prepared to undertake "a particular type of work as a contribution to the war effort". The competition was won by F.H.W. Hawes of Dagenham who finished in less than 8 minutes.

THE TRAGIC LIFE OF ALAN TURING, THE GENIUS OF BLETCHLEY PARK

**Alan Turing slate statue
at Bletchley Park**

Alan Mathison Turing was conceived in Chatrapur in Orissa, British India. His father Julius Mathison Turing, a member of the Indian Civil Service and his wife Sara (*née* Stoney) wanted Alan to be brought up in England: so they returned to Maida Vale in London where Alan was born on 23 June 1912. Very early in life Turing showed signs of genius. He taught himself to read in three weeks and showed an amazing affinity for numbers and puzzles. In 1926 he went to Sherborne School in Dorset. Despite the General Strike, he was so determined to attend his first day that he rode his bicycle over 60 miles, staying overnight at an inn – aged fourteen.

Turing's natural inclination toward mathematics and science did not endear him to his teachers at Sherborne, where emphasis was placed on the classics. His headmaster wrote to his parents, "I hope he will not fall between two stools. If he is to stay at public school, he must aim at becoming educated. If he is to be solely a Scientific Specialist, he is wasting his time at a public school". Nevertheless, Turing continued to demonstrate his remarkable abilities. Aged sixteen he encountered Albert Einstein's work: not only did he grasp it but he extrapolated Einstein's questioning of Newton's laws of motion, from a text in which this was never made explicit.

He graduated from King's College, Cambridge; and in 1935 was elected a fellow, on the strength of a dissertation on the Gaussian error function. In a momentous paper *On Computable Numbers, with an Application to the Entscheidungsproblem* (submitted on 28 May 1936), Turing reformulated Kurt Gödel's 1931 results on the limits of proof and computation. He substituted Gödel's universal arithmetic-based formal language with what are now called "Turing machines". He proved that such machines are capable of performing any conceivable mathematical task, if represented as an algorithm.

> Turing fell in love with his friend Christopher Morcom but this was not reciprocated. Morcom died suddenly, a few weeks into their last term at Sherborne, from bovine tuberculosis contracted as a child from drinking infected cow's milk.

A SIMPLE FLOW CHART

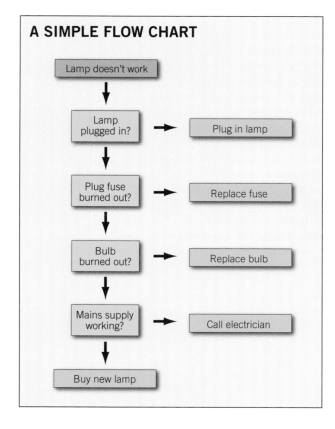

Al-Khwarizmi, the Persian astronomer and mathematician, wrote a treatise in Arabic in 825: *On Calculation with Hindu Numerals*. The text was translated into Latin in the 12th century as *Algoritmi de numero Indorum* – where "Algoritmi" was a rendition of the author's name. The word "algorithm" now means a "method of calculation".

In simple terms, an algorithm is a "tick list" of questions to be answered with a "yes" or "no". The methodology began as a way of recording procedures for solving mathematical problems. It was formalised in 1936, through Alan Turing's machines and Alonzo Church's *lambda calculus*. Algorithms are the basis of all computer science.

Su Doku puzzles require the use of a primitive algorithm, with a pencil and eraser acting as a *bombe*.

• **A simple flow chart, a 3–rotor Enigma**

Turing spent most of 1937–38 at Princeton University, studying under Alonzo Church; returning to Cambridge in 1939. On 4 September 1939, the day after Britain declared war on Germany, he reported to Bletchley Park, the wartime station of GCCS.

At a top-secret meeting in the Pyry Forest near Warsaw at the end of July 1939, Polish cryptologists handed over details of their success in decrypting German military signals, and demonstrated an *Enigma* machine to French and British agents. Knowing that the Nazis were on the point of invading Poland, the Poles managed to deliver working models of the machine to each country via diplomatic channels, a fortnight later. This farsighted and unselfish Polish contribution to the Allied war effort was of enormous value – and this is, most unfairly, often overlooked.

A 3–rotor Enigma G

Turing designed an electro-mechanical *bombe* (an improvement on the rudimentary Polish *bomba*). The *bombe*, with a further refinement suggested by the mathematician Gordon Welchman (1906–85), was the most important tool used to decipher *Enigma* – the very possibility of which the Germans seem never to have considered.

In the spring of 1941, Turing proposed marriage to Hut 8 co-worker Joan Clarke. The engagement was broken off by mutual agreement in the summer.

Turing's ingenious device searched for the correct settings of the *Enigma* rotors. A "crib", a piece of matching plain text and ciphertext, was needed. For each possible setting of the rotors, the *bombe* performed a chain of logical deductions based on the crib, implemented electrically. The *bombe* detected when a contradiction had occurred, ruling out that setting and moving onto the next. Settings that caused contradictions were discarded, until only a few were left to be investigated in detail. The first *bombe* was installed on 18 March 1940. By the end of the war there were over 200.

Conway Berners-Lee, one of the Manchester team, was the father of Sir Timothy (Tim) Berners-Lee OM (born 1955), who invented the 'World Wide Web' in 1989.

In December 1940, as head of Hut 8 (which read German naval signals), Turing solved the complex naval *Enigma* indicator system. He also invented a "Bayesian" measurement [of probability] he called *Banburismus*, which could rule out certain orders of the *Enigma* rotors, reducing the time needed to test settings on the *bombe*s.

A bombe machine

In July 1942 Turing devised a technique termed *Turingismus* or *Turingery* for use against *Fish*, a Lorenz teleprinter cipher; and introduced the *Fish* team to Tommy Flowers, who went on to create *Colossus*, the world's first electronic computer. It is often said that Turing designed *Colossus* – this was not the case, though clearly he was closely involved.

In the latter part of the war, teaching himself electronics at the same time Turing, assisted by engineer Donald Bayley, designed a portable machine codenamed *Delilah* to allow secure voice communications. However, *Delilah* could not be used for long-distance radio transmissions; and was completed too late to be used in the war.

From 1945–47 Turing worked on the design of the ACE (Automatic Computing Engine), at the National Physical Laboratory at Teddington in Middlesex; and in 1946 he presented the first blueprint for a stored-programme computer in Britain. In late 1947 he returned to Cambridge for a sabbatical year (while he was at Cambridge, the ACE was completed and ran its first programme, on 10 May 1950). In 1949 he became deputy director of the computing laboratory at the University of Manchester, programming the software for the earliest proper computer – the Manchester Mark I. In *Computing Machinery and Intelligence* (in *Mind*, October 1950) he proposed the "Turing test", to measure "sentience" (the level of artificial intelligence).

Turing worked from 1952 until his death on morphogenesis (mathematical biology). In *The Chemical Basis of Morphogenesis* he proposed reaction-diffusion equations which are now central to the study of pattern formation. His later papers were published in 1992, as the *Collected Works of A.M. Turing*.

> Turing was a world-class marathon runner. His best time (2 hrs: 46 mins: 3 secs) in 1947, was only 11 minutes slower than the winner's in the 1948 Olympic Games.

Turing was homosexual at a time when homosexuality was illegal in England and regarded as a mental illness. In 1952 Arnold Murray, a nineteen year-old recent acquaintance, and an accomplice broke into Turing's house. As a result of the police investigation, Turing acknowledged a sexual relationship with Murray. They were both charged with gross indecency. Turing was unrepentant and was convicted. He was forced to choose between imprisonment and probation, provided he accepted hormonal treatment designed to reduce libido. He was given oestrogen injections for a year, with side effects that included the development of breasts. His security clearance was removed, which terminated his consultancy with GCHQ.

> Leaving aside the bigoted, cruel insensitivity of the treatment inflicted on Turing, the stupidity of it is mind-boggling. His genius was an irreplaceable national asset – one only has to imagine the loss to science if Newton had been hounded to death in such a way. The Russians would simply have provided Turing with a stream of "rent boys".

He died, aged forty-one on 7 June 1954. A cyanide-laced apple was left half-eaten. Though his death was ruled as suicide, he may have killed himself in an ambiguous way deliberately, to spare his mother. The US Apple Computer company is believed to have been so named in honour of Turing. Since 1966, the A.M. Turing Award has been given annually by the Association for Computing Machinery for technical contributions to computing. It is considered the computing world's equivalent of the Nobel Prize.

On 23 June 1998, 86 years after his birth, an English Heritage Blue Plaque was unveiled on his house in Warrington Crescent, London – now the Colonnade Hotel.

William Stephenson

"THE QUIET CANADIAN"

Sir William Samuel Stephenson CC (1896–1989) was the senior British intelligence officer in the western hemisphere during WWII, with the code-name "Intrepid".

He was born near Winnipeg of Scottish and Icelandic ancestry. He left school at fourteen to work as a telegrapher. In January 1916 he sailed to England with the Canadian Expeditionary Force. In August 1917 he was commissioned into the RFC and posted to 73 Squadron. Known as "Little Bill", he was 5 foot 5 inches tall – an ideal size for a fighter pilot, fitting snugly into the cramped cockpit of the dangerous, yet highly manoeuvrable Sopwith Camel biplane. He had already shot down at least six German aircraft before he was accidentally shot down himself in July 1918 and captured. He was released in December with the rank of Captain, having been awarded the Military Cross and the Distinguished Flying Cross, for "conspicuous gallantry".

Stephenson returned to Winnipeg and started a hardware business. When the business failed he returned to Britain. In 1924 he married an American tobacco heiress, Mary French Simmons. Her financial support, with his flair and energy had made him a millionaire before he was thirty: with supposed interests ranging from the electrical, automotive and steel industries to construction and real estate. He is also said to have invented a device for sending photographs by wireless. Little confirmation of this exists.

By April 1936, using information acquired on his business travels, Stephenson had begun to pass German intelligence to Winston Churchill. In June 1940 as Prime Minister, despite the protests of the head of the Secret Intelligence Service (SIS), Sir Stewart Menzies, Churchill sent Stephenson to New York to establish a covert intelligence office: the British Security Coordination (BSC). It was more than a year before the US entered the war – his cover was as a British Passport Control Officer.

By 1945 the BSC (telegraphic address: *Intrepid*), had become an umbrella organization representing MI5, MI6 (SIS), SOE (Special Operations Executive) and PWE (Political Warfare Executive) throughout North and South America and the Caribbean. Stephenson's initial instructions for BSC were first, to investigate enemy activities; second, to institute security measures against the threat of sabotage to British property; and finally, to organise US public opinion in support of Britain. Later this was expanded to include, "the assurance of American participation in secret activities throughout the world in the closest possible collaboration with the British".

Stephenson became an advisor to President Roosevelt and recommended his friend William ("Wild Bill") Donovan (1883–1959) to him as the chief of all US intelligence services. Donovan founded the US wartime Office of Strategic Services (OSS) – which eventually became the Central Intelligence Agency (CIA). He made it his business to stay close to J. Edgar Hoover, the powerful head of the FBI. Whatever else, Stephenson knew how to cultivate important friendships – which paid great dividends to Britain.

The BSC directly influenced the US media, most importantly well-known syndicated US journalists, towards consistently and strongly pro-British, anti-Axis comment.

Not least amongst Stephenson's contributions to the war effort was the establishment by BSC of Camp X at Whitby in Ontario, the first training school for clandestine wartime operations in North America. Camp X trained over 2,000 agents, including five future directors of the CIA, to operate across Europe, Africa and the Far East. One of his trainees was Ian Fleming.

This much is true: sadly, later in life Stephenson embellished his biography ridiculously. He claimed twenty more air victories, the French *Légion d'Honneur* and *Croix de Guerre*, two extra bars to his DFC, the world amateur lightweight boxing title – and participation, if not a leading role, in increasing the production of the Spitfire, decoding Enigma messages, developing the atom bomb and promoting the jet engine. His fantasies explain why it took the Canadian government so long to honour him – a great pity, as his contribution to winning the war was real enough.

Stephenson, later known as "the Quiet Canadian", was one of the few people authorised to view raw "Ultra" transcripts from Bletchley Park. He was trusted by Churchill to decide what information to pass on to US and Canadian agencies.

Stephenson was unpaid. He hired hundreds of people to staff his organization and paid for much of the expense himself. Among his employees was the future advertising mogul David Ogilvy, who founded Ogilvy and Mather in 1948.

In Fleming's novel *Goldfinger*, the raid on Fort Knox was inspired by a Stephenson plan to steal $2.9 billion in Vichy gold reserves from the French Caribbean island colony of Martinique. It was never carried out.

**Francis Bacon by
Ruskin Spear (1984)**
National Portrait Gallery, London

**Lucian Freud OM by
Sir Jacob Epstein (1949)
Bronze head**
National Portrait Gallery, London

**David Hockney OM in his
studio with his self-portrait
and painting My Parents
by Bernard Lee ("Bern")
Schwartz (July 1977)**
National Portrait Gallery, London

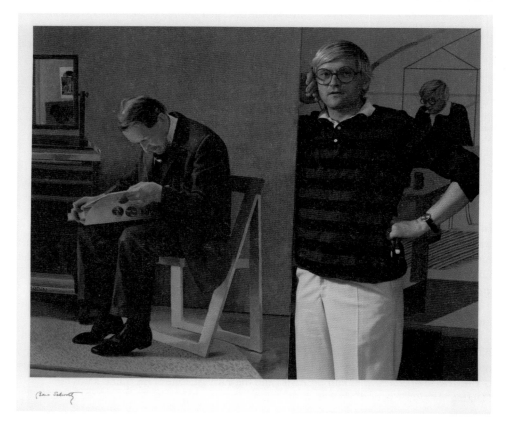

Stephenson was knighted in 1945: Churchill wrote, "This one is dear to my heart". In 1946 he was the first non-US citizen to receive the Presidential Medal for Merit, the highest US civilian award at the time. The citation paid tribute to Stephenson's "valuable assistance to America in the fields of intelligence and special operations". "The Quiet Canadian" was at last recognised in his native land and invested as a Companion of the Order of Canada in 1980. He died in Bermuda aged ninety-three.

Ian Fleming wrote that: "James Bond is a highly romanticised version of a true spy. The real thing is …. William Stephenson". Fleming however, was fooled as much as everyone else, except the wily Stewart Menzies – there was nothing "real" about Stephenson at all. In this at least he was indeed, the perfect secret agent.

THREE GREAT MODERN BRITISH ARTISTS ALREADY AT WORK IN 1965

Born Damien Brennan in Bristol on 7 June 1965, Damien Hirst was adopted and brought up in Leeds. A "conceptual" or "installation" artist, with death as his central theme, Hirst was claimed in 2009 to be the richest living artist in the world.

Francis Bacon was born in Dublin on 28 October 1909. An Anglo-Irish figurative painter, he was a collateral descendant of the brilliant Elizabethan philosopher and Lord Chancellor Francis Bacon. His painting is known for bold, austere artwork and often grotesque or nightmarish imagery. On 15 May 2007 his *Study for Innocent X* (1962) was sold for $52,680,000. He died in London on 28 April 1992.

Lucian Freud OM, grandson of Sigmund Freud (1856–1939), was born in Berlin on 8 December 1922; but came to Britain in 1933 and was naturalized in 1938. He was educated at Bryanston School in Dorset. Freud's first solo exhibition, at the Lefèvre Gallery in 1944, featured the now celebrated *The Painter's Room*. His portrait of Sue Tilley, *Benefits Supervisor Sleeping* (1995) was sold for $33,640,000 on 13 May 2008. He died 20 July 2011.

David Hockney OM, R.A. was born in Bradford in Yorkshire, on 9 July 1937. He was for long based in Los Angeles – and has used the brilliant Californian light and colours, especially in swimming pool scenes with acrylics, to great effect. He was a founder of the Pop Art movement and is a superb draughtsman. Known as the "playboy of the art world", he is the most influential British artist of his generation. One of his early paintings, *The Splash* (1966) was sold for £2,600,000 on 21 June 2006.

Field Marshal Smuts

FIELD MARSHAL SMUTS OM CH KC FRS

Smuts was the only man to sign the treaties which ended both WWI and WWII. As the architect of the League of Nations and the author of the preamble to the United Nations Charter, he was also the only signatory of both charters. Of greatest significance perhaps, by redefining the relationship between Britain and her Empire, he proposed the British Commonwealth. Smuts's importance within the Imperial War Cabinet in WWII was such that a suggestion was made in late 1940 to appoint him as Prime Minister of Britain, if Churchill died or became incapacitated. The idea was first put by Sir John Colville, Churchill's private secretary to Queen Mary, then to King George VI; both of whom endorsed it.

Fortunately Churchill lived for another twenty-five years – but his closeness to the British establishment, to the King and to Churchill made Smuts even more unpopular amongst Afrikaners in South Africa than he already was.

Cecil John Rhodes (1853–1902), son of the Reverend Francis William Rhodes, was born in Bishop's Stortford in Hertfordshire. A sickly child, he attended the local grammar school instead of following his brothers to Eton or Winchester – and was then sent to join the eldest Herbert in Natal to improve his health.

He followed Herbert to the new diamond fields at Kimberley in Griqualand, which had recently been annexed by Britain: where his acumen and managerial skills enabled him to make £10,000 (over £5 million today) in a remarkably short period of time. Hoping to become a barrister, he was accepted by Oriel College, Oxford in 1873.

However, at the end of his first term, following his mother's death and with consumptive lungs he returned to Kimberley – to turn a modest fortune into an enormous one. In April 1880 Rhodes and C.D. Rudd established the De Beers Mining Company, after amalgamating a number of individual claims. De Beers today controls 60% (once 90%) of the world's diamonds.

Rhodes became Prime Minister of Cape Colony. He was a supreme imperialist, saying: "I contend that we [the Anglo-Saxons] are the first race in the world and that the more of the world we inhabit the better it is for the human race". He is also supposed to have said that, "to be born an Englishman is to win first prize in the lottery of life". If he did not say this, Rhodes certainly declared: "all of these stars .... these vast worlds that remain out of reach. If I could, I would annex other planets".

Rhodes's British South Africa Company annexed Mashonaland and Matabeleland to form the state of Rhodesia which was named after him. Rhodesia (later Northern and Southern Rhodesia) eventually became Zambia and Zimbabwe respectively. He had hoped that his new country would straddle the route of his dream: a Cape to Cairo railway that ran only through British or British controlled territory.

In his will he established Rhodes Scholarships. The programme enables students from territories once under British rule, from the USA or from Germany (all Anglo-Saxon, as Rhodes saw it), to study at Oxford University.

• **Cecil John Rhodes by George Frederick Watts (1898)**
National Portrait Gallery, London

Jan Christiaan Smuts was born on 24 May 1870 at Bovenplaats, near Malmesbury in Cape Colony (now South Africa's largest province). His family were prosperous, traditional Afrikaner farmers, long established and highly respected. Jan was a quiet, delicate child and strongly independent – often exploring the surrounding countryside on his own. He retained a passion for nature throughout his life.

Smuts graduated from Victoria College, Stellenbosch in 1891 with double First Class Honours in Literature and Science. Having also won the Ebden scholarship for overseas study, he left South Africa to read law at Christ's College, Cambridge. While at Cambridge Smuts wrote a book, *Walt Whitman: A Study in the Evolution of Personality*, although it was unpublished. The thinking evident in this book developed later in his life into a belief in holism ("The whole is more than the sum of its parts").

Smuts graduated from Cambridge in 1893 with another double First. Over the previous two years, he had won numerous academic prizes and other accolades. One of his tutors, Professor Maitland described Smuts as the most brilliant student he had ever met. Lord Todd, the Master of Christ's College said in 1970, that "in 500 years of the College's history, of all its members, past and present, three had been truly outstanding: John Milton, Charles Darwin and Jan Smuts". Einstein was later to say that Smuts was "one of only eleven men in the world" who fully understood his *Theory of Relativity*.

In 1894, Smuts passed the bar examinations and entered the Middle Temple. Christ's College also offered him a fellowship in Law. However Smuts turned his back on a potentially distinguished legal future; and in June 1895, returned to South Africa.

Smuts found it difficult to make money from the law. Intrigued by the idea of a united South Africa, he turned to politics and journalism; and joined the Afrikander Bond. Its leader, Jan Hofmeyr introduced him to Cecil Rhodes who owned the De Beers mining company.

Map of Africa, showing the colonial boundaries in 1913: A map of Africa, showing colonial boundaries in 1913 (the "Scramble for Africa"). In southern Africa: German South West Africa is now Namibia, Bechuanaland is Botswana, Basutoland is Lethotho, Northern Rhodesia is Zambia, Southern Rhodesia is Zimbabwe, Mozambique is Maputo and Nyasaland is Malawi. Only German East Africa, later Tanganyika (now Tanzania), stood in the way of Rhodes's dream – a Cape to Cairo railway, across British or British-controlled territory.

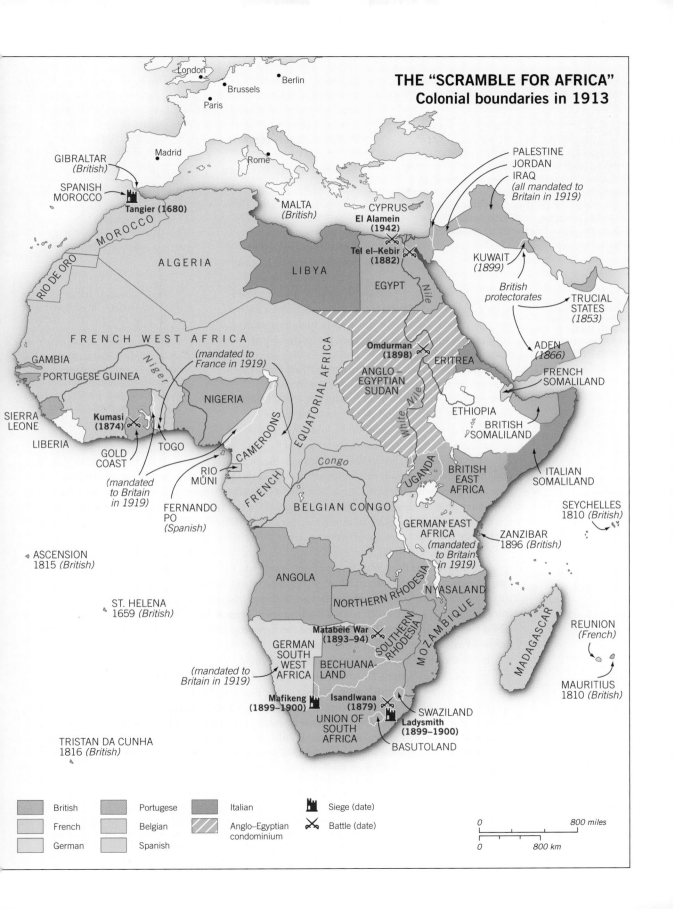

THE "SCRAMBLE FOR AFRICA"
Colonial boundaries in 1913

GIBRALTAR
(British)

SPANISH
MOROCCO

Tangier (1680)

MOROCCO

RIO DE ORO

ALGERIA

MALTA
(British)

LIBYA

EGYPT

Nile

CYPRUS
El Alamein
(1942)

Tel el–Kebir
(1882)

PALESTINE
JORDAN
IRAQ
(all mandated to
Britain in 1919)

KUWAIT
(1899)

British
protectorates

TRUCIAL
STATES
(1853)

ADEN
(1866)

FRENCH
SOMALILAND

London
Brussels
Paris
Berlin
Madrid
Rome

FRENCH   WEST   AFRICA

(mandated to
France in 1919)

GAMBIA

PORTUGESE GUINEA

SIERRA
LEONE

LIBERIA

Niger

NIGERIA

Kumasi
(1874)

GOLD
COAST

TOGO

(mandated
to Britain
in 1919)

FERNANDO
PO
(Spanish)

RIO
MUNI

CAMEROONS

EQUATORIAL AFRICA

FRENCH

Congo

BELGIAN CONGO

ANGLO–
EGYPTIAN
SUDAN

White Nile

Omdurman
(1898)

ERITREA

ETHIOPIA

BRITISH
SOMALILAND

ITALIAN
SOMALILAND

UGANDA

BRITISH
EAST
AFRICA

GERMAN EAST
AFRICA
(mandated
to Britain
in 1919)

ZANZIBAR
1896 (British)

SEYCHELLES
1810 (British)

ASCENSION
1815 (British)

ST. HELENA
1659 (British)

ANGOLA

NORTHERN RHODESIA

NYASALAND

MOZAMBIQUE

SOUTHERN
RHODESIA

Matabele War
(1893–94)

GERMAN
SOUTH
WEST
AFRICA

(mandated to
Britain in 1919)

BECHUANA-
LAND

Mafikeng
(1899–1900)

Isandlwana
(1879)

UNION OF
SOUTH
AFRICA

Ladysmith
(1899–1900)

SWAZILAND

BASUTOLAND

MADAGASCAR

REUNION
(French)

MAURITIUS
1810 (British)

TRISTAN DA CUNHA
1816 (British)

British

French

German

Portugese

Belgian

Spanish

Italian

Anglo–Egyptian
condominium

Siege (date)

Battle (date)

0   800 miles

0   800 km

The Jameson Raid into Paul Kruger's Republic was carried out by Dr Leander Starr Jameson (1853–1917) and his Rhodesian and Bechuanaland policemen, over the New Year weekend of 1895–96. It was intended to trigger an uprising by the primarily British expatriate workers (known as *Uitlanders*) in the Transvaal. The raid was a disastrous failure and no uprising took place: but it did much to bring about the Second Matabele War – and the Second Boer War.

Rudyard Kipling said that his famous poem *"If–"* was written in celebration of Jameson's courage in bouncing back from his absurd adventure.

Mohandas Karamchand ('Mahatma') Gandhi by Elliot & Fry (1931). Gandhi served as an ambulance driver in WW1
National Portrait Gallery, London

Rhodes hired Smuts as his personal legal advisor. Smuts trusted Rhodes implicitly in spite of harsh criticism of him in the hostile Afrikaner press.

When Rhodes launched the Jameson Raid on 29 December 1895, Smuts was outraged and resigned from De Beers: and seeing no future in Cape Town, moved to Johannesburg in August 1896. However he was disgusted by what seemed to be a gin-soaked mining camp: and realised that his new law practice would do little business in this environment. Smuts moved to Pretoria, capital of the independent South African Republic.

Smuts's politics had been turned on their head. He was transformed from being Rhodes's most ardent supporter into being the most fervent opponent of British expansion. In late 1896 and 1897 Smuts toured South Africa, condemning Britain, Rhodes and anyone opposed to the Transvaal President, the autocratic Paul Kruger.

After the Jameson Raid, relations between the British and the Afrikaners steadily deteriorated: until, in early 1899 war was inevitable. The Orange Free State President, Martinus Steyn called for a peace conference at Bloemfontein on 31 May. With an intimate knowledge of the British, Smuts led the Transvaal delegation. However the German-born British High Commissioner, Sir Alfred Milner (1854–1925) was intransigent. The conference collapsed, Kruger left in tears and war was inevitable.

On 11 October 1899 the Boer republics invaded the British colonies in South Africa, sparking the Second Boer War. At the outset Smuts was Kruger's amanuensis: handling propaganda, logistics, communication with generals and diplomats – and anything else that was required. As the war turned against the Afrikaners, Smuts organised the successful retreat from Pretoria. The British offered the Boers an olive branch, but Smuts refused to negotiate whilst there was still hope. He restructured the surviving Afrikaner units into elite fast-moving mounted infantry units called "commandos".

In the second phase of the war Smuts served under Koos de la Rey, who led a 500–strong commando in the Western Transvaal. Smuts excelled at hit-and-run warfare. The Commandos evaded and harassed a British army, known by the Boers as the "Khakis", forty times its size.

Now called *Oom Jannie* ("Uncle Jannie") he took the war to Cape Colony with a small force of 300 men, while another 100 men followed him. By the time of the Peace Conference in May 1902 he had 3,300 men under his command.

To bring an end to the war, Smuts decided on a final flourish – to take a major target, the copper-mining town of Okiep in the Northern Cape. With a full assault impossible, Smuts

Smuts's raid was to prove one of the most influential military adventures of the 20th Century. It had a direct influence on the creation of the British Commandos and all the other special forces which followed. With these practical developments came the evolution of the military doctrines of deep penetration raids, asymmetric warfare and today, the tactics of terrorism.

packed a train full of explosives; and tried to push it downhill into the town. Although this failed, Smuts had proved that he would stop at nothing to exasperate the British. Combined with their failure to pacify the Transvaal, Smuts's success persuaded Britain to offer a ceasefire and a peace conference, to be held at Vereeniging.

Before the conference, Smuts met Lord Kitchener at Kroonstadt station to discuss the terms of surrender. Smuts then took a leading role in the negotiations between the representatives of all of the commandos from the Orange Free State and the South African Republic (15–31 May 1902). Although he admitted that, from a purely military perspective, the war could continue, he stressed the importance of not sacrificing the Afrikaner people for that independence. He was very conscious that more than 20,000 women and children had "already died in the Concentration Camps of the enemy". He felt it would have been a crime to continue the war without the assurance of help from elsewhere. Representatives of the Boer Governments met Lord Kitchener: and at 11:05 on 31 May 1902, they signed the Peace Treaty.

Nothing could mask the fact that the Afrikaners had been defeated and humiliated. Lord Milner, who had been elevated to the peerage in 1901, had full control of all South African affairs: and had established an Anglophone elite, known as Milner's Kindergarten (the author John Buchan was his personal assistant). As an Afrikaner, Smuts was excluded. Defeated but not deterred, in January 1905 he decided to join other Transvaal generals to establish a new political party, *Het Volk* (The People's Party), to fight for the Afrikaner cause. Louis Botha was elected leader and Smuts his deputy.

When the Conservative government under Arthur Balfour collapsed in December 1905, Smuts joined Botha in London to seek support for *Het Volk* and full selfgovernment for the Transvaal, within a British South Africa. Exploiting the thorny issue of Asian labourers ("coolies"), the South Africans convinced Prime Minister Sir Henry Campbell-Bannerman, his cabinet and Parliament.

Smuts prepared a constitution for the Transvaal: and, in December 1906,

The British have been castigated for introducing "Concentration Camps" and treating their inmates badly. It is true that to start with, they failed to control disease and malnutrition and many died. But conditions quickly improved, to such an extent that Botha came to say, "One is only too thankful nowadays to know that our wives are under English protection". In fact he said that it was the women and children not in the camps who were "in the most pitiable state". More than anything else, it was this, not defeat in the field, that forced the Boers to negotiate a surrender. Furthermore, a dark truth not much discussed until recently, is that by 1902 over a fifth of the Afrikaners still in the field were fighting for the British.

John Buchan was born on 26 August 1875 in Perth, son of a Free Church of Scotland minister. He won a scholarship to Glasgow University and then to Brasenose College, Oxford. He won the Stanhope Essay Prize in 1897 and the Newdigate prize for poetry in 1898. In 1901 he became a barrister in the Middle Temple; but went to South Africa as private secretary to the High Commissioner, Lord Milner (1901–03). *Prester John*, published in 1910, was based on his South African experiences. During WWI he wrote for the War Propaganda Bureau and was a correspondent for *The Times* in France.

In 1915 he published his most famous book *The Thirty-Nine Steps*, a spy thriller set just before the outbreak of war, featuring his hero *Richard Hannay* whose character was based on [Field Marshal] Edmund Ironside (1880–1959). The following year he published a sequel *Greenmantle*, in which the hero *Sandy Arbuthnot* was inspired by another friend, an intelligence officer and key member of the Arab Bureau, Aubrey Herbert (1878–1967). In 1916 Buchan joined the British Army Intelligence Corps where, as a 2nd Lieutenant he wrote speeches and communiques for Field Marshal Sir Douglas Haig (1861–1928).

Buchan wrote over a hundred books, of which about forty were fiction. *The Thirty-Nine Steps* was filmed, greatly altered, by Alfred Hitchcock (1899–1980) in 1935 – and even less accurate versions followed, in 1959 and 1978.

From 1927–35 Buchan was a Conservative M.P. for the Scottish universities; and Lord High Commissioner of the Church of Scotland (1933–34). He died, as 1st Baron Tweedsmuir of Elsfield, Governor-General of Canada (1935–40) and Chancellor of Edinburgh University, in Montreal on 11 February 1940.

• **John Buchan, 1st Baron Tweedsmuir by Bassano (1883)**
National Portrait Gallery, London

elections were held for the new parliament. Despite being shy and reserved, unlike the showman Botha, Smuts was returned for the Wonderboom constituency, near Pretoria. *Het Volk* won a landslide victory and Botha rewarded Smuts with two key cabinet positions: Colonial Secretary and Education Secretary.

Smuts proved to be effective, if not much liked. Although he had once been a dedicated member of the Dutch Reformed Church, as Education Secretary he challenged the church's right to impose Calvinist doctrine on schools. As Colonial Secretary, he was forced to confront Asian workers, the very people whose plight he had exploited in London, led by Mohandas Karamchand Gandhi. Despite his unpopularity, as South Africa's economy continued to boom, Smuts became the Afrikaners' brightest star.

Following British victory in the war South African unification was inevitable. It remained though, to decide what sort of country would be forged – and how. Smuts favoured one state, with power centralised in Pretoria and English as the only official language – and with an electorate that included women, many Asians and even Africans. To press his ideas he convened a constitutional conference in Durban in October 1908.

The Orange Free State delegation refused every one of his demands. Smuts compromised on the location of the capital, the official language and suffrage: but refused to budge on the fundamental structure of government. Eventually they agreed that Smuts should draft the new constitution: which was duly ratified by all the South African colonies. Smuts and Botha took it to London: where it was passed by Parliament and signed into law by King Edward VII, in December 1909. Smuts's dream had been realised.

The Union of South Africa was born. The Afrikaners however, now united as the South African Party, formed the largest part of the electorate. Botha was appointed Prime Minister and Smuts was given three key ministries: those for the Interior, the Mines and Defence. He was now the second most powerful man in South Africa.

The Cullinan Diamond, found by Frederick Wells, surface manager of the Premier mine in the Transvaal on 26 January 1905, is the largest gem-quality diamond ever found, at 3,106.75 carats (although a carbonado found in Brazil weighed more than 3,600 carats, no gem-quality material could be extracted from it). The stone was named after Sir Thomas Cullinan (1862–1936), owner of the mine.

Premier has yielded the majority of the largest diamonds in the world – as recently as September 2009 a 507 carat stone was found. It is still the only significant source of blue diamonds. Sir William Crookes OM (1832–1919), a distinguished chemist and physicist, examined the colourless diamond and observed a black spot in the middle. The colours around the spot were vivid and changed as the analyser was turned, pointing to severe internal strain. Such strains are not uncommon in diamonds – and have actually caused stones to explode when reaching the surface, or even when exposed to body warmth in the pockets of miners.

The diamond was bought by the Transvaal government and presented to King Edward VII. It was cut into three large parts by Asscher Brothers of Amsterdam; and eventually into a further eleven large gem-quality stones, with some smaller fragments. Cutting technology had not yet evolved sufficiently to be sure of the outcome and the procedure was considered very risky. To enable Joseph Asscher to cut it, an half-inch deep incision was made. Then a specifically designed knife was used to split the diamond with one heavy blow. It duly split precisely through the defective spot, which was shared between both halves of the stone. Asscher, the greatest cutter of his day, is said to have had a doctor and nurse standing by. When he struck the diamond and it broke perfectly in two, he fainted.

The largest polished gem from the stone is named Cullinan I or the *Great Star of Africa*. At 530.2 carats it was the largest polished diamond in the world – until the 1985 discovery of the brown *Golden Jubilee* diamond (545.67 carats), also from the Premier mine. Cullinan I is part of the British crown jewels, mounted in the head of the Sceptre with the Cross. Cullinan II or *Lesser Star of Africa*, at 317.4 carats, is part of the Imperial State Crown. Both gems are on display at the Tower of London.

In 1905 detectives from London were stationed on the steamer that was rumoured to be taking the stone to Britain, but this was a diversionary tactic. The stone on the ship was a fake – the actual diamond was sent in a plain box via parcel post.

• **The Great Star of Africa**

Harmony and cooperation soon ended. Smuts was criticised for his all-embracing powers and reshuffled. He lost the ministries of Defence and the Mines, but gained the Treasury. This was still too much for his opponents: at the 1913 South African Party conference, Botha and Smuts narrowly survived a vote of confidence: but the Old Boers (Hertzog, Steyn and De Wet) stormed out, leaving the party for good.

With the schism in internal party politics came a small-scale miners' dispute which flared into a full-blown strike. In 1914 a railway strike turned into a general strike; and threats of a revolution caused Smuts to declare martial law. Smuts acted ruthlessly, deporting union leaders without trial and using Parliament retrospectively to absolve him and the government of any blame. The Old Boers formed the National Party, urging their supporters to arm themselves, and civil war seemed inevitable. In October 1914 an open rebellion led by Lieutenant Colonel Manie Maritz was crushed by Botha and Smuts before it could escalate into a Third Boer War.

In 1914 Smuts had formed the South African Defence Force. His first task was to suppress the Maritz Rebellion, which was accomplished in November. With the other Dominions, the country had declared war on Germany in August: now he and Louis Botha led the South African army into German South West Africa (Namibia) and quickly overran it. In 1916, as a General in the British Army, Smuts was put in charge of the war in German East Africa. While the East African Campaign went tolerably well, the German forces were by no means destroyed. Early in 1917 however, he was invited to join the Imperial War Cabinet in London by David Lloyd George. In 1918 Smuts helped to create the Royal Air Force, independent of the British army.

Smuts and Botha were key negotiators at the Paris Peace Conference. Both favoured reconciliation with Germany and limited reparations. The Treaty of Versailles (28 June 1919) gave South Africa a mandate over Namibia – which was exercised until 1990. When Botha died in 1919, Smuts became Prime Minister: until he received a shocking comeuppance in the 1924 election, at the hands of the National Party. The Old Boers had taken their revenge.

After nine years in opposition and academia, Smuts returned as Deputy Prime Minister in a "grand coalition" government under Barry Hertzog. When Hertzog advocated neutrality towards Nazi Germany in 1939, he was deposed by a party caucus: and Smuts again became Prime Minister. Having served alongside Winston Churchill in WWI, he had developed a personal and professional rapport: and was again invited to join the Imperial War Cabinet, as the most senior South African in favour of the war. On 28 May 1941 Smuts was appointed a Field Marshal in the British Army, the first South African ever to hold that rank. He had been elected to the Royal Society in 1930.

As Prime Minister Smuts was opposed by the majority of Afrikaners, who wished to continue and further the *de facto* "apartheid" of the inter-war years. After WWII Smuts had set up and then supported the Fagan Commission: which advocated the abandonment of all segregation in South Africa. However Smuts lost the 1948 general election, which was won by Daniel François Malan's pro-Apartheid National Party. Although his defeat was widely forecast, it is a credit to Smuts's political acumen that it was only by a narrow margin: and that he actually won the popular vote. Smuts retired from politics – and forty shameful years of Apartheid followed.

He died on 11 September 1950 at Doornkloof, his family farm near Pretoria, aged eighty. His ashes were scattered on Smuts's Koppie, near the farm.

In May 1945 Smuts represented South Africa in San Francisco at the drafting of the United Nations Charter. As at Versailles in 1919, Smuts urged the delegates to create a powerful international body to preserve peace. He was determined that, unlike the League of Nations, the United Nations would have teeth. Smuts signed the Paris Peace Treaty on 10 February 1947, nearly two years after the end of the war.

Statue of Smuts (in Parliament Square) by Jacob Epstein

Smuts had set out his philosophy in *Holism and Evolution*, published in 1926. His far-reaching political vision had much in common with his view of life in general: small units must develop into bigger ones – and they in their turn, must grow unceasingly into larger and ever-larger structures. Thus the unification of the four provinces into the Union of South Africa; then the Union into the British Commonwealth of Nations; and finally into a great whole, resulting from the combination of the peoples of the earth in a great league of nations, was simply a logical progression.

It is an irony that the only words human beings can employ to describe their dealings with ethnic or religious differences are "annihilate", "segregate" or "integrate": all of which rhyme with "hate". The first two approaches having failed miserably, only co-existence is left.

Smuts collected plants from all over southern Africa. He went on several expeditions in the 1920s and 1930s with John Hutchinson, once Botanist in charge of the African section of the Herbarium at Kew – and a distinguished taxonomist.

In 2004 Smuts was named by voters in a poll held by the South African Broadcasting Corporation as one of the ten greatest ever South Africans. The final positions were to be decided by a second round of voting, but the programme was cancelled due to political controversy. Based on the first round of voting, Nelson Mandela came first: Jan Smuts came sixth, despite many Afrikaners still hating him – surprisingly, Rhodes was in the list: unsurprisingly, he was voted 56th.

Already a Bencher of the Middle Temple, in 1931 he became the first foreign President of the British Association for the Advancement of Science. He was also elected Lord Rector of St Andrews University: after Fridtjof Nansen, only the second foreigner to be so honoured. In 1948, he was the first foreigner ever to be elected Chancellor of Cambridge University, a position that he held until his death. He is remembered also for coining the terms "holism" and "holistic": abstractions clearly linked to his political vision. The earliest use of the word *apartheid* (meaning "separateness" in Afrikaans) is also attributed to him, in a speech made in 1917.

The international airport at Johannesburg was known as "Jan Smuts Airport" from its construction in 1952: until, in 1994 it was renamed "Johannesburg International Airport", to remove any political connotations. In 2006 it was renamed yet again: "Oliver Tambo International Airport".

In 1932 the kibbutz *Ramat-Yohanan* in Israel was named after him. Smuts was a vocal proponent of the creation of a Jewish state: and spoke out against the rising anti-Semitism of the 1930s. This was another bond with Churchill, though for different reasons.

Cynical opinion has suggested that Smuts was suborned by his years at Cambridge and in Britain: and spent the rest of his life scheming to become an accepted member of the Establishment. Britain in return, such sceptics would add, was delighted to welcome so distinguished an ex-Boer "Uncle Tom": and showered him with honours. It is true that both Britain and Smuts had good reason to see the merit and utility in each other – and furthermore, Churchill would have empathised with a fellow "outsider". To most people however, Jan Smuts was quite simply a remarkable and very gifted man.

KHAKI

Many Urdu and Hindi words encountered by the British in India are in common English usage today.

The word khaki comes from the Urdu *khak* (soil), derived from Persian, and came to English through use by the British Indian army.

Adele Campbell of Utley in Gloucestershire bred the first "Khaki Campbell" duck in 1901. A mallard + Rouen + Indian runner cross, the breed is a prolific layer.

Khaki means "earth-coloured", referring to the colour of uniforms introduced by the British in the 1880s. More accurately, the correct shade of "Khaki" is the colour of "Multani Mitti", meaning "the mud of Multan" – a city and old military cantonment, now in Pakistan.

Elsewhere the hidebound British army replaced its celebrated and respected red coats with khaki uniforms reluctantly – but quickly, once it was perceived that it saved its soldiers' lives. In various colour variations, it was rapidly taken up by other armies.

RUDYARD KIPLING, THE "BARD OF EMPIRE", WROTE THE POEM "IF—"

Kipling was born on 30 December 1865 in Bombay, British India. Lockwood and Alice Kipling (*née* MacDonald) had moved to India earlier that year. They had courted each other at Rudyard Lake in Staffordshire and named their son after it. Lockwood Kipling was a sculptor and pottery designer.

Kipling won the 1907 Nobel Prize for Literature, but refused the Order of Merit. He died on 18 January 1936 – his ashes were buried in Poet's Corner in Westminster Abbey.

In his autobiography *Something of Myself*, published in 1937, Kipling avers that *If—* was inspired by Dr Leander Starr Jameson, who had led an incursion into the Transvaal in 1895. The inevitable fiasco increased the tensions that ultimately sparked the Second Boer War. The British press and Kipling thought that Jameson was a romantic adventurer and described his raid as a British "victory".

Though *If—* was written in 1895, it was first published in 1910 – in *Rewards and Fairies*, a collection of short stories and poems. It is an evocation of Victorian stoicism and "stiff upper lip". In 1995 *If—* was voted Britain's favourite poem. Smuts would have been far more worthy of Kipling's admiration than the foolhardy Jameson.

If you can keep your head when all about you
    Are losing theirs and blaming it on you,
If you can trust yourself when all men doubt you,
    But make allowance for their doubting too;
If you can wait and not be tired by waiting,
    Or being lied about, don't deal in lies,
Or being hated, don't give way to hating,
    And yet don't look too good, nor talk too wise:
If you can dream – and not make dreams your master;
    If you can think – and not make thoughts your aim;
If you can meet with Triumph and Disaster
    And treat those two impostors just the same;
If you can bear to hear the truth you've spoken
    Twisted by knaves to make a trap for fools,
Or watch the things you gave your life to, broken,
    And stoop and build 'em up with worn-out tools:
If you can make one heap of all your winnings
    And risk it on one turn of pitch-and-toss,
And lose, and start again at your beginnings
    And never breathe a word about your loss;
If you can force your heart and nerve and sinew

(Joseph) Rudyard Kipling by Sir Philip Burne-Jones, 2nd Bt. (1899)
National Portrait Gallery, London

Kipling was desolated by the loss of his only son, John at Loos in 1915. He was also wracked by guilt as he had urged him to join the army (the Irish Guards), despite having eyesight so poor that he could easily have avoided military service. Despairingly, Kipling wrote, "If any question why we died: tell them, because our fathers lied".

To serve your turn long after they are gone,
And so hold on when there is nothing in you
  Except the Will which says to them: 'Hold on!'
If you can talk with crowds and keep your virtue,
  Or walk with Kings – nor lose the common touch,
If neither foes nor loving friends can hurt you,
  If all men count with you, but none too much;
If you can fill the unforgiving minute
  With sixty seconds' worth of distance run,
Yours is the Earth and everything that's in it,
  And – which is more – you'll be a Man, my son!

THE LEAD IN YOUR PENCIL

A pencil "lead", or even a line drawn by a pencil, will conduct electricity. It is made from graphite, the low density allotrope of carbon. For 327 years pure graphite was almost as valuable as carbon in its purest form – diamond. Flaunted adornment will always have a market amongst the rich, or those who aspire to be thought so. The humble pencil however, has a larger market: the billions of people who use one every day.

Pure graphite

In 1564 an enormous deposit of graphite was discovered in Seathwaite Fell, near Borrowdale in Cumberland (Britain's wettest inhabited spot, with an average yearly rainfall of 140 inches). The graphite (or plumbago, a soft form of carbon combined with a small amount of iron) was pure and solid. It remains to this day the only such deposit ever found, anywhere in the world. If the graphite at Borrowdale had been slightly more compressed by geological forces, it would have become actual diamond – but as one "wad" (graphite deposit) alone yielded £43,000 (£120 million today), it was almost as precious.

Legend has it that a large tree blew over and shepherds noticed a black material clinging to the roots. They tried to burn it, thinking that it was coal – but it would not burn. They found though, that it was very useful for marking sheep. Borrowdale graphite could also easily be sawn into sticks and bound by string, which could be unwound as the point became worn. Within a few years the pencil industry was born, in nearby Keswick. The first hand-made modern pencils were known as *Crayons d'Angleterre*. In 1832 a pencil factory was established; and in 1916 it became the Cumberland Pencil Factory. It produced the Derwent pencils that were for many years the finest in the world. The mine was eventually worked out and closed in 1891.

A pencil is an extraordinarily useful instrument: it is entirely self-contained, using no messy liquids such as ink, it can write a continuous line for over 20 miles, it makes a well-defined mark that is relatively smudge-proof – and it is easy to erase.

Other graphite mines in Scotland, Spain, France and Germany were unable to match Borrowdale for the purity of its "black lead" – and the size of the pieces which it produced. From the 16th to the 19th centuries, the best pencils in the world were made using Borrowdale graphite. Today most of the world's (inferior) pencil lead comes from Sri Lanka, Madagascar, Mexico and Siberia.

Once the value of the material was realised, the mines were taken over by the Government. The graphite was transported from Keswick to London by armed stage coach. It was used for medicinal purposes: but, as it is unaffected by heat, its chief use from Elizabeth I's reign onwards was in making moulds for the manufacture of cannon balls. This led to a new Act in 1752: stealing or receiving wad became a felony, punishable by whipping and twelve month's hard labour, or seven years' transportation.

Nowadays glasses are made of plastic, tins are made of aluminium and golfing irons are made of titanium. It is not so odd therefore, that pencil "lead" is made from graphite.

GOLF

Golf, like tennis, is another of the five great international spectator sports that originated in the British Isles. When amateurs with the same handicaps (even if thirty years apart in age or stones different in weight) play on level terms, golf is technically a game: when played without handicaps, it is a sport. Conversely tennis, though described as a game but having no handicapping system, is in fact a sport.

The origins of golf are uncertain. The Romans played *Paganica* ("country dweller") where a stick was used to hit a leather ball stuffed with feathers. In the Netherlands, a club and ball

Elm or beech golf balls were replaced in the 17th century by boiled feathers forced into a leather pouch. In 1848 feathers were replaced by gutta-percha (a golf ball is often still called a "gutty"), a tough thermo-plastic material made from the coagulated latex of the Malaysian *Palaquium gutta* tree. Until recently the modern golf ball was surfaced with balata (the resin of another tropical tree) and made with a waterfilled core wrapped in rubber yarn. Dimples, to speed the flight pattern, were patented in 1908 – modern golf balls have between 250–450.

The first recorded game of golf between named players took place in 1503. King James IV of Scotland played the Earl of Bothwell – and lost 42 shillings (£1,000 today). On 3 February 1504 the Lord Treasurer of Scotland recorded an outlay of nine shillings: "Items to Golf Clubis and Ballis for the king that he play it with". James V was a keen player, as was his daughter Mary Queen of Scots who was censured for playing within days of the murder of her husband Lord Darnley.

Their son James VI of Scotland and 1st of England (1566–1625), on his accession to the English throne, travelled down to London with his clubs. His sons Henry and Charles (later King Charles I) were taught to play golf as boys.

The Links at Leith, common ground grazed by sheep and rabbits near Edinburgh, was the first popular centre of golf in the British Isles. In 1724 the first match reported in the press, between Alexander Elphinstone and Captain John Porteous (who later opened fire on an Edinburgh crowd and was lynched by the mob) was played for a stake of twenty guineas (over £30,000 today).

Charles I was playing at Leith when he received news of the Irish rebellion which triggered the events that ended with his execution. He used the news as an excuse to abandon the game. His Victorian biographer, Sir Walter Simpson explained that: "The King acted on this occasion with his usual cunning. At the time he was being beaten and that he hurried away to save his half-crown rather than his crown".

game called *Colf* was played from the late 13th century. In Scotland, which enjoyed close trading links with the Low Countries, a game recognizably similar to the modern game of golf, was played by shepherds knocking stones and later wooden balls along "fairways" of grass clipped by sheep, into rabbit holes. The first place identified with the game was along the links (dunes) of Fife, on the east coast of Scotland. Today, it is the home of the Royal and Ancient Golf Club of St Andrews.

By the middle of the 15th century golf had become sufficiently popular in Scotland that, with "Futeball", it was banned from time to time to prevent distraction from the archery practice needed to do battle with "our auld enemies of England".

The first known golf "professional" was a shoemaker, John Paterstone, recommended as a partner to King James II, then Duke of York and Lord High Commissioner of Edinburgh, at Holyrood in 1681. They duly won their match and Paterstone was rewarded by James, who had put up the stake, with half the winnings. He built himself a fine house which he called " Golfers

Land". A plaque near the site bears Paterstone's crest: a *dexter* (right) hand grasping a golf club, with his motto "Far and Sure"; and below, the words " I hate no person" – an anagram of I (in place of a "J") Paterstone.

In 1744 "several Gentlemen of Honour" founded the Honourable company of Edinburgh Golfers – the world's first golf club. They invited the City of Edinburgh to furnish a Silver Club as a prize for an annual competition to be held on the five-hole links at Leith, to be open "to as many Noblemen or Gentlemen or other Golfers from any part of Great Britain or Ireland". There were thirteen rules, the first ever drafted. In 1754 the citizens of St Andrews founded what became The Royal and Ancient Golf Club, usually referred to as the R & A, which now has a world-wide membership of 2,400.

There was still no set number of holes: at St Andrews there were twelve, one after the other along the foreshore. A "round" was played to the furthest hole and back again playing only ten, making twenty-two holes in all. In 1764 the club converted the first four holes into two, making a round a total of eighteen holes. When St Andrews drafted the rules of golf 133 years later, the committee members naturally chose eighteen holes for the standard course.

In 1833 the Perth Golfing Society was the first to be given Royal status – by King William IV. He granted the "Royal" prefix to St Andrews in the following year.

Blackheath is the oldest golf club in England, which claims to have been founded in 1608, by Scottish courtiers attending King James VI and I at Greenwich Palace. It was not until 1818 that the next English club was founded, the Old Manchester Golf Club. England's first links course by the sea, the North Devon at Westward Ho! opened in 1864. In 1888 all the leading golf clubs in Britain agreed to abide by the rules drawn up by the R & A. This code was refined in 1897, when all Scottish and English clubs asked St Andrews to codify and and regulate the game nationally.

Until 1857 there were no matches played between clubs: only private matches arranged between individuals. The Prestwick Club in Ayrshire proposed a tournament between clubs – which was a triumph. On 17 October 1860 Prestwick held a competition for professionals. It was the first "Open", although only eight Scotsmen took part. In 1861 Prestwick declared the prize, a Challenge Belt "to be open to all the world".

The ninth Open in 1868 was won by seventeen year-old Tom Morris, who won the next three championships too – acquiring the Challenge Belt outright. Prestwick asked the R & A to provide a new prize. St Andrews commissioned a silver claret jug – still awarded every year. "Young" Tom Morris was the son of "Old" Tom Morris (1821–1908), who had won the Open four times in the first nine years of its existence. Young Tom's career ended in tragedy. He was only 24

The R & A is the world's leading golfing authority other than in the US and Mexico which instead recognise the United States Golf Association (USGA).

In 1867 the first recognised ladies' golf club was established at St Andrews. The first Ladies Championship was played at Lytham & St Anne's in 1893.

In 1970 Tony Jacklin (born in Scunthorpe in 1944), who won the Open in 1969 at Royal Lytham & St Annes, was the first Briton to win the US Open since 1920.

The Ryder Cup, a gold trophy, was donated in 1926 by Lancashireman Samuel Ryder (1858–1936), who was the first man to sell garden seeds in "penny packets". The first official match was held at Worcester, Massachusetts in 1927.

when he lost both his wife and first-born in childbirth. He was found dead in his bed on Christmas day 1875.

The first golf club in the US, the Oakhurst opened in White Sulphur Springs, West Virginia in 1884. The St Andrews Golf Club of Yonkers, New York was next: founded in 1888 by Robert Lockhart, a Scottish textile merchant. By 1895 there was sufficient enthusiasm for the launch of both a US Amateur and, in October, a US Open Championship (held at Newport, Rhode Island). In the early years it was dominated by British, usually Scottish, professionals who won all of the first 16 competitions – until 1911, when nineteen year-old John J. McDermott became the first American-born winner. Willie Anderson (1879–1910) from North Berwick is one of only four men to have won the tournament four times (the others are Bobbie Jones, Ben Hogan and Jack Nicklaus) – and the only player to win three times consecutively (1903–05).

The US has dominated the Open, winning every year from 1924–33. Since WWII players from the US have won 30 times; from South Africa, Australia and Britain, 9 times each; from Spain, 3 times; from Ireland, twice; and once each from Zimbabwe, New Zealand and Argentina. The Ryder Cup, until 1979 a biennial competition between the US and Britain and Ireland, proved equally one-sided. From 1927 to 1978, the British and Irish won only three times. In 1979 Europeans were invited to join the British and Irish. The effect was immediate: Europe has won eight and the US seven of the subsequent sixteen matches (with a tie in 1989).

The number of golf courses worldwide is increasing rapidly. The first golf course in the People's Republic of China opened in 1984 – by 2008 there were 376.

Henry Vardon (1870–1937) was born in Grouville on the Channel Island of Jersey. His record remains unequalled by a Briton – he won the Open six times before WWI and the US Open in 1900.

The most successful British golfer after WWI was Henry Cotton (1907–87), who was born in Congleton in Cheshire. He won the Open in 1934, ending a decade of US victories, and again in 1937 and 1948. He also won 11 European Opens – and represented Britain in the Ryder Cup four times. He died on 22 December 1987 and was awarded a knighthood posthumously.

AN UNUSUAL TREATMENT OF ZEBRAS CROSSING

Edward John Moreton Drax Plunkett, 18th Baron Dunsany (1878–1957), an eccentric Anglo-Irish contemporary of Churchill, fought in the Boer War before becoming a successful writer, poet and dramatist. His passion was collecting trophies for his game book. He took up the post of Byron professor of poetry in Athens eighteen months late – by travelling to Greece via India, to shoot tigers.

In the 1930s John Lobb & Co., the gentleman's boot-maker in St. James's, advertised its premises by driving a trap drawn by two zebras round Westminster. A story circulated in London's club-land that Dunsany, never having bagged a zebra, took up a fire-position between Fortnum & Mason and Hatchards, the bookshop – and shot them both dead as they trotted down Piccadilly.

WHY, WHEN AND HOW BRITAIN DEVELOPED NUCLEAR WEAPONS

Despite British scientists having proved critical to the success of the US *Manhattan Project* to develop an atom bomb in WWII, the US was prevented by the McMahon Act of 1946 from continuing nuclear cooperation with the UK after the war.

In October that year Prime Minister Clement Attlee called a small cabinet meeting to discuss building a gaseous diffusion plant to enrich uranium. The meeting was about to decide against it on grounds of cost, when Ernest Bevin (1881–1951) arrived late and said "We've got to have this thing. I don't mind it for myself, but I don't want any other Foreign Secretary of this country to be talked at or to by the Secretary of State of the US as I have just been .... We've got to have this thing over here, whatever it costs .... We've got to have the bloody Union Jack on top of it". The first UK weapon (*Operation Hurricane*) was detonated below the frigate HMS *Plym* in the Monte Bello Islands (80 miles off north-western Australia's Pilbara coast) on 2 October 1952.

In 1992 it was disclosed that the success of Britain's first 'H-bomb' tests in 1957 (*Operation Grapple*), held at Maiden and Christmas Islands in the Central Pacific, was exaggerated. The US was fooled into giving Britain the means to make her own thermonuclear devices, in exchange for access to British designs for future weapons. The deception was kept secret by top nuclear scientists and civil servants for many years.

SIR ALAN PATRICK (A.P.) HERBERT

A.P. Herbert M.P. (1890–1971) was born in Ashstead in Surrey. He served in the Royal Navy during WWI. Called to the bar in 1918, he never practised. He became instead a novelist, playwright, law reformer and humorist – using humour to make serious points. He also wrote bawdy verse as a diversion. He is believed to have written the pornographic ballad of *Eskimo Nell*, in a parody of *The Songs of a Sourdough* by Robert Service (1874–1958). Whether he did or not, he certainly wrote this informative piece:

The portion of a woman that appeals to Man's depravity
Is fashioned with considerable care.
And what, at first, appears to be a simple little cavity
Is really an elaborate affair.
For doctors of distinction have examined these phenomena
In a number of experimental dames;
And listed all the things they found in feminine abdomina,
And given them delightful Latin names.
There's the Vulva, the Vagina, the jolly Perineum
And the Hymen that is found in certain brides;
And lots of little gadgets you would love if you could see 'em –
The Clitoris and God knows what besides.
What a pity it is then, that when we idle menfolk chatter
Of the mysteries to which I have referred,
That for such a very wonderful and complicated matter
We use such a short and unattractive word.

A JOKE AT HIS OWN EXPENSE

James Abbott McNeill Whistler (1834–1903) was an increasingly highly regarded American painter and etcher who required dozens of sittings to paint his mother. He lived most of his life in Britain.

In 1878 Whistler sued John Ruskin (1819–1900) for libel, after the critic condemned his painting, *Nocturne in Black and Gold: The Falling Rocket*, in

James Abbott McNeill Whistler Nocturne in Black and Gold, the Falling Rocket (*c*.1875)

print: "For Mr Whistler's own sake, no less than for the protection of the purchaser, Sir Coutts Lindsay (founder of the Grosvenor Gallery) ought not to have admitted works into the gallery in which the ill-educated conceit of the artist so nearly approached the aspect of wilful imposture. I have seen, and heard, much of Cockney impudence before now; but never expected to hear a coxcomb ask two hundred guineas for flinging a pot of paint in the public's face".

Having sued for £1,000 (£528,000 today), Whistler won only a farthing in damages (55 pence today). Ill-advisedly, with the same mistaken sense of occasion displayed by Oscar Wilde in his own trial in 1895, Whistler made the jury laugh – but not the pompous judge: who asked him irritably, "Mr Whistler, do you believe that genius is inherited?". Whistler replied, "I have no idea my lord, I have no children".

DNA WAS DISCOVERED IN THE YEAR CHURCHILL WON HIS NOBEL PRIZE

Research into DNA has continued to be a fruitful field for British inventiveness. In 1984 Sir Alec Jeffreys FRS (born 1950) was the first in the world to develop the technique of DNA "fingerprinting", which has subsequently secured the conviction of many murderers. In 2002 Sir John Sulston FRS (born 1942) and Sydney Brenner FRS (born 1927) were each awarded a one-third share of the Nobel Prize for Medicine, for their roles in the international Human Genome sequencing project.

Francis Harry Compton Crick OM FRS (1916–2004) was a molecular biologist, physicist and neuroscientist. In 1953 he was the most important co-discoverer of the structure of DNA: and together with an American, James Watson and a fellow Briton, Maurice Wilkins was awarded the 1962 Nobel Prize for Physiology and Medicine. The award was made "for their discoveries concerning the molecular structure of nucleic acids and its significance for information transfer in living material".

Crick was educated at Northampton Grammar School and University College, London. He was refused entry to Cambridge, because he lacked the requisite Latin. During WWII Crick played an important role in the development of magnetic and acoustic mines for the Royal Navy. After the war he studied biology. He had to "adjust from the elegance and simplicity of physics to the elaborate chemical mechanisms that natural selection had evolved over millions of years". He discovered that a "codon" (a group of three bases) on one DNA strand identified the position of a precise amino-acid on the spine of a protein molecule – determining the codon code for each amino-acid found in a protein.

DNA double helix

Francis Crick

This revealed how a cell uses DNA to build proteins. Crick coined the phrase "central dogma" for the flow of genetic information in cells from DNA to RNA to protein.

Crick's last years were spent as a Distinguished Research Professor at the Salk Institute at La Jolla in California, researching human consciousness. He died, aged eighty-eight, while editing a manuscript: "a scientist to the bitter end". He had refused a knighthood.

TWELVE PRACTICAL BRITISH INVENTIONS MADE IN CHURCHILL'S LIFETIME

Finger-printing	Sir Francis Galton FRS (1892)
Vacuum cleaner	Hubert Booth (1901)
Marmite	Frederick Wissler (1902)
Crossword puzzle *(at the time a US resident)*	Arthur Wynne (1913)
Stainless Steel	Harry Brearley
Electric kettle	Arthur Large (1922)
'Cat's Eyes'	Percy Shaw (1934)
Holograms *(he won the 1971 Nobel Prize for physics)*	Dennis Gabor FRS (1947)
'Float' glass	Sir Alastair Pilkington FRS (1952)
Ultrasound *(for obstetric examinations)*	Ian Donald (1958)
Hovercraft	Sir Christopher Cockerell FRS (1959)
'Baby Buggy'	Owen Maclaren (1965)

THE PILL AND ITS AFTER EFFECTS

Herchel Smith (1925–2001) was born in Plymouth, the son of a bookmaker. He took a double first in Natural Sciences at Emmanuel College, Cambridge, before continuing his research at Oxford from 1952–56. Whilst lecturing in organic chemistry at the University of Manchester, he devised important new methods of synthesising steroids, which he patented – before joining Wyeth Pharmaceuticals in Pennsylvania in 1961. His development of Norgestrel, a potent contraceptive, led to the first commercial production of a wide range of oral and injectable drugs.

Holding all the patents for his work, Smith made a fortune. He retired in 1973 to cruise the oceans in his yacht, named *Synthesis* – and spent the rest of his life giving most of his money away. He donated well over $250 million, principally to fund research at Cambridge and Harvard, before dying in his sleep at his home in the US. This unsung hero has made "more of a difference" to the modern world than most – to the health and freedom of women; and in mitigating the inexorable increase in population.

Earlier birth-control treatments used hormones sourced from prohibitively expensive Mexican yams. Doctor Smith was the first to find an affordable way of making them. Orval, the first "pill" using his synthetic hormones was marketed in 1968.

IN 1874 PHYLLOXERA WAS RECOGNISED AS A PROBLEM IN SOUTH AUSTRALIA

The Phylloxera and Grape Industry Board was established in 1899 under an Act of the South Australian Government. Its origins trace back to 1874, the year of Churchill's birth, when South Australian vignerons first lobbied the government to protect the state from the deadly pest sweeping through Europe and Africa.

Phylloxera, *Daktulosphaira vitifoliae*, was originally native to the eastern US. Tiny, pale yellow sap-sucking insects, related to aphids, feed on the roots of vines – gradually depriving them of nutrients and water. It was inadvertently introduced to Europe in 1860. Grape species in the US are resistant to it – but the European wine grape, *Vitis vinifera* is very susceptible. In 1863 vines in the southern Rhône region of France showed signs of stress. The pest spread rapidly across the continent. The area used for growing vines in France peaked in 1875, at over six million acres (1.7 times the size of Yorkshire); with total wine production of 8,450 million litres. It fell in only a few years to 2,340 million litres. Some 80% of all European vineyards were destroyed.

Resistant US rootstock was used in Europe to combat the insect: had it not been, whatever the niceties, there would be no *Vitis vinifera* wine industry in Europe at all, or almost anywhere else – other than Chile, Washington State and parts of Australia. The only European grape that is resistant to Phylloxera is the *Assyrtiko* grape on the island of Santorini in Greece, though this may be due to the volcanic ash on which it grows.

In France today two million acres are used for viticulture, producing 6,000 million litres of wine. The 2008 figures in Britain were paltry in comparison: less than 3,000 acres, producing 1 million litres. The UK however, is the largest importer of wine by value in the world – and is the hub of the international wine trade.

YORKSHIRE IS FAMOUS FOR RHUBARB AND LIQUORICE

Rhubarb crumble is a much loved British pudding. Edible (as opposed to medicinal) rhubarb comes from the banks of the river Volga, in Russia. The Volga was called *Rha* by the Ancient Greeks, while *barbarum* means "foreign" in Latin. Rhubarb arrived in Britain in the late 16th century, though it was 200 years before it drew much attention. Counter-intuitively, rhubarb is a vegetable while the tomato is a fruit.

The procedure of 'forcing' rhubarb, or growing it in the dark, was introduced by Joseph Myatt (1772–1855), a London nurseryman. He left a chimney pot over one of his plants and found that depriving it of light made the stems shoot upwards, searching for light, making it more succulent and delicate. Around 1808 Myatt sold bundles of his Russian cultivar in Covent Garden – encouraging his customers to cook the rhubarb with sugar. His sales grew dramatically as sugar became cheaper.

Rhubarb needs water, nitrogen and a cold climate. The "Wakefield Triangle", a nine-square mile 'frost pocket' near Leeds, proved perfect: with the right kind of soil; abundant water from the Pennines; nitrogen sourced from "shoddy", a waste product from the wool industry; and later, coal from local pits to heat the forcing sheds. This small area of West Yorkshire used to produce 90% of the world's forced rhubarb. Until the 1960s the "Rhubarb Express" train would take crates of rhubarb from nearly 200 growers to be sold at Covent Garden. Today there are very few growers left – imported exotic fruit has become affordable, while rhubarb is rather old-fashioned and expensive to grow commercially.

Rhubarb has been used in China for 2,000 years as a laxative. The leaves from any variety however, are toxic – due to high concentrations of oxalic acid, an organic poison and corrosive. Ten or eleven pounds of the leaves are a lethal dose to a human.

Pontefract lies 14 miles south-east of Leeds. Crusaders or Dominican monks introduced the liquorice plant to the town in the 14th century. Liquorice roots can run to 5 or more feet in length; and the deep clay soil of Pontefract proved ideal for growing it. The sap was extracted from the roots of the plant and used medicinally by the monks, to ease coughs and stomach cramps.

Around 1614 Sir George Savile (whose great-grandson, a Restoration statesman became 1st Marquess of Halifax) stamped a small impression of Pontefract Castle on lozenges of the extract, which he called Pontefract Cakes – although it was still used as a medicine. In 1760 George Dunhill, a Pontefract apothecary, added sugar to the recipe to produce the first "Pomfret Cakes" commercially, as a sweet. Within a few years Dunhill became the best known English manufacturer of liquorice confectionery.

Liquorice was last harvested in Pontefract around 1970. It is now imported from Spain, Italy and Turkey. Where there were once 13 liquorice factories in the town, there are now only two: Haribo (formerly Dunhills) and Cadbury Trebor Bassett.

The liquorice bush is related to the pea family. The root is one of the sweetest substances known to man – fifty times sweeter than sugar cane.

THE END OF THE BRITISH RAJ AND THE PARTITION OF INDIA

India and Pakistan came into existence at the stroke of midnight on 15 August 1947: Pakistan however, celebrates independence a day earlier. Ceremonies were held on 14 August in Karachi, then the capital of the new state of Pakistan, and on 15 August in Delhi – enabling the last British Viceroy, Earl Mountbatten to attend both. This also made it clear that a sovereign Muslim Pakistan was not seceding from a secular India.

"West" and "East" Pakistan (now Pakistan and Bangladesh) adopted new standard times after partition: 30 minutes ahead of and 30 minutes behind India. At midnight on 15 August , when India became independent, it was still 23:30 the day before in Karachi.

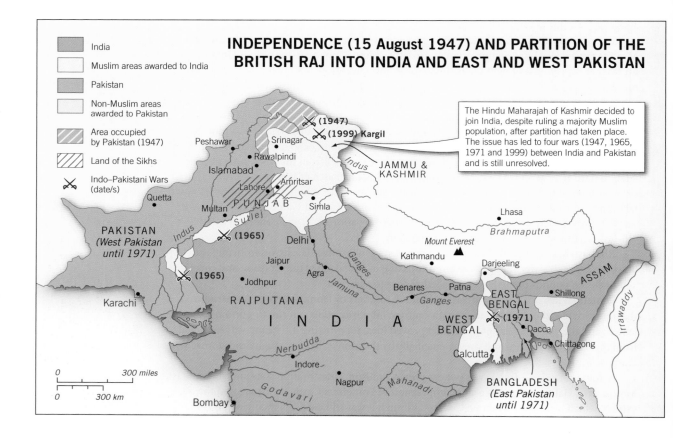

Map of India and Pakistan following independence and partition: Cyril, later 1st Viscount Radcliffe (1899–1977) was given just five weeks by Earl Mountbatten to draw the borders between India, West and East Pakistan (a name coined by Rahmat Ali in 1932). The main problems were the Punjab, mostly Moslem but also the land of the Sikhs; and West Bengal, for Calcutta could not be alienated from India. Some two million people died as a result (1947–48). Kashmir was not included at all.

TWELVE BRITISH INVENTIONS OR DISCOVERIES IN CHURCHILL'S LIFETIME THAT HAVE CHANGED THE WORLD (* NOBEL PRIZE WINNER)

Telephone *(hence to give someone a "bell")*	Alexander Graham Bell (1875)
Malaria parasite	Sir Ronald Ross FRS (1897)*
Splitting the atom	Lord Rutherford OM FRS (1917)*
Insulin *(with Sir Frederick Banting of Canada)*	John Macleod FRS (1921)*
Television	John Logie Baird (1926)
Penicillin	Sir Alexander Fleming FRS (1928)*
Jet engine	Sir Frank Whittle OM FRS (1930)
RADAR	Sir Robert Watson-Watt FRS (1935)
Programmable Computer *("Colossus")*	Tommy Flowers (1943)
DNA	Francis Crick OM FRS (1953)*
Birth control pill *(Norgestrel)*	Herchel Smith (1961)
LCD crystals	George Gray FRS (1962)

THE ORDER OF MERIT (OM)

The Order of Merit, based on the Prussian *Pour le Mérite*, was established in 1902 by King Edward VII. It was intended to be a reward to British or British Empire, now Commonwealth, citizens for distinguished service: in politics, the armed forces; to science, art and literature; or for the general promotion of culture. It is in the sole gift of the monarch and is limited to the Sovereign and 24 members.

There have been only 176 ordinary members and 11 foreign "honorary members", including Mother Teresa in 1983 and Nelson Mandela in 1995, since inception. At present there are 21 members and 3 vacancies. The most recent ordinary member, appointed in 2009, was Jean Chrétien (born 1934), the Prime Minister of Canada from 1993–2003. The Order of Merit is the most prestigious British honour still in regular use.

THE FIRST NATIONAL HEALTH SERVICE IN THE WORLD

The National Health Service (NHS) is the collective name given to the four public health services of England, Scotland, Wales and Northern Ireland. Its creation in 1948 was based on the proposals of the 1942 "Beveridge Report". The Report of the Inter-Departmental Committee on Social Insurance and Allied Services was commissioned in May 1941 by Ernest Bevin (1881–1951), Minister of Labour in the WWII National Government, and chaired by William Beveridge. It identified five "Giant Evils" in society: squalor, ignorance, want, idleness and disease. It proposed the "Welfare State" to address them.

In England and Wales the NHS was created by the National Health Service Act 1946, and in Scotland by the National Health Service (Scotland) Act 1947.

William Henry, 1st Baron Beveridge (1879–1963), the eldest son of Henry Beveridge, an Indian Civil Service officer, was born in Rangpur in British India (now in Bangladesh). After Charterhouse School and Balliol College, Oxford, he practised law. A Fabian socialist, he made himself an authority on unemployment insurance; and in 1908

William Henry Beveridge, 1st Baron Beveridge by Helen Muspratt (1938)
National Portrait Gallery, London

Though the report was worthy and far-reaching, its cost to the UK economy over the next 60 years was enormous. In accepting its recommendations, Britain diverted resources from the investment needed for industrial regeneration after WWII – in contrast to the rest of Western Europe, notably France and Germany. Within 25 years the decline in Britain's industrial competitiveness had become irreversible.

joined the Board of Trade to introduce a national system of labour exchanges. In WWI he organised industrial manpower – becoming permanent secretary to the Ministry of Food, now with a knighthood. He was appointed director of the London School of Economics and Political Science (LSE) in 1919 and left the Civil Service.

In 1933 he helped to establish the Academic Assistance Council, to enable prominent German-Jewish academics escape Nazi persecution.

In 1937 Beveridge became Master of University College, Oxford, by now generally recognised as a brilliant scholar and economist. Though conceited, opinionated and difficult to work with, he was the outstanding candidate to chair Bevin's committee. His greatest accomplishment was in persuading even Conservatives that a healthier and more motivated workforce would increase Britain's industrial output.

Beveridge was no bleeding-heart. A strong believer in Eugenics, he argued in 1909 that: "those men who through general defects .... are to be recognised as 'unemployable' .... with complete and permanent loss of all citizen rights, including not only the franchise but civil freedom and fatherhood".

His last words, as he sat up in bed whilst working on his monumental *History of Prices*, were: "I have a thousand things to do". He is buried at Thockrington in Northumberland.

Sir John Cowperthwaite (1915–2006), blessed with the financial acumen and lack of sentimentality inherent in a Yorkshireman educated in Scotland, took a very different line to Beveridge when he was appointed Financial Secretary of Hong Kong in 1961. He was a liberal in the tradition of the "Scottish Enlightenment", a free-trader influenced especially with the ideas of Adam Smith. He described his approach as "positive non-intervention". Personal taxes were kept at a minimum of 15 per cent; government borrowing of any sort was unacceptable; there were no tariffs or subsidies. Red tape was so reduced that a new company could be registered with a one-page form.

The effect of Cowperthwaite's ten-year term of office was long-lasting and dramatic: average earnings in Hong Kong, which had been only one quarter of those in Britain in 1961, had risen to exceed them by 1990. Asked what is key to an emerging country's economic success, he remarked: "They should abolish the Office of National Statistics".

When the Hong Kong Executive offered to refurbish his official residence, he refused: saying that as other citizens did not receive that sort of benefit, he did not see why he should. In his first speech as Financial Secretary, he stated: "In the long run, the aggregate of decisions of individual businessmen, exercising individual judgement in a free economy, even if often mistaken, is less likely to do harm than the centralised decisions of a government, and the harm is likely to be counteracted faster". Cowperthwaite's policies were later adopted with great success by the People's Republic of China.

A contemporary of Adam Smith, another remarkable contributor to the Scottish Enlightenment (an outpouring of intellectual and scientific accomplishments in the 18th century) was Henry Home (1696–1782), an advocate raised to the bench as Lord Kames in 1752.

A philosopher, who wrote extensively about laws protecting the private ownership of property, and their importance to society as a whole, he was also a merciless judge with a biting wit. This was often expressed in coarse language. On one occasion he is said to have greeted the verdict against an old chess partner found guilty of murder, with the words: "…and that Matthew, is checkmate to you!".

THE ROYAL BACCARAT SCANDAL

On 8 September 1890, while Winston Churchill was a schoolboy, Sir William Gordon-Cumming, 4th Bt. (1848–1930) and the Prince of Wales, later King Edward VII (1841–1910) were guests of the Hull shipping magnate Sir Arthur Wilson at Tranby Croft, for the Doncaster race meeting. That evening the guests played baccarat, a game which was illegal in England but a favourite of the Prince. Several players observed Sir William apparently cheating by altering the bets he had on the table – after he had won or lost a hand. They watched him closely the next evening: and became certain. Sir William won a total of £228 (£108,000 today) in the two days.

On the morning of 10 September six of the guests decided to inform the Prince and to confront Sir William. Sir William denied any wrong-doing but finally agreed to sign a pledge that he would never play cards again, in exchange for an agreement that the matter would be kept secret. However it did not remain secret: and quickly became common knowledge within the social circles that Sir William moved. Undoubtedly one of the people spreading the tale was Lady Daisy Brook, a notorious gossip known as the "Babbling Brook". She was also the Prince of Wales's current mistress.

Sir William was ostracised by society. On 1 June 1891, to defend his reputation, he sued his accusers. The Prince of Wales was naturally reluctant to testify: but was given no choice. Article 42 of the Queen's Regulations was invoked: that as an Army officer, which technically he was, and as Sir William was an officer in the Scots Guards, the Prince should have reported the offence. Sir William stated he had only signed his pledge to prevent the Prince's involvement in a public scandal.

The trial ended on 9 June; and the jury deliberated for only ten minutes before finding against Sir William. He was dismissed from the army and retired to his Scottish estate, the site of Gordonstoun School today. He never re-entered society and remained bitter about the incident for the rest of his life. One happy note was that his fiancée, American heiress Florence Garner, supported him throughout the scandal. The couple wed the day after the trial ended, had four children and lived happily everafter.

The Prince changed his behaviour, but only somewhat. He continued to gamble, albeit more discreetly, and ceased to play baccarat altogether. He also replaced Daisy Brook with a new mistress, Alice Frederica Keppel, *née* Edmonstone (1869–1947), the mother of Violet Trefusis – and great-grandmother of the present Prince of Wales's second wife, the Duchess of Cornwall. Alice had a breath-taking reputation for adultery.

The Tranby Croft scandal is mentioned in *Flashman and the Tiger*, by George MacDonald Fraser (1926–2008), and in *Moonraker*, the third *James Bond* novel, by Ian Fleming.

Alice Frederica Keppel (*née* Edmonstone) by Frederick John Jenkins; after Ellis William Roberts (*c*.1900–1910)

National Portrait Gallery, London

Sir William was descended from John II Comyn, Lord of Badenoch, known as the "Black Comyn", a claimant to the Scottish throne in 1292.

IAN FLEMING

Ian Lancaster Fleming, born in Mayfair on 28 May 1908, was the son of Valentine Fleming M.P. and the younger brother of travel writer Peter Fleming (1907–71).

He was the grandson of the Dundee-born son of a shopkeeper, Robert Fleming (1845–1933), a City financier who founded the merchant bank Robert Fleming. Ian was educated at Eton (where he was *Victor Ludorum* two years running) and the Royal Military College at Sandhurst (it became an Academy in 1947) – which he disliked. He failed the Foreign Office examination; worked for the Reuters news service; and for Rowe and Pitman, a City stockbroker.

He married Anne Geraldine Charteris (1913–81) in Jamaica in 1952. Their only child, Caspar (1952–75), committed suicide with a drug overdose.

In 1939 Fleming was commissioned into the RNVR, promoted to Commander and joined Naval Intelligence. During WWII he devised ingenious schemes to frustrate the Nazis, none of which were adopted, and met many of the characters and travelled to many of the places later portrayed in his books.

Ian Fleming

Israel Beer Josaphat, later Baron Julius von Reuter (1816–99), born in Kassel in Germany but naturalized British in 1857, founded his agency in Aachen (historically Aix-la-Chapelle), Germany's westernmost city, in 1849. He used homing pigeons to bridge the 76-mile gap in the telegraph between Aachen and Brussels, to speed up the dissemination of news from Berlin. He moved to London in 1851, to take advantage of the new undersea telegraph cable from Dover to Calais by providing London Stock Exchange prices to Paris and prices from Continental *bourses* to London. Reuters is now Canadian-owned; and operates in at least 200 cities in 94 countries, supplying news text in some 20 languages.

Over 100 million copies of Fleming's James Bond (agent 007) twelve spy novels and two volumes of short stories have been sold. The first, *Casino Royale* in 1953 was followed by *Live and Let Die* in 1954, *Moonraker* in 1955, *Diamonds are Forever* in 1956, *From Russia, With Love* in 1957 and *Dr No* in 1958 – which was located in Jamaica, where Fleming owned a house called *Goldeneye*. He wrote a new book every year.

Goldfinger in 1959, *For Your Eyes Only*, a collection of short stories in 1960, *Thunderball* in 1961, *The Spy Who Loved Me* in 1962, *On Her Majesty's Secret Service* in 1963, *You Only Live Twice* in 1964, *The Man With The Golden Gun* in 1965 and *Octopussy and The Living Daylights* in 1966 complete the list – all of which were made into hit movies, beginning with *Dr No* in 1962.

The second to be filmed, *From Russia with Love* in 1963, was the last that Fleming saw. The short stories in *Octopussy*, published after his death, and the manuscript for *The Man with the Golden Gun* had been delivered to his editor, William Plomer – along with the comment: "This is, alas, the last Bond and, again alas, I mean it, for I really have run out of both puff and zest".

He also wrote *Chitty Chitty Bang Bang: The Magical Car* for his son Caspar, in 1964. A film based on the book, scripted by Roald Dahl and Ken Hughes and starring Dick Van Dyke and Ann Howes, was made in 1968.

As a world traveller and gambler with a fondness for fast cars, vodka, hand-made cigarettes and women, Fleming's own life was reflected in the fictional adventures of his hero. He died of a heart attack in Canterbury on 12 August 1964, aged fifty-six, and was buried in Sevenhampton churchyard, near Swindon in Wiltshire.

Sean Connery (born 1930)

SUITS FOR PLAYING CARDS

James Bond looked his best in a dinner jacket, practically the only item of informal dress from the late-19th century that is still in fashion today. It was invented by Henry Poole in 1860 for the Prince of Wales, later King Edward VII.

Henry Poole & Co is acknowledged as the "Founder of Savile Row". The company was established in 1806 by James Poole, who specialised in making military uniforms, an especially profitable business in the years leading up to the Battle of Waterloo. After his father's death in 1846, Henry Poole moved to splendid new premises in Savile Row; and, by the time he died in 1876, the firm had virtually every European crowned head as a customer. Under the ownership of his cousin Samuel Cundey, whose family still manage the business five generations later, Poole & Co. grew to become the largest bespoke tailor in the world, with branches in Paris, Berlin and Vienna.

THE PROFUMO AFFAIR

John ("Jack") Dennis Profumo (1915–2006), the son of Albert Profumo, a prominent barrister of Italian origin, was the central figure in a scandal that rocked the Conservative government headed by Harold Macmillan in 1963. The youngest M.P. in the House of Commons and a serving soldier when elected in 1940, he was at his death the last of the forty Conservatives who voted against Chamberlain in May that year.

In 1960 Profumo was appointed to the Cabinet as Secretary of State for War (Minister of Defence today). In July 1961 his worthy but unremarkable career was destroyed when he met an attractive young call girl, Christine Keeler at Cliveden (a large country house overlooking the Thames, west of London). She caught his eye while swimming naked and he conducted a brief affair with her – while she was also "seeing" Yevgeny Ivanov, a senior naval attaché at the Soviet Embassy. It was later alleged that this had posed a risk to national security. Though unlikely, this had brought the liaison to the attention of the security services and rumours circulated in Westminster.

When challenged in the Commons by Labour M.P. George Wigg in March 1963, Profumo denied any "impropriety" in his relationship with Miss Keeler. On 5 June he had to admit that he had lied. He resigned his office and from the Privy Council; and disappeared from public view, supported loyally by his wife, the beautiful actress Valerie Hobson – known best for her role in the 1949 Ealing comedy, *Kind Hearts and Coronets*.

Deeply penitent, he volunteered to clean lavatories at Toynbee Hall, a charity in the East End of London and raised large sums of money for the organisation over the next 30 years. He made no published comment ever again in his life and expiated his moment of madness with years of silent and selfless service. He received royal recognition of this with an award of a CBE in 1975. He was placed next to the Queen at Margaret Thatcher's 70th birthday party in 1995. Outraged public prurience however, contributed to the four-seat Conservative defeat in October 1964.

Profumo's lapse seems rather trivial, and his self-abasement extreme, in the light of the far worse behaviour and lack of truthfulness deemed acceptable, even the norm in parliamentary life today. It must however be seen in the context of the exemplary conduct expected then from establishment figures in a more deferential society. It was lampooned anonymously but memorably at the time:

> *"Oh what have you done?", cried Christine.*
> *"You've wrecked the whole party machine.*
> *To lie in the nude may be terribly rude,*
> *but to lie in the House is obscene".*

Harold Macmillan resigned as Prime Minister, having been diagnosed incorrectly with inoperable prostate cancer, on 18 October 1963. Harold Wilson (1916–95) replaced Sir Alec Douglas-Home (1903–95) as Prime Minister in the Labour interest a year later, on 16 October 1964 – just three months before the death of Sir Winston Churchill.

The "14th Earl of Home", in Wilson's term of contemptuous dismissal, made way for the "14th Mr Wilson", in Sir Alec's less pejorative riposte. Mr Wilson was to become the first (and last) Lord Wilson of Rievaulx. Sir Alec, who had renounced his title in order to return to the House of Commons, was the last patrician to head a British government. He was replaced by a wily, unprincipled political operator whose administration proved to be cynical, divisive and incompetent. But Jack Profumo's dalliance started the rot.

In 1886 James Potter of Tuxedo Park in New York, stayed with the Prince at Sandringham and, having admired his evening wear, was told that Henry Poole could make him a similar suit. He wore it with great pride at the Tuxedo Park Club on his return home. It was swiftly copied – and became known thereafter in the US as a "Tuxedo", or "Tux".

Christine Keeler

Profumo took refuge with his family first at the House of Tongue in Sutherland. Tactfully, the owner sent the housekeeper on holiday. Her first name was Christine.

THE END OF EMPIRE

No maritime power can last beyond its ability to protect its lines of communication and to dominate the hinterland of its overseas possessions. Athens, Phoenicia, Venice and Portugal were all eventually overtaken by distance, military atrophy and a shortage of treasure: and were pecked away at until there was nothing left. So it would have been for Britain at some point. Sooner or later, it would have become obvious that the emperor had no clothes.

Rudyard Kipling, the "Bard of Empire" wrote his *Recessional*, on the eve of the Second Boer War in 1899. The third verse is eerily prophetic:

Far-called our navies melt away –
On dune and headland sinks the fire –
Lo, all our pomp of yesterday
Is one with Nineveh and Tyre!
Judge of the Nations, spare us yet,
Lest we forget – lest we forget!

(James) Harold Wilson, Baron Wilson of Rievaulx by Rex Coleman
National Portrait Gallery, London

Macmillan was rewarded with the Order of Merit and the last hereditary peerage to be created for a commoner in Britain. He became the 1st Earl of Stockton on 24 February 1984. It is unlikely that there will be another.

Any country would surely prefer, however humiliating the circumstances in the short run, to be cut back to size honourably, peacefully and with the fabric of nationhood intact: by a friend (who spoke the same language and shared much of her history, culture and institutions), than by a monstrous Continental tyranny.

Britain could not have administered India in the modern era; and others of her colonial possessions would have caused intractable problems shortly after the Suez fiasco in 1956. But it was the exhaustion of specie, manpower and vigour in one terrible World War, followed twenty years later by another, that brought Britain to her knees so abruptly.

Britain bowed to the inevitable and dismantled her Empire within fifty years; and is now left in the lee of much the same relationship with the US as that of Athens with Rome. Britain, the first industrial nation, is now the first to be almost post-industrial: still eccentric, presently muddled by a lack of purpose and sense of belonging, even rather chaotic. But the country is still deeply civilised and abidingly tolerant. This included the single-handed abolition of the slave trade: which should be celebrated, rather than its unattributable and opaque origins be bemoaned. Britain's record of scientific achievement and magnificent literary and cultural heritage remains unmatched by any other country since classical antiquity. English is the world's second language, used in most means of communication, from cyberspace to air-traffic control. Countless international boundaries drawn by the British are still acknowledged, Mountbatten's miserable legacy to India and Pakistan excepted. English law is the preferred medium of international arbitration; and her democratic processes are mimicked to some extent in every country with pretensions to humanity. Britain's ties of kinship with her old dominions have

China is roughly the same size as the US, with nearly 20% of the world's population. Without sufficient landmass, people and natural resources to sustain it, an empire is doomed – China possesses all three. Furthermore, the ethnic, religious and cultural homogeneity of the population is crucial: China's is over 90% Han. The British Isles are only a thirtieth of the size of China; and there are over 20 ethnic Chinese for every Briton. This is why there has been a Chinese empire of one sort or another for nearly 4,000 years. The British Empire lasted for about 300.

On 29 May 1953, two years into Winston Churchill's second and final administration and four days before the coronation of HM Queen Elizabeth II, Sir Edmund Percival Hillary ONZ (1919–2008), born in Auckland in New Zealand, and Sherpa Tenzing Norgay GM (1914–86) became the first men known to have reached the summit of Mount Everest. News of their success reached Britain on the day of the coronation.

Less than a year later, on 6 May 1954 Sir Roger Gilbert Bannister (born in 1929) became the first man ever to run a mile in less than four minutes – his time was 3:59:4. He was watched by about 3,000 spectators, at Iffley Road Track in Oxford.

been loosened but not broken, her moral compass is intact, her institutions are the model of many across the globe. Even her monarchy is a source of fascination to billions who have nothing similar of their own to admire and enjoy.

Britain today, despite the worst efforts of self-serving and incompetent politicians, remains a wise and benevolent society; and a country that many others instinctively look up to.

Pax Americana has replaced *Pax Britannica*, in a seamless transfer of power: but it is the latter that history will judge to have had the greatest and most enduring impact on the world since *Pax Romana*. To a far greater extent than realised, Britain retains the respect, often affection of many of her former colonies. The Commonwealth, a colourful and inoffensive association, is the living proof of this. Britain is still "the lucky country". As with parenthood, she will live forever in the memories of her progeny – Australia, Canada, New Zealand, even South Africa – and above all, the US. Britain, now a somewhat reluctant member of the European Union, is the preferred destination of many from its newly joined member states; and London has become one of the most cosmopolitan and dynamic capital cities in the world.

> The priorities for most 19th century British colonies were golf courses, cricket pitches, race courses, botanical and zoological gardens; and, where appropriate, a stock exchange – legacies that are greatly appreciated by their present owners.

WISHFUL THINKING

The shared history of the countries that comprise the British Isles, glorious as it has often been, has one terrible stain upon it – an alienation that still exists between the United Kingdom and the Republic of Ireland. Unquestionably, blame for this lies mostly with Britain, principally England, and her often brutal treatment of a smaller neighbour. Though relations have been too damaged over the centuries to be repaired overnight, cultural links are where reconciliation might be found – focusing on a common language and wonderful literature. The Irish have produced some of the finest poetry and prose ever written in English.

Might it be possible to refer to the 'Atlantic' Isles in future: and to build on that gesture a forum to heal the wounds inflicted over the centuries? Eight hundred years of union, forced or not, have spread English literally around the globe.

A Council for the Isles might be created: nonpolitical, nonjudgemental and unsentimental, to promote the use and enjoyment of English; and to establish what might become a colloquy for the only truly global language. Eighty years after separation, the Republic is now too prosperous and confident to feel patronised – and membership of the EU has at least the merit of blurring boundaries.

By an accident of geography and history, one of the islands in the British archipelago is outwith the UK, the Republic and the EU. It is equidistant from England, Ireland and Scotland and not much further from Wales. If a saltire of diagonals were to be drawn, one from Banba's Crown, the northernmost tip of the Irish mainland, through Burr Point, the furthest east, to the Channel Tunnel; and the other from Dunnet Head, the most northern point of mainland Britain, to the Lizard, the southernmost, they would intersect on this island too. Legend has it that Finn McCool scooped earth, from what became Lough Neagh, and tossed it at a Scottish rival. He missed and it landed in the Irish Sea: so creating the Isle of Man, a perfect name and an ideal place for the islanders to come together again.

Illustration and Map credits

By special permission of the City of Bayeux 82, 89

© BARC, Archaeological Sciences, University of Bradford 171

Berger Collection at the Denver Art Museum 187 (top)

© Birmingham Museums and Art Gallery — All rights reserved 239 (left), 358

By kind permission of Bridgeman Art Library on behalf of Detroit Institute 590

© The British Library Board: Cotton Claudius B.IV.f.59 66; 74236 159 (top)

The Cobbe Trust 15, 53

© Daily Herald Archive/Science & Society Picture Library 60

Courtesy of DoctorMacro.com 483 (centre), 484 (both), 568, 598

© English Heritage Photo Library/Apsley House: 406, 418

By kind permission of the Trustees of The Highlanders' Museum: Scotland/Bob Simpson 279, 423 (bottom)

Angelo Hornak Photograph Library, London: 21 (bottom left), 101, 165 (bottom), 427

© Ian Fleming Publications Ltd, London 597

© IrishViews.com 76

© Nick Jenkins/FotoLibra 118

Courtesy of The King's Lynn Museum, Norfolk 21

Lambeth Palace, London, UK/The Bridgeman Art Library 190 (bottom)

© Collection of the Earl of Leicester, Holkham Hall, Norfolk 228 (bottom), 229 (top)

Courtesy of Lloyds Banking Group Archives 372

Photograph by kind permission of the Trustees of the Long Shop Project Trust 360 (centre)

Mehrangarh Museum Trust, Jodhpur/Neil Greentree 464 (left)

© The National Archives, UK 418

The National Archives/Heritage-Images/TopFoto 508, 514

Courtesy of the Council of the National Army Museum, London 28 (bottom), 135, 351, 429 (bottom), 449

© National Gallery, London: Wilton Diptych Reverse 143; Wilton Diptych 150; Turner, The Fighting Temeraire 441; Stubbs, Whistlejacket 553

© National Maritime Museum, Greenwich, UK 206, 208, 236 (bottom), 249, 292, 300, 301, 309, 321, 325, 326, 330, 395

National Portrait Gallery [NPG] 28 (top right), 81, 87, 88, 102, 112, 123, 132, 140, 148, 149, 152, 159 (bottom), 164, 172, 175 (both), 176, 179, 180, 181, 186 (both), 187 (bottom), 198 (both), 190 (top), 192 (centre & bottom), 193, 198 (both), 199 (both), 201 (top), 203, 205 (both), 209, 210, 212 (centre), 220, 224, 225 (centre), 226, 227 (both), 228 (left), 229 (bottom), 233 (centre), 234 (top), 235 (both), 238, 241 (both), 246, 247, 250, 251 (centre), 252, 254 (bottom), 257, 258, 259, 260, 262, 263, 267, 269 (top), 270, 271, 272, 273 (both), 276 (bottom), 277, 278 (both), 280, 281, 282, 287, 289, 291, 293, 303, 310, 311, 315, 317 (top), 333 (right), 337 (all), 338 (bottom), 339 (both), 342, 344 (bottom), 347, 348, 353, 354, 355 (top three), 357, 358, 360 (top), 360 (bottom), 362 (both), 364, 366, 367, 369 (both), 370, 371, 373 (top), 375, 379 (bottom), 381 (both), 387 (centre), 389, 390, 394, 396, 402 (top), 405, 407, 408, 410, 412, 417, 423 (center), 426, 428, 432, 434, 435, 438, 439 (centre), 444 (bottom), 445, 447, 448 (both), 451, 452 (both), 453, 454, 455, 456, 458, 459 (bottom), 464 (right), 469 (centre), 471, 472 (bottom), 483 (top & bottom), 485 (bottom), 486, 487, 488, 489, 490 (bottom), 491 (centre), 493, 494, 496, 497, 503, 507, 509 (top & bottom), 512, 513 (bottom), 514 (bottom), 522, 524 (both), 529, 530, 534, 538 (top & centre), 539, 542 (both), 543, 545, 549, 553 (top), 550 (both), 566, 559, 560, 562, 563, 566, NPG/ © 2010 E.O. Hoppé Estate Collection / Curatorial Assistance Inc 567, 576 (all), 578, 580, 581, 595 (bottom), 597 (top), 600

© National Trust/The Gap Studio 338 (top)

© ® The Nobel Foundation 544

Bill Norton 185

Courtesy of Peter Harrington Books 538

Private Collection/Photo © Bonhams, London, UK/The Bridgeman Art Library 296

Private Collection/Nicola Jennings 409

Courtesy of Pyms Gallery, London 425

Richard Raynsford 104, 430

The Royal Collection © 2011, Her Majesty Queen Elizabeth II 183, 188, 232 (bottom), 469 (bottom)

Courtesy of Scotavia Images 570

ScotlandImages.com/Crown Copyright 2007 The National Archives of Scotland 288 (bottom)

Courtesy of Sotheby's 325 (bottom)

© Tate, London 2011 295, 314 (bottom), 332 (both), 349 , 440 (both)

Courtesy of the Thomas Cook Group 474

TopFoto 514, 599

Courtesy of the Victorian Web 461

War History Collection, Alexander Turnbull Library, Wellington, N.Z. 352

Courtesy of Daniel Weinstock 335

Maps drawn by Helen Stirling (www.helenstirlingmaps.com). All maps have been created from material in the public domain with specific acknowledgment to: The University of Texas Libraries, The University of Texas at Austin; Ordnance Survey Data © Crown copyright and database right 2010; Association of British Counties; Eric Gaba (African Colonies in 1913)

Index

Montagu, Lady Mary Wortley
375
Montrose *see* Graham, Charles
Moore, Sir John 297, 411, *412*,
412
More, Sir Thomas 173, 189, *189*;
Utopia 184, 189
Morocco, Agadir Crisis 548
Morris, Tom 588
Morris, William 490–491, *490*
Morris, William Richard, 1st
Viscount Nuffield 564
Morte d'Arthur, Le (Malory) 26,
167, 539
Mortimer, Roger, 1st Earl of
March 126, 132, 134
Mortmain, Statute of (1279) 127
Morton, John 184
Mortough O'Neill 35
Moseley, Sir Oswald, 6th Bt
561–567, 562, 565
Moseley Memorandum 564
Moslems 108–109
Mousetrap (Christie) 542
Mowbray Dukes of Norfolk 117
Moyle, Sir Thomas 177
Munich settlement (1938) 512,
527
Munro, Sir Hector 314
Munros 29
Munster, kings of 76, 78
Murmansk 218
Murray, John, 4th Duke of
Atholl 334
Muscovy Company 218
mustard gas 79, 397

N

Nájera (*or* Navarrete), Battle of
(1367) 137
Namibia 583
Napier, Sir Charles 464–465
Naples 296–297
Napoleon Bonaparte *420*;
birth of 294; the
"hundred days" and
Waterloo 418–425;
proposed invasion of
Britain 92, 299; on St
Helena 340; and war in
Spain 414
Napoleonic Wars (1803–15)
298–302, 395–397; in Spain
(Peninsular War) 411–418,
413 (*map*), *see also* French
Revolutionary Wars
Naseby, Battle of (1645) 236, 242
National Blood Transfusion
Service 376
National Health Service
595–596

National Insurance Act (1911)
546–547
National Parks, New Forest 95
National Trust 538, 539
Naval Construction Yard,
Barrow 500–501
Navarino, Battle of (1827) 400
Nazi Germany 498, 523
Nelson, Fanny (Frances) 294,
298, 302
Nelson, Horatia 298, 301, 302,
458
Nelson, Horatio (Lord Nelson)
293, **293–304**, *300*, 308, 349,
354
Nelson's Column 348
Nemesis (ship) 338
Nennius 25
Neolithic settlers 19
Netherlands 204, 504, *see also*
Anglo–Dutch Wars;
Dutch East Indies
Neville's Cross 133 (*map*), 137
Nevison, Kohn (*aka* William)
267
New Forest 95
New Model Army 241
New Party 564, 565
New York 218, 271
New Zealand 323, 323 (*map*),
325, 371–372; All Blacks
480
Newfoundland 218, 322–323
Newgrange 19, 20, *20*
Newmarket 256
Newton, Sir Isaac **261–266**, *263*,
322
Newton, Revd John 367
Ney, Marshal Michel 419,
423–424
NHS 595–596
Nicot de Villemain, Jean 217
Niger River Basin 373–375, 373
(*map*)
Nightingale, Florence 342, *448*,
448
Nile, expeditions to source 465
Nile, Battle of (1798) 296, *296*
Ninian, St 39
Nixon, Richard 115
Nizariyyah (Assassins) 108
Nobel prizes 544; Laureates
from English universities
120, 121; for Literature 55,
486, 543–544, *544*, 585; for
Medicine 366, 591;
Quakers awarded 1947
Peace Prize 247; Royal
Society Laureates 260
Nonconformists 246–247,
438–439, 545
Norfolk, Dukes of 117
Norman Church 95
Norman Conquest 84–85,
90–95, 91 (*map*)
Norman Kings 77, 151

Norman-French (language) 49,
58, 62
Normandy 31, 67, 90, 97
Normans 62–64
Norse (language) 49, 54, 65
North America: discoveries of
31, 34, 184; early voyages
and settlers 206, 217,
218–219, 226–227, 229, 257;
Darien scheme 277;
surveys and charting of
322–323, 326, 384–387, 385
(*map*); New York 218, 271;
War of Independence
(1775–83) 293–294,
381–382, 386; emigration
to 382, *see also* Canada;
Quebec; United States
North Nibley 52
North West Company (NWC)
384–385, 385 (*map*), 386, 387
North-West passage 218–219,
326, 386–387
Northampton, Treaty of (1328)
76, 131, 134
Northern Ireland 527
Northern Rugby Football Union
480
Northumbria, Kingdom of 36,
63 (*map*), 71, 73, 75 (*map*);
early Christianity in 41–43
Norwegian Vikings 20, 21, 33
Norwich 156
Nuclear Weapons programme
589–590
Nuffield Foundation 564
nursery rhymes 214–217, 289

O

Oastler, Richard 368
Oates, Titus 254
OBE 552
Odo, Bishop of Bayeux 89, 92,
94
Offa, King of Mercia 37, **65–66**,
73, 104
Offa's Dyke 65, 65, 158
O'Higgins, Ambrosio 398
Olaf, King of Dublin 27, 73
Old English (language) 30, 54,
69
Old Pretender (James Edward
Stuart) 278, *278*
Old Trip to Jerusalem, Ye,
Nottingham (public
house) 142
Oldcastle, Sir John 160–161
Olivier, Laurence 177, *484*
Omai 325, *325*
Omdurman, Battle of (1898)
473, 510

O'Neill family 32, 35, 39, 78, 219
Opens (golf championships)
588, 599
Opus Anglicanum (needlework)
84, 92, *92*
Orange Free State 581, 582
Orange Pippin apple 142
Order of the British Empire
(OBE) 552
Order of the Garter 38, 134, 135
Order of Merit (OM) 594
Ordinance of Labourers (1349)
147
Orient (French flagship) 296,
296, 303
Origin of Species (Darwin) 496,
497
Orkney 19, *19*, 20, 48, 97, 133
(*map*)
Orosius, Paulus 72
Osborne College 526
Osburh, Queen of Æthelwulf of
Wessex 70
Ostrich, The, Colnbrook (public
house) 143
Oswiu, King of Northumbria
41, 42, 43
Otterburn, Battle of (1388) 133
(*map*), 160
Ottoman Empire 555–556
Ottoman Turks 166
Outremer 108, 111 (*map*)
Owain ap Gruffydd 105
Owain Glyn Dwr (Owen
Glendower) 153, 159–160
Owen, Margaret 545
Oxford, Provisions of 122–123,
125
Oxford Martyrs 216–217
Oxford University 103, 120, 121,
*see also names of colleges
e.g. Balliol College*

P

Pacific Ocean 206
Packenham, Catherine (Kitty)
(*later* Lady Wellington)
410
Paddington Station *461*
Paget, Henry William, 1st
Marquess of Anglesey *423*
Paine, Thomas 381, *381*
Pakistan, East and West 594, 595
(*map*)
Palestine 511, 556
Palmerston, Henry John
Temple, 3rd Viscount
447–448, *448*, 504
Pankhurst, Emmeline 457
Paradise Lost (Milton) 259, 260
Park, Mungo 373–375, *373*

© Adelphi Publishers, 2011
Text and Maps © Adrian Sykes 2011

First published in 2011 as *Made in Britain*
New revised edition *They Made Great Britain* 2014
Adelphi Publishers
Northburgh Street
10 Northburgh House
London
EC1V 0AT

ISBN 978 0 9562387 3 3

Designed by Isambard Thomas with Zara Frith
Jacket designed by Judith Brugger at Peter Willberg Ltd.
Maps designed by Helen Stirling
Printed and bound in Germany

10 9 8 7 6 5 4 3 2